*to my sweetie E on
his 34th b-day.*

Hitler's Spies ♡-M

7/7-01

ALSO BY DAVID KAHN

The Codebreakers

Hitler's Spies

German Military Intelligence
In World War II

DAVID KAHN

DA CAPO PRESS

A CIP record for this book is available from the Library of Congress
ISBN: 0-306-80949-4
First Da Capo Press Edition 2000

Published by Da Capo Press
A Member of the Perseus Books Group
http://www.dacapopress.com

1 2 3 4 5 6 7 8 9 10——04 03 02 01 00

To my Birdie

Contents

III. THE WEIGHERS

IV. THE CASES

V. EPILOGUE

Preface

INTELLIGENCE has always interested me, and the German army—that glittering exemplar—has always fascinated me. At the junction of the two lies German military intelligence. I thought it might be of value to see how an army widely regarded as the best in the world handled this task in the greatest of all wars. Was its information as good as its arms? Were its intelligence operations as efficient as Germans are reputed to be? Were its results as solid as the vaunted Teutonic scholarship?

These were among the questions I wanted to investigate. But I sought to do so under three aspects that had never before been used together in a book on intelligence. The study would encompass not just spies but all forms of information gathering. ("Spies" is used metaphorically in the title to represent all these forms.) It would base itself not on the writings of other authors on intelligence, but on primary sources. And it would not stop with the intelligence coups, but would complete the story by telling how the information was used—or ignored—by the generals.

Such a study, interestingly enough, could be done on the German side only for World War II. The Prussian-German army documents for World War I and before were destroyed in a 1945 air raid. It could also be done best for World War II. Although many records were destroyed, both accidentally and deliberately, enormous quantities survive. Repetition and corroboration within them lead me to believe that they accurately outline the whole topic, despite inevitable losses of detail, and that no major episode has been lost. Allied postwar prisoner-of-war interrogations, historical commissions, and war-crimes trials generated vast quantities of additional information. Finally, many of the participants survive and can be interviewed, often with the help of the documents.

People often ask whether the documents are available and whether the interviewees can be believed. The documents are available. After the war, the Americans and British microfilmed the military, ministerial, Foreign Office, and SS records while they were in their possession. These microfilms lie in drawers—in effect, on open shelves—at the National Archives in Washington, D.C., accessible to any researcher. The originals have since been returned to the three chief German depositories—the Military Archives in Freiburg-im-Breisgau, the Federal Archives in Koblenz, and the Foreign Office's Political Archive in Bonn—where they are in general available to scholars. As for the interviews, they are not, I believe, reliable when the subject tells about his anti-Nazi attitude, how he saved Jews, how he knew where and when the OVERLORD invasion was coming, and how Hitler lost the war by not listening to him. But I have not used the interviews for such things. I have used them for low-level factual data or "color," such as what the subject's office looked like, how he came to his intelligence job, and what the course of a typical day was. In such matters, I believe, an informant can be trusted.

In looking into World War II German military intelligence, I naturally concentrated on the army. It dominated because of its size and the importance of its results, though, in the last analysis, the intelligence of all the other agencies sought to assure victory on the battlefield, which alone was decisive. The study excludes some areas—weather, mapping, radar—either because they do not deal with enemy intelligence or because the story is rather technical and has been told elsewhere. Likewise, all counterintelligence aspects have been rigorously eliminated, such as the Communist Red Orchestra spy ring and the anti-Hitler resistance, which sometimes fed intelligence to the Allies. The book deals with information coming into Germany, not with information leaving it.

What has come out of all this? First of all, a good deal of material that has, to the best of my knowledge, never seen print before. The work describes the personalities in German intelligence, not only the world-renowned Admiral Canaris but also the obscure naval codebreaker who helped Germany fight the Battle of the Atlantic, not just General Gehlen but also the total unknown who became head of armed forces intelligence. It recounts the exploits of the aerial reconnoiterer who flew high over Suez to bring back aerial photographs of a British naval concentration, of the line-crosser spy who, at the risk of his life, obtained information about an enemy division opposite, of the military attaché whose information Hitler loved, of the statistician who computed Soviet armor production from brass plates taken from the underside of tanks. It provides close-ups of the well-oiled operation of Gehlen's intelligence branch, of the work of the document forgers who provided agents with faked credentials, of the struggles for power among the intelligence chiefs, of how they got money to pay their spies abroad. It examines the effectiveness of German intelligence at three critical junctures in the war: the attack on Russia, the Allied invasion of North Africa, and the cross-Channel assault on Normandy. It compares German intelligence at many points with Allied.

In a more general sense, what has emerged is a picture of Hitler's intelligence apparatus and its results. Or, in other words, the information-gathering mechanism of an entire nation. No one seems to have done this before (and now that I've finished, I know why). In view of the importance of intelligence in the world today, this may be of some use. The investigation of the problem, which troubles all intelligence organizations, of why intelligence is often treated as a stepchild enjoyed the advantage of having as its case history the German army, in which this problem was more severe than in any other. In the comparative operation of intelligence systems, a surprising contrast has emerged: that of the relative effectiveness of the supposedly efficient dictatorship and the traditionally bumbling democracy. In these three matters, the book aspires to contribute to political science.

It hopes to contribute to history as well. It seeks to explain why intelligence rose to its modern importance. It tries to answer why the man who manipulated reality so well that he became master of Europe later petulantly swept unwanted intelligence papers off his desk. It investigates the effect of German arrogance on German intelligence and looks for the roots of that arrogance. And since what was happening in intelligence in the Third Reich was also happening in other sectors of its society—the economic, political, military—the intelligence microcosm may help illuminate the Nazi whole.

Finally, the book offers some theories about military intelligence, and may alert the public to the dangers of unrestricted intelligence operations. During the Third Reich, the party intelligence service began taking over foreign policy, usually with counterproductive results. Parallels with present-day agencies will spring to many a mind.

But the main thing that has come out of all the research and writing is a book that may appeal to any man or woman who likes stories about intelligence, or Nazi Germany, or World War II.

The writing of this book posed an unusual problem: every victory for German intelligence and German guns was a defeat for justice and freedom. I could not sanctify these deeds with a positive outlook or soaring eloquence; I could not end the stories about them with the sense of moral order triumphant that I could have done had I been writing about the Allies. Many times a glorious phrase came to mind or I knew of some vivid image that I could use, such as the one from *Paradise Lost* so perfect for aerial reconnaissance: ". . . and Satan there / Coasting the wall of Heaven on this side Night / In the dun air sublime." But I could not grace the villains or the nonheroes of Nazi Germany with this ennoblement. Even to equate Hitler with Satan would imply that he was once an angel. So I have left out the great words and the trumpet-tongued grandeur that can close a chapter so well. I have ended my chapters on downbeats, with flattened prose.

The reading of this book likewise poses a problem. Many operations of intelligence are antiseptic. They involve the passing back and forth of pieces of paper. But the reader must always remember that in Hitler's Germany they existed against a double background of horror. One was the war itself, whose reality was less that of parades and medals and gratifying movielike explosions than of fathers and sons bleeding, going blind, freezing, starving, dying. The other was Naziism, whose ultimate reality is not to be found in the autobahns but among the uncounted millions murdered in the gas chambers.

So the colors of this book are not crimson and gold, its sounds are not of trumpets, its images not of glory. Its color is brown, the color of the Nazi party and dirt. Its sounds are the screams of men with their legs just blown off, and the crying of children as the SS machine-guns first their mothers, then them. Its images are those of mountains of shoes taken from the dead, of emaciated zombies that are Russian prisoners of war, of a little boy wearing a yellow star holding his hands up. These matters will seldom push to the foreground in a book on German intelligence. But they must never be forgotten.

Many people have helped with this book, often simply by acting as a sounding board to my ideas. But some have been especially kind, and it is a pleasure for me to record my indebtedness to them.

Foremost are the Warden and Fellows of St. Antony's College, Oxford, who for two years permitted me to enjoy their hospitality as a senior associate member, and thereby to gain immeasurably through so many conversations with so wide a range of stimulating people. In particular, Anthony J. Nicholls, head of the German seminar, provided friendship and enlightenment. Anne Abley, then the librarian, let me work in her domain and use the as yet uncatalogued collection of Sir John Wheeler-Bennett.

H. R. Trevor-Roper, the Regius Professor of Modern History in the University of Oxford, guided this work through its dissertation stage successfully enough for it to have been accepted for the doctorate of philosophy. I am deeply grateful to him for his encouragement.

Michael Howard, now the Chichele Professor of the History of War at All Souls College, Oxford, deepened my knowledge on many points of military history. Nicholas Reynolds did likewise in our innumerable discussions about the German army. Timothy W. Mason opened my eyes to aspects of German history I had never even thought about.

Ladislas Farago kindly lent me his valuable microfilms of the Abwehr's Bremen outpost records on spying in Britain and America. David Irving told me of many useful tidbits that I otherwise would never have seen.

The staff of the Militärarchiv provided not only quantities of documents, usually with exemplary speed, during the year I was there, but friendship as well. Especially kind was my advisor, Helmut Forwick. Also helpful were Friedrich-Christian Stahl, Gerd Sandhofer, Alfred Bottlar, Hansjoseph Maierhofer, Martin Ziggel, Wulf Noack, Erich Kroker, Robert Moser, and Oswald Binger.

At the National Archives outstanding performance is routine in the shop of Robert Wolfe. Helping him—and me—were John Mendelsohn, George Wagner, John Taylor, and Timothy Nenninger. At the Army's Center for Military History, Maurice Matloff, Charles MacDonald, Detmar Finke, and Hannah Zeidlik were quick to put their resources at my disposal.

Werner Pix and the late Richard Bauer of the Berlin Document Center made things very easy for me there. Franz Seubert of the Working Group of Former Abwehr Members generously provided me with many addresses. Of the many former soldiers and civilians, in intelligence and out, who responded to my letters and consented to be interviewed, I want to express special thanks to General Gerhard Matzky, General Walter Warlimont, and Captain Heinz Bonatz. Dr. Gerd Brausch gave me many insights.

Without the resources of the New York Public Library, this book would be a great deal poorer. And without the friendliness of its Frederick Lewis Allen Room, where I worked, I would be much the poorer. I remember with thanks the support of my fellow authors: Robert A. Caro, Susan Brownmiller, Joseph P. Lash, Nancy Milford, Lawrence Lader, David Lowe, Waldemar Hansen, Ruth Gross, and the others.

I often blessed my typist, Edgar Stecher, for magically converting an indecipherable draft into a clear, clean, and even beautiful typescript.

I am grateful to all these people. But my gratitude to my wife, Susanne, who has lived with German generals and dusty documents and many a useless idea on intelligence since the day of our marriage is, in feeble words, inexpressible.

D AVID K AHN

Great Neck, New York
September 1977

I
PROLOGUE

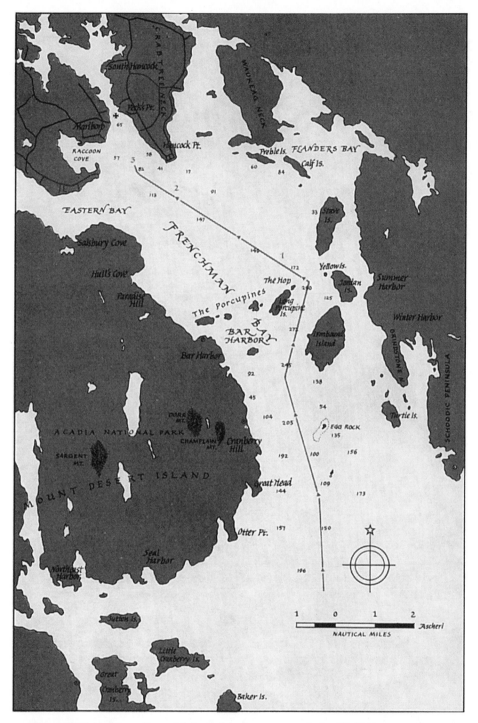

Map of Frenchman Bay, Maine, showing route of the U-1230 to land two German spies at Peck's Point with position of morning stop at 1, of afternoon stop at 2, and of disembarking of the agents at 3

1

The Climax of German Spying in America

AT about 4 o'clock in the afternoon of Tuesday, 28 November 1944, the screws of U-1230 began turning. The submarine rose slowly from the murky Atlantic seabed off the Maine coast. Staying submerged, it moved north, toward the hulking American continent—and the culmination of its secret mission.

On the darkening surface the wind whipped the sea. The temperature stood in the low twenties. After several hours, the U-boat's master, 27-year-old Lieutenant Hans Hilbig, saw through his periscope the sweeping flashes of lighthouses, for, though it was wartime, these continued to operate. They helped him navigate into the five-mile-wide mouth of Frenchman Bay, a body of deep water that indented the land to a depth of 10 miles. With first light, Hilbig steered for the red can buoy before Egg Rock, in the mouth of the bay. To port, Mount Desert Island thrust up a succession of peaks; to starboard loomed the hills of the mainland. Submerged to periscope depth, the U-1230 slipped undetected between the naval patrol base at Bar Harbor and the little naval reserve station across the way at Winter Harbor. Moving at only one or two knots even with the push of the rising tide, Hilbig threaded his way past Egg Rock, past Ironbound Island, past The Porcupines, The Hop, and Yellow Island. Mostly he had plenty of water—more than 200 feet—but in one dangerous place a rocky ledge pushed up to 54 feet from the surface. When he rounded the last island of the chain in the bay's mouth, he headed northwest to near the middle of the inner bay before lowering his vessel into the muck of the bottom. He had to wait for the light to fade.

It was freezing in the U-boat, for to save electricity Hilbig kept the heating off. It was silent, for the officers and men spoke only when they had orders to give, and then as quietly as possible. But though enemy territory encircled the vessel, an air of confidence pervaded it. The crew was tough and well-trained, and Hilbig felt secure in his careful preparations.

Late in the afternoon of what was now Wednesday, 29 November, while there was still light, Hilbig raised his vessel to periscope depth and moved it a few miles closer to a peninsula, Crabtree Neck, that jutted into the upper end of the bay. Then he put it on the bottom again.

Inside the U-boat, two men bustled quietly about. They shed the submariners' uniforms that they had been wearing for the past seven weeks and put on civilian clothes. From a briefcase containing $60,000 in American money wrapped in packets of plain brown paper, they took out $8,000 and divided it equally, each putting a thick sheaf of bills into his wallet. They checked the contents of their airplane suitcase. They spoke in English, one in native American tones, the other with a German accent. They discussed whether to take with them a 10-pound package including a microscope that they had brought across the Atlantic with them, and decided to leave it behind.

Some time after 10 p.m., Hilbig started his motors again and lifted U-1230 until its glistening conning tower barely emerged from the water. Snow was falling. Mostly submerged, the submarine glided with extreme caution up the western side of Crabtree Neck into a kind of inlet. Now the water shelved rapidly—87, 67, 41 feet. Finally, about 500 yards from the shore, not too far from the wharf at Peck's Point, the U-boat stopped, then swiveled to face south, ready for a fast getaway. The waves splashed against it. Some crew members clambered out and readied a rubber boat with oars, to which was attached a light line for pulling it back to the submarine. Into it they put the two men's suitcase and briefcase.

Then the pair emerged, hatless, and wearing light topcoats. The one with the American accent was six feet two inches tall, weighed 150 pounds, and had brown hair and eyes. He bore papers identifying him as William C. Caldwell, but he was in fact William C. Colepaugh, born 26 years earlier in Niantic, Connecticut. The other spoke a native German to the crew members. His real name was Erich Gimpel, though false documents said he was Edward G. Green. He stood six feet one inches tall, but was rather heavier at 177 pounds, with blue eyes and a fair complexion. He was 34, eight years older to the day—25 March—than Colepaugh.

During the launching of the rubber boat, the light line parted and two sailors got in to row the boat back to the submarine. Colepaugh and Gimpel shook hands with Hilbig and the crew, spoke their farewells in hushed voices, and climbed into the boat. The sailors pushed off. The tiny group rowed away from the submarine over the slapping black water. The wooded shores ahead gave no sign of life. In a few moments, their boat scraped a pebbly beach. It was around 11 p.m. Colepaugh and Gimpel sprang onto the shore. The waves lapped at their feet; the wind blew the snowflakes past them. The vast gloom of the enemy land menaced them. But though lights twinkled here and there, they could see no other sign of life. The woods seemed empty. The sailors handed them their luggage, then jumped onto shore themselves so that they could boast that they had invaded the United States. They heiled Hitler, bade farewell to the two men, and quickly returned to their submarine.

Colepaugh picked up the suitcase, Gimpel the briefcase. They turned their backs to the sea and began walking up the beach. Soon the snow and the woods had swallowed them up. Two German spies dispatched by the highest authorities of the Third Reich had begun their secret mission inside the United States of America.

The impetus for the mission had come from the Reich foreign minister. Joachim von Ribbentrop, a former champagne salesman, was pompous, not especially bright, and concerned above all to protect his prerogatives from the abrasions of other and mightier Reich ministers. He had conceived the mission in part to reinforce some of his powers, which dealt with foreign propaganda. He had some say in this, although the main effort was that of Josef Goebbels's Ministry for People's Enlightenment and Propaganda. German radio broadcasts had sought to disaffect the Irish, Polish, Czech, Yugoslav, and Italian minorities in America. Ribbentrop particularly wanted to test the effect of this propaganda during the 1944 presidential election. More generally, he wanted to know what was being done right and what wrong in German broadcasts to America so that he could increase their effectiveness. The best way to do this, he reasoned, was with spies.

The idea occurred to him at the end of 1943. It was a time of incessant German defeats. Early in the year, just after the agonizing loss of Stalingrad, Goebbels had demanded of an audience in the Sports Palace in Berlin, "Do you want total war?" The people had roared back a thundering "Ja!" But although a year of full commitment and of economic control by Albert Speer had indeed improved war production, Germany's military situation had worsened. Her Axis partner, Italy, had defected, and the Allies were advancing up the boot. Her last great offensive in the east had failed at Kursk, and now the Red Army was hammering the Wehrmacht back inexorably toward the borders of the Reich. Her cities were bombed-out wastelands.

The leaders of the Third Reich professed no concern, however, about its ultimate victory. Adolf Hitler told a visiting statesman that he wished the British and Americans would attack in the west so that he could destroy them. To his armies and his people, he spoke of the ancient Hellenes against the Persians and Germany against the Asiatics, of holding out like Frederick the Great until the enemy gave up from exhaustion, of glorious new cities springing from the ruins of the old, of weapons of revenge, of the war's leading ultimately "to the greatest victory of the German Reich."

His soldiers and his subjects were not always so optimistic. Letters from the front spoke despondently of regiments reduced to company strength, of severe shortages of ammunition. At home, people ate turnips and made comments like "I'm not so easy to shake up. But now the situation in the east is starting to get really nasty." An increasing number no longer believed in a final German victory. Cynical lines circulated.

"What's the shortest joke?"

"I don't know. What is?"

"We're winning!"

This sort of thing was, however, kept down by the fear of the SS and the police, both of whom were commanded by the schoolmasterish Heinrich Himmler. A businessman once remarked to an acquaintance that things were going to get even worse because the country's leaders "are all incompetent: Göring's a dope fiend, Goebbels a sex maniac, Adolf a hysteric, and Keitel [head of the Armed Forces High Command] an old aunt." He was sentenced to a year in jail. During 1943 and 1944, the SS spread its dominion over increasingly large areas of German life—including the concentration camps—and tightened its hold on them all.

Its Security Service, the Sicherheitsdienst, or SD, was the Nazi party's only permitted intelligence organ. The SD had a domestic and a foreign arm. Both were incorporated with government police agencies into a party-state amalgam called the Reichssicherheitshauptamt, the RSHA, or Reich Security Administration. Its Department III, for example, was the domestic SD; Department IV was the Gestapo, the secret state police. SD foreign intelligence was RSHA VI. Its head was a boyish, charming SS brigadier, who looked well in his black SS uniform with silver trim: Walter Schellenberg. He was only 34, but his brains, his flair, and his loyalty had gained him the post three years earlier. He commanded not only VI's headquarters in Berlin, but also its outposts throughout the Reich and the conquered territories and, after June 1944, a major new element. This consisted of the foreign sections of the military espionage agency, the Abwehr, long headed by the almost legendary Admiral Wilhelm Canaris. After one of its members defected to the Allies, Hitler, fed up with its incompetence and corruption, ordered it merged into his party's more aggressive, more trustworthy agency. Canaris was fired; Schellenberg came to control all German espionage, military as well as political.

It was to Schellenberg that Ribbentrop passed his request for a spy to gather political intelligence in the United States. But RSHA VI had no sources for this. A few former Abwehr agents sometimes radioed bits of military data. In South America, a well-organized ring provided some technical information from the north. Schellenberg had long considered sending agents to the United States, but a bad experience and a difficulty had deterred him. The experience was the failure in 1942 of an Abwehr sabotage mission to the United States. Canaris had had a submarine land eight men near the eastern tip of Long Island. They were to blow up some factories in Philadelphia and elsewhere. But within days all eight had been captured. This gave Schellenberg pause.

The difficulty was in obtaining recruits. SS Major Dr. Theodor Paeffgen had long sought them. A tall man with an absurdly small head, Paeffgen was head of RSHA VI's Group D, which directed spying in the Anglo-American sphere of influence. He had himself spoken with about 15 or 20 repatriates from the United States, whose names he had gotten from the Nazi party's Auslandsorganisation, the branch to which all party groups abroad belonged. The repatriates had sometimes provided their fatherland with valuable intelligence. Two men from New York, a civil engineer and a tunneling expert, had revealed the sensitivity of the New York City water supply to sabotage. One offered to show where aqueducts and pipelines lay exposed, most vulnerably in nearby White Plains. Another repatriate reported that President Roosevelt had recently asked Congress for $2 million to reactivate and enlarge a disused helium plant in Alabama; he connected it with the possibility that the helium might be used to produce uranium for atomic fission. But though the repatriates were glad to help out in Germany, they were not inclined to return to the United States.

Finally, however, a number of possibilities hove onto the horizon. Among them were Colepaugh and Gimpel. They had set foot years before on the paths that had taken them into Paeffgen's view.

Colepaugh had been born and raised in Niantic, Connecticut, on the shores of Long Island Sound. He was regarded by the townsfolk as dour and taciturn, a loner who roamed the woods by himself or had his nose in a book. By his teenage years he was getting into scrapes. Perhaps to discipline him, his father sent him to Admiral Farragut Academy in Toms River, New Jersey. His classmates considered him "a swell fellow" and "an obscure little gentleman with the big castles in the air" who spent "too much time studying." Afterward he went to the Massachusetts Institute of Technology near Boston, where, in addition to studying marine engineering before flunking out, he did considerable drinking—although, his fraternity brothers at Phi Delta Beta said, he held his liquor badly.

Colepaugh's maternal grandparents had come from Germany, and with this as a start he soon gained an exaggerated respect for the Third Reich and its armed forces. He read avidly of Hitler's blitzkrieg through Poland in September of 1939. The next month, he visited the Hofbrau, a German bar in Boston. There he struck up a conversation with an official of the German consulate and the captain of an interned German tanker. The next day he visited the ship, the *Pauline Friedrich,* and later worked on it, lived aboard, and invited its sailors for weekends at Niantic. He devoured news releases and brochures from the German consulate in Boston, whose consul general, Dr. Herbert Scholz, propagandized energetically.

In May of 1941, Scholz asked Colepaugh, who was a member of the

U.S. Naval Reserve, to ship aboard a British vessel as a crew member and bring back information on the operation of British convoys. Colepaugh consented at once to this invitation to spy. He traveled to Halifax, Nova Scotia, and without any difficulty landed a job on the freighter *Reynolds.* On 9 May, the *Reynolds* sailed for Scotland, with Colepaugh assiduously noting what patrols accompanied the convoys and how they guarded them. He did the same on its return trip, which ended in Boston at the end of July. But his spymaster was gone: all German consulates in America had been closed.

He persisted in his attempts to help Germany. He signed on with the Swedish ship *Anita* and sailed for South America. In Buenos Aires, capital of pro-German Argentina, he jumped ship and sought permission to go to Germany to join the German army. But German officials there told him that they had no way for him to get to Germany.

Disappointed, he took a couple of jobs as a sailor. During a trip to Philadelphia, agents of the Federal Bureau of Investigation picked him up for failure to notify his draft board of his change of address. Eventually he was allowed to join the navy. But in January of 1943, after only a few months of duty, he was honorably discharged. The official reason was "for the good of the service"; the real one was his pro-German sympathies. And indeed, through 1943, while he worked first for a watch manufacturer and then for a poultry farmer, his German plan still revolved in his mind. In January 1944, at just about the time that Ribbentrop's request was reaching Schellenberg, he joined the crew of the Swedish ship *Gripsholm,* sailing for Portugal. This time he duly notified his draft board. But it became academic when he got to Lisbon, for he jumped ship there.

A few days later he was telling the German consul that he was a friend of Scholz's and wanted to join the German army. That was a Monday. On Friday, after the consul had gotten approval from Berlin, Colepaugh, using an alias, boarded a train to Germany, accompanied by a Gestapo agent.

In Biarritz, France, the first major stop in German-occupied territory, he had his first contact with German intelligence. An SS officer met him and asked why Colepaugh wanted to join the German army. Colepaugh answered that he had always wanted to and liked the way it was organized and run. The officer asked if Colepaugh wanted to go back to the United States. "No," he replied. The officer then left Colepaugh in charge of one of the repatriates, who took the young American to Saarbrücken. After two weeks there, Colepaugh went on to Berlin. The SS officer who had met him in Biarritz put him up in the Hotel Excelsior. He also introduced Colepaugh to an SS sergeant from RSHA VI.

Schellenberg's department was quite interested in Colepaugh. He could be the ideal agent for the mission to America. He was a native. This meant that he spoke the language without accent, he knew his way around, he might have well-placed friends. This constellation of qualities both decreased the risk of his being caught and increased the chances of his providing useful information. But if Colepaugh's being an American enhanced him as a possible spy, it also encompassed a grave danger. He might be a double agent, dispatched by American counterintelligence to penetrate SD foreign intelligence. So for three months RSHA VI checked up on him, tested him, and watched him.

The SS sergeant questioned him repeatedly about why he had left the United States, why he wanted to join the German army, what he intended to do after the war, what he thought of the German government and of Hitler. He stayed with him almost constantly, only allowing Colepaugh to go out occasionally for an hour or two. He pumped the American about rationing in the States, the coming presidential election, the attitude of the people to the war. Behind the scenes, Schellenberg was probably checking up on him with Scholz, with the sailors of the *Pauline Friedrich,* and with any other sources he could find.

Finally, SS Major Otto Skorzeny himself interviewed him. Skorzeny was a giant of a man with an open, pleasant face who had become a legend in the SS. A year before, Schellenberg had appointed him to form a new group of RSHA VI. Group S, for sabotage, was to handle all sorts of special assignments, such as infiltrating enemy lines in enemy uniforms, and would train men for these and other VI assignments. In September 1943, Hitler selected him for the mission that made him famous. Benito Mussolini had been deposed as dictator of Italy and was being held captive in a swank hotel atop the Gran Sasso, the highest peak in the Appenines. Skorzeny and his paratroops descended onto the ski resort with gliders and a light plane, surprised Mussolini's captors, freed the grateful Duce, and flew off with him. The delighted Führer awarded Skorzeny the Knight's Cross for this spectacular success.

It was Skorzeny who told Colepaugh that he would be permitted to serve the SD. And at the end of June 1944 the young American found himself in the spy school near The Hague where Skorzeny taught. It was there that Colepaugh met his future fellow spy, Erich Gimpel.

Gimpel had been born in Merseburg, a smallish town 100 miles southwest of Berlin. After graduating from high school, he studied high frequency and then designed electrical transformers. In 1935, when he was 25, he decided to take a job with the German radio corporation Telefunken in remote, romantic Peru, home of the mysterious Inca civilization. Under Hitler's reinstatement of compulsory military service, however, Gimpel could not leave Germany without permission. He obtained it from his military district on condition that he present himself to the German legation in Lima upon his arrival. This he did. An attaché there directed him to observe the ships and cargoes coming into port. It was the modest start to what would become a more serious spying career.

Following the rupture of diplomatic relations between Peru and Germany in January 1942, Gimpel and other Germans were interned. Repatriation procedures via the United States were started, and in June he was taken to a holding camp in Texas, leaving his wife and two children in Peru. In Jersey City, New Jersey, he embarked on the neutral Swedish ship *Drottningholm,* which brought him to Göteborg, Sweden, whence he arrived in Germany early in August of 1942.

Under the terms of the repatriation, he could not serve in the German army. He took a job in Hamburg designing radio transmitters. The massive air raids of July 1943, which caused the fire-storm destruction of the ancient Hanseatic port, bombed out his firm, and he went to Berlin. The Foreign Office heard of his knowledge of Spanish, and employed him three or four times as a courier between Berlin and Madrid. Once he carried 250,000 Swiss francs to the Germans in Spain. Other times he sought to get klystron tubes from Allied planes that had crash-landed in Spain, but without any luck. While not on such trips he worked in Berlin listing repatriated Germans, checking their political reliability, and helping them get jobs. From about February of 1944 he translated technical material dealing with aeronautics in Spanish-language newspapers and magazines. This intelligence work led, in the summer of 1944, to a proposal to spy abroad for Germany.

Like Colepaugh's, the proposal came from RSHA VI. A member of the department asked Gimpel to go to Portugal, to Spain, or to Sweden to gather technical information, particularly on Gimpel's specialty, radio. Voicing one of Schellenberg's chief concerns, the man explained that not enough technical data was coming in and that much of what did come in was late and inadequate. Germany needed someone on the spot who could visit libraries and exploit other sources to increase and speed the flow of this material to Germany. Gimpel agreed to help. He went to visit Department VI.

Separate from the other departments of the RSHA with their dreaded Prinz-Albrecht-Strasse 8 address in the heart of Berlin, VI was located somewhat off to the southwest, at the corner of Berkaerstrasse and the wide Hohenzollerndamm. Its offices were in a curvilinear four-story brick-and-concrete building constructed in 1930 as a Jewish old folks' home; RSHA VI took it over in 1941 and kicked out the inhabitants. Across the way were some vegetable gardens. Inside, the RSHA personnel mostly wore civilian clothes, but many gray-uniformed army officers went in and out. Gimpel walked down the long corridors, passing rooms bearing only the name of the official within, until he came to Paeffgen's office.

The tall SS man began by telling Gimpel that the war was becoming increasingly technical and that the side that made the better weapons would have an enormous advantage. But gradually he shifted the talk to the political situation in the neutrals and in the United States, and finally he urged

Gimpel, who had been in the United States, even though only as an internee, and had improved his English, to go there for political spying. Gimpel declined. Paeffgen redoubled his efforts. He said that if Gimpel were a soldier in the army he would have to obey but that he realized that as a repatriate he could not be forced. He warned Gimpel, though, that if Germany lost the war, Gimpel, as a technician, would be taken off to the Soviet Union by the Russians. Gimpel conceded the force of this argument, and finally consented to at least sample the spy training. He got travel expenses from RSHA VI, and within a few weeks entrained for the spy school near The Hague.

Gimpel was met at the station by an SS man who took him to the school. Called the A-Schule West, probably for "Agent School West" (its eastern counterpart was in Belgrade), it was located between The Hague and Scheveningen on an estate called Park Zorgvliet. Built in the 1600s by a poet, the main house later fell into disuse until wealthy businessmen renovated it and added small outbuildings, a swimming pool, and a wall. Many of the instructors had been with Skorzeny on the Mussolini rescue. Inside, Gimpel was presented to the camp commandant, an SS major, then given a room and issued a workingman's shirt, trousers, coat, and boots as his training clothes.

It was here that he and Colepaugh met. They did not, at first, know one another's name, for like all students and instructors, they had adopted aliases. Colepaugh's was WILHELM COLLER.

Everyone was enjoined not to speak about the school on the outside. The students could only go out at night if accompanied by a member of the staff, who picked up the checks. They received no salary, only spending money for their out-of-pocket expenses. Training took place in small groups. Colepaugh's had five or six men, Gimpel's three, counting himself. The length of the course varied. Some students had been there three months when Gimpel arrived. He himself stayed only four weeks, because he already had much of the technical knowledge required, but Colepaugh studied there for eight. The other students included two South Americans and a fake Irishman, who did much of the interpreting for Colepaugh, who did not speak much German.

Both men spent a great deal of time in physical training. They learned to ride motorcycles. They practiced gunnery, firing different makes of pistols and German and English submachine guns, with the left as well as the right hand. Gimpel already knew radiotelegraphy; Colepaugh, who did not, learned to receive 80 words a minute. He studied sending for two days, but never really learned it. He and Gimpel were taught to spot and shake shadows. They got some political indoctrination. Because of its origin in the sabotage group, the school spent a great deal of time on explosives training—though neither man was intended for operations using them.

Nevertheless, they learned to handle two kinds of plastic explosive. P.E.2 stuck to objects, exploded in all directions, and often was used on railroad tracks. The other, 808, sought the weakest path and thus was good on masonry and brick buildings.

The RSHA decided that Colepaugh and Gimpel should go to America as a team in what it dubbed Unternehmen ELSTER, or Operation MAGPIE. The agency felt that a pair would work better than individuals: the men could support and complement one another. Gimpel, who was the more critical and serious of the two, did not blindly accept Colepaugh as his partner. But when he heard that Colepaugh wanted to become a German national, saw his enthusiasm for Germany, and learned that his mother had been a German, he decided that "he would be a good man to go with me." He expected Colepaugh to front for him in America, while he himself gathered the information and transmitted it. He seems not to have been above making up some stories to impress his younger and more credulous partner. He said that he had been sent to Munich to investigate a countess who had spoken out against the regime and that, on his word only, she had been shot. He told how he had broken into a British consulate in North Africa, using explosives, and stolen some papers. He hinted that, while in Spain, he dated girls at the American embassy and got war information from them. And Colepaugh believed him.

After completing his course, Gimpel took a final examination. He had to find out the name of the commandant, the number of troops, and other details about the German garrison at The Hague and then radio this information to Berlin without being caught. He passed. Then he went back to Berlin, living on his *RM*500 a month for expenses.

While he was there waiting for Colepaugh, and as the Allies invaded Europe and—contrary to Hitler's assurances—refused to let themselves be pushed off, he had long, rambling discussions about his assignment over several days with an SS colonel who dealt with foreign politics. It would be interesting, the colonel told Gimpel, if the United States knew what was going on in Germany and Europe. He repeated the basic Hitlerian prophecy: if Germany lost the war, Europe would go Communist. The real interest of the United States therefore lay in joining forces with Germany to exterminate the Red bacillus. If America did not do this, she would soon be involved in another war—one with the Soviet Union. And this would be fought once again over the prostrate territory of a ruined Germany. No real cause for conflict existed between America and Germany, the Nazi said; Germany never really saw the United States as an enemy, and the war between them had started merely because of some clashes between German submarines and American destroyers. Some hints of the fundamental conflict between the United States and the Soviet Union had emerged recently, he said, when it was learned that the United States had stopped Lend-Lease deliveries of tanks, airplanes, and other matériel on 1

September 1944. The reason—which was highly significant—was a Soviet request for an American military mission in Rumania to leave. (In fact, neither of the stories was true.) The colonel seemed to want Gimpel to get in touch with high authorities in the United States and show them the light, then report his success to Germany. Gimpel protested that he knew nobody in the United States with enough influence. This aspect of the mission was never resolved, and Gimpel never did know exactly what the man expected him to do.

A short while later, Colepaugh joined Gimpel in Berlin. They received training in photography for about a week and a half in one of the SD buildings. Using Leicas given them, they learned how best to take pictures and how to develop and print them. Next they went to Dresden, a china-doll city southeast of Berlin. For two days, they practiced microphotography, reducing Leica photographic negatives of printed or written pages to microdots—images little larger than a period. These they checked by reading them under a microscope.

Up to this time, Colepaugh had no idea of where he would be sent, but during his stay in Dresden he was told that he was going to the United States. At the time, however, he learned nothing more.

They returned to bomb-struck Berlin, and then went to Halle, near Gimpel's birthplace of Merseburg, for a weekend at Gimpel's family home. After a day-long course in secret ink back in Berlin, they were finally briefed on their mission.

The briefing took place in the home of a high SD officer, only two blocks from the Berkaerstrasse headquarters. Gimpel and Colepaugh also met two SS colonels in uniform who were engineers. They told them what RSHA VI had originally told Gimpel. What was needed was technical data on shipbuilding, airplanes, rockets, and any other information, particularly from the engineering field, that would be of value to Germany. The spies were not expected to get this information by the classic means of espionage —theft, bribery, seduction, or force. Rather they were to exploit the openness of American society, picking up what they needed from newspapers, technical magazines, radio, and books. Some of this material was already reaching Germany, but only after intolerable delays. *The New York Times,* for example, usually arrived no earlier than four weeks after publication, and it both cost a lot—generally around $7 per copy—and depleted foreign exchange. With newspaper information, the spies' function was to accelerate its transmission to Germany. Books and many magazines, on the other hand, did not reach Germany at all. Here the spies were to ensure that this information did get to the Reich. They were to radio essential material. If the material was too voluminous to send by radio, with its danger of counterespionage direction-finding, the spies were to reduce the articles or book passages to microdots and mail them to Germany via cover addresses in neutral countries. The original aspect of their mission, the testing of American political opinion in the light of German propaganda, was not mentioned at this meeting, and in fact Colepaugh was never told of it. The mission was to last for two years, after which the pair would be withdrawn.

Final preparations began soon after this briefing. Gimpel and Colepaugh each received a .32-caliber Colt automatic pistol loaded with clips of seven bullets. They were given a special document-copying lens for their Leica; for proper use, the document had to be 53 centimeters (21 inches) from the camera. They had already received their two Krahl wristwatches. They got two bottles of what appeared to be ordinary blue-black ink but was in fact a secret ink, as well as powder to develop any secret-ink messages from Berlin. Colepaugh reduced to microdots instructions to Gimpel for building a radio and for transmitting messages to Berlin. These included the call signs (oxz for the two spies, wk5 and vk7a for Berlin), their radio cover names (WALTER for Colepaugh, EDGAR for Gimpel, DAVID for Berlin), and the times of transmission for both ends. Colepaugh also put into microdots the names and addresses of the mail drops, one in Lisbon and one in Madrid, that Gimpel would use if necessary. At the same time, the two were furnished a microfilm bearing the names of about 20 American prisoners of war. The spies were to write their secret messages in invisible ink and then address an innocuous cover text to the prisoners; the German authorities would intercept the letters and pass them to RSHA VI. Gimpel and Colepaugh also memorized a cipher whose key phrase was the easily remembered advertising motto: "Lucky Strike cigarettes—they're toasted!"

Finally, on 22 September, with all preparations complete, they said good-bys in Berlin and headed north to Kiel. In this long and narrow harbor, filled with sailboats whose halyards rattled against their masts in the fresh Baltic wind, the starting point of many a U-boat's first cruise, the two men boarded the Hamburg-Amerika liner *Milwaukee* to await their submarine. Here they received their last supplies from two young SS lieutenants.

They got their false papers. Colepaugh's were made out in the name of William Charles Caldwell. They consisted of a birth certificate showing Caldwell to have been born in New Haven, Connecticut, a Selective Service registration card showing him to be registered at Local Board 18 in Boston, a Selective Service classification card from the same board, a U.S. Naval Reserve discharge certificate, and a Massachusetts driver's license. Gimpel had essentially the same papers, made out to Edward George Green, born in Bridgeport, Connecticut. The two also had several additional fake forms signed and sealed by the "American" authorities but with the spaces left blank so that the spies could fill in whatever they might need. RSHA VI F, the false-documents group, had predated some of these forms "1946" in case they were needed in the last half of the spies' two-year mission.

The SS lieutenants provided them with two tiny compasses, about ¾ inch in diameter, and with two kits of concentrated food, taken from American pilots downed in Germany. And the spies got the money they needed to live on. Gimpel had already been given 99 chip diamonds, which he was to convert to cash in case he discovered upon arriving that the United States had changed its currency in some way, such as shifting to a

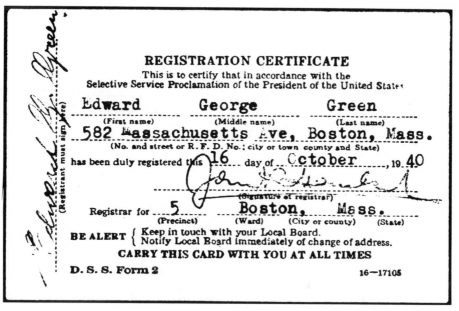

Forged draft card made out to "Edward George Green" for spy Erich Gimpel

bill of a different size, or in case they ran out of funds. And they received cash. Colepaugh had fast-talked the Germans into believing that a single man in America needed $15,000 a year to live on (in a year when the average family income was $2,378). For two men on a two-year mission, then, the total needed was $60,000. Schellenberg had to obtain permission from the head of the entire RSHA, the scar-faced SS general Ernst Kaltenbrunner, to expend such a sum, but he did. The gullible Germans furnished it, in packets of fives, tens, twenties, and fifties wrapped in thin parchment paper and with plain brown wrapping paper around that, each neatly tied with string. On each package was written its amount. Gimpel put them into his brown leather briefcase.

After two days aboard the *Milwaukee* in Kiel harbor, Gimpel and Colepaugh transferred to the U-1230. It was a Type IXC submarine, the newer, larger, and longer-ranged of the two standard classes of Atlantic submarines.

Displacing 1,120 tons over a length of 252 feet, it could cruise 16,000 miles on one load of fuel. Its speed was 18¼ knots on the surface, 7¼ under water. The U-1230, built at Hamburg by the Deutsche Werft, one of the three chief makers, had been launched on 8 November 1943. Normal complement for a Type IXC was 48 men, but the U-1230 carried only 36 on this cruise.

Blank draft card, forged in 1944 and bearing a fake 1946 postmark, for one of the spies to fill out with a false name if required near the end of their mission, which was expected to last for two years

No sooner were the two spies aboard than it headed out of the harbor. Outside, it hove to for a couple of days, waiting for a convoy headed for Norway. Once there, it underwent almost a week of tests at Horten, in the Oslofjord. Then it proceeded to Kristiansand, at the southern tip of Norway, where it loaded fuel and supplies. Two days later, it cast off and headed west into the autumnal desolation of the North Atlantic.

For almost two months, Gimpel and Colepaugh, wearing the uniforms of the German submarine service, shared the discomforts of the dank, close, smelly cruise. Once the snorkel, which brought air from the surface to the submerged submarine's diesels, malfunctioned; water got in and toxic gas from the engines overcame some of the crew. But one sailor managed to switch on the electric motors, enabling Lieutenant Hilbig to bring the boat up. Otherwise its crossing was uneventful.

Finally, it neared the coast of North America. On Friday, 10 November, off the Grand Banks, the vessel took radio bearings on three major New England cities: Boston, Portland, and Bangor. Then, near Mount Desert Rock, a wave-splashed islet 50 miles south of their destination, the crew discovered that the sonic depth-finding gear did not work. It was essential if the submarine was to safely navigate the bay entrance and approach the shore. The submarine sank to the floor of the sea, and specialists began to repair the gear. Meanwhile, the Allies were driving into Germany. The Russians crossed the Danube in a major offensive. American bombers dropped 1,581 tons of high explosives on factories in Gimpel's birthplace of Merseburg. Though President Franklin D. Roosevelt had just defeated Republican Thomas E. Dewey in the 1944 U.S. presidential election, eliminating one of the original motives for the mission, the need for technical intelligence had intensified. In the radar war, the Allies had learned to blind the German night fighters, so that more and more Allied bombers escaped their guns. Colepaugh and Gimpel, whose specialty was high-frequency radio, might help reverse this trend. But they had to get to America first. And for a week they waited on the bottom of the Atlantic while the experts worked on the depth gear. Everyone moved about as quietly as possible, for trawlers fished on the surface nearby; one even anchored directly above. Only by night did the U-boat stir, rising to near the empty surface to poke its snorkel out and run its diesels to recharge its batteries.

Lieutenant Hilbig had been instructed to land the men on a beach near Frenchman Bay because of the bay's deep water, its desolation, and its ingress to main road and rail routes. But one day Berlin radioed that because a U-boat had been sunk not far away carrying two other German spies on a similar mission, the U-1230 was to put the men ashore elsewhere. Gimpel, Colepaugh, and Hilbig discussed other landing places near Newport, Rhode Island; Portsmouth, New Hampshire; Portland, Maine; and the northernmost coast of Maine, all of which have deep water close inshore. Hilbig finally concluded, however, that Frenchman Bay was the safest of all and that he would disregard the instructions, when, as finally happened, the depth-finder was fixed.

At about 4 p.m. on Tuesday, 28 November, U-1230 started its motors. Its propellers lifted it from the muck and pushed it slowly north. Next morning it entered Frenchman Bay. Hilbig approached the landing point in a succession of slow advances. Colepaugh and Gimpel changed into their civilian clothes, and checked over their luggage. When the U-boat surfaced, approached the shore of Crabtree Neck, and stopped, they got into their rubber boat and were rowed over the choppy water to the shapeless mass of the land. They leaped onto the little beach, said their farewells, picked up their luggage, and mounted the slight incline leading to the woods. Behind them, the sailors paddled the rubber boat back to the submarine and went aboard, taking the boat with them. At once U-1230 churned the waters, putting the land and danger behind it. Soon it submerged. Hilbig steered carefully past the islands at the mouth of the bay into the open Atlantic.

Behind him, Colepaugh and Gimpel walked through the snowy woods until they reached a dirt road. They had walked only about a hundred yards when a car passed them. It moved slowly and pulled far over so it wouldn't hit them. In it was Harvard Merrill Hodgkins, a high-school senior and Life Scout, who was returning home from a dance. His was one of six families that lived on the lower end of Crabtree Neck all year round. He did not recognize the two men, who turned their faces as he approached, and he was struck by the fact that they had on such light clothing.

"No one around here wears a topcoat in the winter," he thought to himself, especially on a night like this. He drove along their tracks in the snow. They soon turned off the road and went into the woods. Hodgkins was aware that many people were concerned about spies landing on the coast, so he stopped his car, got out, and followed the footprints down to the shore. But he saw nothing else.

Hodgkins's father, Dana, was a deputy sheriff of Hancock County. But he was away on a hunting trip. Young Hodgkins and his mother decided to wait for him to come back the next morning and tell him about it.

Meanwhile, Colepaugh and Gimpel continued walking. They spoke little. At a house, they turned onto another dirt road and finally came onto a macadam highway. As they trudged along the side, Mrs. Mary Forni, 29, another local resident, drove by and saw them, but thought nothing of it. Suddenly, the handle of the suitcase that Colepaugh was carrying broke. He opened the bag and fixed it; then he and Gimpel took their Colt automatics from their pockets and put them in the suitcase. Hatless, they walked with heads bowed against the increasingly heavy snowfall. After about five miles, they came to U.S. 1, the main road from Maine to Florida. They turned onto it and walked some more.

At about 12:30 a.m. on Friday, 30 November, a car pulled up a few feet ahead. Colepaugh ran up, found it was a taxi, and arranged with the driver to take them to Bangor, about 30 miles away, for $6. They arrived there at about 1:30, changed a $10 bill in a restaurant to pay the cab, and walked to the railroad station, where at 2 a.m. they caught a train for Portland, arriving at 6 a.m. Here Gimpel had his first scare.

He and Colepaugh went into a restaurant for breakfast. Gimpel ordered ham and eggs.

"What kind of bread do you want with it?" the counterman asked.

Gimpel hesitated. Were there different kinds of bread in America? This was something he hadn't been prepared for. What kinds were there? What should he ask for?

"Oh, anything," he said finally.

"Toast?"

"Yes," said Gimpel, relieved. "Toast will be fine."

After breakfast, they caught another train that got them to Boston around 10 a.m. At about this time, Deputy Sheriff Hodgkins and his son were going down to the spot where Harvard had seen the men and the footprints. But the snow had turned to rain, and this had washed away all traces of their landing. The lawman, who thought the pair were probably burglars, did not investigate the matter any further.

In Boston, Gimpel had his second scare. The pair went into a haberdashery to buy hats. Gimpel also bought a tie. The salesman glanced at Gimpel's brown gabardine topcoat and remarked that it wasn't from the States. Gimpel started.

"I can see that right away from the fabric and the cut," the salesman said. Gimpel mumbled something about his having bought it on a trip to Spain, which he had—and thereafter never wore it again.

They had some trouble in wartime Boston in finding a hotel room, but finally registered at the Hotel Essex shortly after noon. They spent the night there, and early next morning entrained for New York. Upon arrival, they checked the suitcase at Grand Central Station. For security's sake, they put the briefcase containing the money in a locker in Pennsylvania Station across town. Then they found a room at the Kenmore Hall Hotel at 145 East 23rd Street. By 3 p.m. Friday, 1 December, they had checked in under their false identities. Their insertion had succeeded.

Gimpel's and Colepaugh's primary need was to find an apartment. It would serve as a headquarters and as a radio station. This latter requirement excluded all buildings with steel construction—in effect, most of the apartment houses in New York. The two spent days telephoning real-estate agents, answering classified ads in the newspapers, and looking at apartments. To establish credit, Colepaugh had opened an account in a bank at the corner of Madison Avenue and 42nd Street with a deposit of $300. They looked at several apartments, but the steel problem compelled them to turn them all down, until on Friday, 8 December, they finally found a studio on the top floor of a town house at 39 Beekman Place, on Manhattan's East Side. It was a sublet. They rented it for $150 a month. At 10 a.m. the next morning, they took a cab from the Kenmore Hall Hotel. Gimpel got out on First Avenue, forgetting a pair of black shoes in the cab, and waited there, not wanting to draw attention to the fact that two men were renting the apartment. Mrs. Julieta del Busto, the sister of the man who had sublet the apartment, was cleaning it when Colepaugh entered with two suitcases. He introduced himself as Caldwell and said he was from New England. After a little while the apartment lessor came in, and he and "Caldwell" discussed the care of the plants that were being left in the apartment. "Caldwell" said that he had learned to take care of plants at his mother's home in Connecticut and would be glad to take care of those in the apartment. He paid two months' rent in advance. After a while, Gimpel came over.

Meanwhile, a British freighter, the 5,000-ton *Cornwallis,* had been torpedoed at 6 a.m. on 3 December 8 miles northwest of Mount Desert Rock while en route from the British West Indies to Saint John, New Brunswick. An explosion in the starboard bow caused the vessel to sink in less than 10 minutes. The sinking was the first off American shores in months. But the F.B.I. had been told by the navy that a U-boat sunk in August off the American coast had been carrying a spy, who had survived. This suggested to the Federal Bureau of Investigation that the submarine that had sunk the *Cornwallis*—which was in fact the U-1230—might also have deposited spies on this ideal portion of the American coast. At once the F.B.I. mounted a manhunt. The Boston field division dispatched agents to Maine, where they formed a coastal patrol and began questioning inhabitants of areas which the navy had indicated as potential landing places. They struck pay dirt when they spoke to young Hodgkins and Mrs. Forni. It now seemed likely that two spies had indeed invaded the United States. But no one else had seen anything. No one had boarded the only bus operating that night along U.S. 1 between Machias, Maine, and Bangor. No unexplainable long-distance calls had been made from the exchange covering Crabtree Neck. Neither the ticket agents of the Maine Central Railroad nor truckers had noticed anything untoward. The F.B.I. did not think to ask any taxi drivers. Widespread questioning of law-enforcement agencies and all other sources of information elicited no additional details. Nevertheless, the investigation continued.

In New York, the targets of the F.B.I. search left their four-story brick town house early in the morning every day and returned late at night as if they were businessmen. They made some preparations for their spying. The day that they moved into their apartment, they went downtown to buy a radio. At a store at 124 East 44th Street, just east of Lexington Avenue, Gimpel saw what he wanted. He waited outside while Colepaugh went in and bought a secondhand commercial radio broadcast receiver. Gimpel planned to convert this into an 80-watt transmitter-receiver, which he could do without the quartz crystals often used to stabilize sending frequencies. The following Tuesday, 12 December, the two walked along a row of radio stores on Greenwich Street in lower Manhattan. They followed their earlier procedure, Colepaugh doing the actual purchasing while Gimpel waited outside. Colepaugh bought a combination ammeter-ohmmeter-voltmeter for about $30, two small milliammeters, a No. 616 tube, and a *Radio Handbook,* 1944 edition, to help in building the radio. They also bought a magnifying glass to read the microdot instructions for building the radio set. (It later proved to be too weak and so useless.) All this they took back to Beekman Place, from where, in a month or two, Gimpel would contact RSHA VI's radio unit in Berlin. The next day, they retrieved the briefcase containing the bulk of the money from the locker at Penn Station.

But they did not work hard at digging up the technical information they had been sent over to get. They spent most of their time going to restaurants and shows, spending a total average of $100 a day. At Radio City Music Hall, Elizabeth Taylor was starring in *National Velvet,* while on the great stage the Christmas show, *The Nativity,* glittered. At the Astor, Judy Garland sang her way through *Meet Me in St. Louis.* The top night clubs—the Copacabana, El Morocco, the Stork Club—packed in customers. Though the Sixth War Loan Drive was on, and government agencies urged people to save their waste paper, tin cans, and fat, though meat and gasoline rationing continued, the war seemed all but won. Everyone had plenty of money. Gimbels advertised that it was "open every night till 9." Men's stores offered business suits at $40 to $50, name-brand raincoats at $25.50 to $50. This tempted the two spies. Gimpel, who needed American clothes to replace his treacherous European garb, bought a pair of brown shoes on the Bowery and an army officer's raincoat. At Rockefeller Center, he ordered a suit and an overcoat at a Robert Reed store; Colepaugh ordered a suit at a Roger Kent near by.

Colepaugh continually pressed to go out on the town. He was far less serious about the spying than Gimpel was, apparently seeing it mainly as a chance to live it up in New York without having to work. Gimpel sensed this, and since he dominated the younger man, was able to keep him under control most of the time. Sometimes, though, he yielded to Colepaugh's importunings and let him out for an evening, which Colepaugh spent drinking and picking up girls.

The skinny American also spent much time reflecting on what he was doing. It was dangerous—there was no doubt about that. It could cost him his life. Moreover, it did not appear especially important or urgent. His partner seemed in no rush to build a radio transmitter and to find intelligence to send back to Germany. Doubts grew in his mind.

Then an unexpected event shattered the city's Christmas gaiety and confidence. Hitler's western armies flung themselves upon the American forces in Belgium—and sent them reeling. Somber thoughts filled the minds of many citizens. Stomachs knotted when people heard about it on their radios: Hitler might win the war after all. Colepaugh heard of the Ardennes offensive as well. He was a confused young man. He wanted Germany to win the war, but he did not want America to lose it. Now the Battle of the Bulge was forcing him to face this contradiction. Finally he decided to resolve it.

On Thursday, 21 December, the pair were to pick up their suits. *The New York Times* that morning had bannered a story by Drew Middleton:

NAZI PUSH MOUNTS IN POWER, 13 DIVISIONS USED;
FOG BALKS AIR BLOWS AT RAMPAGING COLUMNS;
AMERICANS TIGHTEN FLANKS OF 45-MILE BREACH

About 5 p.m., the two spies arrived at Rockefeller Center. Shoppers thronged the sidewalks. Olive-drab and navy-blue uniforms abounded. Civilians in fedoras wore overcoats that reached below the knees. Fifth Avenue's elegant bronze traffic lights, topped by miniature statues of Mercury, flashed red and green—almost the only color on the dimmed-out street. In front of Radio City, skaters whirled around the sunken rink, flanked by its French and English restaurants and encircled by towering skyscrapers. Crowds looked down at the skaters, admired the huge Christmas tree, and listened to the loudspeakers blare out "The Trolley Song," "White Christmas," "Silent Night."

Colepaugh and Gimpel first picked up Colepaugh's suit at Roger Kent. Then they went over to the Robert Reed store. But Colepaugh did not go in. He told Gimpel that it would embarrass him because he was carrying a box from a rival firm. He would wait for Gimpel outside, watching the ice-skaters and listening to the carols, he said.

Gimpel went in. It was between 5:15 and 5:30. The temperature hovered just above freezing. All over the city, housewives were listening to "Portia Faces Life" on WEAF and teenage boys were vicariously living the exploits of Dick Tracy on WJZ. In Rockefeller Center, a young American spy for Germany was making a momentous decision. Colepaugh did not go over to the skating rink. Instead, he melted into the crowds and caught a cab to Beekman Place. He had the cab wait while he went upstairs and got his suitcase and a new one that he and Gimpel had recently purchased to hold the briefcase with the money. On the way down he met Mrs. del Busto. She was returning to her own apartment, and Colepaugh—whom she knew as Caldwell—chatted briefly but cordially with her. He put the two suitcases down to shake hands and wish her a merry Christmas, saying that he himself was going to Connecticut to spend the holidays with his family. Then he left.

The taxi took him to Grand Central Station. There he checked the suitcases at the baggage room. He did not have their keys because Gimpel held them, and, not wanting to lug the bags around, thought to leave them in a safe place. Then, carrying his new suit, he took the Lexington Avenue subway uptown two stops to 59th Street. After buying some toilet articles, he registered at the swank St. Moritz Hotel on Central Park South as "Mr. and Mrs. William C. Caldwell" in anticipation of a date and paid for his room in advance.

When Gimpel came out of the Robert Reed store with his new suit and overcoat, Colepaugh was nowhere to be seen. Gimpel understood at once what had happened. He returned immediately to 39 Beekman Place, and saw that the two suitcases were gone. Mrs. del Busto told him that Colepaugh had left an hour ago to visit his family. Gimpel thanked her and went out.

Colepaugh was merely trying to make off with the money, he thought. He also thought that the young man would probably live it up in New York before going to Connecticut and would not want to be burdened by suitcases that he could not open. On a hunch, Gimpel went to Grand Central Terminal, from where trains leave New York for New England. There, in the checkroom, he could see the two bags. For three hours he hung around, hoping that perhaps Colepaugh would return to pick them up. Finally, at midnight, he spoke to one of the checkers, saying that he had given in two bags but had lost the tickets. The checker let him in; Gimpel picked out his bags, produced the keys to them, and opened one for the checker. Inside was dirty clothing and a Leica camera. Gimpel signed a receipt for each bag, took them, and returned to Beekman Place, where he spent the night.

He did not at first think that Colepaugh would betray him—and he read his companion exactly. Colepaugh spent his first two days and nights enjoying himself. But Gimpel soon grew nervous, and about 1:30 p.m. the next day, Friday, 22 December, he quit the Beekman Place apartment, leaving his radio behind. Carrying two cardboard boxes under his arm, he implied to Mrs. del Busto that he was going to spend the holidays with "Caldwell." Instead he returned to a neighborhood he knew and, as Edward Green, checked into the George Washington Hotel on the corner of 23rd Street and Lexington Avenue, half a block west of the Kenmore Hall Hotel. But by now he had grown more nervous. He began to fear that Colepaugh would talk, giving away his cover name. He worried about moving back to a neighborhood in which he might be recognized. So he never stayed at the George Washington. He went to the Pennsylvania Hotel, on 33rd Street and Seventh Avenue opposite Penn Station, and checked in as George Collins, a name for which he could provide identification with his forged papers.

Again he had read Colepaugh's mind correctly. After spending two nights at the hotel, Colepaugh went, at around noon on Saturday, 23 December, to see an old friend, Edmund F. Mulcahy, who had gone to Admiral Farragut Academy with him. At the Mulcahy home at 91-13 111th Street, Richmond Hill, a section of New York City's borough of Queens, Mulcahy's mother told Colepaugh that her son was working at a shoe store in Jamaica. Colepaugh went there, and the two old friends had lunch and talked over old times. They made another date for 11 that evening at Mulcahy's house. While Mulcahy was shaving, Colepaugh came into the bathroom.

"Edmund," he said. "Remember you said that I could never get into any real trouble? Well, I am in a lot of trouble now."

"What sort of trouble, Bill?" asked Mulcahy.

Colepaugh hesitated. Finally he got it out.

"I just came back from Germany."

"You mean you were in Germany?" said Mulcahy, incredulously.

Colepaugh repeated that he had been, and then explained that he had come back to the United States to get information. Mulcahy asked how he would get this back to Germany. Colepaugh told him about the radio, about his fellow agent, and then the whole story: the trip to Lisbon on the *Gripsholm,* his entry into Germany, his attendance at the school at The Hague, his instructions, and his trip back by submarine. But only when he showed Mulcahy his microdots, his strip of film with the names of American prisoners of war, his false identification papers for Caldwell, his wristwatch made in Germany, and finally the more than $1,900 that he still had, did his old chum believe him. Mulcahy asked where Gimpel was now.

"I don't know," said Colepaugh. "I ditched him."

They agreed that the best way to get in touch with the authorities was for Mulcahy to telephone an F.B.I. agent whom he knew. Then they went out and had a few drinks. Colepaugh stayed over. The next day, he had a date in New York, but that evening, Christmas Eve, he and Mulcahy bar-hopped in Greenwich Village. Mulcahy went home around 4 a.m. with a friend, but Colepaugh continued on to a party with some new friends. He got back to Queens around 9 a.m. on Christmas Day. He and Mulcahy slept during the day, went out to dinner, and talked more about contacting the F.B.I. On Tuesday, the 26th, Colepaugh bought a suitcase at the Mark Cross leather goods store on Fifth Avenue, went to the St. Moritz, packed his things, checked out, and returned to the shoe store in Jamaica. He and Mulcahy had an early dinner. Afterward, at around 6 p.m., Mulcahy finally called the F.B.I. office in New York. He said that he had important information that he could not discuss over the telephone and that he wanted an F.B.I. agent to come to his home. At 7:30 Special Agent William O. McCue was there, and Colepaugh told him his story, producing the same evidence that had convinced Mulcahy.

McCue took Colepaugh back to headquarters, and there he reported in detail about Gimpel. Colepaugh told the F.B.I. what Gimpel looked like, what he was wearing, how he spoke, that he used the alias Edward Green, that he wore a squarish ring with an Inca design, that he frequently bought Peruvian newspapers at a subway newsstand in Times Square, and that he had a habit of taking money from and putting change back into the breast pocket of his jacket. Within hours, a massive manhunt for Gimpel was under way, not only in New York, but throughout the country.

F.B.I. agents in every office in the country checked hotels, rooming houses, railroad stations, bus terminals, airports, and general-delivery windows at post offices for a man fitting Gimpel's description and using either his true name or his alias. In New York, agents went immediately to 39 Beekman Place. They found only the radio Gimpel had left behind. Then they canvassed every known hotel and rooming house. They placed a 24-hour surveillance on the Times Square subway newsstand. They went to the Robert Reed store where Gimpel had bought his suit and overcoat. Records there showed that an Edward Green had purchased two items: a single-breasted three-button suit of gray-blue material with chalk stripes an inch apart and a faint blue stripe between them and with flap pockets and three black buttons on each sleeve, and a dark-blue double-breasted overcoat with a faint herringbone pattern, six black buttons on the front and four on each sleeve, a left top pocket and two side flap pockets, and a plain back. The store made duplicates of the apparel available to the F.B.I., which distributed photographs of them.

Colepaugh had given the F.B.I. the checks for the two suitcases he had left at Grand Central. Agents questioned checkers at the baggage room and discovered that "Green" had taken away the bags. They posted a watch in case he returned to contact Colepaugh when Colepaugh came back for the suitcases. The massive survey of hotel rooms turned up the fact that an Edward Green had registered at the George Washington Hotel at 4:20 p.m. on 22 December. But a hotel maid said that the room had apparently not been used. Here too the F.B.I. set a watch.

Gimpel, meanwhile, was nervously trying to stay one step ahead of any pursuers. His new alias and change of hotel protected him for a while. But the net was tightening. A little before 9 on Saturday evening, 30 December, Gimpel went to the Times Square subway station newsstand at the Seventh Avenue and 42nd Street entrance to buy some newspapers. Two F.B.I. agents, maintaining a surveillance there, noticed his resemblance to the man they were looking for. His blue double-breasted overcoat and his suit matched the description of the clothes bought by Gimpel. But they could not see if he wore an Inca ring, and he neither asked for nor went near the South American newspapers. Instead he just perused the English-language newspapers and magazines. He finally bought a pocket edition of a book on Russia. At the cash register, he spoke a few words to the clerk in English with a foreign accent. And when he paid, he reached inside his coat and took out a bill apparently from the breast pocket of his jacket.

The agents nodded to one another. One left the store ahead of Gimpel and started up the subway stairs. The other followed him as he began to climb the steps. On the stairway, the first agent turned to him and identified himself and the other agent as federal officers. Both displayed their badges and requested his name.

"What's this all about?" he asked.

One of the agents told him that they were from the F.B.I., that it was a routine investigation, and that they just wanted his name. He hesitated. Again they asked. Finally he replied, "Green."

The agents then asked for his full name and home address. He said that he was Edward Green and that he lived in Massachusetts. He went with them to a room behind the newsstand, where they searched him. On him they found a Selective Service classification card made out to Edward George Green of 582 Massachusetts Avenue, Boston, a U.S. Naval Reserve discharge made out to the same person, $10,574 in cash, and the 99 small diamonds wrapped in tissue paper. In his hotel room, the agents found $44,100 in cash, blank Selective Service registration and classification certificates, blank U.S. Navy discharge forms and birth certificates, two loaded Colt automatics, Leica camera film, and two small bottles of secret ink.

Gimpel and Colepaugh were accused of espionage and tried by a military court on Governor's Island. They were found guilty and sentenced to death, but President Harry S Truman later commuted the sentence.

Thus ended the final spasm of the German secret service in America. It had cost the Nazis $60,000 in cash, the value of 99 diamonds, the time of a U-boat, the effort of spymasters in Berlin, Dresden, and The Hague, and the hopes of high officials of the Thousand Year Reich. And it had produced absolutely nothing.

2

Protozoa, Speech, and History

FOR eight years, Hannibal, the Carthaginian military genius, had lain waste to the Roman provinces in the southern part of Italy. His father had made him swear eternal hatred to Rome, and Hannibal, in the Second Punic War between Rome and Carthage to rule the Mediterranean, had beaten the Romans at Cannae and other battles and now ravaged their wheatfields and pastures. He was awaiting the arrival of his brother Hasdrubal, who, in the spring of 207 B.C., had crossed over the Alps with 48,000 infantry, 8,000 cavalry, and 15 elephants. Their forces would unite and rout the Romans.

Soon after his arrival in the north of Italy, Hasdrubal drafted a message to his brother in the south. It said that he would meet Hannibal in Umbria, on the eastern coast of Italy. He dispatched four Gallic and two Numidian horsemen to carry the letter to Hannibal. They traversed the length of Italy without finding him, then turned around to follow him as he moved northward. Uncertain of the roads, they were captured by a party of Roman troops and brought before the praetor. At first they evaded his questions, but under threat of torture they acknowledged that they were carrying a letter from Hasdrubal to Hannibal.

The praetor sent it, still sealed, to one of the consuls of Rome, Gaius Claudius Nero, commanding near by. Nero (not the notorious emperor) had an interpreter read it. He recognized at once the danger if the two brothers combined forces. Sending the letter to the senate with a request for more troops, he promptly marched north against Hasdrubal. At the Metaurus River, his legions attacked Hasdrubal, who was unsupported by his brother and outnumbered by the Romans. They decisively defeated him. The victory erased forever the threat of a Carthaginian conquest, and Rome advanced to become the mistress of the western world.

The battle of the Metaurus holds a unique place in military history. It is the only one of Edward S. Creasy's *Fifteen Decisive Battles of the World: from Marathon to Waterloo* that had intelligence as a precondition of victory. For in the 4,000 years from the dawn of civilization to World War I, military intelligence had little effect on warfare.

To be sure, it had always been an essential element. In the biological struggle for survival, even a protozoan must have mechanisms to receive stimuli and to judge whether they are good or bad for it. An animal must see or feel its quarry to kill it. But intelligence was like breathing: vital to the functioning of an organism, but not to its dominance. To the animal capacity for deriving information from the observation of physical objects, man then joined the ability to derive it from words. The addition of time- and distance-conquering verbal intelligence to physical expanded information's range and powers. But even these did not at first enable intelligence to win many victories. In the main, there were not many to win. Strategies for conquering a country in ancient and medieval times were so vague, so imprecise, that information about them would bring only vague and diffuse benefits to the target nation. Intelligence had little opportunity to concentrate one's own strength enough to overcome enemy force.

This is not to say that tribes and nations spurned it. Often they gathered and used it. The primitive Jibaro of Ecuador crept into enemy villages to count houses and estimate the number of fighting men they had. The ancient Egyptians interrogated prisoners of war. Julius Caesar dispatched scouts to reconnoiter enemy forces. Medieval rulers paid spies. The Mongols flung out mounted patrols to scour the land. Codebreakers in Renaissance Venice solved the esoteric dispatches of foreign diplomats. And sometimes the intelligence produced victories. When Caesar learned from a prisoner that an enemy barbarian had assembled 6,000 infantry and 1,000 cavalry for an ambush, he counterplanned and defeated the chieftain. When spies told Richard the Lion-Hearted about a caravan bringing supplies to the Saracens, he concentrated his cavalry and raided it.

But most often intelligence did not control the course of events. The pharaoh Ramses II won at Kadesh despite having dribbled away the advantage gained from a prisoner interrogation. Venice's knowledge, derived from an intercept, that the commander of the army of the Holy Roman Empire was requesting either 20,000 ducats or the presence of the emperor did not help her win any victories. Cannae, the classic victory of warfare, in which Hannibal encircled a larger Roman force and defeated it, owed nothing to intelligence. Nor did the innumerable sieges, successful for one side or the other, of the Middle Ages. Nor did Creasy's 14 other decisive battles, such as Marathon, in which the Athenian hoplites defeated the Asiatic armies of Xerxes; Tours, where Christendom turned back the Moorish tide of Islam; Hastings, in which William of Normandy conquered England; Blenheim, which undercut the designs of Louis XIV for European domination; Saratoga, which all but decided the American Revolution, and the others. In these and all the other cases that comprise the vast majority of engagements in the long history of warfare, the issue was decided not by intelligence but by tactics, resolution, and strength.

Intelligence only began finding the opportunities and the powers it needed to become a significant factor in war in the industrial and the French revo-

The first recorded interrogation of a prisoner of war: Egyptian soldiers beat two Hittites, captured near Kadesh, to compel them to tell the truth

lutions. They created railroads, the telegraph, good maps, mass armies, and a general staff. These made it necessary and possible to draw detailed plans for the mobilization of an army and the invasion of an enemy. At the same time, industrialization made new aspects of society factors of importance for intelligence. The ancient Greeks did not care how much coal and iron a nation's mines could produce; it was a question of vital importance to a modern country—and to its enemy. At last intelligence had targets that gave it a chance to play a major role in war.

The same revolutions also furnished intelligence with the tools that would enable it to gain more knowledge of another country. A daily press emerged. Diplomacy evolved the military attaché. Bigger armies yielded more prisoners for interrogation, more documents for seizure. Tapping telegraph wires, and later intercepting radio transmissions, provided far greater volumes of enemy messages than the occasional waylaying of couriers. The balloon, the Zeppelin, and the airplane saw more and faster than the deep-est-driving cavalry. The camera fixed fleeting impressions in greater detail than the eye and reproduced them for others. In all of these ways, intelligence amplified its ability to gather information.

At the same time, it was enhancing its evaluation of information. The proximate cause of this was the evolution of the general staff.

Though commanders of ancient times and feudal lords had called their lieutenants into council for military advice, these bodies were ad hoc and dissolved upon completion of their service. A permanent staff began to develop when the rise of capitalism enabled monarchs to cease relying on foraging and to supply their professional armies themselves, with the greater flexibility that this brought. In the 1600s, the Great Elector of Brandenburg assigned his quartermaster and some assistants to plan ahead for the next day's march and encampment—to reconnoiter and draft orders. In this planning lay the germ of a general staff.

During the next century, as the operations of war grew more complex, commanders gathered groups of specialized assistants around them to serve throughout a campaign. They channeled to him the information he needed to make his decisions, and they then elaborated these broad decisions in the detailed orders for march and supply needed to realize them. "Attack on the right flank," orders the commander, and his chief of staff barks out commands for the 2nd Regiment to advance, for the 3rd to change its direction of march from the left flank to the right and to go into reserve, for the artillery chief to begin firing, for the supply officers to bring up ammunition, and so on. Staffs vary as do commanders. Frederick the Great had a small staff, Napoleon a large and rather badly organized one. The generals of the newly created division of combined arms soon had small staffs of their own, called a "general's staff."

But these were all temporary wartime organizations. It remained for Prussia, in 1803, to establish the first permanent general staff—a body to plan war even in peace.

Prussia's general staff constituted a separate corps, like, for example, the engineers. Originally it had its own uniform, which was later abbreviated to dark red stripes on the trousers of the army's field gray. It consisted of officers of the Prussian army who had been admitted to the War Academy on the basis of brains and who, after graduation, had been called to the general staff by its chief. Only about 2 percent of the officer corps attained this eminence—some 200 men in 1870, 600 in 1914. They divided their staff time between the central headquarters in the red brick building at Berlin, the Great General Staff, and the smaller staffs at corps, regiment, and fortress headquarters, known collectively as the Troops General Staff. At any one time, somewhat more than half were working in Berlin. In addition, at regular intervals they suspended their staff service to command troops in the field. This alternation sought both to keep them in contact with practical problems and to disseminate the concepts and the control of the general staff throughout the army. Their basic intellectual ability, their training, their selection, and their rapid advancement made the staff into an élite. Its reticence ("General staff officers have no names," said one chief), the secrecy of its work, the seeming mechanical unrolling of its victories over Austria in 1866 and over France in 1870, the German awe of the military—all these combined to create the legend of mysterious invincibility, of dark control of the cords of destiny that has always enveloped the German general staff.

The basic task of the Great General Staff was to prepare the plans that the German army would follow in case of war with a particular nation. This naturally required a modicum of information, just as on the individual level: a country has to "see" its enemy to strike it. "The work of the department [meaning the general staff]," stated the opening words of an 1816 order on the staff's basic duties and organization, "must aim at the most exact knowledge of this country and of the other European states in military matters and must prepare all that is necessary in an emerging war." Because this staff was permanent and its functions uninterrupted, it gave intelligence a continuous institutional existence for the first time in its history. This enabled it to improve its abilities in evaluation.

Nevertheless, intelligence in the Great General Staff did not crystallize out as a separate activity. It blurred into planning. Raw data about a foreign country went to one of the two war-plans sections—one for the eastern theater, one for the western. Officers there blended it with all other factors in devising their strategy. The Great General Staff in Berlin did not create a permanent separate section for the general evaluation of intelligence. Likewise, no officer in the Troops General Staff worked solely on it.

The reason was a basic antagonism to intelligence that paralleled the opposition to any technical innovation. The aristocratic officer corps feared that it would lose its quasi-monopoly of commanders' jobs to the new technicians. Such concerns frightened Germany's officer corps more than those of other European countries. Consequently, while France had a G-2 section for the general evaluation of intelligence and England set up an Intelligence Division, Germany had neither.

She did bow slightly to the new realities however. With the outbreak of hostilities in 1866 and 1870, the army mobilized. The Great General Staff converted into a General Headquarters. Its duties compelled it to organize, not geographically like its peacetime parent, but functionally. It thus included, for the only times during the existence of the Great General Staff up to 1914, a section for the general evaluation of intelligence. The job of this Intelligence Branch mainly consisted of receiving the immense flow of data, which is far greater in war than in peace, of picking out the important items, of judging their probable veracity, of assembling them into overall reports, and of passing them to the Operations Branch, which issued the orders of the chief of the general staff of the field army. With the return of peace, the objections to intelligence resumed their sway. The Intelligence Branch was dissolved, and intelligence reverted to its indeterminate and subaltern status.

In one area, however, it preserved in peace the gains made just before the start of Prussia's war with Austria. The area was espionage; the organization became the forerunner of World War II's legendary Abwehr.

On 25 March 1866, Helmuth Count von Moltke, chief of the general staff of the army, established an Intelligence Bureau on an emergency basis to get information he lacked about his prospective enemy. At the end of May, a few days before hostilities began, the bureau received from a young south German officer then in Vienna news that Austria was setting up a Northern Army under the command of Ludwig von Benedek. This suggested to Moltke that the Austrians would advance in a unified force in a single direction, not in any encircling or pincer movement. He perfected his own plans. A couple of weeks later, another agent brought to Berlin the order of battle of the Austrian army, together with some profiles of its more important commanders. This agent was destined to become the greatest in Germany's history.

He was Baron August Schluga, 25, slim, blond, blue-eyed. Born in Zsolna, Hungary (now Zilina, Czechoslovakia), he had studied at the Polytechnical Institute in Vienna, had joined an Austrian infantry regiment, and had fought "very bravely" at Magenta and Solferino in 1859. He had been described as a capable officer suited for a general staff post. But he resigned in 1863 just before taking the examination for the Austrian War School, saying he wanted to marry and to manage personally the estates he would gain. His credentials apparently enabled him to penetrate the Austrian headquarters as a journalist and obtain the information he brought to Berlin. Moltke thrashed the Austrians in a seven-weeks' war. Afterward, evidently having found the Intelligence Bureau valuable, he made it permanent and subordinated it directly to him.

During its first half-century, the Intelligence Bureau bounced back and forth from one unit of the Great General Staff to another. In 1889, with the creation of a layer of deputy chiefs of the general staff called, in an apparent historical allusion, "Oberquartiermeister," it went to the IIIrd Oberquartiermeister, or O. Qu. III. Thenceforth it carried the designation by which in World War I it became famous—III b. The constant rise in its funds during those same years to an amount greater than any European country's except Russia enabled what had been a tiny office to enlarge. By 1901, 124 officers and men directed agent activities from War Intelligence Posts in Belgium, Switzerland, England, Italy, Spain, Luxembourg, Denmark, Sweden, and Rumania.

They aimed above all at the most secret enemy documents—those disclosing the enemy's deployment plans to concentrate his armies for the first, decisive battle. And with France, Germany's chief enemy, they partly succeeded.

Schluga had, after the war of 1866, gone to Paris, where he delivered information to the Prussian military attaché before the Franco-Prussian War. III b designated him "Agent 17."

The embodiment of Germany's Great General Staff: its chief, Helmuth Count von Moltke, as caricatured in a humor magazine

He came to be regarded by the Germans as "the ideal of a major agent." A charming, well-educated, aristocratic man whose head resembled Bismarck's, he remained somewhat of a mystery to III b, who never knew his sources, his other activities, or even whether he lived in Paris under his own or another name. He fended off such inquiries, arguing that III b could be concerned only with his performance. During the 40 years of peace between the wars of 1870 and of 1914, III b kept him virtually on ice. Though he continued to report, often amusingly, the agency spoke to him only once a year, preserving him from suspicion, and for service in a catastrophe.

The plan worked to perfection. Some time before the outbreak of World War I, Agent 17 furnished Germany with a document of which spymasters dream. It detailed how the French would deploy some of their forces on the fifth day of their mobilization. With this coup, one of the greatest in the history of espionage, III b seemed to justify its existence and all the money that it had spent, for it had provided Germany with what appeared to be a key for the defeat of the counterattacking armies of France in a cataclysm that was sure to come.

A pistol shot in Sarajevo in 1914 detonated that cataclysm.

The German army's *Field Service Regulations* of 1908, in force when World War I began, declared—as previous editions had done—that the most definite intelligence comes from visual observation and that obtaining this falls chiefly to the cavalry. But the army's 10 cavalry divisions failed to push deeply beyond the enemy foreposts at the start of the war and find out what was going on behind her front. Trench warfare then quashed any new hopes for it.

During such warfare, the bulk of enemy intelligence was acquired—as it always has been—by the visual observations of the fighting troops. Most of it was physical evidence. The men in the trenches reported the digging of new trenches and the installation of machine-gun nests. They sent out patrols to look more closely, to capture prisoners, and perhaps to obtain documents. And during the battle itself, they could spot new enemy positions, detect new tactics, take prisoners, capture new weapons.

Their basic information was supplemented by new sensing devices. Sound- and light-ranging units, for example, fixed the location of an enemy gun, enabling the German artillery to bombard and destroy it.

The tool of reconnaissance that made the most spectacular progress during World War I was, of course, aircraft. This activity expanded so rapidly that it had to be centralized at General Headquarters after only eight months of war. Where speed was paramount, as in artillery spotting and during the progress of a battle, reconnaissance was visual. The observers radioed in the fall of shot, or dropped notes about enemy actions.

But it was photography that gave aerial reconnaissance its greatest meaning. The introduction of vertical photographs during 1915 made it evident that they could yield far more information than the naked eye. By 1918, German cameras were photographing from the air each week an area larger than Connecticut. Aerial photography became Germany's chief single means of military reconnaissance. The great influence that this new source of intelligence had on the operations of both sides was shown most dramatically in a single datum. After 1917, both Allied and Central powers so feared it that neither dared move troops in daylight hours.

In the opening days of the war, the radio station of the German fortress at Königsberg, in East Prussia, intercepted several Russian army radiograms in the clear. They disclosed the intentions of the Russian forces moving ponderously into East Prussia in such detail that the German commander in the east, Paul von Hindenburg, and his chief of staff, Erich Ludendorff, gained a knowledge of enemy intentions unprecedented in the whole of military history. With it, they enveloped, cut up, and destroyed an entire Russian army in the battle of Tannenberg, one of the few decisive victories of the war. It gave Russia its first great push toward defeat. And it opened German eyes to a form of intelligence they had never really considered.

After Tannenberg, the high command established radio intercept posts. The new source of information was nurtured mainly by Captain Ludwig Voit, the father of communications intelligence in the German army. When, at the end of 1914, aged 32, he became chief of the General Headquarters radio station, he set up the Cryptanalytic Station West within it. Though it could never quite overcome France's superiority in this area (France solved German diplomatic codes, for example, though the Germans never broke the French), in the east radio intelligence played a role of high importance. "We were always warned by the wireless messages of the Russian staff of the positions where troops were being concentrated for any new undertaking," said one high German commander. And with the help of these warnings, the Germans defeated Russia.

More verbal intelligence came from enemy trench telephones. Early in 1915, a 32-year-old telegraph inspector, Otto Arendt, devised an apparatus to overhear these conversations by picking up and amplifying the return earth current. By 1918, 292 such apparatuses were in service.

Major Walther Nicolai, an energetic, blondish general staff officer of medium height, in his mid-thirties, headed III b throughout World War I. He ran the spy agency exactly as he would have led a regiment in the field, for he was a Prussian officer, who did his duty wherever he was assigned. He was far from being a mysterious spymaster, and indeed he claimed, "I myself have never seen a spy and never spoken to one." It was his way of saying that he believed his own main job was less in supervising espionage than in advising his superiors of its results.

By 1917, he commanded about 150 officers. Many served directly under him at General Headquarters, but others worked in Berlin, in regional posts, at lower headquarters on the western front, and in the headquarters for the eastern and southeastern theaters. Most of the agents were run by the nine regional War Intelligence Posts. Of these, Antwerp's, headed from early 1915 by Dr. Elsbeth Schragmüller, the famous "Fräulein Doktor," was perhaps the most effective. In mid-December 1915, Antwerp controlled 62 of III b's 337 agents in the west; three months later, Dr. Schragmüller had almost doubled the number of her agents and had raised the fraction of active ones from two-thirds to three-quarters.

III b's best-known spy was, of course, Mata Hari. The idea of using the famous dancer came from a III b officer stationed in Kleve, Baron von Mirbach. Nicolai met her in the Domhotel in Cologne, apparently early in 1916. He put her up in the hotel Frankfurter Hof in Frankfurt-am-Main for her training. Captain Roepell, then leader of the War Intelligence Post Düsseldorf, who prudently stayed in a different hotel, instructed her in political and military matters. Dr. Schragmüller laid out her trip for her and taught her how to make observations and write reports. Herr Habersack of the Antwerp post showed her how to use invisible ink. Then, designated Agent H-21, she vanished into enemy territory. Roepell received two or three letters in secret ink from her at cover addresses; they contained nothing important. Early in 1917, the French intercepted and solved a message from the German military attaché in Madrid requesting that she be paid. They caught her, and shot her at dawn in the courtyard of the forbidding fortress of Vincennes.

Though Mata Hari became an eponym for "spy," the most successful German agent of the war remained undetected throughout his lifetime and unknown for years afterward. This was Agent 17—Baron Schluga. He had, just before the outbreak of war, delivered to the German high command information on the deployment of some French forces on the fifth day of mobilization. This information had not realized the great hopes placed in it by Germany's spymasters. For the German commanders were unclear as to whether or not a suspected variant of France's Plan XVII had been activated, and this worry prevented them from exploiting Schluga's intelligence.

Disappointment over the failure of his supreme effort may have contributed to the break in health that Schluga, then 73, suffered soon afterward. He went to Germany for a rest, but by May of 1915 was back in Paris in full activity. He sent in reports every second day through a messenger system tailored to the weaknesses of the border controls between France and Switzerland; they usually reached III b's Report Collection Station South at Lörrach, in southwestern Germany just across the border from Switzerland's Basel, within 48 hours. His report of 9 June 1915, which arrived on the 11th, disclosed: "English complaining over lack of munitions. They regret that the promised support of the French attack north of Arras is not possible on account of munition insufficiency."

Schluga's sources consisted mainly of members of the legislature and personnel in the war ministry. But their information was incomplete, mainly because Joseph Joffre, the commander in chief, and Alexandre Millerand, the war minister, kept their plans secret from the legislators. In general

Schluga could throw light only on tactical matters. Moreover, his reports were sometimes true, sometimes false, reflecting his lags in reporting the constant changes of view in high French quarters. On the political, economic, and psychological situation, however, Schluga was well informed. His reports seemed accurate, as far as they went. And this very accuracy nearly bred disaster.

The presence of so veteran, so reliable, and so well placed an agent as Schluga overimpressed the then chief of the general staff of the field army, Erich von Falkenhayn. He insisted upon seeing Schluga's reports himself. He then read them, not as contributory, as part of the whole intelligence picture, but as determinative. And Schluga, whether consciously or not, repeatedly emphasized French weaknesses in character and in government. This reinforced Falkenhayn's inclination to underestimate the French will and ability to attack. Consequently, in the summer of 1915 he discounted clear indications of a threatening offensive: the bringing up of troops, the construction of installations for an attack, even the definite statements of prisoners. The inactivity of the Allies in midsummer and Schluga's reports confirmed his view of the general situation as hopeless for the Allies. Had he continued to rely solely on Schluga, he might have suffered a serious defeat. But finally the authoritative tone of the heavy guns overruled the spy. Falkenhayn moved to repel the Allied advance.

Schluga continued in his work until ill health forced him to quit. His final report arrived 5 March 1916. He then went to Germany, where, after a year of receiving his pension from III b, he died, regarded by his chiefs as "the most important phenomenon in the entire history of espionage, so far as that history is known to us."

But if III b succeeded with Schluga, it failed in three critical areas. One was the United States. Nicolai held the astonishing view that it was "no business of the intelligence service" to obtain information about U.S. strength that might be brought to bear in Europe. It did not even begin to prepare espionage against its new enemy until several months after the entry of the United States into the war. And in the end, its total espionage effort against the nation whose efforts would eventually defeat Germany consisted of the massive total of seven agents.

III b's second failure lay in inadequate economic espionage, during a war in which economics increasingly determined the outcome. Third, it failed to learn in advance and warn the troops and the high command of the frightening appearance on the battlefield of a new and epoch-making weapon—the tank.

The Imperial German Navy naturally utilized intelligence as well. The Admiralty Staff had four sections for it: an Intelligence Branch for reconnaissance and agents, an Observation and Cryptanalytic Service, a Military-Political Branch, and a Foreign Navies Branch to evaluate the material.

Communications intelligence in particular evolved into an effective organization. Lieutenant Martin Braune, a north German in his early forties, recognized the importance of the work. He created a 458-man organization with headquarters in Neumünster, the north German site of a major radio station, and supplemented by almost two dozen intercept and direction-finding posts along the German coasts and inland and by floating units aboard German naval vessels. During the Battle of Jutland, his code-breakers fed the High Seas Fleet information on the position and movements of the British Grand Fleet, and in mid-October 1917, a team aboard the cruiser *Brummer* solved parts of an English message that disclosed the sailing of a convoy from Norway to Scotland guarded only by two destroyers. The *Brummer* and another cruiser sank both destroyers and 9 of the 12 merchantmen.

No commander had the time to read all the intelligence that came in. The first half of 1917 produced 32,000 prisoner-of-war interrogation reports from just a single post in Berlin. Sometimes 800 Arendt reports reached an army headquarters in a day. To pick out the useful reports, to fill in an incomplete picture from one source with material from another, to build up an image of the enemy forces and predict what they would do —this was the task of the agencies that evaluated intelligence.

Since no intelligence officers had existed in peacetime at the Troops General Staff, wartime commanders found it necessary to assign this work. At the level of division, army, and army groups, which had not existed in the prewar army, their designations varied widely: I e, I d, M.S.O. (for Melde-Sammel-Offizier, or Report Collection Officer), I b. Only at corps, which had existed in peacetime, did some uniformity appear: I c. (The roman numeral I indicated the staff's first, or command, section; the appended small letter designated a subsection.) All these officers focused mainly upon the enemy unit at the corresponding level opposite them.

The general evaluation of operational and strategic intelligence for the entire German army fell upon the Intelligence Branch of General Headquarters, formed upon mobilization and renamed after 20 June 1917 the Foreign Armies Branch. From shortly after the beginning to the end of the war, Major von Rauch, "an experienced and careful General Staff officer," headed it. The branch's staff of 5 officers and 2 officials plus clerks at the start of the war rose to 21 officers and 10 officials at the end. They sifted the enormous mass of incoming data to determine the enemy's activities and capabilities and possibly his intentions.

Some of Foreign Armies' reports served background purposes: studies of the English and French replacement situations, a 23-page overview of the war organization of the French army. More valuable to the high command were its predictions of Allied moves. One dealt with the mighty Allied offensive on the Somme in the summer of 1916.

As early as the end of February, German pilots had observed the construction of new barracks and other offensive installations in the area. Soon thereafter the number of British divisions increased. Patrols and other reconnaissances showed that these divisions stayed at the front only briefly; apparently they were being blooded for future use. By the end of April more than eight British divisions stood opposite four German in a certain sector. Air reconnaissance showed that the offensive would not be limited to the British forces but would also include French. On 23 June the Allies began to shell German batteries. The next day a more general heavy fire began. Allied mining activity increased. A prisoner reported that an infantry attack would begin in a few days. And at 8:30 a.m. on 1 July, after the drumfire preparation, the storm broke "in full accord with the observations, expectations, and reports."

But Foreign Armies could also err. When the French mounted their great offensive in July of 1918, they were stronger by almost a fifth than the Germans knew. And the attack succeeded.

World War I, a watershed in so many ways, proved one in intelligence as well. In her previous wars, Germany had distracted the chiefs of the Intelligence Branch with secondary duties: political matters in 1866, political and press in 1870. In World War I, after a single blunder at the start of the war, the branch chief concentrated strictly on his work. In 1870, Prussia had employed—outside of the cavalry—only a handful of men in intelligence: some balloonists, a 20-man field photography detachment, III b's spymasters. Between 1914 and 1918, Germany assigned thousands of men to intelligence. She evidently found them more useful doing this work than firing rifles from trench parapets.

The reason for this new importance of intelligence lay in the rise of verbal intelligence to preponderance over physical. An understanding of this and its effects requires making the distinction between the two clear.

Basically, verbal intelligence derives from words, physical intelligence from things. If the object of intelligence is a stolen plan, a report on troop morale, or an intercepted order—that is, if it is words—the intelligence is verbal. If the object of intelligence is not words but other entities, the intelligence is physical. Among the objects of physical intelligence are bodies of troops, aerial photographs of fortifications, the noise of tank motors.

It is important to note that the difference between the two does not rest on how the stimulus is acquired: the eye both reads a report and sees enemy troops. Nor does it rest on the method of gaining the information: a spy or a prisoner can verbally report on the presence of tanks or an enemy plan. Nor, finally, does it rest on the method of transmission: the presence of tanks can be passed by telephone, an enemy plan by photographs. The difference rests solely on the objects of intelligence itself.

Verbal objects mean verbal intelligence; nonverbal mean physical. This distinction has perhaps little value in intelligence operations. But it is the key to understanding how intelligence evolved, why some forms are superior to others, and consequently why countries who exploit these forms best enjoy intelligence supremacy.

The explanation starts from the observation that war has both a physical and a mental component. All actions of war therefore affect the combatants physically or mentally or both. Artillery can kill or demoralize. Because war is, as Clausewitz said, "an act of force," the elements of "physical force"—men and guns—exert the most influence on the outcome. Killing is more decisive than demoralizing. The psychological elements, such as morale and tactics, though "among the most important in war," are less determinative. The best disciplined company cannot stop an army. As with artillery, the impact of intelligence takes two forms, depending upon whether the physical or the mental component transmits it.

In the physical realm, intelligence magnifies strength. Knowing where an enemy will attack enables a commander to dispose his men more efficiently. Psychologically, intelligence improves command. Knowing that a town ahead is free of the enemy relieves a commander of anxiety and facilitates his direction of his advancing troops. These are the ultimate purposes of military intelligence.

It might seem that verbal evidence should serve the mental component of war and physical, the physical. But in fact they cross. To begin with, war is a physical encounter. The men, guns, supplies, and so on must be present, waiting to kill the enemy and occupy his land, for the encounter to take place at all. The presence of these objects of physical intelligence affirms the likelihood of the encounter with greater probability than a plan, for men cannot move guns or troops as easily as they can rewrite orders. This relative certainty helps the commander make better decisions. Thus physical evidence serves the mental component of war.

The plans and orders that are objects of verbal evidence, on the other hand, cannot kill. The enemy must realize them in physical form first. This step gives the commander who obtains verbal intelligence time. With this time he can shift his soldiers into the most endangered sectors, in effect adding to his forces. Thus verbal evidence serves the physical component of war, and because that component is the more important, verbal evidence possesses greater importance than physical.

The time that verbal intelligence gives a commander puts his knowledge of the enemy ahead of the present situation—in effect, it foretells what the enemy will do. Physical intelligence, on the other hand, just reports on the present situation. The fundamental difference between them is that physical evidence merely confirms enemy intentions, while verbal evidence predicts them.

For the first 4,000 years of warfare, physical intelligence supplied nearly all information. World War I changed this. The conditions of the war fostered the new kinds of verbal information-gathering engendered by the French and industrial revolutions—many prisoner interrogations, a daily press, above all radio and telephone intercepts. Verbal intelligence became more important than physical. It gave enough commanders enough time in enough cases to win perceptible numbers of victories. It awarded Germany her greatest triumph—Tannenberg—and contributed substantially to the defeat of Russia. Largely because of it, intelligence became what it had never been before: a significant instrument of war.

At last it convinced the German generals of its value. They finally acknowledged this in the single most important event in the history of German military intelligence. In contradistinction to their disbanding of the intelligence branches of General Headquarters at the end of the 1866 and 1870 wars, in 1919 they set up a permanent unit for the general evaluation of intelligence for the first time. Intelligence had arrived.

It had done so in the pattern of World War I, and it persisted in this pattern. Almost all the sources of information of World War II had existed in World War I, and the German army of 1939 reproduced many of the organizations for exploiting these sources that were operating in 1918. In the same way, the heightened acquisitiveness of intelligence, its potential for victory, its recognition (though reluctant) by the generals as an essential factor in war—these characteristics, forged in the original total war, endured in its successor. The First World War shaped German military intelligence in the Second.

The Institutions of Control

BERLIN. The Bendlerstrasse. A modernistic concrete office building. The tan of its stucco warmed its impersonal façade, with its four rows of identical windows, and made it less forbidding. Behind, innumerable wings branched out and crossed, forming a multitude of large and small light courts.

This was the structure that housed the Armed Forces High Command. It should have formed the focal point of German military power and hence of its World War II intelligence organization. It did neither; indeed, the Armed Forces High Command never even had its own unit to evaluate intelligence until halfway through the war. Better than any other fact, this epitomizes the German attitude toward military intelligence in World War II.

Contrary to the image of a monolithic state that emanated from Nazi Germany, no single high-level body controlled intelligence. The various collecting agencies went their own ways. And their findings streamed together only in the mind of Adolf Hitler.

Germany's intelligence apparatus was extensive and varied. All the information-gathering mechanisms of a modern industrial state, including those normally serving peaceful or domestic ends, such as the Foreign Office or political parties, strained to aid the war effort. But this apparatus was also, in Hitler's dictatorship, somewhat disorganized and unregimented. Sometimes several agencies had the same function and so competed against one another; sometimes an agency that belonged to one command sent its output to another.

The complex had not sprung into life full-formed in 1939. Some parts had evolved during the industrial revolution. Much of the military intelligence pattern had emerged during World War I. In the first decade following her defeat, Germany, undeterred by the restrictions of the Treaty of Versailles, restored her military intelligence organs in that pattern; after

Hitler assumed power, restoration became expansion for these organs as for the armed services as a whole. The newest elements of intelligence were the agencies of the Nazi party, which came into being only in 1930 and later.

During World War II, the intelligence complex existed within four areas of society: the armed forces, government ministries, the Nazi party, and the private sector.

A survey of the individual agencies and of the institutions within which they operated will photograph the whole mechanism in a unique snapshot. And it will chart their interrelationships, without which their working cannot be understood.

In the Weimar Republic, the president, the head of state, nominally held the supreme command of the armed forces. Under him the Reich defense minister exercised the actual command power. This situation existed on 30 January 1933 when Adolf Hitler, leader of the plurality party in the Reichstag, became chancellor and thus head of government. Upon the death the following year of the president, Field Marshal von Hindenburg, Hitler merged the office of president into that of chancellor. He thereby became nominal head of the armed forces. It was his first step in gaining absolute control of them. On 4 February 1938, after the Gestapo providentially discovered that the war minister (the new title of the defense minister) had married an ex-prostitute, Hitler abolished the war ministry, arrogated to himself "direct personal" command over all the armed forces, and elevated the ministry's main office into a new Oberkommando der Wehrmacht (OKW), or Armed Forces High Command. He directed that, "as my military staff directly under my command," the OKW handle "the unified preparation of Reich defense in all areas according to my directives." It was the second step.

General Wilhelm Keitel became chief, OKW. Thickset, sixtyish, Keitel was an indefatigable mediocrity, a tireless clerk. When Hitler, seeking someone to head his new staff, asked about him, the war minister replied, "Oh, Keitel, there's no question of him—he's just the man who runs my office." Hitler seized upon this. "That's exactly the man I'm looking for!" Believing in Hitler as Germany's savior and grateful to him for his advancement, constantly in Hitler's presence and so under his influence, Keitel became utterly devoted to him. After the bomb that was intended to kill Hitler exploded on 20 July 1944, Keitel picked himself out of the dust and wildly embraced his chief, crying, "Mein Führer! You're alive! You're alive!" Later that year, when it became legal for members of the armed forces to join the Nazi party, he joined. Keitel regarded it as his job to support Hitler and smooth things for him. At situation conferences, he constantly interjected words or phrases of agreement with Hitler. He never opposed him, except perhaps once, never supported commanders

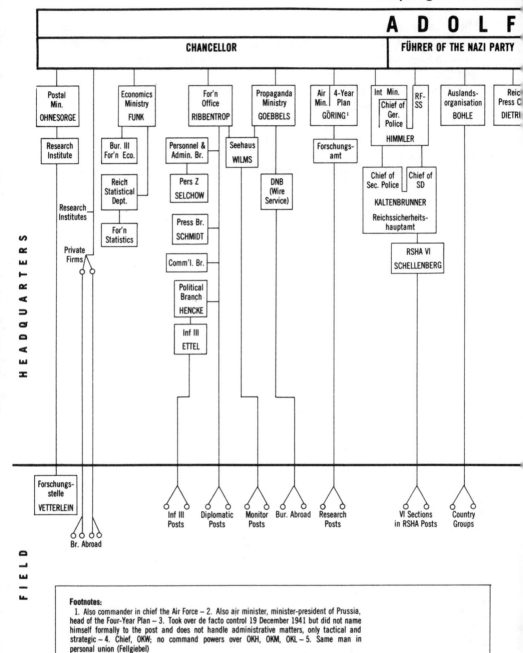

Footnotes:
1. Also commander in chief the Air Force – 2. Also air minister, minister-president of Prussia, head of the Four-Year Plan – 3. Took over de facto control 19 December 1941 but did not name himself formally to the post and does not handle administrative matters, only tactical and strategic – 4. Chief, OKW; no command powers over OKH, OKM, OKL – 5. Same man in personal union (Fellgiebel)

Abbreviations:

Adm. Administration	Comm'l Commercial	For'n Foreign	Ofc. Office
B'n Battalion	Comms. Communications	Ger. German	Prod. Production
Br. Branches	Dep't Department	Gr. Group	Recon. Reconnaissance
Bur. Bureaus	Div. Divs. Division, Divisions	Int. Interior	RF-SS Reichsführer SS
Ch. Chief	E. East	Intel. Intelligence	Sec. Security
Cmds. Commands	Eco. Economy, Economies, Economics	Interrog. Interrogation	S. South
C in C Commander in Chief	Eval. Evaluation	Min. Minister, Ministry	SE. Southeast
			W. West

Germany's intelligence organization

Foreign Intelligence at End of 1943

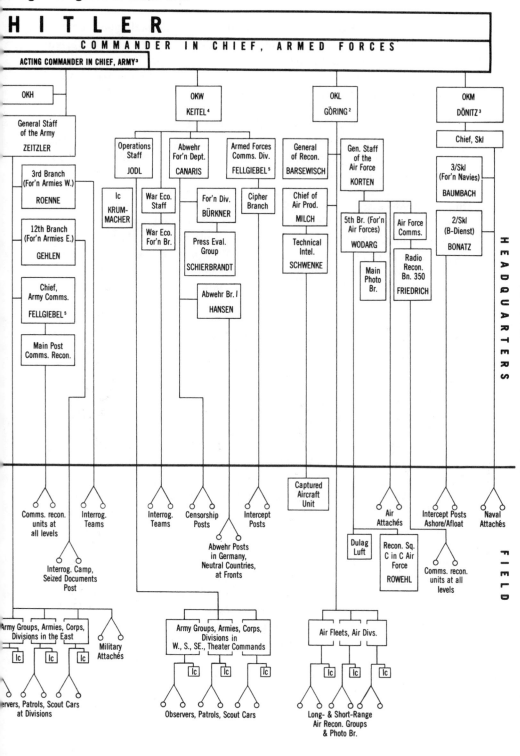

who opposed him. He shielded him from unpleasant intelligence on the ground that it would only disturb him. Keitel did whatever Hitler bid, even if he himself thought it harmed the military effort, or if it contradicted some other order just given out. He had, an observer summarized, loyalty but no character. But if he had been otherwise, he would simply have been replaced.

The most important unit under him was the OKW's Operations Staff. Its head was General Alfred Jodl, thin-lipped, narrow-faced, taciturn, and highly intelligent. If anyone could be regarded as Hitler's chief of staff, it was he. In 1936, he had turned down an offer to become chief of the general staff of the new Luftwaffe to remain in the Operations Staff's embryonic predecessor. He too believed in Hitler, but not as unreservedly as Keitel. He sometimes joked caustically about him, and sometimes argued stiffly with him. Usually he proceeded more diplomatically. At the situation conferences at which he reported on the OKW matters, he slipped the unpleasant news of divisional withdrawals in between colorful accounts of individual episodes. He skirted difficult matters and only later brought them up and persuaded Hitler to yield or even to reverse himself. In 1944 he too joined the party. He wrote well, and many of Hitler's war directives and the Wehrmacht communiqués came from his pen. One of the last things he put it to was the surrender document in the schoolhouse at Rheims.

The mandate of the OKW would seem to have enabled it to prepare controlling war plans for all three services in a coordinated strategy, rather like the Joint Chiefs of Staff in the United States. But it did not do so. In the first place, as a staff it had no command functions. Keitel's powers ran only within the OKW itself; he could not issue orders to the commanders in chief of the services. Only Hitler could do that—though he often issued them through Keitel. In the second place, each commander in chief jealously maintained his independence, each with his reasons. The army was the most powerful and, for continental Germany, the most important service. The navy could not let a landlubber handle its special problems. The air force was commanded by Hermann Göring, whose party closeness to Hitler gave him far more power than Keitel. Never did the three meet to plan operations jointly. Third, Hitler wanted to reserve for himself the prerogative of drafting such important plans; he feared the concentration of authority that that might give others. So he basically used the OKW, specifically its Operations Staff, as a megaphone to elaborate his ideas. He busied it with current projects that left no time for long-range planning and kept it small—some 50 to 60 officers. The imposing title of the High Command of the Armed Forces in no way matched its powers.

Then, in a series of decisions in 1941, Hitler divided the fronts into eastern and other theaters. He assigned the west (France), the south

(Italy and Africa), and the southeast (Balkans) to the OKW and the east (Russia) to the OKH, the Oberkommando des Heeres, or Army High Command. This meant that the OKH fought the war against the Soviet Union and the OKW that against Britain and America. In effect Hitler reduced the Armed Forces High Command to another Army High Command, making two uncoordinate agencies in a sense equal and therefore rival. It short-circuited the lines of command for army intelligence agencies concerned with the western Allies and thus servicing the OKW.

Within the old war ministry, several agencies had performed intelligence functions. These the OKW inherited, and during the war it added others.

- Military espionage was run by Abwehr I—Branch I of the Abwehr. (This word means "defense"; here it implies defense against spies, counterintelligence, which was one of the functions of the Abwehr— but not the only one.) The Abwehr consisted of three branches (II dealt with sabotage and minority uprisings, III with counterespionage), which in turn formed part of the Amt Auslandsnachrichten und Abwehr, or Foreign Information and Counterintelligence Department. Its head was Admiral Canaris. Owing to the department's being an element of the OKW, everything to do with spies—recruiting, insertion, control, communications—was run centrally by Abwehr I for all three armed services.

- Various groups of the Foreign Information Division, generally called "Ausland," the other part of Canaris's department, gathered, evaluated, and distributed reports, especially from the foreign press, on the domestic and foreign affairs of other countries that might affect the military situation.

- The Cipher Branch intercepted foreign press, diplomatic, and military transmissions, cryptanalyzed those in code or cipher, and distributed the results. It belonged to the Armed Forces Communications Division, another element of the OKW. It was commonly referred to as "OKW/Chi" or just "Chi," from its German title, Chiffrierabteilung.

- Postal censorship was conducted during the war by posts subordinated to the Foreign Information and Counterintelligence Department.

- Foreign economic intelligence bearing on military matters was controlled and evaluated by the War Economy Branch of the War Economy and Armaments Department. Starting in 1942, the department lost functions to Albert Speer, the new minister for armaments and munitions, and changed its name several times, as did its foreign intelligence section.

- A tiny intelligence staff was created within the Operations Staff in January of 1943 to pick out items of importance to the OKW and present them to Jodl. It did little evaluation of its own, basing its own reports on the digests supplied by the service intelligence agencies.

Berlin, showing the headquarters of the main intelligence agencies

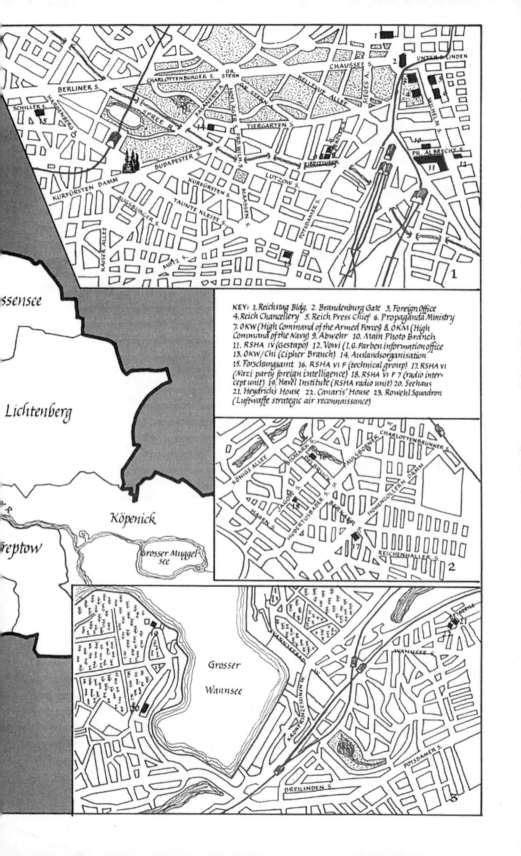

KEY: 1. Reichstag Bldg. 2. Brandenburg Gate 3. Foreign Office 4. Reich Chancellery 5. Reich Press Chief 6. Propaganda Ministry 7. OKW (High Command of the Armed Forces) 8. OKM (High Command of the Navy) 9. Abwehr 10. Main Photo Branch 11. RSHA IV (Gestapo) 12. Vowi (I.G. Farben information office 13. OKW/Chi (Cipher Branch) 14. Auslandsorganisation 15. Forschungsamt 16. RSHA VI F (technical group) 17. RSHA VI (Nazi party foreign intelligence) 18. RSHA VI F 7 (radio intercept unit) 19. Havel Institute (RSHA radio unit) 20. Seehaus 21. Heydrich's House 22. Canaris' House 23. Rowehl Squadron (Luftwaffe strategic air reconnaissance)

All of these organizations except that within the Operations Staff maintained field units in addition to their headquarters, which were located at or near the Bendlerstrasse or Führer Headquarters.

Under Hitler stood, in addition to the OKW, the individual services. Each had its own command. In 1935, the same year that Hitler reintroduced compulsory universal military service and began his vast enlargement of the army, two important administrative developments took place. As of 1 March, Hitler publicly established the Luftwaffe, or air force, as the third branch of the Wehrmacht. And on 1 June the high commands of the three services got their uniform titles: Oberkommando des Heeres (OKH), or High Command of the Army; Oberkommando der Kriegsmarine (OKM), or High Command of the Navy; and Oberkommando der Luftwaffe (OKL), or High Command of the Air Force. Each had its commander in chief; the Luftwaffe's, Hermann Göring, was simultaneously aviation minister, among other important posts.

After Hitler's assumption of personal command in 1938, these commanders in chief, who had previously reported to the war minister, now reported to Hitler. One major change occurred in this subordination during the war. On 19 December 1941, a few days after the failure of his Russian blitzkrieg became clear, Hitler fired Field Marshal Walther von Brauchitsch as commander in chief of the army and himself took operational command, though he did not formally assume the title. This was the third and final step in Hitler's conquest of the army. Henceforth, in absolute and direct control, he issued battle orders to commanders at the front.

Immediately beneath the head of the army ranged the commanders in the field and office heads at headquarters. In peacetime, the latter included, among others, the chiefs of the Army Ordnance Department, the Army Administration Department, and the Army Personnel Department, the inspectors of the several arms and services, and—the first among these equals—the chief of the General Staff of the Army. Upon mobilization, he went into the field. At home, a commander of army equipment and of the replacement army came into being to take over from him the massive task of raising, training, and equipping troops for the wartime army. All of the headquarters offices except personnel became subordinated to this commander. Like the chief of the general staff, his only superior was the commander in chief of the army or, later, Hitler.

The general staff moved into its field headquarters, codenamed ZEPPELIN, in two semicircles of A-roofed, reinforced bunkers, at Zossen, 20 miles south of Berlin. From there it directed the fighting forces.

Despite changes in name, this agency descended directly from the old Great General Staff of Moltke and Schlieffen. World War I's General Staff of the Field Army demobilized on 1 February 1919 back to the Great General Staff. The Treaty of Versailles ordered that it "shall be dissolved and may not be reconstituted in any form." The day after the army "abolished" it, it reformed it on 1 October 1919 as the Troops Department. "The form changes; the spirit remains the same," said the army chief. Throughout the 1920s evasion of Versailles, the Troops Department preserved the forbidden traditions of the general staff. Its 3rd branch, T 3, handled intelligence. On 1 July 1935, the Troops Department shed its disguise and reappeared as the General Staff of the Army. This title held throughout the war. T 3 became the 3rd branch, Foreign Armies, of the General Staff of the Army.

The chief of the general staff in 1939 was Franz Halder. An artilleryman, short, crew-cut, pince-nezed, reflective, quiet spoken, he was a Bavarian heading what had once been the Prussian general staff. Though he lacked the fire of greatness—he had to work things out on paper rather than, as the Germans say, "shaking it out of his arm"—he was the complete master of his job, with a good strategical brain, revered by his subordinates. At the situation conferences he personified the highest traditions of the general staff in knowledge, judgment, and style, but Hitler's vulgar dynamism apparently threw him off and left him somewhat flustered. His internal conflict between his hatred for Hitler and his obligation to Germany tended to incapacitate him. His arguments with Hitler grew more frequent, but Halder never had the courage to resign. He waited until Hitler kicked him out, on 24 September 1942. Because of his later resistance, he ended the war in Dachau.

His successor was Kurt Zeitzler, much more the man of action and at first much more pliable. He had performed with brilliance and energy in solving complex supply problems during the French and Russian campaigns. Insensitive and straightforward, he spoke in a loud voice and carried out his orders with energy. As chief of staff to the commander in chief west, he "buzzed back and forth," Hitler said, "like a hornet." The Führer saw the Canadian test landing at Dieppe in the summer of 1942 as an invasion attempt and ascribed the Allied failure largely to Zeitzler. So after he fired Halder, he jumped Zeitzler several ranks to make him chief of the general staff. His overwhelmed gratitude, his diminished authority compared to that of Halder, and his lack of knowledge about the Russian front made it difficult for him to oppose Hitler much at first. But later he too increasingly disputed Hitler's military plans—sometimes losing his temper. Hitler's manner grew more distant, and early in July 1944 he fired him.

Next came the famed panzer general, Heinz Guderian. In 1941 Hitler had relieved him of his command; now he called him back. Though the appointment seemed to some the climax to the career of the shaper of Germany's armored forces, it shocked others, who regarded Guderian as a one-sided specialist and a battlefield bull without the temperament to be a chief of the general staff. He was impetuous and gruff and spoke roughly even at the briefing conferences. Though he, like Zeitzler, urged the general staff to prove its faith in National Socialism, he was not afraid to argue with Hitler, once even shouting at him before a large group. But none of it mattered. Hitler had long since taken the detailed direction of the war into his own hands. A month before the end, when Guderian talked of peace, Hitler replaced him with Hans Krebs.

Such were the men who led the General Staff of the Army during World War II. They were the immediate superiors of the heads of the 12 branches of the general staff—operations, organization, mapping, among others—and of the agencies attached to it at mobilization, such as transportation, communications, and weather forecasting.

Two of the branches evaluated intelligence. These were the 3rd, Foreign Armies West, and the 12th, Foreign Armies East, whose most successful and famous head was General Reinhard Gehlen. (The odd numeration came about because originally only the 3rd branch existed for intelligence, called Foreign Armies. As German and foreign rearmament progressed, its work increased. So on 10 November 1938, a second branch was created. It took a new number; the other retained the old.) The two divided the world on the principle that "People who wear their shirts inside their pants belong to the west, those who wear theirs outside, to the east." To them flowed information on foreign armies from all sources—spies, codebreaking, prisoner interrogations, front-line observations, and so on. These they weighed as to their probable truth or falsehood and their meaning and then assembled into a picture of the organization, strength, and intentions of the armies of other nations, particularly antagonists. They were the key high-level agencies. A superior once summed up their task by saying, "What I want to know from you is: What is the enemy doing?"

On the same day that the two branches came into being, an Oberquartiermeister IV (O Qu IV), or fourth assistant chief of the general staff, was also created as their superior. He sought to maintain the unity of intelligence evaluation and to produce a balanced overall picture. It didn't work. For a variety of reasons, some administrative, political, and personal, others stemming from the separation of the OKW and OKH theaters of war, which rendered half the O Qu IV's work of no interest to the chief of the general staff, who dealt only with Russia, Zeitzler dissolved the post on 9 November 1942. Thenceforth, the two branches stood immediately beneath him.

Other units subordinate to the chief of the general staff also produced or evaluated intelligence. The signal corps command contained the radio intelligence headquarters. Military attachés collected information in foreign countries and transmitted it via the Foreign Office to the general staff.

The forces in the field likewise gathered and evaluated intelligence. Some elements specialized in this collection, such as patrols, reconnaissance troops, artillery observers, interrogators of prisoners of war, translators of captured documents, and signal intelligence units. Others did it as a by-product of their fighting. They captured prisoners, removed papers from the dead, reported what they saw. All this went to the intelligence officers of the staffs of the field commands.

Such staffs began formally at the division level and extended upward through corps, army, and army group. Though they varied in size, they were essentially organized alike. At army groups, armies, and corps, a chief of staff directed the staff and deputized for the commander. The chief of staff's principal assistant, the I a, or first general staff officer, handled troop operations. Division staffs had no chief; the I a post included that job. The staffs' intelligence officer was the I c, or third general staff officer. (Among the other officers on the staff were the I d for training, the III for judge advocate affairs, the IV c for veterinary matters, the signal officer, the artillery staff officer, and the VI, or Nazi guidance officer. Home staffs in Germany had an I b for supply, but at the front a staff quartermaster handled this.) The chief of staff, the I a, and the I c (except at divisions and sometimes at corps) were normally members of the general staff.

The air force and the navy did not require the massive intelligence input that the army did because their contacts with the enemy were neither so broad nor so continual. Consequently their intelligence services were smaller, just as they themselves were.

The air force's organization greatly resembled that of the army, from which it sprang. Its central evaluation agency, Foreign Air Forces, was the 5th Branch of the Luftwaffe general staff. During the war an Air Force Operations Staff precipitated out as a leading element of the general staff, and the 5th Branch became widely called the Operations Staff/I c. On the other hand, its two geographic subdivisions were called Foreign Air Forces East and Foreign Air Forces West. Regulations assigned it the task of evaluating foreign intelligence touching on the air war. This included gathering material on bombing targets. A photo center evaluated aerial photographs of strategic import. The air force's special prisoner-of-war interrogation center, Dulag Luft, was a field unit of the 5th Branch.

The Oberkommando der Luftwaffe embraced other units that gathered or evaluated intelligence. The headquarters of the communications intelligence organization stood under the chief of Air Force Communications. A special long-range reconnaissance squadron filled the OKL's requirements in strategic aerial photography. Air attachés supplied information from abroad.

Like the army, the air force maintained intelligence units in the field. About one of every seven of its airplanes were reconnoiterers. The long-range squadrons worked mainly by camera; the short-range mainly by eye. Their photographs were developed and interpreted at photographic sections at the various field headquarters. Liaison officers at army commands transmitted the ground troops' requests for aerial reconnaissance to the squadrons and reported back the results. At OKL headquarters, a general officer, whose title changed during the war, supervised the air reconnaissance organization.

Field radio intelligence units listened to opposing air units. The air force staffs with the fighting forces, patterned largely after the army's, included I c officers for intelligence evaluation; the heads of the photographic sections and of communications, which controlled radio intelligence, served on these staffs.

The navy centralized its intelligence organization tightly within its high command in Berlin. A few months after the start of the war, the OKM, in a reorganization, created the Seekriegsleitung, abbreviated "Skl," the Naval War Command. Three subordinate sections produced and/or consumed intelligence:

- The 1/Skl, the first branch of the Seekriegsleitung, the Operations Branch. It made the enemy-situation judgments during the course of reaching command decisions.
- The 3/Skl, the Foreign Navies Branch, which evaluated incoming raw intelligence and passed it to the 1/Skl. One of its most important sections kept track of all foreign commercial vessels.
- The B-Dienst, short for Beobachtungs-Dienst, or Observation Service, the usual name for the naval communications intelligence unit. Together with naval communications, it formed the Marinenachrichtendienst, a title that was convenient, if sometimes confusing, for the German word "Nachrichten," which basically denotes "news" or "information," also means both "communications" and "intelligence." The Marinenachrichtendienst was originally the 2/Skl. But the immense growth of the B-Dienst raised it from a branch to a division. Later in the war, after the U-boat section took over the 2/Skl slot, the division became in effect the 4/Skl. The B-Dienst was technically the division's Radio Reconnaissance Branch.

Two men ran the Kriegsmarine during the war. Grand Admiral Erich Raeder, who had commanded since 1928, was succeeded on 31 January 1943 by small, narrow-faced Grand Admiral Karl Dönitz, a devoted admirer of Hitler. As commander of submarines, he had developed the wolfpack tactics that almost won the Battle of the Atlantic for Germany. He retained the U-boat post when he became commander in chief of the navy.

Though the armed services naturally concentrated more than any other sector of German society on military intelligence, several ministerial bodies also contributed information.

The Foreign Office stood first among these. Its diplomats abroad swept up news in the traditional way of foreign services. Much of it dealt with the crucial questions of peace and war. The Political Branch received and evaluated this. The Commercial Branch handled economic intelligence. The

Foreign Office also had its own codebreakers, concealed in the Personnel and Administration Branch as Pers Z. Its Press Branch read the foreign press for political and economic news.

The foreign minister was Joachim von Ribbentrop. He had impressed Hitler with his knowledge of foreign countries and his fluency in English and French, gained through his work as a champagne salesman. He became Hitler's chief advisor on foreign affairs and scored a diplomatic triumph by negotiating the Anglo-German naval treaty of 1935, which Hitler thought freed him from the danger of British interference in his aggressive plans. Soon afterward he became foreign minister. He quickly became regarded by all, Germans and foreigners alike, as stupid, vain, and pompous. Once, when he received an American diplomat, he harangued him for two hours, never stopping except for translation, all the time sitting with his arms extended on the sides of his chair and with his eyes closed. He jealously but in wartime rather unsuccessfully guarded his bureaucratic empire from attrition, spending half his time in these internecine squabbles.

A grasp for power was one of the motives for his creation of an intelligence agency unconventional for diplomats: a spy service based on the missions abroad. It was called Inf III, short for Informationsstelle III or Information Post III (Inf I and II being propaganda units). The same motive led him to start up a radio-news monitoring service, the Sonderdienst Seehaus, or Lake House Special Service. But here he lost a little: he had to share it with Josef Goebbels, the propaganda minister. Goebbels also had, as a source of foreign news, the official press agency, DNB, or Deutsche Nachrichten Büro, a government organ.

Another ministerial body incorporated offices for intelligence, chiefly economic. The Reich Economics Ministry had a Foreign Economy Bureau and the ministry's quasi-independent Reich Statistical Department had a Central Desk for Foreign Statistics and Foreign Research. They fed much material to the OKW's War Economy and Armaments Department.

One of the most successful of Germany's intelligence agencies was a quasi-ministry, the Forschungsamt (Research Department). Set up in 1933, it tapped telephones, intercepted diplomatic, commercial, and press radio messages, and broke codes. Though operating independently, it maintained, for secrecy, the most numerous and complicated administrative links in Germany. It was a national agency, getting its money from the national budget, but it was administratively responsible to a state government—that of Prussia, which, however, did not give it its assignments. In addition, it tacked onto its title, as camouflage, "of the Reich Air Ministry," though it had nothing to do with that body. Later it carried its officials on the lists of the Four-Year Plan. It could tangle its lines so because they all led to one person: Hermann Göring. He was simultaneously the minister-president of Prussia, the Reich air minister, and head of the Four-Year Plan.

Göring alone controlled the work of the Forschungsamt. Indeed, it seemed at times to serve as his personal communications intelligence service.

Political power in the Third Reich lay, of course, with the NSDAP, the Nationalsozialistische Deutsche Arbeiterpartei (National Socialist German Workers' Party), or Nazi party. It had an intelligence service of its own, the SD, the Sicherheitsdienst (Security Service) which included an arm for foreign intelligence. Except for the Forschungsamt, it was the only major German intelligence service to come into being only long after World War I.

The SD's primary function was to alert the Nazi party to threats to it. It delivered these warnings to its parent organization, the black-uniformed SS, the Schutz-Staffel, or protection squadron. The SS had originated in 1923 as Hitler's bodyguard and had expanded the concept of protection to the entire party. Heinrich Himmler, crew-cut, bespectacled, a brilliant organizer, ruthless, totally dedicated to Hitler and his anti-Semitic mission, became chief—Reichsführer SS—in 1929; he was destined to preside over the entire totalitarian apparatus of secret police, concentration camps, slave labor, gas chambers, and SS military units: a state within the state.

After the Nazis had suddenly emerged as a major party in the elections of September 1930, the national and state governments tightened their surveillance of it. Himmler soon recognized that he needed an intelligence unit to warn him of their activities. At the same time, a young ex-naval officer, cashiered on a matter of honor involving a girl, was looking for a job. A letter recommending him wound up in Himmler's hands. The letter spoke of him correctly as a former "Nachrichtenoffizier," meaning "signals officer," but Himmler took the word in another sense to mean "intelligence officer." He also liked the young man's Nordic good looks in an accompanying photograph, and had him summoned.

The tall, big-hipped, blond man of 27 arrived at Himmler's chicken farm outside Munich on 14 June 1931. "I need an I c man," said the SS chieftain, using army terminology. He gave him 20 minutes to write out how he thought such a service should operate. The young job-seeker had never had anything to do with intelligence, but he organized his essay on military lines and sprinkled it with military jargon. Himmler hired him on the spot. Thus began the skyrocket career of Reinhard Heydrich. In its ruthless elevation of might and intelligence to virtual control of the nation, it was one of the most significant careers of the Third Reich, and in its effect on German foreign intelligence, one of the most baleful.

It began inauspiciously enough on 10 August 1931 in a shared office in party headquarters in Munich with Heydrich sorting clippings and other incoming information. But he lost no time. On the 26th, he lectured at Nazidom's Brown House headquarters on "battle methods of the enemy." On 4 September he issued an order that SS formations set up an information net. In November, he won his first important victory. Discovering that a long-time party member in the Bavarian police was spying for the police, Heydrich "turned" him so effectively that not only did the police lose their information on the party, the party gained intelligence about police activities. The next month, Heydrich was twice promoted, was given three clerks for his card indexes of informers, and got married.

But the SS was not the only party body to have an intelligence organ. The brown-shirted SA, or Sturmabteilung (storm battalion), the party's street army, had set up an intelligence unit in 1930. The party's organization management, a local propaganda head, and a local party branch all had their own intelligence units. But various indiscretions and police actions all but eradicated the SA's unit, and by mid-1932 the others had also faded away, perhaps in the face of competition from Heydrich. On 19 July 1932, Heydrich, who until then had technically only been "with" the intelligence service—Himmler having retained the headship for himself—became the leader of what was thenceforth called the Sicherheitsdienst. Ten days later, he won yet another promotion, to SS colonel.

By September, the infant SD had outgrown party headquarters. After a brief stay in the newlyweds' two-room flat in Munich at Türkenstrasse 23, near the university and not far from the Bohemian center of Schwabing, the SD central office moved across town to a villa near the Nymphenburg Palace, at Zuccalistrasse 4. Heydrich and his wife lived in a separate building on the grounds. Luxurious it was not: one of the now seven employees worked at a round iron garden table with a broken saucer as an ashtray. For since the SD was a party organ, its money, for salaries as well as supplies, came from the Nazi treasury. These funds flowed more copiously after Hitler became chancellor, with the concomitant increase in members, but they were never large enough. Once Heydrich requested a monthly budget of *RM* 700,690; the party treasurer indignantly replied that the total monthly membership income was only *RM* 710,000! In fact the SD was getting *RM* 350,000 a month, of which only *RM* 80,000 came from the party treasury, the remaining *RM* 270,000 being supplied by the office of the Deputy Führer, Rudolf Hess.

The Nazi takeover of the national and then of the state governments offered government posts to party officials, and they grasped them with the alacrity of party winners seizing the spoils in any parliamentary system. On the March day in 1933 that demonstrations forced the Bavarian government to capitulate to the Nazis, Himmler became police president of Munich. Under him, Heydrich grabbed his own power base. With this as a start, Himmler went on to seize control of the political police in all the states, completing this by April 1934. Heydrich took police posts under him, the most important that of head of the secret state police in Prussia.

Paradoxically, however, the Nazi assumption of power jeopardized the existence of the SD. Its job was to help protect the party. But the party was merging with the state: Hitler's official government style included his party title of "Führer" and a 1933 Law for Securing the Unity of Party and State proclaimed the party "the bearer of the German state-idea" and named party officials to the government cabinet. The enemies of the party became the enemies of the state, and they could be fought with the means of the state. The SS and the SD had lost much of their reason for being. But Himmler and Heydrich were not anxious to surrender any power, much less that which had brought them to where they were. They preserved their party organs.

The retention of the SD side by side with the government secret police soon duplicated efforts and muddled responsibility. Heydrich resolved this problem in two ways. One was to make distinctions without differences in defining jurisdictions for the rival agencies. He decreed that the police would handle individual cases, while the SD was to keep watch for ideological dangers. That such dangers present themselves as individual instances mocked his effort. Confusion constantly arose as to which of Heydrich's agencies would perform a particular task. But he preferred a confusion that doubled his power base to a clarity that would have halved it.

Heydrich's other solution for the problem of the superfluity of the SD was to attack. He would not let party intelligence wither in the shade of government bureaucracy. On the contrary. He would engross state prerogatives for his party agency. This would legitimize its powers and—just as important—would add to them.

Before he did this, however, he would have to secure his own position within the party. He had expanded his net of secret informants, who reported on anti-Hitler statements by members of the population and on other antiparty trends. He had organized the SD into four administrative levels to channel and evaluate this information. Himmler had elevated the SD to a department of the SS. Heydrich had won an important victory when Hitler, not wanting to see this strong support of his regime buckle, extended his protection after the SD had suffered a minor defeat in Braunschweig. He ordained that it was to take over a rival party intelligence service, apparently the only one still existing.

This was within the party's Foreign Political Department, which was headed by the party's chief ideologue, Arthur Rosenberg, author of *The Myth of the Twentieth Century,* the most important Nazi book after *Mein Kampf.* Rosenberg's intelligence chief was Arthur Schumann, 32, who had originally joined the party in 1922 under membership number 7,956, had fought for it—and had intelligence ambitions of his own. Schumann had headed the intelligence unit of the party's organization management until Heydrich had crushed it. He himself had nimbly danced over to Rosenberg's department. Here he organized party members in 60 countries into a network of agents, thus again threatening Heydrich's hegemonial ambitions. Now, with Hitler's order, Heydrich had apparently defeated him a second time. But Schumann did not hasten to comply. And meanwhile the party's German Labor Front had developed a counterintelligence office of its own.

By June of 1934, however, several counterforces were helping Heydrich. Himmler had gained the post of political police chief in the last of the German states. Hitler was planning the Night of the Long Knives—the assassination by the SS of the homosexual leaders of the SA, the burgeoning radical power of whose 2 million members menaced him. He perhaps wanted to block any flow of information to the SA, or to induce the SD to supply him with further evidence of brownshirt crimes, or to reward Himmler, or to do all of these. Whatever the reason, he granted the SD its long-sought monopoly in party intelligence. An order of 9 June 1934, signed by the Deputy Führer, Rudolf Hess, required the transfer of Schumann's "apparatus" to the SD by 15 July and decreed that "apart from the Sicherheitsdienst RFSS [Reichsführer SS], no intelligence or counterespionage service of the party shall exist." Heydrich had, at 30, won exclusive control of all Nazi intelligence.

With his rivals eliminated, he returned to his goal of having his party organ invade governmental duties. A first step came when on 4 July 1934, four days after the Night of the Long Knives, Himmler's Bavarian police recognized the SD as the "single political and counterespionage intelligence service"—this recognition was not limited to the party—and forbade others from operating in Bavaria. Less than three weeks later the SD intruded upon an area hitherto exclusively governmental: counterintelligence. Two official bodies, the Abwehr and the Prussian secret state police, were already handling different aspects of this work. But even though Heydrich was head of the Prussian agency, he contended that it and the Abwehr "did not appear to guarantee sufficient security." So on 28 July, the SD, in the form of a single new official, Heinz Jost, assumed the task of protecting Germany against foreign spy services. It was the start of the SD's fateful involvement in foreign intelligence.

Signs began to accumulate that Heydrich's looting of government power was succeeding. The Bavarian police acknowledged that "the SD participates in fulfilling all duties of state protection." The SD headquarters moved from Munich, the party headquarters, to Berlin, the national capital. No one objected when, some time before 1936, Heydrich institutionalized his party encroachment into the governmental terrain of foreign intelligence; he expanded Jost's section into a whole new branch of the SD for that work. This was Branch III, Ausland, of the central SD Administration. (Branches I and II handled administration and domestic intelligence.) Heydrich's invasion of government accelerated. A few months later, on 17 June 1936, Hitler created a national police within the Interior Ministry and named Himmler Reichsführer SS und Chef der Deutschen Polizei. Under him, as chief of the German police, stood offices for both the uniformed and plainclothes police. The latter, consisting of criminal police (detectives) and political police (Gestapo), formed the Security Police Administration. Its head was Reinhard Heydrich—still also the head of the SD. In 1935 and again in 1936, he signed agreements with Canaris. In theory they delimited their conflicting areas of competence; in actuality they legitimized Heydrich's. By the following year, the party's organization book was labeling the SD "the political information unit of the movement and the state." In 1938, even the bureaucracy, whose rationalism melted before the party's zeal, conceded that the SD would thenceforth be "active in government assignments."

At the same time, Heydrich was moving into another government domain: that of the Foreign Office. He concluded police accords with more than half a dozen countries and attached Gestapo liaison men to two German missions. Shortly after the war started, he and Himmler won from Ribbentrop an exemption from a Führer decree that "for the duration of the war, all representatives of the civil authorities or the party offices [abroad] . . . are to come under the authority of the head of the German [diplomatic] mission." They could thenceforth send their own agents abroad and control them there without Foreign Office interference.

These pressures and movements culminated on 27 September 1939 in the creation of an agency that combined Heydrich's party and government organs. This was the Reichssicherheitshauptamt, or RSHA, the Reich Security Administration. It laminated the Security Police Administration and the SD Administration. For example, Branch III, Ausland, of the SD Administration became Department VI, foreign intelligence, of the RSHA. (The RSHA's other departments were: I, personnel; II, administration; III, domestic intelligence; IV, Gestapo; V, detectives; VII [added much later], ideological research and evaluation.) Reinhard Heydrich headed it with the rank of SS lieutenant general and the title of Chef der Sicherheitspolizei und des SD (chief of the security police and of the SD).

The RSHA formed one of the 12 SS administrations. (Among the others were those for the uniformed police, for economy and administration [which ran the concentration camps], for eastern resettlement, for personnel, and for the Waffen-SS, which fought at the front.) Within and without it, the SD persisted. The members of Department IV remained members of the SD and continued to receive their pay checks from the party to the end of the war. The Gestapo and the detectives, on the other hand, were government employees. Field units of the RSHA, established in many cities of the Reich and the occupied territories, had the same hybrid organization. Abroad, police attachés in the German missions included RSHA VI personnel. Outside the RSHA, SD informers continued to rat.

The formation of the RSHA carried Heydrich to a peak of his power. Tall, blond, and blue-eyed, with a high forehead and spidery hands, a high-pitched voice and nervous staccato speech that seldom finished a sentence but always made its meaning clear, Heydrich, then in his late thirties, exuded a chill that caused many who feared him to hate him as well. He had no friends. Men drew back when he appeared. While many of Himmler's subordinates thought the Reichsführer SS personally kind, none of Heydrich's did. They did not enjoy accompanying him, as they sometimes had to, on his drinking and whoring expeditions through garish Berlin back streets. His handwriting was twisted and his prose contorted. But the exposition was logical. He was a passionate sportsman. He loved fencing especially, but he also liked to ski and to ride; he served as SS inspector for physical training. His "hardness" was the model for many an SS man. He was an outstanding violinist, who sometimes brought tears to the eyes of his listeners—and himself—with his delicate and sensitive playing.

His power, through his control of the Gestapo, was immense. But it did not satisfy him. Part of his program of adding government powers to his party ones was the assimilation of the military espionage service into his political one. An element in this program was his replacement in 1941 of the mediocre head of RSHA VI, Jost, with the energetic, polished, and youthful Walter Schellenberg. Another was his pursuit of Admiral Canaris. Though he maintained outward cordiality with the head of the Abwehr, who had been his superior on the training ship *Berlin* in the 1920s, he never ceased hounding the older man. When Canaris bought his squarish house at Betazeile 17 in southwest Berlin, Heydrich bought an angular one just around the corner, at Reifträgerweg 14. He pressed Canaris on 1 March 1942 to a revision of their 1936 agreement, nicknamed the "Ten Commandments." It had been evenly balanced; the new one disadvantaged the Abwehr. It granted powers to the security police and the SD, but only promises to Canaris's agency.

Heydrich's drive to ingest government powers continued to move forward against the Foreign Office. His SD fomented an unsuccessful revolt in Rumania and planned large-scale subversion in Iraq. He urged that police attachés be established within the German missions abroad. Ribbentrop counterproposed that they become part of the foreign service—in other words, that he control them. Heydrich simply overrode this, and on 8 August 1941, Ribbentrop signed an agreement permitting police attachés to join the missions and to remain in effect under SS control. Their reports, for example, went to Himmler directly. Very soon such attachés—nearly all of them Gestapo officials—were being built into the missions.

But the excesses of Heydrich's ambition thwarted completion of his plan. Eager to gain a territorial base of power, he had Hitler name him governor of rump Czechoslovakia. His official title was acting protector of Bohemia and Moravia; his unofficial—the butcher of Prague. On 4 June 1942 the Czech resistance rolled a bomb under his car and assassinated him. Hitler called him "irreplaceable" and in revenge wiped the town of Lidice from the face of the earth.

For six months Himmler ran the RSHA himself. Then, in January of

1943, he placed Ernst Kaltenbrunner at its head. Kaltenbrunner was a doctor of law from Linz, the Austrian industrial town in which Hitler had grown up, and had joined the SS at the end of 1931. Among his services was that of recruiting family friend Adolf Eichmann for the SS. Kaltenbrunner became SS leader of Austria in 1933, and after the Anschluss in 1938 became the senior SS and police commander in Vienna. He remained there for the next five years, doing his work adequately but showing no remarkable administrative ability. He was an ox, the combined stereotypes of a villain and a lumberjack with his thick neck and scarred, wooden face, slightly roughened speech, and coarse manner; only his viperlike eyes betrayed some flickerings of inner power. He chain-smoked and drank heavily. His IQ of 113 was one of the lowest of the Nazi leaders. But he had unquestionable abilities in deviousness and in sniffing out conspiracies, undoubted ruthlessness in quelling them, and a driving instinct for power.

He continued, for example, Heydrich's encroachment onto Foreign Office territory. The number of police attachés and assistants had risen, by October of 1943, to 73 in 19 missions. This naturally did not suffice, and the SD demanded—and got—more, including one in the Vatican. Sometimes SD meddling ruined things. When an SD agent's arms negotiations with Argentina were exposed, that country broke diplomatic relations with Germany and cost Hitler his last toehold in the western hemisphere. The next year, 1944, Kaltenbrunner pressured Ribbentrop into signing another agreement with Himmler. It basically reaffirmed the existing relationships. The first sentence of its point 4 expressed the pious assurance of cooperation between the two paladins of the Nazi dictator: "The foreign intelligence that comes from the RSHA will, insofar as it is of interest to the Führer, be submitted by the foreign minister to the Führer as RSHA material." The second sentence, however, made clear where control really lay. For it conceded that the Reichsführer SS could, "in his competence . . . himself tell the Führer about a report."

Kaltenbrunner demonstrated his own capacity for power most clearly when, a year after he took office, he realized one of Heydrich's oldest dreams. He wrenched the Abwehr from the military and subjugated it to his RSHA. On 12 February 1944, Hitler decreed the creation of "a unified German secret intelligence service" under SS control. Canaris was ousted. The new combined agency came into being on 1 June 1944; Abwehr I (espionage) metamorphosed into the main part of a new Military Department of the RSHA's Department VI. The Nazi party had finally conquered all German espionage.

Two other party elements also contributed to German military intelligence. The AO, the Auslandsorganisation (Foreign Organization) consisted of members of the Nazi party living outside Germany. Its cells sent information to Germany, mostly on the political situation in their host countries, but occasionally including military information. Its chief contribution, however, was in providing the names of potential spies.

The Nazi party press chief, who was also state secretary in the propaganda ministry, set up a special service to assemble the more important items from the wire services and the newspapers and to send them to him wherever he was, which was where Hitler was. He then gave them to the Führer.

Foremost among the collectors of intelligence in the private sector were the giant cartels and arms manufacturers. Such firms as I. G. Farben and Krupp scoured the technical press and had their representatives abroad keep their eyes and ears open for information of value to their commercial enterprises, which in a rearming Germany often meant military devices and supplies. They maintained elaborate information offices that often passed raw data and finished reports to the military authorities.

Less important were the numerous private research institutes. These usually analyzed economic data and submitted reports on them to the military. Near the end of 1943, they were placed under the supervision of Group G of the RSHA's Department VI. It did not much improve their output, always rather insignificant. In September of 1944, most were suspended.

This gigantic, jerry-built apparatus, Germany's intelligence system, consisting of numerous uncoordinated and often competing mechanisms, sucked up torrents of information—some of it duplicated—through its remote and multiform termini. Each unit refined its information, passing it either through special evaluating agencies, as with the military, or through the general bureaucracy, as with the Foreign Office. Then the jealous ministers, the arrogant party officials, the proud warlords of the high commands all scrambled to bring their tidbits to the Führer.

Hitler wanted it that way. The disunity and the rivalries remitted control of the intelligence apparatus to him. And, as the only person with access to all intelligence, he could judge it as he alone saw fit. He would not readily abdicate these powers to anyone else, and he never did. But this afflicted German intelligence with two fatal flaws: inefficiency, and subjugation to a madman.

II
THE FINDERS

Cylinders

THE room was large and pompously furnished. Its windows looked out upon a semitropical park planted with firs. Inside, a small, sinewy man with sharp features sat at a big desk and drafted a cable. He was the minister plenipotentiary and envoy extraordinary of the Deutsches Reich to Iran, and the message he was composing in his legation in Teheran that summer's day of 1941 contained urgent information.

To many people, Iran seemed the target of pincers. From Libya, Axis forces menaced Egypt, which alone barred the western route to Iran. From southern Russia, German armies crashed forward, seemingly invincible. The two appeared destined to link up in the Middle East, enabling Hitler to seize the oil there. He might then advance via Iran to India, to shake hands with the Japanese and complete the Axis conquest of the world.

But on that 3rd of July 1941, both tongs were still thousands of miles from Teheran, and the Iranian oil wells were mainly pumping for the British. The Abwehr, assigned earlier to sabotage these installations, had done little more than make plans, but the large German population of technicians still threatened the wells, and the shah showed no inclination to expel or intern the aliens.

Now the main function of a diplomat is, in addition to negotiating, to report. The minister, Erwin Ettel, was not a career professional, though he could wear the striped trousers and top hat—"Zylinder," in German—with aplomb enough. Like many others in the Third Reich, he owed his eminence to his party reliability. He was a mere clerk when he joined in 1932, but he rose rapidly to become an SS brigadier, and he served as country leader of the party in Italy for three years before Hitler named him minister to Iran late in 1939. But he understood the reporting aspect of his job well enough, and at his desk that day he was carrying it out.

The day before, he had received critical information bearing on the situation in Iran. The British had decided to occupy the country.

The Egyptian ambassador had brought Ettel this information at the direction of his king, the tubby, pornography-loving Farouk, who like other Egyptians resented the British overlords of his country and who may have regarded a German victory as likely. Farouk was passing it along as proof of his good faith toward Germany. Though the ambassador did not say how Farouk had gotten wind of this, he did stress several times that it involved not rumors but actual knowledge of a British decision. The British general staff was requesting 500,000 men for an occupation of Iran and two months to prepare it. The actual takeover of the oil concession area, including the Persian Gulf ports, was expected to be completed in only three weeks. Ettel set all this down, and added still more specifics of the enemy plans.

He had his dispatch encoded. Next morning, when the telegraph office opened, it was transmitted to Berlin, where it provided the first solid news of British plans for Iran. It was immediately forwarded to Hitler. He considered it but took no action. A few days later, Ettel, continuing to report, wired that Iran was preparing to defend itself against the British—news that perhaps lulled the Führer. Next month, however, danger signs began to mount. From a "reliable source," Ettel had discovered that the British had "recommended the removal" of the Germans. A few weeks later, a "most urgent" cable stung Hitler into action. Ettel reported an hour-long conversation with the Iranian minister-president which indicated that the Iranians were starting to cave in under the British demands. Thoroughly alarmed now, the Führer frantically urged the shah to resist the British until the German armies from Russia could rescue him. But words meant little against guns, and when, two days later, British and Russian troops entered Iran from south and north, Hitler could but rage impotently. Ettel had done what he could with his precise and timely dispatches but military realities had overwhelmed desires. It was the story of the Foreign Office in the war.

Why must diplomats do this work at all? Cannot a government collect information on another nation from at home? Not as well, obviously, as from within the other nation. Men on the spot can meet more people, read more of the general and special press, attend parliamentary debates, visit constructions, and, simply by walking the streets, buying food and clothes, taking trains, and going to the theater, sense the economic and intellectual vitality of the country. In the larger missions, specialists, usually called "attachés," concentrate on political, economic, cultural, and military affairs. They collect information mainly by talking with officials of the host government and reading the newspapers. This information they compile into reports, which they transmit by mail, cable, or wireless to their foreign offices.

In Berlin, this was housed in an eighteenth-century town house of gray stone, sober in design with the exception of two sphinxes flanking its entrance, in the heart of the city, at Wilhelmstrasse 76. Inside, officials working at geographic desks in the political or commercial branches read the diplomats' reports and sought to use them to propose Germany's foreign policy to the one maker of it, Adolf Hitler.

For the Foreign Office, the war meant mainly the closing of post after post and the decline of its influence. But the war also forced it to work in an area that it traditionally eschewed: the military. Diplomats normally preferred to let their military attachés grub about for news about armies and armaments, while they themselves pursued their lofty aims of conciliation between nations. But Nazi aggression diverted them from their benign to a malignant task. Even before the war started, the state secretary of the Foreign Office instructed all major missions abroad, not to redouble their efforts to preserve the peace, but to "collaborate . . . in the obtaining of military intelligence."

The German consuls in America sprang eagerly to the task. In New York, Eduard Lurtz clipped newspapers and bought maps of England and its overseas territories. Erich Windels in Philadelphia, Dr. Georg Krause-Wichmann in Chicago, and Karl Kapp in Cleveland all sent clippings to the military attaché in Washington. Dr. Georg Gyssling in Los Angeles covered the local press thoroughly—his office read 10 southern Californian papers, as well as other publications, including the special reports of the chamber of commerce. He also dispatched a man from his office twice a week to drive around and count how many airplanes each of the virtually open-air factories was producing.

During the war, the diplomats sought above all to find out what the other side intended to do. For them, as for all humans, this probe of the future was one of their most difficult tasks. Sometimes they, or their sources, succeeded. Ettel's forewarning of the British moves in Iran is a case in point. So was the 1943 report of the German ambassador in Spain. He messaged on 25 May that his old friend, the Spanish ambassador to the United States, who had been received by President Roosevelt three weeks before, said that FDR would run again in 1944 and that only a major American military defeat would diminish his chance of reelection.

But more often the diplomats, or the sources to whom they had access, were wrong. In 1940, the chargé in Washington predicted that the chances of a deal giving Britain 50 American destroyers for rights to use bases in the western hemisphere were "slight." Several weeks later, it went through. In Tangier, the Foreign Office representative cabled Berlin the gist of a conversation he had had with the Spanish chief of staff a month after the Axis forces in North Africa had surrendered. The Spaniard had just visited the American general, Mark Clark, and found that the Americans made "a very bad impression. . . . He did not think that General Clark's troops would be in condition before two months to undertake a major attack on the European continent." A month later, the Americans landed on Sicily.

One of the most consequential failures of prediction occurred in Yugoslavia in the spring of 1941. The Foreign Office, in common with the Abwehr and the SD, had utterly failed to learn in advance of the coup that ousted a pro-Axis government and set up an anti-Axis one. This shift led Hitler to attack and conquer Yugoslavia, delaying his onslaught on Russia for a month and, so he said in retrospect, costing him the war. He fulminated at his spy chiefs and at Ribbentrop for the intelligence failure.

This embarrassment coincided with others. Ribbentrop had just lost a bid to take control of the SD foreign spy apparatus and so remained dependent upon it and the Abwehr for secret intelligence. Hitler was voicing suspicions that a spy in the Soviet embassy, an informant of a Ribbentrop underling, was a double agent. He was constantly criticizing Ribbentrop's diplomats—an expression of his general distrust of experts and professionals. Just at this moment, a proposal from an entirely different quarter came to Ribbentrop's attention that he generalized into a way out of all these difficulties. Iraq was beginning to revolt against British control, and the director of his political branch suggested that the Foreign Office give an anti-British leader there a radio transmitter and ciphers; he could then send political intelligence from there direct to the Foreign Office independently of the Abwehr. Ribbentrop approved this and expanded the idea into an entire espionage service of his own.

His idea was almost original: in eighteenth-century France, Louis XV had a secret foreign reporting and negotiating service that duplicated and often contradicted his recognized diplomats. Ribbentrop felt that spy information might impress Hitler more; it would certainly accord better with Hitler's views that foreign intelligence could best be gathered by seducing the daughters of foreign envoys and politicians. That an espionage service might have contravened long-existing diplomatic convention did not deter him. On 9 April, three weeks after the Yugoslavian coup, the head of the political branch set down Ribbentrop's decision that day

> immediately to organize for the Foreign Office an intelligence service of its own in North Africa and the Middle East, independent of the Abwehr and of the SD. For that purpose he [Ribbentrop] made available every possible financial assistance, both in gold and in foreign exchange, and said that he intended to direct Minister Luther [Martin Luther, head of the internal German affairs department] to provide all the most modern technical aids necessary, such as radio equipment, etc. This service was later to be incorporated into a new intelligence service to be organized by the foreign minister that would be independent of other departments.

Two weeks later, Ribbentrop named as its head Andor Hencke, a 45-year-old career official then serving in Berlin, a party member since 1935.

Hencke established his central within the information section, perhaps as a disguise. It was called Information Post III, soon abbreviated to Inf III; posts I and II, and later IV to XV, issued information in the form of foreign propaganda. Hencke then traveled about setting up the acquisition posts. Sometimes he dispatched people from Berlin; sometimes he used personnel on hand. In every case, the head of the post was a member of the German mission in that country. They employed as their informants correspondents of German newspapers or the German wire service, businessmen, Germans resident there. In possible contravention of Ribbentrop's wishes, Hencke forbade "active espionage. . . . We were to keep to legal methods and do nothing that would imperil good relations. We were not to break safes or steal diplomatic pouches!" The informants aimed less at specific items than at general reports about the feeling in a country, the stability of its government, the reliability of key individuals. Hencke had it running in a few weeks.

The mission chiefs naturally disliked this rival service, but mostly they raised no fuss, especially since they could read the reports, though they could not change or withhold them. The SD was tougher: once it actually arrested some Inf III informants. A greater problem arose from Inf III's attachment to the foreign service. This limited it in practice to Germany's allies and neutrals, and these mostly in Europe, though it did have one informant in Shanghai and others in South America. It mainly emphasized the Balkans.

The chief of each Inf III post sent his reports to Berlin in an envelope marked for Hencke personally. There his staff—only two officials and three or four clerks—evaluated and edited them. In this tightened form they went to the state secretary, to Ribbentrop, and to the interested desks. Ribbentrop had about 5 percent of them submitted to Hitler. On 1 December 1941, for example, Hitler received two Inf III reports, one on the political and military situation in Iran, one on the situation in Egypt.

Such reports were sometimes as erroneous as they were imprecise. An Inf III agent in the puppet Croatian state that Germany and Italy had molded out of the torso of Yugoslavia pointed at several of its ministers as "Italophiles." An Inf III man in Iraq declared that the situation in the capital was not critical for Germany—four days before the pro-Axis cabinet quit and fled. An informant in Turkey reported that the British-Soviet occupation of Iran "has caused surprise and even alarm in influential Turkish circles." There followed three pages equally newsy and detailed.

In 1943, Hencke was promoted to head the political section of the Foreign Office. He retained Inf III under him but put first Ettel, back from Iran, and then Marschall Adolf Baron von Bieberstein, son of a former state secretary of the Foreign Office, in immediate charge. But the quantity of reports, as well as their quality, had begun to decline noticeably, in part because of courier difficulties. The service was abandoned in 1945 before the end of the war. Even Hencke admitted it had "attained no great importance."

Like all organs with intelligence functions, the Foreign Office served as a gigantic filter. It screened out enormous quantities of data to let only the most important get through to the men at the top. Each day hundreds of pages of reports poured in by cable and mail to the Wilhelmstrasse. Officials forwarded only about a third of them to the state secretary, who in turn passed only a few dozen of the most vital to Ribbentrop, on his special train near the Führer, usually far from Berlin. The Foreign Office liaison man then submitted an average of about four documents a day to Hitler.

Ribbentrop, however, entertained a particular view of his job as foreign minister. He believed that his chief duty, aside from executing the Führer's wishes, was to shield him from doubts and from considerations that might instill doubts. He urged his officials to share his faith and forbade them to submit reports that might shake it. Consequently, though his subordinates often reported unpalatable truths, the reality that reached Hitler through him was less objective than subjective.

The Military Attaché

I3 HUNGERED. The intelligence section of the Troops Department, proscribed by Versailles from sending "to any foreign country any military, naval, or air mission," was starving on the thin gruel that its sources were providing. It believed that only its own specialist, full-time observers could gather the fare it required. So, starting in 1925, it prodded the army command to reestablish the military attachés. But not until 5 January 1933 did the government feel it could finally authorize them. They would take up their posts on 1 April.

The army named seven men, and accredited four of them to several posts at once. It was thus represented in 14 countries: the United States, Britain with Belgium and the Netherlands, France, Italy with Hungary and Bulgaria, Poland, Czechoslovakia with Yugoslavia and Rumania, and the Soviet Union with Lithuania. The navy sent attachés to London, Paris, and Rome. Air matters were handled by the army until the Luftwaffe began dispatching its own attachés. After 1938, one attaché in each capital was designated Wehrmacht attaché to handle matters dealing with the host nation's armed forces as a whole. By 1939, 18 military, 12 naval, and 13 air attachés and assistants served in 30 countries.

Despite the long period of agitation for attachés, the services had not trained men specifically for the job, nor did they ever. Selection seemed to be rather haphazard. The Army Personnel Office recommended names on the basis of its general knowledge of officers' capabilities to the commander in chief of the army. He discussed them with the head of Foreign Armies and with the head of the Troops Department, or, later, the general staff, and made his choice. He picked them on such qualities as good character, military knowledge, social skills, and handsome appearance.

For exotic countries, for which specialists were harder to find, he would reach outside the élite of the general staff corps. Thus, the longest-serving

[73]

attaché in Moscow, General August Köstring, was not a member. But he had been born and raised in Russia, had fought at Tannenberg, and had represented the German army to the Soviet Union in 1931. A later chief of Foreign Armies called him "far the most knowledgeable man about Soviet Russia that Germany had before 1941." Colonel Hans Rohde, assigned to Turkey, Greece, and Iran, though likewise not a member of the general staff, knew the Near East well and had written half a dozen books on it.

But generally the army took its attachés from that corps. The main reason seemed to be that the men choosing the attachés were themselves members of the general staff and so knew the candidates. This could lead to less than the best selections. An old friend of Enno von Rintelen headed the Army Personnel Office. Rintelen knew no Italian and not much more about Italy. But his friend had him named attaché in the key post at Rome anyway. His preparation for the job consisted of a month's brushing up on French, as the language of diplomacy, together with some background reading on Italy, followed by three weeks on the Italy desk of Foreign Armies. It was not entirely successful: the chief of the Italian general staff once had to tell him to learn Italian so that they could talk more freely.

Sometimes not friends but foes controlled appointments. Eugen Ott, a follower of the politically minded General Kurt von Schleicher, who served briefly as chancellor before Hitler, fell with his mentor. Hitler kicked him out of his job as a department head and halfway round the world into Japan, where he became military attaché. Moriz von Faber du Faur, a rather astringent personality who was not in the general staff corps, always felt that his enemies had banished him to Belgrade.

Usually, however, saner criteria reigned. Three of the first seven attachés had served as chiefs of Foreign Armies: General Friedrich von Boetticher in Washington, General Erich Kühlenthal in Paris, and Colonel Herbert Fischer in Rome. Both Boetticher, who had visited the United States for four months in 1922, and the first attaché in London, Colonel Leo Baron Geyr von Schweppenburg, spoke English.

An attaché post was a plum. It offered freedom, prestige, and fun with an undemanding job. "A military attaché is free to set about his task in any way he chooses," wrote Geyr. Faber du Faur stepped off the Orient Express in Belgrade on 1 October 1935 to independence for the first time in a 30-year military career. "I had only one superior, the chief of the general staff. I was well paid. I could wear mufti and had to appear in uniform only in the presence of the Prince Regent. The minister was not my superior, I was only attached to the legation; my office consisted of a single clerk, I had obligations only when I gave them to myself. It sufficed if I reported from time to time and punctually sent in my expense account every other week." The attachés' allowances enabled them to keep up a house, servants, and the necessary social engagements. They had a government car. Traveling expenses were paid. In the bigger countries, they had a captain or two as assistants. This life lasted on an average of three to four years, and then the attachés returned to regular service, distinguished by their glamor, their sophistication, and their new expertise.

The chief of the diplomatic mission either co-signed the attachés' reports or wrote dissenting opinions of his own; he could not change or withhold the original report without the attaché's permission. The reports went by wire or courier to the Foreign Office, where they were decoded, copied if necessary, and sent over to the armed services. For particularly secret matters, the attachés had their own cipher machines held only by the armed services. Though these were seldom used, the attachés often supplemented their official reports with personal letters to the chief of the general staff or to his intelligence chief. Here they could express their opinions more freely, since only a few eyes would see them, and those excluded the civilian diplomats.

Before the war, the military attachés returned to Berlin once a year for an 8- or 10-day meeting. They caught up with the latest developments in their own army, talked individually with superiors, met the attachés from their host countries, and spoke at a general assembly for about 10 to 15 minutes about their host countries. Faber du Faur painted a sardonic picture of the 1935 meeting, which Hitler attended. To the attaché it resembled a Nazi party rally at the Hofbräuhaus in Munich. He found no trace of protocol and little of military objectivity. "The military attachés . . . depicted everything in the rosiest colors. Everybody loved us and admired National Socialism. Ethiopia was just the thing. What a success for the Führer's theory that one only had to have guts and then even the impossible became possible!"

In Berlin, the four high commands had units that handled the paperwork for its attachés. They received the attaché reports from the Foreign Office, distributed them to interested parties, collected questions that German units wanted answered and forwarded them to the attachés, kept the attachés informed, did the accounting, and provided supplies. They also managed all business with the foreign attachés in Berlin.

An attaché gathered his information about the host country's army in open ways. He accepted information distributed by the host force both on its own initiative and in response to his questions. He observed maneuvers and parades. He attended lectures. He read newspapers and technical literature. He talked with officers of the host army and exchanged information with other attachés and with newspapermen. The amount of information that the host country gave out largely depended upon how much Germany gave to that country's attachés in Berlin. That is why Boetticher urged Berlin in 1940 to let the American attachés there visit the front. The German attaché often had to consider whether Germany would be willing to answer the questions he wanted to ask. To help him, the attaché unit sent copies of all questions from the host country's attaché in Berlin and the German answers to them. And since news was an attaché's currency, the attachés were constantly demanding, and Berlin was constantly sending, information that they swapped.

The intelligence technique varied according to the country. In the Soviet Union, which gave out no information, the smallest detail became a usable item. The naval attaché, Commander Norbert von Baumbach, tracked ship movements by gleaning the appearances of their officers' names from the national and provincial press and comparing them with their previous locations. He could travel, after getting permission, and—with luck—could see the warships, but he could never visit them. He never carried a camera. Once, though, he got a photograph of a new kind of vessel from a young English archeologist with whom he became friendly on a voyage to Russia. The closing of the German consulates in 1938 reduced the military attaché, Köstring, to depending almost exclusively on the observations of German diplomatic couriers for information outside of Moscow. In the United States, on the other hand, said Boetticher, "It was so easy, the Americans are so broad-minded, they print everything in their papers. You don't need any intelligence service. You have only to be industrious, to see the papers and what they print!"

In the major countries, the attachés practiced no espionage. Geyr was told by the war minister, "Get those ideas right out of your head." Boetticher not only refused to handle spies himself, he even tried to keep the Abwehr from placing agents in the United States, for fear that their exposure could damage his relationships with Americans and hence his effectiveness. The Abwehr called attachés like these, who had no assignments from it, "spotless." It called the others "somewhat stained."

These tainted attachés served mostly in smaller or friendlier countries, where Germany had little to lose from or little fear of expulsion or retaliation. In some cases they handled spying only against a neighbor: the attaché in Franco's Spain ran agents against France. But in some countries they directed the spies against their own hosts. The military attaché in Belgrade after Faber du Faur, the naval attaché in Turkey, and, most blatant of all, the major attachés in Latin America did so. Until Brazil's break with the Axis, the German military attaché, General Günter Niedenfuhr, headed Abwehr espionage for the southern part of the western hemisphere. After he departed, Captain Dietrich Niebuhr, the naval attaché in Argentina, who had once headed the Abwehr's naval espionage section, picked up the threads. He contacted agents, paid them (up to $8,000 in one case), received their reports, and passed these to Berlin, sometimes by couriers. The pressures for attachés to do this work mounted throughout the war as other sources of information dried up, and by 1943 at least 13 attaché assistants were handling Abwehr matters. Many attachés disliked this, however, and they kept fighting the demands.

The attachés expressed their findings in reports that ranged from t. minutiae of weapons to the broadest political generalities. The attaché in France reported in December 1935 that Spain would resist a transshipment of French troops from Africa in case of a Franco-German war; Berlin marked this "worth reading." Boetticher sent in four pages in November 1936 on the testing of cannon in airplanes and on parachute bombs. At about the same time, one of Geyr's assistants reported on a talk he had with a lieutenant colonel in the War Office who advocated infantry tanks and would soon take over a new tank division. One of the most precocious reports of the era came from Boetticher on 7 January 1936. He dealt in four excellent pages with the rocketry experiments of Professor Robert H. Goddard—experiments that blossomed eight years later in Germany in the V-1 and V-2. Boetticher covered the background (Goddard "has worked for decades with the problem of rocket flight"), finances ("considerable support from the Daniel & Florence Guggenheim Foundation as well as the Carnegie Institution"), latest success ("the first practical really usable rocket"), technical details ("altitude of 2,400 meters and a speed of about 1,100 kilometers/second . . . 3.64 meters long . . . reportedly can be filled with 27 kilograms of fuel"), and problems ("certainty that the rocket will be automatically maintained in a vertical course").

Much of the attachés' work consisted of answering questions from staff units at home. On 9 September 1936, General Heinz Guderian requested information about communication means between infantry and tanks in the British army. Geyr responded with a report of the tank referee at maneuvers the year before.

Reports sometimes profiled important personalities. Geyr sketched Major General John Dill, director of military operations and intelligence in the British War Office, on the eve of Dill's visit to Germany in 1935 during which he was to meet the commander in chief of the army. Dill, said Geyr, had a lively interest in horses because he was an Irishman and even though he was an infantryman, made a good appearance, was "an extraordinarily interesting person—as such much more than the Chief of the [Imperial] General Staff," knew little about Germany despite a pre-World War I visit to Weimar, and could be assumed free of prejudices about Germany. But Geyr said nothing about Dill's military interests, the theories he favored, how others viewed him, his prospects. Geyr provided some tidbits for a superficial conversation but failed to supply his chief with elements that would help him judge the personality and perhaps the probable tactics of the potential enemy opposite him—a man who, during World War II, became chief of the Imperial General Staff.

In the years before the war, the attachés constituted the most valuable intelligence source for the army. But when hostilities commenced with a country, the attaché there packed his bags and came home. Sometimes Germany put their experience to use. The air attaché in England gave lec-

Deutsche Botschaft.   Washington,D.C.   7. Januar 1936
Der Militärattaché.
Der Luftattaché.

                                                    4 Ausf. RKM

Betr.: Raketenversuche in den Vereinigten Staaten.

Vorgang: 1.) Anlage 10 zu Nr. 975/geh./Att. vom 15.11.35
         2.) Anlage 9 zum Bericht Nr. 40/1935 vom 4.12.35.

Professor Robert H.Goddard ist Lehrer an der Clark University in
Wooster, Massachusetts. Er beschäftigt sich seit Jahrzehnten mit
der Frage des Raketenfluges. Im Jahre 1919 hat er in den Veröffentlichungen der Smithsonian Institution einen Bericht erscheinen
lassen, der als Grundlage seiner Arbeiten anzusehen ist : "A Method
of Reaching extreme Altitudes."

Die Versuche des Prof. Goddard finden in der Nähe von Roswell in
Neu-Mexiko statt. Bis vor kurzem finanzierte die Smithsonian Insti -
tution seine Versuche. Als von da nicht ausreichende Mittel zu er-
halten waren, hat sich Oberst Lindbergh ins Mittel gelegt und durch
Vermittlung von Harry F.Guggenheim erhebliche Unterstützung aus der
Daniel & Florence Guggenheim Foundation sowie der Carnegie Institution beschafft.

Soweit bis jetzt festzustellen, ist die neuste Raketenkonstruktion
des Prof. Goddard als ein erheblicher Fortschritt anzusehen. Ein in
den Zeitungen erschienenes Bild wird in der Anlage beigefügt. Nach
Ansicht von Vertretern der Smithsonian Institution hat Prof.Goddard

An das   damit

Reichskriegsministerium,
Oberbefehlshaber des Heeres,
      Attachégruppe,

              Berlin.

The military and air attaché in Washington, D.C., General Friedrich von Boetticher, transmits a detailed report about early U.S. rocket experiments to the
Reich War Ministry and the commander in chief of the army in Berlin

tures on targets to bomber crews. Boetticher wrote reports for the OKW on such topics as American war aims and "Problems of Coalition War at the United Nations." Other attachés rejoined the fighting troops. During the Normandy battles, Geyr headed the Panzer Group West.

Attempting to fill the gap left by their return home were the attachés to the remaining neutrals, such as Sweden, Switzerland, Spain, and Portugal, and the attachés of those countries in Berlin. They never provided anything vital, however, and sometimes their information was misleading.

In the spring of 1944, the Wehrmacht waited tensely for the Allied invasion. All sources of information strained to learn where and when it would come. The attaché contribution to this was insignificant. The man in Stockholm, for example, could provide only indirect clues. Hitler was constantly concerned about Sweden's repeated call-ups of its home guard because he feared a possible attack on his rear in the event of an Allied invasion of Norway. At his situation conference in the afternoon of 6 April, he heard a report of the attaché about a new call-up. It might have been regarded as foreshadowing an Allied move against Norway. But it was, at best, extremely tenuous, and in the end no such move occurred. The Bern attaché energetically forwarded information from spies, from other attachés, from Swiss civilians and general staff officers about the invasion. None of it helped.

Nor did the information supplied by neutral attachés in Berlin after the invasion.

DIARY ENTRIES OF A GERMAN MILITARY ATTACHÉ
Bern, Switzerland, 1944

15.5.   Report on Swiss mobilization measures.

19.5.   Report on agent report on invasion questions and intelligence from England.

20.5.   Report on statements of Hungarian military attaché on invasion questions.

25.5.   Confidential note on land preparations in England.

25.5.   Report on discussion with Swiss personalities (among other topics on invasion intentions of the Allies: mid-June at the latest).

31.5.   Report on lecture tour of General Theiss.

30.5.   Report on return of Italian prisoners of war to Italy.

2.6.   Report on stay of the Soviet Russian Lieutenant Colonel Baeleff in Switzerland.

2.6.   Report on intention of Polish internees to join with French resistance group at a suitable moment.

5.6.   Report on interview with Colonel Müller of the general staff on probable landing of the Allies on the coast opposite England.—No

Balkan operations by the Allies.—Further on enemy shifting of forces on the northern part of the Eastern Front. Supposed major push against the Baltic provinces.

5.6.   Report on enemy distribution of forces according to statements of Finnish military attachés.

5.6.   Confidential report of the German consul in Lugano over the military occurrences in Ticino and intended innovations in the military arrangements of Corps Commander Constam.

7.6.   Telegram on reports of Kriegsorganisation [the Abwehr post] on total mobilization of the Swedish air force.

7.6.   Report on troop identifications (among others new war organization).

7.6.   Report covering various matters (among others the present active strength of the mobilized Swiss forces).

The Spanish military attaché, Colonel Marin de Bernardo, received mail by courier on 6 July 1944 and hastened to the Attaché Branch that very day. He told them that a traveler from England reported that the V-1 flying bomb had done great damage and reduced morale. Other travelers said that the Allied invasion force consisted of 90 divisions, 30 of them in the bridgehead. A landing was possible on the southern French coast soon, since 25 divisions were in Africa, 5 in Malta, 3 in Corsica. The item about the southern France landing was almost six weeks premature, the invasion figures were double what they should have been, and the Mediterranean figures were wildly exaggerated. So much for the help of the neutrals.

General von Boetticher in Washington was the most interesting German military attaché, for he influenced the war more than any other. His reporting was disastrous, yet Hitler read it, liked it, and acted upon it.

Of average height, blond, heavy-set, genial, with a round head and a peasant nose, Boetticher was one month short of 58 when the war broke out in September 1939. Unlike many of his fellow generals of World War II, such as von Kleist, von Stulpnagel, von Manteuffel, whose ancestral names recur with startling frequency in German military history, Boetticher came from neither a military nor a noble family. His father was a physician, who only received his patent of nobility in 1903, when Friedrich was 22. The "von" that they could now put before "Boetticher" perhaps made some people think later that Friedrich was a cousin or nephew of Karl-Heinrich von Boetticher, a trusted deputy of the revered Bismarck, with a consequent increase in prestige. In fact the families were unrelated. Friedrich joined the army in 1900, became a member of the general staff in 1913, and during World War I handled transportation questions in Bulgaria and served as I a of a division. After some international service, he became head of Foreign Armies. He took such good care of American officers that they invited him to visit America. During his trip, he sought to learn how the United States could create the great army of 1918. He discovered the secret in West Point, the National Guard, and the Reserve Officers' Training Corps. Back in Germany and reassigned, Boetticher served with troops, at the League of Nations, and as head of an artillery school, and wrote works on former chief of the general staff Alfred Count von Schlieffen, France, and Frederick the Great. He owed his appointment to Washington in part to his knowing President von Hindenburg. He regarded his attaché period as "the happiest time of my life" and said that his proudest moment came when the American Historical Association asked him to lecture. But he also detested many things in America.

In Washington, he exploited the standard sources of newspapers, troop visits, and official contacts. These included three successive chiefs of staff, generals Douglas MacArthur, Malin Craig, whom he had met in 1922, and George C. Marshall, and Secretary of War Harry Woodring. He also, through aviation journalists close to Charles A. Lindbergh and other members of an isolationist group of officers, tapped into the rich information sources available to this military clique. After the war began, Boetticher extended his coverage to include the British Commonwealth, insofar as he could do so through the press.

He sent off his military dispatches every three or four days. They reported the destination of ships sailing from New York, New Orleans, Mobile, and Beaumont, the arrival of Australian troop transports in Egypt, a speech in Ottawa by Air Chief Marshall Sir Hugh Dowding that a "detector" in airplanes that spots enemy planes would soon overcome the danger of night attacks, anti-German propaganda. He transmitted detailed figures on the November 1940 exports of American airplanes based on official statistics. From time to time he gave reasonably specific figures on army size. On 12 July 1941, for example, he cabled: "On July 1 the American army, including its air force, had a strength of about 1,400,000 men, consisting of 4 armies, 9 army corps, 27 infantry divisions, one of them motorized, 2 cavalry divisions, and 4 armored divisions, which will be increased to 6 in the near future, under one commander of armored troops. . . . At the moment the equipment is still inadequate. Only 2 divisions can be considered as fully equipped, and a total of 5 as being ready for immediate use." Most of this came from the *Biennial Report* of Chief of Staff Marshall, which had made headlines a few days before.

But it was not the accuracy of his statistics that won him Hitler's admiration and a telegram of recognition. It was that his views coincided with his Führer's.

Boetticher, like Hitler, believed that the Jews ran America. Cable after cable contained such phrases as "the fatal control of American policy by the Jews." The naming of Presbyterian Henry L. Stimson as secretary of war and Congregationalist Frank Knox as secretary of the navy satisfied him that "The Jewish element now controls key positions in the American armed forces." President Franklin D. Roosevelt was "the exponent of the Jews" and "operated within the framework of the true Jewish conception regarding the power of money and business."

The two also perceived American political goals in the identical way. At about the same time that Hitler was saying that in the postwar world the United States would take over "the inheritance of England," Boetticher was cabling that "After the war, American money economy and American imperialism will rule the world." Boetticher's views that the United States had a "large-scale imperialist policy in the Atlantic" matched Hitler's comments that Roosevelt intended to "take possession of or gain control over the islands in the Atlantic."

And they felt the same certainty about the outcome of the war. "People are already beginning to become resigned to the idea of the defeat of France and the overthrow of England," Boetticher wired on 24 May 1940. Air attacks had struck "London's heart like an earthquake" and had made life more difficult, hindered production, and caused optimism to disappear. An attack on Malta caused heavy damage. Hitler liked these reports: he called specifically for the one about Malta. A month after Boetticher had cabled that America could not make any immediate large deliveries to Britain, Hitler was saying that U.S. aid to Britain was "greatly overrated." All these reports constituted good evidence for his view that England was defeated and must soon surrender.

Of course, they told him little new. He was sure before he read a word of them that the Jews ran America, that the nation was imperialistic, and that England would fall. But they persuaded him of the trustworthiness and perspicacity of his military observer in the distant giant, and facilitated his acceptance of that observer's reporting on current American affairs. Here, too, a gross misconception clouded Boetticher's thinking. And Hitler, accepting Boetticher's views, made one of his most critical decisions.

For Boetticher believed that, unlike in 1917, the United States did not endanger Germany. He arrived at this conception through two complementary arguments. The first held that the United States was so preoccupied with Japan that it was focusing its strength on the Pacific. This left the Atlantic—and Germany—undisturbed. The second held that, even if the United States did turn against Germany, it could not bring its strength to bear in time to have any effect.

"The Pacific Ocean and the need of adequate defense preparations occupy the foreground," stated Boetticher a month after the outbreak of the war. He never deviated from this theme. September 1940: "The first aim of the United States continues to be to bring the situation in the Pacific Ocean to a military or diplomatic solution." July 1941: "American war policy regards as its most important task the elimination of the danger threatening from the Pacific." November 1941: "Now as before the key to America's conduct lies with Japan."

Boetticher maintained this view by denying or distorting the mounting evidence of a shift to an Atlantic priority. When, contrary to his predictions, America exchanged 50 destroyers for British bases in the western hemisphere, he suppressed the news: he never mentioned the deal or its implications in his subsequent dispatches. Lend-Lease was to him a "trick" and an "empty gesture"; an estimate of $7 billion of it meant nothing because immediate deliveries were not possible. The Roosevelt-Churchill meeting that produced the Atlantic Charter did not, for Boetticher, demonstrate solidarity against Germany but constituted "the greatest admission of Anglo-American military weakness."

The attaché never displayed his fixation more remarkably than when he refused to acknowledge his error in the face of black-and-white proof to the contrary. He could not know that American strategists had, early in 1941, shifted the primary effort of the United States in a war with the Axis away from Japan and onto Germany. But on 4 December 1941, the isolationist *Chicago Tribune* and its sister publication, the Washington *Times-Herald,* disclosed this plan in a sensational news story. The story quoted the plan as proposing that " 'the first major objective of the United States and its associates should be the complete military defeat of Germany ... while holding Japan in check' "—exactly the opposite of what Boetticher had been saying. He and the chargé d'affaires agreed that the story was "apparently authentic" and "doubtlessly authentic." The chargé had no trouble in discerning that in the plan "Military measures against Japan ... would be of defensive character" and that "America will, in the event of a two-ocean war, make its main offensive effort in the direction of Europe and Africa." But Boetticher, though saying that in the Far East the United States would remain "watchful and defensive," and though conceding that an invasion of Europe was planned, disregarded entirely the key point that the offensive against Germany would comprise the main American effort. For him, somehow, the entire war plan merely "confirmed our prevailing situation estimate." Handed gold on a silver platter, Boetticher refused to surrender his dross.

His geographical argument Boetticher clinched with his temporal one. American power did not matter because it could not be brought to bear in time. Boetticher never made this point outright. In fact, he forwarded quantities of information on the growth of American manpower and armament. He reported the official strength figures given by General Marshall, for example, as well as the government intention of raising army and navy air strengths to 20,000 and 5,000 airplanes respectively. He warned against underestimating American efficiency and determination. He called attention to the "high requirements" of the officer corps and the military's "excellent" equipment and high morale. He noted that war industry was overcoming its bottlenecks. But he nullified all this by asserting that it would take effect too late. Boetticher implied that Germany would have won the war before America could exert its strength. As the war went on, however, he had to keep pushing his dates back. He did not do so because of any expansion in American programs, for his timetables bore no relation to what the army was then planning, but because Germany's expectations of victory receded. By thus shifting his date of American effectiveness, he preserved his suggestion that it meant nothing.

In December 1939, after the war had just begun, he cabled: "No land and air armaments adequate for an aggressive war policy by the United States are to be expected before the late summer of 1940." In the late summer of 1940: "Before the middle of 1941 at the earliest the army and air force will not have the necessary forces at their disposal for undertaking any important aggressive maneuvers outside the western hemisphere." In the middle of 1941: The United States will not have "in the course of this year an adequate army and a suitable air force."

In this way, Boetticher obliterated America's smoking factories, its vast wheat fields, its millions of military-aged men. Hitler liked this, as he liked Boetticher's Pacific view, and he drew the inference clearly enough. "America, however, considering her present state of armaments," he said in the fall of 1940, "could play no significant role prior to 1942. By that time, England would be occupied or turned into a waste of rubble."

Thus freed by his attaché of any fears about America, Hitler saw "no danger of an intervention by the United States." A few months later it was still "a matter of indifference." Ten days before Pearl Harbor, he said once again that an American entry into the war "would no longer signify any danger" for Germany. So, on 11 December 1941, he considered that he had nothing to lose and perhaps something to gain—cutting England's lifelines, destruction of a hated nation, bringing things to an ideological conclusion—by declaring war on the United States. With Boetticher's reassurances at the back of his mind, he took that fatal step.

6

Private Sectors, Public Secrets

O N a spring day in Germany in 1938, Frank A. Howard, the hooded-eyed president of the research subsidiary of the Standard Oil Company (New Jersey), walked into the offices of I. G. Farben, the giant international chemical cartel. He was seeing Dr. Fritz ter Meer, the tall, handsome, silver-haired chemist and Nazi who headed Farben's Division II, which produced poison gas, dyes, pharmaceuticals, chemicals, and synthetic rubber.

The two men had things in common. They knew one another, having met both in Germany and America. Ter Meer was a chemist; Howard directed an army of them. They were both at the top of their field. And they were both aware of the agreements signed in 1929 and 1930 between their firms to share development and divide exploitation of new products in their areas.

One such product was a form of synthetic rubber, called "butyl rubber." Farben had synthesized this early in the 1930s from a highly volatile liquid, isobutylene, readily available as a by-product of oil refining. But this original rubber was too soft and weak for commercial use, and anyway Germany did not refine enough oil to produce large quantities of isobutylene. Standard did, however, and it had development laboratories of its own. So under the agreement, Farben had told Howard about butyl rubber on one of his earlier visits to Germany.

During the next few years, working in the malodorous laboratories in Bayway, New Jersey, two of Standard's chemists discovered that, by the addition of another compound, isobutylene could be cooked into a strong and useful form of butyl rubber. Particularly impermeable to gases, it proved valuable for inner tubes and for hoses. This opened up vast commercial prospects. But Standard feared that Farben might create the improved butyl independently. This would jeopardize Standard's rights as the

[85]

inventor, for the agreement stated that "the party which first acquaints the other with the technical details of a new chemical process . . . shall be considered the originator." So Howard went to Germany to disclose his new secret to ter Meer.

In March of 1938, just after the tumultuous days in which Hitler annexed Austria, the two men met. Howard brought with him reams of technical details concerning the new product, and handed them over to ter Meer. In return for facts he got a promise: ter Meer said he would obtain the consent of the German government, which had been financing much of the German research, for the exploitation of "rubber-like products" in the United States. It never came.

So the Germans got early information on the invention of a substance critical to motorized warfare without giving anything in return.

Nor was this an isolated case. In 1933 and 1934, the Sperry Gyroscope Company of Brooklyn, makers of an automatic pilot, a directional gyroscope, and an artificial horizon, licensed Askania Werke A. G. of Berlin, the foremost German precision instrument firm, to manufacture and sell the Sperry devices. Sperry furnished technical data and know-how to Askania. It sent over tool and production drawings and details of manufacturing methods. For a while assembling and mailing this information to Berlin took up practically the full time of a Sperry employee. In addition, the Brooklyn plant was visited by four technical representatives of Askania in successive months. Askania soon began producing the artificial horizon; the other products followed later.

What was Sperry getting out of all this? It was certainly not equivalent information, for Askania long ignored Sperry's requests for data on the German system. Sperry was getting protection in Germany: Askania had promised not to produce anything competitive. But it wanted information as well. The Germans kept stalling for years until, in June of 1939, with Hitler on the brink of his war, they released to Sperry a model of their single-axis automatic pilot. It was then three years old—three years in which the Germans had had time to install the superior Sperry devices into the fighters and bombers of their expanding Luftwaffe.

The Bendix Aviation Corporation made similar agreements with two other German firms. It faithfully sent designs of its aviation instruments to Siemens Apparate und Maschinen G. m. b. H.—but never got full data in return. And as late as 1940, it was still supplying Robert Bosch G. m. b. H. with designs and manufacturing information on starters for aircraft and diesel engines.

In still another field, the Germans patted themselves on the back for getting much from the honest and trusting Americans while giving them little:

> As a consequence of our contracts with the Americans, we received from them above and beyond the agreement many valuable contributions for the synthesis and improvements of motor fuels and lubricating oils, which just

now during the war are most useful to us, and we also received many other advantages from them.

Primarily, the following may be mentioned:

(1) Above all, improvement of fuels through the addition of lead-tetra-ethyl and the manufacture of this product. It need not be especially mentioned that without lead-tetraethyl the present method of warfare would be unthinkable. The fact that since the beginning of the war we could produce lead-tetraethyl is entirely due to the circumstances that, shortly before, the Americans had presented us with the production plans complete with experimental knowledge. Thus the difficult work of development (one need only recall the poisonous property of lead-tetraethyl, which caused many deaths in the U.S.A.) was spared us, since we could take up the manufacture of this product together with all the experience that the Americans had gathered over long years. . . .

(3) In the field of lubricating oils as well, Germany, through the contacts with America, learned of experiences that are extraordinarily important for present-day warfare.

. . . Particularly in the case of the production of aviation gasoline on an iso-octane basis, hardly anything was given to the Americans, while we gained a lot.

Thus did Hitler's Germany obtain, in a perfectly legal way, and without the need of any industrial spies, information of considerable value to its war effort.

To harvest information systematically in the inventive fields of American business, which teemed with new ideas, Farben in 1928 created an organization specifically for that. Max Ilgner, nephew of the chairman of the managing board of directors, came to New York to set it up. He soon had it running so well that he could turn it over to his brother, Rudolf, and return to Germany to further his ambitions there. Chemnyco, Inc., as the firm came to style itself, after its parent's business and its location, worked out of a narrow, five-story office building at 520 Fifth Avenue, between 43rd and 44th streets. It was corporately independent of Farben, but Farben supported it by contracting for its services at $84,000 a year, plus charges for extra work.

Chemnyco swept up everything it could find from open sources. Its subscription list to technical and other publications covered 16 single-spaced typewritten pages; the magazines alone cost $4,000 a year. It obtained maps of the mineral industries of Ohio, of oil and gas fields, of shore lines and pipelines. From the chambers of commerce of cities and towns it learned about the industries there and the economic advantages of the localities. Royalty payments on industrial processes enabled it to calculate production in these areas. In 1937, Farben asked Chemnyco for the carbide capacities of certain plants; Chemnyco supplied figures for 3 out of 10. The next year it got 56 chemical samples for Farben, 8 of them "difficult to obtain." It assisted the numerous German visitors who toured U.S. plants, such as one who during his six-month visit mailed hundreds of pages of reports back home, especially on synthetic chemicals and rubber. Each week Chemnyco sent scores of clippings and a report to Germany. When the war supervened, and Britain made such direct transmission impossible, Farben gave Chemnyco cover addresses in Portugal for it to use. And Chemnyco operated up to the day Hitler declared war on America.

Chemnyco's hundredweights of blueprints, clippings, reports, and photographs flowed mainly into a Farben economic-information branch at Unter den Linden 78, Berlin. Other Farben units, notably a post for Wehrmacht liaison and one for other government liaison, were quartered in this office, known throughout the Farben organization as "N. W. 7" from its postal zone and headed by the ambitious and arrogant Max Ilgner.

The economic-information branch had originated in 1929 as the brainchild of three men, all of whom wanted a research institute like those in the United States, but each for his own purposes. A former top government official, involved in the League of Nations, wanted it to investigate the economic preconditions needed for a peaceful development of Europe; one Farben chief wanted it to investigate international finance and currency for Farben's benefit; another Farben boss wanted its information to help settle labor-management disputes, perhaps favorably to management. At first Farben merely financed the unit, which was independent, but in 1936 its personnel became employees of the trust, or Interessengemeinschaft (I. G.).

Dr. Anton Reithinger, an employee of the Reich Statistical Department and an adjunct professor at the University of Berlin, took charge. Farben placed at his disposal the small library and clipping service that had existed for several years at N. W. 7. His main job was to provide information that would help Farben executives decide such questions as whether a license agreement should be made on a dollar, pound, or other basis. Under Reithinger's energetic direction, the service very rapidly flowered and was renamed the Volkswirtschaftliche Abteilung (Public Economy Branch), or Vowi, for short. Vowi scored a great coup by anticipating the devaluation of the dollar in January 1934 and enabling Farben to save *RM*30 million. This helped it grow from around 10 people at the start to 100 during the war and its budget to rise correspondingly from *RM*100,000 to *RM*1 million. Early on, Reithinger began to collect information not merely on markets and currencies, on chemical developments, and on rival firms, but also on the economies of foreign countries, especially those regarded as possible Farben growth areas. Moreover, unlike the other economic research agencies, which only began to look into a subject when they received a request to do so, Reithinger assembled material on products, markets, persons, as soon as they came to public notice. This enabled him to answer demands for information much more rapidly than other agencies with no loss of quality. As a result, many "customers," such as Karl Ritter, long-time head of the Foreign Office commercial branch, preferred to ask Vowi for information.

Reithinger's information came mostly from the press, technical as well as general. Much of the rest came from exchanges with economic research institutes in Germany, with major banks and government ministries, and with other leading firms, including foreign, such as America's Du Pont and Britain's giant Imperial Chemical Industries. Many of the foreign companies were headquartered in Frankfurt, and Vowi established a branch there to facilitate getting their material. Finally Vowi information low in quantity but high in quality came from permanent Farben representatives abroad, who reported regularly to Germany on conditions in their host countries, and from men sent out specially from Germany to observe particular conditions. Vowi worked this up into reports, bound in green, numbered consecutively, and lithographed in editions of 20 to 500. Volume 4 of the East Asian report, for example, went on 6 September 1938 to almost 100 people, including General Georg Thomas of the OKW's War Economy and Armaments Department, Martin Bormann, head of the party chancellery, the ambassador in Tokyo, and the head of Krupp.

It was Max Ilgner who decided on the distribution. He realized that Vowi's information could be of value, and soon after the Nazis took power he peddled it to the Gestapo, to the infant SD, and to Thomas. Thomas's was the most immediate interest, since he was charged with Germany's economic mobilization and with investigating foreign war economies. His contacts with Vowi were sometimes direct, sometimes through the military liaison post that Farben had set up in 1935 under N. W. 7. One of this post's officials, Dr. Heinrich Diekmann, a chemist who handled intelligence affairs among his other duties, met with some of Thomas's people on 2 May 1939. He told them about nitric acid and nitrogen plants in Great Britain—key elements of the explosives industry there. He cited two new factories built in Scotland, listed some older ones, mentioned the conversion of another. Farben calculated the capacity of one of the new ones at 40,000 tons on the basis of its construction cost. Diekmann also corrected the Abwehr's 1938 figure of nitric acid production capacity in Great Britain.

In August, as war appeared imminent, Reithinger visited Thomas's office and placed his archives at its disposal. Soon thereafter, he received from it a batch of requests for specific studies and for raw material. Eventually Reithinger had to assign 10 of his then 35 men just to handle the military material. Sometimes Thomas's men would simply ring up and ask a question that Vowi might be able to answer from its files. Sometimes they assigned Vowi full reports. In 1940, for example, they asked for a study of the American production capacity in explosives and nitrogen. Vowi complied. By then it and the other N. W. 7 units had expanded so much that they had to move twice, finally settling at Kochstrasse 73.

During the war with Russia, Vowi produced reports on the Soviet economy for Thomas's foreign war economy branch. One, on military chemical production, told of industry's shift to the east. The northwestern area of Russia, which produced 24.66 percent of Russia's military chemicals in 1937, produced only 14.73 percent in 1942, while western Siberia's percentage rose in the same time from zero to 4.25. In 1943, Vowi drew upon analyses made by Farben's laboratories of 90 captured Russian shells to determine the effect of the German invasion on the Soviet explosives industry. While shells produced before the war were mostly filled with TNT, it reported, those produced in 1941 and later had increasing percentages of the much poorer ammonium nitrate compound. Vowi attributed this to Russia's loss of two-thirds of her coke works to the Germans in the summer of 1941.

Other Vowi reports had a more direct and baneful impact on the war. Thomas's office asked it for photographs and maps of industrial plants in enemy countries. Vowi did not have many of these, and had to photostat the illustrations in its technical publications. At the request of the military, Vowi once explained, with the help of an aerial photograph and the advice of a Farben employee who it knew was familiar with the factory, the use of the various buildings of the Clifton Magnesium Works in England. It was the preparation for an air raid.

Farben's direct links with Thomas's office had the grave inconvenience, from the Abwehr's standpoint, of bypassing it. The Abwehr had economic sections of its own, called I Wi, the I for its espionage branch, the Wi for "Wirtschaft," or economy, because without them it could not claim to be a well-rounded intelligence-gathering agency. Probably the most active of these was precisely the one that dealt with Farben.

The reason was Major Albrecht Focke. He had served as an active officer in the artillery from 1914 to 1920, had risen in industry to an executive post with a freight-car factory, and then, during summer reservist training with the Abwehr, had let a friend, Major Ernst Bloch, head of the Abwehr headquarters I Wi, talk him into returning to active service because of his business background. The Abwehr subpost at Cologne had included, since around 1936, one of the first I Wi desks in an Abwehr outstation, perhaps because only a few miles down the Rhine, at Leverkusen, was Farben's big pharmaceutical plant for Bayer Aspirin. But the unit had done little, in part because it consisted of only one officer. Focke became the second in the second half of 1938 and immediately began to build it up.

A small round nimble man with a thousand bright ideas, Focke sped about in the Rhine and Ruhr areas contacting Farben and other firms for information. Although he sometimes contacted the Bayer representatives abroad directly, normally he dealt with the Leverkusen plant manager, the assistant manager, and the pharmaceutical sales chief, all of them Farben directors. Focke's assistant, a young man whose brusque and stubborn manner elicited complaints from the sales chief, then picked up the actual documents from a younger Farben official. These consisted of Bayer correspondence and of extracts from the reports of Bayer sales representatives abroad. The Focke-Bayer relationship paralleled one on a higher level between Max Ilgner and Bloch, who had overcome what some Germans called the "birth defect" of being a half Jew by being made an honorary Aryan.

Despite this, Farben always fiercely resisted giving out information. In 1939 the Abwehr called a conference in Frankfurt of all the Farben executives who represented its interests in the various factories. One purpose was to improve the flow of information. But "Except for a good Farben meal, not much came out" of the conference, remarked Focke afterward. In two years, things degenerated to the point where he summoned some of the board members—among Germany's most powerful industrialists—to his office and lectured them on their national duty. It didn't help. One day he gave a pep talk to some Farben people in which he mentioned how their information helped improve the Abwehr's. Afterward, one executive came to him and, instead of offering to provide more material, asked whether Farben couldn't subscribe to the Abwehr reports! Ilgner himself played the double game.

"I don't understand," he told Focke once. "Surely you must have gotten my travel reports."

When Focke denied it, he called in one of his subordinates and bawled him out. The man squirmed like a worm. As the man and Focke left the room together, he told the Abwehr officer:

"You see how he is. He knows perfectly well that you didn't get them."

Farben used anything as an excuse not to give out information. In the spring of 1944, while the transfer of the Abwehr to the SD was being prepared, an Abwehr officer appeared at a company office for some data. "You're supposed to be working for the SS," the Farben executive said to Berlin, "and here's a man from the Wehrmacht come to us. What's the story?" That, said Focke, was "typical Farben." He felt that all big firms were far less helpful to the war effort than the average individual, and that Farben was the worst of all. He thought the cartel was just protecting its pocketbook, but the cause reached deeper than that. A giant business enterprise was again placing its own interests above those of anybody or anything else, including its country.

The Abwehr sucked on other firms as well. On 20 March 1935, Major Gustav Bode of the Abwehr post in Dresden wrote to August Kotthaus, manager of the optical giant, the Carl Zeiss firm, in Jena, not far from the Czech border. After first politely thanking Kotthaus "for your willingness to support me in my assignment, economic reconnaissance," Bode fired seven requests at him. The first asked, "In which factory of the Skoda concern are crankshafts produced? Latest plans of the factory with exact indication of the factory buildings in question." Other questions dealt with electric monitoring apparatuses produced by a Prague firm and with maps. Four weeks later Kotthaus sent in the answers. Abwehr officers from two other posts likewise contacted Zeiss for information, and the firm cooperatively delivered material on the optical and precision-tool industries in Czechoslovakia, Poland, Russia, France, and the United States. In the summer of 1937, Zeiss executives visiting the largest precision-tool and optical plant in Warsaw learned that this factory had installed the artillery fire-control system at the fortress on a peninsula protecting Danzig. They sent in a report.

The Abwehr also approached one of the largest and most notorious of German firms: the armaments manufacturer, Fried. Krupp A. G. On 12 October 1937, the Abwehr's Lieutenant Commander Hermann Menzel conferred in Essen with a Krupp representative.

"Menzel asked for intelligence on foreign armaments (but not including matters published in newspapers) received by Krupp from their agents abroad and through other channels to be passed on to the Abwehr," the representative noted. "On our part we undertook to supply information." Near the end of their talk, Menzel soothed the evident concern of the businessman. He promised not to pass on to Krupp's competitors any foreign information that Krupp had picked up for the Abwehr.

One of those competitors was already working for the Abwehr, and producing more: Rheinmetall-Borsig, the big gun company. The reason for the greater success? The Abwehr had taken in a former Rheinmetall employee.

Nazi party intelligence likewise sought the cooperation of major industries. Long before he took over in June 1941 as head of the RSHA's Department VI (foreign intelligence), Walter Schellenberg had thought about the need for economic intelligence. He had dealt with economic matters earlier in the thirties and with firms on counterespionage during his SD assignment in the Ruhr later. Soon after he became head of RSHA VI, he went to see the Reich economics minister, the effeminate Walther Funk. Funk was said to have had a certain weakness for the 28-year-old Schellenberg, and let him establish within his ministry a liaison unit whose main function was to help RSHA VI gain entrée to major firms. At the same time, Schellenberg founded within his Department VI an economic-intelligence group, VI Wi.

He then made contact with virtually every important firm in Germany, in many of which an officer was assigned as liaison to VI Wi. At the

Dresdner Bank, for example, VI Wi spoke with Dr. Karl Rasche, a party member. Schellenberg's men talked with insurance firms, with Telefunken and Standard Elektrik, with the Hamburg shipping firm Hapag and other corporations with foreign connections, with industrial associations such as the Reichsgruppe Industrie. The information that they obtained flowed into VI Wi, where it was digested and then fed to such clients as armaments minister Albert Speer.

Independent and government research agencies also contributed to the German intelligence effort. Nearly all had been created long before the war to study economic affairs. The Institute for Market Analysis, for example, had begun in 1925 as a small work group within the Reich Statistical Department. By the time the war started, it had 180 employees, 25,000 volumes in its library, and its own building on the Fasanenstrasse in Berlin. To it, and to other agencies like it, flowed quantities of data, which the staffs analyzed, refined, and worked up into reports. These went to military and party posts either on demand or on the institutes' own initiative. The reports usually just implied military conclusions, but sometimes they stated them outright.

Before the attack on the Netherlands, for example, the Reich Department for War-Economic Planning issued an 87-page report on the economic structure of the Netherlands. It went into great detail about the population, the land, agriculture, and various industries, pointing out that economically the country "divides into the industry-poor north and the mainly industrial south," and not forgetting to note that "Commerce and transportation are . . . to a great extent dominated by Jewish elements." But its conclusion said nothing about the strategic importance of the country to Germany. On the other hand, the same department's 23-page report of about the same time, "The British Tonnage Problem in the War," predicted: "If it is, for instance, possible to maintain or even to increase ship sinkings at or above the rate struck in the first two weeks of the war, in other words to sink 500,000 gross tons a month, for a long time—for example, two years—then the fate of Great Britain will probably be sealed. Such losses can be recovered neither through recourse to neutral tonnage nor through raising the new construction activity, unless the U.S.A. actively enters the war."

Dozens of institutes, from the largest and most respected to what appeared to be one-man operations, sent material to the military agencies. The famous World Economic Institute, attached to the University of Kiel, reported in June 1943 on the organization of the British blockade of Germany. From Vienna, Dr. Ivan Karl Turyn, working out of Suite 9 at Doblhoftgasse 5 in the center of the city, submitted 2- and 3-page reports almost daily late in 1941 and early in 1942. Report No. 129 of 18 September 1941 reported that despite a rise in Hungarian oil taxes, the oil

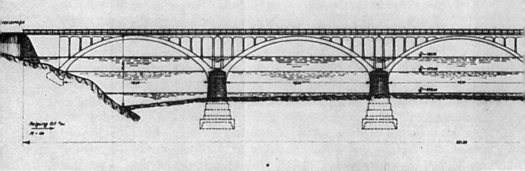

The Marienbad Research Institute furnishes a drawing of the railroad bridge over the Euphrates River in Turkey that could be dynamited to disrupt shipments of chrome to the Allies

producers had decided to maintain their price. The Reich Statistical Department's foreign research section produced an economic atlas of the Soviet Union in 1942, mapping the sources of such vital raw materials as petroleum, coal, wood, iron, and manganese. Just after the invasion of Russia, the Gmelin Institute provided figures on Soviet phosphate rock production. After Turkey broke off diplomatic relations with Germany, the Marienbad Research Institute showed, with photographs and diagrams of bridges and with highly detailed railroad maps, that shipments of the 12,000 tons of chrome that went to America every month could best be disrupted by destroying a certain railway bridge over the Euphrates River.

Seldom were the reports that specific, however. Most were far more vaporous. In Germany, an estimated 380 institutions crowded the research scene. Some were purely academic, such as the one dealing with the dictionary of German spoken abroad. Many others had potential for national defense. Various scholarly associations and government and party offices held sway over groupings of these institutions. There existed, for example, the Reich Research Council, the Reich Research Association, the research branch of the Ministry for Science, Education, and People's Culture, and the Interior Ministry's Branch VI, which controlled many cultural matters. These agencies often conflicted with one another, lacing the usual snide battles of the Nazi period with a dash of academic bitchiness.

At the end of 1943, some months after displacing Frick as interior minister, Himmler rearranged assignments within his enlarged sphere. He transferred the supervision of the research institutes previously handled by Branch VI of the ministry to RSHA foreign intelligence. He put in charge a

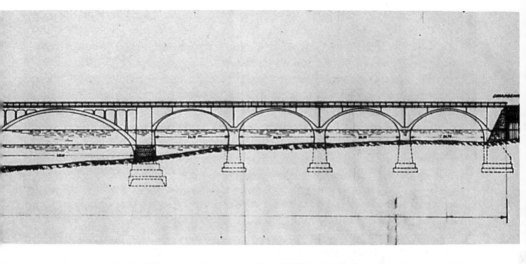

six-foot, two-inch Viennese historian, Dr. Wilfried Krallert, a 31-year-old SS lieutenant who had previously handled publication of research works in Vienna for the ministry. Schellenberg created a new group in his Department VI, Group VI G, with Krallert at its head.

Krallert's main work seemed to be to coordinate and standardize the work of the research institutes. At a conference in Prague on 9 and 10 March 1944, for example, Krallert urged closer cooperation among the institutes. He had already begun to unify map symbols and colors, he said. At least one participant was pleasantly surprised by Krallert's lack of the dictatorial aggression customary among officials with power in Germany.

But the system was already doomed. The payments of the OKW's War Economy and Armaments Department to research foundations, which had risen to a peak of *RM*305,763 ($122,305) in 1941–42, fell back in 1943–44 to *RM*121,869 ($48,747). In September 1944 most of the research institutes were suspended for the duration of the war. There is no evidence that the German war effort suffered greatly as a consequence.

Intelligence also arrived in Germany from other co-belligerents, but it was merely a trickle. Hungary, Rumania, Finland had neither the means nor the motivation to make great contributions. The Japanese were half a world away; the Italians dropped out of the war halfway through.

The exchange of information between the German armed services and their foreign counterparts did not operate on an organized basis before the war. At best, each passed some details to the other from time to time.

Before Germany invaded Russia, Finland sent over some material based on her experience in the Winter War. Later, at the battlefronts, where, for example, Rumanian and Hungarian armies fought under German command, front-line intelligence was routinely passed back and forth. But though exchange channels were formalized during the war, and liaison posts created where the attachés did not suffice, higher levels still only sent bits and pieces to Germany. Vichy France's Admiral Darlan offered the German navy information on British naval dispositions; the Führer was pleased to accept. On 3 August 1942, the chief of the general staff—then directing the German advance on Stalingrad—got a report, via Stockholm, from the Japanese military attaché in Russia: "West of Stalingrad 3 armies. Very weak in number of divisions. Unified army command no longer assured. Army groups operate without connection." The Balkan satellites seem not to have forwarded their intelligence estimates to Foreign Armies East and West—probably in part because the eastern information was already incorporated in the German army group reports to Foreign Armies East and because they had nothing of value to say about the United States and Great Britain, with whom they were not in contact.

Intelligence cooperation among the Axis countries was most extensive, paradoxically, in the most secret area: radio intelligence. It produced the most voluminous and most concrete results, and technical cooperation was easy and fruitful. The B-Dienst began as early as 1934 to work with the Finns on Soviet naval traffic. With Franco's permission, it set up posts in Spain to monitor British and French naval communications in the Mediterranean. Before the war, it swapped French intercepts with the Italians, then moved to British intercepts as well, and finally to a close cooperation on cryptanalytic techniques and results. The army's codebreakers were approached by the Japanese to trade cipher material over Russia. A little while later they gave the Italians a French cipher key, for which they expected in return some material out of the Mediterranean. At the height of the war, the SD's young spymaster-evaluator in Vienna for southeast Europe, Wilhelm Höttl, made contact with a Hungarian army radio-intelligence unit. By giving it some money, he obtained from it quantities of its solutions, notably those of the Turkish ambassador and military attaché in Moscow. These he passed back to Schellenberg in Berlin.

The Abwehr and Italy's Servizio Informazione Militare traded information, largely as a result of the good relations between Canaris and General Cesare Amè. Other espionage material was passed between the allies via diplomatic channels. In London, for example, American embassy code clerk Tyler Kent copied hundreds of confidential documents and gave them to a woman friend, who in turn passed them to the Italian military attaché (this was before England and Italy were at war). As a result, on 23 May 1940 the German ambassador in Rome was telegraphing Berlin that President Roosevelt had told Winston Churchill that "It would be possible to hand over 40 or 50 destroyers of the old type," among other matters of high policy.

And occasionally the heads of government themselves brought intelligence to one another. They embedded it in their communications—usually to support a point they were making. "It is my conviction that America will intervene in the war," Mussolini wrote Hitler on 6 November 1941, "and this time with an expeditionary corps, to be based in Egypt. This is logical. I am in possession of a cable intercepted by my service, announcing the arrival at Cairo of a mission headed by General Maxwell." The other Axis dictators could seldom provide even minutiae like this. Representatives of states puny beside Germany, and terrified of offending her, their sole intelligence function in their groveling conferences with Hitler was to reflect back to him his views of the situation. They nodded, they concurred, they repeated his arguments in new words or with new facts. The effect was anti-intelligence, for it reinforced the unreal and distorted visions by which Hitler sought to guide the German war machine.

For centuries Germans had emigrated and established colonies or settlements all over the world. In some places, such as the United States, they assimilated relatively quickly. Elsewhere, they segregated themselves in cultural and linguistic enclaves. The biggest of these was in Russia, where the Soviet regime established the German Volga Autonomous Soviet Socialist Republic for them.

Seventy-four organizations connected the 4 million German emigrants with their homeland. Some, dating as far back as 1880, served mainly economic and cultural goals. The newer Nazi agencies sought to extend party influence over the expatriates or to use them abroad for party foreign-policy purposes, giving rise to the legend of the 5th column. Both old and new also obtained information from the residents abroad.

Of the several pre-Nazi organizations, the most important was the Deutsches Ausland-Institut (DAI). It was founded in 1917 as a propaganda agency, but, perhaps because it was in Stuttgart, center of an area that had contributed a high proportion of German emigrés, it changed its function after World War I. To help Germans find opportunities overseas, the DAI collected information on other countries, in particular on their industries and on jobs. This work continued after Hitler assumed power and the agency was Nazified.

Most of its information came from newspaper clippings, which it filed by country. Some came as well from travelers or residents asked to write reports. Much of this was rather general, and, while usually accurate in details, was mistaken in larger impression. It erred badly, for example, on American attitudes. For its informants were nearly always Germans or of German descent living in or visiting German communities, and their views were often one-sided. Even the clippings were selected, consciously or not, to support German preconceptions. This kept the DAI from providing any kind of corrective to prevailing German judgments about the United States.

Sometimes, however, the DAI's files and influx of newspapers and magazines proved useful to government agencies seeking specific facts. Among

those agencies was the Abwehr. For the German occupation of the Sudetenland, the German-populated border districts in Czechoslovakia, the DAI
furnished the OKW with a 1:200,000 map of the boundary between the
Czech and the German areas. Admiral Canaris wrote the lord mayor of
Stuttgart on 11 February 1938 noting that the DAI "had often rendered
valuable services to the Wehrmacht" and sending *RM5*,000 ($2,000) to
pay for future cooperation with the Abwehr post in Stuttgart. The DAI
used *RM3*,000 of this to start a newspaper- and magazine-clipping service
and the rest to buy membership in the organization for several officers of
the OKW and of the local military district. With the outbreak of the war,
the Abwehr post there assigned the DAI to produce a daily military press
information service for the OKW and the OKM. And when the Abwehr
needed men to send by U-boat to America on what became the eight-man
sabotage mission of 1942, it found their names in the files of the DAI.

By far the most important Nazi agency for gathering foreign information was the Auslandsorganisation, or AO. This was the party "district,"
or Gau, for all members abroad. Its head, or Gauleiter, was Ernst-Wilhelm
Bohle. He was only in his late twenties when he founded the organization
in Hamburg in 1931, but he possessed the impressive credential of having
been born in England. He guided the AO's growth from 3,350 members
early in 1933 to 52,648 in 1939 and was rewarded in 1937 with being
made a state secretary in the Foreign Office. In the summer of 1935, Bohle
and Ribbentrop, not yet foreign minister but only the head of Hitler's main
party foreign-affairs advisory body, agreed that this army of supporters
should help advance the foreign policy of the Reich by supplying pertinent
information on local affairs.

So every month each Nazi country group leader wrote and forwarded
to AO headquarters in Germany four or five pages on the political situation of his host country. Sometimes he included economic or military tidbits. Bohle bragged that his men kept him better informed than the diplomats
did the Foreign Office. He did not give the reports to the foreign minister but to his party superior, at first Hess and then Bormann. Himmler too
saw them. Hitler, however, seldom did. The reason is that, despite Bohle's
boast, the quality of the reports was not particularly high, nor did they
often furnish the party with any valuable foreign secrets. The country group
leaders abroad mainly scratched them together from the local press, rarely
even adding any information or comments of their own. Their selection
naturally suited Nazi preconceptions. As a result, Himmler, who seldom
read anything longer than two pages, pored over the voluminous AO reports and annotated them with approving comments such as "very interesting" and "good observation." But their superficiality and lack of substance
meant that they played almost no role in the making of foreign-policy
decisions.

The AO, however, performed another and more sinister function. It provided a pool of potential spies. As early as 1937, the AO was maintaining liaison with the Abwehr. The liaison officer was Captain Heinz Cohrs, a World War I artillerist and AO member who had won an instant of notoriety in 1933 by being sensationally kicked out of Austria for pro-Nazi activities. Later Bohle deputized the head of his personnel department as liaison to the SD. This was Erich Schnaus, a slender man in his early thirties who had served as party leader in Madrid and whom Bohle regarded as unimaginative but industrious.

One of the AO's greatest spy successes came in the Netherlands. The Nazi leader there, a dentist named Otto Butting, was a formidable type who terrorized the German minister and who had had himself named an attaché to the legation to prevent Dutch prying. He used one-half of a house under diplomatic immunity in The Hague. The other half was occupied by the Abwehr, which had its own agents. Butting supplemented these paid spies with the numerous members of his German Citizens' Association—the disguised Nazi country group—scattered throughout Holland. In February 1939, he suggested using German girls working as servants in the homes of prominent Dutchmen to spy on them. This seems to have come to naught, as did his proposal to use the members of his association to spy on Netherlands shipping: Cohrs told him the Abwehr had already arranged for this. Finally, Butting simply directed the local functionaries of his organization to send him all data that might be of military importance.

Dozens of items came in. There were descriptions of fortifications, of airfields, of road obstructions; there were reports of overheard telephone conversations and of troop movements. Butting gave some of these to the local Abwehr chief, who boasted that there was hardly a stone or tree in Holland that he didn't know about. The others Butting put into envelopes addressed to Cohrs and, using his diplomatic immunity, took them across the border to Kleve to mail them. Unfortunately, one day in April 1940, he somehow lost one of these envelopes, It was filled with 15 pages of reports, some typed, some handwritten, some on German legation letterheads, some signed by Butting as attaché, some by JONATHAN, the codename of the Abwehr chief. A bicyclist found it on the side of a street in Voorburg, a suburb of The Hague. The Dutch opened it—and promptly kicked Butting out. But his work was done. Bohle wrote that he had successfully fulfilled his assignment to get information on the Dutch army and the defense system and its installations.

The AO also recruited spies in South America. The names of many members of the espionage rings in Chile and Argentina had first been found on the party rolls. In Switzerland, scores of AO members worked for the Abwehr post in Stuttgart. This form of recruitment made spies a little more prominent than they ought to be, but ease or necessity led the

Germans to it. It worked better in some places than others. The pro-Axis attitude of some Latin American governments long protected the spies, but Switzerland arrested several dozen of the AO recruits in August 1942.

In the United States, however, fear that a similar episode would damage relations kept both the AO and the Abwehr from recruiting agents among the German-American Bund and its predecessors. Indeed, the Nazi party and the German government fought shy of those organizations and discouraged individual Nazi political activity. Nevertheless, individual Nazis did spy, such as the physician who had once been president of the Friends of the New Germany, a forerunner of the Bund. A ring sprang up around him, which was broken in 1938. Despite the innumerable rumors, no connection was shown between the Bund and the ring because none existed. Indeed, Fritz Kuhn, leader of the Bund, loudly declared, "If they was spies, they should be shot." They were not, but although the Abwehr, with the reluctant consent of the Foreign Office, continued to spy in the United States, it tapped neither the Bund nor the AO for agent candidates.

During the course of the war, however, Bohle grew dissatisfied with the subservient position of the AO in supplying hard-won manpower to other agencies, which in effect aggrandized themselves at his expense. He had his own empires to maintain.

And these were crumbling. In 1941, he had been booted out of his Foreign Office post. Like so many others in the Third Reich who had lost real power, he turned to intelligence as an indirect source of it.

So he built up his information networks. But in the summer of 1942, he collided with the authorities who had gotten there first. In Turkey, the ambassador, former chancellor Franz von Papen, fought bitterly against the AO, and finally succeeded in getting Ribbentrop to order the local AO leader home. At the same time, Schellenberg got Himmler to warn the AO leaders in the various countries not to maintain their own intelligence services. Schellenberg believed he had won the battle, and he and Canaris then again used the AO to get the names of prospective agents, particularly from among Germans returning from having lived overseas.

But administrative victories under Hitler were seldom clean-cut and total. More than a year later, the AO still clung to a private and secret intelligence service of its own in Turkey, undamaged by a defection there that had led to the downfall of the Abwehr. A Luftwaffe intelligence officer characterized its agents as "dilettantes lacking completely in know-how and experience." But it mattered not whether their reports were good or bad, objective or partisan. The time had passed when intelligence could stay or divert the inexorable mandate of events. Bohle's hopes of intelligence that would let him pull off a diplomatic coup and so restore his power died when, on 2 August 1944, Turkey broke relations with Germany.

7

Before the Main Body

THE oldest, simplest, and most basic form of military intelligence consists of the sensing of the enemy by the individual soldier. He watches him. He listens to him. He may even smell him. In hand-to-hand combat, he feels him. He senses his enemy beginning to thrust with his bayonet, and dodges. In aiming his gun, a soldier uses intelligence.

This is of course physical intelligence at its most rudimentary. But such observation by troops constituted the primary and most voluminous means of reporting enemy activity for German military intelligence; it formed the basis of I c reports, though it did lose in importance relative to other sources as they rose in the command structure. Sometimes individual observations offered clues to enemy intentions. If Soviet soldiers wore caps, they would probably remain on the defensive; if they wore helmets, an attack was likely. In Normandy in 1944, the Germans watched the British put up bridges over streams in their cramped lodgment area and saw supplies pouring into it. They recognized that these were preparations for an attempt at a breakout.

More often, not one but a succession of observations enabled the Germans to detect a trend—and consequently to deduce enemy intentions. They did so successfully in central Russia in 1942.

Flat, open farming land spread out before the 102nd Infantry Division. Bushes speckled the uncultivated fields. Here and there grew scraggly woods of mixed hard and soft wood. To the north stood a few low hills. Innumerable little Russian villages, each with its single street lined by houses, dotted the area, seldom more than half a mile apart. The division's lines ran north and south. Through them diagonally to the northeast cut the Osuga River, a steep-banked, meandering stream, some 75 feet wide,

INDICATIONS OF RUSSIAN INTENTIONS

offensive	*defensive*
wearing of helmets	wearing of caps
artillery firing for adjustment	harassing fire of uniform density at regular intervals, as morning and evening
increased observation posts without noticeable increase in fire	roving pieces firing at intervals from many positions
clearing of mine fields and barbed wire	laying of mine fields and setting out of barbed wire
construction of lightly built dugouts	construction of heavily built dugouts
construction of real artillery positions unoccupied or with dummy pieces just behind the front lines, especially for antiaircraft artillery	construction of dummy artillery positions with no point of concentration; antiaircraft artillery only at traffic centers
inconspicuous traffic near front	sporadic appearances of tanks in same sectors
continuous visible traffic in open columns and motor noises toward the front for long periods	no increase in traffic
increase in enemy patrols	no increase in patrols
nervous behavior of soldiers with movement across areas under fire, indicating new arrivals	no change in behavior
change in mess and guard hours	no changes in schedules
new faces and languages in front lines	same faces and languages
carrying of packs but not gas masks	carrying of gas masks but not packs

which was soon joined, behind the Russian lines, by the similar Vazuza River; the two then spilled into the Volga.

From field fortifications and from the hills, the troops could look over into the enemy territory between the two rivers. They could see the Russian troops eating, walking, digging; sometimes they could hear them, and their vehicles, as well. These observations reached the division's I c. He sought to pull them into a coherent picture and passed the important ones on to the corps command.

The strategic picture in that November of 1942 made a Soviet attack likely. The 102nd was part of Army Group Center, whose front bulged toward Moscow, 120 miles to the east. The Russians had, during the summer, tried to reduce this salient. It still irritated and threatened and tempted them; the higher German commands expected that they would renew their assaults upon it. But to defend it well, the Germans had to know where on its long perimeter the attacks would fall.

Much of the answer came from simple observation of the Russians and their activities. On Thursday, 5 November, the Germans spotted several hundred Russians marching toward the front before the division and its neighbor to the south. The Russians had long been harassing the 102nd with long-range artillery fire; that same day, this included for the first time shells of all calibers and salvos of 16 rounds, which suggested the arrival of a "Stalin organ" rocket gun. The Russians appeared to be strengthening their artillery before the division as well as trying to soften up the Germans. That night, the Russians probed the 102nd's lines for weak spots in an attack supported by three or five tanks. In the clear sunny weather of the next day, Friday, the Germans saw 600 to 700 Russians march toward the front in company-sized groups. Saturday saw normal Russian trench traffic and only slight movements in the rear. Artillery continued to harass the 102nd. The Germans watched with amusement as the Russians tried to smokescreen a shifting of two antitank guns in a gully.

All of this activity was compared by corps, army, and army group I cs with that in other areas of the front. It appeared to be greater before the 102nd. This pointed to it as a possible target. Shortly thereafter, however, all activity ebbed as the fall rains turned the Russian roads into mud that all but immobilized vehicles. Only when the ground had frozen hard enough to support tanks did the Russians resume operations.

On 18 November, they shattered the calm with a peppery artillery and rocket fire onto the wings of the 102nd. For the first time, the division observed skiers and sledge parties in winter clothing. It heard the enemy digging and hammering. The Russians again reconnoitered the 102nd's left wing in a raid against Hill 207.3 that cost them 26 dead. In the following days, traffic grew heavier between the Osuga and Vazuza rivers. The regular 10-day artillery check showed that Russian guns had become denser before the 102nd and its neighbors. Scouts felt out the 102nd and neighboring divisions. The Russians again struck at Hill 207.3. They reinforced their front-line troops. They put up new bridges across the Vazuza, which, German officers scrutinizing them through their binoculars noted, were capable of carrying tanks.

The I cs at the higher levels spiced this basic information with more exotic intelligence from radio intercepts, spies, and prisoner and deserter interrogations. But the solid facts of enemy troop reinforcements and artillery concentrations, of men sacrificed in reconnaissances and of matériel and effort expended in construction, most persuaded the Germans. It helped convince them that the Russian intentions against the 102nd were not a sham. The Red army needed guns and men too desperately to squander so many just for show. Their much greater concentration opposite the 102nd compared to other areas indicated to the Germans that the major Russian attack would fall on that unit.

And, at 7:30 a.m. on 25 November, after an hour and a half of artillery bombardment, it did. Wave after brown wave of Russians, supported by 25 thundering, spitting tanks, charged against the 102nd. The Germans were ready. They flung them back, repulsing, right at "the presumed point of main effort," the strongest assaults of the "anticipated" Soviet winter offensive.

The Germans gained the intelligence that enabled them to win this defensive success mainly through passive observation. But they did not wait just for information to come to them. They went out and actively sought it. Most frequently they did this by means of patrols. Company, battalion, and regimental commanders dispatched small groups of men to sneak into the enemy lines, usually at night, to investigate the enemy situation in detail.

One commander, for example, wanted his patrols to discover:

1. Are the Russians preparing a defense near the front or in a line further back (while leaving weak infantry elements with strong artillery in the front)?
2. Where are enemy positions (foxholes, trenches, dugouts, connected constructions, strong points, machine-gun nests, concrete bunkers)?
3. Where has the enemy erected barricades and obstacles?
4. Where have mines been laid?
5. Where are close-combat defenses?
6. Where are antitank defenses?

Patrols varied in size with the difficulty of their task. Sometimes only a handful of men moved into enemy territory. In early 1940 such a patrol of the 289th Infantry Regiment, 98th Infantry Division, reported on its operations near the Maginot Line on two successive nights like this:

A patrol under the leadership of First Lieutenant Winkler, 10th Company, crossed over the Lauter [from Germany into Alsace, a German-speaking region of France] opposite the playing field west of Scheibenhardt the night of 2 March 1940 and discovered a machine-gun position (unoccupied) on the Scheibenhardt-Niederlauterbach railroad stretch and a dugout (unoccupied) on the Heidenberg. The patrol came back without being fired upon.

On 3 March 1940 First Lieutenant Winkler with Lieutenant Liepart, Corporal Medrisch and Private Wehrle went to the same place over the Lauter with the intention of reconnoitering along the railway embankment to the east. Near the rail line the patrol fell into a hand-grenade trap, in which two hand grenades exploded. Since the patrol was known to the French through the explosion, it returned. First Lieutenant Winkler was lightly wounded.

Larger than these were the fighting patrols. In addition to reconnoitering enemy positions, they often sought to take prisoners for interrogation and to seize documents. In Italy, such patrols of the Ist Parachute Corps stayed as far as 10 miles behind American lines for up to three days, observing the defense system, supply routes, and reserves. In Russia, a raiding party of Grenadier Regiment 320 investigated the enemy territory:

> The raiding party departed from the German main line of resistance at 3:55 p.m. on 16 January 1943 under the command of Noncommissioned Officer Steffler with a force of 2 noncoms, 5 men, and 3 engineers with 2 covering troops of 10 men and Lieutenant Federer (Signal Battalion 212) with a radio and attained the enemy barbed wire at 4:50 p.m. Since the cloudiness rapidly diminished to complete cloudlessness, the start of the operation was delayed. The preparatory work in the biting cold wind and crunching snow required the greatest exertion. The approach took place unnoticed; the Russian machine-gun outpost was firing out of the embrasure in another direction; the barbed wire was 5 feet high and set up in 3 rows as a 15-foot-deep apron obstacle. In front of this were tank mines, which stuck up out of the snow about 4 inches and were immediately recognizable, with an intermediary distance of 35 feet. A little way in front of the wire barrier were cylinder-shaped tension-wire mines of cast iron. Engineer-Corporal Probst cut through the barrier and the tension wires, then he stuck a distributed charge, to which a dazzle bomb was also fastened, into the machine-gun embrasure. One engineer and one man at once secured about 100 feet north and south of the break-in point and each laid a warning mine. At this a sentry of the next bunker just to the north called an alarm.
>
> The turf wall was barbed-wired and the battle position surrounded with an all-around barrier. On crossing the barrier a mine went off, which caused no damage. It turned out that the bunker broken into was a heated, one-room battle position. On the previous days it had always smoked and created the impression that it comprised a living bunker with an attached battle position. The position was already badly destroyed by the distributed charge, the Russian and the machine gun annihilated. Other occupants were not in it.
>
> In between came a counterthrust from the north, inside the Russian wall, in strength about 30 to 40 men, which was first turned back by the raiding party at about 35 feet with hand grenades, machine pistols, and rifle grenades. Undoubted enemy losses were occasioned by the warning mines. According to statements [our men] agreed upon, 12 to 15 men were casualties. Simultaneously one Russian ran toward the break-in position; he was blown into the air by the other warning mine. During the counterthrust 3 men were slightly wounded by enemy hand grenade fragments. With another demolition of the entire bunker the raiding party vacated the break-in position. The fire of the heavy weapons was ordered by light signals, since the radio was not understandable because of the battle noise. On the way from the turf wall to the Russian barbed wire the raiding party commander was wounded by a grazing shot and another member by hand grenade fragments.
>
> The fire of the heavy weapons came immediately and lay remarkably well, so that it may be assumed with certainty that further enemy losses were occasioned by the interdiction fire, which was drawn toward the break-in point and lay directly upon the line of main resistance.

Ascertainments:

1. The battle stand was heated and created the impression of a living- and combat-bunker.

2. The sentry post is barbed-wired and mined inside the enemy line of main resistance.

3. In every operation of the battalion, the Russian counterthrust has started immediately.

4. After the pulling out of the raiding party the Russians replied with heavy mortar and antitank fire, in contrast to the last operation.

5. The Russian positions were heavily wired at the point of break-in.

6. About 200 feet east of the break-in point were ostensible living shelters.

7. On the basis of the previous raiding parties the Russians are the strongest opposite the 6th Company.

Results:

The raiding party leader, 2 members and 2 engineers slightly wounded.

One battle position with one machine gun and one sentry blown up.

Twelve to 15 Russians brought down in the counterthrust.

The information improved the regimental commander's picture of the enemy and so helped him lead his troops more effectively.

Patrols, even fighting patrols, went on foot. In static warfare, this satisfied the basic idea of reconnaissance: that it be out ahead of the main body, to give it warning of the enemy. But with troops on the march, this requirement could be fulfilled only by having a reconnaissance organ that moved faster than the main body. For infantry, this meant mounted troops. Infantry regiments thus had mounted platoons of 33 horse to scout ahead for them.

Because divisions, which combine the several arms, can fight independently, they need a more self-sustained reconnaissance unit. Each German infantry division had a reconnaissance battalion. Essentially, it consisted of a main operational element and several support elements—rather like a miniature division itself.

Its normal form was found in the 48 divisions mobilized together in the first, second, and twelfth "waves" of mobilization. In their reconnaissance battalions, the reconnaissance elements comprised a cavalry squadron for reconnaissance, a bicycle squadron for manpower support, and a heavy squadron with guns and two light scout cars. Most of the other divisions substituted a bicycle squadron for the cavalry squadron, though motorized infantry divisions had all motorized elements. Altogether, these battalions had about 600 men; the normal ones, 200 horse as well.

They reconnoitered for the divisional commander and reported to him, not the I c. Starting very often before dawn, the mounted units rode out, generally in three groups. The middle one trotted along the main advance road of the division, the others on roads to the right and left in a total width of 5 miles. If they encountered enemy resistance, the bicyclists and heavy weapons squadron sped up, dismounted, and provided the strength to break through. The riders reconnoitered up to 15 and 20 miles ahead of the division, sometimes not returning in the evening but staying out and getting their next day's orders via the mounted radio troop. They reported not only on enemy location but also on topographic conditions. During the French campaign, for example, the reconnaissance of the 3rd Infantry Division reported that the bridges leading over the Semois to Hautes Rivières were too narrow. The commander sent engineers ahead to build their own.

The turn in the war that shifted Germany from offense to defense and the often static nature of the fighting in Russia doomed the reconnaissance battalions. They were needed less than during the great advances. Many lost their mounted squadrons to the cavalry regiments that were formed to fight partisans on the difficult terrain. In October 1943, the army drew the logical conclusion. It converted the reconnaissance battalions into fusilier battalions—infantry battalions with somewhat stronger firepower and greater mobility than the ordinary. Divisional commanders used them as a reserve that they could throw in wherever the situation was especially difficult. They had become, the former reconnoiterers ruefully said, the divisional fire department.

The principle that reconnoiterers must stay out before the main body excluded horses as scouts for tanks. Only armored cars would serve. Captain Heinz Guderian recognized this when, in the 1920s, he disregarded the Versailles Treaty, which forbade Germany from having "armoured cars, tanks, and all similar constructions," and began building up a German armored force.

To tell the divisional commander of a fast-moving panzer division where the enemy was, the armored cars frequently had to travel fairly far and often had to cross rough terrain. They needed considerable range and the ability to traverse fields, ford streams, climb hills, cross trenches, and maneuver with agility. Sometimes they had to punch through enemy resistance and see what was behind the outposts. So they carried armor and weapons. But—as was historically characteristic of them—reconnaissance troops were not a combat outfit. If they ran into overwhelming enemy forces, they were not to stand and fight but were to pull back to where they could safely observe them and report. To facilitate this, the German heavy scout cars had separate rear-facing controls with their own driver so that they could rapidly pull backward out of danger. (The rear driver's job while the car was moving forward consisted of little more than watching the scenery disappear.)

The German army began developing armored cars to fit these requirements in 1926. Its original ambitious specifications for an 8- or 10-wheeled

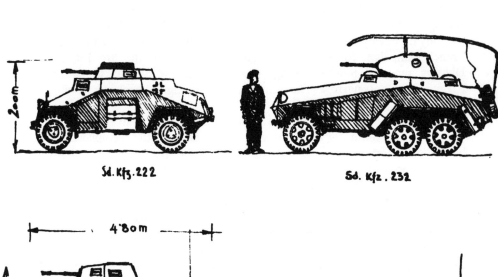

Sd. Kfz. 222

Sd. Kfz. 232

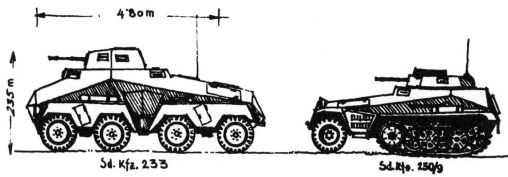

Sd. Kfz. 233

Sd. Kfz. 250/9

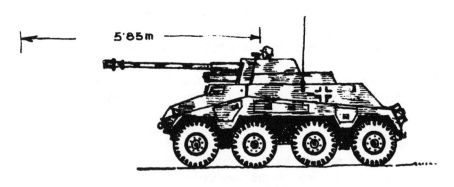

Sd. Kfz. 234 /4

The various armored scout cars used by the German army

vehicle proved too expensive, and in 1929 the army issued specifications for a 6-wheeled car. Early in the 1930s this entered mass production. It formed the backbone of the armored reconnaissance battalions that the army was then setting up. This was the Sd.Kfz. 231 (Sonder-Kraftfahrzeug, or special motor vehicle, 231). Though it had rearward controls and other special capabilities, it was basically an armored body on a truck chassis. Advancing standards soon impeached its cross-country performance, and in 1935, with money available and rearmament getting under way, development began on an 8-wheeled replacement that took over both its function and its Sd.Kfz. number.

This elegant vehicle had independent suspension and drive for each wheel and independent steering for each axle. It thus had a cross-country ability comparable to that of a tracked vehicle but much greater speed—50 miles an hour. It had half-inch armor, a three-quarter-inch gun, and a machine gun. Carrying a crew of four, including a rear driver, it ranged almost 200 miles. It came in three models: the Sd.Kfz. 231 (8-wheel) with a movable turret, the Sd.Kfz. 232 (8-wheel) with a radio but a fixed turret, and the Sd.Kfz. 233 (8-wheel) with a heavier gun and open top. In 1937, it began replacing the 6-wheeler, and by 1941 it had become the standard heavy armored scout car of the German army.

But not for long. Russian mud and poor roads bogged even it down. In December 1942 Hitler stopped its production. He replaced it with another, more modern 8-wheeler, designed in 1940 for the tropics with an air-cooled 12-cylinder motor. This became the Sd.Kfz. 234, which entered mass production in July of 1943. It not only proved capable of operating under some of the worst Russian conditions, but also met the new demands of warfare. It had a long-barreled gun up to 3 inches in caliber and armor up to an inch thick. In addition to this 8-wheeler, the Germans converted the half-tracked chassis of the armored troop carrier Sd.Kfz. 250 into the Sd.Kfz. 250/9, a heavy ground reconnaissance vehicle for the most difficult conditions.

Complementing these long-range vehicles was the light scout car. The 4-wheeler that first went into service in 1937 came in three models: the Sd.Kfz. 221, with a crew of two and a machine gun in its open-top turret, the Sd.Kfz. 222, with a three-man crew and a three-quarter-inch cannon, and the Sd.Kfz. 223, the radio version. Though relatively fast (up to 40 miles per hour), well armored (up to half an inch), and maneuverable, with independently driven and suspended wheels, it did not go cross-country as well as the troops had expected from such a vehicle. Nevertheless, it became the most widely used light scout car and served throughout the war.

These heavy and light scout cars formed the core equipment of the armored reconnaissance battalions. Within each battalion, at the start of the war, they were formed into two armored-car squadrons. Each squadron had one heavy and two light platoons. The heavy platoon comprised six of the larger armored cars. At the direction again not of the I c but of the divisional commander, these cars thrust like spears deep into the unknown territory ahead of the main body of the division. They sought to discover where in general the enemy was. They radioed back about obstacles, barricades, antitank guns—and contact with the enemy.

When contact was made, the commander released his two light platoons, with their total of 12 of the smaller cars. They swarmed densely around where the bigger cars had seen the enemy. With a patter of little feelers, they located him at more points and so with greater precision. This information naturally grew in urgency as the clash of the main bodies neared. Supporting the cars were a motorcycle squadron, which, arriving fast, provided firepower in case a skirmish developed, and a heavy squadron. This comprised an artillery platoon, to back up the motorcyclists, and an engineer platoon, to help the cars and guns cross streams and other obstacles. (These elements played a large role in the battalion's other main duties: advancing to, seizing, and holding important points, and screening its division's movements from the enemy.) A staff with a communications platoon and supply troops completed the battalion.

This equipment, this organization, and some names changed during the war. In preparation for the Russian campaign, the army expanded from 10 panzer divisions in May of 1940 to 21 a year later. Tanks had priority in production, and the output of armored cars fell behind. Consequently, for many of the new panzer divisions the reconnaissance battalion had instead of two scout car squadrons only one and a platoon. During 1943, however, Hitler and Guderian reorganized the panzer leadership in the hope of going once again onto the offensive. They renamed the squadrons, a word too reminiscent of slow-moving horses, "companies," a term long used by the tank arm. They raised the number of scout-car companies to the original two or even three per battalion. And they converted the motorcyclists, who had constantly gotten stuck in Russia, into infantry riding in armored personnel carriers. All battalions were not, however, identically organized or equipped: in particular, the late-arriving Sd.Kfz. 234 and 250/9 were distributed where most needed, and so unequally.

The reconnaissance battalions usually investigated the most immediate and local—the most tactical—situations. At 5:30 p.m. on 24 December 1941, Reconnaissance Battalion 3 in North Africa reported enemy armor advancing 10 miles north of Agedabia on the coastal road. The group consisted of armored cars, men, and artillery. The 15th Panzer Division, forewarned, drove it off. Occasionally ground reconnaissance results reached the Führer's situation conferences.

"The enemy," Jodl told Hitler on 5 March 1943, "has appeared for the first time eastwards of Sbeitla, that is, he was spotted by ground reconnaissance in the area of Sidi bou Zid. Some tanks and other movements. The southern area is now entirely clear."

Ground reconnaissance did not guarantee certainty of knowledge, for commanders sometimes drew wrong inferences from its reports. In November 1941, Rommel heard from the reconnaissance battalion of the 21st Panzer Division about considerable British armored-car activity. He thought it was just a reconnaissance in force. In fact it was the start of a major British offensive.

Other forms of ground reconnaissance were as highly specialized in their way as the armored cars. A dozen special engineer platoons set out acoustical sensors at a few points on the Russian front. These sensors, or sounding pots, were cylindrical or conical in shape, about 16 inches high and 5 inches in diameter. They were buried in the ground. Wires connected them to central listening stations. Experienced personnel there could tell, from the volume and type of noise, what kind of activity the enemy was engaged in.

These sensors mostly detected enemy sapping or bomb clockworks. But they could also hear a single infantry scout approaching. The range depended upon the ground: 15 to 20 yards on soft earth, 30 to 35 on hard, 80 to 100 on ice. When several enemy infantrymen were heard, the central would explode mines near them. The platoons covered 1 to 2 miles of front, but since they were always being stretched, their efficiency decreased. Moreover, enemy artillery fire often cut many of their wires, so that in combat the platoons seldom got a chance to fire their mines. Finally, the continuous retreats during the latter part of the war reduced their opportunities to set out their sounding pots and mines. The entire acoustic sensor program remained little more than experimental—not least because it was entirely defensive and could never promise much in the way of victory.

A far more important kind of special ground reconnaissance was the spotting of enemy guns. During her rearmament, Germany established artillery observation battalions within many of her artillery regiments to do this. They included sound- and light-ranging units. The light units took bearings on enemy muzzle flashes from three points a half-mile apart and, drawing the lines on a map, saw where they converged. Sound-ranging complemented this system, working in fog and rain and over ridges. It fixed a gun's location by measuring the time difference between the arrivals of a shell's air compression shock and the gun's muzzle clap at four microphones.

In a typical case, an observation battalion before Sevastopol spotted 15 Russian guns, 8 of them for the first time, in the 24 hours starting at 7 p.m. 25 November 1941. Four of the new ones, with "h" for "horizontal coordinate" and "v" for "vertical coordinate," were:

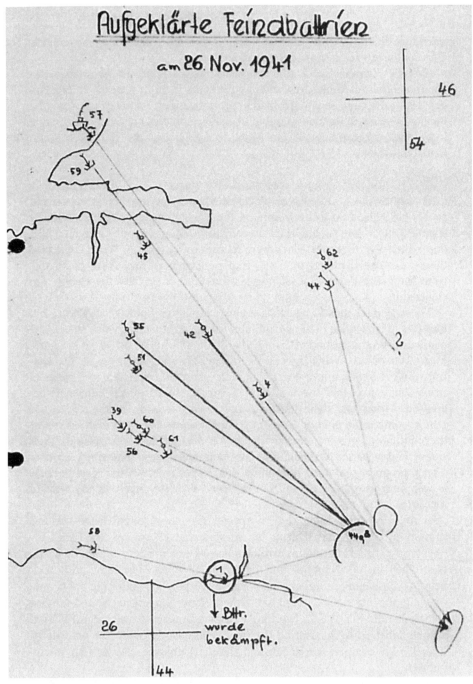

An artillery sound- and light-ranging battery map of "Reconnoitered Enemy Batteries" south of Sevastopol in the Crimea. Each enemy gun or battery—including one aboard a ship—is numbered; one battery is being counterbombarded by the Germans

Target 655   h 43 500   v 37 140   uncertain (180 by 300 yards) fired 60
             shots on 25 November from 4:15 to 7 p.m. into unknown area
             3 guns, medium caliber
Target 656   h 43 655   v 33 385   exact
             fired 6 shots from 10:55 to 11:25 p.m. into unknown area
             1 gun

Usually this information went to the artillery commander so that he could counterfire upon the enemy guns. During the campaign in the west, Observation Battalion 14 sustained some accurate, long-range enemy artillery fire. After some difficulty, it located the enemy guns about six miles away, just southwest of Wareghem. It relayed this information to the German batteries, which began to fire. The observation battalion noted the fall of shot, enabling the guns to correct their aim. They began firing for effect. Shell after shell flew over. The French battery fell silent. Later the Germans discovered that their shells had landed right in among the French guns—one directly on a gun—destroying them.

The intelligence about enemy gun locations also went to the I c. He observed where they were thickening or thinning out. This helped him decide whether the Russians were planning to advance or to withdraw.

Battle itself is the ultimate reconnaissance. Only then does the enemy disclose his full strength. Before the engagement, he does not fire all his guns all the time, as much for economy as for concealment. During it, however, he often needs them all. So he uses them—and reveals them. He also discloses his will to fight, his tactics, his strength. To gain this information during the critical moments of an engagement, regulations stated, "Combat reports are indispensable." The regulations summed up the German army's philosophy in a sentence that had barely changed since it appeared in the *Field Service Regulations* of 1887: "Battle furnishes the most trustworthy basis for judging the enemy."

8

The World from the Sky

ON a clear spring afternoon in 1942, Luftwaffe Captain Siegfried Knemeyer lifted his Junkers Ju 88 off a runway in Crete and headed east. The sun sparkled on the blue Mediterranean. Near Cyprus, he banked to the right and headed south, still climbing. In the cabin behind him, the crew chief–engineer monitored instruments and the radioman-observer re-checked his two big cameras. The converted bomber grew colder as it gained altitude, but the crew did not: they wore electrically heated suits that kept them warm enough, but that sometimes gave them little burns where the wiring had short-circuited.

The two engines droned, as they had that morning. On that mission, Knemeyer and his two crewmen had flown the Suez Canal from north to south, photographing it. The British had filled it with ships, apparently in preparation for an attempt to force their way through a hostile sea to beleaguered Malta. Even as Knemeyer was flying in the afternoon, dozens of his morning pictures, each about 12 inches by 12, were being evaluated by photo interpreters. They examined what looked like splinters in the thin streak of the canal with magnifying glasses and loupes to determine what each vessel was and what the total tonnage assembled there was.

This second flight was intended to complete the German coverage by providing information on the ships in the harbor of Alexandria. About an hour after take-off, Knemeyer saw, gradually emerging from the indistinct rim of the horizon, the historic city founded on the Canopic mouth of the beneficent Nile by the conquerer who had named it for himself and whom Knemeyer's Führer was seeking to emulate, where Euclid had taught, where the great library had burned, where Antony had abandoned an empire for Cleopatra. No pharos guided the twentieth-century pilot to it, but soon he was over the great metropolis and its harbors, soaring at 37,500 feet, far above the reach of antiaircraft fire and enemy fighters.

The Ju 88 banked to the right. Knemeyer ordered the cameras started. Every several seconds, they automatically snapped pictures. One camera, with a focal length of about 12 inches, provided broad coverage. The other, with a focal length of about 20 inches, furnished the details in a narrower area. Knemeyer held the craft steady and peered out the cockpit window. Far below in the transparent air, silhouetted against the tawny ground, British fighters swung helplessly back and forth, tethered at their ceiling. "It was like looking down into an aquarium and seeing the fishes swimming," Knemeyer said later.

But as he continued westward along the coastline, the situation changed. The fighters gave up the chase, but flak exploded under him. None seemed to hit the Junkers, but a little while later a propeller went bad and the engine had to be turned off. The plane sank lower. Knemeyer began losing control. For the first time in more than two years of aerial reconnaissance, he grew anxious. But fortunately he saw no more enemy airplanes. Soon he reached Tobruk, south of Crete. He turned north and flew home with his pictures.

They and the others revealed some 1.5 million tons of enemy shipping assembled in Egypt. Knemeyer's mission had brought strong evidence that the British were planning to mount a major operation of some kind or another. And when, in June, they did attempt to force a passage to Malta from both east and west, the Axis was ready: only 2 of the 17 freighters and tankers got through, and the island remained in jeopardy.

Siegfried Knemeyer was no ordinary reconnaissance pilot. He was flying for the Luftwaffe's élite strategic reconnaissance group. Knemeyer was a good enough airman to have been chosen as the personal pilot of the commander in chief of the army during the Polish campaign. And he was bright enough to have devised, before the war, a triangular course reckoner of particular value in navigating during long flights. These were among the reasons that a friend had recruited him for the special group.

This was the brainchild of lanky, easygoing Colonel Theodor Rowehl. A native of the lovely university town of Göttingen, Rowehl had been a reconnaissance pilot in World War I; he had several times crossed the Channel in his Rhomberg C 7 to reconnoiter targets in England. His group grew out of a solution he thought he saw, a decade or so after the war, to a problem of national defense. The re-creation of Poland as a nation had, after the First World War, gravely weakened his fatherland. The Polish Corridor separated Germany into two parts: East Prussia, the sacred homeland of the Junkers, and the main portion of the country. Exacerbating this strategically and emotionally intolerable situation was the hostility of the Poles and their alliance with France, Germany's antagonist. And now rumors began to flit that the Poles were building fortifications along the frontiers. But the German army was unable to gain much information about these. Aerial photography of them seemed excluded. The commercial flights that crossed Poland to and from East Prussia had to follow routes that kept them far from the construction. The military planes could at best scout over the neutral Baltic, from where they could not see much. Rowehl got the idea of photographing the forts by flying so high that no one could see him.

Entirely on his own, he tried it. On clear Sundays and holidays, he hired a private plane and flew it at 13,000 feet over the forbidden areas. No one caught him. When he had enough pictures, the 26-year-old airman showed them to the authorities. They were dumbfounded—and pleased.

"I can do more, if you provide the money for it," Rowehl told them. "I don't have a thick enough wallet myself."

"All right," they replied. "We'll do it. If you do the flying, you'll get the money from us."

So it began. It was 1930. Rowehl remained a civilian paid by the Abwehr, which was then intended to be Germany's central military intelligence collection post. He had one chartered plane. But it was an exceptional one: the single-engined Junkers W.34 that on 26 May 1929 had set a new world altitude record of 12,739 meters (about 41,800 feet). Though on many of his missions, Rowehl stayed inside Germany, flying along the border and taking oblique photographs of the fortifications, on others he overflew Polish territory. These flights violated the 1929 treaty that Germany had signed with Poland, which prohibited military aircraft or private ones used as such from entering one another's air space and required special permission for aerial cameras. This raised no moral scruples within the German commands. But after Hitler signed a nonaggression treaty with Poland in 1934, which broke the ring of French treaties that hemmed in Germany, the Rowehl flights jeopardized this stroke of politics. So they were halted—at least for a while.

By then Rowehl had assembled a handful of expert pilots and five airplanes. He had rejoined the military. He moved his unit, now with the camouflage title of Experimental Post for High-Altitude Flights, from Kiel to the Staaken airfield in western Berlin. He remained under Abwehr control. In that same year, his unit flew its first missions over Russia. Its twin-engined planes soared unseen over the naval base of Kronstadt, over Leningrad, over the industrial areas of Pskov and Minsk. At about the same time, it began to survey the border fortifications that Germany's neighbors were building. For France's, Rowehl zoomed along the Rhine, taking oblique photographs that looked down the throats of the guns in the concrete bunkers of the Maginot line. Over Czechoslovakia, he employed stereophotography—one of the first in Germany to do so—to get pictures of the deep-set fortifications.

These pictures reached Göring, commander in chief of the air force. One day in 1936, Canaris, as head of the Abwehr Rowehl's superior, summoned the flyer and took him over to Göring. The fat Nazi was lying on his big belly with Rowehl's pictures spread on the floor all around him.

"You've got to come over with me," he said.

And soon it was done. The Experimental Post changed its name to Squadron for Special Purposes. It was subordinated to the General Staff of the Luftwaffe's 5th Branch (intelligence). Rowehl soon had reason to be satisfied with the change. Göring disposed of far greater means than Canaris, and he was generous to Rowehl, obtaining promptly the high-

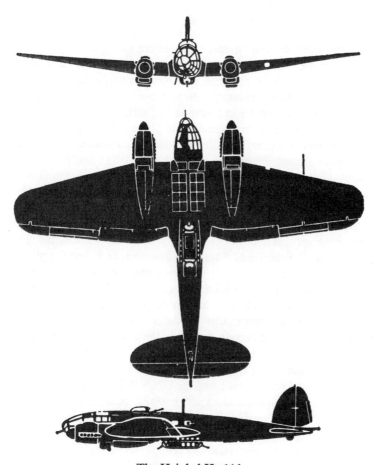

The Heinkel He 111

quality personnel, aircraft, and equipment the flyer requested. Rowehl recruited pilots who had worked for aerial-photography firms, for international commercial carriers, and for airplane manufacturers; captains Count Hoensbroech and Count Saurma, who had flown as air adventurers abroad in the 1920s and early 1930s, joined his team. With his advice, the optical firm of Carl Zeiss developed advanced aerial cameras; these became standard in the Luftwaffe during the war. As his first basic aircraft, he got the new twin-engine low-wing monoplane developed by Ernst Heinkel in the mid-1930s as the fastest passenger plane in the world—and as a speedy medium bomber. This was the He 111, which could carry a four-man crew to a normal range of 2,000 miles, but was also heavy enough to lie stable in the air and so facilitate photography.

In the late 1930s, Rowehl and his pilots flew missions against Poland, France, Czechoslovakia, the Soviet Union, and England. In good weather, five or six airplanes were always flying. Not all flights started from Germany. In 1937, some planes were stationed in Budapest, the capital of friendly Hungary, whence they flew against southeastern Europe. They were fulfilling assignments given them by Josef "Beppo" Schmid, head of Luftwaffe intelligence. Nearly all the jobs provided photographs of potential bomb targets. Many such targets were strategic, such as armaments factories. Others were operational, such as border fortifications and interior road nets. If the target was open, as a city, Rowehl disguised his planes as commercial craft, with civilian markings and crew in mufti, and his pilots pretended to be proving out new airline routes. They were to say that they had lost their way if they got caught—but this never happened. If the target was secret, Rowehl sent his planes so high—up to 32,000 feet—that they were invisible to observers on the ground in those preradar days. People could hear the faint drone of the engines, but the spy plane was gone before binoculars could locate it in the blue immensity. If the planes made condensation trails, the flight was usually broken off. Sometimes it was not, however, and then the pilots hoped that the trails were either not seen or not recognized as being from spy planes. Rowehl tested all sorts of colors as camouflage on his planes, painting the craft and then watching for them as they circled high over the Staaken airfield. But he found no point in this: all colors lost much of their hue at that height, and all glinted at certain angles in the sun. Though the flights over Czechoslovakia and England, where harbors, including London's, were photographed, violated air treaties that Germany had signed with them (no such treaties existed with France and the U.S.S.R.), no nations protested the overflights, either because they had not detected them, or because they could not ascribe them with certainty to Germany, or because they feared Hitler's wrath. Even the loss of an He 111 over Russia during a mission did not occasion diplomatic repercussions. Perhaps its disguise as a passenger plane gave the Russians an excuse not to press the matter.

The unit continued to grow. While many of its planes were hangared at Staaken, headquarters moved to nearby Oranienburg, a section of Potsdam, where the Luftwaffe general staff was quartered. The air force's Main Photo Center was briefly put under Rowehl. From it flowed a stream of glossy prints. Some went into the Luftwaffe target folders. Others went to

Abwehr I's air section, perhaps to help orient it to espionage targets: Canaris and Rowehl sometimes conferred on what areas should be photographed. The photo center assembled the shots of Czechoslovakian border areas into a photomap at 1:75,000 that the German forces took with them when they marched into the Sudetenland in the fall of 1938.

With the outbreak of war a year later, the Squadron for Special Purposes quickly grew to three squadrons of 12 planes each. It changed its name to Reconnaissance Group of the Commander in Chief of the Air Force. The photographs of Polish bridges and antitank obstacles and field fortifications that it had taken were distributed to the ground commanders, who used them to achieve the astonishing success of the first blitzkrieg the world had ever seen. Early in 1940, a squadron of the group, based in Bulgaria, sailed high toward the Caucasus, Syria, and Turkey, surveying the oil regions on Göring's order. When Hitler decided to attack Norway, the OKW discovered that it had no up-to-date maps of the country: the general who was given only a few hours to prepare a plan of attack had to buy a Baedeker "to find out what Norway was like . . . what all the harbors were." Rowehl was called in. Very soon his group had provided fresh pictures of the ports at which the Wehrmacht might land and of many of the coastal batteries and airfields that protected them, contributing to the success of the invasion. During it, pilot Cornelius Noell twice made the long flight from Königsberg in East Prussia to Narvik in a four-engine Focke-Wulf 200 Condor to see whether the British had yet occupied that northern Norwegian port. Rowehl's work was not perfect, however. His photographs, or the evaluations of them, led to underestimation of some batteries, overestimation of others, and a complete miss of others. Similarly. Luftwaffe intelligence regarded his work over France as "unsatisfactory," for it covered airfields and industrial installations only in the areas bordering Germany.

For the invasion of Yugoslavia, a squadron was based at Wiener Neustadt in southeastern Austria for 10 frantic days of pre-attack photography. The photographs went, not to Oranienburg, but to a photo unit in Göring's special train, which always had steam up and could pull into the famous tunnel of the Semmering mountain in case of an air raid. When the attack began, the airplanes had their civilian markings painted over with military insignia and the pilots changed into uniforms.

At the same time, Rowehl was continuing his major effort: against the Soviet Union. He had created a fourth squadron for this in January of 1941, a few weeks after Hitler issued his directive to war on Russia. Altogether, his craft violated Soviet air space several hundred times between October 1939 and the German invasion of Russia. Twice airplanes came down during these preinvasion incursions. One emergency-landed; the other —a Ju 86 with pressurized cabin, enabling its crew to fly at great heights— sustained motor trouble at 39,000 feet and sank to 16,000, whence Russian fighters forced it down. On the ground in both cases, the Russians found the telltale maps of the Soviet Union, the cameras, and the film. Göring, when he heard of it, raged and bellowed in his train on the Semmering. But the Russians, who had been spotting and tallying the flights, perhaps ever since they had been alerted by the crash of the He 111 several years before, merely protested. Except for a couple of isolated cases, they never fired upon the Rowehl craft.

So Rowehl's planes penetrated the Soviet Union both shallow and deep from Cracow in Poland, from Bucharest and Plovdiv in Rumania, from Kirkenes on the Arctic shores of Norway. Some flights reached as far as the Black Sea—a round trip of 1,500 miles. They brought back photographs of industrial targets and of the newest construction on Soviet field fortifications. Flights continued when the campaign began. On 26 June 1941, four days after the Germans attacked, Noell took off in his Ju 88 from a forward fighter airfield and headed toward Moscow, homing in on its broadcasting station. Soaring godlike over the city in the cloudless summer sky, he looked through the angular braces and panes of his cockpit window down onto the world capital of communism and saw the trolleys, like long, thin insects, crawling through the craze of streets. Noell, as always, felt secure in his altitude. He calmly photographed the airfields surrounding the city. He was not nervous when the Russian fighters rose to meet him and the black puffs of the antiaircraft shells exploded; both remained, as he had expected, far below his Olympian height and without effect. When he was finished, he turned and sailed unscathed for home.

By now, at its maximum, the Reconnaissance Group had some 200 or 300 men and about 50 planes (though about 200 passed through its hands altogether during the war). The He 111 had been supplemented by the Dornier Do 215 and the Ju 86 and Ju 88, and later by the Do 217 and the Henschel Hs 130—all of them twin-engine converted bombers—and by the Heinkel He 410, a small, speedy, four-motored craft.

These planes were distributed all over Europe, flying against different targets. From Fontainebleau and Belgium, they worked southern England. (These flights were important since the normal reconnaissance planes were often shot down. Rowehl's planes carried a special oxygen-nitrogen mixture that, pumped into the engines, would improve their performance for 20 to 25 minutes between 25,000 and 35,000 feet and enable them to escape the British fighters.) From Stavanger, at the southwest point of Norway, Knemeyer and other pilots reached Scapa Flow in 40 minutes, swooping down from a different direction each time in 1940 and 1941 to photograph the Home Fleet. From Crete, in 1942, Rowehl's men—including Knemeyer —investigated the Allied-held areas of North Africa. Indeed, this had become his main effort. From 29 May to 17 July, his group flew against North Africa 44 times, for a total of 170.5 hours. One mission that summer was an eight-hour marathon circling from Rhodes over parts of the Near East and then back again. Knemeyer's view of the enemy fighters like goldfish beneath him was the only contact with the enemy that Rowehl's planes had. Elsewhere, his daring pilots winged high above the corners of the Allied and the neutral world: Iceland, Glasgow, the Red Sea, Iraq.

Around 1941, a watcher at one of the Rowehl-used airfields would have seen these preparations for a typical flight: Crewmen attach film cassettes with a capacity of 180 pictures each onto the three heavy cameras. These they then fit into the tail of the Do 215, which carries no signs of nationality, only the registration symbol L 2 OS. The biggest camera, with a focal length of about 29½ inches, will shoot vertically. The others, with a focal length of 19½ inches, will aim to right and to left. They can be set at angles of 30° or 60°, depending upon whether the photographs are to provide greater precision (by overlapping) or greater coverage. The crewmen fix them at the desired angle and set the shutter stop and exposure time.

The pilot, Lieutenant Diedrich Wilmar, who had flown over Yugoslavia, gets in, followed by the other two members of his crew. He warms up the two engines, trundles the twin-tailed monoplane to the end of the runway, and, upon a signal, starts forward, picks up speed, and lifts into the air. He turns toward the target, climbing steadily. All goes smoothly; the flight is almost boring. At 26,000 feet, over his target, he sets the plane onto a straight course. The observer starts the cameras. Automatically they click, photographing a strip of land 17 miles wide. They could rise higher and cover more ground in a run—27 miles at 42,000 feet. But they would have to pay for it in picture quality: not only does resolution drop, but the steering grows soft and tends to smear the picture line.

After several runs back and forth, the target has been photographed. No enemy planes have bothered them, but Wilmar is nevertheless relieved when he turns for home. Immediately upon landing, the cassettes are removed from the cameras and flown to Oranienburg, where the film is developed. The oblique images are rectified to eliminate the distortion of perspective and then are fitted together into a continuous photomap. Photo interpreters scrutinize them under magnifying glasses, turning what appear to be tiny spots, smudges, and hairlines into commercial buildings, factories, antiaircraft batteries, streets, and railroads. Then they are rushed to air force intelligence headquarters for evaluation.

Rowehl himself, creator of this whole organization, flew from time to time to keep his hand in and to show his men that he had not grown old and frightened. But mainly he took care of his men, whom he had welded into a high-morale team, and decided when a mission could fly: this decision was his alone, though others told him what to look at. And he dealt with the higher-ups. This was often disappointing. Like all consumers of intelligence, they always wanted more. They rarely told Rowehl that he had done a good job or that he had discovered something they had not known before. Far more frequent were comments to the effect that other air reconnaissance units had spotted something: how come Rowehl had missed it? Rowehl felt that the high commands simply did not understand the value and the limitations of aerial photographs. Worse was Göring's reaction when Rowehl brought him some photographs revealing uncomfortable facts. It might seem impossible to reject evidence as solid as that of aerial photographs, which show the actual objects, but Göring managed it. "That's not possible!" he would say when Rowehl told him that a picture showed something. The photo interpreters might have erred, he would argue. Or Rowehl had not covered areas that might have furnished different intelligence. Or the Reichsmarshal would simply ignore the photographs. He would thank Rowehl for them, but he would not question him on them, and in the end would simply exclude them from his consideration.

Long before the end of the war, the situation was clear to the tall reconnaissance pilot, who had a good sense of humor, and hence a good sense of proportion. The Reich had been forced onto the defensive. The Luftwaffe was busy defending German skies from Allied bombers and had little use for aerial photographs of strategic bombing targets of Allied industry. The Nazi empire had shrunk drastically. No one was calling for information about foreign countries soon to be invaded. Indeed, there was no real need for strategic aerial reconnaissance at all. "Our homeland we knew," said Rowehl dryly. This loss of purpose, together with the death of his wife in an air raid, which left him to care for two small children, led him to resign in December 1943.

New needs changed his organization. Renamed Bomber Wing 200, it expended its crack pilots and special planes on nonreconnaissance missions, such as dropping secret agents over enemy territory. There was even talk of hurling its skilled airmen as kamikazes against critical enemy targets. The organization's original function—to spy without spies—flickered and died. The impulse that had made Rowehl's one of the earliest and most successful organs of strategic aerial reconnaissance in the world vanished as completely as, years before, his planes had done in the vast and listening sky.

Rowehl was, in a sense, preaching to the converted when he first proposed his aerial reconnaissance. The value of this form of intelligence had won acceptance even before World War I: the first German military airplanes were all reconnoiterers. After that war, a desire to have men and machines for aerial reconnaissance in part motivated the violations of the Versailles prohibition against an air force. Air officers in the military districts covertly taught the World War I lessons of aerial warfare, including reconnaissance. Their small photography units utilized aerial photographs from that war for training. They got sports pilots to fly them and their trainees about as they practiced anew taking pictures from the air. In a few years, the lack of uniformity of this dispersed work led the army in 1924 to create a chief air photographic officer with a Main Photo Center under its air desk at headquarters. The desk developed specifications for two reconnaissance airplanes, one short- and one long-range, and let the contract to Heinkel.

Development and training continued during the 1920s at Germany's secret air base in Lipetsk, Russia. The three tiny squadrons in three cities that, in 1930, constituted the first military airplanes that Germany dared to fly at home were all reconnoiterers. These formed the nucleus of the air reconnaissance element in the expanding German air force. In parallel with this, civilian firms, often staffed with former military observers, pursued aerial photography, chiefly for mapping and surveying.

The advent of Hitler gave aerial reconnaissance its greatest spur. The Luftwaffe ordered new airplanes, with greater range and speed to suit tank warfare. In 1937, the post of Luftwaffe general to the commander in chief of the army was created. A major part of his job was to pass high-level army reconnaissance needs to the air force and to submit the air force's results to the army. The analysts of the Main Photo Center, who now scrutinized their shiny prints in the reading and hearing rooms of the now defunct Prussian legislature because their work had outgrown the Reich air ministry, marked factories and military installations on the square photographs. Some of its employees and other personnel in German aerial reconnaissance gained valuable experience under Franco in the Spanish Civil War. One photo interpreter gained something more: he had earned so much in Spain that, though only a corporal, he drove to work in a luxury car that was the envy of his colleagues.

By the outbreak of the war, the three reconnaissance squadrons of 1930 had multiplied to 53. Their 602 airplanes constituted one-seventh of the Luftwaffe total of 4,103. Each squadron theoretically consisted of 12 airplanes, but sometimes they lacked one or more craft of the 3-plane reserve flight.

These squadrons maintained the distinction between long- and short-range units that had begun in the 1920s. The 30 short-range units with 342 airplanes served the army for tactical and battle reconnaissance. The 23 long-range units totalled 260 planes.

Rowehl conducted the strategic air reconnaissance for both the army and the air force. But each service had, at the start of the war, its own long-range squadrons for operational reconnaissance. In the Luftwaffe, one such squadron was assigned to each air fleet and each air division. Among its chief assignments were to observe enemy airfields, thereby locating enemy air concentrations, and to photograph operational bombing targets. This supported the basic tasks that regulations set for the Luftwaffe: to defeat the enemy air force and to attack the enemy army's sources of strength and their connections to the front. A long-range squadron was likewise assigned to each army group and army. Their operational reconnaissance, regulations declared, "embraces the surveillance of the enemy's concentration, especially his railroad concentration, the advances or withdrawals, transports forward or to the rear of enemy army components, the improvement of enemy field and permanent fortifications." Operational reconnaissance was usually carried out by aerial photography at from 15,000 to 30,000 feet in planes flying deep into enemy territory, usually to observe important road and rail lines, though orders seldom set out specific areas of observations.

Its results usually determined where tactical reconnaissance was to be carried out. Often the tactical concentrated on the strips over which a particular corps or armored division would advance during the next two or three days—about 20 to 40 miles into enemy territory. Short-range squadrons were attached to infantry corps and panzer divisions for this work. Panzer corps had several such squadrons, assembled into groups. (Infantry divisions had no aerial reconnaissance units.) They reconnoitered visually from heights of 7,000 to 15,000 feet. Observers sometimes snapped pictures, but developing and evaluating usually took too much time. Regulations explained: "Tactical reconnaissance embraces the closer observation of the enemy's assembly, his advance, the organization, distribution, extension of his forces in breadth and depth, his supply, his supporting installations, his air situation, especially new airfields and his anti-aircraft. The timely reporting of enemy motorized forces is important."

Merging into this was the battle reconnaissance that these short-range flights also carried out. Flown at under 7,000 feet to see details as closely as possible, it "gives information about the distribution of enemy forces, especially his artillery, about the layovers and movements of reserves, tanks and other such occurrences behind the enemy front. It watches the course of battle." A major element of battle reconnaissance was spotting for the artillery. It picked out targets, such as enemy guns, tank formations, and marching columns, and then noted the fall of shot to help the artillery zero in. In these cases, the observers usually reported by radio or by dropping a note or map.

Each reconnaissance unit had a photographic section right at the airfield. Its darkrooms, evaluation areas, and reproduction sections were housed in half a dozen trucks to make it as mobile as the air unit itself, which moved from airfield to airfield as the army advanced or retreated. The photo section was self-contained, with its own 100-gallon water supply, light tables, enlargers, celluloid triangles, graduated steel rules, loupes, magnifying glasses, slide rules, colored pencils. They handled the tactical and operational photographs. Strategic material was evaluated at the photo unit of the Air Force General Staff's Intelligence Branch. The unit had been hived off what had been the Main Photo Center and had become the Main Photo Branch at the start of the war; this photo branch, working now out of converted apartment houses on Columbiastrasse in Berlin, developed new techniques, wrote training and recognition manuals, and cleaned African sand and Russian dust from the film from the front—then stored it in barges on a lake to preserve it from fire when, later in the war, air raids became heavy.

All these units—airplanes, observers, evaluators—belonged to the Luftwaffe. But the army controlled those assigned to it, giving them specific tasks and receiving their reports. To coordinate this work between the two services, the Luftwaffe attached liaison officers and staffs to the headquarters of the various army units. These staffs and their tasks grew larger and more important as the level of the army unit rose, until they culminated in the Luftwaffe general to the commander in chief of the army.

This arrangement worked well for the first two years of the war. But the Russian campaign strained it. New squadrons were required by the many new corps and panzer divisions. But their activation had so outstripped airplane production that most squadrons had only 7 planes instead of the established 12—inadequate to meet the demands. The transfer of a factory from Bremen near the North Sea far inland to Prague to protect it from British air attacks cost the Luftwaffe its production of a new reconnaissance airplane for half a year. And the warfare in Russia proved more costly than expected. By 6 December 1941, when the Russians launched their big counterattack, more than 300 reconnaissance planes had been lost. Some squadrons in the Army Group South area had only a single aircraft. In addition, manpower had grown tighter, and the campaign had shown that reconnaissance entailed some fighting with enemy ground troops and that consequently reconnaissance planes should be accompanied by fighters for defensive purposes. This further worsened the situation.

So on 8 December 1941, the very day that Hitler suspended his offensive and it became clear that the war would last for some time, the Luftwaffe general to the commander in chief of the army, Paul Bogatsch, met with the army chief of staff, Halder, to discuss a "complete reorganization" of the army's air reconnaissance. Agreement was reached after several months of discussion. Control of all reconnaissance would shift to the Luftwaffe. The army could no longer order reconnaissance, it could merely request it. The luxury of separate army and air-force long-range reconnaissance flights would be abandoned. A single mission would henceforth carry out both. The large liaison staffs at army and army group would vanish, as would that of the Luftwaffe general to the commander in chief of the army. They had lost much of their reason for being with the shift of control of army reconnaissance and with a simultaneous transfer of control of the Luftwaffe's antiaircraft units from army to Luftwaffe; they had also grown so big that they had tended to lose touch with the front. The post of Luftwaffe general to the commander in chief of the army would be downgraded into a general of reconnaissance.

To carry out the change, Bogatsch was replaced by General Günther

Lohmann, who had, however, fewer powers, reflecting the transfer of the army-controlled squadrons. Himself a former aerial observer, Lohmann replaced the large liaison staffs with young (and low-ranking) Luftwaffe officers, usually of a captain's grade, who had often served as a squadron leader, and a few assistants. These were attached to the I c staffs at army and army group as I c/Lw. He assembled the dispersed reconnaissance

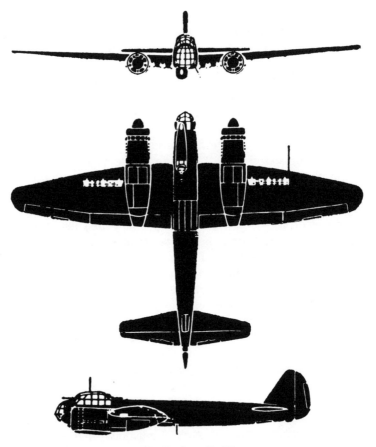

The Junkers Ju 88

squadrons into groups of three squadrons each, or about 36 planes, under a Luftwaffe corps. Army corps and panzer divisions now dealt with them. This saved personnel, but cost flexibility. Lohmann, however, whom some regarded as unimaginative and a do-nothing, lasted only nine months. In December of 1942, he was replaced as head of the air reconnaissance organization by his I a, General Karl-Henning von Barsewisch, an airman who had the trust of the younger pilots, had pushed the idea of reconnaissance by fighter planes, and was the originator of the entire reorganization. He remained in the post to the end of the war.

For each reconnaissance plane flying in 1943, about four had preceded it—lost through enemy action or other causes. This was not as severe a loss ratio as fighter planes, which were then in their eighth "generation," but it was worse than bombers, which were only in their second. Through-

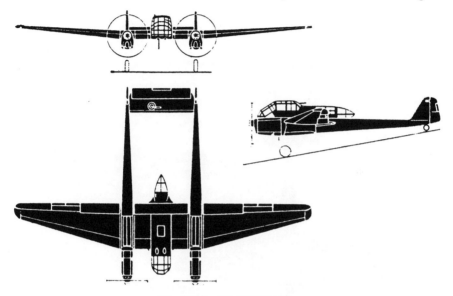

The Focke-Wulf FW 189

out the war, Germany built 6,299 reconnoiterers—5.5 percent of its total production of 113,515 airplanes. The ratio of all reconnoiterers to the Luftwaffe strength as a whole continued its historical decline from 100 percent at the start of World War I to one plane in three near its end, and from one plane in seven at the start of World War II to one in eight and a half as its end became clear.

At any one time, however, the number of reconnoiterers in service remained fairly constant. The figures for the long-range planes ran: 260 in September 1939, 412 in January 1942, and 377 in May 1943. The numbers of short-range craft on the same dates stood at 342, 294, and 402.

The airplane models, however, naturally varied. At the start of the war, the chief long-range reconnoiterer was the Dornier Do 17 F, an adaptation of a medium bomber, originally designed about 1935. It was a long-fuselage, twin-engine, twin-tail machine that carried a pilot, an observer-cameraman, and a radioman-gunner. But its service ceiling, at 18,000 feet, was rather low. For the Russian campaign, the Luftwaffe replaced it with the Junkers Ju 88 D, a photo version of one of the basic medium bombers. It soared almost 50 percent higher—26,000 feet—and faster and very much farther—3,000 miles compared to 1,000. It basically flew Luftwaffe long-range reconnaissance to the end of the war, though other models also served.

The short-range planes went through three phases. The Henschel Hs 126, a single-engine, high-wing, two-seater monoplane, started the war. Early in the Russian campaign, the Germans began displacing it with the Focke-

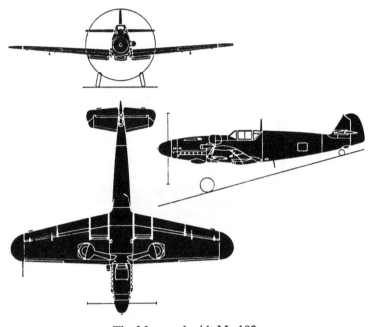

The Messerschmidt Me 109

Wulf FW 189 A. This was a twin-engine utility plane that carried a crew of three at a top speed of 213 miles an hour—almost 60 more than the Hs 126. For two years it served as an ideal plane for battle and short-range reconnaissance. But the increase in the speed of the Russian fighters finally doomed it. Though it flew night reconnaissance to the end of the war, the Luftwaffe turned for daytime flights to the only craft fast enough to avoid enemy fighters: German fighters. It built cameras into several versions of the Messerschmidt Me 109. This speedy little plane, with its liquid-cooled motor in a pointed nose, darted over enemy territory at 37,000 feet at up to 380 miles an hour, dodging enemy fighters and flak and getting pictures that slower planes could not. But it had two chief disadvantages. As a one-seater, its pilot had to double as an observer, making reconnaissance of individual points, as railroad stations and bridges, very hard. And it could not carry the taller cameras that would produce the same resolution at great heights as shorter ones at lower altitudes. It thus lost some detail.

In part this may have been due to the German failure to improve their cameras during the war as much they did their airplanes. They felt that their apparatus was good enough. Examination of captured cameras showed them "how far behind the enemy is in the development of this area." The main camera was the Rb 75/30. This automatic camera (Reihenbild-apparat, or Rb) had a focal length of 75 centimeters (about 29½ inches) and made negatives 30 centimeters (about 12 inches) square. It mounted a cassette with 60 meters (almost 200 feet) of film, for 180 shots. For low-level close-ups the Luftwaffe used the Rb 20/30 (focal length 8 inches, image 12 inches square) and the 50/18 (focal length 20 inches, image 7 inches square). Where extra detail was needed, as on very high altitude flights, the Luftwaffe photographed with focal lengths of 40, 50, and even 60 inches. With their excellent Zeiss lenses, the whole system was good enough—under laboratory conditions—to attain a resolution of 30 lines per millimeter (more than 750 per inch) on the film.

Like the cameras, the film underwent no basic refinements during the war. Experiments with color film showed that hues did not add very much information to high-altitude photography, and so it was not introduced. In-frared and ultraviolet film were not even discussed very much. The Germans never came up with anything like Kodak's color infrared Ektachrome, which showed the chlorophyll green of plants as crimson and the painted green of camouflage as violet, allowing photo interpreters to distinguish easily between them.

For a mission, the reconnaissance pilots would not simply leap into their cockpits, rev up their motors, and take off to see what they could see. Their squadron captain gave them assignments after the I c of the army or air force combat unit ordered or requested information to fill in his picture of the enemy. As the Germans assembled for the invasion of Greece, the I c of the XXXth Army Corps set down what one short-range flight was to do: "Battle reconnaissance is to be carried out with point of main effort at first along Road IV towards Kemontini . . . to determine: Where is the enemy effecting resistance? Where is the enemy retiring? Where is the ad-vance battalion of the 50th Infantry Division? Where are roads and bridges destroyed? Where are enemy artillery positions?"

The pattern for a reconnaissance flight, laid down on the first day of the war, never varied. For the assault on Poland, one observer, Lieutenant Hutter, was assigned to see (1) whether the enemy had fortified a certain town for a strong defense, (2) whether a trench system and barricades had been set up along a particular chain of lakes, and (3) whether the enemy was assembling or marching between the town and the lakes. Hutter was due to overfly the frontier at 4:30 a.m. Shortly before take-off at 4:20, he and his pilot clambered into their Hs 126. The pilot, for some reason called "Emil" in reconnaissance jargon, merely chauffeured; the observer—"Franz"—was in charge, sitting behind the pilot in the semiopen cockpit. Right on time Hutter's plane and five others of the flight roared off into the graying east. The others soon turned away and vanished, heading for their own target areas. Looking down, Hutter at first saw little more than inky smudges, punctuated by the flash of a stream or the pinpoint of a farm light. But as the day grew brighter, forms began to take shape. He began to watch more carefully for troop movements, for field fortifications.

What could he expect to see from the air with the naked eye? He could spot men, standing or lying, from a maximum of 2,500 feet, from up to 4,000 if they were moving. Closed march columns and vehicles would be seen from up to 13,000 feet, depending on the ground and the dust they raised. A sharp-eyed observer could detect machine guns and antitank guns from 4,000 feet, but troops usually camouflaged these well and so made them hard to see even from lower down.

Hutter's plane droned on. No Polish fighters troubled them; no Polish guns fired on them. Hutter compared the terrain, with the map on his lap, now flecked with oil from the motor. Suddenly, ahead of them, he spotted the town and the nearby chain of lakes. At 3,000 feet, the Henschel swung over them as Hutter looked in vain for barricades or enemy assemblies near the lakes. But around the town he saw many trench systems wriggling across the land. He sketched them in quickly on his map and photographed them with his hand camera. Then—flak! The Henschel turned and raced for home with its precious results.

A day in North Africa demonstrated the effects of short-range reconnaissance. It was 26 December 1941. Rommel had just pulled back to Agedabia, and British troops were moving up to launch a frontal attack on his defensive position there. On that day after Christmas, German and Italian airplanes flew half a dozen missions. The German early morning reconnaissance showed about a thousand vehicles, mostly at rest, in a particular area, while at the village of Solluch it found only 35 tents, presumably British. The Italian air reconnaissance spotted 500 vehicles around Msus between 9 and 10 a.m. Later that day, Captain Veit, observing with his 1:400,000 map from an airplane piloted by Lieutenant Lams, swung in a wide circle over eight villages but saw only one thing of importance: 300 to 400 vehicles at El Haseiat at 12:30 p.m. At 4:40 p.m., First Lieutenant von Weyrauch dropped a note from his plane. Near Solluch and Scindima he had seen only tents, no vehicles. These and other aerial observations, combined with additional intelligence, disclosed to Rommel a gap between two advancing British formations. He exploited it in three days of tank fighting to outflank, maul, and repulse the British. This enabled him to end the danger to his position and ready his next advance.

Artillery reconnaissance provided more immediate satisfactions to the

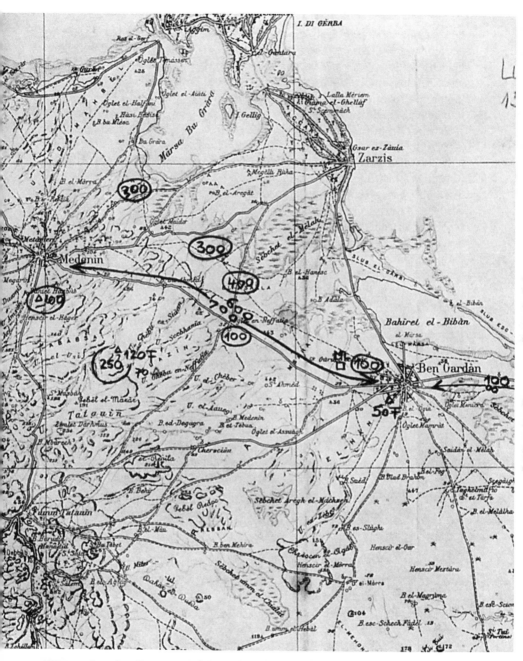

The results of a German aerial reconnaissance mission over North Africa are marked on the map: 100 Allied vehicles going in both directions on the road east of Ben Gardan, 50 tanks south of that town, 100 vehicles parked on its western edge, 600 moving on the road west of it, and concentrations of 100, 400, and 300 vehicles air reconnoiterers. In Russia once, Lieutenant Hutter spotted an enemy battery supporting a Russian breakthrough attempt with fire from uncamouflaged positions. By voice radio, he reported its location, then dodged back over his own lines. When the German battery radioed "Ready to fire," the plane returned, notifying the ground station with the word "Fire!" At the moment the battery reported "Strike!" the flier saw black mushrooms rise 100 yards from the Russian guns. Hutter gave the correction. The second salvo landed in the middle of the enemy battery. "On target! Fire for effect!" cried Hutter. As the plane cruised in ellipses over the Russian positions, shell after shell exploded in them, flinging bodies about, upending gun carriages. Within a few moments, Hutter called out, "Battery destroyed." And the artilleryman replied, "New target!"

Not every mission was successful. During the French campaign, Lieutenant Pape, an artillery observer, had been assigned to watch for enemy columns along a particular road. But French fighters drove him off. Next day the artillery requested reconnaissance near Mooreghem in Belgium. Pape spotted a long column of troops, marching openly. Presumably they were French—but they would have had to be crazy to expose themselves like that. Perhaps they were German. Unable to find out, he got another job. But enemy camouflage, the dust and smoke, and some clouds made it impossible to achieve any results. In addition, bad weather frequently prevented any flying at all. On an average, however, squadrons flew about two missions a day.

Long-range reconnaissance was sometimes flown visually. During the French campaign of 1940, two sorties went out early on 28 May. One returned on account of bad weather. The other observed by eye heavy rail traffic on the Joinville-Brienne stretch at 6:55 a.m. with five trains, and, 15 minutes later, on the Dijon-Nuits St. Georges stretch—Burgundy's famous Côte d'Or, with some of the greatest vineyards in the world—two heading north and five south, or away from the front.

In the east, timely flights penetrated enemy secrecy measures from time to time.

The Russians sought to conceal the approach of troops by sometimes unloading them 100 miles behind the front. This eliminated telltale train traffic to the points of main effort. They then marched the troops to the front at night and in small groups, often avoiding roads and going cross-country. But sometimes the marches were so long that they began and ended in twilight, and dawn and sunset reconnaissance could spot the trudging men. Even when this did not work, the reconnoiterers could find them. The soldiers bivouacked out, and from their campfires thin gray columns of smoke rose like giant fingers into the windless morning sky.

But most long-range missions were photographic, chiefly because of the great heights that planes had to fly when penetrating so deep into enemy territory. The pilot had the choice of route to his target, which was usually a road or a rail line. Depending upon the overlap required in the pictures —typically 30 percent—and the speed and height of the plane, the camera was set to automatically take pictures, say, every six seconds. As the pilot followed the road and the camera clicked, the observers looked around with naked eye and with telescope in case of camera failure and to supplement the photographs.

When the plane landed, the crew of the photo unit fell upon the film cassette, unscrewed it from the camera, and rushed it to their mobile darkroom. Ten minutes after the film was developed, coarse evaluations could be ready. Made from the wet negatives, with the naked eye and perhaps a magnifying glass, these showed trains and armored columns—the indications of enemy concentrations. The detailed evaluations, made with loupes, could be ready within two hours, but usually took longer. The photo interpreters had learned the differing visual characteristics from above of enemy artillery positions, covered machine-gun nests, positions for heavy infantry weapons such as antitank guns, small field fortifications, mine fields. They counted freight cars in railroad yards and ships in harbors. With the help of a handbook that thumb-indexed enemy planes according to the number of motors and the type of tail—stabilizer tips pointed, squared, round— and then gave their measurements, the interpreter could determine what kind of enemy aircraft and how many occupied an airfield. A sequence of shots would tell whether a train was moving; the position of horses and wagons, which way a troop column was going. The shadows of the column would betray what kind of a unit it was: the shadow of a gun differed from that of a supply wagon. If railroad flatcars headed toward the front were carrying guns or tanks, reinforcements were coming up. If they were empty, a relief or withdrawal was probably beginning. Trains that mixed passenger, freight, and flat cars were probably troop trains.

The interpreters could distinguish between the firing position of a Russian 76.2-millimeter antitank gun and that of a 125-millimeter howitzer, because, they had discovered, the Russians adhered closely to their manuals in constructing them and they prescribed different forward openings, antifragmentation walls, location of ammunition niches, and so forth for different types. Some photo interpreters became so expert in the nuances of Russian camouflage that they could tell from it alone when the Russians were planning an attack. It was Soviet practice to have the troops at the front prepare their positions for the fresh troops who would actually carry out an attack. But troops camouflage positions that others will occupy much less carefully than those they are occupying. The practiced eye of the German photo interpreters could recognize the lapse from the usual superb Russian camouflage technique—and thereby the imminence of an attack.

Generally the photo units just made a print or two of each photograph for the use of the I c and the commander. But sometimes it distributed photographs to the lower commanders to show them the terrain over which they would be advancing, the enemy fortifications, the roads, the bridges that the enemy might destroy. From the preparation period for the Balkan invasion to the end of the brief campaign, the photo units of the 12th Army reproduced 11,048 small photographs (one foot square), and 20,360 large ones (two feet square). They bragged that for this they needed the equivalent of about two acres of photographic paper.

Aerial reconnaissance delivers some of the most psychologically satisfying evidence that an intelligence officer can get—what a man sees with his own eyes. Nothing convinces like a photograph. It owes this sense of certainty to its furnishing physical evidence. And of all forms of physical evidence, it provides the longest lead time, since it penetrates farther behind enemy lines than the others do.

"Under favorable conditions, the reconnaissance pilot can quickly win a comprehensive picture of the enemy and report the results in the shortest possible time," declared the army's handbook for troop commanders. But the source was far from perfect.

"Air reconnaissance furnishes only snapshots; continuous observation of one area is generally not possible. Weather, ground cover, and enemy reaction produce further limitations," the handbook said.

To these may be added those of human failure. The photo interpreters sometimes erred. Natural growth over old installations, camouflage with nets, woods or shadows concealing defense positions—all prevented them from seeing things. More common and more serious than these were the observers' errors. They got lost and mistook one place for another, resulting in totally false information. They forgot to say when and in what direction a movement was taking place. They misspelled place names, making them unfindable on maps. They reported in terms so general as to be useless: What does a "large" or "small" march column mean? They exaggerated, reporting as "destroyed" rail stations that had to be attacked again a few days later. They repeatedly confused friend and foe.

And the evaluating officers compounded these difficulties. Late in the afternoon of 4 September 1944, a reconnaissance flight in Rumania spotted a mounted Russian advance unit followed by motorized elements and tanks advancing far to the west of Bucharest. The Germans flew along the road 150 feet up. They photographed a tank with a hand camera. But at headquarters no one wanted to believe them. It was not possible for so strong a formation there to be Russian troops! Even the picture of the tank did not convince them: it could have been captured. Only after a flight the next day confirmed the report did headquarters believe it.

All this diminished the value of some of the hardest intelligence available. It normally gained its full value only with correction and completion, as one element in the intelligence picture. It alone could seldom foretell enemy intentions. But sometimes it did, with dramatic effects.

In the first days of November 1943, the advancing Russians cut off the German-held Crimea from the German forces on the mainland. Soon thereafter, German aerial photographs disclosed that the Russians were building a dam across an inlet of the Sea of Azov, between the Crimean peninsula and the mainland. This would give them a second route of attack; the primary route ran over the connecting isthmus. Interpretation of the photographs showed that the dam would be completed in about 10 days and would be wide enough to allow T-34 tanks to cross. The Germans at once bombed it, delaying its completion until early March 1944. This helped forestall the Russian attack for several months.

After the Normandy invasion, Göring commented at a Führer situation conference that the latest aerial photographs suggested that the Allies were shifting the center of their unloading operations from where mine fields had been laid to where they had not. This would be taken into account in future mining operations, he said. In February 1945, Dönitz noted that since aerial photographs of the Thames showed lively convoy traffic, his midget submarines should attack there. And in a few weeks, he did send a small fleet of them into the Thames.

The curve of the effectiveness of German aerial reconnaissance matched that of the rise and fall of German arms in general more closely than that of any other form of intelligence. In seeking physical evidence, it depended more upon strength—control of the air—or speed to obtain this evidence than almost all other forms of intelligence. This strength was naturally a function of the overall German strength. For the first half of the war, German air superiority permitted German aerial reconnaissance, and it in turn helped German arms win their victories. But with the German defeats on the ground and in the air, reconnaissance became sparser and less effective. Toward the end it became almost nonexistent. In December 1944, an air force officer noted that no air reconnaissance of British industry had taken place for three years. German aerial reconnaissance made no great discoveries, as the Allies' did of the V-1 sites. It could not get planes over London to correct the fake reports of turned-around agents about the impact points of these flying bombs. It failed to spot the bringing-up of the troops from Siberia that stopped the Germans at Moscow. A mournful comment by the navy on 22 May 1944, while the Germans were trying desperately to discover where the expected invasion of Europe would come, may serve as its epitaph: "Especially on account of the lack of constant comprehensive air reconnaissance, the [enemy's] main transport effort in one sector or another of the Channel coast is not ascertainable."

9

Questioning the Foe

SECOND Lieutenant Howard G—— of the U.S. Army Air Corps stationed his Piper Cub 1,000 feet over the ground near Trier in southwest Germany. He was relaying radio messages. Suddenly, light flak disabled his plane. G—— managed to land between the lines. He fired the little monoplane with a match and set out for the American side. Upon reaching a radio post, he called his unit and waited along a road for a jeep to pick him up. Instead a German patrol emerged from nowhere and captured him. Within a few days, the 34-year-old Texan found himself at the Luftwaffe's Dulag Luft—the best-run, the cleverest, and by far the most successful interrogation center in all the German armed forces.

Dulag Luft comprised a cluster of low barracks in Oberursel, a town in the hilly country a few miles north of Frankfurt-am-Main. It had 200 individual cells, each soundproofed and with its own electrical heating unit to prevent prisoners from communicating by tapping on the pipes of a steam-heating system. During the war, its formal name became Evaluation Center West, but since it still contained a Dulag—"Dulag Luft" means "transit camp, air"—for temporarily holding prisoners before they were sent to a Stalag, or permanent camp, everyone kept calling it Dulag Luft. Like Evaluation Center East, which interrogated Red air force prisoners, it was subordinated to the Luftwaffe's Foreign Air Forces Branch. Evaluation Center West had outstations at Budapest and at Verona. But its Oberursel station was far the most important.

Prisoners arrived there several days to several weeks after being shot down. G—— got there in 18 days. Usually an airman, upon being downed and captured, was immediately taken to an air force base for preliminary search and questioning. If he was a fighter pilot, the German interest lay less in intelligence than glory: the pilots were seeking credit for the kill. The preliminary interrogations of bomber crews, on the other hand, often yielded immediate indications of forthcoming raids.

From his capture point, the prisoner and any papers found on him or in his aircraft were sent on to Dulag Luft, often arriving via the trolley that ran right by it, for questioning on longer-range and technical matters. After reception, he was placed in an individual cell. Here he was given a form with a red cross at the top and "Printed in Switzerland" at the bottom. It was not an official Red Cross form but a German trick. Some prisoners refused to fill it out. Lieutenant Colonel A. P. Clark, a fighter pilot downed in a dogfight over northern France in 1942, was one such prisoner. Moreover, he carried no papers. He thus denied the interrogators many clues that would have helped them break down resistance. His experiences were typical of many prisoners in the same situation:

> The first thing they did when I entered the cell was to take away my leather jacket and my pink trousers, declaring that they were not uniform. They put me in very ill-fitting British battle-dress army trousers with suspenders—about size 50. The entire time I was at Dulag Luft, about three weeks, I spent negotiating for the return of my uniform. Taking it from me was a gimmick, of course, to damage my morale and self-respect; it also gave them bargaining leverage to seek information from me.
>
> I was prepared for the first round of official interrogations, for I had been warned to expect the little officer with the Red Cross armband who really was not working for the Germans, but rather "simply for the prisoners' best interests." He told me that the Red Cross would inform my loved ones at home that I was alive and well. He had the usual card, which we had been warned of, which sought more information than we were authorized to give, including squadron identification and other items. I went through the standard little routine about not being authorized to fill it out. He countered with the comment that every prisoner filled out the card, and that it was to my advantage to give this information so it could be processed to insure prompt mail deliveries and the receipt of Red Cross parcels. The most pressing anxiety of prisoners was the fact that they didn't know whether their families knew that they were alive; the Red Cross overture was a rather clumsy attempt to capitalize upon this anxiety.
>
> This anxiety was indeed a fearful thing. The initial period of captivity involved a very difficult readjustment for every prisoner of war. I had to convince myself that I was in fact a prisoner. The impact of this realization was stunning, and it affected various individuals in different ways....
>
> Later I was confronted by some highly skilled interrogators who employed a wide variety of techniques to gain information. One of these Sonderführers [specialists with officer rank], a man named von Schilling, was a quiet type who tried to establish a casual rapport with the prisoners. He ignored rebuffs, and calmly pursued his objectives. I recall one day he asked me if the name "Bolero" meant anything to me. BOLERO was the codename of the operational project for flying the fiirst American wings to Europe.... I merely shrugged

my shoulders. But I specifically recall that he was watching me very closely for a reaction. . . .

In general, the Germans did not press prisoners who declined to talk. So many passed through that it was more profitable to find one who would talk than to batter down a tough customer. Besides, they felt torture was ineffective. So they generally abided by Article 5 of the 1929 Geneva Convention on prisoners of war. Germany, Britain, and the United States had all signed it: "Every prisoner of war is required to declare, if he is interrogated on the subject, his true names and rank, or his regimental number. . . . No pressure shall be exerted on prisoners to obtain information regarding the situation in their armed forces or their country. Prisoners who refuse to reply may not be threatened, insulted, or exposed to unpleasantness or disadvantages of any kind whatsoever."

Occasionally the Germans violated this. Some prisoners they threatened with being shot as spies, or withheld food or washing facilities from for a few days, or subjected to mild torture. When British warrant officer Robert Trumbull L—— drew a line through his fake Red Cross form, the interrogation officer grew furious. After he left, L——'s cell grew so hot that he had to lie on the floor in his underclothes, face to the door, trying to get a breath of cool air. He finally told an interrogator his squadron number, and the heat was turned off. But the Germans did not resort to anything stronger. They had methods more refined and more productive.

These began with any documents found on the prisoner or in his aircraft, or with the information on the fake Red Cross form, if he had filled it out. Major Heinz Junge, who as head of the intelligence branch was in charge of interrogation, assigned the prisoners to his interrogators on the basis of this information. His interrogators specialized. Some were experts on fighter planes, others on bomber pilots, bombardiers, gunners, radiomen; some concentrated on four-engine planes, others on fighters. Junge matched them to the prisoners on the basis of this specialization, or similar backgrounds, or civilian jobs. Dulag Luft owed much of its success to Junge, who had thoroughly organized the interrogation process. Regarded by a subordinate as a man of "extreme good humor," in his late forties, a World War I aviator who was shot down in 1918 and imprisoned first by the French and then the British, then a representative of the German air industry in South America, he had been recalled in 1942 from a brief wartime stint as assistant air attaché in Buenos Aires to Oberursel at the request of the commandant, a prewar friend.

Upon receiving the phony Red Cross form filled out by the prisoner, which now had the number assigned to the plane crash on it, the interrogator took it to the casualty recording branch. There he would see whether Dulag Luft had any other prisoners from the crash and whether the branch had any information of value to give him. Next he went to the document evaluation branch, gave the crash number, and again asked for information.

From there he went to the intelligence room, where the information from the documents and interrogations was coordinated. Files containing interrogation and evaluation reports lay on the table. Charts showing recent attack techniques and lists of participating crews were tacked on the wall. The interrogator read all relevant information. If he suspected that a prisoner belonged to a particular squadron, he might call for its history from the squadron history branch. These named its commanders, told of incidents in the life of the squadron, specified where it had been committed, and contained miscellaneous information, often in the form of clippings from the press branch, about it.

At noon each day Junge briefed his 65 interrogation and evaluation officers. He told them about the night's bombing attacks, which had been reported to him in the 100 teleprinter messages he received a day. He told them what new questions were to be asked. These had come from the OKL, from the intelligence officers of fighter squadrons and antiaircraft artillery regiments, and sometimes from industry. On 11 May 1944, for example, Foreign Air Forces West told Oberursel that agent reports had put the British 85th Fighter Group in the Wash, subordinated to the Tactical Air Force, and equipped with Typhoons, Spitfires, and Mustangs. It required confirmation through prisoner interrogations.

After the briefing, the interrogators went to talk to the prisoners. Most were interrogated only once. The highly refined probings started from the vast quantities of information collected about a prisoner and his squadron. With his apparently inexplicable knowledge of intimate matters, the interrogator surprised the prisoner into conceding the truth of some innocuous item, such as his parents' names or his home address. Once he was talking, the interrogator first got him merely to confirm known information and then gradually led him to produce new material. Afterward, prisoners often rationalized their loquacity on the ground that the Germans knew everything anyway. They seldom asked themselves why the Germans were then asking questions. The subtlety of the technique, repeated if necessary at difficult points in the interrogation, disarmed suspicion, and this, plus the flattery implicit in being asked about something and the pleasure of talking shop with a knowledgeable fellow from the other side, especially after several days alone, produced remarkable results.

The report on G—— ran to five single-spaced pages. It dealt with artillery pilots, and covered in brief his personal background, his training and shipment to Europe, and then, in detail, the organization, duties, radio equipment, and aircraft of artillery observation pilots. As extras it threw in sections on G——'s judgment of German field artillery ("considerably inferior to the American in fire control") and on a prisoner-of-war camp near G——'s home in Texas about which he happened to know. The interrogator let nothing go past: "The 'Piper-Cub' is equipped with the S.C.R. 600 radio. The apparatus is quartz-controlled and has B, C, and D

Luftwaffenführungsstab Ic
Fremde Luftwaffen West
Auswertestelle
B.Nr. VE 04935/44 geh.

Bohra./Kg.

ε 6589/44

Oberursel, 11.10.1944

Sondervernehmung - Artillerieflieger.

Abschuss-Nr.: KU 1027 - A.　　　　　G e h e i m .

An Verteiler gemäss Entwurf.

Betr.: Vernehmung des 2nd Lt.　G　　　　　(Flugzeugführer)
abgeschossen am 15.9.1944, nachmittags, SW Trier, mit einer
"Piper Cub L 4 B" der Kurier- und Artillerieflieger-Staffel
Nr. 1090.

Bezug: Br.B.Nr. VE 04665/44 geh.v.22.9.1944.
(Artillerieflieger-Vernehmung).

1. Militärischer Werdegang.

2nd Lt. Howard　G　　　　　(S.-Nr. 0-204 501 5)
geb.26.3.1910 zu Cullmen (Alab.), verheiratet, Tank-Kontrolleur.
Februar 1944 zum Offizier befördert.
Der Kgf. ist im Zivilleben Angestellter bei den Gross-Tank-Anlagen
der Standard Oil Comp. in Baytown, 30 km O Houston, Tex., am
Kanal Galveston-Houston gelegen. Er ist 34 Jahre alt, aufge-
schlossen und natürlich. Er besitzt Erfahrung in fliegerischen
Dingen und zeigt ein für amerikanische Verhältnisse überdurch-
schnittliches Interesse an Fragen des öffentlichen Lebens.
　Im August 1942 meldete er sich freiwillig zur Luftwaffe, da er
bereits den Zivil-Fliegerschein für leichte ein-mot.-Flugzeuge
besass. Nach kurzer Grundausbildung in R a n d o l p h
F i e l d (Tex.) wurde er in November 1942 der Artilleriefli-
gerschule F o r t　S i l l (Okl.), die meist mit L a w t o n
bezeichnet wird, überwiesen, wo er bis Januar 1943 verblieb.
Seine Einsatzschulung erhielt er darauf bei den Manövern ver-
schiedenster Heeresverbände entlang fast der gesamten Atlantik-
küste. Am 8.Okt.43 erfolgte die Überfahrt von Boston nach
Southampton in stark gesichertem Geleit von 8 grossen Truppen-
transportern. Dauer der Überfahrt: 11 Tage. Kein U-Boot-Alarm.

　Nachdem die Einheiten der 28. Infanterie-Division eingetroffen
waren, wurde Kgf. zusammen mit weiteren 9 Piper-Cub-Besatzungen
zur L i a i s o n - S q d. Nr. 1 0 9 0 (Kurier- und Be-
obachtungsstaffel) zusammengefasst und obiger Division zugeteilt.
Im Rahmen dieser Einheit wurde die 1090.Sqd. Anfang Juli nach
Frankreich überführt. Erste grössere Gefechtshandlung der 28.Divi-
sion: 30.Juli bei St. Sever, W Vire, Normandie.

2. Kampfauftrag und Abschuss.

Kgf. war am 15.9. als Relais-Flugzeug ohne Beobachter eingesetzt
und wurde von leichten Bodenwaffen (FlaMG oder 2-cm) aus 300 m Höhe
abgeschossen. Ihm gelang zwischen den Fronten eine Notlandung.
Nachdem er sein Flugzeug mit einem Zündholz in Brand gesetzt hatte,
lief er zu den USA-Linien, gab bei der nächsten Funkstelle seinen
Verbleib an seine Einheit und wartete auf ein Kfz, das ihn abholen
oder mitnehmen sollte. Während er am Strassenrand wartete, kam ein
deutscher Stosstrupp und nahm ihn gefangen. Nach Durchlaufen mehrerer
Gefangenen-Sammelstellen und Heereslager (Limburg) wurde er am 3.10.
bei der Auswertestelle West eingeliefert.

*Dulag Luft writes up the detailed results of an interrogation of a
downed American pilot*

channels. The frequencies lie between 40–50 kilohertz. To the objection of the interrogator that this must be megahertz, the prisoner stuck by his assertion, but added that anyhow as a pilot he was not enough of a radio specialist to swear to it."

In another case, the interrogator used G—— to test his inference from a document: "According to statements of the prisoner, each infantry division disposes of a liaison squadron of 10 'Piper-Cubs.' Despite a hint on the part of the interrogator, based upon a distribution list for an artillery-observer pamphlet that had come in as a captured document, according to which each corps would receive only 10 copies, the prisoner stuck to his statement that each infantry division disposes of a liaison squad of 10 airplanes of the above-named type." This report, mimeographed, then went to Foreign Armies West, where a reader of it noted "Correct!" in the margin next to the sentence about 10 Piper Cubs per divisions.

Many other reports went equally into full detail. Platoon Sergeant William F. C—— provided order-of-battle information about his airborne division and gave, down to the number of men in the bazooka teams, the table of organization of his paratroop battalion. An extract from a report specified how American artillery observation planes signaled fire corrections to be made (raise nose one time = 100 yards short). Once a prisoner cleared up a mystery for the Luftwaffe. What kind of fighter-plane weapon was producing the 1½-inch holes in German airplane armor over Africa, and why was there always only one hole? An interrogation brought out that the Royal Air Force had armed some Hurricanes with wing cannon, but to save weight had dispensed with reloading equipment and had given each gun but a single shot.

Dulag Luft spewed out a hundred reports a day. It fed the Air Force Operations Branch with vital information, and the Luftwaffe appeared satisfied with its work: Göring personally commended the camp commandant at Christmas 1943. A memorandum from an officer of Foreign Air Forces West set forth the value of the Dulag Luft interrogations:

> Knowledge of new battle methods of the enemy and the use of new types of airplanes and weapons is won almost exclusively through questioning of prisoners. Knowledge of this kind is immediately taken into consideration in German battle conduct and in air defense. It increases our defense success and saves the troops personnel and material. . . . A thorough interrogation supplies the Luftwaffe with trustworthy information on transfers and assembly changes, which permit the drawing of conclusions about enemy intentions in regard to shifts of points of main effort and preparations for attack. On the basis of the judgment of the enemy thus obtained, decisive conclusions for the entire Wehrmacht leadership have been reached in the highest quarters.

Dulag Luft enjoyed a remarkable and ever-increasing success as a major source of Luftwaffe intelligence. But a bitter anomaly attended that success. In large measure it reflected the flow of prisoners and documents. The number of p.o.w.s passing through rose from 500 in 1941 to 3,000 in 1942, to 8,000 in 1943, and finally to 29,000 in 1944, when there were so many that only half were questioned. The number of interrogators likewise rose from 4 in 1941, after two years of existence, to about 65 in 1944. For the air war had shifted to German skies. Dulag Luft could produce better intelligence only as the Allied bombers destroyed more of Germany.

This situation contrasted with interrogation results at the fronts in many ways. Better intelligence was produced not during the later but during the earlier days of the war, when the advancing German armies were capturing hundreds of thousands of prisoners and attracting tens of thousands of deserters. The interrogators depended not upon elaborate Byzantine sleight of hand to dissolve the prisoner's resistance but upon a far more powerful flux: fear of death. And the intelligence generated seldom possessed broad, long-range, or background value, but instead usually applied directly to the immediate tactical situation. The case of deserter Ivan Kotschov exemplifies this.

On the evening of 4 January 1942, he and a friend quit their posts and came over to the Germans. The 3rd Battalion, 1st Regiment, of the 4th SS Police Division received and interrogated them. The friend said little more than that they had belonged to the 4th Company of Rifle Regiment 296. Kotschov, speaking more freely, said that he had been stationed at a forward post previously unknown to the Nazis. The 3rd Battalion commander, Major Korn, dispatched a patrol which found the post, confirming Kotschov's statements. The next morning, Korn had the Russians brought to the front to look over the Russian forward post situation. He then formed a combat patrol to destroy these outposts. Chiefly on the basis of Kotschov's statements, aided by his own observations, Korn instructed the patrol about the posts' strength, the best route to them, and the way to attack them. And when it set out at 11 p.m. that night, Kotschov went along.

Moving silently in their snow suits, passing the Russian tanks destroyed two weeks before, they penetrated half a mile into the bushy terrain, where they found Russian paths. They ripped up a section of telephone cable and then came up on the outposts from behind. At 11:50 a Russian machine-gun post challenged them. Kotschov and a Russian-speaking German answered "Patrol!" in Russian, which satisfied the machine-gunners. The Germans took them with cold steel without resistance. But in the next three bunkers, short fire fights developed. The Germans quickly overcame the surprised Russians, killing 10 and capturing 6. They seized weapons and documents, blew up the bunkers, and returned without loss of men or matériel.

The episode illuminates the chief characteristic of prisoner and deserter intelligence: its intensity of detail combined with its extremely narrow focus. Most prisoners have a worm's-eye view. The movements of an army, the plans of higher commanders, technological advances lie beyond their ken. They know what touches them. They know their units, their position, their commanders, their combat experiences, their weapons, their route to the front, their peacetime jobs and factories, their life at home. But not all they know is of the same military urgency. Consequently, the German army—like others—interrogated a prisoner at successive levels of command to extract information of value to that level.

During the war, as the Germans learned or relearned the value of promptness in interrogation, and as more interpreters became available, interrogation expanded downward—closer to the battlefield. Prewar regulations, and those from before the attack on Russia, foresaw the headquarters at army level conducting the main interrogations. They had, in 1939, the only really qualified interpreters. The interpreters at division, though possessing linguistic ability, lacked military knowledge. After Poland, three-month training courses corrected this. The Russian campaign then demonstrated that interrogations at division headquarters produced the most useful results. This was probably due mainly to the greater closeness of the interrogation to the moment of capture, secondarily to the now adequate interpretation and the direction of an intelligence officer. Throughout the war, the most important interrogation took place at division. Forward of division, still closer to the combat, the tiny staffs had, early in the war, usually been too busy to bother with prisoners. Even when they found time, their interrogations had been rather cursory, handled by anyone at the regiment, battalion, or company command posts who knew a little Russian. But after the conquests of 1941 had won new quantities of interpreters and the stabilization of the fronts reduced the fighting, the Germans apportioned less qualified interpreters to many posts forward of division and often assigned an adjutant or special-missions officer there to seize papers and to direct and evaluate the questioning. This remained limited compared to that at division, but it had greater immediacy.

Such great emphasis was placed upon promptness in interrogation because fear makes prisoners talk, and fear decreases the longer a prisoner remains alive after he is taken. It overwhelms him at the moment of capture. He is terrified that he might be bayonetted on the spot. Fear still rules him a few minutes later. As he stumbles along, prodded by hard-bitten soldiers who have just been trying to kill him, his sole thought is, "What are they going to do with me now?" He is in the complete power of an enemy who minutes ago jerked him from sleep at the point of a gun, or bombarded him with a rain of hell, or overran his trenches with gigantic armored monsters, or shot at him with their rifles or machine guns. They might well do now what they just missed doing before if he does not do what they want. But as the hours pass, and he moves out of the fire zone into the calmer atmosphere of headquarters, confidence returns that he will live after all, and with it declines the compulsion to save his life by talking.

Other benefits accrue from promptness. One is usefulness of information —only speedy questioning can elicit facts in time for them to serve. Another is accuracy. A prisoner still stunned by his capture, realizing that he is naked to his enemies, separated from his friends, cut off from his family —a man in such a state cannot master himself sufficiently to invent deceptions. His proximity to the front and the consequent ease of checking on his statements further restrict lying. In the Italian theater, intelligence officers regarded p.o.w. interrogations from divisional interrogations as 80 percent reliable. In the east as well, p.o.w. information was regarded as highly trustworthy.

Battle usually produced prisoners or deserters in quantities sufficient for intelligence purposes. When it did not, as on quiet fronts, the Germans got what they needed by raiding parties or propaganda.

Upon capture, the Germans disarmed their prisoners, separated officers, noncoms, and men, and took their papers. At the posts forward of division, a selected few were asked which units they belonged to and where antitank and machine-gun positions and mine fields were, what heavy guns were where, whether any tanks were present, and other matters pertaining to the battle situation. The posts did not write down the results, though they telephoned important information to division headquarters. Then they sent the prisoners and their documents to division.

At this command, the first with an intelligence officer, the first thorough and systematic interrogation took place. Except when overburdened, the division normally interrogated all prisoners fairly thoroughly. Depending upon circumstances and personal inclination, either the I c, his assistant, or, fairly often, the interpreter questioned prisoners or deserters, nearly always singly. Both parties were usually seated in a room at divisional headquarters. The interrogation techniques varied between the theaters.

In the east, no real technique was needed at first: fear did the work. The Russians well knew that the Geneva Convention did not protect them from the aggressor's atrocities, and the Nazi contempt for the Russian Untermensch led to mishandling, beating, torture, and shooting in the combat zone and to mass and individual killings behind it. It is therefore not surprising that early in the Russian campaign about 97 percent of prisoners spoke freely, in the hope of winning clemency, nor that others, reasoning to a different conclusion, at first remained silent in the hope of postponing the expected execution. Only by 1943, with the change in the tide of the war, did very many more Russian prisoners remain silent, and only then did the Germans cultivate their interrogation technique.

In the west, most prisoners' fear seemed to be dissipated soon after capture by more humane treatment. A racist feeling of equality with the western nations governed this treatment. Consequently there the Germans obeyed their regulation that "The prisoner is obligated to give his correct name and rank. He may decline further statements." Even an SS division ordered that the handling of prisoners "is regulated strictly by international convention." Many Allied prisoners gave little more than name, rank, and serial number. British soldier Edward George Best told the interrogator of the 10th Panzer Division in North Africa on 1 December 1942 that his serial number was 6922109 and that he had been inducted in 1941, but "made no statements." Soldier David Melner, serial number 6916635, inducted 1940 to the infantry, "refuses to make any statements at all."

But some there were who talked, and for them probably the iron fist of fear shattered their resistance, while the velvet glove of mildness eased the information out of them. Sometimes an interrogator gave them food or cigarettes to relax them. Though the interrogators' techniques varied as their natures and those of the prisoners, most agreed that a quiet and objective tone produced the best results. Severity made many prisoners obstinate; excessive friendliness, suspicious. Occasionally interrogators resorted to refinements or tricks. During a walk, they sometimes guided conversation from the themes of "We're all soldiers together" or "Poor men fight, the rich make money" to a comparison of Allied and German army methods. Inviting an officer to dinner placed him under a subtle obligation to talk. Prisoners might be told that if they did not want to name their troop unit, it would not be possible to report their capture to their families through the Red Cross. But these ruses served only rarely. Direct questioning, perhaps beginning with some personal matters to get the prisoner talking, were the rule. The vastly superior position of the interrogator—his power over the prisoner, his usually greater mental ability, his broader knowledge, his relative tranquillity—sufficed to exploit the weakness of the prisoner and elicit the information wanted.

For the first few years of the war, divisional intelligence officers based their interrogations on standard, rather simple OKH questionnaires. In October 1941, the 50th Infantry Division had a one-page form asking name, rank, political participation, regiment, division, previous regimental and divisional designations, where first employed in combat, regiment's route to the front, division's route, armament, battle assignment, morale, supplies, clothing, and miscellaneous. From prisoner Vasilli Krasnichin, however, it got only his rank (soldier), regiment (20th Cavalry), division (2nd Cavalry), route (from Odessa), and staff location.

After the lower staffs took over the preliminary combat questioning, the divisions expanded their interrogations, guided, from the summer of 1942, shortly after Gehlen took command of Foreign Armies East, by exceedingly comprehensive questionnaires from that body. This began with the prisoner's home life and job, induction, and training and ran through his combat activities, touching not only on such basic matters as unit mission, composition, strength, condition, replacements, commanders, chain of command, and locations of artillery, rockets, mines, ammunition dumps, and fuel depots, but also asking about effects of German fire, losses of units in each action, and preparations for gas warfare. Foreign Armies West also put out such questionnaires, though its were not quite so detailed. In addition, many commands maintained lists of questions that they wanted answered.

These interrogations ascertained mainly tactical and organizational mat-

The German 5th Infantry Division briefly notes Soviet prisoner Vasilli Krasnichin's regiment, division, and route to the front

ters, usually enemy order of battle, that were of value to the division. The 56th Infantry Division, protecting Orel in the summer of 1943, discovered from a Russian lieutenant who deserted that Mortar Regiment 475 had been committed near the Russian 269th Rifle Division under the control of the 3rd Army. An attack by the German 299th Infantry Division brought in 165 prisoners who confirmed the presence of Rifle Regiment 102, among other units. In North Africa in February of 1943, Private James S——, a 26-year-old Tennessee farmer, described the organization and equipment of his battalion, an element of the 1st Armored Regiment. A comrade, a 24-year-old Ohioan, Private Robert D——, said that the regiment be-

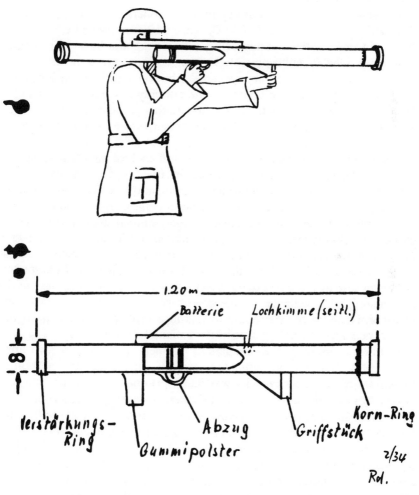

On the basis of information obtained in a 15 January 1943 interrogation of a captured American non-com, the intelligence officer of the 10th Panzer Division in North Africa makes one of the earliest sketches of a new American antitank weapon, later to be called the "bazooka"

longed to the 34th Infantry Division. This was false—one of the cases that kept p.o.w. information at a reliability of about 80 percent. But the private may not have been lying. Both the 34th Infantry Division and the 1st Armored Division, to which the regiment actually belonged, were scattered throughout the same sector. Either a temporary subordination may have taken place, or the private may have thought from their proximity that it had.

In North Africa in January 1943, the intelligence officer of the 10th Panzer Division reported on a "new American antitank weapon." The information was obtained, he said, on the 15th from a captured American non-commission officer. According to the prisoner, American forces in the prisoner's sector had first used it in December 1942 in the battle for Hill 295 north of Medjez el Bab. "It apparently is a rocket gun, which can be fired by individual riflemen and reportedly has an enormous armor-breaking force. The weapon consists of a thin, light steel tube about 1.20 meters long and 8 centimeters diameter," the I c wrote, and not only described it in detail, but sketched it as well. It was the bazooka, and this prisoner information gave Germany some of its earliest news about this surprising and powerful American weapon.

Each division normally made five copies of each of the interrogation results. It retained one and passed the others up. Corps and army each got one; army group two. The thorough interrogation at division practically obviated the need for further tactical questioning. Corps headquarters seldom interrogated. Army headquarters largely limited itself to prisoners of particular importance, such as high-ranking commanders, general staff officers, and specialists. The army I c himself often participated in these interrogations. Because of the far superior linguistic abilities of interpreters at this level, plus the much fuller information it could bring to bear in the questioning, the reliability of prisoner-of-war intelligence at army headquarters jumped to 90 percent. Army groups received and evaluated this intelligence, generally doing little interrogation of its own.

In France, however, the commander in chief west, who had two army groups under him, set up, after the invasion, an interrogation station at Châlons-sur-Marne. Its capacity was 6,000 prisoners, but in the first days of July 1944 it held only some 400. Prisoners were isolated in one of its 30 individual cells during their interrogations. Interrogators on the staff of his I c questioned them first on military and tactical matters. Sergeant Arnold F. C——, a farmer, 34 years old, captured near Aachen on 12 October, detailed the equipment of his 9th Reconnaissance Troop, 9th Infantry Division: five officers, about 150 men, two half-tracks, two jeeps, one 2½-ton truck, a 1st Platoon with nine jeeps, three .30-caliber machine guns, three 2-inch mortars, three bazookas, and so on for the other platoons.

Prisoners with special knowledge were then made available to the specialist interrogators: two from the Foreign Office and two from RSHA VI Wi, the economic-intelligence element of party foreign intelligence. After the Allied advance compelled the removal of the Châlons camp, the commander in chief west set up at Diez, near Koblenz, a special interrogation group of 36 men—10 for administration and evaluation, 12 interpreters, and 14 guards.

Above this level, Foreign Armies East and West created their own interrogation units to obtain information of particular use to themselves. Foreign Armies East's Desk III a had a small interrogation camp for some 80 important prisoners, such as higher officers or officers reduced in rank, first near Lötzen (now Gizycko, Poland), in East Prussia near Führer headquarters, then at Luckenwalde, near Berlin. In December 1944, its staff of 8 Germans and 19 Russians conducted 63 interrogations. Some of the prisoners wrote detailed reports on subjects about which they were knowledgeable and on which the Germans wanted information. Major Senikev produced a table of organization for a rifle replacement regiment and a list of intelligence personnel. Corporal Borodin described the medical services and training in the Red Army.

Foreign Armies West preferred mobile teams. Such a team submitted a report on the morale of British soldiers in Tunisia in 1943. Another, named Kommando Fritz, produced information on operations of the U.S. Office of Strategic Services. It questioned First Lieutenant Peter S—— of the O.S.S. about his mission to spring Allied prisoners from German camps in Italy. S——, a 32-year-old Newark tree surgeon, parachuted with a small team into the Gran Sasso area 2 October 1943 carrying, in addition to a U.S. first lieutenant's insignia, a false identity card, and two rolls of cigarette paper (which the Germans tested for secret ink), tens of thousands of lire. He and his men were to lead the prisoners to the Adriatic coast. But they never found a single camp, and at the end of October S—— ordered his group to break up and pass individually back through the lines. He himself lived for six months in the mountains, sleeping in huts and eating bread and potatoes, until German soldiers captured him on 26 April 1944 on the road toward Bisenti. In addition to Kommando Fritz, three mobile interrogation teams questioned Allied soldiers early in the Normandy invasion in a holding stockade at Alençon. By December of 1944, there were four such teams, each immediately subordinated to the chief of Foreign Armies West, operating in the western theater, each assigned to an army headquarters.

The Abwehr, early in the war, included interrogation for combat intelligence among its duties. During the campaign in France, when the Germans were halted at the Aisne River, one Abwehr officer discovered in interrogating two prisoners that the French had been in their positions for 14 days, had not been relieved, and were very tired. This report contributed to the German decision to advance promptly—and within three days they were over the river.

Later, combat intelligence faded away, to be replaced by interrogation for economic and technical information. In Russia in 1943, the Abwehr had four teams, one with each army group, and a camp, about a mile from Harnekop, for this work. The camp was equipped with an extensive reference library, Luftwaffe target folders with their detailed information on individual enemy factories, and rooms to write reports. It fed these to the foreign-intelligence branch of the OKW's War Economy and Armaments Department, which also had specialist teams of its own in the east. One of these was headed by Major Prince Reuss, scion of a family dating from the twelfth century with territories in central Germany, of whom it has been said that its genealogical history was as complicated as its territories were small. His Royal Highness's team and another produced the department's most valuable information.

Economic interrogations in the west were less fruitful. An Abwehr I Wi (economics) officer was first granted permission by the Italians to interrogate p.o.w.'s when they had been held more than a year. Most had paid no attention or had forgotten the harbors and roads through which they had passed; even maps did not jog their memories. Later, when 108 Americans arrived in the Capua camp after capture in Tunisia, they proved to be too young and too insignificant—farmer, laborer, student—to yield any useful information.

The greatest contribution of prisoner-of-war intelligence to the higher levels of command was its simplest: the identification of units. Individually, these meant little. Indeed, no single interrogation seems ever to have provided intelligence critical to the high command throughout the war. But the assemblage of the many individual identifications helped I cs and Foreign Armies East and West to build up an enemy order of battle.

At most times, this merely enabled them to know what the enemy had just been doing and to infer what he was capable of doing. Thus, the knowledge from a prisoner that the U.S. 88th Infantry Division was not in French North Africa as the Germans thought but had been fighting in Italy since mid-March 1944 showed that the Americans had more power and so greater potentialities there than previously believed. In some cases, however, order-of-battle knowledge helped the Germans draw strategic conclusions. In March 1944, a prisoner revealed that the U.S. 1st Infantry Division was now in Great Britain. This shift of a battle-tested division from the Mediterranean theater to Britain pointed yet again to the forthcoming invasion. But even in this sort of determination, prisoner intelligence remained a secondary source for the higher commands. Of the 123 Allied divisions that Foreign Armies West located during the French campaign of 1940, only five were ascertained through prisoners. At Hitler's situation conferences, prisoner information was mentioned rather less than other sources.

Why, then, was so much effort devoted to it? One reason was its vital assistance at the tactical level. Troop commanders in the east regarded it as the most important source of enemy intelligence. Another reason lay in a peculiar advantage it has over other sources.

All sources of intelligence depend upon how much material the enemy places at their disposal. Radio intelligence hangs on how much he is radioing, aerial photography on how well he camouflages. Prisoner-of-war intelligence is subject to these limits as well. It cannot exceed what captured soldiers know. But the limits are much more elastic with interrogations. Unlike radio monitors or aerial photographs, interrogators can ask the enemy questions.

Betrayers in
Paper and Steel

THE most solid, most indisputable form of intelligence is a captured enemy document. It offers physical guarantees that it is authentic, all of them testable: the paper, the typewriter, the ink. The Germans did not employ such examinations, however, because where the document was found usually attested to its genuineness well enough. Nevertheless, despite their superior validity, seized documents never became a primary source of intelligence, mainly because they too seldom provided advance information about enemy plans. They had other uses, however. Most common was to help question prisoners.

Identity cards, pay books, distribution lists on orders or reports, all gave the interrogator clues to the prisoner's units and its neighbors. He could then ask questions that merely required a confirmatory answer, and so get the prisoner talking, and he could often check the truthfulness of volunteered information. This sort of work reached its apex at Dulag Luft. Its documents section, headed by a professor of sinology from Heidelberg, extracted information from papers and photographs found on the prisoners or in the airplane.

Letters gave a great deal of personal data about an airman, enabling the interrogator to seem to know all about him. The envelope often carried his complete address, including the name of his squadron. The service newspapers that airmen brought along to read during the long flight confirmed old units and revealed new ones. They gossiped about personnel, equipment, installations, and activities. Officers' identity cards showed where they had been commissioned and occasionally where they had been trained. A card issued at Langley Field, Virginia, or Boca Raton, Florida, indicated that its owner had probably taken blind bombing training. The diary of the leader of a flight of Marauders, which strayed en route to England from America and lost three planes over France, listed the names of all the crews in the entire group and reported the serviceability of every plane.

Even nonverbal documents talked. Though all men in the European Theater of Operations had the same type of ration card, the post-exchange clerk at the 100th Bomb Group always cancelled them on a rough board counter with a heavy black pencil that picked up the wood grain. The Germans identified members of that unit with ease. The fake identity photographs given airmen to facilitate their escape via the underground sometimes helped the enemy more. The photographs of the 91st Bomb Group had a peculiar brown tint. The personnel of the 95th Bomb Group all wore the same checkered coat when they had their pictures taken.

At the fronts, documents found on prisoners served in the same sort of way, though naturally without the refinements permitted by Dulag Luft's painstaking collation. Troops found documents everywhere—on prisoners and deserters, on the dead, in tanks and downed airplanes, in trenches and field works, in military headquarters, in radio stations, in railroad towers and rolling stock, in post, telegraph, and telephone offices, in mailboxes, in government bureaus, in newspaper offices. They picked up maps, orders, reports, regulations, pay books, pay lists, war diaries, personal diaries, notebooks, tables of organization and equipment, supply lists, leave lists, casualty lists, personnel lists, leaflets, newspapers, photographs, letters, lists of radio codenames and call signs, codes.

Divisions and corps that captured some low-level maps, as of enemy mine fields or trenches, or some personal papers of value in interrogation, sometimes retained them. But the more important they merely skimmed, seeking items for battle information such as the numbers of the troop units opposite them. They had neither the time, nor enough good interpreters, nor the correlative information that would allow a productive evaluation. For this, they sent the documents back to army headquarters, where they underwent their main examination and, often, translation. Army, after its study, passed the documents of more general application, such as manuals, to army group and Foreign Armies East and West. These translated many and reproduced them for distribution.

On 16 January 1942, for example, the 16th Army sent to its subordinate corps the translation of an order of 9 January from the Red army general staff concerning the use of ski battalions. They were mainly to carry out deep battle reconnaissance of enemy flanks and rear, to insure constant security against enemy surprises, to fall upon enemy staffs, destroy enemy communications, blow up his bridges, and mine roads in his rear, and the like. When a British document referred to a "dual purpose" antiaircraft battalion, Foreign Armies West warned that "now heavy antiaircraft batteries may also be used for ground fire." On 13 August 1943, Foreign Armies West published "The Landing of the Reinforced 3rd American Infantry Division at Licata [Sicily] on 10 July 1943," based on a captured partial landing order of the division and on the landing order of a reinforced infantry regiment of the division. It reported, for example, that the division was to capture the harbor, listed the units with which it had been reinforced, told of the BLUE, YELLOW, GREEN, and RED battle groups into which it had been divided and of their assignments, and gave minute-by-minute details of the operational timetable:

x minus 4 days to x minus 1—night bombing attacks;

x minus 30 minutes to x minus 4—ship gunfire on coastal batteries and battle installations;

x minus 2 minutes—mortar screen from incoming landing ships;

x minus 1 minute—air bombing attacks on beach;

x—first wave lands, occupies and secures artillery formation areas, prepares for advance on Licata;

x to x plus 3 minutes—ship's artillery fires on targets at will, after x plus 3 only on request;

x plus 10 minutes—second wave;

and so on up to x plus 7½ hours—eleventh wave, with its components. Such a document would, the Germans hoped, tell the troops what to expect in the event of another Allied invasion so that they would be prepared, psychologically and physically.

Of more immediate value were the papers, usually evaluated at lower headquarters, that gave current information. They dealt in most cases with organization and order of battle. A captured order in France in May 1940 corrected a belief about which of two French armies was which; Foreign Armies West directed that on maps the designations for "1st Army" and "9th Army" were "to be reciprocally interchanged." When the artillery commander of the Russian 3rd Armored Guards Army was killed in battle, the Germans found on him the complete table of organization of his army. In Normandy, the presence of the U.S. 3rd Army, suspected from signal intelligence, was confirmed when the 18th SS Panzer Grenadier Division found a list of the codenames of the components of the 12th Army Group, which included that army.

Documents that provided directly usable tactical intelligence were much rarer. An order captured by the Germans on the first day of their offensive in France on 10 May 1940 disclosed that the two enemy divisions in southern Belgium were to retreat while fighting delaying actions against the German attack on Neufchateau-Arlon. This eased the decisions of the German commanders opposite. On 4 September 1941, the Germans shot down a Russian plane attacking the headquarters of the 3rd Panzer Division. The pilot parachuted out, landing not far from the command post. The I c buzzed over on a motorcycle. The pilot tried to escape but was shot by soldiers rushing up. In his pockets the I c found a detailed map of the Soviet troops lying in front of the division. This showed that the division was aiming directly at the boundary between the two Soviet armies—always a point of weakness. On the basis of this, the divisional commander ordered an attack for the next day.

The seizure of a document indicating enemy future intentions was the rarest case of all. And even this treasure was not unalloyed. It might have been a plant. Even if it was genuine, the enemy might have changed his plans. Or the tactical situation, or enemy strength, might have prevented its exploitation. In January 1943, the chief of staff of the Russian 1st Guards Army, then part of a major offensive that was driving the Germans back, drove to the front with a general. They lost their way and, in the fluid situation, blundered into German artillery. The general was killed; the chief of staff was captured with the maps they had been carrying. The most important of these, an operations map, listed the Soviet units with their numbers, boundaries, direction of advance, and objectives for the next four days. The divisional and army commands, with commendable alacrity, rocketed it up to army group and Foreign Armies East. All the intelligence helped the Germans not a whit. The Russian juggernaut simply rolled on.

Were none of the documents ever plants? Did none ever trick the Germans?

In one critical case, the most important and dramatic involving this source, they did.

British deception concocted false documents and played them into German hands through the Spanish by means of a corpse, ostensibly a courier killed in an air crash at sea. It happened in April of 1943, when it was becoming clear that the Allies would soon conquer all of North Africa and would thereafter undertake some further offensive in the Mediterranean. Roosevelt and Churchill had decided at Casablanca that, to shake Italy loose and to open the Mediterranean to shipping, the next target would be Sicily, in the center of that middle sea. So the fake documents—letters between high commanders floated ashore on a body given a fake identity as a Royal Marines major—pointed away from there. They referred obliquely to forthcoming operations in the eastern Mediterranean, especially Greece, and in the western, mainly Sardinia.

Months earlier, Hitler and the OKW had concluded, apparently on the basis of little more than their own fears, that the Allies would next attack Greece, to menace the eastern front, frighten Germany's Balkan allies into quitting, deprive Germany of Turkish chrome and Rumanian oil. The documents, when the Germans got them, reinforced these preconceptions. Berlin had no way of detecting them as fakes, in part because they only had photographs to work with, but chiefly because the main letter, at least, had been drafted by the commander who signed it and had been typed by his secretary on his own stationery. Prevented thus on the one hand from discrediting them, and incited on the other to accept them because they said what the Germans wanted to hear, the Abwehr, Foreign Armies West, and the 3/Skl swallowed the bait eagerly. All believed the documents were genuine. And all drew the exact inferences from them that British deception wanted. Admiral Canaris, who several weeks previously had been saying that the Allies might attack Sicily and Sardinia, now argued that they would advance against Greece and Sardinia. Foreign Armies West issued an appreciation saying practically the same thing.

The documents strengthened Hitler's original views. The day after the Axis forces surrendered in Africa, Mussolini predicted that the Allies would next invade Sicily, because the freeing of the sea route would release 2 million tons of shipping. Hitler rejected this contention. "The discovered Anglo-Saxon order," he said, "had solidified" his belief in a Balkan attack. This never changed. On 9 July the OKW warned again of attacks east and west. The next day the Allies fell with all their strength on Sicily. The battle was not easy, but it was not as hard as if the Germans had been expecting them.

Marks not only on paper spoke to the Germans. Those on tanks and guns also provided intelligence.

In the 6th Army area in February 1945, captured weapons revealed that the Russian IVth Guard Mechanized Corps used animals as insignia—a deer for the 13th Brigade, a horse for the 14th, an elephant for the 15th. This and other information helped the Germans determine the number of enemy formations opposite them and to identify many that had been shifted there from distant portions of the front. Analysis of the serial numbers of the weapons disclosed enemy formations, estimated the rate of replacements, suggested the refitting time of a unit, specified where and when the weapon had been produced, and computed the likely production volume. And many times, the weapons themselves provided some of the most valuable intelligence of all. The Germans inspected and ran a captured U.S. Sherman tank at their tank testing area at the Berlin suburb of Kummersdorf to see both its weak points, enabling troops to know where to cripple it, and its strong points, helping German industry to improve its own armored vehicles. In 1942 Hitler ordered a gunfire test against the Russian T-34 tank. Foreign Armies West reported in September 1943, "A hitherto unknown apparently English mine has been captured in Russia." Its description—diameter and height 20 inches, tapering to a point that is stuck in the ground, seemingly 11 smaller mines inside—helped German troops to recognize and so avoid or destroy it.

The Luftwaffe enjoyed especially favorable conditions for obtaining enemy equipment: aircraft often crashed or landed within the Reich or occupied territories. Badly damaged ones the Luftwaffe examined on the spot. A week after a Russian TB-7 belly-landed in East Prussia, a Luftwaffe chief expected a report that, on the basis of an analysis of the parts, would provide even such details as the plane's range. With other planes, the Luftwaffe often expended considerable effort to get them flying. When a Stirling bomber emergency-landed in Holland, the Luftwaffe built a runway, filling in several trenches to do so, delivered a new motor to replace the one that was damaged, and flew the plane off to a research station at Rechlin, north of Berlin. It was the first of this important English four-motored model to fall into German hands in impeccable condition with all its equipment. Norden bomb sights, found in fallen bombers, were cleaned, repaired, and examined. German experts regarded them as one of the factors of American bombing accuracy. Captured and repaired Allied fighters were flown to German airfields, where pilots flew them to gain a better feel for how these enemy planes handled.

This captured material came under the control of Colonel-Engineer Dietrich H. Schwenke, in charge of technical intelligence under Field Marshal Erhard Milch, the head of air armament. Schwenke was a smart, tough pilot with an engineering background and lots of foreign experience: he had served as an assistant air attaché in Britain and had toured Soviet air plants just before the German attack. During the French campaign of 1940, he systematized the collection of captured enemy airplanes, sending them to the booty center he created at Rechlin. Eventually Schwenke had 200 Russian prisoners of war cutting the aircraft apart so his experts could analyze them in detail. He issued the results in reports to the troops and Foreign Air Forces and in oral presentations at conferences with Milch, other high Luftwaffe officials from Göring on down, and German manufacturers.

The Germans seemed to be especially interested in the Boeing B-17, the Flying Fortress. In August 1942, one of the first crashed on the eastern front. The Luftwaffe sent in a team of men to get it out. But it lay under artillery fire too near the Russian lines, gradually disintegrating, and despite an eight-day attempt, the team could not salvage it. A few weeks later, however, the Germans succeeded in examining another shot down. It showed by its equipment that the Americans were shifting to daylight bombing. Schwenke himself piloted one and found that it flew "extraordinarily easily. You can talk normally in the cockpit with the co-pilot." A comparison of the B-17 F with the earlier B-17 C showed that the later model carried a ton and a half more armor. This, and the fact that German fighters had fired long bursts at these planes without any apparent effect, led to a discussion at one of the air-armament conferences about how best to bring down this and other bombers. Here Schwenke's careful examinations came into their own.

"If I may show this," he said, "here is a presentation that I've had made on the various installations of the [fuel] tanks in the six four-motored models that are present in England and in the U.S.A. and in a Russian."

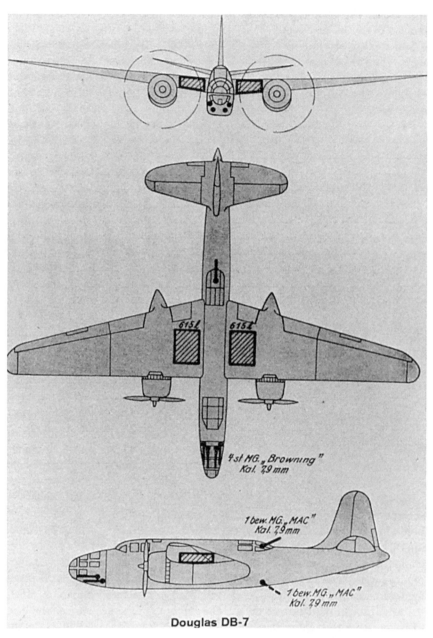

Douglas DB-7

A diagram of an Allied bomber shows in cross-hatching—in red in the original —where the fuel tanks lie so that German fighter pilots will know where to aim. Such information often came from careful German examination of downed enemy aircraft

Milch picked this up. One promising form of air attack, he said, is: "Where are the tanks? Here you can say: in the four-motored airplanes, between the two motors. Only the [American B-24] Liberator has nothing there."

Milch also wanted to know which munition would pierce the B-17's armor. Schwenke explained that "According to experience so far, with the larger calibers the inertia of the shot is greater, the deflection possibility lesser. The greater the caliber, the greater the probability that no ricochets will occur but that it will go through."

"What are the calibers?" Milch persisted. "Will two centimeters [1 inch] punch through?"

"Not always, but two centimeters is pretty good."

"Three centimeters [1½ inches] seems to me to be always more substantial and better," Milch said. "I would propose that, when we have enough armor plates, we have them shot at in Rechlin with various kinds of munition and invite the general of fighter planes and men whom he suggests, doing this at various angles of fire. We'll get the original armor plates from the Tommies and from the Americans!"

The Overt Factor

THE cheapest and fullest of all sources of information has always been the press. So before the war everybody used it. Officers of the Foreign Armies Branch of the general staff spent their mornings reading the general and technical press of their target countries. Diplomats in the Wilhelmstrasse perused *The Times* of London and *Le Temps* of Paris. Nazi party units scanned foreign newspapers for bits that would be useful to higher-ups. Agencies sprang up specializing in press intelligence.

Up until the outbreak of hostilities, they had little difficulty in obtaining the newspapers and listening to the radio broadcasts they needed. The propaganda minister, the brilliant, ratlike Dr. Josef Goebbels, had had the power since 1936 to prohibit the import of foreign newspapers into Germany and to have the Gestapo seize them. After the war started, he exercised it more often. At the same time the government prohibited the general public from listening to foreign radio stations. *The Times* suspended its deliveries to Berlin, and after the fall of France, Britain banned the export of all newspapers to the Continent.

Under these circumstances, official bodies that needed foreign press information had to make special efforts and use special agencies to get it. One such agency was Foreign Newspaper Trade, Inc. of Stolkgasse 25, Cologne, which had been granted a monopoly on the import of foreign newspapers. Neutral newspapers never posed much of a problem. The OKW, for example, got 51 copies of nine papers, including 17 of the *Neue Zürcher Zeitung*, 10 of the *National-Zeitung*, and 6 of the *Basler Nachrichten*, all from Switzerland.

Enemy newspapers—the more interesting—presented greater difficulties. Often government posts had to turn to unorthodox channels to get them. Many English and American newspapers came from Portuguese and Dutch fishermen. They made a tidy side profit by getting them from British fishermen at sea and then reselling them when they got back to the Continent. They charged up to *RM*100 ($40) for a copy of *The New York Times,* though £1.10.0 ($7.50) was more usual. The German embassy in Portugal set up a special unit to buy these papers. Through this and other routes, British papers arrived in Berlin a week after publication, American ones four to six weeks after.

Dr. Paul K. Schmidt, the youthful head of the Foreign Office's Press Branch, who had energetically built it up as a news-gathering body, found a way to get American newspapers faster and cheaper. The State Department supplied the American embassy in Portugal with many newspapers. Since the originals would have taken up too much space and weight on the transatlantic Clipper, they were microfilmed. In Lisbon, the Americans had a local photographer enlarge them. Schmidt, hearing of this, paid the photographer to make an extra set for him. When Schmidt received it in Berlin, he had additional copies made in his own branch and distributed to interested agencies and individuals.

The turn of the war's tide against Germany compounded all of her problems, including that of obtaining foreign press information. Spies helped some. They forwarded such technical journals as *Iron Age* from Latin America in microdot strips. An I. G. Farben subsidiary in Portugal supplied many items; the firm's agents abroad acquired newspapers and books. To make the limited number of periodicals available to more people, and to save foreign exchange, a Hamburg Information Service sold photocopies of foreign newspapers and magazines to authorized subscribers. The World Economic Institute at the University of Kiel also tried to make foreign publications available to a wider circle. So, finally, did the RSHA. It set up a German Society for Documentation in Berlin, which inventoried all foreign printed matter that had come into Germany since 1 January 1939. In December 1943 the society issued its first, 29-page list, giving locations of such magazines as *Electrical World.* But of course no one revealed his most valuable publications. Nor could this system replace the inflow of many issues of the magazines themselves. By 1944, when the Allied invasion of France cut off the press supply from Lisbon, the Germans turned to Sweden to get their English and American newspapers. So acute was their hunger that the OKW had to set up a special unit just to try to get these vital intellectual provisions.

Unlike print, radio waves propagate freely across boundaries, and they do so at the speed of light. To snare the information they carry, scores of official posts of all sizes monitored foreign news transmissions. The army alone had dozens. The Reich Commissar for the Occupied Netherlands Area had his own in The Hague. The Reich Radio Corporation, working out of two low small humid rooms in a private house near the center of Berlin, supplied only the corporation's news staff. DNB, the Deutsche

Nachrichten Büro, the German wire service, distributed mimeographed—and censored—excerpts from its monitors' activity to its clients. The Foreign Office's post, a part of its Press Branch, distributed reports throughout the day as they appeared important enough to do so. It also telephoned officials with flashes: the Foreign Office first heard of the Pearl Harbor attack from it. The Forschungsamt and the OKW Cipher Branch both had posts monitoring press transmissions. And there were others.

Then, in 1940, a new agency joined these, ostensibly to close a gap in their coverage. They listened only to easily receivable stations in common European languages. The new agency would concentrate on distant stations and rarer languages, such as Chinese, Arabic, and Hindustani. But the real dynamic was crude ambition.

The first person to profit was the creator of the organization. Kurt Alexander Mair had come to Stuttgart from Austria in 1935 and become head of Hallwag, a well-known publisher of maps and books on motoring; Mair himself wrote two books on cars. In 1938, claiming that he had worked for the Nazi party during its period of illegality in Austria, he was granted party membership, and soon thereafter joined the Foreign Office's radio desk. In 1940, he stole the idea for the news-monitoring service from an official of the propaganda ministry, who had wanted to unify the many other agencies, and sold it to Ribbentrop. The foreign minister became the second chief gainer of power, which he expected to swipe from Goebbels, to whom the Foreign Office had lost a number of functions when the propaganda ministry was founded in 1933.

Mair, a charming, versatile man with a gift for organization, envisioned things on a grand scale and began at once seeking a suitable home for his new agency. Reichspost technicians tested various locations in and around Berlin for good reception. In a wooded section of southwest Berlin, on the Wannsee, a bay of the Havel River, they found a large former hotel and restaurant, the Swedish Pavilion, at Am Grossen Wannsee 28–30. Mair rented it in July 1940, and within three weeks monitoring had begun. From its location, the new agency took the name of Sonderdienst Seehaus (Lake House Special Service). Within a few months it had almost 500 employees.

Almost at once Goebbels began grabbing for it. The battle reached Hitler. He ordered Goebbels and Ribbentrop to settle their squabble themselves. So on 22 October 1941, they agreed to set up a combined agency, the German Foreign Broadcast Company Interradio, Inc. This would primarily broadcast propaganda but would also incorporate the Seehaus as an "interministerial institute." Probably as a result, the Seehaus absorbed the Foreign Office's monitoring post and, later, the Reich Radio Corporation's.

Mair had equipped the Seehaus headquarters with an omnidirectional antenna with special amplifiers. Since foreign broadcasts often went out simultaneously on several frequencies to reach as many listeners as possible, each monitor controlled two short-wave receivers so he could hear a broadcast on two wave lengths and so reduce errors caused by static. For more complete coverage, Mair established outposts. At one time or other, the Seehaus had major listening stations in Paris, Bucharest, Marseilles, Rome, Graz, Pforzheim, and Merano and minor ones elsewhere, and cooperated with the stations of other authorities in Oslo, Copenhagen, The Hague, and Shanghai. At the start of 1942, the Seehaus was listening regularly to broadcasts from 33 countries and occasionally to 14 more in a total of 37 languages, including Afrikaans, Icelandic, Hindustani, Persian, Gaelic, Maghreb, and Latin (for the Vatican). In February 1942, it heard five new stations: WCBA appeared on the ether on the 13th, for example. A New York station controlled by the Columbia Broadcasting System, it transmitted news in Polish, French, German, and English from 9:45 to 11 p.m. at 17,825 kilocycles for Europe and 6,170 kilocycles for South America simultaneously with WCBX and WCRC. Though a check at The Hague later that year showed that because of the coupling of short-wave with medium-wave emissions the Seehaus was picking up all British broadcasts, it estimated it was missing 20 to 30 percent of the North American overseas broadcasts. Despite this, the Seehaus heard, in January 1942, 8,266 news broadcasts plus 646 statesmen's speeches and major commentaries.

The constant increase in targets led to a constant growth in personnel. In February of 1942, the Seehaus had 527 employees. In March of 1943 it had 630, and in August of 1944, more than 700. Ideally, the monitors had to know a foreign language with its current expressions, be familiar with the politics and geography of the target country, and be able to translate the text into German. As much as possible, therefore, the Seehaus employed Germans who had lived abroad.

One monitor in the American department, Frederick W. Linge, had been born of German parents in Jersey City. During the Depression, they returned to Germany, where Hitler was solving the unemployment problem by arming for war. Their son joined them in 1937. Former U.S. resident George W. Dasch also worked as a Seehaus monitor—until the Abwehr plucked him from that assignment and sent him by submarine as a saboteur to America, where he was quickly arrested and, after trial, executed. But Germans who had lived abroad were a rarity, and the Seehaus had to resolve its personnel problems in different ways. One was to hire foreigners. The case of Dagmar Geissler demonstrated another.

Frau Geissler, a commercial artist, was bored with her job of drawing production charts for the Hermann-Göring Works. Friends told her about their jobs at the Seehaus, which sounded much more glamorous and lucrative than her own. At a card party, she met an official of the agency. Frau Geissler knew no foreign languages, had never been abroad, had no interest in politics or foreign affairs, and had no journalistic background. But she was 23, tall, slender, blonde, and recently separated from her husband. The official offered her a job in his group, which prepared the condensed Seehaus report for the Reich foreign minister, Ribbentrop himself. And so a totally inexperienced girl was hired on totally irrelevant grounds for the Seehaus unit that had one of the greatest responsibilities of all.

The Seehaus knew the foreign broadcast and news transmission schedules, just as did the intended listeners, and it assigned its monitors to listen to the main ones. The demands upon it always exceeded its capacity. When Goebbels asked for reports on Latvian, Lithuanian, and Estonian broadcasts from Moscow, the Seehaus said it could furnish them but would have to drop eight other transmissions. An officer at a control desk could shunt incoming transmissions to various monitors, who usually sat two to a hotel room, each with his own radio sets. They listened to broadcasts live and also recorded them. If the broadcast was important, the monitor transcribed it verbatim. Otherwise he dictated notes to a typist. Urgent intercepts were telephoned to a distribution point. The Seehaus estimated that a monitor could report on six broadcasts in his eight-hour working period, assuming there was time in between to dictate before the information grew stale.

Dagmar Geissler worked on the second floor of the rather shabby hotel, in three interconnected rooms that overlooked the water. Two things recalled their former use: a large, lovely easy chair into which she gratefully slumped, and a reversed annunciator so that the monitors downstairs could summon the evaluators to a particular language group for a flash. She began at 9 a.m. for five days, then had five days off; then she began at 9 p.m. for five days, then had five days off; then she repeated the cycle. When she arrived she normally stopped at the canteen for something to eat, then went to her office to read up on what had gone out on the previous shift. This brought her up to date and prevented her sending out anything that had already been dispatched.

Working with her on her shift was another evaluator, there mostly in case she got sick, or vice versa. Their main job was to compress the pages and pages of boring, repetitious transcripts of news broadcasts, announcements, and speeches into brief reports for Ribbentrop. Three a day were teleprinted to his headquarters, which was usually with Hitler's in East Prussia. The main report, three or four pages long, went out at 7 a.m. Shorter reports went out at 3 and at 7 p.m. Copies also went to the higher officials in the Foreign Ministry. The reports were expected to accentuate the positive. If a news item asserted, "The Germans are by no means through; they still have a lot of reserves left," this topped the report. Before they were dispatched, Dagmar's immediate boss, Helmut Albrecht, a Nazi who had once lived in the United States, edited it—adding, in the manner of editors everywhere, mistakes as he did so. Others in the unit supported the evaluators with the correct spelling of the names of the islands the Allies had invaded and other background. Head of the entire Report Group, as Frau Geissler's was called, was Dr. Markus Timmler, a member of Ribbentrop's staff. He often gave the evaluators pep talks.

The group's most dramatic moment came on 25 July 1943. It was a slow night. Suddenly the annunciator buzzed. The Italian group was summoning them. This was strange: they had never done so before. Frau Geissler and another evaluator rushed to their office. A single girl was there. She was green.

"Mussolini has resigned," she stammered.

The evaluators didn't believe it at first; false reports were as common on the air waves as flies in a stable.

"Who says so?" they demanded.

"Rome," the girl said.

No reaction—then a double take.

"Rome!" they yelled. They rushed back to their rooms and passed the news on the teleprinter to Ribbentrop, elated that for once they had beaten the press agencies, who usually got the news first.

Timmler's group issued the Seehaus's most condensed report. Only the occasional flashes telephoned to important officials were briefer. The Seehaus also put out a daily digest, the *Radio Mirror,* of a few pages, and a *Weekly Radio Mirror,* for government agencies that did not need complete coverage, as well as reports on individual topics. But its basic publication distributed the texts, verbatim or abbreviated, of all important intercepts. This was the daily *Radio Intercept Reports: Transmissions of Foreign Radio Broadcasters,* printed at the Seehaus's own plant behind the hotel. During most of the war, it ran to more than a thousand pages a day. It had six parts and its pages were color-coded according to the source:

Vol.	*Title*	*Content*
I	Enemy Transmitters, Part 1	English transmissions out of London (red)
II	Enemy Transmitters, Part 2	Transmissions out of London and other enemy transmitters in various languages, insofar as they do not appear in Vol. III and Vol. IV (red)
III	Enemy Transmitters, Part 3	Transmissions out of Russia (blue)
IV	Enemy Transmitters, Part 4	Transmissions out of the U.S.A. (green) and Latin America (yellow)
V	Allied and Neutral Transmitters	Transmissions out of Italy (ivory), Spain, Portugal, and Latin America (yellow), and other countries (white)
VI	Foreign-Language Original Texts	Literal reproduction in foreign languages (colors as in Vols. I to V)

Each inch-thick volume arranged its reports alphabetically by transmitter and language and by time of transmission. The reports were mostly news broadcasts, including the radiotelephone transmissions of radio news correspondents, such as Edward R. Murrow and Charles Collingwood, for use on their home networks.

Trucks brought the Seehaus reports to Reich offices in Berlin every morning. At the end of 1941, the Seehaus was distributing 88 sets of the *Radio Intercept Reports* a day. Both the daily and the weekly digest circulated to 430 recipients. Then in 1942 came a number of changes. Mair rose to head Interradio. (Later it was discovered that he had failed to mention in his party application that in 1932 he had been convicted of fraud and sentenced to two years in prison. He was kicked out of the party and out of his job.) Dr. Hans A. Wilms, 41 years old, a lawyer who was a member of the Seehaus since its start, took over as head of the Seehaus. But he lasted only two years before suffering a nervous breakdown. Albrecht replaced him.

At the same time that Wilms took charge, Hitler reduced the number of persons entitled to receive this contaminating foreign information—a veritable fountainhead, as Goebbels put it, of "defeatism." The Foreign Office, which had gotten 28 full sets and 204 daily digests, dropped to 18 and 107. Later, Goebbels reduced the number of full sets to 13 for the entire government and specified to whom they were to go. But by January 1945, the number of sets had climbed back to 50. Among the takers were navy head Dönitz, spy chief Schellenberg, and the Japanese embassy.

In comparison with the other monitoring services, one recipient summed up, the Seehaus was "not as fast but more comprehensive than the DNB-blue [the wire service's confidential reports to trustworthy officials], not as complete and reliable as the Forschungsamt, but again faster than this. It is at a midpoint that makes it quite useful for the needs of press evaluation."

Many agencies did that evaluation. Each examined the press in the light of its own interests. The party's Reich Press Center had 15 readers scanning 200 newspapers and magazines to spot "the journalistic expression of the party's work in the domestic and foreign press." Goebbels and his assistants avidly studied the foreign press to exploit weak spots in their propaganda. Unnumbered research institutes, government bodies, professional associations, and businesses sieved enormous quantities of economic nuggets from the foreign press. In the Foreign Office, 10 readers at Schmidt's Press Branch's Desk X clipped, clipped, clipped foreign newspapers. These they indexed by country and by topic. Desk XII, with 125 employees, distributed, to the ministry officials who it thought needed them, these clippings, pasted on special forms, as well as the "Foreign Press Report," the "Special Service for Political Information," the "Special Service for Military Information," and yet others, all tailored to the needs of foreign policy. Some of this material came from the press attachés in the

25. Jañar 1943

N e w (Tag) Y o r k

von Algier für CBS   Tele-Sendung   englisch   23.55 Uhr

(Sender)   (Welle)   (Sprache)   (Zeit)

HeB-7 ADi-78

Text:	Stichwort:
C o m m e n t a r y Charles Collingwood This is Charles Collingwood in North Africa. The Tunsian front is quieter tonight as it becomes evident that the German offensive southwest of Pont du Fahs have been checked. I left Allied Headquarters two days ago. At that time the Germans were attacking along the .. Valley running more or less southwest of Pont du Fahs. This German offensive was important because it was so obviously designed to protect the Axis communications in the Sfax coastal belt into which Rommel intends to bring his somewhat dented Africa Corps. When I left there the Germans were at the gate of the .. Valley and close to ... Valley and beginning to occupy the northern ridges (unverständlich) But in the last 2 days their advance has been checked and pushed back. The British Fleet from the north and the Americans from the south had come to the aid of the French who were bearing the brunt of the German attack and they have held, and have in fact pushed back the German spearhead into the ..Valley. Of course the main feature of this African campaign at the moment is the progress of Rommel and the 8th Army towards Tunesia. That is not my story to tell. I could tell you how we ...... Yesterday American forces raided .. down in southern Tunesia and (unverständlich) and captured 80 prisoners and	Collingwood

The Sonderdienst Seehaus, chief German agency for monitoring foreign press broadcasts and transmissions, distributes the text of a Charles Collingwood report missions abroad, who sent in daily reports, some from Desk X, some from the Seehaus, a great deal from the DNB and such other wire services as Transozean and Europapress, which issued news reports to government agencies, not by a "ticker," as in the United States, but by distributing mimeographed sheets. Foreign Office officials sometimes came to the Press Branch when they needed information. State Secretary Ernst von Weizsäcker, whose son, Carl, a nuclear physicist, was working on a German atomic bomb, asked the branch on 6 October 1941 whether it had found any information in the foreign press, especially the American, on "the use of uranium for blasting purposes." Schmidt forwarded some reports out of Sweden but said that he had not yet found anything from the United States.

Military agencies likewise exploited press material. Some of them were abroad: the attachés. Boetticher in the United States supped on American newspaper stories for much of his intelligence nourishment. At home, the Ausland part of Canaris's department maintained a Foreign Press Group as part of its charge to report on the politico-military situation for the OKW. Lieutenant Colonel Hans von Schierbrandt, a former journalist, headed its 15 to 20 translators and evaluators all through the war. In contrast to the Foreign Office, which dealt with broader issues, his unit emphasized speed.

Thirty or forty papers arrived every morning. Schierbrandt scanned those in English and French, marked important stories, and passed them over for translation. Other newspapers were evaluated by specialists in their languages. Schierbrandt also received the intercepts of OKW/Chi. He assembled all this and then dictated extracts that formed his Foreign Press Report. It came in two editions. The shorter, just two pages, reported news almost in telegraphic style, preceded by the source: " 'O' Secolo': Several hundred American airplanes flew over the Azores Monday." The longer edition, about a dozen pages, spelled these items out: "Airplanes for the Western powers under way? The Portuguese newspaper 'O' Secolo' reports that passengers of a Portuguese steamer have said that early Monday several hundred American airplanes flew over the Azores." The Foreign Press Group also issued an afternoon update.

Once Schierbrandt had such important news that he was ordered to report it to Hitler himself. In January 1940, two German officers, carrying the plans for the offensive against France and the Low Countries, crashed in Belgium. The great question was whether they had burned the papers. The first stories reassured the Germans. The *Gazet van Antwerpen,* for example, ran a short story near the bottom of an inside page the day after the crash saying that the officers had immediately burned all the papers that were on board. But the next day, as a shirttail to the lead story that the Belgian government was protesting the infraction of its air space, the newspaper reversed itself. The officers had indeed tried to set fire to the papers, but Belgian soldiers had seized them only slightly damaged.

Schierbrandt brought the newspaper to the chancellery and told his Führer what it said. Hitler asked Schierbrandt whether he thought the papers would have actually burned or not. Hitler had a package of typing paper brought in and tried to light it. It did not catch. Hitler thanked Schierbrandt and dismissed him. Next day he issued the Basic Order No. 1 that so limited the dissemination of information in the Third Reich and after the war served as an alibi for so many: No one must know more than he has to for his work. The offensive itself was put off, and when, in May, it finally began, its tactics bore an entirely different character.

Schierbrandt normally limited himself to news items. But sometimes he appended extracts of important texts. He did this with Churchill's speech girding Britain for the expected invasion. The magniloquent ending of this, the greatest oration of the century, greatly impressed the Germans. They evidently intended to give the translation into German in full, but for some reason made some odd excisions and abbreviations:

German version	*Original*
We want to conduct ourselves so, that if the British Empire becomes 1,000 years old, men will still have to say: That was its finest hour!	Let us therefore brace ourselves to our duties, and so bear ourselves that, if the British Empire and its Commonwealth last for a thousand years, men will still say: "This was their finest hour!"

Schierbrandt sent the morning and the afternoon Foreign Press Report to about 30 military posts, including the four high commands. But Hitler's restriction on press material affected it as well: after 1942, it went only to a few top officials.

Much of its work was duplicated by another OKW agency, Chi, the Cipher Branch. Its Group IV (later II) monitored broadcasts at four listening posts and boiled down the interceptions into a half a dozen pages. Called the Chi-Nachrichten (Chi-News), these came out twice a day in two editions: one on the military, one on the political situation, each at 8 a.m. and 11 p.m. Like Ausland's, it went to 30 agencies, some also on the Ausland list. Often both reports carried the same items. On 19 May 1942, for example, both gave official Russian statements on the battle of Kharkhov, Chi attributing it to the Russian information bureau, Ausland to the Soviet army report. Because the Chi-Nachrichten relied exclusively on radio news, they were more current and covered more areas than Ausland's, which in its turn was more thorough and detailed in its individual reports.

The navy and the air force had centralized press-evaluation units. The army's was more spread out. Foreign Armies East's Desk III h listened to Russian broadcasts; III d read Russian newspapers. After major battles, these often listed the names of the meritorious commanders and their troop units—a windfall for the order-of-battle specialists. But the agency that undoubtedly gained the most from its press evaluation was Foreign Armies West. It had the "negligent" American press to mine in. This was filled with stories one of whose purposes was to build morale in the home front and fighting formations. Mostly the censors or the reporters themselves had purged them of secrets. A *New York Times* story by Hanson Baldwin on the training of parachutists and one from the *Washington Post* on a three-dimensional relief map gave away no real information to the Germans.

But some military detail leaked through, such as details about the 50-foot LCM, or Landing Craft (Mechanized), with its crew of four plus machine gunners and its capacity. The statement by Secretary of War Stimson that by the end of 1943 the total strength of the American army would be 8.2 million men probably helped Foreign Armies West calculate the number of American divisions. Later, British broadcasts mentioning the arrival of convoys, announcements that General Montgomery had quit the Mediterranean theater for a new assignment in Britain, an American official's statement about an increase in landing-boat production—all pointed to a build-up in Britain for invasion.

Army groups and armies monitored the foreign press as well, and their results sometimes helped their troops indirectly. When the Allied press reported that King George VI had lunched at the headquarters of a Canadian corps after visiting the Cassino battlefield, the Germans rightly inferred that the corps was resting in the rear of that front. When the I c of the 14th Army in Italy learned from the press of the arrival of a Negro division, and then heard from the same source that General Mark Clark had visited it, he deduced that it would soon be put into action.

The most avid reader of foreign press information was probably Hitler himself. All of it had to be translated into German, since he knew no foreign languages, and mangled them when he tried to speak them: one of his subordinates, who knew English, winced when Hitler mispronounced, as he invariably did, "United Press."

Many people brought him his favorite of all kinds of information: the large illustrated magazine, such as *Life*. These often printed huge photographs of Allied equipment, sometimes in the color advertisements for Camel cigarettes, which he liked to look at and comment upon. Schmidt, the head of the Foreign Office Press Branch, knew that he could catch Hitler's interest whenever he arrived with a copy of the *London Illustrated News*. Often Hitler flipped through it while standing and had the captions translated. Dönitz fed both this interest and Hitler's weakness for news of enemy failings at a situation conference on 1 January 1945 when he produced a copy of the British *Picture Post* of 28 October 1944. An illustrated article on the battle of the Atlantic mentioned how the "hastily-built" Liberty ships "literally couldn't move forward against a storm."

Foreign press reports, on the other hand, which were one of his most important sources of information, were passed to him through a single conduit. This was Reich Press Chief Otto Dietrich. They came to Dietrich, in Berlin, in Berchtesgaden, or in the Führer headquarters, via a service he had begun rather informally.

In 1936, he had had a 23-year-old DNB stenographer, Heinz Lorenz, accompany him on his trips with Hitler to take the news by telephone from DNB and type it up for submission to the Führer. Before the war this Führer Material Service operated only outside Berlin, because while Hitler was in the capital Dietrich supplied him. With the start of the war, and the increase in the volume of material, Dietrich had Lorenz and a couple of other men get the material in Berlin as well and give it to him. When he and Hitler were at the Führer headquarters, Lorenz sent the information to him by radio and teleprinter. DNB selected the stories on the basis of general news judgment and items wanted by Dietrich: political declarations of leading statesmen, important debates in Parliament or Congress, comments of serious newspapers. Dietrich read these and made the final decision on what was to go to Hitler. Each morning he gave this material to Hitler's valet, who had to place it outside the Führer's bedroom door, so that it would be there if he awoke early. Usually, however, the press reports were presented to him with the newspapers immediately after breakfast. These were translations of the original reports, though they were sometimes cut. Throughout the day, Hitler continued to read the new ones. Dietrich gave them constantly to the valet, who always stood near the Führer and gave them to him when he asked for them, which was often. Many days he read 100.

These reports, and the picture magazines, furnished him with interesting and sometimes significant facts. But he could no more extract vital military or political secrets from the newspapers than could his subordinates. The man who tightly controlled his own press recognized that wartime newspapers do not tell the full story.

"It would be very useful to me at this moment, for example, to be informed concerning the importance of the opposition in England, who belongs to it," he said once. "As it is, all I know on the subject is what I've learned by reading the newspapers."

And he saw quite clearly one of the great dangers of relying too much on the press. Talking about the Italian front at a situation conference one day, he pointed to a spot on the map and said, "The English are putting out reports that in this area they have set up the prerequisites to drive forward here. Those are just the kind of reports that obviously are prattled out by journalists."

12

Hearing Diplomats Chatter

IN a converted youth hostel on the Dutch coast, 200 yards from the sea, engineers tended the electronic equipment that produced one of Germany's most sensational World War II intelligence coups. It snared the very voices of Franklin D. Roosevelt and Winston Churchill flashing in scrambled form through the ether and restored them automatically and instantaneously to their pristine form. Translations of its tape recordings of these intimate talks then went to the Führer himself.

This apparatus belonged to the Research Institute of the Deutsche Reichspost. During the 1930s, the Research Institute had been studying voice privacy methods for the German post office, which, like most European post offices, ran the nation's telephone system. At the start of the war, its head decided that descrambling enemy conversations would help Germany more. He shifted Kurt E. Vetterlein, a 29-year-old engineer, from scrambling to descrambling. Vetterlein felt that the transatlantic radiotelephone connection between Great Britain and the United States was the most interesting, and he concentrated on that.

To prevent anyone with a short-wave receiver from listening to the conversations that passed over this circuit, the American Telephone & Telegraph Company and the British post office mangled the voices upon transmission and demangled them upon reception with an electronic mechanism called the A-3. AT&T housed its A-3 in a locked room at 47 Walker Street, New York, and all radiotelephone transmissions passed through it before being propelled into the ether for the long leap across the Atlantic.

Since the Deutsche Reichspost also had an A-3 for radiotelephone communications with America, Vetterlein knew the principles of its operation. But he did not know the variables that enshrouded the American messages in secrecy. Using transmissions from America intercepted near Bordeaux in occupied France, Vetterlein and his assistants, working in the big brown

Deutsche Reichspost building on the Ringstrasse in Berlin, attacked the problem with oscilloscopes and spectrographs, filters and patience. By the end of 1940, they had reconstructed the A-3's secret parameters—the widths of the subbands, their division points, their inversions, and their intersubstitutions, which changed 36 times every 12 minutes.

For the day-to-day solution of the conversations, Vetterlein wanted to construct a mechanism that would descramble them as they were being spoken. This demanded an extremely exact time standard, because the A-3 shifted its enciphering pattern every 20 seconds in the 36-step cycle, but it was the only way to cope with the volume of communications. In looking for a place to set up his intercept post, Vetterlein found that near Noordwijk on the coast of the Netherlands gave the best reception. It could pick up both the ground wave of the transmitter in England and the back lobe of its beam toward America. Vetterlein took over the youth hostel and began installing his equipment—enough to fill a couple of living rooms: three or four single-sideband receivers, filters, modulators, switching equipment, tape recorders, the timers. Based on a quartz-stabilized watch, these held his descrambler so close to the A-3 that even if no messages passed for an entire day, the equipment woud lose only a fraction of a syllable when communication started up again.

By the fall of 1941, Vetterlein's unit—sometimes called the Forschungsstelle (Research Post)—was intercepting and descrambling messages. On 6 March 1942, the postal minister, Wilhelm Ohnesorge, a kindly-looking elderly gentleman who held Nazi Party Card No. 42, notified Hitler of its coup and sent along a sample intercept. Soon the dozen or so engineers under Vetterlein were monitoring the Allied conversations 24 hours a day. The calls were intercepted by the two rhombic antenna in scrambled form, instantaneously disentangled by the apparatus, and tape-recorded in the clear. Often as many as 60 calls a day came in, and never fewer than 30. A half-dozen highly qualified interpreters listened to them and selected those of intelligence value. At first they translated them on the spot and teleprinted the German in cipher to Berlin. But scrambling degrades the quality of speech, and this, plus static and the occasional imprecisions of translations, led to the messages being sent on in English. Because of Ohnesorge's friendliness with SS General Gottlob Berger, they passed through RSHA VI, with Schellenberg forwarding them to Hitler, the Foreign Office, or the OKW. A direct line also existed to the Führer headquarters.

The operation was not entirely cut and dried. Once the AT&T engineers changed the subband widths, compelling Vetterlein to repeat some of his analyses. In 1943, after commandos captured some coastal radars, the Germans feared that this might happen to the Forschungsstelle as well. So it moved to Valkenswaard, a small town in the southeast Netherlands. Here a compact brick-and-concrete bunker, in the shape of an L, was built for it in woods at the intersection of Nieuwe Waalreseweg and De Hazelaar streets at the north of the town. The men worked in areas guarded by inch-thick steel doors, cooked in their own kitchen, slept in rooms with dormer windows, and relaxed in a living room with a fireplace. A fence topped by barbed wire surrounded the bunker. In the fall of 1944, the unit retreated to Bavaria. But here the distance from the transmitter considerably impaired its results.

Most of the intercepts revealed middle-level bureaucrats discussing middle-level problems. Many dealt with requests for reinforcements, aircraft, and other supplies. A typical intercept is that of 4:50 p.m. 28 February 1944 among three officials of the British Board of Trade: Herbert Tout, assistant secretary, Industrial Supplies Division, and John Stirling, assistant secretary, Commercial Relations and Treaties, both in Washington, and Ralph Nowell, principal assistant secretary, Commercial Relations and Treaties, in London. In part, the transcript reads, in the original English, with the Germans' use of B for Britain and A for America, where Stirling apparently did the talking:

A. Yes, the main reason I called you up was that there is but a month to an unshakeable conviction on the American side that the Empire estimates of requirements on Lend-Lease are ... as follows[:] each Empire country sends to London an estimate of its total requirements. London then says we can or we can not supply so much of that ... and the requirement on Lend-Lease is the balance. Have you got that?

B. Yes.

A. ...I want confirmation from you that this is simply not the case.... We sent you a telegram the other day, the 917 about subsidization.

B. Yes, I got that.

A. Well, you can *forget* it.
    . . .

A. 917. Now the next point is this: Saunders gave me a note before I left, which ... on the method of allocation of iron and steel by the material committee. There was a note at the end by Lane (?) suggesting that it ought not to be communicated to the other side. Well I can not for the life of me see, *why* it shouldn't be, ...

Schellenberg puffed this up in his covering letter to the Foreign Office. "Mistrust and dissatisfaction rule on the American side, because the Lease-Lend matériel requirements are requested without data on their own production," he said. But even with Schellenberg's exaggerations and falsehoods, the intercepted document is hardly of very vital importance.

Nor did the conversations of the top officials provide much more. The Forschungsstelle intercepted many high Allied officials: Churchill, Roosevelt, General Mark Clark, British ambassador to the United States Lord Halifax. It overheard W. Averell Harriman, in London on his way to taking up his new post as ambassador in Moscow, talking to Leo T. Crowley, who had just been named foreign economic administrator. It listened to

British Foreign Secretary Anthony Eden talking to his new minister of state, Richard Law, in the United States to discuss monetary problems. But the results remained thin.

The Germans eavesdropped on Harry Hopkins, President Roosevelt's closest advisor, speaking with Churchill at 5:05 p.m. 9 October 1943. (Churchill used the codename JOHN MARTIN, but the German interceptors knew who he was anyway.) The President and Churchill had been discussing the question of Italy's imminent declaration of war on Germany, and the Hopkins-Churchill talk perhaps referred to that. But no definite clue leaked out:

B. John here.
A. Yes.
B. Can you give me any hopeful answer?
A. Yes.
B. Good.

Churchill then said that something "could be free, open, and . . ." Hopkins replied, "Yes," which Churchill had to have repeated several times. Then:

A. The report (or note) has not yet gone, but it will be sent.
B. I see, good.
A. Is that all right?
B. Yes.
A. All right. Good bye.
B. Good bye.

Fully as revealing was a Churchill talk of 23 July 1942 with an official in New York. A translation of it went to Hitler. It had as its most pregnant sentence, "You will accelerate the greatest exertions."

The lack of substance in the talks stemmed almost certainly from the general recognition that the scrambler was insecure. The circuit's operators constantly warned the speakers of this. The speakers mostly used it despite this insecurity when they needed a quick answer to a question or had to rapidly settle a matter that required some discussion but would not give anything away, or sometimes when they just wanted to hear one another's voices.

Nevertheless, Churchill and Roosevelt were not always as careful as they should have been. Churchill was practically addicted to the telephone, picking it up at all hours of the day and night to call Roosevelt, who in his turn surprised the Germans with his indiscretions. He, Churchill, and a few other high officials were not given the warnings about insecurity that the lower officials were—an indication to the Germans, when this was omitted, that an important person was coming on the line. Partly because of this, partly because of their rank, some of the Roosevelt-Churchill conversations disclosed matters of more import than the other intercepts. One suggested a build-up for the cross-Channel invasion, indicating that it was coming yet closer. On 29 July 1943, another suggested to the Germans that the Allies had been dealing with the new non-Mussolini Italian government. Though these suspicions were false, the intercept hardened Germany's three-day-old decision to get troops into Italy as quickly as they could and deny the Allies advantages from Italy's flip-flop.

But these results were at best marginal and corroboratory. And toward the end even they fell off. The spectacular technical feat of tapping into the top-level Allied radiotelephone conversations produced no great results. They did not give the Germans any extraordinary insight into Allied plans. As a Foreign Office official noted disappointedly on a sheaf of intercepts, "There is in general not much to be gotten from them."

The Forschungsstelle constituted but one element of Germany's communications-intelligence effort. Indeed, at the height of World War II no fewer than nine major agencies tilled this rich acreage:

1. the Forschungsstelle
2. the Forschungsamt, an independent agency under Hermann Göring that tapped wires, intercepted radio messages, and solved codes in the entire gamut of political and economic intelligence
3. the Foreign Office's Pers Z, which solved diplomatic telegrams
4. the OKW's Cipher Branch, which steered armed-forces cryptology and broke high-level military and diplomatic codes
5. the army's radio intelligence organization
6. the air force's radio intelligence organization
7. the navy's radio intelligence organization
8. RSHA VI's Radio Observation Post, which solved diplomatic telegrams until it was disbanded in 1943
9. the censors of mail and telegrams

Why did so many agencies work this field? One reason was specialization: the army solved military codes, the navy, naval; censorship requires a different organization than that for intercepting transatlantic radiotelephone calls. Another was greed for power: Göring, Ribbentrop, and the military held tightly to agencies that to a considerable degree produced the same intelligence. Still another was Hitler's unwillingness to allow a single source to control his information—he always preferred to have it come from several, preferably rival, agencies, despite duplication of effort. The multiplicity further presupposed the relative cheapness and ease of communication intelligence, compared to other forms of intelligence such as espionage, as well as the freshness and reliability of its information. The agencies cooperated fairly well in technical matters, even though rivalries and old resentments in some cases kept relations cool.

The largest of these agencies contributed the least to German foreign intelligence. Censorship had thousands of employees in its—at times—more than two dozen postal and telegraph control stations in Germany and the occupied territories. Censorship came under the Abwehr, later the RSHA. The station at Frankfurt-am-Main, which opened the mail between Germany and Switzerland and Germany and occupied France, had 97 officers, 120 officials, and 2,580 employees in November 1941 to examine 120,000 to 150,000 letters a day. By September 1944 the daily average

A German "opened by censor" sticker

had fallen to fewer than 20,000 letters, and the number of workers had likewise dropped.

Censorship sieved bits and pieces of information from its massive surveillance of mail, including neutral post transiting Germany, which went from spot checks to total coverage in June of 1942. Each station sent items it thought potentially useful to a central evaluation post in Berlin. This separated them into political, military, and economic material and forwarded them to interested agencies. On 11 September 1942, it told the OKW's economic-intelligence branch, Canaris's Ausland Department, and naval intelligence that the British war transport minister had taken over the French steamer *Commandant Dorise*. On other days it reported on a Portuguese export of carob bread to England, the lack of a shortage of mercury in the United States, and the Allies' great difficulties about supplies of hemp. The economic-intelligence branch called the information it obtained from the couple of hundred items it received each day "valuable."

Three days after the war started, the foreign branch of the Nazi party's SD called in 39-year-old Josef Gottlob for a talk. Gottlob had served as a teenaged radioman at the front in World War I, and through subsequent employment as an export representative with electrical and other firms had built up a rare combination of technical expertise, language ability, and firsthand knowledge of foreign countries. The SD knew of this because he had, since 1937, worked as a translator and language instructor for various Nazi agencies.

The SD wanted him to set up a radio intelligence post. This he did. With the formation of the RSHA a few weeks later, his post became RSHA VI's Desk A 6, later redesignated F 6, F 7, and then F 2, but always called the Radio Observation Post. Gottlob himself rose from SS first lieutenant to SS major.

The core of the unit consisted of Austrian cryptanalysts. Chief among these was Colonel Andreas Figl, the grand old man of Austrian codebreakers. Figl had founded the cryptanalytic service of Austria-Hungary's Royal and Imperial Army back in 1911 and played a key role in its World War I successes, later doing the same work for the Interior Ministry. His name had been suggested by another Austrian cryptologist, Dr. Albert Langer, who had joined the SD after the Anschluss. Eventually Gottlob's unit consisted of 47 specialists and assistants, housed in Berlin at Jagowstrasse 18.

Their intercepts came from a propaganda ministry listening station in The Hague, which in 1942 was turning over 10 pages a day of foreign diplomatic messages. Langer, a mathematician and physicist, left around 1941 to work on the counterfeiting of English pounds. The Radio Observation Post still scored some successes with the systems of minor nations—especially when Figl took the intercepts that had stumped others into a rear room with a pot of black coffee. But it made no memorable solutions, and Walter Schellenberg, the head of RSHA VI, had to beg other agencies for intercept results. Moreover, he did not trust Gottlob, whom many regarded as an enigmatical personality. These factors, plus Gottlob's ineptness as a leader of men, led to the dissolution of the post in 1943. Gottlob went to Madrid; the cryptanalysts switched from breaking codes to making them.

The richest, the most secret, the most Nazi, and the most influential of the nine agencies was the Forschungsamt. At the peak of World War II it had 6,000 employees, half of them party members, in its special quarters in Berlin, where raw intercepts poured in over hundreds of wires. But it had started in 1933 with half a dozen men working in an attic.

Gottfried Schapper founded it. A small, energetic, impulsive redhead in his forties, he had long cherished the dream of an objective central communications intelligence agency for Germany. The idea had come to him first in World War I, after he succeeded Ludwig Voit, the founder of German military radio intelligence, as chief of the General Headquarters' radio station, with its cryptanalytic unit. He proposed it to Ludendorff for after the war, but Germany's defeat quashed it. Schapper himself, sometimes unemployed, concentrated on keeping himself alive until, in 1927, he was hired by the Defense Ministry's Cipher Center. He disliked its intrusion into political cryptanalysis, and, when Hitler came to power, he saw an opportunity to realize his dream. A Jew-hater, Schapper had joined the Nazi party in 1920, had quit after the failure of the 1923 putsch, but had rejoined in 1931. In February 1933, with two other Nazi Cipher Center employees, he took his idea to Göring, whom he knew from World War I.

He had hoped to attach the agency to the chancellery, which had no ministerial special interests, but Hitler's fear of intelligence monopoly ruled this out. Göring, instantly perceiving personal advantage, took over the proposal for himself. He granted Schapper's conditions of making the agency independent of any ministry and of subordinating it to him not as a minister but as an individual. He liked Schapper's suggestion of "Forschungsamt" (Research Office) as the agency name because "You indeed research the truth." Schapper's only disappointment came when Göring asked him to nominate a chief: he could not propose himself, so he suggested—and Göring accepted—Lieutenant Commander Hans Schimpf, a sunny, likable man who was naval cryptology's liaison to the Abwehr, then the central for all German intelligence, and who was an old acquaintance of Göring's. He promptly quit the navy and joined the party.

On 10 April 1933, the Forschungsamt began work in the attic of Göring's air building. By July it had attracted some 20 radiomen, telephone technicians, cryptanalysts, and evaluators. It began using a postal radio station to monitor wireless transmissions, and it snatched telephone wiretapping from the Defense Ministry, which had had this activity since at least 1925. By the end of the year it had to move into a former hotel, and in 1934 and 1935 into a converted housing complex, the Schiller Colonnades, set back from the street at Schillerstrasse 116–124. The former apartments became its offices, and the basement was filled with rows of teleprinters and festoons of pneumatic tubes. The agency stayed there until bombings destroyed many of these buildings and forced a series of moves to dispersed locations.

The organization had six branches, raised to bureaus in 1941: I, administration; II, personnel; III, distribution of incoming requests and sifting of incoming reports; IV, cryptanalysis; V, evaluation; VI, technical equipment development and management. Its chief, Schimpf, committed suicide as a result of a love affair in 1935 and was replaced by Prince Christoph von Hessen, younger brother of a crony of Göring's and a member of one of the oldest families in Christendom. He volunteered for war service in 1939, and Schapper, head of administration, served as acting chief. When Christoph was shot down over Italy in 1943, Schapper finally achieved his ambition and, in February 1944, became chief.

The Forschungsamt's information came strictly from telecommunications. (A brief venture into espionage failed ignominiously, and no further attempts were made.) In some areas, such as press or diplomatic radiograms, the Forschungsamt picked up as much as it could. But in areas where the information flow was too great, such as telephone calls, it selected its targets on the bases of requests for information from other agencies. Sometimes these specified the person or organization whose communications the Forschungsamt was to monitor. Sometimes they were more general—as when the intelligence section of the OKW's war economy office asked on

2 June 1944 for political-military material connected with economics. When the requests involved telephone taps, Göring had to approve them. Usually he did so within a day by putting his "G" on them, but sometimes he denied them with a "Nein." Some of the Forschungsamt's acquisition organs were in Berlin, but many were scattered around the country for better radio reception or to tap calls to and from organizations in the provinces.

The agency's telephone-tapping organs were its A research posts. In the middle of the war, the Forschungsamt had 15 in cities in greater Germany and 15 in cities in occupied territory. In Germany alone, they maintained about 1,000 taps, half in Berlin, half outside. Cables led from the telephone connections of the post offices to these posts, most of which were in rented rooms, though some were in the post office buildings themselves. In Berlin the A research post was in the Schillerstrasse; in Cologne, at Konstantinstrasse 1; in Düsseldorf, on the second floor of the post office building; in Danzig, on the third floor of police headquarters. In some occupied countries, the Forschungsamt simply took over existing monitoring agencies, as in Paris and Copenhagen.

Each A research post had a number of listening stations that handled up to 20 lines apiece. When a call passed through a tapped line, a bulb lit up and a monitor, called a Z man, listened through earphones and took notes on the conversation. If it were too fast, he could wire-record it. If it were in a foreign language, or if he were busy, he could pass it to another Z man. Between calls, he transcribed his notes into a Z report, usually using indirect quotations but keeping to direct for specially important or questionable parts. These went by teleprinter to the report-sifting center in Berlin, which sent it to the proper evaluation unit. At night and on Sundays and holidays, all incoming messages were recorded to be played back when the staff returned to work.

The B research posts were radio receiving stations, owned and operated by the post office, which the Forschungsamt rented. From the original post at Beelitz, the Forschungsamt expanded until it had seven in Germany and five abroad. They concentrated on three kinds of traffic: diplomatic (insofar as it was recognizable), news (dispatches of Associated Press, Reuters, Havas, and other wire services), and economic (these usually on specific order). Within the latter, they focused on the transmissions of the big international banks, armament firms, merchant ships, and firms involved in major commercial agreements.

The radio intercept stations of the C research posts monitored broadcasts, such as the speeches of important politicians. Speed was particularly important in the area of public policy statements: sometimes an evaluator was working on the head of a speech while the tail was still coming in.

In a large room in the cellar of one of the Berlin buildings, 50 teletypewriters pounded out intercepted teleprinter messages day and night. Cut into particular lines—including the Anglo-Indian cable, which touched Germany—they printed out everything that passed over them. Similar units were set up later in Vienna and within some of the telephone-monitoring units. The teletypewriter interception—D 1 research posts—required the smallest number of personnel, nearly all mechanics. The personnel for telegram interception, the D 2 research posts, who had to know languages, mostly picked up telegrams inside local telegraph offices, working with a name list supplied by Forschungsamt headquarters. Berlin alone went through some 34,000 domestic and 8,000 to 9,000 foreign telecommunications a day. Nearly all the material served for economic evaluation.

Material in code went to Bureau IV for solution. It had more old-timers than any other department of the Forschungsamt. Its chief, Georg Schroeder, a man who would have loved to have solved the mathematical riddle of breaking the bank at Monte Carlo, was one of Schapper's two original associates. The unit naturally worked mainly on diplomatic codes and secondarily on private ones. Its 240 members, helped by Hollerith machines, cracked about three-fourths of all the codes it worked on, enabling them to read—before the war—about half the diplomatic telegrams that passed through Berlin. During the war, they solved about 3,000 intercepts a month. Among the solved codes—at least for a while—were high French, Italian, and British diplomatic systems—though the top British code was never solved. The Forschungsamt could not break the Russian diplomatic traffic, any more than anyone else could, but it counted as one of its greatest successes the solution of a Russian system used between armament centers behind the Urals, which produced considerable valuable information.

The flood of material from all these sources poured into a giant sorting unit in Bureau III, which sifted out the chaff and directed the rest to the various branches of Bureau V for evaluation and writing up into reports. Branch 11, foreign politics, got each month at the peak of its activity: 2,400 cryptanalyzed messages, 42,000 cleartext radio and wire messages, 11,000 broadcast transcripts, 14,000 Z reports, and 150 newspapers, plus Reuters and Havas copy. Branch 12, economy, received some 20,000 messages a day out of an estimated 100,000 intercepted. These plus Branch 13, domestic politics, sent about 1,000 items daily to the chief of Bureau V, Walther Seifert. He had these compressed to between 60 and 150 reports—some short individual intercepts, some studies several pages long. They sought to maintain a scrupulous objectivity, noting in parentheses when words were questionable. Some looked almost scholarly, with their footnotes referring to previous reports. Multigraphed in purple on the light brown paper used for external distribution, these became the Forschungsamt's famous Brown Sheets. Brown was, of course, the Nazi party color.

The reports went first to Göring, who read them all—except when they were too long—including the jokes about him, which were often very nasty. The reports then went to the agencies that had requested the information and to others that could use it. But their flow was sometimes troubled. Göring himself sometimes blocked them. In the RSHA, Schellenberg sought to trade his information as head of Nazi foreign intelligence for the Forschungsamt reports. But he delivered nothing, and Schapper, who also felt that he was too young and too ambitious, gave him almost nothing. Ribbentrop hated it when Göring's agency gave Hitler reports on foreign affairs that he had not seen. Sometimes he had the Brown Sheets retyped on white paper and stamped as coming from the Foreign Office! The Brown Sheets themselves moved under heavy control. Forschungsamt couriers brought them in locked pouches to the ministries, where an official designated by the Forschungsamt signed for them. After a month, they had to be returned for destruction.

Much of the information gathered by this gigantic apparatus was economic. Its intercepts on foreign industrial activities helped the Luftwaffe keep its dossier of factories as potential bombing targets up to date. The Luftwaffe file on Soviet aircraft factory No. 447 included an inference drawn from a Forschungsamt report on the factory's call of 21 March 1944 for materials: the factory prefabricated parts. Forschungsamt intelligence also aided the OKW's war-economy section in drawing a picture of enemy production capabilities.

While the economic reports probably enjoyed the best reception of the entire Forschungsamt output, they could not match the diplomatic intercepts in drama—or in importance, which Schapper estimated as in the ratio of 9:1.

During the Czech crisis of 1938, when Hitler was demanding the Sudetenland, the Forschungsamt took advantage of the fact that the London-Prague telephone lines ran through Germany to intercept the talks of both British and Czech diplomats. It often listened to the Czech minister in London, Jan Masaryk, conferring with his president, Eduard Beneš. In a conversation of 11:24 a.m. 24 September 1938, as the most acute international crisis since 1918 approached its peak, the Forschungsamt heard:

Masaryk: I said here that we have gone as far as we possibly can and are further ready to do everything for peace. But we absolutely cannot pull back from our positions.

Beneš: It is completely out of the question that we yield our positions.

And at the end of the talk, a little health advice:

Beneš: You simply cannot imagine what I have gone through.
Masaryk: Yes, that must have been bad, but are you still sleeping well?
Beneš: Yes.
Masaryk: The main thing is good sleep and regular bowel movements.

Göring gave these intercepts to the British in an apparent attempt to sow dissension with the Czechs, since some of the passages seemed to indicate that Masaryk was in contact with the opposition to the party in power.

Masaryk denied it, but the Forschungsamt also listened to the comments of Britain's special envoy indicating that Britain had withdrawn its support from the Czechs and would let the militarily vital Sudetenland go to the Germans. A sneering and satisfied Hitler read the report in which Masaryk told journalists that "There's nothing more to do . . . it's all lost." And with this knowledge he pressed Neville Chamberlain at Bad Godesberg and at Munich to the notorious appeasement of "peace in our time."

The last-minute flurry of negotiations over Hitler's demands upon Poland in August of 1939 provided the Forschungsamt with good insights into British, French, and Polish diplomacy. These came from its Berlin telephone taps on embassies, on the homes of the higher diplomats, and on foreign correspondents. It heard the British ambassador talking with his home office, arguing with the French ambassador, and trying frantically to contact the Polish ambassador. It picked up the French ambassador just after meeting with Hitler expressing pessimism about peace as well as determination about war to his premier: "And if the Germans strike? Then I place my trust in the strength of the [French] nation."

Though such opportunities practically vanished at the outbreak of hostilities, cryptanalyzed telegrams, whose volume grew considerably during the war, filled the gap. One of the most dramatic proofs of Forschungsamt ability and efficiency in this area came, however, on the last day of peace.

Birger Dahlerus, a Swedish businessman and amateur diplomat, was seeking to negotiate the differences between Germany and Poland, France, and England. At 1 p.m. on 31 August 1939, while he was talking with Göring at the latter's country home, Karinhalle, a messenger rushed in with a red envelope, used for urgent state matters. Göring ripped it open and read therein a Forschungsamt solution of a message that the Polish government had sent an hour or two before to its ambassador in Berlin. It forbade him to enter into any actual negotiations. Though Göring recognized that disclosure would spoil " a real and important source of information," he showed it to Dahlerus for transmission to the British ambassador because, he stormed, it proved the Poles' bad faith and thus justified Germany's attitude. This did not affect Hitler's plans one way or the other, but it provided a good propaganda point.

The Forschungsamt's more important solutions went to Hitler. Thus he saw Churchill's message to the Japanese foreign minister urging peace on the same day—12 April 1941—that it was delivered to its rightful recipient. He read the report of the British ambassador in Teheran on his interview with the Iranian prime minister concerning a plan for an alliance between Iran, Great Britain, and the Soviet Union. On 21 January 1942, he saw a Turkish report from Moscow on the military situation, together with Soviet plans and preparations, and, a few months later, a Forschungsamt report, compiled from its secret sources, on the Allies' diplomatic and military situation in the Middle East.

Sometimes the agency gave clues to the future. "I have received from the Forschungsamt," Goebbels noted in his diary on 17 April 1943, "secret information supporting the belief that Roosevelt is planning to meet Stalin somewhere. It must be said that this information is still quite unsubstantiated." This report, perhaps based on Roosevelt's inconclusive correspondence with Churchill and Stalin in November and December of 1942 concerning this possibility, may have further alerted the Germans to the general likelihood of a Big Three conference. Sometimes the agency saw things clearly. "From the Forschungsamt I have received material on the object of Churchill's visit to Washington," Goebbels wrote on 23 May 1943, while the meeting was still under way. "From this too it can be seen that Churchill's intention is to mediate between Stalin and Roosevelt." But not even the Forschungsamt's powerful communications intelligence could pry open the Allies' strategic plans.

Though the Forschungsamt did not hesitate to paint dark pictures—it told Goebbels, for example, how shocked the diplomatic corps in Russia was by the German defeat at Stalingrad—its consumers obstinately picked out the highlights they preferred. "I am reading," observed Goebbels on 8 December 1942, a month after the North Africa landings, "a detailed memorandum put together on the Darlan case, in which this French admiral's treachery is depicted from its earliest beginnings. It proves quite clearly that Darlan hightailed it to North Africa just for the purpose of defecting." But this was not true. Darlan, a pro-Nazi, switched sides after he saw where the wind was blowing.

Thus, despite all the Forschungsamt effort, despite all the care and all the objectivity that went into the Brown Sheets, despite even the agency's party trustworthiness, when its material countered the wishful thinking of Hitler and the Nazi leaders, it could be neglected. "I felt," said Walther Seifert, head of evaluation, "that they [the Brown Sheets] were indeed read, but that the proper conclusions were not drawn."

The Foreign Office also solved diplomatic cryptograms. "I am bound to say we found it very useful," said a high official.

I remember how we knew that a certain foreign ambassador in Berlin, who on the surface was always profuse in expressions of respect and admiration for Hitler and the Nazi regime, was in fact reporting to his government in quite the opposite sense and more than that was committing inaccuracies and positively misrepresenting certain things. Knowing the exact contents of his reports, we could be guided in what we said to him and shape our instructions accordingly; and then it was a help in formulating instructions to the German representative to this man's government. We knew what points would need to be especially treated, or emphasized, in conversations with that Foreign Office. Then, of course, it is always very helpful if you can know in advance what instructions a foreign representative has had and so be fully prepared to talk with him when he calls at the Foreign Office pursuant to these instructions.

The Foreign Office had begun this work on an order from the Reich chancellor issued less than a month after Germany signed the armistice of 11 November 1918. The first and only chief was a retired signal corps captain, Curt Selchow, 32, like Forschungsamt chief Schapper a successor of Voit as head of the radio station at World War I General Headquarters, and a good organizer. By 1933, his unit had about 30 civil servants; in 1936, after a reorganization of the Foreign Office, it got its title of Pers Z, meaning the Z section of the Personnel and Administrative Branch (the Z perhaps indicating mystery and the seclusion of the cryptanalysts from the rest of the branch).

At its peak in the middle of the war, Pers Z employed some 300 workers in a garden apartment and a nearby girls' school in the Dahlem district of southwest Berlin. Only about 50 were cryptanalysts; the others were clerks and support staffers. Among the latter was an information group headed by a pastor. It collated data from radio broadcasts, Foreign Office memoranda, Allied newspapers, and the Pers Z output itself so that it could give the answer when the cryptanalysts asked them, "Who beginning with *w* spoke with somebody ending with *n* in a place with a kind of *po* on Thursday?"

During its existence, Pers Z solved the codes of 34 nations, though not every code of those countries. They included all the major powers except the Soviet Union—Britain, France, Japan, Italy, Spain, the United States, the Vatican. At first it concentrated on French cryptograms, solving some 15,000 to the defeat of France in 1940. Then these slackened off, despite the continuing importance of France and its North African holdings, and Italian solutions picked up. Whereas from the start of its numbering to the end of November 1940, Pers Z had solved only some 6,700 Italian cryptograms, in the next 16 months it read almost 3,700 more—a significant index of the trust placed by one dictator in another. American solutions remained at a tenth of these levels. Curiously, Pers Z solved many more American cryptograms in the four months before Pearl Harbor than in the four months following—540 compared to 129. The latter figure constitutes barely one message a day of the scores that the State Department must have been transmitting.

Between these extremes in quantity, but apparently above others in quality, lay Pers Z's solutions of Turkish cryptograms. After the German invasion of Russia in June 1941, these intercepts formed the great bulk of the Pers Z material that the Foreign Office submitted to Hitler. The need for the Turks to know as much as possible about their powerful and dangerous neighbor, and the excellence of their diplomatic and attaché representation in Moscow, obtained for them detailed and accurate reports about events in the Soviet Union. The solution of these dispatches gave the Germans access to an acute and comparatively unbiased observation post in the enemy capital.

The Turkish intercepts from Russia that went to Hitler included reports on war matériel seen at a 1941 October Revolution anniversary parade, Stalin's pleasure with the situation on the front just after the stopping of the German offensive before Moscow in December 1941, the results of the Stalin-Eden talks, Soviet demands for a Moscow conference and for a second front in Europe, plans for a Soviet attack around Smolensk, which in fact was then under way, and the arrival of American tanks and aircraft in Russia.

In 1940, Pers Z began to break into one of the major U.S. State Department codes. And by August 1941 it could hand the foreign minister fully solved telegrams of American diplomat Robert Murphy, then pursuing delicate negotiations with the French in North Africa. One message transmitted a request of an aide of French general Maxime Weygand, commanding in French North Africa, for an American promise of military aid. The Germans knew that Weygand was no friend of theirs, but it was not until they had what a Vichy source called "documentary proof" of his dealings with the United States that they forced Vichy to dismiss him. Thus Pers Z's solution damaged American diplomatic efforts and won time and advantages for Germany.

In the fall of 1941, Pers Z read and sent to Hitler two American messages involving top statesmen. In one, the shah of Iran told the American minister in special audience that he "has no sympathy for the Germans." This could hardly have surprised Hitler, however, since just a few weeks earlier British and Soviet troops had virtually occupied his country and neutralized any German power there. In the second, telegraphed triple priority on 29 September 1941 in confidential code, Roosevelt promised Stalin in a "personal message" that "ways will be found to provide the material and supplies necessary to fight Hitler on all fronts." On 8 October, two days after Hitler read this communication between his archenemies, the German press agency utilized it—perhaps on Hitler's orders—to strike a propaganda blow. It published the message, obtained "from a reliable source," to demonstrate "the will of the U.S.A. president to deliver all of Europe and thus the entire European culture and religion to Bolshevism."

Though this episode must have suggested that the Germans had solved an American confidential code, the State Department did not then change its system, and so Pers Z continued to peer into American diplomatic secrets. On 16 December 1941, five days after Hitler declared war on the United States, it passed to him a six-day-old message of Roosevelt's to Marshal Henri Pétain, head of the Vichy government, that bore on the naval war in the Atlantic. Roosevelt was urging that Pétain personally order that no French ships be permitted to sail from any French colonies in the western hemisphere. The following day, Darlan, then acting premier and

French naval minister, agreed to issue such instructions. But Roosevelt had less success with a later attempt. On 27 March 1942 he warned Pétain that the United States would "discontinue its existing relationships" if Pétain brought the strongly pro-Hitler Pierre Laval back into the government. Four days after someone in Washington had stamped "This cable was sent in confidential code. It should be carefully paraphrased before being communicated to anyone" on the triple priority Telegram Sent form, Hitler was reading it. The threat failed to impress either him or Pétain, for a few weeks later Laval became premier. The United States recalled its ambassador but did not break off relations; in the end it was Vichy that did this, after the North African invasion—with Laval generously telling the American chargé in Vichy that the United States "would be free to use its codes for the time being."

Toward the end of the war, the Pers Z results fell off. Though Turkish messages continued to be read, such as one out of Sweden detailing Soviet troop organization, the Americans replaced their code with the so-called strip cipher system. Pers Z managed to crack this, but it took so long that the solutions were obsolete when attained. When the strips were changed, Pers Z lost out altogether.

In a sense it did not matter. For the Nazi leaders often ignored disagreeable intelligence. Though Pers Z marked messages important enough for the Führer with a green F, Ribbentrop did not always give him bad news. The intercepts that Hitler did see, he did not always appreciate. Across the face of one long dispatch that bore importantly on agricultural conditions in Russia, Hitler scrawled, "This cannot be." As one of the Pers Z cryptanalysts later mourned, "Even if we had a plum, it was not considered as one."

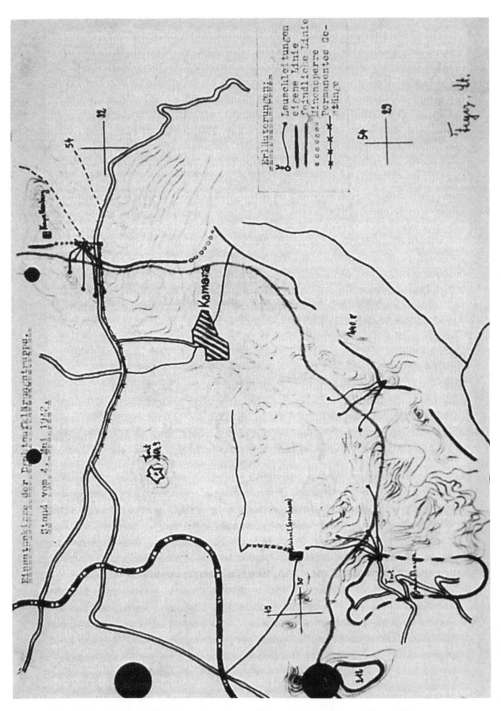

The 24th Infantry Division lays three "loops" of wire south of Kamara, on the Crimea near Sevastopol, and several north of it, to intercept Russian trench telephone conversations

Electric Probings

A GERMAN interpreter hunched over and listened intently to the Russian voice in his earphones. It came from a loop of wire that members of a wiretapping squad had set out two weeks before to intercept Soviet field telephone conversations.

All around him, that winter's day early in 1942, German forces tightened their steel grip around Sevastopol, a key port on the Black Sea. But the Russians defended their Crimean fortress with toughness and tenacity. Like a bear swiping at his tormentors with his paws, they struck out at the Germans in a series of counterattacks. The interpreter's unit, the 24th Infantry Division, had suffered many of these for the past week.

In this positional warfare, it was the chief duty of the wiretapping squad to preclude surprise attacks by eavesdropping on enemy talk that would give hints of Russian intentions. To this end, members of the squad had, after the suspension of the first systematic German offensive against Sevastopol, when Russian counterattacks might be expected, crawled to the Russian lines on 7 January and left there a loop of wire. One of three such loops, it did not actually connect to the enemy wires, but detected the return speech currents in the earth, like the Arendt apparatus of World War I. It thus picked up, not the distinct conversations of a single line, but some 20 telephone stations with consequent cross-talk and hum. For the first week, it produced general intelligence on enemy equipment and supplies, replacements and their instructions, observations, morale, losses, and battle measures. Twice it enabled the Germans to save their scouts, once from enemy gunfire, once from encirclement, by alerting them that the Russians had spotted the patrols.

On 15 January the Russians began a week-long series of attacks aimed particularly at winning observation posts that would overlook the German rear, as well as at tying down and weakening German forces. The German wiretappers provided clues that helped alert their division to Russian activities. They heard a speaker asking "Where am I going to get some schnapps?" and another promising to fire "very, very much" on a bunker. On 21 January, the attacks started early in the morning. The battles flamed in close combat along the main trench line, and at one point the Russians broke through, only to be quickly thrown back. During the early afternoon a pause set in. The infantrymen waited uncertainly, not knowing whether they were through fighting for the day or whether the Russians would suddenly rain shells upon them and follow with a renewed onslaught.

At 4 p.m. the interpreter heard Russian Post 21 calling all company commanders to the telephone. After some indistinct expressions, he heard the commander at Post 21 say clearly:

"Forty-five minutes left till then."

Ten minutes later, a Russian telephone speaker asked another:

"Usina! When are we supposed to begin again?"

To which the reply came:

"In thirty-five minutes."

The interpreter reported this to the divisional I c, who correctly interpreted it as another attack. The troops were alerted. As the Russians assembled their companies, the artillery of the 24th, of the neighboring 50th Infantry Division, and of the corps brought them under fire. When they finally attacked in battalion strength, only weak leading elements even reached the main German lines, and the infantry repulsed them with their light weapons. The Russians returned to the attack in several uncoordinated pushes but were repeatedly thrown back. At 6:45 they finally gave up, returning to their original positions and leaving the Germans firmly in control of their main lines.

The I a declared the next day: "Wiretap reconnaissance again achieved important results in the enemy attacks on 21 January, creating the basis for their successful warding off. In defense, wiretap reconnaissance is of controlling importance, which is widely recognized by the combat troops."

Unlike political circles, the military welcomed communications intelligence. In fact, in the field it became the most important source of enemy intelligence.

To produce it, the army, the navy, the air force, and the armed forces high command each had its own organization, adapted to its own needs. The oldest of these, and in theory the coordinator of all the others, was the OKW's Cipher Branch.

The end of World War I wrecked the German army's communications intelligence organization. It also threw many of its members onto the streets. To preserve this valuable instrument, as well as to give people jobs, a rawboned, open-faced lieutenant only 24 years old founded a radio intelligence unit within the Free Corps, the quasi-official military units that fought the Communists in Germany and coming from Russia. Erich Buschenhagen, a telegraph officer since 1915, had been in charge of traffic analysis at general headquarters in World War I and had worked at radio intelligence with the Austrians on the Italian front. His Volunteer Evaluation Post, on an upper floor of the house at Friedrichstrasse 203 in Berlin, began work early in 1919. At first it merely translated plaintext material intercepted from Russian, French, English, and American sources, as well as press reports sent by radio. In the spring, cryptanalysts joined it, and by May of 1919 the unit was distributing cryptanalytic results, as the partial solution of a Russian field code. Soon thereafter the defense establishment took it in. In a praiseworthy attempt to centralize intelligence collection, the army attached it to the Abwehr group in T 3, the Troops Department's intelligence branch. It took the name of Cipher Center, and moved to the army headquarters on the Bendlerstrasse.

It had grown to 32 persons by the fall of 1925, when Buschenhagen left. His successors were military administrators who, with one or two exceptions, did not know much about communications intelligence. The permanent professional chief was Wilhelm Fenner, a tall, deliberate professor type. Born in St. Petersburg in 1891, he had gone to school there and then had served as a Russian translator and as one of III b's intelligence officers at various staffs in World War I. Afterward, he served briefly as a German agent in the Near East but was captured by the British and imprisoned for a year. Through his connections with intelligence, he joined the Cipher Center in 1922 and the following year became head of cryptanalysis, a post that he made into the effectual technical chief. An organizational genius, he nevertheless overemphasized his cryptanalysts' work to the detriment of the service as a whole. One subordinate attributed his refusal to cooperate to a basically negative attitude, likening him to Goethe's Mephistophelean "spirit that always denies." But he also called him the "soul and inspiration" of German cryptanalysis.

In 1928, a new defense minister, seeking to augment his power, brought the Abwehr to his office and centralized all intelligence under it. The Cipher Center, which had long broken codes for the ministry as well as the army, moved with the Abwehr from the Army Command to the ministry. It became the Abwehr's Group II. The navy's codebreaking agency, which had no ministerial functions, maintained only a liaison with the Abwehr. This arrangement lasted only until Abwehr reorganizations in the 1930s abolished both links. The Cipher Center remained in the ministry, though independent of the Abwehr. The navy retained its agency. The army was now establishing its own communications-intelligence headquarters, so the Cipher Center could now concentrate on its ministerial work. In 1938, when the OKW took over the ministry, the Cipher Center became a part of its Armed Forces Communications Division. Near the start of the war, it rose to become the Cipher Branch, or Chiffrierabteilung, commonly called OKW/Chi or simply Chi.

Chi's office had its entrance at Tirpitzufer 80—one of many private homes that the armed forces had taken over on the street bordering the tree-lined Landwehr canal just around the corner from the OKW headquarters. After the big bombing raid of 23 November 1943 destroyed this house, Chi headquarters moved to a modern semicircular office building at Potsdamerstrasse 56. Its name gave rise to many bad jokes, since the building's German name, Haus des Fremdenverkehrs, not only meant a tourist information office but could also mean a house for sexual intercourse with foreigners.

Chi maintained intercept posts outside of Berlin. Some were especially secret, like those hidden in private homes in Madrid, Seville, and Sofia, with a dozen men in each. During the war many secondary posts sprang up in Germany and the occupied territories, but the main ones were at Treuenbrietzen, 25 miles southwest of Berlin, and at Lauf-an-der-Pegnitz near Nuremberg. Here, six radio towers stood in a circle on a slope surrounded by broad fields outside a lovely medieval town. Radiomen—a total of 150—sat in the tree-shaded low stucco buildings and tuned their receivers round the clock to the transmissions of the countries assigned them: Egypt, Argentina, Brazil, France, Italy, the Vatican, Switzerland, Spain, and the United States. Treuenbrietzen monitored Great Britain and Russia and backed up Lauf on Egypt, the United States, and Switzerland.

At its peak, OKW/Chi employed some 3,000 men—about 800 percent more than its prewar planned mobilization strength of 374. Most worked in the intercept posts, the rest at headquarters. This was organized into eight groups—a central group for administration, Group I for steering, VI for evaluating foreign broadcasts and press transmissions, VII for distribution and archives, II and III—assembled into Office A—for German cryptography, and IV and V for codebreaking. Group IV researched new methods of solution. Group V comprised 22 national sections that actually solved the foreign messages. These groups were combined into Office B, which was headed by Fenner.

He sought constantly to expand its powers. As early as 1937, he had begun to mechanize this work by using Hollerith machines (a form of punched-card sorting device). During the war he had special devices made out of teletypewriter and electrical parts. These clattered loudly as they sought statistical anomalies in messages. He shone light through translucent graph paper with holes punched in it and cross-hatched disks piled up on it; the locations of the lightest and darkest spots indicated mathematical relations that helped solve superencipherments. He brought in mathematicians to develop new cryptanalytic techniques. Topologist Wolfgang Franz cracked a cipher used by the U.S. embassy in Bern based upon distances between letters in a mixed alphabet. The first plaintext he recovered was one telling Washington that Bern was out of cigarettes and would they please send some more.

Chi's assignment called for it to solve the cryptograms of "foreign governments, military attachés, and agents." But in addition to military messages, which would seem its proper domain, it attacked diplomatic cryptograms. This traced back to a prewar agreement with the Foreign Office. Chi purportedly worked on diplomatic traffic in preparation for war, while Pers Z did so for current information. Behind this arrangement lay two facts. Only diplomatic traffic could be intercepted in sufficient quantity for the Chi cryptanalysts to practice on, and the defense ministers liked getting this information. During the war, inertia, a desire not to lose bureaucratic ground, and Hitler's refusal to be locked into a single source kept Chi turning out diplomatic solutions. In view of the extreme rarity of good cryptanalysts, this duplication of the work of Pers Z and the Forschungsamt stands out as the most wasteful operation of the entire German intelligence effort.

Chi's greatest success came with the American military attaché code. The Americans called it the BLACK code, from its binding. The Italians had stolen a copy of it from the embassy in Rome and were reading messages in it, but they did not give a copy to their Axis partner (though they sometimes did pass over decryptments). The Germans cracked the BLACK code analytically (and in their turn did not give it to the Italians). By the fall of 1941, they were reading with particular interest the messages of the American military attaché in Cairo, Colonel Bonner Fellers.

The British and the Germans, under Rommel, were then fighting their seesaw war back and forth across the North African desert. Colonel Fellers, the representative of a nation whose help the British desperately wanted, had access to all aspects of British operations. As befits a good attaché, he went everywhere and saw everything—and reported it back in long and detailed radiograms to the War Department so that it could learn the lessons of desert warfare.

But as the dots and dashes raced overhead, a German monitor in the tree-shaded buildings at Lauf and another at some other post—to ensure that no parts of the precious message were lost—listened to them, translated them into letters, and wrote these down. The intercepts were then teleprinted to OKW/Chi in Berlin, where they were rapidly converted into English, and then into German. From here they went, for security's sake usually in a disguised form, to a variety of intelligence posts, among them the I c at Rommel's headquarters, where they were known as "the good source."

With good reason. Fellers's messages provided Rommel with one of the broadest and clearest pictures of enemy forces available to any Axis commander throughout the war. During January and February of 1942, as he was rebounding 300 miles across the desert, he was getting information like this from the Fellers messages:

> January 23: 270 airplanes and a quantity of antiaircraft artillery being withdrawn from North Africa to reinforce British forces in the Far East.
>
> January 29: Complete rundown of British armor, including number in working order, number damaged, number available and their locations; location and efficiency ratings of armored and motorized units at the front.
>
> February 1: Forthcoming commando operations, efficiency ratings of various British units; report that American M-3 tanks could not be used before mid-February.
>
> February 6: Location and efficiency of the 4th Indian Division and the 1st Armored Division; iteration of British plans to dig in along the Acroma–Bir Hacheim line.
>
> February 7: British units stabilized along the Ain el Gazala–Bir Hacheim line.

In May, when Rommel rolled forward in his supreme effort to conquer Egypt and punch through Palestine to join the German forces that would be driving down from Russia, the intercepted messages told him where the British were first planning to anchor their defense line, and about their later changes of mind.

But without fuel even the most daring general could not move. The greatest danger to his lifeline was Malta. This tough little island, a British bastion in the Mediterranean between Sicily and North Africa, served as a base from which British ships and planes attacked his supply vessels. The Axis sought to batter Malta into submission with air raids night and day; the British, to strengthen and arm it. Though the Germans were well aware of its importance, they were glad to hear Fellers report at the end of April that lack of munitions kept half the antiaircraft guns from firing, that air raids had exhausted the civilian population, and that if German air attacks were continued and no convoys arrived, "the fall of Malta is to be expected."

In June of 1942 the British determined to make a large-scale attempt to relieve the island. They planned to pass convoys through from the east and west simultaneously. (Earlier that spring, Siegfried Knemeyer of the Rowehl air reconnaissance squadron had photographed some of these ships assembling in the Suez Canal.) To neutralize Axis forces that might attack the ships, the British bombed a key naval base and planned bombing and commando raids against air bases. On 11 June, the day the eastern convoy sailed from Alexandria, Fellers drafted his message No. 11119:

> Nights of June 12th June 13th British sabotage units plan simultaneous sticker bomb attacks against aircraft on 9 Axis airdromes. Plans to reach objectives by parachutes and long range desert patrol.
>
> This method of attack offers tremendous possibility for destruction, risk is slight compared with possible gains. If attacks succeed British should be pre-

pared to make immediate use all R.A.F. [Royal Air Force] to support coordinating attacks by army.

Today British making heavy troop movement from Syria into Lybya.

Fellers

He encoded it and filed it with the Egyptian Telegraph Company in
Cairo for radio transmission to Washington. The intercept station at Lauf
snatched it from the ether at about 8 a.m. June 12. By 9 a cryptanalyst was
working on it; by 10 it had been decrypted; by 11:30 Rommel had it in
plenty of time to warn his airfields.

On the night of the 13th, as expected, commandos roared in from the
east in North Africa and climbed out of submarines off Crete. The waiting
German and Italian forces massacred them. Some planes were destroyed,
but in general the operation failed. The next day, airplanes saved from destruction by the timely warning delivered heavy attacks upon the convoy
and turned it back. The approach to Malta remained sealed. And Rommel's
pipeline remained open.

Within a couple of weeks, the Germans stood practically at the gates of
Alexandria. Hitler and Mussolini ordered its capture. A few days later,
Hitler commented after dinner that "the capture of Alexandria would in-
furiate the entire English people—only the moneyed classes were directly
interested in the fall of Singapore—and [make them] rise in a putsch
against Churchill. It was only to be hoped that the American minister
[meaning the attaché] in Cairo continues to inform us so well over the
English military planning through his badly enciphered cables."

But at just about that very time, the Americans, having somehow gotten
wind of the Axis reading of the Fellers messages, replaced the BLACK code
with a new cipher, which defied all Chi's efforts to break it. Rommel, deprived of his main source of information, and without enough supplies now
to press on the next 60 miles to Alexandria, went over to the defensive.
The British began building up their forces in secrecy. Rommel, unenlightened
by his old "good source," remained in such ignorance of this assembly that
he went back home for a rest. While he was there, General Bernard Montgomery opened fire with a thousand guns at a railway junction called El
Alamein. It was the start of the offensive that Churchill later said marked the
turning of the Allied hinge of fate.

The hinge turned as well for the Cipher Branch. Increased Allied crypto-
security reduced its successes with American and British codes and ciphers;
it had never, since the early 1930s, made any entry into the higher-level
Soviet codes. Toward the end of the war, its solutions—called "VN" from
those two big red letters at the top of each sheet that stood for "Verlässliche
Nachricht" (trustworthy report)—were reduced to near trivia. Perhaps
typical is the VN of 29 December 1944, the solution of a U.S. State Depart-

TELEGRAM SENT

Department of State

TO BE TRANSMITTED
SECRET
CONFIDENTIAL
RESTRICTED
CLEAR
RESTRICTED

Charge Department: X

Charge to

Washington,

AMERICAN CONSUL,

TUNIS, (TUNISIA).

56

Marcel E. Malige is designated Counselor for Economic
Affairs near the Government of Poland, now established
in London. Should proceed upon arrival of his successor,
traveling via Department for consultation en route. This
transfer not made at his request nor for his convenience.

His transportation expenses and per diem, Tunis to
London, via Washington, D.C., transportation expenses
and per diem for his family and shipment effects direct
authorized, subject Travel Regulations. Travel via any
feasible route and means, including military aircraft,
authorized. Per diem granted on consultation accordance
Note 15, Accounts Supplement E. Expenses chargeable
"1950515.001 Transportation, Foreign Service, 1945".

Submit estimate and report dates.

DCR - Per. Unit

DRS/CR
DEC 23 1944

FA:DJ   FP   BF   WE   EE   AF
12/21/44

Accompanied by hectograph.

Travel Order
No. 5 2870

State Department original, graded restricted, the lowest category of secrecy
classification, of a message solved by the OKW Cipher Branch

VN

Sofort an Chef Chi zurück!
Weitergabe, auch innerhalb des Hauses,
selbst in veränderter Form und mit
Verschleierung der Quelle, verboten!

V.N.Nr. 1482/12.44(USA)
F.24.12.44(wif-thd2)
Eingeg. 27.12.44

29.Dezember 1944

Betrifft: GROSSBRITANNIEN - Ernennung eines USA-Beraters für
die Londoner Polenregierung

Von: Staatsdepartement Washington
An: USA-Konsulat Tunis
Nr.56

23.12. 2200 h.
Marcel E.Malige wird zum Berater für Wirtschaftsangelegen-
heiten bei der jetzt in London aufgestellten polnischen Regierung ernannt. Er hat die Reise bei Eintreffen seines Nachfolg
gers anzutreten und zwecks Rücksprache beim Staatsdepartement
über Washington zu reisen. Diese Versetzung geschieht weder
auf sein Ansuchen hin noch zwecks seiner persönlichen Annehm-
lichkeit.

Seine Beförderungskosten und Tagegelder von Tunis nach
London und während seines Aufenthalts in Washington D.C. sowie
die direkten Beförderungskosten und Tagegelder für seine Fami-
lie und die Transportkosten für seine Privatsachen werden ent-
sprechend den Reisevorschriften genehmigt. Die Reise wird für
jegliche geeignet erscheinende Route und für jedes verfügbare
Verkehrsmittel einschließlich Militärflugzeug genehmigt. Tagegelder werden für die Zeit der Rücksprache gemäß Anmerkung 15,
Abrechnungszusatz E, gewährt. Die Kosten sind unter "1 950 515,
001, Beförderungsgelder für den Auswärtigen Dienst 1945" zu
verbuchen.

Reichen Sie einen Veranschlag ein, und melden Sie die tat-
sächlichen Daten.

Stettinius.

A VN, Verlässliche Nachricht, or Trustworthy Report—a solution by the
OKW's Cipher Branch of the unimportant personnel transfer message shown
on the preceding page. The branch marked it, like all VNs, "secret" and
ordered "Return at once to Chief of Chi!"

ment message of six days earlier. A cabled travel order marked "restricted," the lowest grade of security classification, it told the American consulate in Tunis that one of its staffers, Marcel E. Malige, had been named as counselor for economic affairs with the government of Poland in London and specified how his travel expenses were to be paid. Chi graded it, like all VN, "top secret" and directed its recipients to send it back at once.

Though this message seemed hardly worth the effort of solving it, others may have proved more valuable. The Mexican embassy in Moscow was reporting that Czechoslovakia and Yugoslavia were recognizing the provisional Polish government. The Japanese foreign ministry was informing its embassy in Moscow about a new Chinese cabinet. Yet such solutions could hardly have affected the course of Germany's strategy.

In only one place does the Treaty of Versailles mention intelligence agencies. Its table listing German infantry division strengths allowed the signal detachment to include an intercept section. The German army did not use the men for the low-level work that had been intended, but assigned them instead to the army's 12 major radio stations. In 1925, with Germany increasingly departing from the Versailles restrictions, the army set up six posts specifically for interception. Each had three or four receivers served around the clock by about 20 radiomen. The difficulty of following foreign maneuver traffic from these fixed locations led in 1928 to the erection of mobile direction-finders near the borders, and two years later to the creation of mobile intercept units which evolved into mobile intercept companies. Directing this work was first the Cipher Center and then the new agency organized by about 1936 in the army command: the Main Intercept Post.

The intercept organization was part of the signal corps, which was headed by General Erich Fellgiebel. He was subordinated in wartime to the chief of the general staff; he served simultaneously as head of armed-forces communications, making him also the superior officer of OKW/Chi. A bespectacled, kindly, well-liked officer in his early fifties, divorced and remarried, a former chief of the Cipher Center, Fellgiebel won high praise from the OKW chief, Keitel: "In his field a pronounced leader type with broad vision, a gift for organization, full of energy . . . satisfied even the most unexpected and difficult requirements." But Keitel added that Fellgiebel inclined to an "unconsidered mania of criticism" toward Naziism. And indeed Fellgiebel participated in the 1944 attempt to kill Hitler. His hesitancy in sealing off communications to the Führer headquarters after the bomb went off contributed to the failure of the plot, for which the conspirators, including himself, paid with their lives. He was succeeded in both his army and armed forces offices by General Albert Praun, 49, a short, pleasant, extremely capable signal officer who had also led an infantry division and who was, Chief of Staff Guderian wrote, a "good National Socialist."

These two men, especially Fellgiebel, presided over the remarkable expansion of German army communications intelligence in World War II. It provides a classic case history of how an intelligence organization develops in response to the requirements of intelligence consumers and its success in satisfying them.

At the start of the war, army communications intelligence operated on four levels: the Main Intercept Post at Zossen, 10 fixed intercept posts that passed their information to Zossen and to the army groups, 7 mobile intercept companies attached to armies, and intercept platoons within the divisions. But communications intelligence scored only minor successes during the Polish campaign. Fellgiebel traced this in part to the distance of the Main Intercept Post from the action. But bringing control closer to the front implied a dispersal of control, and all the lessons of radio reconnaissance taught that strong centralization was essential for success. Fellgiebel compromised. He created commanders of intercept troops to handle communications intelligence for each of the three army groups getting ready to attack France.

This organization worked well on the higher levels in the French and Russian campaigns. But the tactical results continued to be poor. So in 1942 Fellgiebel centralized this work. He pulled men out of the intercept platoons of the divisions, which were left with only a squad, and assembled them in short-range communications reconnaissance companies. He gave one to each army headquarters. The company scattered its platoons throughout the army's area: two platoons for message interception, two for short-range direction finding, five for wiretapping. To rationalize the terminology, Fellgiebel renamed the armies' intercept companies "long-range communications reconnaissance companies," the Main Intercept Post the "Main Post for Communications Reconnaissance," and the commanders of intercept troops "commanders of communication reconnaissance."

Each army then had a short-range company and either a long-range company or a fixed intercept post. Again centralization promised improvement. On 15 December 1943, Fellgiebel united each army's organs into a communications reconnaissance battalion. The 17 that existed were in turn grouped into 8 regiments for communications reconnaissance, each under a commander of communications reconnaissance at army group or theater command. Finally, early in 1944, the only field level that did not have its own agency, corps, set up small, 10-man units to evaluate the material that came in from the divisions and from any nearby platoons of the short-range companies.

In the fall of 1944, Praun carried all this to a logical conclusion. At the very peak, he created a general of communications reconnaissance to assure cooperation among the various units and to improve personnel and equipment. General Fritz Boetzel, a man of some charm and broad cultural interests and a one-time head of the Cipher Center, was named to the post. This gave communications intelligence its sixth and final level and completed its evolution into a highly articulated organization that effectively served all commands and delivered the most valuable enemy intelligence that came to German army generals during World War II.

The work of many of the officers in many of these posts can be illustrated by the daily routine of a young lieutenant, who despite his low rank became in effect the commander of Communications Reconnaissance 2, the regiment that served Army Group Center. He was Fritz Neeb, a bright, stubby Viennese who had been interested in cryptology as a teenager. He read everything he could find on it in the Austrian National Library and cracked the cryptograms that friends made up for him. Through some blunder on the part of the German army, he was actually put into the kind of work for which he was best suited. He served in communications in the Polish and French campaigns and the first part of the Russian—early in which, while a member of the 137th Communications Battalion, he captured 130 Russians 20 miles behind their lines. One day his major met an old friend, the colonel commanding the Army Group Center communications reconnaissance regiment. The colonel told the major of some of his problems, and the major responded that he had a young lieutenant who had resolved those same problems within his battalion. Three days later Neeb was at the regiment's headquarters. Code-named HEINRICH EAST, it was located on two floors of a former Russian secret police building in Smolensk. Neeb was at first just one of several able evaluators, but as first one and then another of the officers departed, and eventually the chief himself was transferred, Neeb became virtually the commander of HEINRICH EAST, with its 400 men, and made the daily reports to the army group I c, Colonel Rudolf-Christian Baron von Gersdorff.

His day began when he got up about 11 p.m., after the most important reports from the subordinate companies came in. He looked through these, gave assignments as to how they were to be handled, and from about 3 to 5 a.m. assembled the daily report, either by dictating it or by simply assembling the rewritten drafts of the subordinate companies' reports. Between 5 and 7 a.m. these reports were teleprinted to the Main Post for Communications Reconnaissance and to the subordinate armies' communications reconnaissance companies. Five or six copies went to the I c and other officers of his own army group. If no immediate questions came in, Neeb could then go to sleep about 6 or 6:30; otherwise, 7:30. He awoke again around noon, ate in the officers' mess, put out a short so-called "advance report" of four or five pages with the most important new information, then prepared for the I c afternoon situation conference in Gersdorff's office. This began at 4 p.m. and sometimes lasted three hours. Here the leaders of the various organs of specialized reconnaissance submitted their results and compared them. Often the discussions were very lively. Neeb had to advance communications intelligence entirely on its own, without recourse to any other source. At about 6 or 6:30, or sometimes 7, he went home, grabbed a bite to eat, and went to bed to try to get some sleep.

Sometimes instead of sleeping Neeb went to or gave instructional lectures, for he realized that for him and others on the same schedule it often didn't pay to try to sleep a few hours in the early evening. He also prepared tests for potential cryptanalysts and evaluators, and during the course of time tested more than 1,500 persons to try to cover his personnel needs. Twice he gave information out over the telephone in his sleep. He had no recollection of it when he awoke, but was told of it—and found to his relief that the information had been correct. Thereafter he had a wire recorder attached to his telephone.

The production of communications intelligence began with an assignment from an intelligence officer. Sometimes this simply called for general information, sometimes for specifics on, for example, artillery or armored formations. The communications reconnaissance commander disposed his units to obtain the raw material he needed to fulfill the assignment. In the west, Colonel Maximilian Baron von Oer, the higher commander of communications reconnaissance (called "higher" because he had two regiments under him), sought simply to get as much information about the Anglo-American forces as possible. Before the invasion, his Communications Reconnaissance Battalion 12 concentrated on radio traffic in and with the United States. After the invasion, he shifted 10 receivers of its Fixed Intercept Post 3 at Euskirchen to cover Great Britain. He divided British army traffic between Fixed Intercept Post 2 in Port Marly, which listened from 4,500 to 7,500 kilocycles with a search up to 10,000, and Post 12 in Louveciennes, which listened from 3,000 to 4,500 with a search from 100 to 3,000 kilocycles. Within each post or company, the commander might further divide up these bands into subbands and assign one to each of his approximately 36 receivers. The monitoring radioman would tune slowly up and down, sometimes listening to two frequencies at once, until he heard a transmission. He notified the direction-finding team. If they told him the transmitter was outside of the interception area, he continued his patrolling of the other. If it was within the area, he continued to listen. He observed the tone of the transmitter and the "fist" of the radioman—his way of sending, which is as distinctive as handwriting. These alone could often identify a particular radioman, whose moves from one place to another—and by implication the moves of his unit—could therefore be followed. The monitoring radioman also noted

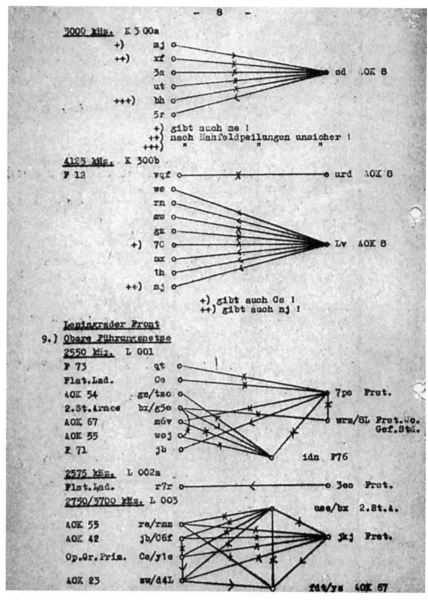

German radio reconnaissance diagrams Soviet radio communications. *At top,* in a network called K300a, on 3,000 kilohertz, a station with call letters *ed,* identified as belonging to the Russian 8th Army, communicates with forward stations using call letters *mj, xf, 3a,* etc.; these stations do not intercommunicate. *Lower,* top command nets of the Leningrad Front (the army group) includes one, designated L001, on 2,550 kilohertz. Its two rear stations, *7pc,* the front's staff, and *wrz,* also *8L,* the front staff's battle post, communicate with, among others, stations *woj,* identified as the 55th Army, and *bx,* also *g5e,* the 2nd Shock Army, which radio to one another

other details, such as the wave length of the transmission, the calling station's sign, the called station's sign, and cipher recognition groups as he wrote down the intercept.

These intercepts poured out of the radio room, where the monitors sat with their headphones on, into an evaluation center. Each command level had such a center, corresponding in size to the volume and complexity of its work. The centers divided into subsections for traffic evaluation, direction-finding evaluation, contents evaluation, and final evaluation. The raw data could often reveal much. Long wave lengths often meant higher staffs; short waves, corps and division staffs; ultrashort waves, armor. Since not every unit held every cipher, the cipher recognition groups helped define communications nets and so, by implication, command organizations.

Supplementing this was direction-finding. Monitors in widely separated locations turned the movable antennas of their specialized radio sets until they heard an enemy transmitter at its quietest. A calculation indicated in which direction it was. They reported this direction to the direction-finding evaluation subsection. It plotted, on a map, the bearings given by several monitors. Where these lines crossed marked the location of the enemy transmitter.

The traffic evaluators then listed on cards all stations using a certain frequency, all stations called by a particular call sign, and all known locations of the different stations. They diagramed these relationships and saw what patterns emerged. One station addresses messages to many others, which seldom intercommunicate; direction-finding shows it further to the rear. The evaluators deduce that it represents a higher echelon commanding the others. A higher volume of traffic on one circuit may portend an attack, a withdrawal, a relief, perhaps only a disciplinary problem, but almost certainly something. The evaluators followed the movements of the stations. Often they were extremely acute. Once the Russians sent an armored army toward Stalingrad while leaving some of the army's radiomen in its old location to give the impression that it was still there. But on the march, one of the radiomen who had gone along inadvertently transmitted. The Germans picked up his transmission, recognized him, and concluded that the armored force was moving south, probably toward Stalingrad.

Valuable as these inferences from the traffic patterns were, they could seldom provide the insights that the actual contents of the enemy messages could. Many of these were unenciphered. Indeed, at the lowest level, such cleartext radio or wire intercepts provided about 95 percent of communications intelligence. Sometimes they shocked with their revelations of enemy attitudes. In Russia on 17 February 1944, the 17th Panzer Division overheard a conversation on 1,960 kilocycles at 10:30 a.m.:

Rokot: Thirty minutes ago my patrol came out of Oktyabr and reported that no one is there. It found only our own wounded.

Tochka:	Why was it shot into? You're dogs, bastards, traitors.
Rokot:	The battery commander fired without an order.
Tochka:	Arrest him and shoot him with his own pistol.
Rokot:	Acknowledged.

Other times the cleartext messages provided helpful background information. In May 1943, radio reconnaissance of a landing practice of the Royal Marines near Southampton shed light on amphibious tactics. The Germans learned that the Marine division landed on a width of 10 miles in the morning hours, attacking with three brigades in the forward lines. Despite strong "enemy" counterattacks, by 5 p.m. it had reached the line Totton-Ringwood, two-thirds of the way to its objective 12 miles inland. Most rarely, cleartext intercepts revealed actual enemy intentions. In November of 1944, the 26th Panzer Division in Italy intercepted an order for a bombing mission naming in clear the village that headquartered the neighboring 278th Infantry Division. It sent a warning, and the 278th suffered only minor casualties. Similar cases in Russia led a commander of communications reconnaissance to declare in mid-1943: "The monitoring of the radio voice traffic (short-range intelligence coverage) brings valuable results."

Wiretapping produced a lower volume of intercepts than radio, and seldom overheard anything but front-line conversations of limited concern. The German troops crawled from their own to the enemy trenches and either tapped directly into the enemy telephone lines or set out loops that picked up ground currents, which were then amplified.

During the Russian campaign, the wire reconnaissance team of the 72nd Infantry Division, advancing into the Crimea, hooked into the wires on the permanent telephone poles along the main road. Through these during a German attack, the team heard the Russian defenders being told that it was absolutely necessary to hold a certain position and that reinforcements were on the way. The conversation included details about the Russian guns and their locations. All this enabled the Germans to rush up their own reinforcements and to take the position.

Cleartext messages like these nearly always outnumbered cryptograms. In September of 1944, for example, the commander of Communications Reconnaissance 7, in Italy, picked up 22,254 cleartexts and 14,373 cryptograms. This preponderance stemmed from the enormous number of short local messages within a division. At the higher echelons, where orders live longer and therefore allow more time for encipherment, the proportion of cryptograms increased, until at the top, practically all messages were enciphered. They were obviously of far greater importance than those in clear. To get to their contents, the Germans had to crack open their cryptographic armor. As the enemy improved his cryptographic protection during the war and extended it to more classes of messages, the German army's cryptanalytic establishment grew to keep pace.

The Main Intercept Post had only a handful of cryptanalysts at the beginning of the war—five for all Britain, for example. By 1942, it had 200, divided into country sections and such service sections as those for Hollerith machine processing and for archives. It attacked not only the enemy high command systems but also those unsolvable by field echelons, which worked on the simpler cryptosystems of the enemy units on their level opposite them.

At first the Germans had relatively good success with the Russian codes. The solved messages, said the cryptanalysts of Army Group North in 1944, "contain operational combat reports, statements about assembly areas, command posts, loss and replacement reports, reports about chain of command and positions prepared for the attack (e.g., messages of the 122nd Armored Brigade on 14 and 17 February)." These results came from only a small proportion of the intercepts. In the thirteen months from 1 May 1943 to 31 May 1944, Army Group North intercepted 46,342 Russian cryptograms. It solved 13,312, or less than one in four. Its commander of communications reconnaissance explained why:

"It is only infrequently possible to get enough identically enciphered messages from the same net to be able to solve the current systems." Later

	3	6	2	9
8			К	Ø
5		А	Л	Х
1		Б	М	Ц
4		В	Н	Ч
0		Г	О	Ш
2		Д	П	Щ
9		Е	Р	Э	Ы
7		Ж	С	Ю	Й
3		З	Т	Я	Ь
6		И	У	.	
	I	II	III	IV

A simple Russian cipher, valid for 5 March 1942, solved by the Germans. In this, 39 means E, 93 means 6; the roman numerals merely assist the cryptanalyst he adduced additional reasons: ". . . a growing complication in the systems used by the enemy . . . a greater care in enciphering . . . (avoidance of identical addresses and signatures; names and phrases with characteristic endings and patterns, which must be given in code form in individual letters or syllables, were either enciphered abbreviated or were inserted in cleartext)."

In other words, as Russian code construction and discipline improved, German cryptanalytic success declined. Whereas from May to August 1943 the Army Group North codebreakers always solved more than 34 percent, of all intercepts, from January to May 1944, with even greater monthly volume, they never solved more than 33 percent. These almost never included the top-level command systems. It was the same for the western Allies. In general, the Germans failed to read the messages moving in the higher command nets.

The cryptanalysts passed their solutions to the contents evaluators, who passed their conclusions in turn to the final evaluators. They combined these conclusions with those of the traffic evaluators. Often their analysis could precipitate precious observations. The evaluators of Intercept Company 3./N.7 (3rd company of Communications [Nachrichten] Battalion 7) did so for the 11th Army in March of 1942.

In its drive to conquer the Crimea, the 11th Army had split the Russian forces on that peninsula. It had penned some in Sevastopol in the west; it had not yet swept away those in the eastern portion, an elongated peninsula ending in the city of Kerch. These Russian eastern forces, controlled by the Crimean Front, continued to assemble troops for a counteroffensive. The intercept company concentrated much of its effort at determining the composition of these forces, since this would help the Germans know how many of their own troops they might have to use to repel the Russian attacks in their rear.

This was the situation when, at 7:16 a.m. on 13 March, the company intercepted a message to an unknown radio station with call sign SOTÖ. It was addressed "To the chief of communications of the 44th Army." This indicated pretty clearly that SOTÖ was the 44th Army, and since company's records showed that direction-finding had located SOTÖ transmitting from near Kerch, the company could report a few hours later to the intelligence officer of the 11th Army, "44th Army definitely on the Kerch Peninsula." It was one more element in his picture of the enemy.

Though these chains of hypotheses might seem to have led to frequent error, constant observations corrected wild reasoning and kept the results close to the facts. A few days after the intercept company identified the 44th Army, it assigned radio station ÖPWCH to the air staff of the enemy's 51st Army on the similar basis of a message address. But the following day, it recognized that the net to which ÖPWCH belonged was in fact identical to a net of the 44th Army "according to the net construction, frequency notifications, and statements of the monitoring radiomen." ÖPWCH was therefore a station of the 44th Army, the company concluded, and had probably merely accepted the message for forwarding to the 51st Army.

Through such detailed and often wearisome activity, German radio intelligence units contributed enormously to German tactical and operational intelligence. In these low and middle echelons, it warned of enemy attacks, provided solid information on enemy order of battle and enemy weaknesses, and saw through both radio silence and radio deceptions.

In Russia, for example, the Main Post for Communications Reconnaissance issued a report each day listing all enemy troop units recognized or confirmed through communications intelligence. A typical such report ran 14 pages for Soviet army units, 2 for partisan forces, and 2 for air units. From the south to the north of the long Russian front, it dealt with the major commands, as far down as divisions. "5th Guards Army. Direction-finding for the army command from 24 August [1944] indicates the area southeast of Staszów [Poland]. According to a message of 7:30 a.m. 25 August it is changing its location," read one entry. Another entry, based on a Moscow broadcast praising heroic units, listed a score of divisions, their commanders, their location, and their subordination. This top-secret report, produced in 37 copies, went to Foreign Armies East, where it joined other sources in creating a picture of the Soviet forces opposite the German.

In France in 1944, the higher commander of communications reconnaissance likewise achieved good accuracy in determining American order of battle. Between D-Day and 25 June, it recognized the presence of the U.S. 1st Army, 4 corps, and 15 divisions or parts of divisions. Under the VIIIth Corps, for example, it correctly listed the 101st and 82nd Airborne Divisions and parts of the 90th Infantry Division. Much of this information later appeared in the order-of-battle reports of the I c of the commander in chief west. Toward the end of June 1944, the breaking of a logistical code used by the senior officer, Ferry Control, in the area of the British 2nd Army in Normandy gave the Germans exact figures on the personnel and equipment brought in there for the bridgehead. They learned, for example, that in the 24 hours starting at 6 p.m. 1 July, the Allies unloaded 4,371 tons of supplies, 1,232 vehicles, and 1,700 men.

Of more direct value were those results that told of upcoming enemy measures. On 14 June 1944, German radio reconnaissance in Normandy ascertained the bringing up of the U.S. XIXth Corps and concluded the following day that a major attack would take place in that area. The attack did occur—and was halted that same day well short of its objectives by stubborn German resistance. On the 19th, radio reconnaissance intercepted orders for Allied air units to take aerial photographs west and southwest of Caen, with a deadline of the 25th. This told the Germans of the probability of an attack and its location; they prepared themselves accordingly. This attack too came as predicted, and likewise met strong opposition, with the result that three weeks later the Allies stood in virtually the same position as when they had started.

The front-line troops in France most acclaimed those results that warned of enemy bombings. The Germans intercepted and solved British calls for air support for ground forces. They then broadcast, in cipher, warnings based on these intercepts. At each divisional headquarters, a noncommissioned officer stood by constantly at the wave lengths assigned for these broadcasts. When he received one, he passed it to an officer, who deciphered the message and had it to his commander or I a in half an hour. At 9 p.m. on 10 August 1944, for example, the western theater command warned subordinate units in this way that "In a short while the armor 2 kilometers southwest of Soignolles (15 kilometers northwest of Falaise) will be bombed." Between 20 and 30 such warnings were broadcast every day, and since the bombings usually took place at the exact time reported or within an hour of it, the German intelligence, which proved 90 percent correct, greatly reduced casualties and damage. A signal officer reported from the front that "great worth was placed upon the broadcasts" and that they were "thankfully accepted."

One of the most valuable operational results of signal intelligence in the west came during the Battle of the Bulge.

After Hitler had struck in the Ardennes in December 1944, the Americans brought up troops to push the Germans back. The military police battalion in the U.S. 1st Army zone controlled much of this traffic, which moved according to itineraries fixed by higher authority. The Germans soon discovered that the battalion broadcast these itineraries in cipher to all its control points—the Germans knew of 35 of these and located 22, many at the intersection of two French national highways. The messages gave the name of the unit, its time and place of departure, route, average speed, numbers of vehicles and of march blocks, and destination and time of arrival. The radio reconnaissance unit estimated that it intercepted about 90 percent of these broadcasts and so ascertained almost 100 percent of all units with itineraries. Those without itineraries and those going around this area were not spotted, it said. This gave the German command on the western front an accurate picture of which enemy forces were coming up and where, enabling General Hasso von Manteuffel to shift his 5th Panzer Army and so sidestep the Allied blow.

But communications intelligence did not invariably enable the Germans to win victories. Sometimes its information, though correct when delivered, was falsified by enemy plan changes that it did not detect. For example, in 1943, the commander of communications reconnaissance of Army Group North reported: "An intended Russian attack on Staraya Russa was recognized on 25 June, which was to begin at 2300 hours 25 June and in which 6 armored battalions, among others, were to take part. The attack, however, was not carried out, probably because of the unfavorable weather conditions."

Communications intelligence was also often nullified by any of the host of nonintelligence factors that determine success and failure in battle. On 9 August 1944, the Main Post for Communications Reconnaissance disclosed in its report that "11th Guard Army gets order to improve clothing, get new underwear, all airplanes to be overhauled and prepared for flight, provisions to be improved and three hot meals a day served." The next day, the Germans, who were preparing a relief operation, learned through radio intelligence that two of the 11th Guard Army divisions were ordered to be ready to go into action against enemy attacks by 5 p.m. When the Germans began their drive on the 16th, the 11th Guard Army responded with a counterthrust, just as predicted. But this forewarning did not enable the Germans to stop the Russians, one of whose platoons carried the ground war, for the first time, onto the soil of the Reich.

And sometimes communications intelligence simply failed. The evidence on which it rested was ethereal—peepings in radiomen's earphones—and could be suppressed or faked. Occasionally the Germans turned radio silence against its users: the 7th Army I c declared in France in November 1944 that radio silence suggested Allied attack preparations. But in North Africa, the British concealed a division very close to the front by shutting off their radios for several weeks. Radio silence also preserved surprise for many Allied landings in Sicily and Italy. Radio deceptions sought to fool the Germans. The Russians tried this every few weeks, but the Germans always seemed to see through them. On the other hand, the British successfully covered the transfer of three armored divisions from one point in the line to another during the Normandy battles through radio deception.

Perhaps the most common failure was simply misevaluation. In November 1940, the chief of the general staff, Halder, thought that an intercepted message referring to a transfer of headquarters might mean that the English were about to occupy all of Ireland to get the western harbors. He was all wrong. Before Leningrad in June of 1943, the commander of communications reconnaissance in Army Group North reported: "The [Russian] 8th Army had only a little radio traffic in the early days of May and soon afterward complete radio silence ensued. . . . Together with the radio silence of the 8th Army, the irregular and opaque traffic of the 2nd Shock Army and the change in location of the command post of the Leningrad Front . . . , it is concluded that a Russian attack of considerable magnitude is imminent." It never came.

But the many successes counteracted these occasional failures. Moreover, communications intelligence produced great quantities of information about the existence, locations, and movements of enemy formations—the basic enemy order-of-battle intelligence that says so much about enemy capabilities and intentions. Consequently, by 1943, commanders in the field, who in 1939 had mistrusted communications intelligence—particularly when it came, not from the contents of messages, but from inferences based on traffic volume and routing—came to look upon it as their best source of intelligence. The I c of the XXXXth Panzer Corps noted that through the "outstanding" communications intelligence in February 1943 the corps "always knew almost exactly the enemy situation, location and strength. This knowledge contributed considerably to the complete annihilation of the Popoff armored army." During Normandy, the I cs in the west drew about 60 percent of their information from radio intelligence, 40 percent from all other sources combined. The chief of staff of the western theater called it "the most important means for clarifying the enemy picture." A head of Foreign Armies West called it "the darling of all intelligence men"; the head of Foreign Armies East, Gehlen, listed it as the most important of his sources. And Halder flatly declared it to be "the most copious and the best source of intelligence."

Virtually the entire Luftwaffe had to be created out of the whole cloth, and its radio intelligence organization participated in this magical evolution. In May of 1934, while the air force was still shrouded in official secrecy, it established the post of head of signal communications, naming Major Wolfgang Martini to it. He set up within his office a Branch 3, radio, whose Desk c handled radio intelligence. Its head was Captain Kurt Gottschling. His first job was to create a radio intelligence organization.

By the start of the war, he had set up 10 mobile intercept companies and 14 fixed intercept posts. The latter, cover-named "weather stations," usually operated out of a single-story stone building accompanied by a garage and barracks. At ground level were the radio-receiving rooms, direction-finding control, and data-evaluation, communications, and administrative offices. The attic held a conference room, an emergency kitchen, resting rooms, and storage areas; the cellar had the power and heating units and workshops. All about stood the tall wooden towers that supported the shining cobwebs of the antennae. Each post monitored an assigned area. Trier, for example, in the southwest corner of Germany, watched France, Belgium, and Holland.

The Luftwaffe carried out its operational mission through its four air fleets, each equivalent to an army group. Each received a radio reconnaissance battalion, consisting of two mobile companies, which operated in the field with the air fleet, and a back-up fixed post in Germany. The increasing value of radio intelligence during the war led to the expansion of three of them to radio reconnaissance regiments. Regiment 353 worked Russia, 352 the Mediterranean—where one of its companies established a listening post at Cape Sounion, the southernmost tip of Attica, on whose bluff the ruined temple of Poseidon stands high above the ruffled waters of the Aegean. Regiment 351 focused on the Allied air forces in the west. It divided its work—which was mostly at night—among its specialized battalions, such as 357, which concentrated on heavy-bomber traffic.

Steering the entire Luftwaffe radio intelligence organization was Battalion 350, which included the Cipher Center of the commander in chief of the Luftwaffe, located in the former royal stables of the New Palace at Potsdam, and the Central Battle Station for Radio Reconnaissance, located near the Luftwaffe's Ist Fighter Corps at Treuenbrietzen. Head of this battalion, and thus of the entire 5,000-man Luftwaffe radio intelligence organization, was first Major Ulrich Freudenfeld, who later died at Stalingrad after winning the coveted Knight's Cross to the Iron Cross for bravery in action, and, after 1942, Colonel Rudolf Friedrich, who was, in his off hours, a passionate hunter.

The organization sought basically to ascertain enemy air organization, supplies, and operations—which for most of the war in the west meant warning of Allied bombing raids. Usually the Germans determined the latter by listening to the Allied bombers' radiomen testing their sets before take-off. On the evening of 25 June 1941, for example, the monitor sets of one German unit, tuned to Royal Air Force bomber frequencies, gradually came alive with a manifold whistling and chirping. The Germans soon determined that about 16 bombers would take off from Hemswell and about 24 from Waddington. They alerted their night-fighter group.

Occasionally, the Allies sought to deceive the Germans by testing sets on more planes than would fly. But the Germans usually saw through this. Radiomen's chatter sometimes revealed the target, and direction-finding fixes every two or three minutes gave the route of the flight. Off Norway, one radio reconnaissance company installed a radioman-interpreter in place of an aerial gunner on long-range patrols. These flying monitors provided early warning of many an R.A.F. raid. But casualties ran high, and replacements for the 10-man cadre had to be continuously trained.

One of air radio reconnaissance's greatest successes came during the American bombing of the Rumanian oil fields at Ploesti. On 1 August 1943, 178 four-engined Liberators lumbered into the air at Bengazi in one of the longest-range and potentially one of the most important air strikes in the war, for Ploesti was Hitler's chief source of oil for his thirsty war machine. A Luftwaffe radio reconnaissance unit in Greece detected this and alerted all defense commands that a large formation of bombers had been taking off since early morning in the Bengazi area. This gave the defenses at Ploesti, the strongest in Europe, plenty of time to get ready. When the bombers roared in at derrick-top height over the oil field, with its wells, refineries, and tanks, they were met with the heaviest antiaircraft fire encountered by American bombers during the war. Fifty-three planes, or almost one out of every three, were downed, and dozens of Americans died. And the wells kept pumping.

German air force radio reconnaissance gave advance notice of many Allied raids, and indeed provided 70 percent of and the most valuable intelligence about the enemy that the Luftwaffe received. But German flak and fighters were often too weak to do much against the broad and endless streams of Allied bombers. In the end, air radio intelligence did little more than to prove once again that knowledge without power is worthless.

The glowing testimonials that many high-ranking officers gave to military communications intelligence referred only to tactical and operational results. For on the strategic level, German communications intelligence failed utterly. In contrast to the Allies, who could read all levels of German cryptosystems up to those enshrouding the command messages of the Führer himself, the Germans—though they sometimes read diplomatic messages of Roosevelt and Churchill—never cracked the high- and top-level military ciphers of the Allies. Thus, unlike the Allies, who often knew German plans for the overall direction of the war, the Germans never knew the Allies'. Probes of high-level Allied messages showed that they could not be solved analytically. Testing them all statistically for a possible cipher clerk's error that might have permitted the solution of a dozen or so would have taken too many cryptanalysts away from work that, though lower in echelon, was more certain of results. So the Germans did not seek to crack these high-level messages, and after a while they even gave up intercepting them. This was their unacknowledged admission of defeat in the most vital sector of the secret war.

The Codebreaker Who
Helped the U-Boats

I F one man in German intelligence ever held the keys to victory in World War II, it was Wilhelm Tranow.

A man so bursting with energy that he sometimes seemed to skip instead of walk, he was a middle-level civilian official for the navy. He had been doing the same work since World War I, steadily advancing in grade. He was one of those rarities in bureaucracies: a man who both performed the technical aspects of his job in exemplary fashion and administered the men under him effectively. He was tall and erect, with firm features and a compelling way of talking. But the most impressive thing about him was his memory, his brain. Knowledge of foreign warships was helpful for many Kriegsmarine personnel; Tranow, in the 1930s, had at his fingertips the movements, the ports of call, and the destinations of every capital ship of the major fleets of the world, especially of the Royal Navy. It contributed greatly to his success. Tranow was the head of the English-language section of the German navy's codebreaking unit.

He had gotten into the work by breaking the rules. As a young radio-man on watch aboard the three-stack battleship *Pommern* in the summer of 1914, he picked up a coded message from the cruiser *Breslau* in the Mediterranean and forwarded it to the fleet command. After a few hours the command reported that it could not read it; a repeat would be necessary. Tranow did not have the key, but had become interested in cryptology during previous maneuvers, and he attacked the code's encipherment. Within a couple of hours he had solved it, enabling the command to read the message. The immediate reaction demonstrated the blindness of the Imperial Navy. It took steps neither to correct its superencipherment nor to see whether British messages could likewise be solved. Instead it told Tranow to keep his hands off secret matters.

During the war, however, Lieutenant Martin Braune set up a naval intercept and codebreaking organization. Tranow had been in his squadron, and Braune soon sent him to its headquarters at Neumünster. There he participated in solving British messages in the Royal Navy's 3-letter code that told of the location of elements of the Grand Fleet after the Battle of Jutland; the information was passed to the U-boats, but they could not make contact.

With the loss of the war, the navy dismantled the codebreaking unit. The High Seas Fleet had been interned at Scapa Flow, and having no ships, the navy needed no cryptanalysts. But by the spring of 1919, things seemed less black, and the navy, remembering the value of this intelligence, began recalling its codebreakers. Tranow, who had not yet been demobilized, let Braune persuade him to stay on. The staff of the new agency, which formally began work on 28 April 1919 in Berlin, numbered eight.

The changes in foreign radio procedure since wartime made it impossible for them to resume where they had left off, but they eventually broke into a number of systems. Helping them was the fact that the naval radio stations had no ships to communicate with; they could therefore devote that much more time to interception. Under the several officers who successively administered the unit, three men emerged as the chief cryptanalysts: Tranow, who concentrated on English material, Lothar Franke, for French intercepts, and Paul August, for Italian.

The first major solution came surprisingly quickly. Tranow reconstructed Britain's enormous Government Telegraph Code. The Germans were interested because it carried reports to and from the Admiralty about the movements of foreign warships. Later in the 1920s it enabled the Germans to follow the British gunboat activity in the Yangtse as they fired upon anti-British demonstrations in Shanghai and Canton. Tranow's next success was a 4-letter naval code that let the Germans peek into Royal Navy maneuvers, especially in the Mediterranean and with convoys in the Atlantic. In particular in 1932 he followed a British convoy maneuver in the Atlantic down to the last ship's position. Meanwhile Franke cracked three French codes: the TBM, for Tous Bâtiments Marines (all naval vessels), the BDG for Bâtiments de Guerre (warships), and the Signaux Tactiques (tactical signals).

The early successes led gradually to an enlargement of the unit, which was now commonly called the B-Dienst, for Beobachtungs-Dienst (observation service). To better intercept naval messages from the Mediterranean, it established in 1925 a listening post far to the south, in the Black Forest town of Villingen. It slowly added people. One of them, Wilhelm Schwabe, a former radioman, first broke into a French superencipherment with the help of Tranow's knowledge of the movements of the *Duquesne*. Progress was not undisturbed. One of the original team departed: August, whose superior regarded him as unsuitable for the work.

His specialty—Italy—was dropped. But the B-Dienst was still so small that it had to send the intercepts of Poland, one of its main targets, to the Defense Ministry's Cipher Center for solution. And when the Reichstag insisted that the navy reduce the size of its headquarters, the naval command banished the B-Dienst to the Inspection of Torpedoes and Mines in Kiel, where it scrounged offices in the naval academy. For 10 years starting in 1928, though, it maintained a liaison officer with the Abwehr Branch in the Defense Ministry.

In the fall of 1933, after four years in exile, the B-Dienst returned to Berlin and close contact with the command authorities. It became one of the three elements of the naval command office's communications and intelligence branch. In 1934, it got an energetic new chief, Lieutenant Commander Heinz Bonatz. Under him, as part of the rearmament, it added men and listening posts and put teams aboard ships during cruises. And the international situation began to tauten, increasing the importance of intelligence.

For the Kriegsmarine, the main target remained, of course, the major potential opponent: the Royal Navy. But this clashed with Hitler's conceptions. He viewed England racially as a potential ally, and when, in mid-1935, he agreed with her to limit his navy's size to a third that of Britain's, he believed this would allay British fear and hostility and free him for his other designs. He wanted his naval staff to redirect its planning energies against the more probable enemy, France. So he forbade the preparation of war plans against Britain, and he likewise ordered that the main codebreaking effort be transferred from England to France. Tranow laughed when he heard this order, and did nothing. A little while later his chiefs asked him how he was doing with the shift. He said he hadn't begun yet. "But it's about time!" they cried.

"Gentlemen," replied Tranow, "I don't want to delve into high policy, but I do want to say one thing: You know that the English report their worldwide ship movements through these codes. Suppose their Mediterranean Fleet pours out through the Strait of Gibraltar and goes into the Atlantic or the Channel or even into the North Sea. Don't you want to know about this in advance?"

The higher gentlemen of the German navy, envisioning the ruin of their strategy, their turreted gray warships, and their careers, quailed. They reconsidered. They ceased insisting on their Führer's order. They let Tranow pursue his researches.

Later that very year, he made one of his major advances. He and his assistants had solved the Royal Navy's most widely used code, the 5-digit Naval Code—in part by comparing the coded reports of merchant vessel movements with their routes as printed in *Lloyds Weekly Shipping Report*. But the B-Dienst had not been able to make much progress with the much more tightly held Naval Cypher, a 4-digit code with a superencipherment (a superencipherment consists of a layer of cipher atop the code to make it harder to break). Now, for greater security in the messages of a squadron patrolling the Red Sea to keep watch on the Italian invasion of Ethiopia, the British began superenciphering the Naval Code as well. Apparently out of logistical simplicity, they used the superencipherment of the Naval Cypher. Since Tranow had solved the Naval Code, he could easily strip off the superencipherment. He could then remove it from the Naval Cypher. Then, with the help of such external factors as his knowledge of what the ships were doing there and their names, he could crack the Naval Cypher as well. This gave the Germans control over the main Admiralty cryptosystems and insight into Royal Navy phraseology and traffic routines, and, of course, into British ship dispositions.

These successes, and the attacks in 1937 on four other English, five French, four Russian, and three Danish cryptosystems enlarged the B-Dienst. The 30 men in its Berlin central in 1936 became 90 by the summer of 1939. In 1937, its 14 intercept posts picked up a total of 252,000 messages, or some 700 a day. Two years later, two more posts had been added. Each of the 16 concentrated on the fleets closest to it. Counting the workers here, by the summer of 1939 the B-Dienst employed more than 500 persons.

Tranow, meanwhile, was growing constantly in influence. The naval chiefs changed every two years—Bonatz, for example, left in 1936—but Tranow remained. The increasing importance of his specialty naturally played a major role in his rise, but personality helped as well. The other major desk leader, Franke, for France and Italy, was somewhat vain and a bit of a loner. A professor type, he kept his work pretty much to himself. His co-workers felt that he had perhaps studied a little too much and grown a little unworldly. Though a good cryptanalyst, he increasingly lost contact with his men. Tranow, on the other hand, seemed to be the ideal boss. He pressed his men to keep their work coming. He was courteous. He was full of ideas. He always had time for his subordinates. And of course he knew the name of the British cruiser that had crossed the Atlantic the previous summer, or the former commands of a particular admiral. His technical expertise was unquestionable. All this led eventually to his taking charge of all the cryptanalysis, even though he was not a Nazi and Franke was an old one.

Owing to Tranow's ability, on the day the war started the Germans read the major British naval codes and knew the locations of the major fleet forces. The work bore immediate fruit. On 11 September, with the war barely a week old, the B-Dienst read a British radio message specifying the assembly points of a convoy in the Bristol Channel. The U-31 sighted it soon thereafter and on the 16th torpedoed and sank the steamer *Aviemore*. Soon thereafter, B-Dienst intelligence suggested that the British had instituted the convoy system, as in World War I, to protect their shipping. The Germans concentrated U-boats in the busy zone south of Ireland and sank a couple of big ships. Then, when further information hinted that convoys in this area had been rerouted, the Germans sent their submarines to lurk near Gibraltar. A first concerted attack was driven off by alert Royal Navy destroyers. But another in mid-November, in which the B-Dienst interception of messages located a convoy, resulted in a sinking. On 17 February 1940, a solution revealed that two convoys totaling 24 ships were to join up west of Oporto, Portugal. U-boats sank two of them. On 30 August, the B-Dienst intercepted and solved a report that convoy SC 2, coming out of Sidney, Canada, would be at 57°00′ north latitude, 19°50′ west longitude at noon on 6 September. This information, passed to the U-boats, enabled them to spot the convoy and sink five of its ships. Dönitz praised the B-Dienst as a "major help" in the operation.

These successes aided the expansion of the B-Dienst. Its intercept and direction-finding posts followed the German conquests. Eventually 44 dotted the map of the Grossdeutsches Reich and its occupied territories from Kirkenes at the uttermost tip of Norway to Montpellier in sunny Provence and from Brest at the end of Brittany to Feodosia in the Crimea. Its personnel eventually soared to a total of 5,000, about 1,100 of them in Berlin. Tranow's English section, with some 700 clerks, evaluators, and cryptanalysts by day and 200 by night, worked behind steel bars on an entire floor of the navy's headquarters, a sober sandstone building with three portals and a swash carved W for Kaiser Wilhelm II, under whom it was built, at Tirpitzufer 72–76, just around the corner from the OKW headquarters on the Bendlerstrasse. It was a branch of one of the offices of the Seekriegsleitung, the Naval War Command of the OKM. Which office it belonged to varied with the incessant reorganizations and renumberings: it started with the 3rd section of the Seekriegsleitung, or 3/Skl, became part of the 2/Skl, then stayed with the 2/Skl when it rose to a division and when the division became in effect the 4/Skl. Technically it was the Radio Reconnaissance Branch of the Naval Communications Service Division.

Early in 1940, the B-Dienst helped the successful assault on Norway. It kept track of the British forces, which could have blown the weaker German invaders out of the water, thus enabling the Germans to avoid them and land with surprise. An intercept detachment on board the *Gneisenau* helped alert the German task force. Tranow's omniscience often assisted in such situations. In general he could follow the movements of every English battleship. One morning his work caused him to arrive a little late at the 10 a.m. situation conference. A chorus greeted him.

"Herr Tranow, where is the *Queen Elizabeth?*" At the start of the war, this battleship had been in dry dock, undergoing a major renovation. No radio intelligence had come to light suggesting that the work had been completed and that the ship had rejoined the fleet. But suddenly word reached higher OKM circles that an agent had reported that the *Queen Elizabeth* lay in Gibraltar.

Many of the older officers trusted agents' sightings more than crypt-analysts' deductions. They raged at Tranow.

"You and your deciphering! Who needs it?"

Tranow remained calm.

"Gentlemen," he replied, "I don't care what your agents say. The *Queen Elizabeth* is not there."

The question remained temporarily unresolved—until later the Germans discovered a document showing that sailing from Gibraltar as a home port was a little fishing boat named the *Queen Elizabeth*.

Later in 1940, on 20 August, the B-Dienst suffered a setback when all Royal Navy cryptosystems changed. Naval Code, for example, became a 4- instead of a 5-digit code. The consequent blackout perhaps con-tributed to the OKM's coolness to an invasion of Britain. But Tranow and his group came back fast. Making the first break into a code is the most difficult step, but in just seven weeks they had discovered the meanings of 850 code groups—400 of the general vocabulary, 450 ships' names—in Naval Cypher. By the start of 1941, this had expanded to 700 ships' names and 1,200 vocabulary words. The B-Dienst had by then begun nicknaming the British systems after German cities, partly for ease of references, partly for security. Naval Cypher was COLOGNE. The new Naval Code, which was also crumbling under B-Dienst attack, was MUNICH. It had two variants, BROWN and BLUE.

The entry of the United States into the war increased both the work and the opportunities of the B-Dienst. The number of radio reconnaissance target areas rose from 136 at the start of 1942 to 237 at the end. By 1943, intercepts had soared to a total of 3,101,831 for the year—8,500 a day, though probably many were duplicates. Just to sort them as they arrived by teleprinter from the intercept posts required 8 to 10 men. To help in registering, counting, and statistically analyzing the tens of millions of code groups, the B-Dienst employed Hollerith sorters and tabulators. At first it had used the machines in the OKW's war-economics department. But these were never quite right. Finally, in 1943, Tranow set up his own unit. Eventually he had 130 men working six machines. They could print out in six to eight hours a difference catalogue of code numbers, a necessary first tool in stripping superencipherments. In theory several hundred men could have done the same thing in the same time, but the B-Dienst did not dispose of such manpower. Only the Hollerith unit enabled the Germans to solve intercepts in time for the command to be able to use them.

But neither the increase in intercepts nor these machines helped with the wartime American systems. Before the American entry, the B-Dienst, like the rest of the world, was reading American codes. On the very first day of the war, the U-30 torpedoed the steamer *Athenia,* costing 28 American lives. Admiral Raeder called in the U.S. naval attaché to deny that they had done it, and on 16 September the attaché dutifully reported this to Washington. Four days later the B-Dienst passed a solution of his message to Raeder. And in November 1941, hope sprang when the B-Dienst discovered some repetitions that seemed to promise solution of another American cipher system. It was soon deceived. In April 1942 a new system appeared. Long, time-consuming statistical work showed that this was a machine cipher, and that solution could not be kept up to date. Intercept material from 10 days would require four weeks of Hollerith work. Moreover, up to the end of 1942 B-Dienst statisticians had discovered no repetitions numerous enough to break into the system. These results never changed with this major American cipher.

These failures contrasted sharply with B-Dienst successes against the British systems. It read London's messages to British naval attachés and thus got the Admiralty figures on the sinkings of British ships. Despite a change of the basic codebooks both for COLOGNE and MUNICH on 1 January 1942, the B-Dienst broke relatively quickly back into MUNICH, the less important system, and into COLOGNE a little later. The British were, however, constantly increasing their cipher security. Some top holders of COLOGNE, for example, got as their superencipherment the only cipher that is unbreakable both in theory and in practice: the one-time pad. This reduced the areas in which the B-Dienst could crack COLOGNE messages—and these areas were naturally the more important. But mitigating these difficulties was the B-Dienst's success with a new system, a 4-digit Anglo-American code, which the Germans called FRANKFORT. The B-Dienst attacked it with heavy manpower at the end of January 1942, and by the end of March could already read a major portion of intercepts in it. In late summer the Allies began using different superenciphments in different areas and then changed them at rapid intervals to render solution more difficult. Tranow's group soon overcame these, so that by December the results were proving of great value, "especially in the U-boat war." For FRANKFORT served mainly in the transmission of convoy messages.

Both Axis and Allies recognized the fundamental importance of the struggle for control of the sea lanes. "The Battle of the Atlantic was the dominating factor all through the war," wrote Churchill. "Never for one moment could we forget that everything happening elsewhere, on land, at sea, or in the air, depended ultimately on its outcome, and amid all other cares we viewed its changing fortunes day by day with hope or apprehension." Intelligence was vital in this battle. The U-boats had to know where the Allied shipping was to sink it. The B-Dienst provided much of this information, and in this agency Tranow was far and away the most important individual. Hitler had said, less eloquently than Churchill, "The moment England's supply routes are severed, she will be forced to capitulate." Had that severance succeeded, a substantial share of the credit would have gone to Tranow.

On 30 October 1942, the B-Dienst submitted an XB report—a report based on cryptanalysis—reporting that Convoy SC 107, eastward of Cape Race (at the tip of Newfoundland), would steer 45°. At the same time, a U-boat sighting gave its exact position. Admiral Dönitz, commander of U-boats, at once sent a wolfpack to intercept it. "The timely arrival of the radio reconnaissance report on the route of the convoy," Dönitz wrote later to the B-Dienst, "made it possible to pull the U-boat formation together so narrowly that within a few hours after the first sighting several U-boats made contact," and soon sank 15 steamers. An addition on Tranow's copy of this memorandum commended him specially for his part in the success.

No one knows what a coded message will say until it is broken. To make sure that useful FRANKFORT intercepts got to the command while they were still "alive," all or nearly all of them had to be solved. To do this, Tranow had doubled the personnel working on them. He took them from the COLOGNE group, leaving this system not worked on, since a new encipherment of its recognition groups had prevented the B-Dienst from getting almost anything of military value from it. Even this new manpower did not suffice, and Tranow had to triple the original number, and then force through additional work on the Hollerith machines. Eventually there were 360 working during the day and 200 at night under the leadership of Schwabe.

To help further, he pressed his case with higher authorities. He had known Dönitz since before the war, having worked in an office next to his, though he did not get along with him as well as he had done with Raeder. Shortly after Dönitz became commander in chief of the navy, he heard that things weren't quite right with Tranow, and summoned him to a meeting.

"So, Tranow," he said. "What's the problem? You can speak freely—from the heart." The other officers present listened with interest.

"Well, Herr Grossadmiral," replied Tranow, "the navy could help me a little more by getting the Luftwaffe to reconnoiter more for us." He explained that knowing the positions of convoys that radioed these positions in code would help him break those codes.

"Tranow," replied Dönitz, "you're forgetting Reichsmarshal Göring. 'The Luftwaffe is mine,' he says. As long as he's on vacation, I can do something for you with the Führer, but as soon as he comes back . . ." Dönitz did bring up the matter at his first conference with Hitler, who promised to do whatever possible.

To squeeze as much intelligence out of the intercepts as possible, Tranow himself would sit down at a desk in the evening and seek to tease out some new meanings or strip off a new superencipherment. In this work he was helped by the introduction into the convoy service of Canadian destroyers with Indian names, all of which had to be spelled out syllable by syllable.

It particularly helped in the greatest convoy battle of the war. This came in March of 1943, shortly after Roosevelt and Churchill had decided at the Casablanca conference to make the antisubmarine campaign their first priority in the war, when Dönitz finally had the number of U-boats at sea that he thought would be needed to cut England's lifelines, and when the B-Dienst solutions of FRANKFORT were at their peak of efficiency.

On 5 March the slow convoy SC 122 departed New York harbor, and on the 8th, the faster HX 229. On the 12th and 13th, as SC 122's 51 vessels steamed majestically in 13 columns, and HX 229's 38 in 11, both toward the northern Atlantic, the Allies heard heavy U-boat radio traffic, which they located directly in the path of the two convoys. They ordered them to steer around the U-boat–infested areas. At 8 p.m. 13 March, SC 122, then at 49° north, 40° east, was directed to steer a course of 67°.

This order the B-Dienst intercepted, solved, and passed to Dönitz. Now one degree of longitude represents about 70 land miles, and one of latitude there, about 45. This meant that, even if the convoy knew exactly where it was, and the U-boats knew exactly where they were, the submarines could still be scores of miles from their target. To enable them to spot their prey, then, Dönitz instructed 17 submarines to stretch out in a north-south picket line ahead of the convoy. When the B-Dienst provided information on the HX 229 route, he repeated the maneuver with 11 submarines against this convoy.

Green seas, mountain high, and visibility averaging only 500 yards made the actual contact largely a matter of chance. The B-Dienst reported another HX 229 course change. This solution later proved to be in error: the cryptanalysts had evidently filled in some words on the basis of rather thin probabilities, rather as a crossword-puzzle player will try at some words that seem likely, only to find later that he was guessing wrong. But this did not then much affect events at sea. The wolfpacks had congregated in the fatal area, the faster convoy had overtaken the slower to form "a large mass of shipping in a relatively confined space of ocean," and the imprecision of locations at sea minimized the harm of the false course report. The submarines, Dönitz exulted, "hurled themselves like wolves" on the convoys. In a three-day battle, marked by the shocking explosions of torpedoes and the sudden heelings of ships, the screaming of men drowning in icy waters, the rumbling geysers of depth bombs, and the silent sweating tension of submariners facing death encased in tons of compressed and pitiless liquid, the U-boats sank 21 ships with a loss of only one of their own. It was the greatest U-boat success of the war, and the Allies feared that they might have lost the basic battle of the war.

The fear turned out false, for within the next few months additional

Allied escorts, better radar, and improved Allied codebreaking turned the tide of the Battle of the Atlantic. And at about the same time, the B-Dienst lost ground. On 10 June, the basic codebook for FRANKFORT changed. It was never possible to break into it again.

With other systems, things were only slightly better. COLOGNE had been dropped. A MUNICH BLUE codebook had been captured on 14 September 1942 at the British landing attempt at Tobruk, probably from the destroyer *Sikh,* which sank close inshore. It arrived at the B-Dienst the 29th. By 10:15 the next morning the cryptanalysts had ascertained the current locations of nearly all Royal Navy battleships and aircraft carriers. Tranow reduced the forces working on the other systems to exploit this. This enabled him to keep up despite the introduction on 15 December of a superencipherment to complicate the system. The basic captured code went out of service on 19 April 1943, however. Thereafter it took the B-Dienst seven months with heavy personnel commitment to break into the new system, and then it still served only to report the locations of heavy British warships—in a war without any major fleet actions.

Though MUNICH BROWN could still be read easily at the end of 1943, the situation grew grimmer. A heavy air raid on Berlin in November 1943 destroyed many of the B-Dienst's records, which were invaluable in its work, and forced it to move to an encampment near Eberswalde, a village some 25 miles northeast of Berlin. The British rendered their systems increasingly difficult. Instead of giving locations by latitude and longitude, they introduced a special indicator system. They increased the tempo of their key changes, from every 15 days to every day. They used one-time pads in more and more areas. Even the salvaged coding instructions from the Canadian destroyer *Athabaskan,* sunk off Brittany, did little more than confirm the impotence of the codebreakers. When, a month before the Normandy invasion, Hitler asked the B-Dienst which English system could be read and which not, it had to reply that it could read only a number of secondary systems and a convoy system for stragglers, but that "The two main English systems cannot be read, the one since the start of 1944 and the other since the start of June 1943." On orders from above, the B-Dienst began attacking Swedish, Turkish, and Italian cryptosystems. This helped little in a war against the English and Americans, and anyhow by then many of Tranow's team had been pulled out to fight at the fronts. They no more defeated the enemy there than they had at their desks in the OKM. But the B-Dienst, Dönitz said, had contributed half the operational intelligence that the Kriegsmarine used in fighting its war. It was a record unmatched by any other intelligence agency of the Third Reich.

The Admiral and
His Abwehr

THE 176th Infantry Division called for a spy. It was defending the very frontiers of the Reich against the advancing English, who in that December of 1944 had taken Sittard, across the border in Holland. The division had just delivered a counterattack so hard that the Tommies were saying that by Christmas they would no longer be in Sittard, a flat, spread-out town dominated by a church tower with horizontal red and white stripes. But were they in fact pulling out, or shifting their forces, or just talking? The 176th needed to know, and it could only find out by injecting an agent behind the enemy lines.

In the twilight of Hitler's Germany, the SS controlled spies. The division applied urgently to the liaison officer of the SS leader west. On 20 December, he came up with an agent codenamed PAN, and assigned him to head into Sittard to see what the English were doing. That very evening, an SS man gave PAN the proper identification card and brought him to the 176th. They passed from the regimental combat command post to the battalion near Susteren, north of Sittard. PAN then vanished into the darkness.

On the road to Sittard, he noticed three English tanks in position west of the railroad line. In the houses along the railroad tracks west of Sittard, where he stayed with an acquaintance, he counted 32 medium tanks. He also discovered two light batteries south of the Sittard-Limbruch road. The next morning he twice bicycled out of Sittard and then back again, seeing medium and heavy tanks on both sides of both roads—300 altogether, he estimated. He observed many English cars and trucks in the so-called Villapark, and then laid low at his friend's house, waiting while the British searched Sittard for German spies. On the way back that evening, he coolly questioned an English soldier about a heavy gun in position north of the town and learned that it was a 42-centimeter howitzer.

He reported what he had seen to the 176th, giving them a sketch of it as well. Though he brought back no specifics of the British intentions, his information perhaps helped the I c draw his own conclusions as to what the enemy planned, for the division declared itself "very satisfied with the results of his ascertainments."

PAN's story epitomizes in many ways German military espionage during World War II. It is a story of success only at the tactical level, of distinctly minor contributions to the German military commands, and of administrative absorption by a rival agency at the end. It perhaps inherited this smell of failure from its unsuccessful father, III b, the espionage branch of the Great General Staff. For it descended directly from that body, without the discontinuity to which Versailles subjected so many other organs of the army.

Six days after the armistice of 11 November 1918, the chief of the General Staff of the Field Army transferred III b, now called the Intelligence Branch, to the Acting, or caretaker, General Staff in Berlin. Its duties included espionage and counterespionage. After demobilization, it was reduced to an Intelligence Group and attached to the Foreign Armies Branch of the Great General Staff. III b's old chief, Lieutenant Colonel Walther Nicolai, whose propaganda activities had made him politically unacceptable, went on permanent leave into obscurity. The head of the Intelligence Group was Major Friedrich Gempp, a III b veteran. With the Treaty of Versailles, a number of disguises went into effect. The Great General Staff became the Troops Department. Foreign Armies became its third branch, or T 3. And the Intelligence Group became T 3's Abwehr Group.

The term "Abwehr" does not refer in any way to concepts of intelligence or information. One element, -*wehr,* which traces back to an Indo-European form, is akin to the English word "weir," a dam. It means essentially "defense, protection" and serves in such words as "Wehrmacht" (defense force). The *ab-* is cognate with English "of" in its sense of "from." It means "away" or "off" and here intensifies the idea of rejection in -*wehr.* "Abwehr," then, denotes a "warding off." It can legitimately serve as the name for a counterespionage organization. The German army adopted it partly because the Abwehr Group did defend against foreign espionage, but mainly because the word camouflaged its own espionage functions. The term stuck.

The four officers in the tiny unit sought first to clarify the troubled situation in the east, where the Poles and the Red and White Russians were fighting one another, and then to build up a spy network, presumably first against France. It also steered the intelligence operations, though not the administration, of the army's codebreaking unit, the Cipher Center, and received its solutions. Gempp remained in charge until 23 June 1927, when advancement to general promoted him out of the job. Major Günther

Schwantes succeeded him. He was a cavalryman, assigned to the Abwehr a little more than a year before.

Meanwhile, intrigues and power struggles within the Defense Ministry were about to have a profound effect on the Abwehr's organizational position. A new defense minister had come to office, and he was succumbing to the influence of one of his subordinates, Kurt von Schleicher, a World War I friend and an energetic, conniving, and ambitious officer with an eye on the chancellorship. Schleicher was urging him to increase his power —and, not inconsequentially, Schleicher's own—by expropriating some of the subordinate services'. One area in which this could be done was intelligence; its information could also bring additional benefits. So, as of 1 April 1928, the minister pulled the Abwehr Group out of T 3 and the naval espionage unit out of the naval command and united them in an Abwehr Branch subordinated directly to him. The Cipher Center came along, and the minister further ordered that all naval radio intercepts be sent to the Abwehr Branch. This centralization of information-gathering functions enabled him to declare the Abwehr Branch to be "the Defense Ministry's sole intelligence-acquisition post." Naturally, this did not slake Schleicher's thirst for power. Less than a year later, as of 1 March 1929, the minister assembled several offices that had previously stood immediately beneath him, including the Abwehr Branch, into a Minister's Department. Its head was, to no one's surprise, Schleicher. Since the Minister's Department ultimately evolved into the OKW, these two steps made the Abwehr into the supraservice agency that handled spying for Germany's army, navy, and air force that it was in World War II.

Schleicher perceived the advantages of full control of an information-gathering organ, and at the end of the year he replaced Schwantes with a close friend, Lieutenant Colonel Ferdinand von Bredow. Bredow had served as a field Abwehr officer in 1921, but this probably helped Schleicher more as excuse than as reason to put him in charge of the Abwehr. He was a husky, jovial man, always ready for a party, and with a certain need to make himself appear important that conflicted with the reticence essential to the chief of a secret service. He reorganized the Abwehr and expanded it somewhat, traveling to France and Belgium to do so, in particular recruiting representatives of German armaments firms as agents. But his real job was to serve Schleicher, in part through the connections that he was said to have had through his wife to the press lord and right-wing politician Alfred Hugenberg. Schleicher eventually became defense minister. He promptly made Bredow head of the Minister's Department. Three days after that, on 7 June 1932, Schleicher broke with a 66-year tradition. He appointed a naval officer as head of the Abwehr.

Commander Conrad Patzig, an upright officer with bright blue eyes, had been sent to head the naval group of the Abwehr in 1929. He was replacing a man who could not get along with Bredow and had cost the navy influence. Admiral Raeder, the navy's commander, who knew Patzig from service together in Kiel, felt that Patzig's affable manner would eliminate this problem. He was soon proved right. Though Patzig would have preferred to stay at sea, he worked hard at the Abwehr assignment. Indeed, when Bredow left, Patzig was regarded as more suitable to run the entire Abwehr than any of the other five section heads, all army men. This capability, together with Schleicher's need to mollify the navy by giving it some post to replace one it had just lost to the army, led Schleicher to name Patzig chief of the Abwehr. The Abwehr was not, however, considered very important; its command was not a key post: if it had been, the army—in a continental power, the largest and most influential service—would have kept it for itself and the navy would have been thrown some other scrap.

Patzig continued to build up the Abwehr. His benign ways warmed the Abwehr into a familylike body. But the information that he submitted to Schleicher every day consisted normally of two or three solid intercepts of the Cipher Center, while spy reports were rarer and flimsier. His charm failed, moreover, with the Prussian secret police and with the SD after Hitler's takeover of power. Their powers rivaled one another too closely. In particular, Patzig clashed with the head of the counterespionage branch of the secret police. This did not please the new defense minister, Hitler's choice, the "Rubber Lion," Field Marshal Werner von Blomberg. Then Blomberg learned that Rowehl's high-altitude reconnaissance planes, flying under Abwehr contract, had photographed Polish harbors and forts. This, if discovered, would have endangered Hitler's most brilliant foreign stroke to date: the surprising nonaggression pact with hated Poland, which covered Hitler's rear for action in the Rhineland. The aerial indiscretion provided the excuse Blomberg needed to placate Himmler. As of 31 December 1934, he fired Patzig, who became commander of the new pocket battleship, *Graf Spee*. In Patzig's place, Raeder nominated as head of the Abwehr a man who became a legend, Captain Wilhelm Franz Canaris.

Canaris was born on 1 January 1887 in Aplerbeck, then a suburb of Dortmund in the Ruhr Valley. Though he later liked to pretend that he was descended from the daring nineteenth-century hero of Greece's war for independence, Admiral Konstantios Kanaris, his family had in fact migrated to Germany from Italy in the 1600s. His father, director of a foundry, moved to Duisberg, where Canaris attended high school. At 18, he joined the navy as a cadet. He was only about five feet four inches tall, with light-blue eyes and fine hair. His superiors said that he was, "despite a certain shyness, well liked." He spoke "pretty good English"; to this were later added French, some Russian, and then, during cruises in the Caribbean, Spanish, in which he became fluent.

At the start of World War I, he was serving aboard the light cruiser

Dresden, which became the only German ship to escape destruction in the Battle of the Falkland Islands. It raided commerce in the Pacific until, cornered by an English cruiser, it scuttled itself in Chilean waters. The crew was interned on Quiriquina Island, about halfway down the coast of that stringbean country. About five months later, on 4 August 1915, Canaris, with his commander's permission, disguised himself as a native, rowed ashore, and, using his language ability, escaped. He went first south 300 miles to Osorno, then crossed the Andes by horseback 300 miles to Neuquen in Argentina. From there he rode a railroad 600 miles to Buenos Aires. With a false Chilean passport made out in the name of Reed Rosas, he boarded the Dutch steamer *Frisia.* The voyage tested Canaris's nerves: the last port of call before its destination, neutral Amsterdam, was the enemy one of Falmouth. He arrived back in Berlin on 4 October 1915, two months to the day after he escaped.

The following year the German admiralty sent him back to Spain on the same passport. Under the supervision of the naval attaché, he chose secret agents for special tasks. During this year he not only gained experience in espionage but laid the foundation of relations that, 20 years later, proved helpful for German negotiations. But Canaris yearned for combat, and so Reed Rosas daringly headed back for Germany through hostile France and Italy—where he was arrested. Influential friends freed him for a return to Spain. This time he was not to risk the land route back to Germany: the navy sent a submarine for him.

He shook his shadows on the train from Madrid and laid low in the Mediterranean port of Cartagena. A first attempt to pick him up, at the end of August 1916, failed. The U-35 was dispatched for the second attempt, arranged for the nights of 30 September or 2 October five miles from the lighthouse on nearby Cape Tiñoso on a bearing of 180°. Canaris and some other Germans who were also to go back to Germany put out to sea in a small boat without being stopped by the Spanish patrol vessels. About midnight they transferred to a larger sailboat with a Spanish crew and papers cleared for Palma de Mallorca. For two and a half hours he made the Morse recognition signal with dimmed light to seaward—with no result. At the same time, the U-35 had come close under the lights of Tiñoso and had picked out, from the many fishing boats whose lights dotted Salitrona Bay, one whose top lantern flashed the recognition signal. The U-boat stood 300 yards off and repeated the Morse K at least 10 times. But Canaris failed to see it, and at first light on 1 October flew a red pennant. Shortly thereafter, Canaris reported,

> I observed a steamer in the west which I soon made out as an enemy trawler. It lay stopped at first, and then came toward us. I had hauled down the red pennant upon recognizing the trawler, and then, to appear less suspicious, at slow speed gradually laid course for Mazaron. The trawler came rapidly nearer. We hid ourselves in the sand ballast inside the boat. The trawler

stopped close by our stern. Since it saw only the Spanish crew, it gradually continued to travel southeast toward a vessel coming into sight there, . . . the crew of the trawler wore French naval uniforms.

Canaris returned the boat to the rendezvous line. At the same time, the U-35 arrived there under water, spotted the sailboat, and caught up with it. Someone on the sailboat sighted the periscope off the port stern. Canaris had the boat laid on a westerly course and showed the red flag behind the sail so that the trawler would not be able to see it and repeatedly dipped the mainsail, as agreed upon. Then, 50 yards away, in an always astonishing moment, the U-35 appeared where moments before only the vacant sea was running. Water poured from her uppers as the two vessels closed. At 6:40 a.m., Canaris and the others sprang aboard. They entered. The submarine dived and headed for home.

Canaris himself finally got to command a submarine, the UB-128. But the location—the Mediterranean—was too poor, and the time too late, for him to win any laurels.

In the confusion of post-Armistice Germany, Canaris pursued a resolutely right-wing course of some importance. He served on the court-martial that largely exonerated the murderers of the Communist leaders Karl Liebknecht and Rosa Luxemburg, and later he helped one of the defendants, convicted for dereliction of duty, to escape. While an aide to the defense minister, he sided against him and with the short-lived army putsch of Dr. Wolfgang Kapp. For this he spent a few days in a police jail. When conditions stabilized, and when, in 1919, he married, he calmed down. But he still moved along hidden corridors as one of the secret agents in the rebuilding of the German navy. Late in the 1920s, he wrote a memorandum on the use of torpedo boats that so interested the king of Spain that he built a torpedo factory in Cadiz with German money that let the Germans advance their knowledge of this weapon. Through his personal relations with the king and his dictator, Miguel Primo de Rivera, Canaris set up the basis for the construction of a new type of U-boat in Cadiz. Later, he visited Buenos Aires in an attempt to win Argentinian help for the German U-boat project.

During these years, he rose in rank, alternating sea and land duty and collecting unanimously good fitness reports: "possesses in rare high quantity all characteristics that make up an excellent officer in an important post . . . tireless . . . clear judgment . . . greatest capability" (1921); "outstanding" (1927); "his subordinates trust him" (1928); "fastest perception, excellent brain" (1931). One of his superiors observed in 1926 that his strength lay in the "naval-military-political direction" and raved: "With a finest feel for foreign psychology and mentality, together with uncommon linguistic ability, he knows in exemplary fashion how to deal with foreigners (from the lowly to the prominent), whose trust he then soon possesses. If he were to have such a duty, there would be no obstacle for him, no illness would hold him back, no area is so closed off that he would not get in and get to the person in question, in order then in amazingly short time to run the show, with a childish innocent face." Yet many officers—including Karl Dönitz, a future commander in chief of the navy—did not like him. He was sly, they felt.

In October 1932 he became captain of the battleship *Schlesien,* and soon after Hitler assumed power began giving lectures to his crew about the virtues of Naziism. "By thorough, very diligent preparation and generally intelligible execution he had an exemplary influence on this area," wrote his superior. He seized opportunities to play up to power brokers in the new Nazi hierarchy: when one of his subordinates, a paymaster, wrote to Himmler, Canaris passed along his regards. (The subordinate was Oswald Pohl, later head of concentration camps.) Canaris served two years on the *Schlesien,* and then, in the most important step in his sea career, he failed. He did not advance to the next command, that of commander of ships of the line. His superior gave him the weakest possible positive recommendation—"Canaris must be adjudged fit"—and nullified much of even this by suggesting that his "talents and perhaps his inclinations direct him more to the military-political than to the purely military area." For Canaris, though brave and capable, simply did not possess the ruthless driving personality needed by a higher commander. Moreover, Raeder did not like him. So the post went to someone else, and Canaris was put on the shelf as commander of the naval station at Swinemünde on the Baltic to await retirement.

But a few weeks after he got there Patzig was fired. As his replacement, Patzig recommended Canaris. His rank was right. His service record was excellent. He knew foreign countries. His superiors had repeatedly emphasized his abilities in politico-military affairs, and he had experience in espionage work. His pro-Naziism would help eliminate the friction that had made things difficult for Patzig. He was perfect for the job in every respect but one: Raeder's dislike of him. Raeder turned Patzig's suggestion down. Only when Patzig pointed out that the navy would then have to surrender the Abwehr Branch to the army, since there was no suitable navy successor in the branch, did Raeder relent. Late in the fall of 1934, he summoned Canaris from Swinemünde and sent him to Berlin to familiarize himself with his new assignment. On 1 January 1935, his 48th birthday, Captain Canaris became head of German espionage and counterintelligence.

His hair was prematurely white, and so they called him "Old Whitehead." His manner was unmilitary. He moved softly and inconspicuously. In his office, the "Fox's Lair," he would suddenly appear: no one had heard him come. He preferred mufti to his uniforms, and when he did wear one, it was usually his shabbiest. He placed little value on appearances. He threw his decorations into a drawer with other odds and ends. When his subordinates heard that he had gotten the German Cross in gold, they could get no confirmation from him. They learned of his promotions to rear and vice and full admiral from other sources. His wife and two daughters felt as he did, and it typified the family's attitude when one daughter remarked, as he returned in full dress one evening from a large reception, "Oh, you poor thing!" On the other hand, he placed great value on social form. He was always extremely courteous and always early for appointments.

He never seemed warm enough. Even in the summer he sometimes wore an overcoat. When he played tennis, he wore a thick sweater. He was a bit of an insomniac and a hypochondriac. He rose at 6 a.m., and when he met his neighbor, the pianist Helmut Maurer, in the street, he would ask almost enviously, "Did you sleep well?" He himself got his few hours with an enormous quantity of Phanodorm and Bromural. He urged on others the pills and medicines that he constantly took. He relaxed by riding horseback and playing tennis, basing his strategy on surprise.

He led a harmonious family life, though during the war his wife and daughters lived on the Ammersee, a lake in Bavaria, while he stayed in Berlin, visiting them a couple of times a year. He was kindly and took an interest in his personnel. One Sunday he asked a young clerk to type a memorandum for him. She put on her glasses to do so, whereupon he said, "Child, what do you need glasses for?" She replied that she was shortsighted, and he said that she shouldn't need glasses at her age. It wasn't much of a conversation, but it showed her that he cared for his subordinates as people, that they were not just so many workers. A further indication of his friendliness was his readiness to use the intimate "du" form of address.

He loved animals. In addition to the parrot at his home, he had a pair of dachshunds that trailed him about the office. He spoke to them constantly. He sometimes seemed more concerned about them than about his men and his job. Once, in Italy, he telephoned to Berlin to ask about one of them, which was sick. Some of the Italians thought the conversation, which went into great detail, was a code, but it was the real thing. He believed that if a man didn't like dogs, he couldn't be trusted. He himself said that he could trust animals above people. Hitler made the same remark.

His basic attitude toward life was pessimistic. He usually wore a sad mien and spoke little, except when he was with friends. To spare his strength for his enormous burden of work, he regularly quit the numerous affairs he had to attend at 10 p.m. sharp. Once he explained to a subordinate, "No one says anything worthwhile after ten o'clock anyway." Murmured the officer, "Not before ten, either, Herr Admiral." He retained an interest in many intellectual areas, reading widely, especially in foreign affairs, but also belles lettres; as presents, he gave books on philosophy and prehistory to his acquaintances. Everyone regarded him as intelligent. He grasped ideas quickly and disliked long conferences.

He had a nasty side, but it seems not to have struck to the heart of an individual's sensibilities. At his daily conference, the "Column," he often stage-whispered one sarcastic comment after another while a subordinate delivered a report. During tennis matches, he loved to place his deputy Hans Oster, who was fastidious in his dress, in a damp corner of the clay court behind his house and then keep after him until he finally got Oster to slip and stain the seat of his freshly pressed long white trousers. When he received an oral report, he sometimes probed into it with persistent exactitude and stopped only when the subordinate admitted doubts.

But his subordinates seemed to sense the lack of harshness in his sardonicism and to see an innate humor and kindliness behind it, for they liked and even loved him. They enjoyed hearing him tell how he used to deal with an irritated superior. The prescription was always to repeat his last word. "Your deck officer is a complete blockhead!" the superior might shout. "Blockhead, sir!" Canaris would reply. "Everything the man does is shit!" "Shit, sir!" And so on, until the superior had cooled off.

The technique was pure Canaris. Like him, it used indirection and nuance, it turned the superior's force against himself. Canaris seldom gave a clear yes or no. Often he answered a question with a question. His remarks were frequently elliptic and obscure. He disliked force. Not surprisingly, he was inept as an administrator. He could not delegate responsibility. He issued contradictory instructions to different subordinates. He created chaos when he visited his branches. He chose some bad subordinates and tolerated lightweights. On the other hand, he defended them vigorously against outside criticism. Yet in general his characteristics led one immediate subordinate to call him the most difficult superior he had ever worked with in his military career. One head of air force intelligence called him a good agent, but no outstanding leader.

Among the first problems that he faced upon taking command of the Abwehr was the one that had cost his predecessor his job: the friction with the party and the agencies it controlled. He resolved it in a simple way. He broke with Patzig's views and began cooperating with Himmler's men. On 17 January 1935, two and a half weeks after he took command of the Abwehr, he and a subordinate met from 3 to 6 p.m. in the Defense Ministry with Heydrich and three of his officials and agreed upon a division of labor between the Abwehr, the Gestapo, and the SD. Five days later, Defense Minister Blomberg was urging the interior and finance ministers to adopt some measures that Heydrich would have liked—probably at Canaris's urging. Heydrich, in his turn, replaced the anti-Abwehr Gestapo official with a rather more diplomatic one, who got along well with Canaris. Two years later, on 21 December 1936, Heydrich and Canaris signed the

"Ten Commandments," which reclarified the respective areas of counter-espionage competence between the Abwehr and the Gestapo.

The superficial smoothness at the top between these rival organizations was due largely to the personal relation between their chiefs. Canaris had been first officer of the cruiser *Berlin* when Heydrich had served aboard as a cadet in 1923 and 1924, and Heydrich always maintained at least outward respect for and friendliness to the older man. They lunched together. They lived near one another in a residential section of southwestern Berlin. The Heydrichs often invited the Canarises for croquet; the Canarises had the Heydrichs over for dinner, with the host himself cooking such exotic dishes as saddle of boar in a dough of black bread crumbs and red wine. Frau Canaris played violin with Heydrich. Once the Canarises spent a week with the Heydrichs in Prague.

But Canaris recognized the danger that the ambitious Heydrich posed. One day his neighbor Maurer was walking to the railroad station when a man and a dog appeared on the corner. The dog charged him. Though the man whistled it back, Maurer, furious, told the man that the next time this happened he would shoot not only the dog but him. A few days later Canaris introduced Maurer to the dog owner: "Herr Heydrich." Heydrich said he had already met Maurer: he was the man who wanted to shoot him. Promptly Canaris asked: "Yes? When?" But the white-haired admiral seems not to have found the force of personality to fight Heydrich's primitive drives. Once Heydrich told him that a Protestant pastor, whom Canaris knew, was continuing his anti-Nazi activities. Canaris could have asked how the man could do this from a concentration camp, but he remained silent. In the same way he said nothing when Heydrich told him he had been opposed to the anti-Semitic riots of the Night of Broken Glass and was only following his orders.

Another of Canaris's immediate problems was the growth of the Abwehr. Less than 11 weeks after Canaris took command, Hitler announced the resumption of conscription and the expansion of the army. The number of military districts jumped from 7 to 12, and each had an Abwehr post. Not only did the number of posts rise, but each one expanded. In the 1920s each had one or two officers. By 1937, the Munich post, as an example, had 10, plus soldiers, officials, and employees.

Canaris also oversaw the reversion of the Abwehr from the military's "sole intelligence-acquisition post," which it had been since 1928, back to a pure spy agency. In his first year, before this process began, the Abwehr Branch had six groups: I, army espionage; II, the Cipher Center; III, counterespionage; IV, sabotage and uprisings; V, naval espionage, including the liaison with the B-Dienst; VI, air force espionage. The departures of the Cipher Center and the Rowehl air reconnaissance group began stripping the branch of its non-espionage functions. A 1936 reorganization strengthened the espionage aspect by centralizing it. This placed Groups

I, V, and VI under the command of the Group I leader. At the same time, Group IV was renumbered VII and the B-Dienst liaison became Group IV. Group II was vacant. The trend toward espionage specialization culminated in a new organization of the agency on 1 June 1938, when it rose from a branch to a division—advanced in rank with other organs of the OKW, apparently to give the new command more prestige. Army, navy, and air force espionage became sections of a new branch, Abwehr I, which handled all spying for the armed forces. Group VII, sabotage and uprisings, became Abwehr II; Group III, counterespionage, became Abwehr III. The old Group II was abolished. Group IV, the B-Dienst liaison, moved to the Ausland (foreign) Branch, which was appended that same day to Canaris's division. Ausland originally handled international law and treaties affecting the armed forces. Gradually it added functions. It mainly distributed information on the foreign political situation, insofar as that touched on military matters, to the OKW. It evaluated the foreign press for the OKW. It maintained the OKW contact with the Foreign Office and served as liaison for Wehrmacht attachés abroad and foreign armed forces attachés in Berlin. Its chief from the summer of 1938 to the end of the war was Captain (later Vice-Admiral) Leopold Bürkner. In 1939, Canaris completed his internal arrangement by adding a Central Group at headquarters under Colonel Oster, he of the stained tennis pants, who thereby became Canaris's chief of staff. This group handled personnel, finances, and other administrative matters. One of its desks, for example, maintained the central agent files—large metal tubs whose covers opened at the top. Each agent was represented by a card or, if the file was voluminous, by an envelope.

Canaris's work embraced more than the internal running of his agency. Hitler used him as a personal emissary and information-gatherer. Canaris talked to the dictator of Rumania in Bucharest, the Spanish chief of staff and Franco in Madrid, Mussolini in Rome, and the Italian intelligence chief after Mussolini's fall. He argued for his agency against other units of government. After the fall of France, the Italians sought exclusive control of the French Mediterranean coast; Canaris urged German participation because ports there offered the best communications with North Africa and the rest of the world, needed by his agents. He lost that fight, but won another. An interministerial conference contended that Abwehr agents ought not visit North Africa disguised as businessmen because this increased French resistance to German economic activity. Canaris disputed that on the superior need for information about Allied activities to the south—and the Foreign Office relented.

Within his own sphere, assignments for the non-intelligence-gathering sections of the Abwehr distracted him from that phase of his work. He conferred with the Grand Mufti of Jerusalem on sabotage. He personally assumed the armed forces–Foreign Office liaison task of his Ausland unit when he reported to Army Chief of Staff Halder on a top American diplomat's visit to Rome and Berlin. Indeed, it sometimes seemed as if he provided information from spies less often than he did anything else. His frequent reports to high OKW officers seldom dealt with spy intelligence. He reported to Halder from time to time on the general situation, and he saw Hitler dozens of times. He attended a two-and-a-half-hour conference

Canaris's signature

to discuss the attack on the Belgian forts, such as the "impregnable" Eben Emael. He reported on Dutch uniforms for sabotage troops. During the Polish campaign Hitler asked what information there was from the west. Canaris said that the French were planning to attack at Saarbrücken, but Hitler rejected the news. "I cannot believe that the French would attack just in the Saarbrücken area, where our positions are the strongest." He was right. Another time he bawled out Canaris for telling the Italians something he shouldn't have.

Canaris, for his part, felt that "You can talk to the man. He is reasonable, and sees your point of view, if you point it out properly." For he was, until 1938, an exponent of Hitler. In an article published that year, he said semiautobiographically that "As the officer before the World War was naturally a monarchist . . . so it is naturally understandable today . . . to be a National Socialist. . . . The Wehrmacht is become the tool of the National Socialist will for development." A month before Hitler's Anschluss of Austria, he personally directed deception measures that created the impression of serious German military preparations for this aggression. A few weeks later, he told assembled I c officers that he expected them to act in a Nazi fashion and in effect told them that they would be punished if they crossed the party.

But then he began to turn from Naziism. His nature may have revolted against the humiliations of the Jews. He criticized the "degrading way" in which the SS had interrogated the army commander in chief on suspicion of homosexuality. Later he probably discovered that the charges, which compelled the man to resign, were actually a despicable party frame-up to get a more pro-Nazi man in. Perhaps most decisive was the arrival of two strongly anti-Nazi officers, one of them Oster, as two of his four immediate subordinates. Later, on the evening that England declared war on Germany, Canaris, with three subordinates, was visiting the home of the Gestapo official who handled counterintelligence. The official and his wife feared a long war; the Abwehr subordinates thought Germany would win quickly. Canaris said nothing. But it became evident to colleagues in the following weeks that he was deeply pessimistic about the war, probably because he regarded Germany as unready and doomed. This apparently clinched his opposition to the author of the destruction. He was soon counted as a member of the anti-Hitler resistance.

But he did nothing about it. For though he detested Hitler, he loved Germany. Working for Germany, however, meant furthering the Führer. This dilemma tormented him, changing him from a charming and sociable personality to a gloomy, nervous wreck, who took increasing refuge in his dogs and began drinking more than usual. His despair sometimes expressed itself indirectly, as was his fashion, when, after questioning a subordinate so thoroughly that the man came to doubt his information, he would say: "See, son, when you look at things very closely, nothing makes sense." He often compared himself to the Russian admiral who sailed bravely halfway around the world to battle the Japanese at Tsushima in 1905 though he knew defeat was certain. But he never faced his dilemma. He fled from it —physically and psychologically. He seized any pretext to rush across half the continent from one capital to another, from one field office to the next. Criticisms of his "constant absence" did not keep him at home. For in Munich or Madrid, Venice or Algeciras, he could not attend the daily conference at which he would have to decide whether to help Hitler or harm Germany, nor face the same problem in administrative matters, nor bring reports to the Führer and hate himself whether he won praise or blame. And when he was in Berlin and these problems confronted him, he evaded them. By 1942, he had delegated the task of making situation reports to the high OKW types to a subordinate. He avoided Hitler, never seeing him after the middle of the war, declining even the usually undeclinable invitations to dinner. He twisted, he turned, he dodged the basic decision. "He remained hesitant to the end," said one observer. Though one acquaintance likened him to Odysseus and another to the Wandering Jew, a profounder student saw him more clearly: "He was the Hamlet of conservative Germany."

His indecision led to professional and personal disaster, one because of inaction, the other in spite of it.

Even though his secret agency afforded innumerable opportunities, he never conspired to kill Hitler, or even to depose him. (At most he sheltered some resistance people.) He never betrayed secrets to the Allies. Yet his mere association with the opposition meant his arrest on 23 July 1944, three days after the bomb attempt on Hitler. For months his life, unlike that of the active conspirators, was spared. Only as the Third Reich itself neared its end did Hitler involve him in the general destruction. He was executed on 8 April 1945 at the prison in Flossenbürg, north of Munich, after having spent his last hours in reading Ernst Kantorowicz's magisterial life of Frederick II of Hohenstaufen, the greatest German emperor of the Middle Ages, the strongest battler against the power of the papacy and one of the most learned and lascivious men of his day, called "Stupor Mundi," the Amazement of the World, whose life contrasted so sharply with Canaris's own.

For his paralysis had destroyed his organization. His failure to build the Abwehr into a successful organization permitted its absorption by the RSHA in February 1944, with his dismissal and demotion to head a special staff for economic warfare. Canaris's good qualities, which at the start had seemed so valuable, never served or proved irrelevant. The highly touted cunning never once concocted a successful scheme of insurrection in enemy territories. The celebrated politico-military judgment did not operate within the scope of the Abwehr, and especially not under a Hitler. What the Abwehr needed for success were forceful leadership and managerial flair. It needed a chief who would fight other organizations for the best man instead of allowing his own to become a haven for dissidents, who would recognize the wastefulness of overlapping targets and assign each substation specific geographic areas, who would investigate his agents' ciphers and improve them, who would push the communications inspectorate to reduce the size and increase the range of agent radios. Canaris did none of these, or did them far too weakly. Instead he let his agency drift, especially in comparison with the zealous SD. The result was that long before the end the Abwehr had failed, and at the end it had even ceased to be.

For nearly all of the eight years that Canaris served as Abwehr head, his Branch I chief was Colonel Hans Piekenbrock, who thereby had the chief direct responsibility in the Third Reich for obtaining military information through spies. Piekenbrock was a grand seigneur. Scion of a rich Catholic family of Essen, he had joined the army as a cavalryman early in World War I and managed to stay in the post-Versailles army, serving in T 3 in 1928 and 1929. He came to the Abwehr as a major to head the old Group I on 1 October 1936, when it began supervising all spy activities, and half a year later, still optimistic over the Abwehr's potential, toured the Mediterranean with the military attaché in Belgrade, Faber du Faur, an old regimental comrade. When the war started, he was a month short of his 46th birthday, tall and dark, with a thinning hair and prominent ears, intelligent and cheerful, worldly, broad-minded. His irony covered his lack of energy. He was Canaris's closest collaborator and possibly his best friend: Canaris told him things that he said to no one else, and Piekenbrock caught on to his subtle jokes long before the others. He called

Canaris "Excellency," a title to which general officers had a right under the Kaiser. He seems to have concentrated on running his office, leaving to Canaris the external contacts, since only once in three years of war did he describe his work to Halder and only a handful of times did he appear at the OKW's Operations Staff. He occasionally got special assignments. Five days before the German invasion of Norway, he met Vidkun Quisling in Copenhagen. Piekenbrock was promoted to lieutenant colonel in 1937 and colonel in 1940, but to rise to general he had to command troops at the front. So toward the end of March 1943 he left the Abwehr, commanding first an infantry regiment and then the 208th Infantry Division, winning the coveted rank by August. He remained on the eastern front to the end.

Succeeding him as military spymaster was Colonel Georg Hansen, a quite different type. He was 38, blond, tall, slim, good-looking, who in contrast to the elegant Piekenbrock often buddied up to the enlisted men. He was sometimes loud and self-important and claimed to be able to do anything. Some thought him excessively ambitious. Helmut Maurer, Canaris's neighbor, was one, perhaps because of an incident when he was sent to get Hansen. It was at Piekenbrock's house in Berlin, and Hansen was sitting with the chauffeurs, swilling drinks. Suddenly he bellowed, "Maurer, I'm going to run you all down."

Hansen had been in intelligence since 1937, working in Foreign Armies, where he headed the desk studying the armies of the British Commonwealth, the United States, and others, and then in Foreign Armies East. From 1939 to 1941, he headed its Group I, which included most Balkan and Near Eastern countries. During May and June 1941, when German paratroopers invaded Crete, British forces attacked Vichy-controlled Syria, and anti-British elements revolted in Iraq, winning Hitler's promise of support, Hansen visited Syria and Iraq and reported directly a number of times to Halder and the OKW. In 1942, he was transferred to the Russian area, by then much more important, giving figures on Soviet battle strength to Halder. He retained a cool judgment. In Athens, during the victory celebrations that followed the German breakthrough of the Stalin line, he remarked to an Abwehr officer, "And how many Stalin lines are still to follow?"

After taking over from Piekenbrock, he ran Branch I for almost a year, until Canaris was removed. He was then named to command the entire Abwehr as a caretaker while it was being prepared for absorption by the RSHA, retaining his command of Branch I. When the RSHA took over in June 1944, he stayed as head of the rump Abwehr. But Hansen had actively conspired to kill Hitler. He met with some of the younger plotters on 16 July 1944 in the house of the man who, four days later, placed the bomb that exploded under Hitler's conference table. Four days after that, when he was in Würzburg visiting his wife, who was expecting their fifth child, a telegram summoned him to Kaltenbrunner's office. He lived six and a half weeks more.

The Abwehr had its offices in a block of former elegant houses on the Tirpitzufer, a tree-lined street on the north side of the Landwehr Canal. Their official entrance was through the adjacent four-story sandstone building at Tirpitzufer 72–76 that housed the OKM and had housed defense ministries since Kaiser Wilhelm II's reign. All the structures had rear corridors connecting with the rambling armed forces headquarters on the Bendlerstrasse, which ran north at right angles from the Tirpitzufer. The Abwehr buildings comprised a warren of hallways, staircases, former dining rooms, kitchens, maid's rooms, bedrooms, and living rooms—quite unsuited for offices. Canaris, however, never wanted to move. His own office, guarded by an outer office with two secretaries, had a balcony that faced the canal. Of modest size, the office was furnished sparsely with a desk, a sofa, a few filing cabinets, and a cot. On the wall hung a map of the world, photographs of his predecessors and of Francisco Franco, with a long inscription, and a Japanese painting of a grimacing demon given him by the Japanese military attaché. Here Canaris worked, held his meetings of the "Column," and here he sometimes napped after lunch. But increasing bombing of Berlin compelled the Abwehr, like so many other agencies, to quit the capital. On 19 April 1943, it moved out to the army headquarters at Zossen, some 20 miles south of Berlin.

The Abwehr headquarters completed its organizational development on 18 October 1939, a month and a half after the outbreak of the war. It rose to a full department. Its three Abwehr branches remained individually subordinate to Canaris but were generally referred to collectively as the Abwehr.

Branch I, espionage, was the largest and most important. In March of 1943 it had 63 officers in the Berlin central as compared to 34 in Branch II, sabotage, and 43 in III, counterespionage. Seven of its groups oversaw espionage in the enemy areas for which they were named: I H Ost (I Heer Ost, or I army east) and I H West, divided on a line running east of Norway and Italy according to the countries in which the agents worked, not according to the countries the information dealt with, I Ht (Heerestechnik, or army, technical), I M (Marine), I L (Luftwaffe), I T/Lw (Technik/Luftwaffe), and I Wi (Wirtschaft, or economy). Branch I did not, except very occasionally, run agents, nor did it generally direct the operations of the espionage units in the field. Basically, it coordinated. It forwarded requests for information from other agencies to the proper Abwehr field unit for spying out. When the answers came in, it sent them to the requesting agency. It did not evaluate them except to throw out the blatantly useless ones. It did decide questions beyond the competence of the field units: it might order the reorganization of a ring if its chief was suspected of being in danger; it sometimes decided on whether a ring should be allowed to buy a car, or inquired whether certain jobs were finished and whether others were possible, or questioned rings on expenses, or arranged passwords between agents of different field units. It took care of the requests of the field units for personnel and for supplies. In this work, it had the support of two groups: I G (Geheim, or secret), which forged documents and produced invisible inks, microdots, and other paraphernalia of espionage, and I i for communications.

It was the Abwehr field units that really ran the spying. Each of the 21 military districts had its Ast, short for "Abwehrstelle," or Abwehr post, usually housed in the district headquarters building, such as the three-story gray concrete structure near the dead end of the tree-lined Sophienterrasse, in the quiet residential section of Harvesthude, for Military District X, Hamburg. The bigger Asts had three kinds of subsidiary units: subposts, which were really smaller Asts; outposts, whose functions were more limited; and, during the war, report centers, which helped the agents of an Ast reach their areas of operation and report from them. During the war, this system expanded to the occupied territories. New categories of units sprang up. In theaters, the Abwehr post was called a main post. Very small units were called "outstations" or "suboutposts." By the spring of 1942, at approximately the time of Nazi Germany's greatest conquests, the Abwehr had 33 posts (including two main posts), 26 subposts, and 23 outposts. (This excludes the organization, headed by the Abwehr Main Post East, in the only combatant zone then to have an Abwehr organization—the eastern front.) Posts rose and fell in rank during the war. Cherbourg, in 1942 a three-man counterespionage outstation, was elevated to an outpost with the threat of invasion in 1944. Thessaloniki, once a full post, fell to a suboutpost. And as Germany lost territory, units were dissolved.

The organization of the Abwehr posts and of the subposts reproduced that of Abwehr headquarters. Each had elements I, II, and III for espionage, sabotage, and counterintelligence, and its subdivisions likewise corresponded to those at headquarters. On an average, each Ast and its dependencies had 150 persons working in it, though the individual figures for each geographically separate unit ranged from 3, as at Cherbourg, to 382 at Paris.

Though these Asts were attached administratively to their local military authorities, for operations they were subordinated directly to Canaris himself. The inability of any one man to effectively supervise 33 widely scattered units, and Canaris's disinclination to do so, virtually left the posts on their own. Some did not even dispatch agents: Königsberg, Kassel, Posen, and Danzig, for example. The only coordination of the others came from the loosely observed principle that Asts operate against the foreign territories opposite them. Dresden worked against Czechoslovakia, Stuttgart and Wiesbaden against France, Hamburg against Great Britain and the United States. But personal interests dislocated even these crude guidelines. The officers at Munich sought economic intelligence in the Balkans to the exclusion of almost everything else, though neither Munich's geographical

ABWEHR POSTS, SUBPOSTS, AND OUTPOSTS

Spring 1942

Army District	Abwehr post	Subpost	Outpost[1]
I	Königsberg[2]		Ziechenau[3]
			Bialystok
II	Stettin[4]		
III	Berlin[5]		
IV	Dresden		
V	Stuttgart	Lörrach	Säckingen
		Bregenz	Constance
		Strasbourg	
VI	Münster	Cologne	
VII	Munich		
VIII	Breslau[6]	Kattowitz[7]	
IX	Kassel	Frankfurt-am-Main	Weimar
X	Hamburg	Bremen	
		Flensburg	
XI	Hanover		
XII	Wiesbaden	Metz	Kaiserslautern
			Saarbrücken
			Luxembourg
XIII	Nuremberg		
XVII[8]	Vienna		
XVIII	Salzburg		Graz
			Klagenfurt
			Innsbruck
XX	Danzig		Bromberg
XXI	Posen[9]		Litzmannstadt[10]
—	Kiel[11]	Swinemünde	
—	Wilhelmshaven[11]		
—	Prague	Brünn	
—	Cracow	Warsaw	
		Lemberg[12]	
—	Copenhagen	Aarhus	
—	Norway	Bergen	
		Drontheim	
		Tromsoe	

nor its economic position justified this. At Dresden, the energetic I Wi leader, Lieutenant Colonel Thilo Daehne, gained so much economic intelligence through his agents in Spain and Turkey that he soon won promotion. With his departure the Ast's work collapsed.

Army District	Abwehr post	Subpost	Outpost[1]
—	Netherlands		
—	Brussels	Lille	
		Boulogne	
—	Paris[13]	Orleans	
—	Angers		Brest
—	——	Bordeaux[14]	Biarritz
			Poitiers
			Angoulême
			La Rochelle
—	Dijon	Nancy	
—	Lyons	Toulouse	Limoges
—	Athens[13]		Crete
—	Saloniki[15]	Mytilene	Dimotika[16]
—	Belgrade		
—	Estonia	Reval[17]	Kauen[18]
			Minsk
—	Ukraine	Nikolayev	Kiev

1   may depend from either Abwehr post or subpost
2   now Kaliningrad
3   now Cieche; formerly also called Züchen
4   now Szczecin
5   not the same as Abwehr headquarters
6   now Wroclaw
7   now Katowice
8   no army districts XIV, XV, XVI, or XIX; the numbers had been used before the war for training staffs
9   now Poznan
10 now Lódź
11 not attached to any army district; worked with navy
12 now Lvov
13 Abwehr main post. The Abwehr post rose to an Abwehr main post in theaters —technically those areas in which authority was vested in a commander in chief, as distinguished from those areas in which it was vested in an armed forces commander, an army group commander, or a civilian agency. Paris served the commander in chief west; Athens, the commander in chief southeast. The commander in chief south, in Rome, employed, instead of a main post, a liaison officer to Italian military intelligence. The eastern theater, which was run by the OKH, also had a main post.
14 apparently independent
15 local name: Thessaloniki
16 local name: Didymoteikhon
17 now Tallin
18 now Kaunas

These fluctuations, plus the overlapping that stemmed from the almost total lack of central control, precluded any orchestration of the Asts. Each played its own tune, on its own instrument.

Berlin (the Ast, not Abwehr headquarters): Mainly Jewish and Swiss agents for both military and economic espionage, in no particular area; its agents worked against widely spaced targets. When its active Branch I head was transferred to Paris in 1944, its operations rapidly fell apart.

Stuttgart: Able officers and local business houses with good foreign commercial contacts (Stuttgart was the "capital" of Germans abroad) gave it high-grade agents. After the fall of France, it built up a network in Spain and Portugal for economic and military espionage.

Münster: Military and air-technical intelligence. It maintained a unit at Hendaye on the French-Spanish frontier for collecting reports from agents in Spain. But its subpost at Cologne, which concentrated on economic intelligence and was run by Lieutenant Colonel Focke, overshadowed it.

Breslau: Czechoslovakia and Poland; then some economic espionage in the Balkans and Turkey.

Hamburg: Great Britain and British territories and the United States, chiefly for naval, secondarily for military and technical-economic intelligence. Its naval emphasis stemmed from its location in a port and the navy membership of the versatile, erudite, and reliable leader of the post, Captain Herbert Wichmann, and of the leaders of the subposts. Its Anglo-Saxon targets derived in part from a tradition going back to World War I, in part from the expertise of its radiomen in overseas communications. In addition to agents in the United Kingdom and the United States, it maintained networks in Latin America, reporting on Allied shipping and war effort, in Turkey, reporting on British military dispositions in the Near East, and in Spain and Portugal, and later in Spanish Morocco, the Balearics, and the French Riviera. It operated on a larger scale than any other Abwehr post and was therefore larger than most.

Vienna: Balkans and Middle East; penetrated Rumanian political and military circles through local Germans; used tobacco firms in Turkey as espionage cover.

Salzburg: Almost totally ineffectual.

This inefficient and rudderless system had but one advantage: security. Penetration of one Ast's net of agents would not lead to the heart of the organization. But this was bought at a heavy price.

The Abwehr posts in the occupied territories primarily recruited agents for the others, dispatching them rarely. Their work never attained the importance of that of the domestic Asts.

In only one allied country did the Abwehr have an Abwehr post: in Rumania, which was legally independent but virtually occupied, with half a million German troops in it to enforce its cooperation. (Another special case was Vichy France and its colonies and dependencies overseas, especially North Africa. The Abwehr operated against them from a section within the German armistice commission in Wiesbaden, with outstations in French territory.) In all other allied and neutral countries, the Ast, with its open military affiliations, did not exist. The Abwehr station was called a Kriegsorganisation (War Organization), or KO. One of the first began when Canaris went to Spain on 5 February 1937—in the middle of the civil war —to raise an Abwehr organization there. A small post came into life in Shanghai around the end of that year because of the Sino-Japanese War. One was set up in the Netherlands in 1938. But most of the KOs apparently started during the war.

By May 1942, 10 existed: the KOs Portugal, Spain, Switzerland, Sweden, Finland, Bulgaria, Zagreb (for a puppet Croatian state), North Africa (in Casablanca), Near East (in Ankara), and Far East (in Shanghai). Like the Abwehr posts, their internal organization reproduced that of Abwehr headquarters, they depended directly from Canaris, and they maintained outside units. The KO Spain had a total of 30, a few large but mostly small sections in Spanish harbors.

In an overlap that typified the confusion and duplication of Abwehr work, the KOs did not have exclusive control of Abwehr activities in their territory. The Abwehr posts often dispatched their agents through a KO country to their ultimate destination. Sometimes Ast officers would accompany them. Many posts and outposts maintained permanent representatives in KO countries, working under commercial cover, such as the representatives of Cologne in Madrid and Lisbon, of Vienna in Turkey. Some worked closely with the KO; some remained independent, with their own connections to the parent post. Moreover, both Asts and Abwehr Branch I—especially their economic and air-technical sections—sent businessmen on short trips to KO countries to carry out espionage assignments there. The KOs may not have liked this interference in their own territories, but they put up with it and lent assistance as long as they were informed. Later in the war, however, they clashed increasingly with the Asts and forced them to curtail their activities in neutral countries more and more.

For the KOs faced a problem different from all other agencies of the Abwehr: they depended upon the clemency of the host country. Canaris and the Foreign Office had agreed to "build in" the KO personnel to the diplomatic service. This openness gave them immunity and other privileges. The KO quartered itself in the German embassy, for example, sometimes, as in Spain, spilling over into other buildings having diplomatic protection. Its larger outposts were frequently housed in consulates. KO Spain's worked out of the German consulates in San Sebastian, Barcelona, Seville, Tetuán in Morocco, and Spanish Morocco. Though the personnel were mostly servicemen, they wore civilian clothes.

Early in the war this caused no difficulty. The host countries did not

PERSONNEL DISTRIBUTION OF ABWEHR POST HAMBURG
1 April 1942

	officers	officials	noncoms	men	employees
Command Group					
post leader	1				
office chief	1				
paymasters		2			
registry chief		1			
registry personnel					4
office supervisors					2
cashiers					2
index chief					1
index personnel					3
technical employee [photography, drawing]					1
photographer's assistant					1
draftsman					1
telephone personnel					4
teleprinter personnel					4
clerks					36
noncommissioned officer for transportation			1		
drivers				7	
motorcyclist				1	
bicyclists				2	
Group I [espionage]					
leader	1				
assistant officer	1				
specialists	7				
assistants	11				
air force engineers		3			
specialist for ship inquiry service	1				
chief radioman			1		
assistants					2
economic inquiry specialist					1
translator and assistant					1
technical radio employees					2

Radio Center					
leader	1				
assistant (also translator)	1				
I M [navy] worker	1				
first sergeant			1		
chief radioman			1		
radiomen			20	72	
drivers				2	
motorcyclist				1	
radio maintenance man					1
[*no Group II*]					
Group III [counter-intelligence]	26			4	15
Bremen Subpost					
leader	1				
specialists	4				
assistants	5				
paymaster		1			
state police official		1			
adjutants (also for person surveillance)				4	
drivers				3	
assistants					2
translator and assistant					1
cashier					1
registry and office work					3
assistant with language ability					1
photographer					1
telephone personnel					3
clerks					10
Flensburg Subpost					
specialists	2				
driver				1	
clerks					2
TOTALS:	64	8	24	97	105
GRAND TOTAL: 298					

PERSONNEL AND THEIR DUTIES IN KO SPAIN
June 1944

Number of people

Kriegs-Organisation Leader　　　　　　　　　　　　3
Commander Gustav Leisner (command of the organization)
Fräulein Häupel (secretary, mail)
Frau Obermüller (agent card catalogue, secret documents, visitors)

Group I [espionage]　　　　　　　　　　　　　　3
Lieutenant Colonel Eberhard Kieckebusch (leadership of Group I
　and subordinated posts, basic intelligence assignments, process-
　ing of incoming I-area information)
Reserve Lieutenant Wilhelm Oberbeil (adjutant, assistant for spe-
　cial duties)
Fräulein Meyer-Quittlingen (secretary, mail, registry).

Kühlenthal Desk　　　　　　　　　　　　　　　6
Specialist-Captain Karl-Erich Kühlenthal (recruiting and con-
　trol of the most important KO links—England, U.S.A., Canada,
　Portugal, North Africa, Gibraltar, France)
Corporal Gustav Knittel (office manager, main interpreter, chief
　translator)
Private Knappe (leader of the external service; control, prepara-
　tion, and recruiting of agents)
Private Zierath (processing of incoming reports, interpreter, ex-
　ternal service)
Fräulein Mann (secretary, secret ink developer, cipher work)
Fräulein Heinsohn (correspondence)

Subgroup I Army　　　　　　　　　　　　　　4
Reserve First Lieutenant Dr. Schöne (control of assignments, eval-
　uation and forwarding of incoming reports from agents in all
　enemy countries, situation map)
Specialist-Captain Constantin Canaris [a nephew of the admiral]
　(evaluating and forwarding of incoming reports from France
　and North Africa)
Fräulein Preusse (registry of all enemy troop units, correspon-
　dence)
Fräulein Spindler (correspondence)

Subgroup I Navy　　　　　　　　　　　　　　10
Commander Baltzer (leader of the subgroup and of the outposts
　in Spanish harbors)
Lieutenant Commander Gaber (support of and deputy to the
　leader, especially in agent matters and emergency interro-
　gations)
Corporal Bugge (evaluator, office chief, guard duty)

Number of
people

Corporal Steinbrüggen (card catalogue of agents on land and on
all Spanish ships, guard duty)
Private Otto (handling of convoys, guard duty)
Private First Class Kuttner (evaluation of incoming reports, guard
duty)
Private Sick (correspondence, guard duty)
Fräulein Walters (secretary)
Fräulein Goldel (preparation of courier post)
Fräulein Brumm (clerk)

Subgroup I Technical/Luftwaffe   3
Air Staff Engineer Dr. Weiss (technical air inquiries in U.S.A. and
England, investigating emergency-landed enemy airplanes in
Spain)
Special-Lieutenant Collmann (running technical agents)
Frau Bakker (clerk)

Subgroup I Air   (*attached to
air attaché*)
Colonel von Wenckstern

I i Desk [communications]
radiomen   34
female cipher clerks   10

I G Desk [fake documents]   3
Dr. Künkele (processing of documents, preparation of rubber
stamps and copies)
Employee Lamprecht (photo laboratory, photocopy laboratory,
training of agents in secret inks, development and testing of
inks)
Frau Kirschner (assistance in secret inks, photographs, repro-
ductions)

Group II [sabotage]   3

Group III [counterintelligence]   5

Administration   3
Senior Staff Paymaster Franzbach (supplying the KO with all
necessary foreign currencies, checking of accounts, payments,
purchases, passport matters, and leader of the administrative
staff at the Barcelona, Tetuán, and Seville outposts)
Staff Paymaster Zimmer (cashier and deputy of the chief)
Private First Class Pfau (checking of all accounts of the central
post and 30 outposts; car pool)

TOTAL   87

protest when the local KO worked almost openly, because they feared Germany. The German missions did not mind the small Abwehr units. When Piekenbrock, noting in December 1941 that the entry of the United States into the war had reduced the reporting base, warned the Foreign Office that the Abwehr might request the building-in of more personnel, the Foreign Office consented. But it did not expect the enormous expansion that followed. The growing threat of Allied offensives swelled the Abwehr. Eventually the KO Spain had 87 members in Madrid alone—every one carrying a diplomatic passport. In addition, various other agencies, such as OKW radio intercept teams, attachés, and the RSHA, raised the number of built-in diplomatic personnel in Madrid to 315—almost double the embassy total of 171!

This caused friction, at first within the missions. In 1944, the minister in Stockholm protested against the swollen Abwehr organization on the ground that it was endangering his work. Half the KO command staff of 10 men could go without endangering intelligence results, he said. Elsewhere, mission chiefs complained that they did not always hear of Abwehr personnel before they arrived, did not always know the full extent of the local Abwehr organization, and did not always see the Abwehr reports—all of which they had the right to do.

Gradually the negative side of diplomatic immunity became apparent: the KO personnel had no cover and, unlike secret operatives, could be expelled simply on demand of the host country. As the war turned against Germany, and as the Allies exerted increasing pressure against the neutrals, such demands increased. The KOs spent more and more of their time arguing with the host foreign ministry. But the result was inevitable. By October of 1944, Spain had ousted 82 of the 149 persons on a list submitted by the Allies. In the end, the KO's chief advantage—working from neutral territory—had largely vanished, and with it disappeared much of the organization's value.

The Berlin headquarters, the Asts, and the KOs did not yet exhaust the Abwehr organization. It put units into combat areas to run front agents—those who collected information within the combat zone and its dependent areas.

The Abwehr set up such units with the start of the war against Poland. It found them effective there as well as in France and Yugoslavia. Their activities extended beyond agent control to seizing caches of enemy documents and interrogating prisoners. But in the Russian campaign the Abwehr generally restricted itself to spying. Canaris ordered that "columns" of 25 agents be attached to each army group and army. The columns consisted of two troops, one short- and one long-range. The short-range line-crossers reconnoitered up to 30 miles behind enemy lines and brought back tactical information. The other agents, chiefly Poles, Russians, and Ukrainians, wearing enemy uniforms and traveling in captured cars equipped with radios, drove 30 to 200 miles behind the front seeking operational intelligence.

To control all Abwehr work on this front, Canaris founded an Abwehr Main Post East. At the head of its espionage, or I, branch, he put Major Hermann Baun, a short, thin, chain-smoking ex-infantryman who had been born in Odessa in 1897, spoke Ukrainian as well as Russian, and had come to Abwehr I at the start of the war. After several months of preparation, Baun took up quarters three days before the German attack in the village of Suleyovek near Warsaw. His post was codenamed WALLI I (WALLI II and III handled the Branch II and III aspects of Abwehr work). WALLI I advanced with the German armies, but later settled down in a sprawling former vacation boarding house on the wooded shores of Lake Spirding (now Lake Sniardwy, Poland), close to the Führer headquarters at Rastenburg (now Ketrzyn). Eventually WALLI I had some 500 men, including the Russian volunteer assistants.

By that time the Abwehr front organization had, after some changes, evolved into two levels. Each army group had an Abwehr command. It mainly ran the long-range agents, who by now did not drive into but were parachuted deep into enemy territory to obtain information requested by the army group I c. Each army had an Abwehr troop for the line-crossers. These units were designated by 3-digit numbers beginning with 1, indicating that the unit worked in the Abwehr I domain. (The Abwehr II and III units had 3-digit numbers beginning with 2 or 3.)

Similar organizations later existed in Italy (southern theater) and in Greece (southeastern theater). In France (western theater), Canaris converted the stationary Abwehr posts and their subunits to movable elements on the eastern pattern in February of 1944, as the invasion threat loomed. The Abwehr main post in Paris added the word "West" to its name to parallel WALLI I's formal title and so became the Abwehr Main Post West. The Abwehr posts and outposts in France became Abwehr commands and troops. From Paris on down, they shifted to the operational control of the I cs of the commander in chief west, the army groups, and the armies. Their agents were divided. Those in German-occupied countries remained under the control of the units in France; those in neutral or enemy lands were shifted to the Asts in Hamburg, Cologne, Wiesbaden, and Stuttgart. The units in France now concentrated on finding, training, and placing agents who would stay behind and radio back information when the Allies advanced past them. About the middle of May, with the invasion nigh, the intelligence officers ordered the Abwehr units to their battle stations. Army Group B's Abwehr Command 130, for example, moved from Paris west to Mantes-la-Jolie on the Seine.

In June 1944 most of the Abwehr was attached to the RSHA. The frontline espionage organizations in all theaters, however, remained in the

Wehrmacht. They were administratively subordinated to the OKW's Operations Staff I c. At first they were just in its Branch I, later under a fancier chief of front reconnaissance and troop counterintelligence. In the summer, after the invasion, and after a name change that replaced the defensive-sounding element "Abwehr-" with the more neutral "Frontaufklärungs-" ("front reconnaissance"), 1 front reconnaissance main post, 5 commands, and 13 troops flecked the map of France. But together with the front reconnaissance units in the east, these last Wehrmacht holdouts were transferred to the RSHA on 1 December 1944 as Branch F of its Military Department (the former Abwehr).

About 9,200 officers and men worked in these units. When to this was added the several hundred at Abwehr headquarters, an estimated 1,000 in the KOs, the 5,000 at the Abwehr posts (less the 2,000 in the west who became front reconnaissance personnel), the number of persons in the Abwehr on an average totaled more than 13,000. This was, in military terms, a little less than a division. But it was surely more than the number of Abwehr spies.

Apparat

O N 28 July 1934, an utterly average man became the first member and first head of Nazi party foreign intelligence.

His height and weight were ordinary: five feet six inches, 154 pounds. His looks were unprepossessing. His personality was unobtrusive: a bit reserved but friendly. He was easily influenced and did not stand up to superiors. His creative abilities were not outstanding. No great ambition drove him. Capping these qualifications was the fact that he had never once been outside Germany.

He was Heinz Maria Karl Jost, 30 years old, a lawyer. He had been born in a village some 60 miles north of Frankfurt, Holzhausen, where his father was a druggist. He was a boy of 10 when all Germany celebrated the euphoric start of what became known as World War I; he was an impressionable adolescent of 14 when the German defeat mocked his dreams. "The experiences of the First World War, the loss of that war, and the postwar years awakened my interest in all questions concerned with my fatherland," he said later. Jost's political ponderings crystallized in his last year of law school. He concluded that the working class, whom he believed he had come to know while playing sports with them in high school, had been excluded from German society by his own "exclusive, narrow, and conceited" bourgeoisie. At the same time that he saw this rift, he first became aware of the National Socialist German Workers' Party—the Nazis. Other political parties had long ago seen this and other ills of German society, but Jost turned away from their more moderate solutions and embraced instead Hitler's extreme, nationalist, anti-Semitic program. He became a Nazi on 1 February 1928 with the relatively low membership number of 75,946.

He performed various volunteer chores for the party—distributing leaflets, handling cash, administering local affairs, running local propaganda—

while working at various legal jobs in several town courts. He had passed his bar and had risen to a lawyer's post, still in the Hessian civil service, when Hitler became chancellor. Six weeks later, when the Nazis took over the government of the province of Hesse, a Nazi friend of Jost's, who became a top Hessian police official, named Jost to the job of police director in Worms, a historic but smallish German city. Soon the friend transferred him to Giessen, much closer to home. But the friend lost a battle with a higher Nazi and was fired. So, later, were many of his friends, including Jost—he on the excuse that he could not quell a fight in Giessen between the police and the brown-shirted SA, the party's street army which he had joined in 1929. The party soon found him a job in Berlin with its German Labor Front.

His friend, meanwhile, had gone to work for the Sicherheitsdienst, the SD, the Nazi party intelligence organization. Its head was the sinister Reinhard Heydrich, whose career was then gaining irresistible momentum in its rocketlike rise to the pinnacles of Nazi power: in the summer of 1934, soon after Jost had come to Berlin, he had won for his SD a monopoly as the sole party intelligence service. His next step was to augment his power by seizing areas of government responsibility for this party organ. The area he chose to invade first was that of protecting against foreign intelligence services. That the Abwehr and one of his own agencies, the Prussian secret state police, were already doing this work did not faze him. While casting about for someone for the new assignment, he heard about Jost from Jost's old friend. Jost was university educated, a lawyer—just the kind of bright young man that the expanding SD, with its pretensions to being the élite of the élite, was hiring. He was still a bachelor—free to put in long hours. He had joined the party before it had come to power; he was pleasant and intelligent enough. But he had neither drive nor creativity nor experience abroad. Why then did Heydrich choose him? Precisely because Jost lacked these things. He threatened Heydrich the less: Heydrich's apparatus was not yet the omnipotent terror it was to become and he did not want to risk losing control to anyone. So he offered the job to the utterly average man, and on 28 July 1934 Jost joined the SD as an SS major and embarked in a most modest way upon a most momentous enterprise.

His ostensible task was not—at first—to send spies abroad. It was to hinder foreign intelligence services. For this he was to study "their history, their organization, their modus operandi, their methods, job assignments, and similar questions." Industry, regarded as the most likely target, provided most of the actual protection from these putative enemy agents; the SD merely advised. The thinness of the work did not stop Heydrich from creating, sometime before 1936, Branch III, Ausland, of the SD under Jost's actual, if not formal, command, which came later. This thinness probably stemmed from the dependency of the SD on the party treasury, never as brimming as the government's. It also suggested that Heydrich was less interested in forestalling foreign agents than in amassing domestic power. For he had assigned Jost other tasks as well. He gave him a government job in the Gestapo office: deputy chief of counterintelligence (the chief was Jost's old friend from Hesse). He made him leader of the commission that sailed to Spain and concluded a cooperation agreement with Franco's police. Later he put him in charge of a combined SD-Gestapo unit for the march into Czechoslovakia. Though these jobs kept Jost from devoting full time to counterespionage, they fortified his position, and hence Heydrich's.

The internal power struggles so occupied Jost that, during the first five years of what was then the SD Administration's Ausland Branch, it mounted no major effort to spy on foreign countries. At best, some SD posts near Germany's frontiers set up informer networks run by acquaintances in foreign countries. Stuttgart, for example, had a Branch III desk for this. Whatever coordination there was of this by Branch III was handled by Jost's chief assistant, Dr. Alfred Filbert, a law-school comrade of Jost's and another of the SD's generation of young intellectuals.

On 1 September 1939, Hitler invaded Poland. Heydrich at once dispatched Jost on yet another special mission: to serve with an army staff as civil administrator for the occupied territories. But hostilities suddenly made espionage important and exposed the inadequacies of Branch III. Though Heydrich had himself been largely responsible for these, he nevertheless sharply criticized Branch III. The foreign reports, he told Filbert, who was deputizing for Jost at a meeting of department heads during the Polish campaign, were nothing more than a poor conglomeration of newspaper clippings and broadcast reports. He demanded that the work be improved and that only information gleaned directly from intelligence activity be submitted to him.

Upon Jost's return in mid-October, he found that his counterespionage function had been discontinued, that he no longer had his Gestapo post, and that his Branch III had been transformed into Department VI of the new Reichssicherheitshauptamt (Reich Security Administration), or RSHA, a half-party (SD), half-government (security police) agency, headed by Heydrich.

Impelled then by the outbreak of hostilities, released from his Gestapo duties, strengthened by the new organization, liberated by a Himmler-Ribbentrop agreement from diplomatic control, and spurred by Heydrich, Jost began in the middle of a war a task enormously, heartbreakingly difficult even in peace: creating an espionage organization to spy in belligerent countries. He reorganized his department, RSHA VI, dividing it into uncoordinate groups and desks. To these he assigned characters in the arcane numerology of the Third Reich. Thus VI G 2 referred to the U.S. desk —the VI for RSHA Department VI, the G for the northwest group in that department, and the 2 for the American desk in that group. Jost had five geographic groups, while Group A, headed by Filbert, had supervisory, liaison, and radio intelligence functions, Group B handled technical matters, such as communications and false papers, and Group H reconnoitered "conceptual enemies abroad"—Jews, Freemasons, political churches, Marxists, monarchists, and emigrants.

The Department VI pay checks, signed—since it was a Nazi agency—by the party treasurer, were smaller than those for equivalent government posts. Since the men with experience in handling informants all held government jobs in various police departments and were disinclined to give them up for something paying less, Jost had to fill his office with clever university graduates who, bewitched by the Nazi philosophy and attracted by the SD's intellectual nature and promise of status, would work for idealism instead of money. Many such earnest young men had streamed to the SD in the 1930s. Jost himself was one; so was Filbert.

Their youthful inexperience and know-it-all superciliousness, as well as their administrative training and background, often led, however, to dilettantism and inadequacy in SD foreign intelligence. Compounding the problem of obtaining realistic information from abroad were the qualifications that Himmler had required of SD men since 1938. The first three were: "1. German or similar blood; 2. Possession of German citizenship; 3. Unconditional political trustworthiness." Never mentioned was objectivity in evaluating information. Heydrich intensified this attitude when he declared that the goal of training was "an SS attitude in word and deed" and that "Purely scientific and military training stands second to this." To these obstacles to intelligence success were added insufficiency of time, men, and money, the handicaps created by hostilities, such as closed frontiers and spy fever in enemy countries, and, finally, the personality of the SD foreign intelligence chief, Jost himself. The negative characteristics that Heydrich had first wanted could not attain the positive results that Heydrich now needed. Nor could they achieve victories in the vital battles for dominance within the Reich. In particular, Jost had not provided Heydrich with enough support in an invasion of Ribbentrop's turf. Heydrich had just gotten rid of Jost's old patron from Hesse, whose legalisms had hampered Heydrich's power drives. Now it was Jost's turn.

As this became clear, the vultures of the RSHA began to peck. Heinrich Müller, the head of the Gestapo, which was Department IV of the RSHA, sought to get Department VI to work for it. Jost refused, saying that was not his job. Müller impugned him as "separatist" and "politically unreliable." In June 1940, the RSHA personnel chief, with whom the Gestapo head used the intimate "du" form of address, came to Jost's office and cut off funds. Heydrich supported the attacks, since he had a protégé whom he wanted to put into Jost's job. In February or March of 1941, as Jost still hung on, Heydrich told him that if he could not assure the political reliability of his wife, a non-Nazi, he certainly could not assure that of his department. Under this bombardment, Jost's work further deteriorated—and so did his health. Heydrich and the others told him that, really, he wanted to get out. He definitely wanted to get away from Heydrich, but he was reluctant to relinquish his power. A few days before the invasion of Russia, Heydrich, claiming that Jost's health made it impossible for him to carry the burdens of his duties, assigned his young protégé as Jost's deputy and acting chief of the department. It was the end for Jost, though he remained nominal department head for a while. He later left Berlin to command an einsatzkommando, one of the Nazi units that cleansed the conquered eastern territories for Germany by liquidating thousands of subhumans— Jews, Poles, and Russian partisans.

The protégé who replaced him was Walter Schellenberg. At 31, he had become head of the party foreign intelligence service and the youngest department chief in the RSHA. He was the Benjamin of the SD. Who was he, and how had he achieved such power?

Walter Schellenberg was born in Saarbrücken, in the southwestern corner of Germany that touches Luxembourg, on 16 January 1910. He was the seventh child of a piano manufacturer. The Allied occupation of the Saar at the end of World War I drove his family to Luxembourg, and the depression badly hurt his father's business and compelled young Schellenberg to abandon the study of medicine for that of law, which promised more immediate and more regular pay in a government job. Like Jost and many others of the future young SD generation, he had been deeply affected by Germany's loss of World War I and its disastrous economic consequences. Unlike them, however, he did not join the Nazi party before it came to power—a delay that later blemished his prestige. Only when he sought a government-supported job did he realize the importance of membership. He applied for membership in both the party and the SS, which he regarded as an élite for "elegant people." Curiously, he was accepted first in the SS, and a month later, on 1 May 1933, in the party, with membership number 3,504,508.

At his university, Bonn, he spoke at Nazi party meetings. After one of his lectures, two professors in SS uniform recruited him for the SD. His reports on "professional, political, and personal associations" at the university attracted Heydrich's attention. In 1935, Heydrich brought him to SD headquarters in Berlin. At first he still wanted to become a lawyer for one of the giant industries of the Ruhr and dealt a lot with economic questions. He came to appreciate the need for information from abroad. He began to collect books on espionage. Gradually he began to aim at becoming head of the SD's foreign intelligence service. But Jost, only a few years older than he, was there. So Schellenberg moved instead into counterespionage. This was a government police job; he was a middle-level civil servant. He viewed it, however, merely as an apprenticeship. In 1934, he got his first foreign-intelligence assignment: Paris, to check on a professor's political views. Three years later, he went to Italy. Though this trip was a police assignment—he was in charge of security for a forthcoming Mussolini visit to Berlin—Schellenberg took the opportunity to gather some intelligence on Italian foreign policy. During the Mussolini visit, he drew attention to himself by doing an excellent job in security. The following year, he created for Heydrich's use during the occupation of Czechoslovakia units that, for the first time in Nazi Germany, combined government and party personnel; Jost headed one in the invasion of Czechoslovakia. Perhaps inspired by this, Heydrich a few months later ordered preparations for the massive application of this principle that would so increase and solidify his power: the merger of the SD and the plainclothes political and criminal police into the Reichssicherheitshauptamt. He had Schellenberg suggest ways of organizing the proposed new agency, and Schellenberg came up with arrangements having five and seven departments before evolving the final one, with six.

This work also gave Schellenberg an opportunity to think about intelligence work systematically. He once wrote, for example, that SD intelligence comprised three activities. Gathering intelligence, done through agents at "the front line of the SD," called for "special skill in handling men" on the part of the SD member. Evaluation required "above all political maturity and experience." Scientific research used specialists to investigate an area purely objectively, "without being informed of the political-intelligence intention and goal." Schellenberg wrote his memoranda in a calm, well-organized, and fairly clear style, with little of the clotted phraseology typical of Heydrich and Canaris and without the shrillness common to much of the Nazi rhetoric: his anti-Semitic comments seem almost pro forma.

During this time, however, Schellenberg was suffering from marital difficulties. While a 21-year-old student, he had met Käthe Kortekamp, a sweet-faced seamstress three years older than himself. They began living together, and her needle helped support him while he was going to university. Finally, after seven years, they married. But Schellenberg was rising in the world, and a socially inferior wife did not help. He complained of her slovenly attitude, her dowdy dress, her poor handwriting, her bad spelling and grammar, her deliberate attempts to disparage him. His colleagues' wives deprecated him because of her, he said. She had complaints of her own, and on the evening of 3 March 1939 it all came to a head. He had told her that he would be coming home only around 10:30 after a conference and had asked her to have something for him to eat. When he arrived, nothing was on the table. He went into the kitchen and opened the icebox to get out a plate of tomatoes. Suddenly, his wife hit him in the side and shouted:

"You stinker, I've had it with you!"

The future chief of German intelligence wordlessly put his coat back on and started to leave the house. She forcibly locked the door. For half an hour they argued, until he was able to get her to listen as, seated on the edge of the bed, he explained the difficulties in the marriage. Finally she agreed to a divorce. Schellenberg spent the night in an armchair. The argument resumed the next morning, with Frau Schellenberg threatening suicide. But by promising to buy her a fashion business that was going to be "aryanized"—seized from Jewish owners—he calmed her down and got her to agree to a divorce.

Still the irritations persisted, and, Heydrich noted, they had Schellenberg, "one of my best and . . . most trustworthy supports," working at half draft. So, one afternoon a few weeks later, he had one of his men pick Frau Schellenberg up for a 50-minute conference in his office. He made little headway in getting her to leave Berlin until he said that he would have Schellenberg transferred. Suddenly she said that she would leave Berlin herself—she'd made all kinds of sacrifices for her husband and she'd do this as well.

"None of you know my husband," she cried. "He's selfish. He can never stick to what he says." A few months later, she wrote to Himmler himself, asking if she could see him about the matter. But it had no effect. The divorce went through, and soon thereafter the young man on the make married a socially more desirable woman, Irene Grosse-Schönepauck, daughter of an insurance executive. But here too he found problems. He only had to hang his pants on the bed, he ruefully told his co-workers, for her to get pregnant.

His career proceeded upward. With the establishment of the RSHA, he took charge of Group IV E. Department IV was the Gestapo; Group E handled defense against foreign intelligence agencies. (It was the job once held by Jost's old friend from Hesse, whose deputy Jost had been.) In this capacity Schellenberg engineered a coup that gave him his biggest boost thus far. He kidnapped two British secret service officers.

Calling himself "Major Schemmel" and representing himself as a member of an anti-Hitler generals' plot that wanted to overthrow the Führer and make peace with England, he met the two officers several times. With a quick, decisive manner and a ready answer to their questions, he took them in completely. Finally he set up a meeting at the Café Backus near the Dutch town of Venlo. As the two arrived by car on the morning of 9 November 1939, they spotted "Schemmel" on the second-floor terrace of the Backus, along whose backyard ran the Dutch-German border. He gave a sweep with his arm. They interpreted it as a signal to come up. Instead, to an outburst of shouting and shooting, a large green car crashed through the frontier barricade and raced up to the café. Out tumbled a number of Germans, who snapped handcuffs on the two surprised Englishmen and, in the midst of a pistol battle with one of the Englishmen's aides, whisked them, with Schemmel, back across the border into Germany. Though the kidnapping did not enable Heydrich to crack the embryonic opposition to Hitler, it did virtually paralyze the British espionage service

Perſonal-Bericht

des **Walter Schellenberg**   **SS-Oberscharführer.**
　　(Vor- und Zuname)　　　(Dienſtſtellung und Einheit)　　　(Dienſtgrad)

Mitglied-Nr. der Partei: **3.504.508**　　　SS-Ausweis Nr. **124.817**

Seit wann in der Dienſtſtellung: .... Beförderungsdatum zum letzten Dienſtgrad: **13.9.36**

Geburtstag, Geburtsort (Kreis): **16.1.1910 zu Saarbrücken**

Beruf: 1. erlernter: **Juriſt**　　　2. jetziger: **Angeſtellter**

Wohnort: **Berlin SW 68**　　　Straße: **Wilhelmſtr. 102**

Verheiratet? **nein** Mädchenname der Frau: **-----** Kinder? **---** Konfeſſion: **gottgl.**

Wirtſchaftliche Verhältniſſe: **geordnet**

Vorſtrafen: **keine**

Verletzungen, Verfolgungen und Strafen im Kampfe für die Bewegung: ....

....

....

Beurteilung:

I. Raſſiſches Geſamtbild: **Rein nordiſch.**

II.　1. Charakter: **Offener, einwandfreier, lauterer Charakter; er iſt SD-Mann.**

　　2. Wille: **Feſt, zäh, beſitzt Energie.**

　　3. Geſunder Menſchenverſtand: **Sehr ſcharf denkend.**

　　Wiſſen und Bildung: **Aſſeſſorexamen: gut; überdurchſchnittliche Allgemein-bildung.**

　　Auffaſſungsvermögen: **Erfaſst überraſchend ſchnell das Kernproblem.**

　　Nationalſozialiſtiſche Weltanſchauung: **Durchaus gefeſtigt.**

III. Auftreten und Benehmen in und außer Dienſt: **Soldatiſches Auftreten in und auſſer Dienſt.**
　　(Beſondere Neigungen, Schwächen und Fehler)

....

....

First page of SS master sergeant Walter Schellenberg's personnel report of 27 March 1937. Under Evaluation, his "Overall Racial Picture" is "pure Nordic"; he has an "open, irreproachable, reliable character; he is an SD man"; his will is "firm, tough, possesses energy"; his common sense is "very sharp thinking"; his National Socialist philosophy is "thoroughly fortified" in Germany. And it enormously increased the prestige of young Schellenberg, who was awarded the Iron Cross first class a few weeks later from the hands of Adolf Hitler himself!

Schellenberg's success in the Venlo incident probably led Ribbentrop to summon him for a similar mission in Portugal. This time, however, the person involved was possibly the most famous man in the world: the former King Edward VIII of England, who had given up his throne to marry the woman he loved and was now the duke of Windsor.

During a 1937 trip to Germany, the duke had expressed some pro-Hitler statements, and after the outbreak of the war both the British and the German governments regarded him as the possible nucleus of a peace movement. This was fine for Hitler, who had by then conquered his Poland, but not for Britain, which had gone to war over that very issue. The British government therefore appointed the duke to the distant and trivial post of governor of the Bahamas. But while the British wanted him on the other side of the Atlantic, the Germans wanted him in Europe. So as he passed through Spain and then Portugal on his way to the Caribbean in the summer of 1940, Schellenberg went to the Iberian peninsula to prevent his departure. He proposed the same border-kidnapping technique that had worked so well at Venlo, coupled with "psychologically adroit influence" on the duke. This latter would exploit the duke's alleged anxiety about the British intelligence service and would hold out the prospect of free political activity. Under Schellenberg's scheme, the duke and duchess, then in Portugal, would be invited to hunt near the Spanish border. A Portuguese border official, who owed a favor to a Spanish minister, would be won over. "At a precisely designated place at a particular time," the Germans planned, the ducal pair would cross into Spain. Schellenberg's group, assisted by Spanish forces, would guarantee security.

But after a week or so, it became obvious that the duke had decided not to return to Spain. Schellenberg then sought at least to stop him from sailing. He tried everything. He listed the Jews and emigrés sailing on the same ship and got the Portuguese counterespionage police to state that they could not guarantee the duke's security. He had a Portuguese official's wife call on the duchess begging her not to go since, if anything happened, the official would lose his job. He sent flowers with an anonymous warning note to the duchess. He bribed the duke's English driver to remark about the danger and to refuse to go to the Bahamas. He persuaded the Portuguese police to search ostentatiously for a bomb on the ship. But nothing worked. The duke and duchess loyally followed instructions and sailed as scheduled.

The episode did not help Schellenberg, but it did not harm him much either. He had other routes to power. He was working closer to Heydrich. He fenced with him—both were passionate about the sport. He accompanied him on his all-night drinking bouts. He visited him frequently at his home, where he conversed with his wife about cultural affairs. He penned Heydrich's replies to Jost's patron, whose pettifogging legal arguments had stood in Heydrich's way. He handled touchy assignments for him, such as the negotiations with the army to support the SS murder squads operating in its rear areas.

He was effective in such matters. He had a quiet way about him, quite different from the bullying pretentious hardness of most SS types. He spoke softly, almost shyly, in a clear tenor with exceptionally precise enunciation and with a boyish charm that was one of his greatest assets. For, wrote one student, "He believed not in force, nor in nonsense, but in subtlety; and he believed that he was subtle." Not everyone liked him. Some of the older, street-brawler types of the SS despised him as effete; some officials regarded him as too pushy. But he did win over many top Nazis. They perhaps recognized in his brisk gait and lively gestures the energy boiling behind his low-pressure manner. They probably liked his "pure Nordic" racial type and the dueling scars on his cheeks, though these could not toughen his pasty features. Nevertheless, his five-foot, nine-inch body was well proportioned, and he wore the black SS uniform with elegance. He was bright and perceptive: people meeting him often had the impression that he could form a clear picture of people and events on the basis of a few key facts. He was a hard worker and a good superior.

But his greatest asset of all was Heydrich's trust in him and preference for him. Schellenberg's ambition was great, but he never gave Heydrich the slightest cause for worry by eyeing the domestic sector. He limited his desires strictly to foreign intelligence. Though Jost was equally trustworthy, he did not shine as did the new young protégé. In comparison with other members of the RSHA, Schellenberg seemed relatively sophisticated. He could lunch smoothly with foreigners and befriend young officials in the Foreign Office and the propaganda ministry. He was credited with understanding foreign affairs. All this could create a far glossier image for Heydrich's external intelligence service than ever before—and a better one than Germany had ever had. As early as mid-1940, Heydrich had apparently determined to make Schellenberg head of RSHA VI. It took a year to oust Jost, but finally, on 21 June 1941, the day before the start of the great war of conquest in the east, SS Major Walter Schellenberg achieved "the goal toward which I had striven for years" and was named acting chief of the Nazi party's foreign intelligence organization. Whereupon Heydrich took him to lunch with Canaris at a fine Berlin restaurant so the two could meet—the kindly, fiftyish, uncertain admiral and his new counterpart, respectful, perhaps even awed, but ambitious, single-minded, and 23 years younger.

The next day, 22 June 1941, after three minutes of direction from Heydrich, Schellenberg took up his new job. Jost stayed on for a few months to help him, and Schellenberg, faced with the task of reconstructing Nazi foreign espionage at the height of the war, did not rush into it. "I decided first to feel my way into the routine work of the organization, then gradually to approach the larger problems. I had been considering these for a long time, of course, and theoretically had worked out clear solutions, but these were not quite so easy to put into practice."

He visited an old boss from the SD office, then administering the conquered territories in the east, and spent several days in the open spaces of a Polish estate riding, fishing, and thinking. He devised a 10-point program for Department VI. His experience in the Nazi jungle led him to cover himself in case of failure with his very first point: "Great changes in organization and personnel are necessary, but unfortunately, because of the advanced stage of the war, only a limited reconstruction is possible." The last one boded ominously for the rival Abwehr: "The long-range goal of my work is the creation of a 'unified' German Secret Information Service." In between were chiefly commonplaces. "(2) The question of staff is of decisive importance.... (3) The administration must be divided between: (a) The collecting sector ... and (b) the evaluating sector.... (5) The Secret Service must become a respected and valued department of state."

He moved rather slowly in implementing this program. For example, it took a year to issue a directive for the relatively simple point 7 ("A filing system must be set up, arranged under subject headings, as well as under individual persons"). With Teutonic precision, this specified an elaborate arrangement: personal files of each agent, a card index of all agents, a file of personalities, arranged both by name and by field of activity, a similar card index of personalities, and a subject file. Each agent's personal file would begin with his code designation, consisting of the letter V (for "Vertrauensmann," or "confidence man"), the number of the country in which he operated (according to a list running from Afghanistan = 1 to Yemen = 182), a virgule, and a personal number assigned by the country desk. Thus an agent in England might have the number V 45/85. His file would contain a short biography, his security checks, his assignment, a short record of his reports, and his evaluation on a five-number scale: 1, excellent; 2, good; 3, medium; 4, bad; 5, useless. The subject file was divided into five main headings, such as A, foreign policy, and B, internal affairs, each of which was subdivided into roman numeral headings (under B, IV was political influence), with further elements indicated by 3-digit Arabic numerals (215 was military circles, 216 aristocratic circles). But this complicated plan never flowered completely. The several groups each maintained its own files, and they did not attain the full complexity envisaged by Schellenberg.

Schellenberg also reorganized the department. He swept away Jost's overseeing deputies. He elided the five geographic groups into four and re-lettered them. He pushed the technical group further down the alphabet and oversaw the expansion of its radio unit into a full-fledged service for agent communications, the so-called Havel Institute. He added new groups —G for coordinating the work of the research institutes in the Reich, Wi (Wirtschaft) for economic intelligence. By January of 1945, at its greatest elaboration, Department VI had 12 groups and 48 desks.

Schellenberg also put his own men into his department. For some posts it was easy, since Jost had let three of his five group-leader positions fall vacant. With others, Schellenberg moved more cautiously. Filbert, Jost's right-hand man, stayed on until 1943. But his function shrank under Schel-

---

THE ORGANIZATION OF RSHA VI IN JANUARY 1945

Group	Desk	Function	Leader
A		Organization	SS-Lt.Col. Sandberger
	1	Organization	SS-Capt. Reichert
	2	Currency, Finance	Chief Insp. Wiesinger
	3	Personnel	SS-Capt. Buchmann
	4	Instruction, Training	SS-Capt. Janssen
	5	Travel, Visas	SS-Lt. Geppert
	6	Inspection	SS-Capt. Reichert
	7	Central Interview Post for Returnees	—
B		[West Europe]	SS-Col. Steimle
	1	Italy	SS-Maj. Wolff
	2	France, Belgium, Holland	SS-Lt.Col. Bernhardt
	3	Switzerland	SS-Maj. Wolff
	4	Spain, Portugal	SS-Capt. Fendler
	Vat.	Vatican	SS-Capt. Reissman
C		[Russia, Far East, Near East]	SS-Lt.Col. Tschierschky
	1–3	Russia	SS-Maj. Dr. Hengelhaupt
	4–6	Japan, Manchukuo, Thailand	SS-Maj. Weihrauch
	8–10	China	" "
	11	India	" "
	a–c^1	Turkey, Iran, Afghanistan	SS-Maj. Schuback
	13	Syria, Transjordan, Iraq, Palestine, Egypt	—
D		[North and South America, Great Britain, Scandinavia]	SS-Lt.Col. Dr. Paeffgen
	1	North America	SS-Capt. Carstenn
	2	Great Britain	SS-Maj. Dr. Schüddekopf
	3	Sweden, Finland, Norway, Denmark	SS-Capt. Grönheim
	4	South America	SS-Capt. Gross

lenberg to a strictly administrative one, and in this he proved somewhat inefficient. So to run Group A, administration, Schellenberg brought in a man who had made a reputation in RSHA I, personnel. This was Dr. Martin Sandberger, 32, a one-time assistant judge and administrator in southern Germany who had joined the SA in 1931 and the SD in 1936. When the RSHA was formed, he served successfully for a year and a half in Department I handling training matters. At the start of the war with Russia, he left Berlin for einsatzkommando work in Estonia. He had risen to

Group	Desk	Function	Leader
E		[Southeast Europe]	SS-Lt.Col. Waneck
	1	Slovakia	—
	2	Hungary	SS-Capt. Frühlich
	3	Croatia, Serbia	SS-Capt. Kleber
	4	Albania, Montenegro	SS-Capt. Pratsch
	5	Greece	—
	6	Bulgaria	—
	7	Rumania	—
F		[Technical Support]	SS-Maj. Lassig (acting)
	H[2]	(Havel Institute) radio	SS-Maj. Siepen
	3	Chemical and Mechanical Sabotage	SS-Maj. Lassig
	4	Forgeries, Photography	SS-Maj. Krüger
	5	Technical Means of Assistance	SS-Capt. Weideling
	6	Instruction	SS-Maj. Dr. Fesel
	P	Personnel, Administration	SS-Capt. Nötenberg SS-Capt. Faulhaber
G		[Scientific-Methodic Research Service]	SS-Capt. Krallert
Wi/T		[Economics and Technology]	SS-Col. Dr. Schmied
	Wi 1	Acquisition	Lt.Col.[4] Daehne
	Wi 2	Evaluation	SS-Maj. Abandroth
	Wi 3	Building-in of personnel	Capt.[4] Ulrich
	Wi 4	Building-in of personnel[3]	Dr. Rénard
	T	Technology	SS-Maj. Dr. O'gilvie
S		[Sabotage]	SS-Maj. Skorzeny
Kult		Nonscientific [Cultural] Domestic Acquisition Service	SS-Capt. Carstens
Z		[Military Counterespionage and Personnel Checks]	Lt.Col.[4] Freund
Abwehr		[Civilian Counterespionage and Personnel Checks]	SS-Maj. Otten

[1] so given; no Desk 12
[2] Desks 1 and 2, dealing with radio matters, were absorbed into the Havel Institute
[3] same title as Wi 3
[4] army officer

commander of the security police and of the SD there when Schellenberg summoned him near the end of 1943. Able and ambitious, he managed the reorganized Group A efficiently, generally gained his way in personnel disputes with other groups, and kept the complicated books of the extensive domestic and foreign funds straight to the last pfennig.

Other Jost men vanished more quickly than Filbert. Jost's chief of the Anglo-American group, Hans Daufeldt, a playboy type whose chief qualification was his ability to speak English, lasted little more than a year. Schellenberg replaced him with an old college pal, Theodor Paeffgen, 32, who had recruited Gimpel and Colepaugh for their mission to America. Paeffgen, "racial type: Nordic," was a doctor of law, unexcitable and undynamic, but strong in " 'methodical' work," with knowledge "far above the average" and with his political philosophy "in order." He had studied at Bonn with Schellenberg, who in 1938 recruited him for the SD and then kept track of him as he served in a series of posts in Germany and the occupied territories. Paeffgen did not "entirely fulfill the requirements in leadership respects" during antipartisan activity with an einsatzkommando in Russia, a superior noted. In fact his technical qualifications to head Group D of Department VI were little better than his predecessor's. But before the war he had studied in Bordeaux and Geneva for a year and in Edinburgh for a summer, and this provided Schellenberg with a rationale. On 21 September 1942, after booting out Daufeldt, he installed Paeffgen.

Schellenberg's choice for the England desk showed that he could make unorthodox selections if he felt the man was good enough. One day one of his chief assistant's assistants ran into a friend on the Berlin subway. The friend was Dr. Otto-Ernst Schüddekopf, a fast-talking, 29-year-old historian. He had already published a book on English naval policy and was then working in the Luftwaffe's historical section in Potsdam. He was a member of neither the party nor the SS, but his qualifications seemed good. The wheels began turning, and on 21 June 1942 he began working for Department VI. On the same day, he joined the SS as a second lieutenant —a considerable improvement over the rank of corporal that he had held in the air force. But he never joined the party; in this respect he was like the head of the Gestapo, also a member of the SS but not the party. Shortly after his arrival at the RSHA, Schüddekopf bombarded Schellenberg with entirely rational but somewhat impracticable suggestions: a central evaluation group with subcommittees, a monthly report on the political situation in England (with contents outlined in detail), a staff for Schellenberg. But he soon settled down, came to understand the utter worthlessness of most agent reports and the relative value of open sources, recognized the pointlessness of intelligence in the Nazi-charged atmosphere, and simply plugged away at his desk work.

Another choice exemplified what has been called "Hitler's social revolution." This was the far greater opportunity than ever before in Germany for unprivileged persons to rise on the basis of ability—and political reliability. Eugen Steimle proved one of the most capable and gifted of VI group leaders. A farmer's son, he came, like Sandberger, from southwest Germany. He joined the Nazi party in 1932, when he was 20 and studying German and history. Soon he became head of the Nazi student league for his university and then for the entire province. His SD activity began when he met a party official in a Stuttgart square one day who convinced him to join what he described as a young, promising organization. Steimle proved so effective that the SD very quickly advanced him to head of its Stuttgart post. This post, relatively close both to France and to Switzerland, had, in those prewar years, one of the few desks for foreign intelligence. The fitness report that a superior made out for him then set a pattern that barely changed: "fanatically fortified National Socialist attitude . . . Steimle has proved a remarkable success and has built up a first-rate [SD] sector. He has created a hegemony for the SD in all enemy questions and won the esteem of the entire district, above all that of the Gauleiter and the old party members. . . . Advancement is especially desired." In 1941, instead of combat service, he was given command of an einsatzkommando unit. This was followed by service back in Stuttgart, after which he returned to Russia to again command a killing squad. Here he demonstrated "outstanding qualities in leading and handling the men assigned to him." In February 1943, Schellenberg, who knew of his work and had met him, and had grown discontented with the head of VI B, the western Europe group, summoned Steimle to the post. He quickly satisfied the chief. "He possesses an above average intellectual talent, an adroit gift for negotiation, and an extremely polished style. Equipped with a good political instinct and corresponding psychological capabilities, he worked into the problems of the secret intelligence service in a relatively short time and above all attacked the difficulties of procuring information with great success." He was not perfect. Schellenberg thought him a little too intuitive and requiring direct supervision and a bit of a bully. But he was good enough for Schellenberg to gain his advancement to SS colonel two years before he had reached the prescribed age of 36.

Helping Schellenberg fill Department VI with his own men was the normal attrition of personnel through transfers, firings, deaths. When the leader of Group C (Russia and the Near East) was killed in a car accident, Schellenberg naturally named a successor. Such events apparently turned over most of VI's personnel during the nearly six years of the war, though probably to a greater degree at the lower levels than among the group leaders, where Schellenberg initiated more of the shifts. For the group leaders were his immediate subordinates.

These men, in their mid-thirties, ranked in the SS as what an army would call field-grade officers: majors, lieutenant colonels, and colonels. They advanced to that level in compliance with the regulations for promotion within the SS. These called, of course, for "irreproachable character and model National Socialist life," as well as for service at the front. But, the regulations said, since RSHA members were all deferred as essential, they could substitute for front service an assignment in an einsatzkommando. And, to get their promotions, many did: Paeffgen, Sandberger, Steimle, Albert Rapp, a man with a face like a steel trap who was second head of VI C, and his successor, Karl Tschierschky. Department VI was thus riddled with killers, and Nazi Germany depended for the honest, unbiased information that alone can guarantee success in intelligence upon amoral, compliant men.

The Berlin personnel did not exhaust VI's roster. The SD had divided Germany and the occupied territories into regions, and in some of these, especially those closer to the enemy, the SD offices had representatives of Department VI. In Paris, for example, the VI section sought intelligence on all areas, but its VI B 2 desk—covering France, Belgium, and Holland—was naturally the largest and most important. It consisted of a chief, a deputy who handled personnel, a chief of collecting and editing, two editors, two evaluators with two clerks, and three clerks for subject, personality, and reports files.

These outposts handled the spies. Berlin, where between 400 and 500 persons worked in the middle of the war, dealt mostly with paper—reading reports, evaluating and annotating them, answering letters, studying newspapers, approving funds, passing on requests for equipment, recruiting personnel. Possibly the same number worked for VI in the outposts as in Berlin, making a total of 1,000 in the Nazi espionage service.

Department VI was quartered by itself in Berlin in a four-story modernistic brick-and-concrete building at Berkaerstrasse 32, on the corner of the Hohenzollerndamm, a main street in the southwest-central section of the city. (The rest of the SD was in the center of town at Wilhelmstrasse 102 and 106, the Gestapo around the corner at the dread address, Prinz-Albrecht-Strasse 8.) Schellenberg had his own office in here, with, he boasted, a desk with two hidden machine guns, ready to cut down anyone foolhardy enough to try to assassinate him.

Here he worked day and night, up to 20 hours at a time. He was reaping Jost's harvest. He mastered the stream of information that poured in upon him, apparently reading every intelligence report that came in and forwarding it to the proper user, often with a covering letter. Sometimes he personally brought reports to the users; occasionally he attended Hitler's military situation conferences. He conferred incessantly with his group chiefs and with individual desk officers. He interviewed important spies when they were in Germany. He approved all major expense items. He traveled to the outposts of the department—Stockholm, Madrid, cities in Germany—to inspect and to boost morale. He ran his own agents as a check on the regular nets. He made contact with outside agencies to improve VI's output. He lunched with a head of the German news service. He asked the Forschungsamt and OKW/Chi to intercept and solve certain radio traffic for him. He visited Oslo to talk with the Reich protector of Norway. He had, a subordinate thought, "an ear at every wall."

The infighting among various agencies and personalities absorbed a great deal of his time and energy. He kept up an elaborate sham with Canaris. They went horseback riding together. Their families socialized. They swore not to talk shop on these occasions, but did anyway. It all meant nothing, since neither side ever gave the other anything of importance. But each handled the relationship in his own way. Canaris was paternal and solicitous to the younger man, plying him with the pills and medicines that he himself always took. Schellenberg was the one who, following orders after the 1944 plot to assassinate Hitler failed, arrested Canaris.

At the same time, he was cementing his own position in the Nazi hierarchy. What had happened to Jost loomed ever before him. But a new situation made things easier for Schellenberg. A few months after he took office, Heydrich had had himself named acting protector of Bohemia and Moravia. This reduced the time he had for foreign intelligence, in which he was not particularly interested anyway, and so he left the work increasingly to Schellenberg. Moreover, Heydrich's new rank now granted him direct access to Hitler. He could thus himself bring intelligence tidbits to the Führer. Heydrich's boss, Himmler, did not like this loss of influence. Schellenberg seized upon this situation. He ingratiated himself with Himmler by helping to restore the lost influence: he delivered his foreign intelligence not to Heydrich, who was often in Prague, but to Himmler. The technique worked. He gained the Reichsführer's confidence, and he never lost it.

Schellenberg gained and held power effectively enough. But the Reich's master in this treacherous game was Heydrich. None of Hitler's murdering ministers reached out for mastery as relentlessly, as purposefully, as he. His SD and security police had helped stoke the fires for the SS's expansion into the most powerful agency of the state, the agency that, more than any other, stamped Hitler's Germany into its characteristic image. While other German leaders attended, at least to some degree, to winning the war, Heydrich concentrated on the one conflict, that, to him, mattered: the struggle for power in the Reich.

He attacked on many fronts, in particular that of the Abwehr. He pointed out to Himmler and Hitler the renewed indications that the Abwehr and Canaris were in league with the resistance. And the Abwehr played into his hands. It bumbled. After a British raid on a German radar installation at Bruneval on the Channel coast, which cost the Germans the advantages of a new secret radar, Hitler raged about Canaris's failure to provide good information about British radar. He demanded some from

Himmler. But Schellenberg hadn't any either, and this kept the SS from following up its advantages that time. Nevertheless, Heydrich exploited such events and the continuing frictions between the SD and the Abwehr to wear Canaris down. In their agreement of 1 March 1942, Heydrich got much and gave little. Three months later, as he seemed on the verge of his goal, he was dead, assassinated by Czech nationalists.

For the half a year that Himmler ran the RSHA himself in addition to his other duties, the drive on the Abwehr slackened. Then Himmler named Ernst Kaltenbrunner head of the RSHA, to take over on 30 January 1943. Among Kaltenbrunner's first acts was to elevate Schellenberg on 24 February from acting chief of Department VI to chief. Thus fortified, Kaltenbrunner resumed Heydrich's advance against the Abwehr. And that agency played into his hands.

Two of its high officials were arrested for illegal currency transactions. A Gestapo investigation that scented resistance tendencies led to the resignations of Colonel Oster, Canaris's chief of staff, and of Hans von Dohnanyi, another Abwehr member. Reports of Abwehr peace feelers in Turkey and the Vatican came to Hitler. In January 1944, the Gestapo arrested an officer of Canaris's department as part of a resistance circle. It learned that an Ausland official and an officer of Abwehr III had warned this circle that the Forschungsamt was tapping its telephones. These deviations might have been tolerated but for the Abwehr's repeated failures in its main job: foretelling what the enemy would do. Time after time the Allies completely surprised the Germans. North Africa, Sicily, Anzio—these battered the Abwehr's reputation. The SD, on the other hand, basked in the glow of the greatest spy coup of the war: photographs of secret documents from the British embassy in Turkey.

The break the SD needed came near the end of January 1944. A member of the Abwehr post in Istanbul, Dr. Erich Vermehren, an opponent of the Nazi regime, greatly influenced by his wife, a devout Catholic 13 years older than he, defected to the British. On 10 February, the British officially confirmed the episode to the press.

Hitler exploded. Two days later, he signed a decree that abolished the Abwehr as an independent organization, subordinated it to the RSHA, and gave the Nazi chieftains the total control over foreign intelligence for which they had so long conspired:

Top Secret Military
Senior Officers' Material
By Officer's Hand Only

Der Führer

Führer Headquarters
12 February 1944

Chief OKW No. 1/44 Top Secret Military—Senior Officers' Material
2 copies
1st copy

I order:

1. A unified German espionage service is to be created.

2. I entrust the Reichsführer SS [Himmler] with the command of this German espionage service.

3. Insofar as the military intelligence and counterintelligence service is hereby affected, the Reichsführer SS and the Chief, OKW [Keitel], will take the necessary measures by mutual agreement.

signed: Adolf Hitler

Six days later, Canaris was removed from the post he had held for nine years. The head of Abwehr Branch I, Colonel Hansen, took charge of the Abwehr for its dissolution, simultaneously continuing to head Abwehr I. Negotiations began in Zossen early in March for the absorption of the Abwehr into the RSHA. General August Winter, chief of the OKW central office, represented Keitel, assisted by Hansen and the chiefs of Abwehr II and III. Kaltenbrunner, Schellenberg, and Heinrich Müller, head of the Gestapo, which would get Abwehr III (counterintelligence), handled the RSHA side.

Difficulties appeared at once. Not a quarter as big as Abwehr I, RSHA VI was faced with the same problem as a tiger who wants to swallow an elephant. Kaltenbrunner thought Abwehr I should dissolve immediately and entirely into RSHA VI; Schellenberg and Hansen wanted it to remain an entity during an interim period. Many of the Abwehr personnel were officers and enlisted men. Would they lose their status as soldiers? The Abwehr front-line units worked in intimate contact with the combat troops. Would a transfer hinder their work? It took months to hammer out agreements on details such as these.

Finally, in the middle of May, with the work all but completed, Himmler and Keitel assembled members of the RSHA and of the Abwehr at the Mirabell Castle in Salzburg for two days to orient them on what was going to happen. Some 300 RSHA and 400 Abwehr officers and officials attended. The high point was a 2½-hour speech by the winner.

Himmler began with a historical survey that praised the intelligence service that the Aryans must have had to make conquests as far as India. Today, however, he said, the Russians have, next to the English, the most powerful intelligence service. "The German intelligence service and apparatus was, corresponding to our unhappy, fragmented, and perpetually self-destructive German history and our historical advance, very meager and poor." This had been true in World War I and in the 1920s. But times were changing. "Observe the word 'Abwehr'! It came out of the conditions of the years 1933–34 . . . because we were defending. . . . For the future, that must never be our motto. . . . Through the Führer order of 12 February 1944 a single great intelligence service, corresponding to the greatness of the Reich, corresponding to the greatness of today's war demands, and corresponding to the greatness of the coming German-European peace duties, will now be created."

After iterating that an intelligence service "must found itself upon a race, upon a people of the same blood," Himmler told the assembled specialists "what I expect from this great intelligence service." The main thing was not honesty in reporting. "First of all, an unconditional loyalty to the Führer. . . ." He also wanted "unconditional obedience . . . comradeship . . . unconditional veracity . . . clear reports . . . certainty of German strength and the final German victory." Near the end he gave them some practical advice: Keep your word to agents. "Believe me," he declared, "in the long run that will bring us the most trustworthy supporters, even among the colored people and the Untermenschen."

Having thus placed his new intelligence service on a firm ideological footing, Himmler issued the agreement that he and Keitel had signed on 14 May. It covered four single-spaced pages. In its most important point, it ordered Abwehr I and II to be formed into a Military Department, whose "gradual merger" with RSHA VI "is foreseen and is to be systematically prepared." The actual deadline would be fixed by Keitel. The Abwehr posts in Germany, in the occupied territories, and in neutral countries likewise fell under the SD. The Abwehr front-line units, however, stayed subordinate to the OKW, specifically to its Operations Staff's intelligence officer. Soldiers remained members of the armed forces, but civilian employees moved to the SD. The Abwehr budget was to be transferred to the RSHA.

A week later, Kaltenbrunner issued his detailed regulations for the actual incorporation of the Abwehr into the RSHA. Its first specification set the death date of the 78-year-old German military espionage organization. The Abwehr, it ordered, "is dissolved as of 1 June 1944." It repeated the provision that Branches I and II would constitute a Military Department, which Schellenberg was to gradually amalgamate into RSHA VI. The Abwehr posts, which incorporated the negative term "defense" ("Abwehr") in their titles, changed their names to Command Report Area plus the name of their headquarters town. The SS regional inspectors and commanders supervised them. Intelligence channels were set up. General reports went to Kaltenbrunner; individual military reports went, as before, directly to military commands, with copies to Kaltenbrunner. In both cases the reports passed through Schellenberg.

Hansen became head of the Military Department—Amt Mil, in the jargon of German military abbreviations. But he had served less than two months when he was arrested as a conspirator in the 20 July 1944 attempt on Hitler's life. Schellenberg then took over the running of Amt Mil.

The new department's basic operation sections were Branch B, for the west, with about 50 people, and Branch C, for the east. Each was divided into acquisition and screening sections. Mil B's acquisition sections were numbered 1 to 4. Each handled a geographic area: 2, for example, gathered information from France and Belgium through the Command Report Area Cologne and the Command Report Area Wiesbaden. Its screening section, Mil B/S (the S for "Sichtung," or "screening"), was divided into army, navy, and air intelligence sections. It sorted the incoming intelligence, sifted the useful from the useless, and routed it to the military commands. It also received their requests for information and passed them to the acquisition sections. Most of the heads of Amt Mil units came over from the Abwehr. C, for example, was headed by Lieutenant Colonel Werner Ohletz. Branch B, however, went to the efficient Eugen Steimle, group leader of RSHA VI B, western Europe, who then headed both. Other Amt Mil branches were: A, for organization, planning, personnel, and training; D, sabotage and subversion (the old Abwehr II); E, radio communications (the old Abwehr I i); and G, secret inks and false documents (the old Abwehr I G).

Half a year after this new organization had come into being, the party concluded its conquest of military intelligence. Under an addendum to the Himmler-Keitel agreement, the Abwehr front-line espionage units, which had remained under OKW command, moved on 1 December 1944 to Amt Mil as its Branch F. Colonel Georg Buntrock, a slender young general staff officer who had had considerable I c experience on the eastern front, became head of front reconnaissance as Branch F chief that same day.

With this, the chain of command led down from Hitler, who was chancellor, party leader, commander in chief of the armed forces, and in effect commander in chief of the army, through Himmler, leader of the party's SS, minister of the interior, chief of the German police, and by then commander of the Replacement Army and also commander of Army Group Upper Rhine, through Kaltenbrunner, head of the party intelligence service and the government security police, to Schellenberg, an SS major general and government civil servant who had under him, in addition to the party foreign espionage department, elements of the armed forces. The organizational chaos of the German spy service was complete.

Operations of the Infrastructures

Spies do not sprout in the enemy's lands like soldiers grown from dragon's teeth. They have to be found, trained, equipped, assigned missions, disguised, inserted, communicated with, paid, and sometimes withdrawn. Their reports must be evaluated and forwarded. Their files must be maintained. All this was the work, the raison d'être, of those vast, rambling infrastructures, the Abwehr and the SD.

They began, of course, with recruitment. This task sometimes racked the spymasters' brains more than any other, for a secret approach to the public is practically a contradiction in terms. Both agencies therefore developed recruitment techniques that occasionally bordered on the bizarre.

The Abwehr advertised. Before the war, notices appeared in newspapers outside Germany offering loans to salaried persons, especially government employees. From the debt-ridden who applied the Abwehr selected the most interesting—usually officers, noncoms, or officials in military agencies—and proposed a loan. If anyone could not pay it back on time, the Abwehr offered him an extension in return for information. Many agreed. As they got in deeper, the Abwehr escalated its demands. One French cavalry lieutenant, whose mistress cost him too much, at first delivered some elementary facts about his regiment. When he continued to live extravagantly and could not repay his debt, the Abwehr had him apply for the general staff course. He passed the examination and soon was delivering higher grade material, such as the annual report on the Belgian armed forces. Later he won a transfer to Paris, where he continued to support his girl friend by giving still more information to the Germans. Only the outbreak of war broke off the relationship.

The Abwehr also employed scouts to spot prospects. The Hamburg Abwehr post's economics expert doubled as one. By keeping his eyes and ears open for persons with suitable qualifications as he moved through occupied Europe, he discovered several who, he thought, might pass in Britain as refugees from Naziism. Before the start of hostilities, some German sympathizers abroad, unable or unwilling to spy themselves, likewise watched for potential agents. In Wales, for example, where Welsh nationalism provided a reservoir of England-haters, the manager of a German engineering firm, a factory manager, and a visiting lecturer at Cardiff University passed names to the Abwehr. During the 1944 invasion of France, members of the front reconnaissance units recruited agents from supporters of such pro-Nazi movements as the Partie Populaire Française, the Milice, and the Belgian Rexists. Front Reconnaissance Command 120 had two especially astute and successful recruiters, codenamed MARÉCHAL and CHARLIE, who interviewed prospects in French labor camps and in Sigmaringen in southern Germany, headquarters of the Vichy French government in "exile."

During the war, at the border between occupied and unoccupied France, guards sometimes steered French soldiers who wanted to make prohibited visits to friends and relatives in occupied France to the Abwehr. The post in Bordeaux helped the soldiers if they promised to bring in some information. A few years later, as the Allied invasion began to loom, the same post paid a man in an army office in contact with the public to ring it whenever a good prospect appeared in his stream of callers. An Abwehr officer then met the prospect to sound him out. Many turned out to be former foreign legionnaires.

Special circumstances contributed agents. On the German frontier with France and Luxembourg before the war, the Abwehr often captured French spies—and freed them at the price of their turning double agent for the Germans. When the Wehrmacht invaded the Channel Islands in 1940, they persuaded at least one of the criminals in prison there to spy for them.

By far the greatest number of agents came from the prisoner-of-war camps. When the Abwehr needed 500 agents for a massive commitment in North Africa, it found Arabs who had served with the French army and were languishing in prison camps in France. It offered them a trip home by parachute if they would spy. In the east, the Abwehr garnered hundreds of agents from among the Russian p.o.w.s.

The same held true for the SD. Schellenberg's massive Operation ZEPPELIN catapulted hundreds of former prisoners of war into Russia as spies. Since many of these men simply reported to Russian authorities upon reaching their homeland, especially after the course of the war became clear following the German defeat at Kursk in 1943, the Germans began accepting as agents only those whose way back was blocked by a crime, such as desertion. If a candidate could not demonstrate this, the Germans forced them to prove themselves by mass executions of Soviet citizens; they were then photographed in front of their victims. Only after that were they accepted. For individual agents, however, the SD, smaller and newer than the Abwehr, sometimes had to transfer informants from its domestic to its foreign service. One Heinrich Schlie, for example, worked for SD-Inland for several years in Berlin and then for SS Major Adolf Eichmann in Vienna before transferring to the foreign service there under SS Captain Wilhelm Höttl, head of the VI desk of the SD office in Vienna. Schellenberg also sought agents in the volunteer SS contingents from Sweden, Switzerland, and Finland. At the foreigners' SS camp at Sennheim, one of his Department VI officials, pretending to be an instructor in political philosophy, observed the men for agent possibilities. A second official, ostensibly a censor, read their mail for other clues.

Less scrupulous than the Abwehr, the SD could employ more creative methods. One of Schellenberg's thoughts was hardly original: let's use whores! The head of RSHA V (detectives) issued an order to his station houses, which licensed the girls. "I ask that you look around in your areas . . . for suitable women . . . very good looking . . . who have flawless manners, intelligence, and tact and if possible knowledge of foreign languages. . . . Report them . . . to Department VI." But whether he found any such paragons leaning against the lampposts of the Third Reich remains one of the mysteries of the Second World War.

Himmler demonstrated a little more imagination in his recruiting idea, which was both callous and desperate. He sought to coerce fiancés into spying for him under threat of withholding permission for them to marry. (He held this power as interior minister for part-Jews and as head of the SS for SS members.) On 16 December 1944, he asked Schellenberg to see if the half-Jewess Friederike Deutsch, who planned to marry an Italian nobleman, Giovanni Enrico Count Sizzo-Noris, could and would spy for the SD. At the same time, he ordered Schellenberg to set up a desk where similar marriage applications could be screened for the same purpose. Schellenberg told him how promising the idea looked and dispatched it and four other cases to outstations for investigation.

One couple was Hazar Hazarian, a 29-year-old Bulgarian working as a translator at a Waffen-SS regiment, and Erna Dangler, a 44-year-old German who was living with him in Vienna. Hazarian declared himself ready to work as a secret agent—to get out of the army. But he declined to serve in Bulgaria, the one place his knowledge of language and country would be of use, because, he said, he would run too much of a risk there. The interviewer reported that anyway he "makes no trustworthy impression." Berlin decided that he was unsuitable for spy work, approved the marriage, and closed the matter. Only one case appeared promising: that of Schauki Omiera, a 26-year-old Transjordanian who had fought for Arab independence against the French and had served briefly as an Abwehr radioman, and his fiancée, Elisabeth Rose, 25, seven months pregnant by him. But though the interviewer, who carefully avoided mentioning his intelligence connections, found him "usable" for spy work, Berlin somehow concluded that he was not really suitable.

The other couples likewise failed to qualify. One man was judged "very cowardly and untrustworthy," another lay hospitalized with blood poisoning. In the original case, Count Sizzo-Noris decided to wait a bit to marry and vanished into Italy. Not one of the attempts succeeded, and no others were tried. Thus ended the queer attempt of the Reichsführer SS to divert love into the service of spying.

In their recruiting efforts, both Abwehr and SD naturally sought the ideal—an agent who was intelligent and quick-witted, emotionally stable and with good nerves, physically strong, and who possessed a thorough knowledge of the target country's geography, customs, language, and army. Seldom did they find such perfection. Indeed, the vast majority of agents had only two chief qualifications: their youth—nearly all spies were in their twenties or thirties—and a willingness to serve.

That willingness itself reflected a variety of motivations, of which four were the most common. Leading the list by far was the lure of easy money. The prospective spy envisaged an easy life. He would sit about in cafés, under the very posters warning people not to talk carelessly, and pick up vital, war-winning secrets. He would stroll past a factory or an antiaircraft gun position or two, would radio an occasional message, perhaps would even seduce a secretary in the line of duty. He saw it all—quite correctly— as much more pleasant than fighting at the front or working in a factory, and as much more lucrative, for he would be paid for this relative leisure, and would also get cash for expenses.

Danger enticed some men. The perils of the fronts were too ordinary and too uncomfortable to attract them. Their blood raced at visions of stealing documents, photographing fortifications, dodging counterintelligence agents. This motive often mingled with the first. In both cases, the hidden psychological pressures were sometimes less healthy than the overt motives: a megalomaniac feeling of secretly pulling the strings of history, or a schizophrenic satisfaction in assuming a false persona.

A third motive was idealism. Some spies believed in National Socialism. More hated the governments that controlled their homelands. Most of the Russian prisoners who became spies did so because they opposed the Communist regime. Many Algerians wanted to see their country freed from France.

Finally, some who said they would serve as agents never intended to. They merely wanted to escape from Germany.

Once recruited, these men could not be simply sent abroad. They had first to learn what facts were wanted, how to find them, and how to report them. The Abwehr and the SD taught these skills at spy schools. At least a score existed at different times, varying greatly in curriculum and in appearance.

Because for reasons of security the older schools taught each spy individually, they scattered their "classrooms" about the city disguised as business firms. The Abwehr posts at both Stuttgart and Hamburg did this. Stuttgart made sure that its offices were in buildings with considerable traffic to make surveillance more difficult, and it changed their locations from time to time. Hamburg gave instruction in radio construction and invisible inks at legitimate but Abwehr-connected factories. Both posts put up their students at local hotels, Hamburg favoring a boarding house called the Klopstock, after the eighteenth-century poet.

The training of agents for operations against the Soviet Union expanded considerably in 1941, with schools in Königsberg, Stettin, Berlin, and Vienna. After the start of hostilities, mass combat-zone espionage compelled the Abwehr to convert its instruction in the east from individual to group, and to reduce the duration for non-radio spies to as little as six weeks. It could permit this because most of its spies, as former Russian soldiers, were familiar with the country and with Red army equipment, insignia, and regulations. By 1943, the Germans had set up nine schools for such agents on conquered Russian territory with a capacity of 10,000 spies and saboteurs. Other schools sank to this mass level. Outside Vienna, Major Franz Seubert taught 40 to 50 Rumanian fascists in a three-month course of 8 to 10 hours a day in preparation for commitment behind Russian lines.

In the west, too, the same development took place as Germany was thrown increasingly on the defensive and the demand for intelligence grew. The SD and its captive Abwehr, now the Military Department, abandoned —reluctantly at first—their policy of individual instruction. They feared the loss of security. The Cologne post, for example, while conceding that a simultaneous commitment of agents called for common training, never assembled more than five in a class. But after the Normandy invasion, security objections vanished—though the worries did not—and mass-instruction schools sprang up like mushrooms. Two new RSHA VI B agent control posts, WALTER and SIEGFRIED, set up several. SIEGFRIED, which specialized in Belgian agents, had two schools near its headquarters in Marburg. WALTER established one on the island of Mainau in Lake Constance, one in the town of Constance itself for agents recruited from the Partie Populaire Française, one in Woelfingen castle near Sigmaringen for agents recruited from the Milice, and others elsewhere in southwestern Germany for agents from other sources. Front Reconnaissance Command 120 and its subordinate front reconnaissance troops had camps in or near Leistadt, Eitorf, Haan, Bad Neuenahr, Velberg, and Kirchzarten. The Command Report Area Munich trained its Italian agents at a house in Verona, giving out as cover that they were working for armaments minister Speer. Later it moved the camp to a hilltop house overlooking Merano. Here it hinted that this was a convalescent home and that the agents were wounded soldiers.

The instructors in these schools were mostly German army officers. They taught their specialties. Signal officers taught radio, for example. Usually they spoke in German, though in some cases they had to use the trainees' native language. Sometimes the agents' countrymen taught. North African agents, who lived and studied in three camps under the jurisdiction of the Command Report Area Stuttgart, had one such instructor, and the Italians at Merano were taught by an Italian army officer.

At the older schools the instruction was multifaceted and thorough—especially at Hamburg, which, because of its overseas responsibilities, ran perhaps the most elaborate school. Agents studied Morse code, radio construction and repair, cipher systems, invisible ink, microdots, spotting and shaking shadows, and recognizing aircraft types. Instruction was nearly always individual. So time-consuming and costly was this training that only about 200 young men attended the Hamburg school throughout the entire war.

In contrast to this, the quality of instruction declined in the newer schools. More agents were taught in larger groups for shorter periods of time. They learned little more than to recognize basic military equipment and the unit insignia worn by many soldiers. But if their instructors were good, they were taught to observe with precision.

Major Seubert walked through the woods with his Rumanians. "What is that?" he would ask them.

"A sheep," they would say.

"What?" he would ask, more sharply.

"A white sheep," they would say, catching on.

"No," Seubert would say. "You have to be more exact in your reports. What you must say is that at 1643 hours on 28 September 1944 on the right side of the road from Vienna to Breitenbrunn you saw a sheep that was white on the side that faced you."

Flunk-outs seemed to be fairly rare. Probably the Abwehr felt that, since agents were pretty expendable anyway, it might as well send them abroad in the hope that they might collect some information as retain them in Germany, waste all that training, and have another mouth to feed. The camps run by Munich did send back for use as workers trainees who were politically unreliable or who talked too much. But another camp found that both its schooled and unschooled North African agents worked with equal effect.

It was during his training period that the agent came to know well the man who would become his chief link to Germany when he was abroad: his handler, his spymaster. This man, who had sometimes recruited the agent, had the difficult task of ensuring that the agent, when on assignment, would continue to work well—and for Germany. This was no easy problem, for the agent would then no longer be under the Abwehr's observation and physical control, and would have ample opportunity to lie, malinger, or desert.

The spymaster sought to bind the agent mainly by instilling in him respect or affection toward himself. He hoped that the spy, who was nearly always younger than he was, would then not want to cause him pain—or worse—by letting him down but would repeatedly perform despite difficulties, danger, fatigue, even laziness. The handler imbued this feeling by demonstrating a strong personal concern for the agent. He showed how he was making sure that the spy got the right false papers and clothing, that he got good food and cigarettes at the agent compound, that he had been trained well enough to succeed. He went with him to the departure point. Negative sanctions, often unspoken, also played a large role: the implied threats to cut off funds or to take reprisals against family members in German-controlled areas. Once the spy was in the enemy camp, the spymaster maintained the link. He sat with the radiomen when the spy's message came in and drafted replies, got him decorations, tried to get money to him when it was needed, and kept up a constant flow of encouraging messages. The theory was sound, for this personal connection was the best way of assuring a spy's reliability, upon which the success of a mission largely depended. And often it worked well in practice. But frequently, too, an agent was trapped by forces beyond his control, and then he could do little more for his spymaster than regret that he had to betray him.

After training and before insertion, the spies had to be given cover identities. These came from legitimate and from fake business firms that could put the spy on their rolls. In neutral countries, real German and neutral firms could serve; in enemy countries, only neutral firms. Among the German enterprises that provided "employment" for Abwehr agents were the Schenker & Company bank, the national railroad, the national airline, some steamship companies, I. G. Farben's Bayer aspirin—all offering a plausible reason to be outside of the fatherland. In Spain, Johannes Bernhardt, the German businessman who in 1936 had delivered a letter from Franco to Hitler that led to German support of the Falange, placed his Sociedád Financiera Industriál, or Sofindus, at the disposal of the SD, which utilized these opportunities to the full.

The fake firms ranged from large companies to single-owner enterprises. They were fake only in the sense that they existed not to make money but to facilitate espionage, for all of them actually operated. In France before the war, for example, the Abwehr founded a firm that was to publish brochures describing the sights along the trunk rail lines; this gave its agents good excuses for travels, photographs, questions. It also set up resident agents in newsstands or tobacco stores, since these offered good opportunities for inconspicuous meetings with subagents. In Portugal and South America, its more important agents got import-export firms as their cover. For smaller traveling agents, the Abwehr found that in western Europe a cover as a postage-stamp dealer worked well, while in the Balkans a traveling tobacco and wool merchant blunted suspicion. One agent in unoccupied France pretended to represent a manufacturer of cigarette cases and cosmetic boxes, samples of which he carried with him as he traveled about noting where French troops lay.

In Latin America, full-sized firms, some of them incorporated, flourished to conceal Germany's extensive espionage. Three major ringleaders in neutral but pro-Nazi Argentina each had his own cover firm. Hans Napp pretended to the world that his meetings, his travels, his telephone calls, his mail, merely concerned the normal business of his Compañía DIN, with offices in rooms 162 and 163 of Calle Reconquista 331 in Buenos Aires. In fact, all this activity involved Napp's real work as head of one of the busiest spy groups in South America. Friedrich Tadeo von Schulz-Hausmann used Bromberg y Compañía at Calle Moreno 970 in Buenos Aires to cover his spy activities. Ottomar Müller's ring passed the information it had collected in Argentina to a cover firm in Rio de Janeiro, Brazil, Informadora Rapida Ltda., for transmission to Germany by its clandestine radio. In Chile, a former branch of Norddeutscher Lloyd, the Compañía Transportes Maritimos, Prat 828, Valparaiso, which with the war's strangling of German shipping had lost almost all its business, kept its seven remaining employees active collecting information—some of which came in through its post-office box—and passing it to a spy radio for forwarding to Germany. The Abwehr and the SD stood what were usually the losses of these businesses as part of the cost of espionage, though one Abwehr cover firm, Transmare in Argentine, turned such a profit in its import-export affairs that it defrayed all the agent's costs!

The faking of the documents attesting to the false identities of the agents fell to special sections of the Abwehr and RSHA VI. The Abwehr's was Group G of Branch I. Albert Müller headed it throughout the war. A small, pudgy chemist, he had done similar work in World War I. In 1937, with rearmament in full swing, the Abwehr dug his name out of the archives and, since he was a reserve officer, reactivated him. He was then a captain, aged 50.

His office in Abwehr headquarters embraced all Abwehr scientific work, including long-range photography and devices for the censorship's mass checking of letters for invisible ink. Of its six desks, only 1 and 6 dealt with false documents. Desk 1 manufactured the papers, seals, and stamps.

Desk 6, which grew out of 1 during the war, filled them out and distributed them; it also supervised the work of the G sections of the Abwehr posts and of the army group I cs in Russia.

While Müller was embarking upon his duties, the SD was moving into the same area. Heydrich faked documents to discredit Red army officers, which perhaps played a minor role in the great purges of 1937 to 1939. Assisting in this scheme, in part by finding a trustworthy engraver-forger, was a 28-year-old SD man, a street brawler from Kiel who had gained Heydrich's attention by ratting on his chief. This was Alfred Naujocks. Soon after what he regarded as his Russian successes, Heydrich decided to establish a section to produce false documents and other aids for his agents on a full-time basis. He gave the job to Naujocks, by then an SS major who had proved himself by sabotaging an anti-Nazi radio station near Prague. Energetically, Naujocks assembled the necessary manpower and matériel and installed the unit in a large gray stone building at Delbrückstrasse 6a in a residential neighborhood in southwestern Berlin. Like the Abwehr's I G, it handled more than false documents. Thus it developed and manufactured agent radio sets and miniature cameras, communicated with SD agents by radio, and supervised the RSHA's tiny communications-intelligence unit. Within about a year, Naujocks had it running so well that, though he remained its nominal head, Heydrich freed him for other capers: faking a Polish attack upon a German radio station to give Hitler his excuse to attack Poland, helping Schellenberg kidnap the British secret service officers at Venlo, setting up a bugged brothel, called "Salon Kitty," to try to learn the secrets of diplomat johns.

With the creation of the RSHA, his unit became VI B, later redesignated VI F. But early in 1941, Naujocks, who incurred Heydrich's displeasure because he forgot to turn off the tape recorder during a Heydrich visit to the brothel, and who disliked Schellenberg, who, all signs indicated, was about to become his boss, accepted Jost's offer of a transfer to The Hague. His replacement was an old buddy of Schellenberg's: Walther Rauff, an SS lieutenant colonel, who had attended Heydrich's attempt to persuade Schellenberg's first wife to be gone. He apparently took the new job just temporarily, for he retained his post as head of RSHA II D. This group dealt with technical matters for the entire RSHA and devised the efficient vans that asphyxiated Jews and others with exhaust gases while transporting them to their mass graves. And in fact, after little more than a year, Rauff departed Berlin for more important assignments: rounding up Jews in Tunis and Italy. His replacement, SS Major Hermann Dörner, 34, took over on 20 July 1942. He had served on Himmler's personal staff since 1935 with the exception of nine months early in the war commanding an engineer platoon with the SS Death's Head Division. Schellenberg regarded him as being imaginative in his work and as trying hard. But he was no leader, and after a year and a half he was transferred to an SS corps at the front as I c. SS Major Rudolf Lassig, the head of VI F 3, the sabotage desk, became acting group chief.

These choices and changes, perhaps indicative of the basic triviality of SD espionage, affected the group less than they might have, partly because its individual desks had rather disparate functions and seemed to run themselves well, partly because of the continuity of service of Naujock's original chief assistant, whose aptitudes and experience covered all the desks. He was Bernhard Krüger, a former locksmith who had run a radio station for the SD for several years. On 1 September 1943, he took provisional charge of the false documents desk, VI F 4.

The work of both VI F 4 and the Abwehr's I G fell into the same two areas: generating the physical documents and printing and filling them in. The pieces of paper that constituted the material basis of the documents came in three forms. By far the most desirable were blank originals. Around 1940 a pro-German secretary at the American consulate in Antwerp turned over a quantity of blank U.S. passports to an Abwehr officer, who forwarded them to Berlin. The overrunning of an enemy headquarters could furnish blank originals. But they were normally hard to come by, and were limited in quantity. The second form of document was the filled-in original. On the Russian front, most of these came from prisoners of war; elsewhere, they were stolen or taken from persons who had died or been sent to concentration camps. Such papers had the advantages of being genuine and of having legitimate stamps in them from previous actual trips. Their disadvantage lay in that their alteration to fit the agent could never withstand careful scrutiny. Most nations attached passport pictures with methods that betrayed their removal. They used ink that ate deep into the paper and whose mechanical or chemical erasure left traces. Because of their unreliability, altered documents served mostly agents whose papers could be expected to be given only the same cursory glance as the majority of travelers'.

The third form of document was the counterfeit. It avoided the problems of alteration and of limited quantity. But producing it demanded a lot of time and trouble. Red army documents might not pose much of a problem, but passports, with their special watermarked papers, their laminated covers, and sometimes their secret markings, presented considerable difficulties. Both the Abwehr and the SD had paper made to the necessary specifications. The SD had batches cooked up in huge tubs by a handful of men in a paper factory in Spechthausen, a tiny town some 20 miles northeast of Berlin. When problems arose concerning the cellulose coating on passport covers, the SD consulted outside research laboratories as well. Since all this work might be rendered useless by a nation's changing its passports, both agencies undertook such forgeries only in the rare cases of exceptionally important and trustworthy agents. Between 1941 and 1945, for example, Berlin produced only two passports for the Prague Abwehr post—a Bulgarian and a Turkish.

An essential part of the paper base was the intricate background guilloche imprinted into it and the gold seals stamped into the covers. The Abwehr had 20 engravers and graphic artists reproducing these. But equally important was what the documents said.

The forms printed on them and the rubber stamps that covered them had to conform to current enemy usage. Their serial numbers could not exceed current ranges. To ensure this, I G had its subordinate G sections at the Abwehr outposts photograph passports and other important foreign documents and send in the pictures with descriptions of ink and paper colors. VI F kept up to date by having SD outposts photograph passports and identity cards collected by the police from travelers registered at hotels. From these, the Abwehr and SD workshops reproduced rubber stamps and dyed ink pads with the proper tints. I G had a thousand stamps for foreign visas, border posts, and other authorities.

Filling in the particulars posed many problems which, if not resolved properly, could mean the death of an agent. These data had naturally to employ the terminology of the "issuing" country. It would not do, in a purportedly American or English passport, to give an agent's height as 172 centimeters. Consequently, I G specified, in the form that outposts used to apply for a document, that details about the agent be given in that country's language. Since a brand-new passport would arouse too much suspicion, I G stamped in entries and exits. It had to plan these notional trips with care, basing much of the route on information from a 4-page questionnaire that the agent's spymaster had to fill out. It could not follow an impossible route, showing, for example, a border crossing at a post that was closed on the stamped date. It could not show entry into a country for which a visa was required if it did not have the visa stamp. When things got too difficult, I G fudged by smudging impressions or overstamping to make them illegible.

Its greatest problem was keeping up with the unimaginably great variety of documents that agents required. Paper is a bane of modern civilization, and red tape proliferated in wartime, with new documents, such as ration books, constantly coming into existence. Even the legitimate possessors were burdened. How much greater must the task have been for I G and VI F 4, which had to prepare up to 10 documents per agent. A list of some of the 146 Red army counterfeits that I G 6 kept on file suggests the magnitude of the problem: Russian passport (monolinguistic, without numbers), Russian-Ukrainian passport (with number and series), Russian-Ukrainian passport (without number), military driver's license, hospital discharge certificate, Caucasus area receipt for a surrendered pass, Communist party book, deferment certificate for workers in war industry, the same for workers on the railroads, letterheads of the Central Administration for Equipping Armored Troops, of the Staff of the Southern Front Operations Section, and of the Political Command of the Leningrad Front, ordinary travel orders (both on normal and on thin paper), travel orders for a pilot of the Voronezh Front (both in yellow and in white), certificate of decoration (war edition), a birth certificate in Lesginer, one in Avar, six kinds of hospital discharge certificates (ordinary, small white, medium white, large brown, and large long white and from the naval hospital in Archangel), and no fewer than 16 kinds of officer's identity cards (not to be confused with the four kinds of personal identity cards for officers).

In many cases, I G and VI F 4 did their jobs adequately. To test one of its new fake passports, which had already withstood an ultraviolet examination, VI F 4 ordered a young soldier to use it to cross into Switzerland. It then alerted the Swiss that a spy might be coming through at that point. The border guards scrutinized the soldier's passport and supporting papers with the greatest of care—and passed him. One Abwehr agent was equipped with I G–furnished papers identifying him as a Soviet lieutenant ordered to an air force school. He attended for several months, constantly reporting what he was learning. Another agent was given papers that, playing on his sickly appearance, certified him as unsuitable for the army, and, exploiting his real-life profession, showed him as a teacher. With them, he got a job in a school in central Russia, from where he spied on the Red army.

The Abwehr posts and, from June 1942, the I cs at army groups had their own small I G units for local purposes. Usually they did little more than fill in the prepared forms. That at Army Group Center issued about 500 a month. During the war, the entire I G organization issued more than 400,000 false documents.

Not surprisingly, therefore, its forgers sometimes overlooked one or another of the minutiae. And sometimes the Russians spotted the errors. Forged Communist party books with serial numbers above 3,800,000 left a blank space for the year of the member's financial contribution, whereas in the real books the year dates were printed. In other fake party books, the loop over the "i" in "Chlenski" ("membership") appeared as two dots. Certain counterfeit stamp impressions were in violet ink, while the genuine ones were black. German rubber-stamp impressions were in general sharper and darker than the Russian. The Germans used chromium-plated wire for stapling which, unlike the Russian staples, left no rust marks on the paper. And in preparing a cédula, or identification paper, for a spy going to Argentina, I G merely pressed the thumbprint onto the page instead of rolling it as was normally done, omitted the date of the photograph, which was regarded as an important detail in cédula records, misspelled "comerciante" (businessman) with two *m*s, used too coarse a watermark and had it too low on the page, and gave the title of the signing official, not as the correct chief of police, but as prefect general of police, an office that had never existed in Buenos Aires!

To the fake documents the Germans had to fit fake identities, or "legends." One agent dropped in Ireland, Sergeant Günther Schütz, adopted the identity—and the South African passport, suitably doctored—of a school friend, Hans Marschner, who had stayed on in Germany at the start of the war. This was an easy legend for an agent to learn. Others, more remote from their experiences, were harder both to construct and to remember. Moreover, they were not always easy to sustain under capture. The Russians tested the speech of suspected agents against the dialect of the region from which they ostensibly came. They called in local residents to help question the suspects about the terrain there. Similar difficulties in homogeneous Britain occasionally led the Abwehr to abandon attempts to get real agents in as fake businessmen and to try instead to get real businessmen to work as agents.

To further back up their legends, the Germans gave their agents appropriate family photographs, letters, bills, receipts, cards, clothing, and equipment. The spy agencies generally avoided errors that would betray the agents. Sometimes they got the genuine articles from the enemy himself. The English-made clothing that the Allies parachuted into France for the Maquis occasionally fell into Abwehr hands.

But at times the Germans erred. Their Russian spies wore fake uniforms with minor tailoring errors. Their shirts had side slits in their tails, whereas the real ones did not. Their buttons were covered with material, while the genuine ones were not. In an excess of thoroughness, they sewed the shoulder tabs down onto the sleeve. The Russians just let them hang. The flaws were slight, but for some they proved fatal.

To gather information, Germany's spies had to be in enemy territory. But how could they get there? Battle lines lay athwart land routes. Strict controls at seaports and airports throttled entry from neutral countries. Yet only three possibilities existed—by land, by sea, and by air. Hitler's spies had to find and exploit the tiny interstices that penetrated these three kinds of boundary. In many cases they did so, and succeeded in seeping through them into the target country.

Land boundaries in peacetime, or wartime boundaries with neutrals such as Switzerland, could sometimes be crossed quite simply at legal border posts by spies showing their false papers. This did not invariably work. Perhaps their papers could not withstand the inspection of a sharp-eyed official. Perhaps they had to cross frequently, or to take money or equipment through. In such cases, spies often traversed the "forested frontier." Typical of these was that with France.

No fences entirely closed the hilly, wooded, twisting border from the

Rhine to Luxembourg. The Abwehr spymasters from Trier sent their agents into France on one of the many paths that snaked through the woods across the border—spies were not the only people who avoided the immigration and customs officials. The Germans called this technique "Schleusung," a word, cognate to English "sluice," that means "passing [ships] through a lock." To inject agents into the United States, the Abwehr bought them sea passage from Lisbon to South America; from there they went to Mexico, whence they entered by wading and swimming across the Rio Grande like wetbacks. The process was long: often it took a year before the agents reported back. Schleusung also served to infiltrate agents through the front lines in the east. Under cover of darkness, front-line soldiers brought the agents from their own lines out into no-man's-land and then showed them routes that, skirting enemy positions, led into the enemy rear. The agents, sneaking past the enemy sentries, then silently hastened as far as they could from their point of entry.

A quite different method served when the German armies were in retreat: Überrollung. Agents remained in place and let the advancing enemy armies "roll over" them. The Germans used this in the east during their periodic winter retreats and in the west during the OVERLORD invasion.

The dangers of these procedures could be avoided, and the advantages of deep penetration gained, by aerial insertion.

Early in the war, Rowehl's reconnaissance squadron lent its long-range planes and navigationally experienced pilots for this purpose. Luftwaffe Captain Karl Edmund Gartenfeld specialized in this work. As the need for it grew, especially after the invasion of Russia, Gartenfeld added more pilots and airplanes, until by the summer of 1942 he formed his own squadron, the 2nd Test Formation of the commander in chief of the Luftwaffe. In the next two years it grew to a group with four squadrons, of which 1 and 4 worked the west. In March of 1944, Gartenfeld's 2nd was united with the 1st Test Formation, a true research unit. The combined outfit, under the command of one of the leading German pilots, Lieutenant Colonel Werner Baumbach, was called Battle Wing 200, though the two parts curiously reversed numbers: the 2nd Test Formation became the first group of the battle wing. About the same time, Gartenfeld was replaced by Major Adolf Koch.

The unit strewed its airplanes all around Europe in response to its needs. It flew from Simferopol to Iran, Iraq, and the Caucasus, from Athens-Kalamaki to Egypt, Transjordan, and Libya, from Marseilles to Tunisia, Algeria, and Morocco, from Rennes and Paris to England, and, after OVERLORD, from Echterdingen and other airfields on the right bank of the Rhine to the western front. It used the tiny Fieseler Storch as well as the Focke-Wulf FW 200 and the Junker Ju 188. And it did not disdain captured foreign aircraft. During a conference of the air production chief, at which the officials discussed a Russian four-motored TB-7 that had belly-landed near

Köningsberg and that had a very great range, one official said, "Canaris is wild to get as many such machines as possible. . . . We must give them to the I c at once." Other Russian types flew in the east. In the west, the squadron used B-17 Flying Fortresses, cover-designating them Dornier Do 288s, a nonexistent German type.

The timing of agent flights depended mainly upon the weather. Often they had to be postponed two or three times, adding to the anguish of the agent. Sometimes flights actually started, only to be forced back by bad weather or enemy action. Gartenfeld's men nearly always flew at night and preferred no moon and thick cloud cover. The unit painted its planes black and dyed the agents' parachutes dark brown. Early in the war, when agents' radios were still bulky and heavy, they had to be dropped on a separate parachute. Agents sometimes lost them, like Hermann Goertz, who spent the whole night looking in vain for his after jumping into Ireland. This led the Abwehr to put the radios into phosphorescent bags until a later reduction in their size enabled agents to carry them on their jumps.

Agents were naturally to be dropped as close as practicable to where they would work. Thus, for one agent, an Englishman, the area about Wisbech, some two train hours north of his destination, London, was chosen, because the pilot could fly in over the flat terrain with ease, the surrounding countryside was sparsely populated, and the spy knew the area. The squadron estimated the accuracy of its drops as within 5 miles of the target point, depending upon wind, altitude, and enemy fighters. But the planes could stray considerably. Once Gartenfeld, who intended to drop an agent near Dublin, flew 60 miles to the south instead. The Irish promptly captured the man.

During the flights, the poor agent squeezed into an uncomfortable corner of a plane never intended for spy transport. Weighed down by his parachute and equipment, he stared at the tiny hole cut in the fuselage through whch he would jump, he thought, to fortune or to death. Going to England, the pilot often skimmed the surface of the water to avoid radar detection. That danger past after he crossed the coast, he then zoomed high to make it harder to see and hear him. Often the agent got airsick. He grew sicker as the pilot took evasive action against enemy fighters. Sometimes the pilot made him jump from high up, sometimes the plane swooped low, with throttled motors, to let him go. Some agents hesitated at the last moment and were "helped" out. One had a different problem. He was too fat. As he wriggled frantically, stuck in the exit hole with legs flapping in the windstream, the plane flying further and further from his target, crew members stomped on him until they forced him through.

Aerial insertion continued in the east throughout the war. But Britain's growing mastery of her own skies forced the Germans to abandon agent flights there after June of 1941. They switched instead to the sea.

Shakespeare said that it served his "sceptered isle" "in the office of a wall / Or as a moat defensive to a house." But the sea also is, as Homer said, the highway of the gods, and though the spies of Nazi Germany were anything but divine, they too used it as a route of infiltration into England. Some agents pretended to be refugees from occupied Europe. Sailing secretly from Holland, they landed openly in England. Few, if any, got past the watchful British port security, however, which sometimes even put native Englishmen, returning home by devious routes after having been trapped by the fall of France, into protective custody for weeks until their statements could be checked. Other spies crossed the Channel or the North Sea in motorboats or trawlers for most of the way and rowed the last short distance in dinghies.

For very long-range insertions, as into the western hemisphere, the sea afforded the only possibility. Several times the Germans used submarines to North America. At least twice they sent some of their agents to Latin America on neutral vessels with the help of stewards. In one case, a steward on a Spanish vessel, the *Monte Amboto,* had been befriended by a German returning to Europe after being expelled from Ecuador for spying. Later, in Spain, he persuaded the steward to help a German stow away aboard his ship on a trip to Argentina. The spy, Hans Zweigert, was intended to be one of Germany's few agents in place: he was to burrow into Argentine society but was not to activate himself and send radio messages until and unless Argentina broke relations with Germany. Zweigert spent the entire seven-week voyage in a hold filled with steel, the first few days without food or water. The steward carried his money, blueprints of the radio he was to build, and microfilms of ciphers and other instructions: the Germans assumed, correctly, that crew members passing through the British control point at Trinidad would not be searched. Upon arrival in Buenos Aires in May 1943, Zweigert managed to debark unnoticed. But the police, tipped off somehow, arrested the steward. He confessed that he was to meet Zweigert and give him his money and other papers at 8 p.m. a day or two later at the Confitería La Armonía at Avenida de Mayo 1002. When Zweigert appeared for the rendezvous, the police picked him up

The Germans also transported agents across the Atlantic in their own 50-foot sailboat. The Abwehr outpost in Le Havre had purchased a yawl, the *Passim,* built on the lines of a tuna boat for private cruising. It was slow but comfortable and had a crew of three in addition to the captain, Lieutenant Heinrich Garbers, who had apparently been chosen because in 1938 he had sailed solo across the Atlantic. The *Passim* took saboteurs to South Africa in 1942, and then, on 9 June 1943, it stood out of the little harbor of the wealthy resort of Arcachon, France, just south of Bordeaux, with two spies aboard: Wilhelm Heinrich Knopff, a former leader of the German community in Peru, who was heading back to that country, and— a rarity in German espionage—a black man, William Marcus Baarn, a native of Netherlands Guiana, just north of Brazil. He had been in Amsterdam when the Germans occupied it and had volunteered for spy duty, receiving training in radio telegraphy and ship identification. He and Knopff carried $12,500 in U.S., French, Argentine, and British currency and a portable radio, with which Baarn was to send back shipping information. For this trip the *Passim* bore the name *Santa Barbara* and wore Portuguese colors. For two months it sailed southwest, through the choppy green seas of the North Atlantic and the glinting glassy swells of the South. Early in August, Garbers spotted the lighthouse at Cape Frio, just north of Rio de Janeiro. He turned back north until he came opposite Sao Joao da Barra, a village isolated on the coastal plain 150 miles north of Rio. Here, at midnight, the two spies paddled ashore in a rubber boat. But the Brazilian authorities were awaiting them, and they were arrested at once.

Undaunted, the Abwehr tried again. Later that year, General Friedrich Wolff, the military attaché in Argentina who had taken over the espionage duties with the expulsion of the naval attaché Niebuhr, instructed one of the German agents, Wilhelm Seidlitz, to seek out a place on the Atlantic coast of the province of Buenos Aires for spies to land. Seidlitz got in touch with Gustav Eickenberg, who owned a ranch near the coast southeast of Buenos Aires. The two toured the area and agreed that a spot halfway between the lighthouses of Miramar and Necochea, where a road led to Eickenberg's ranch, was the best. Near the end of April 1944, the *Passim* again set sail. It carried Walter Burckhardt, an expert radioman, and Alphonse Chatrain, a microphotographer, together with $20,000 in cash and *RM*80,000 ($32,000) worth of pharmaceuticals to be sold for additional cash. This time, as the yawl splashed its way across the ocean, an Allied patrol stopped it. Sailors boarded it for inspection, but it carried no contraband, and its papers, and those of the crew and passengers, seemed in order. They let the vessel go. Soon it approached the South American coast. An exchange of radio messages with the local spy ring shifted the landing site from south of the Miramar lighthouse to north of it—about 3 kilometers south of the lighthouse at Punta Mogotes. On the night of 5 July 1944, the crew saw lantern signals on the coast at the agreed-upon point. Burckhardt and Chatrain rowed ashore in a rubber boat. They were met by German spies in three cars who drove Burckhardt to one ranch, Chatrain to another, successfully concluding Germany's longest-range insertion in the entire spy war. Garbers won the Iron Cross 1st and 2nd Class, the German Cross in gold, and the Knight's Cross for his successes. They made him probably the most decorated man in the entire German intelligence effort.

Once in their target country, agents often had to contact others, in particular the ringleader. To assure one another that they were legitimate, spies exchanged prearranged passwords. A message from Germany told an agent in Latin America in 1941 that a new spy would say to him in German: "I bring greetings from Germany." The agent would reply: "Surely from Königsberg." "Thereupon," concluded the instructions, "do business."

Arranging meetings, which was more complicated than merely recognizing someone, required more complicated codes. Dusko Popov, a Yugoslav regarded as one of the Abwehr's top spies, telephoned his German spymaster, who was in neutral Portugal, when he wanted to meet him. If Popov said, "I shall come by train," it meant he was to be picked up in Lisbon at a prearranged spot on the Avenida da Liberdade. If he said he was coming by taxi, it meant that he wanted to be met a mile outside Estoril on the main road to Lisbon. Making the date for "Monday" meant meeting at 6:10 p.m., "Tuesday," 7:10, and so on. Normally the meeting was the following day, but if Popov said it was "urgent" the meeting was for the same day. Popov's spymaster got in touch with him by having a girl call, give any name, and say, "I'm sorry I behaved so stupidly the other night." Popov and she agreed upon a meeting that night or the next at a certain nightclub. But in fact the spymaster's blonde secretary (and mistress) met Popov at the Estoril casino. "She would go to a roulette table; I following," said Popov, "and would play three times, the numbers indicating consecutively the date, hour, and minute of our rendezvous. Then she would play 0 or 36. Zero meant the pickup was to take place in Lisbon, 36 meant Estoril at prearranged locations. It was an expensive code."

An agent who collects information is useless if he cannot report it. Communications are therefore the vital link of espionage. And these links took many forms.

To Piekenbrock, head of Abwehr I, by far the best was for an agent to meet his handler. The agents naturally gave more details in a conversation than in a letter. They answered questions then and there. The handler could test the agent anew, satisfy himself as to the man's sources, reinspire him, give him new instructions. Interviews ran marathon-length, with a secretary taking it all down in shorthand. Such talks took place from time to time during the war when agents sailed from England to Portugal. But they were rare. Mostly, agents had to transmit their messages by courier, post, or radio.

Couriers, who usually worked on ships or planes, carried original or microphotographed letters and documents from the spy or his contact to a neutral country or to Germany. Spies in America before Pearl Harbor used 11 couriers on ships and airplanes. In October 1939, one of them, a blonde named Lilly Stein, brought money and a microphotograph from Sweden to New York on the SS *Drottningholm*. A net in Argentina sent its reports and photographs of strategic places to Germany via the courier Benjamin Juan Roson, the brother-in-law of an employee of the Siemens-Schuckert firm; Roson frequently traveled on the *Cabo de Hornos* to Spain, where a German official presumably picked up the material and forwarded it to Germany through official channels. A courier line is usually the most certain form of communication, but it is also very expensive, fairly slow, and, in wartime, quite difficult to set up.

Letters, on the other hand, are the cheapest form of communication and the most secure, since they are almost impossible to trace; they permit greater volume than radio, which must keep its transmissions short to avoid goniometric detection, but they are less certain to reach their destination, because of enemy censorship, and they are slow.

Naturally, spymasters did not mail letters direct to spies, nor did the spies post their letters to their bosses c/o the Abwehr. Individuals at innocuous residences or offices received the letters and then handed them to the true recipient. The Hamburg post directed its agents in Valparaiso, Chile, on 13 February 1942 to "address letters to Hanno von Halem, Schaan, Lichtenstein." Two other agents got "Simon Simon, Travessa Rio de Janeiro 73, Lisbon," as their cover address.

To slip illicit information through censorship, a barrier designed specifically to block it, the spies concealed it in their letters. German agents during World War II resorted in the main to three techniques, two of which dated from the days of the Caesars.

The first was the jargon code, which veils real meanings under business or personal terms. Cicero used it, and so did a German spy in 1940. Finding it difficult to fulfill an assignment given him in message 5, he wrote, "Your order No. 5 is rather large, and I with my limited facilities will never be able to fill it completely." More common was the second technique: invisible ink. Pliny the Elder gave a formula for one in his *Natural History,* and secret agents from the Renaissance to World War I employed them. Now chemists bubbled liquids in retorts and poured the contents of one test tube into another in the laboratories of VI F and I G 3 as they sought new formulae. Müller defined a good secret ink as one that was clear, left no traces, was able to withstand heat, cold, and sunshine, and defied development by any reagent except the intended chemical. The Abwehr divided its invisible inks into groups numbered I to V, starting with the best, which had most of the qualities Müller considered important; these were given only to top agents. Within each group there were three kinds of ink: 1, dry; 2, alcoholic; 3, water-based. The inks bore codenames: one III 1 ink, a yellow pill, was named GEORG; another, a white pill, was HEINRICH. The agent stuck a toothpick into the pill and wrote on a sheet of paper that he had previously cleaned with cotton. To develop a GEORG message, the recipient dampened the paper, sprinkled it with a red powder containing naphthalene, heated it to 60° centigrade, and irradiated it with ultraviolet light. PURAL was a laxative tablet containing phenolphthalene. The agent dissolved it in a 50 percent solution of schnapps for writing. The spymaster developed it into pink writing with a mixture of water and cigarette ashes. Another common Abwehr ink was the headache remedy pyramidon, sometimes dissolved in alcohol. The Abwehr concealed the ink for some of its spies to Ireland by impregnating it into a cloth wad, which turned yellow, and sewing it into clothes as shoulder padding. To make the ink, the agent soaked the wad in water. VI F invented an invisible ink of which an essential component was hemoglobin: the agent pricked a finger and used a drop of blood to make his ink. Its development likewise involved biological processes, turning the message up in green.

The two German spy agencies sought ways of counteracting the two main techniques of Allied censorship to spot invisible ink. In one technique, which used four or five brushes wired together and dipped simultaneously into four or five developers for common inks, the censor painted stripes diagonally across pages and watched to see whether anything came up. To defeat this, I G 3 invented an ink that required three repeated applications of developer with waits of three hours between each application and then a third delay of three hours before writing would appear. The censor's second technique employed iodine vapor. The violet fumes settled differentially into the fibers of the paper that had been disturbed by the fluid of the invisible ink and so showed up the writing without the need to ascertain the specific reagent. The SD taught Gimpel how to avoid detection this way. He was to write his secret-ink message normally on a blank piece of paper, and then press this tightly—using weights, if possible—against a second sheet, to which some ink would migrate. He would discard the first sheet, cover the second with an innocuous message, and mail it to Berlin, where a laboratory would develop the traces of secret ink. The writing would come out backward, but that difficulty was insignificant.

If the first two techniques for hiding messages in letters were ancient, the third was as modern as precision photography. This was the microdot. Microphotography had served communications as long ago as 1871, when it reduced letters to the size of postage stamps for the balloons and carrier-pigeons out of Paris, besieged by the Germans. But Heinrich Beck, a chemist with I. G. Farben pulled into I G 2, determined to improve on this. With the help of Agfa and other German firms, he developed lenses of extra high resolution. He adapted film emulsions based on aniline dyes, which could distinguish light and dark at the molecular level instead of at the much coarser granular level of normal silver emulsions. Eventually Beck managed to reduce a printed page to the size of a printed period. Then he squeezed the size of the equipment needed for this, which originally filled a whole room, down to that of a small trunk. The SD adopted his work.

This technological triumph suffered, however, from practical drawbacks. It was extremely expensive, and the apparatus was bulky and hard to conceal. Consequently it mostly served from Germany to send instructions to agents, who needed only a powerful microscope to read the microdots. Only a very few major agents, such as some in relatively safe South America, received sets to produce microdots, usually not as circles but as tiny squares of film. Many of these used them to good advantage, sending over whole issues of such hard-to-find magazines as *Iron Age* hidden as infinitesimal strips of film camouflaged against the shininess of the gum of the factory-sealed flaps of letter envelopes. But not every agent thought too highly of the microdot system. When Gimpel landed in Maine, he left his set aboard the submarine because it was too heavy to carry.

A report that arrives too late is about as useless as one that is never sent or never arrives. And during World War II, mail, even airmail, moved too slowly. Both the Abwehr and the SD thus relied increasingly on radio as their chief means of communication.

For this the Abwehr equipped its agents with special transmitter-receivers called "Afus," from "Agentenfunk," or "agent radio." Developed during the 1930s, this was a hand-keyed Morse apparatus, about the size of a suitcase, tuned by quartz to a single, preset frequency, and powered by batteries that gave it about 10 watts.

The agents transmitted their messages according to a radio plan. This gave them their call signs, cipher keys, and times of transmission, which were usually quite simple, such as "Mondays 8 p.m." But agents did not have to radio if they had nothing to report, and on the other hand they could transmit at other times if they had something important. In general, they had to keep their messages as brief as possible to avoid enemy monitors. Most agent messages were very short, only about 50 to 100 letters, which took an average agent about a minute to transmit, or twice as long as a good radioman. Overseas messages ran longer, and were often broken into parts. Agent BOBBI in Canada radioed three message-parts of four-and-a-half typewritten lines each, which arrived in Germany on 5 February 1943 at 4:55, 4:58, and 5:04 p.m.

Receiving the messages were the various Abwehr and RSHA radio posts. The Abwehr's constituted Group i of Branch I. Lieutenant Colonel Kurt Rasehorn, who had been an engineer in World War I but then became a graduate engineer in high frequency and was reactivated in 1936, led it until 1943, when a signal corps officer, Colonel Theodor Poretschkin, replaced him. The group's 2,000 men were formed into Signal Regiment 506. It had four battalions, headquartered in Hamburg, Wiesbaden, Vienna, and the Abwehr headquarters on the Russian front, WALLI. The men worked in various communications posts distributed throughout Germany and the occupied areas and in the KOs abroad. They handled much traffic from one Abwehr post to another. Of the Madrid traffic, for example, about three-fifths constituted intelligence reports; the rest was administrative. This went via the Madrid-Paris-Berlin teletypewriter line until 1943, when bombings compelled a shift to radio. Thenceforth the I i transmitter, located in the embassy annex, established contact with Berlin every hour, and with other posts, such as Rome or Bordeaux or its own outposts, every four hours. The Abwehr also used other routes. The outpost in Algeciras, for example, radioed its observations of ships in Gibraltar to a station at Dax, in south-western France, which forwarded it to Berlin.

Which stations agents radioed to depended upon where they operated. Thus Abwehr agents in Switzerland, France, Spain, and North Africa sent mainly to the stations subordinated to Wiesbaden. That station, a specially built installation with lodgings for the men, was actually located at Eiserne Hand, a village in the low mountains north of Wiesbaden, for the Abwehr sought to locate its transmitters and receivers in remote or quiet areas, away from large or numerous electrical installations that created static. Wiesbaden had subordinate radio stations in the village of Krum, just across the Rhine from Cologne, in a villa in Neuilly, next to Paris, which had grounds large enough for the antennas, and in an elaborate compound on the hills around Sigmaringen. This had two transmission sheds, one with 8 to 10 transmitters, the other with 19, each of which could be connected to each of the 20 working tables. Actual transmission took place by remote control over an underground wire to the towers a mile away. The transmitters ranged up to 750 watts.

Overseas traffic to Britain, Ireland, Iceland, and the western hemisphere was handled by the Hamburg station. Major Werner Trautmann had come from the Stettin Abwehr radio post in 1937 to set it up. He took over as his headquarters a graceful Renaissance-style stucco house that a merchant had built before World War I as a wedding present for his daughter. A lawn in front, a pond behind, it stood at Kupferredder 45 in a still un-developed area of the extreme northeast of the proud Hanseatic city. Trautmann erected his receiving antennas in the meadows across the road and his transmitting ones half a mile away on the north side of Diestelstrasse, keying them, as at Sigmaringen, by remote control. Those of his 120 men who were receiving messages worked four-hour shifts day and night in the receiving room on the second floor of the house. To pick up overseas messages that propagation characteristics made hard to hear in Hamburg, he set up subsidiary reception stations near Stettin, Oslo, and Bordeaux.

Each radioman listened for two different agents on different frequencies in each of his earphones, for although the agents had prearranged transmission periods, circumstances sometimes made them early or late. Much of the time, the radioman was straining to hear the faint chirpings of an Afu through the loud crackle of static. When he finally did detect "his" agent's call sign, he responded with a go-ahead and then, listening hard for each dot and dash, took down the message with great care, for I i did not wire-record transmissions in case of error. If, as was not unusual, the radioman had trained the agent, he watched for the agent's peculiar sending characteristics—his "fist," which is as distinctive as handwriting. He then deciphered the message and made sure it contained its security check. This was a peculiarity in the text, such as an X in the 15th and 20th positions, or a misspelling of the third word, that assured the Abwehr that the mes-

UNIT CASE # SA-2-7-111448   WASHINGTON CASE # 68
             N. CHARLESTON, S. C.
DATE   : APRIL 5, 1941
OBSERVER : F. STEWART JONES

CALL   : STATION CALLING "AOR" AND STATION ANSWERING TO "AOR".
FREQUENCY : 14,558 & 14,568 KCS. AND 14,385 KCS., (MEASURED)
EMISSION : A-1
BEARING   : NONE
RECORDING : NONE   (PAGE5)

GMT
1713   (14,385 KC.) VVV OK OM GA GA K   VVV VVV VVV RR OK OK GA GA

        K   VVV VVV VVV VVV VVV - RRR QTC OK GA GA K

1714   (14,568 KC.) VVV VVVV - QSA8 PSE QSV K K

1715   (14,385 KC.)VVV VVV VVV VVV VVV VVV VVV VVV VVV VVV VVV

        VVV VVV VVV VVV OK OK OK VVV VVV VVV

1716   (14,568 KC.) RPT RPT RPT

1716   (14,385 KC.) OK QTC OK GA K VVV GA GA OK OK QTC OK

1718   (14,568 KC.) - - SRI RPT ALL KA - YENOV (GROUP MISSING)

        ERILJ EGBRI PHEBR ENELE TIUNO ITACQ GYOFB EEEE GYOFB

        XHMAY QTXME INUDR TISHI MYYSN TXLXO FSL   MQRIX   NUS

1722   LRXFX YOEYE QAUME GERXA SEION   AR CODE OF 3 OK? QSV K

1722   (14,385 KC.) VVV VVV VVV VVV VVV VVV VVV VVV VVV VVV VVV

        OK OK GA GA K

1722   (14,568 KC.) R GLAD GLAD NW KA KA DYRE DYRE ILIC ILIC

        SUA SUA ILL ILL - - GLDTG GLDTG TTELR TTESR XTSRI XTSRI

        IPEIN IPESS TXAEX TXAEX GRLUD GRLWB EGZMC EGZMC ORAWW

        ORAWW FTNLH FTNLH SRREI SNREI FSIKE FSIKE SOIEU SOIEU

        BOELP BOELP SNERS SNERS LAHNB LAHNB NAXSA NAXSA GHISB

        GHISB ZARVC ZARVC BUERS BUERS NRAIA NRAIA PTFXM PTFXM

        AWERU AWERU SLNGB SLNBZ HECHE HECHE ZRWEG ZRWEG EEHEN

(CONTINUED PAGE 6)

Radio dialogue between a German spy station, on 14,560 kilocycles, and the Abwehr radio station in Hamburg, here using call sign AOR on 14,385 kilocycles, as intercepted by an American monitor. The repeated vs enable each station to tune in exactly to the other and let the operators warm up. At 1714, the spy, using conventional three-letter Q signals, sends: "What is my signal strength, please? Send a series of vs." Hamburg complies, then, at 1716, using the Q signal, asks, "How many messages do you have to send?" The spy replies "all" and then begins transmitting his first. After erroneously keying GYOFB, he sends a series of dots, or ES, to indicate an error, then retransmits correctly. He completes the message in four minutes. After receiving an acknowledgment, he begins his next, repeating each group to make sure it is received correctly. In the abbreviations, GA means "go ahead"; RPT, "repeat"; K, "over"; RR and RRR, "I have copied and received okay"; KA as a unit indicates the beginning of a message and AR as a unit, the ending. The groups GLAD, DYRE, ILIC, SUA, and ILL are probably private abbreviations or cipher indicators sage was genuine, for the agent was to omit the security check if he had been caught and made to send under duress. The radioman handed the deciphered message to his chief, who had it re-enciphered either in the Enigma cipher machine for radio transmission to Berlin or in a cryptographic teletypewriter for transmission by landline.

The greatest difficulty in agent radio communication was hearing the spy's first message. Often a quarter of a year would pass between the agent's departure and his reappearance on the air waves. Sometimes several men would listen for an agent. To keep them alert and concentrated for the call signs all that time was Trautmann's greatest problem. He motivated them by awarding a goose to the first radioman to hear a call.

Procedures were essentially the same in the much smaller establishment of RSHA VI. This had begun as part of VI B under Naujocks. By 1941 it had become VI F. The large-scale commitment of VI agents into Russia the following year, Operation ZEPPELIN, impelled Himmler to order the creation of a radio unit to handle communications with them. To head it, the RSHA snatched away on 13 August 1942 a 31-year-old radioman and SS major who was serving as communications chief of the Organization Todt, the party's construction agency. This man, Peter Siepen, found quarters for the unit not far from the press-monitoring Seehaus in some low yellow outbuildings of a villa on the edge of the Wannsee, a bay of the Havel River in southwest Berlin, and named it the Havel Institute.

With an annual budget of *RM*3 million ($1.2 million), he had, by the end of 1943, scraped up 160 technicians, installing most of them in the four outposts he had established, each for a specific agent area. Together they had 18 transmitters and worked 50 circuits. Berlin, with 42 men and women, handled long-range communications. In addition, it trained agents, especially for ZEPPELIN: in December 1943, some 200 were under instruction. Siepen developed an agent radio the size of four cigar boxes that successfully covered the 3,000 miles from Iran to Berlin.

The military and the party radio agencies continued to exist even after the takeover of the Abwehr by the RSHA. The Havel Institute absorbed desks VI F 1 and 2, which had dealt with radio matters. Abwehr I i became Branch E of the RSHA's Military Department. But their agent radio activity remained astonishingly low to the end. The Havel Institute, the busiest because of the mass insertion of ZEPPELIN agents, handled between 4,000 and 7,000 words a day. But the Abwehr Wiesbaden post seldom gathered in, from its agents in France, North Africa, and Spain, more than a dozen messages a day. And Trautmann in Hamburg thought it was quite noteworthy when, from agents scattered over a quarter of the globe, the number of messages he received in an entire week rose to ten.

Agents had to be paid. Even those who worked out of ideological conviction had expenses. Both the Abwehr and the SD used three forms of payment: the advance, the retainer, and what might with but slight cynicism be called the "honorarium."

The advance served the long-range agent who was expected to be out of physical contact with Germany for a long time. In 1941, spy Hans Napp presented himself to Captain Niebuhr, the naval attaché in Buenos Aires. Niebuhr had received a credit of 500,000 pesos ($125,000) from the embassy at the start of the war, which he promptly converted into cash and kept in 1,000-peso ($250) notes and change in his safe. Upon hearing the password "My cousin sails on the *Gneisenau*" from Napp, Niebuhr gave him, as instructed, 5,000 pesos ($1,250). In 1942, the Rio embassy paid $50,000 as an advance to Johann Siegfried Becker, head of SD espionage in Latin America. It followed that the next year with *RM*50,000 ($20,000). Gimpel and Colepaugh took $60,000 in cash plus 99 small diamonds across the Atlantic with them. Long-term agents for Britain also enjoyed financial security. One got £4,000 ($19,200), a top agent £20,000 ($96,000). (Altogether the Abwehr paid an estimated total of £85,000 [$408,000] to its agents in Britain.)

Though in general the Abwehr would not enter into contracts with agents, it paid a few what amounted to a salary plus expenses, and even gave favored ones a kind of unemployment compensation. Some of these agents reported regularly, either after trips or from a stationary position. The Abwehr outpost in Luxembourg paid *RM*120 ($48) to V-Mann 934 in June and in July 1941. Agent MARCEL, who was unable to work for a while in 1942 and 1943, nevertheless got his regular *RM*120-a-month retainer. In Argentina, Niebuhr paid spy Ottomar Müller 700 pesos ($175) a month starting in the middle of 1941. Other retainer agents were expected to go to ground but remain loyal and report after the enemy had overrun their areas.

The vast majority of agents received a fee for each report they brought in. The fees varied greatly. In the Abwehr's Bremen outpost in January 1940, they ranged from $14 for V-10002 to $1,000 for V-10038. These amounted to almost half Bremen's total payout of *RM*5364.24 ($2,145.70) for that month.

The spymaster of an English agent codenamed JOHNNY paid him £20 ($96) for most of his reports, chiefly on British air matters, but sometimes gave him £50 ($240) for an especially valuable one. During the battles in France in 1944, line-crossers on short-term missions got *RM*200 ($50), radio agents, who worked much farther away and much longer behind enemy lines, from *RM*2,000 to *RM*5,000 ($500 to $2,000).

As early as 1943, however, many agents began to prefer more substantial methods of payment than the paper tokens of perishable governments. Many demanded medicine. Those so paid, the Abwehr central conceded even while urging restraint in such disbursements, "tackle their work with far greater interest." By 1945, many agents were refusing money as payment. Instead they accepted jewelry—often for front-line agents—or goods in short supply, such as tobacco, alcohol, clothing.

Occasionally, payments were made in adventurous, spy-story style. The RSHA parachuted money for its agents in Iran onto airports marked by red lights or onto geographical points in the desert region of Gaichgais. In France in 1945, a spymaster hid 200,000 francs near Granville on the Normandy coast, from where two agents retrieved it.

But in the vast majority of cases, the agents were simply handed their money by their spymasters or the pay clerks at post headquarters. Both Abwehr and SD accounted for these payments as much as possible. It was not always possible. One agent in South America had slipped a large sum in pounds under a local notable's napkin at a dinner party. "And now I've got to produce his receipt for the money!" he shouted in the age-old exasperation of the man in the field against the imbecile strictures of the home office. And in some cases accounting was not even desirable. Some spymasters felt that financial reports endangered their work by letting too many people in the administration learn about their agents. Schellenberg did not demand an accounting of his agents in Iran, preferring to use the radio links for more substantive reports. But such uncontrolled distribution of money opened the way to abuses—mainly, that the spymaster would himself pocket funds intended for spies. This happened in South America: agent Josef Starziczny spent 20,000 pesos ($5,000) on himself instead of a ship-reporting ring. It was not rare in the Abwehr. Consequently, the two espionage agencies instituted some controls. At the SD outposts, accounting took place monthly. Individual payments up to $RM3,000$ ($1,200) could be approved at the Prague outpost by the chief of espionage, and payments of up to $RM15,000$ ($6,000) by the post chief. Amounts above that went to the RSHA, where the group chief approved them and passed the form up to Schellenberg for his countersignature. Payments above $RM50,000$ ($20,000) could be passed on only by Kaltenbrunner himself.

To handle this work, both agencies had financial units. The Abwehr's lay in its Central Branch's Group Z F (for Zentralabteilung, Finanz). Chief Commissary Martin Toeppen at first headed the 30-man group, but he was jailed at the end of 1941 for taking presents from agents and giving them extra funds. Succeeding him was Dr. Georg Duesterberg, a reserve officer who had done the bookkeeping for an infantry division before his transfer to the Abwehr. In the RSHA, Department II handled finance and administration. From mid-1944, Josef Spacil there dealt with—among other agencies —RSHA VI on money. Spacil had failed when he had gone into business for himself, and his chief qualifications for his work seemed to be his intimate friendship with Kaltenbrunner, his long-time membership in the Nazi party, his specialization in finance in the SS since 1931, and his year's experience in doing the accounting for the Dachau concentration camp. His incompetency drove Schellenberg to control the day-to-day agent payments from within his own department under a former Abwehr official, Dr. Joerges.

Among the matters that these men supervised was the flow of money from the central offices to the outposts and to the agents. In January of 1945, the chief of front reconnaissance appropriated for the Main Post West for Front Reconnaissance about $20,000, £5,000, 3 million French francs, 30,000 Belgian francs, and 20,000 Dutch gulden. The spy agencies transferred these funds sometimes by bank, sometimes by messenger, sometimes (to KOs abroad) by diplomatic pouch, and sometimes by smuggling. The outposts often disposed of considerable money in many currencies. At the end of the war, Prague, for example, had *RM*15,700, $2,569, £498 (198 in gold), 4,900 Swedish kronor, 1,000 Swiss francs, 8,090 Turkish pounds, 6,200 Hungarian pengö, 46,000 Rumanian lei, 15,000 Russian rubles, and an estimated *RM*68,000 worth of valuables.

The main financial problem of the espionage services was foreign exchange. Agents abroad seldom accepted reichsmarks; they wanted gold or local currency, or at least easily convertible, nonsuspicious currency. But these items were tightly controlled; by law, the Reichsbank had to hold gold and foreign currency "at such a level as it deemed necessary in order to settle balances with foreign countries and to maintain the value of the currency." Resolving this conflict constituted "one of the major bottlenecks" for Schellenberg, and for Duesterberg, "my hardest task," even though he claimed to get one-sixth of all the foreign currency available in Germany. The two agencies obtained what they needed in a variety of ways.

Often the Abwehr simply drew on Reichsbank stocks, having the amounts charged to it sometimes in foreign currencies, sometimes in reichsmarks. On 3 December 1940, for example, it asked permission to pay out $25,000 to a representative in Buenos Aires without the money's being charged against its foreign currency account; three days later, the request was granted. The RSHA got more foreign currency more easily from Germany's biggest holder of it, Göring's Four-Year Plan, and from the Ministry of Economics than from the red-tape-bound Reichsbank. Only when the ministry's funds were down did the minister, Walther Funk, who was also president of the Reichsbank, grant gold and foreign exchange from the bank. For a mission to Iran in 1943, Funk authorized the Reichsbank to give the RSHA, in return for the equivalent amount in reichsmarks, $150,000, 26 kilograms of gold bars, and 25 kilograms of French napoléons d'or, which the tribes there desired.

In addition to getting foreign funds in Germany, both agencies tapped German-owned foreign funds abroad. In 1940, the Abwehr got permission for a Berlin firm that was working with it, the Tobis-Tonbild-Syndikat, to pay out $10,000, which it held on the account of the Mitteldeutsche Montan-Werke in the Bankers Trust Company, New York, to one of its board members, then in the United States. The money was ostensibly to buy patent interests in Tobis's field of narrow movie films and photographic appliances. But in fact it was for Abwehr purposes. In a similar way, Schellenberg once had the Argentine branch of Telefunken pay his agents there in pesos while he reimbursed the firm *RM*50,000 ($20,000) in Berlin.

And both agencies quite legally generated some foreign exchange on their own. Schellenberg gave Johannes Bernhardt *RM*50,000 a month to invest in his Sofindus or another firm he controlled in Spain, thereby producing pesetas. The Abwehr's 20 to 30 cover firms abroad converted currencies, sometimes making money as they did so.

But these legitimate methods did not cover the constantly increasing demand for foreign exchange. Duesterberg was driven to run an illicit business with the help of four businessmen, a German, an Austrian, a Hungarian, and a Swede. When he badly needed a certain currency, he would give one of them the equivalent in reichsmarks, half a dozen passports of various countries made out in the man's name, and an order to return in two months with the required funds. The man could keep whatever profit he could make on the money-changing in between. Usually the men began in Greece, where the rate was most favorable. At borders, they either had to fling bags full of bills over fences in woods or fields, or get help from an Abwehr officer. Because, Duesterberg thought, he trusted them, they never betrayed him, and time after time he got the foreign currency he needed.

Behind these transactions and conversions operated the vast and sometimes obscure organs that brought in the Abwehr and SD wealth in the first place. Some of them were normal. The Abwehr, as a part of the armed forces, got its funds from the government. RSHA VI, as a party agency, was paid mainly from the Nazi treasury—partly in the normal budget, partly with special appropriations that had, by January 1941, already soared to *RM*1.5 million ($600,000). The successive heads of the RSHA, Heydrich and Kaltenbrunner, also got some money paid to them out of governmental funds. Late in 1944, income from customs duties began going to the combined espionage service.

Other means could be regarded as wartime measures. In 1942, the Reichsbank confiscated 200 tons of Belgian gold locked in the vaults of the Banque de France. During the war, captures of enemy agents yielded millions of reichsmarks, dollars, rubles, and Swiss francs.

Still another means was utterly cynical. It violated German and international law and betrayed Germany's agents. Yet a demigod's precedent sanctioned it: Frederick the Great had employed it during the Seven Years' War to cause an inflation and thus to help him pay for that conflict. This was counterfeiting of foreign currencies. The SD's Naujocks had begun this work. It was disregarded during the years of victory, but at the end of 1942 was restarted under Bernhard Krüger of RSHA VI F 4, the false documents desk. The project was named for him: Operation BERNHARD. Krüger's engravers and printers were prisoners in Blocks 18 and 19 of the Sachsenhausen concentration camp. His chief technical aide was Dr. Albert Langer, a former Austrian codebreaker with training in physics and mathematics who had briefly served in the RSHA's Radio Observation Post. Langer doped out the proper serial numbering system and resolved the final, most recalcitrant problem of the project. The color of their English pound notes was not quite right. He concluded that the water used in the paper and printing had something to do with it. The English money was printed in Hull. He ascertained the chemical composition of the water there, duplicated it—and had the satisfaction of seeing his counterfeit color match the original exactly.

Operation BERNHARD produced 8,965,080 5-, 10-, 20-, and 50-pound notes with a total value of £134,610,810 ($645,131,888). Mainly they were intended to cripple the British war economy. But though both Schellenberg and Duesterberg generally felt that they would imperil missions and so refused to use them, in some cases the spy agencies could not refrain from utilizing this free and easy source of funds. Walter Simon, inserted by the Abwehr into Ireland in June 1940, carried 120 fake £1 notes among his funds. Another spy, set down by seaplane off the Scottish coast in 1943, was captured with false banknotes. An Irishman, John Francis O'Reilly, parachuted in to give information on the forthcoming invasion, carried the counterfeits. SD representatives in Sweden sometimes paid their informants with the same falsifications. Line-crossers late in the war also got fake pounds. And the best spy of the war, CICERO, who photographed documents from the dispatch box of the British ambassador in Turkey, ostensibly was paid more than any other spy in history for his information. But the Bank of England notes apparently totaling £300,000 ($1.84 million) that he received proved afterwards to be counterfeits, and utterly worthless. Thus did the Nazi intelligence service reward those who risked their lives for it.

The biggest source of espionage funds was, however, far more criminal, far more vicious than mere counterfeiting. It dripped with blood. It was the "final solution" of the Jewish problem.

The Nazis confiscated the property of the Jews they uprooted. In the western occupied territories alone, they had, as of 31 July 1944, expropriated from Jews currency and securities worth RM11,695,516 (more than $4.6 million), as well as 674 trainloads of goods. They did not stop there. At Auschwitz, Treblinka, Mauthausen, and elsewhere, the Nazis stripped the prisoners of earrings, necklaces, brooches, gems, wedding bands, gold frames for eyeglasses, and cash—sometimes in $1,000 notes. After these men, women, and children had been murdered in the gas chambers, but before their bodies went into the ovens, the Germans yanked the gold teeth from their mouths. These they melted into bars and trucked them, with the other items, in chests to Berlin. There, the Prussian state mint smelted the gold, which then became part of the Reichsbank reserves— subject to SS needs if required.

And it was required. Kaltenbrunner financed his intelligence service in large measure from this gore-encrusted gold. Once Himmler specifically directed that some death-camp gold, which he was turning over to the Reichsbank, be made available for bribery or intelligence operations if the SS wanted it. And the jewelry that front agents were given as payment for their services during the latter part of the war had, in many cases, once bedecked some slaughtered innocent. In the end, German espionage, like so much of that vile regime, ran on blood and stank of burnt flesh.

18

Battalions of Spies

O N New Year's Day 1937, a medium-sized, blondish man walked for the first time into a bare office containing a desk, two chairs, and an empty safe in a gray concrete building in Hamburg. The building was the headquarters of the German army's Military District X; the rooms, those of its Abwehr post; the man, Nikolaus Ritter, a former career officer and for many years a textile executive in the United States. He had come to start Abwehr air espionage against Britain and America.

This duty fell naturally to the Hamburg post. It had handled similar assignments in World War I, and its position as a port, with its international connections, facilitated that work. Ritter was its I L—I for Abwehr I, the espionage branch, L for Luft, or air.

Soon after Ritter's arrival, one of the older Abwehr officers handed him a notice about a potential spy. He was Arthur Owens, a tiny Welsh electrical engineer who professed to hate the British. Unknown to the Germans, Owens had actually begun his spying working for the British. On his business trips to the continent, he picked up technical information which he reported to the Admiralty. But he grew discontented with the pay and the condescending treatment, and he thought he might sell information to the Germans. He began frequenting a club in London for German au-pair girls, in part to pick them up, in part in hopes of making a German contact. The latter, at least, worked: the manager of the club was a recruiter for Ritter's colleague. On one of his next trips to Europe, Owens met the man, who began to run him as a spy. When Ritter joined the staff, the officer passed Owens along to him. Ritter codenamed him JOHNNY, gave him number 3504 (the 3500 series for Hamburg's I L agents, the 4 a serial number), cultivated him with drinks and food, and received from him—in return for cash, of course—some moderately interesting information dealing with R.A.F. electrical equipment.

During the two years before the war began, Ritter also managed to insert a few other agents into Britain. Ritter regarded one of them as "the perfect spy."

One day soon after Ritter had started his job, an official of the Hamburg chamber of commerce, who scouted for agents for the Abwehr, asked Ritter whether he was interested in a former freighter captain who was looking for work and who could perhaps be used against England.

"Naturally," replied the spymaster. "If you think he's suitable, I must meet him."

They agreed that the official and the prospect would have a drink in the first-class dining room in the main Hamburg railroad station, where Ritter would be at a separate table. The official would have the man walk around, as if he were looking for someone, and Ritter would be able to observe him. A few days later, as Ritter was seated before a glass of Moselle wine in the dining room, he saw the official and a thin, wiry man in his late fifties come in and take seats at a corner table. After a while, the man circulated through the room. As he passed Ritter's seat, the spymaster was impressed by his way. His walk was light and unhurried. He seemed confident and at ease. He was about six feet tall, neatly shaved, with a bold chin. Ritter decided he could use him. He went over to their table.

The official introduced the man, Walter Simon, to Ritter, using Ritter's cover name of Dr. Rantzau.

"How you do you, Herr Doktor," said Simon, in a hoarse and toneless voice—the result, Ritter later learned, of a larynx operation. "I am at your disposal. What can I do for you?"

"First we have to see who you are and what you know," said Ritter, laughing. "Tell me about yourself."

Simon related how he had left home at 15 and had sailed around the world, gradually rising in rank until he finally became captain of a freighter. He spoke fluent English, in part because he had been interned in Australia during World War I. Ritter tested this by continuing the conversation in that language. The talk confirmed his first favorable impression. Only the rough voice, which drew attention to the man, gave him pause. He told Simon that he would be in touch the following week.

A security check confirmed all of Simon's statements. His advantages outweighed the voice problem, and Ritter took him on, training him himself. He felt that Simon knew more about England than he did, so he concentrated on the assignment the agent would have: exact observations of airfields, including occupancy, types of airplanes, and defenses, and reports on certain munitions and arms factories. As practice, they visited German airfields and factories, while Ritter showed him what to look for and how. Ritter also explained how to dredge information from local newspapers.

Simon learned fast, and in March of 1938, after a handshake from Ritter in his downtown office, he departed for England, using his own seaman's passport, which had been stamped all over the world.

In four weeks he was back. Spy and spymaster met again in the same office, this time with a secretary to take notes for his report. He astonished the two Abwehr employees by pulling out a notebook, but calmed them by saying that it included only some addresses and dates. Then he dictated clear and precise details on five new airfields, of which the Abwehr and the Luftwaffe knew only that they existed. He told of a number of factories that were new to the Luftwaffe, and specified the production of one in Winchester, which figures he had gained from a worker there whom he had met. Berlin liked the report, and Ritter dispatched the tall seaman in May on another trip to a different area of England.

This mission lasted six weeks, and proved fully as successful as the first. The Luftwaffe's appetite increased. It wanted Simon to go yet again. But Ritter feared that so many trips in so short a time would awaken the suspicions of British immigration. He shelved his good agent for a while. Eventually, however, the pressure grew too great. In the fall of 1938, he decided to commit him again. This time Simon took with him as cover a friend's manuscript, which he was offering to British publishers, about his Robinson-Crusoe–like life on a small, isolated southern island. The immigration officer at Harwich was surprised to see him again so soon. The manuscript seemed to satisfy him, however, and he passed Simon. But he apparently reported him to the counterintelligence authorities.

Simon took a room in a seaman's hostel in Whitechapel, a section of London east of the Tower and near the giant floating West India docks. From here he traveled around southeastern England, spying out new airfields and reporting regularly through a cover address in Rotterdam. He also recruited a few Welsh nationalists as potential saboteurs. But in February 1939, he forgot to register as an alien in a hotel in Tonbridge, Kent. Police arrested him. Instead of a light fine, he was sentenced to a total of six months in jail. He was interrogated often but gave away nothing. The police took his notebook, but returned it when he was freed.

Shortly after his return to Hamburg, war broke out. Ritter naturally could not send him back to England, but he kept him with pay on the waiting list, until, early in 1940, the navy asked to "borrow" him. They needed convoy and weather reports from Ireland. Though neither Simon nor Ritter liked the idea, they consented. He was taught radio and the standard Abwehr agent cipher, a simple columnar transposition. His key was the first verse of Schiller's "Glocke." Before he left, he was given a yellow pad, impregnated with invisible ink, which he could sew into the lining of his suit, fake papers showing that he was Karl Anderson, a Swede naturalized in Australia, $1,910 and £215.15.10 (of which £120 was fake), and a few details about Ireland, where he had never been. At the end of May 1940 he departed Wilhelmshaven in a U-boat.

On the night of 12 June, the submarine slipped cautiously into lovely Dingle Bay, at the southwest tip of the Emerald Isle. Simon was rowed ashore in a dinghy. He buried his radio set, then hiked until he reached a railway, and began walking east along it. In the morning, he met some workmen and asked them when the next train ran.

"The last train here ran fourteen years ago," said one. But nothing happened, and Simon continued on foot to the station at Tralee. As he walked up and down the platform, he noticed three men watching him. They chatted with him and rode in the train to Dublin with him. When they asked if he were waiting for someone from the Irish Republican Army, he mockingly asked, "Are you from the I.R.A.?" They took this as a sign that he was involved with the outlawed organization; with this as an excuse, and because his boots were suspiciously wet and muddy, they arrested him. Inside the brown paper parcel he carried the police found his money; later they dug up his radio set. He was convicted and jailed in Mountjoy Prison, Dublin.

It was the end for Simon—and for Ritter it meant the loss of "an ideal agent. Simon had carried out all his assignments with discretion, élan, and pluck. He was for me the perfect classical secret agent, the deliberate, intelligent, and trustworthy scout, of whom every intelligence officer dreams."

Ritter still had JOHNNY, however. In the summer of 1939, he had brought the little Welshman—and his much taller, much younger blonde girl friend—to Hamburg for training. The Abwehr post's radio officer, Major Trautmann, taught him Morse code and how to build a radio transmitter and conceal it well. Owens returned to England just when the war broke out. He picked up his radio at the Southampton railroad station, where it had been deposited by a crew member of a fishing boat that had brought it from Germany. Soon thereafter he tested the radio link with his first message. Trautmann watched as his assistant raised his hand, saying, "Here he comes!" when, punctual to the second, JOHNNY's message began arriving. The assistant wrote it down on a pad. Suddenly they roared with laughter. The letters spelled out JOHNNY's only words of German, which he had learned in several lively evenings on Hamburg's notorious Reeperbahn: "Ein Glas Bier!"

The following messages were more serious. JOHNNY transmitted data on ship movements, R.A.F. concentrations in England and France, deliveries of war matériel from the United States, strengthening of coastal defenses, the use of balloon barrages, and the location and camouflage of oil tank farms, which served as reference points for air reconnaissance. He even told the exact location of major radar stations in England, though he did not know and could not say what they were for. But this tended to bolster

German confidence in him, for aerial reconnaissance had revealed these positions, and a prewar spy flight of a zeppelin had disclosed a few clues to their use.

JOHNNY also recruited additional agents for Ritter. Once the spymaster sought to meet him and a new man on a trawler in the middle of the North Sea, as they had arranged before the war. But the rendezvous failed. Shortly thereafter the two did meet in Lisbon. Ritter was suspicious. He did not believe that a man in Owens's position—in defense work—could have got out of England without the knowledge of British counterespionage. But he suspended judgment until Owens could bring the new agent—a former R.A.F. officer, he said—from England in another visit.

Several weeks later, JOHNNY reappeared in Lisbon and introduced a Mr. Brown to Ritter. He proved to have been an R.A.F. airman, a Communist. But instead of working for Ritter he disappeared. Ritter could not blame this entirely on Owens, and as Owens's reports continued to come in, be checked by Luftwaffe intelligence, and found accurate, his suspicions dwindled. Finally he concluded that although the British may have suspected Owens, the little man had cleverly persuaded them of his loyalty, when, in fact he was basically loyal to the Germans. JOHNNY's information, Ritter said, "was of the greatest value for Germany."

The most famous German agent in the west was indirectly a creature of Ritter's as well, since one of his subordinates had developed him. The agent's codename, JOSEFINE, became legendary in army, air force, and OKW circles. JOSEFINE was an unwitting agent; he did not himself realize that he was delivering information to Germany. His reports from London to his neutral home government, Sweden, were being stolen in Stockholm for the Ritter subordinate, one of the prodigies of the Abwehr.

He was Dr. Karl-Heinz Krämer, a very tall, very good-looking, very active young lawyer. Born 24 December 1914 in Obernkirchen, a village in Hanover, where the best German is said to be spoken, he went to university in Hamburg. In 1937, while still a student, he joined the party, receiving membership number 4,174,743. For a little while, he worked in London for Ribbentrop. He was drafted into the air force at the start of the war with the rank of specialist lieutenant and was assigned to the Hamburg Abwehr post under Ritter. He handled espionage in the Low Countries, in Budapest, and in Istanbul, where he recruited one of the Germans who had helped build the Turkish telephone net to tap British embassy telephones. Back in Hamburg, he managed to obtain, perhaps with some help from Ritter but mainly through agents and connections in Sweden, the monthly production summary of the society of British aircraft constructors. By September of 1942, the information had become "of the greatest importance" to the Luftwaffe. It called his reports its "most valuable target documents for the commitment of the Luftwaffe against English armament works."

Krämer had previously traveled to Sweden from time to time to meet his contacts, but travel was growing more difficult, and the Luftwaffe, which did not want his reports interrupted, urged his transfer there. The OKW had promised the Foreign Office that it would not ask to build any more Abwehr personnel into the missions, but this was deemed a special case. Ribbentrop himself gave permission. Ten days later, on 29 October 1942, Krämer arrived in Stockholm. His wife, Eva, and their 11-month-old daughter, Heidi, followed a few weeks later. Krämer was given the rank of secretary of legation, attached to the press section.

Almost at once, his dynamic energy generated results. His reports in Hamburg had dealt largely with British air production, and his first ones in Stockholm did, too. He sent his first to Abwehr I L only 11 days after he arrived. It was his first "mantle report"—a report that included a variety of items under a single cover. An average mantle report had about 20 items; one reached 35. In addition, he dispatched uncounted individual reports covering everything from shipments of strategic material to Britain to tactical and strategic intelligence out of that island.

Krämer ascribed the shipment reports to SIEGFRIED A, who was catalogued as V-3569 in the list of Hamburg air agents. This source had originally been developed in 1940 by a representative of Lufthansa, the German airline, who was also an Abwehr agent. Working at Bromma airport, he monitored the movement of vital war matériel to England. Then he enlisted two Swedes, a freight manager named Svahlwink and a mechanic, to help with this, paying each 7,400 kronor. Krämer took these men over when he came to Sweden, and forwarded to Germany the information he got from them. On 13 April 1943, for example, he reported on seven shipments that the Swedish ABA airline had readied for England on 6 April and five on 12 April. Among them were 75 packages of high-speed steel drills weighing 1,549.2 kilograms addressed to Bruce & Brown Ltd., 21 Rochester Road, Coventry. Another of Krämer's contacts was the shrewd, publicity-minded head of ABA, Karl Florman. But he dribbled only minor items to Krämer.

That there was a SIEGFRIED A implied other SIEGFRIEDs, and indeed Krämer had a SIEGFRIED B. Under this rubric he carried a variety of sources. Some were contacts in England, who sent most of their material in via pilots and other employees of the ABA airline. Krämer steadfastly refused to name these contacts to his superiors, but he hinted that they were well-placed individuals in England and Swedes who traveled there. They also sent material in by mail and through sailors acting as couriers on the ships that plied between Sweden and Britain. The information arrived with a delay of two to four days. Krämer himself dealt only with the middlemen who brought it to him, and did not meet the actual sources in Britain.

In Sweden, though, he met sources. While in Istanbul, he had made contact with an Italian who worked for the Japanese secret service; this man had moved to Stockholm, and through him Krämer met the Japanese military attaché there, reputed to be the chief of Japanese intelligence in Europe, the able General Makato Onodera. Thereafter they frequently exchanged information, to their mutual benefit. Krämer also dealt often with Major Laszlo Voeczkoendy, assistant military attaché to the Hungarian legation in Stockholm. They became quite friendly—Krämer once took Voeczkendy's wife to the airfield and saw her off for him. Their business consisted chiefly of comparing what information they had gotten from the Japanese. Another Krämer source was Anton Bela Grundboek, owner of the Swedish Trading Company. This firm sold oriental rugs, radios, and other hard-to-get items to German diplomats in Sweden at reduced prices. Though Krämer insisted that Grundboek produced some of his most important intelligence, other intelligence personnel felt that he was not in a position to provide this, and that, in return for various favors, Krämer carried him as his agent, facilitating the man's travel on his business trips through Europe.

A source that the blue-eyed giant tended to keep from his superiors was the press. Every morning he spent several hours at the embassy, where his press job afforded a perfect cover, going through the Swedish, British, and technical newspapers and magazines. From time to time, he would send off a report based, for example, on the fitting of a story in one paper to an item in another, and would attribute it to SIEGFRIED B. He could get away with this because he got the papers about four days before they reached the various evaluating posts in Germany.

SIEGFRIED B reported both on Allied intentions and on Royal Air Force organizations. For example, on 23 December 1942, six weeks after the North African invasion, Krämer told Berlin that it did not have to worry about an Allied landing in Norway—one of Hitler's main concerns:

SIEGFRIED B reports on 22 December 1942, report time 18 December: From the English side rumors of a major Allied action in northern Norway are being deliberately started. Also such reports are being brought to the Swedish legation in London, so that the same thing will be reported to Stockholm. Purpose of these rumors is said to be to annoy Germany and apparently to delay an expected German action in Spain. Speaking against a Norwegian operation is that again fighter formations have been pulled out of the 13th and 14th Fighter Groups as well as formations of the Coastal Command out of the 18th Group. Report of SIEGFRIED A of 8 December 1942 confirmed by SIEGFRIED B. Moreover empty tonnage in northern England and Scotland is viewed as completely insufficient for such an undertaking. Said to be expected is intensified commando activity.

Auswärtiges Amt

Dr.Krämer
Tagebuchnr.40/43.   Stockholm, den 17.8.1943.

                        An das Oberkommando der Wehrmacht
                        Amt Ausland Abwehr I Luft/E
                        z.H.Herrn Oberstltn.i.G.Kleyenstüber o.V.i.A.
        Abdruck: Auswärtiges Amt, Berlin   1x nebst Anlage.
                 Deutsche Gesandtschaft, Sthlm.   1x nebst Anlage

                          G e s e h e n .
                        Stockholm, den 17.August 1943.
                          Der Deutsche Gesandte
                          gez. Thomsen.

_____

Anliegend wird überreicht: Mantelbericht Nr.40/43

Anl. 1) Produktion von Spitfire im Juni 1943.
     2) Produktion von Lancaster im Juni 1943.
     3) Produktion von Halifax im Monat Juni 1943.
     4) Produktion Hawker Hurricane im Juni 1943.
     5) Produktion von Typhonn im Juni 1943.
     6) Produktion von Short-Stirling im Juni 1943.
     7) Produktion von Wellington im Juni 1943.
     8) Produktion von Miles Training Flugzeugen im Juni 1943.
     9) Produktion von Mosquitos im Juni 1943 bei de Havilland.
    10) Produktion von Cygnet und Owlet im Juni 1943.
    11) Bristol-Produktion im Juni 1943.
    12) Produktion von Sunderland im Juni 1943.
    13) Produktion von Bombay und Flamingo im Juni 1943.
    14) Produktion von York im Juni 1943.
    15) Produktion von de Havilland Schulflugzeugen im Juni 1943.
    16) Brief an Abw.I Luft/E.

Dr. Karl-Heinz Krämer, who obtained information from JOSEFINE, Germany's
most famous secret source in the west, lists the reports he is attaching to this
cover sheet and signs it

The reports of still another of Krämer's agents—HEKTOR—dealt mostly with Allied air production. Some sources considered them the most valuable on this matter that Germany received.

Krämer expanded his knowledge by energetic legwork to keep from falling into any traps and to feed his masters what they wanted. He traveled at least one week every month, going variously to Switzerland, France, and Copenhagen, and he visited Berlin every other week. While there, he saw Dr. Giselher Wirsing, publisher of the *Münchner Neueste Nachrichten,* an aide to Schellenberg, and author of special RSHA intelligence compilations called the Egmont Reports. Wirsing and Krämer exchanged information, which Wirsing found valuable because of Krämer's ability, his location outside Germany, and his doing his own thinking.

In addition to bringing in unsolicited information, Krämer also answered the questions that the Luftwaffe fired at him through the Abwehr: "Which formations of the Army Air Corps have been transferred to the Middle East?" "Does the creation of four new fighter flights involve British or American formations?"

All of this was, however, but as lagniappe to his main information: that supplied by JOSEFINE.

Who was JOSEFINE? As his fame grew in intelligence circles, his identity gradually percolated into some of them as well. JOSEFINE—whose codename meant nothing—was not one man but several: the Swedish military and naval and air attachés in Britain. Though as representatives of a power that was regarded as somewhat pro-German, they were not warmly welcomed everywhere, and were certainly not privy to the secrets of the Allies, they nevertheless moved with the relative freedom of neutrals in a belligerent capital, and their mere presence enabled them to pick up quantities of information not available elsewhere. They compressed it into reports to their defense ministry in Stockholm. And these Krämer obtained.

But how? That was Krämer's great mystery. His social contacts did not exceed what was considered normal for an officer of the legation. He did not give many parties and had few Swedish friends. He himself refused to say what his sources were. He threatened to resign instead of disclosing them. In an attempt to find out, Schellenberg even had him shadowed.

"With no result," he said. "He would not do anything during the day. He would not make any contacts but maybe a couple of times a week he would go out to some party and he always knew how to disappear for three or four hours and then the next morning he would be back and start dictating."

Some of these times he apparently vanished to one of the three safe apartments he maintained in the northern part of Stockholm. Part of his ability to disappear was due to his breakneck driving in his souped-up DKW. On the other hand, he usually parked his car directly in front of one of his apartments, making it easy for the Swedish police, who had been tailing him since three months after he arrived, to identify them and recognize his contacts.

Among these were three young Swedish women who worked in the defense ministry. Krämer wined and dined them at his favorite restaurants in the center of Stockholm and at a cozy inn in one of the western suburbs. And sometimes he took one of them to a tryst where she handed over to the charming foreigner the reports of the attachés in London, and perhaps some other secret documents as well.

With a pipeline into an enemy belligerent's capital, Krämer could submit reports that seemed to the information-starved Germans to peer direct into the Allies' minds. On 1 September 1943, for example, JOSEFINE reported on the just-ended Quebec conference. At this, Roosevelt and Churchill had concluded major plans for the cross-Channel invasion, now that Italy had all but left the war. Said JOSEFINE:

> In principle nothing has changed in the conception held up to now. A major action in northern France, which is supposed to bring a decision in the war, is not to be expected before the spring of next year. Creation of points of main effort in North Africa, Sicily for operations against Italy and Mediterranean islands.

All this was accurate, though not very newsworthy. Every armchair strategist knew that the assault on Europe would require a summer for campaigning and so could only come in the spring. And the Germans had evacuated Sicily two weeks before: the Allies were hardly likely to leave it at that. Nevertheless, a spy report on it was better than mere surmise, and the Germans were glad to have it. Some of JOSEFINE's later dispatches were less accurate. On 19 June 1944 he passed word that eight airborne divisions had been created in the United States. Only five had been. On 29 October he declared that by the end of the month the main part of the U.S. 14th Army would be in France. It had never existed.

But while many of Krämer's recipients appreciated his intelligence, other agencies looked askance at his activities. Major Friedrich Busch, the assistant air attaché and the representative of Abwehr I L in Stockholm, who envied Krämer his trips, his girls, and his restaurants, felt that the handsome spymaster ran many agents less to get information from varied sources than to collect big expenses and to protect himself by being able to jettison any single source in whom the Luftwaffe might lose confidence. Busch believed that Krämer was faking much of his information and that some Abwehr officials were protecting him because he helped them with their shady currency dealings. The Gestapo, too, suspected him of double-dealing. It perhaps felt that he could not have done as well as he did in any other way. One of its best operatives compiled an 80-page dossier on the tall agent. He thought that Krämer had sold papers of the Luftwaffe operations staff and other secret German material to the Russians in Stockholm and had received English or American intelligence in return; the deal was supposedly arranged through Onodera.

So one day in December 1944, the Gestapo chief, Müller, sneeringly asked Schellenberg at a meeting of RSHA department chiefs: "Are you also a British agent? You're going to have trouble with that Krämer of yours. You'll have plenty of explaining to do." Soon thereafter, he summoned Krämer to Berlin for a four-hour interrogation. Krämer denied all the allegations; Müller was unable to prove them. Schellenberg assumed direct responsibility for Krämer, who returned to Stockholm. And there he remained—highly regarded in some quarters, suspect in others—to the end of the war.

While the most famous German spy in the west was JOSEFINE, in the east the most famous was MAX. Both were shrouded in mystery. Just as most intelligence officers knew only that JOSEFINE was a source in England, so they only knew that MAX was a source in Russia. But MAX had an extra piquancy. For while JOSEFINE's German contact was a certified Nazi, MAX's was a Jew.

He was tubby Fritz Kauders, born in Vienna on 23 June 1903. His mother was a Jewess; his father, he said, had been born an Aryan, had converted to Judaism, and then had had himself baptized a Christian. At 24, Kauders left Vienna for Zurich, where he worked for a while as a sports journalist. He did the same in Paris and then in Berlin, where he also handled some private business. When Hitler came to power, he went to Budapest as a reporter, but he also pursued an activity that seems to flourish in certain societies: he provided introductions to the right Hungarian officials for people who needed them and could pay for them, and he obtained such sometimes hard-to-get papers as residence permits and visas. He was able to do this, he claimed, because he had been introduced to the best private and the highest official circles in Budapest, especially those of the Foreign Ministry. On the side, he changed money.

While in Budapest, he became acquainted with the head of the Abwehr unit there, who gave him assignments. Some of the most fruitful involved an American consul, John J. Meily, stationed in Zagreb, Yugoslavia. Kauders had met him at a dinner given by the head of the press section in the Hungarian Foreign Ministry, who had known Meily from the time he, the Hungarian, had also been a consul in Zagreb. Kauders exploited this opportunity to the utmost. Passing himself off as a Dutchman, he helped Meily in many little ways on the shopping trips that the consul and his wife made to Budapest. Kauders converted currency for Meily; he helped him find antique pistols and swords, which Meily collected. Kauders hoped to benefit from this friendship by obtaining American visas for rich Jews who wanted to get out of Budapest.

But Kauders also utilized the friendship to steal documents from Meily.

In the spring of 1941, during one of his numerous trips to Zagreb, Kauders lifted English propaganda material and a report on the lack of gasoline in Yugoslavia and gave them to the Abwehr. Later he appropriated American reports on war armaments, rapidly photocopied them and returned them to Meily's office, then delivered the photocopies to German intelligence. When Meily gave him a letter to bring to the American consul in Budapest, Kauders opened it and provided the Abwehr with photocopies. He even-handedly did the same with the Budapest consul's reply. Probably his most useful theft was that of State Department regulations about giving out visas: this perhaps ended up in Abwehr I G, which produced false documents.

Kauders perhaps was furnishing some of this material to the SD as well, for he was in contact with Wilhelm Höttl, who was one of the RSHA Balkan experts, on a matter involving Meily. He tracked Höttl from Vienna to Berlin once on this. While there he engaged in one of his major occupations: skirt-chasing. He met an RSHA employee, Fräulein Thiel, with whom he took a little trip, getting her in a little trouble for going out with a Jew. Höttl had not been pleased to see Kauders, but nevertheless gave him a letter to take back to Zagreb to give to Heinrich Schlie, one of Höttl's agents. In Zagreb, Kauders combined pleasure with business, and, while making a long-distance telephone call from the armed forces communications center, picked up Fräulein Holthaus. Things didn't seem to go so well with her; he only met her twice, both times with a friend. Back in Budapest, however, he had more luck. Miss Belosevič, of the embassy of the newly founded Croatian state, seemed to like him. She gave him some information, and planned to visit him in Zagreb. But then he got into some kind of a scrape and was detained, and that put an end to that.

Much of this happened around the start of Hitler's attack on Russia. At the same time, certain links to the interior of that country were being transmuted.

They had originally belonged to the White Russian general Anton Turkul. Turkul had commanded a division in the Russian Civil War and, after the Communists had consolidated their power, found asylum, at least for part of the time, in Hitler's anti-Communist Germany. He became a head of the White Russian emigrés. While awaiting the fall of the Red regime, he maintained contacts in Soviet Russia, and even sent in some of his officers to propagandize for him, getting the help of the Polish general staff for this. After Hitler's onslaught, some of his people in Russia apparently made contact with the Germans and offered to provide information to them by radio. The offer was accepted; the assignment was given to the Abwehr. It found some White Russian radiomen, provided them with equipment, and established regular communications. The Germans codenamed the Russian transmitters, one supposedly in the Kremlin and one behind the Urals, MAX and MORITZ. Eventually MORITZ dropped out and MAX, in the Kremlin, gave his name to the entire operation.

Canaris entrusted the work to one of his closest associates, Colonel Rudolf Count von Marogna-Redwitz, head of the Abwehr post in Vienna, one of the centers of espionage against Russia since the intrigue-laden era of the Austro-Hungarian empire. Around the end of 1941, this post moved its Turkul work to Sofia, perhaps because the Bulgarian capital was closer to Russia, affording better radio connections, perhaps because someone hoped to gain supplementary information from the huge Soviet embassy there. To handle this work, Marogna-Redwitz established an outpost of his post. He installed it in a villa on one of the main streets of Sofia, Patriarkh Evtimiy Boulevard. The lower floors had offices; in the attic, the radiomen worked their technological mysteries. This outpost operated independently of the KO Bulgaria, headed by the able Colonel Otto Wagner, whose headquarters were down the street.

As head of the outpost there appeared Kauders. How and why he was chosen remained obscure for the Abwehr personnel in Sofia. What was, on the other hand, crystal clear was that he enjoyed the absolute support and complete protection of the higher echelons of the Abwehr, starting with Canaris himself. This came out in Canaris's comments to Wagner.

Like most Abwehr personnel, Kauders used a cover name. His was Klatt. He called himself "engineer," a title which, it must be admitted, in Austria did not always correspond to the profession. He was of middle height, with a round face, well fed and well dressed, a bit on the chubby side, alert and intelligent but not physically active; some thought him rather greasy. His weakness was women. But, Wagner observed, he mastered this trade and didn't go under like many others. He was always on the qui vive, always eager to know what was coming, what would be said to him. Soon after his arrival, he began throwing his money around. He spent his days in his office and on the move, apparently also doing some private business and paying off the Bulgarian police so he would not be bothered. He spent his nights in restaurants and cafés dining well and dating women.

Despite these nonprofessional activities, the MAX reports poured in. Kauders passed them to Vienna. From there they went to Abwehr headquarters, thence to Foreign Armies East and Foreign Air Forces East, which agencies in turn sent them down to the army groups and the air fleets. A message arrived almost every day. Many dealt with troop movements. On 4 June 1942, for example, MAX reported:

> On 2 June one rifle division, one artillery regiment, one medium tank regiment coming out of Astrakhan arrived in Tikhoretsk, supposedly going on towards Rostov. On 3 June one transport of 200 heavy and medium tanks arrived in Krasnodar out of Stalingrad, intended for the Taman peninsula.

But some of the messages were far more consequential than this. They seemed to come from sources at the very heart of Soviet power—inside the Kremlin itself. On 14 or 15 July 1942 he had reported:

FINLAND

U. S. S. R.

miles

0   100   200   300   400

Front - 4 November 1942

Leningrad

L. ILMEN

VOLGA R.

POLAND

Kalinin

Rzhev ● Moscow

FRONT LINE

Orel

Voronezh

Stalingrad

Kiev

DNIEPER R.

Astrakhan ●

Rostov

FRONT LINE

HUNGARY

Tikhoretsk

Krasnodar

Grozny

CRIMEA

CAUCASUS MTS.

RUMANIA

●Bucharest

BULGARIA

●Sofia

GREECE

Samsun

TURKEY

●Ankara

Ascherl

Russian front on 4 November 1942 when MAX, Germany's most famous spy on
the eastern front, forwarded a report about a Kremlin war council that day
presided over by Stalin that disclosed Soviet plans for the winter offensives

Military council in Moscow, with among others Shaposhnikov, Molotov, Voroshilov, and the English, American, and Chinese military attachés present, ended in the night of 13.7. Shaposhnikov announced a withdrawal as far as the Volga, so that the Germans must spend the winter on the Volga.... Attacks will apparently be tried at two places, one north of Orel, the other north of Voronezh; air fleets and armored troops will apparently be committed in this. As a diversion a drive near Kalinin will supposedly be carried out.

Foreign Armies East commented that "The development of the overall enemy picture in the last few days lets the report appear believable."

Four months later, as the Russians were gathering their forces for hammer blows against Army Group Center and against the German spearhead into Stalingrad, MAX seemed to have attained the pinnacle of German espionage in World War II. He disclosed the decisions taken at a military conference run by Stalin himself the very same day. Agents in the west, such as JOSEFINE, indeed claimed to reveal the results of Roosevelt-Churchill meetings. But none came close to the speed and the apparent precision of MAX's astonishing message of 4 November 1942:

On 4 November war council in Moscow presided over by Stalin. Present: 12 marshals and generals. In this war council the following principles were set down: a) Careful advance in all operations, to avoid heavy losses. b) Losses of ground are unimportant.... f) Carrying out all planned offensive undertakings, if possible, before 15 November, insofar as the weather situation permits. Mainly: from Grozny [out of the Caucasus] ...; in the Don area at Voronezh; at Rzhev; south of Lake Ilmen and Leningrad. The troops for the front will be taken out of the reserves. ...

This remarkable advance notice of Moscow's four major planned winter offensives tallied with the views of Foreign Armies East, which distributed it two days later with its judgment of the situation.

Such sensational reports soon had the intelligence and command personnel buzzing. Rumors flew. Some thought that MAX was a doctor on Stalin's staff. Another thought he was a Rumanian whose network tapped into Russian telephones and listened even to Kremlin conversations. Others believed that he got his information from a Japanese newspaperman who had long worked for Japanese intelligence—Japan was not at war with the Russians—via intermediaries in Turkey.

But they all loved his reports, which they believed. The commander in chief of Army Group Center often asked his I c what MAX had said that day. When Guderian was chief of staff, he told Schellenberg, then head of the combined RSHA and Abwehr, that no other agent was as valuable as MAX. A story was current that when Hitler heard that MAX was a Jew, he refused to accept the information anymore, but Guderian declared that MAX's reports, especially on the Red Air Force, were unique, and that to close him down would be an act of criminal irresponsibility. This attitude never changed in the higher echelons.

Some intelligence officials, however, suspected Kauders-MAX of being a double agent. KO chief Wagner found his behavior very questionable. Around the end of 1942, Kauders complained to him that his request to be aryanized had not been acted upon. He urged that it be expedited, saying that he had important connections in the Red air force that kept the Germans up to date on its strength and organization. Wagner told him outright that he didn't believe him. He had learned that the MAX outpost was not radioing to Russia—though it was, curiously, communicating with Vigo, Spain. This was true, Kauders retorted; he used the radio section of the Bulgarian police to communicate with Russia because their mentality suited the Russians' better. Wagner acknowledged the point, then checked with the Bulgarians. They told him they weren't radioing for Klatt. He summoned the man, who coolly responded that he had deliberately misled Wagner to protect his secret radio links, which actually went to Russia via Turkey. Radios on board cutters off the ancient Black Sea port of Samsun in Turkey relayed the transmissions, he said. The Abwehr leader in Istanbul told Wagner this was not possible. Wagner now felt certain that, if Kauders was not a double agent, he was certainly a fraudulent one. At a meeting one day with Canaris, Piekenbrock, and Marogna-Redwitz, he voiced his suspicions. Silence fell over the room. Then Marogna-Redwitz said that the Luftwaffe called Kauders's reports the best, decisive for the war, and that was why he could do what he wanted. Canaris backed up his Vienna chief. "You can watch him," he told Wagner about Kauders, "but don't disturb him in his work." So to the end Kauders kept it up, and to the end he was believed.

In but one area of the world did the Germans spy as readers of spy novels would have them do: in Latin America. They did well in Mexico, where they had at least 40 agents with others in the United States, all organized into three rings which sent at least 500 microdots of information to their controls in Hamburg, Berlin, and Cologne. But their most extensive and elaborate organization operated in Argentina, one of the strongest nations of the region and the most anti-Yankee.

It began there in 1939 when a traveling Abwehr representative recruited Ottomar Müller as an agent. Müller, 38, had emigrated to the pampas 15 years before, during Germany's disastrous postwar inflation. He proved an energetic spy. Once he negotiated with an Argentine army officer to buy a bombsight. He told about cattle bought by England and gave monthly reports on the exports of important raw materials and foodstuffs to Britain and America. He organized a ring of agents. He dispatched numerous messages about ships arriving, sailing, loading. And the OKW told him that his time as a spy would count as military service.

But Müller's patriotism exceeded his discretion. While head of the spy ring, he was broadcasting German propaganda over Radio Callao. The

Abwehr deposed him, although—inexplicably—it let him continue as a member of the ring.

One of his agents took over the ring. He was Hans Napp, 40, an agronomist who had come to Latin America in 1921. At first he ran a small farm in Uruguay, then he managed a business, and in April of 1939, apparently fulfilling a dream, he opened the Adlon Tea Room Bar in Buenos Aires with a local shoe manufacturer as partner. Within five months, it had failed. Napp went bankrupt. But the next month the war fortuitously provided employment. Napp became a spy.

He did well enough to be appointed as Müller's successor in October of 1941. Through the ring's radio link via the clandestine transmitter of a cover firm in Brazil, the Hamburg Abwehr post directed him to go to the office of the naval attaché in Buenos Aires, give the password, "My cousin sails on the *Gneisenau*," and receive 5,000 pesos ($1,250). Half the money was for a "single special payment" for himself. The other half was to help buy and operate the ring's own radio transmitter. (Hamburg had authorized 10,000 pesos [$2,500] for this, but only after closely questioning the spies: "How high are total costs up to readiness to operate radio?" "How high current message charges independent of current month's payment?") Napp's first job was to supervise installation of this transmitter.

Afterward he gathered information and ran his ring, covering his activities with his Compañía DIN (most probably standing for Deutsche Internationale Nachrichten, or German international information). One of his spies, who was a former waiter, shared office space with him. Napp often lunched with his agents at the Bar Central, Calle 25 de Mayo 357. Among them were a long-time friend who recruited seamen on Spanish vessels as couriers—he was a Spaniard himself—and who often lent Napp one of his cars for days on end, a Paraguayan of German descent, and a Swiss businessman kicked out of the Swiss chamber of commerce in Buenos Aires because of his Nazi proclivities. Napp did well enough at his spying to move from his cramped quarters in the Hotel Viena to a rather luxurious home at Calle Pedro Goyena 1259 in the northwestern suburb of Martínez.

Napp continued Müller's emphasis on shipping information. On 7 December 1941, for example, he radioed in message No. 430:

> Arrived in Buenos Aires: on the 2nd, the *Ogna*, and on the 3rd, the *Delane* from Santos. On the 3rd the *Thorstrand* departed from Buenos Aires for Rio. On the 3rd the *Thalia* arrived at Montevideo from Libertad. . . .

The naval attaché, Captain Dietrich Niebuhr, looked with a jaundiced eye on all this. The spies' shipping reports merely duplicated those he sent in routinely from his office overlooking the port. He believed that their military-political reporting, which he regarded as the most important part of the work, merely rehashed street gossip because they did not have the access to the high informed circles that he had. Nevertheless, on instructions from Berlin he supported them, paying Napp, for example, several hundred pesos a month.

And he ran a little spy ring of his own. Though some of the personnel overlapped with Napp's, the intelligence targets differed somewhat. Niebuhr's ring reported on 1 January 1942 that "Curtiss Columbus factory [in the United States] will begin May mass production series SB 2 C single-seater dive bomber for Navy." Germany bombarded it with requests ("Can you get U.S. Field Manual No. 3-154 'Chemical Warfare' "), and also showered it with compliments ("Drawing attention to investigation order concerning torpedo protective nets which was sent in M49-50-1 [probably messages M49, 50, 51], reports on equipment of English and American cruisers and auxiliary cruisers with technical details were unusually correct").

The German declaration of war on America was followed, within eight weeks, by Brazil's rupture of diplomatic relations with the Axis. Within eight more weeks, authorities there had crushed three major German networks. Some spies were jailed, but some of the important radio technicians fled to Argentina and to Chile. Unlike Brazil and most of the other Latin American countries, Chile long retained its diplomatic links with Germany, Italy, and Japan. As in Argentina, this facilitated German espionage. For not only was the spying sheltered by Chilean neutrality, but German diplomats could furnish sustenance.

In Chile, the air attaché did the helping. But the man in charge of the ring was Heinrich Reiners, a German national and Nazi party member who had a small shipping concern at Prat 773, Valparaiso. In the late summer of 1941, he visited various ports in Chile, recruiting agents to report on ship movements.

Some of these apparently sent their reports to Reiners at Post Office Box 1545. But Hamburg had forbidden him to pick up his mail there, specifying that only a trustworthy middleman could do this. So it was gotten by a partner in a firm that shared office space with Reiners. Some of the other harbor spies sent their reports to a Chilean who functioned chiefly as the ring's mailbox. He sometimes received letters in secret ink from the United States, and he subscribed to the *New York Maritime Register,* which provided many details on American shipping.

Clerical channels served as well. Out of Quito came intelligence of a secret report to the president of Ecuador. It spoke of a $37 million loan by the United States and the provision of 5,000 rifles, 250,000 machine guns, and a naval cruiser. (It was slightly exaggerated: the Lend-Lease agreement was for only $17 million and included no cruisers.) A pro-Nazi priest, Father Viane, forwarded it in a prayer book to a Catholic theological student at the seminary in La Cisterna, just outside Santiago. The Germans picked up the prayer book from the student, Tullio Franchini, who may have known nothing about the spy material.

The intelligence that went out from Chile dealt largely with shipping. "Chilean *Tolten* loading here for U.S.A.," it told Germany. The ring also passed along weather reports, which Hamburg had requested, presumably at the instance of the Luftwaffe. The recipients appreciated the information. "Provide Christmas gifts value each one hundred marks," Hamburg ordered spy chief Reiners.

Such messages were naturally exchanged by radio—otherwise the material would have arrived far too late to be of use.

The ring's transmitter had been built about mid-1940 by a radio store owner who had no connection with the spies. He had been told that the transmitter was for amateur use, which was legal at the time. It could be partly dismantled and fitted into a large wooden box.

At first one of the ring's members, Wilhelm Zeller, a licensed amateur, transmitted from his home at Avenida Alemana 5508 in Cerro Alegre, near Valparaiso. These illegal emissions attracted the attention of U.S. monitors. They alerted the Chilean police, who raided the house on 25 June 1942. They did not find the transmitter. But they had taken the precaution of tapping Zeller's house telephone, and shortly after they left, they heard Zeller tell another ring member:

"Luckily they did not search very well, especially in the basement."

The police promptly got another warrant and nine hours later knocked again on Zeller's door. They saw the box with the transmitter, but did not look into it. Nevertheless, twice was enough for the Germans. They moved the main element of the transmitter in its box to an Italian grocery store and hid some of the other parts in a bar. Until October they refused to radio.

Then, with the heat off, they reassembled the transmitter in the shacklike house of Hans Hofbauer at Calle Carrera 1150 in Quilpue, about 15 miles east of Valparaiso. The tile-roofed structure was screened by high hedges, though a tall pole lifted the antenna above them. Its windows were heavily draped; the ground lead was covered with a small box. The operator was Reiners's second in command, the wavy-haired, 32-year-old Johannes Szeraws, formerly second officer on a German ship which he jumped to enter Chile illegally. Szeraws lived in the house, which was kept locked at all times. He transmitted from a back room, using the call letters PYL. In replying, Hamburg tried to hide its signals by operating very close to the same frequency as that of the scrambled transatlantic radio circuit.

It lasted only a month. With the help of the American monitors, some of them on the spot, the Chileans smashed the PYL ring in November 1942. Many members were arrested, but some—Reiners and Szeraws among them—escaped to Argentina. With a temporary exception or two, German spying ended in Chile. At the very same time, the Argentine government, yielding somewhat to American pressure and to the disclosures of its own legislative Investigating Commission on Anti-Argentine Activities, swooped down on its local spies. Napp and Müller and others were arrested.

It appeared that this had shattered German espionage there. But in fact German espionage was not merely to continue, but to increase. The main reason was an exceptionally able and courageous young man sent by the SD to take charge of what became a cooperative Abwehr-SD operation. His name was Johann Siegfried Becker.

Becker was born in Leipzig on 21 October 1912. Immediately after graduating from high school there, he joined the Nazi party. The following year, 1931, he was admitted into the SS. He worked for a tobacco wholesaler, a lignite producers' association, some volunteer party posts. In one of these, said a superior, "The organization and surveillance of the entire German–foreign exchange of youth lay in his hands. . . . Party Comrade Becker fulfilled this assignment independently and to our complete satisfaction." After another year's work in Germany for a party-related organ, he quit. A few weeks later, on 20 April 1937, he was named an SS 2nd lieutenant, and on 9 May he arrived in Buenos Aires aboard the *Monte Pascoal*. He appeared as the business representative of the Berlin firm Centro de Exportación del Comercio Alemán with an office in the Banco Germánico building. He went back to Germany briefly early in the war, around 1940, and came back as a diplomatic courier. Then, after Germany declared war on the United States, he was summoned to the Reich. His trip took several months, since he was delayed in Rio de Janeiro as a result of difficulties with the Italian transatlantic airline, whose flights were being suspended. He only arrived in Berlin in May of 1942. There, promoted to SS captain, he was instructed on reorganizing and directing the espionage services in South America, particularly to prevent loss of contact in the case of war between the several countries and Germany. His work dealt with political intelligence; the Abwehr's, with military.

In December, he stowed away on the *Rita García* in Sagunto, Spain. When ship's officers discovered him, he produced false Argentine identity papers, made out to José Luschnig, a baker. In Buenos Aires, the crew helped him evade the authorities, and he sneaked ashore on 3 January 1943.

At once he contacted one of the SD's men, Wilhelm Seidlitz, a weak-chinned, mean-looking travel agent who had spied for the Germans since the start of the war. Through the embassy, the SD had sent Seidlitz $50,000, which he gave Becker. Seidlitz also put Becker in touch with the 36-year-old advertising chief of Bayer Chemicals in Argentina. Becker set up a general representative's concern with this man at rooms 609 and 611, Calle Cangallo 439, Buenos Aires. The staff was to stop work every day at 4 p.m. to leave the office free for the spy work.

Becker next reorganized the spy nets into three groups. The embassy, or blue, group was headed by the naval attaché, Niebuhr, who was later replaced by the military attaché, General Wolff; this communicated with the Abwehr station in Hamburg. A green group was directed by Johann Leo

Harnisch, an attorney in his mid-forties long resident in Argentina. He had gone back to Germany in 1941, when he entered Abwehr service, returning the next year to set up a ring under Becker. He was a close friend of an Argentine colonel and boasted that he knew Hitler personally. His net, which communicated with the Abwehr post in Cologne, collected economic espionage—particularly on the U.S. arms industry—for the energetic Major Focke there. Becker's own group, the red, an SD unit, included Seidlitz and the Bayer man, who took charge of the organization of Becker's concern and himself supplied information gained through his contacts. Becker communicated with the RSHA through couriers and by radio to the Havel Institute in Berlin, which called this its Line 23.

Serving all three groups was the Orga T, or technical organization. This handled the vital radio and microdot communications with Germany.

Its head was Gustav Utzinger, a gifted, moustachioed 29-year-old Ph.D. in chemistry. The Abwehr had sent him to Brazil early in the war as an employee of the giant Telefunken communications company to set up radio communication to Germany. When Brazilian authorities broke up the German spy rings there, Utzinger escaped, though he was later sentenced in absentia to eight years in prison. Eventually he reached Argentina, where Niebuhr introduced him to the local espionage units. Utzinger bought or rented small, isolated farms around the city where he could undertake the long and difficult attempts to make transatlantic radio contact with Germany. He changed farms from time to time, either for security or convenience.

As his second in command, he had Szeraws, who had radioed from the locked shack and had escaped from Chile. Ulrich Daue, 25, a former merchant-marine radioman, actually sent most of the messages. Daue's ship had arrived in Montevideo at about the time the pocket battleship *Graf Spee,* chased into that harbor by the British, was scuttled by the crew; Daue, with other Germans, was interned. In 1942, he escaped down the River Plate to Buenos Aires in an outboard motorboat and wound up in the espionage organization. In it he carried false identity papers in the name of Carlos Mario Barredo.

In June of 1943, Utzinger took him to a farm called Guerrico in Bella Vista, near Buenos Aires, and installed him there. Within a few days Utzinger brought a small transmitter in a wooden case that operated off the regular house current. Daue transmitted a few messages by Morse to Germany. Meanwhile, to conceal the espionage activities on the farm, the German sympathizers who lived there planted trees, bought 350 chickens, and installed an incubator. Daue dug a pit in the chicken coop and hid the transmitter in it, covering the pit with a board scattered with straw. Every week or so, Utzinger, who had the code name of DON ANTONIO, brought about a dozen coded telegrams of about 50 groups each which Daue sent off to Germany. When they discovered that the transmitter was not working properly, DON ANTONIO brought out another one, smaller but of equal power, and built into a suitcase of dark maroon leather.

The Orga T also had a microphotography laboratory in a country house called La Choza at Calle Corrientes 550, also in Bella Vista. For 200 pesos ($50) a month and the use of the house, a 27-year-old Austrian off-set photolithographer and his wife turned out quantities of microdots, frequently of American publications. These Becker sent by mail or courier to Germany.

After his reorganization, Becker stepped up his information-gathering. Early in 1943, he sent a man to Uruguay with $3,000 worth of Argentine pesos to start espionage there. The man did not succeed as well as Becker thought he should have, and around June he summoned him and a few other agents to a meeting in a house at Calle Oro 2168 in Buenos Aires that his network had bought to board agents and to hold meetings. He bawled the man out, then gave him $1,200 more, and sent him back to Montevideo to complete his mission. Through friends, the man recruited several Uruguayans, at least one of them because he was a nationalist and an anti-Yankee. This agent was asked to obtain statistics on Uruguayan imports and exports and a copy of the magazine *Orientación,* which explained how to get United States import permits.

Becker got his information by analyzing American newspapers and technical magazines, by monitoring radio broadcasts, from personal observation, and in particular from diplomatic and military personnel who visited or were trained in the United States and from the group of colonels, including Juan Perón, who really ran the country and with whom Harnisch and other members of the rings were friendly. The foreign minister, one of that group, who thought the Americans were "Yankee bastards," promised a German agent that he would keep Germany apprised of current happenings because the destiny of Argentina depended upon a German victory. Much of the information consisted of data on American armaments production and the U.S. political and economic situation; much was on Argentine domestic and foreign policy.

For his first year as head of the combined Abwehr-SD spy nets in eastern Latin America, Becker enjoyed the support of the embassy. Niebuhr and Wolff were there with advice and funds and courier services, though not with telecommunications—the Axis diplomats being in effect prevented, by American pressure on Argentina, from sending code messages. Thus the Orga T was at first financed entirely by the embassy; later, it received $7,000 monthly from the embassy and $3,000 a month from Becker's group and the same from Harnisch's, plus extra money for expenses when needed. Moreover, Becker's spying flourished in the benign pro-Axis political climate.

This all changed at the start of 1944. Argentina had long been trying to get arms from Germany in order, it said, to protect itself from aggressive and pro-Yankee neighbors, especially Brazil. Toward the end of 1943, it intensified these efforts. Ultimately, perhaps at the suggestion of Harnisch, it decided to bypass cumbersome diplomatic channels and deal directly with Himmler's SD. The SD, always seeking to expand its powers, moved gladly into foreign affairs. Schellenberg agreed to deal with the Argentine negotiator, an Argentine citizen of German descent who was a close friend of Harnisch. He sailed for Spain, but at the Trinidad control point the British, who had got wind of these moves, detained him. Fear of exposure of this move and of Argentine subversion in neighboring Bolivia and possibly elsewhere, together with U.S. pressure in the form of warships dropping anchor at Montevideo and a threat to freeze funds, led Argentina to break diplomatic relations with Germany on 26 January 1944.

This shut down the blue, or embassy, net. And since the government had given as its reason for the rupture of relations that it had discovered extensive German espionage on Argentine soil, it arrested masses of German agents and subagents in February. The green group, headed by the discredited Harnisch, was a main target. Harnisch, Seidlitz, the Bayer aspirin advertising chief, the microdot man, and many others were swept into custody.

Now the whole burden of German espionage on Argentina and neighboring countries landed on Becker. The easy times were over. Real spying began.

Undaunted, Becker rallied what was left of his red group. He replaced those arrested and those whom he thought to be under suspicion. He put a former Royal Rumanian Legation chancellor into the Bayer man's place, for example. He found a new microphotographer. He shifted the finances. One morning in the middle of 1944 he had some of his agents meet him in the Café D'Huicque on Calle Maipú in Buenos Aires.

"The pesos are gone and it's now necessary to change dollars," he told them. "I have changed some in the past but don't want to continue to do this myself. Inside this newspaper are $2,000. If you get three pesos per dollar [the official rate was four], it's all right, but don't do it all at once, but rather go to several places. I'll wait for you at one p.m. at Corrientes and Maipú—and be careful."

The dollars were in 20s, 50s, and 100s. The agents changed them to Becker's satisfaction, and he gave them $4,500 more to convert.

Some of this went to pay agents. Szeraws, the second in command of the Orga T, got $500 a month, in pesos. An average agent got about $300. Some money went for a kind of spy unemployment benefit: when an agent was arrested, Becker gave his family cash to live on. Other funds went to pay for the ring's seven cars, two boats, its typewriters, and rent on its apartments, boarding houses, and offices. Some cash probably went to pay for false papers and for bribes for information. But the big money went to Orga T. Not only was it constantly buying expensive equipment to build its

33 transmitters and 27 receivers, as well as custom-made wooden boxes to transport and hide them in, but its purchases and rentals of farms required a considerable cash flow. Utzinger estimated that it spent in pesos the equivalent of $62,000 from the time it began operating.

As the figures suggest, communications consumed much of the ring's energy. Fortunately, in Utzinger it had an exceptionally capable chief. He knew his specialty and he knew his men. He chose them carefully and organized them in a cell system by which they did not know each other but only their immediate superior. He himself used several aliases, possessed numerous sets of false papers, drove several cars, and lived in various residences.

Soon after the rupture of diplomatic relations, Utzinger ordered that the transmitter at the farm Guerrico be dismantled and moved to a farm named Mi Capricho near San Miguel, which Utzinger had rented as a reserve. Beneath the kitchen the Germans dug a cellar in which they installed the transmitter. When Daue arrived, Utzinger gave him two or three telegrams in 5-letter groups to send. This time, however, Utzinger told him that if he received no reply after a minute or two to his series of *V*s, which warms up the operator's hand and lets his correspondent tune in his transmissions exactly, he was not to call any more that day but to wait two or three days more. Daue supposed that this was to hinder radio direction-finding. When Daue could not raise Germany that week, Utzinger took back the messages, presumably to give to another radioman.

In April 1944, the ring rented yet another farm. This was near San Justo, like San Miguel a western exurb of Buenos Aires. Daue and Utzinger installed a two-foot radio in the dining room. Utzinger brought 15 messages that Daue was to transmit within a few days. He also told Daue that they would not meet any more; another agent would bring him the messages. The government crackdown was complicating things for the ring.

Szeraws now mainly brought the texts Daue was to encipher and transmit. Daue met him at different places in and around Buenos Aires, often street corners. He transmitted his messages at specific times and frequencies: 11,550 kilohertz at 5:30 p.m., 11,130 at 6:10, 10,400 at 6:40, and so on. The correspondent station always worked 10,600. Once he delivered a transmitter to another farm and sent 20 messages from there. Near the end of June, Utzinger told him that he was in charge of radio transmissions. Daue now listened with his receiver to check the sendings of other agents.

Not all messages went by radio. Becker had four men who found sailors on Spanish vessels who would carry envelopes to Spain, whence they would mail them to cover addresses in Germany. One of the four, Alfredo Villa, worked in a bar in Buenos Aires that was frequented by the crew members of Spanish ships. Another, Father Alfredo Fernández, a priest at the church of San Miguel on Calle Bartolomé Mitre at the corner of Suipacha, had fought with Franco in Spain; he often gave messages, including microdots, to Spanish sailors. Once an agent handed him a watch with microphotographs hidden in it for sending to Spain, and Father Fernández passed it to Villa to give to a sailor

Becker feared that additional arrests would be made, and he asked Germany to send him two additional communications men and more money. They responded by dispatching the yawl *Passim* with Burckhardt and Chatrain, expert radioman and microphotographer respectively, who brought with them in July of 1944 money and drugs that could be converted to money.

At the end of that same month, Becker's fears were realized. Daue had once noted two persons in front of the farm at San Justo, and another day a car had stopped in front. A little while later, to separate himself as much as possible from the incriminating transmitter, Daue moved back to Buenos Aires, living in a house at Zapiola 1451 with the maid from the farm, Luisa Matthies. On the afternoon of 29 July, when he went out to the farm to transmit, he told Luisa to burn or secrete the papers in his yellow briefcase if anything suspicious happened, since he thought he might be picked up at any moment. He was at the transmitter, keying messages, when the police broke in at 6:30 and arrested him.

Other arrests followed. Within a few weeks in August, Utzinger, Szeraws, Chatrain, Burckhardt, and many others were seized. Dozens of radios, the microdot apparatus, and three Enigma cipher machines (apparently inherited from the embassy) were confiscated. The ring was all but broken. But Becker evaded the net, and so did Father Fernández, the barman Villa, and a few others.

Becker now had to spend increasing amounts of time simply dodging the police. He would rent a furnished apartment, live there for a few months, and leave before the lease expired. Often he even left valuable articles behind. If a person who knew of his whereabouts was arrested, another person would notify him. He had one of his agents buy *La Prensa* and *La Nación* for him; he then gave the man clippings of classified ads for apartments that he wanted him to look at. The agent located a two-bedroom apartment at Tucumán 672, second floor, apartment 2. A German woman acquaintance rented it knowing that Becker would be staying in one of the bedrooms. The agent took Becker to the apartment in a taxi; he brought no clothes with him, but had the woman buy him new clothes little by little.

He rarely left the apartment, sometimes staying in it for a month at a time. If he did go out, which was only to meet an agent, he waited until after 10 p.m. The agent who had brought him there visited him twice a week, always arriving after 6:45 p.m., when the German woman was at home, so that the porter would not suspect that another person was living in the apartment. The agent always rang one long followed by three short rings, then paused and gave two short rings.

Becker almost always had the letters he gave the agent ready. He put each into an individual envelope, which he initialed, and then put them all into a larger envelope. If he had to answer a message, he did so at once, using a portable typewriter or dictating to the woman.

The messages to go to Germany were passed to Villa, together with the money, usually 50 to 100 pesos ($12.50 to $25), that he was to give to the Spanish seaman as payment for bringing the letters across the Atlantic. But a little hitch developed here. Instead of doing this, Villa spent the money himself and threw the messages in his closet in his home. When police arrested him in February 1945, they found there the watch that Father Fernández had given him as well as some bits of paper with typed messages from Becker to "Theo," his superior in Germany—SS Lieutenant Colonel Theodor Paeffgen, head of RSHA VI D, the Anglo-American group. Thus was much of Becker's brave and idealistic work frustrated by greed.

Like Villa, Father Fernández and the few remaining members of the ring were arrested early in 1945. Only Becker remained at large. He was finally captured near the end of April, only a few weeks before the Reich for which he had worked so hard itself collapsed.

What had he accomplished? Very little. Paeffgen noted that—perhaps near the end—a month often elapsed between Becker's messages to Germany, and he often wished that they were longer. The reports that came in via the seamen's courier service were fuller, but they always arrived too late to be of use. Kaltenbrunner said that the only important spy report that he got out of South America predicted the rupture of diplomatic relations with Argentina—about which Germany could do nothing. The one area in which spy intelligence might have had an effect—the reporting of enemy ship sailings—sank not a single vessel. Five ships of the dozens reported as sailing from the Atlantic Coast were indeed torpedoed: the *Rodney Star,* the *Solöy,* the *Palma,* the *Azalea City,* and the *Andalucia Star.* But this owed nothing to the spies, for not one of the U-boats that sank them received any messages about them. The enormous efforts of Germany's Latin American spies had, in general, gone for naught.

Danger to Germany lay, however, less in the southern than in the northern hemisphere. The United States had, only 20 years earlier, provided the fresh manpower and the tons of supplies that had crumpled the Second Reich; it similarly threatened the Third. The task of spying out its intentions and capabilities fell at first to the Hamburg post of the Abwehr.

Its first spy came to it. He was Ignatz T. Griebl, a bespectacled physician who was one of the most notorious womanizers in, and a leader of, Manhattan's German colony of Yorkville. Soon after Hitler came to power, Griebl volunteered his services as an agent in a letter to Propaganda Minister Goebbels, a friend of his brother's. Griebl told how, back in 1922, when he was a medical student in Munich, he had once served the fledgling

Abwehr on a secret mission to France. He noted that he was a lieutenant in the U.S. army medical reserve. His offer was accepted, and eventually led to the creation of a substantial spy ring in the United States, headed by himself and subordinated to Hamburg's I M, or head of naval espionage, Dr. Erich Pfeiffer. By 1935, it was delivering such secret data as specifications of pursuit planes built at the Seversky plant in Farmingdale, Long Island, and blueprints of three destroyers and of a U.S. navy scout bomber.

For three years the spy ring continued to grow. At least one other of its members recruited himself in the same way that Griebl had. Twenty-seven-year-old Guenther Gustav Rumrich had been greatly impressed by the memoirs of Colonel Walther Nicolai, World War I head of German espionage, which he had read in the New York Public Library. He wrote to Nicolai in care of the Nazi party's paper, the *Völkischer Beobachter,* saying that if Germany could use him, a former lieutenant in the U.S. army, the war office should insert an advertisement addressed to Theodore Koerner in the public notices of *The New York Times.* On 6 April 1936, a classified advertisement appeared in that section. "Theodore Koerner—Letter received, please send reply and address to Sanders, Hamburg 1, Postbox 629, Germany." This Rumrich did, later becoming a member of Griebl's ring.

But it was Rumrich who brought the ring down. Eager to get $1,000 that Hamburg had offered for some blank American passports, he imperiously telephoned the chief of the New York office of the State Department passport division, identified himself as "Edward Weston, undersecretary of state," and demanded that 50 passport blanks be sent to him at the Hotel Taft. The suspicious chief put the police on the tail of the caller, and with Rumrich's arrest, the entire ring collapsed. Griebl himself fled to Germany, later surfacing in Vienna as a gynecologist in the aryanized practice of an exiled Jewish doctor. Others were not so lucky: they were convicted and jailed.

Essentially they were small fry, and their intelligence minor. How different it was for Hamburg's I L, Major Ritter! In 1937, he visited the United States—and came home with one of Germany's greatest spy coups.

The second Sunday after his arrival in New York, he met, in the Brooklyn home of a rather inconsequential informant, the man who would become his most important and successful spy. Hermann W. Lang was a broad-faced, quiet, and pleasant 35-year-old with dark blond hair and agreeable features. He had come to the United States from Germany in 1927; at the time he met Ritter his naturalization had not yet been completed. Lang worked in the factory at 80 Lafayette Street in Manhattan that was producing what was then the most famous secret of the American arms industry: the Norden bombsight, reputed to be the most accurate in the world.

Lang was an inspector. For this work, he told Ritter, he had access to some of the blueprints of the apparatus—though, for security reasons, not all. Sometimes he himself was supposed to put them in the safe at the end of the day's work, but on those days he took them to his home instead. He and his wife went to bed early. He waited until she was asleep, then crept out of bed, went to the kitchen at the other end of the apartment, and

The tiny advertisement to Theodor Koerner on page 3 of *The New York Times* of 6 April 1936 is the Hamburg Abwehr office's acceptance of the offer of Guenther Gustav Rumrich to spy for Germany traced the blueprints. These he now offered to Ritter, not for money, but to help the land of his fathers grow rapidly strong and free.

Ritter, amazed, stammered out a thanks, and accepted the first drawings. But how could he get them back to Germany safely? They were too large for his courier aboard the *Reliance* of the Hamburg-Amerika Line to carry folded in his pocket. He finally decided to roll them around the stem of an umbrella and let the courier, a steward on the ship, pretending to have to limp, lean on it as he brought it aboard. It worked. On 30 November 1937, the *Reliance* sailed with the first drawings of the device that, some thought, would give the Luftwaffe a remarkable advantage over other European air forces. Later drawings were cut up and laid in newspapers for the trip abroad. And so in the next few years, one of America's valuable

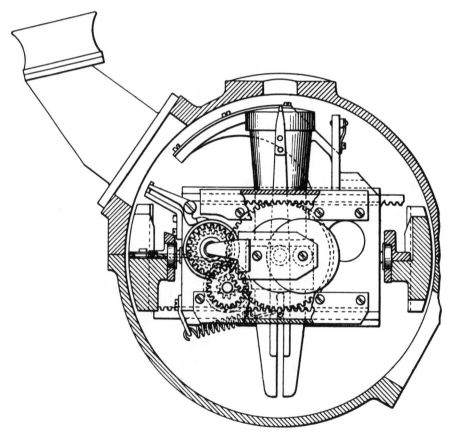

Part of the insides of the Norden bomb sight, America's greatest prewar secret, stolen by German spies

secrets seeped into Germany. There, the Luftwaffe reconstructed the missing parts and built a model of the bombsight.

"The device contains a number of interesting technical solutions, shows a good structural development, and forms the end result of a thorough development," it wrote to the Abwehr. "The target results attained with it in the U.S.A. are extraordinarily good. In Germany such results have not yet been attained. Through the delivery of the documents, considerable experiment costs have been saved.

"Flight testing of the apparatus showed that the principle realized in it worked satisfactorily for bombing. As a result, the documents about the bomb sight delivered by the Abwehr out of the U.S.A. have successfully influenced the development of the German bomb sight." The Norden did not replace the German apparatus, called the Lothfe (from words meaning "long-range pilot"), however, in part because the Lothfe was already in production, was installed in many airplanes, and was familiar to the bombardiers.

This was Ritter's greatest success as a spymaster. But a spy he recruited in Germany was destined to become, curiously, even more influential than Lang—though in quite a different way.

In February 1939, William G. Sebold, 40, a naturalized American who had been born in Germany and had fought as a machine gunner in the kaiser's army, arrived in Hamburg on the way to visit his mother in Mülheim in the Ruhr. Though he had quit his job, he listed it as his occupation on the immigration card: mechanic at the Consolidated Aircraft Company plant in San Diego, California. This information reached the Gestapo, which invited Sebold to visit it in nearby Düsseldorf on a matter that would be of advantage to him and would also serve Germany. Secure in his American passport, Sebold declined. Then the Gestapo pointed out that Sebold had spent some time in jail in Germany for smuggling and other offenses; he had evidently concealed this information from the American authorities in applying for citizenship.

Sebold went to the Gestapo office, where he accepted the German offer to work as a spy. The Gestapo forwarded his dossier to the nearest Abwehr post, Münster. But it was busy with France and sent it on to the "American" post, Hamburg. A few days later, Ritter, using another of his codenames, Dr. Rankin, came down to look Sebold over. Told that the man had volunteered and had been checked out, he "hired" him and arranged for him to attend the spy school in Hamburg.

Sebold did well at the spy school, in particular passing the all-important radio test with flying colors. The day before his departure, under a false name and with a forged passport, one of the post's officers gave him a list of four agents with their addresses whom he was to contact upon his arrival in New York. His job would consist chiefly of radioing their intelligence back to Hamburg or microfilming it for mail transmission.

One of the names was that of Hermann Lang—who, despite his protestations of pure patriotism, had had $3,500 deposited in an account in his name in Germany for his spying. The others were of Everett Minster Roeder, a draftsman who was probably the Abwehr's greatest producer of detailed technical data in the United States; Lilly Stein, a Vienna-born artist's model who recruited agents and served as a cut-out, or special courier; and Frederick Joubert Duquesne, a middle-aged buccaneer of a German publicist and semisecret agent. Sebold met them in the office of a fake Diesel Research Company he set up in the Knickerbocker Building at the southeast corner of Broadway and 42nd Street in Manhattan. The spies' material was dot-and-dashed from a transmitter with the improper call sign vw-2 in a house in Centerport, Long Island, to Hamburg, which also used an outlaw call sign, AOR.

Sebold—codename TRAMP—and his radio channel operated so reliably and rapidly that soon other officers in the Abwehr post in Hamburg asked Ritter to allow TRAMP to transmit messages from their agents. He graciously assented. At the same time, the social propensities of the spies overrode their security prescriptions, and Sebold gradually came to know many of them. There was the cook Paul Fehse, who had been trained in Hamburg and put himself out as the head of the marine division of German espionage in America. He reported on ship movements, summoned the agents to conferences, and developed sympathizers as possible spies or couriers. Carl Reuper, like most of the others a native of Germany who had been naturalized in America, worked as an inspector at Westinghouse Electric Company in Newark, New Jersey; he photographed plans of defense equipment. The smooth, cosmopolitan Edmund Carl Heine, who had served the Ford Motor Company since 1920 in South America, Spain, Detroit, and Germany, where he became manager, and then worked for the Chrysler Motor Corporation, had been asked by Professor Ferdinand Porsche to get some information on automobile matters. Heine got most of his intelligence by openly asking for it. On 22 July 1940, he wrote the Consolidated Aircraft Corporation:

"In one of the recent trade magazines I have read an advertisement stating 'From conception to flight in nine months.' This piece of propaganda has caused quite a conversation among a number of friends, and in order to settle a few disputes could or would you kindly answer the following questions: 1. Was it the B-24 that was conceived and made its first flight in nine months? . . . If any of these questions are not answerable for military reasons, please do not answer same."

On 25 July, Norman Davidson, a public relations assistant at Consolidated, replied to Heine's home at 4447 Baldwin Avenue, Detroit; the answer to the first question was in the affirmative. Heine once sent a long report on "Development of Diesel Engines" to Lilly Stein; she passed it to Sebold, who microphotographed it and sent it to Germany.

Suddenly the entire smooth-working mechanism collapsed. In a series of rapid raids, the F.B.I. arrested the major and minor members of this largest German spy ring on American soil, somewhat after its best work had been done but before it could do any more harm. During the subsequent trial, it turned out that Sebold had contacted the American consul in Cologne while the Abwehr was blackmailing him into its service, and from that time forward had worked with the F.B.I. to expose the German espionage activities. The messages from Centerport had all been sent by an F.B.I. agent after having been screened for truly dangerous intelligence. Sebold's conferences on 42nd Street with the agents had been filmed by F.B.I. cameras through a one-way mirror from the office next door. The whole thing had been, for the Abwehr, and for Ritter, who had started Sebold, a gigantic débâcle.

"The bastard!" said Ritter to Piekenbrock, who showed him the front-page headline in *The New York Times*. "The traitor!"

"But Ritter," said the head of Abwehr I calmly, "by your own principles TRAMP was no traitor, not even a spy. He was a man who worked for his new fatherland."

The F.B.I. also arrested other spies. But a few others continued to operate.

One of the most successful of these was Simon Emil Koedel—A 2011 in the Hamburg files. Koedel was one of the world's colorless men, and he worked in an invisible job: he was a motion-picture projectionist. He had been born in Bavaria on 30 October 1881 and had come to America when he was 22. He served in the U.S. army for three years before World War I and then got his American citizenship. But he could also say that "I love Germany with all my heart" and that he was willing "to give my very life for her." During a trip to Germany in the mid-1930s, he offered his services as a spy, was accepted, trained, and sent back to America as a "sleeper." He rented an apartment at 660 Riverside Drive in Manhattan with his monthly stipend of $200 plus expenses and began burrowing into American society. He established a fake identity and cultivated his sources for the war Hitler was planning.

By enclosing his old army discharge papers and saying that he was a chemical engineer with large stock holdings in major defense industries, he was accepted as a member of the American Ordnance Association, a prodefense lobby with close ties to the War Department. Soon he was writing letters on association stationery to members of the military affairs committees in both houses of Congress. Senator Robert Rice Reynolds of North Carolina replied courteously, inviting this patriot to call on him in Washington, and beginning a relationship that was to prove enormously valuable for Koedel.

On 5 September 1939, a cablegram from Germany signed "Hartmann" and containing the word "alloy" in the text activated the sleeper agent. Koedel, now 57, lean, sinewy, thin-lipped, and humorless, began his spying. He attracted no more attention than a fish that swims in a school as he attended meetings of the American Ordnance Association. He received many War Department press releases. By brazenly walking up to factories and flashing his membership card, he was often admitted and shown around. The occasional rejection he overcame resourcefully. In November of 1939 he tried this trick at the gate of the Edgewood Arsenal, but was turned away. When a later attempt also failed, he telephoned the ordnance association in Washington. It called the War Department, which called Edgewood, which then let Koedel in. His guided tour on 7 December resembled a spy's dream come true. And the long report that he wrote in his hotel room in Havre de Grace, Maryland, detailed storage statistics, suppliers, technical data, and some of the latest developments in the laboratories.

He exploited his other sources as well. In March of 1940, when the Germans were planning their blitzkrieg against France, they needed to know whether the Atlantic ports of Nantes–St. Nazaire and La Rochelle could handle more than tankers and colliers. The query went to the Abwehr, which circularized it to several of its agents, among them Koedel. He coolly put the question to his acquaintance, Senator Reynolds, saying that he needed the information to arrange for shipping supplies to France. Reynolds investigated, and on 9 April Koedel could tell Hamburg that "according to the U.S. Maritime Commission, these ports are not limited in their facilities but are capable of handling ships loading oil and coal as well as general cargo." This report went to Germany both via the German naval attaché in Washington, who enciphered it in his Enigma machine and cabled it over, and by mail via cover addresses unknown to British censorship.

Koedel worked hard at gathering shipping information. He rode the Staten Island ferry, peering through binoculars to determine the names of ships in port. Dressed in old clothes and wearing a cap, he strode through the dock areas as if he were a longshoreman to see the supplies being loaded. By noting the name and address of the manufacturer he could infer the type of material. All of this produced reports like the one he sent 3 January 1940 via a courier on the steamship *Saturnia:*

> Norwegian ship *Berganger* loading great quantity of iron poles, approximate length 20–30 feet, in addition to other cargo.
> Massive supplies piled up on Hamilton Dock, waiting to be loaded on just-arrived *Protopapa,* due to sail for Liverpool; *Emmy* and *Adamas,* bound for Le Havre. According to inscriptions on crates, supplies originated with following firms: Sundsbrand Machine Tool Co. of Rockford, Illinois, shipment consigned to Burton Fils at 68 rue de Marais in Paris, each crate weighing 2 to 3 tons; 100 black-painted metal barrels containing Sadonia oil, to be loaded on *Emmy* for F.A.H. Co., Ltd., in London; . . .

Koedel's 21-year-old daughter, Marie, of 542 West 112th Street, New York, mingled with sailors at waterfront bars to gain information on convoys. One whom she picked up and utilized as a spy, the youthful Duncan Scott-Ford, told her details that enabled her father to submit one of his most valuable items, entitled "Report on the Conduct of Enemy Ships in Convoy at Sea in the Atlantic, Based on Conversations with British Seamen." Scott-Ford pursued his new espionage career in Lisbon, but was eventually caught by the British and hanged 3 November 1942.

Koedel continued to report even in the spy-scare atmosphere of wartime America. Through 1942, 1943, and 1944 his messages continued to arrive in Germany. Ultimately the Abwehr registered some 600 of them. It considered him "tested, very trustworthy." Foreign Armies West, always more conservative, described him as "usable."

Eventually, however, Koedel's fellow employees at the Lyric Theatre grew suspicious of the many letters in foreign handwriting that they saw lying around the projection booth. They grew even more suspicious when a frame from a section of a newsreel about a new airplane was clipped out and vanished—only to reappear when Koedel had had an opportunity to bring it back. Frightened, he left New York and found a job as a projectionist in Harpers Ferry, West Virginia. But the F.B.I., helped by an ex-fiancé of his daughter, tracked him down. In October 1944 they finally arrested him, and then her.

JOSEFINE, MAX, and most of the spies in North and South America worked for the Abwehr. It was a big, old organization, and it fielded many more agents than the SD. The assignments of the agencies differed. The Abwehr's was military intelligence, the SD's, political. But in a war these merged at the top, and Schellenberg took advantage of this. He was striving to improve SD intelligence. So he welcomed the reports on Allied global strategy that his growing numbers of agents brought in. And, as part of his improvements, he ran his own agents. Some were to enhance the quality of SD intelligence by corroborative testing of the output of the ordinary spies. Others increased the quantity by gathering information themselves. With one of these, whose status and access he apparently deemed exalted enough to serve for his own agent, he ventured into society spying.

In 1943 he recruited the Portuguese ambassador's mistress, Irna Baroness von Rothkirch zu Panthen. The widow of a director of a Skoda works annex, also known by her married name of Frau Emden, the baroness was about 45, with a small figure, brown hair, light blue eyes, fine nose, thin lips, and a cultivated voice—she had once been a singer. Thinking she might tease valuable information out of the foreign diplomats in Berlin, Schellenberg paid the rent at a large house in Berlin to which she invited many of them. But though the Portuguese ambassador had sent his wife out of the country because of her, the baroness brought in only tidbits from him and her guests. Schellenberg sent her to Portugal, where she overspent her allowance—mostly on shopping. When she boasted of her contacts with Americans from the time she had spent in America, he dispatched her to Switzerland to see what she could find out. She spent most of her time visiting her son in boarding school, and brought back a report of such utter banality that it proved to Schellenberg that the Americans did not regard her as politically important. He helped her unfreeze some $50,000 that she had in the United States, which she promptly used to buy an estate in Silesia. By then he recognized that she was costing too much and producing too little, and he dropped her.

His less social spies enjoyed greater success. Often they stole diplomatic communications. On 12 November 1942, Schellenberg flashed a message to Himmler. It summarized the contents of two telegrams of Portuguese diplomats in Brazil to their Foreign Ministry. In one, the consul in Recife reported the imminent departure of six U.S. troop transports. In the other, dated 9 November, the embassy in Rio de Janeiro reported that the Brazilian government had placed two more steamers at the disposition of the American government for the transport of troops out of northern Brazil. As soon as these troops and the six transports arrived in Monrovia, an attack would begin on Dakar, the embassy said. Even though this was after the Allies had committed themselves by landing in North Africa, Himmler gave the stolen telegram to Hitler. Its total falsity could not have enhanced his trust in his spy services.

Later, Schellenberg obtained an entire series of messages of the Brazilian ambassador in Spain. They discussed the war situation in ill-informed terms. Another time, his men filched a low-level Spanish code and read some messages with it.

What appeared to be the most sensational of these coups was the theft of several score pages of correspondence of the president of the United States himself. Roosevelt's letters to his minister in Hungary, Herbert Claiborne Pell, as well as Pell's writings to him and to others, were photographed or were removed from the wastepaper basket in Pell's apartment in the Ritz Hotel in Budapest by—the story goes—a fresh-faced young chambermaid who recognized the chance to turn a fast pengö when she saw it.

In fact, however, the success was more apparent than real. For the documents were neither new nor informative. In one, Pell expressed his fears to Roosevelt that Spain might join the Axis and attack England's friend, Portugal. But this letter was two years old and Franco had long since refused to enter the war. Others gave the American ambassador in Vichy some advance details about a German diplomat going there, and expressed to someone in America Pell's views on Charles Lindbergh, then a discredited figure. Roosevelt's replies to Pell were equally significant. "I read with careful attention your letter of June 23 [1941] reporting the first reactions in Hungary to the war between Germany and the U.S.S.R. It is an interesting account of the situation at that critical moment." And even this trivia came to the attention of the SD only some eight months after Roosevelt sent it.

Perhaps on the basis of the Machiavellian principle that one should stretch out good deeds and abbreviate bad, Schellenberg and Heydrich

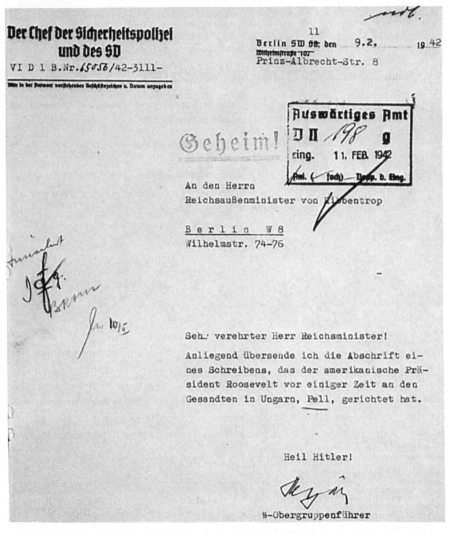

The Chief of the Security Police and of the SD transmits to Ribbentrop "the copy of a letter that the American president Roosevelt sent to his minister in Hungary, [Herbert Claiborne] Pell, some time ago." Heydrich puts his contorted signature between the complimentary close and his rank of SS general. His letter bears the office indication of RSHA VI D 1, the North American desk of Nazi party foreign intelligence

RSHA, den 19. Juli 1944
Ankunft " 19. " " - 4.10

ohne Nummer,

Inl II 4306
eing. 21. Juli 1944

An das Auswärtige Amt z.Hd. des Herrn Vortragen-
den Leg.Rat Wagner o.V.i.A. Berlin.

Als geheime Reichssache zu behandeln.

Betr. : Europareise Präsident Roosevelts.
Bezug : ohne.

Aus absolut zuverlässiger Quelle
wird bekannt, dass Präsident Roosevelt
beabsichtigt, in nächster Zeit nach
England zu reisen und/evtl. auch die
Normandie aufzusuchen.

Verteiler :

1, 1a, 1b LR Wagner
2, 2a, 2b RAM
3, 3a, 3b St.S.
4, 4a BRAM

RSHA Amt VI

gez. Schellenberg,
SS-Brigadeführer

Dies ist Exemplar Nr.

Arbeitsexemplar!

Schellenberg telegraphs the Foreign Office that "Out of an absolutely trustworthy source it has become known that President Roosevelt intends to travel
to England in the near future and possibly also to visit Normandy." Schellenberg addressed it to Legation Counsellor Wagner, whose office, Inland II, dealt
with the RSHA. At the left is the distribution list: Wagner, the Reich foreign
minister, the state secretary, and the bureau of the Reich foreign minister.
Underneath, an official has directed the report first to the under state secretary,
Hencke, whose name is misspelled, for his kind attention, thence to the files

doled out the information to the Foreign Office over six months. But much of it never got to Ribbentrop. Subordinates refused to submit many of the documents because they were outdated and unimportant. The great coup was, in fact, a big nothing.

On the other hand, a lot of the intelligence that flowed in volume through Schellenberg's office did deal with questions of importance, such as Allied global strategy, and many of these arrived well in advance of the events they were predicting. But often their inaccuracy vitiated their virtues. Rarely did a report hit the bull's-eye. On the other hand, seldom were they totally wrong. So many people were making so many plans that even a shot in the dark was bound to hit one of them. Of course, only a few came to fruition, but the German secret service cannot be fairly blamed for not knowing which one would when the planners themselves did not. For example, on 19 July 1944 Schellenberg reported in a top-secret message to the Foreign Office: "Out of an absolutely trustworthy source it has become known that President Roosevelt intends to travel to England in the near future and possibly also to visit Normandy." No such trip ever came about —but one to Scotland was discussed.

Typical of the semiaccuracy was a report of 1 February 1943. Churchill, it said, had flown that day from Adana, in Turkey, to Moscow. Though the prime minister had indeed departed Adana, where he had met the Turkish leaders, he had gone not eastward to Moscow, but westward to Cyprus. This half-right, half-wrong quality especially colored RSHA VI's intelligence on the Roosevelt-Churchill conferences, which made the high decisions for Allied grand strategy in the war. On 1 June 1943, for example, Department VI reported once again on a telegram from the Portuguese embassy in Brazil to the Foreign Ministry in Lisbon. According to this, Roosevelt and Churchill had said during their talks in Washington that they would stick to their decision to mount simultaneous major offensives against Japan and Europe. It was true that the two leaders had conferred in Washington in May. But it was false that they planned a synchronized double offensive. The "Over-all Strategic Concept for the Prosecution of the War" that the president and the prime minister had approved placed Europe first.

Irrational Nazi prejudices sometimes further distorted RSHA reports. This went beyond mere entanglement in one's own preconceptions, to which all intelligence agencies are prone. In August 1944, at the same time that it was pressing for spies to go to America to investigate the effect of propaganda on the upcoming presidential campaign—the mission that Gimpel and Colepaugh eventually undertook—the Foreign Office asked RSHA VI for information on the political and philosophical attitudes of New York Governor Thomas E. Dewey, who had just been named Republican candidate to oppose President Roosevelt's try for a fourth term. The head of the Anglo-American group, Theodor Paeffgen, submitted a short memorandum based on material from "an entirely trustworthy informant in Spain, who has been a party comrade since 1922" and who knew Dewey "personally:"

> The informant held talks of a political nature with Dewey in the year 1938 that had as subject especially National Socialism and the Jewish question. Dewey hereby showed an instinctive antipathy to the Jews, while noting that many Jewish elements were to be found among the gangsters he had fought [as Manhattan district attorney]. This attitude is, according to the informant's view, traceable to Dewey's [distant] Irish ancestry as well as to his defeat in the 1938 campaign against the Jewish-Democratic candidate [Governor Herbert] Lehman. The governor [Dewey] was even then reviled by the Jewish-steered press. As the informant declared, Dewey would, if he is named president of the U.S.A., hardly allow Jews into authoritative and important posts.
>
> Dewey's opinion about Germany is indicated as friendly and appreciative, and the informant mentioned the possibility of an understanding between Germany and the U.S.A. under Dewey's presidency. On the other hand, Dewey appears to be absolutely uncompromising in relation to the Far East war and steadfast for an exclusion of Japan from world commerce.
>
> The governor, like all other Republicans, categorically rejects Bolshevism.

It is astounding that for so basic a question the RSHA had to rely on so questionable a source and had no other additional material with which to supplement or correct it. It is less astounding that such one-sided material served as the foundation for major German decisions. But this kind of bias, and the mixture of truth and falsehood that characterized so many RSHA reports, could not have much helped the Germans formulate very effective policies.

Nazi prejudices did not, however, prevent the RSHA from running the most successful spy of the war. It neither recruited nor trained nor inserted him. He landed by luck into a key position and then offered his services to the Germans.

He was Elyesa Bazna, an Albanian living in Turkey. A former juvenile delinquent, locksmith, fireman, driver, and ultimately valet for foreign diplomats in Turkey, he served first the Yugoslav ambassador, then a German counsellor, who fired him for reading his mail, and next the British first secretary. Bazna was a small, compact man in his forties, with a high forehead, a deep chin, black moustache, and low brows. He lived mainly by his wits. Spying came as an unexpected piece of luck for him. One day, while he was in the bedroom of the British first secretary, the official, called away suddenly, slipped an important file into his desk drawer and left the room without locking the desk. Bazna took the folder out, read it— and got an idea.

A little while later, he became the valet of the British ambassador, Sir

Hughe Knatchbull-Hugessen. A few days after he came to work, Bazna noticed that Sir Hughe kept the most important and secret documents in a locked black dispatch box in his bedroom to pore over late at night. One morning, while the ambassador was taking a bath, Bazna took his keys from the bedside table and made wax impressions of them. He had put them back when he noticed that a bit of wax was sticking to one. He got one of the ambassador's handkerchiefs, cleaned the key with it, and put the key ring back on the table. At that moment Sir Hughe came into the room in his bathrobe. Bazna held up the handkerchief. It was snow-white.

"It ought to be sent to the laundry, Your Excellency," he said.

Sir Hughe nodded, but he was not really listening. With relief he saw his keys still lying on the bedside table, picked them up, dropped them into his pocket, and returned to his bath. Bazna wiped his brow with the handkerchief. Later he thought to himself that if Sir Hughe had not taken the time to put on his bathrobe, he would have caught Bazna redhanded—and would have nipped the war's greatest spy saga in the bud.

A friend of Bazna's made keys from the impressions, and Bazna prepared for mass-production photography of most secret British documents by buying four rods and a ring on which he would mount his camera and a 100-watt light bulb. On 26 October 1943, he visited his former employer at the German embassy. This man summoned the RSHA VI representative, who was built into the embassy staff as a commercial attaché.

Ludwig Moyzisch, a man with swarthy features, heavy eyebrows, dark hair, and narrow eyes, was a Viennese and a member of the Nazi party since 1932. He had attended a technical high school and worked for the Austrian government writing contracts until, he claimed, he was fired for his party activity. He spent some time abroad, and later worked in some party posts. In 1942, while in Ankara as an attaché, he applied to join the SS, but was turned down when he could not learn the identity of his mother's father and so could not prove that he was 100 percent Aryan. He took a supercilious view of Bazna at first. When, at their original meeting in the German embassy, Bazna told him he wanted £20,000 for the photographs, Moyzisch smiled. But he grew more serious as Bazna's confidence began to impress him, as well as Bazna's savvy: Bazna told him that he wanted the Germans to supply him with film because he did not want to be seen buying it. Eventually Moyzisch said he would check with Berlin. A few days later, when Bazna telephoned him, he reported that Berlin had agreed to the deal. Bazna brought over his first rolls of film of British secret documents. Moyzisch developed the 56 photographs, pronounced himself satisfied, and handed over £20,000. Bazna naturally did not know it, but the Germans did not haggle about the price because the deal was not costing them much. The English "money" was all counterfeit, manufactured by the RSHA in the Sachsenhausen concentration camp.

From that time on, Bazna was CICERO, the cover name the Germans gave him because of the eloquence of his information. Regularly he photographed the documents of the British ambassador, and, after arranging a rendezvous with Moyzisch, brought them to a street in Ankara where the attaché picked him up in his car. During these brief rides, Bazna turned over the film in return for more British banknotes. Then Moyzisch dropped him off, and both returned to their respective embassies. Bazna spread out the bills under the carpet in his room, where he felt they would be safe and less conspicuous than in a bank account and where he could tread upon them every day. He spent some of the money on a small house where he and his mistress relaxed. For weeks his routine ran smoothly, broken only once when a car chased him and Moyzisch through the back streets of Ankara. Bazna jumped out of Moyzisch's auto when Moyzisch slowed in turning a corner; the other car sped by, and Bazna glimpsed its driver, a smooth-faced young man. But the terror of the episode soon faded, as all continued normal at the embassy and in his spying.

The first policy-maker to see the documents was the German ambassador, Franz von Papen. To this old smoothie, briefly a chancellor of Germany before Hitler, spying was nothing new: as military attaché, he had

COPY.

MOST SECRET.

REFLECTIONS ON MILITARY CONVERSATIONS AT ANGORA
IN JANUARY 1944.

To what extent has the Turkish attitude during the recent

military conversations been due to genuine fear of the military

consequences of Turkey's entry into the war at this stage and

how far has it been inspired by political motives such as the

desire to avoid a break with Germany if possible, or, if such

a break is inevitable, at least to postpone the evil day as long

as possible and to exact the highest possible price from the

United Nations for Turkey's active cooperation?

2. To be fair to Turkey on the military side, allowance

must be made for three things, (a) that our handling of the

supply problem hitherto has not been such as to give Turkey any

very great confidence;   (b) that Turkish information regarding

Axis strength and intentions comes mainly from Military Attachés

Part of one of the actual documents that the spy CICERO photographed in the British embassy in Ankara (Angora), Turkey been expelled from Washington in World War I for it. Nor was intrigue: he was Germany's ambassador to Austria at the time of the Anschluss. Now Hitler—whose accession to the chancellorship Papen had helped—had sent him to the parlous diplomatic outpost in Turkey, where his main task was to keep that strategic nation in pro-German neutrality and to prevent her from yielding to Allied demands.

The CICERO documents helped him in this. They told him what the Allies were asking and what the Turks were telling them. He learned, for example, that the British had requested that pursuit planes be allowed on Turkish airfields and that the Turks were dodging a reply. The CICERO information about the Cairo conference helped him probe the Turkish foreign minister about Turkish intentions. The photographs also revealed that the Turks were resisting British pressure; this kept him from having to take countermeasures that might antagonize them. Only once did he do so. After he read that the English wanted to put radio stations in European Turkey to help their airplanes bomb the Rumanian oilfields, he threatened the Turks with a reprisal air raid on Istanbul. The stations were not built. On 3 February 1944, a British military mission left Ankara without what they came for. Exulted Papen: "The first round in the battle over Turkey's entry into the war has doubtlessly been won by us."

The CICERO material flowed to Germany both as extracts in Papen's and Moyzisch's telegrams and as film in the diplomatic pouch. Ribbentrop read the glossy prints and brought them to Hitler. Everyone questioned their authenticity. Was Ankara falling for a giant hoax?, Berlin asked.

"The question you raise," Papen replied, "occupies us constantly. We are of the opinion that the content and circumstances of CICERO let one conclude with the greatest probability that it is genuine. Deception is nevertheless not excluded." Eventually, however, nearly everybody believed in the source's validity.

In the Reich, Schellenberg cleverly tried to exploit these documents to expand the flow of intelligence. He thought that the plaintexts of the English telegrams might enable German cryptanalysts to crack the British diplomatic codes. He brought the photographs to the Foreign Office's Pers Z. But they merely confirmed what the experts already knew: that the most important telegrams were enciphered in the one-time pad, the only theoretically and practically unbreakable system. Even knowledge of the plaintext of one one-time pad message does not permit solution of another, so the CICERO photographs proved useless for cryptanalysis.

Policy-makers utilized the CICERO information more directly. During Hitler's conversations with representatives of Hungary and Bulgaria, Ribbentrop commented that he had "precise intelligence" that the Turks were resisting British demands, thus showing that no Turkish declaration of war on Germany was imminent. This remark was intended to bolster the countries' faith and so keep them in the Axis camp.

Hitler himself walked into a situation conference in December 1943 with CICERO photographs in his hand and announced, "I have mostly studied through these documents. There is absolutely no doubt that the attack in the west is coming in the spring." He went on to talk about possible deception attacks in Norway, the Bordeaux area in France, and the Balkans. These views were made more definite by telegram No. 1751 from Britain's Foreign Office to its Ankara embassy. This "immediate" message bore the highest security classification of the times: "most secret" and "BIGOT," a codeword restricting access to the very few allowed to have knowledge of key aspects of the forthcoming cross-Channel invasion. Dated 21 December, it forwarded the text of a message from the British chiefs of staff to Eisenhower. It seems to have first come to Papen about 6 January. After baldly stating, "Our object is to get Turkey into the war as early as possible," the chiefs added, "and in any case to maintain a threat to the Germans from the eastern end of the Mediterranean until OVERLORD is launched." Papen guessed what OVERLORD meant: "Apparently attack out of England," he noted in a cable. A few weeks later, another telegram from the British foreign secretary and the chiefs of staff repeated, "We must now concentrate our main effort on maintaining the threat to the Germans from the eastern Mediterranean." But the term "threat" in both of these dispatches was ambiguous. It could have meant only a scare tactic—a feint. Or it could have meant pressure backed up by force that could be thrown into action if the situation looked favorable. Which was it?

Some military clues suggested the scare tactic. Air reconnaissance showed no build-ups in the harbors of the eastern Mediterranean. Various sources showed that the Allies were continuing to pull their good divisions out of the area. Perhaps influenced by this, General Jodl of the OKW felt that CICERO indicated no major Allied attack in the eastern Mediterranean. Yet Hitler, in the last days of December, repeated time and again his expectation that the Allies would in fact attack in the Balkans.

The reason was that a successful invasion there would have enormous repercussions on the German war effort. Even if it did not immediately roll up the Russian front from the south, it would probably cause Rumania, Hungary, and Bulgaria to defect as Italy had done, costing divisions and ground. It would shut off essential supplies of bauxite, copper, and Rumanian oil. Turkey would abandon her neutrality, giving the Allies additional bases, stopping the shipments of vital chrome to Germany, and opening the Straits to Allied supply vessels sailing direct to Soviet warmwater ports on the Black Sea.

Hitler could not risk these disasters on the interpretation of a word or phrase from a spy, about whom still lingered—as there always does—the odor of suspicion, even if some military indications supported him. Perhaps the memory of the papers that floated into Spain on a corpse and that pointed away from the invasion that came in Sicily made the Führer cautious. Even before the CICERO photographs started to come in, he had begun reinforcing the southeastern theater. From July to December 1943, the number of divisions there rose from almost 17 to almost 25. The successful Allied landing at Anzio on 19 January 1944 increased the likelihood of a Balkan invasion. Though troops were temporarily withdrawn from the southeast to contain this beachhead, others rapidly replaced them. CICERO's information did not affect these decisions at all.

Through January, February, and March, Bazna continued to unlock the ambassador's dispatch box or his safe, take the documents to his room, lay them on the floor under his tripod, photograph them, return them, and bring the undeveloped rolls to Moyzisch. The money continued to flow in. An air raid on Sofia, which the CICERO documents had predicted, seemed to expunge any last doubts of their genuineness. Moyzisch told CICERO that Hitler intended to give him a villa after the war. But Bazna was growing increasingly nervous. The British had installed an alarm system in the embassy that complicated his work: he had to remove a fuse whenever he wanted to get into the ambassador's safe. And soon thereafter, he saw something that convinced him to quit.

Moyzisch had gotten a new secretary. She was a lovely girl, 24 years old, with long hair and long legs, named Nele Kapp. Her father was a consul general, then in Sofia, who had served many years in Cleveland, where, among other things, he had clipped newspapers for the German military attaché, Boetticher. He had gotten her the job, but she had good qualifications: experience abroad and knowledge of English, French, and Italian. Nele had, however, made most of her friends during her late teens in America. In Ankara, this background led her to become friendly with an American. One day, Bazna ran into Moyzisch and Nele in a department store and, in a moment of impudence, naturally without giving a sign that he knew the fuming attaché, helped the girl make some purchases. A few hours later, as he waited for a new girlfriend in the lounge of the Ankara Palace hotel, he saw Nele again. Only this time she was with someone else. And this someone was the smooth-faced young man who had once chased Bazna and Moyzisch through the dark back streets of Ankara.

Fear chilled Bazna like an icy wind off the frozen Anatolian plain. That very night he smashed his Leica and threw the pieces and the support rods into a river. He never took another spy photograph. He had already put much of the money into a bank vault; now he did the same with the rest. He left his villa and took a hotel room. He told Moyzisch that he was quitting. But he stayed on for a while at the British embassy to avoid suspicion.

Then he heard that Nele was missing from the German embassy. She had apparently defected to the Americans, and told them all she knew about Operation CICERO. But it had already ended. Soon thereafter Bazna gave notice, and left Sir Hughe's service. He seemed not to have been missed, either in the British embassy or in German headquarters, where Hitler continued to direct his war without the CICERO documents just as he had with them.

It was by then a war of retreats. In April 1944, Hitler began evacuating the Crimea, across the Black Sea from Turkey. The Turks soon saw that they would face the danger of Russia alone if they neglected their ties to the western Allies. They replaced the pro-German chief of the general staff with a pro-English one. They stopped chrome deliveries to Germany. In August, they broke diplomatic relations, and, the following February, declared war on Germany.

The information furnished by CICERO had served the Germans only in a secondary way. It had helped Papen stave off British demands for a few months. But it had not fully clarified Allied intentions in the Balkans, and, in part for this reason, in part because of Hitler's understandable suspicion of unconfirmed spy information, in part because of his strong concern about southeast Europe, the CICERO documents had not affected his decisions. One of the greatest spy coups of all time did not—could not—fundamentally alter the course of events.

But it was not in Turkey, nor in Latin America, nor even in North America that the German war leaders could discover the secrets that they needed to win, or at least to keep from losing, the war in the west. It was in Great Britain.

Here the Allies concocted their assault plans. Here their troops staged. Here their landing craft assembled. Here, if anywhere, was the flash point.

Yet hardly any of the German agents there had been planted before the war. Nearly all were wartime exigencies. This appears incredibly negligent on the part of the German spy agencies. Several factors, however, explain this behavior, if they do not excuse it.

The chief one was that in 1935 Hitler forbade any spying in Britain. This prohibition paralleled that against breaking Royal Navy codes and was based upon the same reasons. He regarded England as racially akin to Germany and hoped to ally his great land power with her great sea power to dominate the world. In particular, he wanted her to cover his back while he completed his historical work of destroying communism and opening the east to German expansion. In 1935, he took the first step in this program by concluding a naval treaty with Britain. By limiting the German fleet to a fraction of the size of the Royal Navy, he eased British fears of a German threat at sea and of a naval arms race like that preceding World War I. Hitler felt, not without reason, that spying in Britain, if discovered, would endanger his grand policy. The tidbits of information that the espionage might bring in were not worth this risk. So he banned the activity. During the next few years, however, Britain's hostility to his aggression, which threatened the European balance of power and consequently Britain's position as a major arbiter, became increasingly evident. Finally, in 1937, he withdrew the prohibition, and men like Ritter could resume the Abwehr's spying against Britain. But two precious years—Canaris's first as Abwehr chief—had been lost.

Another element in Germany's prewar espionage inadequacy against Britain lay in the set against star agents. The Abwehr—the only agency really engaged in foreign espionage before the war—did not focus its efforts on recruiting and establishing any major agents in place (though it had a few low-level ones). Such an agent would wait silently in a key position, winning the confidence of his hosts, growing in responsibility and in knowledge during the long years of peace so that, when a critical moment came during a war, he could, like a time bomb exploding in the enemy vitals, deliver information that would enable Germany to win a crucial victory. Canaris opposed such a concept. He did not want all his eggs in one basket. He preferred that the Abwehr expend its energies on implanting many lesser agents. These medium- or low-grade agents would report on the existence of airfields, fortifications, or factories in peace, and in war on the presence of troop units—all admittedly useful information.

Still another reason for the German spy weakness against Britain was the inadequacy of Abwehr means and experience. Oswald Mosley's British Union of Fascists formed a natural source of spies. Perhaps Ritter did not think of tapping it, or had no contacts with which to do so; perhaps he did not have the time or the administrative support, for espionage against France—which Hitler regarded as the major enemy and as having the best army in Europe—absorbed much of the Abwehr's effort in the west. In any event, he did not attempt to win any agents from the organization.

So, at the start of World War II, Germany had in Britain, outside of a few sympathizers who delivered information when the whim struck them, only a handful of agents. Among them were JOHNNY—Arthur Owens—and his subagents. But the Abwehr did not capitalize on the opportunity for massive agent insertion into England during the first eight months of the war, when traffic between England and France, Belgium, and Holland remained relatively open and voluminous. The spy agency probably felt, like Hitler, that after Germany had blitzed Europe, Britain would realize the hopelessness of her position and make peace.

Her defiance after Dunkirk clarified these misconceptions. In July 1940, Hitler ordered preparations for a landing in England, which he later set for 15 September. Suddenly, the Abwehr had to get all the spies into Britain that it had not before. All Abwehr posts got orders to find volunteers, who would be inserted into the island by boat or by plane. The training and commitment of the parachute agents—codenamed Operation LENA—was entrusted to Ritter.

Within a few days the first two volunteers arrived. They had been found by an Abwehr recruiter among a group of Scandinavian Nazis. Both appeared to fit the high qualifications that the Abwehr headquarters had set: at least 20 and no older than 30, in best physical condition, intelligent, technically capable. One was a well-mannered Dane with a German mother, Hans Hansen, 26, an industrial draftsman, rather taller than average, with dark blond hair and regular features, who had been a member of the Danish Nazi party. The other, a Finn, Goesta Caroli, was a year older and taller, with pleasant blue eyes; he was a mechanic. Both had worked in Germany and spoke not only fluent German but also good English. Ritter liked them both at once.

"I think you know what you have volunteered for," he said to them. "Let's not play games with each other. You know that you're putting your life in the balance and that after you land successfully you're entirely on your own. I'd like you to consider me as your friend. I'm responsible for your training. I expect from you that you'll cooperate conscientiously. The special course that we've worked out for you requires your all. We don't have much time. We have to try to be ready in six weeks at the latest. We'll start tomorrow morning."

"You can depend upon us just as we must depend upon you," replied Hansen briefly.

They were on. Ritter assigned them their agent numbers—Hansen's was 3725—then gave them some spending money and put them up in the Abwehr boarding house, the Klopstock. When he arrived next morning they were already practicing their Morse code under one of Trautmann's assistants. In the next few weeks, they practiced recognizing aircraft. They visited antiaircraft posts to learn about different calibers of guns. They studied meteorology, since weather reporting from England was vital for the Luftwaffe after Britain stopped all public weather forecasts. They learned air control so that they could report intelligently on airfield operations. All this they did with such diligence that they completed their course in less than the expected six weeks.

They had their legend: they were Scandinavian refugees who had come over in a fishing boat. They received their false papers, their rationing coupons, and their £200. With Ritter, one hot sunny July day, they drove out of Hamburg into—as Ritter thought—the unknown. Near Cologne, they stopped and tested their radio apparatus. Hansen tried, thought he heard the Hamburg station, lost it, ripped the earphones from his head, and exploded: "The damn thing screws up the very first time!" Caroli, more patient, tried a few times and figured out that cars passing on the autobahn disturbed the reception. He moved farther away and established contact. They had passed their first test!

In Brussels, where the two future spies were lodged in a hotel, Ritter met in the Abwehr post with the pilot who would drop them. He and the pilot spread out a map to look for a good landing place; Ritter noted with satisfaction that some of the airfields that one of his first agents, Simon, had discovered appeared on it. They compared geological maps with population maps and road maps, and finally decided upon a point near Salisbury, about which lay much open country. Ritter had large-scale maps drawn from which his two agents could familiarize themselves with the countryside. But for a few days the weather prohibited any missions. Hansen and Caroli saw the sights of Brussels. Caroli picked up a girl and seems to have gotten somewhat romantically involved with her, rousing fears in both Hansen and Ritter that he might have compromised the mission. Ritter had her followed, discovered that she was practically a prostitute, and had her held in protective custody for a few days.

Meanwhile, the weather remained poor, and to relieve the growing nervousness of both spymaster and spies, Ritter took his two agents on trips to Antwerp and to Paris. From here they successfully communicated by radio with Hamburg. This reassured the two young men, for the distance was greater than that between England and Hamburg. They returned to Brussels, got a good weather report, and then went back south again to Rennes, capital of Brittany, where a black-painted twin-engine He 111 bomber awaited them with the pilot at the airfield. Ritter shook hands with Caroli for the last time. The young spy climbed aboard. The plane trundled to the runway and, engines roaring, vanished into the darkness. A day later, Hansen took off the same way. Ritter returned to Brussels, sunk in reverie.

At 4:30 a.m. the pilot reported. He had flown low over the Channel, had soared to 7,000 meters over the coast, and then had dived through the clouds to 150 meters over the jump point. He throttled his motors. Hansen jumped. The pilot saw a parachute open. Then he headed for home.

For Ritter there was nothing to do now but wait. On the second day, he anxiously called the Hamburg radio station several times, only to be told, "Nothing yet, Herr Major." Finally, at midnight of the third day, the telephone at his bedside rang.

"We've got 3725 [Hansen], Herr Major," the station reported. "The circuit is good. Wein [the radioman who had trained them] is working it himself. There's no doubt that it's Hansen who's sending."

"What does he have to say?"

"He is only checking in to let us know that he's alive. He'll call again."

"Good," said Ritter. "Call me as soon as you hear from him, please. Good night."

But the next call came only three days later. Caroli's parachute had caught in a tree and he had been injured. The tall spy was hiding in some farm buildings and didn't know what to do. He had not landed near Salisbury, but north of Oxford, some 65 miles away. Finally Ritter decided to send JOHNNY to help him. After innumerable messages back and forth, one of JOHNNY's subagents met Caroli at the High Wycombe railroad station. He took the Finn to his apartment and nursed him, until in October

Caroli took his own apartment south of Cambridge and radioed from there. In January of 1941, however, his transmitter suddenly went off the air. JOHNNY reported that the police were closing in and that Caroli had cut and run. On instructions from Hamburg, JOHNNY's subagent retrieved the radio set from the baggage room at the Cambridge railroad station, where Caroli had left it.

Hansen, on the other hand, set himself up in Barnet, a northern borough of London, and from there worked hard for Ritter. All told, he transmitted more than a thousand messages to Hamburg. Many were weather reports. Others detailed air-raid damage. In February 1941, bombs struck in Borehamwood, only a mile or so away from Hansen's home in Barnet. He radioed a list of factories that had been destroyed: Standard Telephone & Cables Ltd., Serum Laboratories Ltd., Smith & Sons, Ltd., and so on. A few days later, he was traveling about England reporting on airfields and factories. "Many bombers are supposed to be stationed in the Oxford area, mainly in Abingdon, Beson [Benson], and Breazenorton [Brize Norton]. Reconnaissance follows," he radioed. On 24 February, he transmitted about the Brize Norton airfield: "New are especially large, grass-covered mounds of earth, supposedly underground hangars, about 200 by 75 meters in size." This sounded odd; Hamburg merely noted that they were not marked on Sheet 104 of its map of Great Britain airfields. The next day he messaged:

> Further observation of the Brize Norton airfield. The six mounds reported yesterday are in fact underground hangars. I personally saw how two Defiants were pushed into one of these underground hangars on the northwest side. They had the markings N 3446 and N 3479. The exact position of the hangars is as follows: two hangars lie in north-south direction 100 meters west of the village of Brize Norton and north of the road from Brize Norton to Carterton; two further in the same direction but south of the road and 150 meters distant from the road to Bampton; two further lie 1,800 meters south of Carterton and 350 meters west of the road. Observed anti-aircraft position[s], one about 700 meters east of Carterton and one 100 meters south of Carterton.

The following month Hansen, who was a free agent with no regular employment, traveled about near Salisbury to investigate airfields, and in April in the suburbs and exurbs of London to the west. Sometimes his reports as received contained curious misspellings of place names, caused perhaps by transmission errors, which probably annoyed Abwehr evaluators as they flipped frantically through their atlases and gazetteers to find "Heathron airfield" (Heathrow) or "Roading" (Reading).

They were perhaps further irritated by Hansen's independent manner— he would sometimes announce that he was taking off on a holiday because he did not feel like doing any spying for a while—and by his griping.

"You never let me know what you think of my work. An occasional pat on the back would be welcome. After all, I am only human."

"Don't you have anything more important to ask?" he retorted, when instructed to report on the price and taste of a loaf of bread in rationed Britain. "It tastes all right."

"What is delaying the man with the money you promised? I am beginning to think that you're full of shit."

In fact, the Abwehr had great difficulties in getting money to 3725. They had given him only £200 when he parachuted in, in the expectation that the invasion troops would follow not long after. But as the assault was increasingly delayed, his money ran out. JOHNNY mailed him £100. The Germans originally planned to drop £500 by airplane, but abandoned this plan when, they told him, a friend from Hamburg would bring over the money and a new crystal for his radio. They arranged a complicated series of meetings at the Regent Palace Hotel, the Tate Gallery, and the British Museum. None were kept: the British had arrested the friend. Then Hamburg instructed him to wait at 4 p.m. at the terminus of the Number 11 bus at Victoria Station, and there follow certain directions. Hansen replied that that bus no longer ended its run there, and proposed Number 16. After further messages back and forth, the operation unrolled on 26 October 1941 as planned. Hansen, wearing a red tie and carrying a newspaper and a book, boarded the bus. So did a Japanese, carrying *The Times* and a book in his left hand. After the fifth stop, both alighted. They waited for the next bus on the same route, and boarded it, sitting next to one another. After a while, he asked the Japanese:

"Anything interesting in the paper today?"

The Japanese glanced at him.

"You may have it," he said. "I'm getting off at the next stop."

Inside the paper were eighty £5 notes. The Japanese, an assistant military attaché, hurried back to his embassy. Signaled Hansen:

"Won't be reporting for a couple of days. I'm getting drunk tonight."

Hansen also received more money through a complicated financial transaction arranged by a key German agent in Lisbon, the Yugoslav Dusko Popov. Popov reported that he knew a rich Jewish theatrical agent who wanted to exchange his pounds sterling for dollars, as he feared that Britain was going to lose the war. The Abwehr grasped at the proposal. It dispatched Toeppen, the head of ZF, its finance desk, to Lisbon to examine the idea and then to work out details. Popov was to give the Jew dollars, and he in return was to pay out pounds to Popov's nominee in London. This would be Hansen. It worked out just that way, with the exception that a substantial rake-off on the dollars apparently went into the Abwehr officials' pockets. Hansen picked up £20,000, or almost $100,000, in London.

Though this solved one problem, others arose. The Germans pressured him, now that he was rich, to move in better circles and meet more important people. But the police had questioned him about military service, he reported, and he had gotten an exemption only by having a friend certify that he was doing indispensable work on a farm. Though he could take trips only on weekends now, he expanded his spying through his employer's daughter. She was employed in the cipher department of one of the ministries, and consequently saw a great deal of important traffic, which she sometimes spilled on her visits to the farm. Later, her ministry lent her to the Americans, and Hansen profited in his way from this generosity.

Through 1942 and 1943, Hansen continued to report faithfully. In January 1944, when Eisenhower landed in Britain to take command of the Allied invasion forces, Hansen signaled his presence there a few hours before the wire services broadcast it—a remarkable scoop, his Abwehr controllers thought. And as the invasion approached, they instructed him to begin a search for information on it. Soon his reports about it flowed in. Twenty thousand Canadian troops had arrived in the Dover area. Advance elements of U.S. infantry had arrived in the Ashford-Dover area. These were, he said a few days later, part of the 83rd Infantry Division. In southeast Kent, except for Dover the closest part of England to France, a large mass of English, Canadian, and American troops were bivouacked camouflaged in the woods. And after the invasion, as Allied troops poured from England into the bridgehead, he passed still more information. He told of seeing the U.S. 11th Infantry Division move eastward on the main road through Cambridge. At that university town's railroad station, he saw the U.S. XXth Army Corps heading west and the 25th Armored Division heading south, with tanks on the flat cars. Later, he spotted members of that division in Norwich. On 21 September 1944, he radioed solemnly: "On the occasion of this, my 1,000th message, I beg to ask you to convey to our Führer my humble greetings and ardent wishes for a speedy victorious termination of the war."

Hansen's loyalty did not slacken even after the failure of Hitler's Ardennes offensive in December. He once again met a friend on a minelayer who had given him information earlier in the war, and this man now told him about the new mine fields the Allies were laying to deny areas to the new schnorkel U-boats. The German naval evaluators confirmed the truth and value of his reports when a U-boat reported that it had struck a mine and had been forced to scuttle itself: the location was right where 3725 had reported that mines had been laid. To save its submarines, the Kriegsmarine closed 3,600 square miles of ocean to them. And Hansen's loyalty was reciprocated. He received his last message from his controllers at 5:50 p.m. on 2 May 1945—only a few hours before Hamburg fell to the British. Hans Hansen was the longest-lived German spy in England.

Not all the England agents were as successful. One team involved the classic woman spy, a beautiful Nordic blonde, whose name was given as Vera de Schallberg. She had fled from her home in Denmark and had a series of sleazy affairs in Paris, until she finally met Theodore Druecke, a wealthy idler on the fringes of the underworld, who took her to Brussels. There he promptly lost her to one of Ritter's colleagues, Hans Dierks, who despite his ugly face had such strong sex appeal that women ran after him as if in heat. But Dierks soon tired of the affair, and to rid himself of her suggested that she spy for him in England. At first she resisted, but then, seeing the way things lay, resigned herself and consented. As part of her team, Dierks added Druecke, who was willing to go along to be with her, and a Swiss named Werner Heinrich Walti, who had formerly worked as a chauffeur for the French consul in Hamburg and had spied on him for the Abwehr.

After the customary training, the spy trio and Dierks celebrated with an evening out. One drink followed another, and on the drive home Dierks lost control of the car and died in the ensuing accident. But the others were only slightly injured, and a few days later they flew to Stavanger at the southwestern tip of Norway. From here, a twin-engine He 111 seaplane carried them, with a sausage for food and their false papers, to a northern coast of Scotland. But while transferring to the rubber boat from the seaplane in the predawn darkness, the spies dropped their bicycles into the sea. This meant they would have to use public transportation. A few minutes later, they stepped onto the stony beach of the enemy shore. They kicked their boat away, and split up. Walti went east; Druecke and Vera, who now gave her last name as de Cottani-Chalbur, headed west. At 7:30 a.m., they entered the tiny one-room wooden railway station at the village of Portgordon, which lay on the coastal line between Banff and Inverness.

"What is the name of this station, please?" asked Vera.

Stationmaster John Donald grew suspicious. He grew even more so when he noticed that the cuffs of the man's pants were wet. Telling his janitor, John Geddes, to keep them talking, he called the local constable, who took the two spies into custody.

Their arrest, and the discovery shortly afterward of their boat floating off shore, led to a hunt for others who might have landed with them. Inquiries at nearby stations revealed that a man had purchased a ticket early that morning for Aberdeen. Eventually police found Walti in Edinburgh.

After some months the Germans heard of the execution of the two men. But they remained in the dark about Vera, the Mata Hari of World War II, whose espionage career had lasted perhaps 200 minutes.

Many other spies were likewise caught, often in the same jig time as the Hamburg three. Alphonse Timmermann, a 37-year-old Belgian, arrived as a refugee and was routinely sent for an interrogation. On him the examining officer found an envelope with white powder, some orange sticks, and some cotton. They spelled "secret ink" for the officer and "death" for Timmermann. Johannes Marinus Dronkers, a Dutchman, also masqueraded as a refugee. He and two other men, both legitimate refugees, were picked up as their sailboat approached the coast of England. Dronkers drew suspicion upon himself by his lunatic actions; a counterintelligence officer minutely examined all his effects, and found in his Dutch-English dictionary pinpricks under letters that spelled out cover addresses. He was hanged.

Others lasted longer. Some even rose by luck or by energy to key positions, or cultivated subagents in key positions, whence intelligence of top quality, including occasionally even insights into high Allied strategy, flowed to Germany.

Captain Roman Garby-Czerniawski had fought against the Germans when they invaded his native Poland in 1939 and had lost. He joined a French resistance réseau in Paris—and again lost. The Germans captured him along with a good portion of his net. He had been betrayed by his cipher clerk, a young woman who became jealous of his attentions to another girl in the ring.

The Abwehr realized that sitting in a German jail was a professional officer in his thirties, a pilot, an athlete (he was an expert skiier), with experience in the intelligence branch of the Polish general staff. Soon the counterintelligence group proposed to Garby-Czerniawski that he go to England as a spy for them in return for German handling of the réseau members as regular prisoners of war instead of as irregulars or partisans. At first he refused. But after the German invasion of Russia, he gradually became convinced that Germany was working in his country's true interest against the nation that had so long trod on it, and he agreed.

His agent designation, GV-7167, meaning "Gegen-Vertrauensmann," or "contrary agent," was used for double agents and reflected his original assignment of penetration of the British secret service. But to this the Germans added gathering military information out of England. An escape was faked, and after a circuitous passage through Spain and Portugal, Garby-Czerniawski, codenamed HUBERT, reached England in October of 1942. He withstood the refugee interrogation, in large part because his background was genuine, and was soon flying as a wing commander in a Polish air squadron.

In January 1943 he began transmitting his reports. They soon attained an average frequency of one a day. Early in 1944, his value to the Germans rose when he was appointed Polish liaison officer to the staff of General Omar Bradley, commander of the American ground forces for the invasion. HUBERT's reports, written in French, apparently since he spoke little or no German and Polish would be too difficult for the Abwehr to read, dealt with the details of the Allied assembly for the invasion. On 25 February 1944, for example, he wrote five messages, which, however, he did not transmit until the late afternoon of the 29th. He was then in the Southampton area, and he reported that on the River Hamble he saw about 30 small and 5 medium-sized landing craft. On 10 March, he reported, "According to an English officer the division [with the] bear insignia which occupies region east of Norwich has the number Forty-Ninth Armoured Division." He also griped loudly: "Your two seven one. Very disappointed it is neither dangerous nor difficult for the Luftwaffe. I run most of the risks in the operation. . . . I am greatly limited in my work without help on your part I cannot increase the volume. Prefer to stop rather than to do it badly. Not once have I been encouraged by your help."

Nevertheless, he carried on. On 19 May he was transferred to an even more important post: liaison to General George S. Patton's 1st Army Group headquarters. Liaison men may not make decisions, but they often sit at key junctions. And HUBERT utilized this to the utmost. He told about the presence of the 11th Infantry Division and the XXXIIIrd Corps and passed along the insignia of the 17th Infantry Division. He reported on the use of the 9th Army and about the 21st Airborne Division. He noted: "Brentwood some soldiers of the 35th Infantry Division. Belongs to the XIIth Corps and transferred to Kent. Harwich 28th Infantry Division. Belongs to XIIth Corps. Amphibious exercises there." All this and more he kept up to the moment of the invasion—and even afterward. As late as 29 November, he was reporting, in his message No. 877, "In Nottingham area everything calm. [A] few insignia point to the presence of the U.S. 82nd Airborne Division. The 9th and 21st Airborne Divisions are no longer in this area."

His ultimate "customers" in Foreign Armies West loved it. "Has through some outstanding reports greatly contributed to the clarification of the enemy picture," they raved. "Good." "Very remarkable," commented Major Roger Michael, in charge of the English section. Only occasionally did Michael log unenthusiastic views, and these, in comparison to the acerbic remarks made about other agents, practically praised him: "somewhat unclear," "believable."

But suddenly it all ended. In January 1945, transmissions from HUBERT abruptly ceased. The British had evidently caught him.

Other agents began as free-lance spies, offering themselves to the Abwehr as purveyors of intelligence, and rapidly grew into the managing directors of large-scale spying enterprises, with bewildering thickets of main agents, subagents, financial wizards, and communicators, not unlike the interlocking directorates and dummy corporations of some parts of the business world. Most of these flourished in the sheltered climate of neutrality provided by Spain and Portugal.

One of the earliest was Paul Fidrmuc, a Sudeten German once in the intelligence unit of the Austro-Hungarian army. Codenamed CHB, he developed a worldwide net of agents known as CHB 1, CHB 2, and so on. Some of these had served before as agents of the Hamburg Abwehr post. At least three worked in England; others were scattered here and there over the globe. Canaris himself once presented Fidrmuc with a bejeweled snuffbox that once belonged to Napoleon, and the Abwehr regarded CHB 1, for example, as "tested, very trustworthy." But Foreign Armies West was cooler: "Good; more exact troop details required." And later: "Value has recently dropped," and then: "In general little usable and inexact," and even, "What a swindle!" And CHB 1 was the best of the lot.

Another early entry was a German businessman on the Iberian peninsula codenamed OSTRO. He had 17 subagents, who themselves had numerous informants. He became among the most highly regarded of the spies working against Britain. On 21 July 1942, Colonel Dietrich Schwenke, the technical intelligence officer of the air force production chief, reported at a conference that OSTRO had given production figures for the first time of a new type of aircraft long known from captured documents. Two years later, he was still reporting. In August 1944, he noted that indications, especially from a British air attaché, suggested that a major American operation against Brittany lay immediately ahead. On 30 September, he passed along word from "Parliament and the Carlton Club" that pressure was being exerted on headquarters to carry out a major attack against the north wing of the Westwall before the start of the winter.

But the free-lance who succeeded best was codenamed CATO, after the Roman senator who ended every speech with the vindictive "Carthage must be destroyed"; the name was perhaps inspired by Hitler's ridicule of the British comment that the conflict resembled the Second Punic War. The latter-day CATO was a young Spaniard with a high forehead and angular features who convinced the Germans of his hatred of the modern Carthage that stood in the way of German world domination. He proposed to the Germans that he spy against England for them. He would go to the island as a buyer of machinery for his family's textile firm and also as the representative of a Valencia orange exporter.

The Germans checked up on him. He had hidden from the Republicans for a year, they discovered, and had then been arrested by them and, after apparent conscription into their army, had deserted to Franco's. Once an electrical engineering student, he had learned Morse code during his army service—a valuable asset for an agent. Eventually the KO Spain took him on. His spymaster was Specialist-Captain Karl-Erich Kühlenthal, in charge of recruiting and controlling the KO's most important spies abroad. Kühlenthal trained him, paid him, and on 26 November 1940 sent him to England.

In June 1941, he reported some information that he had overheard from a Polish pilot talking to his English girlfriend in the Brevet Club in London. He would not be able to dine with her on 23 June "because he had been given orders to fly on an important mission with a cabinet minister and his staff as well as a group of officers of the Indian Army General Staff. I gathered that he would be flying via Gibraltar and Takoradi [in Ghana] to Khartoum." Kühlenthal found that agents from Gibraltar had reported that a group of officers wearing red tabs had passed through. Soon it became clear that CATO had given advance warning of the naming of Oliver Lyttelton as minister of state, Middle East, to be stationed in Cairo, as well as of General Sir Claude Auchinleck as the new commander in chief, Middle East.

CATO augmented his personal capabilities by building up a net of subagents. He recruited a steward of the British Overseas Airways Corporation to carry messages from England to Madrid and Portugal, a wealthy Venezuelan living in Glasgow who reported on activities in Scotland, a Gibraltarian waiter in an army canteen in Kent. He found an English conscientious objector who worked on a remote farm instead of serving in the army and who, a fanatic for amateur radio, transmitted messages for CATO because he believed CATO was working for the Spanish Republicans. He found Welsh, Irish, and Scottish nationalists. And he found mercenaries. One such, a retired merchant navy seaman who lived in Swansea, on the southern coast of Wales, became the nucleus of a net of agents who reported on the filling of harbors with landing vessels for the invasion. He brought into his orbit an official at the Ministry of Information who had access to much strategic and political information. CATO never said who the man was, but Kühlenthal could infer that he was the head of the ministry's Iberian section. CATO even managed, in the best tradition of spies, to seduce a secretary. She was, he told Kühlenthal, in her early thirties, "far from beautiful and rather dowdy in her dress"—but she worked in or close to Churchill's war cabinet. And soon she became, he remarked, "delightfully indiscreet."

CATO was a superb head spy. Once when a new agent reported on some activity at Dover, CATO added to the report that the man was as yet unproved and that he would try to check his information. A week later he messaged that the information was confirmed and that the man could be classified as "a good reporter." Eventually he had 14 active agents, most of them in southern ports, and 11 well-placed contacts.

As the invasion approached, he, like HUBERT, began passing over details of Allied order-of-battle information. In March 1944, for example, he wirelessed that the British 52nd Infantry Division, the Lowland Division, was in Dundee, Scotland. Later, like HUBERT, he reported bits and pieces of Allied strategical plans that seemed highly accurate to the Germans.

By August 1944 he had sent some 400 secret-ink letters and 2,000 long radio messages to the Germans, all packed with information, and had received the equivalent of £20,000 from them. And he continued thus right up to the end of the war.

The few long-term strategic agents furnished, in German eyes, the most valuable information that spies delivered. But by far the greatest volume of spy information came from the short-term tactical agent—the so-called front agents.

Thousands were seeded behind the enemy lines during the war. The procedure carried Canaris's no-superspy philosophy to its ultimate, and corresponded to the mass commitment of men in the war's other vast and depersonalized operations. The system naturally developed most on the Russian front, where it came under the control of the Abwehr's Main Post East I—WALLI I. Its spies were all short-term by comparison to those in England, but they were themselves divided into short- and long-range agents.

The short-range agents, run by each army's Abwehr troop, investigated details—often armor and artillery concentrations—to a maximum of 30 miles behind the enemy front. Usually, however, they worked only a mile or so in. They were consequently called "line-crossers." They entered and returned on foot, stayed only about a week, and reported in person. Long-range agents were handled by each army group's Abwehr command. They operated between 30 and 200 miles behind enemy lines, seeking mainly information on enemy reserves, higher commands, and transportation capabilities. Their missions lasted longer, and they reported by radio. They were inserted by parachute and came back only on orders, usually by airplane or when the Germans took the territory, occasionally on foot through the front.

A short-range spy mission generally took between three days and a week to get under way, including bringing the agent to the reconnoitering area. It then took time for him to return and report. Long-range missions demanded still greater preparation. Consequently, the I c used agents only when faster and cheaper means, such as radio reconnaissance or prisoner interrogation, would not work. The I c also had to consider whether the intelligence would be obsolete when the agent returned. But for certain pinpoint reconnaissances and investigations of specific questions, agents alone would do. The I c then had to find out from the Abwehr troop or command leader whether the assignment could be carried out at all. Perhaps no agents were available; perhaps the front had no holes in it; perhaps Soviet air defense precluded an air insertion. But if an agent action were possible, the I c then told the Abwehr leader the primary and secondary assignments, the sector, the military situation, and the desired date of return or, for long-range agents, of the first radio message. The execution in detail was planned by the leader. He chose the agent. The man then had to study maps, memorize routes and place names, learn the armament, insignia, and other characteristics of the Soviet units. He had to get the proper clothing and false papers. Only then was he ready.

Short-term agents were usually inserted by Schleusung. An expert in this work, called a "Schleusender" ("sluicer"), brought the agent—preferably just one, at most three—to a suitable sector of the front. This meant one without a continuous trench system, with low enemy troop density, and as free as possible of barbed wire, mines, and other obstacles. The agent crept through the main battle line, past enemy outposts, sentries, and bunkers, into the black terror of enemy territory. Often he pretended to be an escaping prisoner.

To collect the information that the army I c wanted, the agent both observed in person and asked soldiers and inhabitants. When he had gathered what he had come for, he went back. He had naturally arranged with his handler or the Schleusender to notify the German troops of when and where he would arrive. He was taken immediately to the local division's headquarters, where its I c questioned him on what the agent might have learned about the division's sector. Then he went to his Abwehr troop, where his information was extracted in a detailed interrogation while it was still fresh in his memory. This was telephoned to the army I c. Several re-interrogations followed, to bring out small details which had not appeared to be of primary importance to the agent. Then a complete written report, which included an estimate of the agent's reliability, went to the I c.

Abwehr theory called for an agent to be used only once. In practice many went more than once. A woman agent of Army Group Center, Sonia, the daughter of a Russian nobleman, parachuted behind Soviet lines seven times—and came back seven times. To their surprise, the Germans found women quite suitable as agents. Many were ready for anything, even assassination.

The agents' reports usually dealt with details. Foreign Armies East distributed, in abbreviated form, the highly typical report of Army Group Center's Agent 523 of 26 October 1944: "On 26 October the transport of a [Russian] guards armored corps was ascertained on the Zelechów-Garwolin road [southeast of Warsaw] in the direction of Garwolin. About 120 tanks were counted." On rare occasions, front agents predicted enemy actions. Agent 422 of Army Group Center sent a message on 28 October 1944 that preparations were being made north of Warsaw for a new big offensive; 18 rifle divisions, 4 armored corps, and a number of cavalry units were in the area.

Despite the apparent pettiness of much of the information, these and other reports proved valuable enough for Jodl to write Kaltenbrunner a letter of appreciation for the front-agent service during the Russian Warsaw offensive in January 1945. In the same way, agent information sometimes proved important enough to reach Hitler's situation conferences. On 28 December 1943, for example, Chief of Staff Zeitzler told him that an agent had reported that 33 Russian trains were on the way to the Crimea, which Hitler was then trying hard to hold.

Although the Abwehr used many agents, it remained for the SD to perfect the notion of mass agentry. In February of 1942, after the initial blitzkrieg against Russia had failed, and it became clear that German intelligence there had likewise failed, Schellenberg conceived the idea of large-scale spy operations. The agents would be anti-Communists selected from among the hundreds of thousands of prisoners of war that the German armies had captured. This was his project ZEPPELIN.

Within a short while he had 10,000 to 15,000 candidates in training programs. To pump up their anti-Soviet views, he gave them tours of the best side of Germany: industry, farms, the autobahns. Eventually some 2,000 to 3,000 agents were ready for duty. But lack of airplanes and radio sets reduced the number who were actually committed to several hundred. At the start of 1943, when it became clear that Russia was not going to be defeated, the number of ZEPPELIN volunteers declined so much that Schellenberg had to convert it from a mass to a precision operation. During that year, ZEPPELIN SOUTH inserted 19 agent groups with a total of 115 men behind the Soviet lines. About half of these produced information. Schellenberg also instituted an unusual security measure for the program. Some of the returned agents, who were no longer of use to him, were shot.

Despite the diminution of the ZEPPELIN operation, the number of German agents behind Russian lines rose overall in 1943 to half again as many as in 1942, probably because the Germans had gone over increasingly to the defensive, which calls for greater knowledge of enemy intentions. The number of spy schools reached 60, and, to overcome the improved Soviet counterespionage, training time sometimes lasted months.

In the middle of the war in the east, or from about 1942 to 1944, the German army had from 500 to 800 agents behind Russian lines at any one time. It was not unusual for Army Group Center alone to send in 8 or 10 a day. The attrition rate was enormous. Wrong papers, wrong uniform, wrong accent for the area, lack of knowledge of the locality or of where one was supposed to come from, or merely acting suspicious could result in capture, usually followed by death. On 5 September 1944, a man wearing the uniform of a major in the Red army, carrying papers identifying him as P. I. Tavrin, and with the golden star of a Hero of the Soviet Union, was riding on a motorcycle with a woman in its sidecar when two Soviet security police stopped him near Smolensk. They thought something seemed not right. In the sidecar they found a radio, ciphers, pistols, hand grenades. The purported Tavrin had been brought in by airplane that night; he had not been on Russian soil 24 hours when he was captured—after almost a full year's training. The seven-man ZEPPELIN group ULM landed with an airplane near the Urals in June of 1944. One was killed on landing; the leader shot himself; the radioman did the same; one agent died from exhaustion; another was killed by his comrades; one was caught by the security organs; the other two apparently ran away. In the twelve months from October 1942 to September 1943, Abwehr Command 104 dispatched 150 agent groups in strengths of from 3 to 10 men behind the Soviet lines. Members of only two returned. In view of the extraordinary physical and mental demands on the agents, it was not surprising that so many failed. As one German intelligence officer put it, "If the losses were not over 90 percent, we were satisfied; if we could reduce them to 60 percent, we could call this the acme of success."

In the west, the situation differed only in detail. The Abwehr set up I (for "Invasion") nets of some 35 to 75 agents in the coastal zones of Holland, Belgium, and France and R (for "Restant," meaning "remaining," or for "Rückzug," meaning "retreat") nets with 104 agents deeper inland. But the I net in the Normandy peninsula, where the invasion actually came, barely functioned. The RSHA's Military Department made radio contact with only half a dozen agents in France, who transmitted at first only descriptions of general conditions and then requests for money. The other agents either feared to transmit or were forced to evacuate; a few were killed in the bombings. The Main Post for Front Reconnaissance in Paris, which controlled the front-agent organization, received its first messages about Allied landings from Le Havre on 8 June, two days after the Allies had come ashore. The R nets worked better. Its agents gave good eyewitness accounts—obtained, in one case, through binoculars—of Allied ship landings, troop movements, location of gasoline dumps, and pipelines. The agents in Cherbourg maintained silence during the fighting for the port, but after the Allies captured it they regularly transmitted details about the troops and the matériel that the Allies were landing. One agent in particular, EIKENS, and another, NORMANDIE, in Marseilles, accounted together for almost half of the average of 100 R-net messages a month received by the radio stations at Stuttgart and Wiesbaden, which handled communications for the main post.

Lieutenant Colonel Erich Herrlitz, in charge of the front reconnaissance, foresaw the Allied breakout early. To fulfill his duty, he wanted to pull his front reconnaissance commands and troops far to the rear, so that they would have time to prepare new R nets. But the I cs of the army groups and armies opposed this for fear that they would be called defeatist. Nevertheless, a few preparations were made, without anything coming of them. The major in charge of Front Reconnaissance Troop 123 gave a friend in Paris 500,000 francs for future payments to agents—but he never heard from any of them. When an officer offered money and radios to several trained agents in Paris just before the Allies entered the capital, they refused them, saying things were now too dangerous. One front reconnaissance command buried five radio sets near the Vosges mountains, bordering the Rhine. Not one was ever heard from.

Such failures forced the front reconnaissance units, after the lightning Allied advance through France, to rely mainly on line-crossers. These averaged 15 to 25 a month from the fall of 1944 on. Two-thirds of them were handled by Front Reconnaissance Command 120. It worked for Army Group G in the relatively favorable terrain of the Vosges, billeting its 10 to 20 agents in the school and manor house of the village of Wilgartswiesen, in Germany north of Strasbourg. Its subordinate Front Reconnaissance Troop 133 got agents across the Saar, and Troop 132 slipped several through the Allied lines near the Vosges resort town of Gérardmar.

The line-crossers at first were rather low grade, often untrained and without a specific assignment. Later, better agents in civilian clothes moved behind the Allied lines for two to four days, sometimes tapping telephone wires. The low-grade crossers began to be used mainly to find the most suitable routes for the higher-level ones. Toward the end of 1944, the Germans began parachuting agents—nearly all of them French collaborators—into northern France.

The information that these agents brought back merely added tactical tidbits to the German intelligence picture. NORMANDIE reported out of Marseilles in January 1945 that 20,000 American troops were landing there; the I c of the commander in chief west thought that this was the 78th Infantry Division. GAUTHIER reported out of Metz early in December 1944 that an American armored division, perhaps the 8th, was moving up in a northerly direction. A line-crosser of Front Reconnaissance Troop 134 confirmed the presence of the Polish 1st Armored Division near Breda, inside Germany.

These minor successes were purchased at an awful human price. Only about one line-crossing in four succeeded. In half, the agents were lost. In the other one-fourth, the spies were glad to escape with their lives. The man who ran the Wilgartswiesen camp estimated that only 5 percent of the line-crossers who left ever returned. On the Meuse River front in the fall of 1944, the situation was worse: not one line-crosser ever returned. The head of Front Reconnaissance Troop 134 was wounded while trying to guide an agent through the lines, and the head of Troop 139 was drowned in the Meuse while trying to cross it with an agent. And almost never was radio contact established with a parachute agent.

Frequently the agents had simply deserted, melting back into French society. But often, too, they had been captured. On the night of 3 February 1945, an airplane left Stuttgart with nine agents, all of them well trained. All were dropped from 35 to 95 miles from their objectives—one of them even in no-man's-land—and all were picked up relatively quickly, before they could transmit any intelligence.

Not every front agent was executed. Karl Arno Punzler was not.

Though convicted of furnishing tactical information about American movements to his German countrymen, his death sentence was commuted—because he was only 16 years old. But most captured agents did pay the spy's traditional penalty.

Stefan Kotas and Josef Wende, two Poles drafted into the German army, had been ordered to cross the Moselle River in civilian clothes, posing as Polish slave miners, to observe Allied strength in the area opposite their company. They were to return the same day. Except for the civilian clothes that their company commander gave them, they received no preparation. Early on 24 September 1944, they crossed to the west bank of the Moselle River, occupied by the Americans, and filtered into the rear areas. They began trudging along a road. But they had not gotten far when three Americans on patrol challenged them. Sergeant Robert T. Skarboro of Chicago asked them where they were going.

"Polack, Polack," they mumbled. Skarboro called over Technician 5th Class Frank A. Glowczynski of Chicago, who spoke Polish. One of the two men told him that they were "just poor Polish workers" on their way to a nearby farm to seek jobs. Since there were many Polish laborers in that sector, imported by the Germans to do farm work, the reply seemed plausible, and the Americans let them go. Wende and Kotas started walking again.

But then the Americans had second thoughts. They jumped into their jeep, raced after the men, picked them up, and brought them to a platoon command post. By the next day the two had confessed. On 18 October they were convicted of spying by a military commission, and on 11 November, accompanied by a priest and an impassive American sergeant, they walked, their faces showing that they were in shock, to one end of a narrow whitewashed courtyard where, under a gray French sky hundreds of miles from home, a firing squad extinguished the life of first one, then the other.

How useful were all these agents? How accurate was their information? The answer depended largely upon who was asked.

The Abwehr naturally saw things most rosily. In forwarding its agents' reports, the Abwehr was to reject any that were obviously false. But it did not have the comprehensive knowledge that would enable it to do so; only the evaluating agencies had that. And it did not want to. No spies, or useless spies, meant no Abwehr—and that could mean, for its members, winding up on the Russian front. So often Abwehr spymasters and their superiors pushed agents' reports, even when they knew them to be questionable. As a result, the evaluating agencies regarded much Abwehr material as rubbish.

The difference between their attitude and the Abwehr's showed most clearly in their evaluations of individual agents. The Abwehr's were invariably more positive. Where the Abwehr said of V-314, a transport representative living in London, that he had been "proved over many years" and was "trustworthy," Foreign Armies West dismissed his reports as "unclear and false" and "doubtful." Of V-373, a student in Glasgow, the Abwehr said he was "tested and trustworthy," while Foreign Armies West called him merely "usable."

For the evaluating agencies—and the commanders to whom they reported—felt, in general, that agent reports were among the least valuable of their major sources. The head of the Luftwaffe intelligence group for the American and British air forces regarded agent material "almost humorously"; he ranked it far below radio reconnaissance, prisoner interrogations, and the press. One of his colleagues fretted that "agent reports only impede the work." A chief of naval intelligence declared that "The effectiveness of the spy is small," and the navy noted with asperity in its war diary that Admiral Canaris's two predictions that the Allies would occupy Sicily, Sardinia, and Corsica in March 1943 were not fulfilled. A head of Foreign Armies West complained long and loud about the Abwehr's "failure" in the 1940 French campaign. General Siegfried Westphal, the chief of staff to the commander in chief south, did not forget that a few hours after Canaris had visited their headquarters and told them that no new landing need be feared in the near future, the Allies lodged themselves at Anzio and Nettuno.

Not everyone was always critical. Officers of Foreign Armies West had to depend upon the spies in England for much of their preinvasion Allied order-of-battle intelligence, and they accepted it more readily. On the Russian front, agent intelligence consisted mainly of the fairly reliable visual observations of front agents. Though it did not produce results commensurate with the expenditure of time and effort, I cs nevertheless regarded these results as essential for gaining a proper intelligence picture. In 1942, the OKW's war economy department tabulated the value of 72 Abwehr reports that it had received from Africa during the first five months of the year. It found 37, or more than half, "valuable." The others ranged from "less valuable" through "of interest" and "known" to "improbable."

But though one of its categories implied a test for accuracy, the department did not emphasize this aspect in its evaluation. When agent reports were examined primarily on that basis, they made a much weaker showing.

In the fall of 1944 the navy statistically analyzed 192 reports that the RSHA (which by then included the Abwehr) had sent it concerning the Allied landing on France's Mediterranean coast on 15 August 1944. It found only 15 "accurate." This was 1 in 12. An additional 32 were "partly right." All the rest—75 percent—were "possible (not checkable)," "too general (therefore not usable)," and "wrong." "The overwhelming number of the RSHA reports," said the navy, "was, in relation to either the predicted time of attack or place of attack or both, inaccurate or so general that they were not usable for a judgment of the situation."

A few months later, the navy looked into 173 reports concerning Allied intentions that had come in before the great D-Day invasion. The results again impugned the efficacy of spies: 8 percent were accurate, 14 percent partly right, 15 percent possible (not checkable), 4 percent too general (therefore not usable), and 59 percent—or three of every five—wrong.

On the basis of many such evaluations, Foreign Armies East drew up in November 1944 a listing of 133 agents (including some in the west) in order of their worth:

Rating	Number	Percent
very valuable	18	13.5
usable	19	14.3
limited	15	11.3
very limited	7	5.3
still doubtful	74	55.6

Retrospective examinations like these delineated trends and judged the general trustworthiness of a spy. But they could not say in advance how accurate a particular report was. For this, the evaluating officers had but a single method. They had to place the other information on that subject against the report and see whether this information confirmed or denied it. The chief disadvantage of this method is that a report that may be true but that runs counter to many other items will be discounted, and ironically, the "stranger" and more surprising a fact is, the more valuable it is. Yet probabilities dictate in this area as in much of life, and the evaluating officers had no other way of judging the correctness of a spy report. Their remarks on individual agent reports reflect this.

Agent EVA in London reported that an officer of the 5th Infantry Division had said that the division was south of Belfast. "Good," noted Foreign Armies West, "confirmed through prisoner." On a report of agent GUT-MANN: "XVth Army Corps confirmed by radio situation." When HUBERT reported "59th Infantry Division in Harwich area," Foreign Armies West could check this against the information from the head of radio reconnaissance under the commander in chief west: the 59th was confirmed in its old area of the Southeast Command, which would cover Harwich.

The same method discredited individual reports. An agent of the KO Spain reported in detail on 4 June 1944 about the locations in North Africa and Italy of the Brazilian 51st, 72nd, and 85th divisions. Commented Major Richard Euler of Foreign Armies West: "The report is unusable, since it includes entirely unbelievable information. Brazilian divisions with the given numbers do not exist. The presence of Brazilian troops in North Africa is improbable." Foreign Air Forces West said that it considered a report by OSTRO "entirely unbelievable, since up to now the 3rd Tactical Air Force has without doubt been spotted in the Far East." Other comments sound like tips on horses: "not excluded," "possible," "can be true."

Others were blunt: "worthless," "swindle." And some were rather colorful: "lots of paper but little wool," "an absolutely blooming idiotic report," and—more than once—"full of manure."

The most surgical, the most precise examinations of agent reports were made by Foreign Air Forces West. And the depth and precision of its probes enabled it to find important areas of rot.

One of the Luftwaffe's main agent sources on British aircraft production was OSTRO. Starting in 1943, shortly after Krämer had gone to Sweden, one of Krämer's agents, HEKTOR, likewise supplied these figures. Foreign Air Forces West checked one against the other. For most of 1943 they agreed. But starting in November 1943, they had increasingly diverged, and no statistical "acrobatics" could compose these differences.

In June 1944, the intelligence unit began to scrutinize the reports of these agents more closely. All desks involved commented, and it sought additional information from prisoners. It discovered nothing special against OSTRO, whose production figures had been, it believed, approximately correct in 1943, except that his other reports had become more general lately. But HEKTOR seemed more suspicious.

He told of a Rolls-Royce factory in Belper producing 150 airplane motors a month; a prisoner of war from Belper, who had recently been on leave, denied it. Another p.o.w. told of a factory to assemble Lancaster bombers west of Leicester; HEKTOR did not include it in his list, although he divided up the total Lancaster production among other plants, giving the impression that he knew all of them. He seemed to be giving the Luftwaffe the answers he thought it wanted to its questions. To test him, Foreign Air Forces West invented a story that an aerial photograph had disclosed a new factory, probably for airplane engines, four kilometers southwest of Worcester. They asked HEKTOR what it produced. Two months later he replied that an aircraft engine factory south-southwest of Worcester had been built in 1944, employed 2,000 workers, and turned out Napier-Sabre motors for Typhoons.

Eventually Foreign Air Forces West recalled that when Krämer started work he had been given for his guidance 10 typed pages plus target dossiers on British air production factories—all that was known about them. In addition, he probably had access to the air attaché's material, as well as to newspapers, technical publications, and gossip. It concluded that Krämer could have produced his reports without any serious connection with Great Britain. The reports seemed so believable because they were based upon the Luftwaffe's own data. They were in fact believed, and consequently led the Luftwaffe, it concluded sadly, "to erroneous conclusions on the strength of the R.A.F."

But the same principle of comparison of information from different sources that disgraced Krämer's HEKTOR glorified some of the Abwehr sources in England. Time after time, the details that they reported were confirmed independently by other sources, usually radio reconnaissance, sometimes agents of other rings, sometimes the press. Of all the spies in Britain, HUBERT, CATO, and 3725 (Hansen) withstood this ordeal best, and won the greatest trust from the skeptics of Foreign Armies West.

All in all, the picture of German spy activity in England that developed in Foreign Armies West was one in which many useless agents reported erroneous or invented or even enemy deception material, but a few high-quality agents furnished accurate and valuable intelligence on Allied forces and intentions, making the whole expensive operation worthwhile.

In fact it was all a chimera, a mirage. Not a single German spy in Great Britain was legitimate. Not one delivered wholly straightforward information to the Abwehr or the RSHA. Every single one was a double agent, under the control of the British. They all passed on only the information— real or faked—that the British wanted them to. It was the greatest deception in the history of warfare since the Trojans dragged into their jubilant city a huge wooden horse left by the departing Greeks.

The deception had begun even before the war with one of the first German agents in Britain, Arthur Owens—Ritter's JOHNNY. This man had, in the mid-1930s, begun reporting to the Admiralty information that he picked up in his business contacts with the Germans. In 1936, the Abwehr recruited him, and he eventually told the British about this. They took him on to penetrate the Abwehr, codenaming him, in a reversal and partial anagram of his name, SNOW. Ritter used him as a straightforward source of information, and though Owens did not reveal to the British everything he was giving the Abwehr, he basically worked for them, for he never disclosed his British connection to Ritter. When he returned to England after his training in Hamburg just as the war was starting, the British, still not entirely certain of him, jailed him in Wandsworth Prison. It was from his cell that he transmitted his first message: "Ein Glas Bier." These words formed the first link in what grew to be a vast and comprehensive deception of the Germans, the double-cross system.

Eventually a section, B 1 A, of British counterespionage (M.I.5.), emerged to run the turned-around agents, and a committee, called the Double-Cross, or XX, or Twenty Committee, composed of representatives of the armed services and the Foreign Office, evolved to coordinate the false information that these "spies" fed the Germans. When agents like Hansen contacted Owens for help, Owens delivered them into the hands of the British. When other agents parachuted down, often to be captured on the spot by a police constable alerted by a farmer who had seen the parachute, or a few hours or days later by a suspicious Englishman, they too moved into the penumbra of the Twenty Committee and B 1 A. These bodies offered many of these agents a choice: to betray their German masters by working as a double agent for the British, or to die. (Some agents were unsuitable for the work; a few refused; these, and perhaps others, were executed, in part to reassure the British public—and the Germans—that the counterespionage units were on the job.) Still other agents, who the Germans thought volunteered their services, had actually always intended to serve the Allies. At the first opportunity, they offered themselves to the British. Such were CATO and HUBERT.

The double agents transmitted to their German contacts only such information as the British wanted. Some of it was true. It was allowed because it would build up the bona fides of the agents. The underground hangars at Brize Norton that Hansen told about existed in fact; the British deemed this information harmless, and possibly known to the Germans from aerial photographs, so its transmission would not hurt Britain but would inspire credibility in Hansen as an agent. The young Spaniard called CATO by the Germans and GARBO by the British was likewise permitted to pass his probably false-dated report about Auchinleck's and Lyttleton's appointments because the British had already announced them, and the news, when it reached Germany, would confirm to the Abwehr that their man was well placed and reliable.

But the most important information that the British-controlled double agents sent to the Germans was false. Hansen's reports of the U.S. 11th Infantry and 25th Armored divisions passing through Cambridge were entirely fictitious. Not only did they never pass through, they had never even existed. Why, then, did the Germans believe such reports? Either they came from agents who had been established as reliable, such as Hansen, or they were confirmed by other sources—which, unhappily for Germany, Britain also controlled. When German radio reconnaissance confirmed HUBERT's report about the 59th Infantry Division, the Germans were convinced that it existed. Alas, the Allied radio signals that the Germans heard were as fake as HUBERT—and as the 59th. In this way did the Allies feed quantities of false information to the Germans, who, said Churchill, "firmly believed the evidence we obligingly put at their disposal.

The British did not control every German agent, however. CHB and OSTRO, both working out of Lisbon, remained independent. But they did not help the Germans very much either. For though both told or hinted to the Germans that their subagents had burrowed deep inside the Allied high commands, neither possessed such subagents. Many of them were in fact totally imaginary. CHB and OSTRO collected payment and expenses for these notional spies, and in return cooked up, from newspapers, rumors, and contacts, reports purporting to come from them. Nor were they alone in this practice, which—to say the least—did not bring valid inside information to German intelligence.

What about MAX, on the eastern front? Was he a legitimate German spy, or was he, as some suspected, a double agent? If the evidence cannot prove the latter, it at least points away from the former. There are several reasons.

His reports, which seemed so detailed, were actually imprecise and incomplete. Other agents often gave the numbers of formations they saw. MAX never did. One of his highest-level reports seemed false: that dealing with the war council which the American and British military attachés attended. Neither sent messages home about this—unthinkable if they had been there. His report of the Stalin war council omitted any mention of the Russian pincers attack, then only two weeks off, that encircled Stalingrad and led ultimately to the greatest German defeat of the war. Moreover, the radio connection lasted too long to be true. In England or America, such a spy would have been caught within weeks or even days; MAX survived for years. Finally, when the British, who were reading the Kauders traffic from Sofia to Berlin, told the Russians about MAX, they did not appear interested: it seemed as if they already knew about it.

But if his reports were, upon close analysis, so poor, why did the Germans like him so much? Probably because he dazzled them. He was their pipeline into the Kremlin. He reported on such a cosmic level that they did not question his omissions, if they even went back and looked for them. They fed his tactical reports into their intelligence picture. These were so general that they could not have helped much, but by the same token they could not be found false—relieving the Germans of the possibility of discovering this unpleasant fact. As for the Russians, the advantages of MAX probably included wasting the Germans' time and keeping them so contented that they would not trouble to place another agent into Moscow.

What was the reason for the overwhelming failure of German espionage? The roots lie in long-standing German attitudes toward intelligence and the consequent lack of long-term peacetime preparation. But the immediate answer is simply that the cards are stacked against the spy in wartime. Spy hysteria makes every member of the public into a counterespionage agent. During hostilities, controls restrict the spy's movements and make him more conspicuous. The government can question and hold people more easily and for longer periods. Furthermore, as it became increasingly apparent that Germany was losing the war, more and more spies deserted the sinking ship—just, ironically, when their information was most needed to parry Allied blows.

But were there no honest German spies? Did no one in the Abwehr and RSHA's seemingly vast secret armies deliver accurate information, or information that they believed accurate, to the minions of the Führer? There were some, but not many. Most served as front agents and furnished a few tactical details at best. Some may have worked in Spain or Sweden or Switzerland; a few apparently eluded the F.B.I. and radioed some insignificant intelligence from the United States. Only one agent of stellar rank legitimately served the Germans: CICERO. For most of his six-month career, he passed real high-level British documents to Moyzisch. The British suspected a leak for a while before they discovered the source in an intercept of a German message. A British typist had made a mistake in a dispatch and had corrected it in three of the four copies—but not on the ambassador's. The intercept contained the error, pinpointing Sir Hughe's copy as the one accessible to the spy. The British then fed some deception material in through this pipeline. But Bazna quit soon after this was begun, so it did not have much effect, nor did it counter CICERO's essentially deleterious effect. Even counting CICERO's great coup, however, the effects of strategic German espionage were secondary. At best, they delayed by a few months the possible bombing of the German-occupied Balkans and the suspension of chrome deliveries to Germany. But the real control over events in Turkey was exercised by the major events of the war, and on this CICERO had no effect.

In looking back over the work of their organization during World War II, former members of the Abwehr and RSHA conceded that the agency did not supply Germany with vital intelligence—that, in other words, it did not fulfill the hopes placed in it. But the situation was worse than that. In view of their utter deception by the British, and their delivery of quantities of critical false information, the Abwehr and the RSHA had not merely not helped their country. They had grievously harmed it.

III
THE WEIGHERS

The Military Economists

COLONEL Walther Nicolai had a confession to make. In his memoirs, the World War I chief of German espionage admitted that he had not prepared his agency to spy out enemy economies. And economic strength had, especially after the entry of the United States, contributed to defeating Germany.

That nation thereafter recognized the importance of economic intelligence. How big an army a potential enemy could support and how many arms it could supply them with was a basic question in modern warfare between industrialized nations. In the 1920s, T 3, the intelligence branch of the Troops Department, extended its evaluations to such matters. But by 1934, this work had moved under the aegis of the agency that was preparing Germany's own economic mobilization.

This was the War Economy and Armaments Department, later in the OKW. Its long-time chief was General Georg Thomas, whose greatest claim to fame came from his being replaced by Speer as armaments minister in 1942. One function that Speer did not take over was the foreign intelligence unit. From 1939 to 1942, this War Economy Branch constituted one of the department's five branches, with 73 of the department's 322 desks. The decapitation of its department reduced it too in size, so that by November 1944 it had only 22 desks with 52 people. But in the manner of bureaucracies everywhere, it had managed to promote itself, so that it rose to become the Foreign Bureau of what was then the Field Economy Department.

Its chiefs were always military administrators. The actual analyses were done by his brilliant but unmilitary subordinates, nearly all of them civilian economists drafted into the work. Curt Zinnemann, for example, who headed the Russian section, was a demographer specializing in the Soviet

Union and a wizardlike statistician. Their offices were in barracks built in the courtyard of an old building in the Gneisenaustrasse in Berlin. After they were bombed out in 1943 so thoroughly that all that was left were 50 to 60 safes standing in the ashes, they moved east to Frankfurt-an-der-Oder.

Hostilities complicated the task of the War Economy Branch. War swelled enemy economies and thus increased the potential information available, but it also meant that there was more that it had to know. War further imposed a secrecy that blocked the direct sources of information and forced the branch to quarry facts out by secondary methods. The branch had been accustomed to receiving attaché reports, official statistics, notes of traveling German businessmen, and data-rich publications (it took 100 technical newspapers and magazines and 50 dailies as well as industry handbooks and economic atlases). Hostilities dried much of this up. They also reduced the quality, even if it increased the quantity, of the reports of the Foreign Office's Commercial Branch, the Economic Ministry's Bureau III (foreign economies), the food and finance ministries, I. G. Farben's Vowi, and other private and semipublic research institutes. Much of the

---

THE ORGANIZATION OF THE WAR ECONOMY BRANCH
(FOREIGN INTELLIGENCE) OF THE WAR ECONOMY
AND ARMAMENTS DEPARTMENT OF THE OKW

1 February 1942

I   Central group [organization; personnel; legal questions; steering of intergroup cooperation; liaison to other agencies; judgment of effect of foreign economies on German war strategy]

II   Africa

III/IV   III   Southeast Area (Serbia, Croatia, Montenegro, Rumania, Bulgaria, Greece, Hungary, Slovakia, Italy)

  IV   Netherlands, Belgium, Northern [occupied] France, Switzerland, Spain, Portugal

V   British Commonwealth, Ireland, [unoccupied] France, America

VI   Russia, Near East, Far East, Southeast Asia, Finland, Norway, Sweden, Denmark

VII   War equipment and foreign trade; currency matters

VIII   Information service [evaluation of foreign newspapers and magazines; liaison to scientific institutes; library; sifting and distribution of incoming information]

Wi P   War-economy and economic propaganda, domestic and foreign; publications of the department in the press, broadcast, films, and brochures

Vowi information, for example, was outdated by the time it reached the branch.

But hostilities expanded old and created new organs of intelligence. And on these the War Economy Branch and its successors increasingly depended.

The most voluminous of these by far were intercepted communications. Censored letters revealed in September 1942 that Spain was buying up chrome and manganese in Portugal. Forschungsamt intercepts of domestic Russian communications disclosed such details as that the aircraft factory numbered 447 by the Germans had used 50,000 kilowatt-hours of electricity in the first third of June 1944. The OKW's Cipher Branch passed along on 11 August 1944 a summary of a monitored broadcast reporting a U.S. War Department order to reduce the production of Liberators, Thunderbolts, and transport airplanes and to increase that of Super-Fortresses.

One day in May of 1942, an officer from the branch's Desk V b (France), visiting North Africa, stumbled upon the Luftwaffe's radio inter-

---

ORGANIZATION OF GROUP V OF THE WAR ECONOMY BRANCH

1 February 1942

V British Commonwealth, Ireland, [unoccupied] France, America
  a Overall judgment of the war economy of the British Commonwealth and Ireland
    1 Foreign trade, financial questions, labor questions; armaments position of the armed forces
    2 Food and fodder production and trade; wood and forest economy
    3 Ore, metals, coal, petroleum
    4 Armaments industry; iron and metal industry; war-economy organization
    5 Energy supply; specialized industries
    6 War-economic bases; population; coastal and inland traffic; chemical industry
    St Statistics
    z.b.V. [= for special purposes] Comprehensive study of the "big" England report; preparation of the materials for it (statistics, maps); card index of locations
  b Judgment of the war-economic situation of France; traffic questions
    1 Machine construction; armaments industry
    2 Raw-material supply; wood and forest economy; mining and metal industry; chemical industry; energy supply; foreign trade; colonies
    3 Finishing industries; food and fodder production and trade, financial situation; war-economic organization
    4 Unoccupied France
    St Statistics; population; labor allocation
  c Judgment of the war-economic situation of America; traffic questions
    1 War-economic overall situation (except armaments industry)
    2 Armaments industry; war-economic organization.

cept operation, which had "hitherto remained unknown to the War Economy and Armaments Department." The 9th Radio Reconnaissance Company there amazed and delighted him, for it had "extraordinarily good" information on American supply routes through Africa, on convoy traffic, the strength of enemy air formations, and other details. It reported, for example, that three months earlier at least 150 airplanes had flown from America or Britain to Egypt via Accra, Lagos, Fort Lamy, Khartoum, Luxor, and Cairo. The Luftwaffe intercept head office, in Potsdam, gave out "uncommonly clear" reports each month of enemy supply activities, including graphic depictions, that "are of great interest for the War Economy and Armaments Department." The officer urged requesting these reports, which "far surpass the capabilities of the Abwehr."

He was basically right. "Too general, insufficiently supported, and therefore improbable" read a branch comment on a slew of spy messages from Africa. Nevertheless, the branch did not disdain the Abwehr or, to a lesser extent, the RSHA as sources. On 14 November 1942, it gave Abwehr I Wi its new requirements for information about England. This document, intended to serve as the basis for instructing agents, struck off questions that had been answered and added new ones. The Abwehr reported on 7 September 1942 that 18 American ships carrying war matériel for Egypt had arrived in the Persian Gulf. RSHA VI Wi once passed along a memorandum on the use of vegetable oil as lubrication for locomotives. It said that it worked for the wheels and their pistons, but not for the steam cylinder if it got hotter than 400° centigrade.

Early in the war, the War Economy Branch depended for its raw data mainly upon large drafts from other agencies. Except for its reading of the press, it did not itself acquire information. But in the fall of 1941, General Thomas concluded that the loss of all Russian territory and industry from Leningrad through Moscow to the Crimea "need not necessarily lead to a breakdown" of the Russian war economy. Perhaps to gain more information on the industry that was left, the War Economy Branch dispatched specialists to the front. The first group, under Major Prince Reuss, who had worked in Asia as a businessman, went to Army Group South; others later went to army groups Center and North.

At first they interrogated prisoners of war. Reuss, an excellent organizer, had a list of the most important factories and their locations, and his men picked out prisoners from these towns for questioning. Seven to eight hundred a month talked volubly about matters they knew from their jobs at home—the location, products, output, and needs of factories, mines, and other sources of production. This soon proved the most valuable information of all. The military economists summed prisoners' statements of the daily production of T-34 tanks in the individual factories and multiplied these by 30 to estimate production at 1,000 a month for the spring of 1943 and 1,500 for the summer and fall, making a total of 15,000 for 1943.

FABRIK ZEICHEN

Leningrad: Krassnyj Putilower (M/T) Auf d. hint. Ende des
Molotow: Werk Nr. 172 (Jordan)   Mantelrohres einer JKH 76mm
                                        (Burkart)
WOTKINSK: Werk Nr. 235 ☆ (Burkart)
STALINGRAD: Krassnyj Barrikady △ Auf der rechten Seite
    des Bodenstückes einer FK 76mm SIS 22 UssW (Burkart)
GORKIJ: Werk Nr. 92 (Burkart)
WOTKINSK: Werk Nr. 235   ⊛   Auf dem linken
    Holm einer SISs-3 (Jordan)
UST-KATAW: Werk Nr. 13 ⊔ Auf KWK 85mm SISs-Ss 53
STALINGRAD: Krassnyj Barrikady ◬ Auf 76mm FK 1539 USW (B)
GORKIJ: Werk Nr. 92 ▲ Auf 76mm FK 1939 USW (Burkart)
⊞⊒ LENINGRAD, evak. Tal des Kirowelles, nun rem. Werk in
    MOLOTOW

Other data led Zinnemann's subgroup east to conclude that the Russian coal requirements had reached 101,300,000 tons in 1942 and would probably rise to 123 million in 1943—a figure that it said would probably not be met.

Equally solid, if less copious, material came from the branch's analysis of the serial numbers of captured weapons. The teams at the front had been empowered to offer leaves to any soldier who brought back a brass number plate from the underside of a Russian tank. Soon their quarters, as well as the head office's, were overflowing with the 5-by-8-inch plates; some of the officers used them as paperweights. These plates gave the serial number, factory, and date. One of the branch's young statisticians, Specialist Dr. Jordan, intercalated and interpolated the numbers with series from motor works, gun works, and chassis works, using such tank-plate figures as those from nine T-34s from a factory in Nizhniy Tagil, which went from T 47,068 to T 49,181. He eventually reckoned an annual production of 16,500 T-34s—an improvement in accuracy of 9 percent over the prisoner figure.

The fullness of this intelligence and its refinement through computation enabled the foreign section to determine with astonishing accuracy the quantity of supplies that Lend-Lease sent to the Soviet Union. On 10 August 1944, for example, it stated that the total number of passenger cars, trucks, and prime movers that had gone to Russia under the program as of 31 March 1944 was 202,000. In fact the figure stood at 200,793—an error of only 0.6 percent.

Economic intelligence could not by itself enable the Germans to win any battles. But it contributed to operational decisions.

In the summer of 1942, it helped the navy decide whether U-boats should be committed in the eastern Mediterranean when it reported on Egypt's tonnage requirements for its trade with neighboring countries. It advised the Luftwaffe on the most economically worthwhile bombing targets. In July 1943, the Rolls-Royce motor factories in Derby, Crewe, and Hillington with target numbers GB 73 19, GB 73 20, and GB 73 58 constituted the production bottlenecks, it reported. It warned against trying to halt British air production by attacks against the light metal industry. "The domestic production of raw aluminum [in Great Britain] is estimated at 50,000 to 60,000 tons, divided among three works. Even if all three were completely destroyed, the replacement of 5,000 tons a month by imports from the U.S.A. and Canada poses no problem." Jordan's calculations of tank production, added to the Lend-Lease imports, plus the section's knowledge of how long it took tanks to reach the fronts from factory and port, divided into the Red army's tank strength tables of organization as modified by Foreign Armies East's knowledge of the degree to which they were fulfilled, enabled the bureau time and again to predict almost to the day when Soviet units would be refitted and so ready once again to attack.

But if the section's intelligence was nearly always welcomed at the operational level, it was not at the Führer's. When it fit his ideas, he accepted and even exaggerated it. In the spring of 1943, the unit was demonstrating that it was essential to hold the Axis bridgehead in North Africa because its loss would free some 2 million tons of ship capacity for the Allies. At the same time, Hitler was telling his admirals the same thing—with the figures upped to 4 to 5 million tons. But when the unit's reports countered his views, he ignored or rejected them. A few days after Thomas warned him that conquest of most of industrialized European Russia might not cause the Russian war economy to collapse, Hitler was boasting that Russia was losing 75 percent of her aluminum and 90 percent of her oil and "had reached the end of her strength." Later reports increasingly presented uncomfortable information to him. He could not have been happy to learn that the Allies had enough chromium ore not to have to depend on Turkey. More and more, Keitel refused to pass on such information. He sent back one report dealing with Lend-Lease to Russia with the scrawl, "The Führer . . . will doubt . . . the information." Finally he ordered the section to stop submitting its reports to Hitler at all.

In the Luftwaffe and
the Kriegsmarine

THE reports came in during the night and early in the morning. They were ready for him when Major Herbert Owe arrived for work at his office. This wooden barrackslike building lay idyllically in the midst of the Werder deer park near Potsdam, not far from Berlin. From his window, these early summer days of 1944, Owe could look out on a curtain of green. The war sometimes seemed far away.

On this typical day, a secretary laid the papers before him, and he began to read. Owe was a compact, pleasant-looking man, of medium height, with a calm and well-balanced personality. He was a professional officer, having joined the Luftwaffe in 1936, when he was in his twenties. He had started the war in a bomber squadron, but very soon was injured when the He 111 in which he was flying crashed in a night take-off. This limited his flying abilities, and he was assigned to general staff training at the air academy. He completed this on 30 September 1942 and, as his first general staff position, was assigned as I c of the 1st Air Division, then in Russia. This division consisted of two or three bomber wings and a reconnaissance squadron. Owe's main jobs were to report to the I a on the enemy situation and to tell the I a what kind of information was required for bombing targets so that he (the I a) could best order reconnaissance.

Owe quickly grasped the idea of intelligence work. He proved so effective that word of his abilities reached higher headquarters, and in little more than a year he received an order transferring him to KURFÜRST. This was the codename—meaning "elector [of the Holy Roman Emperor]" —for the Luftwaffe general staff headquarters in the deer park. Owe arrived early in 1944, and soon thereafter took charge of Group D of Foreign Air Forces West. Under him were half a dozen officers, three civilian officials, four or five clerks and draftsmen, and three or four women secretaries. Though Group D included desks for Turkey and the Near East and for the French, Spanish, and Portuguese air forces, it concentrated on the British and American air units flying against Germany. Owe was thus the Luftwaffe's expert on the main enemies of the Reich in the air.

The papers that Owe read on an average morning consisted of prisoner interrogations from Dulag Luft, reports of the radio intelligence units and of spies, and memoranda that his staff had written based on their own detailed study of sources. At about 10:30 he began to prepare himself for the noon situation conference of the chief of the Luftwaffe Operations Staff. He made notes and conferred with his officers. Especially after the Normandy invasion, they sought to determine where the Allied point of main effort was coming. This they did by comparing statistics from aerial photographs of various airfields to see which were more heavily occupied. They analyzed enemy attack tactics, based on reports from their own troops. They selected the most significant new items reported about enemy equipment that had been obtained from shot-down planes. All this Owe brought to the conference.

The chief of Foreign Air Forces did most of the talking about the enemy situation, but his subordinates, the head of the east and west sections, and their subordinates, the group chiefs like Owe, answered questions about details. But Owe and the others did not only supply information. They also listened to the description of the entire situation, which helped them to see what was important in their own work.

The conference normally lasted 45 minutes to an hour. In the slack period that followed, Owe and the others took their afternoon break. At about 4 p.m. they began reading through the new material in preparation for the evening situation conference. This started at 8 p.m. By the time it had ended, most of the reports of the day's activities of the German air units and the dispatches of the Abwehr, of Dulag Luft, and of the other posts had arrived. Owe studied them to form a picture of the day's activities. During the evening hours he and his team drafted reports for distribution to the troops. These went out every few weeks under the title of "Individual Reports of the Air Force I c Service West." No. 76, of 8 October 1944, was a handsome 14-page report, illustrated with photographs, of the disastrous American and British airborne landing at Arnhem, part of Operation MARKET-GARDEN, entitled *New Information on the Commitment of Allied Parachute and Airborne Troops.* Some time between 11 p.m. and 1 a.m., Owe and his men finished their work and left. Next morning it would start all over again.

Unlike most specialist functions of the air force, its intelligence effort was as old as the Luftwaffe itself. On 1 March 1920, the day that the army chief established an air unit within the Troops Department, he also assigned one man to study foreign air forces within T 3, the intelligence branch.

On 1 April 1927, air intelligence moved from T 3 to the expanding air unit, becoming its Desk VI. Its commander, a World War I veteran who was carried on the retired rolls, was Major Hilmer Baron von Bülow. He soon expanded Desk VI. By 1931, it was maintaining a file of bombing targets.

When, in the second half of 1937, the Luftwaffe General Staff emerged from its long and complicated organizational gestation, it included intelligence as its 5th Branch, eventually named "Foreign Air Forces." After consolidating this development, Bülow left, to become air attaché in Rome. But his successor, Lieutenant Colonel Hans Jeschonnek, held the post little more than a year before being promoted in February 1939 to air force chief of staff. It marked quite possibly the only time in German military history that an officer in an intelligence post advanced to so major a position, and it probably reflects the more open attitude toward technical competence that the air force had as compared to the army, where such a thing would never have happened.

Also reflecting this attitude was that his replacement in turn came from the Operations Branch. Broad-shouldered, square-headed, Lieutenant Colonel Josef (Beppo) Schmid was regarded as more cunning than intelligent, but as having great energy and organizational talent. He also enjoyed one rare and valuable advantage. In November 1923, when Hitler staged his beer-hall putsch in Munich, the cadets at the infantry school there marched, fully uniformed, behind him and his chief supporter, Erich Ludendorff, who had run Germany's armies during the Great War. The attempt to take over the government of Bavaria failed miserably, and Hitler was sent to prison, where he wrote *Mein Kampf*. But those who had participated in that critical event, which Hitler commemorated yearly, later received a special decoration. Among them were the former cadets, one of whom was Josef Schmid. This gave him a personal link to the Führer, which could both protect him and give him special access.

Regulations assigned to Schmid's branch the "evaluation of intelligence on foreign states, their military-political appreciation, especially on all questions in connection with the area of air war command," and "target study." It also got sundry secondary jobs—for intelligence in the Luftwaffe, as elsewhere, was often regarded as "anybody's girl."

As war approached in 1939, Schmid had 29 officers to carry out these tasks. Most were former officers, recalled in a "supplementary" status because they knew a foreign language. They divided into five groups—I for administration, V for airplane types, II to IV for various countries. (These did not include the United States until 1940.) The officers' major source was the foreign press and the German air attachés. Major Peterpaul von Donat, head of Group II (France, Belgium, Italy, Spain), often claimed that his best informant was a French Major Longeront, who wrote a column on air matters in the right-wing French daily *L'Intransigeant*. Longeront's notices on personnel transfers and promotions, on shifts of squadrons from one airfield to another, on new airplanes, told Donat more than all the German spies in France. The basic reason, Donat explained, was that Longeront knew what he was talking about and the spies did not.

The most precious work of the 5th Branch reposed in a series of folders. This was its file of potential bombing targets.

Some of the target "folders" were simply huge gray index cards, about 12 by 16 inches, listing the target, its latitude and longitude, and its importance. A factory, for example, would have its product listed. But most of the folders, including all those for the major targets, consisted of manila envelopes also 12 by 16 inches. In addition to the basic information carried on the cards, they contained aerial photographs of the target and a 1:75,000 map sometimes showing approach routes, landmarks, and enemy antiaircraft defenses. Some folders included sketches at a scale of 1:100 showing the sensitive points—boilers and water supply, for example—whose destruction would halt production without the need to raze the entire factory. Each target had an identifying 4-digit number, often preceded by a letter or letters for the country. There were two sets of folders. One was arranged by area, the other by product.

Much information had come from attachés, published handbooks of industry, official maps, the press, sometimes spies. The OKW's war-economy department provided many details. Most of the aerial photographs had been taken by the high-flying Rowehl strategic reconnaissance squadron. The Main Photo Center in Berlin outlined each factory or installation in white on the glossy prints.

Not every factory or defense installation of every country was included. A count in one country revealed 40,000 large- and medium-sized factories. The 5th Branch had to choose as targets those whose loss would most damage the country's war-making capabilities. For Czechoslovakia, it picked 500 and prepared folders on them. For France, long foreseen as the chief enemy, Schmid's target section had, by the time of the Munich crisis in the fall of 1938, dossiers on 100 percent of her oil refineries and major power stations, 90 percent of her airfields, 70 to 80 percent of her munitions capacity, and 60 percent of her fuel dumps.

All this information would not help much if it remained, closely guarded, at Luftwaffe headquarters. It had to be distributed to the bomber crews. Foreign Air Forces reprinted the target folders, at first in 300 copies, later more, sealed them in extra-large envelopes, and had them picked up by hand by the bomber squadrons, which stored them in special archives at their airfields. In addition, the 5th Branch printed books showing the major targets in various countries and summarizing the other information. It distributed them to the squadrons.

It kept this information up to date during the war. In mid-October 1940, for example, at the height of the blitz, it issued a special atlas with new information on, among others, target 73 20, the Rolls-Royce airplane motor factory at Crewe, not far from Liverpool. It had first been photo-graphed from the air a month before, and the pictures corrected a previous misconception about the location of the motor shop. The atlas reproduced one of these pictures, outlining the target with a red line. It also printed a 1:10,560 map, apparently taken from the British Ordnance Survey's fa-mous one-inch-to-one-mile series. This showed approximately the same area as the photograph and also delineated the target in red. "The factory, with its large surface area, offers a favorable target for the Luftwaffe," the written description commented. "Its situation at the extreme edge of the city and near the extensive railroad installations facilitates finding it." For a potentially important railroad bridge at Sedan, where the German pan-zers struck through in their blitzkreig defeat of France, the Luftwaffe pro-vided an aerial photograph and a reprint of a French map showing the bridge and a large-scale sketch defining its location over the Meuse River with great precision.

Later, when Germany attacked the Soviet Union, Schmid shifted his effort to that immense country. Prisoners, reports from Foreign Armies East, and an aerial photograph taken 4 May 1942 told him about a factory under construction 5 miles south of Baku; it received number SU 74 26. Similar sources (though no photos) likewise reported that Factory No. 29, an airplane motor works, had been transferred in August 1941 from the southern Ukrainian city of Zaporozh'ye, which the Germans soon overran, to Omsk, a thousand miles east of Moscow, behind the Urals. This lay far beyond the range of German bombers, and the factory received no target number.

Determining the size and equipment of enemy air forces and the rate of airplane production had always been one of Foreign Air Forces' main jobs. Schmid checked after the German victory over France and found that his figures had been quite accurate. He was far less successful with the Royal Air Force, however, and his failure may have contributed to Germany's loss of the Battle of Britain. After Dunkirk, although radio reconnaissance provided good order-of-battle information on the British fighters, the shift of the air war to the skies over England deprived German air intelligence of such sources as captured pilots and downed airplanes. The Abwehr's spies furnished as good as nothing. As a consequence, the 5th Branch, pos-sibly using as a basis the much more leisurely German airplane production, greatly underestimated British fighter replacements. At the same time, basing its figures on pilots' wildly overoptimistic reports, it overestimated British air losses. Schmid's 5th Branch believed that the R.A.F. had only about 350 Hurricane and Spitfire fighters near the end of August, when in fact it had 700. This assessment perhaps helped Hitler and Göring believe that they had defeated the British in the air enough to suspend their at-tacks on the fighter squadrons. With this they lost the Battle of Britain.

The abandonment of these attacks cost them the air superiority they needed for invasion, the blitz failed to bring England to her knees, and the island kingdom survived. It became the base from which bombers were later launched to carry the air war to Hitler's Germany.

The great Anglo-American bombardments put enormous pressure on the Luftwaffe high command. Friction developed between Göring and his subordinates. To Schmid fell the unenviable task of reporting the renaissance of the Red air force, of debunking the exaggerated Luftwaffe reports of enemy downings, of warning of an increase in Allied bombers over Germany, of confirming the British announcement of the first 1,000-plane raid. Schmid's reports were not appreciated. Göring's cronies began punningly calling Schmid's situation judgments "lie judgments" (changing "Lagebeurteilungen" to "Lügenbeurteilungen"). The arrest as a Communist spy of one of his officers, Harro Schulze-Boysen, a first lieutenant in the attaché group, did not enhance Schmid's reputation. One morning at the beginning of October 1942, he found in his mail an order that the new chief of the 5th Branch was Lieutenant Colonel Josef Kögl. Schmid took command of an air defense unit, leaving the agency he had built up from before the war with "mixed feelings."

Kögl himself survived only a year. It was a most difficult period. The Allied strategic air offensive mounted in fury. Berlin was being destroyed. Hamburg was annihilated in a fire storm. American bombers battered the ball-bearing factory at Schweinfurt while the Royal Air Force killed 750 scientists and workers and damaged installations at the Peenemünde rocket research station, Hitler's pet project. Upbraided by Hitler and Göring, Jeschonnek, the air force chief of staff, committed suicide. Wholesale changes were made in the stratosphere of Luftwaffe command. And Kögl departed.

Colonel Rudolf Wodarg took charge of what was now generally called the "Luftwaffe Operations Staff I c," though neither its designation of "5th Branch" nor its name of "Foreign Air Forces" had formally changed. A former naval officer who had transferred to the air force in 1935, he had actually been deputy chief since 1940. But his work had had little to do with intelligence gathering and evaluating. He served as the Luftwaffe representative to the propaganda ministry, passing information to Goebbels on the air war, and ran the Luftwaffe's own press and propaganda unit. Wodarg was 35 when he became head of Foreign Air Forces; some subordinates found him unpleasant, but most agreed that he possessed a balanced and clear-eyed judgment. Just before Goebbels left to visit occupied France and the Luftwaffe units on the Channel coast in the summer of 1940, Wodarg had told the clubfooted propagandist, "Herr Reichsminister, London will be our Verdun of the air." And he was right.

Wodarg applied his sober vision to the task of penetrating the fog of enemy intentions. The chief mystery facing him was: Where will the invasion take place? Foreign Air Forces had, some years previously, developed a statistical analysis of airfield occupancy and rail traffic to detect the points of main effort in forthcoming Russian attacks. It perhaps attempted to use this same technique to determine the location of the invasion. But largely because of the lack of aerial reconnaissance, it could not do so.

Wodarg departed, his place being taken by Colonel Walter Kienitz, former head of Foreign Air Forces West. Owe was promoted to Kienitz's former post. They still faced the task of predicting Allied moves. One way of doing this was to determine the enemy's capabilities. These, in turn, stemmed to a considerable extent from production. To discover the Allies' output, the 5th Branch utilized three chief sources. One was the analysis of serial numbers of parts of downed Allied aircraft. Colonel-Engineer Schwenke, head of technical intelligence under the chief of air armament, maintained a three-man "deciphering unit" for this at his enemy aircraft testing center at Rechlin. They provided apparently solid data on the airplane production of the Americans and the Russians, whose numbers ran consecutively, less solid on that of the British, who left holes in their numeration.

The branch's second source was the German agent Karl-Heinz Krämer in Stockholm, who worked as JOSEFINE and HEKTOR. Schwenke felt that Krämer's work agreed completely with his; this may have been because Krämer was getting, indirectly, Schwenke's results. The figures from these two sources the branch tested against the third: public statements by Allied officials.

Into its equations the branch then inserted figures from the prisoners at Dulag Luft on the number of airplanes per squadron and from radio intelligence on the number of squadrons. A grand calculation followed. But the margin of error in the data base led to wildly erroneous results. In February 1945 the Luftwaffe Operations Staff I c distributed a report on the strength of Allied air in Europe. It gave 5,010 bombers and fighters as the total in the U.S. 8th Air Force. In fact, there were only 4,307.

But it was not the complexity of the computations that they had to make nor the difficulty of obtaining accurate raw material for their analyses that the intelligence officers in the Potsdam deer park considered their worst problem. It was how to break bad news to the chief of the Luftwaffe Operations Staff. As head of Foreign Air Forces West, Owe often spoke at the situation conferences, and he quickly learned that "There were many things that you could only say in doses." He would present a bit of the information at the morning conference, some more at the evening one. It took months to convince the air force command that the Allies had fighters of such long range that they could accompany bombers deep into Germany and home again. The command always suspected the intelligence units of having succumbed to the enemy propaganda. The intelligence officers themselves were astonished at the speed with which the Americans constructed front airfields—smoothing out whole hills and laying steel mesh runways in three or four days. But although a comparison of dated before-and-after aerial photographs left no doubt of this, the command resisted the knowledge. Once Göring berated an I c officer, "When I look at your charts, I get the impression that there is only an enemy and that no German forces exist!"—and he kicked the man out of the conference.

Near the end of 1944, Owe's successor as head of Group D, Captain Albrecht Zetzschke, a professional officer, highly intelligent, with a rare gift for formulating considered judgments clearly, wrote a bitter, eloquent indictment of the Luftwaffe intelligence work. "The German I c service has in fact, from 1939 to the end of 1944, failed," he began. He offered as reasons that the officers were too old, too poorly chosen, and too few, that spies had deceived them, that effort was duplicated (at least 10 different units worked on high-frequency radio matters), and that excessive optimism in the higher commands inhibited officers from pressing their real views in briefings. He concluded that the commands "did not take the I c service seriously," "practically did not pay attention to the I c findings," and, in the end, "produced their own judgment of the enemy."

Perhaps it didn't really matter. By the time of the invasion, the great German air force in the west, the proud gleaming instrument whose Stukas had a few years before terrorized the world, had dwindled to a few hundred combat-ready airplanes. It was for them that the Luftwaffe intelligence apparatus worked—the 30 or 40 people at Foreign Air Forces West, perhaps the same number at the western field command I c posts, altogether close to 100 people. This meant one person in intelligence for every two to four available airplanes. "We sometimes laughed about it," said Owe.

If air force intelligence had a more limited effect on operations than army intelligence, owing to the more intermittent and transient nature of air warfare, the effect of the naval intelligence branch was even more restricted. In part this stemmed from a situation analogous to the air: no one could possess the sea. In part it was due to the lack of any major fleet actions. And in part it evolved from internal circumstances within the OKM. For the Foreign Navies Branch lost competencies to rivals on both sides.

This depreciation began soon after the branch as such came into being with the creation of the Seekriegsleitung, the Naval War Command, late in 1939 (though the intelligence function had, of course, long existed). Almost immediately, what should have been one of its chief feeder agencies, radio reconnaissance, broke away. For the rest of the war the B-Dienst successfully maintained its independence as a separate and co-equal branch of the Seekriegsleitung. At the same time, the Operations

Branch, which should have been one of naval intelligence's chief receptors, arrogated unto itself a basic intelligence job: judging the enemy situation. Shorn thus of its most vital input and its most critical output, Foreign Navies, the third branch of the Seekriegsleitung, or 3/Skl, shrank to virtual insignificance. It was by far the least important of the three services' intelligence branches.

About all it had left, except for issuing multilithed bulletins to the field commands on such subjects as "Duties of the American Navy and of Naval Air Units in Carrying Out Landing Operations" (five pages, 1943), was generating statistics on enemy merchant ships. This involved the great question of enemy tonnage and its sinking by the U-boats—Germany's years-long attempt to cut Britain's supply lines and so defeat her.

Group FH (Fremde Handelsschifffahrt, or foreign commercial ships) produced the figures under the able and efficient direction of Captain Prause, a World War I flotilla commander. It gleaned data from the B-Dienst, the OKW's war-economy office, and the Forschungsamt, but mainly from a thorough screening of the foreign press. A report about a bill submitted on 24 February 1943 in the House of Representatives to appropriate $6 billion to build ships included as background that the ship construction program now comprehended 4,403 vessels totaling 44 million deadweight tons. This gave FH a solid basis on which it could make its calculations. These were carried out by its battery of Hollerith tabulating machines. They clattered noisily at first in the OKM headquarters in the sandstone building at Tirpitzufer 72, then, after the bombings of November 1943, at a dispersal station at Bad Lautern in Saxony, tended by about 50 men, a third of the entire Foreign Navies detachment. The group used the machines to follow the movements of each individual seagoing freighter, tanker, and transport known to it—thousands of vessels. The machines could also produce summaries showing the ship tonnage on various routes —along America's Atlantic Coast, arriving at different ports in Britain, crossing the North or the South Atlantic. They also totaled the tonnages in service by the Allies and the tonnages being built.

In this the group could, as analysts, be remarkably accurate. On 10 March 1943, FH reported that in 1942 American ways had produced 592 Liberty ships and 62 tankers. The actual figures were 597 and 61. But this was after the fact. In prediction, they did less well—but even the American shipbuilders could not forecast exactly how much would be built. At first the Germans overestimated the American capacity. Late in 1941 and early in 1942, estimates of America's 1942 production fluctuated between 7.2 and 9.36 million deadweight tons. Actually, 7.77 million were delivered. But afterward the Germans seriously underestimated the American capacity. At least part of the cause seems to have been FH's belief that it was "not possible" to maintain the pace reported of 55 days to construct a Liberty ship and that on the average 70 days would be required. In fact average construction time dropped to a little above 50 days. On the basis of its assumption, the Naval War Command estimated in October 1942 that American production would attain 14.1 million deadweight tons in 1943. The dockyards built almost 18 million.

The American construction estimates should have played a role in a number that both Hitler and the OKM kept in forefront of their minds. This was the "fatal tonnage figure." It gave the number of gross tons per month that the U-boats had to sink to exceed new Allied construction and thus to win the Battle of the Atlantic. It fluctuated generally around 750,000, though in 1942 Dönitz, still just commander in chief of U-boats, dropped it to 400,000 in a moment of extreme—and unfounded—optimism. The curious thing is that the fatal tonnage figure seemed to bear no relation to the Germans' estimates of Allied construction. A construction estimate on 14 May 1942 higher than one on 20 October 1942 led to a lower fatal tonnage figure. A reason seems to be that the figure was merely a target, a convenient index, that both Hitler and the OKM inflated or reduced for their own ends in propagandizing visiting statesmen or subordinates or in political infighting.

This figure had no effect on the sea war. Moreover, the erroneous American construction estimates proved to be relatively insignificant in comparison with the two causes of error in the chief problem facing German naval intelligence. This sought to determine how much Allied tonnage was available at a certain time and how much was needed for an operation—basic information for predicting Allied moves. First, the Axis consistently claimed more ships sunk than actually were. The OKM believed, for example, that in September 1942 German, Japanese, and Italian submarines and airplanes had sunk 872,127 gross tons of shipping. In fact, the Allies lost only 567,327. Second, the Germans greatly overestimated the tonnage required to transport troops by sea. Foreign Navies figured that an American infantry division required 300,000 deadweight tons. But only 122,000 were needed. In other words, it thought that almost 250 percent more shipping was required than actually was. This meant that it correspondingly reduced the number of divisions that it believed could be brought to an invasion point—and so dangerously underestimated the enemy capacity for action.

Time after time this led to ruinous misconceptions. "The [Allied] tonnage . . . does not meet the requirements of the transport of a large expeditionary force and its continuous supply," forecast the OKM on 20 October 1942. Three weeks later the Allies invaded North Africa. Raeder had to confess to Hitler that that "proves that there is as yet no shortage of ships for strategic purposes." But several months later the Germans repeated their error. On 20 May 1943, a situation report declared: "The current tonnage situation makes it in any case appear highly improbable that the enemy is in a position to transfer the enormous quantities of personnel and

material required for major actions rapidly out of the assembly areas."
Seven weeks later the Allies landed on Sicily and began the march up Italy
that climaxed in that nation's defection from the Axis.

The statistics on which the Operations Branch based these forecasts
came from Foreign Navies. Captain Norbert von Baumbach, the rotund
former naval attaché in Moscow who was named head of the intelligence
branch in 1942 to succeed Captain Gottfried Krüger, felt that while supplying information on the enemy situation to Operations was his most important work, it was a relatively small part of it. His statistics, in any event,
went uncorrected by any deeper insight into Allied planning that might
have been obtained by spies or intercepts. As a result, Operations sought
to foresee Allied moves geographically on the basis of general principles
of strategy and temporally on the basis of the tonnage figures. But the
former was vitiated by Allied surprise, and the latter proved catastrophi-
cally wrong. The gradual infiltration of Hitlerian conceptions into the situation reports—especially after the replacement of Raeder by the very pro-
Hitler Dönitz—did not clarify the navy's view of the world. It was not the
fact, as Operations stated in 1943, that "The U.S.A. stands equally hostile
to Germany and the U.S.S.R." Baumbach's transfer to liaison with the
army general staff in May 1944, in part for shielding an anti-Nazi, and his
replacement by Rear Admiral Otto Schulze, more palatable to Dönitz,
further testified to this tendency.

The result was that Foreign Navies had an almost wholly negative effect
on the German war effort. Its false tonnage figures, its only major addition
to the enemy picture, led the navy into fatally false conclusions. About the
best that might be said for the 3/Skl is that without it, the OKM might
have erred even more. Perhaps this is what Baumbach meant when, asked
what his branch's contribution to the German war effort was, he replied:
"To have been there."

O Qu IV and
OKW/WFSt/Ic

GENERAL Kurt von Tippelskirch was a short, bull-necked, crew-cut, 45-year-old general staff officer. He came from an old military family—his father, too, was a general—and in 1908 he joined the élite Queen Elizabeth Guard Grenadier Regiment. Wounded and captured at the Marne in 1914, he spent all of World War I in French captivity. Perhaps because of the knowledge of the French he had gained, or was thought to have gained, the army posted him in 1924 to T 3. He left for field service after two years, but returned in 1932 and 1933 as head of the branch's Italy group and as I a, or executive officer. In 1936, he came back yet again, this time as chief. T 3 had then become the 3rd branch of the army general staff. A rather aloof man, Tippelskirch was seen by at least one subordinate as weak but power-hungry and unrealistically optimistic and by a foreigner as not aspiring to more than competent evaluation of enemy forces.

But the man who in 1938 became the new chief of the general staff, Franz Halder, liked and trusted him. So on 10 November 1938, when he divided intelligence evaluation into two branches and created a new assistant chief of staff to supervise both, he named Tippelskirch to the post. The assistant chiefs were called, as they had been since the first was set up in 1882, Oberquartiermeister—apparently alluding to the general staff's origin in quartermaster duties. Three such O Qu already existed; the intelligence post became the O Qu IV. Under it Halder placed the two intelligence branches, Foreign Armies West and Foreign Armies East, the attaché branch, and later a branch that mainly regulated army relations with the Nazi party.

As O Qu IV, Tippelskirch dealt with the higher regions of military intelligence, where it merges into the political. He himself did not evaluate raw intelligence and seldom wrote reports. Rather he sought to assure a uniform standard of work, to handle problems beyond the competency of the individual branches, to coordinate their work and to combine it into a total image. After the outbreak of war, he passed his information to Halder sometimes at the daily situation conferences, sometimes privately. For example, at one time or another Tippelskirch reported to the chief of staff about the picture in general in the east, the apparent lack of Russian intentions in the Balkans, the Hitler-Mussolini conference on the Brenner, French methods in operations and tactics, the transport of apparently three divisions from the east toward Paris the day before the German attack in France, the naming of Lord Beaverbrook as minister for air production in Britain, and the situation in Europe after the fall of France. In addition, nonintelligence duties occupied him. He went to Rumania to see about a German military mission there, made suggestions on propaganda, reported to the army commander in chief on the shooting of women and children in Poland.

Tippelskirch served through the Polish, Norwegian, and French campaigns. But, like many other officers, he really wanted to command a division. Around the fall of 1940, with his headquarters time put in and no operations immediately ahead, Halder told him he could go as soon as his successor arrived from Tokyo, where he was military attaché. The change took place on 5 January 1941.

The new O Qu IV was Colonel Gerhard Matzky, 46, a tall, pleasant infantryman who knew Halder from service together on the staff of a corps in Munich during the 1920s. He had fought on both fronts in World War I and had studied philosophy, economics, history, and international law at several universities. He had served in the League of Nations Branch in the Defense Ministry and become one of the few German officers to attend the Armed Forces Academy in addition to the general staff's famed War Academy. With the start of the Russian campaign, he moved with Halder to the general staff's East Prussian headquarters.

Each morning, after getting information on the enemy situation from his adjutant or his subordinate branch chiefs, he presented this with the branch chiefs at the morning and afternoon conferences of the chief of staff and of the commander in chief of the army. They incorporated this information into their reports at the twice-daily Führer situation conferences. Matzky himself never attended one of these. Like Tippelskirch, he made special high-level reports to Halder: what the English forces totaled, the possibility of Japan's entering the war against England, the expectation that the harvest in the Russian areas conquered by Germany would reach 60 to 70 percent of a normal year, a possible crisis in Vichy France. Since Foreign Armies East and West produced the basic intelligence, he saw his job chiefly as the creation of a balanced picture. He tried to assure, in the face of an overwhelming preoccupation with the eastern front, recognition for information from the west and from politics that could affect German strategy. He failed. Despite his efforts to show that the Mediterranean was also important, Hitler told Halder: "This war on the periphery doesn't interest me."

In September of 1942, Hitler replaced Halder with Zeitzler. The new chief of staff objected to the two remaining Oberquartiermeister—I, for command matters, and IV. Halder had abolished the O Qu II and III positions upon mobilization because he felt they impeded him. They separated him from his branch chiefs. For the same reason, he had moved the Operations Branch from under the O Qu I to a direct subordination with him. During peacetime, the assistant chiefs of staff had reduced his control span from a dozen immediate subordinates to five. But though dissolving the two remaining posts would mean that, formally, the chief would now have some 16 immediate subordinates, in practice he would deal almost entirely with only three—the heads of the operations, eastern intelligence, and supply branches. In war, and with the creation of separate OKH and OKW theaters, the others receded into the background. But Zeitzler also had less disinterested objections. That the O Qu I and O Qu IV were senior to him seemed to embarrass him. He probably felt that, if he fired two of Halder's high appointees, he would reduce the opposition within the general staff to Hitler, in whom he believed. The existence of the OKW theaters meant that half Matzky's work was of no interest to him. Matzky's inability to bring the extra-eastern factors to the command's attention confirmed a general inefficaciousness. Moreover, relations had grown tense between the two men. In July, Zeitzler, then still chief of staff of German forces in the west, had won some glory by playing up the Dieppe raid as a repulsed invasion attempt—a view that accorded with Hitler's. Matzky, however, showing on the basis of captured orders that Dieppe was merely a probe, had clouded this prestige.

As a consequence of all these factors, Zeitzler, on 9 November 1942, the day after the Allies had landed with complete surprise in North Africa, abolished the O Qu IV post. Matzky departed to command the 21st Infantry Division. Foreign Armies East and West and the attaché branch came directly under Zeitzler. The head of the attaché branch, Colonel Horst von Mellenthin, assumed some of the politico-military reporting duties that Matzky had exercised.

The disappearance of the O Qu IV perhaps diminished the weight that the intelligence agencies could, through a high-ranking combined superior, bear on the agencies that procured and on the agencies that used intelligence. Matzky's larger, coordinated view fell away. But these benefits, marginal in any event, vanished in the face of the advantages of the dissolution, the contrast between the fronts, and the difference in the agencies that the two branches served.

Of all the organizational peculiarities that afflicted German military intelligence, the most curious seems the long-time lack at the top of a unit to evaluate enemy capabilities and intentions. For more than half the war, the OKW Operations Staff possessed no such unit of its own. Yet the situation was not quite as irresponsible as it may at first appear.

The OKW had, in fact, an agency for evaluating one kind of intelligence that, like its own functions, extended beyond the parochial interests of the individual services. This intelligence, chiefly politico-military in nature, came from its Foreign Information Division (Ausland), which in turn selected it mainly from the offerings of the acquisition agencies. Before the war, daily conferences between Captain Bürkner, Ausland's head; Canaris, Bürkner's chief; Keitel, head of OKW; Jodl, head of the OKW Operations Staff; Colonel Walter Warlimont, Jodl's deputy; and the other OKW department chiefs assured that the Operations Staff got the broad-based information it needed. The heavier flow of information during the war led to the setting up of a liaison officer from Ausland to the Operations Staff. The conferences continued, though not on a daily basis. If the Operations Staff wanted more specifically military intelligence, it did for information about the enemy what it did for information about German operations, organization, and supply: it procured it from the competent elements of the individual services. In intelligence, this meant chiefly Foreign Armies West, for its field of activity tallied with the theaters of war assigned to the OKW. The staff used the intelligence to draw up plans and to help Jodl report at Hitler's situation conferences.

This arrangement served for the first three years of the war. Some consideration was given to the setting up of a central evaluating agency within the OKW. During 1942, for example, Colonel Ulrich Liss, head of Foreign Armies West, repeatedly urged it. He saw as the ideal solution the subordination of Foreign Armies East and West under Canaris. This would unify acquisition and evaluation under a single intelligence chief in the highest staff. The proposed agency would have served the OKH as well. But though Liss had the support of Matzky, the O Qu IV, he could not persuade Halder, who refused to part with a jot of his empire. At the same time, Bürkner assembled the chiefs of the service evaluating sections to discuss the possibility of an interservice intelligence committee. Luftwaffe antipathy aborted it. But the main reason for the failure to create an I c post in the OKW Operations Staff was that until November 1942 the existing arrangement sufficed.

Then the Allied landing in North Africa exploded large-scale military action in the OKW theaters for the first time. The Operations Staff recognized that it would now be much more closely involved with combat operations and that this in turn demanded more detailed knowledge of the enemy. How should it be supplied?

Two weeks after the landing, Warlimont, an extremely polished and capable officer who was deputy head—and the day-to-day director—of the

Operations Staff, raised this issue with Liss. They agreed that Ausland had neither the organization, the personnel, nor the knowledge for the job. The obvious solution, a more modest form of Liss's earlier proposal, would have been simply to transfer his Foreign Armies West, perhaps bolstered with some air and naval officers, to the OKW Operations Staff. The dissolution of the O Qu IV post had rendered this organizationally more feasible. But the new chief of the general staff, Zeitzler, quashed the idea just as Halder had done. Liss then looked, like Bürkner, into the possibility of a kind of committee of the chiefs of intelligence. He discovered that the Foreign Navies Branch merely furnished what he called "statistical" data to the OKM Operations Branch and did not actually make the enemy situation judgment. And he found that the air force intelligence section with which the army and the navy intelligence branches would have to work, namely, the unit in the Werder deer park, could only have contributed what its frequently absent chief, working with a small "forward" section with Göring at Hitler's East Prussia headquarters, would have permitted—an impossible situation. Liss dropped the committee idea.

The only answer left was that the OKW Operations Staff create its own I c. The choice fell neither on Liss nor on Matzky, probably because both were overqualified for a post seen as merely an adjunct to the Ausland liaison job. Instead Bürkner proposed a new liaison man, who could simultaneously serve as I c.

This was Colonel Friedrich-Adolf Krummacher, then 45. A veteran of World War I, he served in Artillery Regiment 6 in the 1920s with Keitel and Warlimont. In 1929, he went to China as a member of the German military advisory mission to Chiang Kai-shek's government. He stayed there for nine years, traveling, fighting, serving as adjutant to the idolized General Hans von Seeckt, former head of the German army, and gaining a love for China that never left him: back in Berlin after 1938, he sometimes dazzled his colleagues—who nicknamed him Futti-Fu—by appearing early in the morning in colorful Chinese garb. He was a confirmed bachelor, and his enjoyment of the good things of life and his relaxed Oriental philosophy led some of his hyperactive Prussian colleagues to regard him as lazy. But his international experience, which exerted considerable fascination on younger officers, his amiability, his reliability, and his early World War II experience in Ausland I A 3, where he handled the armed forces of western Europe and the British Commonwealth, led Warlimont to accept him as Ausland liaison and as his I c.

At first Krummacher's I c work mingled closely with his liaison activities. Many of the documents that passed over his desk could fit as well into one category as into the other. His more purely intelligence activities consisted at first of distributing the situation report that Foreign Armies West had, in December 1942, started sending over each day.

But with growing experience Krummacher spread his wings. Within a few months he began issuing enemy situation reports of his own every few weeks.

He did not work these up from raw intelligence like the other high-level intelligence-evaluating agencies. Rather he compiled them from the enemy reports of Foreign Armies West, Foreign Air Forces West, Foreign Navies, and Ausland, sometimes touched up with a few fresh details. They were clear and well organized. Often they opened with a concise, one-sentence summary of the situation. On 10 June 1943, for example, a month before the invasion of Sicily, Krummacher began his report: "The overall situation is dominated by the enemy preparations for extensive landing operations in the Mediterranean area." He followed this with half a dozen pages of supporting details.

These reports Krummacher supplemented with memoranda on particular topics. On 18 August 1943, for example, he submitted to Jodl and Keitel a report on the "Possibility of Portugal's Entering the War." Based chiefly on information from the German military attaché in Lisbon and comments of the German mission there on this information, it concluded, totally erroneously, that if the Portuguese government gets no support from the Spanish, "it is certain that Portugal will enter the war against Germany by the end of September at the latest." On 5 January 1944, he got a super-rush request. The Führer had frequently expressed concern about a possible enemy landing in Portugal, and Warlimont asked Krummacher to give him, if possible the same day, for submission to Hitler, maps, information on important Portuguese harbors and transportation routes from them to the east and thence through Spain to the Pyrenees, data on Portugal's armed forces ("three lines"), and information that could help judge the probability of a landing. Krummacher, who by now had three or four

---

A spy report goes up through channels to Hitler. This 1944 message, from a "trustworthy well-informed occasional spy HANS," states that the United Nations will immediately deliver or have just delivered a tough message to the Spanish government pressing for the recall of the Spanish Blue Division fighting the Russians and for the ouster of German agents in Spain. Abwehr I teleprinted it to the I c, or intelligence officer, of the OKW Operations Staff; it went simultaneously to the navy Operations and Intelligence branches and to the Luftwaffe Operations Staff I c. Because it seemed likely to be shown to Hitler, it was copied ("Abschrift") on a "Führer typewriter" with its extra-large type. This copy then came to the adjutant of the deputy chief of the OKW Operations Staff. He marked it to go to the I c (it looks like "T c") and added his "received" mark, the jiggle with downstroke. The Operations Staff I c, Colonel Krummacher, using a red pencil, struck out the "I c" and put his modest initial on (to the right of "Feindmächte"). He apparently brought it to the deputy chief of the Operations Staff, General Warlimont, who, in green, wrote his "W" in Gothic script, followed it by the date, "15/1.," and addressed it to his

Abschrift

Fernschreiben: 15.1. - 16.00
A.Ausl.Abw. I

              An

              WFSt.,Ic
gltd.:   OKM 1.Skl.,
              OKM 3.Skl.,
              Lw.Führ.Stab Ic

Betr.: S p a n i e n ,
        Ultimative Note der Feindmächte.

              Zuverlässiger gut informierter gel.-
V-Mann "Hans" meldet aus feindlicher N.D.-Quelle
unterm 14.1.:

              Ueberreichung befristeter Note ver-
einigter Nationen an spanische Regierung un-
mittelbar bevorstehend oder bereits vollzogen.
Note erinnert einleitend an die von Spanien
übernommene Verpflichtung zur Rückberufung
Blauer Division, Auflösung der Falange und
Ausweisung deutscher Agenten. Gefangennahme
von Angehörigen der Ostfront, ebenso wie das
schleppende Tempo bei der Auflösung der Falange,
wobei die Mitglieder derselben in paramili-
tärische Verbände übergeleitet werden, beweist,

superior, the "Chef WFSt." The chief of the Operations Staff, General Jodl, brought it to Hitler, at one of the twice-daily situation conferences, noting with a fine-pointed pen that "F. hat Kenntnis. Jo," meaning "F[ührer] knows [of this]. Jo[dl]." Jodl's adjutant, Waizenegger, underlined this in his thick blue pencil, drew a large cross to indicate that the document was to go to General Keitel, the OKW chief, dated it "16./1." and initialed it. Finally, Keitel put his large vermilion "K" on it after he read it assistants, got the material to Warlimont, as requested, that day. The three requested lines had, however, swollen to a page and a half, and Krummacher symmetrically balanced each indication for a probable landing with one against it—constituting perhaps less of an aid to decision than the Führer would have wished from his intelligence sources. But Warlimont felt that in general Krummacher quite satisfied his expectations.

When, in the spring of 1944, the RSHA swallowed the Abwehr, some morsels that it could not quite cram down fell from its chops. These included the front-line espionage, counterespionage within the troop units, and enemy deception. Krummacher's unit formed the natural nucleus for these gobbets. By August, however, they had engulfed their host, and Krummacher found himself one element among three in a new section. This dealt exclusively with intelligence matters, and was called the I c of the OKW Operations Staff, the Wehrmachtführungsstab, or, in the cryptogram of German military abbreviations, OKW/WFSt/I c. It had three branches: I, front espionage, a handful of supervisors under Colonel Rudolph, an old Abwehr hand; II, enemy situation, under Krummacher, who in August 1944 shed his liaison function and concentrated exclusively on military intelligence; and III, troop counterespionage and military deception, by far the largest, with almost 300 men.

In charge of all this, with a title—chief I c Wehrmacht—far grander than his powers, was Colonel Hugo Baron von Süsskind-Schwendi, a small, alert general staff officer. He had considerable intelligence experience. In 1936 and 1937 he had served on the French desk of Foreign Armies; during the war, as I c of Army Group North in Russia. His nonintelligence postings included those to the armistice commission with France and as I a for divisions in Africa and Russia.

Süsskind-Schwendi's main job was to make sure that the OKW leadership did not overlook important intelligence. Working mostly at Führer headquarters in East Prussia, he submitted material to Keitel or Jodl once or twice a week, to Warlimont more rarely; occasionally he attended Hitler's situation conferences. He got some of his information from Krummacher, who continued working as before, and he continued to emphasize the results of front espionage, even after that work was transferred to the RSHA's Military Department.

But Süsskind-Schwendi, running what was in a sense the highest intelligence-evaluation agency in the Third Reich, encountered the same obstacle that all the others had: resistance to his information. He discovered late in the war what the other intelligence chiefs had learned earlier in it: that Hitler took notice of his work "more or less reluctantly, for he held that the final victory was certain, and that the enemy forces were strong was something he did not want to know."

22

The Third General Staff Officer

ARMIES fight enemies, and their whole purpose in war is the destruction of those enemies. So it might seem at first glance that the enemy would dominate the thoughts of commanders. Intelligence about him would rule their deliberations, and intelligence officers would virtually control the staff.

But armies cannot win battles without troops to fight with, no matter how much intelligence they may have on the enemy. Getting troops to their positions and seeing that they shoot effectively is therefore the chief job of a commander. His thoughts and decisions deal far more often with his own army's problems than with the enemy's capabilities and intentions. Intelligence is a secondary factor. Of 150 separate items that Chief of the General Staff Halder noted in his diary after discussions with subordinates in August 1941, when his armies were striding victoriously into Russia, only 25 dealt exclusively with intelligence, while 11 more dealt partially with it. In France shortly after the Normandy invasion, telephone conversations between high officers comprised 206 statements dealing with German troops and only 64 on the enemy. In the same way, troop commanders are more important than intelligence officers. That is why one divisional commander once said that, if he had to make the choice, he would rather have a good colonel for one of his three regiments than a good I c for his division.

Because control of one's own forces is of far greater importance than knowledge of the enemy's, operations always governs intelligence. The German army, however, took this rule farther than others. It did not merely regard intelligence as secondary to operations, a feeder of decision-making, as other armies did. It specifically subordinated intelligence to operations. This destroyed the independence that the intelligence branch had within the staff in other armies.

The German army expressed this subjugation most plainly in its basic

Regulation No. 92, *Handbook for General Staff Service in War,* published in 1938. This first pointed out that the operations officer, the I a, handled German operations and could run things in the absence of the commander and the chief of staff. Then it opened its section on the intelligence officer, the I c, with the words, "The I c is the assistant of the I a in determining the enemy picture." In a host of other, more subtle but more deeply ingrained ways, the German army signified further its disdain for intelligence. For example, unlike the French or British armies, it never issued a manual or regulation on the subject until after a year and a half of war. And when it did, that regulation did not ameliorate the subjugation. As if to win acceptance for intelligence in a still distrustful army, the regulation not only affirmed the traditional view but overemphasized it:

> § 16.   The I c is subordinated to the I a and is his helper in working up the enemy picture.
> Estimating the enemy picture is a matter for the commander in cooperation with the chief of staff or the I a.
> The judgment of the enemy situation always proceeds from the command authorities, not from the I c alone.

In practice, this meant that the I c merely filled in the details of an enemy picture already seen in gross by the I a.

This condition represented a middle stage in the evolution of German army attitudes toward intelligence. Before World War I, the army had had, in peacetime, no officers whatsoever assigned to the general evaluation of intelligence. It attributed importance exclusively to the commander, to operations. But World War I compelled the German army to admit intelligence to its staffs. When peace came, it established positions at all headquarters for the general evaluation of intelligence. Yet it did not entirely abandon its former convictions. It continued to exaggerate the importance of the commander's will in piercing the fog of war and of aggressive action in clarifying obscure situations. This prevented it from granting intelligence even a formal equality to operations, with the two officers coordinate— both reporting to the chief of staff. Other armies had done this. The French and Americans, for example, ranged both the G-2, the intelligence officer, and the G-3, operations, under the chief of staff, and even gave intelligence a number closer to 1, though operations naturally retained supremacy in action. The German army could not go that far. It created intelligence positions. But it subordinated them to operations.

These intelligence positions were on the small staffs that the Versailles Treaty permitted the German army to have at its divisional and corps headquarters in the field. The intelligence officers received the sole designation for intelligence that had become uniform during World War I, that at the level of corps, probably because this was a permanent and important element of the prewar German army. This designation was that of third general staff officer, or I c. It stuck.

Because of the suppression of intelligence as a fully independent activity, the German army set out its doctrine on it before World War II in implicit form in regulations devoted principally to superordinate topics—tactics and general staff service. Regulation No. 300, *Troop Command,* a pocket-sized, gray paperbound booklet of 319 pages affectionately called "Aunt Frieda" ("Tante Frieda," from its abbreviated title *T. F.,* for *Truppen-führung*), postulated the basic principles of march, attack, pursuit, defense, and other military operations for German commanders. It related intelligence to the commander's decisions, which he based on his assignment and on the situation; his judgment of the situation comprehended both his own and the enemy's forces.

"One's own assignment is determinative," said the manual, expressing first the need to impose one's will on the enemy that is necessary for any victory. Then, discussing the situation, it stated that a commander, to judge his own, had to know "where the separate elements of one's subordinate forces are located, which are available to carry out one's intentions immediately and which later, whether one can count on further forces and support from neighboring units or whether these will themselves need help. . . . The judgment of the situation on the enemy side has to take place according to the same considerations."

Elucidating the enemy's activities constituted a "self-evident requirement" for the commander. *Troop Command* explained how information about the enemy would first come in as generalities and separate hints, and would solidify with air and ground reconnaissance. An officer would be detailed at each headquarters to handle the flow of information. This would include incomplete and erroneous reports as well as accurate ones, so that uncertainty about the enemy situation would prevail. In trying to determine what the enemy might do, the commander would have to consider "how far the enemy can hinder the carrying out of one's own intentions and how one would act in his place. Such considerations must not lead to bias; rather it is recommended to take as a basis the enemy action that can most damage one's own, insofar as no special reasons are at hand to make another enemy attitude more probable." This principle of most damaging enemy action served as a basic one for German military intelligence. It differed from the French principle, which was to try always to determine the most probable enemy action. This French attitude utilized the intelligence officer; the German in effect dispensed with him, because the commander could judge the most damaging enemy action by himself.

The *Handbook for General Staff Service in War* set out, in general terms, the duties of the I c within the staff. He must keep himself informed of the German situation and intentions. He is responsible for the joint working of all units that produce intelligence. He maintains an enemy situation map. He reports to the I a on important intelligence in the presence of the chief of staff. He makes recommendations for the enemy situation paragraph in orders. (This paragraph was always the first—a tradition dating back to the 1800s. The second paragraph set out the general goal, and the subsequent ones the specific duties of the individual formations.) The I c also made recommendations for the paragraphs ordering reconnaissance.

During the war, the new regulation on *Enemy Intelligence Service,* No. 89, written by Colonel Liss, the head of Foreign Armies West, on the basis of his experiences in the French campaign, did little more than expand these generalities. It spelled out in some detail the characteristics of the various sources and suggested organizations for the I c units at different command levels. It listed the nonintelligence duties that the I c would have. It reemphasized that "The intelligence worker of the command authorities from division upwards can avoid a general staff training only in exceptional cases." It differed from prewar regulations only in two points. Instead of urging a commander to think how he would act in the enemy's place, it warned that the enemy operated not on German principles but on his own and that "his national and racial characteristics also affect his military action." And it permitted the I c at the higher-level staffs to report his intelligence directly to the chief of staff. Thus began in modest fashion the upgrading of the importance of the intelligence officer that was never to stop throughout the war.

Staffs in the sense that they were manned by general staff officers existed in only four levels in the German army: division, corps, army, and army group. Only at these levels, therefore, did a staff officer for intelligence exist. During the war, however, the intelligence function spread further and further downward as Germany was forced increasingly on the defensive. By 1944, it had reached battalion and, in some cases, company level.

Here, virtually at the front lines, intelligence was extremely rudimentary. The battalion commander usually designated the adjutant to handle intelligence as one of several jobs. At some battalions, a noncom who knew the enemy's language would ask prisoners a couple of questions, skim captured documents, and pass back to regiment any enemy information he got from the troops, forward artillery posts, or engineer or antitank units. Other battalions would not even bother to do that, because they were too tired, didn't want to write up reports, and had enough to do with their own problems. At regiment, where the colonel's adjutant handled operational matters, only the assistant adjutant was left for intelligence and supply. He had a couple of interpreters to help in questioning. As at battalion, they had time to ask little more than Where are the guns that are firing at us? and What are your troops trying to do? At this level, the commander and his

The most primitive form of intelligence for the most basic
purpose: A German soldier looks down the barrel of his rifle
to find his foe so he can shoot him

Erich Gimpel, the German who came to spy in America

William C. Colepaugh, the renegade American who came with Gimpel

Park Zorgvliet, the spy school near
The Hague where Gimpel and Colepaugh
were taught

Deputy Sheriff Dana Hodgkins, whose son, Harvard, saw Gimpel and Colepaugh as they trudged along a road shortly after landing on the snowy night of 29 November 1944, points to the small pebbly beach between rock ledges on Crabtree Neck, Maine, where the two spies came ashore from the U-1230

SS Major Dr. Theodor Paeffgen, in charge of Nazi espionage against the Americas

General Friedrich von Boetticher (left) Germany's military and air attaché in the United States, listens interestedly to the commandant of the Monterey, California, Presidio during an inspection of civilian and reserve officers' training activities

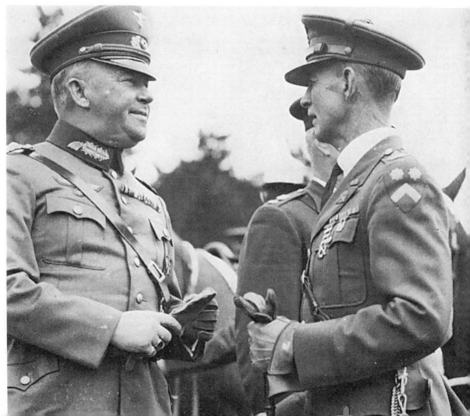

A German soldier strains to peer at the enemy through a telescopic periscope during combat in Russia

General Erich von Mainstein (left), regarded as the most brilliant professional tactician of the German army, visits a front-line post in the Crimea in 1942 to do some basic intelligence work himself: observing where the foe is and what he is doing

Colonel Theodor Rowehl, founder and long-time leader of the Luftwaffe's strategic aerial reconnaissance squadron

A heavy scout car, Sd.Kfz.233 (8-wheel), carrying its antenna over its turret like a scorpion's tail, rolls past a devastated building during the Balkan campaign

Four members of the Rowehl squadron standing in front of one of their spy planes, a Dornier Do 17, on a Hungarian airfield in April 1941 read an early bulletin just after Germany began invading Greece and Yugoslavia. The civilian markings that the squadron had used for its clandestine peacetime flights have begun to be painted over with wartime identification. Two crew members are likewise still in civilian clothes; later all wore Luftwaffe uniforms

The twin-engine Focke-Wulf 189 Germany's standard short-range reconnaissance airplane for the first half of the war in the east

A Dornier Do 17, in its F model the Luftwaffe's first basic long-range reconnoiterer, approaches the English coast. It was replaced by the faster, higher-flying, longer-ranged Ju 88

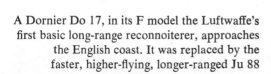

Ground crew readies cameras
for insertion into an Me 109

Some of the larger German
cameras

The Staff Picture Branch of air liaison
of the 1st Army has enlarged to a scale
of 1:400 part of Picture 11 of Film
1701 to show the "Occupied Northern
Spur of the 3-Part Mutterhausen Railroad Gun Position, 7 kilometers southeast of Bitsch"—in the Maginot Line.
Its evaluators have indicated in white
the gun, with a caliber of 28 centimeters (11 inches) and a barrel about
16 meters (53 feet) long, improvements to the roadbed, a switch for
another spur, a munitions and equipment car, and a crane car

iligen
hausen

Verstärkung des Unterbaues

Rohrlänge
etwa 16 m

Geschütz
28 cm

Three key men in Germany's communications intelligence. LEFT, Gottfried Schapper, founder and ultimately chief of Göring's wiretapping Forschungsamt; CENTER, Wilhelm Fenner, technical leader of the OKW's codebreaking agency; RIGHT, Wilhelm Tranow, technical head of the B-Dienst and its English-language specialist

A Russian prisoner of war
talks earnestly to his German captors

Admiral Wilhelm Canaris, head of the German military espionage service, the Abwehr, weary from his wartime work and his anti-Hitler dilemma

Colonel Hans Piekenbrock (shown here as a general), head of the espionage branch of the Abwehr from 1935 to 1943

Colonel Georg Hansen, successor to Piekenbrock and then to Canaris as head of the Abwehr

SS Brigadier Heinz Jost, first head of Nazi party foreign espionage, is pleased to be in full regalia, sword and all

Walter Schellenberg around 1938,
duelling scar still fresh on his chin,
as he began his rise through the SS
hierarchy to oust Jost and become
head of Nazi foreign espionage

The modernistic headquarters of
RSHA VI, Nazi foreign intelligence,
in a former Jewish old folks' home at
Berkaerstrasse 32, corner of Hohenzollerndamm, in southwest
central Berlin

adjutant knew as much about the enemy in front of them as the officer handling intelligence: combat created this intimacy with the foe.

The division was the basic operational formation of the German army; it was the smallest to combine the several arms and be able to maintain itself and fight fairly independently. This demanded a formal staff, including a full-time intelligence officer. The I c here was assisted by a junior officer called the O 3, the third Ordonnanzoffizier, or third assistant adjutant. Under them were a translator or two and a noncom and a couple of privates as clerks. The division basically had to attend only to the enemy forces opposite it. Higher commands, which had geographically more extensive duties, had to know more about the enemy forces, since even somewhat distant ones could affect their operations. Consequently, the higher the command, the bigger the I c staff. At army and army group, the I c formally bore the designation I c/AO, the AO standing for "Abwehroffizier" because the I c at these levels controlled the commitment of the Abwehr troops and commands at the front. At upper levels, the I c had two assistant adjutants as helpers—O 3 and O 6 at corps and army, O 3 and O 5 at army groups. There were usually two translators, a draftsman or two for maps, and half a dozen clerks. These people handled only enemy intelligence.

But all intelligence officers had more than enemy information to occupy their time. The OKH had dumped all sorts of duties upon them, ranging from propaganda to maintaining the morale of German troops by showing movies and bringing in entertainers. In a few areas this included cooperating with the SS murder squads, telling them where Jews were hiding and also occasionally themselves ordering the delivery of Jews to the SS. They also received reports on the numbers killed in or deported from their areas by the SS and their own secret field police; these they filed routinely along with their other military papers.

For the first half of the war, intelligence in the field pivoted on the army level. But by 1943, army group headquarters, which had originally just directed the self-contained armies, gained predominance in command and so in intelligence. They became the most important of the field I cs, with the largest and best-developed organization.

The I c/AO at army group was normally a colonel or lieutenant colonel in the general staff. His O 3 was a rank lower, a lieutenant colonel or major, and his O 5 a captain or first lieutenant. He divided his branch into five groups. Group I, which he himself headed, assisted by the O 3, handled the actual enemy intelligence. Air and communications reconnaissance officers were attached. Group II directed the Abwehr units; III, censorship; IV, secret field police; and V, propaganda, each group with troops subordinated to it. The total I c staff came to only 13 officers and 18 noncoms for a total of 31. In comparison, the G-2 section of the U.S. 6th Army Group consisted of 53, almost twice as many, with a brigadier general at its head.

The Germans made a virtue, not to say a fetish, of the smallness of their staffs. At the higher echelons, they felt that nothing larger was needed, because the identical War Academy training of the general staff officers imparted such uniformity to their work that one of them would know from the briefest of orders or reports what was in the mind of the other. Their staffs had traditionally been small. They believed that smaller staffs worked faster and more efficiently. They got more work out of people. They cut through to the essentials and did not waste time on unnecessary details. They did not tempt the I c to dilate on his information at situation conferences but helped him keep his contribution short, thus sparing the time of the commander for his other, more important duties. High Allied staffs had a meteorologist; the Germans did not. "You can feel that [the weather] yourself," said one I c. "It's just more ballast on the staff. It just lengthens the chief of staff conference." The concept paralleled the German feeling of qualitative superiority. We may have fewer men than the Russians and fewer weapons than the Americans, they told themselves, but ours are better and consequently the equivalent of the enemy's more numerous ones.

In fact the small-staff idea simply rationalized an élite's desire to limit admission. Larger staffs could do far more than smaller ones. When the Allies were planning to invade Sicily, an intelligence staff that eventually numbered in the hundreds worked out four possible enemy reactions to Allied invasion, and selected one as the most likely. It calculated the probable number of enemy prisoners, so the Allied planners would know how many troops would have to be detailed to control them. When Patton was planning one of his "end runs" along the coast of Sicily to outflank the defenders, his intelligence staff spotted possible enemy mine fields and pillboxes, pinpointed machine guns and antiaircraft defenses, plotted drop zones for paratroops—all exactly as an I c would. But the Americans did not stop there. They studied the surf and tides at the landing beaches and drew up new tables of daylight and dark. The I c would have regarded these as unnecessary details, explaining that his commanders would have "felt" about when darkness set in anyway. But the difference is between knowing and guessing, and a general's job is full enough of imponderables to want to rid it of as many as possible. Nor did the large staff necessarily dissipate the commander's time. In Sicily, Patton asked his intelligence officer, Colonel Oscar W. Koch, whether he would bring on a major engagement and thus violate his orders if he attacked Agrigento. Koch, who was backed up by an immense intelligence apparatus, did not explain in detail the location and capabilities of enemy forces, the road and terrain situation, and his reasoning about the probable enemy intention. He just said, "No, sir."

Who were the men who filled the I c posts? For the first part of the war, they were all members of the general staff, that small, tight, and proud aristocracy, alone in the German army entitled to wear the coveted "red trousers"—the wide double carmine stripe that ran down the field-gray jodhpurs and disappeared into the polished, spurred high boots. Even though at first only half the scheduled general staff positions were filled with general staff officers, all the I c positions were. But during 1940, reserve officers who had attended intelligence training courses began being assigned as I cs for the divisions. Though they were doing general staff work, they were not allowed to wear the precious stripes: Chief of the General Staff Halder himself saw to that. Soon reservists alone served in these divisional posts, and within a year, the majority of corps I cs were likewise reserve officers. Often they had done well as divisional I cs; others had served as army or army group O 3s. Many of these reserve I cs, mostly with a major's rank, served in a single post for years, gaining valuable specialized knowledge. For much of the war, the I c ranked lower than the I a. But later, as the importance of intelligence was increasingly recognized, the I c's rank was made the same as that of the I a to raise his status, though it naturally never equalled the I a's.

Army and army group I cs were all general staff officers. The army I c had had experience in one or two staff positions; the army group I c in three or four, one of them the I a at least of a division and if possible of a corps or an army. Colonel Wilhelm Meyer-Detring, the I c of the commander in chief west from mid-1942 to August 1944, had been I a of two divisions before he was promoted to lieutenant colonel and given the job, his first as I c. Colonel Rudolph-Christian Baron von Gersdorff had served successively as O 3 of an army, I c of a corps, and I a of a division before becoming I c of Army Group Center. Though Meyer-Detring held his intelligence job for two years and Gersdorff for three, they both eventually moved on, and both to operational posts, Meyer-Detring in the OKW Operations Staff, Gersdorff as chief of staff first of a corps, then of an army. To get to such a post was the desire of most general staff officers, because here they could do what they had joined the army to do: issue orders to win victories, with all the satisfaction and honor that came with that. These were glories denied to the I c service.

During the war, a general staff officer who was assigned to an intelligence post but who had had no intelligence experience usually went first to Foreign Armies East or West for two to eight weeks. When he arrived at his I c post, his predecessor usually remained with him only a few days before leaving, so that the new man relied in large measure upon his O 3 to work him into the business. Any previous intelligence training would have been a matter of chance or interest. The disguised and dispersed general staff training of the 1920s and early 1930s offered an elective on intelligence evaluation with some exercises in putting together an enemy picture from reports. The War Academy, which was reestablished in 1935, likewise offered a handful of lectures on intelligence, on the Abwehr service, and on foreign armies. No required course on intelligence techniques existed, however. All instruction emphasized tactics. Instructors mentioned intelligence only as an element of the overall picture. But the war changed that. When Halder laid down wartime rules for the instruction of new general staff officers, he ordered that in training at the higher staffs "emphasis is to be laid on I c."

The reserve officers, however, who had not been anointed with the chrism of general staff membership, attended special courses. From 1940 onward, these lasted six weeks and took place at army group headquarters. But the lack of uniformity in the curriculum and the difficulty of making the experiences of one area available to another led in 1942 to Foreign Armies East's decision to institute an intelligence school at Posen (now Poznán). The course lasted three weeks and touched as much upon the current military situation and the enemy forces as on basic techniques. Of the 82 lectures, 24 worked through practical situations. In addition, on active fronts, army groups gave short up-dating courses.

In the west, Army Group B held I c courses. At its second, which ran two weeks in the middle of April 1944, 41 officers from subordinate and neighboring units took part. Among the topics were the I c as the helper of the I a, I c reports, tactical, technical, and organizational innovations of the British and American armies, the aerial photograph and its evaluation, introduction to radio reconnaissance, Nazi leadership, naval matters. Almost every day included a map maneuver. A typical day, Saturday, 15 April, ran like this:

Time	Topic	Instructor
0900–1000	Essentials of the organization and tactics of English and American air fleets	Captain Kirch of Air Fleet 3
1015–1100	Reconnaissance requirements	I c of commander in chief west
1115–1245 1400–1600	Map maneuver (Situation 2, Part C)	I c of commander in chief west
1615–1700	Brief overview of the field of activity of the espionage service	Lt. Col. Waag, Abwehr Main Post West I

Though some officers became O 3s at higher staffs after attending such a course, O 3s for corps and divisions simply learned by experience. The intelligence pamphlets of about a dozen pages issued by Foreign Armies East—the *Pamphlet for Corps and Division I cs* of 1943, and *Troop I c Service in the East* of 1944—as well as the regulation on *Enemy Intelligence Service* further guided and standardized the work. By 1944, the army had recognized the value of intelligence specialists and forbade the use of trained division and corp I cs for other purposes.

The daily routines of the several army group and army I cs in Russia pretty much resembled one another. This was because the staffs operated alike. All commanders held conferences on the situation every morning around 10 in the office buildings or schools or hotels or farmhouses that their staffs occupied. The I c usually attended, coming in from his own room, which was near the I a's office and which had its walls and tables covered with maps and papers. He usually spoke only when spoken to. In addition, all I cs submitted twice- or thrice-daily reports by fixed deadlines to higher authorities. The morning report basically supplied information on the events of the night; it did not attempt any evaluation. Divisions had to send them to their corps by 5 a.m. The corps extracted the most pertinent information, added any from its own reconnaissance organs, and transmitted a consolidated report to army by 6:30 a.m. The armies repeated the process, and so did the army groups, so that their reports reached Foreign Armies East by 9 a.m. The procedure began again at divisions at 4 p.m., ending at Foreign Armies East at 8 p.m. These evening reports were more comprehensive. They often summed up the enemy activities of the past 24 hours. At the lower headquarters they dealt generally with the most important enemy movements observed by the German troops and with the identification or confirmation, usually through prisoners or deserters, of enemy troops opposite. The reports of higher headquarters often concluded with a summary estimate of the enemy situation as it appeared to the I c. Later in the war, armies and army groups added a third report, the daily report. It arrived at Foreign Armies East between midnight and 1 a.m. and included a final situation estimate.

These reports and conferences fixed the rhythm of the I c's day. When Colonel Hans-Adolf von Blumröder, the I c of Army Group South, arrived at his office in Zaporozh'ye about 7 or 7:30 a.m. he found the three or four army I c reports on his desk. He read them, and then began telephoning the I cs. Has anything changed since you transmitted your report? What do you mean by such-and-such? Here we see the situation like this; what do you think? Then he listened in on an extension earphone to the similar conferences of his chief of staff with the army chiefs. He then held a conference with his various specialists—aerial reconnaissance liaison, radio reconnaissance liaison, order-of-battle expert, Abwehr head, and others. They reported their latest intelligence; he told them what information he wanted. This meeting often lasted an hour, sometimes even several hours. While it was in progress, the O 3 would write the morning report and send it off. Then Blumröder gathered up his enemy situation maps, on which the draftsmen had just inked in the new details, and presented his report first to the I a, then to the chief of staff, both in fair detail, and then to the commander, Manstein, who liked these reports as short as possible: Blumröder's seldom took more than five minutes.

Back in his office, he telephoned his neighboring I c, Gersdorff at Army

Group Center, for an exchange of ideas, and the officer at Foreign Armies East who handled his army group. During the rest of the morning and early afternoon he mostly handled paperwork and the nonintelligence aspects of his job. Blumröder flew to the distant front or to the subordinate commands rather infrequently; Gersdorff, on the other hand, very often visited the front units, down as far as battalion, to get his own picture of the situation and to judge the I cs at the lower staffs. This was important, for some were inclined to be too credulous in receiving the reports of their reconnoitering agencies and some overcautious; moreover, some commanders exaggerated enemy activities in order to get more matériel. Knowledge of these situations enabled the higher I c to judge their reports more sensitively.

From about 3:30, Blumröder began again making telephone calls and reading reports and holding conferences. Then came what one I c called the hardest task of all: the assembly of all these various indications into a single comprehensive estimate of what the enemy is doing and, if possible, of what he intends. This comprised the afternoon report. The I c had to submit this to his chief of staff before it could be sent to Foreign Armies East. If an operations order for the next day were to be written, the I c drafted paragraph 1, the "enemy paragraph," summarizing the situation opposite.

In the evening, after dinner, Blumröder made still more telephone calls to keep on top of things, checked to make sure that all was running well in his acquisition organs, sent off his daily report, and finally about 11 or 11:30 left his office to go to bed.

The heart of intelligence work lay in evaluation—in determining the meaning of the various enemy activities. How did the I c do this? How did he move from hundreds of individual observations to a prediction of what the enemy would do, and where and when? Basically, he assembled them and compared this collection with one from a different time or place. The differences offered clues to enemy intentions. That a single Russian spy was captured at Kirov would not mean much. Nor would many arrests scattered randomly within the I c's sector. But if the I c noticed that arrests were clustering at Kirov and not at other points in his area, he could deduce that the Russians were interested in gaining information about Kirov, perhaps as preparation for an attack in its direction.

To automate the assembly of individual items and to facilitate comparisons, the I c noted them on maps. He maintained up to 25 dealing in one way or another with the enemy. Most important was the enemy situation map, which showed the positions of enemy forces. Among the others were the maps showing enemy patrol activity, the results of day aerial reconnaissance, the results of night aerial reconnaissance, the results of radio reconnaissance, enemy agent activity, the enemy air force situation, the enemy artillery situation (both current and at 10-day intervals), the enemy railroad situation, the enemy mining situation, the condition of enemy bridges, the European situation. If on the day aerial reconnaissance map, for example, more trains were drawn in heading toward the front at Kirov than at Vyazma, an attack could be presumed as more likely at Kirov (all other things being equal).

Though the where and the when of enemy action could be shown pictorially and hence most effectively on these maps, further information came from a data bank of another kind. Each I c maintained card indexes of enemy troops, enemy personalities, and enemy field post numbers (to identify units from captured letters). Blumröder called the head of this section "one of my most important people." The troop index included not only the units opposite that German army or army group, but all units identified on the entire eastern front, down to regiments and independent battalions. Each unit's card gave its latest location, its history, strength, commanders, commands to which it belonged, component units, equipment, comments on its battle worth, and so on. Each army group and army kept its file up to date with new identifications on its front, and informed the others via the regular I c reports and by telephone talks between the section heads.

Their most valuable single tool in this order-of-battle intelligence, the most basic intelligence of all, was a thickish pamphlet bound in bright red paper and called the "Red Bible" or the "Red Ass." It listed all known higher units of the enemy army. Different volumes existed for different enemy armies, and Foreign Armies East or West issued new editions from time to time. The August 1944 edition for the Red army, which replaced one of December 1943, ran to 584 pages. The complexity of order-of-battle work is shown by the details that the pamphlet had to include: it carried destroyed units, whose numbers had been freed for reuse, as well as renumbered units, for which it gave both the old and the new numbers. Order-of-battle intelligence served primarily to determine total Soviet strength on the entire eastern front, the datum from which many others flowed. That is why the work was repeated in the several headquarters and at Foreign Armies East. But the cards could also help an individual headquarters. If units suddenly appeared before its sector that had records as Soviet shock troops, the I c could consider that an attack might be in the offing.

The I c could indeed spot indications of enemy action from a single source. But he would have been loath to predict an action to his commander on that narrow basis. He normally made forecasts only when evaluations from one source were replicated by those from another. This was confirmation. Blumröder lived through an almost classical instance.

It was in June of 1944. The southern front swung in a giant curve bending back westward toward the Carpathians in Rumania. The Germans expected a Soviet summer offensive, but where would the blows fall? Would they drive for Stanislav and Hungary beyond it, or would they strike out of their base at Ternopol a bit to the north to punch toward Lvov and Poland? Both possibilities would have been operationally feasible. While Blumröder was pondering the situation, a corps I c reported some visual observations of a small local railroad that ran just behind the Russian front lines. German lookouts at a post on the Strypa River had watched trains on it heading loaded toward the north, crammed full of soldiers, and returning empty to the south.

"Aha," said Blumröder to himself. "They're yanking somebody out of there and bringing him up to Ternopol." The evidence for the movement

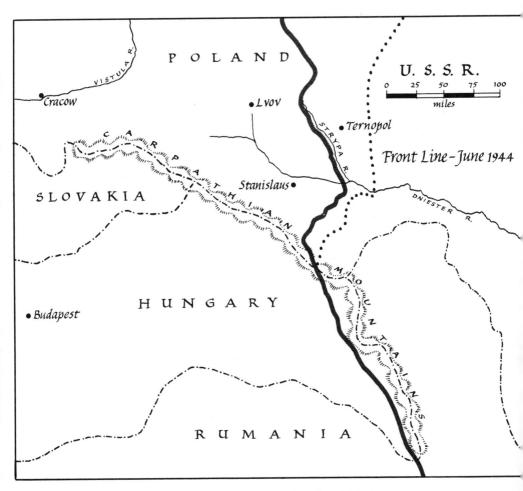

The area of shifting of the Russian 38th Army

was quite solid, but it came from only one source, and the conclusion about Ternopol rested strictly on speculation. Suddenly new information arrived. The Germans had downed a Soviet courier plane. It turned out to belong to the 38th Army, and the artillery officer in it, together with papers he was carrying, corroborated that the Russians were indeed shifting the 38th Army from the southern part of their front, opposite Stanislav, to Ternopol, opposite Lvov. And when, in July, the Russians attacked, the Germans, certain of their confirmed intelligence, were ready. The 38th Army advanced only 10 miles in the first two days, and then, under German counterattacks, even recoiled a little.

This kind of confirmation, of substantiation, is what I cs meant when they spoke of their work as "mosaic work." Bits and pieces of separate and varied items coalesced into a coherent picture. The most valuable information came from verbal evidence. At the tactical headquarters, this was prisoner-of-war intelligence. At the operational, it was radio intelligence. But the greatest volume and the most certain information came from the physical observations of the front-line troops. Foreign Armies East, in its pamphlet *Troop I c Service in the East,* listed some of these that would indicate a Soviet attack: feeling out the German front by increased reconnaissance and raiding-party activity; reconnaissance behind the German front by partisans, explorer troops, and spies; narrowing of the fronts of enemy units (determined by observation of reliefs, changing of the sentry routes, prisoner statements); pushing forward of the trench system as a jumping-off point for the attack; increased air activity (night fighters dropping parachute flares, bombing of individual targets). Higher-level observations offered more clues to Soviet intentions. Radio silence, the appearance of shock troops, stronger air protection over certain areas implied preparations for an attack. The disappearance of known formations, deception attacks, and decreases in artillery firing, air activity, partisan activity, agents, and deserters indicated defensive intentions. Any thickening of any activity in any area would point to the probable place of attack: special density of the radio net, greater depth in troop preparation areas, above all a massing of artillery, mortar, and tank positions. German I cs could often even tell roughly when the Russians would attack from the pattern of their activities. Reconnaissances in force, up to a regiment in strength, began eight to ten days before an attack. Radio silence was broken four or five days before. Heavy weapons arrived in their positions two or three days before the attack. The number of deserters swelled at the same time. And when the Soviet soldiers were given liquor, the attack was soon to come.

Intelligence work is not cut and dried. Different officers can draw different conclusions from the same evidence. In the summer of 1944, the OKH asked Army Group North to shift some of its reserves to Army

Group Center, which the Russians were threatening. North's commander and chief of staff were inclined to consent, for they saw no immediate danger of a Russian attack. The Soviets had thrice failed in an offensive aimed toward Latvia and would probably not try again. In fact, they were now attacking at other points, with partial success. Moreover, air reconnaissance showed enemy forces pulling back 6 miles here and there.

But the I c interpreted these signs differently. That the Russians were pulling back the relatively short distance of 6 miles meant no basic retraction of the front but only that they were resting and refreshing their forces there. The new attacks at the other points were only partially successful because no extra forces were being brought up to follow through. This suggested that they were only deceptions or attacks to bind German forces. The I c also felt that three attempts meant the Russians wanted their goal —the main Latvian port of Riga—very badly. He thought that they would not give up on this prize, even after three failures. After considerable discussion, the I c convinced his superiors of his views. The commander then got permission to hold his reserves for an additional week before releasing them. On the seventh day came the Russian attack. The army group repulsed it.

The I cs based their predictions on the same inductive logic that men use in their daily lives. This rests on probabilities, derived from experience. It holds that when one thing has been found repeatedly associated with another, and never dissociated from it, it will probably also be associated with it in the future. One hundred, one million elephants have gray skins; the chances are that the million-and-first will too. Certain signs have regularly pointed to a Russian attack; the I c expects an attack when he sees them. When the Germans captured a couple of deserters from a single regiment, they inferred the presence of a whole Russian army, for they had found that the Russians generally kept their fighting formations intact, so that divisions (and their regiments) and corps stayed together in an army for long periods of time.

But a gap exists in inductive reasoning that posed a danger to the I cs. Enemy deception can creep through that gap. The philosopher David Hume first analyzed the problem of induction. Nothing in logic requires that future events of a certain kind be like past ones. Differences are thus always possible. The million-and-first elephant may be white. Induction expresses only probabilities. It is true that the more often associations of events have occurred in the past, the more likely they are to occur in the future. But this is not certainty, and the exception can always slip through the rift in induction.

The intelligence officers, though they may not have known the Humean grounds, were as aware of the situation as anyone. They knew that the past did not entail the future. So they wondered in many instances whether a certain set of circumstances represented a repetition of an old pattern or something different—in particular, a deception.

Did they detect any? Did the Russians fool them? The answer in both cases is No. The main reason is that the Russians seem never to have launched a major deception. They did not have the armor and the manpower to march troops about uselessly to trick the Germans; they preferred to use their men to attack. Of course, they often successfully camouflaged their troops and tanks, but this is not the same thing. The Russians did frequently mount radio deceptions. But the acute German radio intelligence as frequently saw through them. Even if the listening teams had missed, the I cs believed, the fine-meshed German intelligence would have spotted the deception by disclosing the lack of the troop and supply movements that it was supposed to be representing.

Though most of the I c's work was directed upward, toward his commander, some of his information went to subordinate officers and men. This forewarned them of enemy characteristics. Shortly after the 2nd Panzer Division had arrived in the west from the Russian front at the start of 1944, its I c issued an 8-page "enemy information sheet" on the British army. He had rewritten it from Foreign Armies West and Luftwaffe I c publications. "The British soldier is brave, tough, and indifferent to setbacks," he began. Further down he evaluated other Empire troops. "The combat value of the Australian and New Zealand troops is not all so good; the inner discipline is considerably inferior to that of the English." The I c discussed the "methodical" leadership of higher officers and the more "flexible" of lower as well as the organization of the several arms and services. He then set out the British attack technique. For an infantry division, the attack "is carefully prepared" and "where possible begun before daybreak. . . . The commitment of the tanks takes places in several waves. The first wave mainly has the assignment of knocking down the enemy anti-tank weapons. If possible, it should not get more than 1,000 yards ahead of the following infantry. . . . If the attack gets stuck at some point, the troops screen themselves with smoke and under this cover change the direction of the push." These specifics sought to inoculate the German troops against surprise and enable them to fight the enemy more efficiently. In the same way, and for the same reasons, the intelligence officer of the 15th Panzer Division distributed to his fighting troops an illustration that showed how best to attack an American tank by pointing out right and wrong places to fire at it.

Much of the effectiveness of intelligence depended, of course, upon the I c himself. Not all were good. An officer on an inspection tour in Normandy in 1944 reported that, in battle at least, the work of the I c of the 2nd Panzer Division "was not very convincing. Insufficient maps, no card index

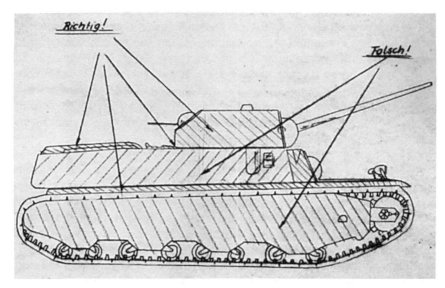

The 15th Panzer Division intelligence officer passes word as to the right and the wrong places to attack an American tank

of enemy units." The I c of the 238th Infantry Division in Italy did little more than keep books on enemy data; the actual evaluations were made by the I a and the division commander. When he was chief of staff of the 7th Army in France during the Allied invasion, Gersdorff, himself a former intelligence officer, had to fire three I cs before he found one who could handle the job properly. Other intelligence officers proved extremely satisfactory. The inspecting officer in Normandy commended the "good work" of the I c of the 17th SS Panzer-Grenadier Division. Of the intelligence officer of the XXXXVIIth Panzer Corps, he noted: "The section is very trustworthy and makes a gratifying impression. There were very detailed and well-taken-care-of situation cards. The I c knows exactly what's what in his sector and shows considerable interest in the enemy forces in the other parts of the bridgehead."

Another determining element in an I c's effectiveness was his relationship to his superiors, especially his commander. The I c's job alone placed him in a difficult situation. More than any other person on a staff, he represented bad news. The commander wanted basically to hear that no enemy would oppose him, but the I c's job was to tell him the opposite. Often a commander felt that the I c was making things appear blacker than they were, and that this might weaken or cripple the all-important will to fight. Moreover, unlike I a reports, good or bad, I c information was uncertain, as shifting as sand, as insubstantial as fog. Yet the commander had to base one leg of his situation judgment upon it to make his decisions. The I c could, in effect, thwart a commander's desires more often than others, could compel him to discard a carefully thought-out plan. His information was negative, pessimistic. Pharaoh slew the bearers of bad tidings. The commander rejected or ignored his I c.

During the campaign in Greece, the chief of staff of the 12th Army simply refused to allow his I c into his presence for days at a time. Other commanders said to themselves, "Here comes the I c with his same old stuff. But I'm going to do it like this anyway." Then they asked him basically to confirm their view of the situation. Often, however, a good intelligence officer could sell himself and thus his product. At Army Group Center, Field Marshal Günther von Kluge was at first not interested in Gersdorff's intelligence. But after the I c presented his material in a professional way several times, Kluge wanted it regularly. No doubt the mutual understanding between general staff officers, similarly trained to think alike, contributed much to this acceptance, but the character and ability of the I c did as well. This led eventually to the most important element in how a commander used intelligence material: his confidence in the man who brought it to him.

When a commander trusted his I c, and in consequence believed the information he brought him, the result was often military effectiveness. This happened with Blumröder and his commander, Manstein, in February and March of 1943. It followed the débâcle of Stalingrad, and the Germans were counterattacking in what was to be their last successful offensive. Manstein, who was considered the most brilliant among the professional tacticians widely regarded as the world's best, told Blumröder, "Tell me what's going on there, and I'll act accordingly." And he did. He listened to what Blumröder told him in his five-minute presentations. Then he used this intelligence to pull his forces out from where the enemy was weak and to throw them in where he needed them to advance across the southern steppes in so dazzling a style that it left not only his own staff but also the Russians gasping in amazement.

But the I cs also learned that intelligence alone cannot win victories. It requires troops and guns. When these were lacking, even the most solid intelligence availed the Germans nothing. The classic case occurred in Normandy on the two days following D-Day, 1944.

On 7 June 1944, as the battle raged to hurl the Allies back into the sea whence they had invaded Hitler's Fortress Europa, Grenadier Regiment 916 got the order to counterattack the American forces that had established themselves in Vierville-sur-Mer, a village just above landing beach OMAHA.

The Germans advanced, and during the fire fight, a youngish American officer, possibly a member of an advance echelon of a staff, was killed. The Germans found his body just to the east of Vierville-sur-Mer, and, in a briefcase he was carrying, they discovered the top-secret operations plan of one of the two main American assault commands, the Vth Corps. Word of this reached higher headquarters at about 10 p.m. Details followed. At about 1 a.m. 8 June, these were telephoned to the commanding general of the LXXXIVth Corps and then to the chief of staff of the 7th Army. When the 100-page document itself came in later that day, it was forwarded to the 7th Army for a more detailed evaluation. By the evening of 8 June, its most important contents had reached Army Group B and the commander in chief west.

The mimeographed order told the Germans the composition and the goals of the Vth Corps: "The V Corps, consisting of the 1st, 28th and 29th Infantry Divisions, with the 2nd and 5th Ranger Battalions and other forces attached, will assault Beach 'OMAHA,' reduce enemy resistance, secure VIERVILLE-SUR-MER–COLLEVILLE-SUR-MER beachhead and advance southward toward St. Lô to cover the landing of other troops and supplies of the First United States Army."

While the Germans were digesting this, they got another windfall. During the early morning hours of 8 June, members of the 914th Infantry Regiment looked into a boat that had drifted ashore in the wide, marshy mouth of the Vire River, which separated OMAHA beach from the other American landing beach, UTAH. In it they found a copy of the top-secret operations plan of the other American assault command, the VIIth Corps.

```
      2.  MISSIONS.  a.  The V Corps, consisting of the 1st, 28th and 29th Infantry
Divisions, with the 2nd and 5th Ranger Battalions and other forces attached, will
assault Beach "OMAHA", reduce enemy resistance, secure VIERVILLE-SUR-MER -- COLLE-
VILLE-SUR-MER beachhead and advance southward towards ST. LO to cover the landing
of other troops and supplies of the First United States Army.  The rate of advance
will be in conformity with the advance of the Second British Army and instructions
issued by Headquarters, V Corps, at the time.  (See Operations Overlay - Annex No.
11).
```

A portion of the invasion orders of the U.S. Vth Corps, captured by the Germans just after the D-Day landings

By 6:40 a.m. the chief of staff of the 7th Army was teleprinting the essential details to the I a of Army Group B: "Assignment: Attack out of the Carentan-Quineville bridgehead in direction north and take Cherbourg from landwards." It was exactly right.

So, within 48 hours of the start of the invasion, the Germans had in their hands the entire order of battle and plan of operations for the American units in the first phase of the onslaught. It was a sensational find, of which intelligence officers can usually only dream. But it was less revelatory than it appeared. The capture of Cherbourg had been foreseen by the Germans as a prime American target; the captured documents, the 7th Army said, merely "confirmed the views of the army about the enemy's operational intentions." The drive on St. Lô was recognizable by the second day of fighting. Most important of all, geography and Allied strength nullified the effects of the information. American air superiority prevented the Germans from bringing up fresh troops or shifting those already there fast enough to block the intended American moves. And the danger of a breakout toward Paris and hence Germany by the British, who were east of the Americans, caused far greater concern than the American moves toward the west and south: the Germans had to guard against this with strong forces.

Thus German intelligence's possession of virtually complete information about American intentions could not and did not affect the German defense in one of the most critical battles of the war. Intelligence is a secondary factor. It is useless without strength. The best I c could be no better than his general's strongest regiment.

Foreign Armies
East and West

THE most important event in the history of German military intelligence took place on 25 January 1919.

Amid the tumult of defeat and Communist uprisings, the chief of the General Staff of the Field Army created as of 1 February the first unit for the general evaluation of intelligence ever to exist in a peacetime German army. He transferred what had been the Foreign Armies branch of the wartime General Headquarters, then being demobilized, to the reconstituted Great General Staff.

When, under the interdiction of Versailles, that staff disguised itself as the Troops Department, Foreign Armies likewise hid behind a less obtrusive title. It was renamed the Statistical Branch, a term that harked back to the nineteenth century, when the collection of information on foreign countries was known as "military statistics." As the third branch of the Troops Department, it was also known as T 3.

In the transition period the branch retained the same chief it had had throughout the war, Major von Rauch. He was succeeded in June of 1920 by Major Friedrich von Boetticher, the future military attaché in Washington. Boetticher first divided the unit into eastern and western desks. Among his successors was Colonel Erich Kühlenthal, later military attaché in Rome and father of the Abwehr spymaster in Spain. During these first years, T 3 averaged 16 officers (not counting the four-man Abwehr unit attached to it). Several later rose to high staff rank: First Lieutenant Hans Jeschonnek, later chief of staff of the Luftwaffe; Captain Dr. Hans Speidel, later chief of staff to Rommel during the Normandy invasion; and Captain Alfred Jodl, later chief of the OKW Operations Staff. But not one member of T 3 achieved fame as a fighting general in World War II—a significant indication of how the general staff kept its best men out of intelligence.

Two months after Hitler took power, Colonel Carl-Heinrich Stülpnagel assumed command of T 3. Stülpnagel was a modest man, who sought less to impress people than to do his work, though some thought him "a bull in a china shop" in blatantly urging some of his anti-Hitler views. With Ludwig Beck, a future chief of the general staff, he wrote the little official manual *Troop Command*—"Aunt Frieda"—that taught tactics to so many commanders during World War II. Stülpnagel commanded an army when Hitler invaded Russia; later he served as military overseer of occupied France; in 1944 he and Beck lost their lives after the unsuccessful plot to assassinate Hitler.

Stülpnagel laid the foundation for the work of the intelligence branch in World War II. It had, several years before, dropped its mask and resumed the blunt title of "Foreign Armies." Now, in the heady years that Germany quit the League of Nations, won back the Saar, denounced Versailles, began to triple its army, and marched into the Rhineland, T 3 expanded.

Former officers, hired as extras, helped handle the flow of intelligence that had increased with the dispatch of attachés, the growth of the Abwehr, the expansion of radio intelligence. Most of its information still came, however, from the daily and military press, which the staff spent its morning reading. The officer responsible for Great Britain and its Commonwealth received the *Daily Telegraph,* the *United Services Review,* the *Journal of the Royal United Services Institution,* the *Army Quarterly,* the *Royal Engineers Journal,* the *Journal of the Royal Artillery,* the *Royal Army Service Corps Quarterly,* and the *Cavalry Journal;* the western group leader took *The Times.* The branch collected population statistics; these would help estimate enemy army size on the prewar principle that every million civilians could furnish the manpower and the support of two divisions. The officers entered these and other details, such as figures for the military budget, into an orientation logbook for each country. In the spring, the branch issued booklets summarizing all this and reviewing major nations' military capabilities and probabilities in a war against Germany. It also watched the current situation. During the Saar plebiscite in 1935, Stülpnagel pessimistically warned of threatening French military movements on the borders—though nothing happened.

The following year, Stülpnagel moved on to the command of a division and a general's rank. Replacing him in charge of what was then the 3rd branch of the army general staff was Colonel Kurt von Tippelskirch—he who was destined to become the O Qu IV. Tippelskirch continued and consolidated Stülpnagel's work. Under him, Foreign Armies comprised an administrative group, an attaché group, a registry, and five geographical groups, assembled into an east and a west echelon. But Hitler's aggression was transforming one nation after another into potential enemies, and his rearmament was giving the army additional manpower. So on 10 November 1938—coincidentally the day after the rest of the world learned with horror of the Night of Broken Glass, an orgy of anti-Jewish beatings and property destruction brutally revealing of Germany's mood—the new chief of the general staff, Franz Halder, doubled his intelligence establishment. He created Foreign Armies West, which retained the designation of 3rd branch of the general staff, and Foreign Armies East, which became a new branch, the 12th. They served as the key intelligence agencies of the Third Reich— those that made the most important intelligence evaluations. Over them Halder placed Tippelskirch as O Qu IV.

Halder also appointed Lieutenant Colonel Ulrich Liss as chief of Foreign Armies West. Liss was a big man, rather imposing, fresh-complexioned, just over 40, unmarried, a bit grumpy in the morning, an artilleryman, and a brilliant horseman who had won some 46 tournament prizes. He had a far broader knowledge of the world beyond Germany than the typical general staff officer. He loved the English, had visited their country several times and spoke their language well. He also knew French and Italian. Liss first came to Foreign Armies in 1931, and, with the exception of the obligatory breaks for service with the troops, stayed with it continuously until 1943. He had risen to be head of the west echelon when he became chief of the entire new branch. He was eventually promoted colonel, the usual rank for a branch chief.

A few days before Hitler invaded Poland, most of the general staff moved from the tan stucco building on Berlin's Bendlerstrasse that it shared with the OKW and the rest of the OKH to its field headquarters at a camp near Zossen, a town 20 miles south. Foreign Armies West remained in Berlin, close to virtually its sole source, the Abwehr. On 1 September, when Hitler spoke to the Reichstag to announce that since 5:45 that morning Germany had returned the fire that regular Polish troops had the night before hurled upon German territory, Liss went to a favorite restaurant to hear him. He drove out the Wilhelmstrasse and through the Brandenburg Gate. The contrast with 1914 was stark. Then, cheering people had packed the streets to welcome the war. Now, just a file of SS men in their black uniforms stood along Liss's entire route. Behind them in the Tiergarten thronged only the silent trees. It was, for Liss, an eerie feeling.

The next day, the French closed their frontier. This reduced the inflow of spy reports, and Tippelskirch permitted the branch to go to Zossen (East was already there). Liss, his men, and his files left in the afternoon and arrived toward evening. Their gasproof bunker had a steep, A-shaped roof, designed so that bombs would skid off it; the cellar, protected by a meter of reinforced concrete, exactly reproduced the ground-floor offices, so that work could continue even during an air raid. Similar bunkers, for the other branches of the staff, stood in two semicircles, called MAYBACH I and II; all were connected by tunnels. The entire camp, with its barracks, stables, and garages scattered on the piny plain, was codenamed ZEPPELIN. Liss's building was not quite ready, and as the branch moved in, drills still echoed and dust hung in the warm summer air. In the officers' mess that evening, he met his former branch chief, Stülpnagel, now the O Qu I, or first assistant chief of staff, who brought him up to date.

During the "Phony War," Foreign Armies West had embarrassingly little to do. Every day at 10 a.m. Liss and the other major branch chiefs assembled in Stülpnagel's office for "morning prayers"—the situation conference. Liss spoke first, but had little to report; he sometimes felt that his picture of enemy forces looked as blank as nineteenth-century maps of Africa. Much of the rest of the day was spent waiting around for the conference with Halder, who was mainly occupied with the campaign in Poland. This gave Liss, who was a lover of French cuisine, time to gripe about the food at Zossen. It consisted of field rations—a good idea in theory, but in practice little suited to the mentally taxing work of a general headquarters, Liss felt. Until the start of the offensive against France in May 1940, the night workers could not even get coffee. Liss swore that no other army in the world treated its key officers in so counterproductive a spartan fashion.

He spent some of his time building up the branch. Two months after the start of the war he had expanded its officer cadre to 16. In recruiting clerks, he seized upon an idea of Stülpnagel's adjutant, in civilian life a banker. He employed bank clerks, who—then, at least—were proficient in languages, were used to quick exact work, and could take dictation on the typewriter—rare in males. For the reserve officers, Liss sought men with broad horizons and foreign experience, such as journalists and businessmen who had lived abroad. He found lawyers less suited for intelligence work, feeling their thinking was too formal and abstract.

But all group heads and officers in key positions were general staff officers. None had received any special intelligence training. The belief was that their studies at the War Academy and their general military experience fitted them for judging the tactical importance and meaning of items of information. They learned their intelligence work on the job. This generally took from three to six months, longer if a man was to be a group head. It was assumed that it would take a year for a newcomer to contribute something of his own.

Chief considerations in selecting a general staff officer for the branch were in the first years knowledge of foreign languages and experience abroad. These qualifications, and those of impartiality and thoroughness which are often found in persons having them, conduce to intelligence success. But they are, rightly, less prized in armies than those required for the more important job of commander—decisiveness, drive, resolution. Consequently, the men chosen for intelligence were often those left after the Operations Branch had taken its pick. Later in the war, however, the branch —like its eastern twin—employed a number of wounded officers who may not have had these intellectual qualities but did have the experience of combat.

Once a man had served in intelligence, he was likely to remain there, for knowledge about enemy armies, which took much time to acquire, was too precious to waste. This specialization was at first anathema to many general staff officers. They saw themselves as military generalists and feared that, as Liss said, they would "gain the good conduct medal instead of the Knight's Cross and the experiences of happier comrades." But many of them got hooked by intelligence work. Captain Lothar Metz arrived "very unwillingly" in 1940, but found that the work soon "fascinated me," in part because he had a much broader view of the war than in a divisional I a post, in part because he felt he could contribute to the decisions of the high command. Liss wrote to a friend:

"Since I came from East Prussia to the 3rd Branch, I have never been, and, except for the job of military attaché in London later, never again will be in a post that so satisfies and fulfills me as the present one. I can utilize my three languages daily, I can employ all the technical and personal knowledge gained over the years . . . and finally my branch can quite often throw its judgment into the scales. . . . Once the intelligence business has grabbed you, it doesn't let go so easily."

Still, to gain at least some broader experience, to maintain contact with the troops in the field, and above all to qualify for promotion, the general staff officers of Foreign Armies West usually left the branch for a year or two for service at the front. Then they returned to where their expertise could best be used.

Liss, who had complained bitterly about the "failure" of the Abwehr to report on French dispositions at the start of the war and was consequently regarded by it as a grumbler, spent part of his time during the months before the German offensive working with the spy agency to improve its work. He attended an Abwehr conference in Frankfurt-am-Main with Canaris. He set up courses at the branch for Abwehr officers to show them how their spy reports fit into the larger picture. In addition, he visited the front a few times. He held conferences at Düsseldorf and at Wiesbaden for the I cs in the west. He told them what he needed and they told him what they wanted. A more memorable result was the "west cocktail." This new drink consisted of equal parts of the liquors typical of the 10 or so countries studied by the branch—gin for England, Campari for Italy, for example. The I cs all liked it, Liss insisted.

He supervised the writing and issuing of new memoranda on the several western enemy armies, new brochures with pictures of enemy tanks and weapons and insignia for the troops, and new maps of enemy fortifications. The branch's output compared favorably, Liss thought, with that of a profitable publishing house.

After the conquest of Norway, Liss was summoned to his second and last audience with Hitler. (The first had been in 1938, when he briefed him on the impression that the French troops had made on him during a review at Versailles in honor of the visiting King George VI.) Hitler was interested in the British prisoners, and he had Liss bring an officer and a noncom who spoke German before him in the garden of the Reich chancellery. After Hitler had questioned them and started to leave, he turned and said: "Well, boys, when you write home, you can write that this war is unnecessary."

Liss's main occupation during early 1940 was to build up a picture of the enemy order of battle. Patrols, prisoners, air reconnaissance brought in tidbits of information. The espionage service, paralyzed at the outbreak of war, revived. Radio reconnaissance, including the solution of French War Ministry cryptograms, shed the most light. The officers of the branch received this flood of minute details and marshaled them into a coherent pattern. Gradually the empty map of enemy dispositions filled in, as did the huge table of the French army elements. The branch provided stereoscopic pictures for the troops who were to descend upon Belgium's Fort Eben Emael, one of Belgium's most modern fortifications. But errors and blank spots still remained. The branch listed the French 9th Army as the 1st, and could not answer a critical question—whether the French had enough reserves around Verdun to counterattack northward against the flanks of the planned German armored thrust out of the Ardennes.

When that thrust came, combat helped Foreign Armies West clear up many of these problems in a performance that its officers regarded as its greatest success. Working out of field headquarters to stay close to the chief of the general staff, who had moved near the front, it spotted 122 of the 123 French and English divisions in France. Its maps showed the bulk of these in northwestern France and Belgium, awaiting the death stroke of the panzers, and indicated that enemy forces were so sparse around Verdun that no counterstroke was likely. It was not perfect: it once lost sight of an entire Belgian army of half a million men. And, in a deeper sense, it was not needed, for Manstein and Hitler had prepared their sickle-cut advance long before this intelligence was available.

Moreover, the branch barely rose above its prewar, quasi-statistical function. Its situation reports merely listed enemy units and their location. It almost never summed up the situation, much less predicted what the enemy might do. It ceded that task to the Operations Branch. This resignation of one of its basic assignments further indicated the total subservience of intelligence to operations in the German army.

Only after fighting had ceased in western Europe, when there was no longer any chance of conflicting with the views of an operations branch directing a battle, did Liss venture to forecast enemy probabilities. At the very end of 1941, for example, he submitted a 17-page report on "Possibilities of the British War Leadership in the Middle East in the Year 1942," which concluded that lack of forces would prevent the British from doing little more than "secure their occupation" in the area.

Liss ran the branch in liberal fashion. If a man showed that he was capable of doing the work well, Liss left him alone. Otherwise he supervised the subordinate closely. He was a tough editor on the written reports. "I can't give that out," he would tell his young staff officers. "You can say that in half the space. Do it again." And they did. He himself was the master of a facile, limpid prose style, with un-Germanically short, uncluttered sentences. He used it after the French campaign in writing secret Army Regulation 89, *Enemy Intelligence Service,* whose 43 pages constituted the first official manual in intelligence that the German army had ever had. He had some organizational problems. Just after Pearl Harbor, when Hitler declared war on the United States, he lost the U.S. desk. It was sent to Foreign Armies East, in part because of a lack of personnel at West, in part because the Japanese specialists were at East and the O Qu IV held that the two countries had to be worked on together, since the Germans expected the Americans to concentrate on the Pacific. But after the Americans and the British landed in North Africa in November 1942, it was hastily returned to Liss. With its restoration, the branch numbered 97 officers, men, and employees.

Early in 1943, Liss departed the agency that he had so largely shaped and built up. He had to serve at the front to be promoted. Zeitzler, the new chief of the general staff, gave him a regiment in Russia. Soon Liss rose to general and the command of an infantry division. On 22 January 1945, he was wounded and captured by the Russians.

His replacement was a former subordinate. Sharp-faced, sharp-minded Lieutenant Colonel Alexis Baron von Roenne had had charge of the big table of French forces during the glorious days of the blitzkrieg into France. Just 40, he had been born in Latvian Russia into one of the noble German families that largely ran the territory; he spoke fluent Russian. Early in 1942, he was transferred to Foreign Armies East, then totally absorbed with the campaign in Russia. As the new head of Group III, which evaluated captured documents, Roenne rapidly upgraded its work, eliminating the translation of outdated papers and concentrating on the active processing of useful material. Foreign Armies East's new chief, Reinhard Gehlen, soon made him his I a, and Liss, when he heard about it, said, "There he has *the* post for which he was born." When Liss departed, Gehlen, who with the elimination of the O Qu IV post had been told to keep an eye on Foreign Armies West, urged that Roenne become chief of that branch. This he did on 1 March 1943. As chief, he was meticulous and somewhat rigid; he could be superior and sarcastic to his juniors; but behind his rimless spectacles and compressed lips there worked a brain as clear as glass.

Liss had failed to predict the Allied invasion of North Africa, and the following year Roenne, in part misled by the fake papers floated ashore at Spain on a corpse, was surprised by the Allied assault on Sicily. Later he was embarrassed by the unexpected Allied landings at Anzio and Nettuno.

Hitler was fully aware of these failures, for he remarked in exasperation a few months later that "the few landings that they have made, we didn't spot at all." Now Roenne faced the most difficult task ever given a German intelligence officer: to discover where and when the Allies would strike in their gigantic cross-Channel invasion.

He and his officers pulled together all the available evidence. Well aware of the possibility of double agents, they agonized in particular over the spies' reports.

FOREIGN ARMIES WEST

1 December 1944

I a
> I a Situation

Group I—Administration
> 3 desks

Group II—France, Belgium, Holland, Spain, Portugal, Switzerland, Italy
> Desks a to f

Group III—British Commonwealth
> Situation Subgroup
>> Desks 1 and 2
>
> Evaluation Subgroup
>> Desks a to d

Group IV—Southeast Area
> Situation Subgroup
>> 2 desks
>
> Desks a and b

Group V—United States of America, Central and South America, Pacific Area
> Situation Subgroup
> Evaluation Subgroup
>> Desks a to d

Fortifications Group

Special Units
> Liaison officers
> Interrogation units

"Ten times the man has reported correctly," Lieutenant Colonel Richard Euler, for a while in charge of the American group, would say to himself. "Is it also right this eleventh time? Or is it backwards? Has something been played into his hands to confuse us?" These determinations, he said, were often "really not simple.

"I always started with the assumption that 'It's not so,' and then I gradually pulled out what perhaps actually could be. Not the other way around: that's too dangerous." Even so, the results were seldom completely solid. "You sit and sit and figure and write it up. And then you can only say, 'It must be something like this.'" Nor did he gain any great sense of success

GROUP V OF FOREIGN ARMIES WEST

1 December 1944

Group V—United States of America, Central and South America, Pacific Area

Group Leader: Major Stolting. Deputy: Captain Ramdohr.

Strength and distribution of the American army. Politico-military questions. Command and tactics. Training and combat worth. Armament and equipment. Military potential of the U.S. Naval situation. Surveillance of the armies of the Central and South American nations. Strength, combat worth, and distribution of the armies of Japan and her allies of Greater East Asia. Observation of the Chinese army. Situation report for the Pacific area and East Asia.

Situation Subgroup—[including] Naval Situation

Subgroup Leader: Lieutenant von Braumüller. Deputy: Specialist Nadermann.

Morning report, evening report, situation report. Evaluation of communications and air reconnaissance and reports from combat troops. Transport surveillance and shipment of troops (in cooperation with V b). Calculations of landing ships' capacity. Naval situation maps. Liaison with 3/Skl.

Evaluation Subgroup—[especially] U.S.A.

Subgroup Leader: Captain Ramdohr. Deputy: Lieutenant Franke.

V a. Captain Ramdohr. Deputy: Lieutenant Franke. U.S. high command. Build-up and total strength. War organization. Distribution at home. Combat worth and training. Card index of troop units, card index of officers. Uniforms and recognition signs. Replacement system. Defense and employment of the population. Evaluation of captured materials (in liaison with V c). Liaison with Communications Reconnaissance West and with Air Force Operations Staff.

V b. [Lieutenant position vacant]. Deputy: Lieutenant Franke. Distribution of U.S. formations outside the U.S. Calculations of strength in the area of commitment. Calculations of the total forces of the Western powers (in liaison with Groups II and III). Evaluation of communications reconnaissance and reports from combat troops. Transport survey (in liaison with V Situation). Judgment of agents, liaison with Abwehr.

V c. Specialist Nadermann. Deputy: Lieutenant von Braumüller. U.S. armament, equipment, and supply, observation of the arms industry, deliveries of war equipment to foreign powers. Military politics. Press evaluation. Captured-material evaluation (in liaison with V a). Liaison to the Arms Department and the Field Economy Department.

V d. (Directly subordinated to the group leader.) Lieutenant Franke. Deputy: Specialist Nadermann. Overall study of the states in the East Asia area, Central and South America. Situation in the East Asian and Pacific area.

from the work. One might get that on the battlefield, he said, "but not in this detail work." Evaluation, he found, was not only a "fantastic mental effort," it was very time consuming. Sometimes he skipped lunch and remained at his desk until 8:30 or 9 in the evening.

The day ran longer for his superiors. Lieutenant Colonel Lothar Metz, the I a, was incessantly meeting with the suppliers or the users of his information, and he often did not end his day until midnight or 2 a.m.

Metz also edited the daily "Situation Report West." Its two or three pages mostly mentioned enemy activity and listed new and reconfirmed enemy unit locations. To it, Roenne added, when warranted, a form of report that he had learned under Gehlen at Foreign Armies East. This "Brief Enemy Estimate West" of a page or two provided a longer view and sometimes predicted enemy intentions.

In addition, the branch issued a number of other reports at greater intervals. Three weeks after he arrived, Roenne started semimonthly reviews of the British and the American armies. The American one, for example, "Survey USA," usually contained in its half-dozen pages reports on new divisions, details of new equipment, names of commanders, the movement of forces to Britain, and a table showing the total number of divisions and their locations. Roenne also published a series of "Individual Reports of the I c Service West." These dealt with such topics as British landing tactics and Allied hand grenades and mines. They went to lower commands to enable their troops to prepare appropriate countermeasures.

All of Roenne's efforts, however, did not help stop the Allies from lodging themselves on the continent of Europe. Six weeks after the Normandy assault sealed the fate of the Reich, a group of officers attempted to assassinate Hitler. Though Roenne did not participate directly in the plot, his anti-Hitler sentiments and associations sufficed for him to be executed.

Succeeding him was Colonel Willi Bürklein. A member of a wealthy wine-growing family in the Palatinate, he had served in Foreign Armies West in 1939 and 1940 as specialist for French commanders and tactics. After a few years at the front, where he received a head wound that pained and enervated him, he returned to command the branch.

It had greatly swollen. Now that German forces in France and Belgium were in actual contact with the enemy, its two basic tactical reports moved from the treacherous preinvasion quicksand of spy messages and radio reconnaissance confirmed only by one another to the firmer ground of captured papers and interrogated prisoners. On the day after Christmas 1944, for example, with the Battle of the Bulge in full sway, "Situation Report West No. 1,491" noted in part:

I. West Front.
    a) Enemy activity ... American 9th Army ... The enemy surrounded in Bastogne had to give up more ground before our attacks. ...

b) Troop identifications . . .
Through prisoners have been confirmed: Parts of the U.S. 7th Armored Division, parts of the U.S. 106th Infantry Division, parts of the U.S. 28th Infantry Divisions, [all] east of the line Stavelot-Vielsalm [in eastern Belgium].

II. Italy . . .

In his "Brief Enemy Estimate West" that same day, Bürklein summed up what he saw the Allies doing:

Eisenhower is recklessly pulling further formations out of the unbroken American front sectors in order to bring the German attack to a standstill east of the Meuse and to hem in the attack wedge through counterattacks forcefully carried out. He is thereby taking into account the risk of considerable front widths for the partly fought-out infantry divisions that he left in place.

But despite occasional verve like that, the evaluations and forecasts of Foreign Armies West rarely had the panache, the sweep, and the punch of those of its ostensible twin on the Russian front.

Many circumstances contributed to the superiority of Foreign Armies East. It could concentrate on a single enemy on a single front, enabling it to organize by function; West had to reduplicate functions among geographic groups following several armies on several fronts. The Russian war was vaster, so that East was larger than West. Combat there flamed continuously, enabling East to gain experience and develop techniques that the intermittent invasions in the west precluded. Warfare in Russia also involved close contact, giving East many more opportunities to collect intelligence; in the west, the combatants were separated by water just before the most important operations. Finally, while both branches were subordinated to the OKH, only East worked for it; West served the OKW, encumbering the transmission of intelligence and perhaps distorting it as well. But important as these background factors were, far more critical was the remarkable personality of the second chief of Foreign Armies East.

His predecessor, the first chief, was the very model of a Prussian staff officer—efficient, monocled, operationally gifted. He was Lieutenant Colonel Eberhard Kinzel, who had served in T 3 in 1933 before becoming military attaché in Poland. Over Kinzel's signature was issued the official handbook that grossly underestimated the Soviet Union's military strength before Hitler's assault. But Chief of Staff Halder did not blame him for the failure of that blitzkrieg, for he retained him in the post for almost a year afterward. Towards the end of 1941, however, Halder became concerned about "symptoms of decline in the I c service," and on 20 March 1942, he fired Kinzel because he "does not satisfy my demands." Kinzel, who was a bit lazy to begin with and who frequently showed up at work tired before the day began—the result, fellow officers thought, of living with a gorgeous blonde—did not in any event incline to intelligence work. He did well in operational posts, however. He rose to a general's rank as chief of staff of Army Group North, where he could act decisively. At the end of the war he surrendered the army group to Field Marshal Bernard L. Montgomery, then shot his blonde and himself.

After firing him, Halder installed Lieutenant Colonel Reinhard Gehlen as head of Foreign Armies East. It revolutionized German military intelligence.

Why? Who was Gehlen?

He was a thin man of medium height with dark thinning hair, a high forehead, blue eyes, big ears, full lips, a down-turned mouth, and a perpetual frown. He was quiet, modest, a poor conversationalist, but friendly with old acquaintances. Three days after he took command of the branch, on 1 April 1942, he turned 40. His father was a sometime soldier, sometime publisher. Young Gehlen had joined the army as an enlisted man in 1920, just after high school, and after attending officer candidate school, gained his commission. He served in the most technical of the three traditional arms, the artillery. In 1931, he married Herta von Seydlitz-Kurzbach, whose family was distinguished in Prussian military annals. His character and ability were outstanding enough for him to be selected to attend, from 1933 to 1935, the leadership courses that substituted for the Versailles-banned War Academy.

This qualified him for the general staff. He began his service in it at its headquarters in Berlin, first as an adjutant, then in the Operations Branch, then in the Fortifications Branch. Halder was working at headquarters at the same time. With the outbreak of the war, Gehlen was transferred to the 213th Infantry Division as I a for the Polish campaign. This reserve division never made it into heavy combat, but Gehlen was nevertheless awarded the Iron Cross 2nd Class for his efforts with it. Afterward, he headed the Fortifications Branch, visited the French front during that campaign as Halder's liaison, and served as Halder's adjutant. Then, in November 1940, as the plans were being prepared for the invasion of Russia, Halder gave him the important post of head of the Operations Branch's Group I, the East, which dealt with "questions of overall strategy." Gehlen stayed there through the Russian war's first summer, first mud period, and first winter, gaining a good insight into the tactics and problems of the vast Russian realm. The excellence of his work—"far above average," his superior wrote, "capable of thinking ahead"—drew attention to him. So when Halder needed a good man for Foreign Armies East, he broke with tradition, plucked Gehlen—to his disappointment—from his career, and inserted an operations man into an intelligence post.

It proved to be his most brilliant appointment. Gehlen produced results that Halder had never dreamed of when Kinzel was in the job. For Gehlen was, first, fantastically hard-working and, second, creative.

Eleven days after taking over, he expanded Kinzel's halting daily report of enemy trends into a full appreciation of probable plans. He tightened relations with Canaris, pulled WALLI I closer to his own headquarters, and assumed operational control of the agents. He ordered that aerial-reconnaissance reports, which were arriving too late, be telephoned in. He instituted intelligence training courses and lectures, both for his own staff and for I cs in the field. He had I c officers given the same rank as their I a in an attempt to raise their prestige and thus their effectiveness. He

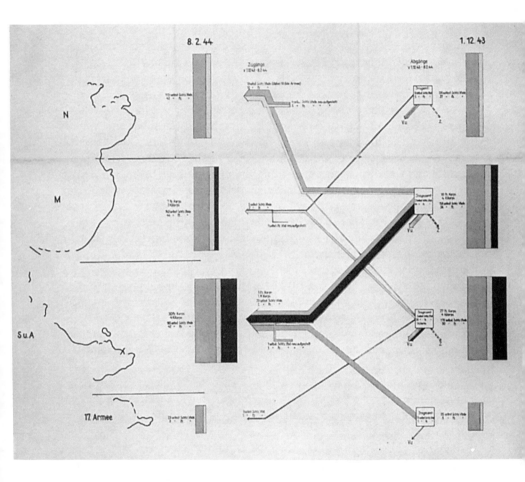

Gehlen's Foreign Armies East graphically shows how the Russians are transferring forces from one part of the front (mainly that indicated by M, for Heeresgruppe Mitte, or Army Group Center) to other sectors (Army Group North and Army Groups South and A). The black represents fast corps (armored, motorized, and cavalry); the dark gray, independent armored formations; the light gray, independent rifle formations

changed the organization of the branch from geographical to functional. He doubled its officer staff, from 24 when he took over to almost 50 by the end of 1944, while the total personnel rose to several hundred. He replaced many of the older officers with younger, more energetic ones, such as Roenne. But the secrets of his success lay less in these administrative re-gearings than in two imaginative innovations.

First, he generated new data. He ordered troops at the front to report every 10 days on the number and location of enemy guns opposite them. This showed where the Russians were building up main artillery efforts. He set specialists to producing such background studies as "The Urals as an Economic and Industrial Area," "Survey of the Higher Military Commanders of the Red Army," "Modern Russian Weapons," and "Experiences in P.O.W. Interrogations and Their Utilization in Questioning Agents." He called for reports on the arrests of enemy agents behind German lines: their concentration in certain areas told where the Russians were seeking information. He sent his "Reconnaissance Requirements East" to lower staffs so that they would concentrate their efforts, especially in prisoner interrogations, on questions he wanted answered. He compared a single activity at different times. Thus an intensification of enemy patrolling in a sector often indicated a forthcoming attack. He compared one source with another—agent concentrations with railway movements—to produce more refined, second-order data. Sometimes these comparisons could penetrate Russian deception. If the sound-and-light artillery results showed more guns than the aerial results, the Russians were firing individual guns from several positions. If the aerial results showed more, the Russians were restraining their fire to conceal their artillery, probably in preparation for an attack. Where he could, he quantified his data. Thus he sought to determine points of main effort by comparing the number of artillery barrels per kilometer on various sections of the front.

Second, Gehlen dramatized his facts. He rendered them in graphic form and so made the innumerable details immediately comprehensible. This usually took the form of maps—of the enemy artillery situation, of railway movements, of enemy armor, patrol activity, air reconnaissance results, the capture places of the enemy agents. These facilitated comparison among activities and between dates. To show the concentration of Russian troop units at one point on the front, his draftsmen made schematic charts with colored blocks representing the troops and arrows their transfers. Once, when he had to present information to Hitler about an expected Russian offensive, he had pictures of blue German and red Russian soldiers, tanks, and ammunition drawn in proportion to the size of the amounts they represented. The reds towered over the blues. Rarely had an officer of the German general staff unbent to use such advertising techniques.

Volume in input and drama in output enabled Gehlen to raise Foreign

Armies East from a unit that did little more than count and locate enemy troops, as it and West long had been, to one in which it offered opinions as to probable enemy actions—opinions that the chief of the general staff came to issue as his own.

Foreign Armies East was quartered in a bunker next to West's at Zossen during the first part of the war. With the invasion of Russia, it moved, with the chief of the general staff and other branches of the OKH, to the Führer headquarters in East Prussia. Its offices occupied one-story wooden barracks ranged under the pines near the Mauersee (now Poland's Lake Mamry), one of the largest of the numerous Masurian lakes in the rolling northern European plain, not far from where in 1914 the Germans beat the Russians in a great victory based in part on intelligence—Tannenberg. The nearest town was Angersberg (now Wegorozo), and scattered in the vicinity were such support elements as the Main Post for Communications Reconnaissance, the Abwehr's WALLI I, and the branch's special interrogation camp. The Führer encampment was only half an hour's shuttle train ride from the branch. Gehlen's office, in a building opposite Halder's, was filled with a big map table in its center, while Gehlen's desk, in an alcove at one end, was illuminated by lamps so strong that people near them perspired.

Most people at Foreign Armies East began their day at 8 a.m. Soon thereafter telephone calls began coming in from the army groups. They went to Group I, charged with the daily enemy situation, each of whose desks handled the enemy before one of the three or four German army groups (one also dealt with the partisan situation). Usually the O 3 or O 6 of the army group spoke with an officer on the appropriate desk while a stenographer took notes. The army group reports covered all forms of enemy activity from all German sources. At the same time, the headquarters of the various German armies sent in summaries of the most important enemy intelligence obtained in the past 24 hours. The desk chief entered all this on a 1:300,000 map, which he brought to the 10 a.m. conference with Gehlen. Gehlen absorbed it for use at the morning conference with the chief of staff.

During the day, information continued to pour in. The head of Group I glanced at each report and passed it to the proper desk chief. WALLI I motorcycled over its agent messages. The Main Post for Communications Reconnaissance sent over its bulky report. The head of Foreign Air Forces East telephoned the head of Group I. The air force liaison staff passed along aerial reconnaissance evaluations. Each desk head talked over the situation with the I c of his army group. Between 7 and 8 p.m., the army groups telephoned in the results of the day's intelligence activities. By this time, the desk heads had formed views of their own on the enemy situation, which they compared with the new material. At about 8:30, Gehlen summoned a conference in his office. The head of Group I, the desk heads, and some specialist officers—a dozen in all—gathered around the map table. Each desk head spoke on enemy activities before his army group and outlined his views on that army group's intelligence summary. The specialists, such as the radio reconnaissance liaison officer, translated the technical jargon of their reports into military German and emphasized the key points.

"On the basis of this briefing," Gehlen said, "I then decided on the general line to be adopted by our overall daily intelligence digest to be issued by Foreign Armies East." The head of Group I wrote the two or three pages of this "Brief Estimate of the Enemy Situation" under considerable pressure, for Gehlen took it with him to the main evening situation conference of the chief of the general staff at 10.

While Group I was pumping out the current evaluations, Group II was dissecting the background factors that helped determine the daily situation. Its Desk II a investigated the primary elements, chiefly the Russian manpower potential, calculating this as best it could from the 1939 census. In May of 1942, for example, it estimated that Russia would create 60 new rifle divisions during the summer if no 18-year-olds, needed on the farms, were drafted. In fact some were, and 64 rifle divisions appeared. Desk II b surveyed the secondary elements, such as morale, food, the political situation, education. It developed this information from captured letters, p.o.w. statements, and newspapers, and presented it in a monthly report.

Desk II c kept track of the enemy order of battle; the whole branch owed the precision of much of its data to this desk. It entered the details that came in about enemy units on one of its 30,000 troop identification slips. Each showed the date the unit was reported, where it was reported, the source of information and its reliability, and—if known—its strength, armament, losses, national composition, field post number, commanders, and history. On the basis of this information, the desk each day issued a "Survey of Soviet Russian Formations." This large sheet, supplemented by maps at 1:1,000,000 and 1:300,000, listed the number of various enemy formations in front of each German army group in three zones: at the front, in front reserve, and in deep reserve. Since not every unit was reported every day, II c assigned nonreported units to zones on several assumptions. Troops that had not been confirmed at the front for 14 days were regarded as in reserve near the front. (The combat situation could modify this. A unit not heard from on a completely calm front might still be there, while a unit not confirmed for just a few days during an enemy attack would almost certainly indicate that it was not involved in the action.) Units carried for a month as "near the front" but not reconfirmed were then shifted to "in the rear." Formations carried there for three months and not further confirmed were marked as "location unknown." Formations not heard of for a year were regarded as dissolved.

These and other rules for determining enemy order of battle appeared in a 32-page directive signed by Gehlen. It bespoke considerable experience. The location of enemy troops on the slips was not to be specified with relation to German forces but exclusively on the basis of geographic location. Russian names were to be printed in block letters. It gave ways of distinguishing between an old formation that reappeared after being refreshed or reformed and a new formation bearing an old one's number (this usually happened when the old one had been destroyed, renumbered, or elevated to the Guards). And the directive set out principles for estimating enemy combat worth. This was done on a quantitative basis. A Russian unit with three-thirds of its table-of-organization strength was called "full," one with two-thirds, "battle-worthy," one with one-third, "battered," and one with one-sixth, "left over." On 26 August 1943, for example, the branch counted 136 Russian rifle divisions before Army Group Center. But in terms of battle worth it estimated them as only 80. II c maintained other indices and issued other documents that permitted rapid retrieval of more refined Soviet troop information: daily force comparison of German and Soviet forces; thrice-monthly survey of fronts (the equivalent of German army groups), armies, and corps; list of all enemy formations; survey of Red army formations that had appeared since the start of the war; survey of Red army formations that had been destroyed and dissolved since the start of the war; monthly Soviet Union armor situation.

Finally, II c made special computations. On 15 October 1943, for example, it figured the total number of Russian guns on the front. It knew that each rifle division should have had 34 guns, each rifle brigade 12, each cavalry division 8. It estimated that units lacked 20 percent of what they should have had and that artillery controlled directly by the armies stood at 50 percent of the divisional artillery. Multiplying by the number of troop units, it arrived at a total of 20,770 guns. This, it noted, was 360 fewer than the 1 August 1943 total. To check its calculations, it reckoned this difference on the basis of other figures:

reported losses of Russian guns from 1 August to 14 October	5,300
reduction for double reports (20%)	1,060
	4,240
reduction for 45-millimeter antitank guns (about ¼)	1,060
actual gun losses	3,180
presumed production in August and September	2,800
	380

The close agreement with 360 confirmed the calculations.

Desk II d analyzed Russian armament production, especially tanks, and II e, Russian tactics and weapons.

Group III, filled with Baltic and Russian Germans, translated the quantities of captured documents, interrogated important prisoners at the branch's camp, monitored broadcasts, and ran the reference library, with its collection of, among other things, 10,000 Soviet military regulations. Gehlen often regarded this bunch of "foreigners" as "shrouded in an air of conspiracy." They threw drinking parties on the slightest of pretexts and gained a reputation for sloth, which Gehlen said was undeserved.

Group IV, operating on a peacetime basis, kept an eye on Scandinavia. Group V's 18 cartographers drew the numerous maps that Gehlen required; the more important of these were printed by the OKH every night. The group's six photo assistants handled photographs, photostats, blueprints. Group VI managed the household affairs—buildings, personnel, movies, Christmas parties, boats for paddling on the lake.

Beside the basic work of the branch coursed its secondary activities. Half a dozen I c officers visited it at a time for five-day briefings after having attended the intelligence course at Posen that Gehlen had set up. Gehlen invited officers of other branches to a lecture on the Red army being given "for internal use." Group VI ran a lecture series on Russian history. The first of the three given starting at 6 p.m. on 28 March 1944 was "Peter the Great and the Europeanization of Russia." Notices appeared on the bulletin board about only the branch chief and his deputy being allowed to give information to posts outside the branch and about officers failing to say where they were going when they left their offices: "What one requires from every clerk and female assistant should be self-evident for an officer." Another notice hinted at tensions within the office. "Fight Noise!" it urged, and was signed by many, including Baroness von Speth-Schülzburg, the chief librarian, in her large green handwriting. Hers was the biggest signature on the sheet, and next to it someone had noted, "Small and modest as always."

Through all this moved Gehlen, supervising, checking, dining with his officers, and sometimes appearing late at night with a friendly word and a pot of coffee for the workers toiling through the early morning hours, for the branch never shut down.

The branch's information flowed both upward and downward. Every day, the army groups received the "Enemy Situation Report East," which summarized that day's enemy activity, and the more important "Brief Estimate of the Enemy Situation," with its forecasts of enemy moves. All I cs in the east received the "Red Bible" listing all known Russian formations, to assist them in determining enemy order of battle. (Foreign Armies West put out similar books for the British and American armies.) East supplied the I cs with how-to booklets on intelligence. Its Desk II e published from time to time the series "Individual Reports of the I c Service East," which alerted the troops to new Russian tactics and weapons. But the branch felt its most important effort was upward.

This meant Gehlen's reports to the chief of the general staff—Halder, Zeitzler, and then Guderian—at the twice-daily conferences. In the morning, Gehlen reported orally to the chief in the presence of the other branch heads attending, of whom the most important was the head of the Operations Branch. In the evening, Gehlen again summarized the enemy situation orally, then submitted the "Brief Estimate of the Enemy Situation." The chief of the general staff incorporated this information into the report he made to Hitler at his midday and late evening situation conferences. The Führer then utilized or ignored it as he made the decisions that ran Germany's war. Gehlen himself resisted going to the Führer conferences. He believed that he could be more effective by letting the chief of the general staff suffer Hitler's displeasure at enemy information instead of himself. Throughout his three years, he only attended four.

How successful was Gehlen as an intelligence officer?

He succeeded in the most basic of his jobs: identifying and locating the enemy forces. Foreign Armies East knew what units stood opposite the German, knew their strengths, knew their commanders.

"The enemy organization has been entirely confirmed by the results of the [German] attack," noted Halder of Gehlen's work in 1942. A year later, as the Germans were retreating after having attacked into the world's greatest tank battle around Kursk, Gehlen passed Zeitzler's praise to his staff:

"The course of the fighting on the eastern front these few days has once again confirmed precisely every detail of the intelligence picture of the enemy we produced despite formidable obstacles that were put in the way of our assessment of the enemy's distribution of forces. The chief of staff expressed particular commendation for this a few days ago."

Gehlen's accuracy was one of the major factors both in fortifying his personal position and in changing the German army's negative attitude toward intelligence. Another was his discreet propaganda. He issued a booklet of his predictions contending that he had "succeeded in correctly recognizing the enemy's intentions—sometimes months in advance." A third factor was circumstance. The Germans were on the defensive, which requires knowledge of the enemy more than the offensive. Moreover, their strength was declining, and since intelligence enables a commander to magnify his available strength, the German generals gratefully accepted Gehlen's assistance.

As a consequence, he converted them from skeptics about intelligence to believers in it. And in persuading them of its importance, he convinced them that he was the dark and indispensable genius who made it possible. Gehlen became one of the few staff officers to reach a general's rank without having served at the front. A little while after his promotion, Guderian defended him against one of Hitler's outbursts. It was early in January

1945. Guderian wanted Hitler to free forces from the western front to defend the eastern. He brought with him figures, compiled by Foreign Armies East, showing the Soviet strength. Hitler flew into a rage. He raved that Gehlen's estimates were "completely idiotic" and that the man ought to be sent to an insane asylum. Then Guderian in his turn lost his temper.

"The man who made these is General Gehlen, one of my very best staff officers," he shouted in a fury. "I would not have shown them to you were I in disagreement with them. If you want General Gehlen sent to a lunatic asylum you had better have me certified as well." He flatly refused Hitler's demand to fire Gehlen—and the intelligence officer stayed on until both he and Guderian were relieved close to the end of the war.

But how well did Gehlen do one of the most important of his jobs: predicting enemy attacks? He himself boasted that he had often correctly done so. Some high officers went so far as to assert that he forecast all major Russian offensives. They saw in him an oracle as accurate as Cassandra and—alas!—as little heeded. Was this reputation deserved?

In a great many, if not most, of the cases, no definite answer can be given. Gehlen's predictions equivocated. In the first place, he seldom specified the timing of an enemy action. Consequently, even if it took place three months later, he could always say that he foresaw it. Second, he listed all possibilities. He deemphasized the less likely ones by saying that they were "improbable" or "not excluded," but if the Russians nevertheless chose one of them, Gehlen could still say that he had predicted it. In the third place, he couched the enemy moves in vague terms. The enemy would seek "limited goals" or the attack might "exceed local proportions." Gehlen could afterward stretch these terms to cover whatever had happened. Finally, when none of these devices would serve, Gehlen would say that the enemy had failed in his original intentions or had changed his mind! In all these ways, Gehlen kept himself from being proven wrong.

His "Brief Estimate of the Enemy Situation" for 18 November 1942, the day before the Russians launched their pincers attack around the tip of Army Group B in Stalingrad, exemplifies these techniques.

1. Army Group A: . . .
2. Army Group B:
   4th Panzer Army, 6th Army, 3rd Rumanian Army: The bringing up of three new armored brigades—supposedly for the [Russian] XIIIth Armored Corps—which is to be expected on the basis of deserter statements, means a further strengthening of the enemy forces before the VIth Rumanian Army Corps [south of Stalingrad]. One may therefore reckon that the expected attacks—even if only with limited goals—may possibly exceed local proportions, though one cannot yet see whether the newly expected armored formations will be committed before the eastern front of the VIth Rumanian Army Corps or in the southern part of the area of Beketovka [also south of Stalingrad].

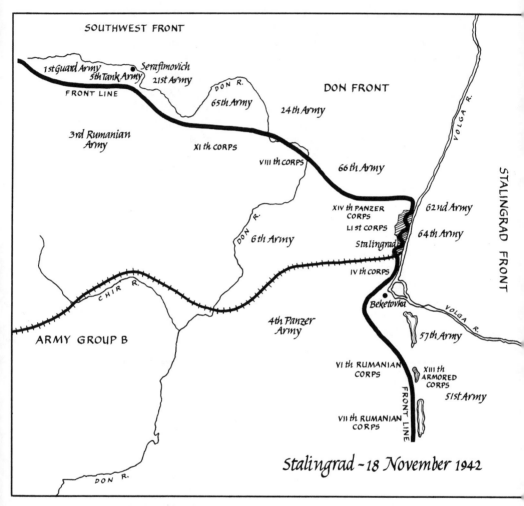

The front around Stalingrad the day before the start of the Russian offensive

With only local combat activity before the 3rd Rumanian Army, the insertion of a further [Russian] division before the center of the army (111th Rifle Division out of the army reserve of the 61st Russian Army—[in front of Germany's] Army Group Center) permits the recognition of a further strengthening of the enemy forces.

Simultaneous attacks out of the area of Beketovka and/or the eastern front of the VIth Rumanian Army Corps [both south of Stalingrad] and on the Don front against the 3rd Rumanian Army [northwest of Stalingrad] do not appear excluded.

8th Italian, 2nd Hungarian, and 2nd [German] Army: Estimate of the enemy unchanged.

3. Army Group Center:

2nd Panzer Army: The appearance, determined by radio reconnaissance, of the 41st Guard Rifle Division (last reported north of Stalingrad in the process of entraining) in the area of the 48th Army may be regarded as a replacement for pulled-out forces and requires no change in the evaluation.

4th Army, 3rd Panzer Army: Estimate of the enemy unchanged.

9th Army: Estimate of the enemy before the east front [of the 9th Army salient] unchanged.

Before the middle of the north front [of the salient] lively movements are worthy of notice.

On the west front further reinforcements before the [German] 7th Luftwaffe Field Division (336th Rifle Division out of the reserves of the 31st Army at the front; 47th and 48th Motorized Brigades, according to deserter statements, in the rear) confirm the previous picture.

11th Army: Enemy situation estimated unchanged.

4. Army Group North: ...

The estimate certainly did not communicate the sense of urgency warranted by the precarious position of the 6th Army, overextended in front and with its flanks held in large part by the weak Rumanian troops, against which Soviet forces were massing. The attacks from north and south that would cut off the 6th Army and end in the greatest German disaster of the war were seen merely as "not ... excluded." Gehlen gave no indication that these onslaughts were frighteningly imminent—less than 24 hours away.

The main reason for this was that Gehlen believed that the Russians would conduct their main winter offensive, not against Army Group B, but against Army Group Center, further north. Its 9th Army salient threatened Moscow. Tactically an attack here posed fewer problems and offered greater chances of success. Though Gehlen had recognized the Russian build-up around Stalingrad, he questioned whether they had enough forces for decisive attacks in both places. He doubted in any event that they would undertake a major operation against Stalingrad at the same time as against Army Group Center. Moreover, while he had said that "one must reckon with an imminent attack against the 3rd Rumanian Army with the goal of breaking the rail line to Stalingrad in order to endanger German troops further to the east" (in other words, in Stalingrad), he had simultaneously said of this possibility that "The available forces may be too weak for more extensive operations." But four days after the attack, the Russian pincers closed. Two days later, the Russians threw whole fronts at Army Group Center, where they rebounded off the waiting Germans. Gehlen maintained his belief in the primacy of this offensive for two weeks after the 6th Army was trapped in Stalingrad. Finally, on 9 December, he conceded that the Russians had placed the weight of their main effort on Stalingrad. Gehlen later asserted that the Russians were surprised by their success at that city of rubble and doom and had changed their minds when this became evident. But Keitel, the chief of the OKW, had his own, simpler opinion: "We underestimated the strength of the Red army at Stalingrad."

Many of Gehlen's predictions were similarly questionable—generally wrong in tone, but with a correct point or two that he could use to prove his perspicacity. On 25 July 1943, two weeks after the failure of the great German offensive at Kursk, and shortly after Zeitzler had commended him, Gehlen predicted that the Russians would continue their summer operations as long as they appeared to offer good possibilities of success. When they no longer seemed so, he said, they would limit themselves to gaining better jumping-off places for the winter offensive. He mentioned the possibility of attacks "beyond the local areas." But aside from that inadequate reference, nothing in the estimate prepared the German high command for the massive attacks against army groups South and Center that started nine days later and that eventually flung the Germans back more than a hundred miles.

A number of Gehlen's predictions erred even more gravely than that. They misfired completely.

On 30 March 1944, for example, he issued a 12-page "Comprehensive Appreciation of the Enemy Situation before the German East Front and Presumed Enemy Intentions in General." Nowhere did it mention the major offensive a week later that hurled the Germans out of the Crimea, with the consequent threat to the Balkans and the loss of Turkish neutrality. On the same day, Gehlen's "Brief Estimate of the Enemy Situation" forecast that the Russians would recognize the extremely satisfactory preconditions for an effective drive over Army Group Center to the west. They would, he said, advance toward Lublin and Brest, cross over the Pripyat Marshes, and throw Army Group North out of its defensive PANTHER position. None of this happened.

Later in the spring, Gehlen considered two possible Soviet offensives. One would drive north to the Baltic to cut off army groups North and Center. The other would strike south through Rumania and Hungary to the Balkans. Believing that the Red army did not have the tactical proficiency to carry out the former, Foreign Armies East decided on the latter —the southern attack. Army Group Center, it promised, could expect a "calm summer." It detected some activity opposite this army group, but unable to penetrate the strong Russian air defenses or to gain intelligence through the curtain of radio silence that had descended on the Russian front, it dismissed these signs as "apparently a deception." Gehlen and Zeitzler continued to believe that the main attack would head for the south, with demonstrations against Army Group Center and elsewhere to precede it as feints. On 22 June 1944, the Red army equivalent of four army groups smashed into Army Group Center, exactly where Gehlen had said nothing would happen. The front collapsed. Before the Germans were able to restore some measure of order, they had lost several hundred miles of territory.

Failures in prediction like these stemmed from two causes. One was the difficulty of peering into the murky future that afflicts all men. More fundamental was an arrogance, a rigid overestimation of German abilities. This damaged Gehlen's predictions in two contrary ways. At times it simply blinded him to Soviet strength, leading him to underestimate the Russians. At other times, projection, or expecting his enemy to do what he would have done, caused him to overrate the Russians, who were operating instead from their own doctrines. Under the impress of events, these tendencies alternated in German thought. They engendered sometimes an unjustified optimism, which failed to foresee major Russian offensives, sometimes an excessive pessimism, which predicted far-ranging attacks that never came.

Gehlen's inflexible conviction of German superiority prevented him from seeing the basic fact of the war in the east: that Germany could lose it. He repeatedly insisted the opposite. In June of 1942, he was writing that "If we are to carry impending operations in the East through to final victory, we shall have to make a supreme effort." In August he was talking of a "surprisingly favorable development" of the military situation. As late as 31 December 1944, he was considering that the eastern front could be saved.

Even neutrals could, early on, see the falsity of this belief. In August of 1942, while Gehlen was envisioning an improvement of the situation, Hans Hausamann, the head of a semiofficial Swiss intelligence agency, grasped the real situation and set down, in eloquent prose, the most remarkable intelligence prediction of the war:

> One way or the other Germany has won nothing decisive in a military-political sense and can win nothing more than space, space, and still more space. Space, which devours forces, in which the German army vanishes, which brings in no gain. And on the other side, constantly heavier Anglo-Saxon air attacks on German cities, without any chance of slowing them down; in the west a "Second Front"; in Africa no possibility of giving Rommel the air and land forces that he needs to drive out the English from the eastern Mediterranean lands; in the south a wobbly Axis partner; in all countries of the European continent discontented people, whose repression absorbs powerful forces.
>
> For the Reich leadership the situation is hopeless! It can do nothing more than battle to the death. If the creation of a "Second Front" comes in the west in the next few weeks, then the collapse will take place sooner; if the "Second Front" fails to come, then later. And all this not least because the

Russians have had the nerve to hold strictly to a strategic plan, to sacrifice land and to save of their strategic reserves for 1943 or even 1944—as the Russians, with stoical calm, say: for the Russian strategic offensive.

Gehlen's vision was in no way as clear. He was not alone in clinging to his belief in the impossibility of a German defeat. Hitler and the whole higher German officer corps felt as Gehlen did. Their careers, their very identities depended on it. One cannot fault Gehlen for thus being a child of his century. But he claimed to be more: a man without illusion, who gazed unblinking at reality, who foresaw all—the perfect intelligence officer. And that he was not.

IV
THE CASES

24

The Greatest Mistake

ENGLAND was still fighting him when Hitler resolved to attack Russia. He had, of course, always intended to do so. He wanted to win for Germany the geopolitical heartland she needed to dominate the world and the Lebensraum to prosper in it. But why do so while England still fought? Why open a two-front war—the terror of the German general staff since it was formed? Hitler decided to attack Russia because he believed that her destruction would compel England finally to surrender. Conquest of the Soviet Union, Hitler said, would eliminate Britain's last hope: that with Russian help on the Continent, Britain would eventually be able to defeat Germany.

He had no doubt that the onslaught would succeed. And for once his general staff, which had argued against his genius at every major point in the war and been proven wrong at every one, agreed with him. In reaching these conclusions the agencies of intelligence played no role. The situation serves as an ideal case history for those numerous episodes in which preconceptions usurp intelligence. Never were the agencies asked their overall views as to the probability of success in an attack on the world's largest country. Never were they asked to ascertain details that might illuminate this basic question. Only after the decision to attack had crystallized on 18 December 1940 in Hitler's Directive No. 21 for the Conduct of the War, "Plan BARBAROSSA," were they called in. The high commands assigned them then to little more than seeking out enemy troop locations so that the Germans could plan a destruction in detail. They were still not asked whether Germany could win such a war. In the planning of the attack on Russia, German intelligence was limited to secondary and technical matters.

It was arrogance that determined this approach to intelligence—a deep-seated but not wholly valid conviction that Germany could defeat any other country in the world. This sense of superiority was compounded in the case of Russia by two additional factors: anti-Slavism and anti-Marxism.

Hitler's officers learned their hatred of communism as boys. It expressed itself chiefly in an abhorrence of the Social Democrats, the German labor party, whose ideals were the ideals of Karl Marx. These boys were sons of the upper middle class or the nobility. Their families hated the socialists because the improvement of the workers' conditions meant a relative decline in theirs, a loss of much of what they had worked for. Though their exponents—Bismarck, the army, industry, the Kaiser—connived to keep the workers down, the socialist political power nevertheless constantly grew. The boys imbibed their families' fear with their milk. When they themselves became young officers, the fear became more intensely personal. They saw that, just as the socialists' economic ideals would rob them of the gifts of the past, the socialists' international and pacifist ideals would rob them of the promise of the future.

They thought they saw these misgivings confirmed in 1918. Four years of awful sacrifice ended, they believed, not with an honorable defeat on the field of battle, but with a stab in the back from the workers and the Jews. On the heads of these traitors could be poured all the officers' woes: the loss of status with defeat and the dissolution of their quasi-feudal link to the abdicated crown, the unprecedented undermining of their authority by the Workers' and Soldiers' Councils, the insurrections that disrupted Germany's domestic stability, and the humiliations and burdens of Versailles, which threw so many brothers in arms out of work.

Their aversion was so extreme that when a captain had to bring a report to the president of the Weimar Republic it marked his first encounter with a Social Democrat—and he imagined that the head of state might be wearing bib overalls and a cap. The establishment of Communist power in Russia after revolution congealed the officers' fear and hatred of what they saw as an international conspiracy. And what they despised, they deprecated.

Another element of the climate of opinion was a racist feeling of superiority toward the Slavs. This view, sown in the first half of the nineteenth century, spread widely in the second. It taught that other races were inherently inferior to the Germanic—poorer in intellect, weaker in willpower, stronger only in the animal aspects of their worthless lives. Many German officers saw this prejudice confirmed by their victory over the Russians in World War I. It hardened as they grew older and as Naziism reinforced it. Colonel Günther Blumentritt, chief of staff of the 4th Army, set it out full-blown in an assessment of 1940:

> The strength of the Russian soldier lies consequently in his unfeeling, half-Asiatic stubbornness, as we as infantry officers with the fighting troops have sufficiently learned, above all in 1914–15. In those days it was taken for granted that one German infantry division had to take on two to three

Russian. In the night attacks, so beloved by the Russians as children of nature, often 10 to 12 lines of riflemen advanced one behind the other against our air-thin positions. The rifles and machine guns fired until their barrels were hot without being able to hold off the dogged masses.

With such views Hitler would have found himself in complete agreement. "The Russian," he said flatly, "is inferior." His own loathing of communism and sense of superiority to the Russians had their roots partly in external circumstances, as did the generals', partly in his own twisted psyche. As early as 1924 he had written that "Russia is ripe for collapse." Nothing occurred to turn him from this view. On the contrary, events seemed to confirm it.

Starting in 1937, Stalin purged some 25,000 officers from the Red army. This loss of about one out of every four of its officers, including the able commander, Marshal Mikhail N. Tukhachevsky, and many who had fought in World War I, virtually decapitated the Soviet Union's armed forces. "The Russian army," crowed Hitler, "is leaderless." Then, in the Winter War of 1939–40, the bear took four months to win a little land and a naval base from tiny Finland. "The Russian army," concluded Hitler, is "a joke."

These attitudes led Hitler and his generals into their certainty of victory and their wildly overoptimistic estimates of how long it would take Germany to defeat the Soviet Union. "When one really gets hold of this colossus, it will collapse faster than the whole world suspects," ranted the Führer. "The Soviet Union will burst like a soap bubble." His generals echoed these thoughts less dramatically but more precisely. Their studies calculated that a campaign would probably take 9 weeks, 17 at the outside. The commander in chief of the army guessed that the initial battles would take up to four weeks, after which only mopping-up operations would be necessary, Blumentritt, overstimulated by his prejudices, predicted that the whole thing would take only 14 days of fighting—admittedly heavy and bloody, but after that the conquest of the largest country in the world would be all but over.

This was the atmosphere in which intelligence operated. Just as this atmosphere affected the views of Hitler and his generals toward a Russian campaign, so it affected the assignments they gave to their intelligence agencies. Though Hitler had always intended to subjugate Russia, and though he had eight years of power to mount a thorough, energetic, sustained reexamination of his original judgment that "Russia is ripe for collapse," he did not do so. Moreover, the widespread sense of superiority toward Russia infected the personnel in intelligence as it did their superiors. Overoptimism made them lazy. It was admittedly more difficult to gather intelligence in Russia than elsewhere. The military links and friendships of the 1920s between the two countries dissolved after Hitler became chancellor. The Soviet press was controlled. Travel there was restricted. The military attaché told Canaris, "An Arab with a flowing burnoose would walk unnoticed through Berlin sooner than a foreign agent through Russia." But this challenge did not stimulate the German intelligence personnel to try harder. Instead they let it blunt their efforts. For, like their bosses, they felt that, when it came to Russia, their work was not really needed.

The military press, for example, forced no reconsiderations upon its readers, cast no new light on Soviet Russia. Although it reported objectively enough on some aspects of the Soviet armed forces, such as the growth of motorization and the air force, the development of paratroops and the modernity of the Soviet military doctrine, it vitiated all this by denigrating the men who would wield these tools. After the purges, the leading specialist weekly, the *Militär-Wochenblatt,* declared that the Red army was utterly without leaders. One military bureaucrat pointed out in a magazine for army administrators what to his orderly German mind was the ultimate corruption of communism: under it, the Russians couldn't even do their paperwork properly. The military press did not tell its readers of an important Communist success—the Russian trouncing of the Japanese during the 1938 border clashes in Mongolia. All it did was soothe them by repeating their assumptions back to them. Never once did it do one of the real jobs of a press: urge its readers to rethink a problem in a fresh way.

From its allies or from friendly neutrals, Germany heard virtually nothing of importance about the Red army. Turkey, a traditional enemy of Russia, seems to have delivered no major evaluations. Japan supplied some information about the critical Soviet Far East army, but the German military attaché in Tokyo regarded this as "often practically worthless." Iran and Afghanistan probably had little more intelligence than that dealing with the Russian troops at their frontiers. From the Fascist regent of Hungary, Admiral Nikolaus von Horthy, came no factual data, merely reflection and encouragement of Hitler's design: "Today there are Soviet republics; if all of them were turned into independent states, the problem [of communism] would be solved. Germany could complete this most important work of mankind, for which history would bless her for centuries to come, in a few weeks. The struggle against England could be continued with airplanes, submarines, etc."

Finland was a potential source of rich intelligence data. She had fought Soviet Russia for three months in 1939–40. She had been an ally in World War I and then had let Germany spy against the Soviet Union from her territory. But the Winter War had begun three months after the Russo-German pact deprived Finland of German support, and Finland was in no mood to reciprocate this infidelity with information of value. Later a number of factors pulled her back closer to Germany: her increasing isolation, first from Britain and France by the German conquest of Norway and Denmark in April 1940, then from the other Baltic countries by their absorption into the Soviet Union a few months later; Germany's need for Finnish nickel from Petsamo and for Finnish rail routes to supply occupation troops in northern Norway; and Finland's own need for weapons, which she could only get from Germany. This rapprochement included the delivery of information on Russia to Germany by Finland in increasing amounts, starting in the fall of 1940. On 29 March 1941, for example, the chief of the German general staff was told that information from Finland showed that the Red army had 15 more divisions in European Russia than previously believed. From Finland too came details of Soviet armor around Pskov and of the Soviet paratroop corps. Solid as it was, however, this information remained uncomplemented by similar material from other areas, raising questions as to whether it accurately represented the entire Red army. The Finns felt, in any case, that the Germans undervalued much of their intelligence.

Theodor Rowehl's long-range air group had begun reconnoitering the Soviet Union in 1934. Various twin-engined craft, fitted with extra fuel tanks and flying at heights up to 30,000 feet, photographed the naval port of Kronshtadt and nearby Leningrad, the industrial areas of Pskov and Minsk in western Russia, and the Black Sea naval port of Nikolayev. The coverage of Kronshtadt, which furnished a sequence of pictures of warships on the ways at intervals of several weeks or months, provided valuable data about the rate of Soviet naval construction. The other pictures seem to have yielded mainly intelligence about Russian factories.

The unit flew against other countries as well, and with the outbreak of the war seems to have shifted its emphasis to them: Poland, Great Britain, France, Norway. But flights continued against the Soviet Union, which detected them—and, in a curious eagerness to please or at least not offend Germany, promised Göring not to fire on these planes as long as the flights were not frequent. At the start of September 1940, Hitler, apparently wanting not to anger Russia just as he was girding up for his invasion of Britain, ordered a stop to all aerial reconnaissance against the Soviet Union. The ban lasted a month. But the army pressed for pictures and early in October, after he had postponed his cross-Channel invasion and had begun to regard the conquest of Russia as one way of forcing England's surrender, Hitler rescinded his order. He now allowed flights to a depth of almost 200 miles into the Soviet Union from the borders of East Prussia and German-occupied Poland. At once the German machines began overflying the Russian border. And again the Russians began spotting them. On 6 January 1941, for example, one crossed the Soviet frontier, flew to a depth of about 15 miles, and then paralleled the border for almost 100 miles before returning to Germany. On 3 March the commander of the Red navy ordered that such craft be shot down. On 17 and 18 March two were fired on over the Latvian port of Liepaja; others soon appeared north-west of the Black Sea. Later Stalin countermanded the navy's order, ap-parently to avoid provoking the Germans, and directed that such planes be forced to land instead.

The flights increased in pace. In the three weeks between 27 March and 18 April, the Russians detected an average of more than three a day. On 4 April, for example, they spotted a plane at 23,000 feet that violated the border near Przemysl at 1:20 p.m. and penetrated 75 miles into Russian-occupied territory before flying back to Germany at 1:50 p.m. They had no illusions as to what the flights were for. In one plane, which landed near Rovno on 15 April, they found a camera, some rolls of exposed film, and a map of the Soviet Union. This may have been the plane that Rowehl sent to photograph Sverdlovsk, the leading industrial city of the Urals, almost a 3,000-mile round trip from Kirkenes in northern Norway, and that never came back. But the Russians merely registered a protest. Even when their fighters forced down a Ju 86 that had lost altitude due to motor damage early in June, recovering the camera and all its pictures, no serious repercussions ensued.

From mid-April to mid-June, the flights became more systematic and remained at about the same rate of three a day. These mainly served to update older photographs, dating from May and October 1940, of Russian fortifications. The priority for the new pictures ran from close to the Russo-German line of demarcation, the most urgently desired, through the areas around Rovno and Lutsk in western Russia, and, last of all, to Kiev in the interior. The photographs looked down the throats of the Russian guns. Some from 4 April 1941, 12 inches by 12, showed artillery emplacements, antitank trenches, and field fortifications in Soviet-occupied southeast Po-land around the small towns of Bobrowka, Wolka Zapałowska, and Buczyna.

None of this contributed much to an overall estimation of the size of the Red army, as by revealing the number and size of its camps, or of the industrial potential of the Soviet Union, as by disclosing its total factory acreage. The size of the country precluded anything approaching complete coverage. So the Rowehl group provided some details of economic intelli-gence, additions to bomber target folders, and indications that the Russian roads were better than the Germans had thought, but mainly operational and tactical information about Russian fortifications in the expected path of the German armies. Valuable, but not fundamental.

Germany's victory over Russia in World War I had been greatly helped by its complete mastery of the Czarist military communications. The great triumph of Tannenberg, which catapulted Hindenburg and Ludendorff to fame and power, had been made possible by German intercepts of Russian army messages. Immediately after the end of the war, the embryonic Ger-man army cipher bureau selected as one of its major targets the messages of the Communist forces fighting in Poland. Though these successes faded as the situation there and in the Soviet Union stabilized, the World War I precedent stimulated Germany's postwar radio intelligence. It focused in particular on the Russian maneuvers, seeking to obtain information about the Soviet armed forces from their radio traffic.

But things were no longer so easy. The Russians had learned their own lesson from Tannenberg, and they had vastly improved their traffic procedures, their cipher systems, and above all their radio discipline. Indeed, their radio camouflage had become the best in Europe. This largely negated the one advantage a foreign intercept organization had: that Russia's size and relative poverty, which kept it from producing as many telephones, telegraphs, and especially as much wire as the West, forced the Red army to radio much more than most armies.

The Germans gradually increased their radio intelligence organization for the east to three intercept companies by September 1939. But direction-finding was only attempted from East Prussia, and this narrow base formed such acute angles in the fixes that the Germans could not accurately locate the Russian transmitters. Furthermore, they could not in general solve the Red army cryptosystems. At best, they gleaned a few crumbs of information during Soviet maneuvers.

Things improved a little after the attack on Poland, mainly because the excitement of war led to violations of the normally rigid Russian service procedures. German intercept companies that had moved into southern Poland picked up the radio traffic of Russian forces entering that country from the east. The Germans ascertained the presence of many individual troop units and their attachment to the army, the air force, or the secret police. But—perhaps because they undertook no cryptanalysis, perhaps because of the excellent Russian radio security, perhaps because of both—they could not discover overall organization. When the Russians occupied the Baltic countries, their short-wave transmissions landed, by a freak of nature, with extreme clarity into the same area of southern Poland. The cleartext chat enabled the Germans to reconstruct the Baltic tactical organization quite well. During the Winter War, the Germans and the Finns followed pretty well the movements of major Russian formations. Later, during the build-up for BARBAROSSA, the Germans boosted to eight the number of intercept units in the east. The older ones—particularly that of Army Group Center—brought the newer ones up to date quickly. But in part they faced a daunting task: their 250 receivers faced an estimated 10,000 Russian transmitters. And in part the Russian radio system remained too hermetic for them. Though they obtained some local information on troops near the border, German radio intelligence failed to obtain solid information on how big the Red army really was.

Soon after Hitler took power, the Abwehr reenergized its somewhat lapsed work against the Soviet Union. This centered in Königsberg, a seaport on the Baltic that was the capital of East Prussia. The Abwehr post there had maintained, since 1927, a liaison officer with the intelligence service of neighboring Lithuania. Germany had no common border with Russia, and the Abwehr hoped to utilize Lithuania's—some 300 miles of forests and swampland—to infiltrate its spies into the Soviet Union. But nothing useful happened. The Abwehr blamed the Lithuanian intelligence service, which it said did not lift a finger either to help Germans or to spy against Russia itself. With the collapse of this feeble attempt, the Abwehr virtually quit trying to inject its agents into the Soviet Union from Lithuania. The absorption of that country by the Soviet Union in June 1940 precluded any future endeavors.

A little while after he assumed his post as Abwehr spy chief in 1936, Piekenbrock had arranged with the espionage services of Austria and Hungary to try to get agents into Russia. He also tried from Rumania, Bulgaria, China, and Japan. Results proved meager. The Königsberg post activated its contacts in Poland. It found an officer who, though he would not betray his own country, hated the Russians. But his efforts, and those of other such agents, foundered on the difficulty of passing the tightly watched frontier. Only from Abwehr spies controlled through Finland and Turkey did any even moderately noteworthy information come.

The Abwehr attempted other tricks. Ships calling at Soviet ports might insert agents. German businessmen visiting the Soviet Union could perhaps be patriotically inspired to observe things closely and then report on them when they returned. Members of Soviet diplomatic and trade missions in German might be subverted. Not one of these techniques produced a significant result. The shipboard agents were caught. Most businessmen either refused to jeopardize their persons and their profits or proved ineffectual as spies. And though a few blackmailed Russians yielded up some military crumbs, they produced nothing of real value.

Only slightly more fruitful were the contacts with anti-Stalin Russian émigré groups. The Abwehr I desk man at Königsberg connected one day with the Danzig branch of a group called the Green Oak. Its members claimed to be in communication with friends who had remained in Communist Russia. The Abwehr checked and then made the head of the Danzig Green Oak an Abwehr agent. He soon produced the names of several high Red army officers ready, he said, for sabotage operations. The Abwehr established that they were former Czarist officers. All seemed proper. But suspicion sprouted when the Green Oak refused to reveal more about their connections to Russia than that they ran through the Baltic countries. A visit to the head of the entire Green Oak organization in Bucharest produced a small pile of reports on, among other things, Russian troop formations. When the Abwehr passed this to Foreign Armies, back came the evaluation: Material already known from Green Oak branches in Paris and Brussels; much of what is true comes from Russian newspapers; some of the rest is false, probably made up. This squelched the Green Oak.

Ukrainian exiles received Abwehr attention. Some of them were friendly because Germany might help again, as it did after World War I, to set up an independent Ukraine. The Abwehr got some of them to obtain military intelligence for Germany. In 1937, Canaris expanded this work by making contact with the Organization of Ukrainian Nationalists. Conferences were held, preparations mounted. But again almost nothing happened, and the intelligence results remained negligible.

One of the greatest potential reservoirs of agents in Russia was comprised by the more than 1.2 million ethnic Germans living in Russia. As Soviet citizens, they suffered the brutal expropriation of their lands and the killings to which Stalin subjected his native kulaks. But they also enjoyed the same opportunities: they had their own autonomous Socialist Soviet Republic of the Volga Germans in the U.S.S.R. Many stayed in touch with the homeland through the Deutsches Ausland-Institut and other agencies for Germans abroad, whose files, however, contained little more on Russia than news clippings. But although the Abwehr thus could learn the names and addresses of these Germans, it never helped one to worm his way into a high central government post or even to subvert a key Russian official into spying for Germany.

The Russo-German pact of August 1939, which freed Hitler from worry about the U.S.S.R., was followed by orders to refrain from spying, which might have irritated the Russians. But as Germany eliminated one enemy after another in the west, fear of Russian interference declined. Interest in destroying communism rose, and espionage activity picked up. Documents captured after the Polish campaign enabled the Germans to make contact with Polish spy nets in White Russia and the Ukraine. The common border that Germany now had for the first time with the U.S.S.R. enormously facilitated slipping agents into that country. The Abwehr created a network of agent support points and training camps near the border and sent scores of agents over it. The first were poorly trained and equipped. Many had identical assignments, because the Germans expected that many would be captured. Dozens were. But others came back with details of Soviet installations. A subagent of agent V-19540 reported on 20 December 1940 an airfield northeast of the little town of Monasterek, in the western Ukraine, with four hangars on its western edge. The agent counted 20 planes and noted that bombing and parachuting were practiced there daily.

Though Hitler had decided on war with Russia in the summer of 1940, and though Foreign Armies East had stepped up its demands for spy intelligence out of Russia in the fall, it was not until after Hitler issued his BARBAROSSA directive on 18 December 1940 that the Abwehr was assigned specifically to participate in the preparations. And then its activities were strictly circumscribed.

At the end of that December or the beginning of January, Canaris and Piekenbrock met in Berchtesgaden with Keitel, head of OKW, and his assistant, Jodl. In his office, Jodl told them that war between Germany and the Soviet Union would come by the summer and that the Abwehr had to assist. It was the first time Piekenbrock had heard about this. Speaking of the war as already won, Jodl said that the general staff needed no specifics about the Red army as a whole. He assigned the Abwehr only to observe the changes in Soviet forces at the frontier. Jodl thus barred the Abwehr from any strategic espionage and restricted it to operational and tactical details. After declaring that Hitler believed that Russia would collapse after the battles at the frontiers, Jodl ended the brief conference.

Within the limits of his assignment, Piekenbrock intensified spying against the Soviet Union. He conferred frequently with Matzky, the O Qu IV, and with Kinzel, head of Foreign Armies East, to define more carefully the espionage assignments required. All Abwehr posts working against Russia were directed to commit more agents. Army group and army headquarters likewise began to send spies across the demarcation line. These agents were more highly qualified than the earlier ones. Many had attended spy schools in Stettin, Königsberg, Vienna, and Berlin; many carried radios. Their numbers rose into the hundreds, but scores of them were captured. In addition, teams of disguised German soldiers occasionally pierced the frontier zone to reconnoiter. In April 1941, a 16-man squad wearing Red army engineer uniforms crossed into White Russia near Avgustov. A Russian border patrol surprised them. In the firefight, 11 Germans were killed, 5 captured.

The penetration of all these agents was shallow. Their job was merely to ascertain the disposition of Russian troops and installations at the frontier. None pushed deep into Russia. None were recruited within the vast bureaucracies of the Soviet state. None were assigned to provide clues to the overall Russian strength. But once one did report on the larger issues. The nature of his report, and the Abwehr's evaluation of it, indicate better than anything else the quality of German espionage against Russia. "When it comes to a conflict of a somewhat strong enemy with the Soviet Union," affirmed the spy, "the ruin of the Communist Party will occur extraordinarily fast, so that it will no longer be capable of mastering the situation, and the U.S.S.R. will crumble into a string of independent countries." This the Abwehr characterized as "specially accurate."

One of the most basic of the German agencies of intelligence in the Soviet Union was the office of the military attaché. General Ernst Köstring, still slim in his early sixties, had been born and raised in Moscow and so was fluent in Russian and familiar with the ways of the country. He had fought against the Czarist army in World War I, and had studied the Red army in T 3 early in the 1920s. He had served from 1931 to 1933 as a military observer in Moscow during the last years of the German-Russian military cooperation before returning there officially as military and air attaché on 1 October 1935. He had a self-deprecating humor: he once referred to the likelihood of getting stuck in the Russian mud as his "hero's death." But he could also be an obnoxious snob, calling the food at an American diplomatic reception "grub out of the Frigidaire" and the Russians there as "of the worst quality." And he lacked what the Germans call "Zivilkourage." Fearing one of Hitler's temper tantrums, he thought it better, when seated next to the Führer at an attaché dinner, not to utter his own views on the Soviet Union.

Six months after his arrival in Moscow, he wrote the head of Foreign Armies to explain, "The experience of several months' work here has shown that it is almost out of the question to get military information or information distantly connected with war industry, even over the most harmless things." Visits to troop units had stopped. Little was to be seen at maneuvers. The Russians seemed to be giving all attachés a mixture of truth and lies. All this was why he could answer only a few of the hundreds of questions put to him from Germany. Nevertheless, he remained hopeful that eventually he would succeed in making "a mosaic of the further development and organization of the Red army." He gave the German consulates lists of questions and photographs of Soviet equipment so that they could obtain at least some crude intelligence by observing the twice-yearly parades in the provincial centers. He visited distant cities of the Soviet Union. Sometimes he flew, sometimes he used his oversized touring car, whose 60-gallon gasoline tank let him get from one consulate to another even if he could not buy gasoline along the way. In June 1937, for example, he drove from Moscow to Tiflis and back, accompanied all 2,000 miles by two Russian secret policemen. This trip generated no new information but confirmed much.

By 1938, however, the German consulates had been closed, no attachés had attended maneuvers for two years, and foreigners had been increasingly cut off from contact with Russians. Parliamentary debates, which in many countries sometimes dealt with military policy, had always been lacking in the Soviet Union, and budgets there spoke only in percentages, never in absolute figures. Köstring was forced back upon three meager sources: his trips and some drives in the Moscow area, the controlled newspapers, which yielded little, and exchanges with other attachés, who knew little more than he.

As a result of these limitations, Köstring's reports almost never furnished hard data about the Red army. They dealt mainly in military generalities, military-political affairs, and economic matters. He expressed his attitude toward the Red army most concisely in a letter to Foreign Armies Branch chief Tippelskirch on 22 August 1938, a year after the purges had begun:

> Through the elimination of by far the greatest number of higher officers, who had in part mastered their skill quite well through a decade of practice and theoretical learning, the Red army has declined in its operational ability. The lack of older and experienced commanders will adversely affect the

training of the troops for some time. The already existing lack of responsibility will now have still further disadvantageous effects.

The best commanders are lacking. But nothing allows one to recognize and prove that the attacking power of the mass has sunk so far that the army does not represent a very noteworthy factor in a warlike quarrel.

On the war economy may be said: Organization, further development of the war economy are, just like industry, strongly affected; a present stagnation is recognizable.

A few months earlier, he had summed up his views in a talk with the British military attaché in a single sentence: "The Soviet army is no longer of international importance."

The military attaché's office began furnishing more concrete data—namely, on the size of the Soviet ground force—as the date for the German attack approached. On 22 April 1941, Lieutenant Colonel Hans Krebs, deputizing for the ill Köstring, wrote Berlin: "The maximum strength of the war army, certainly not yet reached, calculated by us at 200 rifle divisions, was recently confirmed to me by the Finnish and Japanese military attachés." A few weeks later, Köstring and Krebs returned to Berlin to report in person. They told Hitler that the Red army had not much improved. They told Halder that nothing really new had come up. Three weeks later, back in Moscow, Köstring referred in a letter to Tippelskirch, then the O Qu IV, to a Russian army of about 2 million at the western frontiers. But dimming the significance of these figures were the judgments of Köstring and Krebs. The previous September Köstring had declared that the Red army, though improving, would need four years "until it reached its former heights." Now, in May, Krebs said it would take twenty.

All the information acquired was fed into the evaluating agencies of intelligence. One of these was Thomas's armaments office. On 13 February 1941, he issued a memorandum on "The War-Economic Effects of an Operation in the East." It was basically a mouth-watering menu of the riches that would fall to Germany, but a few paragraphs discussed the effect upon Russia of a German conquest of all its territory up to the Urals and the Caucasus. (In his attack, which began 21 June 1941, Hitler planned to occupy at most only this portion of the Soviet Union; the eastern rump would remain as a vassal state.) Thomas rang perhaps the only tocsin in the whole hubbub of German preparations for the attack when he declared, "The industry of the Urals and the Asiatic part [of the U.S.S.R.] can in general exist without the European part of the country." But then he listed deprecatingly what this rump would have left: 18 percent of the U.S.S.R.'s munitions production, 31 percent of its weapons production, 24 percent of its tank production, 10 percent of its oil. In effect this muted the alarm he had previously sounded and let the attack proceed without any real warning of its economic dangers. Not until 2 October 1941, long after the die had been cast, did he advise his superiors that even the loss of virtually all European Russia "need not necessarily lead to a breakdown. This is rather to be expected only after the loss of the industrial areas of the Urals." Thomas was saying that even complete success of the original German war plan would not have achieved its goal but would have left the Soviet Union economically viable. But he was saying it three months too late.

The other major intelligence-evaluating agency was Foreign Armies East. Its staff, under Colonel Kinzel, weighed the details that came in from the various sources, kept an up-to-date count of the number of various Russian formations, so far as its information permitted, and upon request supplied the planners with these details. The summary judgment on the Red army that the navy recorded as that of the German general staff at the end of 1939 stemmed ultimately from it: "Numerically powerful military instrument.—Commitment of the 'mass.'—Organization, equipment, and means of command insufficient.—Leadership principles good, leadership itself too young and inexperienced. . . . —Battle value of the troops in a heavy battle doubtful. The Russian 'mass' is not up to an army with modern equipment and superior leadership."

On 15 January 1941, a month after Hitler had ordered war with Russia, Foreign Armies East issued *The War Forces of the Soviet Socialist Republics,* a 72-page summary. This formed the basis for the intelligence work of lower staffs and the point of departure for revisions by Foreign Armies East. Its "Overall Judgment of the Red Army" held that various improvements would gradually raise the level of the Red army, but "only after years, if not decades." But "the Russian character—heavy, mechanical, shy of decisions and responsibility—does not change." It concluded: "The strength of the Red army rests on the mass and on the number of the masses, on the relative undemanding nature, the toughness, and the bravery of the soldiers. It finds its natural compatriots in the size and the impassability of the country. The weakness lies in the clumsiness of commanders of all ranks, in sticking to the book, in training that does not meet modern requirements, in the avoidance of responsibility and the lack of organization that is noticeable in all areas." This view of the basic insufficiency of the Red army and its leadership Kinzel never altered. In April he reported to Halder that "young majors are commanding regiments and colonels, divisions."

To a great extent these were imponderables. How well did Foreign Armies East determine the size of the Red army and the weapons with which it would fight?

Russian armor, even Hitler recognized, was "numerically the most in the world." The estimate was 10,000 tanks. The Germans had only 3,500.

But the discrepancy did not worry them. They regarded their tanks as superior to the Russian, the vast majority of which they considered obsolete, though they did know of a monster tank much heavier than anything else in existence: the 43.5-ton KV-1, first produced in 1940. In fact, the Germans had underestimated the size of the Russian armored force by almost 2½. At the start of the German invasion, the Russians had 24,000 tanks. The Germans, Keitel felt, never caught up. Equally important, they were unpleasantly surprised by the appearance of the most successful tank of World War II: the T-34. Though several hundred had fought the Japanese in the Manchurian border battles three years before, the Germans had absolutely no inkling of its existence. They met it near the start of the campaign, and it soon spread "tank terror" through the troops, for its thick frontal armor easily deflected the early German antitank fire. One regiment first encountered it southeast of Smolensk.

> We hear loud motor noises. . . . Then with our binoculars we see the bow of a steel colossus push through a row of trees before us, there another and there four T-34s. . . . The light howitzers have no effect on the giants, though their fire is accurate. . . . [Antitank guns] cold-bloodedly let them roll up to 30 yards away. Then they fire. Direct hit—but a ricochet! The tank rolls closer and closer, hit after hit hails against its front—it does no good. Every, but every, shot ricochets away! The tank rolls over the gun and squashes it to a formless lump of iron. [At a range of 2,000 yards, heavier artillery fires.] Our armor-headed shells have tracers, so we can see that the fourth shot is a direct hit. But at this great distance even the 40-pound shell glances ineffectually off. . . . Then behind us we hear a familiar rumble that sounds like music in our ears. It is two German assault guns. . . . We can easily follow the tracer shots. . . . Every shot of the assault gun is a direct hit but—we don't believe our eyes—every shell bounces off!

Not until the T-34s, turning to get into a better firing position, exposed their thinner flanks could the Germans disable some of them. Later the Germans improved their antitank guns and designed tanks of their own to match the T-34. But their unpreparedness for it at the start of the campaign cost them many guns and many men.

The Luftwaffe estimates of the Red air force strength likewise fell dangerously low. One factor in this was perhaps that the Luftwaffe had greatly overrated the French air force and now was overcorrecting. On 1 February 1941 the Luftwaffe I c raised his 1939 estimate of 6,000 airplanes to 10,500. Of these, it figured 7,500 in European Russia. A few weeks later, however, chief of the army general staff Halder counted only 5,655 aircraft in European Russia. Only 60 percent of these were ready for combat, he noted, and only 100 to 200 were regarded as modern. Though the Russians had a 6:1 numerical preponderance in total craft, in combat-ready planes the ratio was 1:1, and in combat the Germans enjoyed,

Halder felt, a decisive superiority: their better training. But on the day of the attack the Soviet Union apparently had many more airplanes than the Germans had calculated: 18,000 of all types, half of them in the western military areas. As Halder ruefully noted: "The Luftwaffe has considerably underestimated the enemy numerically."

The most important of the numerical questions facing the general staff was, of course, How big is the Red army? The Germans consistently underestimated its size.

In January 1941, Foreign Armies East computed the peacetime Red army at 2 million men, the wartime at 4 million. In fact, on 1 January 1941 the Red army already had 4,205,000 men. Halder recognized by the end of April that the Red army stood at what German staffs regarded as wartime strength. But he was even then probably underestimating its current total strength by a seventh, since on the day of the invasion the Red army numbered 5,005,000 men.

These figures included the forces in the Far East, which the Germans discounted, on the ground that Russia would be defeated before they could be brought up. Within the framework of the size of the Red army, the most vital intelligence problem facing the Germans was the number of large formations—divisions and mechanized brigades—available to resist their onslaught.

In August 1940, when General Erich Marcks drew up the first sketches for the attack on Russia, he reckoned with an enemy strength of 171 large formations. This referred to the 117 infantry divisions, 24 cavalry divisions, and 30 mechanized brigades in European Russia. Counted were not only the Russian troops along the German-Russian demarcation line in Poland and along the Rumanian border, but also—cautiously—those troops on the Finnish and Turkish frontiers, even though the Germans thought that they would be tied down by defensive duties. By the beginning of February 1941 the 171 large formations had risen to 180. From then to the start of the attack this figure rose by an average of nearly 6 percent a month. Some of this was no doubt due to new Soviet formations and so reflected a growth of the Red army. But much of it was simply due to German discovery of hitherto unknown Russian formations. On 29 March 1941, for example, Halder noted that the Russians had "15 more divisions than previously thought." In the last 14 days before the invasion, the Germans learned of 14 new large formations—an appalling rate of discovery. On the day before the invasion, the Germans counted 226½ large formations in European Russia. This was a rise of almost one-third since August 1940. The German estimates of the number of formations not guarding against Finland and Turkey and so available to fight Germans rose between August 1940 and 20 May 1941—when there was still time for reconsideration—from 148 to 180. Yet this increase of more than one-fifth in the forces that the Wehrmacht would have to slug its way through did not prod the German generals into altering their strategy in the least or into wondering whether still more unknown units made it unwise even to attack.

The awful truth about the enormity of the miscalculation of the Soviet Union dawned on Halder on the 51st day of the campaign:

> In the entire situation stands out increasingly that the colossus Russia, which consciously prepared itself for the war with the complete lack of restraint that is inherent in totalitarian countries, has been underestimated by us. This determination refers as much to organizational as to economic strengths, to the transportation system, above all to pure military capability. At the start of the war we reckoned with about 200 enemy divisions. So far we have already counted 360.

Two weeks later, Hitler himself acknowledged to Mussolini that "for the first time since the beginning of the conflict, the German military intelligence service had failed." It had not tried very hard in the first place. A few rebuffs and some obstacles sufficed to chill the Abwehr's ardor, never warm, for spying in the Soviet Union. The spy agency never seriously attempted any strategic espionage, despite the presence in that vast and heterogeneous country of elements bitterly opposed to the regime. The radio intelligence organization sometimes did not trouble to cryptanalyze Russian intercepts. It indolently accepted the limited listening areas made available to it by German conquests instead of energetically ringing Russia with intercept stations in Turkey and Finland and the Balkans. One result of all this was the T-34 failure, which took the lives of many young Germans. Another was an inadequacy in ascertaining the number of Russian units. The British, for example, who were not even intending to attack Russia, counted 225 large formations in European Russia on 14 June 1941. Four days later, the Germans had learned of only 220½. Moreover, the British listed many more armored units and fewer infantry—thereby indicating greater power—than the Germans.

Why did German intelligence fail? Why had it not tried harder? For the same reason that the whole failed of which it was a part: German planning for BARBAROSSA. And that planning did fail—disastrously. The high command did not give its troops winter clothing. It did not prepare industry for a long-term production effort. It did not work out important elements of the operations plans. It supplied its advancing armies with only three months' worth of fuel. And it kept fully a third of its divisions in the west.

Why?

Because it was confident that Germany could quickly defeat Soviet Russia. Others felt the same way—even enemies and neutrals. Britain's Joint Intelligence Committee asserted on 14 June: "The Red army is unlikely to offer a successful resistance in open warfare to an army so highly mechanized or ably led as the German army, although its large numbers of tanks might be an embarrassment to its opponents.... the first phase, involving the occupation of the Ukraine and of Moscow, might take as little as 3 or 4 weeks, or as long as 6 weeks (or more)." Diplomatic circles in Moscow did not expect Russia to be able to withstand Germany for more than three or four weeks. A day or so after the German attack, U.S. Secretary of War Stimson sent President Roosevelt his views, which he said coincided entirely with those of Chief of Staff George C. Marshall and the War Plans Division: "Germany will be thoroughly occupied in beating Russia for a minimum of one month and a possible maximum of three months."

But though the German and the Anglo-American views appeared congruent, and though they probably stemmed largely from the same dislike of communism, they differed profoundly. For the English and Americans, a Russian defeat was the more pessimistic, and hence more conservative, assumption. For the Germans, on the other hand, the assumption that they would quickly defeat the Soviet Union was the more optimistic one, hence the more imprudent.

The German confidence in victory over the Soviet Union, which was rooted mainly in arrogance, exacerbated by a blind abhorrence of communism and an invalid racism, debilitated all areas of German planning, including intelligence. The Germans were so certain that the Red army would promptly surrender and that the Soviet government would collapse that elaborate planning and information-gathering seemed pointless. Moreover, intelligence plays a smaller role in the offense, where one's own will is the decisive factor, than in the defense, where the enemy is seeking to impose his will and a knowledge of this will is consequently essential for success. That the Germans were attacking thus further diminished the attention they paid to intelligence. They invested their energies elsewhere. All in all, they simply saw no need to whip their intelligence agencies into questing for still more data.

On the conscious level, at least. Unconsciously, the planning and intelligence failures may have been designed to protect the German assurance of victory. A thorough examination of all the evidence—the details of Russia's industrial capacity, her manpower, her size, the successful tenacity of her rulers in retaining power—followed by detailed forecasts of all the economic and military possibilities, pessimistic as well as optimistic, might well have shown Hitler and his generals that, no matter what, they could not defeat Russia. To preclude this danger, they made sure that intelligence and planning would not touch upon these questions. They limited intelligence to tactics and planning to trivialities.

Thus they preserved their certainty in their victory. But that illusion, and the hatred that sustained it, cost Hitler and his generals their pride, their power, and their despicable war.

The Biggest Surprise

ON 1 March 1942, Colonel Ulrich Liss, head of Foreign Armies West, issued a top-secret document. He had 11 copies mimeographed. Most were addressed to other intelligence units. Liss sent three to command agencies: the OKW's Operations Staff, the chief of the General Staff of the Army, and Army Group B, covering western France.

They went over on one of the quietest days of a lull in the war. Throughout the world, no major actions took place. No campaigns were in progress, except for the generalized Japanese lightning advance over the western Pacific. The Nazi and the Communist armies, sprawled in mortal combat on the steppes of Russia, quivered but did not thrash. The Luftwaffe dropped a few bombs on southwest England. Defeated and half-occupied France shipped gasoline to Rommel from its colonies in North Africa. Everyone waited. In Germany and Russia the pause meant preparation. For the one, it meant readying for an onslaught to succeed where that of the previous year had failed. For the other, it meant girding for a battle for existence.

But what were Britain and America doing? Churchill and Roosevelt had conferred for three weeks in Washington. When Roosevelt told Congress about it, he disclosed no secrets. He said merely that "Powerful and offensive actions must and will be taken in proper time." It was the job of Liss to divine what specifically this meant.

His top-secret document set out his views on this. It was not the first in which he sought to forecast Allied moves. He had, in January, discussed the strategic situation resulting from the entry of Japan and America into the war. The memorandum dealt mainly with Allied moves in Europe, Africa, and the Middle East as repercussions of the war in the Pacific. Perhaps its most noteworthy point was its unexpressed assumption that the initiative had passed to the enemy.

His March document assumed the same thing. But it went further than the older one. Liss now considered "The British-American Operations Possibilities Against Europe and Africa in the Year 1942" as primary operations instead of as secondary effects. He mentioned the possibility that in Allied strategy the destruction of Germany might precede that of Japan. And he incorporated an important new element: the navy's investigation of the Allied shipping problem.

Yet his study added little to German knowledge of Allied intentions. In part this was because the overall war situation, in particular America's unpreparedness, made it evident that the Allies could not mount major offensives against Germany in the near future. In part it was because Liss, like men everywhere who look into the future professionally, admitted all possibilities; no matter what happened, he would be able to refute accusations that he had not foreseen it. This did not help his superiors much. To say, as Liss did, that an Allied attack via Murmansk on the Arctic fringe of Europe was "conceivable" contributed no new knowledge. The main thing that his memorandum did was to solidify the inchoate ideas of the high commanders, to set them down on paper, and to support them with such new details as the tonnage figures.

"In general," Liss declared, "the British-American command is presumably restricted in 1942 to preparing for a major 1943 offensive against Europe by more or less comprehensive individual actions." He had no idea where these raids might come. So he guessed from north to south on the basis of general principles.

An Allied landing on the coast of Norway had both advantages and disadvantages, he observed; he didn't say which would predominate. The Germans had "barely to reckon" with a landing on the Danish and German North Sea coasts, and one on the Dutch and Belgian coasts was "improbable." An assault on the French Channel coast was "barely conceivable" without full air superiority. One on the coast of the Bay of Biscay would be but "slightly effective operationally." The question of a British landing in Spain or Portugal was "primarily a political" one. Swinging round the tip of the Continent into the Mediterranean on his tour d'horizon, Liss wrote that "As long as France maintains her North African empire, the probability of British landings in Italy remains small." Attacks against the Balkans or the Caucasus out of the Middle East needed be considered "only in the later course of the year 1942, if at all." All in all, he concluded, "the great demands placed on tonnage by Japan's entry into the war make major British-American undertakings against the defended coasts of Europe improbable in the year 1942."

But Churchill and Roosevelt had already agreed in Washington on a major offensive: an invasion of North Africa. Among their reasons for this choice, the most important was inability to do anything else. The Allies did not have enough men and ships to win the war the most direct way: by invading Europe and conquering the territory of Germany. But a Mediter-

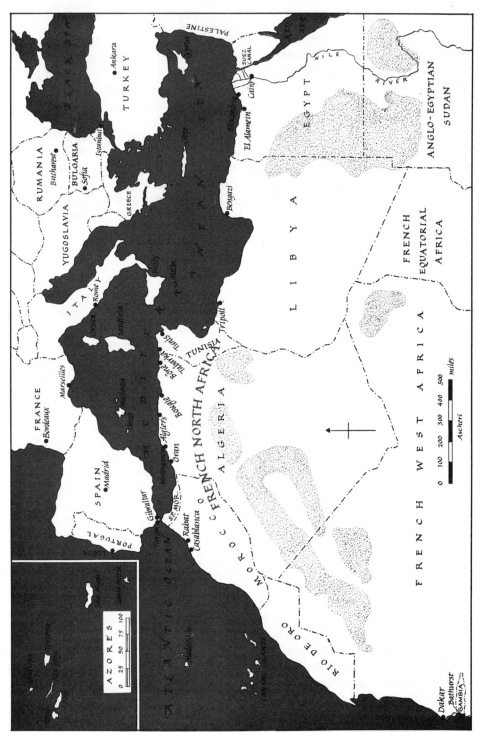

North Africa and the Mediterranean

ranean offensive offered strategic advantages of its own. It might shake
Italy loose from the Axis. It would cause Germany to pull forces out of the
Russian front and so would relieve the U.S.S.R. It would secure the flank
of the eventual cross-Channel attack. It would give the Allies an enormous
boost in morale. Most important at that stage of the war, it would let ships
pass through the Suez Canal to reach the Middle East and Russia instead
of sailing around the Cape of Good Hope. This would, Britain's First Sea
Lord pointed out, release 225 ships for other purposes.

In reaching the North African decision, questions arose about the three
chief Atlantic archipelagoes. Portugal's Azores lay a thousand miles west of
Lisbon. Spain's Canaries clung to the northwestern coast of Africa. Portugal's Cape Verdes stood off the bulge of Africa, on whose westernmost
tip stood France's Dakar. But Churchill felt that it was operationally "not
necessary to take over the Canaries and the Azores" before invading North
Africa. Consequently, aside from making some contingency plans, the two
governments took no steps to occupy the three island groups or Dakar.

Liss, nevertheless, said tentatively, "One must reckon with the possibility
of a successful attack against the Portuguese, perhaps also the Spanish,
islands in the Atlantic and with operations in west Africa." He was more
definite about Dakar. The Allies would not attack it from the sea as they
had in their unsuccessful attempt in 1940 because the forces there had
been increased by 15 infantry and 4 artillery battalions. "Rather it is to be
expected that the attack would be conducted over land from Bathurst," a
British port 100 miles to the south in the colony of Gambia.

As for the actual invasion that the Allies were intending, Liss considered
that, in comparison with a Dakar undertaking, "A British landing on the
Atlantic coast of French North Africa appears less probable." He never
once mentioned the possibility of a landing on the Mediterranean coast.

The lull of 1 March ended abruptly the following day as the entire Soviet
50th Army went over to the attack. Individual actions like this peppered
the spring of 1942. The Germans captured all the Crimea but Sevastopol
and then began their final throttling of that port. The British began to
bomb the Reich heavily. The U-boats enjoyed their "happy time" on the
eastern seaboard of the United States, sending flames and towering columns
of black smoke from torpedoed tankers high into the sky in full view of
watchers on the shores. And on 12 March Hitler listened as navy chief
Raeder discussed the problems of a possible invasion of Norway by the
Allies. The discussion riveted Hitler's attention, for this possibility had
come practically to dominate the Führer's thoughts about the west. Norway's chief importance was to protect the ships bringing the nickel ore
from Finland's Petsamo over the North Cape and down the Norwegian
leads. This ore was essential, Hitler said, "to produce high-grade steels,
mainly for building airplane and submarine motors." Any Allied incursion

that interrupted it would have brought his war machine to a halt. This was why he called Norway the "zone of destiny of this war." There were other reasons as well. He wanted to guard his northern flank, to cover his Atlantic-bound U-boats, to sink the Allied convoys to Murmansk. Consequently, he repeatedly warned his forces of the danger of a British invasion of Norway (which, not so coincidentally, Churchill was unsuccessfully urging). And after his 12 March conference with Raeder, he ordered that the completion of a battle group of surface ships to destroy any enemy landing forces be accelerated.

The Mediterranean interested him far less. It played no similar strategic role in his concept of world conquest, which centered upon the Eurasian land mass. The southern theater had only entered his vision in 1940. Mussolini had belatedly struck France from behind and then had blundered into an invasion of Greece, compelling the Führer to rescue him there and in North Africa. Even then Hitler paid this—to him—secondary theater little attention. De Gaulle's taking of French Equatorial Africa called forth little more than a declaration that it was up to the Vichy French to secure their African possessions. Though Hitler repeatedly toyed with taking Gibraltar and invading Malta, both of which would have had the most profound strategic effects on the war, in the end he dropped both ideas. He saw Rommel and his brilliant campaigns largely as a propaganda tool; the thought of his linking up in the Near East with German forces coming down from the Caucasus remained little more than a daydream.

When from time to time circumstances compelled him to attend to the Mediterranean, he did so briefly and reluctantly. In 1941, a piece of intelligence suggested that the British intended "to establish themselves in North Africa, to occupy the Portuguese islands and overthrow Franco." It stung him into ordering preparations to resist such a move. But nothing happened, and the preparations lapsed. When the Americans replaced the British occupation force on Iceland, and Raeder worried that they might next shoulder their way into one of the Atlantic archipelagoes, Hitler calmed him with some feisty, empty words: "As soon as the U.S.A. occupies the Portuguese or the Spanish islands, I shall march into Spain; from there I shall bring panzer and infantry divisions to North Africa in order to secure it." Later, he read but took no action on a remarkable OKW memorandum. The British and Americans believed, it said, that Germany could not be defeated on the continent and that the strategic situation could be fundamentally altered only in the Mediterranean. To do this, it argued, the Allies would have to eliminate the Axis bridgehead under Rommel, gain possession of the entire North African coast, achieve sea and air mastery, and squeeze Italy with so tight a blockade that she would collapse. This closely paralleled the conclusions that Roosevelt and Churchill would reach several months later. Hitler approved the appreciation and circulated it to his high commands and his foreign minister. Then he forgot about it. For he simply felt no concern about this war on the periphery; nothing that happened there would seriously affect him, he thought. It did not distract him from his great struggle in the east.

This was the situation and Hitler's attitude when Liss, thinking ahead of his Führer, or more globally, or more realistically, or all three, distributed his report.

Three weeks later—perhaps because of Liss's report, but probably not —Hitler issued his Directive No. 40 for the Conduct of the War. "The European coasts are exposed to the greatest extent to the danger of enemy landings in the near future," it began, and then gave some general instructions for coastal defenses. Wisps of news about enemy landings floated in increasingly. On 10 April, Hitler received intelligence that the English and Americans were planning a "great surprise." He thought that it might be either the mass use of small delayed-fuse bombs, which had been reported earlier, or a landing. Two weeks later the possibility of Allied landings in French and Spanish Morocco and in Iberia was discussed by the OKW. Canaris visited North Africa to see things for himself. Returning, he reported that enemy troops were expected to land in west Africa to attack the Axis from the south; support points were already being created. Five days later, on 19 May, Liss told superiors that Vice Admiral Lord Louis Mountbatten, the chief of combined operations, was planning a landing operation—which he in fact was. Sources later pointed to Denmark and to Norway as its targets. Agent F-3197 in Spain reported that Portuguese industrialists said that pro-English circles expected an Anglo-Saxon occupation of Portugal. The Hamburg Abwehr post, for which he worked, noted on his report that its "trustworthy" agent F-3148 had said the same thing six weeks before. Finally, on 29 May, Hitler signed Directive No. 42 for the Conduct of the War. It warned that the situation in France or French North Africa might make it necessary to occupy all of France, that the Allies might attack the Iberian peninsula, and that Germany should prepare countermeasures. Then he turned back with relief to Russia, the theater of his megalomania.

The following month, June 1942, Roosevelt and Churchill conferred again in Washington. They were planning what would be a two-pronged attack on North Africa. Forces would sail from America and land on the Atlantic coast of the French territories. Forces from Britain would pass the Pillars of Hercules and assault the Mediterranean shores of those territories.

During the conference, which newspaper headlines screamed would deal with the creation of the second front for which the Russians had long been clamoring, a report came in to the OKW. Small ships were assembling on the southern coast of England; railroad and cable sabotage was increasing in the area of the commander in chief west. The OKW said this hinted at a forthcoming landing operation. Three days later, the United States announced the creation of a headquarters for a European theater of operations. Named as commander was Major General Dwight D. Eisenhower. Hitler assigned the SS division Das Reich to the west. Then, as the conference ended, Roosevelt and Churchill released, at 11:30 a.m. Saturday, 27 June, their final communiqué. It promised that coming United Nations operations "will divert German strength from the attack on Russia."

Suddenly everything crystallized. Even the deliberately imprecise language left no doubt now that a second front would come. A target existed. Both sides could work toward it, each in its own way.

The next day, Sunday, the OKW reported that the number of small vessels assembled in Britain had risen to 2,802. It was clear what was happening. On Monday, Hitler said that he had to reckon with a major Anglo-American landing to create a second front. He met with Albert Speer and with General Kurt Zeitzler, then chief of staff to the commander in chief west, to discuss the construction of forts. He investigated strengthening the forces in France.

At the same time, Foreign Minister Ribbentrop, stung by the same evidence, was circularizing his major posts. "The main duty set the German foreign representatives throughout the world at present is the trustworthy and prompt transmission of all information on the question whether, when, and where England and America will make an invasion attempt."

At once replies poured in. The tone of urgency and the "main duty" phrase led many diplomats to submit something, anything, no matter how improbable, how trivial or self-evident, from any source that had even the faintest color of authenticity. The man in Lourenço Marques, capital of Portuguese East Africa, passed along the views of an English employee of the local English-language newspaper that Portugal was "not excluded" as the Allied target. Bern reported that the head of the European branch of Unilever believed that the attack would come in the Middle East because Europe and Africa were nuts too tough for the Allies to crack. From his summer resort near Istanbul, the ambassador in Turkey, Papen, cabled that Polish sources were saying that attacks would come first in Holland, then in France—and next week! Buenos Aires, in Portuguese-speaking Brazil, indicated an attack on northern Portugal. A "trustworthy" Spaniard known to the Barcelona consulate pointed to Iberia. Madrid reported that "cabinet circles" there spoke of the Canaries as the Allied target. And the consulate at Santander, the northern Spanish harbor, dutifully noted that rumors among the general public forecast that the invasion would come in Portugal.

German diplomats also reported more thoughtful comments from more solid sources. General Luis Orgaz, the high commissioner in Spanish Morocco, stated that if an attempt were to be made in Spain or Portugal, it would come before September and be on a large scale. The Spanish foreign minister expected no landings in Spain or the Canaries, though he admitted that Spain had sent troops to the islands "because they were always endangered." He predicted that the Portuguese would resist if the Allies landed in that country—but he refrained from saying whether they would land in the first place. The French commander in North Africa, General Alphonse Juin, believed that lack of shipping precluded a second front. An attack on Dakar or Casablanca was possible for prestige reasons, he thought, and perhaps someday a seizure of the Canaries. But in his view the British were simply concentrating on defending Egypt, for they were losing ground to Rommel just then.

One ambassador carried out his assignment in exemplary fashion. Oswald Baron von Hoyningen-Huene, in Lisbon, got his staff scratching for information, visited the northern part of Portugal to get a feel for the situation, and himself interviewed people. His staff's contacts passed along tidbits from the British and American missions in that neutral land. They reported that a "Colonel Donnovan"—probably William Donovan, recently named by Roosevelt to coordinate American intelligence—and the British naval attaché doubted an attack because shipping was lacking. Hoyningen-Huene talked with the Spanish ambassador to Portugal, who had conferred with Portuguese dictator Antonio de Oliveira Salazar the day before. The ambassador, Franco's brother, said that he and Salazar had agreed that no major danger threatened Portugal at the moment. Military men pointed to the total lack of Allied preparations for an invasion. Political circles reckoned with the possibility of an Allied seizure of the Azores if the British were driven from the Mediterranean. But Hoyningen-Huene pointed out that the Portuguese were sending troops to the Azores with the permission of the British.

Throughout the summer, reports continued to stream into Berlin at about two a day. None brought specific indications of a landing. As time went on, the diplomats did less of their own legwork and submitted more press summaries. Spies continued to report. The common denominator of all these reports was that each place usually indicated itself as the most likely area for an enemy landing. Nothing further was heard about the small-ship assembly on England's southern coast; that threat seemed to have faded. In July, Hitler concluded that "no real second front" was imminent. The calm persisted. In August, the OKM summed up the situation as it saw it after Inf III, Ribbentrop's spy service, had urgently telephoned it at 3 in the morning to report a rumor: the American embassy in Vichy had told American newspapermen to stand by their radios because the Anglo-American invasion was imminent. Commented the navy: "If all the talk about the invasion is really only a bluff, as for lack of anything better it might well be, then the sowing of these rumors would be a clue that the enemy side understands how to play that role down to the last little bit."

The army general staff was similarly negative. On 8 August, expressing views probably emanating from Liss, it declared: "Concerning a second front in the west or in Norway, no believable indications (readying of shipping in great volume, stopping of leaves, postal stoppage, increased fighter protection over the English coast, stronger activity of the British air force against France and the German Luftwaffe, preparation of troops) are reported." At the same time, incoming dispatches spoke increasingly of Allied abandonment of plans for a second front.

Suddenly, German hearts leaped. The Allies had landed after all! Early on the morning of 19 August, hundreds of Canadian troops stormed ashore at Dieppe. It was the operation that Mountbatten had been planning. The troops struck the Channel port at eight points. Their purpose was simply to gain experience in landing operations and to obtain information about German defenses, and about 11 a.m., after eight hours ashore, they withdrew as planned, although with much heavier losses than anticipated. Hitler was jubilant. Though he had just said that there would be "no real second front," he chose to view the Dieppe raid, which was essentially a reconnaissance in force, as the actual invasion. Some warned him that this was not so, among them the O Qu IV, Matzky, mentioning perhaps that the B.B.C. had warned the populace that this was not the invasion and it should stay calm. But as usual Hitler believed what he wanted. German propaganda soon blared about a "10-hour second front." And convinced of the fine job that Zeitzler had done in repelling the invasion, he elevated him a month later to chief of General Staff of the Army.

Not everyone agreed with Hitler's view. In Vichy, Marshal Henri Pétain, while expressing his pleasure at the beating of the perfidious English, who had left France in the lurch at Dunkirk, foresaw a renewal of these landing attempts in the fall fogs. Possible was the southern coast of Brittany; improbable, because of the season's strong surf (15-foot breakers) was Morocco, said France's most venerated war hero.

A few days later, Admiral Raeder flew out to the Ukraine to visit Hitler in his advanced headquarters in Vinniza. The Führer was concentrating on his furious advance toward Stalingrad and the Caucasus. Raeder spoke to him of distant horizons. In contradistinction to the soldier Pétain, the sailor saw "the greatest danger to the overall German war command now as before" in an Allied occupation of northwest Africa. "They would attack Italy from there and endanger our position in northeast Africa," where Rommel was fighting, said Raeder.

Was Raeder right? Confirmation and detail could come most concretely by seeing how many ships were in the potential invasion harbors. So from 24 to 28 August, the Luftwaffe flew photographic cover over these ports. It did so quickly so that vessels would not show up twice. Detailed analysis of the photographs showed some 5,000 ships suitable for landings. Large-scale landing operations were entirely possible, decided the OKM. But it did not say when or where or even that one would in fact come.

The flow of intelligence from external sources had by then slowed to a trickle. Though none even hinted at the arguments raging between the

British and Americans on what strategy to follow, individual items of interest sometimes arrived.

General Juin told the Germans: "I do not hold a landing on the African Mediterranean coast as probable, because the rear areas would be too strongly threatened. The catastrophes to the convoys [which sometimes failed to reach Malta, or arrived only with heavy losses] show distinctly how vulnerable all lines of communications in the Mediterranean have become today." And in Madrid, the SD police attaché learned on 28 August that Spanish authorities had two weeks previously obtained a letter carried by an English courier. It suggested Anglo-American landing intentions in northern Spain. The Spanish general staff reportedly confirmed this. The landings, east and west of Santander, would create chaos, free the Reds, and restore the monarchy. The navy, to whom all this was reported, took it with a grain of salt. "This is the second case in which alarming intelligence was gotten in Spain out of allegedly genuine English courier material. [The OKM did not say what the first was.] The suspicion of deliberate distribution of harassing information in this way lies close to hand."

At the end of September, the Germans just missed getting some authentic data. The near leak involved another letter, carried by the hand of an officer.

At least two months before the planned Allied invasion, the governor of Gibraltar invited Eisenhower and General Mark Clark, his deputy, to stay with him during the critical period. On 14 September, Clark accepted on behalf of Eisenhower and himself. "I have already delayed my reply to your invitation until a final determination could be made as to probable dates of arrival. It is expected that I will arrive on D-2 or D-3 [D-Day minus two days or minus three days] by air, followed two days later by General Eisenhower. The target date has now been set as 4th November." The letter did not say anything about the operation. But a careful reader would have construed that some kind of major undertaking, under the American commander of the European theater, and centering on Gibraltar, would take place 4 November.

A Royal Navy postmaster, Lt. J. H. Turner, was given the letter to bring to Gibraltar. He put it into his inner coat pocket and buttoned it for safekeeping. On 25 September, he took off from Britain with two other passengers in a PBY CATALINA that was to avoid enemy or neutral territory. But a violent storm off the coast of Spain sucked it in. It was last seen at 3:30 p.m. flying low near Cádiz. It crashed soon thereafter, killing everyone aboard. The bodies of Turner and some crew members washed ashore. The Spaniards found them on the 26th, kept them for 24 hours, and then turned them over to British representatives. They assured the British that the bodies had not been tampered with. The British found Clark's letter in the inside coat pocket, its envelope's four seals opened by the water and the writing inside quite legible. Had the Spaniards given it to the Germans?

The British had noticed, in unbuttoning the jacket, that sand had fallen out of the buttonhole. It had apparently been rubbed into the buttonhole while the body was on the beach. The British decided that it was highly unlikely that any agent would have replaced the sand when rebuttoning the jacket, and that their secret was therefore safe. And, in fact, it was.

But their suspicions had been partly right. The Spaniards had taken some other documents, perhaps from the plane's wreckage. One of them, in French, dated 22 September, referred to English attacks against French Morocco, Tunis, and other places in French North Africa. An Italian agent learned of this, though not who had written it, and passed the details to the Germans. They quite rightly accorded it no greater importance than any other bit of intelligence, merely noting it like the others.

Most of the information that sifted into Berlin about Allied intentions was even less indicative than this. It consisted largely of spy reports, obtained from the most varied sources. None, however, came from inside Allied commands. Ultimately, many reflected the views of the current strategic situation by persons not in the know. Sometimes these persons were Allied soldiers or civilians, whose useless remarks were dutifully passed on by agents seeking to make a little money. Sometimes they were the agents themselves, who read the newspapers, played armchair strategist, and attributed the results to "observers" or "well-informed circles here." This common dependence upon the overall situation shaped the reports into a common pattern. Like rumors or fads, they moved across the globe and agitated the spy apparatus. Early in the fall of 1942, for example, most spy reports pointed to Norway and to France.

Their very volume endowed them with a certain credibility. But they were insubstantial. A spy report of 3 October from England eliminated this disadvantage at a stroke. Its intensity of details indicated in the most circumstantial way the readying of a possible invasion:

Withdrawal of the entire Fighter Group No. XI from the front, allegedly for maneuvers. New occupancy with bomber squadrons of many airfields in southwest England, among others, Exeter. Almost complete stoppage of transport flights to the Middle East since about 20 September, and pull-back of the ground personnel. General talk on airfields of big air action. Halting of the attacks on Germany since about 10 days ago, which could be attributed to the weather . . . [is actually] announcement of major action . . . [because] terror attacks can take place as well by bad weather. Appearance of especially large armored formations north and northwest of Southampton, nights on many roads. Accelerated conversion of Liberators, Whitleys, and also B-17s [all bombers] to transports. . . . Return trips of ships that have come from the U.S.A. since 17 September stopped. . . . Setting up of offensive depots in various harbors, which can also be intended for 1943. Ban on all vacationers, many columns and supply traffic on all communications routes, turmoil in railroad stations, etc. Can all be intended for maneuvers, but strongly makes the impression of a major action. Though transport possibility over the channel appears insufficient at present in terms of matériel.

Despite its abundance of facts, none or little of this was true. It had all been fed to the Abwehr by one of the agents whom the British had captured and turned. Yet it all sounded so convincing.

A couple of days later, a few more like it came in. One arrived from a spy with connections to Soviet circles in Sweden, whose reports, the Abwehr carefully noted, had not always been confirmed. He indicated 17 October as the date of simultaneous landings in France, Belgium, Holland, Denmark, and Norway. He said that this date was chosen because it was the anniversary of the Russian revolution, but the Abwehr pointed out that the date was wrong. The agent reported that Russian staff officers in England regarded an invasion as not very promising. The training of American soldiers was still incomplete, and so the first attack waves would consist of 80 percent Englishmen. The Americans would handle Norway and Holland. The agent indicated the number of American troops in England as 650,000, but the Abwehr regarded this as exaggerated. It was. By the end of September, only 188,497 had arrived.

Still another spy report named five towns in northern France as landing places, told where the Allied forces were being assembled, and reported an American commitment of 60,000 men and an English of perhaps no more than 40,000 men altogether. Of the 300 bombers, 90 Lancasters would form the vanguard and 75 Flying Fortresses the reserve. And a report of the German embassy in Madrid foretold a double landing in northern France and in central or northern Africa.

The increase in the volume of reports on enemy landings, and perhaps the figures in the most recent, alarmed Hitler. He thought the Allies might repeat Dieppe and land again in northern France. So on the day that the two latest reports came in, 5 October, he set in motion anti-invasion precautions. He ordered the commander in chief west to put his troops on alarm if he thought it necessary and then allotted three divisions for the west.

But nothing happened, and the excitement subsided. Meanwhile, spy interest was shifting away from France and Norway to another area.

At the end of August, Brazil had declared war on Germany—the first country in South America to do so. This new factor dragged spies' attention to the south. Looking at their maps, they saw that the bit of Old World closest to the new belligerent was a tender spot once the target of an unsuccessful Allied assault: Dakar. It rapidly began appearing in the dispatches of the secret agents. One of the first came from a source widely regarded as one of the best informed in the world, but usually not involved with military matters: the Vatican. Circles there said that the Americans would land in Dakar and the English in North Africa in major assaults between mid-October and mid-November. In October, the frequency of reports about Dakar increased.

On the 5th, two came in; on the 6th, another; another on the 9th, and so on. On the 13th, for example, RSHA VI B 2 passed on a spy report. The agent was a former first lieutenant in the French Army who had become a convinced partisan of Franco-German cooperation. He got his information from an officer of what he called the Deuxième Bureau, meaning the intelligence section, of the Vichy colonial ministry. The colonial officer, who had connections with the corresponding section in Dakar, reported that French military circles were increasingly predicting an attack on Dakar. The Allies would launch it overland from their nearby territories to avoid an intervention of the French fleet. Once the port was invested, the French general staff was alleged to believe, Allied divisions would march northward a thousand miles along the edge of the Sahara to take Agadir and Marrakesh in Morocco. The very next day this imbecility was partly reinforced by an Abwehr dispatch out of Portugal. Troop convoys from Gibraltar were on their way to a rendezvous with Americans off Freetown, whence they would move north to take Dakar—this time, in contradiction to the RSHA report, by sea. Another report arrived at the OKM that day from the Foreign Office. The Portuguese ambassador to Brazil had cabled Lisbon that American troops and considerable war matériel had arrived in Natal, Recife, and João Pessoa, three ports on the bulge of Brazil and thus close to Dakar. Their purpose, the ambassador specified, was for an expedition to that strategic city.

This flood of indications drew comment at Hitler's situation conference the next day. And it eventually overwhelmed the OKW and the Italian Commando Supremo. They agreed on 19 October that the Allies were indeed preparing a landing in Dakar.

But not only in Dakar. They envisioned landings as well in Morocco, especially on its Atlantic coast. Less probable were landings at Algiers and especially at Tunis, closer to Rommel's rear. The chief of Italian military intelligence thought the Allies would attack Morocco, but not until the spring. But nobody did anything about all this. And reports continued to come in telling of future attacks on Norway, Denmark, Holland, Belgium, and France. One agent even foresaw an attack on all five at once.

Since any invasion would almost certainly have to come from the sea, the Germans sought to obtain clues to it by seeing where and when the necessary ships were assembling. The Abwehr reported on 17 October that troops and matériel were being readied in the ports of the Isle of Wight, on the southern coast of England. In its harbors lay 42 ships with a capacity of 30,000 men. Another Abwehr report arrived belatedly. Sent in September, it told of a major convoy assembling in the western harbors of

Britain to head eventually for west Africa—Dakar area—and for the Near East. On 21 October, the B-Dienst reported that the number of ships in the radio picture of the Firth of Clyde, on the western coast of Scotland, had risen in six days from 8 to 43.

It could say no more, but this was in fact one of the convoys assembling for the invasion of North Africa. That day it sailed. At about the same time, 100 faster ships carrying men and matériel departed four ports in America. They headed under radio silence and with devious course changes, avoiding areas known to be infested with U-boats, toward the Atlantic coast of French North Africa. A few days later, still more ships passed the bars of England. Far away, a thousand guns flashed and roared in the predawn darkness at a small railway junction in Egypt called El Alamein. As Montgomery leaped forward in what the German naval war diarist recognized as an offensive "of decisive strategic importance," the Russians assembled their forces for blows against Army Group Center and the Germans in Stalingrad. Still more ships crossed the bars of ports of western England. They would later pass through the Strait of Gibraltar and land their English and American troops on the Mediterranean coast of French North Africa.

As these nautical movements proceeded in stealth and secrecy, the German intelligence organs exerted themselves to penetrate the Allied security screen. The B-Dienst was the most valuable of the navy's intelligence agencies. It was not easily fooled. On 3 October it had seen through an attempt to trick it: an increase in deceptive radio traffic in the western part of the Channel. On 22 October, it considered an analysis sent it by the Italian naval intelligence organization. This agency saw a connection between an English convoy with strong protection and a radio message of 1:57 p.m. the day before to all English war ships, which message was later relayed from Gibraltar to Malta. The B-Dienst agreed that the message suggested something unusual, but disagreed that it had something to do with the convoy. The B-Dienst had also picked up some messages to all British submarines in the Mediterranean with two unusual characteristics: they had also gone to a recipient not previously seen in the radio traffic and they were numbered out of the regular series. To the B-Dienst, this indicated special operations orders. A few days later, it concluded that the traffic could merely have emanated from the British offensive in Egypt. On 29 October, it received a Royal Navy code salvaged from a warship sunk off Tobruk on 14 September. This was the code that the B-Dienst called MUNICH BLUE. By the next morning a preliminary work-through by Wilhelm Tranow's teams had given the location of the main warships of the Royal Navy. But from this the B-Dienst drew no inferences about forthcoming operations.

Such inferences might come from the location and movement of Allied ships. Aerial reconnaissance over England, flown almost daily, found, however, that harbors in the southwest were relatively empty. Negative evidence seldom provides clues to positive intentions. But airplanes and submarines furnished some positive information. A U-boat spotted the battleship *Rodney* heading south from Scapa Flow. A carrier formation that had quit Gibraltar on 28 October was seen next day heading west. At noon on 31 October, a German reconnaissance plane spotted two aircraft carriers, a cruiser, and a destroyer racing due south about 300 miles west of Brittany. U-boats saw two large convoys, one heading east toward Gibraltar, on 2 November. But the Germans could see no pattern in these movements.

One pattern, however, was clear. The harbor of Gibraltar was filling up. The Abwehr had long had an observation post in Algeciras. It was in the Villa San Luis, a private house—said to have once belonged to the British air attaché—with a commanding view four miles across the Bay of Algeciras to Gibraltar and its harbor. To this was posted on 1 October 1942 Lieutenant Karl Redl, a Viennese who had served in the Austro-Hungarian navy in World War I and was inducted into the Abwehr after the Anschluss in 1938 because of his language capabilities. These did not include Spanish, however, and he "learned" it in three intensive weeks of study with a niece of the former heavyweight champion Primo Carnera.

Daily Redl and his two noncommissioned officers focused their Zeiss telescope on the harbor and watched the ships, airplanes, and base activities. On 19 October, for example, they observed a landing practice using 8 convoy and 5 landing boats. They spotted the arrival of the carrier *Furious* with three destroyers on the 26th, and its departure heading east two days later. Their radiomen enciphered the messages in the Abwehr hand cipher and radiotelegraphed them to a station in Dax, on the French side of the Pyrenees, which forwarded them to Berlin. During October the count of ships fluctuated, but near the end of the month it began rising steadily. On 3 November, Redl reported that there lay in the roadstead 1 battleship, 3 carriers, 4 or 5 cruisers, 15 destroyers, 28 steamers, 13 tankers, other small ships, and 149 airplanes.

Next day the navy noted that the number of fighter planes alone—Spitfires and Hurricanes—had, in Gibraltar in a week and a half, risen from 59 to 109. A convoy with 14 steamers and 3 destroyers further packed the harbor. What, the Luftwaffe asked the Kriegsmarine, did it all mean?

The navy issued its answer as Allied ships and convoys coursed toward North Africa for the mightiest amphibious operation the world had yet seen.

1. Concentration of strong English sea forces in the last few days in Gibraltar permit one to expect an immediate major enemy undertaking in the western Mediterranean. The kind and number of these forces do not permit definite conclusions about the enemy intention, but correspond to previously observed strengths of security forces for Malta supply convoys; repetition of this kind of operation is, according to the view of the Naval War Command,

the most probable. In a deviation from previous practice of letting the Malta supply convoys with their security forces slip into the Mediterranean unobserved, the present concentration of sea forces lets one conclude that the enemy intends to tie down the Italian fleet and the Axis air forces toward the west to support the English offensive in Egypt.

2. The relatively small number of landing boats (about 50) and of only 2 transport ships does not let an immediate enemy landing operation in the Mediterranean area or on the northwest coast of Africa appear likely.

The next day, Thursday, 5 November, began quietly. The usual spy reports drifted in. From Paris, the Abwehr reported that the Americans would land at Casablanca within 14 days. From Spain and Portugal, it reported that attacks were likely not only against the North African coast but also against Italy. Bad weather prevented aerial reconnaissance over Gibraltar. The ships were still there at 1 p.m.

But at 8 p.m., they began to slip out, heading east—into the Mediterranean. At 10 p.m., as a couple of battleships departed, Redl's observers spotted a big convoy heading into the Mediterranean through the Straits of Gibraltar. An hour later, an Italian agent saw what must have been a different group: 35 dimmed-out ships passing Tarifa, a port west of Gibraltar, also heading east, speed about 14 knots.

Dawn Friday brought little light to the Axis. The German admiral Rome declared that the movements served either a major Malta supply operation or a landing on the coasts of the western or the central Mediterranean—or both. The OKM notified the Führer that it all meant a landing operation, "most probably in the Tripoli-Benghazi area [Rommel's rear], next Sicily, Sardinia, the Italian coast, in last place, French North Africa."

Reports of the sighting of the convoys from the air streamed in. But some of them were as contradictory as the agent reports, and the Germans did not know at first which to believe. They did not credit one sighting of 2:45 p.m. Friday, because it showed the leading convoy heading 100°, or slightly south of east, while previous reports indicated a northeast movement. Not until a second report substantiated the 100° course four hours later did they believe that that direction was right. This conclusion, however, led Rome to consider a landing in Mostagnem, Algeria, just a little to the east of the actual intended landing place at Oran.

By Saturday, the 7th, the German Naval Command Italy had been ordered to send in situation reports every hour. They yielded "no clear picture of the movements of the enemy formations." Aerial reconnaissance began very early in the morning, and at 4:40 a.m. a German airplane spotted a convoy 80 miles south of the holiday island of Ibiza, but did not report its course. Later sightings detected the merger of two convoys. The Italian naval command, Supermarina, concluded at 8 a.m. that the Allies intended a landing in French North Africa—either in the Oran-Algiers area in the morning of that very day or in the area of two ports further east, Bougie and Bône, the next morning. Supermarina did not think a landing in Rommel's rear was likely. But it had no solid information, and was reduced, like its Axis partner, to guessing. On the basis of such flimsy evidence as that the distance between the first two convoys was 170 sea miles and that between the second and third was 100, Supermarina predicted "simultaneous landings by Tabarka [east of Bône], Bougie, and Algiers."

Meanwhile, the German embassy in Madrid added to the confusion by reporting that the Spaniards thought the ships would land in Italy, while the military attaché in Madrid contradicted both his embassy and Supermarina: the goal was Rommel's rear. Reports about an intended landing in French North Africa were, he added, not probable.

Hitler received the movement reports in his headquarters in East Prussia. He thought, like the attaché, that the Allies would land four or five divisions behind Rommel. Then the master politician and strategist acted out his own judgment of how important the convoys and the whole situation in the Mediterranean were. At 1:40 p.m. he quit the WOLF'S LAIR to make his annual speech next day before the old party members.

As the Allied convoys steamed relentlessly eastward into the Mediterranean, and as the convoy from America approached the Atlantic shores of Africa entirely undetected, the chief of military espionage and counterespionage, Admiral Canaris, and his espionage chief, Colonel Piekenbrock, went to Copenhagen for a conference. The OKM wept into its war diary. "These contradictory reports cannot give definite indications of the enemy operational goal or goals." Darkness fell. The Mediterranean night swallowed up the ships. Off the starboard bow the horizon glowed: Oran! Group by group the vessels heeled hard to the right as they turned sharply to head back toward the coast. Five miles off shore the great transports dropped anchor with a splash. Sailors lowered the landing craft into the heaving black water. Assault teams groped into them, and the craft, engines throbbing like thunder in the quiet, set off for the sleeping beaches.

At that very moment, the teleprinter machines in Berlin clattered. Yet another report on Allied intentions was coming in to the Foreign Office from Paris. The French war minister thought the landings would be in Tripoli or in Sicily. It was a guess as wild as all the others. The French, the Italians, the Germans—all had failed utterly to penetrate Allied security. The convoys' radio silence and their dodging of U-boat–infested areas kept the Germans from obtaining information from communications or by observation; the German espionage and cryptanalytic failures barred them from other sources; the sending of some ships direct from America rendered the OKM's calculation of available tonnage still more difficult. As a consequence, the troops clambered onto docks or splashed ashore at Oran and Algiers and Casablanca without the Germans suspecting a thing. They learned about the first great amphibious landing of the war, the first Allied offensive, when, early in the morning, the White House announced it.

The Ultimate Failure

ADOLF Hitler was puzzled. A question was bothering him again that had nagged him off and on for several years. But he did not mention it specifically at the start of his situation conference that Monday, 20 December 1943, in one of the wooden hutlike buildings that formed his headquarters in the thin woods of East Prussia. He merely said:

"There is no longer any doubt that the invasion in the west will come in the spring."

The chief of the general staff, Zeitzler, one of the gaggle of flunkies clustered around the giant tan and blue maps spread out on the big table, parroted his Führer's statement a few minutes later.

"The attack will come; there's no doubt about it," he said.

The conference turned to other matters of the high direction of the war. Then, near its end, Hitler reverted to the Allied invasion and finally voiced the problem that was on his mind.

"It would be good if we could know from the start: Where is a diversion and where the real main attack?" No one denied that this would be good, but no one told him where, either. It was a question that would occupy their attention more and more in the coming months.

Twelve days later and half a continent away to the west, a young officer sat down at his desk in the gray industrial city of Tourcoing, France. He was Captain Hans Colombara, Ph.D., the keeper of the war diary of Germany's 15th Army. This covered northern France and Belgium and so helped shield the Reich from any cross-Channel thrust out of England. Its headquarters were at Tourcoing, just south of the Belgian border, and on New Year's Day 1944 Colombara wrote down the military situation at the start of the year as seen from those headquarters.

"The enemy," he began, "must force a decision in west Europe by an attack."

Captain Colombara's echo of Hitler's thought implied no reading of his Führer's mind, nor any special insights into high strategy. Probably every German soldier had come to the same conclusion. The idea of a forthcoming Allied invasion had long before penetrated everywhere in Europe— even the pathetic attic hiding place of Anne Frank and her family. For the Russians were loudly demanding it, and Roosevelt and Churchill had promised it.

Hitler had, in fact, first mentioned the possibility of an American landing on the continent only six months after he had driven the British off it at Dunkirk. He had then dismissed this idea, quite correctly, as "illusory." But after he invaded Russia, his fears grew. On 29 October 1941, for example, he conceded that the British might land in western Europe to relieve the Russians, though he naturally said that the assault would be repulsed. On 12 December, the day after he had declared war on America, he wondered whether the Allies would turn from Japan to concentrate on Germany, and the next day he again mentioned the possibility of an Allied landing in Europe. Finally, on 23 March 1942, his concern had grown enough for him to issue Directive No. 40 for the Conduct of the War. It warned of "the danger of enemy landings in the near future" and specified the duties of commanders in coastal areas. Three months later, he suddenly ordered the commander in chief west to the highest state of readiness. In the next weeks, reports came in that small vessels were assembling in harbors on the southern British coast. Simultaneously, Roosevelt and Churchill made an announcement after their conference in Washington promising to "divert German strength" from Russia. This clearly meant a second front. But nothing happened. Hitler began to wonder whether it was a deception. Then, on 19 August, the Canadians assaulted Dieppe. The defenders reacted energetically, and Hitler pronounced the long-awaited invasion repelled, even though captured documents told him that the raid was merely a test assault never intended to be permanent. He indirectly acknowledged this during another invasion scare in October—the third that year. But it took the events of the following month to disabuse him at last. The Allies landed in North Africa.

Many said, then, that the cross-Channel assault would take place in 1943. Hundreds of reports poured into Germany assuring Hitler that it would. The generals in charge of defending France thought that the Allies would take advantage of the stretching of their forces, created by their occupation of all of France at the time of the North African invasion, to attack. Hitler did not agree.

"Nothing is going to happen in the west; I'm fully convinced of that," he told his generals at a situation conference on 19 May 1943, a week after the last Axis forces surrendered in North Africa. "If they want to attack somewhere, then they'll only attack in Italy, and in the Balkans, naturally. The Balkans are very dangerous." Things grew tense as the spring and its good campaigning weather advanced. But, as Hitler had foreseen, the Allies struck only in the Mediterranean. They captured Sicily, then advanced up the boot of Italy.

Their strategy worked. Mussolini fell. Italy quit. Shipping eased. And as apple farmers in Normandy plucked their sun-ripened fruit and pressed it to make calvados, and winegrowers in the hot bright fields around Bordeaux cut the luscious purple clusters off their vines, the likelihood of an invasion in Europe receded. The occupation troops drowsed in the mellow golden days. Though the Allied bombing of Europe stepped up and Allied pressure in Italy intensified, the shadows in Paris and Berlin and London lengthened and turned without any invasion. Everyone knew that the assault would have to come the next year. On 3 November, Hitler made it formal, and he emphasized its importance. In his Directive No. 51 he declared:

> The danger in the east remains, but a greater one looms in the west: the Anglo-Saxon landing! . . . In the east, the vast extent of the territory makes it possible for us to lose ground, even on a large scale, without a fatal blow being dealt to the nervous system of Germany. It is different in the west! Should the enemy succeed in breaching our defenses on a wide front here, the immediate consequences would be unpredictable. All signs suggest that the enemy will advance to an attack against the west front of Europe, at the latest in the spring, perhaps even earlier.

But nothing happened "earlier," and the year ran out without the cross-Channel assault.

It would finally come, then, in 1944. Colombara and everyone else saw it. The great questions were where and when. On the third day of the new year, the I c of the OKW's Operations Staff issued, over the signature of General Jodl, chief of that staff, three pages of "Guidelines for Reconnaissance of Enemy Preparations for the Creation of the Second Front in the West." It told subordinate units what intelligence to gather on the expected invasion. Most urgently wanted was information on the number of landing ships and freighters in southern English harbors. Other naval information needs followed, and after them came requests for data on invasion staffs in Britain and "Subordination and organization of formations in south England, which may allow conclusions on jump-off areas." The commander in chief west was to direct this reconnaissance, and all results were to go to the OKW Operations Staff. It was located at the Führer headquarters.

The Allied leaders recognized that a cross-Channel invasion would thrust into Germany to drive a military stake through her heart and defeat her. They had long intended it, but lack of resources had prevented them from carrying it out in 1943. Early in that year, however, they set up a unit to plan for the mighty endeavor that they now scheduled for the spring of 1944.

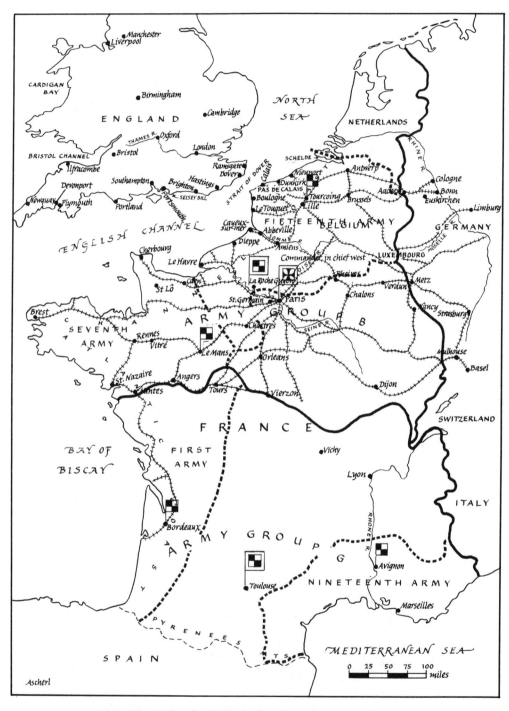

Southern England and Western France: Possible bases and targets for the cross-Channel invasion of the Continent

The basic question that faced it was where to attack. Their choice would be determined by the need to attain preponderance of force. For, as Clausewitz said, "In tactics, as in strategy, superiority of numbers is the most common element in victory." And this meant not only during the initial assault but also during the advance to the objective—the Ruhr, Germany's industrial base.

The most direct way of attaining such a superiority is to concentrate one's forces. This implies a landing site near to both the invader's base and his target. For the closer the fighting is to the men and supplies of home, the more can be brought to the fray in a given time. Air power is an important example of this. The shorter the distance the planes have to fly to the battlefield, the longer they can remain above it. And the nearer the target, the better the troops can focus their efforts. Units will not be diverted, for example, to protect long flanks.

But there is an indirect or negative way of gaining superiority of numbers. Instead of increasing one's own strength, it in effect reduces the enemy forces at the decisive point. It does this through surprise—attacking at an unexpected place. Surprise achieves superiority almost as strongly as direct concentration of forces. Clausewitz said that "Without it, superiority at the decisive point is hardly conceivable."

The Allies naturally wanted the benefits of both ways. Their dilemma was that they could only gain the one at the expense of the other. The planning staff studied landing sites around the coast of Europe in the light of this fundamental issue and of a host of secondary ones. Was there a port nearby? Beaches alone could not handle the enormous quantities of supplies that would enable the Allied build-up to match the enemy's. How strong were the enemy defenses at various points? Could the invading forces easily exit from the beaches and expand inland to form a bridgehead, or did the terrain obstruct their movement? Could airfields be built in the area? Was the potential landing beach firm enough to support heavy trucks carrying tons of cargo? Would prevailing winds and tides excessively hinder landings?

Closest to the Ruhr in a direct line from England were the Netherlands. It had major ports, too. But it lay out of fighter-plane range, its beaches were exposed to the North Sea weather and their sand dunes restricted vehicular traffic, and the land behind could easily be flooded for defense. Denmark and southern France were both relatively poorly defended. But they were too far both from the Allies' base and their target. In the end, the planners decided to land on the Cherbourg peninsula. It offered the best combination of surprise and strength.

This peninsula, the Cotentin, juts northwestward from Normandy, of which it is a part, into the English Channel. The important port of Cherbourg lies at its tip, that of Le Havre near its base. The gently rolling land is divided into small farms, often subdivided into smaller plots, separated by thick green rows of hedges that serve as boundaries and windbreaks The Cotentin was further both from Britain and Germany than other areas, but in consequence offered a greater chance of surprise. This would mean weaker fortifications and fewer and poorer troops. Fighter planes could still reach it—though they could not stay over it long—and the voyage from southern English ports was not excessively long. Nor was the Cotentin as far from the Ruhr objective as other places. Among its other advantages was that the northwest jut of the land sheltered the beaches on its northeastern side from the prevailing westerly weather. The rises behind the beaches would not impede a break-out. The beaches themselves would permit supply over them. This was essential, for the proposed landing area around Caen possessed no major ports for supply in the first days of the landing. To enhance the surprise that the choice of a landing site far from a port would create, and to handle the enormous quantity of men and matériel that would pour across the beaches until the invaders were able to capture either Cherbourg or Le Havre, the Allies boldly conceived two artificial harbors. Ships and caissons sunk in a line off the beaches would form a breakwater protecting a floating pierhead connected with the beach. The Allies codenamed these harbors MULBERRIES and constructed their components in strictest secrecy in Britain's large naval station at Portland, as far as practicable from German reconnaissance sorties.

In choosing the Cotentin, the planners rejected the other chief contender for a landing site, 160 miles to the northeast: the Pas de Calais. This portion of northwestern France bulges out into the Strait of Dover and takes its name from the French term for those narrows: "Pas de Calais" simply means "Strait of Calais." The Pas de Calais lies closer to England than any other part of the continent. Its Cape Gris-Nez approaches to within 21 miles of Dover, and on clear days embattled Englishmen could see its chalk cliffs, the counterparts of their own, gleaming gold in the afternoon sun. This proximity would have helped the Allies concentrate their forces for the invasion and the advance upon the Ruhr. But they saw more disadvantages than advantages. Its obviousness had led the Germans to fortify it more strongly than any other sector of the coast. Its cliffs would let the defenders rake the invaders with gunfire. The few and narrow exits would choke the break-out. The area's ports, Calais and Boulogne, would not be able to handle the tonnage needed for the build-up. The nearest large port, Le Havre, lay much further from the Pas de Calais than Cherbourg did from the Caen invasion beaches; its capture would require a long flank march. But the Allies did not spurn the area's advantages. They would exploit them. They would make the Germans think that the mighty cross-Channel invasion would come in the Pas de Calais.

If the watchword of Allied counterintelligence for the North African assault had been "silence," for the invasion it was "deception." Deception is more complicated than simple security, and it risks more, but it offers greater rewards. Security can compel an enemy to spread his defenses thin all over. Deception can fool him into strengthening them at the wrong point, thus weakening them even more at the right point. In effect, then, deception magnifies one's own resources more than security. It thus especially interests those who have little, or those who want more, which often comes down to the same people.

This had been the case with the British in Egypt in 1940, and it was there that Allied deception was born. The British commander set up a special deception unit that proved so successful that the British chiefs of staff in 1941 ordered similar units set up for all major commands. To coordinate them, to ensure that one deception did not conflict with and possibly disclose another, the chiefs created the London Controlling Station under Colonel J. H. Bevan. When the United States entered the war, Bevan's ideas had to be approved by the British-American combined chiefs of staff.

Soon after Supreme Headquarters, Allied Expeditionary Forces, or SHAEF, was created to prepare for the cross-Channel assault, it set up its Anglo-American Deception Unit. Named as head was Colonel Noël Wild, who was administratively a member of the crack 11th Hussars but who had in fact worked since 1941 as second in command of deception in Egypt. At the end of 1943, he assumed his post in an office in Norfolk House in London, Eisenhower's headquarters.

Much of the ground had been prepared for him. The vital aid was the possession of the main channel for passing the false information to the enemy. This was the German espionage apparatus in Great Britain. From interrogations and especially from their complete control of enemy agent communications, the British gradually grew aware that they had captured every single German spy on the island. Those who would and could cooperate were turned into double agents, working for the British; the rest were imprisoned or executed. All of these double agents fed their Abwehr and SD spymasters the information the British wanted them to. Coordinating these agents was the interministerial Double-Cross Committee, on which Bevan sat. The Double-Cross Committee had not set out early in the war to arrange their double agents into an organization for deceiving the Germans about the invasion of Europe, but the system had evolved into just that, and when Wild arrived he profited from this.

He would also have other channels for displaying the fake details: dummy landing ships and dummy communication networks. He benefited too from the advantages of the strong security measures that curtained off the enemy from what was really going on. Among these were not merely the tight immigration controls of the island nation, but also Allied air superiority, which blocked any comprehensive German aerial reconnaissance, and Allied cryptologic expertise, which denied the Germans any chance of breaking top Allied messages.

The Allies thus possessed the essentials, positive and negative, without which no deception can succeed. But they also possessed another advantage that transcended these, a kind of metasuperiority. This was the Allied cryptanalysis of Abwehr hand ciphers and the main German cipher machines, including the simple version of the Enigma machine used by the Abwehr.

These solutions contributed to British knowledge in two areas key to deception. First, the British specialist in the German intelligence services, Major Hugh R. Trevor-Roper, built up an astoundingly accurate and complete picture of the enemy's organization and operation in this field, extending even to profiles of some of its leading personalities. This enabled the British to avoid blunders in working the agents due to a lack of knowledge of the men and methods of the other side. Second, the German messages told Wild which of the double agents' data was being accepted by the Germans as valid. All in all, the intercepts let Wild run his deception not blind, as he would have had to have done without them, but with considerable insight that let him steer it with maximum effect.

This was the situation when, about 11:15 a.m. 3 January 1944, Wild and Bevan passed through the sober doorway of 58 St. James's Street in London. A little while later, they were admitted to a third-floor conference room with windows onto the street. A dozen men sitting around a large boardroom table looked up as they entered. Bevan introduced Wild. They were the members of the Double-Cross Committee, and they listened with interest as Wild explained how he hoped to use their tame agents in an omnibus plan to deceive the enemy about the forthcoming invasion.

The individuals whom the British wanted to deceive were scattered across the map of Europe. Foremost among them was Hitler, running his war from his isolated encampment in East Prussia. His intelligence on the forthcoming invasion came mainly from Foreign Armies West, headquartered in Zossen, 350 miles away. Here, in one of the double-level A-roofed bunkers, Colonel von Roenne directed his team of general staff officers as they read the weeks-old Allied newspapers, studied the reports of what they believed to be their hard-working agents in Britain, computed enemy strengths, and cross-checked their file cards. Daily, Roenne wrote a situation report. This went to the German commands in the west and to the OKW, responsible for the western theaters of war. The OKW's I c, Colonel Krummacher, passed it to General Jodl, who, on occasion, showed it to Hitler.

The commander in chief west was Field Marshal Gerd von Rundstedt, the very prototype of a German officer, down to his monocle. Rundstedt, then over 70, was one of the senior personalities of the German army. He had led army groups in the blitzkriegs of Poland, France, and Russia, but afterwards went on sick leave. He reported to Hitler in March of 1942 that his health was restored and a week later took charge of the defenses in France, Belgium, and Holland. A touch of dry humor relieved his stern and aristocratic exterior, but otherwise, in manner as well as in thought, he was as correct and as textbook as general staff training could make a man.

He had his headquarters in the beautiful pavilion of St.-Germain-en-Laye, on the Seine just west of Paris. Standing at the ornate balustrade of its splendid mile-long terrace, Rundstedt and his officers could look beyond the gleaming river far below to the gray mass of Paris and see on distant hilltops two tiny domes, the white one of Sacré Coeur, monument to the French dead in the 1870 war that Prussia had won, and the blackened one of the Panthéon, tomb of some of France's greatest heroes. In the pavilion had been born the Sun King, Louis XIV, who had advanced the borders of his country to the Rhine. In this lovely, historic location worked Rundstedt's I c, Colonel Wilhelm Meyer-Detring, a big, smooth, imposing general staff officer who had served in the job since July of 1942. He analyzed the incoming information and frequently exchanged views with Roenne, the next step up the intelligence ladder.

Under Rundstedt were two army groups. Army Group G lay in southern France. Army Group B covered northern France and guarded the most threatened area. Its commander was Field Marshal Erwin Rommel, the Desert Fox, a folk hero and a favorite of the Führer's. His rank gave him direct access to Hitler, thus enabling him to bypass his nominal superior, Rundstedt, in case of differences between them, which in fact soon appeared. He was headquartered in a Renaissance château, La Roche Guyon, in a great northward bend of the meandering Seine about 40 miles west of Paris. La Roche Guyon was the seat of the dukes de la Rochefoucauld, descendants of the author of the famous maxims, and Rommel worked in a study hung with antique tapestries and wrote on the desk on which Louis XIV's minister of war had signed the revocation of the Edict of Nantes, ending religious toleration of the Huguenots in France and starting a crippling exodus of talent not to be seen again in any land until Hitler's persecution of the Jews. Above the château lowered the ruins of a medieval keep. But these omens of error and mortality fazed neither Rommel nor his intelligence officer, Colonel Anton Staubwasser, a heavy-set man who had done exemplary work on the organizational complexities of the British army for several years at Foreign Armies West; he was an intelligence veteran. Rommel's army group embraced the military occupation command of the Netherlands and two armies in northern France, the 15th, in the Pas de Calais, and the 7th, covering the Cotentin and Brittany.

These armies had neither enough time nor enough men to fortify promptly the entire Atlantic and Channel coasts. Their commanders and Hitler thus had to allot priorities, and they would naturally provide the most material to, and station their strongest forces in, the area most likely to be attacked. The determination of this place thus constituted their vital preliminary duty.

The problem was that their intelligence officers enjoyed few of the advantages of their opponents in England. Rundstedt's intelligence, he acknowledged, was "inadequate." The navy admitted: "A judgment on which axis of advance the enemy will choose is hard." But Hitler's officers accepted this difficulty as normal. Had not Clausewitz himself pointed out how "unreliable and transient" intelligence about the enemy is? "Many intelligence reports in war are contradictory; even more are false, and most are uncertain," he wrote. But the great military theoretician did not leave his readers to wonder what a general should do in so bewildering a situation. "The commander must trust his judgment and stand like a rock on which the waves break in vain," he declared. And this his twentieth-century students did.

They based their judgment about the invasion on the universal and immutable principles of strategy. The most important of these was the need for superiority of numbers. Germany's military leaders well knew that this could be achieved either through a concentration of forces or by surprise. They knew, too, that the Allies had thus far in the war chosen the latter, the indirect approach. In North Africa, Sicily, and Italy, the Allies had nibbled around the sea-girt edges of Europe, avoiding a head-on collision. The Germans understood the implications of this perfectly. "The very systematic advance of the Anglo-Saxons . . . makes a threat to the Norwegian area and Jutland appear possible," said the OKW. They admitted that the Allies had surprised them in the previous landings, and their high commands warned that, as Dönitz said, the enemy "is endeavoring to conceal his real main object and to make full use of the element of surprise."

Nevertheless, the German leaders did not think that the Allies would utilize this tactic in the cross-Channel invasion. Instead of using the negative technique of gaining superiority by attacking where deception had weakened the German forces, the Allies would, the Germans thought, pursue the positive technique of concentrating their forces at the decisive point. This meant the Pas de Calais. The invasion would come "across the narrower part of the Channel," Rundstedt said. The Germans found reasons for this view. They believed that the advantages of concentration outweighed the disadvantage that fortifications there would be strongest. The proximity of the Pas de Calais would reduce ships' and airplanes' transit time, in effect multiplying tonnage and airpower. Its closeness to the Ruhr permitted a more concentrated drive. It was "the quickest route to the Rhine," said Rundstedt. The Germans recognized that the Allies might well precede the main attack with diversionary landings elsewhere. But the main attack would come in the Pas de Calais. Anywhere else would weaken the assault and lengthen the advance to the Ruhr which, even Hitler conceded, if successful "would bring the decision." Hitler supplemented these basic strategic arguments for the Pas de Calais with the observation that the Allies would want to eliminate the launching sites there for the V-1 missiles of revenge against England.

Why did Hitler, his generals, and his admirals believe the attack would come in the Pas de Calais despite the known Allied predeliction for surprise away from the central point? Mainly because its directness, simplicity, and orthodoxy agreed with their training and, perhaps, their personalities. "We generals calculated along the lines of our regular military education," said one. "Rather than try to outwit the enemy with complicated schemes," urged Clausewitz, "one should, on the contrary, try to outdo him in simplicity." The soldiers had absorbed the principle of concentration of forces in their youth and then had applied it successfully in battle after battle; it had helped them win their present eminence. Hitler had won his victories, diplomatic as well as military, through force or a threat of force. The principle had proved its validity in the German army far more often than that of deception, which has less scope in land operations than in amphibious. Moreover, it provided an unconscious gratification: it called for the Allies to attack where the Germans were most ready for them.

Consequently no one dissented when Hitler emphasized, in his Directive No. 51, the strengthening of the defenses in the Pas de Calais over those of other areas in the West. "For it is there," he declared, "that the enemy must and will attack, and it is there—unless everything is misleading— that the decisive battle against the landing forces will be fought. Binding and diversionary attacks on other fronts are to be expected. Even a large-scale attack against Denmark is not out of the question." Several weeks later he was still maintaining this view. Finally he took action on it. "Since the front of the 15th Army and the right wing of the 7th Army (Cotentin peninsula) are especially threatened," Keitel said for him, "the mass of the available forces must be assembled behind these fronts." He then ordered four divisions into these positions. Such was the considered and unanimous judgment of Hitler and his high commands. And, as Clausewitz had enjoined them, once having reached it, none of them would budge from the rock.

Their conception dovetailed perfectly with Colonel Wild's deception plan. It was exactly what he wanted to make the Germans believe: that the main assault would come in the Pas de Calais and that the preceding attack in the Cotentin was merely a feint. The first thing he had to do to convince them of this was to demonstrate that the Allies had enough strength to mount both a diversionary and a principal assault. He had, in other words, to invent fake divisions that the Germans would accept as real.

How strong the enemy is is a basic question of military intelligence. It was probably Lieutenant Colonel Richard Euler, Roenne's American expert, who on 12 January 1944 computed the total strength of the U.S.

army as best he could from the public figures available to Foreign Armies West:

Original planning end 1943	8,233,083	official figure, Congress, *Philadelphia Daily News* 18.6.43
Less reduction	562,000	official figure, McNarney
Consequent assumed final strength 1943	7,671,083	
Less air corps troops	2,385,000	Gen. Arnold, 6.1.44
Remainder (army including women)	5,286,083	

Less women			
WAC	60,000		Stimson, 8.1.44
Nurses	57,000		official figure, Congress
	Total women	117,000	
Remaining for ground forces	5,169,083		

Despite its apparent precision, the table contained some serious flaws. It mixed actual figures and estimates. For example, Arnold's figure was correctly reported from a special report he made to Secretary of War Stimson and covered in the press. But it must have been an estimate, projected several months earlier for the end of the year, for the army air corps counted only 2,126,000 men at the end of 1943. Other figures were off for one reason or another. The House appropriations committee, for example, had estimated the total army and air force strength not at 8,233,-083, but at 8,202,881.

Even the U.S. army could not forecast its exact strength figures because of variations in casualty rates and draft call-ups. Foreign Armies West of necessity had to do worse. In fact, the American army, exclusive of the air corps, totalled only 4,878,000 men at the end of 1943. In percentage points, Euler was over by only 6 percent. But the absolute difference of 291,000 had more serious effects. Euler figured that each 175,000 men was equivalent to three or four divisions. This included corresponding air corps troops, as well as support troops attached, for example, to army headquarters. Thus Euler's absolute error meant that he thought that manpower was available for roughly seven more divisions than actually was available—or, if the air corps contingents were eliminated, for perhaps nine divisions. He was thus that much more receptive to deception figures inflating the number of Allied divisions.

A few months later, as the invasion approached, another report seemed to substantiate his calculations. A message to Zossen in April 1944 noted: "According to a report of Secretary of War Stimson, the American army attained its full strength of 7,700,000 men on 1 April, about a month before the time planned." This figure apparently confirmed the earlier one of

7,671,083 for the final strength at the end of 1943. Euler was hardened in his error.

Wild could not have known this, though it eased his task. On the other hand, he did know about another situation that also helped him. This was the U.S. army's system for numbering infantry divisions. It assigned numbers 1 to 25 to Regular Army divisions, 26 to 75 to the National Guard, and 76 and above to the Organized Reserve and to units formed from draftees. In its mobilization, the army exhausted its National Guard units at number 45. Though numbers 46 to 75 should have remained unassigned, the army for some reason gave seven of them to new divisions. This still left 23 of this block available. The army would not use them. But the deception artists might. They could also employ numbers above 106, the highest borne by an existing division.

And they did. One day in 1943, after clearing things with the Quartermaster General, a few deception officers went over to the Institute of Heraldry in southwest Washington, which designed insignia for the army's new units. They told a courtly old gentleman there that they needed patches for some divisions numbered 49, 55, 56, 59, and others. They did not say what the designs were needed for, but the institute produced them anyway. For the 55th Division, for example, it devised a double pentagon —a blue one with a yellow one inside. So when the deception agencies needed legitimate insignia for phony divisions, they had them.

To direct their divisions, armies create higher headquarters. Their presence increases the imminence of military actions. Foreign Armies West got the news of these headquarters, at corps, army, and army group level, from their standard sources. Radio intelligence, for example, told it that the 30th Infantry Division was subordinated to the XIXth Army Corps. This informed them for the first time of the existence of this corps. Perhaps the most important unit that Foreign Armies West discovered was FUSAG. This acronym stood for First U.S. Army Group. It had been activated on 16 October 1943. It was intended to command American ground forces during the OVERLORD invasion, taking charge when two American armies became operational on the continent. Foreign Armies West first heard of it through radio reconnaissance in the first days of 1944. It did not know that the Allies later converted it into a dummy headquarters for deception. Believing it to be a major indicator of Allied intentions, Foreign Armies West kept a close watch on the First U.S. Army Group.

By 1944, radio reconnaissance had become the dominant form of operational-level intelligence in the German army. It delivered more and better information than any other source. The task of obtaining radio intelligence about the invasion fell in the west on Communications Reconnaissance Regiment 5. Its head was Colonel Maximilian Baron von Oer. Of the several commanders of such regiments in the German army, he alone sported the title of "higher commander," because his was the only one to serve, through the commander in chief west, two army groups.

Regiment 5 consisted of three communications-reconnaissance battalions and four fixed intercept posts. Oer assigned each a specific task. Battalion 12, supported by Post 3 and, some of the time, by Post 9, concentrated on transatlantic monitoring of the United States. Battalion 13 listened to units in Great Britain in the frequency range of 1,875 to 7,500 kilohertz, while posts 2 and 13 covered 3,000 to 7,500 kilohertz in Great Britain, Northern Ireland, and Canada. A typical intercept company of Battalion 13 was that of Captain Horst Wiebe, a neat, trim man who, unlike most in signals reconnaissance, had little interest in the work: he had gone into signals only because nothing else was open when he joined the 100,000-man post-Versailles army. He and his company were stationed in Vitré, a small industrial town at the base of the Brittany peninsula. Its scattered listening posts swept up as much of the traffic in England in their frequency range as they could and took direction-finding bearings on as many transmitters as possible. All this information they sent to company headquarters. Here, in a French gendarmerie caserne in Vitré, each of the evaluating sections—intercept, cryptanalysis and translation, and final—had a room of its own. Wiebe transmitted the results both to his local command and to Battalion 13.

Post 3, at Euskirchen, a small town about 15 miles west of Bonn, attained special significance. The U.S. War Department and other army elements used radio to send, in plaintext, messages within the Zone of the Interior—the continental United States—dealing with the training of new formations. The freaks of short wave sometimes propagated such transmissions over extraordinarily long distances. From time to time, they bounced across the Atlantic and tickled the big ear of Post 3. Monitors there could hear Washington order a division from one camp to another, suggesting its training progress.

In the summer of 1943, for example, radio reconnaissance told the Germans that the 17th Airborne Division had been set up at Fort McClellan, Alabama, and that the 69th Infantry Division had been activated at Camp Shelby, Massachusetts. Actually Camp Shelby was in Mississippi, but the Germans might have been led astray by the change of a Morse dot into a dash that converted the "i" in "Miss." to the "a" in "Mass." The 69th, moreover, was not at Shelby, but at Camp Mackall, North Carolina. This error was perhaps created because a message was erroneously sent to Shelby, or had to be sent there for retransmission to Mackall because of static, or because some element of the division was in fact at Shelby. The 17th Airborne likewise was not in Alabama but also at Camp Mackall. But both divisions actually existed, and the German radio intelligence had spotted them. It also ascertained that new American infantry divisions would bear numbers from 46 to 75. In this way, Post 3, further aided by radio newscasts from the States, enabled the Germans to follow almost without a miss the creation of all major American combat formations.

They followed their movements as well. The evaluators of Post 3 knew that when a division got its A.P.O. (Army Post Office) number, it was about to sail. Numbers assigned to a West Coast port meant shipment to the Pacific, to an East Coast port, shipment to the Atlantic theater—despite U.S. army snafus, which the Germans recognized. When the number reappeared in traffic to and from the British Isles or the Mediterranean, the Germans knew that the division had arrived in its theater. In this way, they spotted the movement of the 85th Infantry Division to Italy and recognized that the 37th Infantry Division was on Bougainville, fighting the Japanese. Once the U.S. units were in England, other elements of Regiment 5 listened for them.

And in the two months before the invasion, they corroborated the presence there of many Allied units. The British 50th Infantry Division was spotted "probably in the South-East Command." The 51st Infantry Division, the crack Highland division, was found, on the basis of subsequent evaluations, to have been there since 1 March. They learned accurately enough that the American 1st, 2nd, 4th, and 30th Infantry Divisions, the 2nd Armored Division, and the XVth and XIXth Corps were in Britain.

The assiduous deception organization did not let this opportunity of fooling German radio reconnaissance pass. It had the Signal Corps in the American Zone of the Interior radio messages about divisions that existed only in Allied minds. Through the ether they were transferred to German minds. Thus at about the same time that Euskirchen was discovering the 69th Infantry Division, it also "discovered" the 49th and 59th infantry divisions, neither of which had ever existed. By December 1943, Euler totted up 34 divisions that radio reconnaissance had ascertained. Eleven of these were pure fiction.

Second only to radio intelligence as a source of the basic order-of-battle information were Germany's spies. Like an army of spiders, they fanned out from the centrals of the Abwehr and the RSHA and infiltrated the enemy camps. The antenna cobwebs in the Hamburg meadows and at the Havel Institute in Berlin and inside the clandestine radio station in neutral Madrid quivered to their incoming messages. In the well-provisioned cafés that lined the sunny promenades of the Portuguese resort of Estoril, filled with riffraff and royalty flung there by the upheavals of a Europe at war, other agents reported in person to their spymasters. Pastis or whiskey flowed down their throats as their fictions flowed out. For fictions they were. Everything they said was either a lie approved by the

Double-Cross Committee, or a truth permitted by it to bolster the lies, or a tale invented by a money-hungry raconteur who had never been closer to England during the war than the docks of the Tagus.

HUBERT—the Polish general staff officer who served in liaison posts in Britain—passed messages about the 21st Airborne Division. There never was one. Sometimes the Double-Cross Committee had its spies tell about shoulder patches they had seen soldiers wearing. The committee hoped that this method would persuade German intelligence officers of the information more than a report giving a number, partly because it was more concrete and so presumably more accurate, partly because the officers would themselves draw the conclusions about the identity of a unit by looking the design up in their records, thus in effect convincing themselves of its validity. DRUMMOND sent along the insignia of the American 80th and 28th infantry divisions—a range of three mountains for the former, a red keystone, the emblem of Pennsylvania, its home state, for the latter, a National Guard division.

An agent in New York, KÖHLER, who was partially under F.B.I. control and who had reported some real units, radioed on 4 March 1944 that he had seen some drunken officers in a hotel bar, one of whom was wearing "a pentagonal blue and gold insignia never seen before by me." It was the double pentagon design of the Institute of Heraldry for the 55th Division. KÖHLER added that the officer wearing this patch had retorted to a joking remark about Iceland that "the others shouldn't laugh too soon, since they could also be sent there. When he left there, quarters were being prepared for a lot of men."

This information filtered rapidly into the order of battle maintained by Euler at Foreign Armies West. At the end of April, in his twice-a-month mimeographed "Survey USA," mainly of American army forces, Euler noted:

"According to a believable Abwehr report, another of the formations in Iceland was transported to Scotland. According to many reports it is the 55th Infantry Division. An infantry division of this number has not appeared up to now, but, according to the American activation program, one could have first been set up in the year 1943 and consequently not viewed as a usable formation for the European front. It is consequently possible that the American formation without a number previously assumed to be in Iceland has received the number 55 and now has been transported to Great Britain." But the division had never existed.

The officers in the buildings at Zossen were not dolts. But like journalists, like security analysts or lawyers or detectives, they lay at the mercy of their sources. Since these were tainted and incomplete, the conclusions drawn from them necessarily were as well. German intelligence could not correct this situation through unturned agents, or codebreaking, or aerial reconnaissance. And, on the other hand, the careful Allied

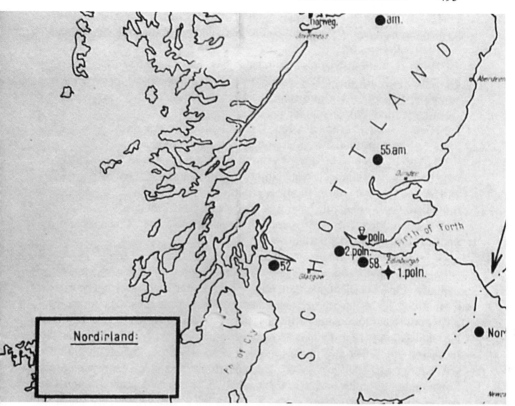

Northern portion of Foreign Armies West's map of the Allied "Distribution of Forces Great Britain/Northern Ireland" for 31 May 1944. In addition to showing the non-existent American 55th Infantry Division northwest of Dundee, Scotland, it gives the wildly false totals of 56 infantry divisions, 5 independent infantry brigades, 8 airborne divisions, 8 paratroop battalions, 15 armored divisions, and 14 armored brigades. The map uses circles for infantry divisions, stars for armored divisions, and circles with superimposed L for airborne divisions

coordination of one form of intelligence with another provided a spurious confirmation. Foreign Armies West was both driven by circumstance and invited by logic to believe what the Allies told them.

But another and quite extraneous factor led it further down this garden path than it might otherwise have gone. This was Baron von Roenne's contempt for Hitler. From his own experience in Foreign Armies East, he well knew that Hitler rejected Gehlen's estimates of Russian strength as defeatist, and indeed prejudged all intelligence men as pessimists. Roenne feared that the Führer's contempt for his estimates of Allied strength would spike German arms. So, in the late summer of 1943, he prepared countermeasures.

He summoned his I a, Lieutenant Colonel Lothar Metz, a man who flashed a broad and frequent smile and who put together the branch's daily situation report.

"From now on," Roenne announced, "we have to exaggerate. The Operations Staff [of the OKW, at Führer headquarters] deducts a certain percentage from everything that we report. So we have to get ready for that in advance. We have to exaggerate."

"Herr Colonel," replied Metz, "I can't do that. I learned as a soldier that you must answer for what you do. It has to be true."

"Think it over—you have twenty-four hours—and tell me tomorrow whether you've changed your mind," said Roenne. "The responsibility will be mine, not yours. If, in good faith, you don't want to do it, I'll understand, but then I'll have to remove you from this job."

Metz, troubled, turned it over and over in his mind. The next day he finally told Roenne: "I'll do it."

From that day on, he and Roenne exaggerated the figures of Allied strength in their reports. They did not invent Allied divisions—that wouldn't have worked. Nor did they involve the individual specialists in their plan. These men, such as Euler, worked with their customary precision and gave the drafts of their sections of the situation report to Metz. He and Roenne then deleted from these many of the qualifications of Allied strength. Euler had put a question mark after the U.S. 55th Infantry Division in his "Survey USA"; Roenne eliminated it on his own enemy forces map. If Euler said that the first third of an American division had arrived in England, Metz made it sound as if the entire division were there. If a formation was still in training, he and Roenne made it seem as if it were ready for action.

This exaggeration, on top of their unwitting acceptance of the Allied faking of divisions, meant that on a day when only 89 U.S. army divisions of all kinds existed, Foreign Armies West counted 98. On 1 June 1944, when only 20 U.S. divisions were in Great Britain, it showed 22. At the same time, for the 23 British and Canadian divisions in Britain, plus 1 Polish and 1 French, all together 25, the branch showed an incredible number of 57—well over double the actual amount. In sum, when there was a total of 47 Allied divisions in the island, Foreign Armies West was figuring on a total of 79. Beyond these, it counted 19 armored brigades and 8 paratroop battalions, approximately equal to 10 more divisions. And its estimates were being accepted by the highest levels. Hitler told the Japanese ambassador that the Allies "have about 80 divisions on their island."

All these calculations pointed to a single great conclusion: the Allies had sufficient manpower to launch both a diversionary and a main attack. The Germans were convinced that the main attack would come in the Pas de Calais. To defend against it they put most of their efforts into building the Atlantic Wall in that sector, where they hoped the Allied assault would shatter like a pane of glass smashed against a concrete pillbox. But any diversionary attack, even though secondary, would also have to be repulsed. For if not stopped at once, it might just break open the German defenses and possibly even turn into the main offensive in a seizure of opportunity. Even if it did not, and the Allies held fast to what the Germans believed would be their chief objective, any diversion, if sustained, could become a festering sore that would drain away German strength. Most important of all, the first attack, even if only a fake, had to be stopped for psychological reasons in Germany and for the disastrous effect this would have upon Allied plans and strength. Its failure might compel cancellation of the main assault. The collapse of an invasion attempt would mean, Hitler said, "that the English and Americans would not advance to battle a second time in the year, as much out of material as out of morale grounds. The shock upon public opinion in England and America of a failed operation of this kind in connection with the giant casualty figures that are certainly to be expected cannot be rated high enough and would probably"—his fancy took wings—"create a turning point in the war. With a single blow great groups of forces would be set free, which could be used in the east not only to stabilize the front, but to take up an offensive action against the Russians."

Hitler's generals probably did not share that overoptimistic view of things. But his two main commanders in the West, Rundstedt and Rommel, agreed upon the necessity of stopping the first attack, even if it was only a feint.

In preparation for the invasion, the Allies were bombing France. Their attacks fell into a certain pattern. German intelligence officers sought to deduce Allied intentions from it. They were alert to the possibility of deception, but they also realized that any ruse takes away from the forces needed for the real—and decisive—operation. In the same way that their commanders preferred a concentration of forces to surprise, they believed that the bombs' destructive effects were far more important than any service as trickery. They therefore concluded that the Allies would attack where they were bombing.

The great majority of bombs fell in what the Germans called the "Belgium–Northern France" area. During the last half of May 1944, for example, the Germans counted 10,701 bombers there and only 5,059 in what they called "Western France," meaning Normandy and Brittany.

Many of the bombs destroyed the bridges over rivers and thus cut the rail lines to the Pas de Calais. This hindered the movement of troops from outside to that area. The destruction of the bridges over the Seine, particularly at the railroad center of Rouen, blocked transport from the Cotentin, Brittany, and all the southern Atlantic coast of France to the

Pas de Calais. The loss of bridges over the Oise and the Somme cut communications between the Pas de Calais and Paris, the southeast, and Italy. Bombs on crossings of smaller rivers and canals at such towns as Arras, the capital of the Pas de Calais department, and Mons and Charleroi in Belgium blocked movement from Germany. To the south nothing appeared touched. The German map of destruction of railroads showed little or no damage to Normandy and Brittany. As early as April, Meyer-Detring, Rundstedt's I c, concluded that the destruction pattern pointed to an enemy main effort on the Channel coast. Though the bombing of the Rouen bridges also hindered the sending of troops to Normandy from Paris and from Germany, the Germans saw only trains passing north, toward the Pas de Calais. On 5 June Rundstedt remarked in his situation report that the bomb pattern could also hint at a Normandy invasion. But this was overshadowed by a repetition of what he had always been saying: "Concentration of the enemy air effort on the coastal fortresses between Dunkirk and Dieppe and on the Seine-Oise bridges could indicate the point of main effort of an intended major landing." In other words: the Pas de Calais.

Attacking troops usually reconnoiter the terrain and the defenses of the point they will storm. Where they probe therefore may indicate where they will attack. The Germans gathered information on whatever Allied reconnaissance of the coast they detected. By mid-April, they had already discovered orders for or had themselves spotted reconnaissances of beach obstacles in seven cases. The most significant intelligence came from an Allied attempt of 18 May.

A group of about 35 men had set out after dark the previous evening in a fast launch from a harbor in southern England. At 2:45 a.m. on the 18th their launch encountered a German boat, fought with it, and got away. But the battle had delayed the mission, and perhaps for this reason two of the men, both first lieutenants, were dropped in their inflatable liferaft much too far from the beach. They lost touch with their launch. After daybreak, they voluntarily surrendered by rowing to shore at 8 a.m. near Cayeux-sur-Mer, a little resort just south of where the Somme empties through a sandy estuary into the sea. An expert interrogator from one of Foreign Armies West's teams questioned them. One man, George L——, 30, a farmer in civilian life, spoke willingly about some things, remained silent about others. The other refused to talk at all. L—— said that their job was to reconnoiter the beach barriers, determining their strength and readiness, and to spot mine fields. They had no electrical mine detectors but used a rod to feel for mines and a shovel to dig them out. Though it was their first assignment, similar tasks had for the past two months been given to Commandos—to which they belonged, as a slip of the tongue indicated. Rumor had it that the coasts of Holland, Bel-

From this shed at 1150 Carrera Street, Quilpe, a small town 15 miles east of Valparaiso, a German spy ring in Chile operated a radio transmitter with call sign PYL to send information to the Abwehr radio station in Hamburg. The radioman, Johannes Szeraws, lived in the house and transmitted from a back room

The Abwehr's radio station in Hamburg, its most important, which maintained its tenuous links with its spies half a world away. Into the radio room on the second floor came the faint Morse peepings of agents in North and South America; from it the Abwehr beamed its orders, requests, and thanks to them

A spy's radio built into a suitcase, used by German agents in South America

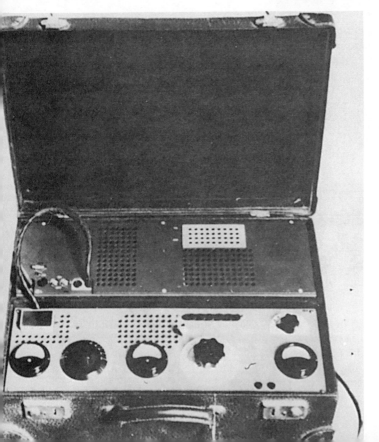

A close-up of a row o microphotographs taped t the inside of an envelop flap and airmailed by Ger man agents in Mexico t a cover address in Lisbo

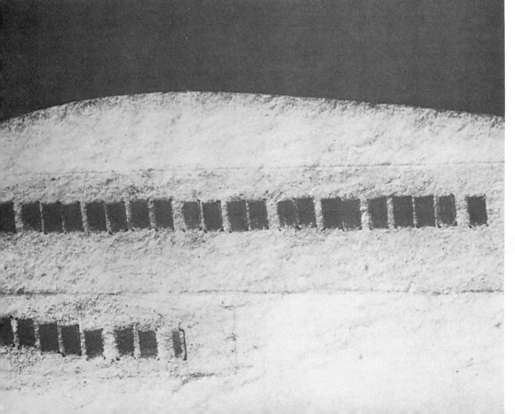

SS Major Eugen Steimle, capable head of Nazi espionage's western European group—and of units of an SS killing squad in Russia

SS Lieutenant Friedrich Carstenn, head of the Nazi espionage desk for North America, all decked out, down to the dagger

Herman Lang, who stole the drawings of the Norden bomb sight and gave them to Germany, photographed by a hidden F.B.I. camera in New York

Johannes Siegfried Becker, effective head of German spy rings in Argentina

Two Poles, drafted into the German army, forced to serve as spies, and captured by the Americans, are tied to the stake in a farm courtyard in Toul, France, 11 November 1944. ABOVE, Josef Wende. BELOW, Stefan Kotas

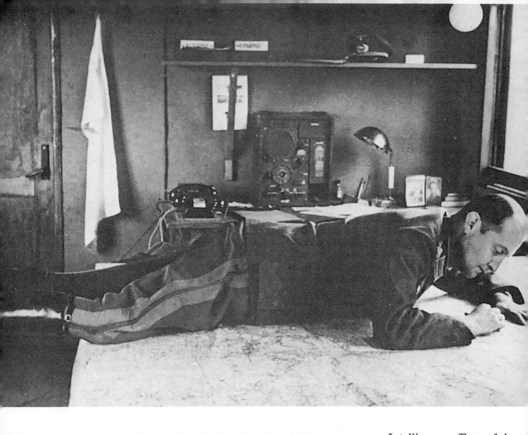

Intelligence officer of Army Group Center Colonel Hans Adolf von Blumröder, though wearing the double stripes of the general staff, doesn't let fear of looking ridiculous prevent him from examining his enemy situation map close up

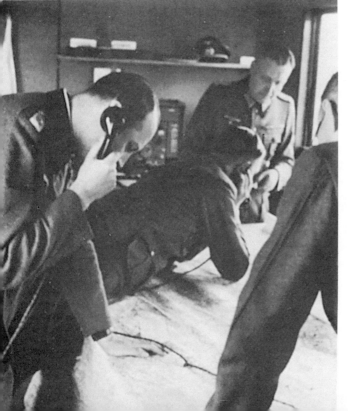

A telephone conference between the intelligence section of the Army Group Center staff and that of another headquarters on the eastern front. AT LEFT, Blumröder

General Gerhard Matzky, the fourth assistant chief of the general staff, for intelligence, emerges from his steel-doored office building at the general staff headquarters in Zossen, south of Berlin

Colonel Hugo Baron von Süss-kind-Schwendi, head of the enlarged intelligence staff of the Armed Forces High Command

The building at Zossen used by Matzky. Those housing
Foreign Armies East and Foreign Armies West were identical

Light shines from one of the converted barracks in East Prussia near
Führer headquarters occupied by Foreign Armies East. Work went on
round the clock at the army intelligence branch

Colonel Ulrich Liss, head of
Foreign Armies West

General Reinhard Gehlen, head of
Foreign Armies East

Colonel Alexis Baron von Roenne, head of Foreign Armies West, the general staff intelligence evaluation agency for Britain, America, and other Western countries. On him fell the responsibility for ascertaining where the Allies would invade the continent

Colonel Josef "Beppo" Schmid, Luftwaffe intelligence chief for the first half of the war

Parts of a Luftwaffe target folder. ABOVE, aerial photograph of the area around Sedan with a railroad bridge over the Meuse River circled. On the following pages, the map and diagram parts

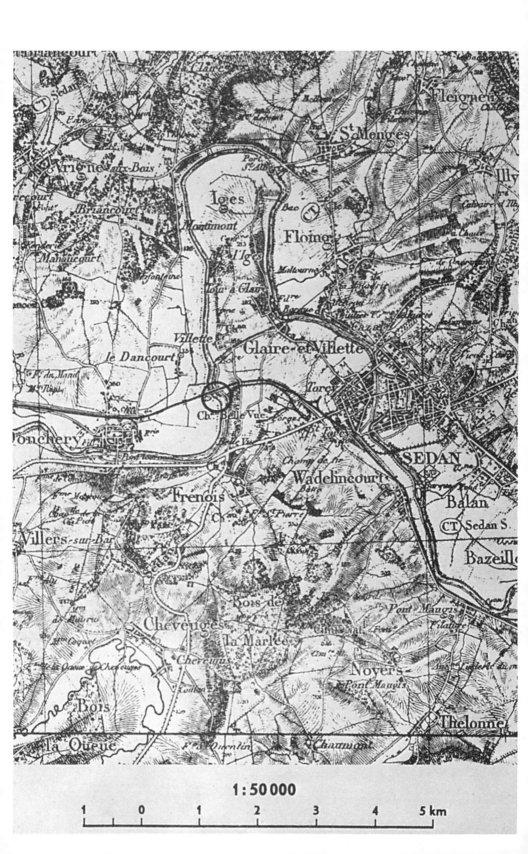

1 : 50 000

| 1 | | 0 | 1 | 2 | 3 | 4 | 5 km |

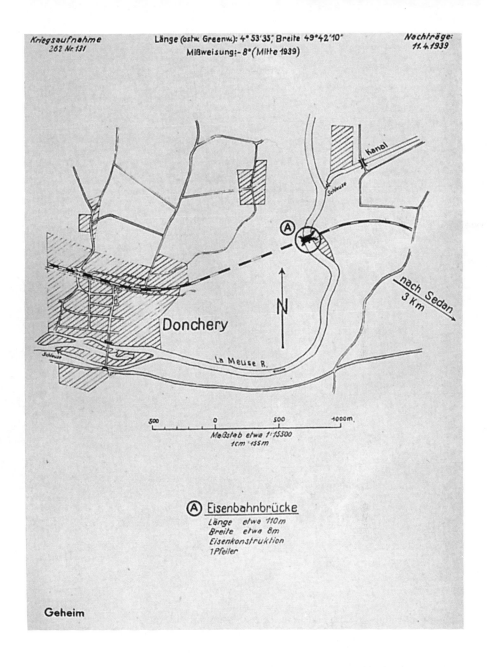

Kriegsaufnahme
262 Nr. 131

Länge (östl. Greenw.): 4° 53'35", Breite 49°42'10"
Mißweisung:-8°(Mitte 1939)

Nachträge:
11.4.1939

nach Sedan
3 Km

Donchery

N

La Meuse R.

Kanal

Schleuse

Schleuse

500   0   500   1000m.
Maßstab etwa 1:15500
1cm = 155m

(A) Eisenbahnbrücke
Länge   etwa 110m
Breite etwa 8m
Eisenkonstruktion
1 Pfeiler

Geheim

Two other parts of the target folder. LEFT, portion of a French map.
ABOVE, large-scale diagram of the railroad bridge, marked "secret" in
lower-left-hand corner, giving a scale of 1:15,500, bridge construction
details (length about 110 meters, width about 8, iron construction, one
support), and an arrow pointing "toward Sedan, 3 kilometers"

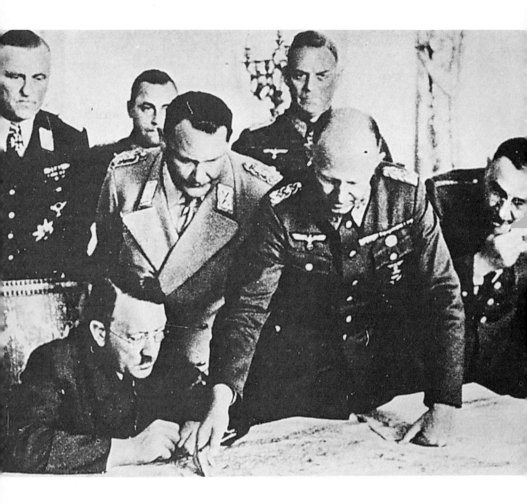

The final arbitor and ultimate consumer of the vast quantities of information pumped out by Germany's intelligence machine: the Führer, Chancellor, and Supreme Commander of the Armed Forces, Adolf Hitler. Here, on 6 June 1941, wearing glasses, he plots his fatal attack on the Soviet Union with, from left, General Karl Koller, air force operations branch chief; General Walter Warlimont, deputy chief of the Operations Staff of the Armed Forces High Command; Reich Marshal Hermann Göring, commander in chief of the air force; General Wilhelm Keitel, chief of the Armed Forces High Command; General Walter Brauchitsch, commander in chief of the army; and a Hungarian general gium, and the Channel, including Normandy, were to be reconnoitered, he said. He knew nothing about the point of main effort and the timing of the invasion, but did not believe that it would take place in the Somme-Dieppe area, in effect the southern flank of the Pas de Calais, since that was too strongly fortified. Asked whether these reconnaissance activities meant that the invasion was imminent, he denied it. That "would overestimate the invasion desire of the English and the Americans," said L——.

Later in the day, another clue was found that, to the Germans, silently bespoke the intent of Allied reconnoiterers. Near the beach barricades east of Calais, just where they had always thought the Allies would attack, the Germans found an apparatus for camera flashbulbs. Jodl told Hitler about it at the situation conference in Berchtesgaden that day.

A major indication of the attack locations would come from the location of landing craft in British harbors. Presumably they would be moored and loaded as close as practicable to where they would land. Thus the presence of many landing ships in the harbors near Dover would indicate a landing opposite that port, namely in the Pas de Calais. Ships farther to the west, as in Portsmouth, Portland, and Plymouth, would suggest an invasion against the Cotentin or Brittany. Spies reported some ship concentrations. They messaged that Norwegian and Swedish seamen said that landing boats, especially for infantry, had constantly moved south from Cardigan Bay in Wales to harbors in the Bristol Channel. They told about landing boats in the small harbors between Newquay and Ilfracombe, both near the southwestern tip of Britain. But these were partial pictures. They didn't tell whether these vessels were more or fewer than those elsewhere.

The surest way of getting this information was by aerial photography. In particular, simultaneous coverage of all ports would ensure a true count of total tonnage, including especially landing craft, and of its distribution. The problem was that Allied air superiority rendered this virtually impossible. The Germans did the best they could, however. They built special cameras into the rump of Me 109 fighters—planes fast enough to have a chance of grabbing pictures before the Allied planes could nab them. Early in the spring, one plane or another made it about every other day. Through April and the first week of May, however, no strong pattern had emerged. On 19 April, the OKM had commented that the reconnaissance of Ramsgate, just north of Dover, and of nearby Sandwich, long ago England's chief military and naval port, resulted in no conclusions about an attack. But on 25 April, air reconnaissance showed 234 LCTs (landing craft, tank), 254 small and 170 auxiliary landing boats, and 15 transports, capable, the navy figured, of transporting 70,000 men, concentrated in Portsmouth, Southampton, and Selsey

Bill—the center of Britain's southern coast. The OKM thereupon suggested that the point of main effort showed in the area from Portsmouth to Plymouth, near Britain's southwestern tip. This tended to infer an attack toward Brittany and Normandy. A 10-day breakdown in aerial reconnaissance in the middle of May did not help to confirm or deny this picture. And when the reconnaissance resumed, though it sometimes penetrated far to the west, it provided only unintegrated details. The Luftwaffe could not provide the full picture that alone could show where the shipping concentrations were. Nor could spies. In the end, the German high commands got no real information from either source on this critical question, and consequently they made no deductions from them as to where the attack might come.

Though this physical evidence did not give the full picture, some verbal evidence claimed to do so. Spies forwarded the purported Allied plans to invade Europe.

Such information had been coming in since before the North African invasion. It poured in throughout the summer of 1943, barely diminishing in acknowledgment of the Allied assault on Sicily. Volume declined during the winter but rose to a new crescendo in the spring of 1944. The duty officers at the Abwehr or the 3/Skl or Foreign Armies West recognized that many of the reports were being fed in by the Allies, for the dispatches of a single night seemed to name every single landing place from Norway to southern France. But they expected that the "organized minority" of the true reports would focus upon the real target while the false reports of the "disorganized majority" would disperse themselves. And they certainly hoped that one of their better agents would obtain and send them at least the essence of the overall Allied plan.

So they scrutinized every message. These were of the most incredible variety. On 22 April, for example, an agent claiming a link to Eisenhower's staff reported that three actions were probably planned: (1) a double operation against southern France from the Mediterranean and from the southern Biscayan coast, meaning the area from Bordeaux to the Spanish border, (2) a secondary action against northern Norway with strong fleet forces having Narvik as its target, and (3) the main action on the Channel coast. (The term "Channel coast" could mean anywhere from the Strait of Dover to the tip of Brittany, and though sometimes it seemed as if it was being restricted to the Pas de Calais and the area just to the south, more often both the spies and the Germans seemed to use it in its broader sense to conceal their ignorance.)

The next day a report arrived from the German diplomatic post at Tangier. "Friendly sources in Algiers" had said that the main invasion attack would come against the area between the mouths of the Schelde in Holland and the Seine in France. This somewhat meant the Pas de Calais.

The Allies would mount secondary attacks against Bordeaux, in southern France, and Brest, at the tip of Brittany, with a simultaneous drive in the Mediterranean against the area around Marseilles and the mouth of the Rhône. The same source mentioned, almost offhandedly, an "expected side attack against Yugoslavia." But the English and Americans would not take part in this, he said, because of Russian-Allied agreements. Instead Italy and other co-belligerents would do the fighting.

On 14 May, an agent of the Stettin Abwehr post, who was still on probation, heard from one of his subagents that the attack would take place against both the southern Atlantic coast of France and the Pas de Calais. Simultaneously, the Allies would attack in Italy and land in the Balkans. The next day, agent KRABBE of the Lyon report center notified his masters that the first attack, against Cherbourg, would be a deception; the main attack would follow, though he did not say where. At about the same time, a neutral diplomat called trustworthy by the Abwehr reported exactly the opposite view after a visit to Vichy. French staff generals foresaw the real landing between the Somme and the Belgium; many smaller operations might take place at the same time on the southern Atlantic coast. Contradictory reports like these kept coming in all spring. One day in May, agent TONY of the KO Portugal warned of commando operations against Dieppe, Abbeville, Boulogne, and Dunkirk. The next day, source ANTON assured his masters that the left wing of the invasion force would rest on Denmark, the right wing on Belgium, and the center, the main effort, on Hamburg.

From these multifarious reports, and the other conflicting bits of evidence, cautious intelligence officers drew no specific conclusions. Their judgments were masterpieces of vagueness.

By 17 April, Meyer-Detring as the commander in chief west was holding that the main attack would come somewhere along the Channel coast. This was equivalent to saying that an attack would come somewhere along the U.S. northeastern seaboard between New London, Connecticut, and Norfolk, Virginia. Four days later, Roenne, at Foreign Armies West, likewise said nothing of value, but said it in more detail. The grouping of Allied forces in Britain, he said, pointed to three main axes of advance: through the area west of the Somme (meaning toward Le Havre and the Contentin), through the area east of the Somme and the Channel coast (here meaning mainly the Pas de Calais), and Belgium-Holland. But he did not say which was the most likely. In effect he had done nothing more than list every possibility. Both reports were useless to plan defenses against the Allied landing. Their only merit lay in restating that no major attack would come elsewhere. This meant: not Norway.

For though the Allies had mounted an extensive deception campaign to suggest that they were planning a Norway invasion, Foreign Armies

West did not fall for it. It came to believe in a few fake Allied units in Scotland, such as the British 4th Army and the American 55th Infantry Division. But it recognized, perhaps through radio reconnaissance, the withdrawal of many divisions from the north of Britain to the south. And most of the energetic Allied radio deception in the north of Britain to simulate the preparations of an invasion force went unheard by the Germans. The reason seems to be that not one of the radio reconnaissance units of the German 20th Army, occupying Norway, was paying the least bit of attention: all were far away in Finland, facing east and listening hard to the Russians. The consequence was that Roenne concluded that any landings in Norway would be secondary; Meyer-Detring concurred. Hitler believed the same thing, since he thought the main invasion would come in France. Yet he never withdrew a single soldier from Norway to oppose this main assault. Why? Because it was his "zone of destiny" in the war owing to its ability to protect his shipments of Finnish nickel ore, his northern flank, and his U-boat departures. But Allied deception had nothing to do with all this. Hitler kept major forces in Norway entirely on his own volition.

If the raw intelligence and the evaluations made from it did not point to a single spot for the invasion, they at least did not contradict the preconceptions of Rommel, Rundstedt, and Hitler. All continued to believe that the main assault would come in the Pas de Calais: they never shifted any divisions out of the area. But Hitler came increasingly to think that a diversionary attack would in fact precede the main one and would come south of the main landing. At first he saw the diversion around Bordeaux, perhaps as a pincers movement from the Atlantic and the Mediterranean. But by March he saw "special incentive for the building of bridgeheads" in Brittany and the Cotentin. He persisted in this view. On 3 May he reckoned "first of all with individual operations for the creation of several bridgeheads. Above all strong bridgeheads will be attempted in Brittany and on the Cherbourg peninsula." He ordered a strengthening of forces there. During a dispute among subordinates three days later as to how this would be done, Jodl, Hitler's mouthpiece in the west, told the chief of staff of the commander in chief west over the telephone that "the Cotentin peninsula would be the first target of the enemy." And two tough armored and two infantry divisions were added to its defenses— one of each in the peninsula and one of each a day's march away.

This move in effect sealed the German views about the location of the Allied assault. Although the intelligence officers still refused to commit themselves, because the evidence did not warrant it, their commanders and Hitler continued to expect the main invasion in the Pas de Calais. Hitler added to this, as a finishing touch, that a first landing could come as a feint in Normandy or Brittany.

The next great question that faced the Germans was when the Allies would strike. Forewarning can save soldiers from the paralysis of surprise. Yet troops cannot be kept permanently on alert; this rapidly decays into not alerting them at all. So the Germans sought by every possible means to determine the time of the Allied landing.

In gross, the availability of men and matériel fixed the date of the invasion for the Allies. When not enough were on hand in 1943, the cross-Channel assault was postponed to 1944. The first target date was May. Lack of supplies, particularly landing craft, put this back to June.

The Allies set the fine timing of the invasion on the basis of three elements: dawn, tide, and moon. The landing would be made about dawn because darkness would cover the arrival of the ships while first light would enable them to aim at their targets in the softening-up bombardment and would help the invaders identify their landing beaches. The tide would be rising, so that the first landing craft could ground, unload, and withdraw without stranding. But how long before high tide should the assault come? The higher the tide, the less risk to troops advancing across the fire-swept beaches—but the fewer ships that could easily unload. The planners decided that three hours before high tide was the least objectionable. The airborne landings, in the first hours after midnight, needed moonlight. The combination of all three factors reduced the number of usable days in each month to just three. In June of 1944, these were Monday, Tuesday, and Wednesday, the 5th, 6th, and 7th of June.

All elements of the German intelligence apparatus strained to learn the date of the invasion. The OKM sought to do so by trying to reproduce the process by which the Allies had in fact determined the fine timing of their landing, based upon its knowledge of previous Allied amphibious operations. The North African invasion had taken place at new moon and at high water. But that was a special situation: stealth against a kind of nonbelligerent. At Sicily, Anzio, and Nettuno, the Allies came ashore against an armed foe. Hitler said that the Allies had always moved in during the night and attacked in twilight; he believed that the Allies would land at dawn. The OKM agreed, merely adding that the attack would take place when dawn coincided with a high tide. As early as April 1943, it charted days on which high tide came at dawn and thus were particularly dangerous. It notified the army commands of these days.

But in 1944, to prevent high-tide landings, Rommel set out foreshore obstacles that would lie under water at high tide and thus snag the landing boats. The navy expected the Allies to spot these and to consider low-tide landings but to opt for the high-tide landings after all. At the same time, the Germans revised their belief that Allied airborne landings could take place only during the day or at twilight. Now they thought that they could occur during bright moonlit nights as well.

On 4 May, British forces practiced an invasion in the south of Britain that the Germans followed through radio reconnaissance. The Naval Group West, a unit attached to Rundstedt's command, analyzed the exercise. It reported that the landing had been made on a flat coast with gradually shelving depth. It had begun two hours after low water, because high water concealed the foreshore obstacles. This required the troops to charge across a beach of hard sand or pebbles 200 to 300 yards wide—considerably more than if the assault had been made at high water. The landing ended two hours after high water. The Naval Group West expressed surprise at the low-tide timing, and the Naval War Command in Berlin saw no advantage in it. But both yielded to the fact. Three weeks later, the Naval Group West dropped all considerations of the tide in issuing its estimates of likely time for enemy landings. It thenceforth based these estimates only on the weather and the naval situation.

One of the sources of foreknowledge about the invasion lay right under the Germans' noses: the French resistance. The resistance in France had grown into a powerful secret army, capable of blowing up bridges, mining roads, disrupting communications. The Allies could be expected to utilize these underground forces to help the invasion. This might well require advance notice—which the Germans could discover.

Penetrating the underground was the job of Abwehr III, counterespionage. In 1942, Major Oscar Reile, a lantern-jawed Abwehr veteran, arrived to take over Group III at the Abwehr Main Post West, quartered in the ornate Hotel Lutetia on Paris's Left Bank. He at once began energetically to seek to inject as many agents as he could into the resistance organizations. His main task was to ascertain what action the French would take against the German occupation forces when the invasion began. If his researches incidentally furnished him with the time and place of the invasion, however, he would not reject the information.

The British agency that supported and directed the resistance organizations in Europe, Special Operations Executive, communicated with them through open code messages broadcast each night by the foreign department of the B.B.C. The open codes were allegedly personal messages—the radio equivalent of personal notices in the classified columns of newspapers. Some were perhaps legitimate, reporting on births, safe arrivals, and other events to people in the oppressed countries. But many were invented phrases: "The elephants are eating the strawberries"; "Catherine is waiting by the well." They announced that a supply drop was set for a certain night, that a report had reached England safely, that the telephones should be sabotaged in S.O.E.'s Region R 3. B.B.C. broadcast them near 7:30 and 9 p.m. They were preceded by the first four notes of Beethoven's Fifth Symphony, the famous V for Victory signal, and—for those for France —by the statement "Voici quelques messages personnels" ("Here are some personal messages"). The announcer then recited them twice in French, once at normal speed, once at a slower dictation speed. All together they usually lasted 15 to 20 minutes.

No cryptanalyst could break these messages, for nothing in the open text implied its hidden meaning. But, like all other secrets, they were vulnerable to betrayal. During 1943, German counterespionage, through questioning of a suspicious person who proved to be an underground courier, had broken up a Resistance net named BUTLER, which had been successfully blowing up railway targets inland from Brittany. Its destruction enabled Reile to learn its invasion open-code message. On 14 October 1943, he reported to the army groups and armies in the area of the commander in chief west that "the English-American invasion will be announced to the sabotage organizations in France that are directed from England through the following verse." It was the first stanza of a poem by the brilliant, suicidal nineteenth-century symbolist, Paul Verlaine:

> Les sanglots longs
> Des violons
>   De l'automne
> Blessent mon coeur
> D'une langueur
>   Monotone.

("The long sobs of the violins of autumn wound my heart with a monotonous languor.")

The British did not suspect that the message had been betrayed, because the Germans played back the BUTLER transmitter as if the net were still operating. Moreover, S.O.E. employed the verse as well for groups that had been associated with BUTLER. Thus the code stayed valid, and the Germans stayed in the know. German agents penetrated other groups and obtained two dozen other messages, such as "Gentlemen, place your bets" and "Electricity dates from the twentieth century." But the Verlaine verse seemed the most widely distributed to the Germans, and they placed the most trust in it. Their radio reconnaissance organizations tuned to the B.B.C. to listen for it and the others, which would disclose to them the start of the long-awaited invasion.

Both Hitler and his generals thought at first that the attack might come as early as February or March. At the situation conference at the end of December 1943, at which Hitler expressed his perplexity over which landing would be the diversion and which the real one, he predicted the invasion for the spring and added, "He [the enemy] has already made landings in April, and he can push it forward; it grows lighter very fast."

But no landings would be undertaken until the Allies were ready. The German intelligence officers at the various levels sought to determine when this would be by the number of combat-ready divisions in Britain, the availability of transport for the sea crossing, the readiness of the air forces. They judged this intuitively, rather than by any mathematical formula. On 1 April, Meyer-Detring noticed that the invasion preparations had entered a new stage. Troops were being pulled out of the north, where they had evidently been assembled for the deception against Norway, to the south, where they would serve in the actual invasion. Air mail and travel to other countries had been embargoed. The bombings of railways in northern France continued. Two days later, Roenne commented on the "readiness" of the units in England. In general, at the start of April, the German high commands sensed that an invasion was militarily possible at any time. Meyer-Detring thought that the Allies were merely awaiting good weather and perhaps a propitious moment to assuage the Russians' demands for a Second Front Now.

Suddenly, evidence began to mount that something was afoot. The B-Dienst, the navy's radio reconnaissance organization, observed that at one minute past midnight on 1 April the old, systematic, LOXO 3-letter cipher system of the Allies was replaced by a new, unsystematic LOXO that was more difficult to solve. At Hitler's situation conference on 6 April the OKM representative reported that although fog and poor visibility had prevented aerial reconnaissance from bringing in results, other sources said they had seen an Allied sortie. General Warlimont, Jodl's deputy, added that the same report came from the north Breton coast. The generals and admirals discussed information "from a very good source" and various Allied command arrangements. It seemed to be adding up to indications of an invasion. But Hitler was skeptical.

"Now I ask myself," he said to his advisors, "must they do that so ostentatiously? Would we do it so ostentatiously, if we wanted to do business? We certainly wouldn't. That is absolutely not necessary. They can assemble their forces here, can load them and bring them over here. We can't determine at all what they're doing over there. . . . I therefore can't get away from the impression that it is probably nevertheless a bold-faced bluff, because the few landings that they have made up to now we didn't spot at all."

He and his generals reached no conclusion about the matter. Next day, however, more evidence came in. Radio traffic in Britain abruptly fell off. It was a customary sign of the imminence of a major undertaking. A "proved" agent said that his trusted subagents warned that the invasion was about to begin. Another, V-319, a Spanish journalist who was a specially trusted spy in England of the KO Spain, held, on the basis of a conversation with the British minister of information at the end of January, that the Allies would attack only when the Russians so advanced that the Germans would have to pull out troops from the west to strengthen the east. Baumbach, the head of naval intelligence, concurred. That very day, the Russians drove forward in their major offensive in the Crimea to regain control of the strategic peninsula. Excitement rose. On 9 April, Easter Sunday, Allied air attacked some airfields in the French rear areas and then began heavy bombing of rail junctions near the coast. The navy notified subordinate units that the great Allied invasion lay immediately ahead. Leaves were reduced or canceled. The army alerted its forces. For two days, the Wehrmacht quivered in anticipation. But nothing happened. On the 11th, radio traffic resumed in Britain. Slowly the Wehrmacht relaxed and returned to its normal state of slight twitchiness, as it continued to seek signs, better signs, of the invasion. By 17 April, Rundstedt, Jodl, and Hitler were all thinking that the invasion would take place in the first half of May.

That very evening a further sign of its approach appeared. The British government imposed unprecedented restrictions on all foreign missions, except the American and Russian. To maintain security in the island, no diplomats or couriers could leave. The missions could not send out any diplomatic pouch unless its contents had been censored. They could cable only in the clear. The measures violated immunities that diplomats had enjoyed practically since the Greek city-states first sent embassies to one another. The ambassadors raised a storm of protest, and Hitler sagely remarked a few days later that, although he did not know when the invasion would come, "the English have taken measures that they can sustain for only six to eight weeks."

More specific, if not more accurate, information about the time of the invasion came from Germany's diplomats and agents. At about the same time that Hitler was forecasting the invasion for the first half of May, the Foreign Office received a message from its consulate in Geneva. Trustworthy sources said that top Swiss circles expected the invasion by 10 May. The very day the message arrived, one of Ribbentrop's close party colleagues in the Foreign Office, Rudolf Likus, passed him one of his "confidential reports." Someone in the Balkans had transmitted a report, stemming originally from an American source in Ankara, allegedly the U.S. naval attaché, that the invasion would take place about the second week in May. This period passed without result, and on 31 May, Likus, unperturbed, gave his minister a new "confidential report." Well-informed circles in Bern, the capital of neutral Switzerland, were certain that the invasion would in no case come before 15 June.

Germany's secret agents were likewise submitting very varied data on the invasion deadline. On 21 April, agent RICARDO was reporting that enemy diplomatic circles in Lisbon expected the invasion at the end of April or the beginning of May. The KO Portugal passed word that the dates 2 to 6 May and, if nothing happened, then 19 to 23 May had "crystallized out" of the many rumors on the timing of the invasion then floating about London. Why these dates? In one of several reasons the KO gave, a U.S. liaison officer to Ferry Command reportedly said that all ferry supplies from America were to be suspended from 2 to 6 May. The agent with links to Eisenhower's staff said that preparations were targeted on the middle of May, or, at the latest, the end. An agent from the Abwehr post in Angers, at the base of Brittany, radioed in the secret he had heard from the Mexican consulate in Barcelona, which had got it from a trustworthy agent of the Spanish general staff. The Allies would land at several points in Europe in the next few weeks to fool and demoralize the German general staff. But the real invasion would only take place in June, when enough fuel would be available for it in England. Lack of fuel, he reemphasized, was what was holding things up.

Some agent reports linked the timing of the attack to external events. From Sweden, the Abwehr reported that the British minister told a large group of co-workers, upon his return from Britain, that the invasion had been delayed, but would come when the Russians threatened the Vistula and thus drew off troops from the west. Since the Russians then stood 500 miles east of the Polish river, the Abwehr prudently noted that the report might be a hoax. Another agent said that the Swedish foreign minister predicted the attack for the summer. It was to give Roosevelt a major victory that he could use as a vote-getter in the November presidential election. Still another argued the contrary: nothing could be done until after the harvest. The high wheat fields disguised the presence of mines in the aerial photographs taken by the Allies, and only when the crops were harvested would the mines be visible and the Allies able to select landing spots for airborne troops.

Communications reconnaissance picked up possible clues to the date of the invasion. The army intercepted a Polish brigade radioing that the Polish government-in-exile in London had called upon all Poles who have weapons to take up the fight against the Germans on 15 May. The Forschungsamt wiretapped a conversation between a French official in Paris and his chef de cabinet in Vichy. It learned that an acquaintance of the official had said that "serious and important events are expected in the night of Tuesday to Wednesday"—9 to 10 May.

In the days that most of these messages were coming in, 21 to 24 April, the army, the navy, and the OKW dotted the *i*s and crossed the *t*s of the intuitions of Hitler, Rundstedt, and Jodl of a few days before that the invasion would take place in early May. Foreign Armies West declared the Allies "militarily ready to jump off." The actual moment was mainly a question of the weather. The OKM commented, "All reports and judgments show clearly that the preparations of the enemy for the invasion are as good as ended." Colonel Krummacher, the OKW/WFSt/I c, wrote that the shifting of the point of main effort toward southern and southeastern England depicted the last phase of invasion preparations. All agreed, in other words, that the invasion was imminent. On the coast, troops strained their eyes as they peered over the water, trying to spot the invasion fleet. The intelligence officers, their commanders, the forces in the west, all waited for the invasion.

So did the people in Germany. Rumors flashed across the land. Hitler had transferred his headquarters to the west, they reported. A clairvoyant, who had proved herself in little experiments during a railroad ride, had said that in April the greatest bloodletting of all time had taken place in the east front, in May the same thing would happen in England, and in June there would be far and wide no human to be seen, since 75 percent of the European population would be destroyed by strange forthcoming events of the war. People complained about the lack of food and feared that rations would be reduced. The ceaseless air raids depressed the population, and the new Allied tactic of strafing individuals in the fields made many farmers afraid to work. When people saw the Allied bombers flying in closed formations undisturbed through the skies of the Reich, only a few thought that the Luftwaffe was husbanding its defenses for the forthcoming battle; most concluded simply that "We don't have much." Bitter jokes were whispered from mouth to mouth.

> An elderly man is called up for military service. The doctor asks him to which branch of service he wants to go. The man answers that he doesn't know enough about it.
> "But you must have served in the First World War," the doctor says.
> "Oh, no," the man replies. "I was too old then."

In May, as the tension rose, people began telling one another that the invasion had already started at Calais, that Allied planes were dropping arms all over France for the underground, that 10,000 British paratroops had come down in southern France to start a partisan action. But the invasion did not come.

The Allies had postponed it for a month because of lack of supplies. During this month, they mainly built up their strength. Indications about their moves shrank to a trickle. Hitler made a judgment on the timing from the nonoccurrence of an event. On 4 May, as the bombings continued heavily in both Germany and France, he observed that the invasion would not come in the next day or so. For, he explained, it would require the Allies to withdraw airplanes from the bombing of Germany to use them in support of the landing. This would abate the air raids in Germany—and this had not happened.

The intelligence officers could do little more in the first half of May than repeat yet again, in different words, their previous estimates. The 3/Skl reasserted that the enemy's assembly of sea forces was approaching completion. The actual culmination would be hard to recognize, it warned, because warships and landing craft could be moved to the departure harbors at short notice. The OKM's air branch reported that the shifting of air units toward the south England coast foreshadowed the invasion. Allied ships and planes attacked German coastal radars and guns, seeking to blind and cripple the defenders. Rundstedt said that the invasion preparations could be regarded as "completed." Naval Group West footnoted that shipping was available for from 12 to 31 divisions and that the Germans had to expect "at least 20 divisions in the first wave." Hitler, who had said in the middle of April that the invasion would come in the first half of May, said near the end of that half that it would come at the end of the month.

Then, on 15 May, a burst of indications suggested that the assault might be on hand. The SD reported that the underground Armée Secrète, which on the previous night had been alerted in the Le Havre area, was ordered to go on full alert 20 May. It concluded that the invasion was to be expected between then and 10 June. And at 10:27 a.m. Allied naval radio traffic came alive with recognition signals similar to those used in the landings in North Africa, Sicily, and Nettuno. The messages were sent blind—without addressee—for the first time, but the B-Dienst thought they were intended for the western Channel, mainly because it had already spotted one of the call signs in the Devonport area. It notified the naval commands. But at 9:30 that evening it discovered from the messages to and from Portsmouth that the traffic was in fact only a practice.

Although this proved a false alarm, improvements in Allied signal security gave further solid evidence of the imminence of the invasion. On 19 May, new recognition signals appeared for various areas of British home waters, and the messages associated with them appeared enciphered in none of the previously standard systems—MUNICH BLUE or BROWN or FRANKFURT. The B-Dienst soon discovered that a special superencipherment, similar to that used in landing practices, had been applied to give them additional security. The following day, a new kind of message, consisting of 5-letter groups, probably generated by a machine cipher, began to appear in Allied naval traffic. Commented the B-Dienst: "It appears entirely possible that the new system is to be seen as a further element in the advance of communications preparations for the invasion." From 4 May, Colonel von Oer's radio reconnaissance battalion had observed no Allied radio traffic reductions in Britain. Then, at 2 a.m. on 27 May, one went sharply into effect. But no alarm went out: the Germans recognized it as a trick. Three days later they were proved right: at 2 a.m. on the 30th, traffic returned to its normal level. Later in the day, Naval Group West issued its estimates of landing possibilities for 31 May on the basis of the weather. On the Atlantic coast, which meant from Brest south to the Spanish border: "satisfactory." On the Channel coast, or from Brest north to Calais: "possible."

On 1 June, the tocsin rang again. This time it had a deeper, more insistent tone. German monitors had heard the B.B.C. transmit 125 personal messages. The RSHA, which that day officially took over the Abwehr, reported that 28 of these were prealarm messages. This meant that the French resistance was to ready itself for sabotage actions, which would presumably accompany the Allied landing. The order to undertake these actions would be transmitted by the B.B.C. any time up to the 15th of the month; the underground agents were to listen for them. If nothing happened by 15 June, the alarm was regarded as canceled. The RSHA commented, "It is consequently possible that the enemy is planning a major attack in the next 14 days." Of the 28 messages, 21 were addressed to groups in Brittany, Normandy, and the Lille-Amiens area (just east of the Pas de Calais). The other seven were scattered all over France. The RSHA answered in advance the natural question of how valid this all was. The Germans had gained control of a number of agent groups and then continued radio communications with Britain as if the groups were still at large; these funkspiele, or radio games, gave them valuable information about the underground and Allied intentions. The RSHA noted that, in the groups whose funkspiele it regarded as solid, prealarm messages came in, while in those the Allies may have spotted, none did.

The most important of the alarms, the one that the Germans apparently believed the most, was the one using the Verlaine poem as the open code. In the almost nine months since he had first learned of its existence, the Abwehr's Major Reile had obtained more precise details about how it would work. The B.B.C. would transmit the stanza in two parts. The first half, when broadcast on the 1st or the 15th of a month, would alert the resistance to the imminence of the invasion. The broadcasting of the second half would mean, "The invasion begins within 48 hours," the count starting at 0000 hours of the day following the transmission.

Among the monitoring units that were straining their electric ears to hear this message was the 15th Army's Communications Reconnaissance Post, located in a concrete bunker at Tourcoing. On 1 June, Sergeant Walter Reichling switched on a wire-recorder when, a little after the end of the 9 p.m. news, the imperturbable voice of a B.B.C. announcer said, "Kindly listen now to a few personal messages." After a brief pause Reichling heard the first half of the long-awaited stanza:

> LES SANGLOTS LONGS
> DES VIOLONS
> DE L'AUTOMNE

He rushed the message to Lieutenant Colonel Helmuth Meyer, I c of the 15th Army, who listened to the recording with him. The intelligence officer informed his chief of staff, who alerted his own army, on which the main weight of the invasion was expected to fall, and then notified higher commands. The communications reconnaissance post attended still more closely to its receivers. The next message, to come within 15 days, would warn of the actual start of the long-awaited landing.

While they listened, however, the weather worsened. One of the severest storms of the century was kicking up high waves in the Channel. Rain pelted the beaches, the fortifications, the German headquarters. Clouds raced over the land. By Sunday, 4 June, Naval Group West called a landing on the Channel coast "improbable." Anyone could see that the seas would prevent the smaller landing craft from crossing the Channel, and the clouds would keep airplanes from supporting any landing. The invasion warning was good for 15 days; nothing would happen for the first few. Indeed, so bad was the storm that the navy canceled its patrols. The next day, 5 June, Rommel departed for a brief vacation at home. Meyer-Detring, Rundstedt's I c, was likewise on vacation, as was Dönitz. Colonel Hansen, now head of the RSHA's new Military Department, had gone to Baden-Baden. He was conferring at the spa with the chiefs of sections I, II, and III of what had been up to then the Abwehr Main Post West. Higher officers of the 7th Army left their posts to attend a map exercise at Rennes. Everyone thought that the weather would delay any landing—everyone except Hitler. After Jodl had once said at a situation conference that the enemy would invade "when the sea is calm and visibility poor," Hitler asked:

"Can he also come out in a bad sea?"

"He can assemble," replied a naval aide.

"Then he doesn't risk much," said Hitler. "He comes out in a bad sea and lands here."

But despite this premonition, and despite the warnings of his counterespionage service, he took no action those first days of June.

Meanwhile, the inadequate German meteorological service, crippled by its loss of weather stations in Greenland and elsewhere earlier in the war, failed to learn what the Allies, with their far more extensive chain of reporting posts, had discovered: that a brief moderation could be expected in the storm. On this basis, Eisenhower, on 5 June, ordered the attack to proceed. His armada sallied forth majestically on its supreme mission.

The German intelligence agencies continued in total ignorance of this. Radio traffic in England stayed at normal levels. The navy had no patrols out because of the weather. Though Roenne had said two days earlier that his branch saw the 5th to the 13th of June as suitable for landings, his "Situation Report West" for 5 June discussed only the Mediterranean area and did not even mention Britain, while an attached evaluation merely iterated the same thing yet again: the forces in England were ready. Rundstedt repeated what he had been saying since 11 April: that his judgment of the situation remained what it was on that date. This merely held that the bombings between the Schelde and Normandy "could be seen as preparations for further events." His weekly review concluded that although the "moment of the invasion has indeed come closer, however according to the tempo of the air attacks [it] is not directly ahead." Rommel's weekly survey, issued 5 June, said that intensification of air raids and minelaying "indicates an advance in the enemy preparations for invasion," while the bombing location "confirms our presumptions as to the area chosen by the enemy for his large-scale landing."

Then at 9:15 p.m., the B.B.C. broadcast the second half of the Verlaine stanza:

> BLESSENT MON COEUR
> D'UNE LANGUEUR
> MONOTONE.

The men in the concrete bunker picked it up. Within five minutes it had been passed to the I c, Meyer, who confirmed it with an officer of the occupation command. By 10 Meyer was giving it to the chief of staff and to the commander of the 15th Army, who ordered his forces on full alert, then returned to his card game, commenting, "I'm too old a bunny to get excited about this."

Meyer messaged his subordinate corps, his superordinate army group, B, and naval and air commands about the message and its significance. He spoke as well by telephone with Staubwasser, I c of Rommel's Army Group B. Staubwasser reported at once to his chief of staff. The chief remembered the false alarm of Easter. So he ordered Staubwasser to ask the commander in chief west to decide whether to alert the troops. That headquarters was skeptical. It felt that the Allies would not "announce the invasion by radio." An officer there conveyed to Staubwasser the decision not to alert the troops. Consequently, the 7th Army, on which the brunt of the cross-Channel attack would fall, was never alerted to D-Day.

While all this was going on, the Double-Cross Committee was putting into practice a somewhat risky plan. It had won Eisenhower's approval for it on the ground that it would pay off greatly later. The idea was to have agent CATO, who by then supposedly had an informant high in the Ministry of Information with access to many military details essential for propaganda, flash a warning of the invasion before it actually began, thus immeasurably enhancing his already good standing with the Germans. Naturally, the report would not leave enough time for the Germans to mobilize their forces. It would have to be deciphered, read, evaluated, reenciphered, and transmitted to Berlin. There it would have to be deciphered, typed up, and sent over to the OKW. Someone there would have to decide to send it on to the commander in chief west. Once this decision had been taken, the message would have to be transmitted to his headquarters near Paris. The same process of decision and retransmission would have to be undertaken here and at each subordinate level of command: Army Group B at La Roche Guyon, 7th Army at Le Mans, LXXXIVth Army Corps at St. Lô, and finally its subordinate 716th Infantry Division with its regiments and battalions on the invasion beaches in Normandy. Even if everyone were at his desk and dealt with the message at once, this process would take several hours.

CATO's message had been enciphered in the Abwehr hand cipher by 1:56 a.m. 6 June. Half an hour later, the Royal Signals radio operator who was impersonating CATO in the ether began trying to get it through. But the KO Madrid had closed down its radio station. Not until 7 a.m. (Spanish time) did it reopen. At once it began accepting CATO's message, which took about half an hour to transmit. When deciphered, it proved to report the embarkation of troops for the assault, the identities of some of the formations, and the direction of the invading force. As the Allied deception organization hoped and expected, it did not have any effect on the defense readiness of the German forces. But it did enormously reinforce the credibiiity of CATO and his ring with his spymaster, Kühlenthal, and with Kühlenthal's superiors.

While CATO's radioman was trying to raise Madrid, the invasion began. American paratroops dropped on the Cherbourg peninsula. Infantry stormed ashore from the sea. Surprise was total. In most places the attackers forced the defenders rapidly back; in a few spots, they made slow and bitter progress. The picture was confused, as it always is early in a battle, but the German staff officers, true to their training, focused their attention upon the main question. At 9:35 a.m., General Günther Blumentritt, Rundstedt's chief of staff, wired a situation report to Jodl. "At present," he said, "it cannot be seen whether [this is] a large-scale feint or the main attack." An hour and a half later, his I a was reiterating this to the general staff's operations branch.

The information on which this report was based came from the front, and Clausewitz had warned that "the effect of fear is to multiply lies and inaccuracies." So the higher commanders in Berlin and the Führer headquarters cleaved to the dictum of a commander's standing on his judgment like a rock in a hostile sea. They had concluded long before that the Allied attack would come in the Pas de Calais. Not only had no information challenged this view, the several elements of the Allied deception had substantiated it. So now, with the attack finally at hand, they reaffirmed that judgment.

At a situation conference that met while Blumentritt's message was passing through army channels, Dönitz and his admirals agreed that they had to "reckon with further landings on other coasts." During the day, Roenne telephoned Staubwasser, Rommel's I c, to tell him that Foreign Armies West thought that this would not be the only landing. Another would come in the area of the 15th Army, he said, and for that reason no troops would be withdrawn from it. Staubwasser passed this to Rommel. Later in the day, Roenne spelled out his reasoning in an appendix to his situation report:

"Not a single unit of the 1st United States Army Group, which comprises around 25 large formations north and south of the Thames, has so far been committed. The same is true of the 10 to 12 combat formations stationed in central England and Scotland. This suggests that the enemy is planning a further large-scale operation in the Channel area, which one would expect to be aimed at a coastal sector in the Pas de Calais area."

In the afternoon of D-Day, Churchill declared in a speech to the Commons that was later broadcast: "There are already hopes that actual tactical surprise has been attained, and we hope to furnish the enemy with a succession of surprises during the course of the fighting." The German monitoring services duly picked this up and passed it to the fighting commands. They viewed it in precisely the way that Churchill had hoped: the navy commented that the main thing was to destroy the present bridgehead and to impede the creation of future ones in other sectors before they became too strong. Rundstedt evidently concurred. On 7 June he ordered two armored divisions into the invasion area and asked Hitler for permission to move a third, the 1st SS Panzer, which was in the OKW reserve. But Hitler, concerned about the possibility that Normandy was a diversion, suspended decision for a time.

In the first days of the invasion, the Germans captured the operational orders of the American Vth and VIIth Corps. They confirmed what the Germans already suspected: that the Allies intended to cut off the Cotentin to gain Cherbourg. But in no way did they tell the Germans that Normandy was the main operation. They left the German preconceptions undisturbed.

These got a further boost when, just after midnight on 9 June, CATO spent two full hours on the air sending a long and detailed report to his spymaster, Kühlenthal. The risk of capture was enormous when an agent transmitted that long, for it gave the direction-finding vans plenty of time to locate him. But this very fact impressed the Germans with the importance of his signal.

"The present operation, though a large-scale assault, is diversionary in character," CATO stated flatly. "Its object is to establish a strong bridgehead in order to draw the maximum of our reserves into the area of the assault and to retain them there so as to leave another area exposed where the enemy could then attack with some prospect of success. . . . The fact that the massive concentration of forces in east and southeast England remains inactive suggests that these forces are being held in reserve for other large-scale operations. The constant aerial bombardment which the sector of the Pas de Calais has been undergoing and the disposition of the enemy forces would indicate the imminence of the assault in this region which offers the shortest route to the final objective of the Anglo-American illusions: Berlin."

The RSHA that day teleprinted a condensed version of this message to Rundstedt's headquarters and to Hitler's, where it arrived at 10:20 p.m. Krummacher noted on it that the report "Underlines the opinion already formed by us that a further attack is to be expected in another place. (Belgium?)" He showed it to Jodl, who showed it to Hitler. Whereupon the Führer made his decision about the 1st SS Panzer Division. He refused Rundstedt's request to put it into action. Instead he sent it behind the 15th Army to defend against what he thought would be the main invasion in the Pas de Calais.

CATO's message was the most decisive single bit of information in the entire Allied deception campaign, for it nailed down the German views so firmly that they would never be changed. But other sources hammered other nails into the Germans' intelligence coffin. Their trust in their spy reports was further sustained by the discovery of divisions in the bridgehead that the turned-around agents of Wild had reported—accurately—as being in England. In April, for example, one such agent had reported the presence of the American 9th Infantry Division in Great Britain. It crossed to France in the second wave. By 9 June, the Germans had spotted it in the invasion front. So they paid attention when, a few days after the invasion, an agent warned that another attack would take place on 14 or 15 June around Dieppe, Abbeville, and Le Touquet—all near the Pas de Calais. Simultaneously, he said, American airborne divisions would drop around Amiens, halfway between Paris and Calais, to capture the city. Roenne's charts showed only two American airborne divisions, and both were known to be in Normandy. But those charts also listed six British airborne divisions still in England. Perhaps the agent had erred on the nationality: this would not necessarily vitiate the basic information.

Information from diplomatic sources also poured into Germany about the expected main invasion. From Madrid, the Japanese minister passed along an interesting report. Two and a half weeks earlier, he said to the German diplomats, he had received information that the main attack would come against Le Havre and Cherbourg, and that three more would follow within eight days: against Italy's Grosseto-Leghorn-Pisa-Genoa area, against the area between Barmes and Cashis, both on the eastern part of France's Mediterranean coast, and against Frontignan and Perpignan, both on the western part. He hadn't believed it himself at first and so had not passed it along. But when the first part proved true he decided to inform the Germans about it. The Japanese had done the same thing after the landing in North Africa. Perhaps both episodes sought to save their face.

The German mission in Bern said that a leading official of the political department of the Swiss foreign ministry said that the attack would come near Perpignan, within several days. Ankara, continuing the tendency of each locale to see itself as the most endangered, foresaw a major action against the Dodecanese or other targets in the eastern Mediterranean. On 12 June, the RSHA VI man in Stockholm, August Finke, passed along word that an American from the U.S. ministry there had said that the attacks would come in Norway and Denmark in the next few days. Finke also reported that the embassy of the Norwegian government-in-exile said an attack would come against Norway on 15 June. Other posts warned of attacks on the Nantes–St. Nazaire area, between Cannes and Ventimiglia, on the French Mediterranean coast, at the Somme mouth or in Holland. One agent attributed to the Yugoslav partisan leader Tito a report that the attack would come against southern France via the Iberian peninsula.

The Naval Group West continued to evaluate the sea conditions for landing. At 3:30 on 8 June it reported the probabilities for that night as "possible" in the Dutch area and as "satisfactory" on the Channel and Atlantic coasts. The navy picked up radio broadcasts from the Allied high command warning fishing ships in the coastal waters of Norway, Denmark, Holland, Belgium, and France that they would have to cease operations in those waters and return home at once from 9 p.m. 8 June to the same time exactly a week later. Wild perhaps chuckled over that little trick; the Germans puzzled over it. On the 10th, Foreign Armies West noted again that the army group in southeast England—FUSAG—had not been used in any way at all yet. The intelligence unit expected an attack in the direction of Belgium, for which, it believed, four to five airborne divisions were available.

Hitler insisted on the emergency laying of mines on the Dutch, Belgian, west French, and Danish coasts—he feared an attack.

The bombings continued in the Pas de Calais. On Sunday, the 11th, 700 planes were counted by the Germans over Belgium and northern France, attacking airfields and transport trains. The next day 1,400 planes attacked 10 airfields in Belgium, while hundreds in western France attacked airfields, antiaircraft positions, and traffic installations.

At the 5:30 p.m. situation conference on 12 June, Keitel and Jodl agreed that the best way of destroying the Normandy beachhead was to block any landing on other places and then return to mop up Normandy. This other landing, if it did come, would probably take place between Dieppe and Boulogne and/or between Calais and the Schelde, they said. In other words, near the Pas de Calais.

That same day, Hitler hurled the first of his revenge weapons, the V-1, the flying bomb, against Britain. The bombs were launched from sites in the Pas de Calais. This, Roenne felt, would further increase the Allies' desire to invade that area. Others concurred. Jodl stuck to his Dieppe idea.

Hitler suffered a brief twinge of nervousness about a Brittany landing as a diversion but never lost sight of the Pas de Calais, fearing that the enemy might want to seize the V-1 bases.

These concerns dominated German strategic thinking in the second half of June and throughout July. Wild made sure they remained alive. On 29 and 30 June and 1 and 2 July, the British suddenly increased the number of French "messages personnels" to the resistance from an average of 50 to 240. The commander in chief west and the navy did not fail to note and to remark that this sudden increase resembled the situation before the 6 June invasion. Meyer-Detring notified Army Group B and others that, according to the Abwehr (he still used the old term), one of the messages was "Berthe jouera au domino ce soir" ("Berthe will play at dominoes tonight") and that messages mentioning Bertha put agents in the area Antwerp and Limburg into alarm phase II. Another message indicated a forthcoming attack on the Antwerp area, he said. His headquarters would not make the same error this time as it had a month before. At 1:10 a.m. it ordered the highest watchfulness and battle readiness in all areas concerned. It reported to the OKW on 3 July that it expected the attack around the middle of the month.

Foreign Armies West noticed withdrawals of forces from FUSAG, but clung to its preconception. It saw the reduction in enemy air activity as a further sign for the imminent new operation. Roenne noted the increase of forces in the Normandy bridgehead to 30 large formations, but warned that this should not deceive the Germans into believing that the enemy was not maintaining all measures for the conduct of a new landing in readiness. He pointed again to FUSAG and the forces attached to it, such as the entirely imaginary 1st Canadian Army. The 3/Skl added its voice: the enemy had enough shipping tonnage to carry it out.

Hitler's views were not dissimilar. At the 1 p.m. situation conference on 13 July, Dönitz warned him of the danger of an Allied penetration of the Skaggerak, which would cut off the iron ore supplies from Norway and render the exit of the U-boats difficult. Hitler replied that the danger was much greater in the Holland-Belgium area or the Pas de Calais.

Meanwhile, three events had led to changes of command of troops and of intelligence in the west. When Keitel moaned "What shall we do? What shall we do?" about the deteriorating Normandy situation, Rundstedt snapped, "Make peace, you fools." Hitler replaced him as commander in chief west with Field Marshal Günther von Kluge. On 17 July, Rommel was gravely injured when his car, racing to avoid British aircraft, crashed into a tree. Command of his Army Group B was taken over by Kluge. Then, three days later, on the fateful 20th of July, Colonel Claus von Stauffenberg placed a yellow leather briefcase with a bomb inside it near Hitler during the afternoon situation conference at Führer headquarters. He went outside, saying he had to make a telephone call. An officer moved the briefcase to get it out of his way. When the bomb went off, a heavy pedestal of the oaken conference table shielded Hitler from the force of the blast, though others were killed. He was stunned but not injured. When he recovered, he instigated a wholesale purge of all possible anti-Nazi elements in the officer corps. Among those who succumbed was Roenne. Bürklein succeeded him. This altered none of Foreign Armies West's strategic conceptions. Like everyone else, it continued to believe in another attack in the Pas de Calais.

During the latter half of July, however, indications suggesting this became less frequent. On the other hand, there were no counterindications: Wild and his team saw no need to disabuse the Germans of their views. In fact, on the 21st, the Allies put up some lively reconnaissance activity in the 15th Army area, throwing a new little scare into the Germans. But the Normandy attack was drawing in more and more units, whose presence the Germans soon recognized. Some came from what Foreign Armies West believed were the FUSAG forces intended for the second landing. Wild's double agents cleverly implied that the tough German resistance had demanded these additional divisions. This fed the German belief that containment of the Normandy assault would best prevent the Pas de Calais landing.

But the withdrawal of forces from FUSAG weakened this body, despite the addition of more notional divisions to it. As early as 10 July Roenne had noticed that it was "qualitatively inferior" to the Normandy force and was consequently "no longer entrusted with the main role." But not until 27 July did he concede that it was "improbable now that it will be used at short notice to attack a strongly fortified coastal sector." On the same day, Kluge's headquarters, while cautiously noting a rise in the total number of Allied formations to 92 as a result of new American arrivals, said for the first time that "the mass of the Anglo-American formations will be put into action in Normandy." Kluge asked for the transfer of a number of divisions from other armies in his area to the bridgehead. Hitler allowed two of them. For the first time, he let one come from the 15th Army in the Pas de Calais. The next day he released two more divisions. One of these was from the 15th as well. But he was still nervous: he ordered that burned-out infantry or armored divisions be placed behind the 15th Army as quickly as possible. Still, the reality of Normandy was beginning to overwhelm the theory of the Pas de Calais. On 3 August, with the Americans pouring out through Avranches, Kluge transferred the LXXXIst Army Corps from the 15th to the 7th Army. Finally, on 7 August, concluding that a second major landing was "improbable," he ordered that all possible formations from the Army Group B area be sent to the battle front.

In a sense, that ended the Allied deception. The German organs of acquisition had failed, and so the intelligence officers and their commanders had fallen into the very trap that Clausewitz foresaw a century before. An officer "is lucky," he wrote, if the contradictions of many incoming reports "cancel each other out, and leave a kind of balance to be critically assessed. It is much worse for the novice if chance does not help him in that way, and on the contrary one report tallies with another, confirms it, magnifies it, lends it color, till he has to make a quick decision—which is soon recognized to be mistaken, just as the reports turn out to be lies, exaggerations, errors, and so on."

This is what happened with the Germans. Only in their lack of recognition of their error did the general staff officers—who may be regarded as novices in intelligence compared to most other armies of the world—deviate from Clausewitz's vision. For the deception had burned itself so deeply into German minds that it smoldered there long after its effects had passed. Foreign Armies West kept FUSAG on its situation map until 31 October, indicating some belief in its existence all that time. Even after it removed FUSAG from that map, it retained on it three nonexistent army headquarters—the English 4th, the American 14th, and the Allied 1st Airborne. Indeed, the chief concept of the deception—a second landing—persisted even into the days when Hitler was preparing his last offensive, which would become the Battle of the Bulge. At a situation conference at 3:30 p.m. 28 November at the Reich chancellery in Berlin, Dönitz brought up the possibility of an Allied landing in Holland. The conditions were poor, he admitted. But the Allied troops assembling south of the Thames, he said, thinking of the nonexistent men, would be able to flow rapidly to the front as soon as the Allied armies opened the Schelde. To this, the last drum tap of the greatest deception of all time, which had cost him the war in the west, Hitler assented.

V
EPILOGUE

27

Hubris, Glory, Charisma, Führer

THUS Germany lost the intelligence war. At every one of the strategic turning points of World War II, her intelligence failed. It underestimated Russia, blacked out before the North African invasion, awaited the Sicily landing in the Balkans, and fell for thinking the Normandy landing a feint. Though in operational and tactical situations it often predicted enemy attacks, it sometimes erred grievously, as at Stalingrad and Army Group Center.

The record appears abysmal. But perhaps this is the best that could be done. Every intelligence service strives to realize the words of the apostle Luke: "For nothing is hid that shall not be made manifest, nor anything secret that shall not be known and come to light." None achieves it. "It will always be a certain tragedy of every intelligence service," wrote General Friedrich Gempp, first chief of the Abwehr, "that even the best results will always lag behind the clients' desires." Is it, therefore, asking too much to expect more of German intelligence? Did it attain the practical, if not the theoretical, limits of any investigation into the dark recesses of other men's minds? Or did other intelligence agencies do better?

Others did. Though the Japanese performed as poorly as the Germans, and though not enough is known of Russian intelligence to evaluate it properly, Anglo-American intelligence far outdid German. It estimated enemy strength more accurately. Throughout the war, for example, the Allies usually knew to within a division the strength of the German forces in France. Their figures were precise when major decisions were being taken at the Washington conference of 1942 and the Casablanca one of 1943, and were off by only one division—58, they said, instead of the actual 59—before the Normandy assault. This error of 2 percent contrasts sharply with the corresponding German error concerning Allied divisions in Britain of 40 percent. And Allied intelligence forecast enemy intentions better. It recognized that Hitler had abandoned his plans to invade Britain and discovered that he intended to attack Russia instead. It learned enough about the German rockets and atomic experiments to delay or cripple both by raids. In a host of individual operations, it foretold enemy moves. U-boats rendezvousing with milch-cows in the Atlantic wastes found themselves being depth-charged by Allied planes that suddenly hove over the horizon. The two American divisions at Anzio were saved from overextending themselves and possibly being cut off when an intercept warned them that Hitler was sending nine divisions from Greece to reinforce the defenders.

The Allies were not perfect. They missed at Norway and Arnhem and the Bulge. Their estimates of German aircraft production fell from 79 percent too high to 33 percent too low—a variation of more than 100 percent. The intelligence reports that the Office of Strategic Services handed President Roosevelt were often quite as devoid of inside information about the enemy and his intentions as those Canaris gave Hitler. But still and all the Allies enjoyed considerable success in their intelligence—much of it due to their superiority in verbal intelligence because of their far better codebreaking. The Germans, in contrast, were glaringly inferior.

Five basic factors bred this failure: (1) unjustified arrogance, which caused Germany to lose touch with reality; (2) aggression, which led to a neglect of intelligence; (3) a power struggle within the officer corps, which made many generals hostile to intelligence; (4) the authority structure of the Nazi state, which gravely impaired its intelligence; (5) anti-Semitism, which deprived German intelligence of many brains.

Sometimes thought to be exclusively a product of Hitler's Germany, anti-Semitism had in fact long wrought its deleterious effects on Germany's armed forces and their intelligence agencies. For it excluded many patriotic Jews who might have contributed a great deal. The Prussian army, for example, simply did not commission Jews as regular officers. The Nazis intensified this attitude and its effects. They "coordinated" scientific, technical, and academic organizations with the party philosophy, squeezing Jews out of them. They enacted a law cynically designated as for the "reestablishment of the professional civil service," which ordered that "Officials who are not of Aryan descent are to be retired." Though this seemed to have little effect on the military establishment because few Jews were there to be fired—in the B-Dienst, for example, none seem to have been let go—the impact elsewhere was ruinous. The Nazis expelled the Jewish rector of the Göttingen Mathematical Institute, beginning the demolition of the foremost center of mathematics in Germany. Such measures, which stripped many Jewish scientists of their jobs, combined with the street humiliations and the hateful atmosphere to drive them from Germany. Mathematicians, scientists, engineers streamed to Great Britain, Russia, above all the United States. Their quality was high. Though Albert

Einstein was in a class by himself, others were highly regarded by their peers: in mathematics alone, about 20 percent were elected to their host country's foremost honorary societies. The Germany of the 1930s did not miss them. Their departure fed her exhilarating sense of renewal and cleanliness and mission. But even the strongest motivation could not make good the replacement of superb intellects by mediocrities.

Anti-Semitism was not confined to Germany. The American and British military establishments suffered from more than tinges of this malady. But they did not systematically exclude Jews, and they did not refuse their civilian assistance. The most dramatic result came when the Allies, with the help of Jewish brains, built the atomic bomb, and the Germans, without them (and for many other reasons), did not. In intelligence, the Allies gained many speakers of German, who proved valuable as interrogators, and they retained such Jews as William F. Friedman, leader of the team that solved the Japanese PURPLE cipher machine, which provided great insight into both German and Japanese policy. German anti-Semitism both seriously depleted Hitler's intelligence potential and vastly increased the Allies', thus doubly damaging the Reich's intelligence.

Germans have often been accused of arrogance, and in the nation's perception of reality—of which perception intelligence is a small and formalized part—the charge is valid. Arrogance distorted the German view of the world to an unreal one, and so led that country into many harmful decisions.

The flaw seems to have been caused by two linked factors. The sense of national superiority was more exaggerated in Germany than in other countries. And a greater rigidity in thought, an expression of an authoritarianism more pronounced in Germany than elsewhere, blocked its correction by reality. This factor, a psychological one, arose from the teachings of Martin Luther. The excessive chauvinism had its roots in Germany's alienation from the West.

In the High Middle Ages, the emperor Frederick II of Hohenstaufen, the "Amazement of the World" whose biography Canaris was reading the night before his execution, who had been born and bred in Sicily, granted powers to his German princes so he could pursue the Italian and Mediterranean policies that interested him more. These powers helped the princes maintain their separate sovereignties for six centuries against the centralizing force of the Holy Roman Empire, the rising dominance of Prussia, and the urgings of intellectuals for political as well as cultural unity. This particularism distinguished the region now called Germany from England and France, where unified nation-states were forming. In these conditions, Napoleon humbled Prussia, subjugated other German principalities, and snuffed out the Empire—the first Reich, which had lasted for a thousand years.

Napoleon called himself the bearer of the great humanistic ideals of the French Revolution. In rejecting him, the people of the German states also rejected the liberty, equality, and fraternity that had become, in one form or another, the ideals of the democratic West. Setting themselves apart, they praised instead German uniqueness, indeed German superiority. The apostle of this nationalism, Johann Gottlieb Fichte, deprecated "the deadly foreign spirit" in his *Addresses to the German Nation* and declared bluntly that "the German, if only he makes use of all advantages, can always be superior to the foreigner." German pride swelled as Napoleon was defeated, as unification approached with Prussia's 1866 victory over Austria and her absorption of several neighbor states, and finally as it was achieved five years later with the defeat of France and the proclamation of a new German empire—the second Reich. It seemed as if Germany was invincible. Her separate development had succeeded. Everything German was better than anything else.

But this was not so. Booming as her economic expansion had been, astonishing as her military victories were, her population and industry compared with those of all her potential enemies could never have sufficed to make her mistress of the world. Her failure to recognize this separated her from reality. Other countries have suffered from the same problem, among them the United ("One American is worth ten Japs") States. But Germany's distance from reality was greater, chiefly because the tardiness of her nationalism exacerbated her sense of superiority. This was indeed dangerous. What made it fatal, however, was its rigidity, its inability to change, to adapt to reality.

This inflexibility stemmed from an authoritarianism that began in the Reformation. Both Martin Luther and John Calvin freed man from papal authority. But while Calvin's theology also permitted resistance to secular authority, as the Puritan revolution in England showed, Luther's opposed it. His teaching that man is saved not by good works but solely by faith raised the specter of anarchy. So he explicitly taught that on earth men must follow the commands of the constituted rulers. "Even if those in authority are evil or without faith, nevertheless the authority and its power are good and from God," he declared. "No insurrection is ever right," he cried. "The answer for such mouths [those of rebels] is a fist that brings blood from the nose." Parents in countries pervaded by Lutheranism, such as Prussia, willingly assimilated these ideas to increase and facilitate their control in the family. The authoritarian personality became established to a greater extent in Germany than elsewhere. Revolution never succeeded there.

The dynamics of an authoritarian person include a need to contain, or at least not to aggravate, an underlying anxiety. One mechanism for this seeks to exclude anxiety-causing events by rigidly controlling the environment. Such a person consequently holds views that meet his needs. And because these views are anchored deep in his psyche, no mere external data can change them. They will not yield to actuality.

It was that way among many Germans with their exaggerated feeling of superiority. Their authoritarian rigidity kept reality from moderating the excesses of that feeling, which reigned unstinted. The result was arrogance. This extreme and stiffnecked overestimation of self skewed Germany's perception of the world far more than the chauvinism of other countries warped their views of the world. Consequently, when she finally collided with reality, the effects proved much more damaging, and sometimes disastrous.

In 1917, considering America as too weak and too far away to do anything, she began unrestricted submarine warfare, which led to America's declaration of war on her. "Germany's policy towards the U.S.A. shows in particularly crude colors the fundamental traits of Germany's world policy at the beginning of the twentieth century," wrote Professor Fritz Fischer, the foremost scholar of the period. "Dazzled by confidence in their own strength, the Germans underestimated the economic and organisatory capacities of America." It cost them the war.

Even after the failure of Germany's supreme offensives in the spring of 1918, however, arrogance kept the German generals from recognizing that they had lost the war. Nor, finally, did the actual capitulation teach them anything. They refused to believe that other armies had beaten the German on the field of battle. To sustain their overestimation of self, they embraced instead the legend that they had been stabbed in the back by Jews and Communists.

Twenty-one years later, arrogance again took its deadly toll. Hitler, with the concurrence of his generals and without even investigating the matter, decided that Germany could quickly conquer the Soviet Union. A few months later, pooh-poohing America's industrial might, he declared war on the United States.

These losses of contact with reality affected the very life and death of the nation. They encompassed and overshadowed anything intelligence could do. But arrogance made itself felt in small things as in great. Albert Speer recognized that Germany could not match Allied production. He held, however, that the qualitative superiority of German weapons outweighed the Allied quantities. It was a delusion. The OKW Operations Staff, in discussing the strategic situation after the Allied landing in North Africa, spoke of equalling the enemy's strength and of the possibility of "a victorious ending of the war." Reinhard Gehlen's irrational view that Germany could not lose the war, which so resembled that of his World War I predecessors, sprang—as theirs did—largely from arrogance.

Arrogance thus predetermined the whole German attitude and directed all German actions. It consequently preempted intelligence. It foreclosed the German mind from even thinking that intelligence might be necessary.

In 1914, the army was so certain of success that many units left their intelligence officers behind. In 1941, Hitler invaded Russia with no real intelligence preparation. Arrogance, which broke Germany's contact with reality, also prevented intelligence from seeking to resume that contact. The other factors that affected German intelligence did not have an impact that, like this, transcended intelligence. They merely damaged intelligence as such.

Hitler decided to solve what he saw as his nation's problems by warring upon other countries. Germany would strike the first blow. She would be —despite grievances, despite rationalizations—the aggressor.

Now offense and defense enjoin different attitudes toward intelligence. It exists, of course, in both. But it is essential to victory only in the defense. The difference between intelligence in the two modes is that between an accompanying and a defining characteristic. All elephants may be gray, but grayness is not a defining characteristic of elephants, merely an accompanying one. Intelligence is a defining characteristic of defense; it is only an accompanying characteristic of offense.

"What is the concept of defense?" asked Clausewitz. "The parrying of a blow. What is its characteristic feature? Awaiting the blow." Now an army can await a blow only if it believes that a blow is planned, and such a belief can be created only by information about the enemy. Defense requires intelligence. There can be, in other words, no defense without intelligence.

Defense also acknowledges that the initiative will come from the enemy. And indeed the offense acts, the defense reacts. The offense prescribes to the enemy; it makes the basic decisions. It is "complete in itself," said Clausewitz. Thus information about enemy intentions, while helpful and to a certain degree always present, is not essential to an offensive victory. (What is essential, Clausewitz said, is surprise, or denying information about one's own plans to the enemy. This further implies that intelligence, meaning knowledge of enemy intentions, is necessary for success in defense.) In other words, while intelligence is integral to the defense, it is only contingent to the offense. As a result—and this is the crucial point—emphasizing the offensive tends toward a neglect of intelligence.

An example will make this clear: the German invasion of France in 1940. According to the plan, a powerful armored force, driving southwest out of the Ardennes Forest, would curve like a sickle to the northwest to strike the Allied armies from the side and then crush them against the Channel and against other German forces. The greatest danger lay in a counterattack by the French reserves. So the Germans protected their long and vulnerable flank by lining it with outward-facing forces. The point is that they did not make these dispositions on the basis of intelligence, of knowing that French reserves were to the south. They made them of their own volition. Where the enemy reserves were or would be was naturally of interest, but it was not essential to German planning. Planning omitted intelligence.

The same conditions held, on a vaster scale, for Hitler's overall planning for his war. He intended to impose his will on other countries. Their fate would lie in his hands. For this he needed no intelligence. He concentrated on what he did need: men, guns, tanks, planes, fuel. "The war will be won with tanks and airplanes, antitank and antiaircraft guns," he said. He poured his energies, his money, and his men into armaments but not into intelligence.

Neither he nor his high commands ever lashed the Abwehr into serious activity, or supported it with the resources and manpower that would allow it to mount serious espionage campaigns against the countries of Europe. Nor did the Abwehr itself seem to feel that it had to dig hard. It lazed along. It sowed some agents here and there, but it implanted none in the high government circles of nations whose attitudes might be critical to Germany—Poland, Czechoslovakia, Belgium, Sweden, Turkey, France itself. Its effort against Britain was tardy, feeble, and utterly ineffective. In other areas, it did gather a few tidbits—mobilization and troop identifications in France, airfield locations along the Soviet Union's frontier, the Norden bombsight, some coastal gun positions in Norway, a minor French naval code. But never once did it score a coup.

Contrast this with Allied espionage. It had its failures, too, but it nevertheless obtained some documents that indirectly but importantly affected the war. French espionage won as a spy a weak and lazy member of the Reichswehr's Cipher Center who sold the operating instructions and some actual keys for the main German cipher machine, the Enigma. With the help of these, Polish cryptanalysts reconstructed the mechanism. When war came, Allied solutions of Enigma messages contributed greatly to the victories of the battles of Britain and the Atlantic, to the control of German spies in Britain, with the deception that that made possible, and to the winning of many combat actions in Europe in 1944 and 1945.

The espionage stroke that ultimately made all this possible was not a fluke, either. France watched Germany carefully, and in particular informed herself in accurate detail about German rearmament: she was concerned about German aggression. The same fear never actuated the Germans into investigating their neighbors. And so they never achieved the same success.

The organization of German intelligence depicts the same negligence. The OKW for years before and during the war did not have an I c branch. On the other hand, the British chiefs of staff established a Joint Intelligence Committee at the very start of the war. Well before the war, the Admiralty established an Operational Intelligence Center that during the conflict became adept at predicting U-boat moves, thus enabling the Allies to sink them and to reroute their own convoys to safety. The OKM never had one.

In the euphoria of Hitler's early triumphs, however, none of these omissions mattered. Poland, Denmark and Norway, France and the Low Countries, Yugoslavia—all justified Hitler's belief that it was the offensive and its armaments that counted. The armed forces naturally had intelligence agencies to tell them where the enemy was, but this information was not essential for victory, since German armies went where they wanted to go anyway. One student has brilliantly epitomized this by commenting that during the first few years of the war the Wehrmacht carried the Abwehr along like a "happy parasite." All German experience in the first part of the war confirmed the insignificance of intelligence.

Then Hitler attacked Russia. He thereupon began losing the strategic initiative. The whole war flopped over. Soon Germany was forced onto the defensive. At once intelligence assumed importance. In a host of ways, Germany began seeking it. Censors, who had previously only spot-checked mail transiting Germany, began in mid-1942 to open it all. Ribbentrop had previously instructed his diplomats to gather information; now it became their "main duty." Halder decided he could no longer afford the lackadaisical work of Kinzel in Foreign Armies East and replaced him with the dynamo of Gehlen. The OKW Operations Staff added an intelligence officer. In their situation conferences, Hitler and his generals and admirals, who earlier had seldom said much about the enemy, talked about him more and more.

But it was too late. Their information remained low-level and sparse. Germany's spies sat in no high councils. Her codebreakers pounded ineffectually upon impregnable walls. The disdain of the previous years had taken its toll.

The situation was just the opposite with the Allies, in particular the British. Their original defensive posture had compelled them to build up their intelligence to warn them of the designs of the aggressor. They put more men into the intelligence agencies and spent more money on them. Intelligence helped them optimize their few resources—especially after Dunkirk, when Britain seemed to have little else but her intelligence. Then, when the German tide of war ebbed, and the Allies seized the offensive, they reaped all the advantages that this extensive organization and greater experience gave them. Their information, in contrast to Hitler's, was high-level, voluminous, and reliable. And they used it to speed their victory.

Germans, however, cannot blame Hitler alone for this disregard of intelligence. The attitude had a long history. Prussia-Germany recognized that her location between potential enemies and her inferiority in natural resources and population made it impossible for her to win a war of attrition. These factors, together with difficult domestic problems most easily suppressed by unification through an aggressive foreign policy, decreed the strategic offensive as her military dictrine. The Schlieffen plan for smashing

France in 1914 by sweeping through neutral Belgium formulated this in its most brutal terms. Germany's defeat in 1918 after four terrible years seared the necessity for a quick offensive victory in the next war into the national consciousness—and into Hitler's. As a result, he created the blitz-krieg, with its dire consequences for intelligence.

In the same way, the World War II leaders of Great Britain do not deserve all the praise for building up their intelligence agencies. Britain's circumstances had given them a big head start. Her island position made it difficult for her to dominate Europe directly, by land forces, as France, for example, had done. She did so indirectly, by being the nation whose strength, thrown to one side or the other, could decide a continental conflict. This balance-of-power policy, which is a reactive, or defensive, technique, requires intelligence to succeed. Intelligence also contributes to economic expansion, which was Britain's other source of power. And so, beginning with Sir Francis Walsingham under Queen Elizabeth I, or, some say, as far back as Edward III in the late Middle Ages, Britain cultivated intelligence.

In a sense, then, each nation's attitude toward intelligence may be seen as an expression of its geography and its internal dynamics. Britain was a sea power, essentially defensive: the Royal Navy is called, not the spear of Britain, but her shield. She needed intelligence. Germany was a continental power with severe domestic tensions. Her armies, attacking, did not require intelligence. And so she failed to develop it.

This fundamental neglect of intelligence perfectly suited the élite of the German officer corps. They believed that the aggressiveness from which it stemmed protected Germany and thus their livelihoods from foreign dangers. Inside Germany, however, in the army, they did not merely ignore intelligence. They fought it. For intelligence threatened their jobs.

The advance of technology naturally creates technicians. In the military, for example, there evolve artillerists, railroad men, and specialists on foreign armies. Their knowledge gives them a certain power. Basically, this consists of the threat of withholding their knowledge, thereby weakening the military forces of their country. Such power enables them to demand at first merely work within the military establishment, then officer posts, then access to the top. The existing officers resist this incursion, for it robs them of jobs once their own.

The Prussian-German officer corps was far more adamant than others. Its Junkers feared displacement more, for, unable to subsist on their lands and unwilling to enter trade, they had no place else to go. Moreover, ever since the Great Elector of Brandenburg had given these rebellious aristocrats commissions in his army to bring them under his control in the late 1600s, they had enjoyed a virtual monopoly of the officer posts. All they had to do to get a job was be born. They contended that only fear of loss of honor prevented cowardice among commanders, that only noblemen had honor, and that consequently only noblemen were entitled to lead troops; bourgeois artillerymen, no matter how well trained, could never do more than lay guns. In fact the Junkers were seeking to ban competition for commissions and to keep it as easy for themselves as possible. In sociological terms, they opposed any shift from an ascriptive to an achievement system of authority.

Like the officer corps as a whole, the general staff fought the threat of specialist competition within its own prestigious domain. In some cases, the pressure of technology proved too great, and it yielded: the railroad expert is a case in point. It opposed intelligence more successfully. Through the nineteenth century, it appeared to have some right on its side. Four millennia of military history had taught that intelligence had played virtually no role at all in war. The staff believed, with some validity, that men, fire, and will won battles. But while the French, the British, and the Americans saw that the French and industrial revolutions were changing things and established special intelligence sections within their general staffs, the Germans did not. Their general staff continued its old and self-serving opposition to intelligence.

It rationalized this view by holding that, since information about the enemy was merely part of the whole, the commander should handle it as part of his overall duties. Intelligence was subsumed under operations. And since the general staff ran operations, it controlled intelligence questions. One of these was whether intelligence should separate out as a speciality, and this possibility the general staff precluded. It required no intelligence courses of students at the War Academy; matters dealing with information about the enemy were amalgamated into the instruction on tactics. It expostulated on the importance of standing above the particular problems of individual branches and seeing them as part of the broad operational picture. When questionable situations concerning the enemy arose during battle, it maintained, energetic operations would clarify them. It ostracized officers who dealt with spies on the ground that association with these deceivers had tainted them; it preferred, one student has said, "honourable ignorance rather than useful knowledge gained by devious means." It belittled intelligence and, in compensation, overemphasized the role of the commander. Thus Chief of the General Staff of the Army Alfred Count von Schlieffen declared that it is "difficult to ascertain where the enemy will go from his assembly area. What cavalry and airships can report about it will generally come in too late. The commander must guess or calculate the intentions of the enemy."

Not even German officers, however, could continue to suppress intelligence after its breakthrough in World War I. To do so, they saw, would jeopardize the nation and hence their position. So they created intelligence officers at the field staffs and an intelligence branch at headquarters. But they did so grudgingly. Their greater conservatism both compelled and enabled them to hang onto as much of their old power as possible. This they did by continuing to refuse intelligence the full status that it had long had in other armies. They institutionalized this attitude by placing the I c under the I a. They safeguarded it by teaching almost no courses on intelligence methods. And they propagandized it when they thought it necessary. The progress of the specialists increased their nervousness and made the army commander of the 1920s, Hans von Seeckt, sharpen Schlieffen's point. "Uncertainty and chance are inseparable characteristics of war. No understanding can control them, no beam out of the brightest and sharpest intellect can illuminate them. Only the will of the commander can dominate them. . . . The clarity of the will is the only light in the darkness of doubt and the future." What was really nagging him was the fear that, if intelligence could win wars, no one would need generals.

Now there is no doubt that intelligence is merely part of the whole and that control of one's own men and resources by the I a is more important than the knowledge of the enemy provided by the I c.

But the German system automatically impaired the quality of its own intelligence. Because the Germans felt that intelligence was part of tactics, they used general staff officers for I c posts, but because the I a was the more responsible job, they put the better men into those posts—and this filled the I c posts with second-raters. A different philosophy would have enabled them to fill the intelligence slots with trained specialists, whose information the operations officer would have fitted into the entire tactical picture. The Allies, for example, used drafted civilians as intelligence officers even of army groups with great success. First-class minds became expert on the enemy; with no worries about a career, they could both be kept in a post for the duration of the war and express their opinions more forcefully. The Germans, with their disdain for technicians and what they called "the burden of technology," which they felt gummed operations (laying telephone wire, for example, delayed commanders and cost them initiative and momentum), did not realize what the collecting and sifting of intelligence detail could yield. The subordination of I c to I a further harmed German intelligence by forcing information to fight through an extra level of command and by reducing the authority with which the I c could express his views to the chief of staff if they differed from those of the I a. The whole German system undervalued intelligence as compared to other armies, in which the G-2 was as much the immediate subordinate of the chief of staff as the G-3.

Two factors somewhat ameliorated this situation. Wartime shortages of general staff officers drove the army to fill many divisional intelligence posts with reserve officers, who developed in effect into intelligence specialists. And Gehlen pressed for making I cs at least equal in rank to their I as. But the first was always regarded as a deviation from the norm and never affected posts from corps upwards, and the latter did not rectify the I a–I c subordination. Only later, when the defensive situation enabled Gehlen and I cs time and again to help commanders save men and matériel, did the army begin to change its attitude to intelligence—slowly, reluctantly, and partially. But this was too little, and by then it was too late.

A quite different factor crippled the high-level organs of intelligence in the Nazi state. This was its authority structure. The Nazis called it the "Führer-Prinzip," but the great sociologist Max Weber had earlier identified it as "charismatic authority." It damaged intelligence by reducing both its quantity and its quality.

The sole source of power in Nazi Germany was Adolf Hitler. It was a purely personal power: his word was law. It emanated from the devotion placed by the masses and the leaders in him as the embodiment of a revolutionary mission. Weber contrasted this authority with two other kinds. Traditional authority maintains the sanctity of immemorial tradition; ancient Egypt and mandarin China typify it. Legal authority strives rationally to fulfill enacted norms; this authority is exerted through specialist officials assigned particular areas of competence—a bureaucracy. The western democracies best exemplify the type.

Charismatic authority is fueled by faith, and Hitler's charisma released torrents of emotional energy among the Germans—far more than either traditional or rationally legal governments would have done. Believing in their Führer, the Germans held gigantic rallies, built autobahns, paraded by torchlight, recreated an army and an air force, conquered most of Europe, and purified the continent of subhumans. Often Hitler boasted of how much his policies had achieved. Devotion to him kept exhausted soldiers fighting even in the hopelessness of 1945.

Charisma thus accomplished much. But it had its disadvantages. Charismatic authority was inefficient and, in the end, ineffective.

From the outside, the principle of strict adherence to the Führer made Nazi Germany appear to be a highly unified state, tightly controlled by an organization whose chain of command ran clearly from Hitler to the lowliest block leader—the cliché was "monolithic." Inside, however, it was a teeming nest of snakes, each seeking to devour the other, with no clearly defined tasks or authority, intent only—and this aspect of the Führer-Prinzip was real enough—on winning the approbation of Hitler and thus enhancing his own power.

For the remission of power by the masses to Hitler had freed him of the restraints of legal or traditional authority. He could arrange his personnel and his organizations as he wanted. And he wanted, basically, to replicate them and to let his subordinates fight among themselves, for two possibly contradictory reasons. First, he believed that competition brought the best man to the top. He employed this social Darwinism within the party and between party and government. Second, by multiplying organizations he would guarantee his power and facilitate his control. To allow any subordinate exclusive authority in an area would cede to that subordinate the power that knowledge confers; Hitler would become the captive of the subordinate in that field. On the other hand, distributing the authority of that function by giving similar duties to several subordinates would force them to come to him for their power. To these ends he assigned Göring to head the four-year plan while Funk was minister of economics, appointed Dietrich his press secretary and Goebbels his propaganda minister, made the OKW into a rival of the OKH, let Ribbentrop set up his own spy service next to the existing ones of the armed forces and the party.

But this technique was inefficient. In intelligence, it dissipated the precious limited expertise of the political cryptanalysts in three agencies. It drove rival organizations, such as the three spy services, to waste time and energy intriguing, backbiting, and defining competencies in the jostle for Hitler's favor instead of concentrating on the enemy. It choked off the very intelligence that was supposed to help agencies make decisions. Hitler refused to allow Speer to transmit information to the OKH; when Dönitz wanted to see the documents of the Foreign Office, he had to get special permission. Hitler decreed in his "basic order" of 11 January 1940: "No one, no post, no officer, may learn about a matter to be kept secret if he does not unconditionally need to know about it." All this diminished the quantity of intelligence.

Charismatic authority was, in addition, ultimately ineffective. It judged policy and information on the basis not of reason but of (Nazi) faith. Himmler told the Abwehr officers at Salzburg that an intelligence service must rest, not upon honest and objective evaluation of the facts, but "upon a race, upon a people of the same blood." Boetticher's reports from Washington seemed right because of his views about Jewish control. The Nazi state practiced such irrationalism. The priority of ideology, which stemmed from its greater emotional force, ensured that, when disputes occurred, the most ideological authority invariably won. Thus Ribbentrop, head of a party post for foreign affairs, ousted the career diplomat von Neurath as foreign minister. Thus the anti-Hitler chief of the general staff, Halder, was replaced by the pro-Nazi Zeitzler. Thus Speer displaced Thomas. Thus Himmler's SS expanded first into foreign policy at the expense of the less ideologically committed Foreign Office, and then into military affairs, with Himmler becoming chief of the replacement army and commander of an army group, at the cost of the unpolitical army. And thus the SD swallowed the Abwehr.

Though this may have worked, at least for a while, within the closed system of Nazi Germany, it failed outside it. Intelligence is better the closer it fits reality. But charismatic authority turns from the most valid route to external reality: reason. It thus becomes dysfunctional. Even a Hitler

Youth's perfect trust in the Führer could not keep Allied bullets from killing him. Even the deepest ideological convictions about Slavic inferiority and Communist weakness did not defeat Soviet Russia. Charismatic authority reduced the quality of German intelligence.

Now charismatic authority no more attained its pure form under Hitler than it did anywhere else in the world. A strong element of legal authority persisted, as Germany's vast bureaucracies made manifest. When disputes occurred within this sphere, as between the Abwehr and the Foreign Office on sending agents to North Africa, they were settled in a reasonable way. Moreover, charismatic authority was not confined to Nazi Germany. Under the Kaiser, the heads of three high army offices and several commanders in the field all had direct access to him as supreme war lord; the same situation existed with the navy. During the early New Deal, Franklin Roosevelt's administrative techniques included overlapping jurisdictions and competitive assignments.

But authority in the democracies was basically legal. This enabled them to shape a unified organization. The Anglo-American coalition is the supreme example. Of course, men wrangled, withheld information, and built empires, but the battles were not the battles to the death that they were under Hitler because law ruled, not men. This increased efficiency. At the same time, the rule of rationality in legislative authority led the Allies to see the world more as it is, despite some wishful thinking, and so to take more effective actions. The contrast is striking between the effect on intelligence of this form of government and that of Nazi Germany.

Charismatic authority fragmented the German intelligence effort and so reduced quantity. It screened the intelligence output in irrational and unreal ways and so reduced quality. Hitler's charisma devastated German intelligence.

For all these reasons, the intelligence that was delivered to the Führer was flawed and insufficient. But suppose it had been perfect. Would he have made better use of it? Would he have exploited its insights to maneuver more effectively?

For Hitler was the ultimate consumer. He stood at the apex of the intelligence pyramid. While he made sure that subordinates saw only part of the intelligence picture, he himself had access to all of it, and he alone evaluated it, making the final decisions on its meaning. More important, he alone decided whether the armed forces would act on it, and so in the last analysis he alone determined its impact on the German war effort.

Hitler wore five hats. He was head of state, head of government, party chief, commander of the armed forces, and acting commander in chief of the army. In one or another of these capacities, quantities of information flowed to him. Every morning the Reich press chief laid not only the German and party papers before his door but also press reports from abroad, such as those from the *Daily Mail,* from Tass, from Swiss and Swedish newspapers. Every day, the Foreign Office liaison to the Führer headquarters, Walther Hewel, submitted three to five documents. On Friday, 19 September 1941, for example, he gave Hitler a telegram from the embassy in Rome, one from the legation in Lisbon, an intercepted Turkish message solved by Pers Z, and a report from an agent of the Foreign Office's Inf III spy service. On other days Hewel gave him reports of the Forschungsamt, memoranda from Ribbentrop and Likus, one of Ribbentrop's chief aides, and clippings from the Foreign Office's press branch. He also reported orally, passing on, for example, the report of a Foreign Office liaison man in North Africa telling how American soldiers had only gone to war to earn money. In addition, Hitler held situation conferences twice a day. At these Jodl and, after the start of the Russian campaign, the chief of the general staff presented the military situation in almost suffocating detail. During the battle for Stalingrad, for example, Zeitzler reported to him:

> At the Fiebig Group is a little town, it's called Kiryevo; enemy cavalry in a strength of about 1,000 men came in there. The following is interesting about this. Prisoners were made from the 40th Guard Division and the 321st Division. These two divisions were formerly on the northwest corner of the [German] 6th Army. The prisoners stated they were brought up in speedy marches for three nights in a row. From this one can conclude that he [the enemy] is now weakening the front of the 6th Army in order to press in this point near Chir. A further indication for this is that the 6th Army was only very weakly attacked today.

Often army commanders reported in person; often Hitler telephoned them for information. Beyond this, Hitler got oral and written reports on various matters from the greatest variety of sources—Göring, Goebbels, gauleiters and other party functionaries, special emissaries such as Philip, Prince of Hesse, or Constantin von Neurath, son of the former foreign minister, who told Hitler how bad the Italians in Sicily were, industrialists, foreign statesmen and diplomats whom he received, even occasionally anonymous letters. In all, he said, he spent eight hours a day just reading reports and memoranda.

Hitler understood a lot about intelligence. He recognized the difficulty of identifying troops from airplanes and knew that intercept operators could recognize individual enemy radiomen. Unlike most laymen, he realized that there was no such thing as "the" English code but that several existed of different strengths and times of service. He knew exactly how intelligence officers put together details into a complete picture: "When I get a report today on a Russian road that leads to a section of the front, in which 36 rifle divisions and armored formations, so many armored regiments and so many other formations are located, and it says that yesterday night 1,000 vehicles travelled on a road, tonight 800 and then 1,200 and 300 vehicles, that is an alarm, then, that runs through the entire eastern front: that says 'Attack imminent.' " He was alert to the possibility of deception, commenting that one report was "too good to be true" and asking of another before the Allied invasion, "Must they do that so ostentatiously?"

He not only understood intelligence, in tactical and operational areas he made good use of it. In October 1942, he deduced from "extensive enemy movements" and "the bridging of the Don" that the Russians would "launch a major attack . . . across the Don in the direction of Rostov." He sent in three divisions. A few weeks later, Luftwaffe aerial photographs showed "that the number of new bridges built across the Don in the sector of the Rumanian 3rd Army is steadily growing. The Führer therefore still expects a major Russian attack across the Don in the direction of Rostov." He ordered the bridges bombed. When in February 1941 the German attaché in Ankara warned that Turkey would go to war with Germany unless German troops in Bulgaria stayed 50 kilometers from the frontier, Hitler issued the necessary orders. When British newspapers announced that American Flying Fortress bombers would "pulverize" Germany, Hitler built up his flak positions and stocked them with quantities of ammunition.

But his use of intelligence ceased at the borders of his strategy. For this issued from his basic conceptions, which had made him what he was and had brought him to where he was. Any admission of error in his racism or anti-Semitism or sense of geopolitical mission would have undermined not only his political power but his very personality. Consequently, these tenets were inaccessible to reason, excluded from argument. No facts could ever have convinced Hitler that he was wrong.

On the other hand, some reassured him that he was right. He had constructed his picture of the world from aspects of reality, and whenever he detected these aspects again, or corollaries of them, he accepted them as confirmation of his views. The impoverished farmers of the motion picture *The Grapes of Wrath,* which he viewed as a documentary rather than fiction, verified for him his image of a "decayed country." These selective corroborations occurred frequently in the years of victory. He had always held that America would eventually absorb the British empire. So he seized upon all reports of friction between the Allies as bearing out his vision and its effects. Feedback intensified this distortion. His subordinates knew what he liked, and supported him with innumerable substantiations of his views. They submitted favorable reports and seconded his remarks during conferences.

But other, less comforting aspects of reality nevertheless impinged. Hitler's mind defended itself from them mainly by denying them. It lightened the burden on itself by selecting a staff that blocked off many of these items before they ever came to Hitler's attention. Reich Press Chief Dietrich censored much of the press material. Keitel prevented Thomas from submitting his reports. These men believed that they were protecting their leader. Once Seifert, head of the evaluation bureau of the Forschungsamt, sent up a report with unpleasant news.

"How can you submit such a report to the Führer at this time?" an adjutant asked him.

"If I hadn't submitted it, you should have had me put up against a wall and shot," replied Seifert.

"No," came the response. "When the Führer has made a decision, we must no longer disturb his intuition."

At the situation conferences, Jodl emphasized minor German successes and soft-pedaled German retreats so that an observer would scarcely realize that major offensives were pounding Germany back. On 6 November 1944, after the Germans had lost a bridgehead over the Moselle, Jodl told Hitler about it like this: German skirmishers south of the Moselle "were suddenly attacked very strongly. It became a very bitter close combat around these little villages. Three [enemy] tanks were shot up. He [the enemy] finally threw our skirmishers back across the Moselle. The southern bridgehead was then given up." Elsewhere the talk stressed the Russian attacks that were thrown back, the German counterattacks under way, the brave resistance of units in tactically meaningless situations. Occasionally, when the soldiers had to admit to a withdrawal, they never spoke of a defeat—the enemy "pressed in," his overwhelming forces compelled the brave troops to yield a little ground. In such ways did Hitler's staff protect him from unpleasant news.

But sometimes bad news did reach him. In some cases, he neutralized it beforehand. If the report showed a preponderance of enemy strength, he charged the submitter with "defeatism"—lacking confidence in Germany's victory. This eliminated him from serious consideration. Or Hitler could tax the report-writer with being an "expert," meaning usually a general staff officer or a diplomat. During his years of diplomatic and military triumphs, the diplomats and the general staff had warned him of dire consequences if he took a certain action; he had dared it anyway and, succeeding, had proved once again his genius and their incompetence. Consequently he could presume their statements to be as wrong now as they were before.

When this procedure was not available, he distorted the information to fit his views. Though Germany had 75 million people and the United States 135 million, Germany was ahead in population because only 60 million of the Americans were of decent racial stock. Sometimes Hitler changed figures to make them more agreeable. A month after the navy had reported to him that the Americans would build 300,000 tons of shipping a month, he was basing arguments on a figure in his head of 70,000 tons. When Jodl told him that a German unit advancing on Rome to arrest the king and the post-Mussolini government was 100 kilometers from the city, Hitler exclaimed: "One hundred? Sixty kilometers!" This process included "underestimation of enemy possibilities," which Halder saw as early as 1942 as becoming "dangerous."

Most often, however, Hitler simply rejected unwelcome news. When England refused to make peace, he "could not conceive of anyone in England still seriously believing in victory." The naval attaché in Russia reported to him about Russian ship construction figures, based on the time ships spent on the ways, obtained from aerial photographs. The size of the figures surprised Hitler, and he concluded, "What we can't do, the Russians can't do either." Across a Pers Z intercept that told him about good agricultural results in Russia, he scrawled, "This cannot be." When an aide wanted to give him information on the destruction of Hamburg from the awesome Allied raids in July 1943, Hitler cut him off: "You don't have to report that—I've already gotten the pictures." Jodl's statement that Allied armor had rolled up part of the Westwall in March 1945 was contradicted: "That's also not so certain. It can be only two or three tanks." Nor was this occurrence rare at his situation conferences. When Guderian submitted Gehlen's figures on Russian troop concentrations, he raved that they were "completely idiotic" and that Gehlen ought to be committed to an insane asylum. When a Luftwaffe officer laid before him a giant composite aerial photograph showing that the Russians had assembled the greatest artillery concentration of all time before Army Group Center, he swept it furiously from the table.

As matters worsened, as the evidence for defeat loomed more and more, Hitler shielded himself from it not only psychologically but also physically, encapsulating himself more and more in his own world. He curtained his railroad car and traveled at night. During situation conferences he darkened the room. He visited the front only once after 8 September 1943, and refused to inspect bombed cities. He would not receive officers who had been in combat. He forbade "pessimistic" and "defeatist" talk.

In a few isolated cases, he seemed to apprehend the true nature of the situation: "We are constantly losing industrial areas"; "The V-1 unfortunately cannot decide the war"; "Our own measures depend upon them [the enemy operations goals]." But in fact these were mere obeisances; they marked no confession of basic error. Nothing, but nothing, could turn him from his Nazi views. While the British bombed German cities and the German British, he envisioned a postwar "durable friendship" between Nazi Germany and England. With Soviet tanks approaching his capital, he saw nothing wrong in his conception of Russian weakness, only in the timing of his attack.

No evidence could penetrate obstinacy like that. So even if Hitler had been served with perfect intelligence, it would have had no essential effect upon him. He would have selectively absorbed what he liked and denied the rest. In the tactical area perfect intelligence might have helped. Strategically it would have mattered not a jot.

The more basic question about Hitler and intelligence is not whether better information would have helped him. It is this: Why did the man who had handled reality so effectively in the 1920s and 1930s that he became the master of Germany and of Europe turn into a creature who petulantly swept unwelcome papers off his desk?

The answer lies less within Hitler than without. External circumstances effected the change. They stripped his defenses from him bit by bit and exposed his neuroticism more and more. The results could be seen not only in intelligence, but in all his actions.

During the early years, Hitler acted largely as he wished, relatively untrammeled by outside forces. His talents—in particular his fierce determination, his rigid will—enjoyed free play. They enabled him to become head of his party and of his country. Expanding these talents onto the world stage, he manipulated other nations to make Germany, and consequently himself, the dominant power in Europe. Hitler acted, molded, led; other men and nations reacted, bent, followed. In psychological terms, he was accommodating to reality by alloplastically altering reality. He was reshaping the world to satisfy his needs. In all this, outside of a few tactical reversals, he was not checked.

Then, in 1939, Britain refused to acquiesce in his program any longer. Her declaration of war seriously limited his freedom of action for the first time. The most direct, simplest, and surest way of resolving this frustration, after Britain spurned his peace offers, was to invade and conquer the island. But Hitler shied from this. He chose instead a solution that promised less to reshape reality than to meet his needs. He attacked Russia. Instead of battling a nation he really did not want to fight, he could destroy one he hated. Instead of fighting at sea, he could fight on land. Instead of sweating in the fear of defeat, he could wallow in the certainty of victory. And all this, he thought, came in addition to depriving Britain of her last hope and thus bringing her to her senses. So instead of facing the objectively more effective solution, he reverted to the subjectively more gratifying one. For the first time in a vital matter, he accommodated autoplastically. Instead of his changing the world, he let the world change him. In psychological terms, he regressed.

Britain's intransigeance was but the first external force to bar him from fulfilling his wishes. As it so often does, an immature response led to greater difficulties. His attack on Russia eventually cost him the strategic initiative, and thereafter events increasingly frustrated him. Increasingly, he responded with regressive behavior. When his blitzkrieg in Russia failed, he declared war on America. When he lost France, he ordered the destruction of Paris. When the enemy occupied Germany, he directed Speer to destroy the country. And when, near the end of the war, generals laid intelligence before him that set forth nothing but more frustration, he swept it out of his sight.

Hitler was not the only leader in the history of the world to prefer pre-conception to uncomfortable intelligence, though his greater power enabled him to assert his more global prejudices much more completely than the others. Long before he arrived, chief of the general staff Schlieffen had analyzed the phenomenon: "The higher commander generally makes himself a picture of friend and foe, in the painting of which personal wishes provide the main elements. If incoming reports appear to correspond with this picture, they are laid by with satisfaction. If they contradict it, they are discarded as entirely false." A few years later, his countrymen repeated the paradigm like sleepwalkers. The Kaiser's government wanted Belgium in 1914 to submit to a temporary occupation—and was surprised when she refused. It overlooked evidence that Britain would not remain neutral in what one scholar has called "a miscalculation bordering on blindness."

Such blindness does not impair only Germans. In 1681, Louis XIV paid no heed to the repeated reports of his ambassador at The Hague that the Swedes were seeking a Dutch alliance because he wanted one with them instead; when the treaty was signed, he refused to take it seriously. Later he dismissed information on Austrian weapons and military successes in order to maintain his previous conclusions. In 1937, Japanese intelligence teams studying the Red army after losing a border clash with Russia found essentially what they wanted to: the fighting was atypical, no conclusions could be drawn, the Russians were as strong as expected, the Japanese had not underestimated them. Next year the Russians sent them reeling again at Khalkhin Gol.

But what about Hitler's opponents? How did Churchill react to bad news? He too was a strong leader; he too not only believed but had to demonstrate his belief in victory; he too could not passively accept obstacles but had to overcome them. Did he then reject unpleasant intelligence? No. He didn't like it. He fumed at it. But he accepted it. He took it into account in his planning.

In part it might be that it was easier for him to do so. The war situation presented him with really bad news less often than it did Hitler. Even in the dark days after Dunkirk, Churchill could hope. Hitler, when the tide turned against him after years of triumph, could not. As he saw his destruction approaching, the psychological pressures became so great that the wonder is not that he swept papers off his desk, but that he did not crack earlier. The different experiences of the two further contributed to their divergent attitudes toward unpleasant information. Churchill had fought elections and, as a child of parliament, had sometimes submitted to opposing views. Hitler had never held office before he became chancellor; opponents, such as Röhm, the SA leader, he assassinated. The whole pattern was far more extreme and unaccommodating. It reflected the basic difference between the two men. Hitler's personality was essentially neurotic, deriving its strength—the inflexible will that enthralled everyone within its range—from its need to maintain its defenses. Churchill, born in a palace, the grandson of a duke, victor over early failures to become an early success, possessed an inner security and confidence that Hitler never had. What clinched their different ways of receiving bad news was their different sources of power. The House of Commons had accorded Churchill his position. If he did not do well—and disregard of reality rapidly leads to inadequate functioning—it would take the prime ministry away from him. Hitler, on the other hand, had total control and was not subject to easy removal, no matter what he did. Only a threat of loss of confidence by the mass of people could perhaps have held him to account, but faith and fear alike precluded that.

In the end, reality overwhelmed Hitler. Unable to avoid any longer the recognition that his life and all that it had stood for had been annulled, he at last annihilated himself. Three weeks later, what was left of his government, the wickedest regime of all time, capitulated. And with it there passed into history the feeble, and rightfully doomed, efforts of German military intelligence in World War II.

Citations, Translations, Abbreviations
Notes
Bibliography
Illustrations Acknowledgments

Citations, Translations, Abbreviations

Citations

To SAVE SPACE, I have condensed the footnotes as much as possible. This mainly means eliminating what a document is—a report by someone to someone, a war diary entry, a memorandum of a conversation. It also means abbreviating them where possible.

Published works listed in the bibliography are cited by author only, followed by page number. Titles are given, usually in short form, for minor works by an author who has several works listed. Thus "Guderian, 100" means page 100 of his memoirs, *Panzer Leader;* "Guderian, *Panzerwaffe,* 20" means page 20 of that work by him. These differences are signaled in the bibliography. Some works issuing from government agencies with long names, such as Reichsministerium für Volksaufklärung und Propaganda, are cited by abbreviations, such as "RMfVuP"; others are cited by their editors, such as "Boberach, ed." Abbreviations and editors are listed under Abbreviations. Works not carried in the bibliography, usually because they relate only to a single point in a single chapter, have full citations in the notes.

The notes for unpublished items utilize a condensed format. Colons separate major elements of the citation in a descending sequence that starts with the archive and ends with the document or page. These notes make considerable use of abbreviations, such as "NA" for "U.S., National Archives." Some bound volumes of documents have been numbered, either by page or by item, sometimes anti-chronologically because later documents have been put on top of older ones and the volume then bound. In these, documents are cited by these numbers. Other volumes or folders are not numbered; in these, items are cited by date. If several items with the same date can be distinguished, as by a time, this is done. Otherwise, the future user will have to check the several documents with the same date. Documents without either dates or numbers are cited by title or description. A sample citation is: "NA:RG242: Schellenberg interrogation:24. Juni 1947:7–9, 12." This means: "National Archives, Record Group 242, the Schellenberg interrogation of 24 June 1947, pages 7 to 9 and page 12." Again, "AA:Pol I M:38:7. August 1941" means "Auswärtiges Amt, Politisches Archiv, documents of the Politische Abteilung I Militaria unit, volume 38 in that series, document dated 7 August 1941."

All documents bear the archival designation with four exceptions: (1) Documents from the Militärarchiv in Freiburg-im-Breisgau. Thus "HGrD:75144/35:85" means "[Militärarchiv], Heeresgruppe D, Volume 75144/35, document or page number 85." Most of the documents cited are from the Militärarchiv and in this form. If clarity demands it, however, as with one of the old naval volumes, the citation will begin with an MA, thus: "MA:F3964:II:2:12.7.1915." (2) The T- series of German records microfilmed by the National Archives. These citations always have three sections preceded by a T-, as T-78:512:6537000, which means microcopy T-78, microfilm reel 512, frame number 6537000. (3) The Foreign Military Studies of the Historical Division, U.S. Army, and the Historical Studies of the U.S. Air Force. The army's are identified by a B-, C-, D-, P-, or T- followed by a single number, a comma, and a page number: D-407, 109. The air force's are USAF-171 and USAF-

191 and others bearing only a title. (4) Documents collected for the second set of Nuremberg trials conducted by the Americans under Control Council Law No. 10. These bear symbols beginning with N, as NG-, NI-, NO-, and NOKW- followed by a document number, sometimes followed by a colon and page numbers: NI-3216:3–4.

Translations

The names of the successive levels in the German administrative hierarchy, both party and government, remained pretty much the same in all ministries. In this book, I have not always given these bodies their formal English translation, but have instead interpreted them as what I believe to be their nearest English-American hierarchical equivalent:

Ministerium	ministry
Hauptamt	administration (an SS term only)
Amt	department (except Auswärtiges Amt)
Amtsgruppe	division
Hauptabteilung	bureau
Abteilung	branch
Hauptgruppe	office (except Foreign Office)
Gruppe	group
Referat	desk
Stelle	post, station, center, central

The following terms, when used, do not refer to any particular bureaucratic level: "agency," "unit," "section," "body," "organ," "element," "service," "secretariat." They are useful when an agency rises from, say, an Amtsgruppe to an Amt during a period under discussion.

I have not translated the names of organizations when they are commonly known under their German name or abbreviation (Abwehr, SS), are understandable to an English-speaking reader (Auslandsorganisation), or, while short, do not indicate their function either in German or in English (Seehaus or Lake House, the press monitoring service). "Strasse" and "Calle" for "street" have been left in the original language; house numbers in these addresses follow the street name.

Ranks are translated according to the tables in *TWC*, 11:703, except that SS Oberführer has been translated as "SS brigadier," Generalfeldmarschall as "field marshal," Grossadmiral as "grand admiral," and generals of all ranks simply as "general." Party and other titles are translated or not depending on their brevity, familiarity, and comprehension by an English-speaking reader. "Führer," "Gauleiter," and "Reichsführer-SS" are not, "Chef der Sicherheitspolizei," "Oberbefehlshaber West," and "Kommandeur der Nachrichten-Aufklärung" are. Translations of regional terms for the NSDAP and the SS are: Gau = district, Leitabschnitt = province, Oberabschnitt = region, Abschnitt = sector, Unterabschnitt = precinct.

Conversions from the metric to the English system have been rounded off. Thus "5,000 to 10,000 meters," which is actually 16,404 to 32,808 feet, has become "15,000 to 30,000 feet."

Reichsmarks (*RM*) are converted at the 1941 rate of *RM*2.50 = \$1, or *RM*1 = 40 cents, pounds sterling at £1 = \$4.80. The dollars are 1941 dollars.

Dates in the text are given in Continental style—"7 February 1942"—because it seems less confusing to follow the form in which they are found in the documents.

Abbreviations and Designations

I	number of the Abwehr branch and of the element in Abwehr posts and KOs that handled espionage
I a	first general staff officer (operations)
I b	second general staff officer (supply)
I c	third general staff officer (intelligence)
1SIIR	first special intelligence interrogation report
1/Skl	first branch (operations) of the Seekriegsleitung
III b	refers to the espionage agency of the Prussian-German Great General Staff from 1866 to 1918, even though designation III b was only given in 1889
3/Skl	third branch (intelligence) of the Seekriegsleitung
VI	number of the department in the RSHA and of the element in subordinate posts that handled foreign intelligence
AA	Auswärtiges Amt: Politisches Archiv
Abw	Abwehr
ADAP	[Germany]. Auswärtiges Amt. *Akten zur Deutschen Auswärtigen Politik 1918–1945*. Serie E.
AG	army group
A.G.	Aktiengesellschaft (corporation)
AK	Armeekorps (army corps)
APWIU	Air Prisoner of War Interrogation Unit
AOK	Armeeoberkommando (army headquarters)
Ast	Abwehrstelle (Abwehr post)
B-	designation for an unpublished report of the U.S. Army's Foreign Military Studies Program
BA	Bundesarchiv
BARBAROSSA	codeword for the German attack on Russia
BDC	Berlin Document Center
BH:KA	Bayerische Hauptstaatsarchiv: Kriegsarchiv
Boberach, ed.	[Germany]. Reichssicherheitshauptamt. Amt III. *Meldungen aus dem Reich.*
C-	designation for an unpublished report of the U.S. Army's Foreign Military Studies Program
CCPWE	(meaning unknown) designation for a series of interrogation reports
CI	counterintelligence
CIC	Counterintelligence Corps
CIR	consolidated interrogation report
CMH	U.S. Army, Center for Military History
COA	Classified Operational Archives
D-	designation for an unpublished report of the U.S. Army's Foreign Military Studies Program
DGFP	[Germany]. Auswärtiges Amt. *Documents on German Foreign Policy 1918–1945*. Series D
DGFP:C	[Germany]. Auswärtiges Amt. *Documents on German Foreign Policy 1918–1945*. Series C

DIS(MIS)/M.	(meaning unknown) designation for a series of interrogation reports
Do	Dornier
Domarus, ed.	[Hitler, Adolf]. *Hitler: Reden und Proklamationen, 1932–1945*
DSDF	NA:RG59: Department of State Decimal File
EAP	Einheitsaktenplan (designation for German documents)
ESM	Berlin (after 1945: Frankfurt am Main): Ernst Siegfried Mittler & Sohn
FA	Forschungsamt
FAK	Frontaufklärungskommando (front reconnaissance [spy] command)
FAT	Frontaufklärungstrupp (front reconnaissance [spy] troop)
FH	Fremde Heere (Foreign Armies)
FHO	Fremde Heere Ost (Foreign Armies East)
FHW	Fremde Heere West (Foreign Armies West)
FIR	final interrogation report
F.O.	Foreign Office (Great Britain)
FRUS	United States. State Department. *Foreign Relations of the United States* (followed by volume designation)
GGVKS	[Union of Soviet Socialist Republics]. . . . *Geschichte des Grossen Vaterländischen Krieges der Sowjetunion*
G.m.b.H.	Gesellschaft mit beschränkter Haftung (incorporated)
GPO	Washington: Government Printing Office
Gren.D.	Grenadier Division
H	Heer (army)
H.Dv.g.	[Germany. Oberkommando des Heeres]. Heeres-Dienstvorschrift geheim (followed by its number)
He	Heinkel
HGr	Heeresgruppe (army group)
HMSO	London: Her Majesty's Stationery Office
HQ	headquarters
Hs	Henschel
HTUSAIC	Headquarters, Third U.S. Army, Intelligence Center
IC	interrogation center
I.D.	Infanterie Division
IfZ	Institut für Zeitgeschichte
IIR	intermediate interrogation report
IMT	International Military Tribunal, *Trial of the Major War Criminals*
Inl II g	Inland II geheim (branch of Foreign Office)
Inf III	Informationsabteilung III (spy branch of Foreign Office)
IR	interrogation report
Ju	Junkers
L	Luft (air)
Lagevorträge	[Germany]. Oberkommando der Kriegsmarine. *Lagevorträge des Oberbefehlshabers der Kriegsmarine vor Hitler*
Lw	Luftwaffe (air force)
M	Marine
MA	Militärarchiv

MFIU	(meaning unknown) designation for a series of interrogation reports
MISC	(meaning unknown) designation for a series of interrogation reports
ML	microfilm library (designation for an NA record series)
NA:RG	National Archives: Record Group
NCA	United States. Chief of Counsel for the Prosecution of Axis Criminality. *Nazi Conspiracy and Aggression*
n.d.	no date of publication given
NG	Nürnberg, government (designation for a document in evidence)
NI	Nürnberg, industrial (designation for a document in evidence)
NO	Nürnberg, organization (designation for a document in evidence)
NOKW	Nürnberg, OKW (designation for a document in evidence)
n.p.	no place of publication given
NSDAP	Nationalsozialistische Deutsche Arbeiterpartei (Nazi party)
O 1	first Ordonnanzoffizier (assistant to I a)
O 3	third Ordonnanzoffizier (assistant to I c)
O 6	sixth Ordonnanzoffizier (assistant to O 3)
OCMH	Office of the Chief of Military History
OKH	Oberkommando des Heeres (High Command of the Army)
OKL	Oberkommando der Luftwaffe (High Command of the Air Force)
OKM	Oberkommando der Kriegsmarine (High Command of the Navy)
OKM, *Denkschriften*	[Germany]. Kriegsmarine, Oberkommando der. *Denkschriften und Lagebetrachtungen*
OKW	Oberkommando der Wehrmacht (High Command of the Armed Forces)
OKW, *KTB*	[Germany]. Wehrmacht, Oberkommando der. Wehrmachtführungsstab. *Kriegstagebuch . . . 1940–1945*
O Qu IV	Oberquartiermeister IV (fourth assistant chief of staff, for intelligence)
OVERLORD	codeword for the Allied invasion of Europe
P-	designation for an unpublished report of the Foreign Military Studies Program
PG	pinched from the Germans (Admiralty designation for German naval records)
PIR	preliminary interrogation report
Pol I M	Politische Abteilung I Militaria (desk of the Foreign Office)
P.R.O.	Public Record Office
Promi	colloquial abbreviation for Reichsministerium für Volksaufklärung und Propaganda
Pz.K.	Panzerkorps (armored corps)
Pz.D.	Panzer Division (armored division)
Rb	Reihenbildapparat (sequence camera)

RM	Reichsmark(s)
RMfBuM, *Rüstung*	[Germany]. Reichsministerium für Bewaffnung und Munitionen. *Deutschlands Rüstung im Zweiten Weltkrieg*
RMfVuP, *Kriegspropaganda*	[Germany]. Reichsministerium für Volksaufklärung und Propaganda. *Kriegspropaganda 1939–1941*
RMfVuP, "*Wollt*"	Ibid., "*Wollt Ihr den totalen Krieg?*"
RSHA	Reichssicherheitshauptamt (Reich Security Administration)
RSHA VI	Department VI (foreign intelligence) of the RSHA
SA	Sturmabteilung (brown-shirted street army)
SAIC	Seventh Army Interrogation Center
SD	Sicherheitsdienst (Security Service)
Sd.Kfz.	Sonder-Kraftfahrzeug (special vehicle)
SIIR	special intelligence interrogation report
Skl	Seekriegsleitung (Naval War Command)
SS	Schutzstaffel (Himmler's organization)
Staatsmänner	[Hitler, Adolf]. *Staatsmänner und Diplomaten bei Hitler,* vol. 2
T	Technik
T-	(when followed by a three-part citation) temporary (NA designation for microfilms of German records)
T-	(when followed by a single number) designation for an unpublished report of the U.S. Army's Foreign Military Studies Program
TWC	[Germany (Territory under Allied Occupation . . .)]. *Trials of War Criminals before the Nuernberg Military Tribunals Under Control Council Law No. 10*
T 3	Truppenamt (Troops Department), 3d Branch (intelligence)
USAF	United States Air Force (designation for an unpublished USAF Historical Series report)
USFET	United States Forces, European Theater
USN	United States Navy
VfZ	*Vierteljahrshefte für Zeitgeschichte*
WALLI I	codename for Abwehr Main Post East I
WFSt	Wehrmachtführungsstab (Armed Forces Operations Staff)
Wi	Wirtschaft (economy)
Wi Rü Amt	Wehrwirtschafts- und Rüstungsamt (War Economy and Armaments Department)
WK	Wehrkreis (military district)
ZS	Zeugenschrift

Notes

CHAPTER 1: THE CLIMAX OF GERMAN SPYING IN AMERICA

Unless otherwise specified, all information comes from the statements of William C. Colepaugh and Erich Gimpel to agents of the Federal Bureau of Investigation on 2 January 1945 and 31 December 1944 respectively, kindly furnished in edited form by the F.B.I., and from an F.B.I. press release of 20 September 1954 entitled "William Curtis Colepaugh—Erich Gimpel: Espionage," which gives many of the names deleted from the spies' statements. Gimpel's ghostwritten book, *Spy for Germany*, must be used with the greatest caution, as it differs in a number of critical points from his statement. The most important are the book's claims that he was assigned to ferret out atomic secrets, that he succeeded to some extent, and that he radioed a message to Germany. None of these are supported by his statement or by Colepaugh's or by the postwar interrogations of his spymasters, and the atomic claim is specifically contradicted by a statement of Schellenberg's (*NCA*, B:1624-5). The book can, however, serve for details of color.

3 low 20s: *New York Times* (30 November 1944), 35:5 (using Portland, Maine).
3 Hilbig: Gimpel, 80; Rohwer, *U-Boot Erfolge*, 187.
3 approach to and entry into Frenchman Bay, conditions in U-1230: Hilbig, letter, 12. November 1977, as well as his drawing in the route on U.S. Department of Commerce, National Oceanic and Atmospheric Administration, National Ocean Survey, Chart 13318, *Frenchman Bay and Mount Desert Island*. The log of U-1230 for this period never reached the German naval archives; the war diary of the commander in chief of U-boats merely records a signal reporting the successful landing (letter, Naval Historical Branch, Ministry of Defence, 4 May 1977).
4 Peck's Point: Herbert Hodgkins (brother of Harvard), telephone interview, 24 April 1977.
4 Colepaugh, Gimpel descriptions: *New York Times* (2 January 1945), 6:4-5.
5 Ribbentrop wanted to test: IfZ:ZS 291:1:8, 12-13.
5 wished for attack: *Staatsmänner*, 2:352.
5 to his armies and his people: Domarus, ed., 2084, 2076, 2072, 2086.
6 "I'm not so easy": Boberach, ed., 485.
6 "What's the shortest joke?": *Wien Wehrt Sich Mit Witz! Flüsterwitze aus den Jahren 1938–1945* (Vienna: Weltweiten Verlag, 1946).
6 "are all incompetent": Boberach, ed., 462.
6 SD, RSHA, Schellenberg: see chapter on them.
6 no sources for political intelligence: NA:RG238:Paeffgen interrogation:15.4.47:6; *NCA*, B:1625.
6 former Abwehr agents: Farago, 645-57, for example: Trefousse, 98; ML-180:passim (reports of A-3778).
6 South America: NA:RG238:Paeffgen interrogation:15.4.47:6.
6 1942 failure: Trefousse, 93-94; Farago, 433; Buchheit, 181-86; Eugene Rachlis, *They Came to Kill* (New York: Random House, 1961), passim.
7 difficulty in obtaining recruits: NA:RG238:Paeffgen interrogation:15.4.47:5-6.
7 New York City water supply: ML-155:7. Januar 1942, 14. Februar 1942: Anlage 1.
7 helium plant: ML-155:29. Juli 1941.
7 Colepaugh personality: *N.Y. Daily Mirror* (3 January 1945); *N.Y. Herald Tribune* (2 January 1945); Francis Biddle, *In Brief Authority* (Garden City: Doubleday, 1962), 342-43.
7 Scholz: *New York Times* (7 June 1941), 4:5.
9 Skorzeny: Skorzeny, 27, 31. 96-97; IMT, 38:83.
9 Gimpel in 1935: Gimpel, 11-15.
10 250,000 Swiss francs, klystron tubes: Ibid., 41, 43.
10 one of Schellenberg's chief concerns: *NCA*, B:1624.
10 Berkaerstrasse: Standortverzeichnis der Dienststellen des Reichssicherheitshauptamtes (7.12. 1943), in BDC:Helmut Möller; Höttl, 1; Gimpel, statement, 20; personal visit, 1 July 1970.
10 Paeffgen's office: My assumption, the name being deleted by the F.B.I. in the Gimpel statement.
11 spy school: L. de Jong, *Het Koninkrijk der Nederlanden in de Tweede Wereldoorlog*. Rijksinstituut voor Oorlogsdocumentatie (The Hague: Nijhoff, 1969-75), 6:88-9.
12 front for him: *N.Y. Herald Tribune* (14 February 1945).
12 final examination: Gimpel, 33-34. The book's picture of training in Hamburg (pp. 29-31) conflicts with that given in Gimpel and Colepaugh's statements, and I have not used it.
15 average family income: United States, Department of Commerce, Bureau of the Census, *Historical Statistics of the United States* (GPO: 1975), Series G-353.
15 Kaltenbrunner permission: *NCA*, B:1625.
15 Type IXC: H. T. Lenton, *German Submarines* (Garden City: Doubleday, 1965), 2:64, 1:95.
17 Allied forces, Russians crossed, 1,581 tons: Hillgruber and Hümmelchen, 136.
17 Allied bombers: Reuter, 143-44.
18 Hodgkins, Forni: *New York Times* (3 January 1945), 9:2-3; *N.Y. Herald Tribune* (3 January 1945).
18 "What kind of bread": Gimpel, 97.
19 "I can see that": Gimpel (German edition), 107-108.

19 Mrs. Julieta del Busto: *New York Times* (8 February 1945), 34:3.
20 *Cornwallis:* Rohwer, *U-Boote Erfolge,* 187.
20 first in months: Ibid., 186–87.
20 carrying a spy: "German Espionage and Sabotage against the United States"; *NCA,* B:1625; NA:RG238:Paeffgen interrogation: 15.4.47:5–6; FDR Library: OF10b: Box 39: 29 August 1944, 31 August 1944, 21 September 1944.
20 124 East 44th Street: *New York Times* (8 February 1945), 34:1.
21 going to restaurants and shows: Ibid.
21 $100 a day: They had $56,474.61 of the $60,000 left. *New York Times* (2 January 1945), 6:4–5.
21 Gimpel dominated: *New York Times* (9 February 1945), 9:1.
21 seemed in no rush: *N.Y. Herald Tribune* (14 February 1945).
21 doubts grew, wanted Germany to win but not America to lose: My assumptions, based on his actions.
22 "The Trolley Song": No. 1 on "Your Hit Parade" for 23 December 1944.
23 Mulcahy: *New York Times* (9 February 1945), 9:1.
26 $10,574: Ibid.

CHAPTER 2: PROTOZOA, SPEECH, AND HISTORY

27 Metaurus: Livy, trans. Frank Gardner Moore, The Loeb Classical Library (1943), XXVII. xliii.1–8; *Appian's Roman History,* The Loeb Classical Library, VII.52; *Cambridge Ancient History,* 8:91–6; Delbrück, 2:377–78; J. Kromayer and G. Vieth, *Antike Schlachtfelder in Italien und Afrika* (Berlin: Wiedmannsche Buchhandlung, 1903–31), 4:429–33; Edward S. Creasy, *The Fifteen Decisive Battles of the World: from Marathon to Waterloo* (1851), ch. 4.
28 protozoon mechanisms: Julius Adler, "The Sensing of Chemicals by Bacteria," *Scientific American,* 234 (April 1976), 40–47.
28 animal capacity: Wolfgang van Buddenbrock, *The Senses,* trans. Frank Gaynor (Ann Arbor: University of Michigan Press, 1958).
28 often they gathered: But not always. In ancient and medieval times, armies did not invariably send out scouts, and sometimes ran into one another by accident (W. Kendrick Pritchett, *The Greek State at War* [Berkeley: University of California Press, 1971], 1:127; W[illiam]. W. Norman, *Cavalry Reconnaissance* [London: Hugh Rees, 1911], 7).
28 Jibaro: Rafael Karsten, *Blood Revenge, War, and Victory Feasts Among the Jibaro Indians of Eastern Ecuador,* Smithsonian Institution, Bureau of American Ethnology, Bulletin 79 (GPO, 1923), 20.
28 ancient Egyptians: Sir Alan Gardiner, *The Kadesh Inscriptions of Ramesses II* (Oxford: printed for the Griffith Institute at the University Press, 1960), 28–30.
28 Caesar dispatched scouts: Julius Caesar, *The Gallic War,* trans. H. J. Edwards, The Loeb Classical Library (1917, reprinted Cambridge: Harvard University Press, 1966), ii.17.
28 Richard the Lion-Hearted: Henri Delpech, *La Tactique au XIIIème Siècle* (Paris: Alphonse Picard, 1866), 2:226–29.
28 other medieval rulers: J. R. Alban and C. T. Allmand, "Spies and Spying in the Fourteenth Century," in C. T. Allmand, ed., *War, Literature, and Politics in the Late Middle Ages* (Liverpool: Liverpool University Press, 1976), 72–101.
28 Mongols: H. Desmond Martin, *The Rise of Chingis Khan and His Conquest of North China* (Baltimore: Johns Hopkins Press, 1950), 29, 38.
28 codebreakers: Kahn, 109–10.
28 Caesar learned: Caesar viii.7.
28 caravan raided: Delpech, 2:229.
28 Ramses II: Gardiner, 28–30.
30 development of general staffs: Hittle; Irvine, "Origin," 161–79.
30 origin of Prussian general staff: Stoerkel, 1–7; Craig, 31; Ritter, 1:209–10; Jany, 1:152–53, 3:411–13; Goerlitz, 20–21; Wheeler-Bennett, 5.
30 2 percent, 200, 600: Förster et al., 80; Jany, 4:254.
30 staff officers and service: E[mil]. von Conrady, *Leben und Wirken des Generals ... Carl von Grolman ...* (ESM, 1894–6), 2:391; Wilkinson, 132–36.
31 legend of invincibility: Goerlitz, 95. Ropp, 155, 176, for impact.
31 staff work: Wilkinson, 139–40; Baron Colmar von der Goltz, *The Conduct of War,* trans. Joseph T. Dickman (Kansas City, Mo.: Hudson-Kimberly, 1896), ch. 8, 4; Julius A. F. W. Verdy du Vernois, *With the Royal Headquarters in 1870–71,* Wolseley Series, 1 (London: Kegan Paul, Trench, Trubner, 1897), 9–11.
31 "The work of": Conrady, 2:263–64.
31 Berlin staff organization: Stoerkel, chart; Jany, 3:411–13, 4:254–55, 294–96; Osten-Sacken, 1:339, 2:231, 3:147–48, 315–16, 490–94; Irvine, "French and Prussian," 192–93.
31 intelligence in the Great General Staff: Bronsart von Schellendorff, *Dienst,* 34, 40–41, 235; [Germany, Grosser Generalstab], *Geschäftsordnung für den Grossen Generalstab und die Landesaufnahme,* Berlin, 18. Dezember 1913 (ESM, n.d.), 2. No source gives a specific picture of how the information that came into the Great General Staff was used, though Schmidt-Richberg, 35, offers a few generalities. I believe that, in the absence of any agency for the general evaluation of all intelligence, and given the organization by geographic area of the Great General Staff, the situation could have been only as I describe it. The catalogue of the now-destroyed archives of the Great General Staff indicates at least that intelligence flowed in and was recorded there (Prussia, Archivverwaltung, *Uebersicht über die Bestände des Geheimen Staatsarchivs zu Berlin-Dahlem,* 2.Teil, Heinrich Otto Meisner and Georg Winter, eds., Mitteilungen der Preussischen Archivverwaltung, 25 [Leipzig: S. Hirzel, 1935], 105).

31 Troops General Staff: Janson, 3, 6–7, for peace; [Prussia, Kriegsministerium], *Felddienst-Ord-nungen* (1908), § 70, for war. Schmidt-Richberg, 36–7, does not mention intelligence.
31 opposition to technical innovation: Janowitz, *Sociology*, 15, 18, 20–21, 26–28; Hayn, 133; Ritter, 2:101; John Ellis, *The Social History of the Machine Gun* (New York: Pantheon, 1975), passim.
31 France's G-2 section: Hittle.
31 England's Intelligence Division: Jock Haswell, *British Military Intelligence* (London: Weidenfeld & Nicolson, 1973).
31 General Headquarters intelligence sections: Stoerkel, 35, 37–38; Paul Bronsart von Schellendorff, *Geheimes Kriegstagebuch 1870–1871*, ed. Peter Rassow (Bonn: Athenäum, 1954), 11, 36; Verdy du Vernois, 24.
32 information lack: *Denkwürdigkeiten des General-Feldmarschalls Alfred Grafen von Waldersee*, ed. Heinrich Otto Meisner (Stuttgart: Deutsche Verlags-Anstalt, 1922–23), 1:24–25.
32 creation of Nachrichtenbüro: Stoerkel, chart; Stoerkel, 33. Prussia also gave secret police official Wilhelm J. C. E. Stieber some espionage assignments in 1866, 1869, and 1870. These, however, were temporary and quite secondary to his basic jobs, in peace, of discovering and suppressing subversion through the Central-Nachrichtenbüro that he headed (not the same as the general staff agency), and in war, of protecting the king and Bismarck against assassination and their headquarters against espionage through field police (Auerbach, 222, 239–40, 248, 251–53; Bronsart von Schellendorf, *Geheimes Kriegstagebuch*, 73, 100, 309; [Friedrich von Holstein], *The Holstein Papers*, ed. Norman Rich and M. H. Fisher [Cambridge: University Press, 1955], 1:48). There seems no basis for claims that he had 40,000 spies nor for the title "the father of Prussian spies" that writers later gave him (Max J. Herzberg, "Memoirs of the 'Father of Prussian Spies'" *The Bookman*, 48 [February, 1919], 744–51).
32 south German officer: Konrad, 4, 7–8.
32 order of battle: Ibid., 9–10.
32 Schluga: Oesterreichisches Staatsarchiv-Kriegsarchiv:Grundbuchblatt: Infanterieregiment Nr. 27, Effektiv, Heft 9, S. 179; Conduiteliste, Faszikel Nr. 301/I:Infanterieregiment Nr. 27–1862; Wiener General-kommando 1863 Abt. 1 68–2/21.
32 bounced: Stoerkel, chart; Stoerkel, 33, 43, 46, 50; Gempp, I:2:15–16, 21–22.
32 funds: Gempp, I:2:28–29, 35; Nicolai, *German Secret Service*, 28, 103; Robert Nöll von der Nahmer, *Bismarcks Reptilienfonds: Aus den Geheimakten Preussens und des Deutschen Reiches* (Mainz: v. Hase & Koehler, 1968), 81–82.
32 amount greater: Great Britain [F.O.], Miscellaneous, No. 6 (1912), *Annual Expenditure on Secret Service by the Governments of Austria-Hungary, France, Germany, Great Britain, Italy, and Russia, according to their Respective Published Budgets*, Cd. 6144, April 1912 (London: HMSO, n.d.), 3–5.
32 124 officers, post: Gempp, I:2:60.
33 Schluga spying: Meisner, ed., 1:25, 53–54; Konrad, 13–25; Gempp, I:1:1, 3–4, II:2:202, 232, II:8A:81, 125, II:8B:39–40. The sources in Gempp and Konrad that affirm that Schluga gave Germany "the" French deployment plan are probably in error. It is questionable whether any one document listed the deployment for the entire French force, since each corps had its own detailed mobilization order, and France's basic strategical Plan XVII does not give a timetable (France, Ministère de la Guerre, Etat-Major de l'Armée, Section Historique, *Les Armées Françaises dans la Grand Guerre* [Paris: Imprimerie Nationale], 1:1 [1922]:33, 1:1:Annexes [1932]: No. 8).
34 most definite intelligence: [Prussia, Kriegsministerium], *Felddienst-Ordnung* (ESM, 1908), §§ 61, 119, 133, 143. Previous editions: (1887), §§ 13, 51; (1894), §§ 43, 82, for example.
34 cavalry failed: [Germany], Reichsarchiv, *Der Weltkrieg 1914 bis 1918* (ESM, 1925–39), 1:122, 123, 126.
34 intelligence from front troops: My assumption.
34 artillery ranging: Cron, 68–70; Jany (Cron), 5:164–67.
34 air organization: Cron, 89–91, 93.
34 airplane reconnaissance growth: Jany (Cron), 5:193, 206, 209; Baron Elard von Loewenstern, *Die Fliegersichterkundung im Weltkrieg* (Berlin: Bernard & Graefe, 1937). For organization: Cron, 91–92; Jany (Cron), 5:206.
34 vertical photographs: Loewenstern, 202.
34 Connecticut: Werner von Langsdorff, "Luftbildwesen, Funkentelegraphie und Wetterkunde in ihrer Bedeutung für die Luftwaffe," in *Unsere Luftstreitkräfte 1914–18*, 79–90 at 83. I have substituted Connecticut (12,000 square kilometers) for Langsdorff's Saxony (15,000).
34 chief means: Cron, 102.
35 no daylight movements: William Mitchell, *Our Air Force* (New York: Dutton, 1921), 84; Baron von Löwenstern, "Bedeutung der Nachtluftaufklärung in den Kriegsmonaten Mai bis Oktober 1918," *Militär-Wochenblatt*, 123 (19.Mai 1939), 3171–75.
35 Tannenberg: Kahn, 622–27.
35 radio intercept posts: Cron, 111; K. Soloff, "Der Funk-Abhör-Krieg," *Militär-Wochenblatt*, 113 (25.April 1929), cols. 1622–25 at 1623.
35 development of German radio intelligence: assembled from Hermann Stützel, "Geheimschrift und Entzifferung im Ersten Weltkrieg," *Truppenpraxis* (Juli 1969), 541–45, Stützel, letters, 15. and 23. Dezember 1969 and 3. März 1972, and interview; Fritz Nebel, "Aus den ersten Jahren des deutschen Funkaufklärungsdienstes," memorandum of early 1970, and letter, 26 Juni 1970.
35 French solution of German diplomatic code: Maurice Paleologue, *Journal 1913–1914* (Paris: Plon, 1947), 15, 36, 44.
35 German nonsolution of French diplomatic codes: Stützel, interview ("Wir kamen einfach nicht durch").

35   "We were always": General [Max] von Hoffmann, *The War of Lost Opportunities* (London: Kegan Paul, Trench, Trubner & Co., 1924), 132.
35   Arendt and his apparatus: Germany, Der Bundesminister für das Post- und Fernmeldewesen, Bundespostmuseum, letter, 19. Oktober 1971; Otto Arendt, "Entwicklung der ersten Abhörstationen," *F-Flagge* (1936), 52–55; Cron, 112; Jany (Cron), 5:234; Praun, *Soldat*, 18–20, 26.
35   Nicolai: Nicolai, *German Secret Service*, 23, 34–35; Müller, interview, 12. April 1970; Heinz, 4, 11–12; IfZ:ZS 207:2:24–25.
35   150 officers: *Rangliste der mob. IIIb*, 1.3.1917 in Gempp, II:9:Anlage 8, shows about 125 officers. I estimate others in posts not included in this list at 25.
35   IIIb units: Cron, 35; Gempp, II:9:3, 23–5, II:7:64–68, 112–17; Nicolai, *Nachrichtendienst*, 11.
35   War Intelligence Posts: Gempp, II:7:43.
36   Schragmüller: Ibid., II:7:43, II:8A:66; Dr. Elsbeth Schragmüller, "Aus dem deutschen Nachrichtendienst" in Friedrich Felger, *Was wir vom Weltkrieg nicht wissen* (Berlin: Wilhelm Andermann, [1930]), 138–55.
36   agent numbers: Gempp, II:7:12, 89, II:8A:51.
36   Mata Hari: Gempp, II:8B:89–90, 118, Anhang zur Anlage 8; Sam Wagenaar, *Mata Hari* (Paris: Fayard, 1965), 198, 200 for intercepts.
36   Schluga: Konrad, 22–30; Gempp, II:2:202, II:8A:81–82, 86, 110–12, 124, II:8B:36–40; *Der Weltkrieg*, 9:21–23, 24, 32, for Falkenhayn inclination and Allied attack.
37   "no business": Nicolai, *German Secret Service*, 227.
37   seven agents: Gempp, II:9:55–57.
37   as troopships arrived: Nicolai, *German Secret Seervice*, 109; Nicolai, *Nachrichtendienst*, 16.
37   inadequate economic espionage: Nicolai, *Nachrichtendienst*, 12–13, 139; Gempp, II:7:26; Heinz, 12.
37   tank intelligence failure: Nicolai, *Nachrichtendienst*, 16.
37   Admiralty Staff: Hubatsch, *Admiralstab*, 252–54.
38   Braune: Wilhelm Tranow, interview, 1 July 1970, 1–2; Tranow, letter, August 1972; Deutsche Dienststelle (WASt), letter, 15. Juni 1976.
38   Neumünster: Bonatz, 18, 22, 24; Tranow, interview, 1–2; BA-MA:F5708:II.9.1:undated chart "Uebersicht über die Gliederung der Fu.E.-und B.Stellen," and II.9.3.:14525 D II:13.September 1918.
38   Jutland: Bonatz, 51.
38   Brummer: Ibid., 56; Tranow, interview, 3.
38   32,000 reports: Gempp. II:9:86.
38   800 Arendt reports: Ibid., II:7:67.
38   Ic, Id, M.S.O., Ib, Ic: Cron, 28, 31, 37, 41; BH–KA:Geschäftsordnungen of: HGr Rupprecht: 26.9.1918; AOK 4:Bd. 39/1; AOK Süd:Bd. 131/1; Generalkommando I. AK:22.9.1917; Generalkommando II. AK:27.3.1918; 1. Bayerische Infanterie Division:28.4.1918; 3. Infanterie Division:10.2.1918.
38   roman numeral and small letters: This system was first used by Blücher in 1813 (Erfurth, 127).
38   Intelligence Branch, Foreign Armies Branch: Cron, 9, 14; Jany (Cron), 5:10.
38   "An experienced": Erich Ludendorff, *Meine Kriegserinnerungen 1914–1918* (ESM, 1919), 14.
38   staff increase: Gempp, II:9:85–86.
38   Foreign Armies reports: BH–KA:M Kr 1777.
38   foresaw Somme offensive: *Der Weltkrieg*, 10:272–73, 341–44.
39   "in full accord": Ibid., 349.
39   stronger by a fifth: von Rauch, "Zur Feindlage auf dem Weltkriegsschauplatz im Sommer 1918," *Militär-Wochenblatt*, 103 (7. Juni 1919), 2677–80 at 2678; Nicolai, *German Secret Service*, 227.
39   secondary duties: Stoerkel, 33, 37–38; Bronsart von Schellendorff, *Geheimes Kriegstagebuch*, 47, 50, 105.
39   balloonists, photography, spymasters: Germany (Federal Republic, 1949–   ), Militärgeschichtliches Forschungsamt, *Die Militärluftfahrt bis zum Beginn des Weltkrieges 1914*, 2d ed. (ESM, 1965–66), 1:1; [Martin] Kiesling, *Die Anwendung der Photographie zu militärischen Zwecken*, Encyklopädie der Photographie, 19 (Halle: Knapp, 1896), 24–28; Stoerkel, 37–38.
40   "an act of force," "physical force," exert most influence, "among the most important": Clausewitz, bk. I, ch. 1, §2, §3; bk. III, ch. iii.
40   relieves a commander of anxiety: cf. Vernon and Bigelow.
41   set up a permanent unit: Stoerkel, "Stellvertretenden," 101.

CHAPTER 3: THE INSTITUTIONS OF CONTROL

42   high command building: visit, 28 June 1970.
42   Treaty of Versailles: published as the law of the land in *Reichsgesetzblatt* (1919), 687–1349.
43   Weimar President: Ibid., (1919), 1392.
43   Defense Minister: Ibid., 1475–76, (1921), 330.
43   Hitler merges offices: Ibid., (1934), 747.
43   4 February 1938: Ibid., (1938), 111. Though this decree refers only to peacetime, Hitler had ordered in an unpublished law of 21 May 1935 (IMT, 30:60–62) that he should take full command if war threatened.
43   War Minister: *Heeresverordnungsblatt* (1935), 83.
43   Keitel: Warlimont, 13, 45, 57, 221; Speer, 239, 243–44, 389; Wheeler-Bennett, 429–30; Davidson, 329, 332, 335, 340; Keitel, passim.

46 OKW Operations Staff: see Schramm in OKW, *KTB*, 4:1746–49 and 1758–59, and Jacobsen in ibid., 1:123E-9E.
46 Jodl: Warlimont, 9, 14, 45, 46, 47, 90, 221; Speer, 239, 242, 244; Wheeler-Bennett, 430; Bullock, 767–68; Davidson, 343–44, 347, 363, 428; Förster et al., 262–63; Hans-Adolf Jacobsen in OKW, *KTB*, 1:189E; Schramm in ibid., 4:1712–14. For his writing as well as his view of Hitler, see his eloquent defense of Hitler written at Nuremberg in ibid., 4:1714–21.
46 no OKW command functions: Warlimont, 11; Davidson, 329; Schramm in OKW, *KTB*, 4:1745; Keitel, 148.
46 no OKW planning: Warlimont, 51; Halder, 1:30.
46 only Hitler, through Keitel: Warlimont, 11; *Hitlers Weisungen für die Kriegführung*, passim.
46 service commanders' independence: Warlimont, 8.
46 commanders do not meet: Ibid., 118.
46 megaphone, small size, current projects: Ibid., 49, 46, 53; OKW, *KTB*, 4:1749.
46 eastern and other theaters: Warlimont, 73, 142, 218; Siegler, 10; Bullock, 665; Speer, 242; Jacobsen in OKW, *KTB*, 1:136E, 170E.
47 OKW: for organization in general, see OKW, *KTB*, 1:113E/114E, 877–946.
47 military espionage: Ibid., 1:886–87.
47 Foreign Information Division: Ibid., 886; OKW:Wi VII/25:1.10.42.
47 Cipher Branch: OKW, *KTB*, 1:883; Kahn, 456–57.
47 censorship: OKW, *KTB*, 1:888.
47 foreign economic intelligence: Ibid., 894.
47 Operations Staff intelligence: NA:RG238:Krummacher interrogation: 28. Januar 1947. Though Warlimont, in *TWC*, 10:287, 288, and Schramm in OKW, *KTB*, 4:1759, give the fall of 1942 as the starting date for this unit, Krummacher, who held the post, says he started in January 1943.
50 armed services under Hitler: implied in the decree of 4 February 1938.
50 compulsory universal service, army enlargement: *Reichsgesetzblatt* (1935), 375.
50 Luftwaffe established: Völker, *Dokumente*, 134–35; *Reichsgesetzblatt* (1935), 609.
50 uniform titles: *Heeresverordnungsblatt* (1935), 83.
50 Hitler assumes army command: PG 32601:239 (English translation); Halder, 3:354; Mueller-Hillebrand, 3:37, 207; Domarus, 1813–14; RMfBuM, *Rüstung*, 127–30. For the awful significance of this Nazi conquest of that which regarded itself as the embodiment of the German nation, see Warlimont, 213; Bullock, 309, 419, 667–68; Wheeler-Bennett, 373, 525; and especially Craig, 495–96, 501–503.
50 subordinates of the head of the army: *Handbuch für das deutsche Reich* (1936), 135–36; Mueller-Hillebrand, 1:116, 172–78; Halder, 1:378 and 3:540.
50 1 February 1919: Stoerkel, "Stellvertretenden," 101.
50 "shall be dissolved": Article 160.
51 reformed it as Troops Department: Stoerkel, "Stellvertretenden," 121. The order dissolving old offices and creating new does not, significantly, mention the Great General Staff (*Heeresverordnungsblatt* [1919], 107–108).
51 "The form changes": Seeckt. Cited in Forster et al., 199.
51 1 July 1935: *Allgemeine Heeresmitteilungen* (1935), 107.
51 Halder: Warlimont, 90, 221, 260; Wheeler-Bennett, 428, 525, 531, 544; Speer, 240; Goerlitz, 331; Manstein, 76; Liddell Hart, 55, 57.
51 Zeitzler: Warlimont, 59, 259, 260; Speer, 240, 421; Bullock, 686; Liddell Hart, 57–59; Goerlitz, 419; Keitel, 184; *Hitlers Tischgespräche*, 405, for "like a hornet."
51 Guderian: Warlimont, 59, 223, 465, 572; Liddell Hart, 60–61, 63; Speer, 421; Goerlitz, 475–76.
52 General Staff sections: Mueller-Hillebrand, 1:116, 172, 177; *Allgemeine Heeresmitteilungen* (1938), 258; Keilig, §55:2; Halder, 1:376, 378.
52 10 November 1938: *Allgemeine Heeresmitteilungen* (1938), 258. This order simply sets forth the organization of the general staff and includes both the intelligence branches and the O Qu IV. But no other orders exist for the separate creation of either the O Qu IV or the 12th branch, and as late as 19 August 1938 no 12th branch existed (OKH:H1/321:20) and as late as 14 April 1938 no O Qu IV (OKH:H1/321:31). Moreover, though Liss, "Erfahrungen und Gedanken," 618, Keilig, §52:IV:1, and P-041i, 3, do not spell out this simultaneous creation of the 12th branch and the O Qu IV, they are fully consistent with it. I therefore assume that they were created together.
52 "People who wear": Liss, *Westfront*, 17.
52 "What I want"; Liss, "Erfahrungen und Gedanken," 618, who says the superior was Fritsch; P-041i, 1, which says the superior was Beck.
52 variety of reasons: Matzky, interviews; Warlimont, 262, 280.
52 9 November 1942: P-041i, 46.
52 other intelligence units: See chapters dealing with them.
53 field general staff organization: H.Dv.g. 92. The prefaces to the National Archives' *Guides to German Records Microfilmed at Alexandria, Va.* dealing with army units give a clear list of the staff offices at various command levels.
53 5th Branch: USAF-173, 72.
53 Air Force Operations Staff: Rieckhoff, Tafel IVb.
53 Operations Staff/I c: Such is the heading on many 1944 documents in RL 2/647.
53 regulations assigned: Völker, *Dokumente*, 163.
53 photo center: NA:RG165:APWIU (9th Air Force):90/1945:7–9; Schreyer, 73–75.
53 Dulag Luft: *War Crimes Trials*, 9:81.
53 other intelligence sections: See chapters dealing with them.
53 long- and short-range squadrons: H.Dv.g.89, §36; H.Dv.300, §§128–30, 144, 150.

53 air force staffs with fighting forces: Völker, *Deutsche Luftwaffe*, 245; USAF-173, 103, 105, 107, 116, 118, Fig. 6; USAF-171, 52; Rieckhoff, 73–74.
54 Skl sections: Lohmann, §32:2–3, 10–11.
54 Foreign Office: *ADAP*, 1:565–75; See also Kahn, 436, for Pers Z.
55 Ribbentrop: Bullock introduction to Ribbentrop; Sumner Welles, *The Time for Decision* (New York: Harper & Brothers, 1944), 91.
55 Inf III: see chapter on Foreign Office.
55 Sonderdienst Seehaus: see chapter on press.
55 press services: Oron Hale, *The Captive Press in the Third Reich* (Princeton: Princeton University Press, 1964), 137–38.
55 Economics Ministry, Reich Statistical Department: *Handbuch für das deutsche Reich* (1936), 157, 162; RWM/20/106:10.Oktober 1944.
55 Forschungsamt links: NA:RG238:Schapper interrogation:15.Januar 1948:6–7. Its officials are not listed in [Prussia], *Handbuch über den Preussischen Staat* (Berlin: R.V. Deckers Verlag), 139 (1935) and 140 (1938).
56 SS origin and duty: Aronson, 48, 264–65; [NSDAP], *Organisationsbuch der NSDAP* (1937), 417, (1943), 417.
56 tightened surveillance: Aronson, 39–40.
56 looking for a job, letter: Ibid., 37.
56 14 June 1931: Höhne, *order*, 169.
56 "I need": Aronson, 37–38.
56 inauspicious beginnings, first important victory: Ibid., 55–56.
57 SA, other intelligence units: Ibid., 40–47; Broszat, 60.
57 19 July 1932: Aronson, 60.
57 Türkenstrasse 23, Zuccalistrasse 4: Ibid., 56, 62.
57 700,690, 710,000: Ibid., 198.
57 350,000: Ibid., 198.
57 police president of Munich: Broszat, 137, 139.
57 political police: Buchheim, 147–52.
57 party merging with state: Bracher, 231–33, 235–36, 348: Buchheim, 127–40.
58 "Führer," "the bearer of": *Reichsgesetzblatt* (1934), 751, (1933), 1016.
58 ideological dangers, individual cases: Boberach, ed., xii.
58 expanded his net, four levels: Höhne, *Order*, 216–18; Aronson, 135, 152, 155; IMT, 38:107; TWC:Case 9:Transcript:2144 (Sandberger).
58 Himmler elevated: Aronson, 140.
58 Hitler ordained: Ibid., 167–68; BA:NS6/215.
58 rival intelligence service: Aronson, 41–42, 140; Jacobsen, 58, 65, 634. It was headed by Arthur Schumann, Party No. 15,292 (BDC). On the Rosenberg department, see also IMT, 25:23–24, 30:164–67, and Seabury, 33–37.
59 German Labor Front: Aronson, 301.
59 "apart from the": BA:NS6/217. Reaffirmed 1938 (IMT, 32:250–51).
59 "the single political": T-580:93:7.Dezember 1934.
59 "did not appear": TWC:Case 9:Transcript:1136 (Jost).
59 28 July: BDC:Heinz Jost:28.Juli 1934.
59 "the SD participates": T-580:93:7.Dezember 1934.
59 SD headquarters to Berlin: Aronson, 201.
59 some time before 1936: An order of 2 January 1936 refers to Jost as "Chief des Abwehramtes im Sicherheitsamt" (BA:R58/239). I am grateful to Dr. George Browder for this information.
59 Branches I and II: Aronson, 202–203.
59 17 June1936: *Reichsgesetzblatt* (1936), 487–88.
59 uniformed and plain-clothes police: *Reichsministerialblatt für innere Verwaltung* (1936), 946–48.
60 signed agreements with Canaris: Berlin: Geheimes Staatsarchiv: Rep. 90:Abt.P/Nr. 1: Heft 2:313–16, 309–12; IfZ:ZS 207:3:19a–19c.
60 "the political information unit": [NSDAP], *Organisationsbuch der NSDAP*, (1937), 442.
60 rationalism melted: Gerth, 539.
60 "active in government": *Reichsministerialblatt für innere Verwaltung* (1938), 1906. The 1933 date given in Buchheim, 171, is a misprint.
60 concluded police accords: T-120:1320:D499946–49.
60 exemption: referred to in NG-4581:3. I have not been able to find the original.
60 "for the duration": *DGFP*, 7:546.
60 27 September 1939: IMT, 38:102–10; Bracher, 352–54; Höhne, 254–56. I believe that the testimony of Rolf H. Hoeppner in IMT, 20:185–210, on the organization of the SD deliberately obfuscates, and have not used it.
60 Branch III to Department VI: BA:EAP 173-b-12-05/45:27 September 1939.
60 12 administrations: [NSDAP], *Organisationsbuch der NSDAP* (1943), 423/424; Höhne, chart opp. p. xii.
60 party and government units, paychecks: NA:RG238:Hoettl interrogation: 2 October 1945: 15–16. Buchheim, 166; Aronson, 153–54, 198; Orb, 87–90.
60 field units: Buchheim, 180; Höhne, 228; NA:RG238:Hoettl interrogation: 19 October 1945; NG-2316; NG-4588.
60 Heydrich: Schellenberg, 11–14; Aronson, 11–38 and passim; Abshagen, 77, 147–48: TWC:Case 11:Testimony:12977(Paeffgen); Speer, 373; Höhne, 171–72, 493–95; *Hitlers Tischgespräche*, 386–87; Reitlinger, 31–36, 213–18; Wighton.
61 Canaris, Heydrich houses: Meurer, interview; personal visit, 30 August 1973. Betazeile is now Waldsängerpfad.

61   1 March 1942: NOKW-3228.
61   Rumania: *DGFP*, 11:1194, 12:12–13, 230, 443–44, 13:171–76, 230.
61   Iran: Schellenberg.
61   proposed, counterproposed: NG-4581:2, 3, 4, 6.
61   8 August 1941: NG-4588. Modified slightly in favor of the SD in NG-4582:344614–16.
61   "irreplaceable": *Hitlers Tischgespräche*, 387.
62   Kaltenbrunner: Schellenberg, 331–34; Aronson, 200, 302; Speer, 391; Davidson, 315–18; Reitlinger, 236–38; NA:RG238:Schellenberg interrogations:12 November 1945:2–8, 7 March 1941, 21–22; G. M. Gilbert, *Nuremberg Diary* (New York: Farrar, Straus, 1947), 31.
62   73 in 19 missions: NG-4582:344632–39.
62   got more, Vatican: Ibid.:344679, 344677.
62   Argentina: United States, State Department, *Consultation among the American Republics with Respect to the Argentine Situation*, Inter-American Series, 29 (GPO, 1946), 6–15.
62   1944 agreement: IMT, 39:575–77.
62   12 February 1944: OKH:H3/1539:12.Februar 1944.
62   1 June 1944: Ibid.:23.Mai 1944.
62   Auslandsorganisation: [NSDAP], *Organisationsbuch der NSDAP* (1937), 143–44, (1943), 143–45; NA:RG59:Poole mission:Bohle interrogation:5–8 September 1945:8; Jacobsen, 90–160.
63   Nazi party press chief: [NSDAP], *Organisationsbuch der NSDAP* (1943), 304; NA:RG165: Schuster Commission:Hoffman interrogation:1–2.
63   cartels, research institutes: see chapter on them.

CHAPTER 4: CYLINDERS

67   room, man: Schulze-Holthus, 13.
67   Abwehr assignment: *DGFP*, 12:498.
67   German population: George Lenczowski, *Russia and the West in Iran 1918–1948: A Study in Big-Power Rivalry* (Ithaca: Cornell University Press, 1949), 164; *FRUS, 1941*, 3:402–403, 405, 415.
67   diplomat to report: Oppenheim, 1:786.
67   Ettel: BDC; George Kirk, *The Middle East in the War*, 2d. ed. Survey of International Affairs (Oxford: University Press, 1953), 131; Hirszowicz, 264. Party No. 952,856.
68   Ettel report to Hitler: *DGFP*, 13:77–78. On Farouk's attitude: Barrie St. Clair McBride, *Farouk of Egypt: A Biography* (London: Robert Hale, 1967), 108–10, 113.
68   defend itself: *DGFP*, 13:103–104.
68   "recommended the removal": Ibid., 272.
68   hour-long conversation: Ibid., 335–38.
68   urges shah: Ibid., 358–59.
68   troops enter: Churchill, 3:481–82.
69   Wilhelmstrasse 76: Seabury, 2, 3.
69   "Collaborate . . . in the": *DGFP*, 2:444–47 at 446.
69   consuls: AA:Pol I M: 28:270597–632; IMT, 34:115–16; *FRUS, 1941*, 2:629; *DGFP*, 12:1034–36; NA:RG238:Gyssling interrogation:8.Mai 1947:3–5. United States, Senate, Committee on Military Affairs, Subcommittee on War Mobilization, *Nazi Party Membership Records*, 79th Congress: 2d Session, December, 1946, Part 4 (GPO:1947), for first names and Nazi party membership numbers of Krause-Wichmann (1,547,946), Kapp (7,054,882), and Gyssling (650,070); letter, Auswärtiges Amt, 31.Juli 1975, for Windels and Lurtz (party no. 7,028,232).
69   FDR would run: AA:Büro des Staatssekretärs: Spanien:1.April 1943–31.Mai 1943:63837–38.
69   destroyer deal chances "slight": *DGFP*, 10:456.
70   "a very bad impression": AA:Büro des Staatssekretärs: Spanien:1.Juni 1943–31.Aug. 1943: 63956–57.
70   Yugoslav surprise: *DGFP*, 12:668. Also lack of warnings in ibid., in Halder, 2:330, and in OKW, *KTB*,1:368.
70   costs war: *Testament of Adolf Hitler*, 72, 74, 97.
70   fulminates: Shirer, 824; NA:RG 59:Poole mission:Hencke interrogation:fair copy:2.
70   lost bid: NG-4581:6.
70   underling informant: *DGFP*, 11:980–81; NA:RG 238:USFET:MISC:OI:IIR;6:2. On the underling, Rudolf Likus: Jacobsen, *Aussenpolitik*, 277, 293, 300, 307, 701; *DGFP*, 12:1088, 1102. Samples of his reports from his informants in AA:Dienststelle Ribbentrop: Vertrauliche Berichte:2b/1, Ibid.:2a/2:Teil 1, Ibid.:Teil 2.
70   double agent: *DGFP*, 12:1049.
70   Hitler criticisms: Craig, "The German Foreign Office," 425–26; *Hitler's Table Talk*, 101; NA:RG 59:Poole mission: Hencke interrogation:fair copy:2; Engel, 101.
70   Louis XV: [Albert], Duc de Broglie, *The King's Secret* (London: Cassell, Petter & Galpin, 1879), 1:iii, 15–16.
70   might impress Hitler: NCA,B:1195 (Ribbentrop); IfZ:ZS 1077:17; NA:RG 238:Steengracht interrogation:18.März 1947:10–11.
70   seducing the daughters: *Hitler's Table Talk*, 102, 539.
70   "immediately to organize": *DGFP*, 12:497–99.
71   Hencke: BDC; IfZ:ZS 1077:1, 4: *DGFP*, 12:1101; Hilberg, 357, 392, 447. Party No. 3,465,491.
71   Inf III, I–XV: IfZ:ZS 1077:17–18; AA:Geschäftsübersicht des Auswärtigen Amtes:1.April 1944:170667.
71   posts set up, personnel, informants: NA:RG 59:Poole mission:Hencke interrogation:fair copy:3; IfZ:ZS 1077:18.
71   "active espionage": NA:RG 59:Poole mission:Hencke interrogation:fair copy:30.

71 Inf III operations: NA:RG 59:Poole mission:Hencke interrogation:fair copy:2–3; ibid.:3 Nov 45:5; IfZ:ZS 1077:18–19; IfZ:ZS 291:36–37; Schellenberg, *Memoirs*, 280–81; IMT, 10:421 (Ribbentrop); *NCA*, B:1195 (Ribbentrop).
71 reports to Hitler: T-120:1073:431710.
71 1 December 1941: T-120:1073:431858.
71 "Italophiles": Ladislas Hory and Martin Broszat, *Der kroatische Ustascha-Staat 1941–1945*, Schriftenreihe der Vierteljahrshefte für Zeitgeschichte, 5 (Stuttgart:. Deutsche Verlags-Anstalt, 1964), 73.
71 not critical: T-120:80:61865–66.
71 "has caused surprise": AA:Büro des Staatssekretärs:Turkei:4:173223.
71 Ettel, Marschall: IfZ:ZS 291:37; IfZ:ZS 1077:19. Marschall party number:2,233,897(BDC). *Gothaisches Genealogisches Taschenbuch der Freiherrlichen Häuser*, Teil A, 90 (1940), 393–94.
72 couriers, end: NA:RG 59:Poole mission:Hencke interrogation:fair copy:3; Ibid.: 3 Nov 45:5.
72 "attained no great": IfZ:ZS 1077:19.
72 hundreds of pages: TWC:Case 11:Transcript:10105.
72 a third, a few dozen: Ibid.:17553.
72 average of four: analysis of liaison man's submissions for September 1941 in T-120:1073: 431776–99. On Hitler's sources in general for diplomatic information: Jacobsen, 347–52.
72 Ribbentrop's chief duty: Craig, "The German Foreign Office," 435.
72 unpalatable truths: Kent, "Britain," 129.

CHAPTER 5: THE MILITARY ATTACHÉ

73 Versailles: Article 179.
73 establishment of attachés: Kehrig, 74, 153–54.
73 attaché posts: Ibid., 202.
73 air matters by army: NA:RG 59:Poole mission:Boetticher interview:6; Geyr, 43; Vagts, *Attaché*, 59. For later air attachés: Völker, *Die deutsche Luftwaffe*, 265, 228, 260; USAF-171, 25–7; Kehrig, 217.
73 Wehrmacht attachés: P-041j, 45–46; P-097, Appendix 1, 5.
73 number of attachés: Kehrig, 217–18.
73 attachés not trained: P-097, 2–5.
73 selection haphazard: P-097a, 4; Vagts, *Attaché*, 57–60.
73 selection process: P-097a, 1–4; P-097, Appendix 1, 3, 4.
74 Köstring: Teske, ed., 327–28; Strik-Strikfeldt, 181–83; Liss, "Entscheidende Wert," 589, for "far the most knowledgeable."
74 Rohde: Books listed in main catalog of New York Public Library.
74 most attachés from general staff: P-097, 10.
74 Rintelen: Rintelen, 13; P-097, Appendix, 1, 2–3.
74 Ott: Wheeler-Bennett, 299; Dirksen, 153–54; *DGFP*, 1:851.
74 Faber du Faur: Faber du Faur, 127.
74 chiefs of Foreign Armies: Kehrig, 203; [Germany], Reichswehrministerium, Heeres-Personalamt, *Rangliste*, 1923, 1924, 1929, 1931; Carsten, 75, 138, 284, 360 for Fischer.
74 Boetticher visit: NA:RG238:Boetticher interrogation:3.
74 Geyr: Geyr, interview; Vagts, *Attaché*, 59.
74 job a plum: Geyr, 15, and Geyr, "Militär-Attachés," 698.
74 "A military attaché": Geyr, 10.
74 "I had only": Faber du Faur: 214–15.
74 allowances and assistants: P-097a, 7; P-097, 9; Rintelen, 14.
75 three to four years: P-097a, 14; P-097, Appendix 1, 5.
75 ambassador co-signs or dissents: P-041j, 5; P-097, Appendix 1, 8; P-097a, 13; B-484, 4; NA: RG238: Boetticher interrogation:6; Geyr, "Militär-Attachés," 702.
75 reports through Foreign Office: P-041j, 5, 26; B-484, 4. Copies were often retained there, as the files of the Foreign Office show.
75 cipher machines: B-484, 4; P-041j, 25; NA:RG59:Poole mission:Niebuhr interview, 7: Farago, 475–76.
75 personal letters: *German Naval Intelligence*, 18; many examples in Teske, ed.
75 Berlin meeting: P-041j, 10–11; P-097a, 9–10. These were discontinued during the war (P-041i, 39).
75 "The military attachés": Faber du Faur, 196.
75 attaché unit duties: P-041j, 1–7, 21. The army's Attachégruppe was subordinated successively to Foreign Armies (OKH:H27/14:10.November 1937), to the Oberquartiermeister IV (P-041i, 4, 29), to the Chief of the General Staff in November 1942 (P-041i, 52; P-041j, 32), and on 23 July 1944 to the Ausland Division in the OKW (OKH:H27/7:23.7.44). For its internal organization, see Kehrig, 233–36, and OKH:H27/57:Februar 1943. The navy's Attachégruppe was subordinated from 1935 to 1945 to the chief of staff of the Seekriegsleitung under his various titles (Kehrig, 239; *German Naval Intelligence*, 8, 17–18). The Luftwaffe Attachégruppe was attached on 1 February 1939 to the 5th Branch (intelligence) of the Luftwaffe general staff (USAF-171, 25–26). For personnel: Völker, *Die deutsche Luftwaffe*, 325; for internal organization: Kehrig, 238.
75 attaché sources: P-041j, 4–5, 6–7; P-097a, 7–8, 10–12; Rintelen, 14; Faber du Faur, 222.
75 amount depends on German information: P-041j, 7–8.
75 Boetticher seeks permission: OKW, *KTB*, 1:70, 106.
75 how much Germany, questions sent: P-097a, 7–8.

76 attachés demand information: Halder, 3:185, 206; OKW, *KTB,* 1:39, 95, 109, 182, 244, 366; *DGFP,* 13:158–59; *FRUS, 1941,* 2:728.
76 Baumbach: Baumbach, interview, 8–11; Salewski, 1:375 for travel, 19, 157, 359–60 for sample reports.
76 courier observations: *DGFP,* 1:915.
76 "it was so easy": NA:RG238:Boetticher interrogation:17.
76 major countries: England, the United States (see citations below), Italy (Rintelen, 14), the Soviet Union (Baumbach, interview, 9–10).
76 "Get those ideas": Geyr, 20.
76 Boetticher opposes Abwehr: B-484, 37; NA:RG238:Boetticher interrogation:14–15; *DGFP,* 9:425–26; Farago, 479.
76 "spotless," "somewhat stained": NA:RG59:Poole mission:Lahousen interview:3. Canaris told the Foreign Office that "service attachés and their helpers and assistant officers may not handle Abwehr questions, unless the officers in question have, in agreement with the Foreign Office, received special assignments of this kind" (AA:Pol I M:13:29.Januar 1943).
76 attaché in Spain: Abshagen, 42.
76 attaché in Belgrade: NA:RG59:Poole mission:Lahousen interview:3.
76 naval attaché in Turkey: Ibid.:Niebuhr interview:15.
76 Niedenfuhr: NA:RG59:DSDF:826.20210/1996:11.
76 scouts landing places: NA:RG59:DSDF 800.20235/421:10.
76 Niebuhr: Ibid.:18, 50, 56, 80; Reile, *Westfront,* 327–28; Party No. 2,640,302(BDC).
76 pressures mount: OKW:H2/120:29.
76 13 attaché assistants: AA:Pol I M:13:1:23.Januar 1943:3–4.
76 attachés fight: OKH:H2/120:[61].
77 attaché in France: OKH:H27/10:17.12.1935.
77 airplane cannon, parachute bombs: OKH:H1/530:2.11.1936.
77 Geyr assistant's talk: Ibid.:26.11.1936.
77 Boetticher on Goddard: Ibid.:7.Januar 1936.
77 Guderian request; Geyr reply: Ibid.:9.9.1936.
77 Geyr profiles Dill: OKH:H27/10:8.August 1935.
77 most valuable source: Kehrig, 41; P-041i, 10, says they provided the most authoritative information on future high foreign commanders.
77 air attaché lectures: IMT, 9:178.
77 Boetticher's OKW reports: NA:RG238:Boetticher interrogation:5; OKW, *KTB,* 2:1061; 3:748, 1032, 1378.
79 Geyr: Though in my interview I asked him three times whether his attaché experience had helped him in fighting the British in Normandy, he never answered the question.
79 6 April: *Hitlers Lagebesprechungen,* 553. This is the only mention of an attaché report in these situation conference transcripts.
79 Bern attaché: OKH:H27/6:22.August 1944.
79 diary entries: OKH:H27/6:22.August 1944.
80 Marin de Bernardo: OKH:H27/6:7.7.1944.
80 invasion and Mediterranean figures: NA:RG165:OPD 320.2 TS (31 August 1945): Deployment of Allied Divisions: 30 June 1944.
80 Hitler read Boetticher reports: NA:RG59:Poole mission:Tannenberg interview:5; Compton, 123.
80 Boetticher biography: *Gothaisches Genealogisches Taschenbuch der Adeligen Häuser,* Teil B, 31(1939), 62; Wedemeyer and Wheeler-Bennett, interviews; NA:RG238:Boetticher interrogation: 1–4, 6, 14; NA:RG59:Poole mission:Boetticher interview:3; works listed in the New York Public Library card catalogue. Families unrelated: comparison with *Gothaisches Genealogisches Taschenbuch der Briefadeligen Häuser,* 2(1908), 92–3.
81 sources: NA:RG238:Boetticher interrogation:6; B-484, 6 and 7; Weinberg, "Hitler's Image of America," 1012; Farago, 477–80; *DGFP,* 9:329.
81 extends coverage: B-484, 48.
81 reports every 3–4 days: examination of OKW:698.
81 reports: Ibid.:15.10.1939 for ship movements, 29.7.39 for propaganda, 13.5.40 for Australian, 2.1.41 for Dowding, 4.1.41 for exports.
81 "On July 1": *DGFP,* 13:125. Curiously, the O Qu IV gave the chief of the General Staff slightly different figures (Halder, 3:57).
81 Hitler's admiration: *Hitlers Tischgespräche,* 352–53.
81 telegram: *DGFP,* 9:232.
81 attaché views coincided: This is also the view of Weinberg, "Hitler's Image of America," 1012, Hillgruber, 175, 375, and Compton, 122.
81 Hitler believes Jews run America: *Hitlers Tischgespräche,* 337.
81 "fatal control": *DGFP,* 10:255. Boetticher's reports contain innumerable repetitions of his views. I have given only a few representative quotations on this topic and on the others mentioned in this chapter.
81 The Jewish element": Ibid., 413.
82 "exponent of Jews": Ibid., 254.
82 "operated within": Ibid., 12:268.
82 "The inheritance of England," "after the war": Ibid., 12:269, 13:904.
82 "large-scale imperialist," "take possession of": Ibid., 11:177, 13:904. These views also convinced the O Qu IV and perhaps the Chief of the General Staff as well (Halder, 2:188).
82 "People are already": *DGFP,* 9:426.
82 "London's heart," made life difficult: OKW, *KTB,* 1:69, 125.
82 Malta attack, Hitler request: Ibid., 1:277, 278.

82   no immediate large deliveries, "greatly overrated": *DGFP*, 12:162, 333.
82   England would fall: Ibid., 10:82, 12:333.
82   unlike 1917: Ibid., 12:266.
82   did not endanger: summarized in ibid., 13:217.
82   "The Pacific Ocean," "The first aim," "American war policy," "Now as before": *DGFP*, 8:179, 9:177, 13:97; T-120:1055:422292.
83   destroyer deal: Compton, 109.
83   "trick," "empty gesture": Ibid., 114.
83   no immediate deliveries: *DGFP*, 12:162, 365.
83   "the greatest admission": Compton, 117.
83   shifted primary effort: Louis Morton, "Germany First," in Greenfield, ed., 28, 39–40.
83   *Times-Herald* publication: Burton K. Wheeler with Paul F. Healy, *Yankee from the West* (Garden City: Doubleday & Co. 1962), 32–34.
83   " 'the first major . . . ' ": I have had to take these quotes from the same story as it appears in the *Times-Herald*'s sister publication, the *Chicago Tribune* (4 December 1941), 1:1–8, 10:3–8, 11:1–6 at 11:1, since I can find no copy of the *Times-Herald* for that date. The first few paragraphs of the *Times-Herald* story (Wheeler, 33–34) are virtually identical to the *Tribune*'s, and in any event the chargé also cites the *Tribune*. Hitler mentioned the plan's publication in his speech declaring war on the United States (Domarus, ed., 1809).
83   "Military measures, America will": *DGFP*, 13:950–51.
83   "watchful and defensive, confirmed our": AA:Büro des Staatssekretärs:Akten betreffend U.S.A.: 10:44725–27. Six months later, he still had not recognized the situation (IWM:Milch:14:856). The admirals held the same view (*Lagevorträge*, 325).
83   20,000, 5,000: OKW:W 01-6/580:13.7.40.
83   warned against underestimating: *DGFP*, 13:126.
83   "high requirements": Ibid., 13:126.
83   "excellent" equipment, high morale: Ibid., 11:78.
83   overcoming bottlenecks: Ibid., 12:267.
83   Germany would have won before: NA:RG59:Poole mission:Dieckhoff interviews:6; Thomas, 278 hold this view also.
84   pushing his dates back: in addition to the key examples below, see also *DGFP*, 11:210, 816.
84   bore no relation: comparison with Watson, 171–72, 175, 177, 184, 188, 333, 337, 340, 343–44. The vagueness of Boetticher's terms—what is an "aggressive war policy" or "an adequate army"?—made it difficult to pin him down to exact timetables, because he could always say that the army was not yet "adequate" or the war policy not really "aggressive." The terms used by the American planners were much more concrete, specifying, for example, exact numbers for an expeditionary force to Brazil.
84   "No land and air": *DGFP*, 8:471.
84   "Before the middle": Ibid., 11:210.
84   "in the course": Ibid., 13:97.
84   "America, however": Ibid., 11:387, repeated 1147.
84   freed of fears: Weinberg, "Hitler's Image of America," 1012; Hillgruber, 196, 374–75; Compton, 122–23; Trefousse, 96–97; NA:RG59:Poole mission:Tannenberg interrogation:3; Farago, 477. Though the last military attaché in England considered Boetticher's reports "sober and realistic" but "disregarded in the high political circles" (P-097a, 14), the German ambassador was much more accurate in his assessment of Boetticher's no-danger-of-war impact (NA:RG59: Poole mission:Dieckhoff interrogation:5–7).
84   "no danger," "matter of indifference," "would no longer": *DGFP*, 11:1147, 12:1068, 13:854. These remarks were made to Mussolini and to the Finnish foreign minister, and I believe that they express one aspect of his divided view about war with America. He expressed contrary remarks to his admirals, whom he wanted to keep on a leash (*Lagevorträge*, 184; *DGFP*, 12:988; Herwig, "Prelude to Weltblitzkrieg," 662, 663), and to the Japanese foreign minister, whose attention he perhaps wanted to direct away from America and toward Russia (*DGFP*, 12:455).
84   Hitler declaration of war: Hillgruber, 553–54; Hillgruber, "Der Faktor Amerika"; Compton, 236; Warlimont, 50; Jacobsen in OKW, *KTB*, 1:103E–110E; Herwig, 666–68; *Lagevorträge*, 193–95, 325.

CHAPTER 6: PRIVATE SECTORS, PUBLIC SECRETS

85   butyl rubber information: United States, Senate, Committee on Military Affairs, Subcommittee on Scientific and Technical Mobilization, *Scientific and Technical Mobilization*, Hearings . . . on S. 702, 78th Congress, 1st Session (GPO, 1943–44), 47, 549–50, 698–99; Frank A. Howard, *Buna Rubber: The Birth of an Industry* (New York: D. Van Nostrand Co., 1947), 35, 47–50, 54–58, 62–63; Dubois, 149–50. On ter Meer, who was later convicted as a war criminal: *TWC*, 7:12, 8:1371, 1206; Mrs. Belle Mayer Zeck, telephone interview, 10 October 1975. Party No. 6,086,456(BDC).
86   Sperry Gyroscope and Askania: *Scientific and Technical Mobilization*, 2089–94.
86   Bendix and Siemens: Ibid., 2102.
86   "As a consequence": NI-10551. For the background of these exchanges, see Gabriel Kolko, "American Business and Germany, 1930–41," *The Western Political Quarterly*, 15 (December 1962), 713–28.
87   Max Ilgner: convicted as a war criminal, *TWC*, 7:13, 8:1207. Party No. 5,382,346(BDC).

87 Chemnyco: NI-10577:5–16, 20, 25; Dubois, 25, 60.
88 brainchild of three, financed, 1936: NI-4875:1; TWC:Case 6:Ilgner Document Book II:Document 34:1–2.
88 Reithinger: NI-6544:11; NI-4875:1; TWC:Case 6:Transcript:13076 (Reithinger).
88 library and clipping service: NI-8149:1; NI-4875:1.
88 main job: NA:RG165:CSDIK/UK:PW Paper 110:§44.
88 renamed: NI-4875:1.
88 dollar devaluation: NA:RG165:CSDIK/UK:PW Paper 110:§34.
88 *RM* 30,000,000: Dubois, 266.
88 growth: NA:RG238:Statement under oath of Anton Reithinger: 1.
88 collects on foreign economies: NI-8149:1; NA:RG165:CSDIK/UK:PW Paper 110:§49.
89 as it came to public notice: TWC:Case 6:Ilgner Document Book II: Document 34:27.
89 Vowi faster, customers prefer: Ibid.:28; NI-6544:17.
89 mostly from press: NI-8149:2.
89 exchanges with research institutes: Ilgner in Richard Sasuly, *I. G. Farben* (New York: Boni & Gaer, 1947), 276–77.
89 DuPont, Imperial Chemical, Frankfurt branch: NA:RG165:CSDIK/UK:PW Paper 110:§71; TWC:Case 6: Ilgner Document Book II:Document 34:28.
89 Farben representatives abroad: NA:RG165:CSDIK/UK:PW Paper 110:§§69–70, 53; TWC:Case 6:Transcript:12913(Reithinger); NI-8149:2; Ilgner in Sasuly, 279.
89 bound in green: NI-6544:17.
89 20 to 500: NA:RG165:CSDIK/UK:PW Paper 110:§49; TWC:Case 6:Ilgner Document Book II:Document 34:28. In the latter document, Reithinger says that from 500 to 1,000 copies of these reports were printed. But Reithinger's testimony changed markedly during the course of the Farben trial. At first his statements tended to incriminate Farben officials, particularly Ilgner. His later, more evasive statements tended to exculpate them. No evidence supports his figure of 1,000 copies, while statements of others and distribution lists contradict it. I therefore disbelieve it. However, an upper limit of 500 copies, which Reithinger uses as his lower limit, seems credible to me.
89 East Asian report: NI-8414.
89 Ilgner decides: NI-8149:2–3.
89 peddled it to Gestapo, SD, Thomas: TWC:Case 6:Transcript:2830–42 (Diels), 4499–510 (Ohlendorf); NI-15132.
89 military liaison post: *TWC*, 7:1046.
89 Diekmann: *TWC*, 8:1363, 7:1047.
89 plants in Great Britain, Scotland: *TWC*, 7:676–81.
89 visited Thomas's office: NI-7493:24. and 25. August 1939.
89 placed its archives: NI-8649.
89 10 of 35: NI-4875:4–6.
89 ring up, assigned: Ibid.; TWC:Case 6:Transcript:3159.
90 explosives and nitrogen: NI-9827.
90 moved twice, Kochstrasse 73: *TWC*, 7:1046–48.
90 Soviet military chemical production: BA:EAP 66-c-12-44/83:Vowi g 124.
90 captured Russian shells: Ibid.:Vowi g 151.
90 photostats, Clifton: NI-8149:3.
90 Focke: NA:RG238:Interrogation of Albrecht Focke:18.8.47:1–2. Party No. 1,241,323(BDC).
90 1936, second man: Ibid.:3; Ibid.:19.8.47:5, 13.
90 small round nimble: IfZ:ZS291:3:37.
91 representatives abroad: NA:RG238:Interrogation of Albrecht Focke: 19.8.47:12.
91 information sources: NI-10422:1–3.
91 assistant: NA:RG238:Interrogation of Albrecht Focke:19.8.47:5, 3.
91 correspondence, reports: NI-10422:1.
91 Ilgner and Bloch: Ilgner in Sasuly, 277, 278, 279; NA:RG238:Interrogation of Albrecht Focke: 18.8.47:4.
91 Farben resisted: Ibid.:19:8.47:10.
91 "Except for a good": Ibid.:2.
91 summoned board members: Ibid.:1.
91 subscribe to Abwehr reports: Ibid.:20.8.47:2.
91 "I don't understand": Ibid.:1.
91 "You're supposed to be": Ibid.:19.8.47:3.
91 far less helpful: Ibid.:11.
91 Farben worst: Ibid.:1.
91 protecting its pocketbook: NI-10422:3.
91 20 March 1935: Schumann, ed., *Carl Zeiss Jena*, 310.
91 Kotthaus: Party No. 5,485,003(BDC).
92 Zeiss: Schumann, ed., *Carl Zeiss Jena*, 514, 515, 527.
92 12 October 1937, two years later, Rheinmetall: IMT, 35:31–36 (partial translation in *NCA*, 6:1069–72); William Manchester, *The Arms of Krupp 1587–1968* (Boston: Little, Brown, 1968), 384–85, 406; Farago, 143.
92 Nazi party intelligence sought: IfZ:ZS291:1:47–51, 59–64, 3:31–42; Schellenberg, *Memorien*, 215–16, 218.
93 Rasche: Party No. 5,919,397(BDC).
93 Institute for Market Analysis: Deutsches Institut für Wirtschaftsforschung, *Beiträge zur empirischen Konjunkturforschung: Festschrift zum 25 jährigen Bestehen des Deutschen Instituts für Wirtschaftsforschung* (Institut für Konjunkturforschung) (Berlin: Dunckcher & Humbolt, 1950), 11–13.

93   87-page report: BA:RWM/20/374.
93   "divides into," "Commerce and": Ibid.:71.
93   "If it is": BA:EAP 66-c-8-18/101:23.
93   World Economic Institute: BA:EAP 66-c-8-46/6.
93   Turyn: OKW:Wi/VI.224. Party No. 7,678,325(BDC).
94   Reich Statistical Office: BA:EAP 66-c-12-44/74.
94   Gmelin Institute: BA:EAP 66-c-44/440.
94   Marienbad Research Institute: BA:EAP 66-c-8-46/6:1, 6.
94   Reich Research Council: *Reichsgesetzblatt* (1942), 389.
94   Reich Research Association, research branch, Branch VI: Germany, *Handbuch für das Deutsche Reich, 1936*, 284, 277, 118.
94   conflicted: Ludwig, 210–71; Helmut Heiber, *Walter Frank und sein Reichsinstitut für Geschichte des neuen Deutschlands*, Quellen und Darstellungen zur Zeitgeschichte, 13 (Stuttgart: Deutsche Verlags-Anstalt, 1966), passim.
94   Himmler rearranged: T-120:1536:D653434–37.
95   Krallert: BDC. Party No. 1,529,315; SS No. 310,323.
95   VI G: IMT, 38:83.
95   conference in Prague: BDC:Wilfried Krallert:undated Vermerk.
95   payments to foundations: OKW:Wi/IF 5.648: undated Zusammenstellung der Aufwendungen für wissenschaftliche Forschungsarbeiten von 1938 bis April 1944.
95   not on organized basis: USAF-171, 92.
95   Finland: Schmid, 23; Halder, 2:333.
95   front-line intelligence: USAF-171, 96.
96   bits and pieces: Ibid., 93.
96   Darlan: *Lagevorträge*, 326.
96   3 August 1942: Halder, 3:498.
96   Balkan satellites: My conclusion.
96   B-Dienst: Bonatz, 89–92.
96   approached by Japanese: Halder, 2:208.
96   French cipher key: Ibid., 1:211; Amè, 195.
96   Hungarian unit: Höttl, *Unternehmen Bernhard*, 238–40; Kahn, 452–53.
96   Abwehr and Servizio Informazione Militare: Leverkuehn, 60–64; Amè, 196.
96   Tyler Kent: *DGFP*, 9:417; DSDF 123/Kent, Tyler: passim; and an unpublished article by Dr. Warren F. Kimball based on DSDF sources. I am grateful to Dr. Kimball for letting me see this.
97   "It is my": *DGFP*, 13:750.
97   to reflect back: my impressions from the conversations in *Staatsmänner*.
97   74 organizations: Smith, 3.
97   4,000,000: Wilhelm Winkler, *Deutschtum in aller Welt: Bevölkerungsstatistiche Tabellen* (Wien: Frans Deuticke, 1938), totaling figures on 79, 100, 111, 114, 142, 143, which, however, omit Great Britain and Latin America.
97   Deutsches Ausland-Institut: Smith 1–25; IMT, 10:49–50; NA:RG59:Poole Commission:Stroelin interrogation:13–14, 19.
97   details accurate, impression erroneous: Smith, 155–57.
98   1:200,000 map: BA:DAI 221:13. Januar 1939.
98   "had often rendered": Ibid.:11.Februar 1938.
98   DAI used: Ibid.:26. August 1938, 1. Dezember 1938.
98   daily military press service: Ibid.:25.10.39.
98   sabotage mission: Eugene Rachlis, *They Came to Kill* (New York: Random House, 1961), 19, 23.
98   Auslandsorganisation: NSDAP, *Organisationsbuch der NSDAP, 1937*, 143–44, *1943*, 143–45; Jacobsen, 90–159.
98   3350, 52,648: Jacobsen, 137, 667.
98   Bohle, Ribbentrop agree: Ibid., 148.
98   monthly reports: Ibid., 149; NA:RG59:Poole Commission:Bohle interrogation: 5–8 September 1945:8; NG-163; IMT, 10:31–32. Sample report in *DGFP*, 6:874–78.
98   military tidbits: IMT, 10:20 (contradicting 10:15).
98   better informed: NA:RG59:Poole Commission:Bohle interrogation:5–8 September 1945:8.
98   quality of the reports, few foreign secrets: Jacobsen, 149, 155.
98   "Very interesting," "well observed": Hoettl, in footnote to NA:RG59:Poole Commission: Bohle interrogation:5–8 September 1945:18.
99   1937: de Jong, 280.
99   Cohrs: Ibid.; NG-3054; Jacobsen, 771; *DGFP:C*, 1:496, 556–57. Party No. 363,179(BDC).
99   Schnaus: NA:RG59: Poole Commission:Bohle interrogation:5–8 September 1945:7, 8, 24; Jacobsen, 651, 657. Party No. 432,273(BDC).
99   Butting: de Jong, 191–92, 67–68; NG-3661; *DGFP*, 9:189–90; L[ouis]. de Jong, *Het Konijkrijk der Nederlanden in den Tweede Wereldoorlag*, Rijksinstitut voor Oorlagsdocumentatie (The Hague: Nijhoff, 1969–75), 2:326, 456; S. B. [Walter Schulze-Bernelt], "Parteistellen der NSDAP Machten in den Niederlanden der Abwehr Konkurrenz," *Die Nachhut* (1. Oktober 1973), 31–33. Butting Party No. 954,618(BDC).
99   Chile, Argentina: See spy chapters; also NG-3402.
99   Switzerland: NA:RG238:Schellenberg interrogation:7 March 1946:16; *ADAP*, 3:443–44.
100 fought entirely shy: *DGFP:C*, 2:5–8, 492; *DGFP*, 1:662, 685–86, 691, 708–709; *FRUS, 1938*, 2:461–62.
100 Bund: Smith, 91–116; Jacobsen, 528–49; Sander A. Diamond, *The Nazi Movement in the United States* (Ithaca: Cornell University Press, 1974), passim.

100 physician: Ignatz T. Griebl. For him and his case: Smith, 75–76; Jacobsen, 532–33; Leon G. Turrou as told to David G. Wittels, *Nazi Spies in America* (New York: Random House, 1939), 100–104, 118, 226–31; Farago, 21–22, 26; ML-37:15.September 1937; *New York Times* (18 October 1938), 28:6.
100 "if they was": *New York Times* (1 July 1938), 8:2.
100 reluctant consent: *DGFP*, 9:30, 491, 13:433–34. This applied only to agents "engaged purely in collecting information." The Foreign Office and German diplomats in the United States vigorously opposed saboteurs (*DGFP*, 8:89–91, 700–701, 9:398–400, 410–12, 425–27, 616, 13: 98–99).
100 booted out: *ADAP*, 1:565–66.
100 Papen fought bitterly: Papen, 481, 489–90.
100 Schellenberg got Himmler, believed: NA:RG238:Schellenberg interrogation:7 March 1946:17–18.
100 Schellenberg, Canaris used AO: Ibid., 19; NG-3054; Schellenberg, *Memorien*, 220.
100 AO intelligence service in Turkey: NG-2209.
100 "dilettantes"; Nielsen, *Intelligence*, 29.

CHAPTER 7: BEFORE THE MAIN BODY

101 primary means: *German Operational Intelligence*, 1.
101 caps, helmets: NA:RG165:USFET:IC:1SIIR:209–10.
101 flat, open farming land: Hagemann, interview; map.
102 table "Indications": NA:RG165:USFET:IC:1SIIR:209–10.
103 several hundred Russians: AOK 9:27970/2:5.11.42:20.30.
103 shells of all calibers: 102.I.D.:26562/4:5.11.42.
103 Russians probed: AOK 9:27970/2:6.11.42:7.30.
103 600 to 700: Ibid.:19.15.
103 normal trench, slight rear, smokescreen: 102.I.D.:26562/4:7.11.42.
103 activity ebbed: from 9th Army I c reports.
103 rains, mud: OKW, *KTB*, 2:818, 821, 823, 836; Seaton, 190.
103 frost: OKW, *KTB*, 2:855, 914, 921, 899.
103 artillery and rocket fire, skiers, digging: 102.I.D.26562/4:18.11.42.
103 26 dead: Ibid.:20.11.42.
103 traffic grew heavier: AOK 9:27970/2:22.11.1942:06.50.
103 10-day artillery check: OKH:H3/199:89:3.
103 scouts felt out: AOK 9:27970/2:24.11.1942.
103 Hill 207.3: 102.I.D.:26562/4:24.11.1942.
103 reinforcements, bridges: AOK 9:27970/2:24.11.1942:18.45.
103 more exotic intelligence: AOK 9:32878/7:17.Januar 1943.
104 attack of 25 November: 102.I.D.:26562/4:25.11.42; AOK 9:31624/3:25.11.42.
104 "the presumed point": AOK 9:32878/7:17.Januar 1943:4.
104 "anticipated": 102.I.D.:26562/4:25.11.42.
104 "Are the Russians": 183.I.D.:32381/1:10.November 1941.
104 "A patrol under": 98.I.D.:8159/2:3.März 1940.
105 "The raiding party": XXXVIII.A.K.:44651/14:28.
106 faster than the main body: Munzel, 90.
106 mounted platoons: "Die Aufklärungszüge der Inf. Regt. 1941/42," 132–33.
106 48 divisions: Mueller-Hillebrand, 2:161–71.
106 reconnaissance battalion organization: Ibid., 2:130; "Zur Gliederung der Div.-Aufklärungsabteilungen," 155–56.
106 reconnaissance routine: *Tag und Nacht am Feind*, 23–26; Stein, 74–75.
107 3rd Infantry Division: Dieckhoff, 49.
107 cavalry regiments: Stein, 52.
107 October 1943: Mueller-Hillebrand, 3:225.
107 fire department: Stein, 74; Wiener, 30–31.
107 "armoured cars, tanks": Article 171.
107 cross country: Guderian, *Panzerwaffe*, 141.
107 punch through: Munzel, 85.
107 historically characteristic: Carl von Clausewitz, *Schriften—Aufsätze—Studien—Briefe*, ed. Werner Halhweg, Deutsche Geschichtsquellen des 19. und 20. Jahrhunderts, 45 (Göttingen: Vandenhoek & Rupprecht, 1966), 1:237–38.
107 not a combat outfit: Mitzlaff, interview; Wiener, 1.
107 1926: Spielberger, 9; Guderian, 26.
109 6-wheeled car: Spielberger, 13; Senger und Etterlin, 226; White, 30–31; Milsom and Chamberlain, 64–67, 72–77.
109 8-wheeled replacement: Spielberger, 59, 13; Senger und Etterlin, 229; White, 33–34; Milsom and Chamberlain, 84–86, 90–107.
109 Hitler stopped: RMfBuM, *Rüstung*, 204.
109 modern 8-wheeler: Spielberger, 59; Senger und Etterlin, 233–35; White, 34; Milsom and Chamberlain, 87–90, 120–27.
109 Sd.Kfz. 250/9: Spielberger, 14–15; White, 73–74; Senger und Etterlin, 225.
109 Sd.Kfz. 221 and 222: Spielberger, 14; White, 31–32; Senger und Etterlin, 221, 223; Milsom and Chamberlain, 22–25, 34–51. For other armored scout cars, see the following works: Ogorkiewicz, 88–89, 427–34, 437, 439–40; Munzel, 87–90; RMfBuM, *Rüstung*, 75, 136, 180, 236.
109 battalion organization: Mueller-Hillebrand, 2:143; Wiener 1 (citing H.Dv. 299/10); Hammerstein, interview.

110 not the I c but the divisional commander: Hammerstein, interview.
110 deep into the unknown territory: *Tag und Nacht am Feind,* 99–100.
110 obstacles, barricades: for a report of a typical mission, see Hammerstein, 96, 108–16.
110 tanks have priority in production: Mitzlaff, letter, 25. April 1975.
110 one and a platoon: Mueller-Hillebrand, 2:183.
110 reorganized the panzer leadership: This mainly involved appointing a general inspector of panzer troops, who was Guderian, and renaming the Schnellen Truppen "Panzertruppen." Mueller-Hillebrand, 2:96, 3:158–59; Wiener, 4.
110 going onto offensive: Guderian, 297.
110 squadrons renamed "companies": Mueller-Hillebrand, 3:158–59; Keilig, §11:112; §103:I:3; Wiener, 4.
110 two or three per battalion: Mueller-Hillebrand, 3:226; Wiener, 5, 25–26; Gerhard Elser, "Zu: Panzeraufklärungsabteilungen," *Feldgrau,* 4 (Juli 1956), 100.
110 motorcyclists into infantry: Wiener, 5.
110 all not identically equipped: Mitzlaff, letter, 25. April 1975.
110 24 December 1941: Deutsches Afrika Korps:22570/2:24.12.41:17.30.
110 "The enemy": *Hitlers Lagebesprechungen,* 162.
111 November 1941: Mellenthin, 59.
111 acoustical sensors: NA:RG165:PW Intelligence Bulletin 2/46:39–44 and Annex II.
111 artillery reconnaissance: Reinicke, "Zielaufklärung" and "Artillerieaufklärung"; P-023; P-041n, 9–15; Froben; Hertel; *Allgemeine Heeresmitteilungen,* 10 (7. Januar 1943), 9–11, (7. August 1943), 392; Keilig, §101:I:6, 8; Mueller-Hillebrand, 2:125, 159, 192–93, 3:218; NA:RG165: SAIC/R/2:8.
111 25 November 1941: XXX.A.K.:13896/2:26.Nov.1941.
113 Observation Battalion 14: Martin Sieber, "Endlich fassten wir den Gegner: Ein Lichtmess-batterie der B.14 an der Schelde im Mai 1940," *Alte Kameraden,* 20 (Mai 1972), 16–17.
113 battle the ultimate reconnaissance: Hauck, interview.
113 "Combat reports": H.Dv.300, §54.
113 *Field Service Regulations* of 1887: §16.
113 "Battle furnishes": H.Dv.300, §54.

CHAPTER 8: THE WORLD FROM THE SKY

I am grateful to retired Luftwaffe colonel Günther Borcherdt for reading an early draft of this chapter and offering corrections and additions.

All material on Rowehl and his squadron comes from Rowehl, interview, and Cornelius Noell, letter, 20.10.77, and memorandum, 30.8.77, unless otherwise noted; the interview is further cited when it is one of several sources.

114 Knemeyer flights: Knemeyer, interview.
115 flight results: Churchill, 4:301–302.
116 paid by Abwehr: Rowehl, interview, 9; Schmid, 3–4: USAF-171, 34.
116 Junkers W.34: Rowehl in USAF-171, 35; Kens, 339–40; *Bulletin de la Fédération Aeronautique Internationale,* 11 (janvier 1930), 46.
116 1929 treaty with Poland: League of Nations, *Treaty Series,* 146 (1934), 333–45 at 337, 339.
116 Poland flights halted: Patzig, interview.
116 rejoined military, camouflage title, Kiel to Staaken: USAF-171, 36–37; Völker, *Deutsche Luftwaffe,* 46.
116 over Russia: USAF-171, 37.
117 Squadron for Special Purposes: Eyermann, 2:36.
117 subordinated to 5th Branch: USAF-171, 36; Rowehl, interview, 5.
117 Hoensbroech and Saurma: Eyermann, 2:36.
118 aerial cameras: USAF-171, 36; Brucklacher, interview, 17; Schumann, ed., 508.
118 Heinkel 111: Rowehl, interview, 5; Green, 288; Kens, 269–75, 524; Brucklacher, interview, 20.
118 late 1930s: USAF-171, 37, 56.
118 Budapest: IMT, 2:467–68.
118 assignments from Schmid: Eyermann, 2:37; Rowehl, interview, 8.
118 commercial craft proving routes: Eyermann, 2:36, civilian markings, mufti: Eyermann, 2:36; Cornelius Noell, letter, 20.10.1977.
118 invisible, could hear: Rowehl, interview, 2.
118 condensation trails: Cornelius Noell, memorandum.
118 not recognized as German: inferred from statement (USAF-171, 37) that Germany received no information that the aircraft had been observed by neighboring countries.
118 treaties with Czechoslovakia, England: League of Nations, *Treaty Series,* 89 (1929), 231–59 at 247, 251, and 71 (1928), 165–83 at 167, 170–71.
118 no treaties with France or Russia: indexes to *Treaty Series* and to Martens collection of treaties.
118 loss of He 111: Green, 228: Ernst Heinkel, *Stürmisches Leben* (Stuttgart: Mundus-Verlag, 1953), 327.
118 Oranienburg, Main Photo Center: Schreyer, 71, 75.
119 Abwehr I, Canaris conference: IMT, 2:467–68.
119 1:75,000 photomap: Schreyer, 76.
119 three squadrons of 12 planes: Schreyer, 71; USAF-171, 34; Kens, 15.
119 Polish photographs distributed: USAF-171, 58.
119 squadron in Bulgaria: IMT, 28:403, 9:402.

119   no maps of Norway: Warlimont, 71; *Hitlers Tischgespräche*, 414–15.
119   "to find out": de Jong, 172.
119   Rowehl Norway photos: USAF-171, 113–14; Schmid, 22; Walther Hubatsch, *"Weserübung"; Die deutsche Besetzung von Dänemark und Norwegen 1940*, 2. Auflage, Studien und Dokumente zur Geschichte des zweiten Weltkrieges, 7 (Göttingen: Musterschmidt, 1962), 40.
119   Noell: Noell, memorandum.
119   "unsatisfactory": USAF-171, 59.
119   Yugoslavia: Schreyer, 98, 99–100; Eyermann, 2:268.
119   fourth squadron: Green, 425.
119   several hundred violations: *GGVKS*, 1:562, states that from October 1939 to the start of the war German airplanes violated Russian territory more than 500 times. The very day of the invasion, the Russians protested that from 19 April to 19 June, the Germans overflew Soviet territory 180 times (*DGFP*, 12:1063). Some of these must have been German non-Rowehl flights, which began either 7 or 13 June (Halder, 2:448, 453) or 16 June (IMT, 34:708). But the vast majority were Rowehl's.
119   two airplanes came down: *DGFP*, 12:602–603; Köstring, 316; Cornelius Noell, letter, 20.10.1977. The dates in Schreyer, 98–100, are wrong.
120   Göring bellowed: Eyermann, 2:268.
120   Russians merely protested: *DGFP*, 12:602–603, 1061–63; IWM:Milch:34:1879.
120   isolated cases, never fired: Bezymenski, 251; Köstring, 316; *GGVKS*, 1:562.
120   flights from Cracow, Bucharest, Plovdiv, Seerappen, Kirkenes: Green, 425; Eyermann, 2:268; Rowehl, interview, 13.
120   Black Sea: USAF-171, 37.
120   industrial targets, newest construction: Ibid.: Halder, 2:426. For additional details about the Rowehl activity against the Soviet Union, see chapter 24, "The Greatest Mistake."
120   Noell over Moscow: Noell, memorandum.
120   airplane types: Rowehl interview, 7; IWM:Milch:15:1765–70.
120   Stavanger: Knemeyer, interview.
120   North Africa, 44 times, 170.5: IWM:Milch:15:1765.
120   eight-hour marathon: Ibid.:34:1874
121   only contact: Ibid.:15:1765.
121   Iceland, Glasgow, Red Sea, Iraq: NA:RG165:APWIU (9th Air Force) 90/1945:3.
121   typical flight: Schreyer, 86, 94–96.
122   "Our homeland we knew": Rowehl, interview, 17.
122   Bomber Wing 200: Schreyer, 113; SHAEF, *German Intelligence Services*, 13.
122   air officers: Völker, *Entwicklung*, 131.
122   sports pilots, Main Photo Center: Ibid., 139–40; "Uberblick über die Tätigkeit und Organisation des gesamten Bildwesens in der Luftwaffe," 5; NA:RG165:APWIU (9th Air Force): 90/1945:2.
123   two reconnaissance airplanes: Völker, *Entwicklung*, 133.
123   three tiny squadrons: Völker, *Deutsche Luftwaffe*, 14–16.
123   civilian firms: Eyermann, 2:23, 32; Prager, 18–20.
123   new airplanes: Völker, *Dokumente*, 406–11; Kens, 255, 256.
123   1937: Völker, *Deutsche Luftwaffe*, 79.
123   Main Photo Center: Schreyer, 73, 75.
123   strength at outbreak of war: Militärarchiv, letter, 25.5.1972.
123   air fleet, air division: LDv. 2 (1938) §2–3; Krahmer, 19.
123   Luftwaffe basic task: Völker, *Dokumente*, 469.
123   army group and army squadrons: Borcherdt, interview and memoranda; Lohmann, memorandum.
124   "embraces the surveillance": HDv. 300/1, §143.
124   aerial photography at 15,000 to 30,000 feet: Ibid., §§144, 146; Harbou, 739–40.
124   corps and armored divisions: Borcherdt, interview and memoranda; Lohmann, memorandum.
124   short-range reconnaissance: HDv. 300/1, §150; Harbou, 120–21; "Gliederung und Aufgaben . . .," 3.
124   "Tactical reconnaissance": HDv. 300/1, §147.
124   battle reconnaissance, "gives information": Ibid., §176.
124   artillery spotting: Harbou, 121, 124: Hutter, *Falken*, 39–42; Halder, 3:527.
124   photographic section: "Ausrüstung der Bildstelle einer H und F Staffel," 1–5.
124   Main Photo Branch: "Uberblick über die Tätigkeit und Organisation des gesamten Bildwesens in der Luftwaffe," 10–14; NA:RG165:APWIU (9th Air Force):90/1945:7–9; Schreyer, 73–5.
125   organization and reorganization of aerial reconnaissance: from Borcherdt, interview and memoranda; Lohmann, memoranda, except for items noted below.
125   new squadrons: Müller-Hillebrand, 2:161.
125   inadequate: OKH:H22/220:84.
125   seven planes: "Die Flugzeuge fuer die Nahaufklaerungsverbaende," 8.
125   300 lost: Hillgruber and Hümmelchen, 56.
125   only a single aircraft: "Die Flugzeuge fuer die Nahaufklaerungsverbaende," 9.
125   reconnaissance entailed some fighting: Halder, 3:335.
125   "complete reorganization": Ibid.
126   unimaginative, do-nothing: Barsewisch, letter, 19.8.1974.
126   Barsewisch: Borcherdt, memorandum.
127   four reconnaissance planes preceded, eighth and second generations: Found by dividing strength figures on 31 May 1943, from "Die Stärke der deutschen Luftwaffe am 5.7.1941, 3.1.1942, und 31.5.1943," *Wehrwissenschaftliche Rundschau*, 11 (November 1961), 641–44, into total production of each type as of that date, the figures for which are given in Baumbach, 313.

568   *Notes*

127 6,299, 113,515: Baumbach, 313.
127 one in three, seven, eight and a half: calculated from figures given respectively in Jany (Cron), 5:209–10; Militärarchiv, letter, 2.5.1972; "Die Stärke der deutschen Luftwaffe am 5.7.1941, 3.1.1942, und 31.5.1943," 643–44.
127 260, 412, 377, 342, 294, 402: Militärarchiv, letter, 2.5.1972; "Die Stärke der deutschen Luftwaffe am 5.7.1941, 3.1.1942, und 31.5.1943."
127 long-range planes: "Die Flugzeuge fuer die Fernaufklaerungsverbaende," 1–2, 8; Kens, 139–43, 512, 682–85, 364–67, 528, 762–68.
127 other models: IWM:Milch:17:3655, 20:5504, 34:3268; Kens, passim.
128 short-range planes: Völker, *Deutsche Luftwaffe*, 132; "Die Flugzeuge fuer die Nahaufklaerungsverbaende"; Kens, 316–17, 526, 752, 202–204, 518, 415–29, 523, 776–81; "Taktische Luftaufklärung," 301–302; IWM:Milch:17:3597.
129 no camera improvement: Brucklacher, interview, 17; Heidelauf, interview.
129 apparatus good enough: IWM:Milch:16:2944.
129 "how far behind": "Unsere Geräte zur Herstellung, Betrachtung und Auswertung von Luftbildern," in National Air and Space Museum Library, Washington, D.C., Captured German Air Technical Documents, Roll 2784, Frames 204–208.
129 cameras: Brucklacher, interview, 15–22 passim; Schumann, ed., 507–508; IWM:Milch:17:3597, 16:2944–45; NA:RG165:APWIU (9th Air Force): 90/1945:3.
129 30 lines per millimeter: Brucklacher, interview, 17. This was approximately the same as American photo systems attained under the same conditions (Irving Doyle, telephone interview, 9 June 1976).
129 films: Heidelauf, interview; Weber, interview.
129 "Battle reconnaissance is": XXX.A.K.:11455/2:Anlage 36.
129 pattern never varied: Fischer, interview.
129 Hutter: Hutter, *Spähtruppe*, 12, 25–28.
130 with the naked eye: Krahmer, 17.
130 26 December 1941: Panzer AOK Afrika:18197/4:26.12.41:11.56, 12.50, 15.15, 16.40, 14.45.
130 Rommel exploited: *The Rommel Papers*, 177.
130 artillery reconnaissance: Hutter, *Falken*, 39–42.
132 Pape: Pape, 256.
132 sorties of 28 May: HGrNord:75136/2:28.5.1940.
132 timely flights penetrated: D-407, 88–89.
133 observers looked around: Fischer, interview.
133 coarse and detailed evaluations: Noack, interview: *German Operational Intelligence*, 28–31.
133 photo interpreters, handbook: LDv.12/1, Beihefte I and V.
133 train direction, gun shadows, flatcars, mixed trains: Zimmermann, interview.
133 firing positions: P-130, 59.
133 attack detection from camouflage: D-407, 90.
133 photo distribution: *German Operational Intelligence*. 31, 63.
134 11,048, 20,360: AOK 12:75991:Stabshildmeldung 3:6.
134 "Under favorable": HDv. 300/1, §128.
134 photo interpreter errors: *German Operational Intelligence*, 32.
134 observers' errors: OKH:RL2/646:6–7.
134 4 September 1944: Prügel, 310.
135 Crimean dam: *German Operational Intelligence*, 49.
135 Göring on mining: *Lagevorträge*, 592.
135 Dönitz noted: Ibid., 660.
135 no air reconnaissance of British industry: OKL:RL2/547:14.12.44:1.
135 no troops from Siberia spotted: Borcherdt, "Die Heeres-Luftaufklärung nach 1918—ein geschichtlicher Rückblick (IV)," 112.
135 "Especially on account": OKM:III M 1000/57:392.

CHAPTER 9: QUESTIONING THE FOE

In this chapter, I have changed the initials of the last names of some of the Allied soldiers who "talked." The German documents, which I cite, naturally have the full names, serial numbers, and other data.

136 G——: OKH:H2/3:11.10.1944:1.
136 Oberursel: Ibid.; personal visit.
136 200 cells, soundproof, individual heating: *War Crimes Trials*, 9:124, 89.
136 formal name: Ibid., 81, 99; heading of the interrogation reports.
136 contained a Dulag; Ibid., 90. "Dulag" is a portmanteau word for "Durchgangslager" ("transit camp"), "Stalag" for "Stammlager" ("permanent camp").
136 Evaluation center East: NA:RG165:HTUSAIC:IR:4:2.
136 time of arrival: based on times of capture and times of interrogations in OKH:H2/3.
136 preliminary questioning: Friedheim, 73; OKL:RL2/558:6.12.1944.
137 longer-range and technical matters: *War Crimes Trials*, 9:125.
137 red cross form: Ibid., 90, 33.
137 "The first thing": Cole, ed., 63–64.
138 so many passed through: Ibid., 64.
138 torture ineffective: *War Crimes Trials*, 9:118, 128, 91, 107.
138 Geneva Convention: League of Nations, *Treaty Series*, 118 (1931–32), 343–411.

138 threatened with shooting: Friedheim. 73.
138 Warrant Officer L——: *War Crimes Trials*, 9:32–35. Such cases were the reason that the camp commandant, Lieutenant Colonel Erich Killinger, Junge, and others were tried as war criminals. Killinger and Junge were both convicted and sentenced to five years in prison—rather heavy, compared to the sentences meted out at Nuremberg.
138 interrogators specialized: Ibid., 90, 95; NA:RG165:HTUSAIC:IR:4:5.
138 Junge: *War Crimes Trials*, 9:117, 107. Party No. 1,121,944(BDC).
138 interrogation preparation: Ibid., 173–74. For a list of the branches, see NA:RG165:HTUSAIC: IR:4:3–11.
139 noon briefing: *War Crimes Trials*, 9:95, 118, 90.
139 65 interrogators: Ibid., 88–89, 125.
139 11 May 1944: OKL:RL2/547:11.5.44.
139 interrogated only once: *War Crimes Trials*, 9:106, 119, 124.
139 interrogation techniques: Basically my surmises from my own experience in interviewing, plus ibid., 174; Friedheim, 16–17; Hammer, ed., 59–60.
139 G—— report: OKH:H2/3:11.10.1944.
141 C——report: Ibid.: 25.10.1944.
141 fire corrections: Ibid.: 28.9.1944.
141 mystery cleared: IWM:Milch:17:3715.
141 100 reports a day: *War Crimes Trials*, 9:124.
141 vital information, Luftwaffe satisfied, Göring: Ibid., 99, 104.
141 "Knowledge of new": OKL:RL2/558:6.12.1944.
142 number of p.o.w.s: *War Crimes Trials*, 9:88–89, 106, 119.
142 two years of existence: It was set up in December 1939 (von Donat, interview, 3–4).
142 better intelligence earlier: P-018a, 31, 35; *German Operational Intelligence*, 3.
142 Kotschev: 4.SS Polizei Div:22371/2:Anlage 190.
142 narrow focus: D-407, 64; Lewal (janvier 1881), 39; [Napoléon], *Maximes de Guerre et Pensées de Napoléon Ier*, ed. Burnod, 5e ed. aug. (Paris: Chapelet, 1900), 35 (LXIII).
143 expanded downward: D-407, Anlage 6; P-018a, 28–29.
143 regulations: HDv.92g., Abschnitt XI:D, table; HDv.89g, Anlage 6; HDv.300/1, §188.
143 qualified interpreters: P-018a, 10.
143 lack military knowledge: Ibid.
143 training courses: Ibid., 12.
143 most important interrogation: D-407, 67; P-018a, 20.
143 too busy to bother: Bottlar, interview.
143 forward interrogations cursory: *German Operational Intelligence*, 61; P-018a, 19–20, 24.
143 new interpreters distributed: P-018a, 33.
143 adjutant, special missions officer: Ibid., 20, 28.
143 emphasis upon promptness: Ibid., 9–10; D-407, 61–62, Anlage 6.
143 fear makes prisoners talk: Manteuffel, interview, 7–8. I believe this to be more credible than all the immediately post-Nuremberg declarations that German kindness made prisoners talk (as P-018a, 10; D-407, 61–62), except as that kindness was backed up by fear, as I explain in the text. The frequent references in the sources to postcapture shock (as D-407, Anlage 6) support this view.
144 usefulness: P-018a, 23.
144 accuracy: Lewal (janvier 1881), 39.
144 80 percent reliable: *German Operational Intelligence*, 3.
144 trustworthy in East: P-018a, 36–37.
144 got what needed: D-407, 60.
144 upon capture: HDv.92g, Abschnitt XI:D, table.
144 posts forward of division: NA:RG165:USFET:IC:1SIIR:153–54; P-018a, 28; *German Operational Intelligence*, 3, 61.
144 first thorough and systematic: NA:RG165:USFET:IC:1SIIR:154; P-018a, 20, 29.
144 all interrogated: P-018a, 24.
144 I c, assistant, or interpreter: Ibid., 20.
144 singly: AOK15:RH27-2/49:21.9.1942:11.
144 seated: D-407, 65.
144 Geneva Convention did not protect: IMT, 36:317–27; Oppenheim, 2:369.
144 beating; torture: IMT, 7:349–95.
144 shooting: Ibid., 431; 3.Pz.D.:19269/18:18.
144 mass and individual killings: IMT, 7:345–437.
144 97 percent: NA:RG165:USFET:IC:1SIIR:156.
144 some remain silent: P-018a, 34.
144 fewer talk after 1943: NA:RG165:USFET:IC:1SIIR:157.
144 "The prisoner is": HDv.89g, 42.
145 "is regulated strictly": 10.SSPz.D.:78014/11:4.7.44.
145 Allied prisoners say little: Hayn, 142; *German Operational Intelligence*, 6.
145 Best, Melner: 10.Pz.D.:RH27-10/63:1.12.1942.
145 mild treatment: D-407, 61–62; P-018a, 9–10, 23–24.
145 tricks: *German Operational Intelligence*, 5.
145 no Red Cross report: AOK15:RH27-2/49:21.9.1942:12.
145 interrogator superiority suffices: P-018a, Supplement.
145 simple OKH questionnaires: P-018a, Appendix 1; *German Operational Intelligence*, 4.
145 50th Infantry Division, Krasnichin: 50.I.D.:16110/11:undated.
145 divisions expand interrogations: P-018a, 29, 31, Appendix 3; NA:RG165:USFET:IC:1SIIR: 154–56.

145   Foreign Armies West questionnaires: *German Operational Intelligence,* 93.
146   commands maintain lists: D-407, Anlage 6; NA:RG165:USFET:IC:1SIIR:24, *German Operational Intelligence,* 4.
146   tactical and organizational matters: P-018a, 23; NA:RG165:USFET:IC:1SIIR:24; AOK15: RH27-2/49:21.9.1942:7.
146   Mortar Regiment 475: AK XXXV:44220/16:Anlage 37:2.7.43:16.00.
147   165 prisoners: AK XXXV:42146/1:5.7.43.
147   Rifle Regiment 102: AK XXXV:44220/16:Anlage 37:5.7.43:15.45.
147   James S——, Robert D——: 10.Pz.D.:RH27-10/63:22.Februar 1943.
148   1st Armored Division, 34th Infantry Division: Stubbs and Connor, 92; Eisenhower, 157.
148   "new American": 10.Pz.Div.:RH27-10/62:16.Januar 1943.
148   5 copies: NA:RG165:USFET:IC:1SIIR:154.
148   corps and army: HDv.89g, Anlage 6; P-018a, 20–21, 26; D-407, 67, Anlage 6; NA:RG165: USFET:IC:1SIIR:95, 127.
148   I c participation: NA:RG165:USFET:IC:1SIIR:127; *German Operational Intelligence,* 69–70.
148   90 percent: *German Operational Intelligence,* 3.
148   army groups: P-018a, 21; NA:RG165:USFET:IC:1SIIR:71–73.
148   Chalons-sur-Marne: OKW:Wi/VIII.11:Anlage 21:2; OKH:H2/3:29.Juni 44.
148   Arnold F. C——: OKH:H2/3:25.Oktober 1944.
148   specialist interrogators: OKW:Wi/VIII.11:Anlage 21:2.
149   interrogation group, Diez: HGrD:75144/33:103/4, 110/6; OKH:H2/3:13.Dezember 1944, 12.2.45.
149   Foreign Armies East camp: OKH:H3/463.2:August 1943:1, OKH:H3/176:3.1.45; P-018a, 22; NA:RG165:USFET:IC:1SIIR:25.
149   Foreign Armies West teams: *German Operational Intelligence,* 93, 118.
149   British soldiers' morale: BA:EAP-175-b-24-10/12:9.4.1943.
149   Kommando Fritz: OKH:H2/3:29.4.44, 25 Mai 1944.
149   Alencon: OKW:Wi/VIII.11:Anlage 21:2.
149   four teams: OKH:H2/124:1.12.1944.
149   Abwehr combat interrogations: Weidemann, interview, 8–9; OKW:1938:4.Juni 1941; Reile, *Ostfront,* 349.
150   four teams, camp: NA:RG165:HTUSAIC:PIR:21 August 1945 (Förster); Ibid.:22 August 1945 (Bahr).
150   specialist teams of its own, most valuable information: Payr, 8–9.
150   held more than a year, most had forgotten, 108 Americans: OKW:Wi/IB 1.145:8, 19, 146. Such interrogations continued in France in 1944 (OKW:Wi/VIII.11:Anlage 21).
150   greatest contribution: My conclusion, based primarily on the repeated mentions of p.o.w. identifications in OKH:H2/107b, the Lageberichte West of 1940.
150   no intelligence critical: A sampling of the p.o.w. intelligence recorded in OKW, *KTB,* shows none such.
150   88th and 1st Infantry Divisions: OKH:H2/9:1.4.44. The 88th actually arrived in Italy on 6 February and the 1st was in fact in Britain when the prisoner said it was (OCMH:Order of Battle of the Army of the United States in World War II:Zone of the Interior:Ch.VIII:Troop Directory).
150   123, 5: Liss, 275.
151   situation conferences: My impression. In only one case was p.o.w. intelligence cited as supplying an item of hard intelligence—the identification of the 233rd Division (*Hitlers Lagebesprechungen,* 689).
151   most important source: NA:RG165:USFET:IC:1SIIR:153; D-407, 59.
151   limits: D-407, 59, says this in different words.
151   more elastic: P-018a, 9.

CHAPTER 10: BETRAYERS IN PAPER AND STEEL

152   most commonly helped question prisoners: My impression from statements in the sources; also *German Operational Intelligence,* 6.
152   Dulag Luft document section: NA:RG238:HTUSAIC:IR:4:8–9; *German Operational Intelligence,* 6–7.
152   letters, service newspapers: *War Crimes Trials,* 9:118; Friedheim, 17, 73.
152   identity cards: Friedheim, 17, 73.
152   Marauders: Ibid., 17.
153   100th, 91st, 95th Bomb Groups: Ibid., 17, 73; *War Crimes Trials,* 9:173–74.
153   where documents found: D-407, 70.
153   kinds found: Ibid., 69.
153   division and corps evaluation: HDv.92g, 24; HDv.89g, 23; D-407, 67–68; NA:RG165:USFET: IC:1SIIR:159–60; *German Operational Intelligence,* 62.
153   main examination at army: HDv.92g, 24–25; HDv.89g, 23; D-407, 67–68; NA:RG165:USFET: IC:1SIIR:92.
153   army group, Foreign Armies East: NA:RG165:USFET:IC:1SIIR:73, 57–58, 59; Strik-Strikfeldt, 60–61. The Abwehr also collected and evaluated documents (Reile, *Ostfront,* 349; Weidemann, interview, 8, 11–12; OKW:1938:4.Juni 1941).
153   ski battalions: II.AK:45114/5:16.1.1942.
153   "dual purpose": OKH:H2/7:1.September 1943:2.
153   "The Landing of": II.AK.:45114/5:16.1.1942.

154   two French armies: OKH:H2/107b:301.
154   3d Armored Guards: NA:RG165:USFET:IC:1SIIR:73.
154   U.S. 3d Army: *German Operational Intelligence,* 7.
154   rarity of directly usable: D-407, 70.
154   divisions in southern Belgium: OKH:H2/107b:300.
154   3rd Panzer Division: Traditionsverband der [3. Panzer] Division, 170–71.
155   1st Guards Army: NA:RG165:USFET:IC:1SIIR:160; Seaton, 343, for success of Russian attack. OKW, *KTB*, 3:33–90, covering the period of this attack, does not mention the captured maps.
155   British deception concocted: Ewen Montagu, *The Man Who Never Was* (Philadelphia: Lippincott, 1954); *FRUS, The Conferences at Washington, 1941–1942, and at Casablanca, 1943,* 584. See Chapter 25 for previous courier losses that may have suggested this ploy.
155   April of 1943; PRO:CAB 79/60:205; Montagu, 105.
155   Sicily: Churchill, 4:692.
155   referred obliquely: Montagu, 52–53.
155   Hitler, OKW concluded: *Lagevorträge,* 429; *Hitlers Weisungen für die Kriegführung,* No. 47; OKW, *KTB,* 2:1061, 3:109, 182; Förster, ed., 101. For disbelief in a move against Crete, *Hitlers Lagebesprechungen,* 112–13; for earlier fears about Sardinia, OKW, *KTB,* 3:55, 178.
155   Turkish chrome, Rumanian oil: *Hitlers Lagebesprechungen,* 205.
155   only photographs: the originals were returned by the Spaniards to the British (Montagu, 114). The use of the term "original materials" by Foreign Armies West (OKH:H22/147:12.5.43) must refer to the photographs in contrast to an earlier report from Spain (Montagu, 128).
155   drafted by commander: Montagu, 52–53.
156   Abwehr: Goebbels, 394.
156   Foreign Armies West: OKH:H22/147:9.Mai 1943:4.
156   3/Skl: photograph in Montagu, following p. 128.
156   Canaris: Goebbels, 324–25, 394.
156   appreciation: OKH:H22/147:9.Mai 1943, repeated in Ibid.:12.5.43 after receipt of the photographs.
156   strengthened: Warlimont, in " 'Der Mann, Der Nie Gelebt Hat,' " argues that the deception had no effect because Hitler believed in an eastern attack anyway, and furthermore that the deception did not affect the Sicily defenses. I feel that the spurious documents hardened Hitler's views, as he himself said, and that had he believed in an attack on Sicily, he would have reinforced it instead of the eastern region.
156   Mussolini, "The discovered": *Lagevorträge,* 500, 502.
156   never changed: *Hitlers Lagebesprechungen,* 205; OKW, *KTB,* 3:1432–34, 1442–45; *Rommel Papers,* 430–31.
156   9 July: OKW, *KTB,* 3:763.
156   marks provide intelligence: OKH:H3/284a:23–24; NA:RG165:USFET:IC:1SIIR:96.
156   deer, horse, elephant: OKH:H3/284a:26.
156   determine formations: Ibid.:24.
156   captured weapons: D-407, 69.
156   Sherman tank: Speer, interview, 2.
156   T34: RMfBuM, *Rüstung,* 68.
156   "A hitherto unknown": OKH:H2/7:1.September 1943.
156   aircraft crashed: MA:RL2/601:Februar 1944:7–8 instructs in their importance for intelligence.
156   TB 7: IWM:Milch:16:2187.
157   Stirling: Ibid.:2185.
157   Norden bomb sights: Ibid.:16:2636, 2941, 18:3987–88, 20:5233.
157   Schwenke, 200 prisoners: Schwenke, interview.
157   team of men: IWM:Milch:16:2186.
157   daylight bombing: Ibid.:2429.
157   "extraordinarily easily": Ibid.:20:5231.
157   ton and a half: Ibid.:16:2429.
157   "If I may": Ibid.:2947.
159   "Where are the tanks": Ibid.:2948.
159   munition size discussion: Ibid.:2949.

CHAPTER 11: THE OVERT FACTOR

160   spent their mornings: Liss, 19.
160   power to prohibit: Joseph Wulf, *Presse und Funk im Dritten Reich: Eine Dokumentation* (Gütersloh: Sigbert Mohn Verlag, 1964), 84–85; BA:R43 II/1150:3. April 1936.
160   he did this: BA:EAP 250-a/221:16755.
160   government prohibited: *Reichsgesetzblatt* (1939), 1683.
160   Britain banned: BA:DAI:176:16.7.40.
160   special efforts: See, for example, Halder, 2:278.
160   Foreign Newspaper Trade: BA:DAI:176:15.Mai 1940, 6. Feb. 1942; RMfVuP, *Kriegspropaganda,* 155, 220.
160   51 copies: BA:EAP 250-a/221:16757.
160   fisherman: Margarete Gärtner, *Botschafterin des Guten Willens: Aussenpolitische Arbeit, 1914–1950* (Bonn: Athenäum-Verlag, 1955), 507; NA:RG242:Interrogation of Anton Reithinger: 18.6.47:6.
161   £1.10.0: NA:RG165:Schuster Commission:Interrogation of Rolf Hoffman:2.

161 a week, four to six weeks: Ibid.; NA:RG 59:Poole Commission:Interrogation of Wilhelm Tannenberg:20 and 21 October 1945:6.
161 special unit: Ibid.; OKW:80:28.3.44.
161 Schmidt built it up: NA:RG165:SAIC/49; Seabury, 75–76; Boelcke, "Presseabteilungen," 46; NG-3590:2.
161 Lisbon photocopies: Paul K. Schmidt-Carell, letter, 12. Juni 1974.
161 spies in Latin America: NA:RG59:DSDF 862.20210/1996:72:18 December 1941; NA:RG59: DSDF 862.20225/620:5-5:four.
161 Farben, Hamburg, Kiel: NA:RG242:Interrogation of Anton Reithinger:18.6.47:7; Ilgner in Richard Sasuly, *I. G. Farben* (New York: Boni & Gaer, 1947), 246.
161 German Society for Documentation: BA:EAP 250-a/221:16827-30.
161 29-page list: Ibid.:16842ff.
161 no one revealed: Ibid.:16828–29.
161 turned to Sweden: BA:R58/123:38.
161 OKW special group: OKW:2166:19; USN:COA:Bürkner interrogation:4, 7.
161 scores of posts: Schnabel, ed., 225.
161 army had dozens: *Allgemeine Heeresmitteilungen*, 6 (7. Oktober 1939), 297; NA:RG165: USFET:IC:1SIIR:96; OKH:H3/463.2:2.Aug.43; Halder, 2:208, 295; D-407, 92.
161 Reich Commissar: BA:R55DC/vorl.465:11.6.42.
161 two low small rooms: Ibid.:14.8.41.
161 DNB: BA:R55/634:203: Boelcke, "Presseabteilungen," 47–48.
162 Foreign Office: Paul K. Schmidt-Carell, letter, 12. Juni 1974; AA:Inland II g:74:22.8.42.
162 Pearl Harbor: IMT, 10:201.
162 to close a gap: Schnabel, ed., 225.
162 Mair: BDC; Boelcke, "Das 'Seehaus,' " 240, 241–42. Party No. 6,199,379.
162 stole the idea: Boelcke, "Das 'Seehaus,' " 239–40.
162 gainer of power: Ibid., 240.
162 Foreign Office had lost: *Reichsgesetzblatt* (1933), 449, and *DGFP*:C, 1:483–85, for example.
162 locations, rented, three weeks: Ibid., 239–40.
162 500 employees: Boelcke, "Das 'Seehaus,' " 246.
162 Swedish Pavilion: Lange, interview.
162 Goebbels began grabbing: Schnabel, ed., 223–24.
162 Interradio: Boelcke, "Das 'Seehaus,' " 253–54; AA:Kult-Pol: Ru 1:5.November 1941:1–2.
162 absorbed: Paul K. Schmidt-Carell, letter, 12.Juni 1974; BA:R55/634:45.
162 omnidirectional, two receivers: Boelcke, "Das 'Seehaus,' " 243.
163 outposts: Ibid., 249–50, 265; NA:RG165:HTUSAIC:IR10:2.
163 February 1942: BA:R55/634:138.
163 WCBA: OKW:732:10.
163 all English broadcasts: BA:R55DC/vorl.465:28.September 1942.
163 20 to 30 percent: BA:R55/733:254.
163 8,266, 646: Schnabel, ed., 237–38.
163 527, 630, 700: Boelcke, "Das 'Seehaus,' " 247.
163 monitor requirements: Ibid., 245.
163 Linge: NA:RG165:HTUSAIC:IR:10:8–9.
163 Dasch: Ibid.:10; NA:RG165:USFET:MISC:O1:FIR:18:3.
163 foreigners: Boelcke, "Das 'Seehaus,' " 245–46.
163 Dagmar Geissler recruitment: Lange, interview.
164 foreign broadcast schedules: OKW:730:15.März 1941.
164 Latvian, Lithuanian, Estonian: BA:R55/733:286.
164 two to a hotel room: Lange, interview.
164 live, recorded, transcribed, telephoned: Boelcke, "Das 'Seehaus,' " 243–44, 252.
164 six broadcasts: Schnabel, ed., 241.
164 Dagmar Geissler work: Lange, interview.
164 three times a day: NA:RG165:USFET:MISC:OI:FIR:18:4.
164 Albrecht, Timmler: Ibid.; NA:RG165:USFET:MISC;OI:FIR:18:Annex:1.
165 25 July 1943: Lange, interview.
165 *Radio Mirror, Weekly Radio Mirror*: Boelcke, "Das 'Seehaus,' " 251.
165 *Radio Intercept Reports*: Ibid.; study of a set in Library of Congress, D731.F8.
166 430: Boelcke, "Das 'Seehaus,' " 251.
166 Mair: NA:RG165:USFET:MISC:OI:FIR:18:6; BDC.
166 Wilms, Albrecht: NA:RG165:USFET:MISC:OI:FIR:18:6.
166 Hitler reduced: RMfVuP, "*Wollt*," 211.
166 "defeatism": Goebbels, 48.
166 28, 204, 18, 107: Schnabel, ed., 229.
166 13: BA:R55/634:82.
166 50 sets, Dönitz, Schellenberg, Japanese: Boelcke, "Das 'Seehaus,' " 267.
166 "not as fast": BA:R55/634:227.
166 Reich Press Center: NA:RG165:Schuster Commission:Interrogation of Rolf Hoffman:1–2.
166 "the journalistic expression": [NSDAP], *Organisationsbuch der NSDAP* (1943), 304.
166 10 readers, Desk X, Desk XII: NA:RG165:Schuster Commission:Interrogation of Rolf Hoffman:2; *ADAP*, 1:573–74; Boelcke, "Presseabteilungen," 47; Paul K. Schmidt-Carell, letter, 12.Juni 1974; NG-3590:8, 10, 11–12.
168 Weizsäcker: *DGFP*, 13:617–18.
168 Foreign Press Group: For the first half of the war this was Group V (OKW, *KTB*, 1:917–18, OKH:H3/1560:12.Juni 1942). After Ausland was raised from a branch to a division in summer

1942, it became Group C of Branch II (OKW:Wi VIII/25:1.10.42, OKW:2165:15.8.43, OKW: 1722: Juni 1944).
168 Schierbrandt: Schierbrandt, interview.
168 15 to 20, procedures: Ibid.
168 Foreign Press Report: OKW:1019:passim.
168 O'Secolo: OKW:WO1-7/248:11.Juni 1940:Kurze Fassung and Ibid.:Längere Fassung.
168 report to Hitler: Schierbrandt, interview; *Gazet van Antwerpen* (11 and 12 January 1940). The paper involved may have been the *Gazet van Mechelen*, where the crash occurred, but no copies of it of that date may survive, since the editors sent me photocopies of the Antwerp paper instead. On the Mechelen affair, see Halder, 1:156, with additional citations.
169 "We want to": OKW:WO1-7/248.
169 few top officials: OKH:H3/1500:4.Juni 1942.
169 Chi: Kahn, 457; OKW;1013:passim; OKW:WO1-7/224:passim.
169 19 May 1942: OKH:H3/1500.
169 navy: *German Naval Intelligence*, 32–34; OKM:PG26674:16–17.
169 air force: Völker, *Deutsche Luftwaffe*, 296; USAF-171, 32–34, 64.
169 Foreign Armies East: OKH:H3/1515; OKH:H3/463.2:2.August 1943:3, 4; NA:RG165:USFET: IC:1SIIR:127.
170 parachutists: OKH:H2/3:21.10.43.
170 relief map: Ibid.:14.Nov.1943.
170 LCM: Ibid.:Auszugsweise Abschrift.
170 Stimson: OKH:H2/9:20.3.43.
170 convoy arrivals: Ibid.:15.12.43, 2.3.44, 31.5.44, among others.
170 Montgomery: P-041h, 14–15.
170 landing-boat production: OKH:H2/9:16.1.44.
170 army groups and armies: D-407, 92.
170 King George VI, Negro division: *German Operational Intelligence*, 54, 70.
170 Hitler mispronounced: Warlimont, 225–26.
170 favorite of all kinds of information: Warlimont, interview; Dr. Paul K. Schmidt-Carell, letter, 12.Juni 1974.
170 *Picture Post: Lagevorträge*, 629; *Picture Post* 25 (28 October 1944), 13–16.
171 one of his most important sources: NG-3705:3.
171 Lorenz, Führer Material Service: NG-4331.
171 bedroom, valet, no condensations: Dietrich, 154.
171 read 100: NG-3590:12.
171 "It would be very useful": *Hitler's Table Talk*, 278.
171 "The English are": *Hitlers Lagebesprechungen*, 418.

CHAPTER 12: HEARING DIPLOMATS CHATTER

In these notes, the interrogations of Gottfried Schapper in NA:RG238 are cited simply as "Schapper" and by number instead of by date according to the following key: 1: 21. Oktober 1947; 2: 8. Dezember 1947; 3: 19. Dezember 1947; 4: 15. Januar 1948; 5: 22 Januar 1948; 6: 23. Januar 1948. Unless otherwise cited, all material on Pers Z comes from Kahn, 436–46, and all on the German postal radiotelephone intercept operation from Vetterlein, interview. This interview is further cited when it is one of several sources.

172 Vetterlein: interview; BDC. Party No. 4,100,140; SS No. 450,689.
172 A-3: Kahn, 554–55.
173 technical solution details: Vetterlein, interview; Lt. Col. E. Schroter, *Research on Speech Scrambling in Germany* (Combined Intelligence Objectives Sub-Committee, 15 March 1946), 3, 5 (in National Air and Space Museum Library, Washington, D.C., Captured German Air Technical Documents, Roll 3787, Frames 457–61).
173 fall 1941, 6 March 1942: Kahn, 555–56.
173 Party Card 42: BDC.
173 Ohnesorge and Berger: NA:RG 238:Ohnesorge interrogation:29.April 1947:4–5.
173 Schellenberg forwards: AA:Inland II g:477f:328440,328455–56, 329063.
173 direct line to Führer: BA:EAP 161-b-12/372A:21.5.42.
173 Valkenswaard: Personal visit, 14 October 1973.
174 most intercepts: My conclusions from those in AA:Inland II g:477f.
174 28 February 1944: Ibid.:329064–66.
174 "Mistrust and dissatisfaction": Ibid.:329063.
174 people intercepted: Ibid.:passim.
175 Hopkins-Churchill: Ibid.:328392 (in German); Churchill, 5:200–201. Sherwood, 840, for "John Martin."
175 23 July 1942: BA:EAP 161-b-12/364 with first page of this intercept bearing notation "for submission to the Führer." Reproduced in Kahn, 557. "You will accelerate" is on page 2 of the transcript. Flicke, 233.
175 scrambler insecurity recognition: Kahn, 560.
175 reasons for speakers' use: Averell Harriman, letter, 15 May 1972; the Earl of Avon (Anthony Eden), letter, 17 May 1972; Sherwood, 440–41.
175 Roosevelt surprises Germans, higher-ups get no warnings: Vetterlein, interview.
175 cross-Channel build-up: Schellenberg, 366.
175 29 July 1943: OKW, *KTB*, 3:854; Colvin, 193. In the conversation, Churchill said he would send a message to the king of Italy urging that Allied prisoners not be given over to the Ger-

mans; in a cable to Roosevelt later that day, in which he mentions the conversation, he reports having sent this message (Churchill, 5:60–61). German suspicions false: Churchill, 5:44; Deakin, 501–502.

176   results fall off: Vetterlein, interview, said that he had the impression that another circuit was in use. In fact, a new kind of scrambler was put into use.
176   "There is in general": AA:Inland II g:477f:328367.
176   nine major agencies: My list. A less complete list, with duties, in OKL:3248:15.6.1944. Two other agencies concentrated on internal security: the OKW/Wehrmachtsnachrichtenverbindungen/Funkwesen, for agent counterespionage (Ibid.; P-041k, 13, 36), and the uniformed police, a branch of the SS, which monitored agent and other illegal transmissions (H. J. Giskes, *London Calling North Pole* [London: Kimber, 1953], 19, 20).
176   specialization: P-041k, 35.
176   cooperated, relations cool: Bonatz, 88; Schapper, 1:9; Seifert, interview, 11; P-041k, 37.
176   more than two dozen: Karl Heinz Riemer, *Zensurpost aus dem III. Reich: Die Überwachung des Auslandsbriefverkehrs während des II. Weltkrieges durch deutsche Dienststellen*, Neue Schriftenreihe der Poststempelgilde "Rhein-Donau" e.v., 61 (Dusseldorff: Neue Schriftenreihe, 1966), iv; Karl Kurt Wolter, *Die Postzensur: Handbuch und Katalog* (Munich: Amm, 1965–66), 2:10, 21–27; OKW:1026:10.Januar 1940.
177   part of Abwehr: OKW, *KTB*, 1:888.
177   Frankfurt station: BA:EAP 173-b-26/3:undated Bericht über die Besuche bei der ABP Frankfurt a/M am 18.11.41 und der APB Köln am 19.11.41.
177   20,000: BA:EAP 173-b-18-41/1:undated Tätigkeitsbericht der chem.-techn. Abteilung der A.B.-Prufstelle Frankfurt/M über die Zeit vom 1.-30.9.1944.
177   number of workers: Ibid., which gives 568 in the chemical-technical section in September 1944; Library of Congress: Manuscript Division:Captured Records Division:Container 328: Kriegstärkenachweisung for the Auslandsbriefprufstelle Frankfurt/Main, 1.5.42, gives 772 in this section.
177   *Commandant Dorise:* OKW:Wi I/52:11.9.42.
177   carob bread: Ibid.:10.9.42.
177   mercury, hemp: OKW:Wi I/51:25.1.43.
177   couple of hundred, "valuable": Payr, 8.
177   Gottlob: BDC. Party No. 8,016,151; SS No. 127,671.
177   A 6, F 6, F 7, F 2: BA:R58/840:1.2.40; BDC:Josef Gottlob:17.11.41, 2.April 1943; IMT, 38:24.
178   Figl: Kahn, 263, 316–18, 446; Dr. and Frau Franz Weber, interview.
178   Langer: Isolde Langer, interview; BDC. Party No. 6,118,206.
178   47 specialists and assistants, Jagowstrasse 18: BDC:Josef Gottlob: 20.1.1940.
178   10 pages a day: BA:R55 DC/vorl.465:18. and 19. März 1942.
178   systems of minor nations, coffee: Wilhelm Höttl [pseud. Walter Hagen], *Hitler's Paper Weapon*, trans. Basil Creighton (London: Rupert Hart-Davis, 1955), 132.
178   no memorable solutions: NA:RG238:Schellenberg interrogations:8 May 1946:3.
178   had to beg: Schellenberg, *Memoirs*, 268–69.
178   Madrid, making codes: NA:RG165:HTUSAIC:IR15:37; NA:RG165:HQ 7th Army:307th CIC Det:FIR:12 Dec 1945:Appendix 3:6–7.
178   6,000 employees: Seifert, interview, 8. He says there were 3,000 to 4,000 at the start of the war. Kittel, 16, says a maximum of 3,500. Schapper, 4:10, says 3,600 at end.
178   half Nazis: Kittel, 17.
178   Schapper: Seifert interview, 6; Schapper, 1:2–3, 3:1, 4:11. BDC. Party No. 536,206.
178   disliked political cryptanalysis: Seifert, interview, 2–3, 13; Schapper, 1:3.
178   Hitler provides opportunity: Seifert, interview, 3; Kittel, 2.
178   to Göring: Schapper, 1:1,3, 4:3.
179   Hitler fear, agency to Göring: Seifert, interview, 4; Kittel, 3.
179   personal advantage: David Irving interview with Erhard Milch, 14 May 1968.
179   grants Schapper's conditions, agency name, leader: Schapper, 1:3–5, 2:6–7.
179   Schimpf: Seifert, interview, 1; Budde, interview; Flicke, 109. BDC. Party No. 2,638,165.
179   10 April 1933: Schapper, 6:1.
179   attic: Kittel, 4.
179   20 men: Seifert, interview, 6.
179   takes over telephone wiretapping: Seifert, interview, 12; Flicke, 93; Kittel, 2; MA:WK XII: 1435:9.Juli 1938:3.
179   locations: Seifert, interview, 6; Flicke, 110–11; Kittel, 5, 8–9; NA:RG165:6824 DIC (MIS)/M. 1170:3; NA:RG165:MIS 0174687:2.
179   6 branches, bureaus: Schapper, 4:9–10; Kittel, 83; NA:RG165:SAIC:CIR:7:3–4.
179   Christoph, Schapper: Flicke, 109; Seifert, interview, 6; NA:RG165:SAIC:CIR:7:2; Schapper, 4:4, 2:1. BDC. Christoph Party No. originally 1,498,608, later 696,176.
179   sources: Schapper, 1:5.
179   espionage failure: Ibid.
179   telephone tapping requests: Ibid., 7; Irving, ed., 187.
179   general requests: Kittel, 26; OKW:Wi/VI.1:2.6.1944:5.
180   Göring approves or denies: IMT, 9:442 (Göring); Schapper, 1:8, 2:7; Seifert, interview, 7, 17.
180   A research posts: Kittel, 30; NA:RG165:MIS 0174687:8–9.
180   1,000 taps, half Berlin: Schapper, 1:14, Seifert, interview, 5.
180   cable connections: Schapper, 2:1, 3:2; NA:RG165:6284 DIC (MIS)/M.1170:5.
180   A research post locations: NA:RG165:6284 DIC (MIS)/M.1170:3.
180   existing monitoring posts: Kittel, 30; Seifert, interview, 5; NA:RG165:6824 DIC MIS/M.

1136:3; Schapper, 2:2. NA:RG238:Steengracht interrogation:3 mentions a telephone intercept made in Denmark.
180 A research post operations: NA:RG165:6284 DIC (MIS)/M.1170:6–7; NA:RG165:MIS 0174687:10–11.
180 B research posts: Kittel, 34–36.
180 C research posts: Ibid., 37–38; NA:RG165:MIS 0174687:7,8.
181 D research posts: Seifert, interview, 5; Kittel, 39; NA:RG165:MIS 0174687:8.
181 Schroeder: Seifert, interview, 2; Schapper, 1:9. Party No. 536,207(BDC). The third original member was Max Böttger (Schapper, 1:4). He quite the Forschungsamt in 1935 to become chief of personnel on the staff of the future Foreign Minister, Ribbentrop (Jacobsen, 226, 276).
181 diplomatic and private codes: Kittel, 44.
181 240 members, Hollerith, 3,000 a month: Ibid., 42, 43.
181 three-fourths of codes: Schapper, 2:3.
181 half the diplomatic telegrams: Weizsäcker, 165.
181 codes solved: Seifert, interview, 10; Weizsäcker, 164; Irving, ed., 17.
181 no Russian diplomatic solutions: Seifert, interview, 10; Schapper, 1:15–16, 2:3.
181 Russian armament solution: Seifert, interview, 9; Kittel, 44. Schellenberg may have been referring to this when he said that the Forschungsamt could pick up Stalin's personal secret instructions (*Memorien,* 217).
181 sorting unit: Seifert, interview, 8.
181 Branch 11 statistics: Kittel, 47.
181 Branch 12 statistics: Ibid., 54.
181 1,000 in, 60–150 out: Seifert, interview, 8. A calculation based on the N numbers in Irving, ed., and in Kahn, 448, confirms this, showing about 113 outgoing reports a day between 11 February 1940 and 13 April 1942, rising to 190 between 21 March 1942 and 19 March 1945. Schapper's figure of up to 500 reports a day (2:6) must reflect an exceptional situation.
181 Seifert: Seifert, interview. BDC. Party No. 4,826,808; SS No. 185,415.
181 objectivity, scholarly: see the pages of the long Forschungsamt report, "Zu der englischen Politik vom Münchner Abkommen bis zum Kriegsausbruch" in AA: Unterstaatssekretär: Dokumente Kriegsausbruch:August 1939–Januar 1940:323510–91. This is the document translated in Irving, ed. Kittel, 63.
181 brown sheets; Kittel, 63; Seifert, interview, 14, says that brown was chosen because all other colors were taken. I don't believe it.
181 reports to Göring: Schapper, 1:8, 4:7; Seifert, interview, 22.
182 Schellenberg: Schapper, 1:12, 2:4; Kittel, 77. One of Schellenberg's reports, however, passed on Forschungsamt surveillance results (BA:EAP 161-b-12/10:6.2.43).
182 Foreign Office: Kittel, 74.
182 distribution control: Irving, ed., 187–88, 190; Schapper, 2:8, 5:3. References to return of documents in OKH:H27/41:Teil 2:27.April 1944, and BA:EAP 173-b-24-10/12:7.9.1944.
182 factory No. 447: BA:EAP 66-c-12-44/464:192966.
182 diplomatic 9:1 important: Schapper, 1:15; Kittel, 48.
182 Sudeten crisis: Kittel, 49.
182 Masaryk-Benes intercepts: PRO:FO371/21742:218–70, at 249 for "I said here" and 252 for "You simply cannot." I am grateful to David Irving for this citation.
182 Göring gives, Masaryk denies: Ibid.: 183, 178, 179.
183 special envoy: *Hitlers Tischgespräche,* 362.
183 "There's nothing more": Wilhelm Treue, ed., "Rede Hitlers vor der deutschen Presse (10. November 1938)," *Vierteljahrshefte für Zeitgeschichte,* 6 (April 1958), 175–91 at 184.
183 insights into British, French, and Polish diplomacy: Irving, ed., passim.
183 Berlin telephone taps: Seifert, interview, 5.
183 British ambassador: Irving, ed., 117, 116, 113.
183 "And if the Germans": Halder, 1:36.
183 Dahlerus: IMT, 9:470 (Dahlerus), 497 (Göring); Birger Dahlerus, *The Last Attempt* (London: Hutchinson, [1948]), 106. The statement in Kahn, 435 and 436, that this message was solved by Pers Z is incorrect.
183 Hitler gets reports: Seifert, interview, 17; Irving, ed., 123–65.
183 Churchill intercept: Irving, ed., 130; Churchill, 3:189–90, 193.
183 British ambassador report: Irving, ed., 139.
183 21 January 1942: Ibid., 152.
183 Forschungsamt compilation: Ibid., 162.
184 "I have received": Goebbels, 333.
184 Roosevelt meeting suggestions: FRUS, *The Conferences at Cairo and Tehran,* 3. The report could not have pointed specifically to the Teheran meeting of November and December 1943, because the first exchanges leading to that only began three weeks after Goebbels got it.
184 "From the Forschungsamt": Irving, ed., 181.
184 no insight into Allied strategy: Seifert, interview, 11.
184 Stalingrad shocks diplomats: Irving, ed., 179.
184 "I am reading": Irving, ed., 178.
184 Darlan: As acknowledged by the OKW on the basis of its own intercepts (OKW, *KTB,* 2:956). Churchill, 4:612.
184 "I felt": Seifert, interview, 10.
184 "I am bound": NA:RG59:Poole mission:Hencke interrogation:5–6.
185 chancellor order: MA:F 5708:II.9.3:4.Dezember 1918; NA:RG242:Pers Z documents:Chiffrierstelle des Reichswehrministeriums:1.10.1919. Selchow: BDC. Party No. 7,910,928.
185 15,000 French cryptograms: extrapolation based on later figures in Irving, ed., 133, 163. I do not know when the numbering started.

185   Italian cryptograms: Ibid., 126, 161.
185   American cryptograms: Ibid., 134, 148, 165.
185   Turkish cryptograms: Ibid., 124–65. Schellenberg, *Memoirs*, 378–79. I have not been able to find these Pers Z solutions in the files of the Büro des Staatssekretärs in the Foreign Office.
185   intercepts to Hitler: Irving, ed., 144, 146, 150, 154, 163. *DGFP*, 13:689; *Staatsmänner*, 2:231.
186   solutions of U.S. messages: Kahn, 496–501; Mäkelä, 153–60.
186   Shah of Iran message: Irving, ed., 136; *FRUS, 1941*, 3:454–55.
186   Roosevelt-Stalin message: Irving, ed., 139; *FRUS, 1941*, 1:836; NA:RG59:DSDF 861.24/638; "Leak Gives Nazis Note," *New York Times* (9 October 1941), 1:7.
186   Roosevelt urges no ships sail: Irving, ed., 146; *FRUS, 1941*, 2:197–98, 198–99.
187   27 March 1942 message: Irving, ed., 161; *FRUS, 1942*, 2:160–61, 170, 201–202; NA:RG59: DSDF 851.00/2699.
187   Turkish message: OKH:H3/68.1:13.2.1945. *Hitlers Lagebesprechungen*, 665.
187   agricultural telegram: Such a message—perhaps the same one—is referred to by Gehlen, 64.

CHAPTER 13: ELECTRIC PROBINGS

189   chief duty: 50.I.D.:22985/4:22.1.42:2.
189   loop 7 January: AOK 11:22279/3:14.3.42:4.
189   15 January start: 24.I.D.:22006/11:19.1.1942:1.
190   helped alert: AOK 11:22279/3:14.3.42:4; Hans von Tettau und Kurt Versock, *Geschichte der 24. Infanterie-Division 1935–1945* (Stolberg: Kameradschaftsring der ehemaligen 24. Infanterie-Division, 1956), 64.
190   "Where," "very": 50.I.D.:22985/4:20.1.42:9.30 and 17.10.
190   battles of 21 January: 24.I.D.:22006/1:21.1.1942.
190   "Forty-five minutes": 50.I.D.:22985/4:21.1.42:16.00.
190   "Wiretap reconnaissance": 50.I.D.:22985/4:22.1.42:1.
191   Buschenhagen: Buschenhagen, interview; Seifert, interview, 1; Keilig.
191   Volunteer Evaluation Post: Buschenhagen, interview; MA:F5709:II.9.4:passim.
191   T 3's Abwehr group: Buschenhagen, letter, 26.11.1972.
191   32 persons: photograph of entire Chiffrierstelle (Cipher Center), in possession of Walther Seifert and identified by Buschenhagen.
191   Fenner: Flicke, 307–308;Ilse Fenner (daughter), letter, 8. Juni 1970.
191   Group II abolished: My conclusions from Seifert, interview; Flicke, 89; USAF-191, 1:123–24; Bonatz, 75–76; Randewig, "50 Jahre," 617.
191   part of OKW: OKW, *KTB*, 1:113E/114E; OKW:224:1:10b; OKW:2165:45; Wildhagen, ed., 106, 107; NA:RG242:*Auszug aus den Dienstanweisungen und Arbeitsplänen von Chef WNV, Ag WNV und unterstellten Abteilungen*, 28.September 1944; OKH:H5/14:12.
192   became Chiffrierabteilung; some time between March 1939, when it was still the Gruppe Chiffrierstelle (OKW:224:12e), and April 1942 (AA:Pol I M:29:Bd.1:26173).
192   headquarters: Flicke, 308.
192   secret intercept posts: AA:Pol I M:K.O. Spanien:Bd. 1:282079–80, 282218; Seifert, interview, 19–20.
192   secondary intercept posts: Schaedel, interview, 1.
192   primary intercept posts: Ibid.; OKW:2047:1.1.44 for assignments; visit to Lauf, 4 August 1970.
192   150 radiomen: OKH:H1/11:895.
192   3,000 men: Kettler, interview, 2.
192   prewar strength: OKW:224:9d, 9e.
192   personnel, organization: NA:RG242:*Arbeitsplan der Abteilung Chi der Ag WNV*. For what is probably a later document, OKH:H5/14:12.
192   Hollerith machines: OKW:Wi/IF 5.2150:29.11.37:1.
192   mechanical devices: Jensen.
192   translucent paper: Kahn, 458.
192   Franz: Franz, interview; *Wer Ist Wer*, 1967/68.
192   Bern solutions: Franz, interview. For other solutions, Schaedel, interview, 2.
193   "foreign governments": *Arbeitsplan der Abteilung Chi der Ag WNV*.
193   diplomatic cryptograms: Kettler, interview, 8; Flicke, 93; Franz interview.
193   agreed with Foreign Office: NA:RG242:Pers Z documents:undated memorandum of a conference on 12.2.34.
193   only diplomatic traffic: Randewig, "Organisation der Deutschen Nachrichtenaufklärung," 2, in Praun, "Eine Untersuchung."
193   defense ministers liked: Seifert, interview, 3.
193   Fellers: Kahn, 472–77; Staubwasser, interview; Schaedel, interview; MA:III M 1000:April 1942:545–46 for "the fall of Malta"; *Hitlers Tischgespräche*, 28.Juni 1942 abends for "the capture of"; Roskill, 2:69.
195   VN: samples in OKW:1707.
195   29 December 1944: Ibid. Original message in NA:RG59. The solution is accurate.
198   other VNs: Ibid.; T-120:2651:E387462–67; *DGFP*, 13:325.
198   Versailles treaty: Part V, Table II, Establishment of an Infantry Division. *Heeres-Verordnungsblatt*, 3 (20.Juni 1921), 257 for its organization. The Germans did not know at first whether this meant wiretapping or radio interception; discussions with the International Military Commissions of Control concluded upon the latter (Nebel, letter, 28 April 1972, 3–4).
198   12 major radio stations: Randewig, "50 Jahre," 616.
198   six interception posts: Ibid., 617.

198 receivers, radiomen: Randewig, "Organisation der Deutschen Nachrichtenaufklärung," 1–2, in Praun, "Eine Untersuchung."
198 1928, two years later, evolution: Ibid., 2–3; Seifert, interview, 2; Flicke, 124.
198 directing: Randewig, "Organisation der Deutschen Nachrichtenaufklärung," 5, in Praun, "Eine Untersachung."
198 Fellgiebel: Wildhagen, ed., passim; NA:RG242: Fellgiebel personnel file; P-132, 61–70.
198 Praun: NA:RG242:Praun personnel file; Praun, interview.
199 four levels: Randewig, "50 Jahre," 685.
199 seven mobile companies: Tessin, *Formationsgeschichte*, 198–205.
199 Polish campaign: Wildhagen, ed., 70–76; P-041k, 42.
199 distance of Main Intercept Post: Randewig, "50 Jahre," 685.
199 creation of commanders: Ibid.
199 tactical results poor: Ibid., 686.
199 divisions' squads: *German Operational Intelligence*, 9, 20.
199 short-range companies: Ibid., 689; Halder, 1:239.
199 company scattered platoons: Randewig, "50 Jahre," 689, 690; OKH, Merkblatt *Die Nachrichtenaufklärungskompanie* (24. Juni 1942), §5; *German Operational Intelligence*, 16–19, 67, 72, 77; OKH:H1/11:865a.
199 renaming: Randewig, "50 Jahre," 690; Tessin, 2:50, 122, 190, 258, 306; HGrNord:75130/31: 333:1.
199 communications intelligence battalions: Randewig, "50 Jahre," 690; Tessin, 2:50, 122, 191, 258, 306; 3:110, 147, 179, 211, 247, 274, 306; OKH:H1/11:813a; P-041k, 34.
199 8 regiments: Hepp, "Funkaufklärung," 292, 293; Randewig, "50 Jahre," 690; *German Operational Intelligence*, 8, 11–12; HGrD:75744/35:untitled organizational chart of communications intelligence.
199 corps evaluation unit: Hepp, "Funkaufklärung," 292; *German Operational Intelligence*, 13–15, 67; OKH:H1/11:860.
199 general of communications reconnaissance: Praun, *Soldat*, 224, 231; Randewig, "50 Jahre," 690; *German Operational Intelligence*, 11–12; OKH:H1/58:55–57.
200 Boetzel: *Das gelbe Blatt* (September 1969), 9–10.
200 to assure cooperation: Randewig, "Verfahren der Funkaufklärung-Empfangs- und Peildienst-Auswertung," 19, in Praun, "Eine Untersuchung."
200 Neeb: Neeb, interview.
201 Oer: HGrD:75144/36:31; Wiebe, interview.
201 Communications Reconnaissance Battalion 12: HGrD:85463:76:Anlage 2.
201 fixed intercept posts 3, 2, 12: HGrD:85463:undated Anlage I:16:81.
201 Euskirchen, Port Marly, Louveciennes: Ibid.:100.
201 individual assignments, 36 receivers, radiomen's techniques: Randewig, "Verfahren der Funkaufklärungs-Empfangs- und Peildienst-Auswertung," 19, in Praun, "Eine Untersuchung."
203 staff wave lengths: Schmidt, interview, 2.
203 direction-finding: Ibid.; Randewig, "Taktische Funkpeilung," *Wehrtechnische Hefte*, 52 (1955), 104–10.
203 card indexes: Randewig, "Verfahern der Funkaufklärung-Empfangs- und Peildienst-Auswertung," 21, in Praun, "Eine Untersuchung."
203 patterns: see, for example, the diagrams of radio nets in HGrNord: 74130/28.
203 Russian armored army: Blumröder, interview.
203 95 percent: Randewig, "Verfahren der Funkaufklärung-Empfangs- und Peildienst-Auswertung," 21, in Praun, "Eine Untersuchung."
203 17 February 1944: III.Pz.Korps:53975/5:25.Februar 1944.
204 Royal Marines practice: OKH:H2/121b:100.
204 26th Panzer Division: *German Operational Intelligence*, 63.
204 "The monitoring of": HGrNord:75130/31:7 July 1943:3.
204 wiretapping: Randewig, untitled insert, 13, in Praun, "Eine Untersuchung"; OKH, Merkblatt *Die Nachrichtenaufklärungskompanie* (24.Juni 1942), §§92, 83, 89.
204 72nd Infantry Division: AOK11:22279/3:14.3.42:6.
204 22,254, 14,373: HGrC:75138/31:10.10.1944:2.
204 proportion increases: *German Operational Intelligence*, 26.
205 handful to 200: Randewig, "Entzifferung," 27a-27b, Anlage 6b in Praun, "Eine Untersuchung."
205 lower staff cryptanalysts: Randewig, "Entzifferung," 27b, in Praun, "Eine Untersuchung."
205 "contain operational combat reports": HGrNord:75130/34:1.3.44:9.
205 Army Group North: Kahn, 648.
205 "it is only infrequently": HGrNord:75130/34:4.4.1944:8.
206 "a growing complication": HGrNord:75130/35:296:10.
206 34 percent, 33 percent: Kahn, 648.
206 command nets unreadable: P-130, 94; Schaedel, interview; Randewig, "Die Beurteilung der Funkdienste . . . ," 124, 127, 128 in Praun, "Eine Untersuchung . . ."; NA:RG242:Pers Z documents:19.Februar 1934.
206 Call sign SOTÖ: AOK11:22409/222:13.III.[1942]:1100.
206 station ÖPWCH: AOK11:22409/223:15.III.[1942]:(2).
207 "5th Guards Army": OKH:H3/245:25.8.1944.
207 American order of battle: HGrD:75144/35:88.
207 Ferry Control code: III M 1000/59 at 54 for 4,371 tons and 77 for 5,336 tons, also 9, 107, 159, 271, 369; *German Operational Intelligence*, 23.
207 XIXth Corps: Ibid.; Harrison, 380–81.
207 photographs, Caen attack: HGrD:85463:28.Juni 1944:89; Wilmot, 337, 342–43; OBWest: Feindlage map:17.7.1944.

208   British calls for air support, stood by, passed: *German Operational Intelligence,* 8–9, 24; HGrD:75144/36:17.Februar 1945, 1.Oktober 1944, 9.Oktober 1944.
208   10 August message: HGrD:75144/4:209/H.
208   20 and 30 warnings: HGrD:85463:219; HGrD:75144/36:17.Februar 1945:45.
208   at exact time: *German Operational Intelligence,* 24.
208   "great worth," "thankfully accepted": HGrD:85459:107, 110.
208   military police interceptions: HGrD:75144/35:6.2.45; P-130, 97; Randewig, "Die Beurteilung der Funkdienste," 128, in Praun, "Eine Untersuchung"; Manteuffel, interview, 1. OKW, *KTB,* 4:1080 may also refer to this.
208   "an intended Russian attack": HGrNord: 75130/31:2.7.1943:3.
209   "11th Guard Army": OKH:H3/245:9.August 1944:7.
209   divisions were ordered: Ibid.:10.August 1944:6.
209   Russian response: Ziemke, 343.
209   7th Army I c: OKH:H2/3:4.November 1944.
209   Germans see through: Neeb, interview; Randewig, "Die Sowjetrussische Funktäuschung in der Schlacht von Tscherkassy," *Allgemeine Schweizerische Militärzeitschrift,* 119 (Juni 1953), 429–37.
209   successful British transfer: HGrD:75820:73/9. OKW, *KTB,* 4:316 implies that the Germans could look through fake messages.
209   Halder: Halder, 2:192.
209   "The 8th Army": HGrNord:75130/31:2.7.1943:4.
210   1939 mistrust: Wildhagen, ed., 74; Hepp, "Funkaufklärung," 288, 297.
210   "outstanding," "always knew": XXXX.Pz.K.:51231/1:2:2.
210   60 percent: *German Operational Intelligence,* 22.
210   "the most important": HGrD:75144/33:4/6.
210   "the darling": Liss, "entscheidende Wert," 585.
210   "the most copious": Halder in preface to Praun, "Eine Untersuchung."
210   Luftwaffe radio intelligence development: USAF-191, 1:193–216, 2:1; Hoffmann, 1:23–25.
210   stone buildings: USAF-191, 1:241–43.
210   radio reconnaissance battalions: Ibid., 2:19–20.
210   radio reconnaissance regiments: Ibid., 27–28; *Luftnachrichtentruppe,* 56.
211   Cape Sounion: B-644, 21.
211   Battalion 350: Kahn, 461, 463; USAF-191, 2:5, 60.
211   5,000: Friedrich, interview.
211   Freudenfeld: Hoffman, 2:2, ix.
211   Friedrich: Friedrich, interview.
211   25 June 1941: Bekker, 209.
211   flying monitors: B-644, 22–23; USAF-171, 22–23.
211   Ploesti: Kahn, 464.
212   70 percent, most valuable: Haenschke, 98.
212   only tactical and operational: Jodl, "Vernehmung," 539.
212   gave up intercepting: HGrC:75138/31:10.10.1944:1.

CHAPTER 14: THE CODEBREAKER WHO HELPED THE U-BOATS

213   Tranow: my impressions; Schwabe, interview, 5.
213   breaking rules: Tranow, interview, 1; Bonatz, 17.
214   Braune: Tranow, interview, 6–7.
214   Neumünster: Ibid., 2–3.
214   Jutland: Ibid., 4; Bonatz, 45–52.
214   spring of 1919: BA:F 5708:II.9.3:Bd.1, passim; NA:Captured Records Branch:Pers Z documents:31.Juli 1919.
214   Braune persuades: Tranow, interview, 7.
214   28 April 1919: Bonatz, 73.
214   three men: Tranow, interview, 8; Tranow, letter, 27. Januar 1974.
214   Government Telegraph Code: Tranow, interview, 9.
214   4-letter code: Ibid., 10.
214   Franke: Ibid., 11.
214   Villingen: Bonatz, 78–79.
214   Schwabe: Schwabe and Budde, interview, 1, 16–17.
214   August departed: BA:II M 62/6:82–85; Tranow, interview.
215   Italy dropped: Bonatz, 117.
215   Poland to army: BA:II M 62/6:82–85.
215   B-Dienst banished: Tranow, letter, August 1973; Bonatz, 74.
215   Bonatz: BA:III M 1006/2:13.11.1941; Lohmann.
215   one of three elements: Bonatz, 75; Hubatsch, *Admiralstab,* 255–56.
215   1935 agreement: *DGFP:*C, 4:323–26.
215   war plans against Britain forbidden: Michael Salewski, *Die deutsche Seekriegsleitung 1935–1945* (Frankfurt am Main: Bernard & Graefe, 1970), 1:30; Cajus Bekker, *Hitler's Naval War,* trans. and ed. Frank Ziegler (Garden City: Doubleday, 1974), 26–29.
215   transfer codebreaking effort: Tranow, interview, 12.
215   Naval Code solved by comparing: Tranow, comments to interview, 2.
216   strips superencipherment: Tranow, interview, 13–14; MacLachlan, 77.
216   control over Admiralty cryptosystems: Tranow, interview, 15–16.
216   1937 attacks: BA:M 26/34128:130.

216   30 men, tripled: Bonatz, 77, 76.
216   14, 252,000: BA:M 26/34128:130.
216   16 posts: Bonatz, 80
216   more than 500: Ibid., 86.
216   Franke and Tranow: Schwabe and Budde, interview, 8; Schwabe, interview, 5–6. Franke Party No.: 19,852(BDC).
216   takes over cryptanalysis: Tranow, interview, 21.
216   11 September, to Gibraltar, mid-November: Rohwer, "Radiotélégraphie," 45, 46, 47.
217   17 February: Ibid., 49; Bonatz, 137.
217   30 August: Rohwer, "Radiotélégraphie," 52.
217   "major help": Bonatz, 138.
217   44 posts: Bonatz, 100.
217   5,000, 1,100; Bonatz, 105, 103.
217   700, steel bars: Tranow, interview, 26, 16.
217   reorganizations: The organizational details in Lohmann, §32, 2, Bonatz, 97–98, and Helmuth Giessler, *Die Marine-Nachrichten- und Ortungsdienst*, Wehrwissenschaftliche Berichte, 10 (Munich: Lehmanns, 1971), 48, conflict at many points with one another, and the information in BA:III M 1006/4:55, 58, and in Militärarchiv, letter, 20.7.1973, is not complete. I have therefore avoided precise details of the B-Dienst subordination.
217   Norway assault: Kahn, 465.
217   *Queen Elizabeth:* Tranow, interview, 15.
218   older officers trusted agents: Ibid., 23.
218   system changeover, come back fast: BA:III M 1006/2:5.
218   nicknames: Tranow, interview, 31. Naval Code and Naval Cypher were also called Secret Code and Secret Cypher.
218   136 to 327: BA:III M 1006/3:231.
218   3,101,831: BA:III M 1006/6:78.
218   Hollerith machines: Tranow, interview, 18; Bonatz, 105, 110; BA:III M 1006/3:229–30.
219   *Athenia* solution: IMT, 35:527–29.
219   November 1941: BA:III M 1006/2:152.
219   April 1942: BA:III M 1006/3:236.
219   no U.S. solutions: BA:III M 1006/4:202–203, 197.
219   naval attaché messages: Tranow, interview, 22; Cf. AA:Pol I M:Mil Politik:2:England:1: 291283, 291296, 291300, 3. Oktober 1941.
219   broke back into MUNICH, COLOGNE: BA:III M 1006/3:233.
219   increasing cipher security: Ibid.
219   FRANKFORT solution, "especially in": Ibid.
219   "The Battle of": Churchill, 5:6.
219   Tranow most important: inferred from BA:III M 1006/6:last page.
220   "The moment": IMT, 37:552. Also Doenitz, 115.
220   SC 107: Bonatz, 141; Doenitz, 274–75; Roskill, 2:215–16.
220   "the timely arrival": Bonatz, 174.
220   Tranow commended: Tranow, interview, 23–24.
220   personnel doubled, tripled: BA:III M 1006/4:199.
220   360, 200, Schwabe: Bonatz, 110; Schwabe, interview, 3–4.
220   pressed case: Tranow, interview, 25–26.
220   Dönitz brings up matter: *Lagevorträge*, 465. Cf. 275, 288.
220   would sit at desk, Canadian names: Tranow, interview, 33.
221   greatest convoy battle: Rohwer, "Die grösste Geleitzugschlacht," 146–47, 149; Bonatz, 142; Dönitz, 329; Roskill, 2:365–66.
222   10 June: BA:III M 1006/4:199.
222   MUNICH BLUE, BROWN: BA:III M 1006/3:179, 233, BA:III M 1006/4, 199–200.
222   current locations: BA:III M 1006/4:197.
222   increased the tempo: BA:III M 1006/6:138.
222   *Athabaskan:* Ibid.:114–16; Roskill, 3:1:290.
222   reply to Hitler: BA:III M 1006/6:169.
222   Swedish, Turkish, Italian: Ibid., 141; III M 1000/60:125.
222   fight at front: Tranow, interview, 21.
222   half Kriegsmarine intelligence: Dönitz, letter, 27.1.1970.

CHAPTER 15: THE ADMIRAL AND HIS ABWEHR

223   PAN: BA:EAP-175-b-24-10/6:22.12.44.
224   IIIb to Intelligence Branch: *Armee-Verordnungsblatt* (1918), 707; Stoerkel, "Stellvertretenden," 93, 95–96.
224   demobilization: *Reichsgesetzblatt* (1919), 1; Stoerkel, 64.
224   Intelligence Group and Foreign Armies: Stoerkel, "Stellvertretenden," 101.
224   Nicolai unacceptable: Nicolai, *German Secret Service*, 236; Reile, *Ostfront*, 46; *Die Regierung des Prinzen Max von Baden*, eds. Erich Matthias and Rudolf Morsey, Quellen zur Geschichte des Parlamentarismus und der politischen Parteien (Düsseldorf: Droste, 1962), 104, 127. For his career after his firing, see Helmut Heiber, *Walter Frank und sein Reichsinstitut für Geschichte des neuen Deutschlands*, Quellen und Darstellungen zur Zeitgeschichte, 15 (Stuttgart: Deutsche Verlags-Anstalt, 1966).
224   Gempp: Stoerkel, "Stellvertretenden," 101; Buchheit, 32.

224   Troops Department, T 3: Stoerkel, "Stellvertretenden," 121; *Heeres-Verordnungsblatt* (1919), 345.
224   Abwehr Group attached to T 3: *Handbuch für das Deutsche Reich* (1922), 170; Kehrig, 39.
224   "Abwehr" etymology: letter, G. & C. Merriam Co., 21 March 1972.
224   four officers: *Rangliste des deutschen Reichsheeres* (1.April 1923), 3. The statement in Leverkuehn, 1, and copied in Reile, *Ostfront*, 47, and Buchheit, 33, that the Abwehr Group had 2 or 3 general staff officers and half a dozen others must refer to a later period.
224   clarifies east: Leverkuehn, 27; Reile, 48.
224   Cipher Center: Buschenhagen, letter, 26. November 1972.
224   23 June 1927: Buchheit, 36.
225   Schwantes: Ibid.; *Rangliste des deutschen Reichsheeres* (1.Mai 1926), 3, (1.Mai 1927), 3.
225   Schleicher's urging: Meinck, 106–107; Bracher, *Auflösung*, 252; Wheeler-Bennett, 182–84, 198.
225   1 April 1928: BA:N42/45:20.März 1928.
225   "the defense ministry's": Ibid.
225   Minister's Department: *Heeres-Verordnungsblatt* (1929), 21; Meinck, 114; Hossbach, 88–93; Bracher, *Auflösung*, 252.
225   Bredow: Buchheit, 38; Carsten, 365–66; *Stellenbesetzung für das Reichsheer* (1. Oktober 1921), 15; Seifert, 2nd interview; IfZ:ZS540:8.
225   expands Abwehr: USN, *German Naval Intelligence*, 9; Buchheit, 40.
225   travels to France and Belgium: *DGFP:*C, 1:210–11.
225   connections: Ott, interview.
225   Patzig: Buchheit, 40–42; Abshagen, 67.
226   Patzig's appointment: Patzig, interview; IfZ:ZS540:1–2.
226   Abwehr unimportant: Ott, interview.
226   information to Schleicher: MA:N97:1:passim.
226   Patzig clashed, fired, Canaris appointed: Patzig, interview; IfZ:ZS540:2–4; Aronson, 228, 306; Orb, 145; Best, 3–4; Abshagen, 67; Colvin, 13–14; Buchheit, 50.
226   Canaris life: unless otherwise specified, details from Krausnick, "Canaris"; Abshagen; Colvin; Schellenberg; Bartz; Leverkuehn; Groscurth; Höhne.
227   route from Chile to Germany: MA:PG75155:5. Oktober 1915.
227   U-boat pick-up: MA:PG61579:21. Oktober 1916 and its Anlagen and Ibid.: undated "Bericht Kapitänleutnant Canaris über Abholung durch 'U-35' von Trefflinie bei Cap Tinoso."
228   torpedo boats, Primo, Argentina: IMT, 34:555, 569, 568.
228   fitness reports: Krausnick, "Personalakten."
229   Dönitz: Dönitz (German ed.), 294.
229   did not like, too sly: Stoephasius, interview, 8.
229   regards to Himmler: Aronson, 290.
229   no ruthless driving personality: Abshagen, 71; Stoephasius, interview, 4.
229   Raeder's reluctance: IfZ:ZS540:4.
229   Canaris personality, incidents: mainly from Maurer, 6–7, 18, 42; Maurer, interview; Best, 7–8; Sachsenheimer, interview.
231   could not delegate: Abshagen, 93.
231   contradictory instructions: Ibid., 95; Lahousen in Gisevius, 439.
231   created chaos: Hoettl, *Secret Front*, 71; Lahousen in Gisevius, 440.
231   bad subordinates; lightweights: Abshagen, 94; Hoettl, *Secret Front*, 70; Bartz, 28.
231   defended them vigorously: Groscurth, 246, despite Barth, 28; Abshagen, 93.
231   most difficult superior: Lahousen in Gisevius, 439; Abshagen, 94, 218.
231   good agent: Schmid, 2.
231   broke with Patzig's views: Letter of Robert Holtzmann, 10.7.35, to Ludendorff, in Holtzmann papers in the Bundesarchiv. I am grateful to Dr. Nicholas Reynolds for this citation.
231   17 January 1935, five days later: Berlin: Geheimes Staatsarchiv:Rep. 90:Abt.P/Nr. 1:Heft 2:313–16, 309–12. I am indebted to Dr. George C. Browder for this citation.
231   Heydrich replaced anti-Abwehr official: Aronson, 306; Best, 4. Out was Dr. Günther Patschowsky, in was Dr. Werner Best.
232   10 Commandments: MA:RW5/v.194:21.Dezember 1936.
232   lunched together: Groscurth, 161.
232   socialized: Höhne, *Canaris*, 174–75.
232   "Yes? When?": Maurer, 20–21.
232   Protestant pastor, night of broken glass: Groscurth, 163.
232   Abwehr growth: Reile, *Ostfront*, 47–48, 175–76; Buchheit, 36.
232   Munich post: MA:WK XIII/7:1.Februar 1937.
232   six groups: USAF-191, 1:74; Buchheit, 39.
232   1936 reorganization: MA:RW5/v. 197:172–66.
233   1 June 1938: OKW: Wi/IF5.450:23 Mai 1938; Müller, 289; Groscurth, 100–101.
233   three branches: OKW: 224:18b, 19b, 20b.
233   Groups II, IV: The reasons for the separation from Abwehr control remain undertermined. I could not get a clear answer despite intensive questioning (Buschenhagen, letter, 26 November 1972; Seifert, interview, 3; Tranow, letter, August 1972; Bonatz, letter, August 1977).
233   Ausland branch: USN:COA:Bürkner interrogation:3; USN, *German Naval Intelligence*, 15. It later rose to a division, reorganized, changed some functions, and, when the Abwehr was taken over by the RSHA, went to the OKW's Operations Staff (OKW:Wi/VIII.25:1. Oktober 1942; NA:RG238:Bürkner interrogation:1–6; Bürkner, interview, 2–3, 7). On 23 July 1944, Keitel attached the OKH's attaché branch to it.
233   Central Group: OKW:1158:21.9.1938.
233   central agent files: Duesterberg, interview.
233   dictator of Rumania: OKW, *KTB*, 1:72.

233 Spanish chief of staff: Ibid., 63, 186; Halder, 2:192; *DGFP*, 10:521.
233 Franco: OKW, *KTB*, 1:196, 211, 219, 222; *DGFP*, 11:782, 816–17.
233 Mussolini: OKW, *KTB*, 2:317.
233 Italian intelligence chief: Ibid., 3:867.
233 Italians sought exclusive: *DGFP*, 10:474–75.
233 Canaris urged: OKW, *KTB*, 1:19.
233 lost fight: *DGFP*, 10:503–504.
233 agents ought not: *ADAP*, 2:240.
233 Canaris disputes, Foreign Office agrees: Ibid., 357–59.
233 Grand Mufti: OKW, *KTB*, 2:1092.
233 handled liaison: Halder, 1:218.
234 frequent reports to OKW officers: OKW, *KTB*, 1:5, 52, 157, 186, 340.
234 general situation: Ibid., 2:286–87, 3:192.
234 "dozens of times": IMT, 15:299 (Jodl). Gisevius, 443; Colvin, 31–32, 158.
234 Belgian forts, uniforms, Saarbrücken, bawled out: Groscurth, 233, 311, 203, 358, 185. Another meeting at OKW:1026:11.Juni 1940.
234 "You can talk": Calvin, 32, 39.
234 "As the officer": Canaris, 49, 52. In *Die Vollmacht des Gewissens*, Europäischen Publikation e.v. (n.p.: Hermann Rinn, 1956), Helmut Krausnick, at 271, says that this article served to camouflage Canaris's anti-Nazi views. I disagree. It fits with other evidence that Canaris was pro-Hitler at the time. See Höhne, *Canaris*, ch. 5. Krausnick is straining a little too hard to find resistors everywhere.
234 deception measures: IMT, 28:367 (Jodl diary); Reitlinger, 119, 121–22, for significance.
234 I c officers: OKW:888:3.3.38.
234 turns from Naziism: Abshagen, 109, 119–20; Höhne, *Canaris*, ch. 8.
234 humiliations of Jews: Halder, 2:79.
234 "degrading way": IMT, 28:368 (Jodl diary).
234 frame-up: Müller, 255–99; Wheeler-Bennett, 362, 367–71.
235 evening England declared war: Best, 9.
235 deep pessimism: Groscurth, 206, 245.
235 member of opposition: Harold Deutsch, *The Conspiracy Against Hitler in the Twilight War* (Minneapolis: University of Minnesota Press, 1968).
235 charming, sociable: NA:RG238:Schapper interrogation:8.12.47:5.
235 gloomy, dogs, drank: USN:COA:Bürkner interrogation:15; Gisevius, 442, 444; Abshagen, 218; Colvin, 187.
235 "See, son," Japanese admiral: Maurer, 6, 5.
235 dilemma: Abshagen, 156; Papen, 481.
235 trips: Abshagen, 119; Weizsäcker, 144; Gisevius, 440; Hoettl, *Secret Front*, 71–72; Sachsenheimer, interview; Bürkner, interview, 5 ("Er fuhr ja dauernd weg"); Groscurth, 203, 240 for "constant absence."
235 never saw Hitler: none of the surviving Lagebesprechungen transcripts include him; these start in December 1942.
235 declines invitations: Picker in *Hitlers Tischgespräche*, 132.
235 "hesitant to the end": Hoettl, *Secret Front*, 73.
235 Odysseus: Weizsäcker, 143.
235 Wandering Jew: Gisevius, 440.
235 "the Hamlet of": Trevor-Roper, "Admiral Canaris," 126. Other summaries of Canaris's personality: Weizsäcker, 143–44; Keitel, 62, 106, 133; Faber du Faur, 132, 121; and in Buchheit, 65, 70, 78–79, 80.
235 never betrayed secrets to the Allies: Cavendish-Bentinck, interview; Vice Admiral Sir Norman Denning, interview; Menzies in Cave Brown, 816.
236 Piekenbrock: Keilig; Abshagen, 85, 115, 217, 223; Heinz, 47; Maurer, 8; Mader, *Spionagegenerale*, 45–46; Bartz, 29; Ritter, 25; Hoettl, *Secret Front*, 69; Faber du Faur, 234; *Rangliste des deutschen Reichsheeres* (1.Mai 1928), 3, (1.Mai 1929), 3; IMT, 28:418 (Jodl diary); Hubatsch, *Weserübung*, 58–59; Halder, 2:122; OKW, *KTB*, 1:22, 194, 391.
237 Hansen: Abshagen, 207, 223–24; Maurer, 8–9; Grosskopf, interview, 4; Gisevius, 425, 479, 582; Bartz, 29, 148; Schellenberg, *Memoirs*, 410; Buchheit, 426; Hoffman, 295, 457, 619; OKH:H27/14:10.November 1937; OKH:H3/4:6.11.39; OKH:H3/4:15.3.41; Halder, 2:399, 434, 450, 3:492, 517; OKW, *KTB*, 1:398, 401; *Spiegelbild einer Verschwörung*, 48, 49, 515; TWC:Case 11: Testimony (Paeffgen):12975, 12981, 12983.
238 offices: Abshagen, 78; Buchheit, 39; Calvin, 11.
238 18 October 1939: Buchheit, 106.
238 63, 34, 43 officers: Count from OKW:2165 (OKW telephone book with Abwehr pages as of 15.3.1943).
238 groups: OKW:2165:58–59; Leverkuehn, 30–31.
238 Norway and Italy: SHAEF, *German Intelligence Services*, 4.
238 countries in which: Kleyenstüber, 4.
238 did not direct nor evaluate: USN, *Espionage—Sabotage—Conspiracy*, 9.
238 occasionally ran spies: *ADAP*, 2:319; SHAEF, *German Intelligence Services*, 2.
238 forwarded, sent: OKW:224:18b; USN, *Espionage—Sabotage—Conspiracy*, 9; SHAEF, *German Intelligence Services*, 2; Buchheit, 101; DSDF 862.20210/1996:passim.
239 reorganization, car, expenses: DSDF 862/20210/1996: passim.
239 I G, I i: Leverkuehn, 31.
239 Abwehr post organization: SHAEF, *German Intelligence Service*, 7–8; Library of Congress: Manuscript Division:German Collection:Box 238 (henceforth cited as Box 238). Subposts were

Nebenstellen; outposts, Aussenstellen; main posts, Abwehrleitstellen; suboutposts, Aussenposten; outstations, Sachbearbeiter or Nachrichtenbeschaffungsoffizier.

239 in headquarters: Weidemann, interview, 7; Ritter, interview; visit to Sophienterrasse, 26 August 1973.

239 33, 26, 23: Box 238, Kriegsstärkenachweisungen for all Abwehr posts, which tally exactly with a distribution list of 5 May 1942 in AA:Pol I M:23:302068.

239 Ast organization: Leverkuehn, 33.

239 150, 3, 382: Box 238 and my calculations.

239 Ast duties and activities: SHAEF, *German Intelligence Service*, 5–7. Buchheit, 111, is incomplete, and like Colvin, 76, not altogether exact. USN:COA:Bürkner interrogation:20, for Wichmann.

240 Abwehr Posts, Subposts, and Outposts: Box 238.

243 Personnel Distribution of Abwehr Post Hamburg: Ibid.:Kriegsstärkenachweisung 3010W.

245 Ast Rumania: Box 238.

245 armistice commission: Ibid.:Kriegsstärkenachweisungen for Deutsche Waffenstillstandskommission, Abteilung Abwehr; Hermann Böhme, *Entstehung und Grundlagen des Waffenstillstandes von 1940*, Quellen und Darstellungen zur Zeitgeschichte, 12 (Stuttgart: Deutsche Verlags-Anstalt, 1966), 151, 377.

245 Kriegsorganisation: Leverkuehn, 33; Buchheit, 127–30, 279–86.

245 5 January 1937: IMT, 28:346 (Jodl diary).

245 Shanghai post: Reile, *Ostfront*, 344–48, 359, 429; AA:Pol I M:Akten betreffend Abwehr-Berichte u. Meldungen des K.O. China:1.Mai 1944–27.Juli 1944.

245 Netherlands in 1938: *Die Nachhut* (15.Mai 1973), 1; (1.Oktober 1973), 32.

245 ten KOs: AA:Pol I M 23:302068.

245 KO organization and dependency: NA:RG59:Poole Mission:Niebuhr interview:3; Buchheit, 127, 106.

245 KO Spain: AA:Pol I M 50:Band 1:282343–9; Ibid.: Band 2:282420–22.

245 Ast operations in KO territories: SHAEF, *German Intelligence Services*, 9.

245 KO quarters: AA:Pol I M 50:Band 1:282334–35; AA:Pol I M 38:318898; SHAEF, *German Intelligence Services*, 8; NA:RG165:HTUSAIC:FIR:19:12.

246 Personnel and Their Duties in KO Spain: AA:Pol I M 30:Abwehr, KO Spanien:September 1940–August 1944:Band 1:282343–49. Some first names from NA:RG165:HTUSAIC:IR:38; Leisner changed from pseudonym Lenz.

248 December 1941: *ADAP*, 1:69.

248 Foreign Office response: T-120:357:264235–40.

248 87, 315, 171: AA:Pol I M:K.O.Spanien:September 1940–August 1941:Band 2:282420–22.

248 friction, Stockholm protest: NG-3402:5; AA:Pol I M 39:Band 1:308211–13.

248 mission chief: T-120:357:264238–39.

248 demands increased: OKW, *KTB*, 3:1184; AA:Inland II g:106:19.Juli 1944, 24.Juli 1944, 3. August 1944.

248 arguing with host: SHAEF, *German Intelligence Services*, 9.

248 82 of 149: NA:RG59:DSDF 862.20252/11:944:23 October 1944.

248 Poland, France, Yugoslavia: Reile, *Ostfront*, 348, 349, 352; Freud, 186.

249 Canaris ordered: OKW:1938:4.Juni 1941.

249 Abwehr Main Post East: Reile, *Ostfront*, 365 (adjusting name); Mader, *Spionagegenerale*, 98; IMT, 7:271.

249 Baun: Gehlen, 41; NA:RG165:HTUSAIC:PIR:16 August 1945; Sayffaerth, interview.

249 Walli I locations: Buchheit, 261; Sayffaerth, interview.

249 front organization changes: BA:EAP 173-b-24-14/4:1.6.42 shows a three-level organization that lasted only from about mid-1942 to mid-1943.

249 long-range agents, line crossers: SHAEF, *German Intelligence Services*, 10.

249 Italy, Greece, France: OKH:H2/120:45, 47, 48; OKH:H3/1539:23.5.1944:2.

249 Canaris converted: Buchheit, 422–23; NA:RG165:USFET:MISC:CI-IIR/48:2.

250 battle stations: NA:RG165:USFET:MISC:CI-IIR/48:3; HGrD:85459:197–98.

250 front espionage in Wehrmacht: OKH:H3/1539:14.Mai 1944:2; OKH:H2/120:51, 28.

250 name change: OKH:H2/120:51.

250 1, 5, 13: Ibid.:45.

250 flecked the map: such a map at HGrD:75144/33:113/6.

250 1 December 1944: HGrD:75144/33:146/6.

250 Branch F: Ibid.:145/6.

250 9,200: Buntrock, 103.

250 1,000: My conservative calculations.

250 5,000: Totaling the Kriegsstärkenachweisungen, mostly dated 1.4.42, in Box 238.

250 2,000: Totaling those of the above in the West.

250 13,000: Maurer, interview, 21, says the Abwehr had 40,000 people in it. I use my figure as more conservative.

250 more than the number of spies: Best, 5.

Chapter 16: Apparat

It should be noted that the International Military Tribunal at Nuremberg found the SD, including specifically the RSHA's Department VI (but not RSHA VI's Military Department), to be a criminal organization. Its employees, except the Abwehr personnel transferred to it, were guilty of crimes against peace, war crimes, and crimes against humanity (IMT, 1:267–68).

Citations here to "Jost testimony" followed by a page number refer to TWC:Case 9:Transcript, the testimony of Heinz Jost in English translation; but since this translation is sometimes confusing and the English transcript has dropped some phrases, it has been checked against the corresponding German transcript (pp. 1151–56) and the quotations as given are sometimes my translations from the German.

I want to thank Dr. George C. Browder for reading this chapter and offering some valuable comments.

251 28 July 1934: BDC: Heinz Jost: 28. Juli 1934.
251 Jost characteristics: BDC; Höttl, *Unternehmen Bernhard*, 67–68; IfZ:ZS 291:2:18 (Ohlendorf interrogation); Werner Best, letter, 24.11.1974; Groscurth, 145.
251 Jost biography: BDC; NA:RG238:Heinz Jost:Affidavit:27.Juni 1947; Jost testimony, 1128–32. SS No. 36,243.
251 "The experiences": Jost testimony, 1130.
251 "exclusive, narrow, and conceited": Ibid.
252 high Nazi friend: Werner Best, letter, 24.11.1974. Best was the friend. On Best: Aronson, 144–52.
252 why Jost was chosen: Höttl, *Unternehmen Bernhard*, 67–68.
252 "their history": Jost testimony, 1136.
252 industry protected, SD advised: Ibid., 1135.
252 Jost's actual if not formal command: Jost is referred to in an order of 2.January 1936 as "Chef des Abwehramtes im Sicherheitsamt," (BA:R58/239), but was only named leader of section 1 of Branch III on 25 January 1936 and of sections 1 and 2 on 27 May 1936 (BDC: Heinz Jost).
253 deputy chief of counterintelligence: BA:R58/840:160; Werner Best, letter 24.11.1974. Jost also served under Best in Heydrich's Security Police Administration, superordinated to the Gestapo, as head of desk V 8, which dealt with the armed forces and Reich defense (BA:R58/840:137).
253 commission to Spain: T-120:1320:D449899–907, D499950–52.
253 combined SD-Gestapo unit: Groscurth, 130, 123; IMT, 39:549.
253 no major spy effort: Jost testimony, 1137.
253 post near frontiers, Stuttgart, Filbert: Höhne, 228; NA:RG165:HTUSAIC:IR 15:22; NA:RG 165:7 Army:307 CIC Detachment:FIR:12 December 1945:appendix 3:6. BDC. Filbert Party No. 1,321,414; SS No. 44,552.
253 civil administrator: Jost testimony, 1137.
253 Heydrich criticism: BA:EAP 173-b-05/2K:81.
253 counterespionage discontinued: Jost testimony, 1137.
253 Jost reorganizes, wartime difficulties: Jost testimony, 1137–38.
253 Department VI organization: BA:R58/840:1.Februar 1940.
254 Jost's university graduates: Höttl, interview.
254 dilettantism and inadequacy: Höttl, interview; Schüddekopf, interview, 17–18.
254 compounding the problem: Schüddekopf, interview, 12–13.
254 qualifications for SD men: *Reichsministerialblatt für innere Verwaltung* (1938), 289–94.
254 "an SS attitude," "Purely scientific": Ramme, 84.
254 rid of Jost's patron: Höhne, 255–56, 257–58.
254 Heydrich ousts Jost: Jost testimony, 1140–47; NA:RG238:Heinz Jost:interrogation:6.Januar 1948:1–4.
255 commands an Einsatzkommando: *TWC*, 4:13. For this he was found guilty and sentenced to life imprisonment (4:587).
255 Schellenberg early life: BDC; Schellenberg, *Memoirs*, 19–20; TWC:Case 11:Testimony:5034, 5038 (Schellenberg):Aronson, 33, 210. SS No. 124,817.
255 SS professors, Heydrich's attention: Schellenberg, *Memoirs*, 22.
255 Ruhr lawyer, came to appreciate: IfZ:ZS 291:3:32.
255 began to aim: NA:RG238:Walter Schellenberg:interrogation:12.November 1945:5; TWC:Case 11: Testimony:5049 (Schellenberg).
255 government police job, civil servant: He was an Oberregierungsrat.
255 to Paris: Schellenberg, *Memoirs*, 25.
256 to Italy: TWC:Case 11:Testimony:5049 (Schellenberg).
256 excellent job in security: BDC:Walter Schellenberg:11.Oktober 1937.
256 government-party units: IMT, 39:549.
256 Jost headed one: Groscurth, 123, 126.
256 Heydrich had Schellenberg suggest: BA:EAP 173-b-05/1A:passim; BA:EAP 173-b-05/2L: passim.
256 five, seven departments: BA:EAP 173-b-05/1A:4.April 1939; BA:EAP 173-b-10-16/2:24.Juli 1939.
256 "the front line," "special skill," "requires above all," "without being informed": BA:EAP 173-b-10:28.Februar 1939.
256 Schellenberg's style: good sample in BA:EAP 173-b-05/2:24.Februar 1939.
256 Schellenberg's marital difficulties: T-175:R257:2748647–700; BDC; Aronson, 304.
257 IV E: IMT, 38:15.
257 Venlo incident: Schellenberg, *Labyrinth*, 63–80; Netherlands, *Enquêtecommissie Regeringsbeleid 1940–1945*, 2B:53, 88, 96, 98. See also L[ouis]. de Jong, *Het Koninkrijk der Nederlanden in de Tweede Wereldoorlog*, Rijksinstitut voor Oorlogsdocumentatie (The Hague: Martinus Nijhoff, 1969–   ), 2:80–115.
259 Duke of Windsor: Schellenberg, *Labyrinth*, 107–24; *DGFP*, 10:187 for peace movement, 317–18 for kidnapping, "psychologically adroit," "At a precisely," 399–400 for Schellenberg's techniques, 397 for duke's sailing; Frances Donaldson, *Edward VIII* (Philadelphia: Lippincott, 1974), 349–56, 383–402.

259 fenced with Heydrich: TWC:Case 11: Testimony:12969, 12977 (Paeffgen).
259 drinks with Heydrich: Schellenberg, *Memoirs*, 237, 239.
259 visited him frequently: NA:RG238:Ernst Kaltenbrunner:interrogation:19.September 1946:7.
260 conversed with his wife: Schellenberg, *Labyrinth*, 17.
260 penned Heydrich's replies: Höhne, 255.
260 negotiations with army: IMT, 32:472–75. Heydrich had prepared the way two years earlier
     (Halder, 1:79). Schellenberg completely suppresses the real reason for the negotiations in his
     memoirs (*Labyrinth*, 196–97).
260 quiet way, boyish charm: Wilhelm Wulff, *Zodiac and Swastika: How Astrology Guided Hitler's
     Germany* (New York: Coward, McCann & Geoghegan, 1973), 90; NA:RG238:Ernst Kalten-
     brunner:interrogation:19.September 1946:7.
260 clear tenor, enunciation: NA:RG238:Disk 519B.
260 "He believed": Trevor-Roper, *Last Days*, 25.
260 despised him as effete: Peis, 113.
260 too pushy: NA:RG242:Gottfried Schapper:interrogation:8.12.47:4.
260 "pure Nordic": BDC:Walter Schellenberg:Personal-Bericht:27.3.1937.
260 brisk gait, well-proportioned body, could form a clear picture: Wulff, 90.
260 Heydrich's trust: NA:RG238:Ernst Kaltenbrunner:interrogation:19.September 1946:7.
260 could lunch, befriend: Ibid.
260 understanding foreign affairs: Ibid.:8; Trevor-Roper, *Last Days*, 25.
260 mid 1940: Schellenberg, *Memoirs*, 160–61.
260 21 June: TWC:Case 11:Testimony:5112 (Schellenberg); *Befehlsblatt des Chefs der Sicher-
     heitspolizei und des SD*, 2 (19. Juli 1941), 140.
260 "the goal toward": TWC:Case 11:Testimony:5105 (Schellenberg).
260 lunch with Canaris: Ibid.:5112 (Schellenberg).
260 the next day: Schellenberg, *Memoirs*, 227.
260 Jost stayed on: NA:RG238:Heinz Jost:interrogation:6.Januar 1948:1, 4.
261 "I decided first": Schellenberg, *Labyrinth*, 208–209.
261 visited his old boss: Ibid., 209.
261 ten-point program: Schellenberg, *Memoirs*, 230–31.
261 Point 7 filing system: *Espionage-Sabotage-Conspiracy*, 47–49; Schellenberg, *Memoirs*, 286–87.
261 groups maintained own files: NA:RG165:7 Army:307 CIC Detachment:FIR:12 December
     1945:Appendix 18.
261 reorganized department: comparison of Jost's organization (BA:R58/840:1.Februar 1940 and
     IMT, 38:17–19, 24) with Schellenberg's (IMT, 38:81–83).
262 Havel Institute: BA:EAP-161-b-12/384.
262 January 1945: OKH:H2/114:9.Januar 1945.
262 puts own men in: NA:RG165:7 Army:307 CIC Detachment:FIR:12 December 1945:Appen-
     dix 14:1.
262 five posts, vacant: IMT, 38:17–19.
262 Filbert to 1943: NA:RG165:USFET:FIR:7:20.
263 Filbert inefficient: NA:RG165:HTUSAIC:IR:15:28.
263 Sandberger: TWC:Case 9:Transcript:2141-8, 2366 (Sandberger); *TWC*, 4:14, 432–34; NA:
     RG165:HTUSAIC:IR:15:28–9. For his einsatzkommando activity, he was sentenced to death
     (*TWC*, 4:588), but the sentence was commuted to life imprisonment (Hilberg, 712).
264 Daufeldt: NA:RG165:HTUSAIC:IR:15:33; NA:RG165:7 Army:307 CIC Detachment:FIR:12
     December 1945: Appendix 8, Appendix 3:3.
264 Paeffgen: BDC; NA:RG59:Poole Mission:Theodor Paeffgen:interrogation: 16 October 1945;
     NA:RG238:Theodor Paeffgen:affidavit:6.August 1947; TWC:Case 11:Testimony:12970–73 (Paeff-
     gen); *Befehlsblatt des Chefs der Sicherheitspolizei und des SD*, 3 (4.April 1942), 14, (8.August
     1942), 991. Party No. 3,965,964; SS No. 324,971.
264 racial type: BDC:Theodor Paeffgen:Personal-Bericht.
264 " 'methodical' work," "far above," "in order"; "entirely fulfill": Ibid.:14.3.44.
264 Schüddekopf: Schüddekopf, interview, 1. BDC. SS No. 455,103.
264 21 June 1942: BDC. This gives 21.6.43 as the date both for his service in the RSHA and
     his rank in the SS, which, on the basis of Schüddekopf's statements and his dated writings,
     I believe should be 1942.
264 suggestions: BA:EAP 173-b-20-20/16:29.9.1942, 29.September 1942, 6.Oktober 1942.
264 agent reports, open sources, pointlessness: Schüddekopf, interview, 4, 14, 12.
264 Hitler's social revolution: Schoenbaum, passim.
265 Steimle: BDC; NA:RG238:Eugen Steimle:interrogation:7.Juli 1947:2–4; NA:RG165:7 Army:
     307 CIC Detachment:FIR:12 December 1945: Appendices 1 and 2; *TWC*, 4:539, 541; Steimle,
     interview. Party No. 1,075,555; SS No. 272,575.
265 "fanatically fortified," "outstanding qualities," "He possesses," bully: BDC:Eugen Steimle:
     16.Dezember 1936, 20.5.44.
265 Group C leader killed: NA:RG165:HTUSAIC:IR:15:31, 33.
266 "irreproachable character," einsatzkommando: *Untersuchungen zur Geschichte des Offizierkorps:
     Ancienität und Beförderung nach Leistung*, ed. Dr. [Hans] Meier-Welcker, Beiträge zur Militär-
     und Kriegsgeschichte, 4, Militärgeschichtliches Forschungsamt (Stuttgart: Deutsche Verlags-
     Anstalt, 1962), 326, 332.
266 Rapp: BDC. Ramme, 269; Hilberg, 188: NA:RG165:7 Army:307 CIC Detachment:FIR:12
     December 1945:Appendix 3:1. Party No. 774,433; SS No. 280,341.
266 Tschierschky: BDC. Party No. 918,746; SS No. 19,984.
266 regions: BA:EAP 173-a-10/17.
266 VI B 2: NA:RG165:HTUSAIC:IR:42:2–5.

266   between 400 and 500: Count of VI personnel in RSHA telephone book of June 1943 (BA: R58/927); IMT, 4:380 (Schellenberg), 11:228 (Höttl).
266   mostly with papers: Steimle, interview; Schüddekopf, interview, 4.
266   possibly same number in outposts: My estimate, since not all the outposts had VI desks. NA:RG238:D-878:3, 4 for RSHA totals in Berlin and out.
266   Berkaerstrasse 32: AA:Inl II g 7:2. Dezember 1943; Höttl, *Secret Front,* 13–14; Gimpel, 45; personal visit.
266   desk with machine guns: Schellenberg, *Memoirs,* 242.
266   worked day and night, reading every report; covering letter: Ibid., 240–47, 258–60, 261; NA: RG165:HTUSAIC:IR:15:26–27; Steimle, interview; Schüddekopf, interview, 7; my impression from the documents.
267   "ear at every wall": Steimle, interview.
267   infighting absorbed energy: Schüddekopf, interview, 7.
267   Schellenberg and Canaris: Schellenberg, *Memoirs,* 204, 215, 399–400, 403.
267   Schellenberg arrests Canaris: Schellenberg, *Labyrinth,* 356–58.
267   cementing his own position: NA:RG238:Ernst Kaltenbrunner:interrogation:19 September 1946:8. He later sought to cement a postwar position with the Allies by seeking to negotiate for peace (Schellenberg, *Labyrinth,* 392–412).
267   Bruneval raid: Schellenberg, *Memoirs,* 398–99; Reuter, 109; George Millar, *The Bruneval Raid* (Garden City: Doubleday, 1975).
268   1 March 1942: NOKW-3228; Schellenberg, *Memoirs,* 405.
268   24 February 1943: BDC:Walter Schellenberg:24.2.43; *Befehlsblatt des Chefs der Sicherheitspolizei und des SD,* 4 (3. April 1943), 94.
268   Kaltenbrunner resumed Heydrich's advance: After the war, Kaltenbrunner said both that he had opposed Schellenberg's pressure to take over the Abwehr (NA:RG238:Ernst Kaltenbrunner; interrogation:19.September 1946:9) and that he had urged amalgamation of RSHA VI and the Abwehr (IMT, 11:240).
268   Abwehr waverings: Abshagen, 356–58, 367.
268   Abwehr failures: Westphal, 240; *Hitlers Lagebesprechungen,* 557; *NCA,* B:1316.
268   Vermehren: NG-2209; *The Times* (9 February 1944), 4:6, (10 February 1944), 4:5. Buchheit's statement (428–29) that Himmler played up the Vermehren defection to cover up a simultaneous one from the SD in Ankara is false: the SD defection did not occur until 6 April (AA:Inl II g:106:8.April 1944; *The Times* [21 April 1944], 3:3).
268   Hitler exploded: Abshagen (German edition), 367.
268   12 February 1944: OKH:H3/1539:23.Mai 1944:Anlage 1. On the drafting of this decree: NA:RG238:Walter Schellenberg:interrogation:12 November 1945:5.
269   Canaris removed: Terence Prittie, *Germans Against Hitler* (London: Hutchinson, 1964), 228.
269   negotiations in Zossen: NA:RG238:Walter Schellenberg:interrogation:12 November 1945:5–6. For OKM views: *Lagevorträge,* 577–78.
269   300, 400, Mirabell: Wagner, 1st interview, 15.
269   Himmler speech: BA:EAP 161-b-12/278.
270   14 May agreement: OKH:H3/1539:23.Mai 1944:Anlage 2.
270   detailed regulations: Ibid.:Anlage 3.
270   Amt Mil: OKH:H2/120:41.
270   Hansen arrested, Schellenberg takes over: TWC:Case 11:Transcript:5208 (Schellenberg); 12975, 12981 (Paeffgen).
270   Branches B and C: OKH:H2/120:77; NA:RG165:7 Army:307 CIC Detachment:FIR:12 December 1945:Appendix 4:1–4; Steimle, interview.
271   VI B and Mil B: Steimle, interview.
271   other Amt Mil branches: OKH:H2/120:77.
271   1 December 1944: HGrD:75144/33:146/6, 145/6; Buntrock, 103; OKH:H2/120:68.

CHAPTER 17: OPERATIONS OF THE INFRASTRUCTURES

272   advertising: Piekenbrock in Mader, *Spionagegenerale,* 54–55.
272   French lieutenant: Ibid.
272   economics expert: Farago, 135, 238.
273   Welsh nationalists: Ibid., 130–31.
273   pro-Nazi movements: NA:RG165:7 Army:307 CIC Detachment:FIR:12 December 1945:Appendix 16:1.
273   MARECHAL and CHARLIE: NA:RG165:HTUSAIC:IR 19:5.
273   guards steered, man called: Weidemann, interview.
273   turning double agent: Wagner, interview.
273   Channel Islands: Owen, 46.
273   500 Arabs: Seubert, interview; NA:RG165:HQ Intelligence Center:6825 HQ and HQ Company:Military Intelligence Service in Austria:IC:1DIR:6.
273   Russian p.o.w.s: Reile, *Ostfront,* 393–94; Seyffaerth, interview, 7.
273   ZEPPELIN: Schellenberg, *Labyrinth,* 261–76; TWC:Case 11:Transcript:5147–8 (Schellenberg).
273   agents with crimes, mass executions: "Die sowjetischen Staatssicherheitsorgane," 1214; T-175: 69:2585634–35.
274   Schlie: BDC:Höttl:84–86; 325–26.
274   SS contingents, Sennheim: BA:EAP 161-b-12/214:Folder 31:21.August 1942.
274   prostitutes: BA:R58/117:24.
274   Himmler permission power: *Reichsgesetzblatt* (1935), 1146–47, 1334.

274 marriage recruitment attempts: BA:R58/117:24:3–64, passim. Sizzo-Noris married Deutsch after the war (*Libro d'Oro della Nobilità Italiana 1969–1972*, 1514–15).
275 money motivations: Gimpel, 61; Weidemann, interview; NA:RG165:USFET:MISC:CI-IIR/ 48:26; Firmin, 77; T-175:461:2980055–62, -75; AA:Inl IIg:72:20.April 1943; Gisevius, 481–82.
275 danger entices: Wagner, interview; Gill, ch. 7, p. 2.
275 idealism: Weidemann, interview; Farago, 256; Gill, ch. 7, p. 2.
275 escape from Germany: Gill, ch. 7, p. 2.
276 Stuttgart offices: BA:R58/116:36.
276 Klopstock: Farago, 320.
276 anti-Soviet agent training: "Die sowjetischen Staatssicherheitsorgan," 1201, 1210–11.
276 Seubert: Seubert, interview.
276 Cologne post: BA:R58/116:64.
276 WALTER, SIEGFRIED: NA:RG165:7 Army:307 CIC Detachment:FIR:12 December 1945:Appendix 14:3, Appendix 16.
276 Front Reconnaissance Command 120: NA:RG165:USFET:MISC:CI-IIR/48:31–32.
276 Munich trained: BA:R58/116:27.
277 instructors: Ibid.:27, 35.
277 Hamburg: Trautman, interview; Ritter, 150, 221.
277 "What is that?": Seubert, interview.
277 for use as workers, schooled and unschooled same: BA:R58/116:27, 37.
277 spymaster, bind the agent: NA:RG165:USFET:IC:1SIIR:111–12, 109.
278 cover identities: *ADAP*, 2:358.
278 Schenker, other firms: NA:RG165:HTUSAIC:IR/15:23.
278 Bayer: NA:RG242:Albrecht Focke:interrogation:19:8.47:6–7.
278 Bernhardt: Craig, "The German Foreign Office," 429–30; NA:RG165:7 Army:307 CIC De- tachment:FIR:12 December 1945:Appendix 5:2, Appendix 7:1–2; T-120:759:348128; Party No. 1,572,819.
278 publish brochures, newsstands: Piekenbrock in Mader, *Spionagegenerale*, 79.
279 cigarette cases: Weidemann, interview.
279 Latin American firms: NA:RG59:DSDF862.20210/1996:7, 16, 8, 24–25; NA:RG59:DSDF862. 20225/620:1, 2.
279 Transmare: Piekenbrock in Mader, *Spionagegenerale*, 90.
279 Müller: Müller, interviews.
279 six desks: Ibid.
280 Heydrich faked documents: Peis; Höhne, *Canaris*, 240–41; Georges Castellan, "Reichswehr et Armée Rouge" in Jean-Baptiste Duroselle, ed., *Les relations germano-soviétiques* (Paris: Colin, 1954), 235–37, 260.
280 Naujocks: BDC; Peis, 103–11; Höttl, *Unternehmen Bernhard*, 71–74; NA:RG238:Naujocks interrogation; Jürgen Runzheimer, "Der Überfall auf den Sender Gleiwitz im Jahre 1939," *VfZ*, 10 (Oktober 1962), 408–26. Party No. 624,279; SS No. 26,240.
280 Rauff: BDC; IMT, 38:19 and 26:103; Hilberg, 219, 429, 432. Party No. 5,216,415; SS No. 290,947.
280 Dörner: BDC; IMT, 38:82 (given incorrectly as Jörner). Party No. 603,788; SS No. 47,639.
281 Lassig: BDC; OKH:H2/114:6.Januar 1945. Party No. 739,497; SS No. 107,190.
281 Krüger: BDC; Höttl, *Unternehmen Bernhard*, 72, 262. Party No. 528,739; SS No. 15,249.
281 blank U.S. passports: Ritter, 135–40.
281 from prisoners: NA:RG165:HTUSAIC:PIR:22 August 1945; Peis, 107.
281 advantages, disadvantages: OKW:106:3/2–3/3.
281 counterfeiting problems: Ibid.:3/4.
281 had paper made: Müller, interview; Peis, 108.
281 outside research: Peis, 110.
282 only to trustworthy agents: OKW:106:3/4.
282 two passports for Prague: NA:RG165:USFET:CI-IIR/11:12.
282 20 engravers and artists: Ibid.:11.
282 G sections photograph: Ibid.: 12.
282 SD outposts photograph: Höttl, *Unternehmen Bernhard*, 73; Peis, 108–10.
282 a thousand stamps: OKW:106:3/6.
282 in that country's language: Ibid.:3/8.
282 notional trips: Ibid.:3/5.
282 questionnaire: Ibid.:4/1–4/4.
282 greatest problem: Ibid.:3/6.
282 10 percent agent: NA:RG165:HTUSAIC:IR/11:19.
282 146 counterfeits: OKW:106:5/1–5/15.
283 cross into Switzerland: Höttl, *Unternehmen Bernhard*, 72.
283 Soviet lieutenant, teacher: OKW:106:3/7, 3/8.
283 small IG units, 500 a month: NA:RG165:HTUSAIC:IR/11:19.
283 400,000: OKW:106:3/7.
283 errors: *Espionage-Sabotage-Conspiracy*, 65–66.
283 cédula: FDR Library:OF10b:37:29 July 1943: Memo:1.
284 Schütz: Stephan, 203, 204.
284 harder legends: Piekenbrock in Mader, *Spionagegenerale*, 87.
284 Russians test speech: *Espionage-Sabotage-Conspiracy*, 44.
284 difficulties in Britain: Piekenbrock in Mader, *Spionagegenerale*, 84.
284 flaws in uniforms: *Espionage-Sabotage-Conspiracy*, 66.
284 at legal border posts: Piekenbrock in Mader, *Spionagegenerale*, 241.

284 "forested frontier," Luxembourg, Schleusung: Ibid.; Wagner, interview. The German term is "grüne Grenze"—literally, "green border."
285 wetbacks: Piekenbrock in Mader, *Spionagegenerale,* 94–95.
285 Gartenfeld, Baumbach units: Piekenbrock in Mader, *Spionagegenerale,* 73, 405; *TWC,* 13:570; SHAEF, *German Intelligence Services,* 13; SHAEF, *The German Intelligence Service,* 24–25.
286 "Canaris is wild": IWM:Milch:16:2187.
286 planes black: Eyermann, 2:38; Schreyer, 113.
286 parachutes dark brown: Owen, 91.
286 Goertz: Stephan, 113–15.
286 Wisbech: Owen, 92.
286 five miles: Ibid., 88.
286 60 miles south: Stephan, 203.
286 tiny hole: Owen, 91.
286 to England: Owen, 218; Stephan, 203.
286 too fat: Gill, ch. 7, p. 6.
286 June 1941: Firmin, 78.
287 sea insertions to England: Firmin, 80; Gill, ch. 7, p. 2; "German Spies in England," *After the Battle,* No. 11 (1976), 1–34 at 17–18, 30.
287 Zweigert: FDR Library:OF10b:37:29 Jul 1943 and memorandum.
287 Garbers: Augier, 123.
288 agents to South America via ships: NA:RG165:USFET:MISC:CI-FIR/73:7; NA:RG238: Paeffgen interrogation:5; *NCA,* B:1627–28; NA:RG165:USFET:MISC:CI-IIR/48:31; *FRUS, 1945,* 9:457, 458; Augier, 125, 144–45, 146, photo following p. 128; FDR Library: OF10b:37:14 August 1943; DSDF 800.20235/421:Enclosure: 10; DSDF 862.20235/4–1045:18–20; DSDF 862.20235/4–2545:6.
289 "I bring greetings": NA:RG59:DSDF862.20210/1996:39.
289 Popov: Popov, 90–91.
289 by far the best: Piekenbrock in Mader, *Spionagegenerale,* 75; Weidemann, interview, 25, 39.
289 marathon-length: Popov, 93.
289 Lilly Stein: NA:Federal Archives and Records Center for New York:Records of the U.S. District Court for the Eastern District of New York:Criminal Docket No. 38425:Indictment: Second Count:Overt Acts:No.3.
289 Roson: NA:RG59:DSDF862.20210/1996:11.
290 cover address individuals: Weidemann, interview, 11.
290 Hanno von Halem: NA:RG59:DSDF862.20225/620:eight.
290 Simon Simon: *FRUS, 1942,* 5:194.
290 jargon code: Kahn, 84, 519.
290 "Your order No. 5": Sayers and Kahn, 34.
290 invisible inks: Kahn, 522–25.
290 Müller regarded: Müller, interview.
290 ink types, PLURAL: NA:RG165:USFET:CI-IIR/11:13.
290 pyramidon: AA:Pol I M:31:292710.
291 hemoglobin: Schellenberg, *Memoirs,* 418.
291 three repeated applications: Müller, interview.
291 Gimpel: FBI:Press Release:September 20, 1954:William Curtis Colepaugh, Erich Gimpel, 25.
291 Beck: Müller, interview; NA:RG165:USFET:CI-IIR/11:11.
291 SD adapted: Müller, interview, which I believe despite Peis, 110–11, which implies that the SD did it, and J. Edgar Hoover, "The Enemy's Masterpiece of Espionage." *Reader's Digest,* 48 (April 1946), 1–6, which attributes the invention to "the famous Professor Zapp," apparently of the Technical High School at Dresden. I cannot determine who this is. RSHA VI F had an SS private, Rudolf Zapp, a former radio store owner in his twenties, SS number 148,935 (BDC), and from November 1943 the head of the SD area for Dresden was Paul Zapp (BDC), probably the former head of Einsatzkommando IIa (T-175:232:2720974; Hilberg, 188, 226, 492). But neither seems to have had the qualifications needed. Hoover's information came from the double agent Popov (Popov, ch. 16, FDR Library:OF10b:28:3 September 1941), who did not get along with Hoover and might have been needling him.
291 served from Germany, few major agents: Müller, interview.
292 microdots, *Iron Age,* envelopes: FDR Library:OF10b:28:3 September 1941; Ibid.:36:18 May 1943; Ibid.:37:11 August 1943:Memorandum:10; Kahn, 326.
292 Gimpel: Gimpel, 90.
292 Afus: Reile, *Ostfront,* 187; Weidemann, interview, 15; Rauh, interview, 2; Gill, ch. 7, p. 3.
292 suitcase size: "German Spies in Britain," *After the Battle,* No. 11 (1976), 15, 22.
292 radio plans: Rauh, interview, 4.
292 50–100 letters: Ibid., 9.
292 BOBBI: ML-180:28/43.
292 Rasehorn and Poretschkin: Poretschkin, letter, 12.7.70.
292 Signal Regiment 506; Rauh, interview, 5: NA:RG165:HTUSAIC:PIR:21 Aug 1945; NA: RG165:HTUSAIC:IR:20:2–8.
292 Madrid: NA:RG165:USFET:FIR/19:6.
292 Algeciras: Redl, interview.
293 station locations: Rauh, interview, 2, 6, 3.
293 Sigmaringen: BA:EAP 173-b-24-16/1.
293 Hamburg: Trautmann, interview; visit, 20 August 1970.
293 radioman duties: Rauh and Trautmann, interviews.
295 quarter of a year, goose: Trautmann, interview.
295 VI B, VI F: BA:R58/840:1.Februar 1940; IMT, 38:19, 82.

295 Siepen: BDC. Party No. 4,690,994; SS No. 222,319.
295 Havel Institut: BA:EAP 161-b-12/384.
295 absorbed VI F 1 and 2: NA:RG165:HTUSAIC:IR 16:12.
295 4,000 and 7,000 words: BA:EAP 161-b-12/384:6.
295 dozen a day: Rauh, interview, 6.
295 ten a week: Trautmann, interview.
295 agents paid: Because the Finance Ministry destroyed all files for the budgets of all Reich ministries from 1914 to 1945, under an order dated 14.7.1943 (BA:R2:12965:14.7.1943), no reliable figures for the cost of the Abwehr and funds spent for its agents exist. (I am grateful to Dr. Peter-Christian Witt for this information.)
296 500,000, 5,000 pesos: NA:RG59:Poole Mission:Niebuhr interrogation:5, 4. NA:RG59:DSDF 862:20219/1996:54.
296 $50,000: NA:RG238:Paeffgen interrogation:5.
296 Gimpel: FBI:Press Release:September 20, 1954:William Curtis Colepaugh, Erich Gimpel: 23, 24.
296 agents for Britain: Masterman, 171, 56, 142, 85.
296 £85,000: Ibid., 17.
296 no contracts: OKW:436:73.
296 Luxembourg agents: BA:EAP 173-b-24-26/10:26.6.41, 30.6.41, 25.6.42, 24.7.42, 6.1.43, 9.2.43, 10.6.43.
296 700 pesos: NA:RG59:Poole mission:Niebuhr interview:5, 4.
296 Bremen outpost: ML-164a:Januar 1940.
296 JOHNNY: Ritter, 43, 216.
296 France in 1944: NA:RG165:USFET:MISC:CI-IIR/48:26.
296 "tackle their work": OKW:436:62.
296 refusing money, accepted jewelry or goods: BA:R58/116:65; Buntrock, 103.
297 parachuted in Iran: IfZ:ZS291:1:3.
297 200,000 francs: NA:RG165:USFET:MISC:CI-IIR/48:30.
297 handed their money: inferences from payment books ML-164a and BA:EAP 173-b-24-26/10 and from NA:RG165:USFET:MISC:CI-IIR/48:25–26.
297 "And now I've": Abshagen, 78.
297 reports endangered: Ritter, 31.
297 radio links: IfZ:ZS291:1:4.
297 Starziczny: *FRUS, 1942,* 5:193.
297 not rare in Abwehr: Höhne, *Canaris,* 470.
297 Prague outpost: NA:RG165:USFET:CI-CIR/11:10.
297 group chief approved, passed: Steimle, interview.
297 above *RM*50,000: NA:RG238:Schellenberg interrogation:12.November 1945:12–13.
297 Toeppen: Abshagen, 77–78. 95; Duesterberg, interview.
297 Duesterberg: Duesterberg, interview.
297 Spacil: NA:RG238:Spacil interrogation:17.Februar 1947:1–3; NA:RG238:Schellenberg interrogation:12.November 1945:11–12; IMT, 33:205–6.
298 Chief of Front Reconnaissance appropriated: NA:RG165:USFET:MISC:CI-IIR/48:25.
298 Prague outpost: NA:RG165:USFET:CI-CIR/11:4.
298 "at such a level": *Reichsgesetzblatt* (1939), 1018.
298 "one of the major": Schellenberg, *Memorien,* 214.
298 "my hardest task": Duesterberg, interview.
298 pay out $25,000: BA:RFM 9:3.Dezember 1940, 6.Dezember 1940.
298 Four-Year Plan: IfZ:ZS 291:1:1–2.
298 Tobis-Tonbild: BA:RFM 9:4.6.40, 28.Mai 1940, 7.Juni 1940.
299 Telefunken: *NCA,* B:1626.
299 Sofindus or Rowak: IfZ:ZS 291:1:19.
299 20 to 30 cover firms: Ibid.:51.
299 illicit business: Duesterberg, interview.
299 sources of RSHA funds: NA:RG238:Spacil interrogation:14.4.1947:7; IMT, 11:310; BA:EAP 161-b-12/149:10.Januar 1941.
299 Belgian gold: IMT, 38:552–53.
299 captures of agents: IfZ:ZS 291:1:8–9.
299 violates law: *Reichsgesetzblatt* (1871), 155: League of Nations, *Treaty Series,* 112 (1931), 377, 378, 386; *Strafrecht der deutschen Wehrmacht,* 3. Auflage (Munich: C. H. Beck'sche Verlagsbuchhandlung, 1940), 123.
299 Frederick the Great: A. O. von Loehr, "Die Finanzierung des Siebenjährigen Krieges: Ein Versuch vergleichender Geldgeschichte," *Numismatische Zeitschrift,* N. F. 18 (1925), 95–110 at 99, 100–101; Friedrich Freiherr von Schrötter, *Das Preussische Münzwesen im 18. Jahrhundert,* Acta Borussica (Berlin: Parey, 1904–13), 3:78–97, 4:191, 195–97.
299 SD counterfeiting: Mader, *Banditenschatz,* 58–59, 70, 72–75; Höttl, *Unternehmen Bernhard,* passim; Anthony Pirie, *Operation Bernhard: The Greatest Forgery of All Times* (London: Cassell, 1961), passim; Dr. Eugen Mauler and Frau Isolde Langer, interviews.
300 Schellenberg, Duesterberg refused: IfZ:ZS291:1:24; Duesterberg, interview.
300 Simon: Stephan, 141.
300 O'Reilly, Sweden: Mader, *Banditenschatz,* 143.
300 line crossers: Buntrock, 103.
300 CICERO: Mader, 139, Bazna, 194–96.
300 *RM*11,695,516: IMT, 38:32.
300 Nazis strip prisoners: Rudolf Höss, *Kommandant in Auschwitz: Autobiographische Aufzeich-*

nungen, ed. Martin Broszat, Quellen und Darstellungen zur Zeitgeschichte, 5, (Stuttgart: Deutsche Verlags-Anstalt, 1958), 164.
301 gold teeth, smelted, Reichsbank: Ibid., 167; Hilberg, 616–17; IMT, 34:112, 33:572, 587.
301 Kaltenbrunner financed: IMT, 11:263 (Kaltenbrunner); Enno Georg, *Die wirtschaftlichen Unternehmungen der SS,* Schriftenreihe der Vierteljahrshefte für Zeitgeschichte, 7 (Stuttgart: Deutsche Verlags-Anstalt, 1963), 136–38.
301 Himmler directed: NO-2208.
301 jewelry: Buntrock, 103; IMT, 33:579–81.

CHAPTER 18: BATTALIONS OF SPIES

To abbreviate the extended references in the section on Latin American spying, I have cited each only by the last digits of their full DSDF designation. Thus "2545" stands for "DSDF 862. 20235/4-2545." The full references are: DSDF 862.20225/620, DSDF 862.20210/1996, DSDF 800. 20235/415, DSDF 800.20235/421, DSDF 862.20235/8-2644, DSDF 20210/3-2944, DSDF 862.20235/ 4-1045, DSDF 862.20235/4-2545.

302 Ritter: Ritter, 15–16.
302 to Hamburg post: SHEAF, *German Intelligence Services,* 6.
302 Owens: Ritter, 19–20, 41–44.
303 Simon: Ibid., 65–68, 128–31, 152–54; Stephan, 137–40.
305 JOHNNY: Ritter, 148–50, 166–67, 198–216, 242–54; Churchill, 1:156, and Reuter, 37–38, for radar.
306 "was of the greatest": Ritter, 320.
306 most famous German agent: my judgment on basis of OKH:H2/114:30168 and OKW, *KTB,* 4:1798.
306 Krämer: BDC; Krämer, interview: AA:Pol I M:38:318933; Farago, 529; NA:RG165:USFET: CI:FIR:67:7.
306 Low Countries, Budapest, Istanbul: Farago, 540, 543.
306 "of the greatest importance," previously traveled: AA:Pol I M:Abwehr-Einbau:Karl-Heinz Krämer:23.September 1942.
307 Krämer arrived, wife followed, rank: Ibid.:29.Okt.1942, 2.Nov.1942, 24.Dez.1942.
307 reports in Hamburg: Ibid.:23.September 1942.
307 first "mantle report": AA:Pol I M:86:307873.
307 reports: Ibid.:passim, and ibid.:86a:passim.
307 SIEGFRIED A, V 3569: Farago, 548: AA:Pol I M:86:307949.
307 Svahlvink: NA:RG165:USFET:CI:FIR:67:8.
307 13 April 1943: AA:Pol I M:86:308029.
307 Florman: Ibid.:308030; NA:RG165:USFET:CI:FIR:67:10–11.
307 SIEGFRIED B: Krämer interview; Farago, 549.
308 Italian, Onoodera, Voeckzoendy, Grundboek: NA:RG165:USFET:CI:FIR:67:10–11; NA: RG238:Schellenberg interrogation:8 May 1946; Farago, 553.
308 press: NA:RG165:USFET:CI:FIR:67:7, Farago, 554.
308 "SIEGFRIED B reports": AA:Pol I M:86:307900.
310 traveled, Wirsing, Switzerland trips: NA:RG165:USFET:CI:FIR:67:7–8, 15. Wirsing: Party No. 8,283,061.
310 "Which formations," "Does the creation": AA:Pol I M:38:318969.
310 Swedish attachés in Britain: OKH:H2/114:30166; Farago, 549–51; *Hitlers Lagebesprechungen,* 545.
310 threatened to resign, "with no result": NA:RG238:Schellenberg interrogation:8 May 1946: 12–13.
310 "In principle": MA:III M 1000/49:132–33.
311 eight airborne divisions, 14th Army: OKH:H2/111:35, 26.
311 Busch, Gestapo: NA:RG165:USFET:CI:FIR:67:9, 13–14; NA:RG238:Schellenberg interrogation:8 May 1946:12–13; Farago, 553.
312 Kauders, Meily: BDC:Wilhelm Höttl:159–64, 168–69; State Department, letter, 20 December 1974.
313 Turkul: Franz Seubert, letter. 3.Februar 1974; B. Orekhoff, letter, 22.12.74.
314 to Sofia: Otto Wagner, letter, 16.Mai 1974; Wagner, 2nd interview.
314 complete protection, Kauders description: Wagner, 2nd interview.
314 "On 2 June": HGrSüd:74124/5:6.Juni 1942; Gehlen, 57–58.
316 "Military council": OKW, *KTB,* 2:1283. It is my assumption that this is a MAX message.
316 "On 4 November": OKH:H3/199:73:Anlage.
316 doctor on Stalin's staff: Bitterl, interview, 5.
316 Rumanian: Gersdorff, interview, 2.
316 Japanese newspaperman: Leverkuehn, 172–75; Rittlinger, 227.
316 what MAX had said, Guderian, Hitler: Gersdorff, interview, 2; Leverkuehn, 172–75: Schellenberg, *Memoirs,* 308.
317 Wagner found it suspect: Wagner, 2nd interview; Rittlinger, 225.
317 the best, decisive, "You can watch him": Wagner, 2nd interview.
317 Mexico: FDR Library:OF10b:40:8 Feb 1945.
317 1939 recruitment: NA:RG59:Poole mission:Niebuhr interrogation:3, 4.
317 Müller: 1996:8–9.
318 Napp: Ibid.:9–10.
318 "My cousin sails," 5,000 pesos: Ibid.:47; NA:RG59:Poole mission:Niebuhr interrogation:4.

318   10,000 pesos: Ibid.:44.
318   "How high are," "How high current": 1996:42.
318   DIN, Bar Central: Ibid.:9.
318   agents: Ibid.:11–13.
318   "Arrived at Buenos Aires": Ibid.:31.
318   jaundiced eye: NA:RG59:Poole mission: Niebuhr interrogation:4–5.
319   spy ring of his own: 1996:17–19.
319   "Curtiss Columbus," "Can you get," "Drawing attention": Ibid.:73, 67, 70.
319   major networks in Brazil crushed: *FRUS, 1942,* 5:188–89.
319   move to Argentina: 1996:17.
319   air attaché, Reiners, Chilean as mailbox: 620:2–3, 4, 5, 8. Reiners: Party No. 3,391,121.
319   clerical channels: Ibid.: 7, one, seven.
320   "Chilean *Tolten,*" weather reports, "Provide Christmas": 620:nine, ten, seven.
320   radio store owner: NA:RG173:Entry 27:Box 11:Folder File No. 1:1 December 1942.
320   Zeller: 620:8.
320   raid, "Luckily they": NA:RG173:Entry 27:Box 11:Folder File No. 1:18 December 1942.
320   shacklike house: Ibid.:13.Nov 1942.
320   Hofbauer: Party No. 3,445,464.
320   Szeraws: Ibid.; 620:6.
320   hide its signals: NA:RG173:Entry 27B:Box 5:Folder:Testimony of George E. Sterling, Section I:14.
320   PYL, Argentine rings smashed: *FRUS, 1942,* 5:237–39, 246, 247.
321   cooperative Abwehr-SD operation: NA:RG59:Poole mission:Paeffgen interrogation:4; 421:Enclosure:1.
321   Becker: Ibid.:4–5, Enclosure:3; 2545:Enclosure 2:2; BDC. Party No. 359,966; SS No. 9,393.
321   Seidlitz: 421:Enclosure:7–8.
321   Bayer advertising chief: Ibid.: 4, 3. He was Johann Harmeyer.
321   reorganized spy nets: 2545:Enclosure:2.
321   Niebuhr, Wolff: Ibid.:4.
322   Harnisch: 421:Enclosure:9; Reile, *Westfront,* 328–29.
322   Orga T: 2545:Enclosure 2: 3, 4.
322   Utzinger: 2644:Enclosure 2:1–2; 2944:Enclosure 1:6, photograph; 1045:50–53; 1996:13; *FRUS, 1942,* 5:252.
322   farms: 2944:Enclosure 5:107.
322   Szeraws: 2944:Enclosure 1:5; 2644:Enclosure 2:4.
322   Daue: 2644:Enclosure 2:3–4; 1045:61–62; 2944:Enclosure 3:5.
322   Guerrico, messages, chickens, suitcase: 1045:62–63, 56.
323   microphotography laboratory: 421:Enclosure:3, 5.
323   man to Uruguay, meeting, recruited: 1045:30, 37–38, 39.
323   Becker information sources: 421:Enclosure:2; IfZ:ZS 291:1:34; United States, Department of State, *Consultation Among the American Republics With Respect to the Argentine Situation,* Inter-American Series, 29 (GPO, 1946), 26; FDR Library:OF10b:39:2 August 1944.
323   Orga T. finances: 1045:40.
323   arms from Germany, break in relations: United States, Department of State, *Consultation,* 6–7, 11–15; Robert A. Potash, *The Army and Politics in Argentina, 1928–1945: Yrigoyen to Perón* (Stanford: Stanford University Press, 1969), 220–23, 230–32; Harold F. Peterson, *Argentina and the United States 1810–1960* (Albany: State University of New York, 1964), 430–34.
324   former chancellor: 2545:Enclosure 2:3.
324   new microphotographer: 1045:14.
324   "The pesos are gone": Ibid.:25; also 32.
324   agents pay, assets, radios, $62,000: Ibid.:60, 22, 17, 16.
325   Mi Capricho, transmissions, April 1944: Ibid.: 63–67.
325   four men, Villa, Fernandez: Ibid.:25, 23.
326   Burckhardt, Chatrain: Ibid., 18–21.
326   Daue sees men, moves, 6:30: Ibid.: 65, 66, 67; 2944:Enclosure 1:5.
326   arrests: dates given in 1045:77–146.
326   Becker dodging: Ibid.:4, 32–34; 2545:Enclosure 2:5.
327   Villa: Ibid.:26.
327   Becker arrested: 2646:1.
327   aften a month, too late: NA:RG59:Poole mission: Paeffgen interrogation:6–7.
327   Kaltenbrunner: NA:RG165:HQ 12 AG:IIR (Kaltenbrunner):28 June 45:26. Kaltenbrunner says "Brazil," but since that rupture took place a year before he became head of the RSHA, I assume he meant Argentina.
327   five ships torpedoed: A check of all the ships mentioned as sailing in the intercepted messages in 1996 against vessels listed in Rohwer, *Die U-Boot-Erfolge,* shows only those five sunk by U-boats. For no messages received by U-boats: Great Britain, Ministry of Defence, Naval Historical Branch, letters, 22 June 1976 and 21 November 1977.
327   Griebl: Smith, 75–76; Jacobsen, 532–33; Leon G. Turrou as told to David G. Wittles, *Nazi Spies in America* (New York: Random House, 1939), 100–104, 118, 226–31; Farago, 21–22, 26; ML-37, 15 September 1937; *New York Times* (18 October 1938), 28:6. Party No. 8,540,674.
327   pursuit planes, destroyers: Farago, 28–29, 63.
328   Rumrich: Sayers and Kahn, 15; *New York Times* (6 April 1936), 3:1; Farago, 63–64.
328   Lang: Ritter, 83–86, 89–91, 121–27; Sayers and Kahn, 26–27; Federal Bureau of Investigation, "Frederick Joubert Duquesne et al., Espionage" (May 5, 1953), 21–22; Farago, 327.

331 "The device contains": AA:Pol I M:28:270475.
331 did not replace Lothfe: Grosskopf, interview.
331 Sebold case: Ritter, 162–64; Farago, 322–29, 455–65; Federal Bureau of Investigation, "Frederick Joubert Duquesne et al., Espionage" (May 5, 1953), passim; Sayers and Kahn, 24–33; *New York Times* (4 November 1941), 27:1.
332 "In one of the": United States District Court for the Eastern District of New York: Docket No. 38425: U.S. vs. Hermann Lang et al.:Transcript:1153–56.
333 "The bastard," "But Ritter": Ritter, 291.
333 Koedel: Federal Bureau of Investigation, "Simon Emil Koedel . . . Espionage-G" (8 June 1945); Farago, 492–502; *New York Times* (24 October 1944), 25:8, (8 February 1945), 21:3, (16 February 1945), 25:7, (20 February 1945), 21:7.
335 Rothkirch zu Panthen: NA:RG238:Schellenberg interrogation:5 February 1946:1–8; Ibid.:8 May 1946:8–10. I believe Schellenberg even though I have not been able to trace such a person either in *Wer Ist's?*, 9 (1928) under Rothkirch and under Emden or in the *Gothäisches Genealogisches Taschenbuch der Freiherrlichen Häuser*, Teil A, 90 (1940), 510.
336 12 November 1942: T-175:124:2599033–34.
336 Brazilian messages: AA:Inl II g:460:19.11.43.
336 low-level Spanish code: Kahn, 449–50.
336 Pell: Farago, 414–23; Leonard Baker, *Brahmin in Revolt: A Biography of Herbert C. Pell* (Garden City: Doubleday, 1972), 219–23.
336 Spain, Vichy, Lindbergh: T-120:307:234403–4, 234398–99, 234368.
336 "I have read": Ibid.:234341.
339 six months: Ibid.:234338, 234596.
339 to and not to Ribbentrop: Ibid.: 234367, 234543; *ADAP*, 2:260.
339 "Out of an absolutely," Scotland: AA:Inl II g:342:EO25055; Sherwood, 812.
339 1 February 1943, Cyprus: AA:Inl II g:357:235846; Churchill, 4:718.
339 1 June 1943, "Overall Strategic": AA:Inl II g:476:1.Juni 1943; Churchill, 4:808.
339 Dewey: AA:Inl II g:342:26. August 1944.
340 Bazna: Bazna, 3–7, 14–18.
341 "It ought to be": Ibid., 40.
341 Moyzisch: BDC. Party No. 1,307,980.
342 Moyzisch-Bazna meetings: Bazna, 60–64, 71–74, 81–83.
342 Papen use of documents: Papen, 511–18; Lothar Krecker, *Deutschland und die Turkei im Zweiten Weltkrieg* (Frankfurt: Klostermann, 1964), 239–48.
343 "The question you raise": T-120:52:41824.
343 English telegrams: Kahn, 451–52.
343 "precise intelligence": *Staatsmänner*, 2:360.
344 "I have mostly studied": *Hitlers Lagebesprechungen*, 440–41. I agree with the editor and David Irving that he is speaking of CICERO documents, which were given to him (AA:Inl II g:7:329722).
344 No. 1751: PRO:FO371/37479:21 December 1943, which is quoted in paraphrased form as a CICERO telegram in T-120:52:41898.
344 "Apparently attack": T-120:52:41898.
344 "we must now": PRO:FO371/44064:12 January 1944, cited as a CICERO telegram in AA:Inl II g:464:296166.
344 air reconnaissance: OKW, *KTB*, 4:620.
344 Jodl: Jodl diary, probably for 10.2.1944 (Foreign Military Studies, P-215, p. 120, giving Warlimont commentary). I am grateful to David Irving for this reference.
344 Hitler expects: OKW, *KTB*, 4:606–607.
345 17 to 25 divisions: Ibid., 3:735, 1402.
345 troops withdrawn, replaced: Ibid., 621, 622–24.
345 Sofia air raid: Papen, 518.
345 Nele Kapp: AA:Inl II g:106:26. Januar 1944; Moyzisch; Bazna; William Gorman, telephone interview, 7 May 1977.
345 Kapp defection: AA:Inl II g:106:8.April 1944, 18.8.44; *The Times* (21 April 1944), 3:3.
346 forbade spying in Britain: Speidel, interview, saying that Canaris had told him this; Speidel was then in Foreign Armies; Staubwasser, interview; Thomas, 118.
346 naval treaty: *DGFP:C*, 4:319–26.
347 no star agents: Schierbrandt, interview.
347 British Union of Fascists: Ritter, interview. Cavendish-Bentinck, interview, thought that Mosley would not have spied against England.
347 LENA: Ritter, 218–19.
348 Hansen, Caroli: Ritter, 219–36; Farago, 256–57; Masterman, 49–53.
349 "Nothing yet," "We've got": Ritter, 234.
350 Borehamwood factories, "Many bombers," "New are," "Further observation": ML-174a:15.2. 41, 17.2.41, 25.2.41, 26.2.41.
350 free agent: Masterman, 93.
350 near Salisbury, suburbs and exurbs: ML-174a:23.3.41, 31.3.41, 5.4.41, 6.4.41.
351 "You never," "Don't you," "What is": Farago, 258–59.
351 money through Japanese: Ibid., 265–66; Masterman, 93–94.
351 money through Lisbon: Masterman, 85–86; Popov, 119–22.
352 better circles, farm, daughter: Masterman, 94–95.
352 Eisenhower: Farago, 595, 600–601; Cave Brown, 409; *New York Times* (17 January 1944), 1:5.
352 Hansen reports: ML-174a:26.4.44, 4.5.44, 10.5.44, 18.5.44, 29.7.44, 31.7.44.
352 "On the occasion": Farago, 259.

352 mine-laying, last message: Masterman, 183–85.
353 spy Vera: Firmin, 69–74; Ritter, 154–60, 254–59; Farago, 238–39, 243–55; *After the Battle*, No. 11 (1976), 17–23. All my attempts to run her down under the various aristocratic names she gave have failed.
354 Timmerman, Dronkers: *After the Battle*, No. 11 (1976), 30; Firmin, 80.
354 Garby-Czerniawski: Cave Brown, 483–85; Farago, 618–21; Masterman, 120–21, 140; Roman Garby-Czerniawski, *The Big Network* (London: George Ronald, 1961), 14; OKH:H2/114:30181; OKH:H2/116:HUBERT.
354 one a day: comparison of message numbers with dates in ML-174a.
355 25 February 1944: ML-174a:1.3.44.
355 10 March: Ibid.: 12.3.44.
355 "Your two seven one": Ibid.:13.3.44.
355 liaison to Patton: Farago, 619.
355 11th, XXXIIIrd, 17th, 9th, 21st: OKH:H2/114:30181.
355 "Brentwood some," "In Nottingham": OKH:H2/111:36, 25.
355 January 1945: Masterman, 191.
356 Fidrmuc and CHB: Piekenbrock in Mader, 85; Farago, 136, 146, 519; OKH:H2/116:CHB 1, CHB 2, CHB 3, CHB 4, CHB 5, CHB 6, CHB 7; OKH:H2/3:V5166/44g; Staubwasser, interview; Höhne, *Canaris*, 190, 191, 490.
356 OSTRO: NA:RG165:HQ7th Army:307th CIC Detachment: FIR 12:Appendix 4:5, Appendix 5:4; OKH:H2/114:30140–43; OKH:H2/115a:OSTRO; OKH:H2/116:OSTRO 6; Masterman, 4.
356 21 July 1942: IWM:Milch:15:1549.
356 Brittany, 30 September: OKL:RL2/647:10.8.44; OKL:RL2/543:8.Oktober 1944.
356 CATO: Delmer, 51–63; Masterman, 114–16.
356 Hitler's ridicule: Domarus, ed., 1411–12.
357 Polish pilot, Lyttleton, Auchinleck: Delmer, 81–82; *New York Times* (30 June 1941), 7:1, (2 July 1941), 1:5, 6:4.
357 subagents: Delmer, 100, 102–103; Masterman, 143.
357 52nd Division: Delmer, 123.
358 400, 2,000, 20,000: Masterman, 142.
358 short- and long-range agents: Moritz, ed., 268–69; NA:RG165:USFET:IC:1SIIR:110–11; D-407, 76–77, 80.
359 short-range spy mission: NA:RG165:USFET:IC:1SIIR:114–16, 109–10; D-407, 77.
359 only once, Sonia, women: *Espionage-Sabotage-Conspiracy*, 25; Gersdorff, interview, 1; D-407, 145, 146.
359 Agents 523, 422: OKH:H3/182:1.11.44.
359 Jodl letter: NA:RG165:HQ 7th Army:307th CIC Detachment:FIR 12:Appendix 20:2.
360 28 December 1943: *Hitlers Lagebesprechungen*, 497.
360 ZEPPELIN: *NCA*, B:1623–4; TWC:Case 11:Testimony:5152, 5153, 5356; NA:RG238:Schellenberg interrogation:13 November 1945:1–3; "Sowjetischen Staatssicherheitsorgane," 1210, 1214.
360 returned agents shot: *TWC*, 13:552, 560–69.
360 half again as much, schools, training time: "Sowjetischen Staatssicherheitsorgane," 1211, 1210.
360 500 to 800, 8 to 10, attrition rate: D-407, 78, 146; Gersdorff, interview; Seyffaerth, interview.
360 P. I. Tavrin, ULM, 150 agent groups: "Sowjetischen Staatssicherheitsorgane," 1215, 1212.
361 extraordinary demands. "If the losses": D-407, 146, 80.
361 I and R nets: NA:RG165:HQ 7th Army:307th CIC Detachment:FIR 12: Appendices 10, 11; USFET:MISC:CI-IIR/48:3, 5, 10; Weidemann, interview, 15, 24, 26; OKH:H2/120:55–57.
361 Herrlitz, preparations: USFET:MISC:CI-IIR/48:7, 6.
362 line-crossers: Ibid.:10; NA:RG165:HTUSAIC:IR:19:4.
362 at first low grade, later better: [United States, Army], 12th Army Group, *Report of Operations*, 4:192–93.
362 NORMANDIE, SCHWAGER, GAUTHIER, Troop 134: USFET:MISC:CI-IIR/48:9–10.
362 human price: Ibid.:4, 10; NA:RG165:HTUSAIC:IR:19:5.
362 3–4 February 1945: 12th Army Group, *Report of Operations*, 4:202.
362 Punzeler: *New York Times* (31 January 1945), 6:2, (11 February 1945), 4:2–3.
363 Kotas and Wende: 12th Army Group, *Report of Operations*, 4:207; *New York Times* (12 November 1944), 37:1; Glowczynski, telephone interview.
363 V-314, V-373: OKH:H2/116:V-314, V-373.
364 "almost humorously": Owe, interviews.
364 "agent reports only": OKL:RL2/547:8.3.45:4–5.
364 "The effectiveness": Baumbach, interview, 13.
364 Canaris's two predictions: OKM:1/Skl:KTB:A:25.4.43.
364 "failure" in 1940: Groscurth, 212, 260, 385.
364 Westphal: Westphal, 240.
364 regarded results as essential: D-407, 79.
364 72 Abwehr reports: OKW:Wi/IB 1.145:29.5.42.
364 192 reports, "The overwhelming number": OKM:1/Skl:KTB:C:14:16.Oktober 1944:4.
365 173 reports: OKM:1/Skl:KTB:A:23.3.45. I am grateful to David Irving for this and the above citations.
365 133 agents: *Espionage-Sabotage-Conspiracy*, 45.
365 EVA, GUTMANN, HUBERT: OKH:H2/114:30188A, 30183A; OKH:H2/111:35; HGrD: 75144/35:83.
365 Brazilian, "The report is": OKH:H2/115a:6.6.44, 6.6.44.
365 "entirely unbelievable": OKL:RL2/649:19784/44geh.
365 other comments: OKH:K2/114:passim.
366 Luftwaffe investigation of HEKTOR: OKL:RL2/547:14.Juni 1944, 25. Sep. 1944, 14.12.1944:5,6; OKL:RL2/649:29.10.1944; OKH:H2/114:16.September 1944.

367 not a single German agent legitimate: Masterman, 3.
367 JOHNNY: Ibid., 36–41.
368 11th, 25th, 59th never existed: Palmer et al., 489–91.
368 "firmly believed": Churchill, 5:596.
368 CHB independent: My conclusion.
368 OSTRO independent: Masterman, 151.
369 other agents gave numbers, not MAX: HGrSüd:74124/5:passim.
369 neither messaged home: P.R.O., letter, 21 May 1974; my checks in various files at the National Archives.
369 CICERO legitimately served the Germans: Hugh R. Trevor-Roper; Victor Cavendish-Bentinck in Constantine FitzGibbon, *Secret Intelligence in the Twentieth Century* (New York: Stein and Day, 1976), 264.
370 typist mistake: Sir Edward Peck (then 3rd secretary in the British embassy at Ankara), interview, 23 February 1974.
370 did not supply Germany: Buchheit, 100–101; Reile, *Westfront*, 290; Abshagen, 159.

CHAPTER 19: THE MILITARY ECONOMISTS

373 Nicolai: Nicolai, *Nachrichtendienst*, 12–13, 139.
373 recognized the importance: Payr, 1; Gempp, II:7:26; Heinz, 12.
373 T 3: Warlimont, letter.
373 by 1934: Thomas, 65; NA:RG165:Schuster Commission:Warlimont interrogation:1.
373 War Economy Branch: Thomas, 66, 116–19, 160, 226, 368–70, 374.
373 73 desks out of 322: Thomas, facing p. 308. Detailed organizational table in OKW:Wi/VIII. 245:1.Februar 1942.
373 22 desks, 52 people: OKW:WiIF5/1923:25.Nov.1944. A 1943 organizational table in OKW: Wi/VIII:216:15.März 1943.
374 Organization of the War Economy Branch: OKW:Wi/VIII.245:1.Februar 1942.
374 military administrators, Zinnemann, barracks, moved: Kirsch, interview. Zinnemann Nazi party membership number: 2,153,419.
374 war dried up: Thomas, 117–18.
374 Foreign Office's Commercial Branch: AA:HaPolIXa:Kupfer:1.Jan.42–Nov.43.
374 Bureau III: Reichwirtschaftsministerium/3/9:Geschäftsverteilungsplan:Dezember 1943:11–16.
374 Vowi, research institutes: see chapter 6.
375 material outdated: Kirsch, interview.
375 chrome and manganese: OKW:WiI/52:10.9.42.
375 Forschungsamt intercept: BA:EAP66-c-12/44:192966.
375 11 August 1944: OKW:Wi/VIII.11:Anlage 8.
375 Luftwaffe's radio intercept: OKW:Wi/IB 1.145:8.5.42.
375 Organization of Group V: Ibid.
376 "Too general": OKW:Wi/IB 1.145:2. Juni 1942.
376 new requirements: OKW:Wi/VI.31:14.November 1942.
376 18 American ships: OKW:Wi/VI.344: Schiffsankünfte Persischer Gulf.
376 vegetable oil: RWM/20/106:21.September 1944.
376 "need not necessarily lead": Thomas, 270.
376 specialists to the front, 700–800 a month, most valuable: Payr, 8–9; Kirsch, interview.
376 tank production: OKW:Wi/VIII.10:5; OKH:H3/284a:142.
378 Russian coal requirements: OKW:Wi/VIII.10:4.
378 leaves, plates: Kirsch, interview.
378 Jordan calculations: OKH:H3/284a:10, 88, 142. For the far more refined American calculations of the same type, see Richard Ruggles and Henry Brodie, "An Empirical Approach to Economic Intelligence in World War II," *Journal of the American Statistical Association*, 42 (March 1947), 72–91.
378 202,000: OKW:Wi/VI.2:10.8.1944:2.
378 200,793: NA:RG169:Entry 514:Part II:Section IX: "Status of the Soviet Aid Program as of March 31, 1944":Sheet 1, totalling cargo and weapons carriers (3/4 ton), trucks (1½ ton), trucks (2½ ton), trucks (5 ton and over), jeeps, and amphibian jeeps, listed as "arrived."
378 helped navy decide: OKW:Wi/VI.31:29.Juni 1942:4.
378 bombing targets: OKW:Wi/VI.399:6.7.1943:3.
378 "The domestic production": Ibid.:3–4.
379 when Soviet units would be refitted: Kirsch, interview; Blumröder, interview. Halder, 3:498.
379 2,000,000 tons: OKW:Wi/VI.399:4.4.43:5.
379 4,000,000 to 5,000,000 tons: *Lagevorträge*, 472.
379 might not cause: Thomas, 270.
379 "had reached the end": *DGFP*, 13:691–92.
379 chromium ore: OKW:Wi/VI.31:7 November 1942:6.
379 "The Führer": Thomas, facing p. 160.
379 stop submitting: Keitel, 183; Speer, 303.

CHAPTER 20: IN THE LUFTWAFFE AND IN THE KRIEGSMARINE

In this chapter, I have converted nearly all German tonnage figures from gross register tons, or gross tons, their customary form, to deadweight tons, the usual American and British form. Leighton and Coakley, 722, say that 1,000 gross tons equals approximately 1,500 deadweight. But backfiguring from equivalent gross and deadweight tonnages given in *Fremde Handelsschifffahrt*, Bericht Nr. 5/43 (OKW:Wi/VI.270:10. März 1943) shows that the Germans converted at an average ratio of 1 to 1.44. As this yields more conservative results, I have used it.

380　Owe, deer park, Group D, daily routine: Owe, interview.
381　"Individual Reports of the Air Force I c Service West": OKH:H2/7:passim.
381　1 March 1920: Völker, *Entwicklung*, 127, 236.
381　1 April 1927: Ibid., 161, 243.
382　Bülow: Bülow in USAF-171, 39–41. But his statement that he had 10 officers in 1930 must be an error, as by 1937 he had only eight (Völker, *Deutsche Luftwaffe*, 260).
382　1931 target file: Völker, *Entwicklung*, 265.
382　5th Branch: Völker, *Deutsche Luftwaffe*, 259, 260; USAF-171, 42. For previous evolution, see Völker, *Entwicklung*, 244, 264–65, 252; Völker, *Deutsche Luftwaffe*, 227, 228, 231, 238, 240, 276.
382　Jeschonnek: Schmid, 2.
382　Schmid: Schwenke, interview; Donat, interview, 10; Rieckhoff, 109. Harold J. Gordon, Jr., *Hitler and the Beer Hall Putsch* (Princeton: Princeton University Press, 1972), 329, 353, for cadets.
382　"evaluation of intelligence," "target study," secondary jobs: Völker, *Dokumente*, 159–66.
382　"anybody's girl": Noack, interview.
382　29 officers, 5 groups: BA:RL2/557:undated officer's list entitled "Generalstab 5. Abteilung," identified by Donat as from shortly before the war.
382　U.S. started in 1940: Schmid, 42.
382　Longeront: Donat, interview, 12.
383　target folders: Deichmann, "Die Zielobjektkartei"; Owe, interview; Schreyer, 75–77.
383　40,000: Deichmann, "Die Zielobjektkartei," 3.
383　500: Schreyer, 77.
383　100 percent, 90 percent, 70 to 80 percent: IMT, 25:386–87.
383　distributed: Schreyer, 77; USAF-171, 53.
383　books: for example, [Germany], Oberbefehlshaber der Luftwaffe, Führungsstab I c, Sonderfolge . . . , 2. Heft, *Britische Flugrüstungsindustrie*.
384　Crewe: Ibid., Lfd. Nr. 9.
384　Sedan:NA:RG242: Cartographic Branch.
384　SU 74 26: BA:EAP 66-c-12-44/464:192969.
384　Factory No. 29: Ibid.:193004.
384　figures on France accurate: Schmid, 6–7, 14, 26.
384　radio reconnaissance: USAF-171, 127–30.
384　no captured pilots: Ibid., 126.
384　underestimated fighter replacements: Ibid., 126, 130.
384　350, 700: Irving, *Rise and Fall of the Luftwaffe*, 101; Wilmot, 49.
384　lost the Battle of Britain: Schmid, 29, does not discuss the question of miscalculation of enemy fighter forces. The charges that the loss of this battle was entirely Schmid's fault (in Georg W. Feuchter, *Der Luftkrieg*, 3. Auflage [Frankfurt: Athenäum, 1964], 99–100; Cajus Bekker, *The Luftwaffe War Diaries*, trans. and ed. Frank Ziegler [Garden City: Doubleday, 1968], 155; and Peter Townsend, *Duel of Eagles* [New York: Simon and Schuster, 1970], 350, 391) are too harsh and exaggerated. Göring and Hitler, after all, made the critical decision to shift to bombing London, and only in part because of overoptimism: they wanted to revenge themselves for the RAF raids on Berlin (Walter Ansel, *Hitler Confronts England* [Durham: Duke University Press, 1960], 247–48; Basic Collier, *The Defence of the United Kingdom*, History of the Second World War: United Kingdom Military Series [HMSO, 1957], 216, 233).
385　friction between Göring and subordinates: Irving, *Rise and Fall*, 147–49; Schmid, 46, 50–52.
385　Schmid reports to Hitler on thousand-plane raid: OKW, *KTB*, 2:400.
385　lie judgments: Schmid, 52.
385　Schulze-Boysen: Ibid.; USAF-171, 100–101; Heinz Höhne, *Codeword: Direktor* (New York: Coward, McCann & Geoghegan, 1971), 137, 157.
385　Kögl: Schmid, 52.
385　Wodarg: RMfVuP, *Kriegspropaganda*, 109–10, 551.
385　chief mystery: Owe, interview, 12.
386　statistical analysis: Halder, 3:374, 400, 410, 416, 419.
386　could not determine invasion location: Owe, interview, 12.
386　Kienitz, Owe promotions: Ibid., 5.
386　Schwenke "deciphering unit": Schwenke, interview.
386　5010: MA:RL2/423:6.2.1944 [actually 1945].
386　4300: United States Air Force, Albert F. Simpson Historical Research Center, 8th Air Force, "Daily Combat Strength as of 2000 Hours 31 January 1945."
386　worst problem: Owe, interview, 12.
386　"There were many things": Ibid., 6.
386　fighters of long range: Ibid., 10.
386　succumbed to enemy propaganda: Ibid., 6.
386　intelligence officers astonished: Ibid., 12–13.
387　"When I look": Ibid., 6–7.
387　"The German I c service," "did not take," "practically did not," "produced their own": MA:RL2/547:8.3.1945:1.
387　"We sometimes laughed": Owe, interview, 9.
387　creation of Seekriegsleitung: Lohmann, §32:1.

387 intelligence function: OKM:PG35533:161–62; *Rangliste der Deutschen Kriegsmarine*, (1. November 1935), 6–7, (1. November 1936), 7; Hubatsch, 255, 256; Bonatz, 74.
387 broke away: Lohmann, §32:2.
387 maintained its independence: Baumbach, interview, 1; Budde, interview.
388 multilithed bulletins: OKH:H2/7:passim.
388 Group FH: OKM:PG26674:17; Baumbach, interview, 2.
388 24 February 1943: OKW:Wi/VI.270:10.März 1943:1.
388 Hollerith machines, locations: Baumbach, interview, 2–3.
388 routes: see map in OKM, *Denkschriften*, 304, for example.
388 592, 62: OKW:Wi/VI.270:10.März 1943:1.
388 597, 61: Gerald J. Fischer, *A Statistical Summary of Shipbuilding Under the U.S. Maritime Commission During World War II*, Historical Reports of War Administration: United States Maritime Commission, No. 2 (n.p., 1949), Table B-3.
388 estimates of America's 1942 production: OKM, *Denkschriften*, 222, 297; OKH:H2/121a:67:7; *Lagevorträge*, 394.
388 "not possible": OKW:Wi/VI.270:10.März 1943:2.
389 construction time dropped: Frederic C. Lane, *Ships for Victory: A History of Shipbuilding Under the U.S. Maritime Commission in World War II* (Baltimore: Johns Hopkins Press, 1951), 174.
389 14.1 million: OKM, *Denkschriften*, 297, subtracting the 5.4 million gross tons for 1942 from the combined 1942–1943 total of 15.8, and converting to deadweight.
389 18 million: Fischer, Table B-3, counting "Major Types" only.
389 fatal tonnage figure: *DGFP*, 12:943; OKM, *Denkschriften*, 207, 242, 280; Halder, 3:420; *Lagevorträge*, 394. I believe that a zero has been dropped in quoting Hitler's statement that 72,000 tons "is more than the Americans can build in a month" (*Hitlers Tischgespräche*, 201). Hitler's use of fatal sinking figures of 700,000 (*DGFP*, 12:943) and of 600,000 to 650,000 tons (Halder, 3:420) suggests to me that he knew at least the range of the production figures.
389 872,127: OKM, *Denkschriften*, 300.
389 567,327: Churchill, 4:879. Dönitz, 221 (German edition), blames the exaggeration on the Luftwaffe and the Japanese.
389 300,000: Great Britain, Ministry of Defence, Naval Historical Branch, letter, 22 June 1976, citing No. 12 in the series Fremde Marinen (Nachrichtenauswertung). That the German navy actually used this figure is shown by backfiguring from transport tonnages given in OKH:H2/121a:67:7, 18, 23. Hitler's statement that the Allies needed double the tonnage for a division that the Germans did (*Staatsmänner*, 2:321) further lends credence to the German use of and belief in this figure.
389 122,000: Leighton and Coakley, 1:647, taking the largest figure (for vehicles on wheels, not boxed) and converting from ship tons to deadweight.
389 "The [Allied] tonnage": OKM, *Denkschriften*, 288.
389 "proves that there is": *Lagevorträge*, 248.
389 "The current tonnage": OKM, *Denkschriften*, 351.
390 most important, relatively small: Baumbach, interview, 3.
390 general principles of strategy: OKM, *Denkschriften*, 376–77, for example.
390 "The U.S.A. stands": OKM, *Denkschriften*, 367. For other Hitlerian conceptions, as peace with Britain, Ibid., 242–43.
390 transfer, Schulze: Lohmann, §32:3.
390 testified: Baumbach, interview, 17.
390 "To be there": Ibid., 12.

CHAPTER 21: O QU IV AND OKW/WFSt/I c

I am grateful to General Walter Warlimont and General Gerhard Matzky for reading drafts of this chapter carefully and making valuable corrections and additions.

391 Tippelskirch: Keilig, s.v. "Tippelskirch"; B. H. Liddell Hart Papers:German Generals File: Ulrich Liss:undated memo; Liss, 82; Strong, 88, 121; Groscurth, 183, 201, 203, 242, 247.
391 10 November 1938: *Allgemeine Heeresmitteilungen* (1938), 258.
391 1882: *Denkwürdigkeiten des General-Feldmarschalls Alfred Grafen von Waldersee*, ed. Heinrich Otto Meisner (Stuttgart: Deutsche Verlags-Anstalt, 1922), 1:216.
391 under the O Qu IV: P-041i, 31–34; Groscurth, 45, 204; Halder, 1:72; Völker R. Berghahn, "NSDAP und 'Geistige Führung' der Wehrmacht 1939–1945": *VfZ*, 17 (January 1969), 17–71.
391 duties of O Qu IV: P-041i, 6; *The German General Staff Corps*, 80.
392 reports to Halder: Halder, 1:63, 142, 232, 244, 296, 374.
392 nonintelligence duties: *DGFP*, 11:126; OKW, *KTB*, 1:179; Groscurth, 278–79, 232.
392 as soon as his successor arrived: USN:COA:Kretschmer memorandum:6.
392 5 January 1941: P-041i, 41.
392 Matzky: P-041i, iii; Matzky, interview.
392 presented information: P-041i, 34; Matzky, interviews; Matzky, memorandum, 30.4.75.
392 special high-level reports: Halder, 2:276, 3:140, 153.
393 "This war on the periphery": Matzky, interview.
393 O Qu IV and O Qu I dissolved: Erfurth, 219.
393 control span, only three: Heusinger, interview.
393 seemed to embarrass him: Matzky, memorandum, 30.4.75.
393 reducing the opposition to Hitler: Erfurth, 219–20.
393 Mellenthin assumed: Matzky, memorandum, 30.4.75.

394   OKW intelligence from Ausland and competent elements: Warlimont, "Kommentar," 201–203; Warlimont, notes on draft of this chapter.
394   for plans, for Jodl: Warlimont, 33, 45.
394   Liss urged: OKH:H2/136:1.Juni [1942].
394   Bürkner assembled: Schmid, 2–3.
394   existing arrangement sufficed: T-101:Annex 3:17.
394   Operations Staff recognized: Warlimont, "Kommentar," 203; Abshagen, 214.
395   Warlimont raised, Liss looked, dropped: OKH:H2/136:30.November [1942].
395   Krummacher: NA:RG238:Krummacher interrogation:1–2: Warlimont, letter, 4. August 1972; Delmer, 13–14; Meier-Welcker, 678, 684; OKW:Wi/VIII.25:1.Oktober 1942; USN:COA:Bürkner interrogation:5, 7.
395   could fit as well: For example, OKW:80:21.1.43.
395   distributing the situation report: NA:RG238:Krummacher interrogation:2.
395   started sending over: OKH:H2/136:18.Dezember [1942].
396   compiled them: OKW, *KTB*, 3:1432; Warlimont, "Kommentar," 205; Warlimont, 591.
396   "The overall situation": OKW, *KTB*, 3:1442–45.
396   "Possibility of Portugal's": OKW:80:18.8.1943.
396   superrush request, that day: Ibid.:5.Januar 1944.
398   satisfied his expectations: Warlimont, letter, 4. August 1972.
398   could not quite cram down: Ibid.; Süsskind-Schwendi, interview, 1.
398   three branches: OKH:H2/120:28.
398   Süsskind-Schwendi: Süsskind-Schwendi, interview, 2; OKH:H10–4/13:5; OKH:H10–4/15:10.
398   did not overlook: Süsskind-Schwendi, interview, 4.
398   submitted material, Hitler's conferences: Ibid., 5.
398   "more or less reluctantly": Ibid.

CHAPTER 22: THE THIRD GENERAL STAFF OFFICER

399   150, 25, 11: count by Susanne Kahn from Halder, 3:137–209.
399   206, 54: count from AOK 7:75106/3.
399   rather have a good colonel: Hauck, interview.
400   "The I c is the assistant": HDv. 92g, 19. A justification at D-407, 5, 19–20.
400   "The I c is subordinated": HDv. 89g, 11–12.
400   filled in the details: MA:RH27-2/49:21.9.1942:1.
400   importance of the commander's will: Rosinski, 305–309; [Hans] v. Seeckt, "Die Willenskraft des Feldherrn," *Militärwissenschaftliche Rundschau*, 1 (15.Dezember 1935), 2–6.
400   aggressive action: Rosinski, 302–303; Meyer-Detring, interview.
400   Versailles Treaty: Article 178 and Part V, Table I.
400   at field headquarters: Goerlitz, 225–26.
400   uniform at corps: Germany (Federal Republic of), Militärgeschichtliches Forschungsamt, *Handbuch zur deutschen Militärgeschichte*, 5: 226.
401   I c: BA-HA:IV:Generalkommando 4:1:4:Geschäftseinteilung Kommando Lüttwitz from mid-1919 and Ibid.:2:5:Bayerisches Schützenbrigade 21 of 25.3.20 show a use of I c for intelligence this early, though ibid.:1:3, staff designations of Generalkommando 4 in August 1919, shows I c for transport and I b for intelligence. (I am grateful to Professor Harold Gordon for these citations.) The designation of I c for intelligence seems to have become standardized during the 1920s. On 20 March 1930, the chief of the army command issued a directive concerning the organization of staffs, in which the divisional I c was assigned "domestic and foreign questions;· Abwehr"—apparently a euphemism for intelligence (WK VII/4082:20.3.1930). On 1 February 1937, the VII Corps staff in Munich included an I c, also handling domestic and foreign questions (WK XIII/7:Anlage 1). In 1938, HDv. 92g fixed the designation and the I c duties. Schmidt-Richberg, 71, does not answer the question of the standardization of the term.
401   bases his decisions: HDv. 300/1, §§36, 37, 59, 61, 62.
401   "One's own," "where the," "the judgment": Ibid., §§60, 61, 62.
401   "self-evident requirement": Ibid., §36.
401   how information comes in: Ibid., §§48, 49, 53, 62.
401   incomplete and erroneous reports: Ibid., §48.
401   "how far the enemy": Ibid., §62.
401   German principle: Ibid.; D-407, 116; Liss, "Erfahrungen," 640. This seems to come more from Moltke than from Clausewitz. Moltke stated that "the most probable thing [in war] is that the enemy will grasp the most correct measure" (Helmuth Count von Moltke, *Gesammelte Schriften und Denkwürdigkeiten* [ESM, 1891–93], 3:69). Clausewitz wrote, on the other hand, "One guards oneself . . . against believing that the enemy will do everything that he is capable of doing. These preconceptions make one incredibly anxious. First one should remember that the enemy cannot do everything at one time that he is on the whole able to do, moreover that he does not know our situation and all its disadvantages as we do, finally that in most cases he does not do everything that he can and should do. . . . The rule is therefore: Always base one's behavior on those things that one knows, rather than on those that one believes he must presuppose" (Carl von Clausewitz, *Schriften—Aufsätze—Studien—Briefe*, ed. Werner Hahlweg, Deutsche Geschichtsquellen des 19. und 20. Jahrhunderts, 45 [Göttingen: Vandenhoeck & Rupprecht, 1966], 413–14).
401   French principle: Liss, "Erfahrungen," 640.
401   duties of the I c within the staff: HDv. 92g. 19, 20, 21.
401   tradition to 1800s: *Felddienst-Ordnung* (1887), §8.

402 expanded these generalities: HDv. 89g, §§35–47, 11–14, Anlagen 1–3.
402 "The intelligence worker": Ibid., §6.
402 "his national and racial": Ibid., §5.
402 to the chief of staff: Ibid., §19.
402 company level: Merkblatt 19/8, 5.
402 battalion adjutant: Merkblatt 19/8, 5.
402 language noncoms: D-407, 19.
402 would not bother: Bottlar, interview.
402 regiment: Merkblatt 19/8, 5; D-407, 18–19, 51–52; Meyer-Detring, interview.
402 division: HDv. 89g, Anlage 3; D-407, 17, 52–53; *German Operational Intelligence*, 57–59, 63–65.
403 difference between division and higher commands: HDv. 92g, 21.
403 I c/AO: HDv. 89g, §12.
403 O 3 and O 6, O 3 and O 5, others: OKH:H2/2:Kriegsstärkenachweisungen (Heer) 9, 11, 12, 51.
403 other duties: Hayn, 139; *German General Staff Corps*, 75, 77; 98.I.D.:8159/2:4.2.1941.
403 murder squad cooperation: Hilberg, 244, 196–98, 213–15, 217, 231, 400, 441, 449, 451–52; NA:RG165:USFET:IC:1SIIR:139.
403 army to army group: D-407, 2–3, 12.
403 army group Ic/AO: Ibid., 13–14; *German Operational Intelligence*, 75–79; NA:RG165:USFET: IC:1SIIR:63–65.
403 13, 18: D-407, 14. This is larger than the 1943 table of organization figures given in OKH: H1/2:Kriegsstärkenachweisung (Heer) 9, but smaller than the figures of about 20 officers and a total of 20 given by Gersdorff, interview, and Blumröder, interview, respectively. Consequently I have used it.
403 U.S. 6th Army Group: [United States, Army], 6th Army Group, Headquarters, G-2 Section, *Final Report: World War II*, 8.
404 smallness of staffs: *German General Staff Corps*, 97–98, 3–4, 8.
404 "You can feel": Blumröder, interview.
404 larger staffs could do more: Implied in *German General Staff Corps*, 95.
404 hundreds, four reactions, prisoners, end runs, "No, sir": Koch, 25, 32, 33, 48, 42, 1.
405 half the scheduled positions: *German General Staff Corps*, 113.
405 all the I c positions: Ibid., 42; P-018a, 11.
405 during 1940, reserve officers: *German General Staff Corps*, 42; *German Operational Intelligence*, 111.
405 no stripes: Halder, 2:230.
405 reservists, majority at corps, previous service, in a post for years: *German General Staff Corps*, 40, 32; *German Operational Intelligence*, 111: P-018, 12.
405 I c's rank made same as I a: Gehlen, 37.
405 army and army group I cs: *German Operational Intelligence*, 111.
405 Meyer-Detring: *Hitlers Lagebesprechungen*, 39.
405 Gersdorff: Keilig, 3:s.v. Gersdorff.
405 two to eight weeks: *German General Staff Corps*, 32; Erfurth, 237.
405 relied upon O 3: *German Operational Intelligence*, 113.
405 intelligence training: Erfurth, 125–27; Model, 34, 37.
405 elective of 1920s and 1930s: Erfurth, 127; Model, 48.
405 lectures on intelligence, Abwehr, foreign armies: Model, 88–89.
406 no required intelligence courses: Ibid., 78–79.
406 tactics emphasized: Ibid., 34, 82.
406 "emphasis is to be laid": Ibid., 124.
406 6-week courses: *German General Staff Corps*, 32; NOKW-2672:2.
406 1942 decision: *German Operational Intelligence*, 114.
406 82, 24: Ibid., 115.
406 updating courses: Ibid., 116.
406 Army Group D course: HGrD:85459:139–45.
406 O 3 courses: *German Operational Intelligence*, 114; HGrD:85459:156.
406 O 3s learn by experience: *German Operational Intelligence*, 114; HGrD:85459:156.
406 intelligence pamphlets: Merkblatt für Korps- und Div. I c, 1.10.43; Merkblatt 19/8, *Truppen-I c-Dienst im Osten*, 1.8.44; HDv. 89g, *Feindnachrichtendienst*, 1.3.1941.
406 forbade I cs in other uses: *Allgemeine Heeresmitteilungen*, 11 (8. Mai 1944), 153–54, (7. Juli 1944), 211.
407 daily routine: Gersdorff, Blumröder, Meyer-Detring interviews; NA:RG165:USFET:IC:1SIIR: 101–102.
407 reports: from NA:RG165:USFET:IC:1SIIR, from D-407, and from *German Operational Intelligence*, all passim.
407 Blumröder day: Blumröder, interview.
408 hardest task: Gersdorff, interview.
408 submit to chief of staff: HDv. 89g, §19; NA:RG238:interrogation of Anton Staubwasser: 29.9.47:6.
408 25 maps: NA:RG165:USFET:IC:1SIIR:149–52.
409 card indexes: Ibid., 126.
409 "one of my most": Blumröder, interview.
409 unit card gives: D-407, 98–99.
409 "Red Bible": 90.1e.I.D.:18014/11:3.
409 "Red Ass" ("Rote Esel"): Dr. Gerd Brausch, conversations, 1969.
409 August 1944: OKH:H3/1361.
409 June of 1944: Blumröder, interview; NA:RG165:USFET:IC:1SIIR:157–58.

411   10 miles, bounced back: Seaton, 446; Ziemke, 332.
411   "mosaic work": Konus, 402.
411   prisoner-of-war intelligence: D-407, 59; *Merkblatt für Korps- und Div. I c*, 3.
411   radio intelligence: Meyer-Detring, Gersdorff, Blumröder interviews.
411   greatest volume: Gersdorff, interview.
411   most certain: my interpretation of "Wichtigste Unterlage" in *Merkblatt für Korps- und Div. I c*, 2
411   Soviet attack indications: Merkblatt 19/8, 9–10; D-407, 107–108.
411   different conclusions: Meyer-Detring, interview; D-407, 115–16.
411   summer of 1944: D-407, 115.
412   inductive logic: Bertrand Russell, *The Problems of Philosophy* ([1912], London: Oxford University Press, 1962), ch. vi.
412   deserters from a single regiment: D-407, 101–102.
412   Hume: *A Treatise of Human Nature* [1789], ed. L. A. Selby-Bigge (Oxford: Clarendon Press, 1888), bk. I, pt. III, sec. VI.
413   no major deception: Blumröder, interview; NA:RG165:SAIC:Notes on the Red Army—Leadership and Tactics:7.
413   small radio deceptions: Neeb, interview.
413   2nd Panzer Division: MA:RH27-2/49:8.2.1944 at 1, 2, 4 for quotes.
413   American tank: MA:RH27–15/37.
413   "not very convincing": HGrD:85459:110.
414   little more than keep books: Hauck, interview.
414   fire three I cs: Gersdorff, interview, 3.
414   "good work," "The section is": HGrD:85459:113, 108.
414   I c relations with commander: Blumröder, interview; Gersdorff, interview; D-407, 6, 114; NA: RG165:USFET:IC:1SIIR:103–104; Liss, "entscheidende Wert," 639; Konus, 399; Wilhelm, 30, citing Schramm.
415   12th Army: Halder, 2:470–71.
415   "Here comes": Blumröder, interview.
415   Kluge: Gersdorff, interview.
415   Manstein: Blumröder, interview; Ziemke, 90–97.
415   troops and guns needed: Meyer-Detring, interview; Hauck, interview.
416   captured orders: B-636; B-637, 2, 4, 7; B-656; B-782, 7, 13–14, 26; B-825, 146; HGrD:85459: 32, 79; AOK7:75106/8:21; AOK7:75106/7:11; NA:RG407:V Corps:Operations Plan Neptune: 26 March 1944:2; NA:RG407:VII Corps:Plan of Operations VII Corps Neptune:1; Harrison, 350–51. Harrison says that the VIIth Corps plan was picked up on the evening of 6 June, but since no other source does and since both AOK7:75106/7 and -/8 give 8 June, I use that date.

CHAPTER 23: FOREIGN ARMIES EAST AND WEST

418   25 January 1919: Stoerkel, "Stellvertretenden," 101.
418   Statistical Branch, T 3: *Heeres-Verordnungsblatt*, 1 (19. September 1919), 107–108, (12. November 1919), 345.
418   military statistics: Stein, *Lehre*, 198–99; Henri Baron de Jomini, *Précis de l'art de la guerre* (Paris: Anselin, 1838), §11.
418   branch chiefs: Those following Boetticher were: Colonel Curt Liebmann, starting fall 1924; Kühlenthal, starting 1928; Colonel Herbert Fischer, starting early 1931; then Stülpnagel. Stoerkel, "Stellvertretenden," 101, 141; Kehrig, 41; Germany, Heeresleitung, *Stellenbesetzung für das Reichsheer*, 1920 and 1921, and *Rangliste des deutschen Reichsheeres*, 1923–33; Erfurth, 191; Halder, 1:386; Meier-Welcker, 689, 326; Great Britain, *Documents on British Foreign Policy 1919–1939*, Series II, 1:478–79.
418   16 officers, high staff rank: Germany, Heeresleitung, *Stellenbesetzung des deutschen Reichsheeres*, 1920 and 1921, and *Rangliste des deutschen Reichsheeres*, 1923–37.
419   Stülpnagel: Keilig, s.v. "Stülpnagel"; Faber, 124–25, 190–91; Reynolds, 195.
419   "Foreign Armies": Germany, Heeresleitung, *Rangliste des deutschen Reichsheeres*, 1. Mai 1931, 3.
419   former officers: Liss, 16–17.
419   press: Liss, "Erfahrungen," 619; OKH:H27/15a:23.November 1938; Kehrig, 40.
419   1,000,000 civilians: *German Operational Intelligence*, 163.
419   orientation logbook, booklets: P-041i, 9, 15–18.
419   Saar plebiscite: Reynolds, 97.
419   five geographical groups: OKH:H27/14:10. November 1937.
419   10 November 1938: *Allgemeine Heeresmitteilungen* (1938), 258.
420   Liss: Strong, 71; Staubwasser, interview; B. H. Liddell Hart Papers:German Generals File: Ulrich Liss:undated memo; OKH:H27/10:25.6.1935.
420   sole source: Liss, 83–84; Groscurth, 257.
420   returned the fire: Domarus, ed., 1315.
420   contrast with 1914: Liss, 85.
420   to Zossen: Ibid.
420   bunkers: Herberg, interview; Staubwasser, interview.
420   drills, dust, Stülpnagel: Liss, 85–86.
421   little to do, "morning prayers," maps of Africa: Ibid., 87, 89, 88.
421   food: Ibid., 89.
421   cadre to 16: OKH:H2/124:8.
421   clerks: Liss, 89–90.
421   reserve officers: Liss, "entscheidende Wert," 640.

421   all group heads, War Academy, on the job: *German General Staff Corps*, 89; *German Operational Intelligence*, 81, 85.
421   take a year: Liss, "entscheidende Wert," 642.
421   chief considerations: My conclusions from interviews with officers in the branch; Liss, "entscheidende Wert," 641; *German Operational Intelligence*, 85.
421   after Operations Branch had taken its pick: Heusinger, interview.
421   wounded officers: Boldt, 25, 29, 44; OKH:H2/136:14.Oktober 1942:3; *German Operational Intelligence*, 85–86.
422   likely to remain: OKH:H2/136:passim; *German Operational Intelligence*, 86.
422   anathema: comments in many interviews about officers' resistance to going into intelligence work.
422   "gain the good": OKH:H2/136:5.Juni 1942:4.
422   "very unwillingly," "fascinated me": Metz, interview, 1, 2.
422   "Since I came": OKH:H2/136:5.Juni 1942:4.
422   service at the front: Euler, interview; Metz, interview; OKH:H2/136:14.Oktober 1942:3.
422   Abwehr "failure," grumbler: Groscurth, 212, 216; Liss, 88.
422   working with Abwehr, visited front, I c conferences: Liss, 104–105, 94, 120–22.
422   branch publications: Ibid., 93–94.
422   Hitler audiences: Strong, 77; Liss, 129.
423   build up a picture: Liss, 96, 105.
423   huge table: Ibid., 104.
423   9th Army as 1st: OKH:H2/107b:301.
423   reserves around Verdun: B-658,1,16; Liddell Hart, 134–35.
423   field headquarters: Herberg, interview.
423   122 of 123: Liss, 255.
423   sparse around Verdun: Halder, 1:299.
423   lost an entire army: Liss, 180.
423   not needed: Manstein, interview; Manstein, 101–102, never mentions any need for knowledge of the enemy; Halder, 1:302; despite Liss, 143–45 and Halder, 1:300.
423   situation reports: Liss, 149.
423   "than secure their": OKH:H2/121a:57:16.
424   liberal fashion: Staubwasser, interview.
424   "I can't give": Euler, interview, 4.
424   *Enemy Intelligence Service:* H.Dv. 89g.
424   U.S. desk: OKH:H2/136:5.Juni 1942, 9.November [1942]; NA:RG238:interrogation of Anton Staubwasser:29.9.47:4.
424   97: OKH:H2/124:24–32.
424   Roenne: OKH:H2/124:1.11.39, 12.8.40, 1.4.43, 1.8.44; Gehlen, 43; Strik-Strikfeldt, 61, 62, 98; Metz, interview; Gehlen, interview; B. H. Liddell Hart Papers:German Generals File:Ulrich Liss:letter:6 September 1957; Höhne and Zolling, 38; *Spiegelbild einer Verschwörung*, 236, 250, 256.
424   "There he has *the* post": OKH:H2/136:14.Oktober 1942:3.
425   "the few landings": *Hitlers Lagebesprechungen*, 557.
425   "Ten times," "I always," "You sit," "But not," "fantastic mental": Euler, interview.
427   Metz: Metz, interview.
427   "Situation Report West": OKH:H2/266a and b.
427   "Brief Enemy Estimate West": Ibid.
427   "Survey USA": OKH:H2/9.
427   "Individual Reports of the I c Service West": OKH:H2/7.
427   Bürklein: OKH:H2/124:1.11.39, 12.8.40, 1.12.44; OKH:H2/136:17.2.40:2; Staubwasser, interview; B. H. Liddell Hart Papers:German Generals File:Ulrich Liss:letter:6 September 1957.
427   greatly swollen: OKH:H2/124:1.12.44.
427   "Situation Report West No. 1491": OKH:H2/266b:26.12.44.
428   "Eisenhower is recklessly": Ibid.
428   circumstances: NA:RG165:USFET:IC:1SIIR:11–13; *German Operational Intelligence*, 136–7; P-041i, 49.
428   Kinzel: Germany, Heeresleitung, *Stellenbesetzung des deutschen Reichsheeres*, 1. Mai 1933 and 1. April 1934; Keilig, s.v. "Kinzel"; OKH:H2/136:31.August [1942]; Heusinger, interview; Ziemke, 257; Francis de Guingand, *Operation Victory* (London: Hodder & Stoughton, 1947), 456.
428   "symptoms of decline," "does not satisfy": Halder, 3:367, 422.
429   Gehlen: Gehlen, 379–80; Höhne and Zolling, 4–9, 12; NA:RG238:SAIC/R/2; Keilig, s.v. "Gehlen"; Gehlen, interview.
429   to his disappointment: Gehlen, 2nd interview.
429   fantastically hardworking: Heusinger, interview.
430   full appreciation, Canaris, telephoned, courses, rank: Gehlen, 35–38, 41, 65; OKH:H3/463.2, Teil 1:399; Ibid., Teil 2:619.
431   organization, staff size: OKH:H3/4:6.11.39, 15.5.43.
431   younger men: E. H. Cookridge, *Gehlen: Spy of the Century* (London: Hodder & Stoughton, 1971), 59–60.
431   every ten days: Gehlen, 65.
431   background studies: OKH:H3/513; OKH:H3/760:12.8.43.
431   arrests of enemy agents: NA:RG165:USFET:IC:1SIIR:37–38.
431   "Reconnaissance Requirements East": OKH:H3/172:28.
431   intensification of patrolling: Ibid.:76–77.
431   could penetrate deception: Ibid.:189.

431   quantified data: Ibid.
431   maps: Ibid.:33–35, 40, 43–44, 45–49.
431   colored blocks and arrows: OKH:H3/1531.
431   blue and red pictures: Boldt, 27.
432   at Zossen: Herberg, interview.
432   in East Prussia: Gehlen, 32–33.
432   at 8 a.m.: OKH:H3/463.2, Teil 2:612.
432   Group I daily routine: Gehlen, 44–46; NA:RG165:USFET:IC:1SIIR:29–30, 33, 37.
433   specialists: Bitterl, interview.
433   "On the basis": Gehlen, 45.
433   Group II: NA:RG165:USFET:IC:1SIIR:51–59.
433   60 new rifle divisions, 64: OKH:H3/595:17.1.1943.
433   "Survey of Soviet Russian Formations": OKH:H3/4:3.10.1944.
434   32-page directive: OKH:H3/463.2:1.9.43.
434   26 August 1943: Ibid.:26.8.1943.
434   other indices, documents: OKH:H3/463.2:Anlage 8.
434   15 October 1943: OKH:H3/612:15.10.43.
435   Group III: NA:RG165:USFET:IC:1SIIR:56–59; Gehlen, 44; Strik-Strikfeldt, 60–61; OKH:
      H3/463.2:August 1943.
435   Groups IV, V, VI: NA:RG165:USFET:IC:1SIIR:43–49, 59–61.
435   boats, Christmas parties: OKH:H3/463.2, Teil 1:408, 573.
435   secondary activities: Ibid.:399, 3.9.44; Ibid., Teil 2:565, 564.
435   pot of coffee: Boldt, 66–67.
435   army groups received: NA:RG165:USFET:IC:1SIIR:41, 42.
435   "Red Bible," how-to booklets, "Individual Reports": OKH:H3/513:Wichtige I c-Unterlagen;
      NA:RG165:USFET:IC:1SIIR:56, 57.
436   reports to the chief of the general staff: Gehlen, 45–46; NA:RG165:USFET:IC:1SIIR:30, 40,
436   resisted going, more effective: Gehlen, 2nd interview.
436   attended four: Gehlen, 47.
436   "The enemy organization": Halder, 3:467.
436   "The course of the fighting": Gehlen, 69.
436   "succeeded in correctly": OKH:H3/185:3.
436   converted them: Heusinger, interview; Blumröder, interview.
436   general's rank: One of the few others was Adolf Heusinger, long-time head of the Operations
      Branch.
436   Guderian defended: Guderian, 387.
436   himself boasted: OKH:H3/185:3.
436   foresaw all major Russian offensives: D-407, 120; Rendulic, "Überraschungen," 356.
436   "Army Group A": OKH:H3/199:85.
439   main winter offensive: OKW, *KTB*, 2:1305.
439   decisive attacks, at the same time: Ibid., 1305–6.
439   "one must reckon," "The available": OKH:H3/199:79:1–2.
439   9 December: Kehrig, *Stalingrad*, 118; OKH:H3/185:37.
440   Russians were surprised, changed minds: Kehrig, *Stalingrad*, 118–19.
440   "We underestimated": "Die Vernehmung von Generalfeldmarschall Keitel durch die Sowjets,"
      659. Similar comment by Jodl in "Die Vernehmung von Generaloberst Jodl durch die Sowjits,"
      539.
440   25 July 1943: Wilhelm, 53–54; OKH:H3/185:118, 120; Ziemke, 155.
440   12-page appreciation: OKH:H3/1531:30.3.1944.
440   drive over Army Group Center: Wilhelm, 59; OKH:H3/185:252.
440   two possible Soviet offensives: Wilhelm, 60–61; Besançon, 96; Ziemke, 313–16; despite Gehlen,
      96–97.
441   blinded him, projection: Wilhelm, 19–20, 58, 66.
441   "If we are": Gehlen, 52.
441   "surprisingly favorable development": OKW, *KTB*, 2:1283.
441   31 December 1944: Wilhelm, 68, 20.
441   "One way or another": Alphons Matt, *Zwischen allen Fronten: Der Zweite Weltkrieg aus
      der Sicht des Büros Ha* (Frauenfeld: Huber, 1969), 305–306.
442   not alone: Wilhelm, 42, 71–72.

CHAPTER 24: THE GREATEST MISTAKE

I am grateful to Prof. Andreas Hillgruber for reading this chapter.

445   eliminate Britain's last hope: Halder 2:49; *DGFP*, 12:1069; IMT, 34:696; Hillgruber, *HS*, 361.
445   Directive No. 21: *Hitlers Weisungen für die Kriegführung 1939–1945.*
446   officers and Social Democrats: Germany (Federal Republic of), Militärgeschichtliches For-
      schungsamt, *Handbuch zur deutschen Militärgeschichte 1648–1939*, 5:111–16, 6:142–46; Gustav
      Adolf Caspar, *Die sozialdemokratische Partie und das deutsche Wehrproblem in den Jahren
      der Weimar Republic, Wehrwissenschaftliche Rundschau*, Beiheft 11 (Oktober 1959), 4–5, 47–48,
      55; Demeter, 189; Höhn, ed., 181.
446   captain brings report: Köstring, 44.
446   racist superiority: Walter Laqueur, *Russia and Germany: A Century of Conflict* (Boston:
      Little, Brown, 1965), 32–34, 38, 71–72.
446   "The strength of": Groehler, 730. Similar at IMT, 34:683, and Waibel, 31.

447 "The Russian is inferior": Halder, 2:214.
447 "Russia is ripe": cited in Hillgruber, "Die 'Endlösung,' " 137.
447 purges: Erickson, 506; Keitel, 124.
447 "is leaderless": Halder, 2:214.
447 "a joke": *DGFP,* 11:770.
447 "When one really": Engel, 86.
447 "The Soviet Union": NA:RG238:USSR-228:2.
447 9 to 17 weeks, up to 4 weeks: Hillgruber, *HS,* 226, 509.
447 14 days: Groehler, 728.
447 more difficult in Russia: Tippelskirch, 206–207; Leverkuehn, 155.
447 links dissolve: *DGFP:C,* 1:609, 875–76.
447 "An Arab with": Köstring, 93.
448 military press: Moritz, "Militärzeitschriften," 309–16: Höhn, ed., 172.
448 Turkey, Iran, Afghanistan: Hirszowicz, 112, 131; Flicke, 143, 147; Hillgruber, *HS,* 56; *DGFP,* 12:237, 242, 324; and inferences from lack of indications in the sources of furnishing information.
448 Japan: USN:COA:Kretschmer memorandum:29; "Die Vernehmung von Generalfeldmarschall Keitel durch die Sowjets," 653.
448 Horthy: Szinai, ed., 180.
448 Finland: Mäkelä, 74; Halder, 2:333; Höhn, ed., 154.
449 early Rowehl reconnaissance: USAF-171, 37.
449 naval construction: inference from Baumbach, interview.
449 promise to Göring, *DGFP,* 12:603.
449 start of September 1940: Greiner, 312–13.
449 army pressed: OKW, *KTB,* 1:72.
449 early in October: Halder, 2:120, OKW, *KTB,* 1:120.
449 6 January: Zhilin, 198.
449 Russians spot, 3 March, Liepaja, Stalin: Bezymenski, 251.
450 three a day, Rovno: *DGFP,* 12:602–603.
450 4 April flight: T-120:279:217956.
450 Sverdlovsk: Rowehl, interview, 13.
450 Russians protested: *DGFP,* 12:602–603.
450 downed a plane: Köstring, 316.
450 no serious repercussions: *DGFP,* 12:1061–63, IWM:Milch:34:1879.
450 mid-April to mid-June: *DGFP,* 12:1063.
450 update: AOK 17:11147/10:Beilage 1.
450 priority: AOK 17:14499/51:overlay in back of volume.
450 4 April photographs: AOK 17:16593/5–10:303, 209.
450 roads better: Halder, 2:308.
450 fortifications: Ibid., 426.
450 World War I victory: Kahn, 622–33.
450 embryonic cipher bureau target: MA:F5709:Bd.II 9–4:1.6.1919:Teil A.
451 Russian radio camouflage: Flicke, 98, 105.
451 radio much more: Praun, "Eine Untersuchung," 90.
451 three intercept companies: Randewig, "50 Jahre," 619.
451 acute angles, no solutions, crumbs: Flicke, 98; NA:Captured Records Branch:AA:Pers Z:19. Februar 1934.
451 southern Poland, Baltic, Finnish, results: Praun, "Eine Untersuchung," 40–41.
451 eight intercept units, 250, 10,000: Randewig, "50 Jahre," 688.
451 no solid information: Moritz, ed., 114.
452 via Lithuania: Reile, *Ostfront,* 226–27, 17.
452 Piekenbrock: Mader, *Spionagegenerale,* 95.
452 Polish officer: Reile, *Ostfront,* 227–28.
452 Finland and Turkey: TWC:Case 11:Testimony:20718 (Halder).
452 other tricks: Reile, *Ostfront,* 227–30.
452 Green Oak: Ibid., 232–33.
453 Ukrainians: Ibid., 234–35; "Die Sowjetischen Staatssicherheitsorgane," 1208.
453 million ethnic Germans: Alfred Bohmann, *Menschen und Grenzen* (Köln: Verlag Wissenschaft und Politik, 1969–70), 3:53–56, 68, 71.
453 Deutsches Ausland-Institut: BA:DAI 789 and DAI 1180, for example.
453 orders to refrain from spying: Höhne, *Canaris,* 430–31. Reile's statement that Hitler ordered the Abwehr in 1933 to concentrate on Russia (*Ostfront,* 226) is unsupported by any other evidence and may represent a misremembering of the cabinet order of 17 October 1933 bearing Hitler's signature that the Abwehr (and not the Gestapo or the SD) controlled in espionage and counterintelligence (MA:RW5/v.195:48).
453 network of support points: *GGVKS,* 1:561.
453 identical assignments: "Die Sowjetischen Staatssicherheitsorgane," 1201.
453 dozens captured: *GGVKS,* 1:561 states that between October 1939 and December 1940 the Russians captured about 5,000 enemy agents and that the number rose in the first quarter of 1941 to 15 to 20 times that of the first quarter of 1940, or about 15,000, and in the second quarter to 25 to 30 times. "Die Sowjetischen Staatssicherheitsorgane," 1208, states that in 1940 and the first quarter of 1941, 1,596 German agents were "rendered harmless." Since these two official figures cannot be reconciled on the basis of available information, since most of the 15,000 were probably internal enemies of the regime, and since many of the others may have been saboteurs and not spies, I have reduced these numbers to a conservative estimate of "dozens" and "hundreds."

453   V-19540: AOK6:15623/104:28.Jan 1941.
453   Berchtesgaden meeting: NA:RG238:USSR-228:1–2.
454   Matzky, Kinzel, more agents: Piekenbrock in Mader, *Spionagegenerale*, 95, 97–98.
454   more qualified agents: "Die Sowjetischen Staatssicherheitsorgane," 1201.
454   hundreds, scores captured: See statistical note above.
454   16-man squad: *GGVKS*, 1:561.
454   only frontier dispositions: NA:RG238:USSR-228:2.
454   "When it comes": Moritz, 164.
454   Köstring: NA:RG165:SAIC/FIR/42:1–2; Köstring, 327, 44; Kehrig, 64.
455   "hero's death": Köstring, 196.
455   "grub," "worst quality": Ibid., 198.
455   attaché dinner: Ibid., 94.
455   "The experience," "a mosaic," consulates: Ibid., 168–69.
455   visited, oversized car, Tiflis: Ibid., 65, 89, 92, 180.
455   consulates closed: *DGFP*, 1:904–905; Köstring, 182.
455   no attachés at maneuvers, foreigners cut off: Köstring, 169, 208.
455   three sources: Ibid., 208.
455   seldom hard data: Ibid., passim.
455   "Through the elimination": Ibid., 202.
456   "The Soviet army": *Documents on British Foreign Policy*, 3d Series, 1:422.
456   "The maximum strength": Köstring, 302.
456   told Hitler: OKW, *KTB*, 1:393.
456   told Halder: Halder, 2:399.
456   2,000,000: Köstring, 311.
456   "until it reached": Halder, 2:86.
456   20 years: Ibid., 397.
456   13 February 1941: Thomas, 514–32.
456   "The industry of": Ibid., 525.
457   "need not necessarily": Ibid., 269–70.
457   "Numerically powerful": IMT, 34:683.
457   15 January 1941: AA:Pol I M:*Die Kriegswehrmacht der Union der Sozialistischen Sowjet-republiken.*
457   "only after years," "the Russian character," "The strength": Ibid., 72.
457   "young majors": Halder, 2:382.
457   "Numerically the best": Ibid., 336.
457   10,000, 3,500: Ibid., 267.
458   Russian tanks obsolete: Ibid., 214.
458   monster tank: Ibid., 336; Senger und Etterlin, *Kampfpanzer*, 386; Ogorkiewicz, 229.
458   24,000 tanks: Sherwood, 336. *GGVKS* gives no totals.
458   never caught up: Keitel, 124.
458   Manchuria: Erickson, 533.
458   start of campaign: Halder, 3:14.
458   "tank terror": Richardson and Freidin, 56.
458   "We hear": Günther Nitz, "Feindpanzer vor der B-Stelle," *Alte Kameraden*, 20 (April 1972), 18–20 at 19–20.
458   6,000 to 10,500: Hümmelchen, 330. Slightly earlier army estimates at OKH:H22/220:31.Januar 1941:52 and Moritz, ed., 83.
458   5,655: Halder, 2:288.
458   6:1, 1:1, training: Ibid., 295.
459   18,000: Hümmelchen, 330.
459   2,000,000, 4,000,000: AA:Pol I M:*Die Kriegswehrmacht der Union der Sozialistischen Sowjet-republiken*:15; OKW, *KTB*, 1:290.
459   4,205,000: Moritz, ed., 167. *GGVKS*, 6:237, gives 4,207,000 for 1941 without a specific day.
459   at wartime strength: Halder, 2:382.
459   5,005,000: Moritz, ed., 167.
459   forces in Far East discounted: Hillgruber, *HS*, 229; *DGFP*, 12:1066.
459   171 large formations: Phillippi, 70.
459   180: Halder, 2:266.
459   "15 more divisions": Ibid., 333.
459   226 1/2: Ibid., 461; OKH:H3/337.
459   148 to 180: Phillippi, 70; OKH:H3/346:20.5.41:1.
460   "In the entire": Halder, 3:170.
460   "for the first": *DGFP*, 13:383.
460   British count 225: PRO:CAB 79-12:87.
460   220 1/2: Moritz, ed., 118. This is the nearest date for which I could find figures summarized.
460   did not prepare industry: Milward, 39–49.
460   omitted elements of operations plans: Leach, 193. See also Hillgruber, *HS*, 373.
460   fuel, a third of divisions: Seaton, 218.
460   "The Red Army": PRO:CAB 79-12:88, 85.
461   diplomatic circles: Butler, 3:89.
461   "Germany will be": Sherwood, 303–304.

Chapter 25: The Biggest Surprise

For brevity in the notes to this chapter, I use the following forms: Numbers like 79321 refer to pages in AA:Büro des Staatssekretärs: Zweite Front:Bände 1–2. Numbers like 38:474 mean BA:III

M 1000/38 (Volume 38 of the Naval War Diary), page 474. *FRUS: CWC* stands for *Foreign Relations of the United States: The Conferences at Washington, 1941–1942, and Casablanca, 1943.*

462   1 March 1942, addressees: OKH:H2/121a:67:title page and Verteiler list.
462   quietest days: Hillgruber and Hümmelchen, 63.
462   Luftwaffe bombs: OKW, *KTB*, 2:302.
462   France shipped: *FRUS, 1942,* 2:147–48.
462   "Powerful and offensive": *New York Times* (7 January 1942), 5:1–2.
462   January document: OKH:H2/121a:67:Vorbemerkung.
463   destruction of Germany, shipping problem: Ibid.:3, Vorbemerkung.
463   "conceivable," "In general": Ibid.:11, 32.
463   possible Allied landings: Ibid.:11–27.
463   "the great demands": Ibid.:Vorbemerkung.
463   agreed on North Africa: *FRUS: CWC,* 78, 262–64, 202, 208.
465   225 ships: Ibid., 585.
465   "not necessary": Ibid., 154.
465   contingency plans: Ibid., 261–62.
465   "One must reckon," Dakar, "Much more is," "A British landing": OKH:H2/121a:67:31, 21, 22.
465   12 March 1942: *Lagevorträge,* 362–64.
465   "to produce": *Hitlers Weisungen für die Kriegführung,* No. 44, §5.
466   "zone of destiny": *Lagevorträge,* 347.
466   secure their African possessions: *Hitlers Weisungen für die Kriegführung,* No. 18, §1.
466   piece of intelligence: *DGFP,* 12:665.
466   "to establish themselves": Ibid.; Churchill, 3:142–43.
466   ordering preparations: OKW, *KTB,* 1:389; *DGFP,* 12:731–33.
466   "As soon as": *Lagevorträge,* 271.
466   OKW memorandum: *DGFP,* 13:422–33.
466   forgot about it: by implication from *Lagevorträge,* 274.
467   on the periphery: Matzky, interview; *DGFP,* 12:42; *Lagevorträge,* 183.
467   "The European coasts": *Hitlers Weisungen für die Kriegführung,* No. 40, §1.
467   10 April: OKW, *KTB,* 2:319, 317.
467   Allied landings discussed by OKW: Ibid., 328.
467   Canaris: *ADAP,* 2:358.
467   19 May: OKW, *KTB,* 2:368.
467   Mountbatten planning: Roskill, 2:240–41.
467   Denmark and Norway: OKW, *KTB,* 2:380, 384.
467   F 3197, F 3148: ML-180:21.Mai 1942.
467   headlines: *New York Times* (19 June 1942), 1:1–8.
467   small ships, sabotage: OKW, *KTB,* 2:442.
468   Eisenhower: *New York Times* (26 June 1942), 1:5–6.
468   SS division Das Reich: OKW, *KTB,* 2:451.
468   "will divert": *New York Times* (28 June 1942), 1:4.
468   2,802, Hitler said, met: OKW, *KTB,* 2:456, 458.
468   "The main duty": *ADAP,* 3:75–76.
468   Lourenço Marques, Bern, Papen, Buenos Aires, Barcelona, Santander: 78973, 78975, 78983, 78977, 78974, 78989.
468   Orgaz, Spanish foreign minister, Juin: 78990, 78996, 78998.
469   Hoyningen-Huene: 79016–18.
469   press summaries: for example, 78986–88, 79037.
469   "no real second front": Halder, 3:471.
469   "If all the talk": 36:4.
469   "Concerning a second front": *ADAP,* 3:294–95.
470   Allied abandonment: 79191, 79202, 79203, 79209.
470   Dieppe: Roskill, 2:240–52; Terence Robertson, *The Shame and the Glory: Dieppe* (n.p.: McClelland and Stewart, 1962); OKW, *KTB,* 2:615.
470   Matzky: Matzky, 1st interview.
470   BBC had warned: 79217.
470   "10-hour second front": *New York Times* (21 August 1942), 5:5.
470   Pétain: 79225–29.
470   "the greatest danger": *Lagevorträge,* 409.
470   photographic cover: 37:85.
471   "I do not hold": 79243.
471   28 August: 79244–45.
471   "This is the second": 37:35.
471   "I have already": Arthur Funk, "TORCH: Allied Deception and Axis Intelligence," unpublished article, based in part on PRO:Premier 3/439/17. I am grateful to Dr. Funk for letting me read this.
472   sand: Arthur Bryant, *The Turn of the Tide* (London: Collins, 1957), 508–509.
472   document of 22 September: 37:565.
472   "Withdrawal of the entire": 38:45.
473   spy reports of 17 October landing, landings in five towns, from Madrid: 38:78–80.
473   Hitler alarmed, ordered: OKW, *KTB,* 2:794.
473   away from Norway, France: 78984–79282, passim.
473   Vatican: *ADAP,* 3:530.
474   5th, 6th, 9th: 38:80, 103, 166.

474   RSHA VI B 2: AA:Inl II g:335:13.Oktober 1942.
474   convoys from Gibraltar, Portuguese ambassador: 38:267.
474   Hitler's situation conference: OKW, *KTB*, 2:828.
474   19 October: 38:381–82.
474   Morocco in the spring: T-77:851:Anlage 194 of 18.10.[1942]. I am grateful to Dr. Arthur Funk for sending me a photocopy of this document.
474   all five at once: 38:78.
474   Isle of Wight: 38:344.
474   major convoy: 38:521.
475   B-Dienst reported: 38:432.
475   convoys for North Africa: Roskill, 2:316, 68–69.
475   "of decisive strategic importance": 38:512.
475   deceptive radio traffic: 38:45.
475   B-Dienst analysis: BA:III 1006/3:178.
475   salvaged code: Ibid.:179; 38:616.
475   aerial reconnaissance flown daily: 38:69, 90, 135, 252, 330, 351, 441, 482, 504, 523, 527, 570, 593; OKW, *KTB*, 2:783–921, passim.
476   harbors relatively empty: 38:649.
476   ship sightings: Roskill, 2:319; 38:669.
476   Algeciras observation post, Redl: Redl, interview.
476   watches ships and airplanes: 38:1, 12, 35, 135, 196, 254, 278, 553–54, 629, 677, 39:10, 34.
476   19 October: 38:397.
476   *Furious:* 38:528, 600.
476   3 November: 39:53.
476   fighter planes, convoy: 39:71, 72.
476   "Concentration of": 39:74–75.
477   Abwehr report from Paris: 39:93.
477   bad weather: 39:91.
477   1 p.m., 8 p.m.: 39:92.
477   10 p.m.: 39:115.
477   Tarifa: 39:92.
477   German Admiral Rome, navy notified: 39:116.
477   in Italy: 79324.
478   military attaché, Supermarina: 39:141–42.
478   Hitler thought, 1:40 p.m.: OKW, *KTB*, 2:913.
478   Canaris, Piekenbrock: Abshagen, 214.
478   heeled hard to starboard: H. R. Knickerbocker et al., *Danger Forward: The Story of the First Division in World War II* (Washington: Society of the First Division, 1947), 22–23.
478   from Paris: 79333–34.
478   White House announcement: 39:151.

CHAPTER 26: THE ULTIMATE FAILURE

As in the notes to the previous chapter, citations of the type 58:162 refer to MA:III M 1000/58:162. III M 1000 is the war diary of the 1/Skl, the operations branch, of the OKM. The volume numbers for the months of 1944 cited here are: 55 for March; 56 for April; 57, May; 58, June; 59, July; 60, August. Some 1942 months are also used. As in the previous chapter, citations like 80050 refer to AA:Büro des Staatssekretärs:Zweite Front:3:80050.

479   "There is no longer": *Hitlers Lagebesprechungen,* 440.
479   "The attack will come": Ibid., 444.
479   "It would be good": Ibid., 449.
479   "The enemy must": AOK15:59364/1:1.
480   Anne Frank: Anne Frank, *The Diary of a Young Girl,* trans. B. M. Mooyaart-Doubleday (Garden City: Doubleday, 1967), 27 February 1943.
480   "illusory": *DGFP,* 11:387.
480   29 October 1941: Ibid., 13:712.
480   12 December: *Lagevorträge,* 325.
480   Allied landing: *Staatsmänner,* 1:686.
480   Directive No. 40, "the dangers of": *Hitlers Weisungen für die Kriegführung,* No. 40, §I.
480   highest state of readiness: 38:108.
480   assembly of small vessels: OKW, *KTB*, 2:422, 451, 456.
480   wonder whether deception: Halder, 3:471.
480   Dieppe and October scare: see notes to them in previous chapter.
480   many said 1943, hundreds of reports: Liddell Hart, 240.
480   stretching of their forces: Ibid., 238.
480   Hitler did not, "nothing is going": *Hitlers Lagebesprechungen,* 217, 219.
481   Directive No. 51: *Hitlers Weisungen für die Kriegführung,* No. 51, introductory section.
481   "Guidelines for Reconnaissance": MA:PG33398:9.
483   "In tactics": Clausewitz, bk. III, ch. 8.
483   "without it": Ibid., bk. III, ch. 9.
483   Allied selection of landing site: Harrison, 56–57, 72; Ellis, 1:16; Wilmot, 170–71.
485   Allied deception: Delmer, 23–50; Cave Brown, 45–50, 268–74; Masterman, 36–45, 60–70.
485   Wild and Bevan: Delmer, 39–42.

486 cryptanalysis of Abwehr Enigma: Kim Philby, *My Private War* (New York: Grove 1968), 38.
486 accurate and complete picture: In SHAEF, *German Intelligence Services,* and SHAEF, *The German Intelligence Service.*
486 avoid blunders: Masterman, 12.
486 Rundstedt: Wilmot, 189–90; Richardson and Freidin, eds., 179–80; Halder, 3:411. The post had been created 25 October 1940 (Mueller-Hillebrand, 2:60).
487 St.-Germain-en-Laye: Visit, 23 May 1970.
487 Meyer-Detring: Interview.
487 Rommel headquarters: Speidel, 30–31.
488 "inadequate"; Ellis, 1:54.
488 "A judgment": OKM, *Denkschriften,* 377.
488 "unreliable," "many intelligence," "The commander must": Clausewitz, bk. I, ch. 6.
488 "The very systematic": OKM, *Denkschriften,* 377.
488 "is endeavoring to": *Brasseys Naval Annual* (1948), 378.
488 concentrating in the Pas de Calais: Ibid., 376–77; Richardson and Freidin, eds., 181; Wilmot, 230.
488 "across the narrower," "It was the quickest": Liddell Hart, 245; Wilmot, 190.
488 "would bring the decision": *Staatsmänner,* 2:418.
489 V-1: Liddell Hart, 246.
489 orthodoxy: Wilmot, 190.
489 "We generals calculated": Warlimont in Milton Shulman, *Defeat in the West* (New York: Dutton, 1948), 97–98.
489 "Rather than try": Clausewitz, bk. iv, ch. 3.
489 soldiers had absorbed: Howard in introduction to Clausewitz, 34.
489 "For it is there": *Hitlers Weisungen für die Kriegführung,* No. 51, introductory section.
489 still maintaining: *Lagevorträge,* 556.
489 "Since the front," four divisions: *Hitlers Weisungen für die Kriegführung,* No. 51a, §§ II and IV A 1.
489 12 January 1944: OKH:H2/11b:IV:1.12.1944.
490 Arnold's figure: *New York Times* (4 January 1944), 8:4.
490 2,126,000: Greenfield, ed., 161.
490 8,202,881: *New York Times* (19 April 1943), 3:5.
490 could not forecast: see *New York Times* (18 April 1944), 4:1.
490 4,878,000: Greenfield, ed., 161.
490 175,000: OKH:H2/9:2.9.44.
490 "According to a": OKH:H2/11b:IV:18.2.44. The report to which this refers, given in *New York Times* (18 April 1944), 4:1, however, says nothing about the 7,700,000 being "full strength."
491 U.S. Army numbering system and assignments: Information kindly supplied by John Wilson of the Center for Military History.
491 to Institute of Heraldry: Maj. Gen. William Baumer, telephone interview, 10 September 1976. None of the fakes appeared, however, in the illustrated article by Gilbert Grosvenor, "Insignia of the United States Armed Forces," *National Geographic Magazine,* 83 (June 1943), 651–722. They were first published in a December 1944 pamphlet of *National Geographic.* But that was too late for the OVERLORD deception.
491 First U.S. Army Group: Harrison, 115.
491 Communications Reconnaissance Regiment 5, Higher Commander: HGrD: 75744/35: untitled organizational chart of communications intelligence.
491 Oer: HGrD:75144/36:31; Wiebe, interview.
492 concentrated on United States: HGrD:85463:Anlage 2 to Tätigkeitsbericht.
492 Battalion 13: Ibid.; AOK15:59369:32; Wiebe, interview.
492 Post 3 at Euskirchen: HGrD:85463:76:undated Anlage I:16:100; HGrD:75744/35:20.Februar 1945; HGrD:85463:Tätigkeitsbericht for 1.4.44-30.6.44:95; Randewig, "Englandaufklärung und Aufklärung gegen USA 1942," 51–53 in Praun, "Eine Untersuchung."
492 17th Airborne: OKH:H2/9:15.7.43; CMH:Order of Battle:Divisions.
492 69th Infantry Division: OKH:H2/9:15.7.43; CMH:Order of Battle:Divisions.
493 from 46 to 75: OKH:H2/9:15.7.43.
493 almost without a miss: Ibid.: 19.6.43, 15.9.43, 15.12.43.
493 APO numbers: P-041h, 9-10.
493 85th and 37th: HGrD:75744/35:95.
493 50th, 51st: Ibid.
493 American formations in Britain: Ibid.
493 69th, 49th, 59th: OKH:H2/9:15.7.43; Palmer, 490.
493 24 divisions: OKH:H2/9:15.12.43.
493 11 of these: Palmer, 490–91.
494 Double-Cross Committee or raconteurs: Masterman, 151.
494 HUBERT: OKH:H2/111:25.
494 DRUMMOND: OKH:H2/114:30190B.
494 KOHLER: ML-180:4. März 1944.
494 "According to a believable": OKH:H2/9:29.4.44.
496 "From now on," exaggerated the figures: Metz, interview; "File on Colonel M," *Interim: British Army of the Rhine Intelligence Review,* No. 19 (4 March 1946), 7–15.
496 Euler question mark, Roenne eliminated: OKH:H2/9:15.5.44; OKH:H22/282:31.5.44.
496 89 U.S. army divisions: Palmer, 489–91.
496 98: OKH.H2/8:1.6.44.

496   20 in Great Britain: NA:RG165:OPD 320.2 TS (31 Aug 1945):Case 15/18 B.P. "Deployment of Allied Divisions" (Monthly Charts):31 May 1944. Henceforth cited as "Deployment of Allied Divisions."
496   showed 22: OKH:H22/282:31.5.44.
496   23 British and Canadian, 1 Polish, 1 French: "Deployment of Allied Divisions."
496   79, 19, 8: OKH:H22/282:31.5.44.
496   "have about 80": *Staatsmänner*, 2:455.
497   "that the English": Ibid., 352.
497   10,701, 5,059: totaling individual figures at 57:295, 326, 344, 364, 381, 400, 413, 431-32, 447, 465, 485, 505, 519.
497   bombing pattern: Ellis, 1:103, Wilmot, 209-12; OKW, *KTB*, 2:298.
498   German map of destruction of railroads: Ellis opp. 112.
498   Meyer-Detring concluded: HGrD:85459:17.4.44.
498   5 June, "Concentration of the": OKW, *KTB*, 4:299.
498   seven cases:HGrD:85459:17.4.44.
498   attempt of 18 May: Ibid.:18.5.44, 19.5.44.
499   flashbulbs: 58:339.
499   Jodl told Hitler: *Hitlers Lagebesprechungen*, 569.
499   from Cardigan Bay: PG33399:46.
499   Newquay and Ilfracombe: Ibid.: 45.
499   about every other day: 56:424, 483, 546, 566, 581, 597; 57:37, 120; BA:RH27-2/49:Bildaufklärung Monat April 1944.
499   19 April: 56:424.
499   25 April: Ibid.: 56:566.
500   Portsmouth to Plymouth: Ibid.
500   ten-day breakdown: 1/Skl war diary lists no aerial reconnaissances from 8 to 18 May.
500   got no real information: 57:392.
500   seemed to name every single place: Baumbach, interview; Weidemann, interview; 56:526.
500   22 April: PG33399:44.
501   "Friendly sources in Algeria": 80050.
501   14 May: PG33399:73.
501   KRABBE: Ibid.:72.
501   neutral diplomat: Ibid., 53.
501   TONY: Ibid.:94.
501   ANTON: ML-180:28.5.44.
501   four days later Roenne: 56:459-60.
501   extensive deception campaign: Cave Brown, 459-68.
502   4th Army: Delmer, 137-38.
502   withdrawal of many divisions: Ibid., 158; OKW, *KTB*, 4:298.
502   Allied radio deception: Ibid., 116-21; Cave Brown, 464-65.
502   far to the east in Finland: AOK 20:58635:21.März 1944.
502   landings in Norway secondary: 56:460.
502   attack against Bordeaux: *Staatsmänner*, 2:347, 390; *Hitlers Lagebesprechungen*, 440-41; PG33397:1; *Lagevorträge*, 572.
502   pincers: Liddell Hart, 239; *Staatsmänner*, 2:457.
502   Brittany: *Staatsmänner*, 2:390, 457; Harrison, 259; OKW, *KTB*, 4:297.
502   "first of all with": 57:37. Iterated at 162.
502   telephone conversation: OKW, *KTB*, 4:302-303.
502   added to its defenses: Wilmot, 201-204.
502   refused to commit themselves: Their reports contain such words as "appear," "seems," and "probably."
502   feint in Normandy or Brittany: OKW, *KTB*, 4:302.
503   Allied timing: Harrison, 189-90; Wilmot, 194, 220-21.
503   Hitler believed dawn landing: *Hitlers Lagebesprechungen*, 441.
503   dawn coincided with high tide: B-675, 15-16.
503   charted days: PG33397.
504   foreshore obstacles, moonlit night: Ibid.; 56:609.
504   Naval Group West analyzed: 57:99.
504   dropped tide considerations: 57:460.
504   Reile: Oscar Reile, "Klärung der Feindlichen Vorbereitungen für die Invasion (Overlord) durch Abwehr III und Frontaufklärung III West," *Die Nachhut*, Nr. 9 (1. Februar 1970), 2-6.
504   open code messages: M. R. D. Foot, *S O E in France: An Account of the Work of the British Special Operations Executive in France 1940-1944*, History of the Second World War (HMSO, 1966), 110-11; Cave Brown, 320-21.
505   BUTLER net: Foot, 388, 335.
505   "the English-American": Reile, "Klärung," 3.
505   groups associated with BUTLER: My assumption from Foot, 388.
505   "Gentlemen, place," "Electricity dates": Kahn, 543.
505   as early as February or March: *Hitlers Weisungen für die Kriegführung*, No. 51a, §I; *Lagevorträge*, 556; B-675, 23.
505   "He has already made": *Hitlers Lagebesprechungen*, 441-42.
506   1 April: HGrD:85459:6.
506   "readiness": OKW, *KTB*, 4:297.
506   good weather, propitious moment: Ibid.; 56:459-60.
506   LOXO: MA:III M 1006/6:98.
506   6 April: *Hitlers Lagebesprechungen*, 557.

506 "Now I ask": Ibid.
506 radio traffic fell off: HGrD:75144 35:85.
506 "proved" agent: PG33399:10.
506 V-319: Ibid.:27; OKH:H2/114:3075.
506 Baumbach concurs: PG33399:28.
507 Allied air attacks: AOK15:59364/1:65.
507 navy notified: PG33399:11.
507 army alerted: OKW, *KTB*, 4:297.
507 radio traffic resumed: HGrD:75144/35:85.
507 17 April: HGrD:85459:13; OKW, *KTB*, 4:297, 298.
507 imposed restrictions: *The Times* (18 April 1944), 4:4; *New York Times* (18 April 1944), 1:8; 56:395.
507 "the English have taken": *Staatsmänner*, 2:418.
507 consulate in Geneva: 80048.
507 Likus: AA:Dienststelle Ribbentrop:Vertrauliche Berichte:2b/1:130621–22.
507 Likus 31 May: Ibid.:130596.
507 RICARDO: OKW:80:23.4.44.
507 KO Portugal: PG33399:35.
508 targeted on middle of May: Ibid.:44.
508 Angers: Ibid.:36.
508 English minister: Ibid.:49.
508 Swedish foreign minister: Ibid.
508 after the harvest: 80085.
508 Polish brigade: PG33399:61.
508 Forschungsamt: Ibid.:62.
508 "militarily ready": 56:459.
508 "All reports and judgments": Ibid.:525.
508 shifting of point of main effort: Ibid.
509 rumors, food, raids, invasion had started: Boberach, ed., 505–506, 508, 509.
509 4 May: 57:54.
509 3/Skl: Ibid.:186.
509 air branch: Ibid.:225.
510 coastal radars and guns: Ibid.:188.
510 regarded as "completed": Ibid.:272.
510 12 to 31, 20: Ibid.:272–73.
510 end of the month: Ibid.:162.
510 Armée Secrète: Ibid.:270.
510 naval radio traffic: BA:III M 1006/6:111.
510 19 May: Ibid.:116–17.
510 five-letter groups, "It appears": Ibid.: 118.
510 radio traffic reductions: HGrD:75144/35:85.
510 "satisfactory," "possible": 57:533, 534.
510 1 June, 28, "It is consequently": PG33399:98, 99.
511 Verlaine code workings, Reichling: AOK15:59365:208/5; Cornelius Ryan, *The Longest Day* (New York: Simon and Schuster, 1959), 30–34.
512 "improbable": 58:62.
512 navy canceled: Ellis, 1:130.
512 Meyer-Detring on vacation: Meyer-Detring, interview.
512 Hansen: USFET:MISC:CI-IIR/48:3.
512 "when the sea": *Hitlers Lagebesprechungen*, 540.
512 radio traffic normal: HGrD:75144/35:86; MA:III M 1006/6:125.
512 suitable for landings: 58:43.
512 Roenne report of 5 June: OKH:H2/266a:5.6.44.
512 Rundstedt repeated, "could be seen": OKH:H22/48:161, 6.
513 "moment of the invasion": 58:80–81.
513 "indicates an advance," "confirms our presumptions": Delmer, 196.
513 9:15 p.m.: AOK15:59365:208/5.
513 10 p.m.: Ryan, 84–85, 96–97.
513 Meyer messaged: AOK15:69365:208/5.
513 Staubwasser reported, false alarm: B-675, 27.
513 "announce the invasion": HGrD:85659:235.
513 CATO: Delmer, 174–86.
514 surprise was total: 58:113; "Die Vernehmung von Generalfeldmarschall Keitel durch die Sowjets," 660.
514 "At present": OKH:H22/48:180.
514 "the effect of fear": Clausewitz, bk. I, ch. 6.
514 "reckon with further landings": 58:96.
514 Roenne telephones Staubwasser: B-782, 46.
515 "Not a single unit": Delmer, 171.
515 "There are already hopes": Churchill, 6:6.
515 to destroy the present bridgehead and impede: 58:113–14.
515 three armored divisions: Ellis, 237.
515 CATO: Delmer, 187–89. Delmer, 17–18, 189, 173, says that on 8 June Hitler had ordered seven divisions from the 15th Army to Normandy and that the CATO message caused him to countermand this order and recall the divisions. The 15th Army war diary shows no such orders (AOK15:59364/1:115–52).

516   1st SS Panzer: OKW, *KTB*, 4:313.
516   9th Infantry Division: OKH:H2/9:15.4.44; Wilmot, 213: HGrD:85459:9.6.44.
516   14 or 15 June: 58:284.
516   Roenne's charts: OKH:H22/282:31.5.44.
516   Japanese minister: 80105.
516   Bern, Ankara, Stockholm: 80111, 80112, 80113.
517   other places: 80116, 80127, 80123, 80131.
517   "possible," "satisfactory": 58:187.
517   broadcasts warning fishing ships: Ibid.: 210.
517   Foreign Armies West: Ibid.:243.
517   emergency laying of mines: Ibid.:246, 274.
517   bombings: Ibid.: 293, 320.
517   Keitel, Jodl: *Lagevorträge*, 589.
518   50 to 240: HGrD:75144/24:142.
518   Commander in Chief West, navy: 59:46, 30.
518   Meyer-Detring notified: HGrD:85459:238.
518   1:10 a.m.: Ibid.
518   middle of the month: OKW, *KTB*, 4:324.
518   Foreign Armies West: 58:306, 59:47.
518   3/Skl: Ibid.:50.
518   Hitler 13 July: *Lagevorträge*, 600.
518   "Make peace": Wilmot, 347.
518   Rommel: Ibid., 357–58.
518   20th of July: The best account is Peter Hoffmann's.
519   lively reconnaissance: HGrD:75144/24:252.
519   tough German resistance: Delmer, 232.
519   "qualitatively inferior," "no longer entrusted": Ibid., 229.
519   "it is improbable now": Ibid. 231.
519   to 92: OKW, *KTB*, 4:326.
519   "the mass of": HGrD:75820:59/9.
519   divisions from and to 15th Army: OKW, *KTB*, 4:327, 329.
519   3 August: HGrD:75144/25:353.
519   "improbable," all possible formations: Ibid.:388.
520   "is lucky," "cancel": Clausewitz, bk. I, ch. 6.
520   31 October, non-existent armies: NA:RG242:Lage West maps.
520   28 November: *Lagevorträge*, 618–19.

Chapter 27: Hubris, Glory, Charisma, Führer

523   "For nothing is hid": Luke 8:17.
523   "It will always": Gempp. II;7:162.
523   Japanese poor: United States Strategic Bombing Survey (Pacific), Japanese Military and Naval Division, *Japanese Intelligence Section, G-2* (GPO: 1946).
523   figures precise: comparing *FRUS: The Conferences at Washington, 1941–1942, and Casablanca, 1943*, 431, 584, with OKW, *KTB*, 2:1377 and 3:8.
523   58, 59: Harry C. Butcher, *My Three Years with Eisenhower* (New York: Simon and Schuster, 1946), 544; Wilmot.
523   40 percent: dividing the 79 of German estimates into the 47 actual and subtracting from unity.
524   abandoned plans to invade Britain: Frederick W. Winterbotham, *The Ultra Secret* (New York: Harper & Row, 1974), 57–58; Patrick Beesly, *Very Special Intelligence* (London: Hamish Hamilton, 1977), 41.
524   to attack Russia: Churchill, 3:354–56.
524   German rockets: Churchill, 5:226–40.
524   U-boats: Beesly, passim.
524   Anzio: General Mark Clark, telephone interview, 20 November 1974.
524   German aircraft production estimates: Charles Webster and Noble Frankland, *The Strategic Air Offensive Against Germany, 1939–1945*, United Kingdom Military Series (HMSO:1961), 4:498.
524   Office of Strategic Service reports: Franklin D. Roosevelt Library:PSF:Boxes 167–170.
524   did not commission Jews: Demeter, 224.
524   "Officials who are not": *Reichsgesetzblatt* (1933), 175.
524   little effect on the military: Hans Mommsen, *Beamtentum im Dritten Reich*, Schriftenreihe der Vierteljahrshefte fur Zeitgeschichte, 13 (Stuttgart: Deutsche Verlags-Anstalt, 1966), 57.
524   none let go from B-Dienst: Heinz Bonatz, letter.
524   Gottingen, 20 percent: Max Pinl and Lux Furtmuller, "Mathematicians Under Hitler," Leo Baeck Institute, *Year Book XVIII* (London: Secker & Warburg, 1973), 129–82 at 132, 142–43.
525   replacement of superb intellects by mediocrities: Joseph Needham, *The Nazi Attack on International Science*, The Thinkers Forum, 14 (London: Watts, [1941]), Alan D. Beyerchen, "The Politics of Academic Physics in the Third Reich: A Study of Ideology and Science," Ph.D. dissertation, University of California at Santa Barbara, 1973; Orlow, 2:487, 492; E.W.B. Gill, "German Academic Scientists and the War," Field Information Agency, Technical, 28 August 1945.
525   arrogance distorted: Fritz Fischer, *Germany's Aims in the First World War* (New York: Norton, 1967), 92.

525 effect of Frederick II of Hohenstaufen: Barraclough, 232–33.
526 Napoleon's effect: Ibid., 407; Bracher, 17.
526 "deadly foreign spirit," "the German": Johann Gottlieb Fichte, *Addresses to the German Nation,* ed. George Armstrong Kelly (New York: Harper & Row, 1968), 101, 60; Bracher, 22–28.
526 authoritarianism that began in the Reformation: Erik H. Erikson, *Young Man Luther: A Study in Psychoanalysis and History* (New York: Norton, 1958), 252.
526 solely by faith: Martin Luther, *On the Freedom of a Christian,* §§8, 10.
526 "Even if those": quoted in Fromm, *Escape from Freedom,* 82.
526 "No insurrection," "The answer": quoted in Erikson, 235, 236.
526 parents assimilated: My assumption. But studies show that German families are authoritarian, and more so than American: Donald L. Taylor, "The Changing German Family," *International Journal of Comparative Sociology,* 10 (1969), 299–302; Donald V. McGranahan, "A Comparison of Social Attitudes Among American and German Youth," *The Journal of Abnormal and Social Psychology,* 41 (July, 1946), 245–57.
526 dynamics of an authoritarian person: These tend to make such a person a poorer intelligence officer than the egalitarian or tolerant personality (Norman Dixon, *On the Psychology of Military Incompetence* [London: Jonathan Cape, 1976], 258, 264–66, 274). Consequently, German I cs may have been poorer intelligence officers than Allied G-2s. But I have no evidence on this point, and the number of variables is so great in the raw data that I do not see how any evidence for or against this hypothesis could be collected. Nevertheless, the authoritarian's desire to control his environment and the consequent rigidity in thought, which in effect means a preference for theory over the uncertainties of reality, may explain what Ralf Dahrendorf called "The German Idea of Truth" and the desire for ultimate solutions in his *Society and Democracy in Germany* (New York: Anchor Books, 1967), 129–71.
527 "Germany policy towards": Fischer, 307.
527 refused to believe: Wheeler-Bennett, 31.
527 qualitative superiority: Milward, 100–106, 129–30.
527 "a victorious ending": Förster, ed., 105.
527 resembled World War I: Wilhelm, 72.
528 left their intelligence officers: Strong, 34.
528 "What is the concept": Clausewitz, bk. vi, ch. 1, §1. Repeated in the German army manual for Troop Command, H.Dv. 300, §41.
528 "complete in itself," active: Ibid., bk. vii, ch. 2. Also in H.Dv. 300, §39.
528 surprise, superiority of numbers: Ibid., bk. iii, chs. 8, 9.
529 planning omitted intelligence: Manstein, interview.
529 "The war will": *Staatsmänner,* 2:299. Somewhat similar quote at *DGFP,* 9:122.
529 French naval code: Bonatz, 93.
529 French espionage: Gustave Bertrand, *Enigma* (Paris: Plon, 1974), 26–28.
529 contributed greatly: Winterbotham; Beesly.
529 French watched Germany: Georges Castellan, *Le Réarmement clandestin du Reich, 1930–1935, vu par le 2ᵉ Bureau de l'etat-major francais* (Paris: Plon, 1954).
529 Admiralty Operational Intelligence Center: Beesly, passim.
530 "happy parasite": Trevor-Roper, *Last Days,* 24.
530 confirmed insignificance: P-041i, 43.
530 censors: *ADAP,* 3:21.
530 "main duty": Ibid., 3:75–76.
530 more and more: My observations from *Hitlers Lagebesprechungen* and the *Lagevorträge.*
530 difficult domestic problems: Michael R. Gordon, "Domestic Conflict and the Origins of the First World War: The British and the German Cases," *Journal of Modern History,* 46 (June 1974), 191–226.
530 decreed the strategic offensive: Halder, letter, 20 January 1972, saw this as a basis of the undervaluing of intelligence in the German army.
531 created the blitzkrieg: Milward, 12–14, 16.
531 power of specialists: Thompson, 6, 12–13; Rosemary Stewart, *The Reality of Organization* (London: Macmillan, 1970), 69–70; Seymour M. Lipset and Reinhard Bendix, *Social Mobility in Industrial Society* (London: Heinemann, 1959), 3, 11.
531 officers resist: Janowitz, *Sociology,* 18, 20; Thompson, 14, 46, 96–97.
531 more adamant: Hayn, 133; *German General Staff Corps,* 3.
531 Great Elector, monopoly: Otto Büsch, *Militärsystem und Sozialleben im Alten Preussen 1713–1807,* Veröffentlichungen der Berliner Historischen Kommission . . . , 7 (Berlin: Walter de Gruyter, 1962), 30–31; Rosinski, 24–25, 36; Howard in Demeter, ix; Demeter, 4, 5; Weber, 3:981, 1:225–26.
532 ascriptive to achievement: Janowitz, *Sociology,* 27–28.
532 general staff fought: Erfurth, 213.
532 men, fire, and will: Michael Howard, interview, 3 November 1972.
532 French, British, Americans: Hittle, passim.
532 intelligence under operations: Rosinski, 299; cf. Thompson, 76, 143; Stewart, 78.
532 amalgamated into tactics: [Louis A.]von Schafenort, *Die Königliche Preussische Kriegsakademie: 1810–15. Oktober–1910* (ESM), 391; Model, 13, 15; Konus, 395.
532 standing above, part of whole: *German General Staff Corps,* 95.
532 "honourable ignorance": Dixon, 293.
532 belittled intelligence: P-041i, 43; Geyr, 7, 8; D-407, 55; Strong, 34; Liss, "Der entscheidende Wert," 592, 643–44; cf. Thompson, 116.
532 overemphasized commander: Rosinski, 305–309.

532   "difficult to ascertain": Generalfeldmarschall Graf Alfred von Schlieffen, *Gesammelte Schriften* (ESM: 1913), 1:8.
533   I c under I a: HDv.g.92, 18; HDv.g.89, 11; D-407, 5, 19–20.
533   no intelligence courses: Model, 34, 48, 78–79; P-041i, 43.
533   "Uncertainty and chance": [Hans] von Seeckt, "Die Willenskraft des Feldherrn," *Militärwissenschaftliche Rundschau*, 1 (15. Dezember 1935), 2–6 at 6.
533   I a more important than I c: Hagemann, interview; Westphal, interview; Hauck, interview; cf. Deutsch, 159–60.
533   I c second-raters: Heusinger, interview.
533   civilians as intelligence officers: Edgar "Bill" Williams, interview.
533   did not realize: *German General Staff Corps*, 95.
533   reserve officers: *German General Staff Corps*, 113; P-018a. 12.
533   equal in rank: Gehlen, 37.
534   army attitude changes: Heusinger, interview.
534   "Führer-Prinzip": Otto Dietrich, "Der Nationalsozialismus als Weltanschauung und Staatsgedanke," 5, in H.-H. Lammers et al., eds., *Die Verwaltungs-Akademie: Handbuch für den Beamten im nationalsozialistischen Staat* (Berlin: Industrieverlag Spaeth & Linde, n.d.), 1:1:2.
534   "charismatic authority": Weber, 1:215. I am indebted to Joseph Nyomarkay's fine book for the illuminating insight about charismatic authority.
534   devotion: Weber, 1:242–43.
534   traditional, legal authority: Ibid., 215.
534   Hitler boasted: Example in IMT, 37:547.
534   replicate, let his subordinates fight: Nyomarkay, 28, 33; Bracher, 212.
534   social Darwinism: Peter Hüttenberger, *Die Gauleiter: Studie zum Wandel des Machtgefüges in der NSDAP*, Schriftenreihe der Vierteljahrshefte für Zeitgeschichte, 19 (Stuttgart: Deutsche Verlags-Anstalt, 1969), 198, 212; Jeremy Noakes, *The Nazi Party in Lower Saxony, 1921–1933*, Oxford Historical Monographs (Oxford: University Press, 1971), 96–97.
535   distributing the authority: Thompson, 87.
535   Hitler refuses Speer: Speer, 316.
535   Dönitz special permission: *Lagevorträge*, 521.
535   "No one": Grundsätzliches Befehl, printed on the inside front cover of many official army manuals.
535   "upon a race": BA:EAP 161-b-12/278:4–5.
535   most ideological authority won: Weber, 3:1115–17; Gerth, 539.
535   charismatic authority rejects reason: Weber, 1:244.
536   Abwehr-Foreign Office dispute: *ADAP*, 2:240, 357–59.
536   under the kaiser: Craig, 230; Rosinski, 240; Hubatsch, *Admiralstab*, 111; Jonathan Steinberg,
536   "Germany and the Russo-Japanese War," *American Historical Review*, 75 (December 1970), 1965–86 at 1968.
536   Roosevelt techniques: Arthur M. Schlesinger, *The Coming of the New Deal* (London: Heinemann, 1960), 516–23.
536   not battles to the death: Cf. Popov, 69.
536   rationality in legal authority: Weber, 1:244.
536   press reports to Hitler: Dietrich, 154; Speer, 298: *Hitlers Lagebesprechung*, 709; *Hitlers Tischgespräche*, 441.
537   Hewel submitted: Average of AA:Vorlagen beim Führer for September, 1941.
537   19 September 1941: AA:Vorlagen beim Führer, 431792.
537   other days: Ibid., 431776–99.
537   reported orally: Speer, 299.
537   liaison man: *Hitlers Lagebesprechungen*, 170.
537   situation conferences: Heiber in *Hitlers Lagebesprechungen*, 12; Warlimont, 219–25; Keitel, 146–47.
537   chief of the general staff: Halder, 3:52, 497; *Hitlers Lagebesprechungen*, passim.
537   "At the Fiebig": *Hitlers Lagebesprechungen*, 58.
537   in person: Ibid., 369–83, 537, 621.
537   telephoned: Gersdorff, interview.
537   greatest variety of sources: Jacobsen, 347–52.
537   von Neurath; *Hitlers Lagebesprechungen*, 221–28.
537   8 hours a day: Ibid., 608.
537   difficulty of identifying troops: Ibid., 106.
537   intercept operators: Ibid., 761.
537   several existed: MA:III M 1006/6:169.
537   "When I get": *Hitlers Lagebesprechungen*, 750.
538   "too good": Ibid., 535.
538   "Must they do": Ibid., 557.
538   October 1942: OKW, *KTB*, 2:864–65.
538   ordered bridges bombed: Ibid., 889.
538   issued necessary orders: Martin L. Van Creveld, *Hitler's Strategy 1940–1941: The Balkan Clue* (Cambridge: University Press, 1973), 122–23.
538   built up flak: *Hitler's Table Talk*, 182.
538   The Grapes of Wrath: *Hitlers Lagebesprechungen*, 170–71.
538   "decayed country": *Hitler's Table Talk*, 188.
538   Americans would absorb: *Hitlers Zweites Buch*, 173; *DGFP*, 13:692.
538   seized upon reports of friction: *Staatsmänner*, 2:306.
538   subordinates support: Speer, 243, 302, 356.
538   Dietrich censored: Jacobsen, 349.

538   Keitel prevented: Keitel, 183; Thomas, 160, 270.
539   "How can you": Seifert, interview, 7.
539   Jodl softpedaled retreats: Boldt, 6.
539   6 November 1944: *Hitlers Lagebesprechungen,* 703.
539   "pressed in," yield ground: Ibid., passim.
539   "defeatism": Ibid., 493; *Staatsmänner,* 2:237.
539   "expert": *DGFP,* 12:940–41; *Hitlers Lagebesprechungen,* 816–17; *Hitlers Tischgespräche,* 238, 396, 443; Gehlen, 23: Speer, 305; Kersten, 83–87.
539   Germany ahead in population: Weinberg, "Hitler's Image of America," 1013.
539   300,000 tons: OKM, *Denkschriften,* 222.
539   70,000 tons: *Hitlers Tischgespräche,* 201.
539   100 kilometers: *Hitlers Lagebesprechungen,* 316–17.
540   "underestimation," "dangerous": Halder, 3:489.
540   "could not conceive": *DGFP,* 10:82.
540   "What we can't": Baumbach, interview.
540   "This cannot be": Kahn, 445–46. Possibly the 1942 Yugoslav intercept cited by Gehlen, 64.
540   "You don't have": *Hitlers Lagebesprechungen,* 201.
540   "That's also not": Ibid., 901.
540   "completely idiotic": Guderian, 387.
540   swept it from table: Primavesi, interview; Warlimont, 1st interview.
540   encapsulates himself: Fest, 925–26; Speer, 245, 299–300, 304.
540   forbade "pessimistic" and "defeatist" talk: Speer, 423; *Staatsmänner,* 2:237; *Hitlers Lagebesprechungen,* 493.
540   "We are," "The V 1," "our own": *Hitlers Lagebesprechungen,* 847, 818, 836, 824.
540   "durable friendship": *Hitler's Table Talk,* 12.
540   timing of the attack: *The Testament of Adolf Hitler,* 97.
541   "The higher commander": Schlieffen, 1:188.
541   1914: Jonathan Steinberg, "A German Plan for the Invasion of Holland and Belgium, 1897," *Historical Journal,* 6 (January 1963), 107–19 at 118.
541   1681: Andrew Lasky, " 'Maxims of State' in Louis XIV's Foreign Policy in the 1680s," in *William III and Louis XIV: Essays 1680–1720 by and for Mark A. Thompson,* ed. Ragnhild Hatton and J. S. Bromley (Liverpool: Liverpool University Press, 1968), at 12–13.
541   dismissed information: Richard Place, "The Self-Deception of the Strong: France on the Eve of the War of the League of Augsburg," *French Historical Studies,* 6 (Fall 1970) 459–73.
541   1937: Alvin D. Coox, "The Lake Khasan Affair of 1938: Overview and Lessons," *Soviet Studies,* 25 (July 1973), 51–65 at 64.
541   Churchill attitude toward intelligence: Cavendish-Bentinck, interview.

Bibliography

This bibliography consists of the following categories:

Laws, Regulations, Official Manuals
Prior and Contemporary Publications
Documents:
    Published
    Unpublished
Diaries, Memoirs, Papers:
    Published
    Unpublished
Official Interviews, Interrogations, Trials:
    Published
    Unpublished
Author's Interviews
Historical and Other Studies:
    Published
    Unpublished

Under published works, it mainly lists those cited in the notes. But it includes some books that made valuable general contributions and a few works that I wanted to show I had not missed. Under unpublished works, it lists all the volumes or folders that I have seen, but not documents ordered as photocopies individually from files that I have not examined.

Laws, Regulations, Official Manuals

Reichsgesetzblatt. 1918–45.
Handbuch für das deutsche Reich. 1922, 1924, 1926, 1929, 1931, 1936.
Heeresleitung (to 1935), Oberkommando des Heeres (to 1945).
    Regulations.
        Allgemeine Heeresmitteilungen. 1934–45.
        Armee-Verordnungsblatt. 1918–19.
        Heeres-Verordnungsblatt. 1919–21, 1933–44.
    Heeres-Dienstvorschriften.
        H.Dv. g. 17. *Aufklärung durch Nachrichtenmittel.* Heft 1: *Die taktische und Gefechtsaufklärung durch Nachrichtenmittel.* 15.3.38. Heft 2: *Die operative Funkaufklärung.* 25.5.38.
        H.Dv. g. 89. *Feindnachrichtendienst.* 1.3.1941.
        H.Dv. g. 92. *Handbuch des Generalstabsdienstes im Kriege.* 1939.
        H.Dv. 300/1. *Truppenführung.* I. Teil. 17.10.33.
    Merkblätter.
        Merkblatt für Korps- und Div. I c. 1.10.43.
        Truppen-I c-Dienst im Osten. 1.8.44.
    Rangliste.
        Heeres-Personalamt. *Rangliste des deutschen Reichsheeres.* 1920–32, except 1922.
        ———. *Stellenbesetzung für das Reichsheer.* 1933–38.
Marineleitung (to 1935), Oberkommando der Kriegsmarine (to 1945).
    Rangliste.
        Marineoffizierpersonalabteilung. *Rangliste.* 1921–44.
Oberkommando der Luftwaffe.
    Luftdienstvorschriften.

L.Dv. 2 and H.Dv. 402. *Der Aufklärungsflieger (Land)*. Teil II: *Luftaufklärung für den Luftkrieg*. 1938.
L.Dv. 2 and H.Dv. 402 and M.Dv. 2. *Die Luftaufklärung*. September 1944.
L.Dv. 12. *Der Luftbilddienst*. Teil I: *Das Luftbild im Dienste der Wehrmacht.* Beiheft 1: *Das Luftbild im Dienste des Heeres: Beispiele für seine taktische Anwendung*. März 1944. Teil V: *Auswertung*. Beiheft 1: *Flugzeuge*. September 1942.
L.Dv. 16. *Luftkriegführung*. 1936.
Nationalsozialistische Deutsche Arbeiterpartei.
Reichsorganisationsleiter der NSDAP. *Organisationsbuch der NSDAP*. Munich: Zentralverlag der NSDAP, Franz Eher Nachf. 4. Auflage, 1937; 7. Auflage, 1943.
Reichssicherheitshauptamt. *Befehlsblatt des Chefs der Sicherheitspolizei und des SD.* 1941–44.

Prior and Contemporary Publications

Auerbach, Leopold. *Denkwürdigkeiten des Geheimen Regierungrathes Dr. Stieber.* Aus seinen hinterlassenen Papieren bearbeitet. Berlin: Engelmann, 1884. 310 pp.
Bronsart von Schellendorff, [Paul]. *Der Dienst des Generalstabes*. 4. Auflage. Handbibliothek des Offiziers, 4. ESM, 1905. 472 pp.
Canaris, [Wilhelm Franz]. "Politik und Wehrmacht." In *Wehrmacht und Partei*, ed. Richard Donnerert. Leipzig: Barth, 1939. pp. 44–55.
Clausewitz, Carl von. *On War*. trans. and ed. Michael Howard and Peter Paret. Under the auspices of the Center of International Studies, Princeton University. Princeton: Princeton University Press, 1976. 717 pp.
"Gefechtsmelde- und -beobachtungsdienst der Infanterie." *Militär-Wochenblatt*, 123 (1. January 1939), 1779–80.
Gehrts, Erwin. *Der Aufklärungsflieger: Seine Aufgaben und Leistungen und die Überraschung im künftigen Kriege*. ESM, 1939. 66 pp.
[Germany. Grosser Generalstab]. *Anhaltungspunkte für den Generalstabsdienst*. Berlin: Reichsdruckerei, 1914. 136 pp.
[————.] *Geschäftsordnung für den Grossen Generalstab und die Landesaufnahme.* ESM. 207 pp.
[————. Reichswehrminister]. D.V.487. *Führung und Gefecht der verbundenen Waffen*. 1. September 1921. Berlin: Offene Worte, 1921. 272 pp.
Grün. "Die Aufklärung der Artillerie." *Militär-Wochenblatt*, 123 (21 April 1939), 2891–95.
Guderian, [Heinz]. "Die Panzertruppen und ihr Zusammenwirken mit den anderen Waffen." *Militärwissenschaftliche Rundschau*, 1 (August 1936), 607–26. Cited as "Guderian, 'Panzertruppen.' "
————. *Die Panzerwaffe: Ihre Entwicklung, ihre Kampftaktik und ihre operativen Möglichkeiten bis zum Beginn des Grossdeutschen Freiheitskampfes*. Stuttgart: Union Deutsche, 1943. Cited as "Guderian, *Panzerwaffe*," 229 pp.
Harbou, von. "Die Luftaufklärung." *Militärwissenschaftliche Rundschau*, 1 (November 1936), 736–45, 2 (Januar 1937), 115–26.
Hitler, Adolf. *Mein Kampf*. Complete and unabridged; fully annotated. ed. John Chamberlain et al. New York: Reynal and Hitchcock, 1939. 994 pp.
Janson, [R. August] von. *Der Dienst des Truppen-Generalstabes im Frieden*. 2. vermehrte Auflage. ESM, 1901. 208 pp.
Krahmer, [Eckard R.]. *Die Aufklärungsstaffel*. Der Dienst in der Luftwaffe, 1. Berlin: Bernard & Graefe, 1937. 199 pp.
Léwal. "Tactique des renseignements." *Journal des sciences militaires*, 8ᵉ serie, 22 (1880), passim, 9ᵉ serie, 1–8 (1881–2), passim.
Nicholai, W[alther]. *The German Secret Service*. trans. George Renwick. London: Stanley Paul, 1924. 298 pp.

————. *Nachrichtendienst, Presse und Volksstimmung im Weltkrieg.* ESM, 1920. 226 pp.
[Prussia.] Kriegsministerium. *Felddienst-Ordnung.* 23. Mai 1887. ESM, 1887. 216 pp.
————. *Field Service Regulations (Felddienst Ordnung, 1908) of the German Army, 1908,* trans. General Staff, War Office [Great Britain]. HMSO, n.d. 214 pp.
Ronge, Max. *Kriegs- und Industrie-Spionage: Zwölf Jahre Kundschaftsdienst.* Vienna: Amalthea, 1930. 424 pp.
Stein, Lorenz von. *Die Lehre von Heerwesen. Als Theil der Staatswissenschaft.* Stuttgart: Cotta, 1872. 274 pp.

Documents: Published

Förster, Jürgen, ed. "Strategische Überlegungen des Wehrmachtführungsstabes für das Jahr 1943." *Militärgeschichtliche Mitteilungen.* No. 13 (1/1973), 95–107.
[Germany.] Auswärtiges Amt. *Akten zur Deutschen Auswärtigen Politik 1918–1945.* Serie E (1941–1945). Göttingen: Vanderhoeck & Rupprecht, 1969– . 4 vols. Cited as *ADAP.*
[————. ————.] *Documents on German Foreign Policy, 1918–1945.* Series C (1933–1936) and D (1937–1941). United States, Department of State, and Great Britain, Foreign Office. GPO and HMSO, 1949–64. 5 and 13 vols. Cited as *DGFP* for Series D, *DGFP:*C for Series C.
[————. Kriegsmarine, Oberkommando der.] *Denkschriften und Lagebetrachtungen.* Vol. 3 of Michael Salewski, *Die deutsche Seekriegsleitung 1935–1945.* Frankfurt am Main: Bernard & Graefe, 1973. 411 pp. Cited as OKM, *Denkschriften.*
[————. ————.] *Lagevorträge des Oberbefehlshabers der Kriegsmarine vor Hitler 1939–1945.* ed. Gerhard Wagner. (Arbeitskreis für Wehrforschung). Munich: J. F. Lehmanns, 1972. 716 pp. Cited as *Lagevorträge.*
[————. Reichsministerium für Bewaffnung und Munition.] *Deutschlands Rüstung im Zweiten Weltkrieg: Hitlers Konferenzen mit Albert Speer 1942–1945.* ed. Willi A. Boelcke. Frankfurt am Main: Athenaion, 1969. 495 pp. Cited as RMfBuM, *Rüstung.*
[————. Reichsministerium für Volksaufklärung und Propaganda.] *Kriegspropaganda 1939–1941: Geheime Ministerkonferenzen im Reichspropagandaministerium.* ed. Willi A. Boelcke. Stuttgart: Deutsche Verlags-Anstalt, 1966. 794 pp. Cited as RMfVuP, *Kriegspropaganda.*
[————. ————.] *"Wollt Ihr den totalen Krieg?" Die geheimen Goebbels-Konferenzen, 1939–1945.* ed. Willi A. Boelcke. Stuttgart: Deutsche Verlags-Anstalt, 1967. 363 pp. Cited as RMfVuP, *"Wollt."*
[————. Reichssicherheitshauptamt. Amt III.] *Meldungen aus dem Reich: Auswahl aus den geheimen Lageberichten des Sicherheitsdienstes der SS 1939–1944.* ed. Heinz Boberach. Neuwied: Hermann Luchterhand, 1965. 551 pp. Cited as Boberach, ed.
[————. Wehrmacht, Oberkommando der. Wehrmachtführungsstab.] *Kriegstagebuch ... 1940–1945.* ed. Percy Ernst Schramm. (Arbeitskreis für Wehrforschung). Frankfurt am Main: Bernhard & Graefe, 1961–69. 4 vols. in 6. Cited as OKW, *KTB.*
Groehler, Otto, ed. "Zur Einschätzung der Roten Armee durch die faschistische Wehrmacht in den ersten Halbjahr 1941, dargestellt am Beispiel des AOK 4." *Zeitschrift für Militärgeschichte,* 7 (1968), 724–38.
[Hitler, Adolf.] *Hitler: Reden und Proklamationen, 1932–1945.* ed. Max Domarus. vol. 1, Privatdruck, 1962; vols. 2 and 3, Munich: Süddeutscher Verlag, 1965. Cited as Domarus, ed.
[————.] *Hitlers Lagebesprechungen: Die Protokollfragmente seiner militärischen Konferenzen, 1942–1945.* ed. Helmut Heiber. Quellen und Darstellungen zur Zeitgeschichte, 10. Stuttgart: Deutsche Verlags-Anstalt, 1962. 971 pp.

[————.] *Hitler's Table Talk 1941–1944: His Private Conversations.* trans. Norman Cameron and R. H. Stevens. 2d. ed. London: Weidenfeld and Nicolson, 1973. 746 pp.

[————.] *Hitlers Tischgespräche im Führerhauptquartier 1941–1942.* ed. Henry Picker. new ed. Percy Ernst Schramm. Stuttgart: Seeward, 1963. 546 pp.

[————.] *Hitlers Weisungen für die Kriegführung 1939–1945: Dokumente des Oberkommandos der Wehrmacht.* ed. Walther Hubatsch. Frankfurt am Main: Bernard & Graefe, 1962. 330 pp.

[————.] *Hitlers Zweites Buch: Ein Dokument aus dem Jahr 1928,* ed. Gerhard L. Weinberg. Quellen und Darstellungen zur Zeitgeschichte, 7. Stuttgart: Deutsche Verlags-Anstalt, 1961. 228 pp.

[————.] *Staatsmänner und Diplomaten bei Hitler: Vertrauliche Aufzeichnungen über Unterredungen mit Vertretern des Auslandes.* ed. Andreas Hillgruber. [1. Teil:] 1939–1941; 2. Teil: 1942–1944. Frankfurt: Bernard & Graefe, 1967–1970. 2 vols. Vol. 2 cited as *Staatsmänner.*

[————.] *The Testament of Adolf Hitler: The Hitler-Bormann Documents, February–April 1945.* ed. François Genoud. trans. Col. R. H. Stevens. London: Cassell, 1959. 115 pp.

Jacobsen, Hans-Adolf, ed. *1939–1945: Der Zweite Weltkrieg in Chronik und Dokumenten.* Darmstadt: Wehr und Wissen, 1959. 538 pp.

Kr[ausnick], H[elmuth], ed. "Aus den Personalakten von Canaris." *Vierteljahrshefte für Zeitgeschichte,* 10 (Juli 1962), 280–310.

Moritz, Erhard, ed. *Fall Barbarossa: Dokumente zur Vorbereitung der faschistischen Wehrmacht auf die Aggression gegen die Sowjetunion (1940/41).* Schriften des Deutschen Institutes für Militärgeschichte. Berlin: Deutscher Militärverlag, 1970. 437 pp.

Schnabel, Reimund, ed. *Missbrauchte Mikrofone: Deutsche Rundfunkpropaganda im Zweiten Weltkrieg. Eine Dokumentation.* Vienna: Europa Verlag, 1967. 506 pp.

Spiegelbild einer Verschworung: Die Kaltenbrunner-Berichte an Bormann und Hitler über das Attentat von 20. Juli 1944. Geheime Dokumente aus dem ehemaligen Reichssicherheitshauptamt. Archiv Peter für historische und zeitgeschichtliche Dokumentation. Stuttgart: Seewald, 1961. 587 pp.

Szinai, Miklós and Laszló Szücs, eds. *The Confidential Papers of Admiral Horthy.* Budapest: Corvina, 1965. 439 pp.

United States. Department of State. *Foreign Relations of the United States: Diplomatic Papers.* Vols. for 1939–45. GPO, 1956–69. Cited as *FRUS* + volume.

Documents: Unpublished

Militärarchiv
Oberkommando der Wehrmacht

OKW:25	OKW:319	OKW:1071	OKW:2091
OKW:79	OKW:436	OKW:1109	OKW:2129
OKW:80	OKW:558	OKW:1134	OKW:2161
OKW:100	OKW:698	OKW:1513	OKW:2161a
OKW:225	OKW:730	OKW:1581	OKW:2165
OKW:226	OKW:732	OKW:1685	OKW:2166
OKW:244	OKW:888	OKW:1689	OKW:2247
OKW:258	OKW:1013	OKW:1707	OKW:2256
OKW:282	OKW:1025	OKW:1938	OKW:2321
OKW:284	OKW:1026	OKW:2047	
Wi/I 26	Wi/VI 1	Wi/VI 344	Wi/VIII 25
Wi/I 51	Wi/VI 2	Wi/VI 397	Wi/VIII 216
Wi/I 52	Wi/VI 31	Wi/VI 399	Wi/VIII 232
Wi/IB 1.145	Wi/VI 224	Wi/VIII 10	Wi/VIII 245
Wi/IF 5.648	Wi/VI 270	Wi/VIII 11	Wi/VIII 254
Wi/IV 5.2150			

Oberkommando der Kriegsmarine

III M 1000/36	III M 1006/1	Case GE 1882	PG 33398
III M 1000/37	III M 1006/2	PG 26674	PG 33399
III M 1000/38	III M 1006/3	PG 31027	PG 33553
III M 1000/39	III M 1006/4	PG 31729	PG 33555
III M 1000/56	III M 1006/5	PG 32052	PG 34425
III M 1000/57	III M 1006/6	PG 33311	M/26/34128
III M 1000/58	Case GE 1639	PG 33397	

Oberkommando der Luftwaffe

E 829/1	RO 60/12	RL 2/547	RL 2/646
E 829/2	RL 2/423	RL 2/557	RL 2/648
L 81–2/1	RL 2/540	RL 2/558	RL 2/649
RO 40/4	RL 2/543	RL 2/601	

Oberkommando des Heeres

H1/2	H2/111	H3/337	H22/57
H1/11	H2/113	H3/344	H22/75
H1/321	H2/114	H3/346	H22/147
H1/463	H2/115a	H3/378	H22/220
H1/530	H2/115b	H3/463.2	H22/228
H2/3	H2/116	H3/513	H22/290
H2/4	H2/120	H3/595	H22/353
H2/7	H2/121a	H3/612	H22/355
H2/8	H2/121b	H3/680	H27/6
H2/9	H3/1	H3/1044	H27/7
H2/11a	H3/4	H3/1048	H27/10
H2/11b	H3/5	H3/1065	H27/11
H2/12	H3/68.1	H3/1073	H27/41 Teil 2
H2/82	H3/172	H3/1149	H27/43
H2/83	H3/176	H3/1361	H28/41
H2/84	H3/199	H3/1460	H28/43
H2/85	H3/245	H3/1500	H28/46
H2/93	H3/261	H3/1515	H29/I B 2.3
H2/107b	H3/284a	H3/1531	H29/VII 20
H2/107g	H3/284b	H22/48	H40/64

HGr B	HGr D	HGr Nord	HGr Süd
65881/8	75144/4	75130/28	39502/57
	75144/24	75130/31	75124/5
HGr Mitte	75144/25	75130/33	W 648, al
75861	75144/33	75136/2	
	75144/35	W 35 30b	
	75144/36		
	75809		
	75820		

AOK 1	AOK 7
13058/11	75106/1
E161/1	75106/3
E209/1	75106/7
E209/2	75106/8
	75106/10

AOK 9

26791/9	27970/5:IV	28878/14	32151/16
26791/14	28878/2	29234/3	32151/17
27970/1	28878/3	29234/6	32878/7
27970/2	28878/7	29234/11	
27970/5:III	28878/11	31624/3	

AOK 11

22279/3	22409/219	22409/222	22409/225
22409/100	22409/220	22409/223	22409/226
22409/218	22409/221	22409/224	22409/227

AOK 12	AOK 15	AOK 16	AOK 17
75991	59364/1	E 138/3	11147/10
	59364/7	W 4819 z 10	14499/51–54
AOK 20	59365		16593/5–10
58631/1–5	59369		25354/89
58635			

Pz. AOK 1	Pz. AOK 2	Pz. AOK Afrika	
45393/3	37075/13	16838/5	18107/4
45393/8	37075/28	16838/6	18197/1
45393/17	37075/182	16838/7	34374/1
		16838/8	34374/6

II. AK	XXX. AK	XXXV. AK	
45114/3	13896/2	42146/1	44220/14
	11455/2	42146/5	44220/15
		42146/6	44220/16
		44220/13	

XXXVII. AK	LXXXI. AK		LXXXIV. AK
44651/14	57791/2	57791/6	44062/6
	57791/4	57793	

XXXIX. Pz. K.	XXXX. Pz. K.	LII. Pz. K.	
26522/18	51231/1	42241/4	48059/2
26522/28	51231/2	42241/28	48621/2
26522/33		48059/1	
26522/38			

Deutsches Afrika Korps

22570/6	22570/26	22926/4
22570/8	22926/1	25570/1
22570/25	22926/3	25570/2

22. Inf. Div.

15821/18	19901/7
19901/6	19901/8

24. Inf. Div.

22006/1	22006/3	22985/1	22985/3
22006/2	22006/11	22985/2	22985/4

50. Inf. Div.	72. Inf. Div.	98. Inf. Div.	102. Inf. Div.
16110/11	21721/13c	8147/2	26562/1
		8159/2	26562/4

126. Inf. Div.	129. Inf. Div.	162. Inf. Div.	169. Inf. Div.
17754/21	17750/2	37813/6	23501/3
		37813/11	

183. Inf. Div.	256. Inf. Div.	257. Inf. Div.	258. Inf. Div.
32255/10	W 5643 i	22966/15	27761/12
32381/1	W 5643 k		

290. Inf. Div.	305. Inf. Div.
45885/4	33410/4
45885/5	42321/4

2. Pz. Div.	3. Pz. Div.	10. Pz. Div.	
III H 50075/3	19269/18	27962	30444/9
III H 50076	19269/22	30444/5	30575/1
	19269/36	30444/6	30575/2
	19269/38	30444/7	
	19269/44		

11. Pz. Div.	15. Pz. Div.		
41070/1	21991/2	30270/4	30270/7
41070/6	30270/2	30270/5	30270/8
41070/9	30270/3	30270/6	30270/9

21. Pz. Div.	15. Pz. Gren. Div.	1. Kav. Div.
18572	76211	13280/21
18572/2	77066/3	

90. lei. Div.	WK VII	WK XIII	
18014/1	1653	7	365
18014/5	2091	352	484
18014/11	2674	362	771
23312/1	3684	364	1435
23312/2	4082		

10. SS. Pz. Div.	12. SS. Pz. Div.	17. SS. Pz. Gren. Div.
78014/11	78016/21–46	78019/13
78013/12		78019/14

Nachlässe
N 18	Wilhelm Heye. Band 1
N 42	Kurt von Schleicher. Band 45
N 97	Ferdinand von Bredow. Bände 1, 2, 3, 8, 9
N 104	Helmuth Groscurth
N 281	Kurt von Tippelskirch

B u n d e s a r c h i v
R2/4915	R55/732	R58/120	R70/Frankreich/1
R3/vorl. 1312	R55/733	R58/123	R158/770
R55 DC/vorl. 465	R58/111	R58/840	NS19/432
R55/vorl. 466	R58/116	R58/927	NS19/2237
R55/634	R58/117	R58/961	

NSDAP
DAI 221   DAI 789   DAI 860   DAI 1180
EAP 66-c-1	EAP 161-b-12/366	EAP 173-b-18-14/1
EAP 66-c-8-46/6	EAP 161-b-12/372a	EAP 173-b-20-14/3
EAP 66-c-12-5/13	EAP 161-b-12/374,	EAP 173-b-20-18/20
EAP 66-c-12-44/74	Folder 61	EAP 173-b-20-18/21
EAP 66-c-12-44/83	EAP 161-b-12/384	EAP 173-b-20-20/16
EAP 66-c-12-44/95	EAP 173-a-10/13	EAP 173-b-24-10/6
EAP 66-c-12-44/464	EAP 173-a-10/20	EAP 173-b-24-10/12
EAP 161-b-12/10	EAP 173-a-10/20a	EAP 173-b-24-14/4
EAP 161-b-12/13	EAP 173-b-01/1	EAP 173-b-24-16/1
EAP 161-b-12/14	EAP 173-b-05/1A	EAP 173-b-24-24/15
EAP 161-b-12/78	EAP 173-b-05/2	EAP 173-b-24-26/6
EAP 161-b-12/132	EAP 173-b-05/2K	EAP 173-b-24-26/7
EAP 161-b-12/149	EAP 173-b-05/2L	EAP 173-b-24-26/10
EAP 161-b-12/214,	EAP 173-b-10	EAP 173-d-01/1
Folder 31	EAP 173-b-10-16/2	EAP 175-b-24-10/6
EAP 161-b-12/250	EAP 173-b-12-05/45	EAP 175-b-24-10/12
EAP 161-b-12/278	EAP 173-b-14/78	EAP 173-b-26/3
EAP 161-b-12/363	EAP 173-b-16-05/53	EAP 250-a/221
EAP 161-b-12/365	EAP 173-b-16-12/93a	

Reichswirtschaftsministerium
3/9	11/15	19/4	20/286
4/23	16/224	20/106	20/374

Reichsfinanzministerium 9
Reichsministerium für Volksaufklärung und Propaganda
  RMfVuP-1
Nachlass Paul Leverkuehn. Bände 6–11, 19

Auswärtiges Amt: Politisches Archiv

Inl II g 7	Inl II g 79	Inl II g 335	Inl II g 463
Inl II g 59	Inl II g 106	Inl II g 342	Inl II g 464
Inl II g 72	Inl II g 107	Inl II g 459	Inl II g 476
Inl II g 73	Inl II g 150	Inl II g 460	Inl II g 477f
Inl II g 74			

III. Politik 15, England, Bd. 1
III. Politik 15, V.8.A., Bd. 1

Pol I M Mil. Politik, 2. England, Bd. 1
Pol I M Mil. Politik, 2. Portugal, Bd. 1
Pol I M Mil. Politik, 2. K. O. Spanien, Bd. 1
Pol I M Mil. Politik, 2. Nordamerika Prozess, Bd. 1
Pol I M Mil. Politik, 2. Nordamerika, Bd. 1

Pol I M 13	Pol I M 28	Pol I M 40	Pol I M 86
Pol I M 17	Pol I M 38	Pol I M 50	Pol I M 86a
Pol I M 23	Pol I M 39	Pol I M 51	Pol I M 185
			Pol I M 196

Büro des Staatssekretärs:Zweite Front:1–3.
Unterstaatssekretär:Dokumente Kriegsausbruch:133
Vorlagen beim Führer (Walther Hewel).
Dienststelle Ribbentrop, Vertrauliche Berichte, 2a/2, Teil 1
Dienststelle Ribbentrop, Vertrauliche Berichte, 2a/2, Teil 2
Dienststelle Ribbentrop, Vertrauliche Berichte, 2b/1

Berlin Document Center

Party Member	Membership Number
Becker, [Johann] Siegfried	359,966
Carstenn, Friedrich	74,557
Cohrs, Heinz	363,179
Dörner, Hermann	603,788
Elling, Georg	3,461,625
Filbert, Alfred	1,321,414
Franke, Lothar	19,852
Gottlob, Josef	8,016,151
Griebl, Ignaz	8,540,674
Hessen, Prinz Christoph von	696,176
Höttl, Wilhelm	6,309,616
Jost, Heinz	75,946
Krämer, Karl-Heinz	4,175,743
Krallert, Wilfred	1,529,315
Krüger, Bernhard	528,739
Langer, Albert	6,143,388
Lassig, Rudolf	739,497
Mair, Kurt Alexander	6,199,379
Möller, Helmut	167,625
Moyzisch, Ludwig	1,307,980
Naujocks, Alfred	624,279
Ohnesorge, Wilhelm	42
Paeffgen, Theodor	3,965,964
Paschke, Adolf	2,649,870
Rapp, Alfred	774,433
Rauff, Walter	5,216,415
Rühle, Gerhard	694
Salisch, Karl-Otto von	4,303,047
Schapper, Gottfried	536,206
Schauffler, Rudolf	8,743,951
Schellenberg, Walter	3,504,508
Schimpf, Hans	2,638,165

Schnaus, Erich	432,273
Schroeder, Georg	536,207
Schulze, Peter	8,858,753
Schumann, Arthur	15,292
Seidlitz, Wilhelm	3,573,913
Seifert, Walther	4,826,808
Selchow, Kurt	7,910,928
Siepen, Peter	4,690,994
Stache, Rudolf	1,433,244
Steimle, Eugen	1,075,555
Szeraws, Johannes	3,758,195
Tschierschky, Karl	918,746
Vetterlein, Kurt	4,100,140
Vietinghoff-Scheel, Paul Baron von	2,642,306
Zuchristian, Walter	149,986

SS Member Only	*SS Number*
Schüddekopf, Otto-Ernst	455,103
Zapp, Rudolf	148,935

Imperial War Museum
Erhard Milch, Handakten (microfilmed): Volumes 13, 14, 15, 16, 17, 18, 20, 21, 23, 34, 62

Bayerische Hauptstaatsarchiv: Abteilung IV, Kriegsarchiv

M Kr/986	M Kr/1151	M Kr/1713	M Kr/1778
M Kr/1000	M Kr/1271	M Kr/1714	M Kr/1779
M Kr/1002	M Kr/1421–1466	M Kr/1775	M Kr/1780
M Kr/1048	M Kr/1630–1668	M Kr/1776	M Kr/1837
M Kr/1150	M Kr/1711	M Kr/1777	

Grufunka 557, Bände 6, 7

National Archives
Record Group 59. Department of State Decimal File. Individual documents
Record Group 173. Federal Communications Commission, Entry 27, Boxes 5–11, 13, 16, 17, 58
Record Group 242. Foreign Records Seized. ML-37, ML-155, ML-156a, ML-164a, ML-165a, ML-174a, ML-180
Record Group 407. Adjutant General's Office. Boxes 1757, 1758, 1760, 5698

Franklin D. Roosevelt Library, Hyde Park, New York
MR Box 136, 63, 71; Container 203
OF 10b, Boxes 20–22, 28–29, 36–43; OF 5613, Acc. 71–31
PSF 163, 167, 170

Federal Archives and Records Center, New York
Records of the U.S. District Court for the Eastern District of New York. Criminal Dockets 38425, 39357, 40120, 40190

Public Record Office, London

CAB 79/12	CAB 86/13	FO 195/2477/166	FO 371/37177
CAB 79/13	CAB 86/14	FO 195/2481/972	FO 371/42449
CAB 79/16	CAB 122/242	FO 195/2482/55	WO 106/3867
CAB 79/19	CAB 122/564	FO 371/21742	WO 106/3874
CAB 79/23	CAB 122/1347	FO 371/30893	WO 106/4361
CAB 79/25	FO 195/2464/170	FO 371/32328	WO 208/1805
CAB 79/91	FO 195/2475/30	FO 371/32340	WO 208/2832
CAB 86/2	FO 195/2475/30.5	FO 371/37069	

Diaries, Memoirs, Papers: Published

Bazna, Elyesa. *I Was Cicero.* trans. Eric Mosbacher. New York: Harper & Row, 1962. 212 pp.

Boldt, Gerhard. *Hitler's Last Days: An Eyewitness Account.* trans. Sandra Brance. London: Barker, 1973. 188 pp.

Churchill, Winston S. *The Second World War.* London: Cassell, 1948–54. 6 vols.

Ciano, Galeazzo. *Diario, 1939–1943.* Milano: Rizzoli, 1946. 2 vols.

[Clark, A.P.] "Dulag Luft Recalled and Revisited." ed. James L. Cole, Jr. *Aerospace Historian,* 19 (June 1972), 62–65.

Dietrich, Otto. *12 Jahre mit Hitler.* Munich: Isar, 1955. 285 pp.

Dirksen, Herbert von. *Moscow, Tokyo, London: Twenty Years of German Foreign Policy.* London: Hutchinson, 1951. 288 pp.

Doenitz, Karl. *Memoirs: Ten Years and Twenty Days.* trans. R. H. Stevens. Cleveland: World, 1959. 500 pp.

Engel, Gerhard. *Heeresadjutant bei Hitler, 1938–1943: Aufzeichnungen des Majors Engel.* Schriftenreihe der Vierteljahrshefte für Zeitgeschichte, 27. Stuttgart: Deutsche Verlags-Anstalt, 1974. 157 pp.

Faber du Faur, Moriz von. *Macht und Ohnmacht: Erinnerungen eines alten Offiziers.* Stuttgart: Günther, 1953. 296 pp.

Geyr von Schweppenburg, [Leo Freiherr]. *The Critical Years.* London: Allan Wingate, 1952. 207 pp.

Gimpel, Erich, with Will Berthold. *Spy for Germany.* trans. Eleanor Brockett. London: Robert Hall, 1957. 238 pp.

Gisevius, Hans Bernd. *To the Bitter End.* trans. Richard and Clara Winston. Boston: Houghton Mifflin, 1947. 632 pp.

Goebbels, (Paul) Joseph. *The Goebbels Diaries, 1942–1943.* ed. and trans. Louis P. Lochner. Garden City, N.Y.: Doubleday, 1948. 566 pp.

Groscurth, Helmuth. *Tagebücher eines Abwehroffiziers 1938–1940.* ed. Helmut Krausnick and Harold C. Deutsch. Quellen und Darstellungen zur Zeitgeschichte, 19. Stuttgart: Deutsche Verlags-Anstalt, 1970. 594 pp.

Guderian, Heinz. *Panzer Leader.* trans. Constantine FitzGibbon. London: Michael Joseph, 1952. 528 pp. Cited as "Guderian."

Halder, Franz. *Kriegstagebuch: Tägliche Aufzeichnungen des Chefs des Generalstabes des Heeres 1939–1942.* ed. Hans-Adolf Jacobsen. Stuttgart: Kohlhammer, 1962–64. 3 vols.

Hammerstein-Equord, Kunrat Freiherr von. "Spähtruppe im Westen." In his *Spähtrupp.* Stuttgart: Goverts, 1963. pp. 95–146.

Hayn, Friedrich. "Aus der täglichen Kleinarbeit der Abteilung I c." In his *Die Invasion: Von Cotentin bis Falaise.* Die Wehrmacht im Kampf, 2. Heidelberg: Vowinckel, 1954. pp. 138–45.

Hutter, Siegfried. *Falken über der Sowjetunion.* Berlin: Steiniger, 1942. 184 pp.

———. *Spähtruppe im Äther: Erlebnisse eines Fliegeroffiziers.* Berlin: Schutzen, 1940. 184 pp.

Kesselring, Albert. *Kesselring: A Soldier's Record.* New York: Morrow, 1954. 381 pp.

[Keitel, Wilhelm.] *The Memoirs of Field-Marshal Keitel.* ed. Walter Görlitz. trans. David Irving. London: Kimber, 1965. 288 pp.

Kersten, Felix. *The Kersten Memoirs, 1940–1945.* trans. Constantine FitzGibbon and James Oliver. London: Hutchinson, 1956. 314 pp.

Koch, Oscar W., with Robert G. Hays. *G-2: Intelligence for Patton.* An Army Times Publishing Company Book. Philadelphia: Whitmore Publishing Co., 1971. 167 pp.

[Köstring, Ernst.] *General Ernst Köstring: Der militärische Mittler zwischen dem Deutschen Reich und der Sowjetunion 1921–1941.* ed. Hermann Teske. Profile bedeutender Soldaten, 1. (Bundesarchiv/Militärarchiv). ESM, n.d. 334 pp.

Liss, Ulrich. *Westfront 1939/40: Erinnerungen des Feindbearbeiters im O.K.H.* Die

Wehrmacht im Kampf, 22. Neckargemünd: Vowinckel, 1959. 276 pp. Cited as Liss.

Manstein, Erich von. *Verlorene Siege.* Bonn: Athenäum, 1955. 664 pp.

Moyzisch, L[udwig]. *Operation Cicero.* trans. Constantine FitzGibbon and Heinrich Fraenkel. London: Wingate, 1950. 209 pp.

Muggeridge, Malcolm. *Chronicles of Wasted Time.* New York: Morrow, 1973–74. 2 vols.

Menge-Genser, M. von. *Das Auge der Armee: Kampf und Sieg eines Fernaufklärers. Nach den Tagebuchblättern.* Berlin: Heinz Menge, 1943. 146 pp.

Pape, Heinz. *Wir Suchen den Feind: Kampf der Aufklärer im Westen.* 3rd ed. Gutersloh: Bertelsmann, 1943. 326 pp.

Papen, Franz von. *Memoirs.* trans. Brian Connell. London: André Deutsch, 1952. 628 pp.

Popov, Dusko. *Spy/Counterspy: The Autobiography of Dusko Popov.* New York: Grosset & Dunlap, 1974. 339 pp.

Praun, Albert. *Soldat in der Telegraphen und Nachrichtentruppe.* Würzburg: Selbstverlag Albert Praun, [ca. 1965]. 287 pp.

Prügel, H[einrich]. "Fernaufklärer—Die Augen der Armee." *Der Frontsoldat erzählt* ... 18 (9/1954), 308–12.

———. "Nachtaufklärung für die Infanterie." *Der Frontsoldat erzählt* ... 18 (2/1954), 52–53.

Raabe, H., ed. *3. (H)12 in Polen.* Essen: National-Zeitung, [1940]. 95 pp.

Raeder, Erich. *Mein Leben.* Tübingen-Neckar: Schlichtenmayer, 1956–57. 2 vols.

[Ribbentrop, Joachim von.] *The Ribbentrop Memoirs.* trans. Oliver Watson. London: Weidenfeld & Nicolson, 1954. 216 pp.

Rintelen, Enno von. *Mussolini als Bundesgenosse: Erinnerungen des deutschen Militärattachés in Rom 1936–1943.* Tübingen & Stuttgart: Rainer Wunderlich Verlag Hermann Leins, 1951. 265 pp.

Ritter, Nikolaus. *Deckname Dr. Rantzau: Die Aufzeichungen des Nikolaus Ritter, Offizier im Geheimen Nachrichtendienst.* Hamburg: Hoffman und Campe, 1972. 327 pp.

Rittlinger, Herbert. *Geheimdienst mit beschränkter Haftung: Bericht vom Bosporus.* Stuttgart: Deutsche Verlags-Anstalt, 1973. 340 pp.

[Rommel, Erwin.] *The Rommel Papers.* ed. B. H. Liddell Hart. trans. Paul Findlay. London: Collins, 1953. 545 pp.

Schulze-Holthus, [Julius Berthold]. *Daybreak in Iran: A Story of the German Intelligence Service.* trans. Mervyn Savill. London: Staples, 1954. 319 pp.

Skorzeny, Otto. *Skorzeny's Special Missions.* London: Hale, 1957. 221 pp.

Strik-Strikfeldt, Wilfried. *Against Stalin and Hitler: Memoir of the Russian Liberation Movement 1941–5.* trans. David Footman. London: Macmillan, 1970. 270 pp.

Thomas, Georg. *Geschichte der deutschen Wehr- und Rüstungswirtschaft (1918–1943/45).* ed. Wolfgang Birkenfeld. Schriften des Bundesarchivs, 14. Boppard am Rhein: Boldt, 1966. 552 pp.

Warlimont, Walter. *Inside Hitler's Headquarters 1939–45.* trans. R. H. Barry. London: Weidenfeld & Nicolson, 1964. 658 pp.

Weizsäcker, Ernst Freiherr von. *Memoirs.* trans. John Andrews. London: Gollancz, 1951. 322 pp.

Zantke, Siegfried. "Bewaffnete Aufklärung über Charkow." *Der Frontsoldat erzählt* ... 18 (3/1954), 71–72.

Zhukov, Georgi K. *Marshal Zhukov's Greatest Battles.* trans. Theodore Shabad. ed. Harrison E. Salisbury. London: Macdonald, 1969. 304 pp.

Diaries, Memoirs, Papers: Unpublished

Buntrock, Georg. "Mein Lebenslauf." 1947–48. Typescript. 140 pp.

Gill, E[rnest]. W. B. "Spies, Science & Staff Officers." [ca. 1950]. Manuscript and typescript. 17 chapters.

[Heinz, Friedrich Wilhelm]. "Von Wilhelm Canaris zur NKWD." Typescript. n.d. 203 pp. (microfilm copy in NA:RG242:ML1078).

Liss, Ulrich. Letters to B. H. Liddell Hart (in B. H. Liddell Hart Papers, German Generals Files).

Maurer, Helmut. "Vom Krieg zum Mord." February 1949 and March 1950. Typescript. 89 pp.

Schwenke, Dietrich H. Untitled memoirs. 18 Juni 1961. Mimeographed. 15 pp.

Official Interviews, Interrogations, and Trials: Published

[Germany (Territory under Allied Occupation, 1945–   , United States Zone), Military Government Tribunals]. *Trials of War Criminals before the Nuernberg Military Tribunals under Control Council Law No. 10.* Nuremberg, October 1946–April 1949. GPO:1950–53. 15 vols. Cited as *TWC.*

[International Military Tribunal]. *Trial of the Major War Criminals before the International Military Tribunal.* Nuremberg, 14 November 1945–1 October 1946. Nuremberg, 1947–49. 42 vols. Cited as *IMT.*

[Jodl, Alfred]. "Die Vernehmung von Generaloberst Jodl durch die Sowjets." trans. Wilhelm Arenz. *Wehrwissenschaftliche Rundschau,* 11 (September 1961) 534–42.

[Keitel, Wilhelm]. "Die Vernehmung von Generalfeldmarschall Keitel durch die Sowjets." trans. Wilhelm Arenz. *Wehrwissenschaftliche Rundschau,* 11 (November 1961), 651–62.

[United States]. Office of United States Chief of Counsel for Prosecution of Axis Criminality. *Nazi Conspiracy and Aggression.* GPO: 1946–48. 10 vols. Cited as *NCA.*

War Crimes Trials, 9. *The Dulag Luft Trial.* Trial of Erich Killinger, Heinz Junge, Otto Boehringer, Heinrich Eberhardt, Gustav Bauer-Schlichtegroll. ed. Eric Cuddon. London: Hodge, 1952. 255 pp.

Official Interviews, Interrogations, and Trials: Unpublished

National Archives

Record Group 59.   State Department Special Interrogation Mission to Germany (De Witt Poole)

Blomberg, Werner von
Boetticher, Friedrich von
Bohle, Ernst Wilhelm
Borchers, Hans
Dieckhoff, Hans-Heinrich
Feldtange, Hanna
Gienanth, Ulrich von
Göring, Hermann
Guderian, Heinz
Hencke, Andor
Hepp, Ernst Adolf
Jodl, Alfred
Keitel, Wilhelm
Klee, Eugen
Lahousen, Erwin

Lammers, Hans-Heinrich
Niebuhr, Dietrich
Ohnesorge, Wilhelm
Paeffgen, Theodor
Prittwitz und Gaffron, Friedrich Wilhelm von
Ribbentrop, Joachim von
Ritter, Karl
Steinhauser, Conrad
Strempel, Heribert von
Stroelin, Karl D.
Tannenberg, Wilhelm Ernst August
Thomas, Georg
Thomsen, Hans
Truetzschler von Falkenstein, Hans

Record Group 165. Schuster Commission Interrogation Reports
Braune, Werner   Keitel, Wilhelm
Göring, Hermann   Warlimont, Walter
Hoffmann, Rudolf   Zinnemann, Curt
Kehrl, Hans

Record Group 165. Interrogations of Prisoners of War
  U.S. Forces, European Theater, HQ, Interrogation Center
    FIR 7.   Arthur Scheidler. 11th July 1945. 42 pp.
    FIR 10.   Ernst Wilhelm Bohle. 26th July 1945. 23 pp.
    1SIIR   "The German G-2 Service in the Russian Campaign (I c-Dienst Ost)." 22 July 1945. 226 pp.

  U.S. Forces, European Theater, HQ, MISC
    CI-PIR/68. Erich Herrlitz. 19 Sep 1945. 2 pp.
    CI-IIR/1.   Karl Ritter. 31 Aug 1945. 12 pp.
    CI-IIR/4.   Conrad Steinhauser. 15 Sep 1945. 10 pp.
    CI-IIR/48   Erich Herrlitz. 20 Feb 1946. 42 pp.
    CI-IIR/49. Franz Ferdinand Alliger. 5 Feb 1946. 8 pp.
    FIR/19.   Friedhelm Baechle. 16 Aug 1943. 18 pp.
    CI-FIR/67. Friedrich Busch. 11 Jan 1946. 15 pp.
    CI-FIR/63. Robert von Tarbuk. 19 Jan 1946. 16 pp.
    CI-FIR/73. Walter Stockmann. 29 Jan 1946. 19 pp.
    CI-FIR/76. Paul Fuchs. 23 Jan 1946. 26 pp.
    CI-FIR/78. Hermann Amende. 22 Jan 1946. 11 pp.
    CI-FIR/84. Ernst Lind. 1 Feb 1946. 9 pp.
    CI-FIR/85. Adalbert von Taysen. 2 Feb 1946. 7 pp.
    CI-FIR/87. Alexander Waag. 1 Feb 1946. 4 pp.
    CI-FIR/88. Werner P. H. Miethe, 6 Feb 1946. 14 pp.
    CI-RIR/12. Jakob Nagel. 7 Jan 1946. 5 pp.
    CI-CIR/11. KdM Prague. 10 Jan 1946. 39 pp.
    CI-CIR/13. Asts in the Balkans, in Poland, and in Wien. 31 Jan 1946. 47 pp.

  12th Army Group, HQ, Interrogation Center
    IIR.   Ernst Kaltenbrunner. 28 June 1945. 49 pp.

  6824 DIC (MIS)/M.
    991   Bruno Bastiansen. 15 Dec 1944. 4 pp.
    1096   Notes on Cartographic Agencies in Wehrkreis X. 29 Mar 1945. 7 pp.
    1136   German Signals Counter-Intelligence, Signals and Other Information. 23 Apr 1945. 6 pp.
    1137   Notes on Chi III/OKW and a Description of HT 2 Dictaphone Recorder. 24 Apr 1945. 7 pp.
    1151   "Transozean" (TO) News Agency. 12 May 1945. 48 pp.
    1160   The Kriegsakademic (OKH) Class of 1931–1934 and Officers of the German Army General Staff. 18 May 1945. 8 pp.
    1170   Notes on the Forschungsamt RLM. 7 Jun 1945. 31 pp.
    1174   Notes on the Reichsamt fuer Landesaufnahme. 4 Jun 1945. 4 pp.
    1177   German Signal Research, Development and Manufacture. 12 Jun 1945. 10 pp.
    1191   The Effects of the German Research and Development Policy. 12 Jul 1945. 4 pp.

  Military Intelligence Service in Austria, 6825 HQ and HQ Company. IC
    1DIR   Franz Seubert. 2 Jan 1946. 20 pp.

  CCPWE 32
    DI-33   Jacob Nagel. 15 Jul 1945. 4 pp.
    DI-36   Hermann Goering Answers Questions Concerning "Forschungsamt" and "Reichssicherheitsdienst." 19 Jul 1945. 4 pp.
    DI-39   Jacob Nagel. 22 Jul 1945. 5 pp.

HTUSAIC

PIR	Erich Müller. 8 Aug 1945. 1 p.
PIR	Theodor Päffgen. 8 Aug 1945. 1 p.
PIR	Herbert Wenninger. 8 Aug 1945. 1 p.
PIR	Herbert Seegers. 11 Aug 1945. 1 p.
PIR	Josef Urban. 13 Aug 1945. 1 p.
PIR	Wilhelm Oberbeil. 14 Aug 1945. 1 p.
PIR	Alexander Waag. 15 Aug 1945. 1 p.
PIR	Robert Arenberg, Prinz und Herzog von. 16 Aug 1945. 1 p.
PIR	Hermann Baun. 16 Aug 1945. 1 p.
PIR	Erna Thurow. 16 Aug 1945. 1 p.
PIR	Walter Stockmann. 18 Aug 1945. 1 p.
PIR	Kurt Auner. 21 Aug 1945. 1 p.
PIR	Friedrich Föster. 21 Aug 1945. 1 p.
PIR	Werner Kapp. 21 Aug 1945. 1 p.
PIR	Otto Müller. 21 Aug 1945. 1 p.
PIR	Hans Nickel. 21 Aug 1945. 1 p.
PIR	Wilhelm Auffermann. 22 Aug 1945. 1 p.
PIR	Ernst Bahr. 22 Aug 1945. 1 p.
PIR	Roland Loos. 25 Aug 1945. 1 p.
PIR	Hedwig Weigelmayer-Sommer. 27 Aug 1945. 1 p.
PIR	Emil Benz. 28 Aug 1945. 1 p.
PIR	Otto Weil. 30 Aug 1945. 1 p.
PIR	Ernst Zölling. 6 Sep 1945. 1 p.
PIR	Heinz Werner Bayreuther. 13 Sep 1945. 1 p.
PIR	Wilhelm Hoettl. 15 Sep 1945. 1 p.
PIR	Willi Otto Ledermann. 20 Sep 1945. 1 p.
PIR	Johann Arnold Quirin. 21 Sep 1945. 1 p.
PIR	Wilhelm Podein. 26 Sep 1945. 1 p.
PIR	Wilhelm Gerlich. 28 Sep 1945. 1 p.
SIR 1	Wilhelm Höttl. 14 Jul 1945. 4 pp.
IR 8	Robert Spies. 14 Jun 1945. 28 pp.
IR 10	§3: The Monitoring Services of the German Foreign Office. 21 Jun 1945. pp. 8–9, 9–13.
IR 11	Frontaufklärungskommandos in the East. 25 Jun 1945. 54 pp.
IR 12	§2: Notes on the Forschungsamt. 29 Jun 1945. 11 pp.
IR 14	§2: Abwehrstelle XII, Wiesbaden. 6 Jul 1945. 17–21 pp.
IR 15	The SD and the RSHA. (by Wilhelm Höttl). 9 Jul 1945. 67 pp.
IR 16	Amt VI of the RSHA. (by Wilhelm Höttl et al.). 13 Jul 1945. 76 pp.
IR 19	Frontaufklärungskommando 120. 16 Jul 1945. 13 pp.
IR 20	[Untitled]. 1. Radio Communications in the Abwehr. 2. The SD in Frankfurt/Main. 3. The Gestapo in Frankfurt/Main. 4. War Criminals. 27 pp.
IR 22	[Untitled]. 1. Frontaufklärungstrupp 318. 2. The Gestapo in Aachen. 3. Note on the Intelligence Service of German Firms. 5 pp.
IR 27	§1: Frontaufklärungskommando 130. 3 Aug 1945. pp. 2–9.
IR 31	§ II: Hungarian Intelligence Agencies. 19 Aug 1945. pp. 29–36.
IR 36	Japanese Intelligence Activities in Europe. (by Wilhelm Höttl). 31 Aug 1945. 3 pp.
IR 38	The Abwehr and the SD in Spain. 9 Sep 1945. 29 pp.
IR 42	Referat VI B 2 (France) of the RSHA. 10 Sep 1945. 7 pp.

SAIC

8	[on Gerhard Rühle]. 31 May 1945. 2 pp.
21	Information on the German Ministry of Posts. 24 May 1945. 9 pp.
23	[on Dr. Sigismund FitzRandolph, of Foreign Press Section of German Foreign Office]. 12 Jul 1945. 8 pp.
29	Brig. Gen. Makato Onodera. 28 May 1945. 5 pp.
47	The German Foreign Office and Its Press Section. 16 Jun 1945. 12 pp.

49	The Press Department of the German Foreign Office. 19 Jun 1945. 6 pp.
CIR/7	Forschungsamt RLM. 19 Jul 1945. 8 pp.
FIR/9	Amtsgruppe Ausland in the OKW. 14 Jul 1945. 4 pp.
FIR/10	Abwehr Personalities. 21 Jul 1945. 5 pp.
FIR/28	German Aerial Photo Service. 21 Aug 1945. 8 pp.
FIR/42	Koestring, Gen.d.Kav. CG of Volunteer Units. 11 Sep 1945. 7 pp.
R/2	Notes on the Red Army—Leadership and Tactics (by Reinhard Gehlen). 21 Jun 1945. 11 pp.
RIR/4	Abwehr Activities in Portugal. 29 Aug 1945. 3 pp.

7th Army, 307th CIC Detachment, Western Military District
FIR   Eugen Steimle. 12 Dec 1945. 62 pp.

US Strategic Air Forces in Europe, APWIU
    A.P.W.I.U.   (9th Air Force) 87/1945. Photogrammetry in the G.A.F. 7 Jul 1945. 7 pp.
    A.P.W.I.U.   (9th Air Force) 89/1945. G.A.F. Photo Intelligence (Field). 26 Jul 1945. 3 pp.
    A.P.W.I.U.   (9th Air Force) 90/1945. Organization of G.A.F. Photo Intelligence. 23 Jul 1945. 10 pp.

US HQ, Berlin District, IC
BDIC/FIR/27.   Mapping and Survey Section of the OKH. 3 Oct 1945. 5 pp.

[Originator not specified]
    AL-47   [untitled]. X. Superior quality of German weapons alleged. XIII. Admiration expressed for accurate Allied intelligence. pp. 1, 6, 7 only. 11 Jul 1944.
    AL-50   Information on the German FLUKO (Flugkommando—Flight Command) Mail and Organization in Italy from a former Italian NCO. 18 Aug 1944. 10 pp.
    AL-57   [untitled]. VII, Personalities allegedly holding high Abwehr (counterintelligence) rank. 4 Nov 1944. only pp. 1, 6.
    AL-70   Information on the Waffen SS, German Intelligence, Artillery Tactics, Delaying Actions and kindred subjects from an SS Standarten Fuehrer (Colonel) P/W captured 3 Jan 1945 in France. 8 Feb 1945. 4 pp.

[Originator not specified] MFIU
    PW   Intelligence Bulletin 2/47. 11. Auslandsbriefprüfstelle Hof. [no date]. pp. 8–9.
    PW   Intelligence Bulletin 2/46. 27. Engineer Listening Units. 21 March 1945. pp. 39–44 + drawings.
    PW   Intelligence Bulletin 2/51. 1. Reich Air Minister, Berlin. 12. US Signal Security. 8 April 1945. pp. 2, 10–11.

[Originator not specified]
PWUS-12.   German Radio Monitoring Service (B-Dienst). 19 Oct 1943. 3 pp.

Record Group 238. Interrogations for Nuremberg trials

Boetticher, Friedrich	Lahousen, Erwin
Bürkner, Leopold	Naujocks, Alfred
Ehlich, Hans	Ohnesorge, Wilhelm
Göring, Hermann	Paeffgen, Theodor
Grundherr, Werner von	Rühl, Felix
Guderian, Heinz	Schapper, Gottfried
Gyssling, Georg	Schellenberg, Walter
Hencke, Andor	Schmieden, Karl von
Höttl, Wilhelm	Six, Franz Alfred
Jodl, Alfred	Spacil, Josef
Jost, Heinz	Staubwasser, Anton
Kaltenbrunner, Ernst	Steengracht von Moyland, Adolf Paul
Krummacher, Friedrich-Alfred	Steimle, Eugen

Record Group 238. Trials of War Criminals before the Nuremberg Military Tribunals under Control Council Law No. 10. Affidavits and Documents

D-878	NG 3402	NG 5351	NI 8414	NO 763
	NG 3494	NG 5352	NI 8649	NO 2208
NG 163	NG 3981		NI 9827	NO 2894
NG 2209	NG 4581	NI 4875	NI 10551	NO 5036
NG 2316	NG 4588	NI 6544	NI 10577	
NG 2479	NG 4852	NI 7493	NI 15138	NOKW 3146
NG 3054	NG 4891	NI 8149		NOKW 3228

Record Group 238. Trials of War Criminals before the Nuremberg Military Tribunals under Control Council Law No. 10. Transcripts (English)

Case 6   (Farben Case)
Huenermann, Rudolf. pp. 3147–52, 13408–10, 13495–522.
Rietlinger, Anton. pp. 3153–66, 12910–53, 13075–92.

Case 9   (Einsatzgruppen Case)
Jost, Heinz. pp. 1128–239.
Sandberger, Martin. pp. 2141–420.

Case 11   (Ministries Case)
Etzdorf, Hasso von. pp. 9586–630.
Grothe, Bruno. pp. 2063–64.
Grundherr, Werner von. pp. 17854–97, 18085–161.
Mackensen, Wilhelm. pp. 11687–725.
Melchers, Wilhelm. pp. 19145–51.
Mirbach, Dietrich Freiherr von. pp. 10104–33.
Paeffgen, Theodor. pp. 12968–83.
Rintelen, Ernst von. pp. 17551–71.
Ritter, Karl. pp. 11743–79.
Schellenberg, Walter. pp. 5034–336.
Schoen, Wilhelm Albrecht Freiherr von. pp. 3196–224.
Selchow, Kurt. pp. 20458–83.
Thomsen, Hans. pp. 18183–89.
Tippelskirch, Werner von. pp. 1935–45.

[United States]. Naval Historical Division. Classified Operational Archives
USFET, MISC, Navy Section. R-3. Report on the Interrogation of P/W Vizeadmiral Leopold Buerkner. 1 December 1945. 20 pp.
ONI. Serial 176-C-48. Interrogation of Ex-Admiral Wenneker, German Naval Attaché at Tokyo. 26 April 1948. 16 pp.

Institut für Zeitgeschichte

ZS 207	Werner Best	ZS 1077	Andor Hencke
ZS 279	Eugen Ott	ZS 1409	Gottfried Schapper
ZS 291	Walter Schellenberg	ZS 1529	Josef Spacil
ZS 540	Conrad Patzig		

Author's Interviews

The post(s) listed for each individual is (are) the most germane for this study. The person rarely held it (them) for the entire war; usually others preceded or followed him.

Andrae, Kurt. Head of army's Main Intercept Post. 26 April 1970.
Baumbach, Norbert von. Naval attaché in Russia; head of naval intelligence. 21 June 1970.
Baumer, William H. Allied deception officer. 10 September 1976 (telephone).
Bitterl von Tessenberg, Max. Liaison of army radio intelligence to Foreign Armies East. 10 September 1973.

Blumröder, Hans-Adolf von. I c of Army Group South, later Army Group Don. 30 July 1970.

Borcherdt, Hans-Georg. Various posts in aerial reconnaissance. 10 October 1973.

Bottler, Alfred. Company and battalion commander. 4 May 1970.

Brucklacher, Walter A. Aerial mapping over Africa and Russia. 1 September 1973.

Budde, Wilhelm. Various posts in naval radio intelligence. 26 June 1970.

Bürkner, Leopold. Head of Department Ausland under Canaris in OKW. 19 June 1970.

Buntrock, Georg. I c of 9th Army; head of Front Reconnaissance (spy) units. 19 September 1973.

Buschenhagen, Erich. Founder and first head of army radio intelligence center. 22 March 1970.

Cavendish-Bentinck, Victor. Chairman of Joint Intelligence Committee, British Chiefs of Staff. 25 July 1974.

Dönitz, Karl. Commander of U-boats; commander in chief of navy. 20 August 1970.

Donat, Peterpaul von. French specialist in prewar Luftwaffe intelligence. 16 August 1970.

Doudot, Joseph M. French army counterespionage officer. 16 May 1969.

Duesterberg, Georg. Abwehr financial officer. 3 October 1973.

Euler, Richard. U.S. specialist in Foreign Armies West. 22 June 1970.

Fischer, Johannes. Aerial observer. 21 November 1969.

Fischer, Peter. Cryptanalyst in German forces in Africa. 15 April 1969.

Flesch, Herbert. Luftwaffe signals officer. Numerous conversations 1967–1974.

Franz, Wolfgang. Cryptanalyst in OKW Cipher Branch. 9 July 1970.

Friedrich, Rudolf. Head of Luftwaffe radio intelligence. 12 May 1970.

Garder, Michel. French army counterespionage officer. 15 May 1969.

Gehlen, Reinhard. Head of Foreign Armies East. 2 August 1970, 22 September 1973.

Gersdorff, Rudolf-Christian Freiherr von. I c of Army Group Center. 11 March 1970.

Geyr von Schweppenburg, Leo Freiherr. Military attaché in Great Britain. 28 July 1970.

Gorman, William. Ex-husband of Nele Kapp. 7 May 1977 (telephone).

Grosskopf, Friedrich. Abwehr specialist in technical air intelligence. 6 October 1973.

Halder, Franz. Chief of the German general staff. 12 May 1970.

Hagemann, Rudolf. Adjutant in 102nd Infantry Division. 7 October 1973.

Hammerstein, Kunrat Freiherr von. Member of an armored reconnaissance unit. 6 October 1973.

Hauck, Friedrich Wilhelm. Commander of an infantry division. 26 April 1970.

Heidelauf, Ulrich. Expert in aerial mapping and photography. 17 February 1973 (telephone).

Herberg, Frederico. Head of administrative section, Foreign Armies West. 24 September 1969.

Heusinger, Adolf. Head of Operations Branch, German general staff. 8 October 1973.

Höttl, Wilhelm. Head of southeast Europe section, Nazi foreign intelligence. 15 September 1973.

Hüttenhain, Erich. Cryptanalyst in OKW Cipher Branch. 5 October 1973.

Kettler, Hugo. Head of OKW Cipher Branch. 30 August 1967.

Kirsch, Johannes. Head of OKW economic intelligence. 12 October 1973.

Knemeyer, Siegfried. Pilot in Rowehl reconnaissance squadron. 27 June 1975 (telephone).

Krämer, Karl-Heinz. Contact man for spy JOSEFINE. 22 August 1970.

Kramarz, Hans. Head of Foreign Office's military liaison desk. 11 May 1970.

Kupfer, Max. Head of naval radio intelligence. 27 June 1970.

Langer, Isolde. Widow of cryptanalyst Albert Langer in Nazi foreign intelligence. 14 September 1973.

Manstein, Erich von. Commander of several armies and army groups. 3 August 1970.

Manteuffel, Hasso von. Commander of armored divisions and of an army. 29 July 1970.

Masterman, John. British counterespionage official. 17 November 1972.

Matzky, Gerhard. Assistant chief of the general staff for intelligence. 9 May 1970, 7 October 1973.

Mauler, Eugen. Cryptanalyst in OKW Cipher Branch. 11 September 1973.

Maurer, Helmut. Neighbor and assistant of Canaris. 27 and 30 August 1973.

Metz, Lothar. Head of French section and deputy chief, Foreign Armies West. 3 August 1970.

Meyer-Detring, Wilhelm. I c to commander in chief west. 3 August 1970.

Mitzlaff, Bernd von. Various posts in armored reconnaissance. 8 October 1973.

Mügge, Karl-Albert. Head of a radio reconnaissance unit. 30 September 1969.

Müller, Albert. Head of Abwehr secret ink and false document section. 22 March and 12 April 1970.

Nebel, Fritz. World War I cryptologist and radio officer. 4 October 1973.

Neeb, Fritz. Operating head, Army Group Center radio intelligence. 30 December 1972.

Noack, Kurt. Staff officer in aerial reconnaissance; air liaison to 9th Army. 10 October 1973.

Ott, Eugen. Officer in Minister's Department; military attaché in Japan. 20 September 1973.

Owe, Herbert. Head of Anglo-American section, Luftwaffe intelligence. 31 August 1973.

Paschke, Adolf. Section head in Foreign Office codebreaking unit. 9 May 1970.

Patzig, Conrad. Head of the Abwehr before Canaris. 24 August 1973.

Praun, Albert. Head of army signals. 30 and 31 August 1967, 4 August 1970.

Primavesi, Ernst. Air force liaison to Foreign Armies East. 12 September 1973.

Ritter, Nikolaus. Spymaster in Hamburg against England and America. 24 August 1973.

Rowehl, Theo. Head of air force strategic reconnaissance unit. 11 October 1973.

Rudloff, Hans-Jochen. Abwehr sabotage officer. 28 July 1970.

Ruef, Hans. Various posts in aerial photography. 15 and 16 September 1973.

Ruge, Friedrich. Various posts in German naval staffs and commands. 22 April 1970.

Sachsenheimer, Rose. Secretary in Abwehr headquarters. 20 April 1970.

Sayffaerth, Gerhard. Abwehr officer at central against Russia. 20 September 1973.

Schaedel, Herbert. Archivist for OKW Cipher Branch. 29 July 1969.

Scherschmidt, Herman. Cryptanalyst in Foreign Office. 22 February 1970.

Schierbrandt, Hans von. Head of press evaluation in Department Ausland of OKW. 10 October 1973.

Schmidt, Herbert. Radio direction-finder. 30 January 1970.

Schüddekopf, Otto-Ernst. Head of England section in Nazi foreign intelligence. 3 July 1970.

Schwabe, Wilhelm. Naval cryptanalyst. 26 June 1970, 21 August 1970.

Schwenke, Dietrich H. Head of air technical intelligence. 18 September 1973.

Seifert, Walther. Head of evaluation in Forschungsamt. 19 August 1970, 10 October 1973.

Seubert, Franz. Various posts in Abwehr. 11 March 1970.

Seul, Helmut. Head of the Army Group Center false documents section. 3 October 1973 (telephone).

Speer, Albert. Friend of Hitler; minister of armaments. 15 August 1970.

Speidel, Hans. Section head in Foreign Armies; chief of staff to Rommel in France. 17 August 1970.

Staubwasser, Anton. British specialist in Foreign Armies West; I c to Rommel in France. 9 March 1970.

Steimle, Eugen. Head of Western Europe section in Nazi foreign intelligence. 2 October 1973.

Stoephasius, Werner. Neighbor and subordinate of Canaris. 25 August 1973.

Stützel, Hermann. World War I army cryptanalyst. 28 January 1970.

Süsskind-Schwendi, Hugo Freiherr von. I c for OKW Operations Staff. 29 July 1970.

Trager, Herbert F. Mapping specialist. 7 April 1972.

Tranow, Wilhelm. Head of cryptanalysis for naval radio intelligence. 1 and 2 July 1970.

Trautmann, Werner. Head of Abwehr radio station for England and the Americas. 20 August 1970.
Vetterlein, Kurt. Head of transatlantic radiotelephone unscrambling. 1 September 1967.
Wagner, Otto. Head of Abwehr post in Sofia. 22 July 1970, 27 June 1974.
Warlimont, Walter. Deputy head of OKW Operations Staff. 10 March 1970, 22 September 1973.
Weber, Franz Konrad. Son-in-law of Andreas Figl, cryptanalyst for Nazi foreign intelligence. 15 September 1973.
Weber, Harvey. Allied aerial photographer. 16 August 1971.
Wedemeyer, A. C. U.S. officer who attended German War Academy. 11 April 1972.
Weidemann, Kurt. Abwehr officer in France. 5 July 1970.
Westphal, Siegfried. Chief of staff to Rommel in Africa and Rundstedt in France. 11 May 1970.
Wiebe, Horst. Head of a radio intelligence company in France. 1 October 1969.
Williams, Edgar T. Montgomery's intelligence officer. 30 November and 15 December 1972.
Zimmermann, Fritz. Instructor in evaluating aerial photography. 21 September 1973.

Historical and Other Studies: Published

Abshagen, Karl Heinz. *Canaris.* trans. Alan Houghton Brodrick. London: Hutchinson, 1956. 264 pp.
Absolon, Rudolf. *Die Wehrmacht im Dritten Reich.* Schriften des Bundesarchivs, 16. Boppard am Rhein: Harald Boldt, 1969– . 3 vols.
Allied Expeditionary Forces, Supreme Headquarters. Office of Assistant Chief of Staff, G-2. Counter-Intelligence Sub-Division. Evaluation and Dissemination Section. *German Intelligence Services.* EDS/G/7. [by H. R. Trevor-Roper]. 4 October 1944. 32 pp.
Allied Expeditionary Forces, Supreme Headquarters. Counter-Intelligence War Room, London. *The German Intelligence Service.* [by H. R. Trevor-Roper]. April 1945. 30 pp.
Aronson, Schlomo. *Reinhard Heydrich und die Frühgeschichte von Gestapo und SD.* Studien zur Zeitgeschichte (Institut für Zeitgeschichte). Stuttgart: Deutsche Verlags-Anstalt, 1971. 340 pp.
"Die Aufklärungszüge der Inf. Regt. 1941/1942." *Feldgrau,* 5 (1957), 132–33.
Augier, Marc. *Les Voiliers fantômes d'Hitler: Aventures vécues.* Paris: Presses de la Cité, 1973. 283 pp.
Bamler, Rudolf. "Der deutsche militärische Geheimdienst bei der Vorbereitung und Durchführung des zweiten Weltkrieges—Tabu der westdeutschen Geschichtsschreibung." In Kommission der Historiker der DDR und der UdSSR. *Probleme der Geschichte des zweiten Weltkrieges.* Protokoll der wissenschaftlichen Tagung in Leipzig vom 25. bis 30. November 1957. ed. Leo Stern. Berlin: Akademie-Verlag, 1958. 2:439–46.
Barraclough, Geoffrey. *The Origins of Modern Germany.* Oxford: Blackwell, 1947, reprinted 1972. 481 pp.
Baumbach, Werner. *Zu Spät? Aufstieg und Untergang der deutschen Luftwaffe.* Munich: Pflaum, 1949. 328 pp.
Bartz, Karl. *The Downfall of the German Secret Service.* trans. Edward Fitzgerald. London: Kimber, 1956. 202 pp.
Benzing, Klaus. *Der Admiral: Leben und Wirken.* Nördlingen: Engelhardt, 1973. 216 pp.
Besymenski, Lew. *Sonderakte "Barbarossa": Dokumente, Darstellung, Deutung.* Stuttgart: Deutsche Verlags-Anstalt, 1968. 352 pp.
Boelcke, Willi A. "Das 'Seehaus' in Berlin-Wannsee: Zur Geschichte des deutschen 'Monitoring-Service' während des zweiten Weltkrieges." *Jahrbuch für die Geschichte Mittel- und Ostdeutschlands,* 23 (1974), 233–69.

————. "Presseabteilungen und Pressearchive des Auswärtigen Amts, 1871–1945." *Archivmitteilungen*, 9 (1959), 43–48.

Bonatz, Heinz. *Die deutsche Marine-Funkaufklärung 1914–1945*. Beiträge zur Wehrforschung, XX/XXI. Darmstadt: Wehr und Wissen, 1970. 174 pp.

Borcherdt, [Hans-Georg]. "Die Heeres-Luftaufklärung bis 1918," *Kampftruppen* (Februar 1965), 16–19; "Die Heeres-Luftaufklärung bis 1918 (II)," *ibid.* (April 1965), 57–58; "Die Heeres-Luftaufklärung nach 1918—ein geschichtlicher Rückblick (III)," *ibid.* (Juni 1965), 83–85; "Die Heeres-Luftaufklärung nach 1918—ein geschichtlicher Rückblick (IV)," *ibid.* (August 1965), 111–12.

————. "Luftaufklärung für das XXIV. Panzerkorps 1941." *Kampftruppen* (März/April 1963), 12–13.

Bracher, Karl Dietrich. *The German Dictatorship: The Origins, Structure, and Effects of National Socialism.* trans. Jean Steinberg. New York: Praeger, 1970. 553 pp.

Brausch, Gerd. "Sedan 1940: Deuxième Bureau und strategische Überraschung." *Militärgeschichtliche Mitteilungen* (2/1967), 15–92.

Broszat, Martin. *Der Staat Hitlers.* dtv-Weltgeschichte des 20. Jahrhunderts, 9. Munich: Deutscher Taschenbuch Verlag, 1969. 473 pp.

Brown, MacAlister. "The Third Reich's Mobilization of the German Fifth Column in Eastern Europe." *Journal of Central European Affairs*, 19 (July 1959), 128–48.

Buchheim, Hans. *Die SS—Das Herrschaftsinstrument: Befehl und Gehorsam.* Anatomie des SS-Staates, I. Olten und Freiburg im Breisgau: Walter, 1965. 390 pp.

Buchheit, Gert. *Der deutsche Geheimdienst: Geschichte der militärischen Abwehr.* Munich: List, 1966. 495 pp.

Bullock, Alan. *Hitler: A Study in Tyranny.* Completely revised edition. New York: Harper & Row, 1962. 848 pp.

Butler, J. R. M. *Grand Strategy, 2: September 1939–June 1941.* History of the Second World War: United Kingdom Military Series. ed. J. R. M. Butler. HMSO, 1957. 603 pp.

Carrias, Eugène. *La Pensée militaire allemande.* Paris: Presses Universitaire de France, 1948. 400 pp.

Carsten, F. L. *The Reichswehr and Politics, 1918 to 1933.* Oxford: Clarendon Press, 1966. 427 pp.

Cave Brown, Anthony. *Bodyguard of Lies.* New York: Harper & Row, 1975. 947 pp.

Chamberlain, Peter; Chris Ellis; and John Batchelor. *German Fighting Vehicles 1939–1945.* Parnell's History of the World Wars Special. London: Phoebus, 1975. 64 pp.

Charisius, Albrecht, and Julius Mader. *Nicht Länger Geheim: Entwicklung, System und Arbeitsweise des imperialistischen deutschen Geheimdienstes.* Berlin: Deutscher Militärverlag, 1969. 632 pp.

Coakley, Robert W., and Richard M. Leighton. *Global Logistics and Strategy, 1943–1945.* United States Army in World War II: The War Department. (Department of the Army: Office of the Chief of Military History.) GPO, 1968. 889 pp.

Colvin, Ian. *Chief of Intelligence.* London: Gollancz, n.d. 224 pp.

Compton, James V. *The Swastika and the Eagle: Hitler, the United States, and the Origins of World War II.* Boston: Houghton Mifflin, 1967. 297 pp.

Craig, Gordon A. "The German Foreign Office from Neurath to Ribbentrop," in *The Diplomats 1919–1939*, ed. Gordon A. Craig and Felix Gilbert. Princeton: Princeton University Press, 1953. pp. 406–36.

————. *The Politics of the Prussian Army 1640–1945.* Oxford: Oxford University Press, 1955. 538 pp.

Cron, Hermann. *Die Organisation des deutschen Heeres im Weltkrieg.* Forschungen und Darstellungen aus dem Reichsarchiv, 5. ESM: 1923. 208 pp.

Davidson, Eugene. *The Trial of the Germans: An Account of the twenty-two defendants before the International Military Tribunal at Nuremberg.* New York: Macmillan, 1966. 636 pp.

Deakin, F. W. *The Brutal Friendship: Mussolini, Hitler and the Fall of Italian Fascism.* London: Weidenfeld & Nicolson, 1962. 896 pp.

Delmer, Sefton. *The Counterfeit Spy.* New York: Harper & Row, 1971. 256 pp.

Demeter, Karl. *The German Officer-Corps in Society and State 1650–1945.* trans. Angus Malcolm. London: Weidenfeld & Nicolson, 1965. 414 pp.

Desai, Makesh M. *Surprise.* The British Journal of Psychology: Monograph Supplements, 22. Cambridge: University Press, 1939. 124 pp.

Deutsch, Karl W. *The Nerves of Government: Models of Political Communication and Control.* London: The Free Press of Glencoe, 1963. 316 pp.

Dieckhoff, Gerhard. *3. Infanterie-Division, 3. Infanterie-Division (mot.), 3. Panzergrenadier-Division.* Göttingen: Borries, 1960. 428 pp.

Dubois, Josiah E., Jr., in collaboration with Edward Johnson. *Generals in Grey Suits: The Directors of the International "I. G. Farben" Cartel, their conspiracy and trial at Nuremberg.* London: Bodley Head, 1953. 374 pp.

"Dulag Luft: The Third Reich's Prison Camp for Airmen." ed. Philip M. Flammer. *Aerospace Historian,* 19 (June 1972), 58–62.

Dvornik, Francis. *Origins of Intelligence Services: The Ancient Near East, Persia, Greece, Rome, Byzantium, the Arab Muslim Empires, the Mongol Empire, China, Muscovy.* New Brunswick, N.J.: Rutgers University Press, 1974. 334 pp.

Eichholtz, Dietrich, and Wolfgang Schumann. *Anatomie des Krieges: Neue Dokumente über die Rolle des deutschen Monopolkapitals bei der Vorbereitung and Durchführung des zweiten Weltkrieges.* Berlin: VEB Deutscher Verlag der Wissenschaften, 1969. 524 pp.

Ellis, L. F. *Victory in the West.* History of the Second World War: United Kingdom Military Series. ed. Sir James Butler. HMSO, 1962–68. 2 vols.

Erasmus, Johannes. *Der Geheime Nachrichtendienst.* Göttinger Beiträge für Gegenwartsfragen, 6 (Institut für Völkerrecht an der Universität Göttingen). Göttingen: Musterschmidt, 1952. 89 pp.

Erickson, John. "The Red Army Before June 1941." *St. Antony's Papers,* 12: Soviet Affairs, 3. ed. David Footman. London: Chatto & Windus, 1962. pp. 94–121.

————. *The Soviet High Command: A Political-Military History, 1918–1941.* New York: St. Martin's, 1962. 889 pp.

Erfurth, Waldemar. *Die Geschichte des deutschen Generalstabes von 1918 bis 1945.* Studien zur Geschichte des Zweiten Weltkrieges, 1 (Arbeitskreis für Wehrforschung). Göttingen: Musterschmidt, 1957. 326 pp.

Ewald, Gustav. "Die Schaffung des Luftlagebildes." *Der Luftwaffenring* (September 1953), unpaged.

Eyermann, Karl-Heinz. *Luftspionage.* Berlin: Deutscher Militärverlag, 1963. 2 vols.

Farago, Ladislas. *The Game of the Foxes: The Untold Story of German Espionage in the United States and Great Britain During World War II.* New York: McKay, 1971. 695 pp.

"La Farce des Services Secrets." *Crapouillot,* No. 15 (1951). 64 pp.

"Fernmelde-Aufklärung." *Allgemeine Schweizerische Militär-Zeitschrift* (1952), 747–57.

Fink, Carl. "Die Entwicklung des militärischen deutschen Luftbildwesens 1911–1918." *Wehrwissenschaftliche Rundschau,* 10 (Juli 1960), 390–99.

Firmin, Stanley. *They Came to Spy.* London: Hutchinson, n.d. 156 pp.

Flicke, Wilhelm F. *War Secrets in the Ether.* trans. Ray W. Pettengill. Washington: National Security Agency, 1954. 305 pp. Reprinted Laguna Hills, Calif.: Aegean Park Press, 1977. 2 vols.

Förster, Gerhard, and Heinz Helmert, Helmut Otto, Helmut Schnitter. *Der preussisch-deutsche Generalstab 1640–1965: Zu seiner politischen Rolle in der Geschichte.* Berlin: Dietz, 1966. 575 pp.

Freud, Hans. "OKW Amt für Auslandsnachrichten/Abwehr." *Feldgrau,* 11 (1 Dezember 1963), 184–87.

Friedheim, Eric. "Welcome to Dulag Luft." *Air Force,* 28 (September 1945), 16–17, 73.

Friedländer, Saul. *Prelude to Downfall: Hitler and the United States, 1939–1941.* trans. Aline B. and Alexander Werth. New York: Knopf, 1967. 338 pp.

Froben, Hans Joachim. *Aufklärende Artillerie: Geschichte der Beobachtungsabteilungen und selbständigen Beobachtungsbatterien bis 1945.* Munich: Schild-Verlag, 1972. 983 pp.

Fromm, Erich. *The Anatomy of Human Destructiveness.* New York: Holt, Rinehart and Winston, 1973. 521 pp.

————. *Escape from Freedom.* New York: Holt, Rinehart and Winston, 1941. 305 pp.

Frye, Alton. *Nazi Germany and the American Hemisphere, 1933–1941.* Yale Historical Publications, Miscellany 86. New Haven: Yale University Press, 1967. 229 pp.

Funk, Arthur L. "Torch: les opérations de diversion alliées et les renseignements de l'Axe." *Revue Historique de l'Armée,* 29 (1973), 78–87.

Gatzke, Hans W. "Russo-German Military Cooperation during the Weimar Republic." *American Historical Review,* 63 (April 1958), 565–97.

"German Aerial Cameras Spy Out the Military Secrets of Britain." *Life,* 7 (18 December 1939), 13–17.

"German Espionage and Sabotage Against the United States." *ONI Review* (January 1946), 33–38.

[Germany.] Militärgeschichtliches Forschungsamt. *Handbuch zur deutschen Militärgeschichte, 1648–1939.* Frankfurt am Main: Bernard & Graefe, 1964– . 4 vols.

[————.] Heeres, Oberkommando des. *Tag und Nacht am Feind: Aufklärungs-Abteilungen im Westen.* Gütersloh: Bertelsmann, 1942. 294 pp.

Gerth, Hans. "The Nazi Party: Its Leadership and Composition." *The American Journal of Sociology,* 45 (January 1940), 517–41.

Geyr von Schweppenburg, Leo Freiherr. "Militär-Attachés." *Wehrwissenschaftliche Rundschau,* 11 (1961), 695–703.

"Gliederung und Aufgaben der Aufklärungsfliegerverbande des Generals der Luftwaffe beim Oberbefehlshaber des Heeres vor und im Zweiten Weltkrieg." *Mitteilungen* (Militärgeschichtliches Forschungsamt), No. 13 (Dezember 1961), 1–4.

"Zur Gliederung der Div.-Aufklärungsabteilungen." *Feldgrau,* 3 (November 1955), 155–56.

Goerlitz, Walter. *History of the German General Staff 1657–1945.* trans. Brian Battershaw. New York: Praeger, 1957. 508 pp.

Graham, Robert A. "Espions Nazis au Vatican pendant la IIᵉ Guerre Mondiale." *La Documentation Catholique,* 68 (5 avril 1970), 331–36.

Green, William. *Warplanes of the Third Reich.* London: Macdonald, 1970. 672 pp.

Greenfield, Kent Roberts, ed. *Command Decisions.* Department of the Army: Office of the Chief of Military History. GPO, 1960. 565 pp.

Greiner, Helmuth. *Die Oberste Wehrmachtführung 1939–1943.* Wiesbaden: Limes, 1951. 444 pp.

Grossmann, Horst. *Geschichte der rheinisch-westfalischen 6. Infanterie-Division 1939–1945.* Bad Nauheim: Podzun, 1958. 318 pp.

Grosvenor, Gilbert. "Insignia of the United States Armed Forces." *The National Geographic Magazine,* 83 (June 1943), 651, 656–714, Plates I–XXXII.

————. *Insignia and Decorations of the U.S. Armed Forces.* rev. ed. Washington: National Geographic Society, 1945. 208 pp.

Gunzenhauser, Max. *Geschichte des geheimen Nachrichtendienstes (Spionage, Sabotage und Abwehr): Literaturbericht und Bibliographie.* Schriften der Bibliothek für Zeitgeschichte, 7. Frankfurt am Main: Bernard & Graefe, 1968. 434 pp.

Gwyer, J. M. A., and J. R. M. Butler. *Grand Strategy, 3: June 1941–August 1942.* History of the Second World War: United Kingdom Military Series. ed. J. R. M. Butler. HMSO, 1964. 783 pp.

Hackworth, Green Haywood. *Digest of International Law.* 4 (Department of State Publication 1756) and 6 (Department of State Publication 1961). GPO: 1941 and 1943. pp. 949 and 655.

Haenschke, Wilhelm. "Die Luftnachrichtentruppe 1944 im Westen," *Wehrkunde,* 4 (März 1955), 91–98, (April 1955), 141–48.

Haas, Gerhart. *Von München bis Pearl Harbor: Zur Geschichte der deutsch-amerikanischen Beziehungen 1938–1941.* Deutsche Akademie der Wissenschaften zu

Berlin, Schriften des Instituts für Geschichte. Reihe I: Allgemeine und Deutsche Geschichte, 29. Berlin: Akademie, 1965. 278 pp.

Hepp, Leo. "Die Funkaufklärung." *Wehrwissenschaftliche Rundschau*, 6 (Juni 1956), 285–98.

Hertel, Werner. *Beobachtungsabteilung 6 1936–1945: Werdegang und Weg einer Heerestruppe.* Dülmen: Laumann, 1965. 178 pp.

Herwig, Holger H. *Politics of Frustration: The United States in German Naval Planning, 1889–1941.* Boston: Little, Brown, 1976. 323 pp.

————. "Prelude to *Weltblitzkrieg:* Germany's Naval Policy toward the United States of America." *The Journal of Modern History*, 43 (December 1971), 649–68.

Heymont, Irving. *Combat Intelligence in Modern Warfare.* Harrisburg: Stackpole, 1960. 244 pp.

Hilberg, Raul. *The Destruction of the European Jews.* London: W. H. Allen, 1961. 788 pp.

Hildebrand, K. "Le Programme de Hitler et sa realisation." *Revue d'histoire de la deuxième guerre mondiale*, 21 (octobre 1971), 7–36.

Hill, Leonidas E. "The Wilhelmstrasse in the Nazi Era." *Political Science Quarterly*, 82 (December 1967), 546–70.

Hillgruber, Andreas. "Die 'Endlosung' und das deutsche Ost-imperium als Kernstück des rassenideologischen Programms des Nationalsozialismus." *Vierteljahreshefte für Zeitgeschichte*, 20 (April 1972), 133–53.

————. "Der Faktor Amerika in Hitlers Strategie 1938–1941." *Aus Politik und Zeitgeschichte*, B 19/66 (11. Mai 1966). 21 pp.

————. *Hitlers Strategie: Politik und Kriegführung 1940–1941.* Frankfurt am Main: Bernard & Graefe, 1965. 715 pp.

———— and Gerhard Hümmelchen. *Chronik des Zweiten Weltkrieges.* (Arbeitskreis für Wehrforschung). Frankfurt am Main: Bernard & Graefe, 1966. 196 pp.

Hinsley, F. H. *Hitler's Strategy.* Cambridge: University Press, 1951. 254 pp.

[Hintze, Otto]. *The Historical Essays of Otto Hintze.* ed. Felix Gilbert. New York: Oxford University Press, 1975. 493 pp.

Hirszowicz, Łukasz. *The Third Reich and the Arab East.* London: Routledge & Kegan Paul, 1966. 403 pp.

Hittle, J. D. *The Military Staff: Its History and Development.* Harrisburg: Military Service, 1944. 201 pp.

Höhn, Hans, ed. *Auf Antisowjetischem Kriegskurs: Studien zur militärischen Vorbereitung des deutschen Imperialismus auf die Aggression gegen die UdSSR (1933–1941).* Schriften des Deutschen Instituts für Militärgeschichte. Berlin: Deutscher Militärverlag, 1970. 478 pp.

Höhne, Heinz. *Canaris: Patriot im Zwielicht.* Munich: Bertelsmann, 1976. 607 pp.

————. *The Order of the Death's Head: The Story of Hitler's S.S.* trans. Richard Barry. New York: Coward-McCann, 1970. 690 pp.

————, and Hermann Zolling. *The General was a Spy: The truth about General Gehlen and his spy network.* trans. Richard Barry. London: Pan Books, 1971. 347 pp.

Hoffmann, Karl Otto. *Ln: Die Geschichte der Luftnachrichtentruppe.* Neckargemünd: Vowinckel, 1965–73. 3 vols.

Hoffmann, Peter. *Widerstand, Staatsreich, Attentat: Der Kampf der Opposition gegen Hitler.* Munich: Piper, 1969. 988 pp.

Horn, Wolfgang. *Führerideologie und Parteiorganisation in der NSDAP (1919–1933).* Geschichtliche Studien zu Politik und Gesellschaft, 3. Düsseldorf: Droste, 1972. 451 pp.

Höttl, Wilhelm [pseud. Walter Hagen]. *Die Geheime Front: Organisation, Personen und Aktionen des deutschen Geheimdienstes.* Zürich: Europa, 1950. 515 pp.

————. *The Secret Front: The Story of Nazi Political Espionage.* trans. R. H. Stevens. New York: Praeger, 1954. 327 pp.

————. *Unternehmen Bernhard: Ein historischer Tatsachenbericht über die grösste Geldfalschungsaktion aller Zeiten.* Wels: Welsermühl, 1955. 291 pp.

Howard, Michael. *Grand Strategy, 4: August 1942–September 1943.* History of the

Second World War: United Kingdom Military Series. ed. J. R. M. Butler. HMSO, 1972. 773 pp.

―――. "Hitler and His Generals." in *Studies in War and Peace*. London: Temple Smith, 1970. pp. 110–21.

―――. *War in European History*. Oxford: Oxford University Press, 1976. 165 pp.

―――, ed. *The Theory and Practice of War: Essays Presented to Captain B. H. Liddell Hart*. London: Cassell, 1965. 377 pp.

Howe, George F. *Northwest Africa: Seizing the Initiative in the West*. United States Army in World War II: The Mediterranean Theater of Operations. (Department of the Army: Office of the Chief of Military History.) GPO, 1957. 748 pp.

Hubatsch, Walther. *Der Admiralstab und die Obersten Marinebehörden in Deutschland, 1848–1945*. Frankfurt am Main: Bernard & Graefe, 1958. 269 pp.

Hümmelchen, Gerhard. "Die Luftstreitkräfte der UdSSR am 22.6.1941 in Spiegel der sowjetischen Kriegsliteratur." *Wehrwissenschaftliche Rundschau*, 20 (Juni 1970), 325–31.

Irvine, Dallas D. "The French and Prussian Staff Systems before 1870." *The Journal of the American Military History Foundation*, 2 (Winter 1938), 192–203.

―――. "The Origin of Capital Staffs." *The Journal of Modern History*, 10 (June 1938), 161–79.

Irving, David. *Hitler's War*. New York: Viking, 1977. 926 pp.

―――. *The Rise and Fall of the Luftwaffe: The Life of Luftwaffe Marshal Erhard Milch*. London: Weidenfeld and Nicolson, 1973. 451 pp.

―――, ed. *Breach of Security: The German Secret Intelligence File on Events Leading to the Second World War*. Introduction by D. C. Watt. London: Kimber, 1968. 216 pp.

Jacobsen, Hans-Adolf. *Nationalsozialistische Aussenpolitik 1933–1938*. Frankfurt am Main: Metzner, 1968. 944 pp.

Janowitz, Morris. *The Professional Soldier: A Social and Political Portrait*. Glencoe, Ill.: Free Press, 1960. 464 pp.

―――. *Sociology and the Military Establishment*. New York: Russell Sage Foundation, 1959. 112 pp.

Jany, Curt. *Geschichte der Königlich-Preussischen Armee*. 5: Hermann Cron, *Geschichte des Deutschen Heeres im Weltkriege 1914–1918*. Berlin: Siegismund, 1928–37. 5 vols.

de Jong, Louis. *The German Fifth Column in the Second World War*. trans. C. M. Geyl. Chicago: University of Chicago Press, 1956. 308 pp.

Kahn, David. *The Codebreakers: The Story of Secret Writing*. New York: Macmillan, 1967. 1164 pp.

Kehr, Eckhart. *Der Primat der Innenpolitik: Gesammelte Aufsätze zur preussisch-deutschen Sozialgeschichte im 19. und 20. Jahrhundert*. Veröffentlichungen der Historischen Kommission zu Berlin, 19. Berlin: de Gruyter, 1970. 292 pp.

Kehrig, Manfred. *Stalingrad: Analyse und Dokumentation einer Schlacht*. Beiträge zur Militär- und Kriegsgeschichte, 15 (Militärgeschichtliches Forschungsamt). Stuttgart: Deutsche Verlags-Anstalt, 1974. 680 pp.

―――. *Die Wiedereinrichtung des deutschen militärischen Attachédienstes nach dem Ersten Weltkrieg (1919–1933)*. Militärgeschichtliche Studie, 2. (Militärgeschichtliches Forschungsamt). Boppard am Rhein: Boldt, 1966. 254 pp.

Keilig, Wolf. *Das Deutsche Heer, 1939–1945*. Bad Nauheim: Podzun, 1956. 3 vols.

Kens, Karlheinz, and Heinz J. Nowarra. *Die deutschen Flugzeuge 1933–1945: Deutschlands Luft-Entwicklung bis zum Ende des Zweiten Weltkrieges*. 2nd ed. Munich: J. F. Lehmanns, 1964. 940 pp.

Kent, George O. "Britain in the Winter of 1940–41 as seen from the Wilhelmstrasse." *Historical Journal*, 6 (January 1963), 120–30.

Kling. "Die Formationsveränderungen der Kavallerie und Reiter-Regimenter im 2. Weltkrieg." *Feldgrau*, 2 (Juli 1954), 79–80.

Koch, Horst-Adalbert. "Die organisatorische Entwicklung der deutschen Panzertruppen." *Feldgrau*, 2 (Juli 1954), 69–74, (September 1954), 101–104; 3 (Januar

1955), 16–18, (März 1955), 38–39, (Mai 1955), 56–57, (Juli 1955), 96–97, (September 1955), 124, (November 1955), 154–56.

Koehl, Robert. "Feudal Aspects of National Socialism." *The American Political Science Review*, 54 (December 1960), 921–33.

König, Walter. "Deutscher Flugmeldedienst am Kanal 1940–1944." *Wehrkunde*, 3 (April 1954), 119–23.

Konus, Kord. "I c-Dienst bei Höheren Kommandobehörden des Heeres im Ostfeldzug." *Wehrwissenschaftliche Rundschau*, 2 (1952), 394–402.

Krausnick, Helmut. "Canaris, Wilhelm Franz." *Neue Deutsche Biographie*, 3 (1957), 116–18.

Leighton, Richard M., and Robert W. Coakley. *Global Logistics and Strategy, 1940–1943*. United States Army in World War II: The War Department (Department of the Army: Office of the Chief of Military History). GPO, 1955. 780 pp.

Lerner, Daniel, with Ithiel de Sola Pool and George K. Schueller. *The Nazi Elite*. Hoover Institute Studies, Series B: Elite Studies, 3. Stanford: Stanford University Press, 1951. 112 pp.

Lettow-Vorbeck, [Paul Emile] von, ed. *Die Weltkriegspionage*. Munich: Justin Moser, 1931. 688 pp.

Leverkuehn, Paul. *German Military Intelligence*. trans. R. H. Stevens and Constantine FitzGibbon. London: Weidenfeld & Nicolson, 1954. 209 pp.

Liddell Hart, B. H. "Hitler as War Lord." *Encounter*, 30 (January 1968), 69–71.

———. *The Other Side of the Hill: Germany's Generals, Their Rise and Fall, with their own account of military events, 1939–1945*. London: Cassell, 1948. 320 pp.

Liss, Ulrich. "Der entscheidende Wert richtiger Feindbeurteilung." *Wehrkunde*, "I: Beispiele aus der neueren Kriegsgeschichte," 8 (November 1959), 584–92; "II: Gedanken zum G 2-Dienst," 8 (Dezember 1959), 638–44. Cited as Liss, "entscheidende Wert."

———. "Erfahrungen im Feindnachrichtendienst aus drei Armeen: III: Erfahrungen." *Wehrkunde*, 10 (Dezember 1961), 649–51. Cited as Liss, "Erfahrungen."

———. "Erfahrungen und Gedanken zum I c-Wesen." *Wehrwissenschaftliche Rundschau*, 7 (1957), 616–27. Cited as Liss, "Erfahrungen." (Pages differ from above.)

Lohmann, Walter, and Hans H. Hildebrand. *Die Deutsche Kriegsmarine 1939–1945: Gliederung, Einsatz, Stellenbesetzung*. Bad Nauheim: Podzun, 1956. 3 vols.

Ludwig, Karl-Heinz. *Technik und Ingenieure im Dritten Reich*. Düsseldorf: Droste, 1974. 544 pp.

Mader, Julius. *Der Banditenschatz: Ein Dokumentarbericht über Hitlers geheimen Gold- und Waffenschatz*. Berlin: Deutscher Militärverlag, 1965. 386 pp.

———. *Hitlers Spionagegenerale sagen aus: Ein Dokumentarbericht über Aufbau, Struktur und Operationen des OKW-Geheimdienstamtes Ausland/Abwehr mit einer Chronologie seiner Einsätze von 1933 bis 1944*. 5th ed. Berlin: Verlag der Nation, 1973. 475 pp.

Mäkelä, Jukka L. *Im Rücken des Feindes: Der finnische Nachrichtendienst im Krieg*. Frauenfeld: Huber, 1967. 206 pp.

Mason, Timothy W. *Arbeiterklasse und Volksgemeinschaft: Dokumente und Materialen zur deutschen Arbeiterpolitik, 1936–1939*. Schriften des Zentralinstituts für Sozialwissenschaftliche Forschung der Freien Universität Berlin, 22. Opladen: Westdeutscher Verlag, 1975. 1299 pp.

Masterman, J. C. *The Double-Cross System in the War of 1939 to 1945*. New Haven: Yale University Press, 1972. 203 pp.

Meier-Welcker, Hans. *Seeckt*. Frankfurt am Main: Bernard & Graefe, 1967. 744 pp.

Meinck, Gerhard. *Hitler und die Deutsche Aufrüstung 1933–1937*. Veröffentlichungen des Instituts für Europäische Geschichte Mainz, 19. Wiesbaden: Steiner, 1959. 246 pp.

Meisner, Heinrich Otto. *Militärattachés und Militärbevollmächtigte in Preussen und im Deutschen Reich: Ein Beitrag zur Geschichte der Militärdiplomatie*. Neue Beiträge zur Geschichtswissenschaft, 2. Berlin: Rütten & Loening, 1957. 87 pp.

638   *Bibliography*

Messerschmidt, Manfred. *Die Wehrmacht im NS-Staat: Zeit der Indoktrination.* Truppe und Verwaltung, 16. Hamburg: Decker, 1969. 519 pp.

Milsom, John, and Peter Chamberlain. *German Armoured Cars of World War II.* New York: Scribner, 1974. 128 pp.

Milward, Alan S. "French Labour and the German Economy, 1942–1945: An Essay on the Nature of the Fascist New Order." *The Economic History Review,* 2nd series, 23 (August 1970), 336–51.

————. *The German Economy at War.* London: University of London (Athlone Press), 1965. 214 pp.

Model, Hansgeorg. *Der deutsche Generalstabsoffizier: Seine Auswahl und Ausbildung in Reichswehr, Wehrmacht und Bundeswehr.* Frankfurt am Main: Bernard & Graefe, 1968. 300 pp.

Molony, C. J. C., with F. C. Flynn, H. L. Davies, T. P. Gleave. *The Mediterranean and Middle East. 5: The Campaign in Sicily 1943 and The Campaign in Italy 3rd September 1943 to 31st March 1944.* History of the Second World War: United Kingdom Military Series. ed. Sir James Butler. HMSO, 1973. 921 pp.

Montross, Lynn. *War Through the Ages.* Rev. and enl. 3rd ed. New York: Harper & Bros., 1960. 1063 pp.

Moritz, Erhard. "Die Einschätzung der Roten Armee durch den faschistischen deutschen Generalstab von 1935 bis 1941." *Zeitschrift für Militärgeschichte,* 8 (1969), 154–70.

————. "Zum Bild der Roten Armee in deutschen faschistischen Militärzeitschriften und Jahrbüchern (1933–1941)." *Zeitschrift für Militärgeschichte,* 5 (1966), 307–17.

Mügge, Karl-Albert. "Einsatz und Arbeitsweise der Fernmeldeaufklärung." *Wehrkunde,* 7 (Februar 1958), 90–91.

————. "Funkaufklärung und Funktäuschung." *Wehrkunde,* 6 (Dezember 1957), 676–78.

Müller, Klaus-Jürgen. *Das Heer und Hitler: Armee und nationalsozialistische Regime, 1933–1940.* Beiträge zur Militär- und Kriegsgeschichte, 10 (Militärgeschichtliches Forschungsamt). Stuttgart: Deutsche Verlags-Anstalt, 1969. 711 pp.

Müller-Hillebrand, Burkhart. *Das Heer 1933–1945: Entwicklung des organisatorischen Aufbaues.* ESM, 1954–69. 3 vols.

Munzel, Oskar. *Die deutschen gepanzerten Truppen bis 1945.* Herford und Bonn: Maximilian, 1965. 352 pp.

Nelson, Otto L., Jr. *National Security and the General Staff.* Washington: Infantry Journal Press, 1946. 608 pp.

Newhall, Beaumont. *Airborne Camera: The World from the Air and Outer Space.* New York: Hastings House, 1969. 144 pp.

Nielsen, Andreas. *The German Air Force General Staff.* USAF Historical Studies, 173. USAF Historical Division, Research Studies Institute, Air University, June 1959. New York: Arno, 1968. 265 pp.

Nyomarkay, Joseph. *Charisma and Factionalism in the Nazi Party.* Minneapolis: University of Minnesota Press, 1967. 161 pp.

Ogorkiewicz, Richard M. *Armour: The Development of Mechanised Forces and Their Equipment.* London: Stevens & Sons, 1960. 475 pp.

O'Neill, Robert J. *The German Army and the Nazi Party, 1933–1939.* London: Cassell, 1966. 286 pp.

Orb, Heinrich. *Nationalsozialismus: 13 Jahre Machtrausch.* Olten: Otto Walter, 1945. 452 pp.

Orlow, Dietrich. *The History of the Nazi Party, 1919–1933.* Pittsburgh: University of Pittsburgh Press, 1969–73. 2 vols.

Oppenheim, L[assa]. *International Law: A Treatise.* 7th ed. ed. H. Lauterpacht. 5th impression [London]: Longmans, 1963. 2 vols.

Owen, Frank. *The Eddie Chapman Story.* New York: Messner, 1954. 242 pp.

Palmer, Robert R., Bell I. Wiley, and William R. Keast. *The Procurement and Training of Ground Combat Troops.* U.S. Army in World War II: The Army Ground Forces. (Department of the Army: Historical Division.) GPO, 1948. 696 pp.

Peis, Gunter. *The Man Who Started the War.* London: Odhams, 1960. 223 pp.

Philippi, Alfred. *Das Pripjetproblem. Wehrwissenschaftliche Rundschau*, Beiheft 2. März 1956. 82 pp.

——— and Ferdinand Heim. *Der Feldzug gegen Sowjetrussland: Ein operativer Überblick* (Arbeitskreis für Wehrforschung). Stuttgart: Kohlhammer, 1962. 293 pp.

Playfair, I. S. O., with C. J. C. Molony, F. C. Flynn, T. P. Gleave. *The Mediterranean and Middle East. 3: September 1941 to September 1942.* History of the Second World War: United Kingdom Military Series. ed. Sir James Butler. HMSO, 1960.

Prager, Stephan. *Das Deutsche Luftbildwesen.* Arbeitsgemeinschaft für Forschung des Landes Nordrhein-Westfalen, 97. Cologne: Westdeutscher Verlag, 1961. pp. 7–52.

Prior, Leon O. "German Espionage in Florida during World War II." *The Florida Historical Quarterly,* 39 (April 1961), 374–77.

R. "Vom deutschen Geheimdienst im zweiten Weltkrieg." *Allgemeine Schweizerische Militärzeitschrift,* 115 (Juli 1949), 486–91.

Ramme, Alwin. *Der Sicherheitsdienst der SS: Zu seiner Funktion im faschistischen Machtapparat und im Besatzungsregime des sogenannten General-Gouvernements Polen.* Militärhistorische Studien, 12, Neue Folge. (Deutsche Akademie der Wissenschaften zu Berlin: Institut für Geschichte: Abteilung Militärgeschichte.) Berlin: Deutscher Militärverlag, 1970. 325 pp.

Randewig, Kunibert. "50 Jahre Deutsche Heeres-Funk-, Nachrichten- und Fernmelde-Aufklärung." *Wehrwissenschaftliche Rundschau,* 14 (Oktober 1964), 615–21, (November 1964), 685–93.

Rauchhaupt, Wilhelm Volrat von. *Die Deutsche Kavallerie zwischen den beiden letzten Kriegen.* 4th ed. Wendlingen a.N.: Im Selbstverlag, n.d. 39 pp.

Reile, Oscar. *Geheime Westfront: Die Abwehr 1935–1945.* Munich-Wels: Welsermühl, 1962. 490 pp.

———. *Geheime Ostfront: Die deutsche Abwehr im Osten, 1921–1945.* Munich-Wels: Welsermühl, 1963. 475 pp.

Reinicke, A. *Die 5. Jäger-Division 1939–1945.* Bad Nauheim: Podzun, 1962. 429 pp.

Reinicke, Adolf. "Artillerieaufklärung und -bekämpfung." *Wehrkunde,* 7 (Oktober 1958), 558–63, (November 1958), 615–19.

———. "Zielaufklärung und Schussbeobachtung." *Wehrkunde,* 7 (Juli 1958), 378–82.

Reitlinger, Gerald. *The SS: Alibi of a Nation.* New York: Viking, 1957. 502 pp.

Rendulic, Lothar. "Die Schlacht von Orel 1943: Wahl und Bildung des Schwerpunktes." *Oesterreichische Militärische Zeitschrift* (Mai–Juni 1963), 130–38.

———. "Ursachen von Führungsfehlern." *Wehrkunde,* 11 (März 1962), 142–47.

———. "Von der Überraschung." *Wehrkunde,* 13 (Juli 1964), 355–60.

Reynolds, Nicholas. *Treason Was No Crime: Ludwig Beck, Chief of the German General Staff.* London: Kimber, 1976. 317 pp.

Rieckhoff, H. J. *Trumpf oder Bluff? 12 Jahre deutsche Luftwaffe.* Geneva: Interavia, 1945. 304 pp.

Richardson, William, and Seymour Freidin, eds. *The Fatal Decisions,* trans. Constantine FitzGibbon. London: Michael Joseph, 1956. 216 pp.

Ritter, Gerhard. *Die deutschen Militär-Attachés und das Auswärtige Amt.* Sitzungsbericht der Heidelberger Akademie der Wissenschaften, Philosophische-historische Klasse. 1959, 1. Abhandlung. Heidelberg: Carl Winter Universitätsverlag, 1959. 52 pp.

———. *Staatskunst und Kriegshandwerk: Das Problem des "Militarismus" in Deutschland.* Munich: Oldenbourg, 1959–68. 4 vols.

Rohwer, Jürgen. "Die grösste Geleitzugschlacht des Krieges: HX.229-SC.122 (März 1943)." *Wehrwissenschaftliche Rundschau,* 18 (März 1968), 146–58.

———. "La Radiotélégraphie: Auxiliaire du commandement dans la guerre sous-marin." *Revue d'Histoire de la deuxième guerre mondiale,* 18 (janvier 1968), 41–66.

———. *Die U-Boot-Erfolge der Achsenmächte 1939–1945.* Dokumentationen der Bibliothek für Zeitgeschichte, 1. Munich: J. F. Lehmanns, 1968. 376 pp.

Ropp, Theodore. *War in the Modern World*. Durham, N.C.: Duke University Press, 1959. 400 pp.

Rosinski, Herbert. *The German Army*. ed. Gordon A. Craig. New York: Praeger, 1966. 322 pp.

Roskill, S. W. *The War at Sea 1939–1495*. History of the Second World War: United Kingdom Military Series. ed. J. R. M. Butler. HMSO: 1954–1961. 3 vols. in 4 parts.

Rowan, Richard Wilmer, with Robert G. Deindorfer. *Secret Service: Thirty-Three Centuries of Espionage*. London: Kimber 1969. 786 pp.

Schafenort, [Louis A.] von. *Die Königliche Preussische Kriegsakademie, 1810–15. Oktober—1910*. ESM: 1910. 397 pp.

Schellenberg, Walter. *The Schellenberg Memoirs*. ed. and trans. Louis Hagen. London: André Deutsch, 1956. 479 pp.

———. *The Labyrinth: Memoirs*. New York: Harper & Brothers, 1956. 423 pp.

———. *Memorien*. Cologne: Verlag für Politik und Wirtschaft, 1959. 422 pp.

Schmidt-Richberg, Wiegand. *Die Generalstäbe in Deutschland 1871–1945: Aufgaben in der Armee und Stellung im Staate*. Beiträge zur Militär- und Kriegsgeschichte, 3 (Militärgeschichtliches Forschungsamt). Stuttgart: Deutsche Verlags-Anstalt, 1962. 121 pp.

Schoenbaum, David. *Hitler's Social Revolution: Class and Status in Nazi Germany 1933–1939*. Garden City: Doubleday, 1968. 336 pp.

Schorske, Carl E. "Two German Ambassadors: Dirksen and Schulenburg." In *The Diplomats 1919–1939*, ed. Gordon A. Craig and Felix Gilbert. Princeton: Princeton University Press, 1953. pp. 477–511.

Schreyer, Wolfgang. *Augen am Himmel: eine Piratenchronik*. Berlin: Deutscher Militärverlag, 1968. 437 pp.

Schumann, Wolfgang. "Zur Beteiligung des Zeiss-Konzerns an der Vorbereitung und Durchführung des zweiten Weltkrieges." *Wissenschaftliche Zeitschrift der Friedrich-Schiller-Universität Jena*, Gesellschafts- und Sprachwissenschaftliche Reihe, 8 (1958–59), 303–14.

———, ed. *Carl Zeiss Jena: Einst und Jetzt*. Berlin: Rütten & Loening, 1962. 942 pp.

Sayers, Michael, and Albert E. Kahn. *Sabotage! The Secret War Against America*. New York: Harper & Bros., 1942. 266 pp.

Scott, J. D., and Richard Hughes. *The Administration of War Production*. History of the Second World War: United Kingdom Civil Series. HMSO, 1955. 544 pp.

Seabury, Paul. *The Wilhelmstrasse: A Study of German Diplomats Under the Nazi Regime*. Berkeley & Los Angeles: University of California Press, 1954. 217 pp.

Seaton, Albert. *The Russo-German War 1941–45*. London: Barker, 1971. 628 pp.

Senger und Etterlin, F. M. von. *Die deutschen Panzer 1926–1945*. 2nd ed. Munich: J. F. Lehmanns, 1965.

———. "Die Feindbeurteilung." *Wehrkunde*, 13 (August 1964), 423–25.

———. *Die Kampfpanzer von 1916–1966*. Munich: J. F. Lehmanns, 1966. 523 pp.

———. "Probleme der Aufklärung." *Wehrkunde*, 6 (Dezember 1957), 672–76.

———. *Die 24. Panzer-Division vormals 1. Kavallerie Division, 1939–1945*. Neckargemünd: Vowinckel, 1962. 400 pp.

Senger und Etterlin, [Frido von]. "Neuzeitliche Aufklärung." *Jahrbuch des deutschen Heeres 1939*. Leipzig: Breitkopf & Hartel, 1938. pp. 131–38.

Sherwood, Robert E. *Roosevelt and Hopkins: An Intimate History*. New York: Harper & Bros., 1948. 979 pp.

Siegler, Fritz Freiherr von. *Die Höheren Dienststellen der Deutschen Wehrmacht 1933–1945*. Munich: Institut für Zeitgeschichte [1953]. 155 pp.

Simon, Leslie E. *German Research in World War II: An Analysis of the Conduct of Research*. New York: Wiley, 1947. 218 pp.

Smith, Arthur L., Jr. *The Deutschtum of Nazi Germany and the United States*. International Scholars Forum, 15. The Hague: Nijhoff, 1965. 172 pp.

"Die Sowjetischen Staatssicherheitsorgane im zweiten Weltkrieg." *Sowjetwissenschaft: Gesellschaftswissenschaftliche Beiträge* (November 1966), 1200–18.

Spaeter, Helmuth, ed. *Die Geschichte des Panzerkorps Grossdeutschlands*. Duisburg-

Rohrort: Selbstverlag Traditionsgemeinschaft Panzerkorps Grossdeutschland, 1958. 3 vols.

Speidel, Hans. *Invasion 1944: Rommel and the Normandy Campaign.* trans. Theo R. Crevenna. Chicago: Regnery, 1950. 176 pp.

Spielberger, Walter J. "Die Entwicklung von Panzerspähwagen für die Deutsche Reichswehr bezw. Wehrmacht 1927–45." *Feldgrau,* 10 (1962), 9–15, 17–20, 57–63.

————. "Die Entwicklung von Strassenpanzerwagen für die deutsche Armee 1905–1919." *Feldgrau,* 10 (1962), 90–93.

Stein, H. R. von. "Die deutsche Kavallerie 1939–1945." *Feldgrau,* 3 (Mai 1955), 49–56, (Juli 1955), 74–76.

Stiftung Luftwaffenehrenmal e.V. *Aufklärungsfliegerverbände.* Celle, 1972. 38 pp.

————. *Luftnachrichtentruppe.* Celle, 1971. 70 pp.

Strong, Kenneth. *Men of Intelligence: A Study of the Roles and Decisions of Chiefs of Intelligence from World War I to the Present Day.* London: Giniger, 1970. 183 pp.

"Taktische Luftaufklärung." *Wehrkunde,* 9 (Juni 1960), 301.

Taylor, Telford. *Sword and Swastika: Generals and Nazis in the Third Reich.* New York: Simon and Schuster, 1952. 431 pp.

Telpuchowski, Boris Semjonowitsch. *Die sowjetische Geschichte des Grossen Vaterländischen Krieges 1941–1945.* ed. Andreas Hillgruber and Hans-Adolf Jacobsen. trans. Robert Frhr. v. Freytag-Loringhoven, Erich F. Pruck, and Hans-Joachim Schunck. (Arbeitskreis für Wehrforschung). Frankfurt am Main: Bernard & Graefe, 1961. 576 pp.

Tessin, Georg. *Formationsgeschichte der Wehrmacht 1933–1939: Stäbe und Truppen des Heeres und der Luftwaffe.* Schriften des Bundesarchivs, 7. Boppard am Rhein: Boldt, 1959. 266 pp.

————. *Verbände und Truppen der deutschen Wehrmacht und Waffen SS im Zweiten Weltkrieg 1939–1945.* ESM, n.d. vols. 2 and 3.

Thompson, Victor A. *Modern Organization.* New York: Knopf, 1961. 197 pp.

Tippelskirch, Kurt von. *Geschichte des Zweiten Weltkrieges.* Bonn: Athenäum-Verlag, 1951. 731 pp.

Toscano, Mario. "Problema Particolari della Storia della Seconda Guerra Mondiale." In his *Pagine di Storia Diplomatica Contemporanea.* Instituto di Studi Storico-Politici, Universita di Roma, Facolta di Scienze Politiche, Nuova Serie. Milan: Giuffre, 1963. 2:75–87.

Traditionsverband der [3. Panzer] Division. *Geschichte der 3. Panzer-Division: Berlin-Brandenburg 1935–1945.* Berlin: Richter, 1967. 602 pp.

Trefousse, Hans L. "Failure of German Intelligence in the United States, 1935–1945." *Mississippi Valley Historical Review* (June 1955), 84–100.

Trevor-Roper, H. R. "Admiral Canaris." In his *The Philby Affair: Espionage, Treason and Secret Services.* London: Kimber, 1968. pp. 101–26.

————. *The Last Days of Hitler.* New York: Macmillan, 1947. 254 pp.

Turney-High, Harry Holbert. *Primitive War: Its Practice and Concepts.* Columbia: University of South Carolina Press, 1949. 277 pp.

[Union of Soviet Socialist Republics]. Institut für Marxismus-Leninismus beim Zentralkomitee der Kommunistischen Partei der Sowjetunion. *Geschichte des Grossen Vaterländischen Krieges der Sowjetunion.* ed. E. A. Boltin & B. S. Telpuchowski. trans. Rolf Feicht, Fred Herms, Georg Kautz, and Arno Specht. Berlin: Deutscher Militärverlag, 1962–67. 6 vols. cited as *GGVKS.*

[United States]. Department of the Army. *The German Campaign in Russia: Planning and Operations (1940–1942).* [by George E. Blau]. Pamphlet 20-261a. [Washington:] March 1955. Department of the Army. 186 pp.

[————. ————.] 6th Army Group. Headquarters. G-2 Section. *Final Report: World War II.* n.p., 10 July 1945. 67 pp.

[————. ————.] 12th Army Group. *Report of Operations (Final After Action Report).* n.d., n.p. vols. 3 and 4.

[————. ————.] European Theater of Operations. Office of the Theater Historian.

Order of Battle of the United States Army: World War II: European Theater of Operations: Divisions. Paris: December 1945. 586 pp.

[————. Navy Department]. Office of Naval Intelligence. *Espionage—Sabotage—Conspiracy: German and Russian Operations 1940 to 1945.* Excerpts from files of the German Naval Staff and from Other Captured German Documents. Washington, D.C.: April 1947. 191 pp.

[————.] Office of Naval Intelligence, Op 32-E. *German Naval Intelligence.* A Report Based on German Documents. 15 October 1946. Washington, D.C. 84 pp.

[————.] *Russo-German Naval Relations 1926 to 1941.* A Report Based on Captured Files of the German Naval Staff. Washington, D.C.: June 1947. pp. 52–73, 112–25 only.

[————.] State Department, European Affairs Division. *National Socialism: Basic Principles, Their Application by the Nazi Party's Foreign Organization, and the Use of Germans Abroad for Nazi Aims.* Raymond E. Murphy, Francis B. Stevens, Howard Trivers, Joseph M. Roland. GPO, 1943. 510 pp.

[————. War Department. Military Intelligence Division]. *The German General Staff Corps: A Study of the Organization of the German General Staff.* Produced at German Military Documents Section by a combined British, Canadian, and U.S. Staff. n.p., April 1946. 276 pp.

[————.] *German Operational Intelligence: A Study of German Operational Intelligence.* Produced at German Military Documents Section by a combined British, Canadian, and U.S. Staff. n.p., April 1946. 164 pp.

Vagts, Alfred. "Diplomacy, Military Intelligence and Espionage." In his *Defense and Diplomacy: The Soldiers and the Conduct of Foreign Relations.* New York: King's Crown, 1958. pp. 61–78.

————. *A History of Militarism.* Rev. ed. n.p.: Meridian Books, 1959. 542 pp.

————. *The Military Attaché.* Princeton: Princeton University Press, 1967. 408 pp.

Vernon, David T. A., and Douglas A. Bigelow. "Effect of Information about a Potentially Stressful Situation on Responses to Stress Impact." *Journal of Personality and Social Psychology,* 29 (January 1974), 50–59.

Vernon, W. H. D. "Hitler, the Man—Notes for a Case History." *The Journal of Abnormal and Social Psychology,* 37 (July 1942), 295–308.

Völker, Karl-Heinz. *Die Deutsche Luftwaffe 1933–1939: Aufbau, Führung und Rüstung der Luftwaffe sowie die Entwicklung der deutschen Luftkriegstheorie.* Beiträge zur Militär- und Kriegsgeschichte, 8. (Militärgeschichtliches Forschungsamt). Stuttgart: Deutsche Verlags-Anstalt, 1967. 339 pp.

————. *Dokumente und Dokumentarfotos zur Geschichte der deutschen Luftwaffe: Aus den Geheimakten des Reichswehrministeriums 1919–1933 und des Reichsluftfahrtministeriums 1933–1939.* Beiträge zur Militär- und Kriegsgeschichte, 9. (Militärgeschichtliches Forschungsamt). Stuttgart: Deutsche Verlags-Anstalt, 1968. 489 pp.

————. *Die Entwicklung der militärischen Luftfahrt in Deutschland 1920–1933: Planung und Massnahmen zur Schaffung einer Fliegertruppe in der Reichswehr.* Beiträge zur Militär- und Kriegsgeschichte, 3. (Militärgeschichtliches Forschungsamt). Stuttgart: Deutsche Verlags-Anstalt, 1962. pp. 121–292.

Vogelsang, Thilo. *Reichswehr, Staat und NSDAP: Beiträge zur deutschen Geschichte 1930–1932.* Quellen und Darstellungen zur Zeitgeschichte, 11. Stuttgart: Deutsche Verlags-Anstalt, 1962. 507 pp.

Waibel, M. "Einschätzung der russischen Kriegsführung durch die deutsche Wehrmacht." *Allgemeine Schweizerische Militärzeitung,* 92 (Januar 1946), 30–36.

Walter, Georg. "Geheime Nachrichtendienste." *Wehrkunde,* 13 (Februar 1964), 59–63.

Warlimont, Walter. "Der Mann, der nie gelebt hat: Das legendare Paradestück des britischen Nachrichtendienstes von 1943." *Die Nachhut,* (1 Oktober 1972), 1–3, (8 January 1973), 1–13.

Watson, Mark Skinner. *Chief of Staff: Prewar Plans and Preparations.* United States Army in World War II: The War Department. (Department of Army: Historical Division.) GPO, 1950. 551 pp.

Weber, Max. *Economy and Society: An Outline of Interpretive Sociology.* ed. Guenther Roth and Claus Wittich. New York: Bedminster, 1968. 3 vols.

Webster, Charles, and Noble Frankland. *The Strategic Air Offensive Against Germany 1939–1945*. History of the Second World War: United Kingdom Military Series. HMSO, 1961. 4 vols.

Weinberg, Gerhard L. *The Foreign Policy of Hitler's Germany: Diplomatic Revolution in Europe, 1933–36*. Chicago: University of Chicago Press, 1970. 397 pp.

————. "Hitler's Image of the United States." *American Historical Review,* 69 (July 1964), 1006–21.

Westphal, Siegfried. *Heer in Fesseln: Aus den Papieren des Stabschefs von Rommel, Kesselring und Rundstedt*. 2nd ed. Bonn: Athenäum, 1952. 355 pp.

————. "Ueber Grosstäuschung im zweiten Weltkrieg." *Wehrkunde,* 3 (Januar 1954), 11–13.

Wheeler-Bennett, John W. *The Nemesis of Power: The German Army in Politics 1918–1945*. 2nd ed. London: Macmillan, 1967. 831 pp.

White, B. T. *German Tanks and Armoured Vehicles 1914–1945*. London: Ian Allan, 1966. 78 pp.

Wiener, Fritz. "Motorisierte Aufklärung—Panzeraufklärung." *Feldgrau,* 4 (Januar 1956), 1–5, (März 1956), 25–31.

Wighton, Charles. *Heydrich: Hitler's Most Evil Henchman*. London: Odhams, 1962. 288 pp.

Wildhagen, Karl Heinz, ed. *Erich Fellgiebel, Meister operativer Nachrichtenverbindungen: Ein Beitrag zur Geschichte der Nachrichtentruppe*. Emden: Im Selbstverlag, 1970. 328 pp.

Wilensky, Harold L. *Organizational Intelligence: Knowledge and Policy in Government and Industry*. New York: Basic Books, 1967. 226 pp.

Wilhelm, Hans-Heinrich. *Die Prognosen der Abteilung Fremde Heere Ost 1942–1945*. in *Zwei Legenden aus dem Dritten Reich*. Schriftenreihe der Vierteljahrshefte für Zeitgeschichte, 28. Stuttgart: Deutsche Verlags-Anstalt, 1974. pp. 7–75.

Wilkinson, Spenser. *The Brain of an Army*. New ed. Westminster: Constable, 1895. 204 pp.

Wilmot, Chester. *The Struggle for Europe*. New York: Harper & Bros., 1952. 766 pp.

Winter, August. " 'Wägbares und Unwägbares bei der Entstehung von Führungsentschlüssen.' " *Wehrkunde,* 14 (März 1965), 116–22, (April 1965), 176–80.

Woodward, Llewellyn. *British Foreign Policy in the Second World War*. History of the Second World War. HMSO, 1962. 592 pp.

Wright, Quincy. *A Study of War*. Chicago: University of Chicago Press, 1942. 2 vols.

Ziemke, Earl F. *Stalingrad to Berlin: The German Defeat in the East*. Army Historical Series. (Department of the Army: Office of the Chief of Military History.) GPO, 1968. 549 pp.

Zhilin, P. *They sealed their own doom*. Moscow: Progress Publishers, 1970. 262 pp.

Historical and Other Studies: Unpublished

Best, Werner. "Wilhelm Canaris." Copenhagen, 10.4.1949. 11 pp.

Gempp, Fritz. "Geheimer Nachrichtendienst und Spionageabwehr des Heeres." Im Auftrag der Abwehrabteilung des Reichswehrministeriums. (T-77:1438–40, 1442, 1507–09).

Jensen, Willi. "Hilfsgeräte der Kryptographie." Dissertation. Flensburg, 1955. 129 pp. + 70 appendices.

Kittel, Ulrich. "Reichsluftfahrtministerium Forschungsamt: Geschichte und Arbeitsweise eines Nachrichtenamtes." (Deutsches Institut für Geschichte der nationalsozialistischen Zeit) [ca. 1951]. 83 pp. (in Institut für Zeitgeschichte, Munich, Archiv. 351/52).

Konrad. "Auswirkungen des geheimen Meldedienstes in der Obersten Heeresleitung 1866, 1870/71 und 1914." [no later than 18.1.34.] 34 pp. (in MA:WK VIII/7).

Payr, von. "Die Erkundung der materiellen Wehrkraft der grossen europäischen und aussereuropäischen Staaten und die sich daraus ergebenden Vorbereitungen für den Wirtschaftskrieg." 24.3.44. 39 pp. (in MA:OKW:Wi VI/397).

Powe, Marc B. "The Emergence of the War Department Intelligence Agency, 1885–1918." A master's thesis, Department of History, Kansas State University, Manhattan, Kansas. 1974. 146 pp.

Praun, Albert, ed. "Eine Untersuchung über den Funkdienst des russischen, britischen und amerikanischen Heeres im zweiten Weltkrieg vom deutschen Standpunkt aus, unter besonderer Berücksichtigung ihrer Sicherheit." 18. Februar 1950. ca. 200 pp.

Steimle, Eugen. "Stellungnahme zu den Memoiren von W. Schellenberg." August 1960. 9 pp.

Stoerkel, A. R. "Die Organisation des Grossen Generalstabes" [no earlier than 30 September 1920]. 65 pp. (in MA:OKH:H35/2). Cited as Stoerkel.

————. "Erste Einführung in die Organisation und in die Tätigkeit des Stellvertretenden Generalstabes der Armee und des Grossen Generalstabes (1919) bis zur Auflösung am 30.9.1919." 162 pp. (in MA:OKH:H35/3). Cited as Stoerkel, "Stellvertretenden."

United States. Air Force. Historical Division.

Historical Studies (Karlsruhe Collection).

USAF-171. Andreas L. Nielsen. "The Collection and Evaluation of Intelligence for the German Air Force High Command." n.d. 224 pp.

USAF-191 (Extra Study). Kurt Gottschling. "The Radio Intercept Service of the German Air Force." 30 August 1955. 2 vols.

"Ausrüstung der Bildstelle einer H. und F. Staffel." 28.6.1955. 5 pp.

"Die Bildaufklärung im Luftkrieg." Studie der 8. Abteilung. 1944. 9 pp.

Deichmann. "Die Zielobjektkartei." n.d. 9 pp.

Fischer, Eberhard. "Die Entwicklung des Luftbildwesens ab 1920." 6.9.1956. 27 pp.

"Die Flugzeuge fuer die Nahaufklaerungsverbaende." n.d. 13 pp.

"Die Flugzeuge fuer die Fernaufklaerungsverbaende." n.d. 2 pp.

Greiff. "Die Aufklärung durch Flugzeuge." 1945. 3 pp.

Kleyenstuber. "Organisation des militärischen Geheimen Meldedienstes (Abwehrdienst)." 27.10.1955. 9 pp.

Mutter, Erwin. "Die Nachtluftbildtechnik: Ein geschichtlicher Ueberblick." 17.8. 1956. 10 pp.

[Schmid, Josef]. "Die 5. Abteilung des Generalstabes der Luftwaffe (I c), 1.1. 1938–1.10.1942." Zum Teil im Auszug. 1945. 53 pp.

"Ueberblick über die Tätigkeit und Organisation des gesamten Bildwesens in der Luftwaffe." Studie der 8. Abteilung/Chef Genst. 1944. 19 pp.

United States. Army. Historical Division.

Foreign Military Studies (now in NA, RG338).

B-336. Guenther Blumentritt. "Military Maps and Military-Geographic Description." 1947. 12 pp.

B-484. Friedrich von Boetticher. "Impressions and Experiences of the Military and Air Attaché at the German Embassy in Washington D.C. during the Years 1933–1941." 24 Apr 1947. 52 pp.

B-636. "Additional Information about the Operational Plan V (US) Corps, captured on 7 Jun 44, in the Sector of 352 Infantry Division." 3 Sep 47. 2 pp.

B-637. Guenther Blumentritt. "V Corps Operation Plan—OB West." 28 Aug 1947. 8 pp.

B-656. Max Pemsel. "Additional Orientation Regarding the American V Corps Plan and Operations, Captured on 7 June 1944." 25 Sep 1947. 4 pp.

B-658. Guenther Blumentritt. "Reconnaissance." n.d. 19 pp.

B-675. Anton Staubwasser. "Army Group B—Intelligence Estimate (1 June 1944)." 15 Oct 1947. 32 pp.

B-825. Anton Staubwasser. [deals with enemy situation 25 Jul–16 Sep 1944]. n.d. 158 pp.

C-020. Percy Ernst Schramm. "The Wehrmacht in the Last Days of the War (1 Jan–7 May 1945)." Part II: Chapters 5 to 8 and appendixes. n.d. pp. 302–674.

C-065a. Helmut Greiner. "Notes on the Situation Reports and Discussions at Hitler's Headquarters from 12 August 1942 to 17 March 1943." n.d. 212 pp.

C-076. Karl-Heinrich Graf Klinckowstroem. "Reproduction Equipment." 1 Apr 1950. 4 pp.

D-024. Hanshenning von Holtzendorff. "Gründe für Rommels Erfolge in Afrika 1941/1942." 27 März 1947. 22 pp.

D-407. Rudolf Langhaeuser. "Studie über die Beschaffung von Feindnachrichten im deutschen Heer während des 2. Weltkrieges an der Ostfront." 10 Sep 1954. 152 pp.

P-018a. Alfred Toppe. "German Methods of Interrogating Prisoners of War in World War II." Jun 1949. 66 pp.

P-023. W. Berlin, C. Roehr, and H. J. Froben. "The Reconnaissance Artillery." n.d. 187 pp.

P-031a, Anlage 33. [Ludwig Beck]. "Einführung in die neue Vorschrift 'Truppenführung.'" 20 December 1933. 39 pp.

P-041h. Kurt von Tippelskirch. "Intelligence on Foreign Armies and the Foreign Intelligence Service, 1938–45." 1952. 16 pp.

P-041i. Gerhard Matzky, Lothar Metz, and Kurt von Tippelskirch. "Organization and Working Methods of the Army Intelligence Division." 1953. 133 pp.

P-041j. Horst von Mellenthin. "The Attaché Branch of the Army General Staff." 1952. 75 pp.

P-041k. Albert Praun. "Signal Services." 28 Nov 1947. 54 pp.

P-041n. Wilhelm Berlin and Gerhard Huether. "Representation of Artillery Interests 1938–1945." 1952. 90 pp.

P-041p. Heinz W. Guderian. "Representation of Armored Interests 1938–45." n.d. 49 pp.

P-041w. Karl-Heinrich Graf von Klinckowstroem. "Mapping and Survey Services in the German Army (1920–45)." n.d. 45 pp.

P-041aa. Walther Guendell. "Headquarters Commandant, Army High Command (1941–45)." 1952. 45 pp.

P-041ii. Kurt Zeitzler. "Stellungnahme zu der Ausarbeitung 'Die Oberste Führung des deutschen Heeres (OKH) im Rahmen der Wehrmachtführung.'" April 1948. 122 pp.

P-041jj. Heinz Guderian. "Stellungnahme zu der Ausarbeitung 'Die Oberste Führung des deutschen Heeres (OKH) im Rahmen der Wehrmachtführung.'" Juni 1948. 1953. 18 pp.

P-044. Hans von Greiffenburg, Erhard Franz-Josef Rauss, and Harald Weberstadt. "Deception and Cover Plans." n.d. 120 pp.

P-093. R. Koch-Erpach. "Auszug aus dem Kriegstagebuch der Div. A.A.161." 162 pp.

P-097. Franz Halder, Enno von Rintelen, Ernst Koestring, and Leopold Buerkner. "Selection and Training of German Officers for Military Attaché Duty." 12 June 1951. 44 pp.

P-097a. Anton Freiherr von Bechtolsheim. "The German Attaché System." February 1952. 15 pp.

P-122. "German Counterintelligence Activities in Occupied Russia (1941–1944)." n.d. 150 pp.

P-130. Wilhelm Willemer. "Camouflage." 1953. 175 pp.

P-132. Albert Praun. "Signal Communications in the East: German Experience in Russia." 1954. 250 pp.

P-149/22. Wolfgang Everth. "Vormarsch, Aufklärung und Kampf einer Panzeraufklärungsabteilung." n.d. 26 pp.

T-31. Peter von der Groeten. "Collapse of Army Group Center and Its Combat Activity until Stabilization of the Front (22 June to 1 Sept 1944)." December 1947. 56 pp.

T-101. "The German Armed Forces High Command—OKW." Ch. B 1 e, "Signal Communications," 34 pp. Ch B 1 f, "Intelligence," 4 pp. Part 2, Annex 3, "The Intelligence Service of the Armed Forces High Command," by L. Bürkner, 29 Feb 1948, 31 pp.

T-111. "The German Army High Command—OKH: Synopsis." December 1949. 118 pp.

ETHINT-49. "An Interview with Genfldm Wilhelm Keitel, Genobst Alfred Jodl: The Invasion." 23 Jul 1945. 7 pp.

Warlimont, Walter. "Kommentar zu T-101: Zu III. Teil, Unterabschnitt B.1-f, 'Die Wehrmachtführung auf dem Gebiet des Feind-Nachrichtendienstes.'" 1949. pp. 201–205.

Wells, Anthony Roland. "Studies in British Naval Intelligence, 1880–1945." A thesis submitted for the Degree of Doctor of Philosophy of War Studies of the University of London. [1972]. 437 pp.

Illustrations Acknowledgments

The author gratefully thanks the following organizations, collections, and individuals for permission to reproduce the illustrations.

Frenchman Bay: Joseph Ascherl; forged draft card: F.B.I.; blank draft card: F.B.I.; Egyptian soldiers: Karl Richard Lepsius, *Denkmäler aus Aegypten und Aethiopien ...* (Berlin: Nicolaische Buchhandlung, 1849–59), 3:154; Moltke: Friedrich F. von Conring, *Das deutsche Militär in der Karikatur* (Stuttgart: Schmidt, 1907), 201; Berlin: Joseph Ascherl; chart: Joseph Ascherl, Otto H. Barz; Boetticher report: MA; railroad bridge: BA; scout cars: *Feldgrau* (1955); light- and sound-battery: XXX.A.K.: 13896/2:26. Nov. 1941; He 111, Ju 88, Me 109: U.S. War Department, *Aircraft Recognition Pictorial Manual*, FM 30-30 (June 1943); FW 189: Kens, 203; aerial reconnaissance map: MA; Dulag Luft interrogation: MA; Krasnichin interrogation: MA; bazooka sketch: MA; Allied bomber: Bibliothek für Zeitgeschichte; Sonderdienst Seehaus: Library of Congress; censorship sticker: author's collection; wiretapping loops: MA; State Department message: NA; VN: MA; Soviet radio nets: MA; Russian cipher: MA; Canaris's signature: MA; Schellenberg's personal report: BDC; radio dialogue: NA; Krämer report: AA; Russian front: Joseph Ascherl; Koerner advertisement: *The New York Times* (6 April 1936), 3; Norden bomb sight: U.S. Patent No. 2,428,678; Heydrich letter: AA; Schellenberg telegram: AA; CICERO document: PRO; tank marks: MA; spy report: MA; 38th Army map: Joseph Ascherl; American tank: MA; Vth Corps orders: NA; movement of Russian forces: MA; Stalingrad front: Joseph Ascherl; North Africa and Mediterranean map: Joseph Ascherl; invasion targets map: Joseph Ascherl; Foreign Armies West map: MA.

Kneeling soldier: Wide World Photos; Gimpel: Wide World Photos; Colepaugh: Wide World Photos; Park Zorgvliet: The Hague, Gemeentearchief; beach: Wide World Photos; Paeffgen: BDC; Boetticher: Wide World Photos; observers, BA; 8-wheel scout car: BA; Manstein: BA; Rowehl: author's collection (Theodor Rowehl); examining papers: author's collection (Cornelius Noell); FW 189: United Press International; Do 17: United Press International; loading cameras: BA; cameras: MA; railroad gun: MA; prisoner of war: NA; Schapper: BDC; Fenner: author's collection (Ilse Fenner); Tranow: author's collection (Wilhelm Tranow); Canaris: author's collection (H.-J. Rudloff); Piekenbrock: author's collection (Frau Piekenbrock); Hansen: author's collection (Isolde Hansen); Jost: BDC; Schellenberg: BDC; RSHA VI headquarters: Landesbildstelle Berlin.

Chile radio transmitter: NA; Hamburg radio station: author's collection (Werner Trautmann); suitcase radio: NA; microphotographs: Franklin D. Roosevelt Library; Steimle: BDC; Carstenn: BDC; Lang: F.B.I.; Becker: NA; Wende: U. S. Army; Kotas: U. S. Army; soldiers aiming: U. S. Army; Blumröder lying on table: author's collection (Hans-Adolf von Blumröder); intelligence conference: author's collection (Hans-Adolf von Blumröder); Matzky: author's collection (Gerhard Matzky); Süsskind-Schwendi: author's collection (Gerhard Seyffaerth); building at Zossen: author's collection (Gerhard Matzky); ramshackle building: Richard Gehlen; Gehlen: Richard Gehlen; Liss: Strong, *Men of Intelligence;* Roenne: Macmillan (Great Britain); Schmid: David Irving; Luftwaffe target folder pictures: NA; Hitler conference: Bibliothek für Zeitgeschichte (Stuttgart).

INDEX

Index

ABA (Swedish airline), 307
Abwehr, 32, 70, 179, 261, 328, 405–406, 530, 535
  absorbed by RSHA, 6, 62, 91, 236, 237, 250, 268–71, 398, 535
  Ausland Division of, 47, 168–69, 177, 233–34, 268
  as branch of Defense Ministry, 191, 215, 225–26, 231
  expansion of, 225, 232, 248, 419
  failures of, 70, 236, 267–68, 284, 422
  and Foreign Armies branches, 420, 422, 426, 430, 432
  and Foreign Office, 100, 233, 245–48, 307, 323, 536
  front organization of, 248–50, 269, 270–71, 273, 276, 298, 398
  KOs of, 245–48, 250, 270, 292, 298, 314, 356
  made central intelligence post, 225
  Main Post East (WALLI I) of, 239, 241n, 249, 292, 358, 430, 432
  Main Post West of, 241n, 249, 298, 504, 512
  as Military Department, 250, 270–71, 276, 512
  nonespionage functions of, 47, 116, 119, 149–50, 177, 249
  Operation LENA of, 347–53
  posts, table of, 240–41 and n
  posts of, 232, 238–45, 249–50, 270, 282, 451–52
  recruitment for, 225, 236, 272–73, 302–303, 306, 317, 319, 331, 347
  reduced to spy agency, 232
  relations with Nazi agencies of, 59, 61, 99–100, 226, 231–32, 236, 252, 267–68, 311–12
  under Troops Department, 191, 224–25, 418
  troops of, controlled by Ic/AOs, 403, 407
  ZF (finances), 297–99, 351
Abwehr I (espionage), 47, 62, 76, 98, 100, 119, 163, 225, 232–34, 236–50, 269–73, 275–99, 302–35, 347–70, 452–54, 460, 467, 469, 472–74, 476, 477, 485–86, 493–94, 499, 508, 514, 529
  G (false documents), 239, 271, 279, 281–83, 290–91, 313
  H Ost (army east), 238

Ht (army, technical), 238
H West (army west), 238
i (communications), 239, 271, 292–95
L (air section), 119, 238, 302–12, 381, 384
M (Marine), 238
Wi (economics), 89, 90–92, 150, 238, 376
  See also Spies
Abwehr II (sabotage), 47, 67, 191, 233, 234, 238–39, 249, 269–71
Abwehr III (counterespionage), 47, 59, 224, 232–33, 238–39, 249, 252, 268, 269, 354, 398, 505
Aerial reconnaissance. *See* Reconnaissance, aerial
Agfa, 291
Aggression in Germany, 524, 528–31
Albrecht, Helmut, 164, 166
Alexandria, Egypt, 114, 194–95
Algeciras, Spain, 292–93, 476
Algerians, 274
Algiers, Algeria, 478
Allied Powers
  air superiority of, 485, 499
  codes of, 206, 219, 506, 510
  cryptanalysis by, 212, 222, 485–86, 524, 525, 529
  deception used by, 367–68, 484–86, 489–99, 500–502, 506, 510, 513–20, 529
  intelligence of, 135, 404, 512, 523–24, 529–30, 533, 536
  intelligence on equipment of, 81, 207, 310, 361, 378–79, 384, 386, 422
  intelligence on strength of, 81, 83, 170, 207, 352, 355, 381, 384, 396, 419, 473, 489–91, 496
  on the offensive, 17, 248, 362, 530, 540
  operations of, centered in Britain, 346, 352, 385, 481, 493, 495, 501, 505–506, 509
  speculation on strategy of, 79, 308, 344, 381, 462–520
  transatlantic conversations of, 172–76
  in World War I, 35, 37, 38–39, 255
  See also Normandy invasion; North Africa; Shipping; individual countries
Amè, Cesare, 96
American Ordnance Association, 333–34